Fodor's 2015

IRELAND

WELCOME TO IRELAND

It's a Celtic mystery: how can a country as small as Ireland be packed with so much majestic history, natural beauty, vibrant culture, and, of course, fun? Norman castles overlook wild, empty beaches, Georgian country houses host impromptu traditional music sessions, excited theatergoers spill out into bustling Dublin pubs. Drama and spectacle lie at every turn, with a pint of Guinness to toast it all. But the real Irish secret is the people: their unique blend of warmth, humor, and irreverence will ensure your trip to the Emerald Isle is a true adventure.

TOP REASONS TO GO

★ **Untamed Nature:** From rugged marshlands to glacial lakes, wild Ireland blows the mind.

★ **Living History:** Neolithic Knowth, Celtic Cashel, Christian Glendalough, and more.

★ **Perfect Pubs:** A fire, chowder, a pint of stout; the Irish pub is a slow, sacred space.

★ **Festivals:** Oysters in Galway, jazz in Cork, St. Paddy in Dublin; celebrate year-round.

★ **Cracking Culture:** Every second native's a poet or a fiddle player—it's in the air.

★ **Hidden Treasures:** Empty islands, silent forests, untouched beaches: serenity abounds.

Fodor's IRELAND 2015

Publisher: Amanda D'Acierno, *Senior Vice President*

Editorial: Arabella Bowen, *Editor in Chief*; Linda Cabasin, *Editorial Director*

Design: Fabrizio La Rocca, *Vice President, Creative Director*; Tina Malaney, *Associate Art Director*; Chie Ushio, *Senior Designer*; Ann McBride, *Production Designer*

Photography: Melanie Marin, *Associate Director of Photography*; Jessica Parkhill and Jennifer Romains, *Researchers*

Maps: Rebecca Baer, *Senior Map Editor*; Mark Stroud (Moon Street Cartography), David Lindroth, *Cartographers*

Production: Linda Schmidt, *Managing Editor*; Evangelos Vasilakis, *Associate Managing Editor*; Angela L. McLean, *Senior Production Manager*

Sales: Jacqueline Lebow, *Sales Director*

Marketing & Publicity: Heather Dalton, *Marketing Director*; Katherine Punia, *Senior Publicist*

Business & Operations: Susan Livingston, *Vice President, Strategic Business Planning*; Sue Daulton, *Vice President, Operations*

Fodors.com: Megan Bell, *Executive Director, Revenue & Business Development*; Yasmin Marinaro, *Senior Director, Marketing & Partnerships*

Copyright © 2015 by Fodor's Travel, a division of Random House LLC

Writers: Paul Clements, Alannah Hopkin, Anto Howard

Editors: Róisín Cameron (lead project editor), Penny Phenix

Production Editor: Carolyn Roth

ISBN 978-0-8041-4272-4

ISSN 0071–6464

SPECIAL SALES

This book is available at special discounts for bulk purchases for sales promotions or premiums. For more information, e-mail specialmarkets@randomhouse.com

PRINTED IN THE UNITED STATES OF AMERICA

10 9 8 7 6 5 4 3 2 1

CONTENTS

MAPS

ABOUT THIS GUIDE

Fodor's Recommendations

Everything in this guide is worth doing—we don't cover what isn't—but exceptional sights, hotels, and restaurants are recognized with additional accolades. **Fodor's Choice** ★ indicates our top recommendations; and **Best Bets** call attention to notable hotels and restaurants in various categories. Care to nominate a new place? Visit Fodors.com/contact-us.

Trip Costs

We list prices wherever possible to help you budget well. Hotel and restaurant price categories from **$** to **$$$$** are noted alongside each recommendation. For hotels, we include the lowest cost of a standard double room in high season. For restaurants, we cite the average price of a main course at dinner or, if dinner isn't served, at lunch. For attractions, we always list adult admission fees; discounts are usually available for children, students, and senior citizens.

Hotels

Our local writers vet every hotel to recommend the best overnights in each price category, from budget to expensive. Unless otherwise specified, you can expect private bath, phone, and TV in your room. For expanded hotel reviews, facilities, and deals visit Fodors.com.

Top Picks
★ Fodor's Choice

Listings
✉ Address
✉ Branch address
☎ Telephone
📠 Fax
🌐 Website
📧 E-mail
🎟 Admission fee
🕒 Open/closed times
[M] Subway
✥ Directions or Map coordinates

Hotels & Restaurants
🏨 Hotel
🛏 Number of rooms
🍽 Meal plans
✕ Restaurant
✍ Reservations
👔 Dress code
▭ No credit cards
[$] Price

Other
⇨ See also
☞ Take note
⛳ Golf facilities

Restaurants

Unless we state otherwise, restaurants are open for lunch and dinner daily. We mention dress code only when there's a specific requirement and reservations only when they're essential or not accepted. To make restaurant reservations, visit Fodors.com.

Credit Cards

The hotels and restaurants in this guide typically accept credit cards. If not, we'll say so.

EXPERIENCE IRELAND

WHAT'S WHERE

Numbers refer to chapters.

2 Dublin. A transformed city since the days of O'Casey and Joyce, Ireland's capital may have replaced its legendary tenements with modern high-rises but its essential spirit remains intact. One of Europe's most popular city-break destinations, it has art, culture, Georgian architecture, and, of course, hundreds of pubs where conversation and vocal dexterity continue to flourish within an increasingly multicultural mix. Get spirited (pun intended) at the Guinness Brewery, "Rock 'n' Stroll" your way through hip Temple Bar, and be illuminated by the *Book of Kells* at Trinity College's great library.

3 Dublin Environs. The counties outside the Pale are a treasure trove of history, monastic settlements, ancient tombs, battlefields, and peaceful valleys only an hour from the hubbub of the capital's center. From the lush greenery of Kildare and Wicklow, to the mythology and traditions of Meath and Louth, the historic timeline encompasses many of the pivotal pre-Christian and early church locales of Ireland's past. Listen for ancient echoes at the Hill of Tara, hike into prehistory at Newgrange, and opt for opulence at Castletown House.

4 The Midlands. Overlooked by many visitors due to the region's relative absence of wow-factor attractions, this verdant oasis of bog and lake harks back to the simpler, and slower, life of Ireland 40 years ago. Friendly, almost shy natives, old-style pubs, unspoiled vistas and walks, plus a wealth of historic ruins make for a relaxing adventure into the way we were. Tree-hug one of the great yews at Tullynally Gardens, lift your spirits at Clonmacnoise, and take a river cruise down the Shannon.

5 The Southeast. Ireland's sunniest corner (with almost double the national average), the coastal counties have long been the favored hideaway of Dublin folk on vacation. Quiet seaside villages, country houses, and some of the nation's best land all offer delightful reasons to tarry. Inland, counties like Kilkenny and Tipperary offer a lion's share of history and important monuments in the main towns, Wexford and Waterford. Follow in the footsteps of St. Patrick at the Rock of Cashel and dig the ducal lifestyle at Lismore.

6 County Cork. After exploring the delights of Cork City—museums, lively pubs, quirky cafés, and lots of good music, trad and otherwise—use it as a base to explore Ireland's largest county, as nearly everyone heads to get the gift of gab by kissing the famous Blarney Stone. Get your fill of five-star scenery by traveling east to Shanagarry—teach yourself good taste at Ballymaloe House, pioneer of the new Irish cuisine. Due south is the "Irish St-Tropez," fashionable Kinsale, while westward lies Bantry, one of Ireland's finest stately homes, which sits atop a breathtaking bluff over Bantry Bay. From here a cliff-top road with stunning views leads to ruggedly beautiful Glengarriff.

MAYO
Achill Island
Clare Island
Clew Bay
Inishturk
Inishbofin
Lou
Oileáin Árainn (Aran Islands)
Galu
Kilrush
Mouth of the Shannon
Listowe
Tralee
Corca Dhuibne (Dingle Peninsula)
Blasket Islands
Dingle Bay
Killarney
Iveragh Peninsula
KERRY
Skellig Rocks
Beara Peninsula
Kenmare Bay
Bantry Bay
Mizen Head

Malin Head

Rathlin Island

Toraigh
(Tory Island)

Portrush

Coleraine

SCOTLAND
(United Kingdom)

Ariann Mhor
(Aranmore Island)

Letterkenny

Derry City
DERRY

ANTRIM

*Gweebarra
Bay*

DONEGAL

Strabane

Ballymena

Larne

Donegal
Town

NORTHERN
IRELAND
(United Kingdom)

Omagh

Cookstown

*Lough
Neagh*

Island Magee
Belfast Lough

BELFAST

Newtownards

*Donegal
Bay*

Ballyshannon

*Lower
Lough Erne*

TYRONE

Dungannon

DOWN

*Killala
Bay*

*Sligo
Bay*

LEITRIM

FERMANACH

*Upper
Lough Erne*

Armagh City

ARMAGH

Newcastle

Sligo Town

Monaghan
City

Newry

Ballina

SLIGO

MONAGHAN

Dundalk

*Lough
Corrib*

Castlebar

ROSCOMMON

Cavan

CAVAN

Dundalk Bay

LOUTH

*Lough
Mask*

Knock

Longford

Drogheda

River Shannon

LONGFORD

MEATH

DUBLIN

GALWAY

[4]

WESTMEATH

Mullingar

Ballinasloe

Athlone

[3]

[2]

DUBLIN

Galway City

OFFALY

Naas

Dún Laoghaire

way Bay

Birr

KILDARE

Bray *Irish Sea*

REPUBLIC OF IRELAND

Portlaoise

WICKLOW

Wicklow

Ennis

LAOIS

Athy

Roscrea

CLARE

Nenagh

TIPPERARY

Kilkenny
City

Arklow

Shannon

CARLOW

Gorey

Limerick
City

Thurles

KILKENNY

LIMERICK

Cashel

[5]

WEXFORD

Newcastle
West

Tipperary
Town

Carrick-on-Suir

Wexford Town

Clonmel

Mallow

Farahy

WATERFORD

Waterford

[6]

CORK

Midleton

Youghal

Cork City

Cobh

St. George's Channel

Kinsale

Skibbereen

0   50 mi

0   50 km

WHAT'S WHERE

7 The Southwest. The counties of Kerry and Limerick have sights that top every tourist's must-see list. The most brazenly scenic coastal drive in the land, the Ring of Kerry, will use up your entire flash card in a jiffy! While there, take a wet and wonderful ride out to the sea-wrapped Skellig islands, whose twin peaks rise out of the sea. The Gap of Dunloe lets you walk through the heart of Killarney's purple mountains and cross the glittering blue lake of Killarney. And don't forget to have your Nikon handy for Ireland's prettiest village, Adare. Everywhere, the glories of Ireland's coastline combine to paint a canvas that still casts a potent spell upon the stranger.

8 County Clare, Galway, and the Aran Islands. Set with postcard-perfect villages like Doolin, the lunar landscape of the Burren, and the towering Cliffs of Moher (they'll give you a new understanding of the word "awesome"), County Clare is pure tourist gold. For a complete change of pace, head to nearby Galway City: one of Ireland's liveliest, it has a compact historic center bursting with artistic energy and a lively pub culture. This is also the place to organize your trip to the Oileáin Árainn (Aran Islands), three outposts of Gaelic civilization, which still have a strong whiff of the "old ways"—and not just the whiff of turf smoke.

9 Connemara and County Mayo. With the most westerly seaboard in Europe, this region remains a place apart—the most Irish part of Ireland. Connemara is an almost uninhabited landscape of misty bogland, studded with deep blue lakes under huge Atlantic skies, and distant purple hills: painters and photographers have strived for generations to capture the ever-changing light. Nearby is the delightful village of Cong, setting for *The Quiet Man*, where fetching ivy-covered thatched cottages contrast with the baronial splendor of Ashford Castle. For bright lights, head to Clifden and Westport, both lively small towns of great charm.

10 The Northwest. Sligo, Leitrim, and Donegal are homelands of rugged, self-sufficient people and roads where wandering sheep and cows are still the norm. Weatherwise, the area gets more than its fair share of the elements—a condition more than compensated for in its warm welcomes. Take a poetry break beside Yeats's grave near Ben Bulben, discover hidden Glencolumbkille, and immerse yourself in Irish in Sligo town.

11 Northern Ireland. This region has positively bloomed since the peace dividend of recent times, which finally nailed the coffin lid upon "the Troubles." From the beauty of Antrim's coastline to the vibrant cultural renaissance of Derry and Belfast, Northern Ireland has finally emerged from the yoke of its sectarian past into a present full of promise and possibility. Cross the Giant's Causeway, relive the glory and tragedy of the world's most famous ship at the stunning Titanic Belfast, and trail after the island's ancient Celtic mysteries in the shimmery Glens of Antrim.

MAYO

Achill Island
Clare Island
Inishturk
Inishbofin

Clew Bay

Oileáin Árainn
(Aran Islands)

Kilru

Mouth of
the Shannon

Listo

Tralee

Corca Dhuibne
(Dingle Peninsula)

Blasket
Islands

Dingle Bay

Killa

Iveragh KERRY
Peninsula

Skellig
Rocks

Beara
Peninsula

Kenmare Bay

Bantry Bay

Mizen Head

IRELAND PLANNER

Safety

Ireland is still essentially a safe country, but you do need to observe some basic precautions.

Don't leave valuables in a rental car: this is advice countless visitors neglect with sad consequences. Most car theft is opportunistic—if there's nothing visible like a pocketbook, a bag, a camera, even maps or guides within the car, most likely your petty criminal will amble past toward more available pickings.

Likewise, when parking in urban areas, use a car park—this also guards against auto clampers (a recent scourge of Irish towns, where fines to release your car cost up to €130).

Carry only the minimal amount of cash with perhaps one credit card when strolling around the streets and shops—while handbag snatching is infrequent, there's no point in making yourself a possible target.

Getting Here

Dublin Airport is the main arrival point for the whole country, with regular flights from most of the world's major destinations. With the new road system, it is relatively easy to get from the airport to even the most isolated area in a few hours. Shannon Airport in County Clare also has direct flights from the United States and is a good starting point if you plan to explore in the West and Southwest. Belfast is the main airport in Northern Ireland and has direct flights from New York. Smaller airports at Cork, Knock, and Waterford have regular flights to the United Kingdom and mainland Europe. Ferries from Britain and France arrive at ports in Dublin, Rosslare, Larne, and Cork.

Getting Around

The Irish bus and rail network made great strides in recent decades, but recent cutbacks have seen a slight reduction in service and routes. All urban centers and towns are now interconnected by bus and rail, and you shouldn't have difficulty crisscrossing the country in any direction.

But if you can, opt for a car—its greater flexibility, combined with the possibility of meandering down byways and country lanes, opens up a great many more vistas than any train will do. Rental rates are on par with most EU countries, and offices are located at all airports, ferry terminals, and town centers. During the summer months, it's wise to book in advance.

FROM DUBLIN TO	BY CAR	BY TRAIN
Belfast	2 hrs 15 mins	2 hrs
Cork	3 hrs 5 mins	3 hrs
Galway	2 hrs 20 mins	2 hrs 10 mins
Kilkenny	1 hrs 30 mins	1 hr 45 mins
Killarney	3 hrs 50 mins	3 hrs 20 mins
Limerick	2 hrs 20 mins	2 hrs
Sligo	2 hrs 50 mins	3 hrs 5 mins

Restaurant Basics

For too many years the restaurant scene in Ireland was a bit of a joke among locals and visitors alike: exactly how many ways can you serve potatoes? One welcome legacy of the short-lived economic boom was an explosion of modern, metropolitan eateries. An influx of immigrants played its part, particularly the Chinese colonization of Parnell Street in Dublin and the sprouting up of real Italian enotecas like Delle Langhe. But Irish chefs also rose to the challenge, using Ireland's nonpareil produce to reimagine Irish cuisine, with places like One Pico in Dublin and the Cliff House in Ardmore, County Waterford, leading the way. The downturn saw a cull of some of the more ostentatious restaurants, but their abandoned premises have been snapped up (at a much cheaper rent) by a host of smaller, cooler, and more innovative eateries such as Wuff in Dublin and Las Rada in Kildare. There's definitely a hint of a restaurant renaissance going on in Ireland.

Overall, there's a return to good food, good quality, and good service. The locavore and slow-food movements have taken root in Ireland and the demand for organic and locally sourced produce is reflected on Irish menus around the country. Visitors are often surprised to find how celiac-friendly Irish restaurants are; look for the "C" for celiac on a growing number of restaurants around the country—there's even a separate line for gluten-free communion in one or two Masses!

Hotel Basics

Determining your budget is the key here—are you content with B&Bs and small hotels, or do you want to splurge on castles and grand country houses? It's best when planning your trip to Ireland to set aside a few hours of Web browsing to familiarize yourself with costs and standards. After a few years of falling prices things are on the increase again, especially in Dublin. But value is there to be had with careful planning, plus a bit of haggling if you are game. As well as our own site (⊕ fodors.com) which should be your first stop—try ⊕ www.ecotourismireland.ie and ⊕ www.visitdublin.ie. The Irish Tourist Board's website (⊕ www.ireland.com), is a mine of information and a good overview of the whole country. For a week's stay in Ireland, consider small city-center hotels in Dublin, Cork, and Galway. For at least one night, consider staying in a castle or country house—it'll be costly, but very memorable. Check out ⊕ www.irelandsbluebook. com for a select listing.

Stretching Your Dollar

At this writing, the dollar is struggling against the euro—($1.37 to €1)—but the situation is pretty fluid. While nobody wants to penny-pinch on vacation, a few changes can yield savings without upsetting your holiday.

For starters, take a bus from the airport—it'll be one-quarter the cost of a cab and will get you into town twice as fast on dedicated bus corridors now operating in all cities.

Stay at B&Bs. They're well located and they'll have comfy bedrooms, good food, and an all-knowing landlady to answer all your questions. Listen carefully to her advice on bargain shopping, as she's got an inside line you'll not find on any website. In restaurants, opt for the house wine—the Irish have become serious wine-drinkers in recent years and the house stuff is no longer just "plonk" for unsophisticated palates.

At lunchtime, why not try a picnic? After all, you're here to see scenery, and given that the changeable weather does allow for some dazzling sunshine most days, why not pack a few sandwiches and some drinks or coffee? Ireland is full of wonderful road pull-ins where you can park, walk a few minutes, and dine in glorious isolation to the sound of gurgling streams, lowing cows, or wind echoing across an open plain.

IRELAND TODAY

Politics

At last there's some light at the end of the tunnel for the Irish economy and the politicians who run it. Fianna Fáil, a center-right party that dominated Irish politics since independence, was cast into the wilderness in a post-economic-crash election. A coalition made up of center-right Fine Gael and the center-left Labour Party swept to power. Handcuffed from the outset, however, by an EU/IMF bailout agreement, the government has had to force through some of the most stringent and cruel budgets in the history of the state. The Irish have suffered this destructive regime of belt tightening with a certain mix of defeatism and stoicism. That doesn't mean the locals don't enjoy a good moan: At any bar, talk of politics will lead directly to the ailing economy or the poor state of the Irish health service—everybody will tell you stories of taking their kid to the local emergency room and waiting five hours for someone to look at a broken finger. But while public services are still suffering, the government has finally regained full control over the national economy and growth is starting to take hold.

Economics

While the green shoots are still quite fragile, there is a growing body of evidence that says the Irish economy has turned the corner. If your only contact with Ireland has been through the international media, you might be moved to pity and fear at the plight of this fragile, little island. In the last few years, the Irish have suffered the classic Greek tragedy (incidentally so have the Greeks). Years of double-digit growth had led to the pride and vanity of the Celtic Tiger, so the fall was far and deep when the international financial crisis swept across the old sod in a tsunami of bad debt.

But now Ireland's exports are climbing at record rates, with food processing and IT two growth areas, and the long dormant domestic market is finally starting to stir. But the recovery is slow and often concentrated in the more urban areas, especially Dublin. So tourism is a vital source of income elsewhere and travelers are valued more than ever, adding greatly to your haggling power.

Media

As the church confessional is no longer the purge-zone of choice for the majority of Irish people, radio and TV talk shows have stepped in to fill the void. Every topic under the sun is squeezed and caressed over the airwaves on a daily basis—the economy, of course, lesbian nuns, love on the Web, or mother-and-daughter double-date rules. The undisputed king of the chattering airways is Joe Duffy and his "must-listen" Liveline show every afternoon on RTE Radio 1. When the Irish are enraged about something, they don't take to the streets like the Greeks, they call Joe for a rant instead. Newspapers include the major three dailies: the *Irish Times* (⊕ *www.irishtimes.com*), the *Irish Independent* (⊕ *www.independent.ie*), and the *Irish Examiner* (⊕ *www.irishexaminer.com*), and these are also the major sources of online news. A host of U.K. tabloids have also entered the market in recent years, with the *Mail*, the *Sun*, and the *Mirror* being the main contenders. So-called freesheets—morning commuter giveaway papers containing a condensed version of the day's news plus heaps of advertising—are similarly flexing their literary muscles.

People

For all of their dangerous propensity to rack up the biggest credit card debt in Europe on BMWs, boob jobs, and second homes on Capri, most Irish were, at heart, as confused by life in Celtic Tiger Ireland as the tourists might have been. It all came to us too fast and too flashy, how could we say no? The Irish, when they have a job, still work some of the longest hours, on average, in Europe, but despite their breezy, world-weary air, they remain largely as enthusiastic and comic about life as they ever were. One caller to a radio show summed up his ideal life: "a two-car garage, sex with my wife twice a week, a 12 handicap, and kids who won't call me a loser to my face." The average Joe is in there somewhere

Religion

Priests and bishops (and even the Pope) continue to hit the headlines through sex scandals and revelations of criminal pedophilia cover-ups that have rocked Ireland for more than a decade. The church has fallen a long way in the estimation of most of the population, and suddenly the media is not afraid to ask some searing questions about the church's past and future. Older people are struggling to come to terms with this national loss of trust in their hallowed institution, while increasing numbers of younger folks are turning their backs on regular Mass-going.

Irish-born men entering the priesthood is down to a handful each year and African priests are often shipped in to fill the breach. A majority of the population will still go to church for births, marriages, and funerals but there is a noted decrease in involvement of priests in the social fabric of Irish life. While the more liberal Pope Francis has stemmed the tide

a little, the Catholic Church in Ireland, it seems, will have to quickly redefine and rebrand itself if it is not to go the way of the Church of England in the United Kingdom and become a minority sideshow.

Sports

In these dark times the enduring love affair between the Irish and their sports has taken on an added importance. Rory McIlroy's surge to the top of the golfing world lifted the nation's spirits, just as the national soccer team's recent failures sent us all to cry into our pints. But on a local level Gaelic football and hurling are still the sports that really matter. With parish pitted against parish and county against county, the passions run deep and every victory and defeat feels personal. Horse racing also holds a special place in Irish hearts—note the bookie's shop on every main street—and we seem to have the uncanny knack for breeding some of the best Thoroughbreds on the planet.

Culture

No amount of technology can dent the nation's fondness for the written word. Although there have been few to match the talent of Shaw, Wilde, and Joyce, the huge-selling works of Joe O'Connor, Roddy Doyle, Colum McCann, and Colm Tóibín underline the country as one of the biggest book-buying populations in Europe. In the theater playwrights like Conor McPherson and Martin McDonagh tell Irish stories to a world audience.

In the movies, time and tide have taken us a long way from John Wayne in *The Quiet Man* to the modern romance of *Once* and writer-directors like Neil Jordan and John McDonagh and their warts-and-all visions of modern Ireland.

IRELAND
TOP ATTRACTIONS

The Rock of Cashel

(A) The center of tribal and religious power for more than a thousand years, it became the seat of the Munster Kings in the 5th century. Handed over to the early Christian Church in 1101, the medieval abbey perched on a limestone mount in Tipperary contains rare Romanesque sculpture and carvings celebrating St. Patrick's visit there in 450.

The Giant's Causeway

(B) Irish mythology claims that the warrior Fionn Mac Cumhaill (Finn McCool) laid the Antrim causeway himself to enable easy crossing to his lover on Staffa Island off the Scottish coast, where similar basalt columns are found. Formed by volcanic eruptions more than 60 million years ago, the area is a magical mix of looming cliffs and thundering surf—and an awesome reminder of nature's power.

Newgrange

(C) Stonehenge and the pyramids at Giza are spring chickens compared to Newgrange, one of the most fascinating sites near Dublin. Built around 5,200 years ago, Newgrange is a passage tomb—a huge mound of earth with a stone passageway leading to a burial chamber constructed entirely of drystone (mortar wasn't invented yet). Steeped in Celtic myth and lore, these graves were built for the Kings of Tara. Untouched for centuries, the main chamber was excavated in the 1960s and revealed itself as the world's oldest solar observatory, where the sun's rays light up the interior on December 21 each year.

Book of Kells

(D) If you visit only one attraction in Dublin, let it be this extraordinary creation housed in Trinity College. Often called "the most beautiful book in the world," the manuscript dates to the 8th or 9th

century and remains a marvel of intricacy and creativity. Fashioned by monks probably based on the Hebridean island of Iona, and worked with reed pens and iron-gall ink on a folded section of vellum, the manuscript demonstrates a sense of sublime balance and beauty in elaborate interlaces, abstractions, and "carpet-pages."

The Blarney Stone

(E) One of the country's most enduring myths, wherein kissing a stone high upon the battlements of a ruined Cork castle bestows a magical eloquence on the visitor, may also be one of its most ludicrous. Grasped by the ankles and hanging perilously upside down to pucker up for an ancient rock, you'll certainly have a tall tale to tell the folks back home. Despite the difficulty, there's generally a long line waiting to scale the skeletal remains of Blarney Castle, a strangely derelict edifice

in the otherwise neatly groomed estate; try to visit in the very early morning.

Ring of Kerry

(F) Ireland's most popular scenic route, the Ring of Kerry is one of Europe's grandest drives, combining mountainous splendor with a spectacularly varied coastline. It's best to escape the tour buses that choke its main road by taking to the hills on foot, by horseback, or by bike.

Aran Islands

(G) Famed for their haunting beauty, these three islands set in Galway Bay have lured artists, writers, and multitudes of curious visitors for decades. On Inishmore, Inishmaan, and Inisheer you'll find a mode of life that reflects man's struggle against nature. Topped with the stone forts and crisscrossed by ancient "garden" walls, they epitomize solitude—one reason Irish bards like playwright J. M. Synge visited them many times.

FESTIVALS AND EVENTS

Make Like a Bird

Happening on the May Bank Holiday Weekend, the **Kinvara Cuckoo Fleadh** (⊕ *www.kinvara.com/cuckoo*) is perfectly timed to welcome in the warmer evenings of early summer. A well-established and richly deserved reputation has ensured that the fleadh has become a showcase for the best in traditional music, attracting musicians from all over the country and beyond. An added bonus is having it in one of the country's prettiest towns in beautiful County Galway.

Sonatas in Ancient Grandeur

Among the architectural grandeur that is Bantry House in Cork, the West Cork Chamber Music Festival (⊕ *www.westcorkmusic.ie*) allows for languid sunsets, picnics on the lawns, and sublime sounds from some of Europe's top classical musicians. The notes may be highbrow, but the vibe is indelibly Irish-mellow. The festival runs from the last week in June until the first week in July.

The Write Stuff

Fancy getting up close and personal with Lawrence Block, Roddy Doyle, Colm Tóbín, Neil Jordan, Anne Enright, and a host of other literary greats? **Listowel Writer's Week** (⊕ *www.writersweek.ie*) is a chaotic and seriously democratic gathering devoted to all things literary—including numerous workshops by the greats where info on writing your own masterpiece is there for the asking. This being Kerry, expect discussions to last well toward dawn. It takes place all over the town of Listowel on the first weekend in June.

Get Your Rugby On

Every spring rugby fever grips the country as the Six Nations Tournament (⊕ *www.rbs6nations.com*) begins. The beloved Irish team take on the might of Wales, France, Scotland, Italy, and the old enemy England in a series of bone-crunching encounters. At least two of the games take place at the Aviva Stadium in Dublin and game weekends are great times to be in and around the capital.

Lark in the Park

Every June, Cork city struts its artistic stuff with the **Midsummer Festival** (⊕ *www.corkmidsummer.com*), a mix of music, film, and theater. Be sure to get tickets for whatever the Corcadorca Theatre Company is doing—in the past they've taken Shakespeare to the local courthouse, the city morgue, and the expansive green spaces of Fitzgerald's Park: a very different experience from a company constantly pushing the envelope. It runs from the 21st of June to the end of the month.

Blooming Forth

Even though it is now reckoned that more Americans and Japanese attend the events surrounding **Bloomsday** (⊕ *www.jamesjoyce.ie*) than Irish people, it hasn't taken away a jot from an event that continues to grow regardless. Most Irish, if they're being honest, will probably admit to "never having actually finished *Ulysses*," but are still happy to discourse at length over deviled kidneys and other Joycean delights on the hidden meanings within this legendary work. Bloomsday is June 16th.

Have a Flutter on the Nags

Galway Race Week (⊕ *www.galwayraces.com*) is one of the country's biggest events with most of Dublin, Cork, and Limerick decamping to the City of the Tribes for an end of July week of celebration centered half around equine excellence and half around pub sessions. Every politician worth his salt hits the races to press the flesh, followed by legions of supporters

and onlookers out for the "craic"—of which there is an endless supply.

Good for the Sole

On the last Sunday in July, join the thousands of pilgrims and adventurers who climb Mayo's **Croagh Patrick** (⊕ *www. croagh-patrick.com*)—and in your bare feet for the full purging of your misdeeds. A ghostly hill, tricky loose stones underfoot, and a Mass overlooking Clew Bay: it all adds up to an experience that is difficult but hugely rewarding.

Acting the Goat

Puck Fair in Kerry (⊕ *www.puckfair.ie*) is the oldest festival in Ireland, dating back to pagan times, where a goat is made king for three days of drinking, dancing, and general abandon. In the town of Killorglin, County Kerry, pubs stay open all night, traveler folk sell horses and cows on Main Street, and up to 100,000 people crowd this tiny town of 58 pubs for a mad three-day weekend. Held on the second weekend in August, all in all, it's truly one of Ireland's most unusual festivals.

Gather Those Boats

Cruínniu na mBád (⊕ *www.kinvara.com/ cruinniu*), or the Gathering of the Boats, is basically a big booze-up and regatta to celebrate the unique and beautiful boat that is the *Galway Hooker*—a sleek, dark little sailing vessel with rusty red sails originally used to transport turf and other necessities along the harsh Atlantic coast of Ireland. The event takes place around the third weekend in August around southern County Galway, with traditional boat races the excuse for a "hooley," or party of trad music and late nights.

Clash of the Ash

Usually the first Sunday in September, the **All-Ireland Hurling Final** (⊕ *www.gaa.ie*), at Dublin's Croke Park, is a uniquely Irish sporting spectacle. Thirty highly amped players clutching ash hurleys whack a heavy leather ball, or *sliothar,* at warp speeds around the pitch as they slug it out for the sport's highest prize. Raw emotions, brilliant color, and geometry-defying skills that you won't see back home make it memorable.

Food, Glorious Food

Long noted for its cuisine innovations, the **Kinsale Gourmet Festival** (⊕ *www. kinsalerestaurants.com*) is all about the happy pursuit of great food and wine plus the excitable bravado of this infectious coastal town. Buy a weekend ticket, have breakfast on a boat, lunch at a pierside pub, and dinner at any of the dozens of great eateries in this amazingly friendly town. It takes place on the second weekend in October.

What a Wonderful World

For jazz lovers, the **Cork Jazz Festival** (⊕ *www.guinnessjazzfestival.com*) on the Halloween bank holiday weekend in October is a perfect antidote to the approaching dark evenings of winter. George Melly, one of the music legends who visits regularly, puts it thus: "I forget where I've parked, where I'm meant to be playing, and, sometimes, even who I am—but it all works out in the end."

QUINTESSENTIAL IRELAND

The Pub: Pillar of Irish Social Life

It's been said that the pub is the poor man's university. If this is true, Ireland has more than 10,000 opportunities for higher education. Even if you only order an Evian, a visit to a pub (if not two or three) is a must.

The Irish public house is a national institution—down to the spectacle, at some pubs, of patrons standing at closing time for the playing of Ireland's national anthem. Samuel Beckett would often repair to a pub, believing a glass of Guinness stout was the best way to ward off depression.

Pubs remain pillars of Irish social life—places to chat, listen, learn, gossip, and, of course, enjoy a throaty sing-along.

Impromptu concerts often break out, and if you're really enjoying the craic—quintessentially Irish friendly chat and lively conversation—it's good form to buy a pint for the performers.

Wherever you go, remember that when you order a Guinness, the barman first pours it three-quarters of the way, then lets it settle, then tops it off and brings it over to the bar.

The customer should then wait again until the top-up has settled, at which point the brew turns a deep black.

The mark of a perfect pint? As you drink the liquid down, the brew will leave thin rings on the glass to mark each mouthful.

"Fleadhs" and Festivals

From bouncing-baby competitions to traditional-music festivals, the tradition of the *fleadh* (festival, pronounced "flah") is alive and well in Ireland year-round.

Before you leave home, check on regional Irish tourist websites or, upon arrival, discuss the local happenings with local tourist boards or your hotel concierge.

Music festivals rule the roost—Kinvara's Cuckoo Fleadh, Galway's Festival

If you want to get a sense of Irish culture and indulge in some of its pleasures, start by familiarizing yourself with the rituals of daily life. These are a few highlights—things you can take part in with relative ease.

of Early Music, the giant Fleadh Cheoil na hÉireann, and the World Irish Dancing Championships (held every April in Ennis) are some major events.

But there are also village festivals dedicated to hill walking, fishing, poetry, art, and food; the Mullaghmore Lobster Festival in August always proves mighty tasty.

Keep A'Clappin' and A'Tappin'

Ceol agus craic, loosely translated as "music and merriment," are not simply recreations in Ireland. They are part of the very fabric of the national identity.

Ask most Irish men or women in exile what they miss most about home and, more than likely, those words "the craic" will be uttered.

And the beat and rhythm that accompany Irish fun are the "4/4" of the reel and the jig. Wherever you go you'll find that every town buzzes with its own blend of styles and sounds.

In its most exciting form, "trad" music is an impromptu affair, with a single guitar or fiddle player belting out a few tunes until other musicians—flute, whistle, uilleann pipes, concertina, and bodhrán drum—seem to arrive out of the pub's dark corners and are quickly drawn into the unstoppable force of the session.

A check of local event guides will turn up a wealth of live entertainment—if you're lucky you'll find a world-class artist in performance whose talents are unsung outside a small circle of friends and fans.

On some nights, Dublin itself—with more than 120 different clubs and music pubs to choose from—almost becomes one giant traditional-music jam session. Where to head first? Just take a walk through Smithfield or the Liberties and keep your ears open.

WHEN TO GO

You don't come to Ireland for the weather. As the saying goes, "If you could put a roof on the country it'd be perfect." That said, in summer the weather *can* be pleasant: the ever-present rain clouds responsible for the ever-green countryside often take a vacation; the sun comes out (and everything in the country comes to a halt to appreciate it!); and the days are long, with daylight lasting until after 10 in late June and July. As British and Irish school vacations overlap from late June to mid-September, vacationers descend on popular coastal resorts in the South, West, and East. There are crowds in popular holiday spots, and prices for accommodations are at their peak. Festival season is also at its peak; in the summer months the country is host to festival events big and small, offering a wide variety of music festivals like Electric Picnic, Castlepalooza, and Spirit of Folk Festival, as well as events celebrating everything from food and comedy, to surfing, goats, and Irish beauty. Local sports also heat up in the summer months as counties battle it out to reach the All-Ireland hurling and football finals in September. In short, if you can afford the flights and peak rates, summer is the time to visit.

If the purse strings are a little unforgiving, it's best to visit Ireland outside peak travel months. Fall and spring are good times to travel (late September can be dry and warm, although the weather can be unpredictable). Seasonal hotels and restaurants close from early or mid-November until mid-March or Easter. During this off-season, prices are lower than in summer, but your selection is limited, and some minor attractions close. St. Patrick's Week gives a focal point to a spring visit, but some Americans may find the saint's-day celebrations a little less enthusiastic than the ones back home. Dublin, however, has a weekend-long series of activities, including a parade and the Lord Mayor's Ball. If you're planning an Easter visit, don't forget that most theaters close from Thursday to Sunday of Holy Week (the week preceding Easter), and all bars and restaurants, except those serving hotel guests, close on Good Friday. Many hotels arrange Christmas packages. Mid-November to mid-February is either too cold or too wet for all but the keenest golfers, although some of the coastal links courses are playable.

Festivals

If you plan to visit the biggest festivals in Ireland, book well in advance. In March, Ireland's major St. Patrick's event is the **Dublin Festival and Parade** (⊕ *www. stpatricksday.ie*), which includes fireworks and bands from the United States. In April, see the spectacular **World Irish Dancing Championships**. In May, the **Fleadh Nua,** the annual festival of traditional Irish music, song, and dance, takes place at a town (on a yearly rotation) in County Clare. August brings a "trad" music highlight: the **Fleadh Cheoil na hEireann** (⊕ *www.fleadhcheoil.ie*), held the last weekend of August or the first weekend in September, an extravaganza across the country. In October, the **Dublin Theatre Festival** (⊕ *www.dublintheatrefestival. com*) puts on about 10 international productions, 10 Irish plays, and a fringe of 60-plus plays. In October, the **Wexford Opera Festival** (⊕ *www.wexfordopera. com*) is high glamour.

IF YOU LIKE

Beautiful Irish Villages

Nearly everyone has a mind's-eye view of the perfect Irish village. Cozy huddles filled with charming calendar-ready cottages, mossy churchyards, and oozing with thatched-roof, pewter-and-china-dog atmosphere, these spots have a sense of once-upon-a-time tranquillity that not even tour buses can ruin. Should you be after medicine for overtired nerves—a gentle peace in beautiful surroundings with a people so warm you'll be on first-name terms in five minutes—these will be your Arcadias. Many are so nestled away they remain the despair of motorists, but then, no penciled itinerary is half as fun as stumbling upon these four-leaf clovers. Here are four of the most famous—but why not summon up courage, venture out on the lesser roads, and throw away the map?

Kinvara, Co. Galway. This village is picture-perfect, thanks to its gorgeous bayside locale, great walks, and numerous pubs. North of the town is spectacularly sited Dunguaire Castle, noted for its medieval-banquet evenings.

Cong, Co. Mayo. John Ford's *The Quiet Man* introduced this charmer to the world and the singular beauty of its whitewashed single-story cottages with tied-on thatched roofs.

Adare, Co. Limerick. Right out of a storybook, this celebrated village of low-slung Tudor cottages is adorned with ivied churches and a moated castle from the days when knighthood was in flower.

Lismore, Co. Waterford. Set within some of Ireland's lushest pasturelands and lorded over by the Duke of Devonshire's castle, dreamy Lismore is popular with both romantic folk and anglers (the sparkling Blackwater here teems with salmon).

Celtic Sites

From rush hour on busy O'Connell Street in Dublin it's a long way to Tipperary's Cashel of the Kings, a group of ancient church relics—the largest in all Ireland—perched high above the plain on its famous rock. The journey is worth it, since it takes you back in time to the legendary days when Celtic Christianity conquered the isle of Eire. Beginning in the 5th century AD, hallowed shrines and monasteries sprung up across the land, often dotted with treasures sacred—the famous High Crosses, inscribed with biblical symbols and stories—and profane, such as the lofty round towers, lookouts for Viking raids. Just north of Dublin, around the Boyne Valley, you'll find two great sites: Tara, where "The Harp That Once Through Tara's Halls" played, and also Newgrange, once seat of the High Kings of Ireland.

Clonmacnoise, Co. Offaly. The isolated monastery at the confluence of two rivers was famous throughout Europe as a center of learning. It's also a royal burial ground.

Glendalough, Co. Wicklow. A monastery founded by a hermit in the 6th century, attacked by Vikings in the 10th century, and plundered by the English in the 12th century—your typical Irish ruins.

Rock of Cashel, Co. Tipperary. A cluster of ruins—cathedral, chapel, round tower—crowning a circular, mist-shrouded rock that rises from a plain.

Tara, Co. Meath. Fabled home of one of Ireland's titular High Kings, the ageless Hill of Tara has fired up people's imaginations from early Christians to Scarlett O'Hara.

Stately Houses

Ireland's stately homes are either proud reminders of a shared history with Britain or symbols of an oppressive colonial past. If you're interested in luxurious pomp and reliving the decadence of yesteryear, there's no denying the magnificence of these country estates and lavish mansions, erected by the Anglo-Irish Protestant Ascendancy in the 17th, 18th, and 19th centuries. The wealthy settlers constructed ornate houses in various architectural styles, with Palladian designs popular in the first half of the 18th century, before the Neoclassical and neo-Gothic influences took over. In the last century, several majestic piles—notably Ashford Castle in Cong and Dromoland Castle in Newmarket-on-Fergus—became hotels, so anyone can now enjoy a queen-for-a-stay fantasy.

Castle Ward, Co. Down. An architectural curiosity, in that it was built inside and out in two distinct styles, Classical and Gothic—perhaps because Viscount Bangor and his wife never could agree on anything.

Bantry House, Bantry, Co. Cork. Set in Italianate gardens and perched over one of Ireland's most spectacular bays, this manor has a Continental air, thanks to its extensive art collection, tapestries, and fine French furniture.

Castletown House, Co. Kildare. Renaissance architect Andrea Palladio would surely have approved of this exceedingly large and grand Palladian country house.

Florence Court, Co. Fermanagh. With magnificent Georgian-period stuccoed salons, this shimmering white mansion is strikingly set against the Cuilcagh Mountains where, legend has it, you can hear the "song of the little people."

Retail Therapy

Once you get past all the traditional Irish leprechauns with "made in China" stickers on their bottoms, you'll find that Ireland has some of Europe's finest-quality goods. Objects like a Donegal tweed hat or a hand-knit Aran sweater, a Belfast linen tablecloth, or a piece of Waterford or Cavan crystal can be pricey but will last a lifetime. In Dublin look for antiques, vintage books, or au courant European and Irish fashions, many showcased at cool shops like Costume and Platform. Galway has its share of galleries and offbeat boutiques and is a great spot for book shopping. Keep an eye open for signs indicating crafts workshops, where independent craftspeople sell directly from their studios. The best of the North's traditional products, many made according to time-honored methods, include exquisite linen, laces, and superior handmade woolen garments. Traditional-music CDs and the unadorned blackthorn walking stick are two good choices at the other end of the price scale.

Kilkenny Design Craft Centre, Co. Kilkenny. Ireland's favorite emporium for Irish-designed crafts includes the best of Irish knitwear, crystal, jewelry, and pottery.

O'Sullivan Antiques, Dublin. Mia Farrow and Liam Neeson are just two fans of this purveyor of 19th-century delights.

Ardmore Pottery and Craft Gallery, Ardmore, Co. Waterford. Home to potter Mary Lincoln, this is one of the most beloved, creative, and cleverly stocked crafts shops in the country.

Avoca, Co. Wicklow. The birthplace of the legendary Avoca mill, you can shop for vibrant throws, rugs, and scarves and meet the weavers at work.

Natural Wonders

It's not always easy to conjure up leprechauns and druids in today's Ireland, but head to any of its famously brooding landscapes and those legendary times will seem like yesterday. With its romantic coastlines, wild bogs, and rugged seascapes, the Emerald Isle is especially rich in rugged, wildly gorgeous spectacle. Around its natural splendors, the countryside is dotted with villages where sheep outnumber residents by 100 to 1. Unfortunately, sheep don't also outnumber tourists.

The Aran Islands, Galway Bay. The islands battle dramatically with sea and storm and now welcome droves of visitors who fall under the spell of their brooding beauty.

The Skelligs, Ring of Kerry. Be warned: these spectacular pinnacles of rock soaring out of the sea will haunt you for days.

The Burren, Co. Clare. A 300-square-km (116-square-mile) expanse that is one of Ireland's strangest landscapes, the Burren stretches off as far as the eye can see in a gray, rocky, lunar landscape that becomes a wild rock garden in spring.

Cliffs of Moher, Co. Clare. One of Ireland's most breathtaking natural sights, these majestic cliffs stretch for 8 km (5 miles). At some points, the only thing separating you from the sea, 700 feet below, is a patch of slippery heather.

Giant's Causeway, Co. Antrim, Northern Ireland. There are equal measures of legend and science surrounding this rock formation—a cluster of 37,000-odd volcanic basalt pillars.

Literary Haunts

Irish literature developed its distinctive traits largely because of Ireland's physical and political isolation. Yet the nation has produced a disproportionately large number of internationally famous authors for a country of her size, including four Nobel Prize winners—George Bernard Shaw, W. B. Yeats, Samuel Beckett, and Seamus Heaney. The list of literary notables is a whole lot longer and includes James Joyce, Oscar Wilde, Sean O'Casey, Seán Ó'Faoláin, Brian Friel, and Edna O'Brien. Indeed, the country's literary heritage is evident everywhere you go. In Dublin you'll find Joyce's Liffey; Dean Swift's cathedral; and the Abbey Theatre, a potent symbol of Ireland's great playwrights. Yeats opens up the county of Sligo; the Aran Islands were the inspiration of J. M. Synge; and Cork inspired the works of Frank O'Connor. Wherever you are in Ireland, its literary heritage is never far away.

Trinity College, Dublin. Founded by Queen Elizabeth I, this university provided the greats—Beckett, Wilde, Stoker—with 30 acres of stomping grounds.

Limerick City, Co. Limerick. Frank McCourt's *Angela's Ashes* had thousands heading here to tour Angela's city and partake of the tearfulness of it all.

Sligo Town, Co. Sligo. Take in the town where William Butler Yeats grew up, then visit his grave in Drumcliff to view his beloved mountain, Ben Bulben.

Aran Islands, Co. Galway. See what inspired the dark genius of Synge's *Playboy of the Western World* and the black comedy of Martin McDonagh's The *Cripple of Inishmaan*.

FLAVORS OF IRELAND

A Food Evolution

You'll hear a lot of talk about a food revolution in Ireland over the last 20 years but in truth much of the country still has some way to go in terms of the quality of the restaurant meals it serves up. Unlike more culinary sophisticated parts of Europe the unsavvy visitor cannot just wander into a local eatery and expect quality. You'll need to use this book and other research to make informed selections. The good news is that there are plenty of exciting choices out there. The best of these have been heavily influenced by the "Slow Food" movement, which has its Irish heart among the artisan producers of the Southwest. Their emphasis on locally sourced produce has helped open the eyes of a new generation of chefs to the world-beating quality Irish produce. Not the packaged and heavily processed food-industry products that the government likes to promote around the world, but the fresh, organic, and wild meat, veg, and dairy that this little island does better than anywhere else. When the food-loving French and Italians come to Ireland, watch them rave over the quality of the game, the oysters and the raw-milk cheeses.

The best of these restaurants, such as The Cliff House in Ardmore and Campagne in Kilkenny, have internationally recognized chefs brave enough to put their own twist and signature on these stunning raw materials. But perhaps even more exciting is the blossoming of a host of great value but inventive smaller eateries in places that were once good-food deserts. For example the wonderful Irish tapas joint Las Rada in Naas has forced the rest of the town to raise its culinary game. At the retail level there's been an explosion in farmers' markets to give an outlet for these artisan producers. The monopoly of

Guinness and the other major beer makers has been challenged by a slew of new microbreweries and small whiskeys labels. So the message is clear, Irish food can be a thrilling experience, but you have to seek out the gems yourself.

Natural Bounty

Dairy. Ireland is a grass-growers dream, and finally has some cheese and dairy producers who know how to lovingly showcase thick, creamy Irish milk. West Cork and Kerry are the epicenters of this new cheese movement. Gubeen, Ardsallagh, and Knockalara are some of the key labels to look out for. Their focus is on traditional methods and organically produced milk from their own farms. These family farms are also expanding to goats cheeses, yogurts, and even ice creams.

Game. Irish chefs are often at their best when working with fresh game, so keep an eye out for in-season partridge, wood pigeon, pheasant, and wild duck and goose during the fall and winter. They are usually roasted and served with minimal fuss, allowing all the focus on the deep, wild, flavor of the meat. Venison on Irish plates is usually farmed, but the quality is still high and it's great in a winter stew.

Seafood. For an island nation the Irish have been surprisingly poor eaters of fish and seafood. But that, too, is changing, with a new appreciation of the glory of our oysters, scallops, lobster, mussels, and the rest. Summer is high season for the best of the sea's bounty. Whitefish stocks have fallen dramatically, so other varieties have come back in favor. The "superfood" mackerel is a great example of a long-overlooked variety that is finally being discovered by chefs and the general public alike. You can buy it fresh off the boat in fishing villages all along the South and West coasts, and it's great with a little gooseberry sauce.

Meat. Grazing cows are the ubiquitous image of the local countryside and it's no surprise Ireland is the world's fifth-largest beef exporter. In Ireland it's not considered a meal unless there's meat on the plate. Look for the organic producers to get the true taste of the gorgeous grass coming through in the Angus and Hereford beef. Eat lamb in spring, when it's fresh off the mountains of Wicklow and the West and still hints of the wild herbs and grasses that grow there.

Beer and whiskey. The bitter, creamy taste of Guinness is the quintessential flavor of Ireland, but a host of exciting small beer and whiskey manufacturers have set about challenging that position. Irish whiskey tends to be smoother and easier to drink than Scotch, and finally the whiskey connoisseur has a full palate of Irish brands to choose from. Makers like Celtic Cask are even producing an Irish single malt. The craft beer phenomena has recently taken off in Ireland, with particular success in making slightly lighter and sweeter stouts, like O'Hara's from Carlow.

Traditional Dishes

Many traditional Irish dishes originate in the poor tenant farmer culture in which no part of the animal or crop could be wasted. The best Irish chefs like to play with these dishes and give them some new life.

Black and white pudding. Traditionally a farmer's breakfast dish, black pudding is a blend of pork fat, onions, oatmeal, herbs, and spices all blended with pig's blood. The white variety is pretty much the same thing minus the blood. In recent years the delicacies have migrated onto restaurant menus, especially in daring starters where their strong tastes are contrasted with something sweet like apple.

Boxty. From the Irish meaning "poorhouse bread," boxty is a traditional Irish potato pancake. Associated mostly with Ulster and the Northwest, it's a mix of grated raw potato and mashed potato, flour, baking soda, and buttermilk fried on a griddle pan for a few minutes on each side. Modern boxty might have a touch of garlic or some spice to liven it up, and it is usually served as a base or wrapping for something like chicken in a creamy smoked bacon–and–leek sauce.

Sausages. Another traditional breakfast staple that has undergone a transformation is the humble sausage. Usually made with pork, you'll now find beef and lamb versions are quite common. But the real change has come in the fantastic variety of flavors on offer, from toasted fennel and chili flakes to apple and craft Irish cider. A lot of the best butchers make their own varieties. A classic Dublin dish is coddle, layers of sausages and rashers (bacon) with sliced potatoes and onions all boiled in a well-seasoned pot.

Corned beef and cabbage. Cabbage is a much-maligned vegetable that the Irish have taken to their heart. Farmers grow different varieties year-round, with a spring York cabbage considered standout. When combined with a quality corned beef, the dish should be slow cooked, with a dash of mustard tossed into the cabbage. A nice piece of bacon can be substituted for the corned beef, and the cabbage should always be cooked in the water used to boil the meat (before putting it in the oven). The whole thing is usually topped off with a creamy leek-and-parsley sauce and, of course, some mashed Irish spuds.

GREAT ITINERARIES

The East and the South

5 to 10 days. Dublin's literary charm and Georgian riches, and rugged County Wicklow and the historic Meath plains are all just a few hours' drive from each other. Here you'll find the Boyne Valley, the cradle of native Irish civilization—no one will want to miss sacred Tara, Kells, Newgrange, and Glendalough, all time-burnished sites that guard the roots of Irishness. More idyllic pleasures can be found at Powerscourt, the grandest gardens in the land. In the south you'll find fishing towns and bustling markets, coastal panoramas, and—just outside crazy Killarney (oh, and it is crazy, an emerald-green Orlando)—stunning mountain-and-lake scenery.

Dublin

1 to 3 days. Dublin's pleasures are uncontainable. James Joyce's Dublin holds treasures for all sorts. Literary types: explore Trinity College, Beckett's stomping grounds, and its legendary *Book of Kells*. Visit key Joyce sites and the Dublin Writers Museum, and indulge in the Dublin Literary Pub Crawl. Joyce fanatics: arrive a week before Bloomsday (June 16) for Bloomstime celebrations. Literary or not, stroll around the city center and take in the elegant Georgian architecture around St. Stephen's Green, austere Dublin Castle, and the national treasures in the museums around Merrion Square and pedestrianized Grafton Street. Check out Temple Bar, Dublin's party zone, and join locals in this city-of-1,000-pubs for a foamy pint in the late afternoon. Pubs are the center of Dublin activity, and the locals never lose their natural curiosity about "strangers." You will frequently be asked, "Are you enjoying your holiday?" "Yes" is not good enough: what they're really after is your life story, and if you

haven't got a good one you might want to make one up. Pay your respects by taking a tour of the ever-popular Guinness Brewery and Storehouse. Night options: catch a show at W. B. Yeats's old haunt, the Abbey Theatre; see some Victorian music hall shows at the Olympia Theatre; or listen to traditional or alternative music at a pub or other venue. Last call arrives early at pubs, even here, so if you're still revved, go to Leeson Street and hit the nightclubs. For a dose of unmitigated Irish enthusiasm, join the roaring crowds at Croke Park and see some traditional Gaelic football and hurling.

Boyne Valley and County Wicklow

2 days. Walt Disney couldn't have planned it better. The small counties immediately to the north, south, and west of Dublin—historically known as the Pale—seem expressly designed for the sightseer. The entire region is like an open-air museum, layered with legendary Celtic sites, spectacular gardens, and elegant Palladian country estates. First head to the Boyne Valley, a short trip north of the capital. Spend the morning walking among the Iron Age ruins of the rolling Hill of Tara. After a picnic lunch on top of the hill, drive through ancient Kells—one of the centers of early Christianity in Ireland—and then to Newgrange, famous for its ancient passage graves. One thousand years older than Stonehenge, the great white-quartz structure merits two or three hours. Spend the rest of your day driving through the low hills and valleys of County Meath and to Georgian-era Slane, a manorial town planned by the Conynghams. Dominating the town are elegant Slane Castle and 500-foot Slane Hill. Backtrack to Kells or continue to Drogheda and spend the night. The following day, head south of

Dublin through the County Wicklow mountains. You might want to stop in one of the small, quiet towns along the Wicklow Way hiking trail and go for a short hike. Drive on to stately Powerscourt House, whose gardens epitomize the glory and grandeur of the Anglo-Irish aristocracy. From the profane to the sacred, head next to the "monastic city" of Glendalough and the medieval monastery of the hermit St. Kevin. Repair to Ireland's highest village, Roundwood, for lunch at the town's 17th-century inn.

West Cork and Kerry

4 days. Head about 250 km (155 miles) southwest to Cork City, filled with tall Georgian houses and old quays and perfect for a half day of walking. The place has few don't-miss attractions, but that's not the point: unlike many other towns, Cork is very much alive. It has a progressive university, art galleries, offbeat cafés, a formidable pub scene, and some of the country's best traditional music. Drive south to Kinsale, once heralded as the gourmet capital of Ireland, an old fishing town turned resort, with many good restaurants. A slow three- or four-hour drive along the coast and up through the small towns of West Cork takes you through the kind of landscape that inspired Ireland's

nickname, the Emerald Isle. Spend the night in the market town of Skibbereen. Next morning, cross into County Kerry and head straight for Killarney, at the center of a scattering of azure lakes and heather-clad mountains. Although it has been almost transformed into a Celtic theme park by a flood of tourists, it's a good base for exploring your pick of two great Atlantic-pounded peninsulas: the strikingly scenic Ring of Kerry and the beloved Dingle Peninsula. Both offer stunning ocean views, hilly landscapes (like the Macgillycuddy's Reeks mountains), and welcoming towns with good B&Bs. To do justice to the fabulous views of the Ring, you need a minimum of two days, especially if traveling by bus. The five-hour drive back to Dublin takes you through Limerick City and the lakes of the Midlands.

The West and the North

7 to 8 days. "To hell or to Connaught" was the choice given the native population by Cromwell, and indeed the harsh, barren landscape of parts of the West and North might appear cursed to the eye of an uprooted farmer. But there's an appeal in the very wildness of Counties Clare, Galway, Mayo, Sligo, and Donegal, with their stunning, steep coastlines hammered

and shaped for eons by the Atlantic. Here, in isolated communities, you'll hear locals speaking Irish as they go about their business. The arrival of peace has opened the lush pastures of long-suffering Northern Ireland to travelers.

Galway and Clare

2 days. A three-hour drive west from Dublin leads straight to the 710-foot-high Cliffs of Moher, perhaps the single most impressive sight in Ireland. Using the waterside village of Ballyvaughan as your base, spend a day exploring the lunar landscape of the harsh, limestone Burren. In spring it becomes a mighty rock garden of exotic colors. The next morning, head north out of Ballyvaughan toward Galway City. On the way you'll pass 2-million-year-old Ailwee Cave and the picture-perfect village of Kinvara. Galway City, spectacularly overlooking Galway Bay, is rapidly growing, vibrant, and packed with culture and history. If time allows, drive west to Ros an Mhíl (Rossaveal) and take a boat to the fabled Aran Islands. Spend the night in Galway City.

North and West to Donegal

3 days. Northwest of Galway City is tiny Clifden, with some of the country's best Atlantic views. From here, head east through one of the most beautiful stretches of road in Connemara—through Kylemore Valley, home of Kylemore Abbey, a huge Gothic Revival castle. After seeing the castle and its grounds, head north through tiny Leenane (the setting of the hit Broadway play, *The Beauty Queen of Leenane*) and on to the most attractive town in County Mayo, Westport. It's the perfect spot to spend the night: the 18th-century planned town is on an inlet of Clew Bay, and

some of the West Coast's finest beaches are nearby. Spend the night in Clifden. Your drive north leads through the heart of Yeats Country in Sligo. Just north of cozy Sligo Town is the stark outline of a great hill, Ben Bulben, in whose shadow poet Yeats wanted to be buried. South of town, follow the signposted Yeats Trail around woody, gorgeously scenic Lough Gill. Continuing north, you pass Yeats's simple grave in unassuming Drumcliff, a 3000 BC tomb in Creevykeel, and small but vibrant Donegal Town. Spend the night here, and the next morning head north through Letterkenny on the tight, meandering roads, into the windswept mountains and along the jagged coastline of northern Donegal. A trip on a fishing boat to one of the many islands off the coast is a must, as is a slow drive along the coast from the Gweedore Headland, covered with heather and gorse, to the former plantation village of Dunfanaghy (Dun Fionnachaid), heart of Donegal's Irish-speaking Gaeltacht region and a friendly place to spend the night.

Northern Ireland

2 days. Begin exploring the province in historic, divided Derry City (called Londonderry by Unionists), Northern Ireland's second city. A few hours are sufficient to take in the views from the old city walls and the fascinating murals of the Catholic Bogside district. Continue on to two of the region's main attractions, the 13th-century Norman fortress of Dunluce Castle and the Giant's Causeway, shaped from volcanic rock some 60 million years ago. Heading south, sticking to coastal roads for the best scenery, you'll soon pass through the Glens of Antrim, whose green hills roll down

into the sea. Tucked in the glens are a number of small, unpretentious towns with great hotels. Early in the morning, head straight to Northern Ireland's capital, Belfast. The old port city, gray and often wet, is a fascinating place, recovering from years of strife. A morning of driving through its streets will have to suffice before you head west through the rustic, pretty countryside to Lough Neagh, the largest lake in Britain or Ireland. It's time to head back to Dublin, but if you're ahead of schedule, take the longer route that passes through the glorious Mountains of Mourne and around icy-blue Carlingford Lough.

BY CAR: SOME TIPS

Road signs are generally in both Irish and English, although in Gaeltacht (Irish speaking) areas new laws now mandate signs in Irish *only* (most such regions are located in the counties along the western coast of the country, Donegal and Connemara in particular). Thus, if traveling in these areas, invest in a good, detailed map with both Irish and English names.

Another new law has mandated that all speed-limit signs now need to be posted in kilometers—not miles—per hour (a bit of a nuisance, as most cars have speedometers in miles). Remember to slow down on smaller, countryside lanes and roads: traffic jams can sometimes be caused by flocks of sheep and herds of cattle, not cars.

Brand-new divided highways are the fastest way to get from one point to another, but use caution: highways sometimes end as abruptly as they begin.

GREAT OUTDOORS IN IRELAND

TOP BOATING TRIPS

Imagine the scene: gentle waves lap at the edges as your boat heads for open water, drawing a perfect silver line across the tranquil mirror-flat surface. Every sound is crystal clear: a dog barks, a kingfisher whirrs past flying low across the water, and fellow-sailors shout a hearty welcome. This magical moment can easily be yours in Ireland, thanks to the wealth of possibilities for either guided tours or private hires.

Coast or Inland?

Ireland's indented western seaboard from Donegal to Cork has many first-class sailing opportunities. The main towns have sailing clubs in scenic areas. The best option is to choose an area such as West Cork and spend a week sailing from port to port. If you want to enjoy the very heart of Ireland, the River Shannon offers an unequalled choice of boating trips from the north Midlands down to Limerick. Cruisers can be hired at Carrick-on-Shannon, Banagher, and Portumna. Crossing the Irish border, the Shannon–Erne Waterway has opened up a little-known area of untamed beauty. And the renaissance of Ireland's canals is a recent regeneration success.

The Five Best Boating Trips?

River Barrow: Hire a traditional steel canal boat at Rathangan in County Kildare for a 120-km (75-mile) trip along the idyllic Barrow—Ireland's oldest navigation—passing through a Chaucerian landscape and dropping anchor at Graiguenamanagh (pronounced *grayg-na-mana* and known as Graig); en route sign up for a canal-ways pub crawl.

West Cork Sailing: The harbors of the ports of call along this coast, such as Kinsale, Glandore, Baltimore, and Bantry, offer delightful overnight stays.

River Shannon Cruising: One of the best places to hire from is the delightful boating town of Carrick-on-Shannon—putter your leisurely way down to Lough Ree or as far as the Lower Shannon.

Fermanagh Lakes: With 700 km (430 miles) of rivers, lakes, and canals, Fermanagh is tops. Upper and Lower Lough Erne are dotted with islands topped with castles or round towers ideal for exploring.

Royal Canal: With its reconstructed locks and bridges, the 145-km (90-mile) canal is perfect for those on narrow boats, and in 2010 it became fully navigable from Dublin to Richmond Harbor in County Longford. Towpaths run from the Liffey all the way to the Shannon.

Guided Tours or Private Hire?

A first-time boater? Get some courses under your belt by contacting the International Sailing Schools Association. If you want to sit back and have it all done for you, book half-day or full-day guided pleasure cruises. *For more info, see "Cruising on the Shannon" in the Midlands.*

Information, Please?

The best websites about boating in Ireland include ⊕ *www.sailing.ie*; ⊕ *www.sailingschools.org*; ⊕ *www.discoverireland.ie/lakelands*; ⊕ *www.waterwaysireland.org*; ⊕ *www.iwai.ie*; Emerald Star Cruisers, ⊕ *www.emeraldstar.ie*; Riversdale Barge Holidays, ⊕ *www.riversdalebargeholidays.com*; Canalways Ireland, ⊕ *www.canalways.ie*; Royal Canal Cruisers, ⊕ *www.royalcanalcruisers.com*.

BEST WALKS AND HIKES

Catch the right day and an Irish hilltop can seem like a slice of heaven. The country is laced with 33 well-marked walking trails. If you're not feeling adventurous, strolls through a forest park or a lakeside wander are wonderful options. If you're going for bragging rights, consider walking the newly added extension to the world-renowned International Appalachian Trail, stretching along the spectacular coastal cliffs of Slieve League in County Donegal. The two best websites for hiking information are ⊕ *www. discoverireland.ie/walking* and ⊕ *www. walkni.com.*

The Top Hiking Regions?

The Wicklow Way: Starting in the suburbs of Dublin, 137 km (85 miles) of trails take you through the heart of the spectacular Wicklow Mountains. Check out some of the gorgeous villages along the way.

The Reeks of Kerry: Munster, in the Southwest of the country, has Ireland's biggest mountains with the MacGillicuddy's Reeks in Kerry (3,414 feet) leading the way in the hierarchy of height. They attract serious hill walkers and serious gongoozlers (those who like to gaze up at the peaks).

West Is Best: Many of Ireland's West Coast walking routes are framed by spectacular Atlantic scenery: Connemara, Sligo, and Donegal are renowned for the allure of their hills with thrilling views.

Ulster Way: Relaunched in 2009, the 1,000-km (625-mile) circular Ulster Way crosses the most stunning upland areas of Northern Ireland including the impressive Mountains of Mourne.

The Top Five Walks?

Burren, Co. Clare: An unforgettable trip into an otherworldly place, this lunar-like landscape is threaded with looped walks, rare flowers, and ancient ruins, many with a backdrop of unbeatable views across Galway Bay. The entire Burren Way is a 123-km (76-mile), pleasure-filled walk.

Silent Valley, Co. Down: Catch a bus from Newcastle and, after a two-hour (undemanding) walk around this idyllic place, you will realize why it was so named.

Glendalough, Co. Wicklow: The gentle, three-hour circular Spink Walk takes you across a wooden bridge, along a boardwalk, through conifer woodland and alongside the Upper Lake with sweeping views over the valley.

Slievenamon, Co. Tipperary: An unmistakable landmark famed in song, there is an easy track to the top where a burial cairn reputedly contains the entrance to the Celtic underworld.

The Barrow Way, Co. Carlow: Follow the Barrow River on a 113-km (70-mile) meander through the forgotten Midlands, where countless historical sights pepper the pastoral landscape. It's a feast for wildlife lovers as well.

Weather or Not?

Irish weather is fickle, mist comes down quickly, and it's easy to get lost. Check the forecast and leave word with someone at your hotel about where you are going. Layers of waterproof gear and fleeces are a good bet so you can strip off when the sun comes out. Even though signposting is generally good in hill areas, bring a map: free walking guides are available from regional tourism offices, but invest in Ordnance Survey Discovery maps available at newsagents for €8.

IRISH FAMILY NAMES

Doherty

O'Hara
Quinn

Friel

McLaughlin
Gallagher
DERRY

McDonnell

McNeill

ANTRIM

Mooney
O'Donnell

Boyle
McSweeney
DONEGAL

Gormley
Quinn
Cahan

Hegarty
O'Neill

Kelly

O'Neil

O'Neill

McGrath
Clery

Donnelly
Murphy
TYRONE

Hagan
McCann
Lynch
White

Flanagan
Corrigan
Cassidy
FERMANAGH
Maguire

McManus
Connolly

ARMAGH

McKenna

DOWN

McGuinness

Clancy
O'Rourke

LEITRIM

McCabe
McGovern

Hanlon

McMahon
Hanratty

O'Dowd
Boland

Rafferty
O'Hara
McDonagh

Boylan

Higgins
Molloy

CAVAN
Lynch
Sheridan
McGowan

McNally

MONAGHAN

LOUTH
O'Carroll

SLIGO

Dugan
O'Malley

Jordan

McDermot
Flanagan

McManus
Hanley

O'Reilly

Plunkett

MAYO

Costello
Madden

LONGFORD
O'Farrell

MEATH
Cusack
Hayes

Dillon
Hennessey

Burke
Kelly
Gormley

Horan
Flynn

ROSCOMMON

Murphy

Quinn

WESTMEATH

Connolly
Plunkett
Quinlan

O'Casey
Plunkett

Joyce

Kirwan
Jennings

Moran

Dalton
Daly

Coffey

O'Flaherty

Kelly

Dillon
Sheridan

GALWAY

French
Blake
Lynch

Madden

McKeogh
Fallon

Kenny

Malone
Coghlan

OFFALY
Molloy
Dempsey

O'Byrne
White

DUBLIN

Daly
O'Loughlin
Boland

Fah(e)y
Clery

Doran
Kelly
Cullen

KILDARE
Fitzgerald
Kelly

O'Toole

Clancy
O'Dea
McMahon

Molan(e)y
O'Halloran

Kennedy

Meagher
(Maher)

LAOISE
Moore

WICKLOW
O'Byrne

CLARE
McInerney
McGrath

Purcell
O'Meara
Fogarty

Ryan
Lynch

Fitzpatrick

Nolan

CARLOW
O'Neill

McKeogh
Doyle

O'Brien
McNamara
Aherne
O'Grady

McKeough
Woulfe

Butler

Redmond
Doran

Lynch
Fitzgerald
Fitzgibbon
O'Brien

O'Dwyer

KILKENNY
Tobin

Kinsella

WEXFORD
Hartley
Kavanagh

LIMERICK

TIPPERARY

O'Carroll

Walsh
Keating

O'Cullane
(Collins)

O'Casey

KERRY

O'Brien
Power
Keane

O'Shea
Moriarty
Galvin

O'Leary
McCarthy

Roche

Phelan
McGrath

O'Donoghue

O'Keefe
Flynn

Barry
Callaghan

Sheridan

WATERFORD

O'Sullivan

Fitzgerald

McSweeney
O'Riordan

Nugent

Scanlon

O'Connell

CORK

Murphy

Lynch
O'Mahony
Hogan

Donovan
Driscoll

Cullinane
Hennessey

1

Antrim
Lynch
McDonnell
McNeill
O'Hara
O'Neill
Quinn

Armagh
Hanlon
McCann

Carlow
Kinsella
Nolan
O'Neill

Cavan
Boylan
Lynch
McCabe
McGovern
McGowan
McNally
O'Reilly
Sheridan

Clare
Aherne
Boland
Clancy
Daly
Lynch
McGrath
McInerney
McMahon
McNamara
Molon(e)y
O'Brien
O'Dea
O'Grady
O'Halloran
O'Loughlin

Cork
Barry
Callaghan
Cullinane
Donovan
Driscoll
Flynn
Hennessey
Hogan
Lynch
McCarthy
McSweeney
Murphy
Nugent
O'Casey

O'Cullane
(Collins)
O'Keefe
O'Leary
O'Mahony
O'Riordan
Roche
Scanlon
Sheridan

Derry
Cahan
Hegarty
Kelly
McLaughlin

Donegal
Boyle
Clery
Doherty
Friel
Gallagher
Gormley
McGrath
McLoughlin
McSweeney
Mooney
O'Donnell

Down
Lynch
McGuinness
O'Neil
White

Dublin
Hennessey
O'Casey
Plunkett

Fermanagh
Cassidy
Connolly
Corrigan
Flanagan
Maguire
McManus

Galway
Blake
Burke
Clery
Fah(e)y
French
Jennings
Joyce
Kelly
Kenny
Kirwan
Lynch

Madden
Moran
O'Flaherty
O'Halloran

Kerry
Connor
Fitzgerald
Galvin
McCarthy
Moriarty
O'Connell
O'Donoghue
O'Shea
O'Sullivan

Kildare
Cullen
Fitzgerald
O'Byrne
White

Kilkenny
Butler
Fitzpatrick
O'Carroll
Tobin

Laois
Dempsey
Doran
Dunn(e)
Kelly
Moore

Leitrim
Clancy
O'Rourke

Limerick
Fitzgerald
Fitzgibbon
McKeough
O'Brien
O'Cullane
(Collins)
O'Grady
Woulfe

Longford
O'Farrell
Quinn

Louth
O'Carroll
Plunkett

Mayo
Burke
Costello
Dugan

Gormley
Horan
Jennings
Jordan
Kelly
Madden
O'Malley

Meath
Coffey
Connolly
Cusack
Dillon
Hayes
Hennessey
Plunkett
Quinlan

Monaghan
Boylan
Connolly
Hanratty
McKenna
McMahon
McNally

Offaly
Coghlan
Dempsey
Fallon
Malone
Meagher
(Maher)
Molloy
O'Carroll
Sheridan

Roscommon
Fallon
Flanagan
Flynn
Hanley
McDermot
McKeogh
McManus
Molloy
Murphy

Sligo
Boland
Higgins
McDonagh
O'Dowd
O'Hara
Rafferty

Tipperary
Butler
Fogarty
Kennedy

Lynch
Meagher
(Maher)
O'Carroll
O'Dwyer
O'Meara
Purcell
Ryan

Tyrone
Cahan
Donnelly
Gormley
Hagan
Murphy
O'Neill
Quinn

Waterford
Keane
McGrath
O'Brien
Phelan
Power

Westmeath
Coffey
Dalton
Daly
Dillon
Sheridan

Wexford
Doran
Doyle
Hartley
Kavanagh
Keating
Kinsella
McKeogh
Redmond
Walsh

Wicklow
Cullen
Kelly
McKeogh
O'Byrne
O'Toole

ANCESTOR-HUNTING IN IRELAND

More than 46 million Americans claim Irish ancestry, and the desire to trace those long-lost roots back to the "auld sod" can run deep. Here are some pointers for how you can make your trip to Ireland a journey into your past.

Before You Go

The more you can learn about your ancestors, the more fruitful your search is going to be once you're on Irish soil. Crucial facts include:

■ The name of your ancestor

■ Names of that ancestor's parents and spouse

■ His or her date of birth, marriage, or death

■ County and parish of origin in Ireland

■ Religious denomination

■ The first place to seek information is directly from members of your family. A grandparent or a great aunt with a story to tell can be the source of important clues. And relatives may have documents stored away that can help with your sleuthing—old letters, wills, diaries, birth certificates, and photos.

On the Ground in Ireland

General Register Office. Civil records—dating back to 1865—are available at the General Register Office. Records for Anglican marriages date from 1845. ⊠ *8–11 Lombard St. E, Dublin, Co. Dublin* ☎ *01/863–8200* ⊕ *www.groireland.ie.*

The Mellon Centre for Migration Studies. For Northern Ireland, you can find information at the Mellon Centre for Migration Studies at the Ulster American Folk Park. ⊠ *Ulster American Folk Park, 2 Mellon Rd., Castletown, Omagh* ☎ *028/8225–6315* ⊕ *www.qub.ac.uk/cms/.*

National Archives. The Curracloe Beach has census records and, like the National Library, provides free genealogy consultations. ⊠ *Bishop St., Dublin, Co. Dublin* ☎ *01/407* ⊕ *www.nationalarchives.ie.*

National Library of Ireland. Ancestor hunters have long traveled throughout Ireland to comb parish church records, but most of these records are now available on microfilm in Dublin at the National Library of Ireland. The library is a great place to begin your hunting; you can consult a research adviser there free of charge. ⊠ *Kildare St., Dublin, Co. Dublin* ☎ *01/661–2523* ⊕ *www.nli.ie.*

Public Record Office ⊠ *2 Titanic Blvd., Queen's Island, Titanic Quarter, Belfast, Northern Ireland* ☎ *028/9053–4800* ⊕ *www.proni.gov.uk.*

The National Archives has paved the way in putting historical census information online, and the websites listed provide information about genealogical research.

If you'd rather not spend your vacation in a record hall, you can hire a professional to do your spadework. The **Association of Professional Genealogists** in Ireland (⊕ *www.irishgenealogy.ie*) will present you with a "package of discovery" upon your arrival.

The *Irish Times* newspaper also has ancestor-hunting resources (⊕ *www.irishtimes.com/ancestor*), and the National Library provides references for professionals.

BEST IRISH GREENS

The wonderfully alive, challenging natural terrain is one of the things that makes Irish golf so remarkable. In a country where mountains and sea so often meet, scraggly coastline and rolling hills of heather dominate the courses here, not the other way around. Real golfers are challenged, rather than deterred, by the vagaries of the elements—the wind, rain, and mist—and the lack of golf carts on courses in rougher terrain. Naturally, links courses tend to be more prevalent in the coastal regions, while parkland courses are found inland. Of the estimated 150 top-quality links courses in the world, 39 of them are in Ireland. Most of these leading courses were designed by celebrated golf architects, such as Tom Morris, James Braid, Harry Colt, and Alister MacKenzie, who capitalized on spectacular landscapes. Others—such as Jack Nicklaus, with his course at Killeen Castle in County Meath—will continue in their footsteps.

Planning Ahead

The top links courses can book up in summer, so if you're after a prime-time slot you might want to book well in advance. At other times you shouldn't have too much problem with a late reservation; pretty much every course in the country now has it's own online booking facility. Keep an eye out for the Irish Tourism Quality Assurance Shamrock when choosing a course. Ireland is such a small country that you can easily sample courses of very different topographies in one visit without feeling like you're rushing around. Pack for dressing smart casual and staying dry. Soft spikes are advised, and don't forget to bring your handicap certificate where possible. A shirt and tie may be needed in a few of the posher club dining rooms.

Keeping The Cost Down

While golf in Ireland couldn't be called cheap, it's often a great value when contrasted with that other links haven, Scotland. There are great savings to be had if you're prepared to come off-season or if you avoid playing weekends on the expensive courses. Focusing on the lesser-known, but equally spectacular, links courses can also cut your costs dramatically. For example, Donegal is a county full of overlooked links golf. You can also save by booking in a group, or buying a golf pass for a number of courses.

The Weather Factor

You see all kinds of weather in Ireland—driving winds, rain, sleet, and sunshine—and you may see it all in one round. There are no rain checks here. You play unless there's lightning, so pack your sweaters, waterproof shoes, and rain gear, especially if you're planning your trip between fall and spring.

The Sunday Bag Factor

If you don't have a golf bag that's light enough for you to carry for 18 holes, invest in one before your trip. Electric carts are generally available only at the leading venues, so you usually have the option of using a caddy or caddy car (pull cart)—or of carrying your own bag. Many courses have caddies but don't guarantee their availability because they're not employed by the course, so you may have to tote your bag yourself. Be prepared with a carryall or a Sunday bag.

The Private Club Factor

Unlike those in America, most private golf clubs in Ireland are happy to let visitors play their courses and use their facilities. It's important to remember, however, that such clubs place members first; guests come second. In some, you'll need a letter of introduction from your club in America to secure your playing privilege. There are often preferred days for visitors; call in advance to be sure that a club can make time for you.

The Downturn Factor

Even though it is experiencing a gradual recovery from the rapid economic downturn, Ireland has seen a few courses close and a slew of them—mostly in the republic—drop their highly inflated prices. A number of premium courses have been snapped up for a song by wily foreign investors. Greens fees for 2015 are a lot more reasonable than during the boom years.

The Perfect Links

Ballybunion Golf Club, Co. Kerry. On the Old Course, one of the country's classics, each and every hole is a pleasure to play. Set on the shore of the Atlantic at the southern entrance to the Shannon River, Ballybunion is famed for tough but pleasant golf, epitomized by the huge dunes—great for a stroll but hellish to play out of.

The K Club, Co. Kildare. You'd have to be a nongolfer and a hermit not to have heard of this course, one of the country's most prestigious and demanding. Arnold Palmer designed the main course, famed for its water obstacles and inland-links feel. The on-site facilities are the best in Ireland.

Portmarnock Golf Club, Co. Dublin. One of the nation's "Big Four" golf clubs (along with Ballybunion, Royal County Down, and Royal Portrush), Portmarnock is a links course near Dublin. Located on a sandy peninsula, it has hosted regular Irish Opens with its 100-plus bunkers ready to trap amateur and pro alike.

Royal County Down, Northern Ireland. A lunar landscape makes this course as beautiful as it is difficult. It has recently ousted St. Andrews as *Golf Digest*'s best course outside the United States. The sea of craterlike bunkers and long rough reward the straight and punish the proud.

Old Head, Co. Cork. Set on a spectacular peninsula jutting out into the wild Atlantic below, the Old Head is the romantic favorite of Irish golf lovers. Often compared to the Pacific sections of Pebble Beach, expect your pulse to race at the stunning views and wildlife.

Royal Portrush, Northern Ireland. This grand old course has made it into *Golf Digest*'s top 10 non-U.S. courses. It's a sea of sand hills and curving fairways, with the White Rocks par-5 fifth set on the edge of a cliff. Word has it (okay, Royal Portrush recommends) that a long carry over the mounds to the right of the white stone will be rewarded with a much shorter approach to the green.

Donegal Golf Club, Co. Donegal. This wild and wonderful course sits between the shores of beautiful Donegal Bay and the shadow of the majestic Blue Stack Mountains. From the 5th to the 9th you enter the "Valley of Tears," a fearsome challenge of four perilous holes made all the more challenging by feisty winds.

Doonbeg, Co. Clare. Recently purchased by Donald Trump, Doonbeg is a relatively new, creative addition to the great tradition of Irish links. Gamblers beware at the treacherous 15th; anything long could run off the green and never be seen again. Making it to the 18th is rewarded with mighty views of the ocean.

DUBLIN

WELCOME TO DUBLIN

TOP REASONS TO GO

★ **Georgian Elegance:** Dublin's signature architectural style makes its most triumphant showing in Merrion, Fitzwilliam, Mountjoy, and Parnell squares.

★ **The Guinness Brewery and Storehouse:** A high-tech museum tells the story of Guinness, Dublin's black blood. At the top, the Gravity Bar has the city's best views.

★ **Toe-Tapping "Trad":** If your head is still throbbing from last night's sing-along at the pub, head to other music-mad venues like the Olympia Theatre for the best in Irish folk music.

★ **Magnificent Museums:** From the Renoirs at the Hugh Lane to the Tara Brooch at the National Museum and the first editions of Joyce at the Dublin Writers Museum, Dublin is one big treasure chest.

★ **Trinity College:** An oasis of books, granite, and grass sits at the heart of the city. Highlights are the exquisitely illustrated *Book of Kells* and the ornate Long Room.

1 The Southside. Between Christ Church Cathedral and Trinity College lies a heavy concentration of famous sights. From the quaint St. Stephen's Green, to the stylish shopping stretch of Grafton Street and west to bustling Georges Street, this is the heart of Dublin.

2 Georgian Dublin. Though there are Georgian enclaves all over the city, Wellington Quay and Dame Street have been transformed into Dublin's trendiest neighborhood. The nightlife doesn't stop at "last call," and on weekends the streets are packed with young people from all over Europe. The spectacular, retractable, giant "umbrella" canopy that now completely covers Meeting House Square makes it a

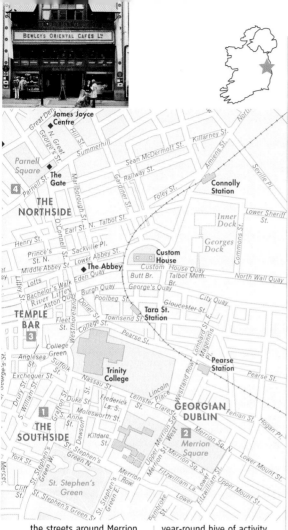

GETTING ORIENTED

Despite the seismic changes of the infamous boom-and-bust Celtic Tiger economy, Dublin happily remains an intimate capital that mixes elegant Georgian buildings, wrought-iron bridges, a battalion of booksellers, and more than 1,000 pubs. The heart of the city is the River Liffey, which runs east to west, splitting Dublin neatly in two. The more affluent Southside has a greater concentration of sights, and it can seem a world apart from the more working-class Northside. North or south, Dublin is compact and easily navigated, making it a great walking city.

Dublin's two great theaters, the Abbey and the Gate.

5 Dublin West. This former industrial district stretches from Christ Church west to that other Dublin shrine, the Guinness Brewery. Imposing Dublin Castle houses the Chester Beatty Library—arguably the most impressive museum in Ireland.

6 Phoenix Park and Environs. Only a 20-minute walk from the city center, Phoenix Park, Europe's largest public city park, hugs the north bank of the Liffey. It's the green lungs of the city, home to Dublin Zoo, and perfect for a stroll or cycle. A handful of other cultural attractions near the park also merit a visit.

the streets around Merrion Square and southeast of Trinity form the city's most important Georgian district; to the west of the square four major museums sit side by side. Farther south lies the Grand Canal and more Georgian splendor in upmarket Ballsbridge.

3 Temple Bar. The cobblestone streets and small lanes bounded by year-round hive of activity and creativity.

4 The Northside. Less affluent but more eloquent than the Southside, this neighborhood was once home to James Joyce; today it's the site of the Dublin Writers Museum and the James Joyce Centre. Other highlights are the grand Custom House, historic O'Connell Street, and

Updated by
Anto Howard

Dublin is making a comeback. The decade-long "Celtic Tiger" boom era was quickly followed by the Great Recession, but we're finally seeing the green shoots of The Recovery. For visitors, this newer and wiser Dublin has become one of Western Europe's most popular and delightful urban destinations. Whether or not you're out to enjoy the old or new Dublin, you'll find it a colossally entertaining city, all the more astonishing considering its intimate size.

It is ironic and telling that James Joyce chose Dublin as the setting for his famous *Ulysses, Dubliners,* and *A Portrait of the Artist as a Young Man* because it was a "center of paralysis" where nothing much ever changed. Which only proves that even the greats get it wrong sometimes. Indeed, if Joyce were to return to his once-genteel hometown today—disappointed with the city's provincial outlook, he left it in 1902 at the age of 20—and take a quasi-Homeric odyssey through the city (as he so famously does in *Ulysses*), would he even recognize Dublin as his "Dear Dirty Dumpling, foostherfather of fingalls and dotthergills"?

For instance, what would he make of Temple Bar—the city's erstwhile down-at-the-heels neighborhood, now crammed with cafés and trendy hotels and suffused with a nonstop, international-party atmosphere? Or the simple sophistication of the open-air restaurants of the tiny Italian Quarter (named Quartier Bloom after his own creation), complete with sultry tango lessons? Or of the hot–cool Irishness, where every aspect of Celtic culture results in sold-out theaters, from *Once,* the cult indie movie and Broadway hit, to *Riverdance,* the old Irish mass-jig recast as a Las Vegas extravaganza? Plus, the resurrected Joyce might be stirred by the songs of U2, fired up by the sultry acting of Michael Fassbender, and moved by the award-winning novels of Colum McCann. As for Ireland's capital, it's packed with elegant shops and hotels, theaters, galleries, coffeehouses, and a stunning variety of new, creative little restaurants can be found on almost every street in Dublin, transforming the provincial city that suffocated Joyce into a place almost as cosmopolitan as the Paris to which he fled. And the locals are a hell of a lot more fun!

Now that the economic downturn seems to be slowly coming to an end, Dublin citizens can cast a cool eye over the last 20 crazy years. Some argue that the boomtown transformation of their heretofore-tranquil city has permanently affected its spirit and character. These skeptics (skepticism long being a favorite pastime in the capital city) await the outcome of "Dublin: The Sequel," and their greatest fear is the possibility that the tattered old lady on the Liffey has become a little less unique, a little more like everywhere else.

Oh ye of little faith: the rare ole gem that is Dublin is far from buried. The fundamentals—the Georgian elegance of Merrion Square, the Norman drama of Christ Church Cathedral, the foamy pint at an atmospheric pub—are still on hand to gratify. Most of all, there are the locals themselves: the nod and grin when you catch their eye on the street, the eagerness to hear half your life story before they tell you all of theirs, and their paradoxically dark but warm sense of humor.

DUBLIN PLANNER

WHEN TO GO

When is it best—and worst—to pay a call on the Irish capital? The summer offers a real lift, as the natives spill out of the pubs into the slew of sidewalk cafés and open-air restaurants. The week around St. Patrick's Day (March 17) is, naturally, a nonstop festival of parades, cultural happenings, and "hooleys" (long nights of partying) throughout the city. Christmas in Dublin seems to last a month, and the city's old-style illuminations match the genteel, warm mood of the locals. The downside quickly follows, however, for January and February are damp hangover months. A warm sweater is a must all year round, as even summer nights can occasionally get chilly. Dublin gets its share of rain (though a lot less than other parts of Ireland), so an umbrella is a good investment—and best to make it a strong one, as the winds show no mercy to cheaper models.

PLANNING YOUR TIME

IF YOU HAVE ONE DAY

Begin with Trinity College—the oldest seat of Irish learning and home to the Old Library, the staggering Long Room, and Ireland's greatest art treasure—the *Book of Kells*, one of the world's most famous illuminated manuscripts. Leave the campus and take a stroll along Grafton Street, Dublin's busiest shopping street and the pedestrian spine of the Southside. Take in a few shops and entertaining buskers on the street and at the end of Grafton you will find yourself at the northwest corner of **St. Stephen's Green,** Dublin's favorite relaxation spot. Head over to the northeast corner of the park to find ground zero for the city's cultural institutions. Here, surrounding the four points of Leinster House (built by the earl of Kildare, Ireland's first patron of Palladianism), are the National Museum, replete with artifacts and exhibits dating from prehistoric times; the National Gallery of Ireland (don't miss the Irish

Dublin Past and Present

Until AD 500, Dublin was little more than a crossroads—albeit a critical one—for four of the main thoroughfares that traversed the country. It had two names: Baile Átha Cliath, meaning Town of the Hurdled Ford, bestowed by Celtic traders in the 2nd century AD; and Dubhlinn, or "dark pool," after a body of water believed to have been where Dublin Castle now stands.

In 837, Norsemen carried out the first invasion of Dublin, to be followed by new waves of warriors staking their claim to the city—from the 12th-century Anglo-Normans to Oliver Cromwell in 1651.

Not until the 18th century did Dublin reach a golden age, when the patronage of wealthy nobles turned the city into one of Europe's most prepossessing capitals. But the era of "the glorious eighteenth" was short-lived; in 1800, the Act of Union brought Ireland and Britain together into the United Kingdom, and power moved to London.

The 19th century proved to be a time of political turmoil, although Daniel O'Connell, the first Catholic lord mayor of Dublin, won early success with the introduction of Catholic Emancipation in 1829. During the late 1840s, Dublin escaped the worst effects of the famine that ravaged much of southern and western Ireland.

The city entered another period of upheaval in the first decades of the 20th century, marked by the Easter Rising of 1916. A war for independence from Britain began in 1919, followed by establishment of the Irish Free State in December 1921 and subsequent civil war. In its aftermath Dublin entered an era of political and cultural conservatism, which continued until the late 1970s. A major turning point occurred in 1972, when Ireland joined the European Economic Community.

In the 1980s, while the economy remained in recession, Irish musicians stormed the American and British barricades of rock-and-roll music, with U2 climbing to the topmost heights.

The 1990s and first years of the 21st century have truly been Ireland's boom time, set in motion to a great extent by the country's participation in the European Union. When Ireland approved the new EU treaty in 1992, it was one of the poorest member nations, qualifying it for grants of all kinds.

Ireland quickly transformed itself into the economic envy of the world, propelled by massive investment from multinational corporations, particularly in the telecommunications, software, and service industries. In 2000 the government announced that Ireland was the world's largest exporter of software. But the later years of the Tiger were fueled by a monumental property bubble, and Dublin, like most of the world, suddenly woke up with one doozy of an economic hangover from which the locals are only now beginning to recover.

Today, roughly a third of the Irish Republic's 4.5 million people live in Dublin and its suburbs. It's a city of young people—astonishingly so (students from all over Ireland attend Trinity College and the city's dozen other universities). Many of them have their eyes feverishly focused on the future.

collection and the Caravaggio *Taking of Christ*); the National Library; and the Natural History Museum.

For a lovely lunch, head back to St. Stephen's Green and the Victorian-era Shelbourne—the lobby salons glow with Waterford chandeliers and blazing fireplaces. From St. Stephen's Green walk west for 10 minutes to pay your respects to St. Paddy—St. Patrick's Cathedral. If, instead, the Dublin of artists and poets is more your speed, hop a double-decker bus and head north of the Liffey to the Dublin Writers Museum. End the day with a performance at the nearby Gate Theatre, another Georgian stunner, or spend the evening exploring the cobbled streets and the many cafés and shops of Dublin's bohemian quarter, the compact Temple Bar area, back on the south bank of the Liffey.

IF YOU HAVE THREE DAYS

Dedicate your second day to the areas north and west of the city center. In the morning, cross the Liffey via O'Connell Bridge and walk up O'Connell Street, the city's widest thoroughfare, stopping to visit the General Post Office—the besieged headquarters of the 1916 rebels—on your way to the Dublin Writers Museum (if you didn't have a chance to visit on your first day) and the Dublin City Gallery, the Hugh Lane. Be sure to join the thousands of Dubliners strolling down Henry, Moore, and Mary streets, the Northside's pedestrian shopping area. In the afternoon, head back to the Liffey for a quayside walk by Dublin's most imposing structure, the Custom House; then head west to the Guinness Brewery and Storehouse. Hop a bus or catch a cab back into the city for a blowout dinner at Restaurant Patrick Guilbaud at the Merrion Hotel. Spend the evening on a literary pub crawl to see where the likes of Beckett and Behan held court, perhaps joining a special guided tour. On the third day tour the northern outskirts of Dublin from Glasnevin Cemetery and the National Botanic Gardens across to the sublime Marino Casino in Marino and the quaint fishing village of Howth. Back in the city, have tea at Bewley's and catch a musical performance at the Olympia Theatre or a play at the Abbey Theatre.

GETTING HERE AND AROUND

AIR TRAVEL

Dublin Airport, 10 km (6 miles) north of the city center, serves international and domestic flights.

Airport Dublin Airport 🖃 *01/814–1111* 🌐 *www.dublinairport.com.*

AIRPORT TRANSFERS: BUSES AND TAXIS
Dublin Bus operates the Airlink shuttle service between Dublin Airport and the city center, with departures outside the arrivals gateway. Journey time from the airport to the city center is normally 30 minutes, but it may be longer in heavy traffic. The single fare is €6 and round-trip is €10; pay the driver inside the bus or purchase a one-day bus pass for the same price. If you have time, you can save money by taking a regular bus for €2.80. Aircoach's comfortable coaches run from the airport to the city center 24 hours a day for €7 one-way and €12 round-trip. The service stops at major hotels. A taxi is a quicker alternative than the bus to get from the airport to Dublin center. A line of taxis waits by the arrivals gateway; the fare for the 30-minute journey to any of the

main city-center hotels is about €20 to €23 plus tip (tips don't have to be large). Ask about the fare before leaving the airport.

BOAT AND FERRY TRAVEL

Irish Ferries runs a regular high-speed car and passenger service into Dublin port from Holyhead in Wales. The crossing takes 1 hour and 50 minutes on the faster *Dublin Swift* and 3 hours and 15 minutes on the huge *Ulysses*. Stena Line has services to both Dublin and nearby Dun Laoghaire port from Holyhead (3½ hours). It also runs a high-speed service, known as HSS, which takes about 2 hours and 15 minutes. Prices and departure times vary according to season, so call to confirm. In summer, reservations are strongly recommended; book online or through a travel agent. Dozens of taxis wait to take you into town from both ports, or you can take DART (electric railway) or a bus to the city center.

Ferry Contacts Irish Ferries ⊠ *Box 19, Alexandra Rd., Ferryport, Northside* ☎ *0818/300–400, 01/607–5700* ⊕ *www.irishferries.com.* **Stena Line** ⊠ *The Ferry Terminal, Dun Laoghaire, South County Dublin* ☎ *01/204–7777* ⊕ *www.stenaline.ie.*

BUS TRAVEL

Busáras, just behind the Custom House on the Northside, is Dublin's main station for buses to and from the city. Dublin Bus runs the city's regular buses. Bus Éireann is the main intercity bus company, with service throughout the country. Aircoach has direct bus connections to Cork and Belfast, and is usually a bit cheaper than Bus Éireann.

In town, there's an extensive network of buses, most of which are yellow and blue double-deckers.

Some bus services run on cross-city routes, including the smaller "Imp" buses, but most buses start in the city center.

Buses to the north of the city begin in the Lower Abbey Street–Parnell Street area, while those to the west begin in Middle Abbey Street and in the Aston Quay area. Routes to the southern suburbs begin at Eden Quay and in the College Street area. Several buses link the DART stations, and another regular bus route connects the two main provincial railway stations, Connolly and Heuston. If the destination board indicates "an lár," that means that the bus is going to the city center.

Museumlink is a shuttle service that links up the National Museum of Natural History, National Museum of Archaeology and History, and the National Museum of Decorative Arts and History. You can catch it outside any of the three museums.

BUS FARES AND SCHEDULES   In the city, fares begin at €1.80 and are paid to the driver, who will accept inexact fares, but you'll have to go to the central office in Dublin to pick up your change as marked on your ticket. Change transactions and the city's heavy traffic can slow service considerably. Most bus lines run until 11:30 at night, but some Nitelink buses run Friday to Saturday until 4:30 am on some major routes; the fare is €6. You can save money by buying a Leap Card which works for the bus, DART, and LUAS (trams). You can even order your Leap card online (⊕ *www.*

leapcard.ie) before coming to Ireland. Otherwise you can get a card at shops throughout the city.

Bus Information Aircoach ☎ *01/844–7118* ⊕ *www.aircoach.ie.* **Busaras** ✉ *Store St., Northside* ☎ *01/836–6111.* **Bus Éireann** ☎ *01/836–6111* ⊕ *www. buseireann.ie.* **Dublin Bus** ✉ *59 Upper O'Connell St., Northside* ☎ *01/873–4222* ⊕ *www.dublinbus.ie.*

CAR TRAVEL

Renting a car in Dublin is very expensive, with high rates and a 12.5% local tax. Gasoline is also expensive by U.S. standards, at around €1.50 a liter. Peak-period car-rental rates begin at around €260 a week for the smallest stick models, like a Ford Fiesta. Dublin has many car-rental companies, and it pays to shop around and to avoid "cowboy" outfits without proper licenses. A dozen car-rental companies have desks at Dublin Airport; all the main national and international firms also have branches in the city center.

Traffic in Ireland has increased exponentially in the last few years, and nowhere has the impact been felt more than in Dublin, where the city's complicated one-way streets are congested not only during the morning and evening rush hours but often during much of the day. If possible, avoid driving a car except to get in and out of the city (and be sure to ask your hotel or guesthouse for clear directions to get you out of town).

TAXI TRAVEL

There are taxi stands beside the central bus station, and at train stations, O'Connell Bridge, St. Stephen's Green, College Green, and near major hotels; the Dublin telephone directory has a complete list. The initial charge is €4.10, with an additional charge of about €1.03 per kilometer thereafter. The fare is displayed on a meter (make sure it's on). You may, instead, want to phone a taxi company and ask for a cab to meet you at your hotel, but this may cost up to €2 extra. There is no charge for luggage.

Hackney cabs, which also operate in the city, have neither roof signs nor meters and will sometimes respond to hotels' requests for a cab.

Although the taxi fleet in Dublin is large, the cabs are nonstandard, and some cars are neither spacious nor in pristine condition. NRC Taxis has a reliable track record. Global Taxis is one of the city's biggest but also the busiest. SCR Taxis has some of the friendliest drivers.

Taxi Companies Global Taxis ☎ *01/872–7272* ⊕ *www.globaltaxis.ie.* **NRC Taxies** ☎ *01/677–2222* ⊕ *www.nrc.ie.* **SCR Taxis** ☎ *01/473–1166.*

TRAIN AND TRAM TRAVEL

As a delightfully compact city, Dublin does not have—or need—a subway system. But its LUAS trams and DART electric railway are a great way to get around the city center and beyond. The DART (Dublin Area Rapid Transit) connects Dublin with the fishing village of Howth to the north and the seaside resort of Bray to the south on a fast, efficient, super-scenic train line that hugs the coastline, providing one spectacular view after another. But this line also runs through the center city with three convenient stations and then continues to such seaside destinations as Dun Laoghaire, Dalkey, and Bray.

As for the LUAS tram service, it runs two lines right into the heart of the city, facilitating easy access to sights like the Guinness Storehouse (James Street Stop), O'Connell Street (the Northside Abbey Street stop), and St. Stephen's Green.

Tickets can be bought at stations, but it's also possible to buy weekly rail tickets, as well as weekly or monthly rail-and-bus tickets, from the Irish Rail Travel Centre. Leap Cards work on the buses, DART, and LUAS.

Train Information Connolly Station ⊠ *Amiens St., Northside.* **DART** ☎ *01/836-6222* ⊕ *www.irishrail.ie/dart.* **Heuston Station** ⊠ *End of Victoria Quay, Dublin West.* **Irish Rail–Iarnod Éireann** ☎ *01/836-6222* ⊕ *www.irishrail. ie.* **LUAS** ☎ *1800/300-604* ⊕ *www.luas.ie.* **Pearse Station** ⊠ *Westland Row, Southside.*

TRAIN AND TRAM FARES AND SCHEDULES — DART service starts at 6:30 am and runs until 11:30 pm; at peak periods—8 to 9:30 am and 5 to 7 pm—trains arrive every five minutes. At other times of the day, the intervals between trains are 15 to 25 minutes. Individual fares begin at €2.15 and range up to €4.70 one way. You'll pay a heavy penalty for traveling the DART without a ticket. LUAS trams run from 5:30 am until 12:30 am Monday to Saturday and 7 am until 11:30 pm on Sunday. They come every 7 to 10 minutes at peak times and every 15 to 20 minutes after that. Fares range from €1.70 to €2.90 according to the number of zones traveled.

TRAINS TO AND FROM DUBLIN — Irish Rail (Iarnród Éireann) runs intercity trains connecting Dublin with the rest of Ireland. Connolly Station provides train service to and from the east coast, Belfast, the north (with stops in Malahide, Skerries, and Drogheda), the northwest, and some destinations to the south, such as Wicklow. Heuston Station is the place for trains to and from the south and west including Galway, Limerick, and Cork. Trains also run from here to Kildare Town, Newbridge, and other west-of-Dublin stops.

For more information on getting here and around, see Travel Smart Ireland.

RESTAURANTS

With the Irish food revolution long over and won, Dublin now has a city full of fabulous, hip, and suavely sophisticated restaurants. More realistic rents have seen new cohort of experimental eateries crop up alongside award-winning Euro-toques and their sous-chefs who continue to come up with new and glorious ways to abuse your waistline. Instead of just spuds, glorious spuds, you'll find delicious new entries to New Irish cuisine like roast scallops with spiced pork belly and cauliflower au gratin topped with a daring caper-and-raisin sauce or sautéed rabbit loin with Clonakilty black pudding. Okay, there's a good chance spuds will still appear on your menu—and most likely, offered in several different ways.

As for lunches or munchies on the run, there are scores of independent cafés serving excellent coffee, and often good sandwiches. Other eateries, borrowing trends from all around the world, serve inexpensive pizzas, focaccia, pitas, tacos, and wraps (which are fast gaining in popularity over the sandwich). And, yes, alas, Starbucks long ago planted its ubiquitous flag in Dublin.

Meeting the Dubs

The most appealing thing about Dublin isn't the sights, or even the great pubs and restaurants. It's the people—the citizens, the Dubs. They're fun, funny, and irreverent, and most of them love nothing better than talking to strangers. So, to get the most out of your visit, make a point of rubbing elbows with the locals. The pub is a natural spot to do this (see "A Trip to the Pub"), but almost any place will do. Ask for directions on a street corner (even if you don't need them), and you might be on your way to a brilliant conversation.

And mind the slag. "Slagging" is the Dubliner's favorite type of humor. It consists of mildly—or not so mildly—insulting a friend or a soon-to-be-friend in sharp but jovial fashion. It's best employed to deflate vanity or hubris, but clearly marks out the victim as well liked and worthy. Packed buses and late-night chip shops are classic slagging venues.

Dubliners dine later than the rest of Ireland. They stay up later, too, and reservations are usually not booked before 6:30 or 7 pm and up to around 10 pm. Lunch is generally served from 12:30 to 2:30. Pubs often serve food through the day—until 8:30 or 9 pm. Most pubs are family-friendly and welcome children until 7 pm. The Irish are an informal bunch, so smart-casual dress is typical.

HOTELS

Dublin hotel prices have been quick to recover from the economic slowdown and are in line with the best hotels of any major European or North American city. Service charges range from 15% in expensive hotels to zero in moderate and inexpensive ones. Be sure to inquire when you make reservations.

As a general rule of thumb, lodgings on the north side of the River Liffey tend to be more affordable than those on the south. Bed-and-breakfasts charge as little as €46 a night per person, but they tend to be in suburban areas—generally a 15-minute bus ride from the center of the city. This is not in itself a great drawback, and savings can be significant. Many hotels have a weekend, or "B&B," rate that's often 30% to 40% cheaper than the ordinary rate; some hotels also have a midweek special that provides discounts of up to 35%. *Hotel reviews have been shortened. For full information, visit Fodors.com.*

WHAT IT COSTS IN EUROS				
	$	**$$**	**$$$**	**$$$$**
Restaurants	under €19	€19–€24	€25–€32	over €32
Hotels	under €120	€120–€170	€171–€210	over €210

Restaurant prices are the average cost of a main course at dinner or, if dinner is not served, at lunch. Hotel prices are the lowest cost of a standard double room in high season, including V.A.T. and a service charge (often applied in larger hotels).

TOUR OPTIONS

Of course, Dublin is a walker's city, and it's a city full of storytellers. Put two and two together, and it's little surprise that Dublin is a particularly good place for guided walking tours.

BUS TOURS

Bus Éireann. Day tours out of Busáras, the main bus station, are run by this company to country destinations such as Glendalough. ☎ *01/836–6111* ⊕ *www.buseireann.ie.*

Dublin Bus. Three- and four-hour tours of the north and south coastlines take in sights such as the James Joyce Tower and the Casino at Marino. The one-hour city tour takes in Trinity College, the Royal Hospital Kilmainham, Phoenix Park, and other city-center sights. The one-hour city tour, with hourly departures, allows you to hop on and off at any of the main stops. Tickets are available from the driver or Dublin Bus. There's also a continuous, guided, open-top bus tour (€18), which allows you to hop on and off the bus as often as you wish and visit some 23 sights along its route. The company also conducts a north-city coastal tour, going to Howth, and a south-city tour, traveling as far as Enniskerry. ☎ *01/873–4222* ⊕ *www.dublinbus.ie.*

Irish City Tours. City-center tours cover the main Dublin itineraries. ☎ *01/898–0700* ⊕ *www.irishcitytours.com.*

PUB AND MUSICAL TOURS

Dublin Discover Ireland Centre has a booklet on its self-guided Rock 'n' Stroll trail, which covers 16 sights with associations to such performers as Bob Geldof, Christy Moore, Sinéad O'Connor, and U2. Most of the sights are in the city center and Temple Bar.

Dublin Literary Pub Crawl. Loveable rogue Colm Quilligan arranges a highly enjoyable evening Dublin Literary Pub Crawl, where "brain cells are replaced as quickly as they are drowned." ☎ *01/670–5602* ⊕ *www. dublinpubcrawl.com.*

Traditional Musical Pub Crawl. Led by two professional musicians who perform songs and tell the story of Irish music, the tour is given April–October, daily at 7:30 pm, and from Thursday to Saturday, at 7:30 pm, the rest of the year; the cost is €12. It begins at the Oliver St. John Gogarty and moves on to other famous Temple Bar pubs. ⊠ *20 Lower Stephens St., Southside* ☎ *01/478–0191* ⊕ *www.discoverdublin.ie.*

Viking Splash Tours. This is a big hit with kids. The amphibious ex–U.S. military vehicle tours the city center before launching onto the water by the IFSC (International Financial Service Center, near the Custom House). Kids get a helmet to wear and love terrifying native pedestrians with the "Viking roar." It runs from February to October and an adult ticket is €22. ☎ *01/707–6000* ⊕ *www.vikingsplash.com* ▣ *€20.*

WALKING TOURS

Dublin Discover Ireland Centre has an iWalk tour with a podcast audio guide narrated by well-known historian and artist Pat Liddy.

1916 Rebellion Walking Tour. This exciting walk outlines the key areas and events of the violent Dublin rebellion that began Ireland's march to independence. The guides are passionately political and the two-hour tour never flags. They meet at the International Bar on Wicklow Street and operate February through October, Monday to Saturday at 11:30 am and Sunday at 1 pm. The cost is €12. ☎ *086/858–3847* ⊕ *www.1916rising.com* ✉ *€12.*

Dawn To Dusk Photography Tours. For around €25, Dawn to Dusk organizes day and night walking tours of Dublin with an expert to help you get some unusual pictures of the capital and its coolest sights. ☎ *086/065–8049* ⊕ *www.dawn2dusk.ie.*

Historical Walking Tours of Dublin. Run by Trinity College history graduate students, these are excellent two-hour introductions to the city. The Tourism Ireland–approved tours take place from May to September, starting at the front gate of Trinity College, daily at 11 am and 3 pm, with an extra tour on weekends at noon. These tours are also available October and April daily at 11 am and November to March, Friday–Sunday at 11 am. The cost is €12. ☎ *87/688–9412* ⊕ *www. historicaltours.ie.*

Trinity Tours. This company organizes walks of the Trinity College campus on weekends from March 17 (St. Patrick's Day) through mid-May and daily from mid-May to September. The half-hour tour costs €10 and includes the *Book of Kells* exhibit; tours start at the college's main gate every 40 minutes from 10:15 am. There are generally nine tours a day. ⊕ *www.tcd.ie/Library/bookofkells/trinity-tours/.*

VISITOR INFORMATION

The main Fáilte Ireland tourism center (known as Dublin Discover Ireland Centre) is in the former (and still spectacular) St. Andrew's Church on Suffolk Street and is open July and August, Monday–Saturday 9–7, Sunday 10:30–3, and September–June, Monday–Saturday 9–5:30, Sunday 10:30–3. There is a smaller Northside branch on O'Connell Street that is open Monday–Saturday 9–5. The Dublin Airport branch is open daily 8 am–10 pm; the branch at the Ferryport, Dun Laoghaire, is open weekdays 9:30–1:15 and 2:30–5.

Dublin Discover Ireland Centre Suffolk Street ✉ *Suffolk St. off Grafton St., Southside* ☎ *1850/230–330* ⊕ *www.visitdublin.com.* **Dublin Discover Ireland Centre O'Connell Street** ✉ *14, Upper O'Connell St., Northside* ☎ *01/605–7700, 1850/230–330* ⊕ *www.visitdublin.com.*

DUBLIN PASS

Like many tourist capitals around the world, Dublin now features a special pass to help travelers save on admission prices. In conjunction with Fáilte Ireland (Suffolk Street Office and at many other Irish tourist offices throughout Ireland), the Dublin Pass is issued for one, two, three, or six days, and allows free (or, rather, reduced, since the cards do cost something) admission to 30 sights, including the Guinness Brewery, the Dublin Zoo, the Dublin Writers Museum, and Christ Church Cathedral. Prices are €39 for one day; €61 for two days; €71 for three days; and €105 for six days; children's prices are much lower (only €19 for one day). You can buy your card online and have it waiting for you at one of Dublin's tourist information offices when you arrive. Another plus: you can jump to the head of any line at participating museums and sights.

EXPLORING DUBLIN

"In Dublin's fair city, where the girls are so pretty"—so went the centuries-old ditty. Today, there are parts of the city that may not be fair or pretty, but although you may not be conscious of it while you're in the center city, Dublin *does* boast a beautiful setting: it loops around the edge of Dublin Bay and is on a plain at the edge of the gorgeous, green Dublin and Wicklow mountains, which rise softly just to the south. From the glass-wall top of the Guinness Storehouse in the heart of town, the sight of the city, the bay, and the mountains will take your breath away. From the city's noted vantage points, such as the South Wall, which stretches far out into Dublin Bay, you can nearly get a full measure of the city. From north to south, Dublin stretches 16 km (10 miles); in total, it covers 28,000 acres—but Dublin's heart is far more compact than these numbers indicate. Like Paris, London, and Florence, a river runs right through it. The River Liffey divides the capital into the Northside and the Southside, as everyone calls the two principal center-city areas, and virtually all the major sights are well within less than an hour's walk of one another.

SOUTHSIDE

The River Liffey provides a useful aid of orientation, flowing as it does through the direct middle of Dublin. If you ask a native Dubliner for directions—from under an umbrella, as it will probably be raining in the approved Irish manner—he or she will most likely reply in terms of "up" or "down," up meaning away from the river, and down toward it. Until recently, Dublin's center of gravity was O'Connell Bridge, a diplomatic landmark in that it avoided locating the center either north or south of the river—strong local loyalties still prevailed among "Northsiders" and "Southsiders," and neither group would ever accept that the city's center lay elsewhere than on their own side. The 20th century, however, saw diplomacy fall by the wayside—Dublin's heart now beats loudest southward across the Liffey, due in part to a large-scale refurbishment and pedestrianization of Grafton Street, which made this already upscale shopping address the main street on which to shop, stop, and be seen. At the foot of Grafton Street is the city's most famous and recognizable landmark, Trinity College; at the top of it is Dublin's most popular strolling retreat, St. Stephen's Green, a 27-acre landscaped park with flowers, lakes, bridges, and Dubliners enjoying their time-outs.

TOP ATTRACTIONS

Bank of Ireland. Across the street from the west facade of Trinity College stands one of Dublin's most striking buildings, formerly the original home of Irish Parliament. A pedimented portico fronted by six massive Corinthian columns dominates the grand facade, which follows the curve of Westmoreland Street as it meets College Green, once a Viking meeting place and burial ground. Inside, stucco rosettes adorn the coffered ceiling in the pastel-hue, colonnaded, clerestoried main banking hall, at one time the Court of Requests, where citizens' petitions were

Reflected in the waters of the Liffey, the Custom House is just one of the many famed Dublin landmarks spectacularly illuminated at night.

heard. Just down the hall is the original House of Lords, with an oak-panel nave, a 1,233-drop Waterford glass chandelier, and tapestries depicting the Battle of the Boyne and the Siege of Derry; ask a guard to show you in. Visitors are welcome during normal banking hours. ⊠ *2 College Green, Southside* ☎ *01/677–6801* ⊕ *www.visitdublin.com* 🖾 *Free* ⊙ *Mon., Tues., and Fri. 10–4; Wed. 10:30–4; Thurs. 10–5.*

Grafton Street. It's no more than 200 yards long and about 20 feet wide, but brick-lined Grafton Street, open only to pedestrians, can claim to be the most humming street in the city, if not in all of Ireland. It's one of Dublin's vital spines: the most direct route between the front door of Trinity College and St. Stephen's Green, and the city's premier shopping street, with Dublin's most distinguished department store, Brown Thomas, as well as tried-and-trusted Marks & Spencer. Grafton Street and the smaller alleyways that radiate off it offer independent stores, a dozen or so colorful flower sellers, and some of the Southside's most popular watering holes. In summer, buskers from all over the world line both sides of the street, pouring out the sounds of drum, whistle, pipe, and string.

QUICK
BITES

Bewley's Oriental Café. The granddaddy of the capital's cafés, and an essential part of the character of Grafton Street, Bewley's Oriental Café, came within a heartbeat of extinction a few years back, after having served coffee and sticky buns to Dubliners since its founding by the Quakers in 1840. Fortunately, the old dame was saved and turned into a combination café, pizza, and pasta joint. Best of all, a revamp brought back some of the old grandeur associated with Bewley's, including the

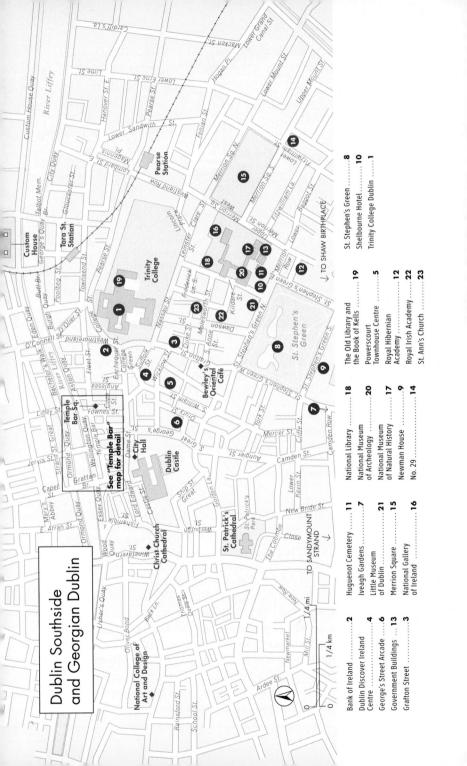

Dublin Southside and Georgian Dublin

0 _____ 1/4 mi
0 _____ 1/4 km

exotic picture wallpaper and trademark stained-glass windows, designed by the distinguished early-20th-century artist Harry Clarke. The place is worth a visit if only to sit in the super-comfortable velvet seats over a cup of quality coffee, and people-watch just like Dubliners have for well over 150 years. There's even a cute little theater upstairs with lunchtime shows. The ticket price (€8–€12) includes homemade soup and brown bread. ⊠ *78/79 Grafton St., Southside* ☎ *01/672–7720* ⊕ *bewleys.com/ bewleys-grafton-street-cafe.*

Fodor's Choice **Iveagh Gardens.** Dublin's best-kept secret has to be this 1865 Ninian
★ Niven–designed "English Landscape" walled garden that shockingly few natives seem to even know about. The architect showed off his dramatic flair in the rustic grotto and cascade, the sunken panels of lawn with their fountains, the blooming rosarium, and wonderful little wooded areas. This public park has no playground, but kids really love the "secret garden" feel to the place and the fact that the waterfall has rocks from every one of Ireland's 32 counties. Restoration of the gardens began in 1995 and has left the city with a Victorian treasure complete with a perfect box hedge and a working sundial. Access is from Hatch Street. ⊠ *Clonmel St., Southside* ☎ *01/475–7816* ⊕ *www. heritageireland.ie/en/dublin/theiveaghgardens* ⊡ *Free* ☉ *Mon.–Sat. 8– sunset, Sun. 10–sunset.*

Fodor's Choice **The Old Library and the *Book of Kells.*** Home to Ireland's largest collection
★ of books and manuscripts, the Old Library's principal treasure is the *Book of Kells*, generally considered to be the most striking manuscript ever produced in the Anglo-Saxon world and one of the great master- pieces of early Christian art. The book, which dates to the 9th century, was re-bound in four volumes in 1953, two of which are usually dis- played at a time, so you typically see no more than four original pages. However, such is the incredible workmanship of this illuminated version of the Gospels that one folio alone is worth the entirety of many other painted manuscripts. The most famous page shows the "XPI" mono- gram (symbol of Christ), but if this page is not on display, you can still see a replica of it, and many of the other lavishly illustrated pages, in library's "Turning Darkness into Light" exhibition—dedicated to the history, artistry, and conservation of the book—through which you must pass to see the originals.

Because of the fame and beauty of the *Book of Kells*, it's all too easy to overlook the other treasures in the library. Highlights include the spectacular Long Room—the narrow main room of the library and home to approximately 200,000 of the 3 million volumes in Trinity's collection as well as one of the remaining copies of the 1916 Proclama- tion of The Irish Republic; a grand series of marble busts, of which the most famous is Roubiliac's depiction of Jonathan Swift; carved Royal Arms of Queen Elizabeth I—the only surviving relic of the original college buildings; a beautiful early Irish harp; the Book of Armagh, a 9th-century copy of the New Testament that also contains St. Patrick's Confession; and the legendary Book of Durrow, a 7th-century Gospel book from County Offaly. You may have to wait in line to enter the library if you don't get here early in the day. ⊠ *Front Sq., Trinity College, Southside* ☎ *01/896–2320* ⊕ *www.tcd.ie/Library/bookofkells/ old-library* ☑ *€9, includes Book of Kells* ⊙ *May–Sept., Mon.–Sat. 9:30–5, Sun. 9:30–4:30; Oct.–Apr., Mon.–Sat. 9:30–5, Sun. noon–4:30.*

Powerscourt Townhouse Centre. One of the finest 18th-century mansions in Dublin, the Powerscourt Town-

WORD OF MOUTH

"At first, the *Book of Kells* doesn't sound fantastic—as my husband told me, we're paying 9 euros to go look at a book?—but this is more than a book. It is a work of art done in the most painstaking fashion." —akila

house Centre has magnificent architecture, quality shopping, and an Irish dancing museum and show. Designed by Robert Mack in 1771, it's a massive edifice that towers over the little street it sits on (note the top story, framed by large volutes, which was intended as an observatory). Inside, there are rococo salons designed by James McCullagh, splendid examples of plasterwork in the Adamesque style, and a shopping atrium filled with high-quality Irish crafts shops, installed in and around the covered courtyard. The mall exit leads to St. Teresa's Carmelite Church and Johnson's Court. Beside the church, a pedestrian lane leads onto Grafton Street.

The Story of Irish Dance (*jig.ie*) is a combination museum and performance space dedicated to traditional Irish dance. The small museum houses old dancing costumes and a multimedia exhibition of the history of dance in Dublin. Jig is a 60-minute virtuoso dance performance held at 6 pm from Wednesday to Saturday inclusive; it includes a free museum visit. Hop Up is a combination performance and dance lesson where you can join in. It lasts one hour and takes place Wednesday to Saturday at 3 pm. You can even get one-on-one dance classes. Check the website for details. ⊠ *59 S. William St., Southside* ☎ *01/611–1060* ⊕ *www.powerscourtcentre.com* ☑ *Jig €17.50, Hop Up €15* ⊙ *Mon.– Wed. and Fri. 10–6, Thurs. 10–8, Sat. 9–6, Sun. noon–6; limited shops open Sun. Closed Jan.*

Fodor'sChoice
★
St. Stephen's Green. Dubliners call it simply Stephen's Green, and green it is (year-round)—a verdant, 27-acre Southside square that was used for the public punishment of criminals until 1664. After a long period of decline, it became a private park in 1814—the first time in its history that it was closed to the public. Its fortunes changed again in 1880, when Sir Arthur Guinness paid for it to be laid out anew. Flower gardens, formal lawns, a Victorian bandstand, and an ornamental lake with lots of waterfowl are all within the park's borders, connected by paths guaranteeing that strolling here or just passing through will offer up unexpected delights (such as palm trees). Among the park's many statues are a memorial to W. B. Yeats and another to Joyce by Henry Moore. In the 18th century the walk on the north side of the green was referred to as the Beaux Walk because most of Dublin's gentlemen's clubs were in town houses here. Today it's dominated by the legendary Shelbourne hotel. On the south side is the alluring Georgian Newman House. ⊠ *Southside* ☑ *Free* ⊙ *Daily sunrise–sunset.*

Shelbourne Hotel. The iconic, redbrick, white-wood-trim Shelbourne Hotel commands "the best address in Dublin" from the north side of St. Stephen's Green, where it has stood since 1865. You don't have to stay to take advantage of the gorgeous location; stop in for afternoon tea in the very opulent Lord Mayor's Lounge, a true Dublin treat, and bask in the history, grandeur, and other tasty dining options available at Dublin's most iconic hotel. In 1921 the Irish Free State's constitution was drafted here, in a first-floor suite. Elizabeth Bowen wrote her novel *The Hotel* about this very place. ⊠ *27 St. Stephen's Green, Southside* ☏ *01/676–6471* ⊕ *www.marriott.co.uk.*

Fodor'sChoice
★
Trinity College Dublin. Founded in 1592 by Queen Elizabeth I to "civilize" (Her Majesty's word) Dublin, Trinity is Ireland's oldest and most famous college. The memorably atmospheric campus is a must; here you can track the shadows of some of the noted alumni, such as Jonathan Swift (1667–1745), Oscar Wilde (1854–1900), Bram Stoker (1847–1912), and Samuel Beckett (1906–89). Trinity College, Dublin (familiarly known as TCD), was founded on the site of the confiscated Priory of All Hallows. For centuries Trinity was the preserve of the Protestant Church; a free education was offered to Catholics—provided that they accepted the Protestant faith. As a legacy of this condition, until 1966 Catholics who wished to study at Trinity had to obtain a dispensation from their bishop or face excommunication.

Trinity's grounds cover 40 acres. Most of its buildings were constructed in the 18th and early 19th centuries. The extensive **West Front,** with a classical pedimented portico in the Corinthian style, faces College Green and is directly across from the Bank of Ireland; it was built between 1755 and 1759, and is possibly the work of Theodore Jacobsen, architect of London's Foundling Hospital. The design is repeated on the interior, so the view is the same from outside the gates and from the quadrangle inside. On the lawn in front of the inner facade stand statues of two alumni, orator Edmund Burke (1729–97) and dramatist Oliver Goldsmith (1730–74). On the right side of the cobblestone quadrangle of **Parliament Square** (commonly known as Front Square) is Sir William Chambers's theater, or Examination Hall, dating from the mid-1780s, which contains the college's most splendid Adamesque interior, designed by Michael Stapleton. The hall houses an impressive organ retrieved from an 18th-century Spanish ship and a gilded oak chandelier from the old House of Commons; concerts are sometimes held here. The chapel, left of the quadrangle, has stucco ceilings and fine woodwork. The looming campanile, or bell tower, is the symbolic heart of the college; erected in 1853, it dominates the center of the square. ⊠ *Trinity College, Southside* ☏ *01/896–1000* ⊕ *www.tcd.ie.*

The Douglas Hyde Gallery. Trinity College's starkly modern Arts and Social Sciences Building, with an entrance on Nassau Street, houses the **Douglas Hyde Gallery of Modern Art,** which concentrates on contemporary art exhibitions and has its own bookstore. Also in the building, down some steps from the gallery, is a snack bar serving coffee, tea, and sandwiches, where students willing to chat about life in the old college frequently gather. ⊠ *Nassau St., Southside* ☏ *01/896–1116* ⊕ *www.*

douglashydegallery.com ✉ *Free* ⊗ *Mon.–Wed. and Fri. 11–6, Thurs. 11–7, Sat. 11–4:45.*

Science Gallery. This kid-friendly museum-slash-gallery occupies a funky building at the rear of Trinity College. Its constantly changing exhibitions aim to allow art and science to meet—or collide, as the case may be, with an emphasis on fun and joining in off-the-wall experiments. Makeshop, on nearby Lincoln Place, is the Science Gallery's sister shop with a drop-in area where you can join in daily "pop-up" workshops on anything from robotics to clock making. ✉ *Pearse St., Southside* ☎ *01/896–4091* ⊕ *www.sciencegallery.com* ✉ *Free* ⊗ *Hrs vary with each exhibition.*

WORTH NOTING

Dublin Discover Ireland Centre. Medieval St. Andrew's Church, deconsecrated and fallen into ruin, has been resurrected as the Dublin home of Fáilte Ireland (the tourism board), and provides the most complete information on Dublin's sights, restaurants, and hotels; you can even rent a car and book theater tickets here. The office has reservations facilities for all Dublin hotels, as well as guided tours, a plethora of brochures, a gift shop, and even a pleasant café. ✉ *St. Andrew's Church, Suffolk St., Southside* ☎ *1850/230–330 in Ireland* ⊕ *www.visitdublin. com* ⊗ *Mon.–Sat. 9–5:30, Sun. 10:30–3.*

George's Street Arcade. This Victorian covered market fills the block between Drury Street and South Great George's Street. Two dozen or so stalls sell books, prints, clothing (new and secondhand), exotic foodstuffs, and trinkets. ✉ *S. Great George's St., Southside* ⊕ *www. georgesstreetarcade.com* ⊗ *Mon.–Wed., Fri., and Sat. 9–6:30; Thurs. 9–8; Sun. noon–6:30.*

QUICK BITES

The Long Hall Pub. With its mahogany bar, mirrors, and plasterwork ceilings, The Long Hall is one of Dublin's most ornate traditional taverns. It's a good place to take a break for a cup of tea or a cheeky daytime pint of Guinness. ✉ 51 S. Great George's St., Southside ☎ 01/475–1590.

Huguenot Cemetery. One of the last such burial grounds in Dublin, this cemetery was used in the late 17th century by French Protestants who had fled persecution in their native land. The cemetery gates are rarely open, but you can view the grounds from the street—it's on the northeast corner across from the square. ✉ *27 St. Stephen's Green N, Southside.*

Little Museum of Dublin. This clever, eclectic little museum sets out to tell the history of Dublin in the last hundred years through the objects and stories of its citizens. The collection includes art, photography, ads, letters, objects, and ephemera relating to life in the capital since 1900. Housed in the first floor of a Georgian building, they even have an interesting section on U2 and how the city shaped them. There's a slightly informal, hodgepodge feel to the place, but that just adds to the pleasure of strolling around and taking it all in. They have regular, free guided tours for visitors. ✉ *15 Stephen's Green, Southside* ☎ *01/661–0000* ⊕ *www.littlemuseum.ie* ✉ *€7.*

Royal Irish Academy. The country's leading learned society houses important documents in its 18th-century library, including a large collection of ancient Irish manuscripts, such as the 11th- to 12th-century *Book of the Dun Cow,* and the library of the 18th-century poet Thomas Moore. ⊠ *19 Dawson St., Southeast Dublin* ☎ *01/676–2570* ⊕ *www. ria.ie* ⊡ *Free* ☉ *Mon.–Thurs. 9:30–5:30, Fri. 9:30–5.*

St. Ann's Church. A plain, neo-Romanesque granite exterior, built in 1868, belies the rich Georgian interior of this church, which Isaac Wills designed in 1720. Highlights of the interior include polished-wood balconies, ornate plasterwork, and shelving in the chancel dating from 1723—and still in use for organizing the distribution of bread to the parish's poor. ⊠ *Dawson St., Southside* ☎ *01/676–7727* ⊕ *www. stannschurch.ie* ⊡ *Free* ☉ *Weekdays 10–4, Sun. for services only.*

Sandymount Strand. South of the city center, a few blocks west of the Sydney Parade DART station, the Sandymount Strand stretches for 5 km (3 miles) from Ringsend to Booterstown. It was cherished by James Joyce and his beloved, Nora Barnacle from Galway, and it figures as one of the settings in *Ulysses;* it's also a popular spot with strolling Dubliners today. (The beach is "at the lacefringe of the tide," as Joyce put it.) When the tide recedes, the beach extends for 1½ km (1 mile) from the foreshore, but the tide sweeps in again very quickly. A sliver of a park lies between Strand Road and the beach, the water of which is not suitable for swimming. At the end of the strand there's a wonderful walk out along the south harbor wall to the Poolbeg Lighthouse, which has eye-popping views of Dublin Bay. ⊠ *Sandymount, Southside.*

GEORGIAN DUBLIN

If there's one travel poster that signifies "Dublin" more than any other, it's the one that depicts 50 or so Georgian doorways—door after colorful door, all graced with lovely fanlights upheld by columns. Today, heading south from Merrion Square all the way to Ballsbridge, visitors can enjoy perfectly planned, tree-lined Georgian streets with some of the most elegant 18th-century buildings in Europe. Included in these are four of the most fascinating and glamorous museums in Ireland, sitting cheek by jowl: the National Gallery, National Library, National Museum of Natural History, and best of all, keeper of the Celtic treasures of ancient Ireland, the National Museum of Archaeology. No part of the city is more uniquely and gloriously Dublin. For convenience we have included the areas slightly farther south, around the Grand Canal and in the heart of the leafy suburb of Ballsbridge, in this section, as they have their own Georgian delights.

TOP ATTRACTIONS

Fodor's Choice ★ **Merrion Square.** Created between 1762 and 1764, this tranquil square a few blocks east of St. Stephen's Green is lined on three sides by some of Dublin's best-preserved Georgian town houses, many of which have brightly painted front doors crowned by intricate fanlights. Leinster House, the National Museum of Natural History, and the National Gallery line the west side of the square. It's on the other sides, however,

Continued on page 70

LITERARY DUBLIN

A PLAYWRIGHT ON EVERY CORNER

As any visit to the Dublin Writers Museum will prove, this city packs more literary punch per square foot than practically any other spot on the planet. While the Irish capital may be relatively small in geographic terms, it looms huge as a country of the imagination. Dubliners wrote some of the greatest works of Western literature, including these immortal titles: *Ulysses*, *Gulliver's Travels*, *Dracula*, *The Importance of Being Earnest*, and *Waiting for Godot*. Today Dublin is a veritable literary theme park: within a few minutes' walk you can visit the birthplace of George Bernard Shaw, see where Sean O'Casey wrote *Juno and the Paycock*, and pop into the pub where Brendan Behan loved to get marinated.

Above, Long Gallery library at Trinity College; Left and right, first editions of Joyce, Swift, Behan, and O'Casey

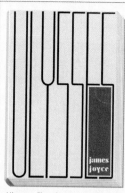

Ulysses, First American Edition

Dublin Writers Museum, Gallery of Writers

A WAY WITH WORDS

As tellers of the tallest tales, speakers of Gaelic (reputedly the world's most perfect medium for prayers, curses, and seduction), and the finest practitioners of the art of blarney, it's little surprise that the Hibernian race produced no fewer than four Nobel prize winners: Shaw, W. B. Yeats, Samuel Beckett, and Seamus Heaney. But what is surprising is that this tiny, long-colonized island on the outskirts of Europe somehow managed to maneuver itself to the very heart of literature in the language of the invader itself, English. And at that heart's core lies Dublin.

A ramble through literary Dublin is a crash course in Irish soul.

FOR BETTER OR VERSE

By the 18th century, the Gaelic tradition was trumped by the boom of literature written in English, often by second- or third-generation descendants of English settlers, such as William Congreve, Richard Brinsley Sheridan, and Oliver Goldsmith. With the establishment of the Irish Free State in 1922, so many Irish writers found themselves censored that "being banned" became a matter of prestige (it also did wonders for book sales abroad, with a smuggled copy of *Ulysses* becoming the ultimate status symbol). Sadly, many writers became exiles; most famously, Joyce was joined in Paris by Beckett in 1932.

DUBLIN B(U)Y THE BOOK

Book lovers know that a guidebook to this city is an anthology of Irish literature in itself. Dublin's Northside is studded with landmarks immortalized in James Joyce's novels. A stone's throw from the Liffey is the Abbey Theater, a potent symbol of Ireland's great playwrights. To the south lies Trinity College, alma mater of Jonathan Swift, Bram Stoker, Oscar Wilde, and Samuel Beckett. And scattered around the city are hundreds of pubs where storytelling evolved as the incurable Irish "disease." They are the perfect places to take a time-out while touring Dublin's leading literary shrines and sites.

THE TRAIL OF TALES

Allowing you to turn the pages of the city, as it were, with your feet, a literary ramble through Dublin is a magical mystery tour through more than 400 years of Irish history.

The view from Front Square, Trinity College

DUBLIN WRITERS MUSEUM. The best place to start any literary tour of the city, this gloriously restored 18th-century mansion was once the home of the Jameson Whiskey family (booze and writers are never too far apart in Dublin). Its Edwardian rooms are filled with inky treasures like the 1804 edition of Swift's *Gulliver's Travels* and the 1899 first edition of Stoker's *Dracula*. ⊠ 18 Parnell Sq. N ☎ 01/872–2077 ⊕ www.writersmuseum.com.

GATE THEATRE. Landmarked by its noble Palladian portico, this magnificent Georgian theater (built 1784) today sees the premieres of some of Ireland's most talked-about plays. Orson Welles and James Mason got their starts here. ⊠ Cavendish Row ☎ 01/874–4045 ⊕ www.gate-theatre.ie.

JAMES JOYCE CENTRE. Now an extensive library dedicated to arguably the greatest novelist of the 20th century,

this sumptuously decorated 18th-century town house was featured in *Ulysses* as a dancing academy. Letters from Beckett, Joyce's guitar and cane, and a Joyce edition illustrated by Matisse are collection highlights. ⊠ 35 N. Great George's St. ☎ 01/878–8547 ⊕ www.jamesjoyce.ie.

SEAN O'CASEY HOUSE. A one-time construction laborer, O'Casey became Ireland's greatest modern playwright and this is the house where he wrote all his famous Abbey plays, including *Juno and the Paycock* and *The Plough and the Stars*. ⊠ 422 N. Circular Rd.

ABBEY THEATRE. Hard to believe this 1950s modernist eyesore is the fabled home of Ireland's national theater company, established on a wave of nationalist passion by Yeats and his patron, Lady Gregory, in 1904. Here premiered J. M. Synge's scandalous *Playboy of the Western World* and the working-class plays of Sean O'Casey. The foyer and bar

display mementos of the theater's fabled "Abbeyists." ⊠ Lower Abbey St. ☎ 01/878–7222 ⊕ www.abbeytheatre.ie.

TRINITY COLLEGE DUBLIN. This 400-year-old college has an incredible record for turning out literary giants like Swift, Goldsmith, Wilde, Synge, Stoker, and Beckett. Majestically presiding over its famous library is the 9th-century Book of Kells, mother of all Irish tomes. ⊠ Dublin 2 ☎ 01/896–2320 ⊕ www.tcd.ie/library.

NATIONAL LIBRARY. Joyce used the 1890 Main Reading Room, with its dramatic domed ceiling, as the scene of the great literary debate in *Ulysses*. At No. 30 Kildare Street a plaque marks a former residence of *Dracula*'s creator, Bram Stoker. ⊠ Kildare St. ☎ 01/603–0200 ⊕ www.nli.ie.

MERRION SQUARE. An elegant mansion, which can be toured, No. 1 Merrion Square is the former Oscar Wilde family residence. A statue of Oscar reclines in

2

Neary's Pub

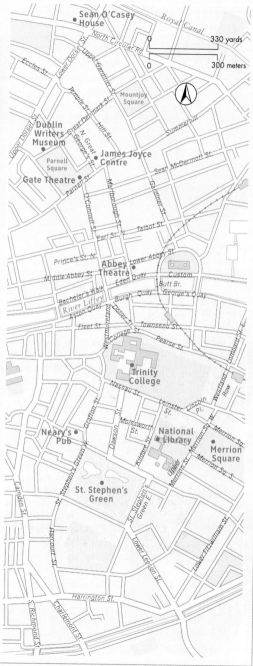

the park opposite. Around the square, note the plaques that indicate former residents, including W. B. Yeats and Sheridan le Fanu, Dublin's most famous ghost-story teller.

ST. STEPHEN'S GREEN. This pretty, flower-filled park is home to a wonderful statue of Joyce.

NEARY'S PUB. The Victorian-style interiors here were once haunted by Dublin's literary set, most notably the raconteur Brendan Behan. ✉ 1 Chatham St. ☎ 01/677-7371.

See main Exploring for full texts on these landmarks.

A DUBLIN PANTHEON

JONATHAN SWIFT
"Where fierce indignation can no longer tear his heart": Swift, one of the great satirists in the English language, willed these words be carved on his tomb at Dublin's St. Patrick's Cathedral. Swift was born on November 30, 1667, in the Liberties area of Dublin. Life would deal him many misfortunes, but he gave as good as he got, venting his great anger with a pen sharper than any sword. His rage at the British government's mistreatment of the Irish was turned into the brilliant satire *A Modest Proposal* where he politely recommends a solution to the dual problems of hunger and overpopulation: breed babies for meat. Best remembered for the brilliant moral fable *Gulliver's Travels*, he died on October 19, 1745, and is buried in Dublin's St. Patrick's Cathedral, where he was dean.

OSCAR WILDE
The greatest wit of his age and arguably any other, Wilde was born on October 16, 1834, at 21 Westland Row in Dublin, the son of an eminent eye doctor. He was educated at Trinity College, where he was a promising boxer and was quoted as saying his greatest challenge was learning to live up to the blue china he had installed in his rooms. Wilde moved to London in 1879, where he married, had children, and became celebrated for the plays *The Importance of Being Earnest* and *Salome* and his titillating novel *The Picture of Dorian Gray*. But his life was always more famous than his work and a scandalous affair with the aristocratic Alfred Douglas finally led to his ruin and imprisonment.

W. B. YEATS
Poet, dramatist, and prose writer, Yeats—winner of the Nobel Prize for Literature in 1923—stands as one of the greatest English-language poets of the 20th century. And yet in Ireland itself he is best remembered for his key role in the struggle for Irish freedom and the revival of Irish culture, including his part in forming the Abbey Theatre (National Theatre). Born in the seaside suburb of Sandymount in Dublin in 1865, his fascination with Celtic folklore and the stories of Cuchulainn can be seen throughout his early poems and plays. But many of his greatest poems are haunted by the dashing figure of Maud Gonne, actress, revolutionary, and unrequited love. He died in 1939 in Paris but his body was buried in Drumcliffe, at the foot of Ben Bulben mountain in his beloved County Sligo.

GEORGE BERNARD SHAW

G. Bernard Shaw—he hated George, and never used it either personally or professionally—was born in Dublin in 1856. His father was a boozing corn merchant and his mother a professional singer. When Shaw was a boy his mother ran away with her voice coach, and it may be no coincidence that his plays are dotted with problem child/parent relationships. In 1886 he went to London where plays such as *Pygmalion* and *Saint Joan* helped propel him to international stardom. Pacifist, socialist, and feminist, Shaw was a true original; a radical in the real sense of the word, his work always challenged the norms of his day. He lived to the ripe old age of 94 and died in 1950 after falling off a ladder while trimming trees outside his house.

SEAN O'CASEY

The first working-class Irish literary great, dramatist O'Casey was born at 85 Upper Dorset Street in the inner-city Dublin slums in 1880. Problems with his eyes as a child kept him indoors where he gleaned a love of reading. An early advocate of Yeats's Celtic Revival, he later found his true faith in the socialism of union leader Jim Larkin. His trilogy of great tragicomedies—*Shadow of a Gunman, Juno and the Paycock*, and *The Plough and the Stars*—all deal with ordinary families caught up in the maelstrom of Irish politics and were performed at Yeats's Abbey in the 1920s. Their playful language and riotous action have made them classics ever since. He spent his later life in England and died in Devon in 1964.

BRENDAN BEHAN

Writer, fighter, drinker, and wit, Brendan Francis Behan was born in Dublin's Holles Street Hospital in 1923 into an educated, political working-class family. Urged on by his fiercely patriotic grandmother, he joined Fíanna Eireann, the youth wing of the IRA and in 1939 was jailed for three years for possessing explosives. In prison he began to write but it wasn't until the 1950s that he hit it big with *The Quare Fellow*, a play based on his prison experiences, and later works *The Hostage* and *Borstal Boy*. But it was in the bars of Dublin that the "demon drinker" Behan delivered many of his greatest lines—alas, lost now forever. A self-proclaimed "drinker with a writing problem," he died in 1964 at the age of only 41.

REJOICE!: The Darlin' Dublin of James Joyce

If Joyce fans make one pilgrimage in their lives, let it be to Dublin on June 16th for Bloomsday. June 16th, of course, is the day Leopold Bloom toured Dublin in *Ulysses*, and commemorative events take place all week long leading up to the big day (and night).

Grown men and women stroll the streets attired in black suits and carrying fresh bars of lemon soap in their pockets, imitating the unassuming hero of what is arguably the 20th century's greatest novel. Denounced as obscene, blasphemous, and unreadable when it was first published in 1922 (and then banned in the U.S. until 1933), this 1,000-page riff on Homer's *Odyssey* portrays three characters—Leopold Bloom, a Jewish ad salesman, his wife, Molly, and friend Stephen Dedalus—as they wander through Dublin during the span of one day, June 16th, 1904. Dedicated Joyceans flock to the weeklong event, now called "Bloomstime," for Bloomsday breakfasts (where they can enjoy, like Bloom himself,

"grilled mutton kidneys . . . which gave to his palate a fine tang of faintly scented urine"), readings, performances, and general merriment.

But don't despair if you miss Bloomsday, because you can experience the Dublin that inspired the author's novels year-round. James Joyce (1882–1941) set all his major works—*Dubliners, A Portrait of the Artist as a Young Man, Ulysses,* and *Finnegans Wake*—in the city where he was born and spent the first 22 years of his life. Joyce knew and remembered Dublin in such detail that he bragged (and that's the word) that, if the city were destroyed, it could be rebuilt in its entirety from his written works.

Left, Joyce Statue, Earl Street;
Top left, a portrait of James Joyce, 1915
Top right, Bloomsday celebrations

IN THE FOOTSTEPS OF A POET: A James Joyce Walk

Begin in the heart of the Northside, on Prince's Street, next to the GPO (General Post Office), where the office of the old and popular *Freeman's Journal* newspaper (published 1763–1924) was once located and where Bloom once worked.

Head north up O'Connell Street down Parnell Square before turning right onto Dorset Street and then left onto Eccles Street. Leopold and Molly Bloom's fictional home stood at 7 Eccles Street, north of Parnell Square.

Head back to Dorset Street and go east. Take a right onto Gardiner Street and then a left onto Great Denmark Street and Belvedere College. Between 1893 and 1898, Joyce studied at Belvedere College under the Jesuits; it's housed in a splendid 18th-century mansion. The **James Joyce Centre** (☎ 01/878-8547 ⊕ www.jamesjoyce.ie), a few steps from Belvedere College on North Great George's Street, is the hub of Bloomsday celebrations.

Go back to Gardiner Street and then south until you come to Railway Street on your left. The site of **Bella Cohen's Brothel** (✉ 82 Railway St.) is in an area

that in Joyce's day contained many houses of ill repute. A long walk back down O'Connell Street to the bridge and then a right will take you to Ormond Quay. On the western edge of the Northside, the **Ormond Quay Hotel,** now under threat by developers,

was an afternoon rendezvous spot for Bloom.

Across the Liffey, walk up Grafton Street to **Davy Byrne's Pub** (✉ 21 Duke St., ☎ 01/671–1298). Here, Bloom comes to settle down for a glass of Burgundy and a Gorgonzola cheese sandwich, and meets his friend Nosey Flynn. Today, the pub has gone very upscale from its pre-World War II days, but even Joyce would have cracked a smile at the sight of the shamrock-painted ceiling and the murals of Joycean Dublin by Liam Proud.

After a stop at Davy Byrne's, proceed via Molesworth Street to the **National Library**— where Bloom has a near meeting with Blazes Boylan, his wife's lover. Walk up Molesworth Street until you hit Trinity. Take a right and walk to Lincoln Place. No establishment mentioned by Joyce has changed less since his time than **Sweny's Pharmacy** (✉ Lincoln Pl.), which though no longer a functioning pharmacy, still has its black-and-white exterior and an interior crammed with potions and vials. Today volunteers maintain the shop as it was in Joyce's time.

Trinity College's Front Square is paved with cobblestones and dotted with statues of its famous alumni, including Oliver Goldsmith and Samuel Beckett.

that the Georgian terrace streetscape comes into its own—the finest houses are on the north border. Even when the flower gardens here are not in bloom, the vibrant, mostly evergreen grounds, dotted with sculpture and threaded with meandering paths, are worth strolling through. Several distinguished Dubliners have lived on the square, including Oscar Wilde's parents, Sir William and "Speranza" Wilde (No. 1); Irish national leader Daniel O'Connell (No. 58); and authors W. B. Yeats (Nos. 52 and 82) and Sheridan LeFanu (No. 70). Until 50 years ago the square was a fashionable residential area, but today most of the houses serve as offices. At the south end of Merrion Square, on Upper Mount Street, stands the Church of Ireland St. Stephen's Church. Known locally as the "pepper canister" church because of its cupola, the structure was inspired in part by Wren's churches in London. An open-air art gallery featuring the works of local artists is held on the square on Sunday. ⊠ *Georgian Dublin* ⊕ *www.merrionsquareart.com* ⊙ *Daily sunrise–sunset.*

Fodor's Choice ★ **National Gallery of Ireland.** Caravaggio's *The Taking of Christ* (1602), Van Gogh's *Rooftops of Paris* (1886), Vermeer's *Lady Writing a Letter with Her Maid* (circa 1670). you get the picture, or rather, you'll *find* the picture here. Established in 1864, and designed by Francis Fowke (who also designed London's Victoria & Albert Museum), The National Gallery of Ireland is one of Europe's finest smaller art museums, with "smaller" being a relative term: the collection holds more than 2,500 paintings and some 10,000 other works. But unlike Europe's largest art museums, the National Gallery can be thoroughly covered in a morning or afternoon without inducing exhaustion.

Dublin's Gorgeous Georgians

"Extraordinary Dublin!" sigh art lovers and connoisseurs of the 18th century. It was during the glorious 18th that this duckling of a city was transformed into a preening swan, largely by the Georgian style of art and architecture that flowered between 1714 and 1820 during the reigns of the four English Georges.

Today Dublin remains in good part a sublimely Georgian city, thanks to enduring grace notes: the commodious and uniformly laid-out streets, the genteel town squares, the redbrick mansions accented with demilune (half-moon) fan windows. The great 18th-century showpieces are **Merrion, Fitzwilliam, Mountjoy,** and **Parnell squares. Merrion Square East,** the longest Georgian street in town, reveals scenes of decorum, elegance, polish, and charm, all woven into a "tapestry of rosy brick and white enamel," to quote the 18th-century connoisseur Horace Walpole.

Setting off the facades are fanlighted doors (often lacquered in black, green, yellow, or red) and the celebrated "patent reveal" window trims—thin plaster linings painted white to catch the light. These half-moon fanlights—as iconic of the city as clock towers are of Zurich—are often in the Neoclassical style known as the Adamesque (which was inspired by the designs of the great English architect Robert Adam).

Many facades appear severely plain, but don't be fooled: just behind their stately front doors are entry rooms and stairways aswirl with tinted rococo plasterwork, often the work of *stuccadores* (plasterers) from Italy (including the talented Lafranchini brothers). Magnificent **Newman**

House (✉ *85–86 St. Stephen's Green, Southside* ☎ *01/716–7422* ⊕ *www. visitdublin.com* ✉ *House and garden €5*), one of the finest of Georgian houses, is open to the public.

The Palladian style—as the Georgian style was then called—began to reign supreme in domestic architecture in 1745, when the Croesus-rich Earl of Kildare returned from an Italian grand tour and built a gigantic Palladian palace called **Leinster House** in the seedy section of town.

"Where I go, fashion will follow," he declared, and indeed it did. By then, the Anglo-Irish elite had given the city London airs by building the **Parliament House** (now the Bank of Ireland), the **Royal Exchange** (now City Hall), the **Custom House,** and the **Four Courts** in the new style.

But this phase of high fashion came to an end with the Act of Union: according to historian Maurice Craig, "On the last stroke of midnight, December 31, 1800, the gaily caparisoned horses turned into mice, the coaches into pumpkins, the silks and brocades into rags, and Ireland was once again the Cinderella among the nations."

It was nearly 150 years before the spotlight shone once again on 18th-century Dublin. In recent decades, the conservation efforts of the **Irish Georgian Society** (✉ *74 Merrion Sq., Southside* ☎ *01/676– 7053* ⊕ *www.igs.ie*) have done much to restore Dublin to its Georgian splendor. Thanks to its founders, the Hon. Desmond Guinness and his late wife, Mariga, many historic houses, including that of George Bernard Shaw on Synge Street, have been saved and preserved.

A highlight of the museum is the major collection of paintings by Irish artists from the 17th through 20th century, including works by Roderic O'Conor (1860–1940), Sir William Orpen (1878–1931), and William Leech (1881–1968). The Yeats Museum section contains works by members of the Yeats family, including Jack B. Yeats (1871–1957), the brother of writer W. B. Yeats, and by far the best-known Irish painter of the 20th century.

The collection also claims exceptional paintings from the 17th-century French, Dutch, Italian, and Spanish schools, and works by French Impressionists Monet, Sisley, and Renoir. If you are in Dublin in January, catch the sumptuous annual Turner exhibition, with paintings only displayed in the winter light that best enhances their wonders. The amply stocked gift shop is a good place to pick up books on Irish artists. Free guided tours are available on Saturday at 12:30 and on Sunday at 12:30 and 1:30. ✉ *Merrion Sq. W, Georgian Dublin* ☎ *01/661–5133* ⊕ *www.nationalgallery.ie* ✉ *Free; special exhibits €10* ⊗ *Mon.–Wed., Fri., and Sat. 9:30–5:30; Thurs. 9:30–8:30; Sun. noon–5:30.*

National Library. Along with works by W. B. Yeats (1923), George Bernard Shaw (1925), Samuel Beckett (1969), and Seamus Heaney (1995), the National Library contains first editions of every major Irish writer, including books by Jonathan Swift, Oliver Goldsmith, and James Joyce (who used the library as the scene of the great literary debate in *Ulysses*). In addition, almost every book ever published in Ireland is kept here, along with an unequaled selection of old maps and an extensive collection of Irish newspapers and magazines—more than 5 million items in all.

The library is housed in a rather stiff Neoclassical building with colonnaded porticoes and an excess of ornamentation—it's not one of Dublin's architectural showpieces. But inside, the main Reading Room, opened in 1890 to house the collections of the Royal Dublin Society, has a dramatic dome ceiling, beneath which countless authors have researched and written. The personal papers of greats such as W. B. Yeats are also on display. The library also has a free genealogical consultancy service that can advise you on how to trace your Irish ancestors. ✉ *Kildare St., Georgian Dublin* ☎ *01/603–0200* ⊕ *www.nli.ie* ✉ *Free* ⊗ *Mon.–Wed. 9:30–7:45, Thurs. and Fri. 9:30–4:45, Sat. 9:30–12:45.*

QUICK BITES

Café Joly. The National Library's light-filled tearoom, Café Joly is usually one of the city's more serene lunchtime spots. There's a light, French-country influence to the fare, with top specials including smoked-fish plates and charcuterie boards. The "Cup and Crust" (small soup, half a

Topped by half-moon fanlights, the brightly hued doorways of Merrion Square are icons of Dublin's 18th-century Georgian style.

sandwich) is a lunchtime favorite. It's open Monday–Wednesday 9–6:30, Thursday and Friday 9–4:30, and Saturday 9:30–4. ⊠ *Kildare St., Southside* ☎ *01/603–0257* ⊕ *www.nli.ie/en/cafe-and-shop.aspx.*

Fodor's Choice
★

National Museum of Archaeology. Just south of Leinster House is Ireland's National Museum of Archaeology, one of four branches of The National Museum of Ireland, and home to a fabled collection of Irish artifacts dating from 7000 BC to the present. Organized around a grand rotunda, the museum is elaborately decorated, with mosaic floors, marble columns, balustrades, and fancy ironwork. It has the largest collection of Celtic antiquities in the world, including gold jewelry, carved stones, bronze tools, and weapons.

The Treasury collection, including some of the museum's most renowned pieces, is open on a permanent basis. Among the priceless relics on display are the 8th-century Ardagh Chalice, a two-handled silver cup with gold filigree ornamentation; the bronze-coated iron St. Patrick's Bell, the oldest surviving example (5th–8th century) of Irish metalwork; the 8th-century Tara Brooch, an intricately decorated piece made of white bronze, amber, and glass; and the 12th-century bejeweled oak Cross of Cong, covered with silver and bronze panels.

The "*Or: Ireland's Gold*" exhibition gathers together the most impressive pieces of surprisingly delicate and intricate prehistoric gold work—including sun disks and the late Bronze Age gold collar known as the Gleninsheen Gorget—that range in dates from 2200 to 500 BC. Upstairs, Viking Ireland is a permanent exhibit on the Norsemen, featuring a full-size Viking skeleton, swords, leather works recovered in

Dublin and surrounding areas, and a replica of a small Viking boat. A newer attraction is an exhibition entitled "Kinship and Sacrifice," centering on a number of Iron Age "bog bodies" found along with other objects in Ireland's peat bogs.

The 18th-century Collins Barracks, near Phoenix Park, houses the National Museum of Decorative Arts and History, a collection of glass, silver, furniture, and other decorative arts. ⊠ *Kildare St. Annex, 7–9 Merrion Row, Georgian Dublin* ☎ *01/677-7444* ⊕ *www. museum.ie* 🖃 *Free* ⊙ *Tues.–Sat. 10–5, Sun. 2–5.*

FAMILY **National Museum of Natural History.** One of four branches of the National Museum of Ireland, this museum is little changed from Victorian times and remains a fascinating repository of mounted mammals, birds, and other flora and fauna. Locals still affectionately refer to the place as the "Dead Zoo." The Irish Room houses the most famous exhibits: skeletons of the extinct, prehistoric, giant "Irish elk." The International Animals Collection includes a 65-foot whale skeleton suspended from the roof. Another highlight is the very beautiful Blaschka Collection, finely detailed glass models of marine creatures, the zoological accuracy of which has never been achieved again in glass. Exhibitions include "Mating Game" and "Taxonomy Trail." Built in 1856 to hold the Royal Dublin Society's rapidly expanding collection, it was designed by Frederick Clarendon to sit in harmony with the National Gallery on the other side of Leinster Lawn. When it was completed, it formed an annex to Leinster House and was connected to it by a curved, closed Corinthian colonnade. In 1909 a new entrance was constructed at the east end of the building on Merrion Street. ⊠ *Merrion St., Georgian Dublin* ☎ *01/677-7444* ⊕ *www.museum.ie* 🖃 *Free* ⊙ *Tues.–Sat. 10–5, Sun. 2–5.*

WORTH NOTING

Government Buildings. The swan song of British architecture in the capital, this enormous complex, a landmark of Edwardian Baroque, was the last Neoclassical edifice to be erected by the British government. It was designed by Sir Aston Webb, who did many of the similarly grand buildings in London's Piccadilly Circus, to serve as the College of Science in the early 1900s. Following a major restoration, these buildings became the offices of the Department of the *taoiseach* (the prime minister, pronounced *tea*-shuck) and the *tánaiste* (the deputy prime minister, pronounced *tawn*-ish-ta). Fine examples of contemporary Irish furniture and carpets populate the offices. A stained-glass window, known

WHAT A CHARACTER!

If you want to size up a real Irish character, check out one of the National Gallery's most eye-catching paintings, Sir Joshua Reynolds's *First Earl of Bellomont* (1773). Depicted in pink silks and ostrich plumes, Charles Coote was a notorious womanizer (leading to his nickname, the "Hibernian Seducer") and was shot in the groin for his troubles by rival Lord Townshend. Famously, Coote gave his inaugural speech as quartermaster general of Ireland in *French*, continually referred to his County Cavan neighbors as "Hottentots," and wound up marrying the daughter of the superrich Duke of Leinster.

as "My Four Green Fields," was made by Evie Hone for the 1939 New York World's Fair. It depicts the four ancient provinces of Ireland: Munster, Ulster, Leinster, and Connacht. The government offices are accessible only via 35-minute guided tours; phone for details. They are dramatically illuminated every night. ⊠ *Upper Merrion St., Georgian Dublin* ☎ *01/619–4249* ⊕ *www.taoiseach.gov.ie* ▱ *Free; pick up tickets from National Gallery on day of tour* ☉ *Call ahead for tour times.*

Newman House. One of the finest examples of Georgian Dublin, Newman House is actually two imposing town houses joined together. The earlier of the two, No. 85 St. Stephen's Green (1738), has two landmarks of Irish Georgian style: the Apollo Room, decorated with stuccowork depicting the sun god and his muses; and the magnificent Saloon, crowned with an exuberant ceiling aswirl with cupids and gods, created by the Brothers Lafranchini—the finest *stuccadores* (plasterworkers) of 18th-century Dublin. Next door at No. 86 (1765), the staircase, set against pastel walls, is one of the city's most beautiful rococo examples—with floral swags and musical instruments picked out in cake-frosting white. To explore the rich history and architecture of the houses you must join a guided tour. At the back of Newman House hides Dublin's "secret garden" (⇨ *see Iveagh Gardens*). ⊠ *85–86 St. Stephen's Green, Georgian Dublin* ☎ *01/477–9810* ⊕ *www.ucd.ie/ campusdevelopment/developmentprojects* ▱ *House €5* ☉ *Tours June– Aug., Tues.–Fri. at 2, 3, and 4.*

No. 29. Everything in this carefully refurbished 1794 home, known simply as Number 29, is in keeping with the elegant lifestyle of the Dublin middle class between 1790 and 1820, the height of the Georgian period, when the house was owned by a wine merchant's widow. From the basement to the attic—in the kitchen, nursery, servants' quarters, and the formal living areas—the National Museum has re-created the period's style with authentic furniture, paintings, carpets, curtains, paint, wallpapers, and even bell pulls. ⊠ *29 Fitzwilliam St. Lower, Georgian Dublin* ☎ *01/702–6165* ⊕ *www.esb.ie/numbertwentynine* ▱ *€6* ☉ *Tues.–Sat. 10–5.*

Royal Hibernian Academy. The Royal Hibernian Academy, an old Dublin institution, is housed in a well-lighted building, one of the largest exhibition spaces in the city. The gallery holds adventurous exhibitions of the best in contemporary art, both from Ireland and abroad. ⊠ *15 Ely Pl., off St. Stephen's Green, Georgian Dublin* ☎ *01/661–2558* ⊕ *www. rhagallery.ie* ▱ *Free* ☉ *Mon., Tues. and Thurs.–Sat. 11–5; Wed. 11–8; Sun. 2–5.*

TEMPLE BAR

Locals complain about the late-night noise, and visitors sometimes say the place has the feel of a Dublin theme park, but a visit to modern Dublin wouldn't be complete without spending some time in the city's most famously vibrant area. More than any other neighborhood in the city, Temple Bar represents the dramatic changes (good and bad) and ascending fortunes of Dublin that came about in the last decade of the 20th century. The area, which takes its name from one of the streets of

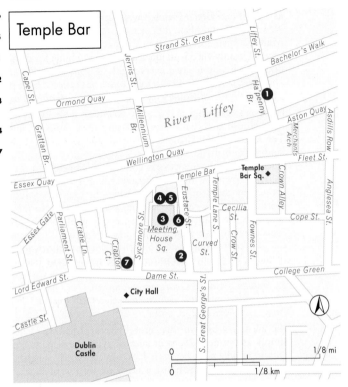

its central spine, was targeted for redevelopment in 1991–92 after a long period of neglect, having survived widely rumored plans to turn it into a massive bus depot and/or a giant parking lot. Temple Bar took off as Dublin's version of New York's SoHo, Paris's Bastille, or London's Notting Hill—a thriving mix of high and alternative culture distinct from what you'll find in any other part of the city. Dotting the area's narrow cobblestone streets and pedestrian alleyways are apartment buildings (inside they tend to be small and uninspired), vintage-clothing stores, postage-stamp-size boutiques selling overpriced gewgaws, art galleries, roaring traditional music bars aimed at tourists, a hotel resuscitated by U2, hip restaurants, pubs, clubs, European-style cafés, and a smattering of cultural venues.

Temple Bar's regeneration was no doubt abetted by that one surefire real-estate asset that appealed to the Viking founders of the area: location. The area is bordered by Dame Street to the south, the Liffey to the north, Fishamble Street to the west, and Westmoreland Street to the east. In fact, Temple Bar is situated so perfectly between everywhere else in Dublin that it's difficult to believe this neighborhood was once largely forsaken. It's now sometimes called the "playing ground of young Dublin," and for good reason: on weekend evenings and daily in summer it teems with young people—not only from Dublin but from all over Europe—drawn by its pubs, clubs, and lively *craic* (good conversation and fun).

TOP ATTRACTIONS

Gallery of Photography. Dublin's premier photography gallery has a permanent collection of early-20th-century Irish photography and also puts on monthly exhibitions of work by contemporary Irish and international photographers. The gallery is an invaluable social record of Ireland. The bookstore is the best place in town to browse for photography books and to pick up arty postcards. ☒ *Meeting House Sq. S, Temple Bar* ☎ *01/671–4654* ⊕ *www.galleryofphotography.ie* ▱ *Free* ☉ *Tues.–Sat. 11–6, Sun. 1–6.*

Ha'penny Bridge. Every Dubliner has a story about meeting someone on this cast-iron Victorian bridge, a heavily trafficked footbridge that crosses the Liffey at a prime spot—Temple Bar is on the south side, and the bridge provides the fastest route to the thriving Mary and Henry streets shopping areas to the north. Until early in the 20th century, a halfpenny toll was charged to cross it. Congestion on the Ha'penny has been relieved with the opening of the Millennium Footbridge a few hundred yards up the river. A refurbishment, including new railings, a return to the original white color, and tasteful lighting at night, has given the bridge a new lease on life.

Irish Film Institute (IFI). The opening of the IFI in a former Quaker meetinghouse helped to launch the revitalization of Temple Bar. It has three comfortable art-house cinemas showing revivals and new independent films, the Irish Film Archive, a bookstore for cineastes, and a popular bar and restaurant-café, all of which make this one of the neighborhood's most vital cultural institutions and *the* place to be seen. On Saturday nights in summer, the center screens films outdoors on Meeting House Square. ☒ *6 Eustace St., Temple Bar* ☎ *01/679–5744* ⊕ *www. ifi.ie* ▱ *Event ticket prices vary* ☉ *10 am–midnight.*

QUICK BITES

Irish Film Institute Café. This buzzing café is a pleasant place for a lunchtime break. Sandwiches are large and healthful, with plenty of vegetarian choices, and the people-watching is unmatched. ☒ *6 Eustace St., Temple Bar* ☎ *01/679-5744.*

Meeting House Square. A spectacular retractable canopy of four 70-foot "umbrellas" has turned this already vibrant square into a year-round playground for Dubliners. The square, which is behind the Ark and accessed via Curved Street, takes its name from a nearby Quaker meetinghouse. Today it's something of a gathering place for Dublin's youth and artists. Numerous cultural events—classic movies, theater, games, and family programs—take place here. (Thankfully, seats can be installed for screenings.) The square is also a favorite site for the continuously changing street sculpture that pops up all over Temple Bar (artists commissioned by the city sometimes create oddball pieces, such as half of a Volkswagen protruding from a wall). The square is also a great spot to sit, people-watch, and take in the sounds of the performing buskers who swarm to the place. There's also an organic food

Continued on page 84

A TRIP TO THE PUB

For any visitor to Ireland who wants to see the natives in their bare element—to witness them at full pace, no-holds-barred—a trip to a busy pub is a must. Luckily for you, a pub is above all a welcoming place, where a visitor is seen as a source of new, exotic stories and, more importantly, as an unsullied audience for the locals and their tall tales.

The term "pub" is shorthand for "public house," which is an apt name for one of Ireland's great institutions. Stepping into a pub (and there seems to be one on every corner) is the easiest way to transport yourself into the thick of Irish life. A pub, of course, is a drinking establishment, and for better or worse the Irish have a deep, abiding relationship with drink—particularly their beloved black stout.

The point, however, isn't what you drink, but where: in the warmth of the public house, in company. It's the place to tell stories, most of them true, and to hear music. It's where locals go to mark the key stages of their lives: to wet a new baby's head; to celebrate a graduation; to announce an engagement; and finally to wake a corpse.

Top, Temple Bar district; Opposite, Dublin pub

HOW TO CHOOSE A PUB

Not all pubs are created equal. Throughout this book we recommend some of the finest, but here are a few ways to distinguish the real gold from the sparkling pyrite:

■ Qualified, experienced bar staff—not grubby students dreaming of the round-the-world trip they are working to save up for. A uniform of white shirt and black trousers is often a good sign.

■ At least one man over sixty (preferably with a cap of some description) drinking at the bar (not at a table). He should know the good bars by now, right?

■ No TV. Or, if there is a TV it should be hidden away in a corner, only to be used for horse racing and other major sporting events.

■ No recorded music. A pub is a place to talk and listen. Occasional live music is okay, especially a traditional session.

■ Bathrooms are clean but not *too* clean. They are purely functional, not polished chambers for hanging out and chatting with friends about your new Blackberry.

THE QUEST FOR THE CRAIC

Pub-going at its best has a touch of magic to it: conversation flows, spirits rise, and inhibitions evaporate. There's a word in Gaelic for this happy condition: the craic, which roughly translates as "lively talk and good times." The craic is the sort of thing that's difficult to find only when you're looking too hard for it. Large crowds, loud music, and one pint too many can also make the craic elusive. When your companions all seem clever and handsome, and you can't imagine better company in the world, that's when you know you've found it.

Top left, pub signs in O'Connell Street, Ennis, County Clare; Right, the Long Hall, Dublin

PUB ETIQUETTE

■ First, if you want to meet people and get into the craic, belly up to the bar counter and pass up a seat at a table.

■ Always place your drink order at the bar and don't heckle the barkeepers to get their attention. They're professionals—they'll see you soon enough.

■ If you do take a table, bring your dirty glasses back to the bar before you leave, or when you order another round.

■ In present-day Ireland, male and female pubgoers usually get equal treatment. At the most traditional places, though, it's still customary in mixed company for the man to order drinks at the bar while the woman takes a table seat.

■ Don't tip the barkeepers, except at Christmas, when you can offer to buy them a drink.

■ Never sip from your Guinness until it has fully settled. You'll know this from the deep black color and perfectly defined white head.

■ Don't smoke in the bar; it's against the law. But feel free to gather outside in the rain and chat with the other unfortunates. It's a great spot to start a romance.

■ You have to be at least 18 years old to *drink* in a pub, but kids are welcome during the day, and nondrinking minors as young as 14 are often tolerated at night.

MAKING THE ROUNDS

You may get caught up in the "rounds" system, in which each pub mate takes turns to "shout" an order. Your new friends may forget to tell you when it's your round, but any failure to "put your hand in your pocket" may lead to a reputation that will follow you to the grave. To miss your "shout" is to become known for "short arms and long pockets" and to be shunned by decent people.

LAST CALL

Technically, pubs have to stop serving at 11:30 Mon.–Thurs., 12:30 Fri.–Sat., and 11 Sun. At the end of the night, ignore the first five calls of "Time please, ladies and gentle-men!" from the barman. You'll know he's getting serious by the roar of his voice.

THE "BLACK STUFF"

Rich, creamy head.

Nearly black in color, with a very slight coffee-like aftertaste.

As you drink, the head will leave "rings of pleasure" down the side of the glass.

THE POUR

The storage and pouring of a pint of stout is almost as important as the brewing. The best quality is usually found in older bars that sell a lot of pints—meaning the beer you get hasn't been sitting in the keg too long and the pipes are well coated.

Pouring a pint consists of two stages: The glass is filled three-quarters full, then allowed to sit. After the head settles, the glass is filled to the top (stage two).

Why the painstaking ritual? Because the barkeeper knows you don't want your first sip to be a mouthful of foam. And because the flavor's that much sweeter for the waiting.

Stout, a dark beer made using roasted malts or barley, originated in Ireland, and it's the country's national drink, consumed in pubs with unflagging allegiance.

GUINNESS. For most Irish, the name Guinness is synonymous with stout. With massive breweries in Africa and the Americas, it really is a world brand, but the "true" pint still flows from the original brewery at St. James Gate in Dublin. While some old-timers still drink the more malty bottled version, draught Guinness is now the standard. A deep, creamy texture and slightly bitter first taste is followed by a milder, more "toasty" aftertaste.

MURPHY'S. The Murphy Brewery was founded by James Murphy in 1856 in Cork City. Murphy's is very much a Cork drink, and often suffers from "second city" complex in relation to its giant rival Guinness. Corkonians say Murphy's has a less bitter, more nutty flavor than the "Dublin stout."

BEAMISH. Another Cork drink, a little sweeter and less dry than either Guinness or Murphy's, and so a little easier on the novice palate. Beamish and Crawford Brewery began making beer in 1792.

Top, Hargadon's pub, Northwest

WELCOME TO IRELAND'S LIVING ROOM . . .

Pub food is a lunchtime thing; the prices are reasonable, and the quality can be quite good. Ask for a menu at the bar. If you're near a coast, look for sea-food specialties, from oysters and mussels to smoked salmon. With beef-and-Guinness stew, you can drink your stout and eat it too.

Although the majority of your companions will be drinking stout, you do have other options.

A lager is always available—Heineken and Carlsberg are the most popular brands.

If you're thirsting for something stronger, take a nip of Irish whiskey, which tends to be less smoky and intensely flavored than its Scotch cousin. Jameson and Bushmills, both smooth blends, are the standard varieties, and you can usually find a single-malt as well.

On the other hand, if the booze isn't your thing, you can always choose tea, soda, or a bottle of water. (Ballygowan is the Irish Evian.) It's fine to order nonalcoholic drinks—many people who drive do so.

"TRAD" MUSIC IN ITS NATURAL DOMAIN

The pub is an ideal place to hear traditional Irish music. Performances can have a spontaneous air to them, but they don't start up just anywhere. Pubs that accommodate live sessions have signs saying so; and they're more common outside Dublin than in the city. To learn more about Irish music, see "Gael Force" in chapter 8.

Top, musicians performing at Gus O'Connor's pub in Doolin, County Clare; Right, oysters and a (half) pint, Galway

market here every Saturday all day. ⊕ *www.meetinghousesquare.ie.*

Olympia Theatre. One of the most atmospheric places in Europe to see musical acts, the Olympia is Dublin's second-oldest theater, and one of its busiest. This classic Victorian music hall, built in 1879, has a gorgeous red wrought-iron facade. The

Olympia has brought numerous musical performers to Dublin, and the theater has also seen many notable actors strut across its stage, including Alec Guinness, Peggy Ashcroft, Noël Coward, and even the old-time Hollywood team of Laurel and Hardy. Big-name performers like Van Morrison often choose the intimacy of the Olympia over larger venues. It's really a hot place to see some fine performances, so if you have a chance, by all means, go. Conveniently, there are two pubs here—through doors directly off the back of the theater's orchestra section. ⊠ *72 Dame St., Temple Bar* ☎ *01/679–3323* ⊕ *www.olympia. ie* ⊠ *Event ticket prices vary.*

QUICK BITES

The Bakery. This no-frills little bakery café at the heart of Temple Bar is bursting with fresh, authentic Irish cream cakes, fruit flans, and apple turnovers. Their coffee is a favorite with in-the-know caffeine junkies. ⊠ *Pudding Row, 2 E. Essex St. W, Temple Bar* ☎ *01/672–9882.*

WORTH NOTING

FAMILY **The Ark.** A self-described cultural center for children, The Ark engages and inspires young imaginations through a variety of creative endeavors and activities like music, poetry readings, film, dance, painting, interactive exhibitions, and more. Its theater opens onto Meeting House Square for outdoor performances in summer. A gallery and workshop space host ongoing activities. ⊠ *11a Eustace St., Temple Bar* ☎ *01/670–7788* ⊕ *www.ark.ie* ⊠ *Free* ☉ *Open only if there's a show, check website.*

National Library Photographic Archive. This important photographic resource holds regular exhibitions in its stylish modern building in Temple Bar. The collection comprises approximately 600,000 photographs, most of which are Irish, making up a priceless visual history of the nation. Although most of the photographs are historical, dating as far back as the mid-19th century, there's also a large number of contemporary pictures. Subject matter ranges from topographical views to studio portraits, from political events to early tourist photographs. You can also buy a print of your favorite photo. ⊠ *Meeting House Sq., Temple Bar* ☎ *01/603–0200* ⊕ *www.nli.ie/en/national-photographic-archive.aspx* ⊠ *Free* ☉ *Mon.–Sat. 10–5, Sun. noon–5.*

NORTHSIDE

"What do you call a Northsider in a suit? The accused." So went the old joke. But faded stereotypes about the Northside being Dublin's poorer and more deprived half were partly washed away beneath the wave of Celtic Tiger development. Locals and visitors alike are discovering the no-nonsense, laid-back charm of the Northside's revamped Georgian wonders, understated cultural gems, high-quality restaurants, and buzzing ethnic diversity.

If you stand on O'Connell Bridge or the pedestrian-only Ha'penny span, you'll get excellent views up and down the River Liffey, known in Gaelic as the *abha na life,* transcribed phonetically as Anna Livia by James Joyce in *Finnegans Wake.* Here, framed with embankments like those along Paris's Seine, the river nears the end of its 128-km (80-mile) journey from the Wicklow Mountains to the Irish Sea. And near the bridges, you begin a pilgrimage into James Joyce country—north of the Liffey, in the center of town—and the captivating sights of Dublin's Northside, a mix of densely thronged shopping streets and genteelly refurbished homes.

For much of the 18th century, the upper echelons of Dublin society lived in the Georgian houses in the Northside—around Mountjoy Square—and shopped along Capel Street, which was lined with stores selling fine furniture and silver. But development of the Southside—the Georgian Leinster House in 1745, Merrion Square in 1764, and Fitzwilliam Square in 1825—changed the Northside's fortunes. The city's fashionable social center crossed the Liffey, and although some of the Northside's illustrious inhabitants stuck it out, the area gradually became run-down. The Northside's fortunes have now changed back, however. Once-derelict swaths of houses, especially on and near the Liffey, have been rehabilitated, and large shopping centers bring the crowds to Mary and Jervis streets. The high-rise Docklands area, east of the Custom House, is pocked with modern high-rise apartments. More importantly, the Daniel Libeskind–designed, 2,000-seat, Grand Canal Theatre and the massive O2 arena have shifted the cultural tectonic plates of Dublin toward this area. In addition, the beginnings of a little Chinatown are forming on Parnell Street, while a swing bridge has been added between City Quay and the Northside. O'Connell Street itself has been partially pedestrianized, and most impressive of all is the Spire, the street's 395-foot-high stainless-steel monument.

TOP ATTRACTIONS

Custom House. Seen at its best when reflected in the waters of the Liffey during the short interval when the high tide is on the turn, the Custom House is the city's most spectacular Georgian building. Extending 375 feet on the north side of the river, this is the work of James Gandon, an English architect who arrived in Ireland in 1781, when the building's construction commenced (it continued for 10 years). Crafted from gleaming Portland stone, the central portico is linked by arcades to pavilions at either end. A statue of Commerce tops the copper dome, whose puny circumference, unfortunately, is out of proportion to the rest of the building. Statues on the main facade are based on allegorical themes. Note the exquisitely carved lions and unicorns supporting the arms of Ireland at the far ends of the facade. After Republicans set fire to the building in 1921, it was completely restored and reconstructed to house government offices. A visitor center traces the building's history and significance, and the life of Gandon. ⊠ *Custom House Quay, Northside* ☎ *01/888–2000* ⊕ *www.visitdublin.com.*

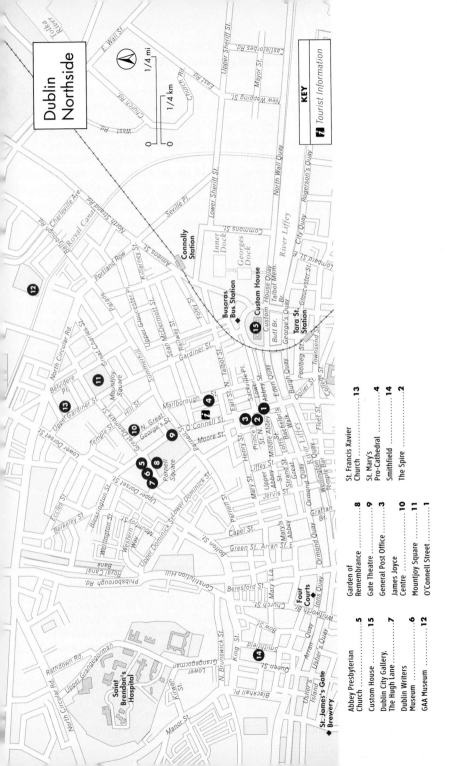

Dublin
Northside

1/4 mi
1/4 km

KEY

🛈 Tourist Information

Abbey Presbyterian Church	5
Custom House	15
Dublin City Gallery, The Hugh Lane	7
Dublin Writers Museum	6
GAA Museum	12
Garden of Remembrance	8
Gate Theatre	9
General Post Office	3
James Joyce Centre	10
Mountjoy Square	11
O'Connell Street	1
St. Francis Xavier Church	13
St Mary's Pro-Cathedral	4
Smithfield	14
The Spire	2

◆ St. James's Gate Brewery

2

Dublin City Gallery, The Hugh Lane. The Francis Bacon studio, reconstructed here exactly as the artist left it on his death (including his diary, books, walls, floors, ceiling, and even dust!), makes this already impressive gallery a must-see for art lovers and fans of the renowned British artist. Built as a town house for the Earl of Charlemont in 1762, this residence was so grand that the Parnell Square street on which it sits was nicknamed "Palace Row" in its honor. Sir William Chambers, who also built the Marino Casino for Charlemont, designed the structure in the best Palladian manner. Its delicate and rigidly correct facade, extended by two demilune (half-moon) arcades, was fashioned from the "new" white Ardmulcan stone (now seasoned to gray). Charlemont was one of the cultural locomotives of 18th-century Dublin—his walls were hung with Titians and Hogarths, and he frequently dined with Oliver Goldsmith and Sir Joshua Reynolds—so he would undoubtedly be delighted that his home is now a gallery, named after Sir Hugh Lane, a nephew of Lady Gregory (W. B. Yeats's aristocratic patron). Lane collected both Impressionist paintings and 19th-century Irish and Anglo-Irish works. A complicated agreement with the National Gallery in London (reached after heated diplomatic dispute) stipulates that a portion of the 39 French paintings amassed by Lane shuttle between London and here. Time it right and you'll be able to see Pissarro's *Printemps,* Manet's *Eva Gonzales,* Morisot's *Jour d'Été,* and, the jewel of the collection, Renoir's *Les Parapluies.*

Irish artists represented include Roderic O'Conor, well known for his views of the west of Ireland; William Leech, including his *Girl with a Tinsel Scarf* and *The Cigarette*; and the most famous of the group, Jack B. Yeats (W. B.'s brother). The museum has a dozen of his paintings, including *Ball Alley* and *There Is No Night.* The mystically serene Sean Scully Gallery displays seven giant canvasses by Ireland's renowned abstract modernist. They also host free classical concerts every Sunday. ⊠ *Parnell Sq. N, Northside* ☎ *01/222-5550* ⊕ *www.hughlane.ie* ⊡ *Free* ☉ *Tues.–Thurs. 10–6, Fri. and Sat. 10–5, Sun. 11–5.*

Dublin Writers Museum. "If you would know Ireland—body and soul—you must read its poems and stories," wrote W. B. Yeats in 1891. Further investigation into the Irish way with words can be found at this unique museum, in a magnificently restored 18th-century town house on the north side of Parnell Square. The mansion, once the home of John Jameson, of the Irish whiskey family, centers on the Gallery of Writers, an enormous drawing room gorgeously decorated with paintings, Adamesque plasterwork, and a deep Edwardian lincrusta frieze. Rare manuscripts, diaries, posters, letters, limited and first editions, photographs, and other mementos commemorate the lives and works of the nation's greatest writers—and there are many of them, so leave plenty of time—including Joyce, Shaw, J. M. Synge, Lady Gregory, W. B. Yeats, Beckett, and others. On display are an 1804 edition of Swift's *Gulliver's Travels,* an 1899 first edition of Bram Stoker's *Dracula,* and an 1899 edition of Wilde's *Ballad of Reading Gaol.* There's a "Teller of Tales" exhibit showcasing Behan, O'Flaherty, and O'Faoláin. Readings are periodically held, and there's a room dedicated to children's literature. The bookshop and café make this an ideal place to spend a rainy afternoon. ✉ *18 Parnell Sq. N, Northside* ☎ *01/872–2077* ⊕ *www.writersmuseum.com* 🎫 *€7.50* ⊙ *Mon.–Sat. 10–5, Sun. 11–5.*

Gate Theatre. The show begins here as soon as you walk into the auditorium, a gorgeously Georgian masterwork designed by Richard Johnston in 1784 as an assembly room for the Rotunda Hospital complex. The Gate has been one of Dublin's most important theaters since its founding in 1929 by Micheál MacLiammóir and Hilton Edwards, who also founded Galway City's An Taibhdhearc as the national Irish-language theater. The Gate stages many established productions by Irish as well as foreign playwrights—and plenty of foreign actors have performed here, including Orson Welles (his first paid performance) and James Mason (early in his career). ✉ *Cavendish Row, Northside* ☎ *01/874–4045* ⊕ *www.gatetheatre.ie* 🎫 *Event ticket prices vary* ⊙ *Shows Mon.–Sat.*

General Post Office (GPO). One of the great civic buildings of Dublin's Georgian era, the GPO's fame is based on the role it played in the Easter Rising. The building, with its impressive Neoclassical facade, was designed by Francis Johnston and built by the British between 1814 and 1818 as a center of communications. This gave it great strategic importance—and was one of the reasons it was chosen by the insurgent forces in 1916 as a headquarters. Here, on Easter Monday, 1916, the Republican forces, about 2,000 in number and under the guidance of Pádraig Pearse and James Connolly, stormed the building and issued the Proclamation of the Irish Republic. After a week of shelling, the GPO lay in ruins; 13 rebels were ultimately executed, including Connolly, who was dying of gangrene from a wound in a leg shattered in the fighting and had to be propped up in a chair in front of the firing squad. Most of the original building was destroyed, though the facade survived, albeit with the scars of bullets on its pillars. Rebuilt and reopened in 1929, it became a working post office with an attractive two-story main concourse. The 1916 Proclamation and the names of its signatories are inscribed on the green marble plinth. The little museum deals with the history of the building, and the role of the Post Office in Ireland. ✉ *O'Connell St., Northside* ⊕ *www.anpost.ie/AnPost/History+and+Heritage/Museum/Museum.htm* 🎫 *€2* ⊙ *Mon.–Sat. 10–5.*

> **THE SCARS OF HISTORY**
>
> Look for the bullet marks on the pillars of the General Post Office—they're remnants of the 1916 Easter Rising.

NEED A BREAK?

The Sackville Lounge. For a classic Dublin pub with a cozy, warm atmosphere, stop in to this place, famously popular with theater folk and old flat-cap Dublin men, for a smooth pint of the black stuff. ✉ *Sackville Pl., Northside* ☎ *01/874-5222.*

James Joyce Centre. Few may have read him, but everyone in Ireland has at least heard of James Joyce (1882–1941)—especially since owning a copy of his censored and suppressed *Ulysses* was one of the top status symbols of the early 20th century. Joyce is of course now acknowledged as one of the greatest modern authors, and his *Dubliners, Finnegan's*

Wake, and *A Portrait of the Artist as a Young Man* can even be read as quirky "travel guides" to Dublin. Open to the public, this restored 18th-century Georgian town house, once the dancing academy of Professor Denis J. Maginni (which many will recognize from a reading of *Ulysses*), is a center for Joycean studies and events related to the author. It has an extensive library and archives, exhibition rooms, a bookstore, and a café. The collection includes letters from Beckett, Joyce's guitar and cane, and a celebrated edition of *Ulysses* illustrated by Matisse. The interactive "James Joyce and Ulysses" exhibition allows you to delve into the mysteries and controversies of the novel. The center is the main organizer of "Bloomstime," which marks the week leading up to the Bloomsday celebrations. (Bloomsday, June 16, is the single day *Ulysses* chronicles, as Leopold Bloom winds his way around Dublin in 1904.) ⊠ *35 N. Great George's St., Northside* ☎ *01/878–8547* ⊕ *www. jamesjoyce.ie* ▧ *€5, guided tour €10* ☉ *Apr.–Sept., Mon.–Sat. 10–5, Sun. noon–5; Oct.–Mar., Tues.–Sat. 10–5, Sun. noon–5.*

O'Connell Street. Dublin's most famous thoroughfare, which is 150 feet wide, was previously known as Sackville Street, but its name was changed in 1924, two years after the founding of the Irish Free State. After the devastation of the 1916 Easter Rising, the Northside street had to be almost entirely reconstructed, a task that took until the end of the 1920s. At one time the main attraction of the street was Nelson's Pillar, a Doric column towering over the city center and a marvelous vantage point, but it was blown up in 1966, on the Rising's 50th anniversary. A major cleanup and repaving have returned the street to some of its old glory. The large monument at the south end of the street is dedicated to Daniel O'Connell (1775–1847), "The Liberator," and was erected in 1854 as a tribute to the orator's achievement in securing Catholic Emancipation in 1829. Look closely and you'll notice that O'Connell is wearing a glove on one hand, as he did for much of his adult life, a self-imposed penance for shooting a man in a duel. But even the great man himself is dwarfed by the newest addition to O'Connell Street: the 395-foot-high Spire was built in Nelson's Pillar's place in 2003, and today this gigantic, stainless-steel monument dominates the street. ⊠ *Northside.*

St. Mary's Pro-Cathedral. Dublin's principal Catholic cathedral (also known as St. Mary's) is a great place to hear the best Irish male voices: a Palestrina choir, in which the great Irish tenor John McCormack began his career, sings in Latin here every Sunday morning at 11. The cathedral, built between 1816 and 1825, has a classical church design— on a suitably epic scale. The church's facade, with a six-Doric-pillared portico, is based on the Temple of Theseus in Athens; the interior is modeled after the Grecian-Doric style of St. Philippe du Roule in Paris. But the building was never granted full cathedral status, nor has the identity of its architect ever been discovered; the only clue to its creation is in the church ledger, which lists a "Mr. P." as the builder. ⊠ *83 Marlborough St., Northside* ☎ *01/874–5441* ⊕ *www.procathedral.ie* ▧ *Free* ☉ *Weekdays 7:30–6:45, Sat. 7:30–7:15, Sun. 9–1:45 and 5:30–7:45.*

The Spire. Christened the "Stiletto in the Ghetto" by local smart alecks, this needlelike monument is the most exciting thing to happen to

Dublin's skyline in decades. The Spire, also known as the Monument of Light, was originally planned as part of the city's millennium celebrations. But Ian Ritchie's spectacular 395-foot-high monument wasn't erected until the beginning of 2003. Seven times taller than the nearby General Post Office, the stainless-steel structure rises from the spot where Nelson's Pillar once stood. Approximately 10 feet in diameter at its base, the softly lighted monument narrows to only 1 foot at its apex—the upper part of the Spire sways gently when the wind blows. The monument's creators envisioned it serving as a beacon for the whole of the city, and it will certainly be the first thing you see as you drive into Dublin from the airport. ⊠ *O'Connell St., Northside*.

WORTH NOTING

Abbey Presbyterian Church. Built on the profits of sin—well, by a generous wine merchant actually—and topped with a soaring Gothic spire, this church anchors the northeast corner of Parnell Square, an area that was the city's most fashionable address during the gilded days of the 18th-century Ascendancy. Popularly known as Findlater's Church, after the merchant Alex Findlater, the church was completed in 1864 with an interior that has a stark Presbyterian mood despite stained-glass windows and ornate pews. For a bird's-eye view of the area, climb the small staircase that leads to the balcony. ⊠ *Parnell Sq., Northside* ☎ 01/837–8600 ⌑ *Free* ⊗ *Hrs vary.*

FAMILY **GAA Museum.** The Irish are sports crazy and reserve their fiercest pride for their native games. In the bowels of Croke Park, the main stadium and headquarters of the GAA (Gaelic Athletic Association), this museum gives you a great introduction to native Irish sport. The four Gaelic games (football, hurling, camogie, and handball) are explained in detail, and if you're brave enough you can have a go yourself. High-tech displays take you through the history and highlights of the games. *National Awakening* is a really smart, interesting short film reflecting the key impact of the GAA on the emergence of the Irish nation and the forging of a new Irish identity. The exhilarating *A Day in September* captures the thrill and passion of All Ireland finals day—the annual denouement of the inter-county hurling and Gaelic football seasons—which is every bit as important to the locals as the Super Bowl is to sports fans in the United States. Tours of the stadium, the fourth largest in Europe, are available. ⊠ *St. Joseph's Ave., Croke Park Stadium, North County Dublin* ☎ 01/819–2300 ⊕ *www.crokepark.ie/gaa-museum* ⌑ *Museum €6, museum and stadium tour €12.50* ⊗ *Jan.– May and Sept.–Dec., Mon.–Sat. 9:30–5, Sun. 10:30–5; June–Aug., Mon.–Sat. 9:30–6, Sun. 10:30–5.*

Garden of Remembrance. Opened 50 years after the Easter Rising of 1916, the garden in Parnell Square commemorates those who died fighting for Ireland's freedom. At the garden's entrance is a large plaza; steps lead down to the fountain area, graced with a sculpture by contemporary Irish artist Oisín Kelly, based on the mythological Children of Lír, who were turned into swans. The garden serves as an oasis of tranquility in the middle of the busy city. ⊠ *Parnell Sq., Northside* ☎ 01/821–3021 ⊕ *www.heritageireland.ie* ⌑ *Free* ⊗ *Apr.–Sept., daily 8:30–6; Oct.– Mar., daily 9:30–4.*

Mountjoy Square. Irishman Brian Boru, who led his soldiers to victory against the Vikings in the Battle of Clontarf in 1014, was said to have pitched camp before the confrontation on the site of Mountjoy Square. Playwright Sean O'Casey lived here, at No. 35, and used the square as a setting for *The Shadow of a Gunman*. Built over the course of the two decades leading up to 1818, this Northside square was once surrounded by elegant terraced houses. Today only the northern side remains intact. The houses on the once derelict southern side have been converted into apartments.

St. Francis Xavier Church. One of the city's finest churches in the classical style, the Jesuit St. Francis Xavier's was begun in 1829, the year of Catholic Emancipation, and was completed three years later. The building is designed in the shape of a Latin cross, with a distinctive Ionic portico and an unusual coffered ceiling. The striking, faux-marble high altarpiece, decorated with lapis lazuli, came from Italy. The church appears in James Joyce's story "Grace." ⊠ *Upper Gardiner St., Northside* ☎ *01/836–3411* ⊕ *www.gardinerstparish.ie* ☎ *Free* ☉ *Daily 7 am–8:30 pm.*

DUBLIN WEST

A cornucopia of things quintessentially Dublin, this area is studded with treasures and pleasures ranging from the opulent 18th-century salons of Dublin Castle to time-burnished St. Patrick's Cathedral, and from the Liberties neighborhood—redoubt of the city's best antiques stores—to the Irish Museum of Modern Art (housed at the strikingly renovated Royal Hospital Kilmainham). You can time-travel from the 10th-century crypt at Christ Church Cathedral—the city's oldest surviving structure—to the modern plant of the Guinness Brewery and its storehouse museum. You can also cross the Liffey for a visit to Smithfield, Dublin's old (but recently revitalized) market area where flowers, fruit, vegetables, and even horses have been sold for generations. Traditional music bars sit side by side here with modern hotels and the Old Jameson Distillery museum.

Keep in mind that Dublin is compact. The following sights aren't far from those in the other city-center neighborhoods. In fact, City Hall is just across the street from Temple Bar, and Christ Church Cathedral is a short walk farther west. The westernmost sights covered here—notably the Royal Hospital and Kilmainham Gaol—are, however, at some distance, so if you're not an enthusiastic walker, you may want to drive or catch a cab, bus, or LUAS tram to them.

TOP ATTRACTIONS

Fodor's Choice ★ **Chester Beatty Library.** A connoisseur's delight, this "library" is considered one of the overlooked treasures of Ireland. After Sir Alfred Chester Beatty (1875–1968), an American mining millionaire and a collector with a flawless eye, assembled one of the most significant collections of Islamic, Early Christian, and Far Eastern art in the Western world, he donated it to Ireland. Housed in the gorgeous clock-tower building of Dublin Castle, exhibits include clay tablets from Babylon dating from 2700 BC, Japanese wood-block prints, Chinese jade books, early papyrus bibles, and Turkish and Persian paintings. The second floor, dedicated to the major religions, houses 250 manuscripts of the Koran from across the Muslim world, as well as one of the earliest Gospels. The first-floor "Arts of the Book" exhibition looks at the different origins and finest examples of books throughout the world. Guided tours of the library

2

are available on Wednesday at 1 pm and Sunday at 3 pm and 4 pm. On sunny days the garden is one of the most tranquil places in central Dublin. ⊠ *Castle St., Dublin West* ☎ *01/407–0750* ⊕ *www.cbl.ie* ⊠ *Free* ☉ *May–Sept., weekdays 10–5, Sat. 11–5, Sun. 1–5; Oct.–Apr., Tues.–Fri. 10–5, Sat. 11–5, Sun. 1–5.*

QUICK BITES

The Silk Road Cafe. A great-value, Middle Eastern delight hidden away in the Chester Beatty Library, the Silk Road Café has a buffet-style menu always full of exotic surprises. The light-filled room (open Tuesday–Friday 10–4:30, Saturday 11–4:30, and Sunday 1–4:30) and serene atmosphere make you want to linger longer than you should. ⊠ *Chester Beatty Library, Castle St., Dublin West* ☎ *01/407–0770* ⊕ *www.silkroadcafe.ie.*

Fodor's Choice ★

Christ Church Cathedral. From its exterior, you'd never guess that the first Christianized Danish king built a wooden church at this site in 1038; because of the extensive 19th-century renovation of its stonework and trim, the cathedral looks more Victorian than Anglo-Norman. Construction on the present Christ Church—the flagship of the Church of Ireland and one of two Protestant cathedrals in Dublin (the other is St. Patrick's just to the south)—was begun in 1172 by Strongbow, a Norman baron and conqueror of Dublin for the English Crown, and continued for 50 years. By 1875 the cathedral had deteriorated badly; a major renovation gave it much of the look it has today, including the addition of one of Dublin's most charming structures: a Bridge of Sighs–like affair that connects the cathedral to the old Synod Hall, which now holds the Viking multimedia exhibition, Dublinia. Strongbow himself is buried in the cathedral, beneath an impressive effigy. The vast, sturdy **crypt,** with its 12th- and 13th-century vaults, is Dublin's oldest surviving structure and the building's most notable feature. The Treasures of Christ Church exhibition includes manuscripts, various historic artifacts, and the tabernacle used when James II worshipped here. But the real marvel are the mortified bodies of a cat and rat—they were trapped in an organ pipe in the 1860s—who seem caught in a cartoon chase for all eternity. At 6 pm on Wednesday and Thursday, and 3:30 pm on Sunday you can enjoy the glories of a choral evensong and the bell ringers usually practice on Friday at 7 pm. ⊠ *Christ Church Pl. and Winetavern St., Dublin West* ☎ *01/677–8099* ⊕ *www.christchurchdublin.ie* ⊠ *€6* ☉ *Mar.–May, Mon.–Sat. 9–6, Sun. noon–2:30 and 4:30–6; June–Sept.,*

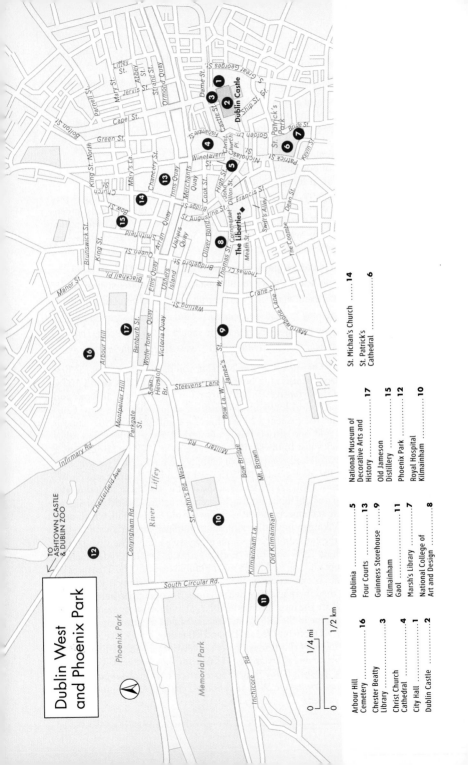

Dublin West and Phoenix Park

0   1/4 mi
0   1/2 km

Mon.–Sat. 9–7, Sun. 12:30–2:30 and 4:30–7; Oct.–Feb., Mon.–Sat. 9–5, Sun. 12:30–2:30.

City Hall. Facing the Liffey from Cork Hill at the top of Parliament Street, this grand Georgian municipal building (1769–79), once the Royal Exchange, marks the southwest corner of Temple Bar. Today it's the seat of Dublin Corporation, the elected body that governs the city. Thomas Cooley designed the building with 12 columns that encircle the domed central rotunda, which has a fine mosaic floor and 12 frescoes depicting Dublin legends and ancient Irish historical scenes. The 20-foot-high sculpture to the right is of Daniel O'Connell, "The Liberator." He looks like he's about to begin the famous speech he gave here in 1800. The building houses a multimedia exhibition—with artifacts, kiosks, graphics, and audiovisual presentations—tracing the evolution of Ireland's 1,000-year-old capital. ⊠ *Dame St., Dublin West* ☎ *01/222-2204* ⊕ *www.dublincity.ie/RecreationandCulture* ⊠ *€4* ⊗ *Mon.–Sat. 10–5:15.*

Dublin Castle. As seat and symbol of the British rule of Ireland for more than seven centuries, Dublin Castle figured largely in Ireland's turbulent history early in the 20th century. It's now mainly used for Irish and EU governmental purposes. The sprawling Great Courtyard is the reputed site of the Black Pool (Dubh Linn, pronounced dove-lin) from which Dublin got its name. In the Lower Castle Yard, the Record Tower, the earliest of several towers on the site, is the largest remaining relic of the original Norman buildings, built by King John between 1208 and 1220. The clock-tower building houses the fabulous Chester Beatty Library. The State Apartments (on the southern side of the Upper Castle Yard)—formerly the residence of the English viceroys and now used by the president of Ireland to host visiting heads of state and EU ministers—are lavishly furnished with rich Donegal carpets and illuminated by Waterford glass chandeliers. The largest and most impressive of these chambers, St. Patrick's Hall, with its gilt pillars and painted ceiling, is used for the inauguration of Irish presidents. The Round Drawing Room, in Bermingham Tower, dates from 1411 and was rebuilt in 1777; numerous Irish leaders were imprisoned in the tower from the 16th century to the early 20th century. The blue oval Wedgwood Room contains Chippendale chairs and a marble fireplace. The Church of the Holy Trinity features carved oak panels, stained glass depicting the viceroy's coat of arms, and an elaborate array of fan vaults. More than 100 carved heads adorn the walls outside; among them, St. Peter, Jonathan Swift, St. Patrick, and Brian Boru.

Enter the castle through the Cork Hill Gate, just west of City Hall. One-hour guided tours are available throughout the day, but the rooms are closed when in official use, so call ahead. The Castle Vaults hold an elegant little patisserie and bistro. ⊠ *Castle St., Dublin West* ☎ *01/645-8813* ⊕ *www.dublincastle.ie* ⊠ *State Apartments €4.50 including tour* ⊗ *Mon.–Sat. 10–4:45, Sun. noon–4:45.*

Four Courts. The stately Corinthian portico and the circular central hall warrant a visit to the seat of the High Court of Civil Law in Ireland. The distinctive copper-cover dome topping a colonnaded rotunda makes this one of Dublin's most instantly recognizable buildings. Built between 1786 and 1802, the Four Courts are James Gandon's second Dublin masterpiece—close on the heels of his Custom House, located downstream on the same side of the River Liffey. In 1922, during the Irish Civil War, the Four Courts was almost totally destroyed by shelling—the adjoining Public Records Office was gutted, and many priceless legal documents, including innumerable family records, were destroyed. Restoration took 10 years. Tours of the building are not given, but you're welcome to sit in while the courts are in session; the locals often pop in to see some of the more interesting trials. ⊠ *Inns Quay, Dublin West* ☎ *01/872–5555* ⊕ *www.courts.ie* ☾ *Daily 10–1 and 2:15–4.*

Fodor's Choice
★

Guinness Storehouse. Ireland's all-dominating brewery—founded by Arthur Guinness in 1759 and at one time the largest stout-producing brewery in the world—spans a 60-acre spread west of Christ Church Cathedral. Not surprisingly, it's the most popular tourist destination in town—after all, the Irish national drink is Guinness stout, a dark brew made with roasted malt. The brewery itself is closed to the public, but the Guinness Storehouse is a spectacular attraction, designed to woo—some might say brainwash—you with the wonders of the "dark stuff." In a 1904 cast-iron-and-brick warehouse, the museum display covers six floors built around a huge, central glass atrium which is shaped like a giant pint glass. Beneath the glass floor of the lobby you can see Arthur Guinness's original lease on the site, for a whopping 9,000 years. The exhibition elucidates the brewing process and its history, with antique presses and vats, a look at bottle and can design through the ages, a history of the Guinness family, a fascinating archive of Guinness advertisements, and a chance to pull your own perfect pint. The star attraction is undoubtedly the top-floor **Gravity Bar**, with 360-degree floor-to-ceiling glass walls that offer a nonpareil view out over the city at sunset while you sip your free pint. One of the bar's first clients was one William Jefferson Clinton. You'll find the Guinness logo on everything from piggy banks to underpants in the Guinness Store on the ground floor. ⊠ *St. James' Gate, Dublin West* ☎ *01/408–4800* ⊕ *www.guinnessstorehouse.com* ⊠ *€16.50* ☾ *July and Aug., daily 9:30–7; Sept.–June, daily 9:30–5.*

Kilmainham Gaol. Leaders of many failed Irish rebellions spent their last days in this grim, forbidding structure, and it holds a special place in the myth and memory of the country. The 1916 commanders Pádraig Pearse and James Connolly were held here before being executed in the prison yard. Other famous inmates included the revolutionary Robert Emmet and Charles Stewart Parnell, a leading politician. You can visit the prison only as part of a very moving and exciting guided tour, which leaves every hour on the hour. The cells are a chilling sight, and the guided tour and a 30-minute audiovisual presentation relate a graphic account of Ireland's political history over the past 200 years—from an Irish Nationalist viewpoint. A new exhibition explores the history of the prison and its restoration. A small tearoom is on the premises. ⊠ *Inchicore Rd., Dublin West* ☎ *01/453–5984* ⊕ *www.heritageireland. ie* ⊠ *€6* ☾ *Apr.–Sept., daily 9:30–6; Oct.–Mar., Mon.–Sat. 9:30–5:30, Sun. 10–6.*

2

Royal Hospital Kilmainham. This replica of Les Invalides in Paris is regarded as the most important 17th-century building in Ireland. Commissioned as a hospice for disabled and veteran soldiers by James Butler—the Duke of Ormonde and viceroy to King Charles II—it was completed in 1684, making it the first building erected in Dublin's golden age. It survived into the 1920s as a hospital, but after the founding of the Irish Free State in 1922, the building fell into disrepair. The entire edifice has since been restored. The architectural highlight is the hospital's Baroque chapel, distinguished by its extraordinary plasterwork ceiling and fine wood carvings. ☎ *01/612–9900* ⊕ *www.rhk.ie* ☉ *Mon., Tues., and Thurs.–Sat. 10–5:30; Wed. 10:30–5:30; Sun. noon–5:30.*

Irish Museum of Modern Art. The Royal Hospital also houses the Irish Museum of Modern Art, which concentrates on the work of contemporary Irish artists such as Richard Deacon, Richard Gorman, Dorothy Cross, Sean Scully, Matt Mullican, Louis le Brocquy, and James Coleman. The museum also displays works by some non-Irish 20th-century greats, including Picasso and Miró, plus recent hotshots like Damien Hirst, and regularly hosts touring shows from major European museums. Café Itsa serves light fare such as soups and sandwiches. The hospital is a short ride by taxi or bus from the city center and there is a Luas stop nearby. ⊠ *Kilmainham La., Dublin West* ☎ *01/612–9900* ⊕ *www.imma.ie* ✉ *Free* ☉ *Tues. and Thurs.–Sat. 10–5:30, Wed. 10:30–5:30, Sun. noon–5:30; tours Tues.–Fri. at 1:15, Sat. at noon and 4, Sun. 2:30 and 4.*

Fodor's Choice
★

St. Patrick's Cathedral. The largest cathedral in Dublin and also the national cathedral of the Church of Ireland, St. Patrick's was built in honor of Ireland's patron saint, who—according to legend—baptized many converts at a well on this site in the 5th century. The original building, dedicated in 1192 and early English Gothic in style, was an unsuccessful attempt to assert supremacy over the capital's other Protestant cathedral, Christ Church Cathedral. At 305 feet, this is the longest church in the country, a fact Oliver Cromwell's troops found useful as they made the church's nave into their stable in the 17th century.

■ TIP➔ **While in the shadow of St. Patrick's Cathedral, head from Patrick Close to Patrick Street; look down the street toward the Liffey for a fine view of Christ Church.**

Make sure you see the gloriously heraldic Choir of St. Patrick's, hung with colorful medieval banners, and find the tomb of the most famous of St. Patrick's many illustrious deans, Jonathan Swift, immortal author of *Gulliver's Travels,* who held office from 1713 to 1745. Swift's tomb is in the south aisle, not far from that of his beloved "Stella," Mrs. Esther Johnson. Swift's epitaph is inscribed over the robing-room door. W. B. Yeats—who translated it thus: "Swift has sailed into his rest; Savage indignation there cannot lacerate his breast"—declared it the greatest epitaph of all time. Other memorials include the 17th-century Boyle Monument, with its numerous painted figures of family members, and the monument to Turlough O'Carolan, the last of the Irish bards and one of the country's finest harp players. "Living Stones" is the cathedral's permanent exhibition celebrating St. Patrick's place in the life of the city. If you're a music lover, you're in for a treat; matins (9:40 am) and evensong (5:45 pm) are still sung on many days. A new "Lives Remembered" exhibition looks at the role of the cathedral during World War One. ☒ *Patrick St., Dublin West* ☎ *01/453–9472* ⊕ *www.stpatrickscathedral.ie* ☒ *€5.50* ⊗ *Mar.–Oct., weekdays 9–5, Sat. 9–6, Sun. 9–10:30, 12:30–2:30, and 4:30–6; Nov.–Feb., Mon.–Sat. 9–5, Sun. 9–10:30 and 12:30–2:30.*

WORTH NOTING

FAMILY **Dublinia.** Ever wanted a chance to put your head in the stocks? Dublin's Medieval Trust has set up an entertaining and informative reconstruction of everyday life in medieval Dublin. The main exhibits use high-tech audiovisual and computer displays; you can also see a scale model of what Dublin was like around 1500, a medieval maze, a life-size reconstruction based on the 13th-century dockside at Wood Quay, and a fine view from the tower. Dublinia is in the old Synod Hall (formerly a meeting place for bishops of the Church of Ireland), joined via a covered stonework Victorian bridge to Christ Church Cathedral. An exhibition on "Viking Dublin" consists of a similar reconstruction of life in even earlier Viking Dublin, including a Viking burial. An exhibition called "History Hunters" puts you in the role of archaeologist with interactive digs and a lab to test your newfound knowledge. There's a guided tour at 2:30 pm every day. ☒ *St. Michael's Hill, Dublin West* ☎ *01/679–4611* ⊕ *www.dublinia.ie* ☒ *Exhibit €7.50* ⊗ *Mar.–Sept., daily 10–5; Oct.–Feb., daily 10–4:30.*

Marsh's Library. When Ireland's first public library was founded and endowed in 1701 by Narcissus Marsh, the Archbishop of Dublin, it was made open to "All Graduates and Gentlemen." The two-story brick Georgian building has remained virtually the same since then. It houses a priceless collection of 250 manuscripts and 25,000 15th- to 18th-century books. Many of these rare volumes were locked inside cages, as were the readers who wished to peruse them. The cages were to discourage the often impecunious students, who may have been tempted to make the books their own. The library has been restored with great attention to its original architectural details, especially in the book stacks. It's a short walk west from St. Stephen's Green and is accessed through a charming little cottage garden. ☒ *St. Patrick's Close off Patrick St., Dublin West* ☎ *01/454–3511* ⊕ *www.marshlibrary.ie* ☒ *€3* ⊗ *Mon. and Wed.–Fri. 9:30–1 and 2–5, Sat. 10–1.*

The National College of Art & Design. The delicate welding of glass and iron onto the redbrick Victorian facade of this onetime factory makes this school worth a visit. A walk around the cobblestone central courtyard often gives the added bonus of viewing students working away in glass, clay, metal, and stone. The glass-fronted new gallery combines work by local, national, and international avant-garde artists. ☒ *100 Thomas St., Dublin West* ☎ *53/1636–4200* ⊕ *www.ncad.ie* ☒ *Free* ⊗ *Weekdays 9–7.*

Old Jameson Distillery. Founded in 1791, this distillery produced one of Ireland's most famous whiskeys for nearly 200 years, until 1966, when local distilleries merged to form Irish Distillers and moved to a purpose-built, ultramodern distillery in Middleton, County Cork. Part of the complex was converted into the group's head office, and the distillery itself became a museum. There's a short audiovisual history of the industry, which had its origins 1,500 years ago in Middle Eastern perfume making. You can also tour the old distillery, and learn about the distilling of whiskey from grain to bottle, or view a reconstruction of a former warehouse, where the colorful nicknames of former barrel makers are recorded. The 40-minute tour includes a complimentary tasting; four attendees are invited to taste different brands of Irish whiskey and compare them against bourbon and Scotch. If you have a large group and everyone wants to do this, phone in advance to arrange it. You can also get tutored—complete with certification—in whiskey tasting. ⊠ *Bow St., Dublin West* ☎ *01/807–2348* ⊕ *www.tours. jamesonwhiskey.com* ☏ *€13* ⊗ *Mon.–Sat. 9–6, Sun. 10–6; tours every 20 mins up to 5:30.*

Smithfield. Bordered on the east by Church Street, on the west by Blackhall Place, to the north by King Street, and to the south by the Liffey, Smithfield is Dublin's old market area where flowers, fruit, vegetables, and even horses have been sold for generations. Chosen as a flagship for north inner-city renovation during the boom, the area saw a major face-lift—with mixed reactions from the locals. Some of the beautiful cobblestones of its streets have been taken up, refinished, and replaced, and giant masts topped with gaslights send 6-foot-high flames over Smithfield Square. Unfortunately, since money's become tight they don't light the gas anymore, and there's the air of a white elephant about the whole thing. But the area is still worth a visit, especially in the early morning, as the wholesale fruit and vegetable sellers still ply their trade in the wonderful 19th-century covered market. It's also home to the wonderful Lighthouse cinema and a twice-yearly horse-trading market. ⊠ *Smithfield, Dublin West.*

St. Michan's Church. However macabre, St. Michan's main claim to fame is down in the vaults, where the totally dry atmosphere has preserved several corpses in a remarkable state of mummification. They lie in open caskets. Most of the resident deceased are thought to have been Dublin tradespeople (one was, they say, a religious crusader). Except for its 120-foot-high bell tower, this Anglican church is architecturally undistinguished. The church was built in 1685 on the site of an 11th-century Danish church (Michan was a Danish saint). If preserved corpses are not enough of a draw, you can also find an 18th-century organ, which Handel supposedly played for the first performance of *Messiah*. Don't forget to check out the Stool of Repentance—the only one still in existence in the city. Parishioners judged to be "open and notoriously naughty livers" used it to do public penance. ⊠ *Lower Church St., Dublin West* ☎ *01/872–4154* ⊕ *www.stmichans.com* ☏ *€5* ⊗ *Mid-Mar.–Oct., weekdays 10–12:45 and 2–4:45, Sat. 10–12:45, Sun. service at 10 am; Nov.–mid-Mar., weekdays 12:30–3:30, Sat. 10–12:45, Sun. service at 10 am.*

PHOENIX PARK AND ENVIRONS

Far and away Dublin's largest park, Phoenix Park (the name is an anglicization of the Irish *Fionn Uisce,* meaning "clear water") is a vast, green, arrowhead-shaped oasis north of the Liffey, about a 20-minute walk from the city center. It's the city's main escape valve and sports center (cricket, soccer, Gaelic games, and polo), and the home of the noble creatures of the Dublin Zoo. A handful of other cultural sights near the park also merit a visit.

TOP ATTRACTIONS

Fodor'sChoice ★ **National Museum of Decorative Arts and History.** Here, in one gigantic treasure chest, is the full panoply of the National Museum's collection of glass, silver, furniture, and other decorative arts. The setting is spectacular: the huge Collins Barracks, named for the assassinated Irish Republican leader Michael Collins (1890–1922). Built in the early 18th century, and designed by Captain Thomas Burgh, these erstwhile "Royal Barracks" were stylishly renovated to become a showcase for the museum, which opened in September 1997. The displays are far ranging, covering everything from one of the greatest collections of Irish silver in the world to Irish period furniture—you'll see that the country's take on Chippendale was far earthier than the English mode. "The Way We Wore: 250 Years of Irish Clothing and Jewelry" and a thousand years of Irish coins are other highlights. Headlining the collections are some extraordinary objects, including the Fonthill Vase, the William Smith O'Brien Gold Cup, and the Lord Chancellor's Mace. ✉ *Benburb St., Dublin West* ☎ *01/677-7444* ⊕ *www.museum.ie* ✉ *Free* ☉ *Tues.–Sat. 10–5, Sun. 2–5.*

FAMILY **Phoenix Park.** Europe's largest public park, which extends about 5 km (3 miles) along the Liffey's north bank, encompasses 1,752 acres, and holds a lot of verdant green lawns, woods, lakes, and playing fields. Sunday is the best time to visit: games of cricket, football (soccer), polo, baseball, hurling (a traditional Irish sport the resembles a combination of lacrosse, baseball, and field hockey), and Irish football are likely to be in progress. Old-fashioned gas lamps line both sides of Chesterfield Avenue, the main road that bisects the park for 4 km (2½ miles), which was named for Lord Chesterfield, a lord lieutenant of Ireland, who laid out the road in the 1740s. To the right as you enter the park is the People's Garden, a colorful flower garden designed in 1864. Rent bikes (including tandems) at the main gate to get the most from the park's hidden corners. ⊕ *www.phoenixpark.ie.*

Phoenix Park Visitor Centre. Within Phoenix Park is a visitor center, in the 17th-century fortified Ashtown Castle; it has information about the park's history, flora, and fauna. Admission to the center is free, and it runs guided tours of the park throughout the year. Hours are April–December, daily 10–6; January–March, Wednesday–Sunday 9:30–5:30. ✉ *Dublin West* ☎ *01/677-0095* ⊕ *www.phoenixpark.ie.* ✉ *Free.*

Dublin Zoo. Founded in 1830, Dublin Zoo may be the third-oldest public zoo in the world but a major renovation completed in 2007 gave new life and luster to the old place. Animals from tropical climes are kept in unbarred enclosures, and Arctic species swim in the lakes close to the reptile house. Some 700 lions have been bred here since the 1850s, one of whom became familiar to movie fans the world over when MGM used him for its trademark. (As they will tell you at the zoo, he is in fact yawning in that familiar shot: an American lion had to be hired to roar and the "voice" was dubbed.) The African Plains section houses the zoo's larger species; the Nakuru Safari is a 25-minute tour of this area. World of Primates is a gathering of the usual suspects from tiny colobus monkeys to big gorillas. In summer the Lakeside Café serves ice cream and drinks. ⊠ *Dublin West* ☎ *01/474–8900* ⊕ *www.dublinzoo. ie* 🎟 *€16.50* ⊗ *Daily Mar.–Sept. 9:30–5, Jan. 9:30–3:30, Feb. 9:30–4, Oct. 9:30–4:30, Nov. and Dec. 9:30–3.*

Farmleigh House. This 78-acre Edwardian estate, situated to the northwest of the park, includes a working farm, walled and sunken gardens, wonderful picnic-friendly grounds, a regular organic food market, and a house full of antique furnishings and historic art. Admission is free. ⊠ *Phoenix Park, Dublin West* ☎ *01/815–5914* ⊕ *www.farmleigh. ie* ⊗ *Wed.–Sun. 10–5.*

NEED A BREAK?

Ryan's Pub. One of Dublin's last remaining genuine late-Victorian-era pubs, Ryan's has changed little since its last remodeling—in 1896. It's right near the entrance to Phoenix Park. The small restaurant upstairs does a mean steak. ⊠ *28 Parkgate St., Dublin West* ☎ *01/677–6097.*

WORTH NOTING

Arbour Hill Cemetery. All 14 Irishmen executed by the British following the 1916 Easter Rising are buried here, including Pádraig Pearse, who led the rebellion; his younger brother Willie, who played a minor role in the uprising; and James Connolly, a socialist and labor leader wounded in the battle. Too weak from his wounds to stand, Connolly was tied to a chair and then shot. The burial ground is a simple but formal area, with the names of the dead leaders carved in stone beside an inscription of the proclamation they issued during the uprising. ⊠ *Arbour Hill, Dublin West* ☎ *01/821–3021* ⊕ *www.heritageireland.ie/en/Dublin/ ArbourHillCemetary* 🎟 *Free* ⊗ *Weekdays 8–4, Sat. 11–4, Sun. 9:30–4.*

WHERE TO EAT

If you arrive thinking you're going to eat potatoes, potatoes, and more potatoes, be prepared to have your preconceptions overturned, and to be enthralled and very happily sated in the process. Ireland has undergone a food revolution, and some of Dublin's chefs are leading the charge—taking advantage of the fact that Ireland has some of the best "raw materials" in the world.

Given that it is a small island on which one is never farther than an hour-and-a-half drive from the coast, it is not only its seaside restaurants that can claim to serve fish on the same day it's caught. In addition, the freshest Limerick hams, tastiest Cork *crubins* (pigs' trotters), and most succulent Galway Bay oysters arrive in the city every day.

Ethnic restaurants now have a firm foothold in the city's foodie culture—thanks to the influx of immigrants during the Celtic Tiger prosperity—so you can indulge your passion for superb French or Italian food one day, then enjoy Korean barbecue the next. A reduction in city center rents and a focus on value has spawned a number of smaller, innovative, and more personalized restaurants putting their own *blás* (Irish for "gloss") on traditional ingredients.

Prices in the reviews are the average cost of a main course at dinner or, if dinner is not served, at lunch. Use the coordinate (✛ 1:B2) at the end of each listing to locate a site on the corresponding Where to Eat in Dublin map.

SOUTHSIDE

$ ✕ **Busyfeet & Coco Café.** This bustling, bohemian café emphasizes good,
CAFÉ wholesome food. Organic ingredients play a prominent role on a menu that's laden with delicious salads and sandwiches. Try the grilled goat-cheese salad served with walnut-and-raisin toast and sun-dried-tomato tapenade on a bed of arugula. The delicious ploughmans sandwich—with Irish cheddar, vine tomatoes, Branston pickle, and mayo served on brown bread—is a must. It's also one of the city center's best-situated spots for a bit of people-watching, as Dublin's young and hip stroll by all day long. **$** *Average main: €9* ✉ *41–42 S. William St., Southside* ☎ *01/671–9514* ⌂ *Reservations not accepted* ✛ *1:C4.*

$ ✕ **Cake Café.** When the former head of the Slow Food Dublin movement
CAFÉ opens a café, expectations are going to be high. Michelle Darmody's
Fodor's Choice dreamy little Cake Café fulfills every one of them. As it is in a plant-filled
★ courtyard at the back of the restored Daintree building, try to snag an outside table if the weather is decent. Then chill out and chow down on simple savory and sweet delights, all made with a loving, homey touch. Local, organic, and seasonal are the words to live by here and the surprising sardines on toast is a typically delicious dish. Save room for the delicate tarts and moist sugar-dusted sponges. This is also the perfect summer spot for a cheeky daytime glass of prosecco with a few nibbles in the courtyard. Ask about the fun cookery classes: they're the talk of the town. **$** *Average main: €11* ✉ *The Daintree Bldg., Pleasants Pl., Southside* ☎ *01/478–9394* ⊕ *www.thecakecafe.ie* ☉ *Closed Sun. No dinner Mon. and Sat.* ✛ *1:B5.*

$ ✕ **Damson Diner.** American–Asian fusion cuisine in a retro-1950s' diner
DINER with a modern twist: it sounds like a disaster waiting to happen, but the Damson Diner has been a hit on the Dublin dining scene. The place looks beautiful—three stories of chrome, glass, banquettes, and flood of natural light. The cool atmosphere is key, with relaxed, humorous but attentive staff, and a lively crowd fueled by to-die-for cocktails and fast but thoughtful dishes. The menu is basically a greatest hits of diner food from around the globe, with the spicy, bite-sized fennel bhajis and the pork chops with Asian slaw nice alternatives to the knockout steaks and burgers. The long bar is a top spot for people-watching and getting experimental—they forage for wild ingredients such as sloes for their cocktails. **$** *Average main: €17* ✉ *52 S. William St., Southside* ☎ *01/677–7007* ⊕ *www.damsondiner.com* ✛ *1:C4.*

BEST BETS FOR DUBLIN DINING

With hundreds of restaurants to choose from, how will you decide where to eat? Fodor's writers and editors have selected their favorite restaurants by price, cuisine, and experience in the lists here. You can also search by neighborhood for excellent eating experiences—just peruse the following pages. Or find specific details about a restaurant in the full reviews, which are listed alphabetically.

Fodor's Choice ★

Cake Café, $, p. 102

Chapter One, $$$$, p. 117

Dunne and Crescenzi, $, p. 104

Enoteca delle Langhe, $, p. 117

Fallon & Byrne, $$, p. 104

The French Paradox, $, p. 112

Hop House, $, p. 117

L'Gueuleton, $$, p. 105

Musashi Noodles and Sushi Bar, $, p. 118

One Pico, $$$, p. 108

Restaurant Patrick Guilbaud, $$$$, p. 113

Thornton's Restaurant, $$$$, p. 109

Wuff, $$, p. 119

By Price

$

Cake Café, p. 102

Dunne and Crescenzi, p. 104

Enoteca delle Langhe, p. 117

French Paradox, p. 112

The Good World, p. 104

Hop House, p. 117

Kingfisher, p. 118

Musashi Noodles and Sushi Bar, p. 118

The Pepper Pot, p. 108

$$

Eden, p. 115

The Green Hen, p. 105

L'Gueuleton, p. 105

The Winding Stair, p. 118

Wuff, $$, p. 119

$$$

Dax, p. 109

One Pico, p. 108

Unicorn, p. 114

$$$$

Chapter One, p. 117

Les Frères Jacques, p. 115

Restaurant Patrick Guilbaud, p. 113

Thornton's, p. 109

By Type

CHILD-FRIENDLY

Cake Café, $, p. 102

Dunne and Crescenzi, $, p. 104

Enoteca delle Langhe, $, p. 117

The Good World, $, p. 104

EXPENSE ACCOUNT

Chapter One, $$$$, p. 117

Restaurant Patrick Guilbaud, $$$$, p. 113

Shanahan's on the Green, $$$$, p. 108

Town Bar and Grill, $$$, p. 114

GREAT VIEWS

Cake Café, $, p. 102

Eden, $$, p. 115

The Winding Stair, $$, p. 118

HOT SPOT

Brother Hubbard, $, p. 116

Cake Café, $, p. 102

Damson Diner, $ p. 102

Fade Street Social, $$ p. 104

Musashi Noodles and Sushi Bar, $ p. 118

Wuff, $$, p. 119

LOTS OF LOCALS

Busyfeet & Coco Café, $, p. 102

Fade Street Social, $$ p. 104

L'Gueuleton, $$, p. 105

L. Mulligan Grocer, $, p. 118

The Pepper Pot, $, p. 108

Roly's Bistro, $$, p. 113

Wuff, $$, p. 119

MOST ROMANTIC

Chapter One, $$$$, p. 117

L'Gueuleton, $$, p. 105

One Pico, $$$, p. 108

DELICIOUS DECOR

Cake Café, $, p. 102

Chapter One, $$$$, p. 117

Restaurant Patrick Guilbaud, $$$$, p. 113

The Pepper Pot, $, p. 108

$
ITALIAN
Fodor'sChoice
★

✕ **Dunne and Crescenzi.** Nothing succeeds like success. So popular is this classy little Italian joint just off Nassau Street that they've expanded into the premises two doors down. Pity the poor little coffee shop in between trying to compete with the unpretentious brilliance of this brother-and-sister restaurant and deli. The menu is extensive but simple: panini (sandwiches), a horde of antipasti choices, a few choice pasta specials, and some evening meat dishes and desserts. The all-Italian kitchen staff work wonders with high-quality imported ingredients. The gnocchi with a slow-cooked ragú of Gilligan's Hereford Irish beef makes a great lunch. A couple of long tables make it perfect for a group, and the hundreds of bottles of wine on shelves cover every inch of the walls. They have opened a second café in nearby Sandymount. $ *Average main: €14* ⊠ *14 S. Fredrick St., Southside* ☎ *01/677–3815* ⊕ *www.dunneandcrescenzi.com* ✛ *1:D4.*

$$
MODERN IRISH

✕ **Fade Street Social.** The latest venture of former Michelin-star celebrity-chef Dylan McGrath, Fade Street Social is a cavernous tapas bar, restaurant, and pub all rolled into one. At 8,000 square feet, the place can seem a bit overwhelming, but if you want a busy, fun, all-in-one dining-and-drinking experience, this place is ideal. Try a seat at the bar, where you can watch the kitchen staff work their magic as they turn out exquisite tapas and hearty but inventive meat dishes, all with a modern Irish twist. The whole squab pigeon poached with thyme and smoked bacon is an original tapas offering, while the braised rabbit leg with white wine, smoked bacon, tarragon, and onion is already a favorite main. $ *Average main: €22* ⊠ *4 Fade St., Southside* ☎ *01/604–0066* ⊕ *www.fadestreetsocial.com* ✛ *1:C4.*

$$
FRENCH
Fodor'sChoice
★

✕ **Fallon & Byrne.** A fresh, one-stop-shop for everything organic and delicious in Dublin, Fallon & Byrne combines a huge deli with a cozy cellar wine bar and expansive second-floor French brasserie. Located on the top floor of a beautiful old telephone exchange building, the high-ceiling, light-filled dining room is always bustling. The menu covers everything from burgers to loin of rabbit, but the grilled fillet of plaice with brandade potato, butternut squash, and basil beurre blanc and the sweet-potato polenta cake with Tuscan bean stew and aubergine (eggplant) caviar are typical. Leave room for the lemon-ricotta cheesecake with ginger ice cream. You can pick up a bottle of wine in the wine cellar and enjoy it for a small corkage fee. $ *Average main: €24* ⊠ *11–17 Exchequer St., Southside* ☎ *01/472–1010* ⊕ *www.fallonandbyrne.com* ⌕ *Reservations essential* ✛ *1:C3.*

$
CHINESE

✕ **The Good World.** When Dublin's growing Chinese population wants a big, uptown night out they come here. The surroundings are modest, with large round tables—ideal for groups—in a somewhat dark but comfortable room. But the food is authentic and inspired—ask for the black-cover Chinese menu, not the standard, dumbed-down one. The dim sum selection is nonpareil in Ireland, with the scallop dumplings a standout, and the chili-salt squid melts in the mouth. It's the perfect spot to order a load of dishes to be shared by an adventurous group. As is often the case with Chinese restaurants in Ireland, the desserts are not really worth trying. $ *Average main: €15* ⊠ *18 S. Great George's St., Southside* ☎ *01/677–5373* ✛ *1:C3.*

$$ ✕ **The Green Hen.** It can be hard to re-create that classic bistro feel out-
FRENCH side of France, but this intimate spot at the heart of busy Dublin has
managed to get the mix of bustle and tranquillity just right. A mix of
warm brick walls dotted with black-and-white snaps of French film
stars from the 1950s and wood paneling with tongue-in-cheek French
movie posters keeps the vibe informal. A quick glance at the gilt-framed,
mirrored menu reveals that this kitchen is all about rich, evocative
French fare—two winners are the poached saddle of rabbit and the pan-
fried hake with Gruyère and crab crust. The rhubarb crème brûlée is a
clever Irish take on the Gallic standard. Lunch is great value, and keep
an eye out for adventurous plats du jour and lively wine list. $ *Aver-
age main: €21* ✉ *33 Exchequer St., Southside* ☎ *01/670–7238* ⊕ *www.
thegreenhen.com* ✛ *1:C3.*

$$ ✕ **Il Primo.** Owners John Farrell and Anita Thoma like to run this little
ITALIAN two-story Italian restaurant like an intimate dinner party. A little quote
board outside offers a daily pearl of wisdom, and old wooden tables
and chairs give the two small dining rooms a casual feel. The friendly, if
cramped, surroundings attract a devoted clientele and John's collection
of contemporary art adds a dash of flair to the walls. The slow-cooked
feather blade beef with winter vegetables and truffle oil is a standout
evening dish. Risotto is a house specialty and the version with panc-
etta, leeks, and taleggio is a must. The wine list—heavy with Italian
influences—is, to quote a local phrase, as long as your arm. $ *Average
main: €22* ✉ *16 Montague St., off Harcourt St., Southside* ☎ *01/478–
3373* ⊕ *www.ilprimo.ie* ☾ *No dinner Sun.* ✛ *1:C4.*

$ ✕ **Jaipur.** Call to mind all the stereotypes of bad, production-line Indian
INDIAN restaurants. Then consign them to the flames, for Jaipur is something
different altogether. A spacious room with a sweeping staircase and contemporary furnishings reflects Jaipur's modern, cutting-edge approach
to Indian cuisine. Mixed with traditional dishes, such as chicken tikka
masala, are more unusual preparations, such as lamb chili fry (lamb mor-
sels with peppers, brown onion jam, and cumin masala). The delightful
karwari is a sweet-and-sour butterfish in a tamarind-flavor broth redolent
of coastal-south-Indian spices. Try the Jaipur Jugalbandi, a selection of
five appetizers. Dishes can be toned down or spiced up to suit your palate, and service is courteous and prompt. Another plus: the wine list is
well thought out. They also have locations in the suburbs of Dalkey and
Malahide. $ *Average main: €17* ✉ *41 S. Great George's St., Southside*
☎ *01/677–0999* ⊕ *www.jaipur.ie* ☖ *Reservations essential* ✛ *1:B4.*

$$ ✕ **La Maison Restaurant.** This Breton-inspired, unpretentious eatery has
FRENCH one of the most inviting and good-value menus in the city. The look is
very much casual bistro, a satisfying backdrop for starters like the hot
smoked-salmon rillette with dill crème fraîche and sourdough toasts,
and such mouthwatering mains as the loin of venison with red cab-
bage and celeriac paste. The chocolate fondant is a must. $ *Average
main: €21* ✉ *15 Castle Market, Southside* ☎ *01/672–7258* ⊕ *www.
lamaisonrestaurant.ie* ✛ *1:C4.*

$$ ✕ **L'Gueuleton.** Dubliners don't do waiting, but you'll see hungry crowds
FRENCH doing just that outside this no-reservations-accepted, exceptional eatery
Fodor'sChoice just off George's Street. L'Gueuleton lost a little of its intimacy when it
★ expanded, but the crowds still come for authentic French food at a fair

DUBLIN'S SEAFOOD BOUNTY

Clarenbridge oysters, Carlingford Lough mussels, Ballina wild smoked salmon, Donegal crab—the menus of the top restaurants in Dublin are now full of some of the most flavorsome seafood on the planet. Surprisingly, Ireland has only recently fallen in love with its own array of briny treasures, and thereby hangs a fish tale.

(above) The Irish treasure of the deep—smoked salmon; *(right, top)* When it comes to fish-and-chips, some say the greasier the better; *(right, bottom)* Seaweed is a chic new condiment.

A somewhat apocryphal story about Ireland joining the EEC (European Economic Community) in 1973 has the government given a stark choice: you can farm or you can fish, but you can't do both. They chose to protect farming, and the result was the massive overfishing by giant Spanish factory ships off Irish waters. This fact may, in part, explain why Ireland—a relatively pollution-free, sea-surrounded nation—is not one of the first places gourmands think of for great seafood. Historically, there was also a certain snobbery about eating fish, as it was seen as peasant food only suitable for fasting Fridays. Well, things have certainly changed in the last two decades.

TOP FISHY JOINTS

Some standout joints in Dublin go that extra mile. The oyster stall at the Temple Bar Farmers' Market every Saturday is something of a Dublin institution, where affordable Atlantic oysters and white wine are downed alfresco. Les Frères Jacques delivers true Gallic panache to its lobsters. The no-frills Kingfisher is noted for its whole rainbow trout.

SMOKED SALMON

From all corners of Ireland small producers are now making some of Europe's finest smoked salmon. Obviously, and perhaps unfortunately, the wild Atlantic salmon still has a richer, more piquant taste than its farmed cousin. The word "wild" in the description will tell you the fish isn't farmed. The traditional smoking method uses only Irish oak, which gives it a very distinctive, subtle flavor, and deep orange color. The best way to enjoy smoked salmon is over some toasted Dublin brown bread with a simple squeeze of lemon and some coarse black pepper to add that little extra tang.

IRISH CHOWDER

It's the pint of heavy cream and density of mussels tossed into the mix that makes Irish seafood chowder such a great snack on the run. It's also a dish that even the most humble of eateries doesn't usually mess up, although the general rule still applies: the nearer to the coast the eatery is located, the better its chowder. Regular fish stock is often used but clam juice—an Irish specialty—also adds to the unique flavor. Enjoy chowders at Ireland's great seafood festivals: the Galway Oyster Festival, the event in Baltimore in West Cork, and the Killybegs festival.

FISH-AND-CHIPS

Every Dubliner will argue about the best place to get their favorite fast-food dish of fish-and-chips, but few will quarrel with the fact that cod, ray, and haddock are the top three battered delights to go for. Interestingly, the descendants of 1950s Italian immigrants—with names like Macari and Borza—are the recognized masters of the battering art, and you'll find one of their eponymously named shops in almost every neighborhood. Tip: a single portion is usually enough to feed two!

SEAWEED

Yes, the Irish are slowly discovering the delights of farming native seaweed for use in the kitchen and elsewhere. Irish seaweed is usually gathered along the western seaboard, dried, and then sold in small packets, a bit like herbs. Look closely at restaurant menus and you'll find dulse, carrageen moss, and various kelps and wracks all turning up to add spice to risottos, salads, soups, breads, and even ice cream. The local spa industry has cottoned on, developing "algotherapies," including wraps, aging creams, and even full-on seaweed baths.

price. Start with 12 snails, fresh herbs, garlic, and pastis butter. For a main course, the sauté rabbit with red wine, sage, and Barolo tagliatelle somehow manages to be hearty and adventurous at the same time. Desserts have a devilishly childish touch to them—passion-fruit cake with white chocolate sauce is a typical example. Although you can't phone in a reservation, you can go there early in the evening and put your name and phone number down for a table, and then pop next door to Hogan's bar while you're waiting. $ *Average main: €22 ⊠ 1 Fade St., Southside* ☎ *01/675–3708* ⊕ *www.lgueuleton.com* ✛ *1:B4.*

$ ✕ **Mao.** Everything is larger than life at this bustling café—which has
ASIAN quickly blossomed into a mini-franchise across the city—from the giant pictures of vegetables on the walls to the eclectic mix of dishes on the menu, which combine Thai, Vietnamese, and other Southeast Asian elements. Top choices include the five-spice chicken on wombok noodles, chili squid, crispy whole sea bass with scallops, and the *nasi goreng* (Indonesian fried rice with chicken and shrimp). $ *Average main: €15 ⊠ 2 Chatham Row, Southside* ☎ *01/670–4899* ⊕ *www.cafemao.com/ restaurant* ⌦ *Reservations not accepted* ✛ *1:C5.*

$$$ ✕ **One Pico.** Chef-owner Eamonn O'Reilly cuts quite a dash, but it's
MODERN IRISH his sophisticated, daring, contemporary cuisine that tends to seduce
Fodor's Choice visitors to his little restaurant tucked away in a quiet lane only a few
★ minutes from Stephen's Green. Try the incredible seared scallops to start. Dishes such as roast rump of veal with fricassee of girolles, pearl onion, and truffle, and *pomme sarladaise* (a southern French version of mashed potatoes) demonstrate a savvy use of native ingredients. Follow this with the mango cheesecake with mango and lime foam. As is usual with Dublin's luxe eateries, the fixed-price lunch and pretheater menus offer great value. $ *Average main: €31 ⊠ 5–6 Molesworth Pl., off Schoolhouse La., Southside* ☎ *01/676–0300* ⊕ *www.onepico.com* ⌦ *Reservations essential* ✛ *1:D4.*

$ ✕ **The Pepper Pot.** The hodgepodge collection of old tablecloths, cutlery,
CAFÉ and cups creates a warm, family atmosphere in this sweet little café on the balcony level of the Powerscourt Town House Centre. Weary shoppers resuscitate with the simple menu, fresh-baked goods, TLC, and people-watching. The soups and sandwiches are top-notch but the salads have a cult following. Tarts are seasonal and cakes are old school; the Victoria sponge and lemon and poppy seed are two standouts. $ *Average main: €8 ⊠ Powerscourt Town Centre, 1st- fl. balcony, S. William St., Southside* ☎ *01/707–1610* ⊕ *www.thepepperpot. ie* ⌦ *Reservations not accepted* ⊘ *Closed Sun. No dinner.* ✛ *1:C4.*

$$$$ ✕ **Shanahan's on the Green.** Glowing with gilded chandeliers and
AMERICAN graced with a few marble fireplaces, this American-style steak house in a restored Georgian town house offers a sleekly elegant setting in which to chow down on some of the most tender Irish Angus beef this side of the Atlantic (they cook it in a special high-temperature oven, searing the outside to keep the inside good and juicy). If steak doesn't float your boat, they also do a mean baked turbot with mussels, clams, and creamed fennel and leek. Oreo-cookie-crust cheesecake is the perfect way to finish off the feast, but many will consider the decor—think sash windows, gilt mirrors, and plush carpets—rich

enough. $ *Average main: €44* ✉ *119 St. Stephen's Green, Southside* ☎ *01/407–0939* ⊕ *www.shanahans.ie* ⌖ *Reservations essential* ☉ *No lunch Sat.–Thurs.* ✛ *1:C4.*

$$$$ ✗**Thornton's Restaurant.** Forget the stretched metaphors: if you're pas-
FRENCH sionate about food, this place is simply a must. Kevin Thornton's cook-
Fodor's Choice ing style is light, and his dishes are small masterpieces of structural
★ engineering, piled almost dangerously high in delicate food towers. Dinner is a set, three-course menu and a highlight is the fillet of Atlantic brill with Jerusalem artichoke puree, curly kale, and champagne sauce. Desserts range from apple tarte tatin to warm clementines with crème patíssíere and lemon verbena; the cheese course is supplied by famed Sheridans of Dublin. The dining room is simple and elegant—there's little to distract you from the exquisite food. ■TIP➔ The Canapé Bar is the perfect spot for a pre- or post-theater snack with a glass of cham-pagne. $ *Average main: €40* ✉ *Fitzwilliam Hotel, 128 St. Stephen's Green, Southside* ☎ *01/478–7008* ⊕ *www.thorntonsrestaurant.com* ⌖ *Reservations essential* ☉ *Closed Sun. and Mon. No lunch Tues. and Wed.* ✛ *1:C4.*

$$ ✗**Yamamori Noodles.** The open plan and family-style tables have kept
JAPANESE Yamamori popular with noodle addicts and the hip crowd. The meals-in-a-bowl are a splendid slurping experience, and although you'll be supplied with a small Chinese-style soup spoon, the best approach is with chopsticks. The seafood *yaki soba*, stir-fried egg noodles with a combination of fresh seafood and seasonal vegetables with *wakame* (an edible seaweed), is a favorite example. You can also get sushi and sashimi, delicious chicken teriyaki, or house specials like baked lob-ster. ■TIP➔ The bento box combo meal is the best value here. $ *Aver-age main: €19* ✉ *72 S. Great Georges St., Southside* ☎ *01/475–5001* ⊕ *www.yamamorinoodles.ie* ✛ *1:B3.*

GEORGIAN DUBLIN

$$ ✗**Chai-Yo.** Watch and learn—and then eat. The Japanese teppanyaki
ASIAN area at this classy pan-Asian restaurant on bustling Baggot Street, where the chef cooks your food right on your tabletop, is a feast for the eye as well as the palate. The white walls and dark lacquered furnishings give Chai-Yo a serene ambience, enhanced by the delicate glassware and fine, green-washed-porcelain plates. The menu picks the best from Chi-nese, Thai, and Japanese dishes, with the Asian tapas a good eat-and-go option. $ *Average main: €19* ✉ *100 Lower Baggot St., Georgian Dub-lin* ☎ *01/676–7652* ⊕ *www.chaiyo.ie* ☉ *No lunch weekends* ✛ *1:E5.*

$$$ ✗**Dax.** When is a wine bar not just a wine bar? When it's one of the
FRENCH city's most talked-about restaurants. Opened as a basement wine bar by Olivier Meisonnave, the former sommelier at stellar Thornton's, Dax has quickly become the choice of discerning Dubliners. You can drink or dine (tapas-style) at the bar, in the lush armchairs of the open-plan lounge, or in the more formal, restrained-modern dining room. The roasted wood pigeon with almond and white chocolate gel and mulled wine syrup is an adventurous starter, while the cold meat plat-ter is a finger-lickin' little bar dish. The wine list is the envy of many a more expensive eatery, and with a couple of dozen wines poured by

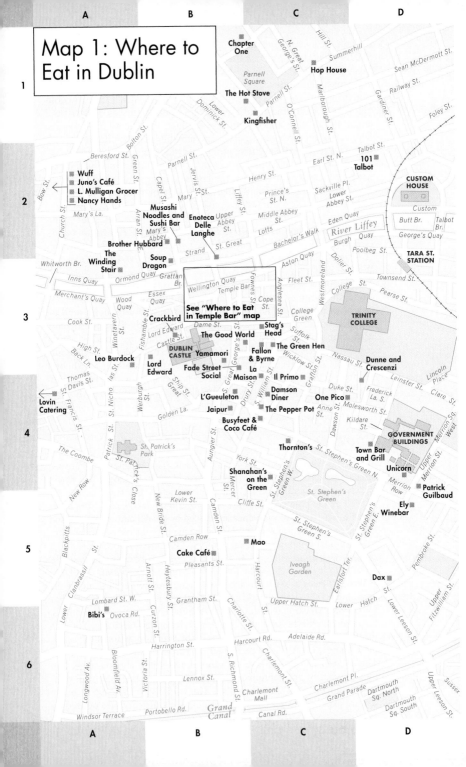

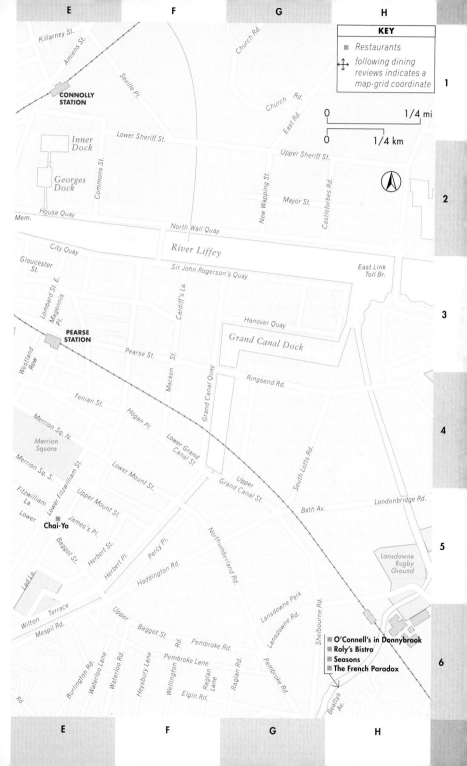

the glass you can dare to try something really special. There's a sister café in the same building with equally scrumptious offerings at a lower price point. $ *Average main: €27* ✉ *23 Pembroke St., Georgian Dublin* ☎ *01/676–1494* ⊕ *www. dax.ie* ⚞ *Reservations essential* ⊘ *Closed Sun. and Mon. No lunch Sat.* ✛ *1:D5.*

$$ ✕ **Ely Winebar.** Almost equidistant
IRISH from the twin dames of Dublin hotel elegance, the Shelbourne and the Merrion, Ely started out as a mere wine bar—and oh, what a selection of wines they have—but it has quickly grown into a wonderful little eatery with organic meat and vegetables from the owner's family farm in County Clare. Dishes such as roast chicken tend to be simple, but incredibly fresh and succulent. The plate of mature Irish and Continental cheeses is the perfect finish—with a glass of wine, of course. $ *Average main: €23* ✉ *22 Ely Pl., Georgian Dublin* ☎ *01/676–8986* ⊕ *www. elywinebar.ie* ⊘ *Closed Sun. No lunch Sat.* ✛ *1:D5.*

$ ✕ **The French Paradox.** Relaxed, simple, but chic would best describe
FRENCH this little restaurant above a wineshop in the heart of Ballsbridge; it
Fodor's Choice also describes the people of the south of France who inspired the place.
★ Wine buffs, Francophiles, and gourmets flock here for the hearty traditional fare and Mediterranean ambience. Share the *assiette le fond de barrique,* a selection of charcuterie, pâté, and cheese, or perhaps indulge in a duck terrine with homemade chutney or a choice from the foie gras menu. Select a nice bottle from the ground-floor wineshop (mostly French labels) and sip it in situ for a mere €8 corkage fee along with a few "French tapas." Seating is limited. $ *Average main: €11* ✉ *53 Shelbourne Rd., Georgian Dublin* ☎ *01/660–4068* ⊕ *www. thefrenchparadox.com* ⚞ *Reservations essential* ⊘ *Closed Sun.* ✛ *1:H6.*

$$$ ✕ **O'Connells in Donnybrook.** When it comes to cooking, pedigree counts.
MODERN IRISH Owner Tom O'Connell is a brother to Ireland's favorite celebrity chef, Darina Allen, famed for her "slow food" Ballymaloe Cookery School in Cork. Tom, now based in the heart of Donnybrook village, follows the family blueprint by showcasing fresh Irish produce and focusing on locally produced meats and game that can be traced to their source (in many cases, an individual farm). Altogether you have the makings of a feast that is deliciously, quintessentially Irish. Spiced beef is prepared according to an old Cork recipe, salmon fillet is "hot smoked" by the restaurant itself, while McCarthy's Black Pudding is handmade in Kanturk, County Cork. Desserts continue the homegrown theme, including a warm chocolate brownie with Gathabawn vanilla ice cream. The cheese board is a Who's Who of Irish farmhouse cheeses, including the Ferguson family's tangy Gubbeen. $ *Average main: €25* ✉ *135 Morehampton Rd., Donnybrook, Georgian Dublin* ☎ *01/269–6116* ⊕ *www. oconnellsdonnybrook.com* ⊘ *No lunch Mon.* ✛ *1:H6.*

$$$$ FRENCH Fodor's Choice ★ 🍴 **Restaurant Patrick Guilbaud.** Also known as "Dublin's finest restaurant," this do-be-impressed place on the ground floor of the Merrion Hotel boasts a menu described as French, but chef Guillaume Lebrun's genius lies in his occasional daring use of traditional Irish ingredients—so often taken for granted—to create the unexpected. The best dishes are flawless: poached Annagassan blue lobster with tonka and lobster jus, or the pressé of game birds with roast salsify, cherry juniper condiment, and crispy potato. Follow that, if you can, with the *assiette au chocolat* (a tray of five hot and cold chocolate desserts). The ambience is just as delicious—if you're into lofty, minimalist dining rooms and Irish modern art (the Roderic O'Conors and Louis le Brocquys are all from the owner's private collection). Nearly as impressive is the 70-page wine list, the view of the Merrion's manicured gardens, and the two-course lunch special for €38. Soaring white vaults and white walls won't make you feel warm and cozy, but you can always go somewhere else for that. [$] *Average main: €55* ✉ *21 Upper Merrion St., Georgian Dublin* ☎ *01/676–4192* 🌐 *www.restaurantpatrickguilbaud.ie* ✍ *Reservations essential* 🕒 *Closed Sun. and Mon.* ✥ *1:D5.*

WORD OF MOUTH

"Probably my favorite restaurant of the whole trip was **Queen of Tarts** (✉ *4 Corkhill St.* ☎ *01/670–7499* 🌐 *www.queenoftarts.ie*). It's a little café right across from City Hall. The interior is small and packed, but we gladly waited for a table after seeing all the amazing, amazing pastries in the display case. I had a potato and onion tart that was to die for, and the first really good salad I'd had in Ireland. The interior here is cozy and adorable. I'd say this is absolutely a restaurant you shouldn't miss in Dublin." —Erin74

$$ BISTRO 🍴 **Roly's Bistro.** While the bistro food at this Ballsbridge stalwart is always top class, it's the jovial atmosphere and superb service that keeps locals coming back. For a starter try the Bantry Bay scallops with braised oxtail beignets. The halibut with Asian spiced consommé, soft noodles, and baby pok choi is a standout main course. They are famed for their wine list, with great options by the glass, and that certainly helps to explain the wonderful buzz that always seems to be about this popular neighborhood place. [$] *Average main: €24* ✉ *7 Ballsbridge Terr., Georgian Dublin* ☎ *01/668–2611* 🌐 *www.rolybistro.ie* ✥ *1:H6.*

$$$$ MODERN IRISH 🍴 **Seasons.** Although the restaurant at the vaunted Four Seasons hotel took a little time to find its feet in and out of the kitchen, it has finally staked its claim in Dublin's dining scene—Sunday brunch here has become a ritual for many well-to-do Dublin Southsiders. Dramatic dishes, served in the large and slightly overwhelming silver-service dining room, creatively incorporate local (and often organic) ingredients. A starter of smoky baby back ribs with crunchy fennel and apple slaw might be followed by Clare Island salmon fillet with warm quinoa salad, mint yogurt, and sauce vierge. The wine list is one of the best in the country. [$] *Average main: €35* ✉ *Four Seasons Hotel, Simmonscourt Rd., Georgian Dublin* ☎ *01/665–4642* 🌐 *www.fourseasons.com/dublin* ✍ *Reservations essential* ✥ *1:H6.*

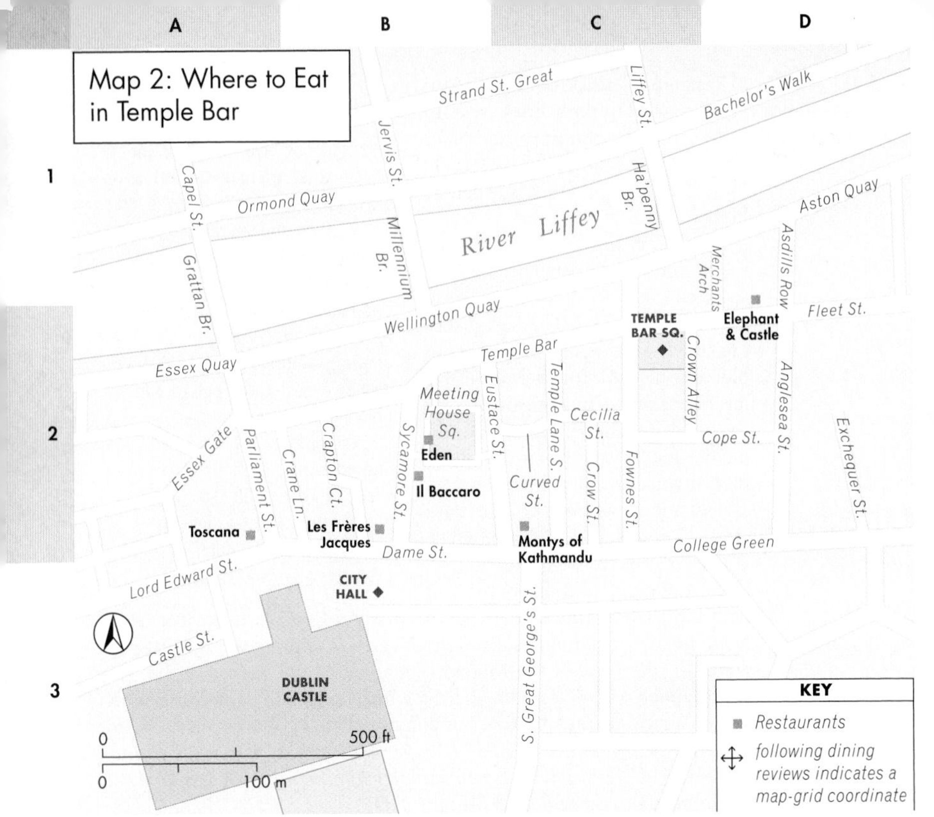
A
B
C
D
Map 2: Where to Eat in Temple Bar
1
2
3
Strand St. Great
Bachelor's Walk
Liffey St.
Jervis St.
Capel St.
Ormond Quay
Ha'penny Br.
Aston Quay
River Liffey
Millennium Br.
Grattan Br.
Merchants Arch
Asdills Row
Wellington Quay
Fleet St.
TEMPLE BAR SQ.
Elephant & Castle
Temple Bar
Essex Quay
Crown Alley
Meeting House Sq.
Eustace St.
Temple Lane S.
Cecilia St.
Anglesea St.
Exchequer St.
Cope St.
Essex Gate
Parliament St.
Crane Ln.
Crapton Ct.
Sycamore St.
Eden
Il Baccaro
Curved St.
Crow St.
Fownes St.
Toscana
Les Frères Jacques
Dame St.
Montys of Kathmandu
College Green
Lord Edward St.
CITY HALL
Castle St.
S. Great George's St.
DUBLIN CASTLE
0
500 ft
0
100 m
KEY
Restaurants
following dining reviews indicates a map-grid coordinate

$$$ MODERN IRISH

🍴 **Town Bar and Grill.** Once an old wine-merchant's cellar, this Kildare Street spot is now a classy eatery with an elegant, New York–vibe dining room, a definite buzz, and a top Irish chef, formerly of the nonpareil Chapter One. Classic dishes are given a new Irish twist; the black cod miso is one of the most exciting starters and for mains try the braised daube of beef with carrot puree, buttered spinach, roasted carrot, and crispy onion. A chocolate tart filled with chocolate mousse and served with almond ice cream, cherry, and lemon is a nice guilty way to finish. [$] *Average main: €26* ✉ *21 Kildare St., Georgian Dublin* ☎ *166/24800* 🌐 *www.townbarandgrill.com* ✍ *Reservations essential* ✥ *1:D4.*

$$$ MEDITERRANEAN

🍴 **Unicorn.** In the art of creating the perfect place to get slightly sozzled over some quality eats, the Unicorn is a master. Posh locals love to head here when they want to let their hair down in some wine-fueled, late-evening craic. The atmosphere is loose and relaxed, especially on the little terrace overlooking Merrion Court, and the menu is scrumptious Italian. Hot antipasti include chicken livers Marsala and calamari fritti, and tempting main courses include linguine with Dublin bay prawns, courgettes, garlic, chili, and white wine. To dine here, you must turn your mobile phone to silent—how cool is that? [$] *Average main: €27* ✉ *12B Merrion Ct., Georgian Dublin* ☎ *91/5998–4874* 🌐 *www.unicornrestaurant.com* ✍ *Reservations essential* ⏲ *Closed Sun. No lunch Sat.* ✥ *1:D4.*

TEMPLE BAR

$ ✕**Crackbird.** Originally a "pop-up" restaurant, this busy fried-chicken
DINER joint has quickly become the hotspot for young Dubliners looking for
something affordable but different. Always bustling, the place thrives
off the energy of its young staff and the over-the-top decor of the fancy
Chinese restaurant that formerly occupied the space. The menu is basically chicken done in a few mouthwatering ways; the buttermilk and soy
garlic being two standouts. The real treat is the wonderfully prepared
sides like the burnt lemon and feta dip or the best potato salad in town.
It's perfect for groups, with large tables and the option to get a bucket
of chicken to share. They're so cool they don't have a phone number,
but you can tweet to reserve (@CrackBIRDdublin)—that is, if you're
cool, too. $ *Average main: €12* ✉ *60 Dame St., Temple Bar* ⊕ *www.
joburger.ie/crackbird* ✛ *1:B3.*

$$ ✕**Eden.** A favorite haunt of arty and media types, Eden has an open
MODERN IRISH kitchen, a high wall of glass through which you can observe one of
Temple Bar's main squares, and patio-style doors that lead to an out-
door eating area—a major plus in a city with relatively few alfresco
dining spots. On weekend nights in summer you can enjoy an outdoor
movie in Meeting House Square while you eat. Seasonal menus are in
vogue here, but standout dishes include Castletownebere scallops with
crispy potato cake, creamed leeks, and prawn bisque. Desserts include a
tempting Belgian hot chocolate pudding. $ *Average main: €21* ✉ *Meet-
ing House Sq., Temple Bar* ☎ *01/670–5372* ⊕ *www.edenrestaurant.ie*
⌂ *Reservations essential* ☺ *No dinner Sun.* ✛ *2:B2.*

$$ ✕**Elephant & Castle.** The Elephant was long established in Temple Bar
AMERICAN before the Tiger (Celtic, that is) came and went and changed the neigh-
borhood forever. Large windows are great for people-watching in the
city's trendiest area, but "nothing fancy" would be a good motto for the
traditional American food. Charcoal-grilled burgers, salads, omelets,
sandwiches, and pasta make up the much-thumbed menu. Sunday
brunch is usually busy. The portions are some of the most generous
in Dublin. When the service is good, the turnover tends to be quick,
although you may be inclined to linger. New Yorkers, take note: yes,
this is a cousin of the restaurant of the same name in Greenwich Village.
$ *Average main: €19* ✉ *18 Temple Bar, Temple Bar* ☎ *01/679–3121*
⊕ *www.elephantandcastle.ie* ⌂ *Reservations not accepted* ✛ *2:D1.*

$ ✕**Il Baccaro.** One of the more romantic locations in the city has to be the
ITALIAN tiny candlelit dining room of this authentic Italian osteria in a vaulted
basement off Meeting House Square. The menu is small and focused,
with classic pastas and traditional starters like the panfried squid with
white wine, garlic, and a hint of chili. Selling house wine by the half
or full carafe is a good-value touch. $ *Average main: €17* ✉ *Meeting
House Sq., Temple Bar* ☎ *01/671–4597* ⊕ *www.ilbaccarodublin.com*
☺ *No lunch* ✛ *2:B2.*

$$$$ ✕**Les Frères Jacques.** Many restaurants call themselves French, but this
FRENCH elegant eatery next to the Olympia Theatre positively reeks of Gallic
panache. Old prints of Paris and Deauville hang on the green-papered
walls, and the French waiters, dressed in white Irish linen and black
bow ties, exude a European charm without being excessively formal.

Expect traditional French cooking that nods to the seasons. Seafood is a major attraction, and fresh lobster is typically roasted and flambéed with Irish whiskey. Also recommended are the seasonal game specialties. A piano player performs Friday and Saturday evenings and on the occasional weeknight. $ *Average main: €34* ⊠ *74 Dame St., Temple Bar* ☎ *01/679–4555* ⊕ *www.lesfreresjacques.com* ⌂ *Reservations essential* ⊗ *Closed Sun. No lunch Sat.* ✛ *2:B2.*

$ ✕ **Montys of Kathmandu.** You might not expect to come to Dublin for
ASIAN good Nepalese cuisine, but this place is a real standout. The decor is nothing to write home about, but the food at this little eatery in the middle of bustling Temple Bar is as authentic as it is unique. *Kachela,* raw minced lamb with garlic, ginger, herbs, and spices, served with a shot of whiskey or Roti (a delicacy among the Newars of Kathmandu) is a more adventurous starter. For a main course try *momos,* dumplings served with momo chutney, a favorite street dish in Kathmandu. It even has a celiac-friendly menu. The wine cellar is surprisingly varied. $ *Average main: €18* ⊠ *28 Eustace St., Temple Bar* ☎ *01/670–4911* ⊕ *www. montys.ie* ⊗ *No lunch* ✛ *2:C2.*

$ ✕ **Toscana.** A genuine trattoria in the heart of crazy Temple Bar, Toscana
ITALIAN buzzes with chatter all evening long and offers a popular pretheater menu. A Mediterranean slant to the simple dining room includes plenty of Italian landscapes, cream tones, and wood. A typical starter is the traditional Tuscan bean soup. The penne entrecôte is strips of Irish beef panfried with onions, garlic, and olive oil and tossed in a plum tomato–and-cream sauce. The meat and pizza dishes are also always reliable, and the Bailey's cheesecake with chocolate sauce is a dessert that will send you home with a smile on your face. $ *Average main: €16* ⊠ *3 Cork Hill, Dame St., Temple Bar* ☎ *01/670–9785* ⊕ *www. toscana.ie* ✛ *2:A2.*

NORTHSIDE

$ ✕ **101 Talbot.** Close to the Abbey and Gate theaters, so there's no dan-
MEDITERRANEAN ger of missing a curtain call, this slightly frantic upstairs restaurant showcases an ever-changing exhibition of local artists' work. The creative contemporary food—with eclectic Mediterranean and Eastern influences—uses fresh local ingredients. The confit of Silverhill duck with sweet-and-sour pickled red cabbage, whole-grain mustard mash, and red wine gravy is popular with the artistic and literary set, as are the versatile vegetarian choices. $ *Average main: €18* ⊠ *101 Talbot St., Northside* ☎ *01/874–5011* ⊕ *www.101talbot.ie* ⌂ *Reservations essential* ⊗ *Closed Sun. and Mon.* ✛ *1:D2.*

$ ✕ **Brother Hubbard.** A delightful slow-food addition to the Dublin din-
MIDDLE EASTERN ing scene, Brother Hubbard is a cozy, elegantly designed Northside café with a stripped-down but standout menu. It's strong on detail, from the muted tones and unobtrusive-but-striking modern design, to the addition of cute little patterns in your cappuccino froth. The healthy emphasis is on fresh salads and soups with delicious twists; dishes tend to have a Middle Eastern feel, with an Irish touch here and there. The pea-and-mint soup with a dash of harissa oil is a perfect lunchtime treat. Try the flourless orange-and-almond cake for dessert. $ *Average main: €10*

✉ *153 Capel St., Northside* ☎ *01/441–1112* 🌐 *www.brotherhubbard.ie* ⏲ *Closed Sun. No dinner* ⊕ *1:B2.*

$$$$ MODERN IRISH Fodor's Choice ★ 🍴 **Chapter One.** This wonderful, culture-vulture favorite gets its name from its location, downstairs in the vaulted, stone-wall basement of the Dublin Writers Museum; the natural stone-and-wood setting makes it cozily cavelike. The contemporary French eatery is currently the culinary king of the Northside. Yeats himself would have loved the Irish sika venison with Jack McCarthy's black pudding and walnut crust, while Synge probably would have fancied the Dublin version of Proust's madeleine: rich bread-and-butter pudding, a favorite of working-class Irish mothers for generations, here turned into an outrageously filling work of art. [$] *Average main: €33* ✉ *18–19 Parnell Sq., Northside* ☎ *01/873–2266* 🌐 *www.chapteronerestaurant.com* ✍ *Reservations essential* ⏲ *Closed Sun. and Mon. No lunch Sat.* ⊕ *1:B1.*

$ ITALIAN Fodor's Choice ★ 🍴 **Enoteca delle Langhe.** Officially called Quartier Bloom in tribute to Joyce's most famous character, this charming little (very little) Italian quarter just off Ormond Quay is a hit with Dubliners long starved of quality, down-to-earth Italian food. It consists of a communal plaza area, a fabulous mural that's a modern take on Leonardo da Vinci's *The Last Supper,* and a couple of places to eat, including Enoteca delle Langhe. Italian-owned and -operated, Langhe serves up the full enoteca experience: quality, affordable Italian wines (more than 75% are sourced from the Langhe district); a limited but enticing selection of appetizers—try the perfect bruschetta with scrumptious toppings like sun-dried-tomato pesto and sautéed zucchini—warm, friendly, family-style service; and a constant buzz in the air. In summer, tango dancers perform outside. [$] *Average main: €12* ✉ *Blooms La., Northside* ☎ *01/888–0834* 🌐 *www.wallacewinebars.ie* ⏲ *Closed Sun.* ⊕ *1:B2.*

$ KOREAN FUSION Fodor's Choice ★ 🍴 **Hop House.** A unique Korean-Japanese standout in the slew of cheap and cheerful Chinese eateries on Parnell Street (the closest Dublin comes to a Chinatown), Hop House is a restaurant and pub in one. Part of the old Shakespeare pub has been transformed into one of the friendliest, best-value restaurants in the city. The dining room is bright and busy, with little table buzzers for service and the sounds of music spilling over from the bar next door. Traditional Korean specialties like kimchi are augmented with a large selection of sushi rolls, including the mouth-watering crunch roll with king-prawn tempura, cucumber, crab stick, and teriyaki sauce. [$] *Average main: €11* ✉ *160 Parnell St., Northside* ☎ *01/872–8318* 🌐 *www.hophouse.ie* ⊕ *1:C1.*

$$ MODERN IRISH 🍴 **The Hot Stove.** Dublin's Northside is undergoing something of a restaurant renaissance and The Hot Stove is a modern-Irish-cuisine standout among the new arrivals. Located in the cozy basement of a pristine Georgian building, the slew of daring, contemporary Irish art on the walls chimes nicely with the nearby Hugh Lane Gallery. For the mid-range prices the food is really top-drawer, with local game and fish featuring strongly and lots of light, inventive touches to make even classics feel original. Parsnip, carrot, turnip, and other traditional Irish vegetables are a constant theme, but certainly not the way your Irish granny might have cooked them. The duck-fat chips are a shockingly good side dish. [$] *Average main: €22* ✉ *38 Parnell Sq. W, Northside*

☎ *01/874–7778* ⊕ *www.thehotstove.ie* ◷ *Closed Sun. and Mon. No lunch Sat.* ✛ *1:B1.*

$

IRISH

✕ **Kingfisher Restaurant.** Don't let the down-at-heel canteen decor put you off—this place has been around for a long time and is a master of the art of fish-and-chips. Their mammoth-value menu is full of seafood surprises like such Dublin favorites as cod and ray (or more unusual choices like halibut) and you can even order a whole sea bass and rainbow trout. Kingfisher's huge Irish breakfasts have won awards with all the meats sourced fresh from the owners' own farm. The Northside locals love this place and give it a lively community atmosphere. Ⓢ *Average main: €14* ⊠ *166–168 Parnell St., Northside* ☎ *01/872–8732* ⊕ *www.kingfisherdublin.com* ✛ *1:C1.*

$

IRISH

✕ **L. Mulligan Grocer.** This gem of an old Dublin boozer—which was once also the local grocer—has been turned into a gastropub and world-beer emporium, without losing too much of its real Dublin feel. Microbrewery beers are hard to come by in Ireland, so the wide selection of small-label ales, lagers, and stouts is reason enough to make the trip to the evocatively named village of Stoneybatter on the Northside. The menu doesn't fuss around with too many choices, but the potted crab with sourdough soldiers is a great starter and the smoked pork boxty burger is the pick of the hearty mains. Mulligan's is the perfect spot for a quick pint of ale and a plate of black pudding (with pear relish and red chard) if you don't feel like a full sit-down meal. Ⓢ *Average main: €16* ⊠ *18 Stoneybatter, Northside* ☎ *01/670–9889* ⊕ *www.lmulligangrocer.com* ◷ *No lunch weekdays.* ✛ *1:A2.*

$

SUSHI

Fodor's Choice

★

✕ **Musashi Noodles and Sushi Bar.** This hot sushi bar on unfashionable Capel Street is the talk of the money-conscious-town because it's finally made the Japanese staple affordable in Dublin. The interior is simple and unfussy; a long, narrow room with dark wood floors and rows of pine wood tables and seats dotted with red cushions. Japanese owned and run, the flair is saved for the fresh and flavorful dishes—all the sushi standards you'd expect but better than anything else in the city. They also do a mean tempura and gyoza for those who don't fancy raw fish. Another treat is the BYOB policy on wine, with a very fair €4 corkage charge. Ⓢ *Average main: €14* ⊠ *15 Capel St., Northside* ☎ *01/532–8068* ⊕ *www.musashidublin.com* ✛ *1:B2.*

$

IRISH

✕ **Soup Dragon.** This tiny café and take-out shop serves an astonishing array of fresh soups daily. They come in three sizes, and you can get vegetarian soup or soups with meat- or fish-based broth. Best bets include pumpkin chili and coconut; fragrant Thai chicken; beef chili; and hearty mussel, potato, and leek. The friendly staff make fine coffee and delicious smoothies. The cost of soup includes bread and a piece of fruit for dessert—excellent value—and they also do a decent grab-and-go breakfast. A second Soup Dragon recently opened around the corner on Ormond Quay. Ⓢ *Average main: €8* ⊠ *168 Capel St., Northside* ☎ *01/872–3277* ⊕ *www.soupdragon.com* ⊟ *No credit cards* ◷ *Closed Sun. No dinner* ✛ *1:B3.*

$$

IRISH

✕ **The Winding Stair.** Once Dublin's favorite secondhand bookshop–café, the Winding Stair now houses an atmospheric, buzzing little restaurant, with old wooden floors, simple decor, a downstairs bookshop, and grand views of the Ha'penny Bridge and the River Liffey. Upstairs, former habitués will enjoy seeing the old bookcases around the walls (some of which are now stacked with wine). Hearty portions of upmarket traditional Irish food rely on locally sourced ingredients; the Goatsbridge Farm sea trout with brown shrimp, almond and caper butter salsify fritters, and mash is a standout. An inventive wine list and a wonderful Irish farmhouse-cheese selection are two more treats on offer, and your sweet tooth insists that you try the rice pudding with melted plums. [$] *Average main: €23* ✉ *40 Ormond Quay, Northside* ☎ *01/872–7320* 🌐 *www.winding-stair.com* ⊕ *1:A3.*

$$ BISTRO Fodor's Choice ★ 🍴 **Wuff.** Locals and critics have been purring about this simple but classy new bistro on a unglamorous street on Dublin's Northside. Gray banquettes, funky pictures, and jovial ephemera liven up the room. Try starting with the deep-fried Camembert with a tangy tomato relish. Follow up with the roasted chicken with black pudding mash and wild mushroom jus. The dessert menu is a real treat, with the rhubarb crumble a standout. It's a great breakfast and Sunday brunch joint, and is open for dinner Thursday–Saturday. [$] *Average main: €19* ✉ *23 Benburb St., Northside* ☎ *01/532–0347* 🌐 *www.wuff.ie* ⏲ *No dinner Sun.–Wed.* ⊕ *1:A2.*

DUBLIN WEST

$ CAFÉ 🍴 **Bibi's.** The small menu at this small café in the middle of a quiet, off-the-beaten-track, residential street emphasizes creative breakfasts and lunch (and brunch on the weekend) with a local twist. The sweet-corn, jalapeno, and coriander fritters with bacon and maple syrup is typical, as is their wonderful spicy cannellini beans with chorizo, crème fraîche, and thyme. **■ TIP→ Don't leave without hitting up their devilishly tempting cake selection.** [$] *Average main: €9* ✉ *14b Emorville Ave., Dublin West* ☎ *01/454–7421* 🌐 *www.bibis.ie* ⏲ *No dinner* ⊕ *1:A6.*

$ IRISH 🍴 **Leo Burdock.** Old man Burdock has moved on and the place hasn't been the same since, but the hordes still join the inevitable queue at Dublin's famous hundred-year-old take-out fish-and-chips shop, right next door to the Lord Edward pub. You can't eat here, but why would you anyway, when you can sit in the gardens of St. Patrick's Cathedral a few minutes way. Fresh cod is a classic, and the battered sausage a particular Dublin favorite, but the real stars here are the long, thick, freshly cut chips, which have a slightly smoky aftertaste. **■ TIP→ Look like a local and ask to season your chips with "crispy bits."** [$] *Average main: €10* ✉ *2 Werburgh St., Christchurch, Dublin West* ☎ *01/454–0306* 🌐 *www.leoburdock.com* 💳 *No credit cards* ⊕ *1:A3.*

$$$ SEAFOOD 🍴 **Lord Edward Restaurant.** Culinary trends and fashions may come and go but Dublin's oldest seafood restaurant remains resolutely traditional. On the cozy top floor above a lovely old bar of the same name, the Lord Edward looks out on the front entrance of Christ Church Cathedral. They do a mean Irish stew but the stars here are definitely the seafood dishes, usually smothered in a totally unhip but delicious, calorie-packed cream sauce. [$] *Average main: €25* ✉ *23 Christ Church Pl., Dublin West* ☎ *01/454–2420* 🌐 *www.lordedward.ie* ⏲ *Closed Sun. No lunch Sat.* ⊕ *1:B3.*

$ 🍴 **Lovin Catering.** This unassuming little shop on Francis Street conjures
CAFÉ up some of the best pastries in town. There's no seating in this powerhouse patisserie, but long counters allow space for perching your coffee and tucking into the finest sweet and savory treats. Try the tomato, basil, aubergine, and goat cheese quiche; or simply take afternoon tea with a pear tartlet or scone. Expect queues at lunchtime, and buy in bulk for the tastiest of take-out picnics. [$] *Average main: €10* ✉ *49 Francis St., Dublin West* ☎ *01/454–4912* 🌐 *www.lovincatering.com* 🕒 *Closed Sun. No dinner* ✥ *1:A4.*

PHOENIX PARK AND ENVIRONS

$ 🍴 **Juno's Café.** At the gates of the Phoenix Park and perfect for a pre- or
CAFÉ post-amble dinner, this café has few culinary frills but delivers plenty of hearty bang for your precious euros. Finnish head chef Juha Salo, formerly of the Mermaid Café and 101 Talbot, adds a little magic dust to some old reliables. His fish-and-chips—with a wafer-light batter and chunky, crisp chips—has to be one of the best in the city. Local produce and seasonal choices predominate, and the rigatoni with Gubeen chorizo, grilled pepper, and olives is a delicious belly filler. Dishes such as the Bellingham Blue Cheese Polenta with roast sweet corn salsa satisfy more adventurous tastes. [$] *Average main: €15* ✉ *26 Parkgate St., Phoenix Park and Environs* ☎ *01/670–9820* 🌐 *www.junoscafe.com* 🕒 *No dinner Sun.–Wed.* ✥ *1:A2.*

$ 🍴 **Nancy Hands Bar & Restaurant.** There's a fine line between re-creating
ECLECTIC tradition and looking like a theme bar, but Nancy Hands just about pulls it off. A galleylike room juxtaposes old wood, raw brick, and antiques with contemporary art to create a convivial, cozy dining area. The bar food is good, but the upstairs restaurant operates on a more serious level. Hearty specialties include ham hock with creamy mash, mustard-seed cabbage, and parsley sauce, and leg of rabbit with steamed dumplings. Numerous wines are served by the glass, and the selection of spirits is one of the most impressive in the country. [$] *Average main: €18* ✉ *30–32 Parkgate St., Phoenix Park and Environs* ☎ *01/677–0149* 🌐 *www.nancyhands.ie* ✍ *Reservations essential* ✥ *1:A2.*

WHERE TO STAY

The economic slowdown abruptly halted the "absolute avalanche of new hotels" as the *Irish Times* characterized Dublin's accommodation boom. But visitors still have an impressive choice of elegant lodgings all over the city, including the visually arresting Marker hotel in the docklands, the totally revamped landmarks of the Shelbourne and the Westbury, and some tempting choices found in Ballsbridge, an inner "suburb" that's a 20-minute walk from the city center. For something uniquely Dublin, you can always stay at one of the elegant guesthouses that occupy former Georgian town houses found on both sides of the Liffey.

Prices have stabilized and are actually on the rise again, but Dublin has a good selection of quality affordable accommodations, including many moderately priced hotels with basic but agreeable rooms. Most guesthouses, long the mainstay of the economy end of the market, have thankfully upgraded their facilities and now provide rooms with private bathrooms or showers, as well as cable color televisions, direct-dial telephones, and Internet connections. The bigger hotels are all equipped with Wi-Fi. If you've rented a car and you're not staying at a hotel with parking, it's worth considering a location out of the city center, such as Dalkey or Killiney, where the surroundings are more pleasant and you won't have to worry about parking on city streets.

Prices in the reviews are the lowest cost of a standard double room in high season. Use the coordinate (⊕ B2) at the end of each listing to locate a site on the corresponding Where to Stay in Dublin map.

SOUTHSIDE

$$ HOTEL 🏨 **Brooks Hotel.** It has nearly 100 rooms, but this hotel—minutes from Grafton Street—likes to describe itself as a boutique property, and it does manage to convey the personal touch of a much smaller establishment. **Pros:** next to Grafton Street; live piano music in bar; rooms refurbished every six years. **Cons:** office-block exterior; business clientele makes for slightly flat atmosphere; standard rooms on small side. [$] *Rooms from: €145* ✉ *Drury St., Southside* ☎ *01/670–4000* 🌐 *www.brookshotel.ie* 🛏 *98 rooms* ⊕ *C3.*

$$ HOTEL Fodor's Choice ★ 🏨 **Central Hotel.** Every city center needs its little oasis, and the Central's book-and-armchair-filled Library Bar—warmed by a Victorian fireplace—nicely fits the bill. **Pros:** central location; original 1887 facade; old-fashioned feel. **Cons:** rooms on the small side; street noise in some rooms; you have to prepay up front. [$] *Rooms from: €159* ✉ *1–5 Exchequer St., Southside* ☎ *01/679–7302* 🌐 *www.centralhotel.ie* 🛏 *67 rooms, 3 suites* 🍴 *Breakfast* ⊕ *C3.*

$$$ HOTEL 🏨 **Conrad Dublin International.** The best thing about the ugly-on-the-outside, seven-story, redbrick, and smoked-glass Conrad is the spectacular views out over the city, so ask for—no, insist on—a room on one of the top three floors. **Pros:** Gary the concierge; great views on higher floors; marble bathrooms; just off St. Stephen's Green. **Cons:** drab, 1970s-style corridors; slightly cramped standard rooms; poor views on lower floors. [$] *Rooms from: €189* ✉ *Earlsfort Terr., Southside* ☎ *01/602–8900* 🌐 *www.conradhotels.com* 🛏 *182 rooms, 10 suites* ⊕ *D5.*

$$ HOTEL 🏨 **Dawson Hotel and Spa.** Overlooking the Mansion House, home to the luxe and popular Dawson Brasserie restaurant, and 50 yards from Trinity College, this intimate town house is one of the classiest boutique hotels on the Dublin scene. **Pros:** great luxury for the price; choice of three quality restaurants; spa oasis in the city. **Cons:** small, so fills up quickly; no parking; one could overdose on the Asian theme. [$] *Rooms from: €150* ✉ *35 Dawson St., Southside* ☎ *01/677–4411* 🌐 *www.thedawson.ie* 🛏 *23 rooms, 5 suites* 🍴 *Breakfast* ⊕ *D4.*

$ HOTEL 🏨 **Grafton Guest House.** A stone's throw from the famous shopping street that gave it its name, this Victorian Gothic–style building has been tastefully transformed into one of central Dublin's best bargains. **Pros:** best value in city center; warm, unfussy service; simple but cool design. **Cons:** some rooms are cramped; can suffer from street noise; no

BEST BETS FOR DUBLIN LODGING

Fodor's offers a selective listing of high-quality lodging experiences at every price range, from the city's best budget options to its most sophisticated luxury hotel. Here, we've compiled our top recommendations by price and experience. The very best properties—those that provide a particularly remarkable experience—are designated with a Fodor's Choice symbol.

Fodor's Choice ★

Central Hotel, $$, p. 121
Four Seasons Hotel Dublin, $$$$, p. 127
Gibson Hotel, $$, p. 129
Kellys Hotel, $, p. 123
Merrion, $$$$, p. 127
Number 31, $$$$, p. 123
Pembroke Townhouse, $, p. 127
Schoolhouse Hotel, $$$, p. 127
Shelbourne, $$$$, p. 123
Westbury Hotel Dublin, $$$$, p. 126

By Price

$

Ariel Guest House, p. 126
Bewley's Hotel Newlands Cross, p. 130
Charleville Lodge, p. 129
Grafton Guest House, p. 121
Jurys Inn Christchurch, p. 130
Kellys Hotel, p. 123
Pembroke Townhouse, p. 127

$$

Brooks Hotel, p. 121
Central Hotel, p. 121
Gibson Hotel, $$, p. 129
Paramount Hotel, p. 128

$$$

The Marker, p. 123
Schoolhouse Hotel, p. 127

$$$$

Four Seasons Hotel Dublin, p. 127
Merrion, p. 127
Number 31, p. 123
Shelbourne, p. 123
Westbury Hotel Dublin, p. 126

By Type

GORGEOUS GEORGIANS

Merrion, $$$$, p. 127
Number 31, $$$$, p. 123
Pembroke Townhouse, $, p. 127

BEST DESIGN

The Clarence, $$$, p. 128
Gibson Hotel, $$, p. 129
The Marker, $$$, p. 123
Number 31, $$$$, p. 123
Shelbourne, $$$$, p. 123
Westin Dublin, $$$$, p. 126

MOST CHARMING

Charleville Lodge, $, p. 129
Number 31, $$$$, p. 123

Pembroke Townhouse, $, p. 127
Schoolhouse Hotel, $$$, p. 127

BEST VIEWS

Gibson Hotel, $$, p. 129
Herbert Park Hotel, $, p. 127
Shelbourne, $$$$, p. 123

MOST ROMANTIC

Dawson Hotel and Spa, $$, p. 121
Dylan Hotel, $$$$, p. 126
The Morrison, $$$$, p. 129
Number 31, $$$$, p. 123

BEST BARS

Central Hotel, $$, p. 121
Kellys Hotel, $, p. 123
Paramount, $$, p. 128
Shelbourne, $$$$, p. 123
Westbury Hotel Dublin, $$$$, p. 126

BEST GRANDE DAME

Shelbourne, $$$$, p. 123
Westbury Hotel Dublin, $$$$, p. 126

elevator. [$] *Rooms from: €104* ✉ *26–27 S. Great George's St., Southside* ☎ *01/648–0010* 🌐 *www.graftonguesthouse.com* 🛏 *16 rooms* 🍴 *Breakfast* ✥ *C3.*

$ HOTEL Fodor's Choice ★ 🏨 **Kellys Hotel Dublin.** With buzzing Hogan's bar and the classy L'Gueuleton restaurant right downstairs, this cool little hotel is at the epicenter of trendy Dublin. **Pros:** killer city-center location; relaxed vibe; great spot to bump into interesting Dubliners. **Cons:** some rooms are small; can suffer from street noise; no elevator. [$] *Rooms from: €119* ✉ *36 S. Great Georges St., Southside* ☎ *01/648–0010* 🌐 *www.kellysdublin.com* 🛏 *15 rooms, 1 suite* 🍴 *Breakfast* ✥ *C3.*

$$$ HOTEL 🏨 **The Marker.** The first big addition to the Dublin hotel scene since the economic crash, the checkerboard facade and sloping, honeycomb ceilings of The Marker make a bold architectural statement, while the view of the docklands from the stunning rooftop bar has quickly become a top Dublin delight. **Pros:** the Burren-inspired rocks and grasses adorning the roof garden and bar; feels new and untarnished; attracts the in crowd. **Cons:** design-heavy in the public spaces; the staff are still bedding in; a little outside the city center. [$] *Rooms from: €190* ✉ *Grand Canal Sq., Docklands, Southside* ☎ *01/687–5100* 🌐 *www.themarkerhoteldublin.com* 🛏 *166 rooms, 21 suites* ✥ *G3.*

$$$$ B&B/INN Fodor's Choice ★ 🏨 **Number 31.** Whether your lodging style is sublime Georgian elegance or cool modern, this one-in-a-million guesthouse, a short walk from St. Stephen's Green, serves up both—as well as the best made-to-order breakfast in town. **Pros:** the king and queen of guesthouse hosts; serene decor and art; fantastic breakfasts. **Cons:** a few rooms can be a little noisy; no elevator; minimum two-night stay on summer weekends. [$] *Rooms from: €220* ✉ *31 Leeson Close, Georgian Dublin* ☎ *01/676–5011* 🌐 *www.number31.ie* 🛏 *21 rooms* 🍴 *Breakfast* ✥ *E5.*

$$ HOTEL 🏨 **Premier Suites Dublin.** Get a top-floor suite at this modernized Georgian town house just off St. Stephen's Green and lord it over the whole Southside. **Pros:** spectacular city views; ground-floor suites have private entrances. **Cons:** decor is motel-functional. [$] *Rooms from: €149* ✉ *14–17 Lower Leeson St., Georgian Dublin* ☎ *01/638–1111* 🌐 *www.premiersuitesdublin.com* 🛏 *30 suites* ✥ *D5.*

$$ HOTEL 🏨 **Radisson Blu Royal Hotel, Dublin.** The sleek glass-and-concrete Radisson, just off South Great George's Street, offers to-the-point business accommodations with a dash of cool contemporary style, proof positive that it is possible to be elegant and functional at the same time. **Pros:** right in the heart of "real Dublin"; stylish, understated decor; landscaped rooftop terrace. **Cons:** looks out over a block of flats; restaurant is hit-or-miss; mostly business clientele. [$] *Rooms from: €167* ✉ *Golden La., Southside* ☎ *01/898–2900* 🌐 *www.radissonblu.ie/royalhotel-dublin* 🛏 *138 rooms, 12 suites* ✥ *C4.*

$$$$ HOTEL Fodor's Choice ★ 🏨 **The Shelbourne Dublin, Renaissance.** Paris has the Ritz, New York has the St. Regis, and Dublin has the Shelbourne—today, newly resplendent in its broad, ornamented, pink-and-white, mid-Victorian facade after a no-expense-spared renovation by new owners Marriott. **Pros:** afternoon tea in Lord Mayor's Lounge; Irish art worth gazing at; new spa and wellness center; all-around luxury. **Cons:** some noise in front rooms; feels a little stuffy at times; pricey. [$] *Rooms from: €379* ✉ *27*

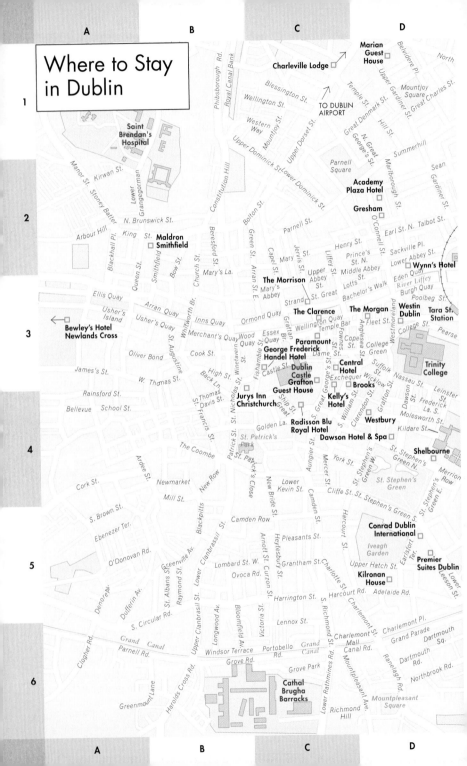

Where to Stay in Dublin

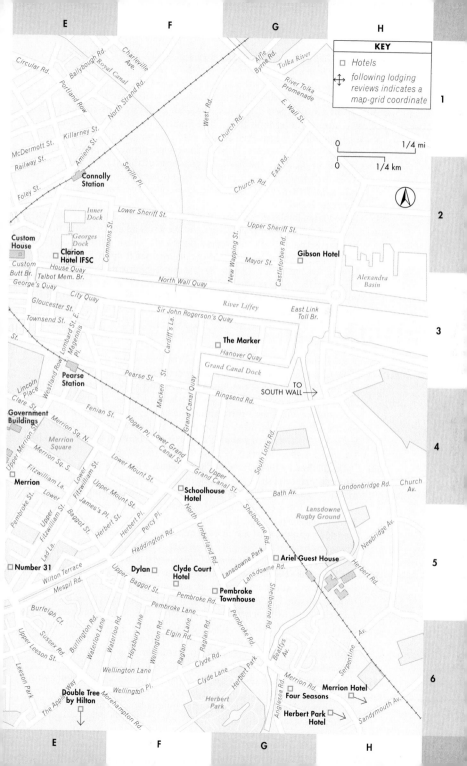

St. Stephen's Green, Southside ☎ *01/663–4500, 800/543–4300 in U.S.* ⊕ *www.marriott.co.uk/hotels/travel/dubbr-the-shelbourne-dublin-a-renaissance-hotel* ⮌ *246 rooms, 19 suites* ✛ *D4.*

$$$$ 🖼 **Westbury Hotel Dublin.** This luxurious, chandelier-filled, modern hotel
HOTEL just off Grafton Street is a favorite with elegantly dressed Dubliners
Fodor'sChoice who stop for afternoon tea in The Gallery, the spacious mezzanine-
★ level main lobby, furnished with a grand piano and a grand view out
onto the bustling streets. **Pros:** great service; prime people-watching;
convenient location; the Art Deco glamour of the Marble bar. **Cons:**
tries a little too hard to be posh. Ⓢ *Rooms from: €260* ✉ *Grafton St.,
Southside* ☎ *01/679–1122* ⊕ *www.doylecollection.com* ⮌ *187 rooms,
18 suites* ✛ *D4.*

$$$$ 🖼 **The Westin Dublin.** Reconstructed from three 19th-century landmark
HOTEL buildings opposite Trinity College, the Westin is all about location, but
the marble pillars, tall mahogany doorways, blazing fireplaces, Palladian marble busts, and period details also set it apart. **Pros:** beside
Temple Bar but not in Temple Bar; in-room spa treatments. **Cons:** on
a busy traffic corner; windowless bar; mediocre restaurants; fee for
Wi-Fi. Ⓢ *Rooms from: €249* ✉ *College Green, Southside* ☎ *01/645–
1000* ⊕ *www.thewestindublin.com* ⮌ *141 rooms, 22 suites* ✛ *D3.*

GEORGIAN DUBLIN

$ 🖼 **Ariel Guest House.** The homemade preserves and oven-warm scones
B&B/INN are reason enough to stay at this redbrick 1850 Victorian guesthouse, in
one of Dublin's poshest tree-lined suburbs and a 15-minute walk from
St. Stephen's Green. **Pros:** four-poster beds in larger rooms; fantastic
collection of Victoriana throughout the house; good price for smaller
rooms. **Cons:** no elevator; a good walk to the city center. Ⓢ *Rooms
from: €109* ✉ *52 Lansdowne Rd., Georgian Dublin* ☎ *01/668–5512*
⊕ *www.ariel-house.net* ⮌ *37 rooms* 🍽 *Breakfast* ✛ *G5.*

$$$ 🖼 **Double Tree by Hilton Hotel–Burlington Road.** The days when Irish and
HOTEL international celebrities partied the nights away at the Burlington hotel
might be gone, but this latest revamp of the old institution is still a
focal point for social events and gatherings on the Southside. **Pros:** a
Dublin institution; large, light-filled rooms. **Cons:** looks a little bit like
a parking garage; staff not as experienced as they used to be; very big.
Ⓢ *Rooms from: €199* ✉ *Upper Leeson St., Georgian Dublin* ☎ *01/618–
5600* ⊕ *doubletree.hilton.com* ⮌ *500 rooms, 6 suites* ✛ *E6.*

$$$ 🖼 **Clyde Court Hotel.** The guest rooms at this modest, contemporary
HOTEL hotel are big and comfortable, if aesthetically uninspired, in muted
tones and soft fabrics. **Pros:** great price for the upmarket location;
facilities of nearby sister hotels available to guests; huge suites are
good value for families. **Cons:** attracts a lot of conferences; service
can be patchy. Ⓢ *Rooms from: €189* ✉ *Pembroke Rd., Georgian
Dublin* ☎ *01/2382700* ⊕ *www.clydecourthotel.com* ⮌ *159 rooms,
26 suites* ✛ *F5.*

$$$$ 🖼 **Dylan Hotel.** A symphony of "Victorian Contemporary Fusion" with
HOTEL Arts and Crafts stained glass, bordello brocades, spray-painted silver
furnishings, and lordly antiques, this unique hotel in an old Victorian
building is a racy addition to the sometimes staid Dublin scene. **Pros:**

great for a romantic weekend; individually designed rooms; property is big enough to ensure privacy, small enough to still feel intimate. **Cons:** hit-or-miss restaurant; prices could be more competitive. $ *Rooms from: €229 ✉ Eastmoreland Pl., Georgian Dublin ☎ 01/660–3000 ⊕ www.dylan.ie ↘ 38 rooms, 6 suites ✚ F5.*

$$$$
HOTEL
Fodor'sChoice
★
🏨 **Four Seasons Hotel Dublin.** Set within the show grounds of the Royal Dublin Society, this Victorian-Georgian hybrid—topped by gigantic eaves and a lovely cupola—looks like the real McCoy but was in fact built during the boomtime excesses of the brash Celtic Tiger era. **Pros:** one of the country's top spas; full range of facilities; Lobby Lounge great for afternoon tea. **Cons:** a bit of an architectural mishmash; room design not the most inventive. $ *Rooms from: €320 ✉ Simmonscourt Rd., Georgian Dublin ☎ 01/665–4000 ⊕ www.fourseasons.com/dublin ↘ 157 rooms, 40 suites ✚ G6.*

$
HOTEL
🏨 **Herbert Park Hotel.** Only a short distance from the city, this hotel nestled next to leafy Herbert Park and the doddering Dodder River feels pleasantly secluded—to maximize enjoyment, you'll want to secure a room overlooking the park, or go for one of the two suites with balconies. **Pros:** independently owned hotel; terrace dining in summer; Sunday jazz buffet. **Cons:** looks a little like an office block; rooms not too exciting; outside the city center. $ *Rooms from: €115 ✉ Merrion Rd., Georgian Dublin ☎ 01/667–2200 ⊕ www.herbertparkhotel.ie ↘ 150 rooms, 3 suites ✚ H6.*

$$
B&B/INN
🏨 **Kilronan House Hotel.** Just a five-minute walk from St. Stephen's Green, this mid-19th-century terraced guesthouse, with its elegant white facade and cozy sitting-room fire, will welcome you home at the end of a long day's sightseeing. **Pros:** great price for location; beautiful, calming facade; cozy sitting room. **Cons:** public areas a bit worn; uncreative room furnishings; no elevator. $ *Rooms from: €149 ✉ 70 Adelaide Rd., Georgian Dublin ☎ 01/475–5266 ⊕ www.kilronanhouse.com ↘ 12 rooms ❄ Breakfast ✚ D5.*

$$$$
HOTEL
Fodor'sChoice
★
🏨 **Merrion Hotel.** Stately and spiffy, and splendidly situated directly across from Government Buildings between Stephen's Green and Merrion Square, this luxurious hotel actually comprises four exactingly restored Georgian town houses. **Pros:** Patrick Guilbaud restaurant; infinity pool; city-center location; attentive staff. **Cons:** you'll pay extra for a room in the original house; some rooms are overdecorated. $ *Rooms from: €260 ✉ Upper Merrion St., Georgian Dublin ☎ 01/603–0600 ⊕ www. merrionhotel.com ↘ 123 rooms, 19 suites ✚ H6.*

$
B&B/INN
Fodor'sChoice
★
🏨 **Pembroke Townhouse.** "Townhouse" does not do justice to the splendor of the place, but it does hint at the cozy, relaxed atmosphere of the Pembroke, a superb example of classic 18th-century grandeur. **Pros:** a Georgian wonderland; big, airy rooms; privately owned. **Cons:** 15-minute trip to the city center; often books out early; no air-conditioning. $ *Rooms from: €114 ✉ 90 Pembroke Rd., Georgian Dublin ☎ 01/660– 0277 ⊕ www.pembroketownhouse.ie ↘ 41 rooms, 7 suites ✚ F5.*

$$$
HOTEL
Fodor'sChoice
★
🏨 **Schoolhouse Hotel.** Excuse the pun, but this converted Victorian parochial school just off the Grand Canal really is A-plus—set in a gorgeous example of 19th-century architecture complete with turrets and soaring nave (now the setting for the restaurant), this may be the most

uniquely upcycled hotel in Ireland. **Pros:** unique building; top-class Irish restaurant; in-room spa treatments. **Cons:** a trip to the city center; fills up quickly; no minibars; no elevator. $ *Rooms from: €179* ✉ *2–8 Northumberland Rd., Georgian Dublin* ☎ *01/667–5014* ⊕ *www.schoolhousehotel.com* ⟿ *31 rooms* ✛ *F4.*

TEMPLE BAR

$$$ ⬚ **The Clarence.** Temple Bar's most prestigious hotel, and occasional
HOTEL home to your potential new best friends/elevator buddies, co-owners Bono and the Edge of U2, this renovated 1852 grand old hotel is the place to sample Temple Bar's nightlife, even if your pals are too busy rocking to hang. **Pros:** stylish Octagon Bar; the owners might be on-premises; Cleaver East restaurant. **Cons:** rooms a bit small; some rooms suffer from street noise; paying a premium for "cool." $ *Rooms from: €179* ✉ *6–8 Wellington Quay, Temple Bar* ☎ *01/407–0800* ⊕ *www.theclarence.ie* ⟿ *44 rooms, 5 suites* ✛ *C3.*

$$ ⬚ **George Frederic Handel Hotel.** Right in the heart of Temple Bar, this
HOTEL basic but well-run hotel somehow manages to feel like something of an oasis from the hustle of this lively neighborhood. **Pros:** ideal location for nightlife; great value; attentive staff. **Cons:** rooms are small; noisy neighborhood; a little short on amenities. $ *Rooms from: €129* ✉ *16–18 Fishamble St., Temple Bar* ☎ *01/670–9404* ⊕ *www.georgefrederichandelhotel.com* ⟿ *40 rooms* ✛ *C3.*

$$$ ⬚ **The Morgan.** A sparkling gem among a lot of very drab hotels in
HOTEL Temple Bar, the Morgan boasts about its chic design and decor, and the excitingly designed bedrooms and luxurious, colorful bathrooms are indeed pleasing to the many fashionistas and photographers who love this place. **Pros:** individually designed bathrooms; great cocktail bar; extended-stay apartments are good value. **Cons:** a little over-designed in places; no parking; no restaurant. $ *Rooms from: €200* ✉ *10 Fleet St., Temple Bar* ☎ *01/643–7000* ⊕ *www.themorgan.com* ⟿ *107 rooms, 14 suites* ✛ *D3.*

$$ ⬚ **Paramount Hotel.** Classic 1930s American movies seem to have been
HOTEL the inspiration for the interior of this medium-size hotel in the heart of Temple Bar—dark woods and subtle colors decorate the bedrooms, continuing the sleek, elegant look. **Pros:** stylish, integrated design; great location; good value during the week. **Cons:** street noise can be a problem; no air-conditioning; fills up on weekends. $ *Rooms from: €152* ✉ *Parliament St. and Essex Gate, Temple Bar* ☎ *01/417–9900* ⊕ *www.paramounthotel.ie* ⟿ *64 rooms* ✛ *C3.*

NORTHSIDE

$$ ⬚ **Academy Plaza Hotel.** This modern, architecturally uninspired Best
HOTEL Western Plus hotel is centrally located just off O'Connell Street and offers lots of comfort at an affordable, slightly unfashionable-neighborhood price. **Pros:** soundproof windows; friendly staff; choice of restaurants. **Cons:** unfashionable location; rooms are not huge; bland exterior. $ *Rooms from: €135* ✉ *10–14 Findlater Pl., Northside* ☎ *01/878–0666* ⊕ *www.academyplazahotel.ie* ⟿ *274 rooms, 12 suites* ✛ *D2.*

$ B&B/INN 🏨 **Charleville Lodge.** If Dublin's city center is a Georgian wonder, a short commute/15-minute walk to the historic Phibsborough area of Dublin's Northside will transport you to the Victorian 19th century and to this lodge comprising a row of completely restored terraced houses. **Pros:** good value; near Phoenix Park. **Cons:** outside the city center; two-night minimum on some rooms in summer weekends; no elevator; few antiques. [$] *Rooms from: €70* ✉ *268–272 N. Circular Rd., Northside* ☎ *01/838–6633* 🌐 *www.charlevillelodge.ie* 🛏 *30 rooms* 🍴 *Breakfast* ✣ *C1.*

$$ HOTEL 🏨 **Clarion Hotel Dublin City (IFSC).** Built with business guests in mind, this high-rise hotel in the middle of the International Financial Services Centre has been a surprise hit with all travelers interested in the business of good value and clean, quiet rooms with good amenities. **Pros:** weekend bargains available; room to swing a couple of cats in big rooms; little nocturnal street noise. **Cons:** room design pretty functional; business clientele; no buzz at night. [$] *Rooms from: €130* ✉ *IFSC, Northside* ☎ *01/433–8800* 🌐 *www.clarionhotelifsc.com* 🛏 *165 rooms, 14 suites* ✣ *E2.*

$$ HOTEL Fodor's Choice ★ 🏨 **The Gibson Hotel.** The terrace bar at the tastefully modern Gibson Hotel has to be the dream spot to view the impressive skyline and shimmering waterways of Dublin's trendy docklands area. **Pros:** stunning views from terrace bar; style at an affordable price; green conscious. **Cons:** slightly off the beaten track; can get busy on concert nights. [$] *Rooms from: €164* ✉ *Point Village, Northside* ☎ *01/681–5000* 🌐 *www.thegibsonhotel.ie* 🛏 *252 rooms* ✣ *G2.*

$$ HOTEL 🏨 **Gresham Hotel Dublin.** Opened in 1817, it's been a while since this was *the* place to stay for visiting dignitaries and local celebs, but the Gresham remains a solid city-center option at a good price. **Pros:** great value for city center; great views down O'Connell Street. **Cons:** bar and public areas can get busy; room design unexciting; it can bump prices on busy weekends. [$] *Rooms from: €135* ✉ *23 Upper O'Connell St., Northside* ☎ *01/874–6881* 🌐 *www.gresham-hotels-dublin.com* 🛏 *279 rooms, 9 suites* ✣ *D2.*

$ B&B/INN 🏨 **Marian Guest House.** A veritable Everest of fine Irish meats, the Marian's mighty Irish breakfast, with black pudding and smoked bacon, is reason enough to stay at this family-run redbrick guesthouse just off beautiful Mountjoy Square. **Pros:** excellent breakfast; family-owned and -run; small. **Cons:** located in a slightly run-down part of the city; gets some street noise; fairly basic rooms. [$] *Rooms from: €70* ✉ *21 Upper Gardiner St., Northside* ☎ *01/874–4129* 🌐 *www.marianguesthouse.ie* 🛏 *6 rooms* 🍴 *Breakfast* ✣ *D1.*

$$$$ HOTEL 🏨 **The Morrison Hotel.** Showcasing new Irish talent in everything from the textiles to the art on the walls and the sculptures in public spaces—there are even famous Irish song lyrics on the walls in some bedrooms—this sleek, trendy spot remains at the top of the Northside lodging charts. **Pros:** people-watching in cocktail bar; intensely designed rooms; near O'Connell Bridge. **Cons:** tries a little too hard to be cool; located on busy road. [$] *Rooms from: €239* ✉ *Ormond Quay, Northside* ☎ *01/887–2400* 🌐 *www.morrisonhotel.ie* 🛏 *120 rooms, 18 suites* ✣ *C3.*

$$ HOTEL 🏨 **Wynn's Hotel.** A few doors down from the Abbey Theatre, Wynn's began its life as a Dublin boardinghouse in 1845, and its beautiful

stained-glass awning has become something of a landmark as a romantic meeting spot for locals. **Pros:** great location for theater fans; feels like a genuine full-service hotel; a touch of history about the place. **Cons:** decor can fell a bit hodgepodge; rooms are on the small side; can be some noise from ballroom downstairs. $ *Rooms from: €129* ⊠ *35–39 Lower Abbey St., Northside* ☎ *01/874–5131* ⊕ *www.wynnshotel.ie* ⤳ *65 rooms* ⦿ *No meals* ✛ *D2.*

DUBLIN WEST

$ 🏨 **Bewley's Hotel Newlands Cross.** This four-story franchise hotel on the
HOTEL   southwest outskirts of the city is, in two words, cheap and cheerful. **Pros:** great value for families; good location for further travels; delicious Bewley's coffee in the morning. **Cons:** mainly business clientele; not convenient to the city center; overlooks the expressway. $ *Rooms from: €69* ⊠ *Newlands Cross at Naas Rd., Dublin West* ☎ *01/464–0140* ⊕ *www.bewleyshotels.com/newlands_cross* ⤳ *299 rooms* ✛ *A3.*

$ 🏨 **Jurys Inn Christchurch.** Expect few frills at this functional budget hotel,
HOTEL   on a hill facing Christ Church Cathedral and within walking distance of most city-center attractions. **Pros:** good value for families; views of Christ Church; near Temple Bar. **Cons:** ugly building; basic, functional rooms; tends to be popular with bachelor(ette) parties. $ *Rooms from: €119* ⊠ *Christ Church Pl., Dublin West* ☎ *01/454–0000* ⊕ *dublinhotels.jurysinns.com/jurysinn_christchurch* ⤳ *182 rooms* ✛ *B4.*

$ 🏨 **Maldron Hotel Smithfield.** On Smithfield Plaza, this snazzy, good-value
HOTEL   hotel is at the heart of Dublin's gentrifying old market district. **Pros:** located on an open plaza; great views from rooms in front on higher floors; under-floor heating in bathrooms. **Cons:** no proper restaurant. $ *Rooms from: €99* ⊠ *Smithfield Village, Dublin West* ☎ *01/485–0900* ⊕ *www.maldronhotels.com* ⤳ *85 rooms, 7 suites* ✛ *B2.*

NIGHTLIFE AND THE ARTS

Long before Stephen Dedalus's excursions into "Nighttown" in James Joyce's *Ulysses*, Dublin was proud of its lively after-hours scene, particularly its thriving pubs. But the now-tamed Celtic Tiger economy, once the envy of all Europe, turned Dublin into one of the most happening destinations on the whole continent. Things have calmed down in the last few years, but the city's pubs are still its main source of entertainment; many public houses in the city center have live music—from rock to jazz to traditional Irish.

Theater is an essential element of life in the city that was home to O'Casey, Synge, W. B. Yeats, and Beckett. Today Dublin has seven major theaters that reproduce the Irish "classics," and also present newer fare from the likes of Martin McDonagh and Conor McPherson. Opera, long overlooked, now has a home in the restored old Gaiety Theatre.

Check the *Irish Times* and the *Evening Herald* newspapers for event listings, as well the *Big Issue* and the *Event Guide* (online)—weekly guides to film, theater, and musical events around the city. Entertainment.ie is another good source for all cultural updates.

NIGHTLIFE

Live music has replaced DJs in a lot of Dublin nightspots, but in Dublin's dance clubs the dominant sound is once again becoming electronic dance music, and the crowd that flocks to them every night of the week is of the trendy, under-30 generation. Leeson Street—just off St. Stephen's Green, south of the Liffey, and known as "the strip"—is a slightly frayed and uncool nightclub area aimed at the over-30 crowd that revs up at pub closing time and stays active until 4 am. The dress code at Leeson Street's dance clubs is informal, but jeans and sneakers are not welcome. Most don't charge to get in.

Despite rampant remodeling during the boom years, the traditional pub has steadfastly clung to its role as the primary center of Dublin's social life. The city has nearly 1,000 pubs ("licensed tabernacles," writer Flann O'Brien calls them). And although the vision of elderly men enjoying a chin wag over a creamy pint of stout has become something of a rarity, there are still plenty of places where you can enjoy a quiet (or not so quiet) drink and a chat. Last drinks are called at 11:30 pm Monday to Thursday, 12:30 am Friday and Saturday, and 11 pm on Sunday. Some city-center pubs have extended opening hours and don't serve last drinks until 1:45 am.

As a general rule, the area between Grafton and Great George's streets is a gold mine for classy pubs. Another good bet is the Temple Bar district (though some of the newer ones are all plastic and mirrors), but things can get a little rowdy there. And if it's real spit-on-the-floor hideaways you're after, head across the Liffey to the areas around Parnell Square or Smithfield. Beware of the tourist-trap, faux-traditional pubs where you can hardly hear the music for the roar of the seven flat-screen TVs.

Most pubs serve food at lunchtime, many throughout the day and into the early evening. This is an inexpensive way to eat out, and the quality of the food is often quite good.

■ TIP→ **If you will need late-night transportation, try to arrange it with your hotel before you go out.**

Use the coordinate (✛ B2) at the end of each pub listing to locate a site on the corresponding Dublin Pubs map.

SOUTHSIDE

IRISH CABARET, MUSIC, AND DANCING

Bewley's Café Theatre. With its intimate nights in this small, Victorian venue, Bewley's Café Theatre has become the atmospheric cabaret hot spot in Dublin. Set in the Oriental Room on the second floor above the glorious, stained-glass jewel that is the Grafton Street restaurant, the unique lunchtime performances here—a one-act play by O'Casey or Wilde with a bowl of soup and soda bread—are also noteworthy. ✉ *78/79 Grafton St., 2nd floor, Southside* ☎ *086/878–4001* ⊕ *www. bewleyscafetheatre.com.*

JAZZ

Ha'penny Bridge Inn. In its tiny but buzzing upstairs room, the Ha'penny Bridge regularly hosts blues and jazz nights and has good comedy on Thursday. ⊠ *42 Wellington Quay, Southside* ☎ *01/677–0616.*

JJ Smyth's. An old-school jazz and blues venue, JJ Smyth's pub hosts live music pretty much every night. ⊠ *12 Aungier St., Southside* ☎ *01/475–2565* ⊕ *www.jjsmyths.com.*

The Mint Bar. A basement venue set in a former bank vault, the Mint Bar is a classic cocktail bar presenting live jazz, lounge, and swing music Thursday through Saturday. ⊠ *Westin Hotel, College Green, Southside* ☎ *01/645–1000* ⊕ *www.thewestindublin.com/the-mint-bar.*

NIGHTCLUBS

Fodor's Choice ★ **Lillie's Bordello.** Once the hot spot for celebs, Lillie's Bordello is now more for regular Joes: a popular hangout for a young late-night crowd. Hot or not, the decor remains a knockout: Victorian brocaded velvets and gilded frames plus pink and purple neon lasers. Take a rest from the dance floor in the gorgeous Library room. ⊠ *Grafton St., Southside* ☎ *01/679–9204* ⊕ *www.lilliesbordello.ie.*

Madison. Slightly cheesy, this big and buzzing nightclub attracts an over-25s crowd with hip-hop and electronic music. ⊠ *6–8 Wicklow St., Southside* ☎ *086/400–5998* ⊕ *www.madison-nightclub.com.*

Rí Rá. Part of the hugely popular Globe bar, Rí Rá has lost some of its shine in recent years, but is still a fun night out. The name means "uproar" in Irish, and on most nights the place does go a little wild. Upstairs is more low-key. ⊠ *Dame Ct., Southside* ☎ *01/677–4835* ⊕ *riraclub.ie.*

PUBS

Cassidy's. Once a quality neighborhood pub with a tasty pint of stout, Cassidy's has morphed into an often overcrowded but very popular spot with a young clientele. ⊠ *42 Lower Camden St., Southside* ☎ *01/475–6540* ✛ *D5.*

Davy Byrne's. A noted pilgrimage stop for Joyceans, Davy Byrne's is where Leopold Bloom stops in for a glass of Burgundy and a Gorgonzola-cheese sandwich in *Ulysses* (and ruminates before helping a blind man cross the road). Unfortunately, the decor—quite an eyeful, with its gaudily painted ceiling, stained glass cupola, and blush pastels—is greatly changed from Joyce's day ("He entered Davy Byrnes. Moral pub."), but it still serves some fine pub grub. ⊠ *21 Duke St., Southside* ☎ *167/75217* ⊕ *www.davybyrnes.com* ✛ *D4.*

Doyle's In Town. A cozy pub, Doyle's is a favorite with journalists from the *Irish Times* and Trinity students. ⊠ *9 College St., Southside* ☎ *01/671–0616* ⊕ *www.doylesintown.com* ✛ *E3.*

The George. Dublin's two-floor main gay pub, The George draws an almost entirely male crowd; its nightclub stays open until 2:30 am nightly except Tuesday. The "alternative bingo night," with star drag act Miss Shirley Temple Bar, is a riot of risqué fun. SaturGays are always packed. ⊠ *89 S. Great George's St., Southside* ☎ *01/478–2983* ⊕ *www.thegeorge.ie* ✛ *C3.*

The Globe. The Globe draws hipster Dubliners who sip espresso drinks by day and pack the place at night. There's live Rockabilly on Sunday and free entrance to the downstairs Rí Rá nightclub every night. ☒ *11 S. Great George's St., Southside* ☏ *01/671–1220* ⊕ *www.theglobe. ie* ✛ *D3.*

Fodor'sChoice
★ **Grogan's.** Also known as the Castle Lounge, Grogan's is a small place packed with creative folk. Owner Tommy Grogan is known as a patron of local artists, and his walls are covered with their work. There's no music or TV, so you can have a proper chat with your pint and toastie. ☒ *15 S. William St., Southside* ☏ *01/677–9320* ⊕ *www. groganspub.ie* ✛ *D3.*

Hogan's. A huge space on two levels, Hogan's gets jammed most nights with a cool, college crowd. But in the afternoons it's a quieter spot and perfect for people-watching out the large windows. ☒ *35 S. Great George's St., Southside* ☏ *01/677–5904* ⊕ *www.kellysdublin.com/food-and-drink* ✛ *D3.*

Fodor'sChoice
★ **Horseshoe Bar.** A recent massive face-lift, along with the rest of the Shelbourne hotel, made the Horseshoe Bar the hottest ticket in town. There's comparatively little space for drinkers around the famous semicircular bar—but this does wonders for making friends quickly. ☒ *Shelbourne, 27 St. Stephen's Green, Southside* ☏ *01/676–6471* ⊕ *www.marriott. co.uk* ✛ *E4.*

Kehoe's. Popular with Trinity students and cynical journalists, Kehoe's has a tiny back room that is nice and cozy, while the upstairs is basically the owner's old living room, open to the public. ☒ *9 S. Anne St., Southside* ☏ *01/677–8312* ✛ *D4.*

Fodor'sChoice
★ **Library Bar.** The place to go when you're ready to get away from all the madness, the Library has book-lined shelves, big armchairs and sofas, and a blazing fireplace—all in all, this first-floor hideaway is one of the most serene nighttime spots in Dublin. ☒ *Central Hotel, 1–5 Exchequer St., Southside* ☏ *01/679–7302* ⊕ *www.centralhoteldublin.com/ library-bar* ✛ *D3.*

The Long Hall. One of Dublin's most ornate traditional taverns, the Long Hall has Victorian lamps, a mahogany bar, mirrors, chandeliers, and plasterwork ceilings, all more than 100 years old. The pub serves sandwiches and an excellent pint of Guinness. ☒ *51 S. Great George's St., Southside* ☏ *01/475–1590* ✛ *D4.*

McDaid's. A landmark that once attracted boisterous Brendan Behan and other leading writers in the 1950s, McDaid's wild literary reputation

---

WORD OF MOUTH

"Here's a cool marketing fact we never knew before: Do you know the *Guinness World Records*? Of course you do. Well, it was originally created as an advertising tool. One of the execs back in the 1950s wanted to settle a barroom bet he made with someone, and didn't have a way of finding an answer—so he came up with the idea to publish a book containing every record imaginable. That way, they could sell them for use in bars around the world, so that the Guinness name would always be there to settle bets. Who knew?"

—Erin74

2

still lingers, although the bar has been discreetly modernized and is altogether quieter. ✉ *3 Harry St., Southside* ☎ *01/679–4395* ✛ *D4*.

Mulligan's. Synonymous in Dublin with a truly perfect pint of Guinness, Mulligan's started life as a *shebeen* (unlicensed drinking venue) and then, publore tells us, was listed as "legal" in 1782. Today journalists, locals, and students flock here for a good pint. ✉ *8 Poolbeg St., Southside* ☎ *01/677–5582* ⊕ *www.mulligans.ie* ✛ *E3*.

Neary's. With an exotic, Victorian-style interior, Neary's was once the haunt of music-hall artists and a certain literary set, including Brendan Behan. Join the actors from the adjacent Gaiety Theatre for a good pub lunch. ✉ *1 Chatham St., Southside* ☎ *01/677–7371* ✛ *D4*.

Fodor's Choice
★

No Name. Considering itself too hip to even have a name when it opened, the Secret Bar/No Name Bar has finally decided to play on its hidden-away vibe. Above the wonderful L'Gueuleton restaurant this open-plan, buzzing bar even has a cute little covered patio. ✉ *1 Fade St., Southside* ☎ *01/675–3708* ✛ *D4*.

The Old Stand. One of the oldest pubs in the city, the Old Stand is named after the now demolished Old Stand at Lansdowne Road stadium, home to Irish rugby and football. The pub is renowned for great pints and fine steaks. ✉ *37 Exchequer St., Southside* ☎ *01/677–7220* ✛ *D3*.

Peter's Pub. The epitome of the cozy little boozer, Peter's Pub hugs a busy corner where people-watching becomes an art at the outside tables in summer. ✉ *Johnson Pl., Southside* ☎ *01/677–8588* ✛ *D4*.

Fodor's Choice
★

Stag's Head. A Victorian beaut, the Stag's Head dates from 1770 and was rebuilt in 1895. Theater people from the nearby Olympia, journalists, and Trinity students gather around the unusual Connemara red-marble bar, study their reflections in the many mirrors, and drink in all the oak carvings. ✉ *1 Dame Ct., Southside* ☎ *01/679–3701* ✛ *D3*.

GEORGIAN DUBLIN

IRISH CABARET, MUSIC, AND DANCING

The Sugar Club. There's a touch of Vegas about this landmark venue with the tables and chairs on tiered levels that look down on the stage. The Sugar Club has regular performance (some touted as "burlesque") nights. ✉ *8 Lower Leeson St., Southside* ☎ *01/678–7188* ⊕ *www.the sugarclub.com*.

PUBS

The 51 Bar. Famous for its collection of whiskies from around the world, the 51 has a beer garden that is always buzzing with activity in fine weather. ✉ *51 Haddington Rd., Ballsbridge* ☎ *01/660–0150* ⊕ *www. the51bar.com* ✛ *G5*.

Doheny & Nesbitt. A traditional spot with snugs, dark wooden furnishings, and smoke-darkened ceilings, Doheny & Nesbitt has hardly changed over the decades. ✉ *4–5 Lower Baggot St., Southside* ☎ *01/676–2945* ⊕ *www.dohenyandnesbitts.ie* ✛ *E4*.

The Horse Show House. A Ballsbridge institution, the Horse Show House is a favorite of the boisterous but welcoming rugby and show-jumping set. A great spot to watch sports of any kind. ✉ *32 Merrion Rd., Georgian Dublin* ☎ *01/668–9424* ⊕ *www.madigan.ie* ✛ *H6*.

Leeson Lounge. This has the look of a classic old Dublin "boozer," with one notable exception: it has a television. The Leeson is known as a place to watch televised sports of all kinds, and it's always pleasant and inclusive. There's often live music; Tuesdays are popular for jazz. ⊠ *148 Upper Leeson St., Georgian Dublin* ☎ *01/660–3816* ✛ *E6.*

O'Donoghue's. A cheerful, tourist-friendly hangout, O'Donoghue's has impromptu musical performances that often spill out onto the street. ⊠ *15 Merrion Row, Southside* ☎ *01/676–2807* ⊕ *www.odonoghues. ie* ✛ *E5.*

Toner's. Though billed as a Victorian bar, Toner's actually goes back 200 years, with an original flagstone floor to prove its antiquity, as well as wooden drawers running up to the ceiling—a relic of the days when bars doubled as grocery shops. Oliver St. John Gogarty, who was the model for Buck Mulligan in James Joyce's *Ulysses*, accompanied W. B. Yeats here, in what was purportedly the latter's only visit to a pub. ⊠ *139 Lower Baggot St., Georgian Dublin* ☎ *01/676–3090* ⊕ *www. tonerspub.ie* ✛ *E5.*

TEMPLE BAR
NIGHTCLUBS

Button Factory. A happening music venue, the Button mixes top DJs and up-and-coming live acts. The place tends to be on the cutting edge of the Irish dance-music scene. ⊠ *Curved St., Temple Bar* ☎ *01/670–9202* ⊕ *www.buttonfactory.ie.*

Club M. Club M is an old-school disco-type venue, popular with the suburban crowd in town for the night. Their theme nights—like "school disco"—tend to pack the place. ⊠ *Cope St., Temple Bar* ☎ *01/671–5274* ⊕ *www.blooms.ie/clubm.html.*

The Turk's Head. The Turk's Head pub/nightclub is known for its extravagant mosaics, Moroccan woodwork, bits of Arabian Nights decor, and its world culture (i.e., Latin, reggae, funk, and flamenco) late nights. ⊠ *Paramount Hotel, 27–30 Parliament St., Temple Bar* ☎ *01/679–9701* ⊕ *www.paramounthotel.ie/turks-head.html.*

The Workman's Club. This no frills, hip spot specializes in Indie club nights and attracts an artistic and hipster crowd. It has three floors of music and live gigs. Check the website for upcoming nights. ⊠ *10 Wellington Quay, Temple Bar* ☎ *01/670–6692* ⊕ *www.theworkmansclub.com.*

PUBS

The Front Lounge. A modern pub, the Front Lounge caters to a mixed crowd of young professionals, both gay and straight. ⊠ *33–34 Parliament St., Temple Bar* ☎ *01/670–4112* ⊕ *www.thefrontlounge.ie* ✛ *D3.*

The Liquor Rooms. This quality cocktail joint under the Clarance Hotel consists of indivudually designed rooms and a huge list of expertly made cocktails. ⊠ *5 Wellington Quay, Temple Bar* ☎ *087/339–3688* ⊕ *www. theliquorrooms.com* ✛ *C3.*

Oliver St John Gogarty. A lively bar that attracts all ages and nationalities, the Oliver St. John Gogarty overflows with patrons in summer. On most nights there's traditional Irish music upstairs. ⊠ *57 Fleet St., Temple Bar* ☎ *01/671–1822* ⊕ *www.gogartys.ie* ✛ *D3.*

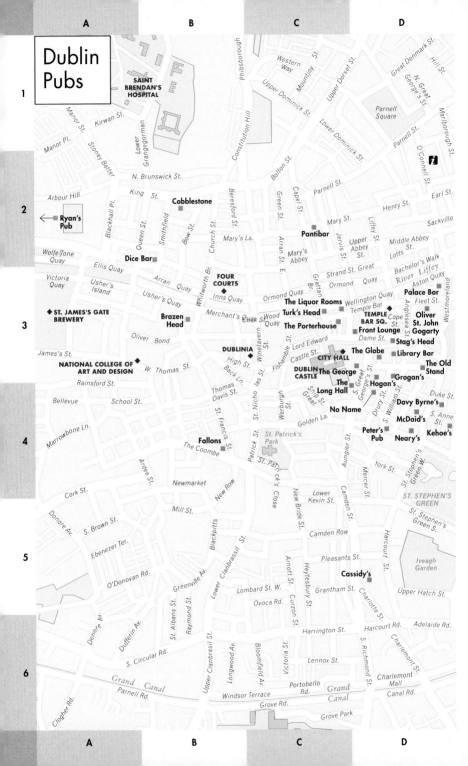

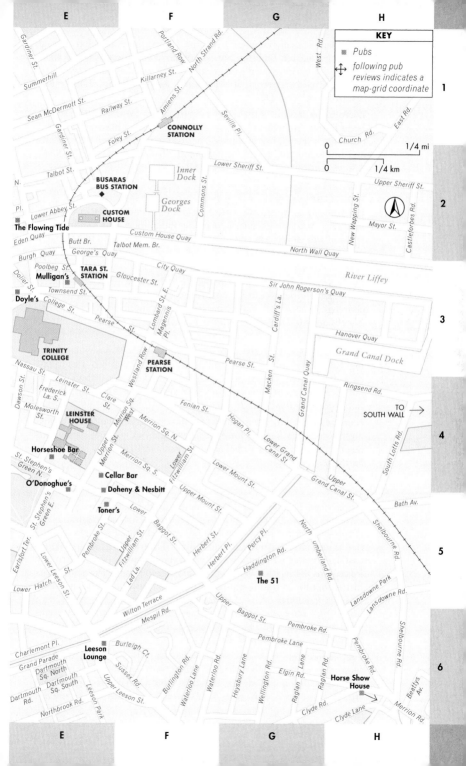

Palace Bar. Scarcely changed since the 1940s, the Palace Bar is tiled and rather barren looking, but is popular with journalists and writers (the *Irish Times* used to be nearby). The walls are lined with cartoons drawn by newspaper illustrators. ⊠ *21 Fleet St., Temple Bar* ☎ *01/677–9290* ✥ *D3.*

The Porterhouse. One of the few bars in Ireland to brew its own beer, the Plain Porter has won the best stout award at the "Brewing Oscars," beating out the mighty Guinness. The tasteful interior is all dark woods and soft lighting. ⊠ *16–18 Parliament St., Temple Bar* ☎ *01/679–8847* ⊕ *www.porterhousebrewco.com* ✥ *C3.*

NORTHSIDE

NIGHTCLUBS

The Academy. A music hub with four floors of entertainment of every kind, the Academy is anchored by big-name local and international DJs and gigs. It attracts a young, dance-crazy crowd who like to party until the wee hours. ⊠ *57 Middle Abbey St., Northside* ☎ *01/877–9999* ⊕ *www.theacademydublin.com.*

The Church. The sacrilege of bopping the night away in a former church might add a little spice at this mainstream weekend club. Non-dancing churchgoers can check out the pub and restaurant upstairs. ⊠ *Jervis St., Northside* ☎ *01/828–0102* ⊕ *www.thechurch.ie.*

PUBS

The Flowing Tide. Directly across from the Abbey Theatre, the Flowing Tide draws a lively pre- and post-theater crowd. No TVs, quality pub talk, and a great pint of Guinness make it a worthwhile visit (although the decor won't win any prizes). ⊠ *Lower Abbey St., Northside* ☎ *01/874–0842* ✥ *E2.*

Pantibar. Fronted by the infamous Dublin drag queen Panti, this amusingly named gay bar has loud music at night but is pretty chilled out during the day. ⊠ *7–8 Capel St., Northside* ☎ *01/874–0710* ⊕ *www.pantibar.com* ✥ *C2.*

DUBLIN WEST

PUBS

Brazen Head. Reputedly Dublin's oldest pub (the site has been licensed since 1198), the Brazen Head doesn't have much of a time-burnished decor—except for one big exception: an enchanting stone courtyard that is intimate, charming, and delightful. The front is a faux one-story castle, complete with flambeaux, while the interior looks modern day (except for the very low ceilings). People love to jam the place not for its history but for its traditional-music performances and lively sing-along sessions on Sunday evenings. On the south side of the Liffey quays, it's a little difficult to find—turn down Lower Bridge Street and make a right onto the old lane. ⊠ *20 Lower Bridge St., Dublin West* ☎ *01/677–9549* ⊕ *www.brazenhead.com* ✥ *B3.*

Cobblestone. A glorious house of ale in the best Dublin tradition, the Cobblestone is popular with Smithfield Market workers. Its chatty imbibers and live traditional music are attracting a more varied, younger crowd from all over town. ⊠ *N. King St., Dublin West* ☎ *01/872–1799* ✥ *B2.*

Some Dubliners now give the Temple Bar district the brush-off; others still find it the pulsing aorta of the city's nightlife.

Dice Bar. Cool students and twentysomethings pack this East Village-style, dark, loud, and lively spot at the heart of Smithfield. DJs keep the crowd happy most nights. ⊠ *79 Queen St., Dublin West* ☎ *01/872–8622* ✛ *B2.*

Fodor's Choice
★

Fallons. Somehow you always get a seat in this tiny sliver of a pub—a warm, old-school boozer at its best—tucked away on a corner near St. Patrick's Cathedral. Pure Dublin class. ⊠ *129 The Coombe, Dublin West* ☎ *01/454–2801* ✛ *B4.*

Fodor's Choice
★

Ryan's Pub. One of Dublin's last genuine, late-Victorian-era pubs, Ryan's has changed little since its last (1896) remodeling. ⊠ *28 Parkgate St., Dublin West* ☎ *01/677–6097* ⊕ *ryans.fxbuckley.ie* ✛ *A2.*

THE ARTS

CLASSICAL MUSIC AND OPERA
SOUTHSIDE

Bord Gáis Energy Theatre. Housed in a brash, Daniel Liebskind–designed building in the growing docklands area of the city, this theater has a 2,000-plus capacity, making it Ireland's biggest theater space. Its calendar includes the best of international ballet, classical music, pop gigs, and even Broadway musicals. ⊠ *Grand Canal Sq., Southside* ☎ *01/677–7999* ⊕ *www.bordgaisenergytheatre.ie.*

St. Stephen's Church. Under its glorious "pepper canister" cupola, St. Stephen's Church stages a tempting program of choral and orchestral events. ⊠ *Upper Mount St., Southside* ☎ *01/288–0663* ⊕ *www.peppercanister.ie.*

GEORGIAN DUBLIN

The National Concert Hall. Just off St. Stephen's Green, the National Concert Hall is Dublin's main theater for classical music of all kinds, from symphonies to chamber groups. The slightly austere Neoclassical building was transformed in 1981 into one of Europe's finest medium-size concert halls. It houses the cream of Irish classical musicians, the National Symphony Orchestra of Ireland. A host of guest international conductors and performers—Maxim Vengerov, Radu Lupu, and Pinchas Zukerman are just a few of the soloists who have appeared—keep the standard very high, and performances continue throughout the year. The concert year picks up speed in mid-September and sails through to June; July and August also get many dazzling troupes. The smaller, more intimate John Field and Carolan rooms are perfect for chamber music. ⊠ *Earlsfort Terr., Georgian Dublin* ☎ *01/417–0000* ⊕ *www.nch.ie.*

TEMPLE BAR

Opera Theatre Company. Ireland's only touring opera company, the Opera Theatre company performs at venues in Dublin and throughout the country. ⊠ *Temple Bar Music Centre, Curved St., Temple Bar* ☎ *01/679–4962* ⊕ *www.opera.ie.*

DUBLIN WEST

Royal Hospital Kilmainham. Frequent classical concerts are hosted by the Royal Hospital Kilmainham in its magnificent 17th-century interior. ⊠ *Military Rd., Dublin West* ☎ *01/612–9900* ⊕ *www.rhk.ie.*

St. Patrick's Cathedral. Along with some regular concert performances, you can catch some beautiful church singing at evensong at St. Pat's most weekdays around half past 5 pm. ⊠ *Saint Patrick's Close, Dublin West* ☎ *01/453–9472* ⊕ *www.stpatrickscathedral.ie* 🎫 *€5.50.*

FILM

TEMPLE BAR

Irish Film Institute. Film-lovers head here for its fascinating schedule of classic and new independent films. ☎ *01/6795744* ⊕ *www.ifi.ie* ⊠ *6 Eustace St., Temple Bar.*

ROCK AND CONTEMPORARY MUSIC

SOUTHSIDE

International Bar. A long-established, tiny, get-close-to-the-band venue upstairs, the International also hosts theater in the afternoon and comedy on weekends. ⊠ *Wicklow St., Southside* ☎ *01/677–9250* ⊕ *www.international-bar.com.*

The Village. Set in a striking, glass-front building, the Village isn't too fussy about the kind of bands it hosts, so long as their amps are turned up full and the lead singer knows how to scream. ⊠ *26 Wexford St., Southside* ☎ *01/475–8555* ⊕ *www.thevillagevenue.com.*

Whelan's. It might look a bit shabby around the edges, but Whelan's is one of the city's best—and most popular—music venues. Well-known performers play everything from rock to folk to traditional music. ⊠ *25 Wexford St., Southside* ☎ *01/478–0766* ⊕ *www.whelanslive.com.*

TEMPLE BAR

Button Factory. A music venue and club rolled into one, the Button Factory buzzes with activity every night of the week. Live acts range from rock bands to world music to singer-songwriters. ⊠ *Curved St., Temple Bar* ☎ *01/670–9202* ⊕ *www.buttonfactory.ie.*

Olympia Theatre. Everything from rock to country is presented at the Olympia, which is noted for its intense atmosphere and great acoustics. ⊠ *72 Dame St., Temple Bar* ☎ *01/679–3323* ⊕ *www.mcd.ie/olympia.*

NORTHSIDE

The O2. Home to the grandest, big-gig concerts by rock stars and dance luminaries, the O2 arena is a high-tech, 14,500-capacity venue. ⊠ *Northwall Quay, Northside* ☎ *01/836–3633* ⊕ *www.theo2.ie.*

DUBLIN WEST

Vicar Street. Across from Christ Church Cathedral, Vicar Street is a venue for intimate concerts. It often plays host to folk music, jazz, and comedy, as well as rock performances. ⊠ *58–59 Thomas St., Dublin West* ☎ *01/775–5800* ⊕ *www.vicarstreet.com.*

THEATER

SOUTHSIDE

Fodor's Choice ★ **Gaiety Theatre.** When this shimmering red-and-gold 19th-century theater is not showing musical comedy, drama, and revues, the sumptuous Gaiety is taken over by Opera Ireland for one of their big shows. ⊠ *S. King St., Southside* ☎ *01/677–1717* ⊕ *www.gaietytheatre.ie.*

Samuel Beckett Centre. Home to Trinity College's drama department, as well as visiting European groups, the Samuel Beckett Centre also hosts dance performances by visiting troupes; the theater was built in 1992 and stands near the center of Trinity's campus. ⊠ *Trinity College, Southside* ☎ *01/608–2266* ⊕ *www.tcd.ie/Drama/samuel-beckett-theatre.*

TEMPLE BAR

The New Theatre. A troupe with a political agenda, the New Theatre often favors productions by Irish working-class writers like Sean O'Casey and Brendan Behan in its renovated Temple Bar space. ⊠ *43 E. Essex St., Temple Bar* ☎ *01/670–3361* ⊕ *www.thenewtheatre.com.*

Project Arts Centre. A theater and performance space in an ugly modern building at the center of Temple Bar, the Project Arts Center is home to fringe and mainstream theater, contemporary music, and experimental art events. ⊠ *39 E. Essex St., Temple Bar* ☎ *01/881–9613* ⊕ *www.projectartscentre.ie.*

Smock Alley Theatre. Smock Alley is a wonderfully atmospheric theater space tucked down a little lane. Now housed in a lovely 19th-century Irish neo-Gothic structure, it stands on the site of a famous 17th-century Dublin theater. ⊠ *6/7 Lower Exchange St., Temple Bar* ☎ *01/677–0014* ⊕ *www.smockalley.com.*

NORTHSIDE

Fodor's Choice ★ **Abbey Theatre.** One of the most fabled theaters in the world, the Abbey is the home of Ireland's national theater company. In 1904 W. B. Yeats and his patron, Lady Gregory, opened the theater, which became a major center for the Irish literary renaissance—the place that first staged works by J. M. Synge and Sean O'Casey, among many others. Plays by recent Irish drama heavyweights like Brian Friel, Tom Murphy, Hugh Leonard, and John B. Keane have all premiered here, and memorable productions of international greats like Mamet, Ibsen, and Shakespeare have also been performed. You should not, however, arrive expecting 19th-century grandeur: the original structure burned down in 1951. A starkly modernist auditorium was built in its place—but what it may lack in esthetics it makes up for in space and acoustics. Some say the repertoire is overly reverential and mainstream, but such chestnuts as Dion Boucicault's *The Shaughran* wind up being applauded by many. Happily, the Abbey's second stage offers more experimental drama. But the Abbey will always be relevant since much of the theatergoing public still looks to it as a barometer of Irish culture. ✉ *Lower Abbey St., Northside* ☎ *01/878–7222* ⊕ *www.abbeytheatre.ie.*

Gate Theatre. An intimate 371-seat theater in a jewel-like Georgian assembly hall, the Gate produces the classics and contemporary plays by leading Irish writers, including Beckett, Wilde (the production of *Salome* was a worldwide hit), Shaw, and the younger generation of dramatists, such as Conor McPherson. ✉ *Cavendish Row, Parnell Square, Northside* ☎ *01/874–4045* ⊕ *www.gate-theatre.ie.*

> **WORD OF MOUTH**
>
> "It is as difficult if not more difficult to get tickets to shows in Dublin theaters than it is to get tickets to shows in London. So good are they, most of the Dublin presentations transfer straight to Broadway and later to Hollywood scripts and the movies. Thus, I would suggest that you jump at the opportunity when you're in Dublin. After all, Irish literature and theater is one of the things that Ireland is famous for. Dramas tend to be deep—reflecting social and historic issues past and present in Ireland—and they give an insight into the country that you will be touring." —Cathy

SHOPPING

The only known specimens of leprechauns or shillelaghs in Ireland are those in souvenir-shop windows, and shamrocks mainly bloom around the borders of Irish linen handkerchiefs and tablecloths. But in Dublin's shops you can find much more than kitschy designs. There's a tremendous variety of stores here, many of which are quite sophisticated—as a walk through Dublin's central shopping area, from O'Connell to Grafton Street, will prove. Department stores stock internationally known fashion-designer goods and housewares, and small (and often pricey) boutiques sell Irish crafts and other merchandise. Don't expect too many bargains here. And be prepared, if you're shopping in central Dublin, to push through crowds—especially in the afternoons and on weekends. Most large shops and department stores are open Monday to Saturday 9 to 6, with late hours on Thursday and Friday until 9. Although nearly all department stores are closed on Sunday, some smaller specialty shops stay open. *Those with later closing hours are noted below.* You're particularly likely to find sales in January, February, July, and August.

SOUTHSIDE

SHOPPING CENTERS

Powerscourt Centre. Once the regal former town home of Lord Powerscourt (built in 1771), this was largely gutted two decades ago to make room for an interior roofed-over courtyard and a space shared by a mix of restaurants, cafés, antiques stores, and boutiques of original Irish fashions by young designers. A pianist often plays on the dais at ground-floor level. ⊠ *59 S. William St., Southside* ☎ *01/679–4144* ⊕ *www.powerscourtcentre.com.*

Royal Hibernian Way. On the former site of the two-century-old Royal Hibernian Hotel, a coaching inn that was demolished in 1983, this complex is home to pricey, stylish shops—about 20 or 30, many selling fashionable clothes and accessories—including Clarke Irish and Celtic Jewellers. ⊠ *Off Dawson St., between S. Anne and Duke Sts., Southside* ☎ *01/679–5919.*

St. Stephen's Green Centre. Dublin's city center's largest and most ambitious shopping complex, St. Stephen's Green Centre resembles a giant greenhouse, with Victorian-style ironwork. On three floors overlooked by a giant clock, the 100 mostly small shops sell crafts, fashions, and household goods. ⊠ *Northwest corner of St. Stephen's Green, Southside* ☎ *01/478–0888* ⊕ *www.stephensgreen.com.*

Westbury Mall. An upmarket shopping mall, the Westbury is where you can buy a stylish range of designer jewelry, antique rugs, and decorative goods. ⊠ *Westbury Hotel, off Grafton St., Southside.*

DEPARTMENT STORES

Fodor's Choice ★ **Brown Thomas.** Dublin's most exclusive department store, Brown Thomas stocks the leading designer names (including top Irish designers) in clothing and cosmetics, plus lots of stylish accessories. There's also a good selection of crystal. ⊠ *Grafton St., Southside* ☎ *01/605–6666* ⊕ *www.brownthomas.com.*

Dunnes Stores. Ireland's largest chain of department stores, all Dunnes branches stock fashion (including the exciting Savida range) and household and grocery items, and have a reputation for value and variety. ⊠ *St. Stephen's Green Centre, Southside* ☎ *01/478–0188* ⊕ *www. dunnesstores.ie* ⊠ *Henry St., Northside* ⊠ *Ilac Centre, Mary St., Northside* ☎ *01/873–0211.*

Marks & Spencer. More affordable than high-end Grafton Street competitor Brown Thomas, Marks & Spencer stocks everything from fashion (including lingerie) to tasty, unusual groceries. ⊠ *Grafton St., Southside* ☎ *01/679–7855* ⊕ *www.marksandspencer.com* ⊠ *Henry St., Northside* ☎ *01/872–8833.*

OUTDOOR MARKETS

George's Street Arcade. Opened in 1881 as South City Markets, this classic Victorian market right in the heart of town is home to a small but eclectic collection of clothes, books, food, and jewelry stalls. It's

CLOSE UP

Dublin Shopping Streets

SOUTHSIDE

Dawson Street. Just east of Grafton Street between Nassau Street to the north and St. Stephen's Green to the south, Dawson Street is full of lively cafés and bars. It's also the address of Hodges Figgis, the best bookstore in the country.

Francis Street. Part of the Liberties, the oldest part of the city and the hub of Dublin's antiques trade, Francis Street and surrounding areas, such as the Coombe, have plenty of shops where you can browse. If you're looking for something in particular, dealers will gladly recommend the appropriate store to you. It's also home to a couple of hot new galleries.

Grafton Street. Dublin's bustling pedestrian-only main shopping street, Grafton Street has two department stores: down-to-earth Marks & Spencer and trés chic Brown Thomas. The rest of the street is taken up by shops, many of them branches of international chains, such as the Body Shop and Bally, and many British chains. This is also the spot to buy fresh flowers, available at reasonable prices from outdoor stands. On the smaller streets off Grafton Street—especially Duke Street, South Anne Street, and Chatham Street—are worthwhile crafts, clothing, and designer housewares shops.

Nassau Street. Dublin's main tourist-oriented thoroughfare, Nassau has some of the best-known stores selling Irish goods, but you won't find many locals shopping here. Still, if you're looking for classic Irish gifts to take home, you should be sure at least to browse along here.

TEMPLE BAR

Temple Bar Cultural Trust. Once dubbed Dublin's hippest neighborhood, Temple Bar is still dotted with small, precious boutiques—mainly intimate, quirky shops that traffic in a small selection of trendy goods, from vintage clothes to some of the most avant-garde Irish garb anywhere in the city. ⊕ *www.templebar.ie.*

NORTHSIDE

Henry Street. Running westward from O'Connell Street, Henry Street is where cash-conscious Dubliners shop. Arnotts department store is the anchor here. Henry Street's continuation, Mary Street, has a branch of Marks & Spencer and the Jervis Shopping Centre.

O'Connell Street. The city's main thoroughfare, O'Connell Street is more downscale than Southside city streets (such as Grafton Street), but it is still worth a walk. One of Dublin's largest department stores, Clery's, is across from the GPO. On the same side of the street Eason's, a large book, magazine, and stationery store.

covered, but feels outdoors, and open every day. ⊠ *S. Great George's St., Southside* ⊕ *www.georgesstreetarcade.ie.*

BOOKS

Books Upstairs. An excellent selection of special-interest books is available here, including Irish literature, gay and feminist literature, psychology, and self-help books. ⊠ *36 College Green, Southside* ☎ *01/679–6687.*

Shop-'til-you-droppers love Grafton Street, a store-lined address custom-made for serious retail therapy.

Fodor's Choice ★ **Hodges Figgis.** Dublin's leading independent bookstore, Hodges Figgis stocks 1½ million books on three floors. Once considered Ireland's oldest, its "independent" claim is a bit bogus, as a giant chain bought it some years ago. That noted, it has a stock, staff, look, and even aroma of an independent bookstore, and might even still please James Joyce (who alludes to it in his *Ulysses*). ⊠ *56–58 Dawson St., Southeast Dublin* ☎ *01/677–4754.*

Hughes & Hughes. This noted bookseller has strong travel and Irish-interest sections (there's also a store at Dublin Airport). ⊠ *St. Stephen's Green Centre, Southside* ☎ *01/478–3060* ⊕ *www.hughesandhughes.ie.*

Reads. Somehow Reads manages to sell best sellers cheaper than any of its rivals. Also, it has a decent Irish section. ⊠ *24–25 Nassau St., Southside* ☎ *01/679–6011.*

Fodor's Choice ★ **Stokes Books.** A gem of an antique bookstore, Stokes has a great used-book section and specializes in Irish history and literature. While on the small side, Stokes is a treasure trove that will turn on most book-lovers. ⊠ *George's Street Arcade, Southside* ☎ *01/671–3584* ⊕ *www.georgesstreetarcade.ie/stokes-books/index.php.*

Fodor's Choice ★ **Ulysses Rare Books.** Head here for a fine array of first editions of Irish literature and many other books of Irish interest, plus old maps of Dublin and Ireland. ⊠ *10 Duke St., Southside* ☎ *01/671–8676* ⊕ *www. rarebooks.ie.*

Dublin à la Mode

The success of shops such as Costume has given young Irish designers the confidence to produce more original and impressive work. One of Costume's most popular designers, **Helen James**, graduated from the National College of Art and Design in textile design in 1992. She went straight to New York, where she worked for Donna Karan, among others. She returned to Ireland in 2002 and developed her line of unique, hand-printed textile accessories. She now designs for major city center stores. Many people say there is a delicate Japanese feel to her work. Check out her work at ⊕ helenjamesdesign.blogspot.ie.

Footwear has long been an area overlooked by Irish designers, but Irishwoman **Eileen Shields** has been living and working in New York since 1988; for almost 10 years she designed footwear for Donna Karan. Her own premiere collection is all about clean, bold lines. Materials include antique kid, fine suede, python, and soft patent leather. Textures are often strongly contrasting, while colors are sensual and sophisticated. You can get the shoes online at ⊕ www.eileenshields.com.

The Tucker family has been a key player in Irish fashion since the 1960s, and new-generation **Leigh Tucker** has quickly established herself as one of Dublin's classiest young designers. Fine tailoring is her trademark—the finish on her eveningwear is nonpareil—and beaded French lace and draped jersey are her favorite materials. She is now designing women and kids clothes for Dunnes Stores in the city center.

CHINA, CRYSTAL, CERAMICS, AND JEWELRY

Appleby Jewellers. This is the best known of the several classy, old-style jewelry shops that line tiny Johnson's Court, a delightful little lane off busy Grafton Street. ⊠ *Johnson's Ct., Grafton St., Southside* ☎ *01/679–9572* ⊕ *www.appleby.ie.*

Fodor's Choice ★ **Barry Doyle Design.** A true original with his Celtic modern jewelry, Barry Doyle is a master who allows you to watch him at work in his adjoining studio as he fashions beautiful wedding rings and his lovely Lilac Collection baubles. It was chosen as one of the top 50 shops in Ireland by *Irish Times* readers. ⊠ *George's Street Arcade, Upstairs, Southside* ☎ *01/671–2838* ⊕ *www.barrydoyledesign.com.*

House of Ireland. For Irish goods and crafts, this is a great one-stop shopping resource with an extensive selection of crystal, jewelry, tweeds, sweaters, and other upscale goods. ⊠ *37–38 Nassau St., Southside* ☎ *01/671–1111* ⊕ *www.houseofireland.com.*

Irish Design Shop. Two young jewelers got together to open this exciting shop dedicated to the best in Irish design and designers. They sell woolen accessories, kitchen stuff, jewelry, and assorted other treasures. ⊠ *41 Drury St., Southside* ☎ *01/679–8871* ⊕ *www.irishdesignshop.com.*

Kilkenny Shop. Specializing in contemporary Irish-made ceramics, pottery, and silver jewelry, Kilkenny Shop regularly holds exhibits of exciting new work by Irish craftspeople and has a wide array of gifts fashioned by Orla Kiely and other top Irish designers. ✉ *6–15 Nassau St., Southside* ☎ *01/677–7066* ⊕ *www.kilkennyshop.com.*

Trinity Crafts. Your one-stop shop for everything kitschy Irish, head to Trinity Crafts for such trashy treasures as "the leprechauns made me do it" mugs and Guinness-logo underwear. ✉ *27 Nassau St., Southside* ☎ *01/672–5663* ⊕ *www.thesweatershop.ie.*

Weir & Sons. Dublin's most prestigious jeweler, Weir & Sons sells not only jewelry and watches, but also china, glass, lamps, silver, and leather. Founded in 1869, its flatiron building has long been a landmark on Grafton Street. ✉ *96 Grafton St., Southside* ☎ *01/677–9678* ⊕ *www.weirandsons.ie.*

CLOTHING STORES

BT2. This is swanky Brown Thomas's impressive attempt to woo a younger crowd. Most of the major labels are present, including DKNY and Paul Smith. ✉ *Grafton St., Southside* ☎ *01/605–6666* ⊕ *www.bt2.ie.*

Carousel. If cute vintage clothing is your thing, husband-and-wife-operated Carousel has a great selection of dresses, skirts, knitwares, and accessories. ✉ *20 Exchequer St., Southside* ☎ *01/677–8713* ⊕ *www. ilovecarousel.com.*

Fodor's Choice ★ **Costume.** A classy boutique for Dubliners with fashion sense and money, Costume showcases local designers such as Leigh, Helen James, and Helen Steele. Temperley and Preen are among the international designers featured among the rails of colorful, stylish clothes. ✉ *10 Castel Market, Southside* ☎ *01/679–4188* ⊕ *www.costumedublin.ie.*

Topshop. The rapidly expanding British fashion chain has its flagship Irish store on Stephen's Green. Its mix of creative and affordable continues to draw the crowds, with designer collaborations including J.W. Anderson and Kate Moss. ✉ *6–7 Stephen's Green, Southside* ☎ *01/633–4803* ⊕ *www.topshop.com.*

MUSIC

Celtic Note. Aimed at the tourist market, Celtic Note has lots of Irish music compilations and greatest-hits formats. ✉ *14/15 Nassau St., Southside* ☎ *01/670–4157* ⊕ *www.celticnote.com.*

Gael Linn. A specialist in traditional Irish music and Irish-language recordings, Gael Linn is where the aficionados go. ✉ *35 Dame St., Southside* ☎ *01/675–1200* ⊕ *www.gael-linn.ie.*

McCullogh Piggott. This is the best place in town to buy instruments, sheet music, scores, and books about music. ✉ *11 S. William St., Southside* ☎ *01/670–6702* ⊕ *www.mcculloughpigott.com.*

Tower Records. With the demise of HMV, Tower is the last big mainstream music store in Dublin. It carries all the latest CDs, DVDs, music books, vinyl, and music merchandise. ✉ *6–8 Wicklow St., Southside* ☎ *01/671–3250* ⊕ *www.towerrecords.ie.*

Waltons. Fancy your own *bodhrán* (Irish hand drum) or tin whistle? Waltons is the place to come for any Irish traditional instrument, or indeed for anything musical at all. ✉ *60–70 S. Great Georges St., Southside* ☎ *01/475–0661* ⊕ *www.waltons.ie.*

SWEATERS AND TWEEDS

Avoca. Avoca is a beautiful store with an eclectic collection of knitwear, jewelry, ceramics, and housewares from contemporary Irish designers. There's a fantastic café in the basement with unmissable cakes. ⊠ *11–13 Suffolk St., Southside* ☎ *01/274–6900* ⊕ *www.avoca.ie.*

Cleo. Hand-knit sweaters and accessories made only from natural fibers are a specialty at Cleo. ⊠ *18 Kildare St., Georgian Dublin* ☎ *01/676– 1421* ⊕ *www.cleo-ltd.com.*

Fodor'sChoice **Kevin and Howlin.** A quintessential Irish store, Kevin and Howlin stocks
★   spiffing fashions, with lots of stylish handwoven tweed men's jackets, suits, and hats, along with an array of treasures woven from tweedy fabrics. All in all, it's a fabulous, one-stop shop for traditional clothes with flair. Wait until you see the whole wall devoted to headgear—eat your heart out, Ralph Lauren! ⊠ *31 Nassau St., Southside* ☎ *01/677–0257* ⊕ *www.kevinandhowlin.com.*

Monaghan's. If you're into cashmere, you should get yourself into Monaghan's. ⊠ *Royal Hibernian Way, 15–17 Grafton St., Southside* ☎ *01/677–0823* ⊕ *www.monaghanscashmere.ie.*

TEMPLE BAR

CLOTHING

Indigo and Cloth. This has quickly become the place where Irish men with a bit of taste come for quality, slightly edgy clothing. Designers like Oliver Spencer and Velour dominate, and they also have a small, but classy, women's section. ⊠ *9 Essex St. E, Temple Bar* ☎ *01/670–6403* ⊕ *www.indigoandcloth.com.*

MUSIC

Claddagh Records. Head here for a good selection of traditional and folk music. They have another shop on Middle Abbey Street. ⊠ *2 Cecilia St., Temple Bar* ☎ *01/677–0262* ⊕ *www.claddaghrecords.com.*

OUTDOOR MARKETS

Cows Lane Market. Held every Saturday from February to September at the west edge of Temple Bar, Cows Lane is home to some of the most innovative young fashion and accessory designers in the country. ⊠ *Temple Bar* ⊕ *templebar.ie/Market/Designer_Mart.*

Meeting House Square Market. Held Saturday morning in the heart of Temple Bar, this is a good place to buy homemade foodstuffs: cheeses, breads, chocolate, and organic veggies. ⊠ *Temple Bar.*

NORTHSIDE

SHOPPING CENTERS

Jervis Shopping Centre. A slightly high-end center, Jervis houses some of the major British chain stores. It has a compact design and plenty of parking. ⊠ *Jervis and Mary Sts., 125 Abbey St. Upper, Northside* ☎ *01/878–1323* ⊕ *jervis.ie.*

DEPARTMENT STORES

Arnotts. Fully filling three floors, Arnotts stocks a wide selection of clothing, household accessories, and sporting goods. It is known for matching quality with value. There is a Gap section downstairs. ⊠ *Henry St., Northside* ☎ *01/805–0400* ⊕ *www.arnotts.ie.*

Debenhams. This U.K. chain store includes a Zara section along with its own clothing and home-ware lines. ⊠ *Henry St., Northside* ☎ *01/814–7200* ⊕ *www.debenhams.ie.*

Eason & Son. Known primarily for its large selection of books, magazines, and stationery, Eason also sells an array of CDs, DVDs, and other audiovisual goodies at its main O'Connell Street branch; all in all, it has about 50 bookstores throughout Ireland. ⊠ *O'Connell St., Northside* ☎ *01/873–3811* ⊕ *www.eason.ie.*

CHINA, CRYSTAL, CERAMICS, AND JEWELRY

McDowells. Popular with Dubliners, this jewelry shop has been in business for more than 100 years. ⊠ *3 Upper O'Connell St., Northside* ☎ *01/874–4961* ⊕ *www.mcdowellsjewellers.com.*

ANTIQUES

Dublin is one of Europe's best cities in which to buy antiques, largely due to a long and proud tradition of restoration and high-quality craftsmanship. The Liberties, Dublin's oldest district, is, fittingly, the hub of the antiques trade, and is chockablock with shops and traders. Bachelor's Walk, along the quays, also has some decent shops. It's quite a seller's market, but bargains are still possible.

DUBLIN WEST

ANTIQUES

Christy Bird. Dublin's oldest furniture shop, Christy Bird was recycling household items before anyone else dreamed of it. You have to hunt for anything that is true quality and most of the goods here are now repro and mass-market. ⊠ *32 S. Richmond St., Dublin West* ☎ *01/475–4049* ⊕ *www.christybird.com.*

Martin Fennelly Antiques. A stalwart of Dublin's traditional antiques quarter around Francis Street, Fennelly's specializes in early furniture and decorative items like candlesticks, tea caddies, and fitted jewelry caskets. ⊠ *60 Francis St., Dublin West* ☎ *01/473–1126* ⊕ *www.fennelly.net.*

Fodor's Choice ★ **O'Sullivan Antiques.** Specializing in 18th- and 19th-century furniture, with a high-profile clientele (including Mia Farrow and Liam Neeson), the O'Sullivan "look" has been so successful that it now runs a full-time sister shop in New York. ⊠ *43–44 Francis St., Dublin West* ☎ *01/454–1143, 01/453–9659* ⊕ *www.osullivanantiques.com.*

OUTDOOR MARKETS

Fodor's Choice ★ **Dublin Food Co-op.** A breath of eco-fresh air on the Dublin food-shopping scene, this member-run co-op has a quality food market in a wonderful old space in Newmarket at the heart of the Liberties district every Thursday and Saturday. It even encourages the use of a few words of Irish among the locals as they shop for organic veggies, flowers, cheeses, and wines. It also holds a world-culture market, a furniture market, and the city's best flea market on the second, third, and last Sunday of the month. ✉ *12 Newmarket St., Dublin West* ⊕ *www.dublinfood.coop.*

Liberty Market. Just minutes from Christ Church Cathedral, this working-class favorite is a great place to get a feel for Dubliners at play. The stalls vary from knickknacks to children's clothing and candy. Open Thursday to Saturday. ✉ *Meath St., Dublin West* ⊕ *www.libertymarket.ie.*

SPORTS AND THE OUTDOORS

FOOTBALL

Soccer—called football in Europe—is very popular in Ireland, largely due to the euphoria resulting from the national team's underdog successes since the late 1980s.

Football Association of Ireland. League of Ireland matches take place throughout the city on Friday evening or Sunday afternoon from March to November. For details, contact the Football Association of Ireland. ✉ *80 Merrion Sq. S, Southeast Dublin* ☎ *01/676–6864* ⊕ *www.fai.ie.*

GAELIC GAMES

Gaelic Athletic Association (*GAA*). The traditional games of Ireland, Gaelic football and hurling, attract a huge following, with roaring crowds cheering on their county teams. Games are held at Croke Park, the stunning, high-tech national stadium for Gaelic games, just north of the city center. For details of matches, contact the Gaelic Athletic Association. ✉ *Croke Park, North County Dublin* ☎ *01/836–3222* ⊕ *www.gaa.ie.*

GOLF

Fodor's Choice   **Portmarnock Golf Club.** The hoo-ha and court battles over Portmarnock's
★   refusal to admit women as full members often overshadows the club's position as the most famous of Ireland's "Big Four" (Ballybunion, Royal County Down, and Royal Portrush are the others). This links course, on a sandy peninsula north of Dublin, has hosted numerous major championships and Tom Watson often used it as a preparation for the Open. Known for its flat fairways and greens and its 100-plus bunkers, it provides a fair test for any golfer who can keep it out of the heavy rough. Greens fees include lunch. ✉ *North County Dublin, Portmarnock* ☎ *01/846–2968* ⊕ *www.portmarnockgolfclub.ie* 🖾 *€175* ⅄ *Championship Course: 18 holes, 7382 yards, par 72; Yellow Course: 9 holes, 3449 yards, par 37. Practice area, driving range, caddies (reserve in advance), caddy carts, club rental, catering* ⊙ *Visitors: daily.*

HORSE RACING

Horse racing—from flat to hurdle to steeplechase—is one of the great sporting loves of the Irish. The sport is closely followed and betting is popular, but the social side of attending races is equally important to Dubliners.

Leopardstown Racecourse. The hub of horse racing in Dublin is Leopardstown, an ultramodern course that in February hosts the Hennessey Gold Cup, one of Ireland's most prestigious steeplechases. Summertime is devoted to flat racing, and the rest of the year to racing over fences. You can also nip in for a quick meal at the restaurant. ⊠ *Leopardstown Rd., South County Dublin* ☎ *01/289–3600* ⊕ *www.leopardstown.com.*

RUGBY

For many years rugby was a "garrison sport" in Ireland, the preserve of "West Brits" and private-school boys. The success of the Irish team internationally, and Ulster, Leinster, and Munster in European club competitions, has changed that somewhat, and you might see an oval ball being tossed around by kids in any area of the country.

Aviva Stadium. The home of Irish Rugby, Aviva's state-of-the-art arena opened in 2010 (on the site of the old Lansdowne Stadium) and can accommodate 50,000 fans. ⊠ *62 Lansdowne Rd., Ballsbridge* ☎ *01/238–2300* ⊕ *www.avivastadium.ie.*

SIDE TRIPS: NORTH COUNTY DUBLIN

Dublin's northern suburbs remain largely residential, but there are a few places worth the trip, such as the architectural gem Marino Casino. As with most suburban areas, walking may not be the best way to get around. It's good, but not essential, to have a car. Buses and trains serve most of these areas.

MARINO CASINO

Take Malahide Road from Dublin's north city center for 4 km (2½ miles). Or take Bus No. 20A or 24 to Casino from Cathal Brugha Street in north city center.

Marino Casino. One of Dublin's most exquisite, yet also most underrated, architectural landmarks, the Marino Casino (the name means "little house by the sea," and the building overlooks Dublin Harbour) is a small-scale, Palladian-style Greek temple, built between 1762 and 1771 from a plan by Sir William Chambers. Often compared to the Petit Trianon at Versailles, it was commissioned by the great Irish grandee Lord Charlemont as a summerhouse. Inside, highlights are the china-closet boudoir, the huge golden sunset in the ceiling of the main drawing room, and the signs of the zodiac in the ceiling of the bijou library. When you realize that the structure has, in fact, 16 rooms—there are bedrooms upstairs—Sir William's sleight-of-hand is readily apparent: from its exterior, the structure seems to contain only one room. It makes a good stop on the way to Malahide, Howth, or North Bull Island. ⊠ *Malahide Rd., Marino, North County Dublin* ☎ *01/833–1618* ⊕ *www.heritageireland.ie* €3 ⊙ *Mid-Mar.–Oct., daily 10–5.*

MALAHIDE

By car, drive from north city center on R107 for 14½ km (9 miles). Or catch hourly train from Connolly Station. Or board Bus No. 42 to Malahide, which leaves every 15 minutes from Beresford Place behind Custom House.

FAMILY **Malahide Castle.** This township is chiefly known for its glorious Malahide Castle, a picture-book castle occupied by the Talbot family from 1185 until 1976, when it was sold to the local County Council. The great expanse of parkland around the castle has more than 5,000 different species of trees and shrubs, all clearly labeled. The castle itself combines styles and crosses centuries; the earliest section, the three-story tower house, dates from the 12th century. The stunning walled gardens are now open to the public. Hung with many family portraits, the medieval great hall is the only one in Ireland that is preserved in its original form. Authentic 18th-century pieces furnish the other rooms. An impressive new addition includes a visitor center, Avoca restaurant, and shop. ⊠ *10 km (6 miles) north of Howth on Coast Rd., North County Dublin* ☎ *01/846–2184* ⊕ *www.malahidecastle.com* ✉ *€12* ⊗ *Daily 9:30–4:30.*

FAMILY **Newbridge House and Farm.** One of the greatest stately homes of Ireland,
Fodor'sChoice Newbridge House, in Donabate, was built between 1740 and 1760 for
★ Charles Cobbe, Archbishop of Dublin. A showpiece in the Georgian and Regency styles, the house is less a museum than a home because the Cobbe family still resides here, part of a novel scheme the municipal government allowed when they took over the house in 1985. The sober exterior and even more sober entrance hall—all Portland stone and Welsh slate—don't prepare you for the splendor of Newbridge's Red Drawing Room, perhaps Ireland's most sumptuous 18th-century salon. Cobbe's son, Thomas, and his wife, Lady Betty Beresford, sister of the marquess of Waterford, had amassed a great collection of paintings and needed a hall in which to show them off, so they built a back wing of the house to incorporate an enormous room built for entertaining and impressing others. That it does, thanks to its crimson walls, fluted Corinthian columns, dozens of Old Masters, and glamorous rococo-style plaster ceiling designed by the Dublin stuccadore Richard Williams. Beyond the house's walled garden are 366 acres of parkland and a restored 18th-century animal farm. The coffee shop is renowned for the quality and selection of its homemade goods. You can travel from Malahide to Donabate by train, which takes about 10 minutes. From the Donabate train station, it's a 15-minute walk to the Newbridge House grounds. ⊠ *Donabate, 8 km (5 miles) north of Malahide, signposted from N1, North County Dublin* ☎ *01/843–6534* ⊕ *www. newbridgehouseandfarm.com* ✉ *House, €7; farm, €5; combined, €10* ⊗ *Apr.–Sept., daily 10–5; Oct.–Mar., Tues.–Sun. 11–4.*

DUBLIN ENVIRONS

Including Counties Kildare, Louth,
Meath, and Wicklow

WELCOME TO DUBLIN ENVIRONS

TOP REASONS TO GO

★ **Newgrange:** Just standing amid these 5,000-year-old tombs (which predate the pyramids), you'll wonder: how did they build them?

★ **A Day at the Races:** The Irish may like a drink, but they really love to gamble, as you'll discover in Kildare, center of the Irish bloodstock world. Punchestown in spring and the Curragh in summer are both unique, passionate racecourse experiences.

★ **Spectacular Georgian Country Houses:** Modesty was not a feature of the Anglo-Irish class, whose propensity to flaunt their riches led to such over-the-top stately homes as Castletown, Russborough, and Powerscourt.

★ **Wicklow Is for Walkers:** There's no better way to meet the locals and see the land than trekking out on the 137-km-long (85-mile-long) Wicklow Way, Ireland's most popular trail.

★ **Early Morning at Glendalough:** Before the tour buses arrive, channel the spirit of the 6th-century, isolation-seeking St. Kevin.

1 **The Boyne Valley.** Set 48 km (30 miles) north of Dublin, this entire area is packed with prehistoric and pagan sites. You don't have to be an Indiana Jones to be awed by the Hill of Tara or Newgrange, a Neolithic burial ground and solar observatory still evocative of the mysteries of pre-Celtic civilization.

2 **County Wicklow.** Set with dense woods and idyllic lakes, "the garden of Ireland" is a favorite day out for Dubliners, thanks to sylvan estates like Powerscourt and Glendalough, a 6th-century monastic site so serene you may be tempted to renounce the profane world.

3 **County Kildare.** After visiting stately Castletown—a monument to Ireland's Georgian age of elegance—check out Derby Day at the Curragh racecourse. The grinning bookmakers are just waiting to take your money.

CAVAN

New Inn

N3

N52

Cloghan

WESTMEATH

Kinnegad   N4

Tyrrellspass

OFFALY

Cherryville

N7

Mountrath

Athy

LAOIS

Abbeyleix

Durrow

0   10 mi

0   10 km

3

GETTING ORIENTED

The Dublin environs include three main regions: County Wicklow's coast and mountains, the Boyne Valley, and County Kildare. The Boyne Valley includes much of counties Meath and Louth to the north and east of Dublin. Kildare and Wicklow are to the southeast and south of the capital. Tour this small region, or opt for day trips from Dublin, especially to the Wicklow Mountains, which rise up suddenly at the fringes of the city.

IRELAND'S HISTORIC HEART

Stone Age, Celtic, early Christian, and Norman: the country is scattered with sites that act as signposts in the long and twisting story called "Ireland." But by circumstance of geography and mystical significance many of the great stone ghosts of ancient Ireland are concentrated in the counties immediately surrounding Dublin.

(top) Newgrange is a spectacular passage tomb; *(right, top)* The Stone of Destiny rests on the Hill of Tara; *(right, bottom)* Graves and High Crosses hallow the grounds of Glendalough.

THE HIGH CROSS

The Celtic High Cross is an endearing symbol of Ireland, and Monasterboice—a former monastic settlement—has more of them than anywhere in Ireland. Dating to AD 923, the 20-foot-high Muireadach Cross is the best preserved, as its panels depicting the slaying of Abel, David and Goliath, and the Last Judgment prove. The nearby 110-foot round tower gives you a view of the once-glorious monastic site.

Here, often so closely thrown together as to make a mockery of the vastness of time and history, stand the man-made wonders that are impressive but slightly melancholic reminders of more heroic and more savage ages. In fact, a tour down the valley of the River Boyne is a trip into the past, back beyond history, to the Neolithic tombs of Newgrange, the Druidic holy place of the Hill of Tara, the monasteries of early Christianity, and the Norman castles of the chain-mailed invaders who brought a bloody end to so much of Celtic Ireland. Not far from Dublin, chart the rise and fall of Irish culture at their glorious monuments.

3

NEWGRANGE

Built in the fourth millennium BC, a thousand years before Stonehenge, Newgrange is not only one of the world's pristine surviving passage tombs but also a great granite reminder of the ingenuity, spirituality, and perseverance of modern Ireland's Neolithic ancestors. How did they move 250,000 tons of stone? How did they align it to perfectly capture the first rays of the dawn sun on the winter solstice? The thrill of visiting and entering the somber tomb at Newgrange lies not only in what you discover but in the awesome mysteries that can only be answered by the imagination.

GLENDALOUGH

A single early-morning hour spent in the isolated and serene Glendalough Valley—a green jewel in the Wicklow Mountains—should be enough to convince you that St. Kevin made the perfect choice when he was searching for 6th-century solitude and peace. The simplicity, separation, and sparseness that were at the heart of early Christianity in Ireland are sublimely apparent in the hermit's cave called St. Kevin's Bed and the ruins of the tiny Church of the Oratory.

HILL OF TARA

First-timers are sometimes disappointed when they finally see the mythical Hill of Tara, spiritual and regal heart of

Celtic and Druidic Ireland. It is now just a hill—300 feet high with awesome views out over the flat central plains of Ireland and all the way to Galway in the West. But with a little reading at the interpretive center and a lot of imagination, you can picture the Iron Age fort that once stood here and the huge *feis*, or national assembly, where Celtic Ireland passed its laws and settled its tribal disputes. It is a place that is both beyond history and made of it.

MELLIFONT ABBEY

As well as war, the Normans brought great stone-church building to Ireland; one of their greatest religious monuments is Mellifont Abbey. Founded in 1142 by St. Malachy, the main parts of the abbey were built a little later in the Norman style, including the two-story chapter house and the octagonal Lavabo, where the monks used to wash. Although much of the abbey is in ruins, it still manages to illustrate the medieval church's rise to wealth and power in Ireland. Incidentally, the term "Celtic" is derived from the tribes that arrived on Irish shores around 700 BC, first called Galli by the Romans and then named Gaels in Ireland.

Updated by
Anto Howard

Walt Disney himself couldn't have planned it better. The small counties immediately north, south, and west of Dublin—historically known as the Pale—seem expressly designed to entertain and enchant sightseers. The entire region is rich with legendary Celtic sites, gorgeous gardens, and the most elegant Palladian country estates in Ireland.

Due to its location on the Irish Sea, facing Europe, the region was the first to attract the earliest "tourists"—conquerors and rulers—and the first over which they exercised the greatest influence. Traces of each new wave remain: the Celts chose Tara as the center of their kingdom; the Danes sailed the Rivers Boyne and Liffey to establish many of today's towns; and the region's great Protestant-built houses of the 18th century remind us that the Pale (originally the area of eastern Ireland ruled directly by the Normans) was the starting point and administrative center for the long, violent English colonization of the whole island.

The Dublin environs include three basic geographical regions. North of Dublin lies the Boyne Valley, with its abundant ruins of Celtic Ireland extending from counties Meath to Louth. In pagan times this area was the home of Ireland's high kings and the center of religious life. All roads led to Tara, the fabled Hill of Kings, the royal seat, and the place where the national assembly was held. Today, time seems to stand still—and you should, too, for it's almost sacrilegious to introduce a note of urgency here.

South of the capital is the mountainous county of Wicklow, where the gently rounded Wicklow Mountains contain the evocative monastic settlement at Glendalough, many later abbeys and churches, and the great 18th-century estates of the Anglo-Irish aristocracy, such as Castletown, Powerscourt, and Russborough.

Southwest of Dublin are the pastoral plains of County Kildare, which stretch between the western Midlands and the foothills of the Dublin and Wicklow mountains—both names refer to the same mountain range, but each marks its county's claim to the land. Kildare is the flattest part of Ireland, a natural playing field for breeding, training, and racing some of the world's premier Thoroughbreds.

Rapid, omnivorous expansion of the capital city in the decade of the Celtic Tiger saw its suburban limits spread deep into the once bucolic areas of Meath and Kildare, so don't be surprised to hear Dublin accents starting to dominate in towns like Navan and Naas. The economic slowdown and a slump in property values disproportionately hit these satellite towns and areas so dependent on the economy of Dublin, though there have been recent cautious signs of improvement.

DUBLIN ENVIRONS PLANNER

WHEN TO GO

While certainly not the wettest part of Ireland (the West gets that dubious distinction), the counties around Dublin do get their fair share of rain. June, July, August, and September tend to be the driest months, and the good news is that the summer showers are usually light and short-lived. Wicklow, with all its hills and valleys, seems to have an obscure microclimate of its own, so don't rely too much on the weather forecast to get it right.

PLANNING YOUR TIME

IF YOU HAVE THREE DAYS

Most people who explore Dublin Environs base themselves in the capital and sample the very different landscapes on day trips. Driving distances from downtown are less than two hours (in decent traffic). Just don't plan on visiting both the north and south of Dublin in the same day—each region is worth its own day or half-day trip.

Visits to Newgrange and Glendalough are musts, and the latter could be combined with a country house visit to Powerscourt. For more active visitors, a one-day walk along the Wicklow Way might pair best with an overnight stay in the cozy Hunter's Hotel.

GETTING HERE AND AROUND

BUS TRAVEL

Bus Éireann links Dublin with towns in the area. Dublin Bus serves some towns and estates in the region as well. All buses for the region depart from Dublin's Busaras, the central bus station, at Store Street. St. Kevin's Bus Services offers regular trips from Dublin to numerous towns and sights in Wicklow, including Glendalough, Roundwood, Laragh, and Bray.

Bus Information Bus Éireann. Guided bus tours are available from Dublin to many of the region's historic and scenic locations during the summer. Trips include Glendalough in County Wicklow; Boyne Valley and Newgrange in County Louth; and the Hill of Tara, Trim, and Navan in County Meath. ☎ 01/836–6111 ⊕ www.buseireann.ie. **Dublin Bus** ☎ 01/873–4222 ⊕ www.dublinbus.ie. **St. Kevin's Bus** ☎ 01/281–8119 ⊕ www.glendaloughbus.com.

CAR TRAVEL

The easiest and best way to tour Dublin's environs is by car, because many sights are not served by public transportation. What service there is, especially to outlying areas, is infrequent. To visit destinations in the Boyne Valley, follow N3, along the east side of Phoenix Park, out of the city and make Trim and Tara your first stops. Alternatively, leave Dublin via N1/M1 toward Belfast. To reach destinations in County Kildare, follow the quays along the south side of the River Liffey (they are one-way westbound) to St. John's Road West (N7/M7); in a matter of minutes you're heading for open countryside. Avoid traveling this route during the evening rush hour, especially on Friday, when Dubliners are making their weekend getaways. To reach destinations in County Wicklow, N11/M11 is the fastest and most clearly marked route. The two more scenic routes to Glendalough are R115 to R759 to R755, or R177 to R755.

TRAIN TRAVEL

Irish Rail (Iarnród Éireann) trains run the length of the east coast, stopping at towns between Dundalk to the north in County Louth to Arklow along the coast in County Wicklow. From Heuston Station, the Arrow, a commuter train service, runs westward to Celbridge, Naas, Newbridge, Athy, and Kildare Town.

Train Information Irish Rail–Iarnód Éireann ☎ 01/836–6222 in Dublin, 041/983–8749 in Drogheda ⊕ www.irishrail.ie.

RESTAURANTS

Dining out in the area is usually a casual affair, but Dublin's top restaurateurs are influencing the cooking—and the prices—at the finer establishments outside the capital. The economic downturn has also encouraged smaller, innovative, and, above all, good-value restaurants like Las Rada to spring up in unlikely places like Naas. Chefs hereabouts have a deep respect for fresh, locally grown and raised produce. You'll find everything from Continental-style meals to hearty ploughman's lunches.

HOTELS

When exploring the region around Dublin, many people opt to stay in the capital and take day trips. A hotel on the south side of the city or in South County Dublin might be a good idea if you're planning to spend time in Wicklow or East Kildare. For Meath and Louth, a hotel on the north side or to the west of the city might work better.

If you don't want to "commute" from the city, the noted country-house hotels around Kildare and Wicklow are great options. They are a surprisingly good value given their unique, luxurious atmospheres. Bed-and-breakfasts are another good option, and though the ones in this region tend to be a little more expensive than in other parts of Ireland, they also are more stylish. Unlike in Dublin, hotel prices have not generally increased again over the last year. *Hotel reviews have been shortened. For full information, visit Fodors.com.*

WHAT IT COSTS IN EUROS				
	$	$$	$$$	$$$$
Restaurants	under €19	€19–€24	€25–€32	over €32
Hotels	under €120	€120–€170	€171–€210	over €210

Restaurant prices are the average cost of a main course at dinner or, if dinner is not served, at lunch. Hotel prices are the lowest cost of a standard double room in high season.

TOURS

Loveireland.com. Guided bus tours throughout the region around Dublin are offered by this company between May and September, including day trips to Wicklow and to Newgrange and Mellifont Abbey. Prices start at €20. ☎ *01/458–0054* ⊕ *www.loveireland.com.*

Railtours Ireland. Take a half-day ride through the Wicklow Mountains with Railtours Ireland. The train stops at Arklow, where a bus takes you through Avoca and on to Glendalough. The cost is €49. ☎ *01/856–0045* ⊕ *www.railtoursireland.com.*

Tourism Ireland. The website for Tourism Ireland has a Grand Tours section that outlines a number of cleverly themed driving tours in the area. ☎ *800/242–473* ⊕ *www.ireland.com.*

Wild Wicklow Tours. For smaller groups, Wild Wicklow Tours uses minibuses that can take you off the beaten track. Day trips to Glendalough also take in Avoca Handweavers and a Dublin coastal drive. Prices start at €28. ☎ *01/280–1899* ⊕ *www.wildwicklow.ie.*

VISITOR INFORMATION

County Kildare, County Louth, and County Meath have offices that offer year-round tourism advice. Some are run by Tourism Ireland while others are locally operated. In summer, temporary offices are open in such towns as Trim in County Meath, Drogheda and Dundalk in County Louth, and Kildare Town in County Kildare.

Tourism Information County Kildare Fáilte ☎ *045/898–888* ⊕ *www. visitkildare.ie.* **County Louth Tourism** ☎ *042/933–5457* ⊕ *www.louthholidays. com.* **County Meath Tourism** ☎ *046/909–7060* ⊕ *www.meath.ie/tourism.* **Wickow Tourist Office** ☎ *0404/69118* ⊕ *www.ireland.com/destinations/ republic-of-ireland/wicklow.*

THE BOYNE VALLEY

For every wistful schoolboy in Ireland, the River Boyne is a name that resonates with history and adventure. It was on the banks of that river in 1014 that the Celtic chieftain Brian Boru defeated the Danish in a decisive battle that returned the east of Ireland to native rule. It was also by this river that Protestant William of Orange defeated the Catholic armies of exiled James II of England in 1690. In fact, this whole area, only 48 km (30 miles) north of cosmopolitan Dublin, is soaked in stories and legends that predate the pyramids. You can't throw a stick anywhere in the valley without hitting some trace of Irish history. The

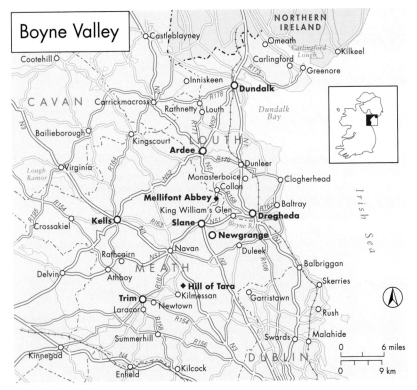

Boyne Valley

great prehistoric, pagan, and Celtic monuments of the wide arc known as the Boyne Valley invariably evoke a sense of wonder. You don't have to be an archaeologist to be awed by Newgrange and Knowth—set beside the River Boyne—or the Hill of Tara, Mellifont Abbey, or the High Cross of Monasterboice. One way to explore this area is to start at Trim, the town closest to Dublin, and work your way north. Keep in mind that Omeath and the scenic Cooley Peninsula are on the border of Northern Ireland.

TRIM

51 km (32 miles) northwest of Dublin.

The historic town of Trim, on the River Boyne, contains some of the finest medieval ruins in Ireland. In 1359, on the instructions of King Edward III, the town was walled and its fortifications were strengthened. In the 15th century, several parliaments were held here. Oliver Cromwell massacred most of its inhabitants when he captured the town in 1649. In the Old Town Hall's visitor center, an audiovisual display depicts the arrival of the Normans and the story of medieval Trim.

GETTING HERE AND AROUND

By car, Trim is just over 48 km (30 miles) northwest of Dublin on the M3 and then the R154. Once in town, parking isn't a problem. There is no train service, but regular Bus Éireann buses head here from Dublin's central bus station. The trip by car or bus takes about an hour.

ESSENTIALS

Visitor Information Trim Visitor Center ⊠ *Old Town Hall, Castle St.* ☎ *046/943–7227* ⊕ *www.meath.ie/tourism.*

EXPLORING

TOP ATTRACTIONS

Cnoc an Linsigh. An attractive area south of Summerhill, Cnoc an Linsigh's forest walks and picnic sites are ideal for a half day of meandering. Many of the lanes that crisscross this part of County Meath provide delightful driving between high hedgerows, and afford occasional views of the lush, pastoral countryside. ⊠ *Intersection of R156 and R158.*

Laracor. In the village of Laracor, 3 km (2 miles) south of Trim on R158, a wall to the left of the rectory marks the now-destroyed building where Jonathan Swift (1667–1745), the satirical writer, poet, and author of *Gulliver's Travels,* was rector from 1699 until 1713, when he was made dean of St. Patrick's Cathedral in Dublin. Nearby are the walls of the cottage where Esther Johnson, the "Stella" who inspired much of Swift's writings, once lived. ⊠ *Laracor.*

Newtown Abbey. East of Trim on the banks of the River Boyne, Newtown contains the ruins of what was once the largest cathedral in Ireland, built beginning in 1210 by Simon de Rochfort, the first Anglo-Norman bishop of Meath. ⊠ *1¼ km (¾ mile) east of Trim, Newton.*

Royal Mint. Facing the river is the Royal Mint, a ruin that illustrates Trim's political importance in the Middle Ages. It produced coins with colorful names like "Irelands" and "Patricks" right up into the 15th century.

St. Patrick's Cathedral. This church dates from early in the 19th century, but the square tower is from an earlier structure built in 1449. Bishops were enthroned here as early as 1536. The stained-glass window on the western side was the first commission of Edward Burne Jones. ⊠ *Loman St.*

Summerhill. One of the most pleasant villages of southern County Meath, Summerhill, 8 km (5 miles) southeast of Laracor along R158, has a large square and a village green with a 15th-century cross. ⊠ *Summerhill.*

Trim Castle. The largest Anglo-Norman fortress in Ireland, Trim Castle dominates present-day Trim from its 2½-acre site, which slopes down to the river's placid waters. Built by Hugh de Lacy in 1173, the castle was soon destroyed, then rebuilt from 1190 to 1220. The ruins include an enormous keep with 70-foot-high turrets flanked by rectangular towers. The outer castle wall is almost 500 yards long, and five D-shaped towers survive. So impressive is the castle that it was used as a medieval backdrop in Mel Gibson's movie *Braveheart*. The admission price includes a house tour. ⊠ *South Bank of River Boyne* ☎ *046/943–8619* ⊕ *www.heritageireland.ie* 🗐 *Keep and grounds €4, grounds only €3*

⌚ *Mid-Mar.–Sept., daily 10–6; Oct., daily 9:30–5:30; Nov.–Jan., weekends 9–5; Feb.–mid Mar., weekends 9:30–5:30.*

Yellow Steeple. On a ridge overlooking Trim Castle, the Yellow Steeple was built in 1368 and is a remnant of the Augustinian abbey of St. Mary's. Founded in the 13th century, it was the site of a great medieval pilgrimage to a statue of the Blessed Virgin. Much of the tower was deliberately destroyed in 1649 to prevent its falling into Cromwell's hands, and today only the striking, 125-foot-high east wall remains. ✉ *Opposite Trim Castle.*

WORTH NOTING

Meath Heritage Centre. If your ancestors are from County Meath, take advantage of the family-history tracing service at this genealogy center. ✉ *Town Hall, Castle St.* ☎ *046/943–6633* 🌐 *www.meathroots.com* 🎟 *Free* ⌚ *Mon.–Thurs. 9–1 and 1:30–5, Fri. 9–2.*

WHERE TO STAY

$ B&B/INN 🏨 **Tigh Catháin.** The "House of O'Catháin" is a Tudor-style country cottage with artfully decorated guest rooms and lovely gardens out back and in front that are perfect for lounging around in the sun. **Pros:** family-owned lodging; hearty breakfasts; glorious gardens. **Cons:** often books up far in advance; half a mile to nearest town; few facilities. [$] *Rooms from: €80* ✉ *High St.* ☎ *046/943–1996* 🌐 *www.tighcathain-bnb.com* 🛏 *4 rooms* 🍴 *Breakfast.*

HILL OF TARA

8 km (5 miles) northeast of Trim, 40 km (25 miles) northwest of Dublin.

GETTING HERE AND AROUND

An hour's drive from Dublin, the Hill of Tara is just off the N3/M3 motorway. From Belfast it's a 1½-hour drive; take the M1 and connect with the N51 at Drogheda. There is ample parking near the site. You can also take a Navan-bound Bus Éireann, which passes within 2 km (1 mile) of the site and walk; ask the driver to drop you at the Tara Cross and follow the signs. A taxi from Navan to Tara costs about €16.

Tours Newgrange Tours. Bus tours run from Dublin Monday through Saturday. The company charges €35, which includes admission to the Hill of Tara and Newgrange. Tours depart from outside the Dublin Tourism office on Suffolk Street, as well as from some major hotels. ☎ *086/335–1355* 🌐 *www.newgrangetours.com.*

EXPLORING

Fodor's Choice ★ **Hill of Tara.** In legends and in the popular imagination, the "seat of the High Kings of Ireland" has taken on mythic proportions. As with much of the Celtic past, it was the 19th-century revival led by W. B. Yeats and Lady Gregory that was responsible for the near-religious veneration of this site, set at the junction of the five ancient roads of Ireland. Today, its ancestral banqueting hall and great buildings (one was the former palace of the Ard Rí, or High King) have vanished except for a few columns. Still, the site is awe-inspiring.

From the top of the Hill of Tara—it rises more than 300 feet above sea level—you can see across the flat central plain of Ireland, with the mountains of east Galway visible from a distance of nearly 160 km (100 miles). In the mid-19th century, the nationalist leader Daniel O'Connell staged a mass rally here that supposedly drew more than a million people—which would be nearly a third of Ireland's current population. At the Interpretative Center, housed in an old church on the hillside, you can learn the story of Tara and its legends. Without this background it will be difficult to identify many of the earthworks outside. After systematic excavations in the 20th century, archaeologists have concluded that the largest remains are those of an Iron Age fort that was ruined in the 19th century by religious zealots searching for the Ark of the Covenant. The "Mound of the Hostages," a Neolithic passage grave, most likely gave the place its sacred air. During the hill's reign as a royal seat, which lasted to the 11th century, a great *feis* (national assembly) was held here every third year, during which laws were passed and tribal disputes settled. Tara's influence waned with the arrival of Christianity; the last king to live here was Malachy II, who died in 1022. But as with so many other prominent sites of the pre-Christian era, Christianity remade Tara in its own image.

> **FIRES OF FAITH**
>
> The Hill of Tara's decline was predicted one Easter Eve in the 5th century when, in accordance with the Druid religion, the lighting of fires was forbidden. Suddenly, on a hillside some miles away, flames were spotted. "If that fire is not quenched now," said a Druid leader, "it will burn forever and will consume Tara." The fire had been lighted by St. Patrick at Slane to celebrate the Christian rites of the Paschal.

Today a modern statue of St. Patrick stands here, as does a pillar stone that may have been the coronation stone (it was reputed to call out in approval when a king was crowned). In the graveyard of the adjacent Anglican church you'll find a pillar with the worn image of a pagan god and a Bronze Age stone standing on end. ⊠ *Off the N3, 12 km (7 miles) south of Navan, Navan* ☎ *046/902–5903* ⊕ *www.heritageireland.ie/en/hilloftara/* ⊠ *€3* ☉ *Late May–early Sept., daily 10–6.*

WHERE TO EAT AND STAY

$$$
MODERN IRISH

✕ **Eden.** One of Dublin's favorite restaurants has set up a second home in the vaulted cellar of Bellinter House. Eden sticks to its seasonal ethos with menus based on locally sourced produce. Boxty (potato cake) salad is an interesting twist on a traditional starter, and the sea bass with cauliflower and cumin puree, baby potato cakes, anchovies, and lemon crème fraîche is a standard main. $ *Average main: €26* ⊠ *Bellinter House, 4 km (2½ miles) northwest of Hill of Tara, Navan* ☎ *046/903–0900* ⊕ *www.bellinterhouse.com* ⚖ *Reservations essential.*

$$$
B&B/INN
Fodor's Choice
★

⌂ **Bellinter House.** Surrounded by 12 acres on the banks of the Boyne, this splendid 1750 country house retains the glories of the original architecture while adding a few modern twists. **Pros:** stunningly authentic original rooms; serene infinity pool; great value. **Cons:** newer rooms not as grand; staff can be a little inexperienced. $ *Rooms from: €200*

✉ 4 km (2½ miles) northwest of Hill of Tara, Navan ☎ 046/903–0900 ⊕ www.bellinterhouse.com ➬ 34 rooms ⦿⦿ Breakfast.

SPORTS AND THE OUTDOORS

GOLF

Killeen Castle. The great Jack Nicklaus had a hand in the design and construction of this championship-level course and golf school set in the serene woodlands of Norman Killeen Castle in Meath. Covering twice the acreage of an average championship course—you might need a buggy to get around—Nicklaus really had room to let his imagination run free, and the natural water features and stonework are a special treat. Check out the wonderful Paul Ferriter sculpture of the great man himself near the first tee box. *✉ 1 Loughmore Ave., Dunsary ☎ 01/689–3000 ⊕ www.killeencastle.com ✉ May–Sept. €80–€90, Apr. and Oct. €65–€70, Nov.–Mar. €60–€85 ⚑ 18 holes, 7700 yards, par 72. Practice area, driving range, caddies, caddy carts, buggies, club rental, shoe rental, catering, golf school ⊙ Visitors: Thurs.–Tues.*

KELLS

67 km (41 miles) northwest of Dublin.

In the 9th century, a group of monks from Scotland took refuge at Kells (Ceanannus Mór), where St. Columba had founded a monastery 300 years earlier. Although some historians think it was indigenous monks who wrote and illustrated the *Book of Kells*—the Latin version of the four Gospels, and one of Ireland's greatest medieval treasures—most now believe that the Scottish monks brought it with them. Reputed to have been fished out of a watery bog at Kells, the legendary manuscript was removed for safekeeping during the Cromwellian wars to Trinity College, Dublin, where it remains.

GETTING HERE AND AROUND

Kells is a 50-minute drive northwest of Dublin on the M3 motorway. There is ample parking in and around the town. Bus Éireann has regular service from Dublin; the trip takes one hour and 25 minutes.

EXPLORING

Kells Heritage Centre. Temporarily located in the tourist office at Kells Town Hall, this center is scheduled to move into the Old Courthouse building sometime in 2015. The prize exhibit is a brilliant copy of the *Book of Kells*—it's a more pleasant, less rushed, and less expensive way to see this medieval masterpiece compared with the madness of Trinity College in high season. *✉ Headfort Pl. ☎ 046/924–8856 ✉ Free ⊙ Weekdays 9:30–1 and 2–5.*

Round Tower. The nearly 100-foot-high Round Tower, adjacent to St. Colmcille's House, dates back to 1076 and is in almost perfect condition. The tower was likely used as a defensive hideout by local monks during an invasion; they would climb up the rope ladder with their valuables and pull it up after them. Its top story has five windows, not the usual four, each facing an ancient entrance into the medieval town. *✉ R163, west of intersection of N3 and N52.*

St. Colmcille's House. Similar in appearance to St. Kevin's Church at Glendalough and Cormac's Chapel at Cashel, St. Colmcille's House is an 11th-century church on a much older site. It measures about 24 feet square and nearly 40 feet high, with a steeply pitched stone roof. ⊠ *R163, west of intersection of N3 and N52.*

St. Columba's. Four elaborately carved High Crosses stand in the church graveyard; you'll find the stump of a fifth in the market-place—during the 1798 uprising against British rule it was used as a gallows. ⊠ *Off Cannon St. and Church St.*

> ### WINTER SOLSTICE AT NEWGRANGE
>
> A visit to Newgrange's passage grave during the winter solstice is a memorable experience. You'll have to get on the nine-year waiting list to reserve one of the 24 places available on each of the five mornings (December 19–23). And then pray that no clouds obscure the sun and ruin the light show the Bronze Age builders intended.

NEWGRANGE

21 km (13 miles) east of Kells, 28 km (17 miles) northwest of Dublin.

Fodor's Choice ★ Expect to see no less than one of the most spectacular prehistoric tombs in Europe when you come to Newgrange. Built in the 4th millennium BC—which makes it roughly 1,000 years older than Stonehenge—Newgrange was constructed with some 250,000 tons of stone, much of which came from the Wicklow Mountains, 80 km (50 miles) to the south. The Brú na Bóinne Visitor Centre, near the village of Donore, is the starting point for all visits to Newgrange and Knowth. Arrive early if possible, because you can't book ahead of time and Newgrange often sells out in high season.

GETTING HERE AND AROUND

From Dublin it's about a 50-minute drive to Newgrange: take the M1 motorway north to the Donore exit before Drogheda; Brú na Bóinne is clearly signposted before the exit. Drive about 6 km (4 miles) to the village of Donore, turn right and travel about half a mile to the visitor center. There is ample parking at the center. The Bus Éireann route from Dublin to Drogheda stops at Newgrange, and Newgrange Tours combines a visit to this site with the Hill of Tara on its bus tour.

ESSENTIALS

Transportation Contacts Over the Top Tours. This company runs a daily shuttle bus from Dublin to Newgrange. ☎ *01/860-0404* ⊕ *www.overthetop tours.com.*

Visitor Information Brú na Bóinne Visitor Centre ⊠ *Off N2, near Donore village* ⊕ *www.heritageireland.ie* 🎟 *€3* ☉ *Nov.–Jan., daily 9–5; Feb.–Apr. and Oct., daily 9:30–5:30; May, daily 9–6:30; June–mid-Sept., daily 9–7; mid- to late Sept., daily 9–6:30.*

Built between 3100 and 2900 BC, Newgrange is strikingly adorned with boulders carved with Neolithic triple spirals and diamonds.

EXPLORING

Fodor's Choice ★ **Knowth.** Under excavation since 1962, the prehistoric site of Knowth is comparable in size and shape to Newgrange, standing at 40 feet and having a diameter of approximately 214 feet. Some 150 giant stones, many of them beautifully decorated, surrounded the mound. More than 1,600 boulders, each weighing from one to several tons, were used in the construction. The earliest tombs and carved stones date from the Stone Age (3000 BC), and in the early Christian era (4th–8th century AD) it was the seat of the High Kings of Ireland. Much of the site is still under excavation, and you can often watch archaeologists at work. Tours of the site depart from the Brú na Bóinne Visitor Centre. ⊠ *Off N2, near Donore village* ⊕ *www.heritageireland.ie* ✉ *€5* ☉ *Nov.–Jan., daily 9–5; Feb.–Apr. and Oct., daily 9:30–5:30; May, daily 9–6:30; June–mid-Sept., daily 9–7; mid- to late Sept., daily 9–6:30. Last tour leaves from visitor center 1 hr and 45 mins before closing*

Fodor's Choice ★ **Newgrange.** How the people who built Newgrange transported the stones to the spot remains a mystery. The mound above the tomb measures more than 330 feet across and reaches a height of 36 feet. White quartz was used for the retaining wall, and egg-shaped gray stones were studded at intervals. The passage grave may have been the world's earliest solar observatory. It was so carefully constructed that, for five days on and around the winter solstice, the rays of the rising sun still hit a roof box above the lintel at the entrance to the grave. The rays then shine for about 20 minutes down the main interior passageway to illuminate the burial chamber. The site was restored in 1962 after years of neglect. The geometric designs on some stones at the center of the burial chamber continue to baffle experts. Tours of the site depart from the Brú na Bóinne Visitor Centre. ✉ *off N2, 2 km (1 mile) west of Donore Village* ⊕ *www. heritageireland.ie* 🎫 €6 🕙 *Nov.– Jan., daily 9–5; Feb.–Apr. and Oct., daily 9:30–5:30; May, daily 9–6:30; June–mid-Sept., daily 9–7; mid- to late Sept., daily 9–6:30. Last tour leaves from visitor center 1 hr and 45 mins before closing.*

SLANE

2½ km (1½ miles) north of Newgrange, 46 km (29 miles) northwest of Dublin.

Slane Castle is the draw at this small Georgian village, built in the 18th century around a crossroads on the north side of the River Boyne.

GETTING HERE AND AROUND

Slane is 46 km (29 miles) northwest of Dublin on the N2 major road. There is plenty of parking around the town and at the castle. Bus Éireann runs a regular service from Dublin; it takes about an hour and 10 minutes.

EXPLORING

Hermitage. The 16th-century Hermitage was constructed on the site where St. Erc, a local man converted to Christianity by St. Patrick himself, led a hermit's existence. All that remains of his original monastery is the faint trace of the circular ditch, but the ruins of the later church include a nave and a chancel with a tower in between. ✉ *Slane Castle Demesne.*

FAMILY **Newgrange Farm.** A two-hour tour of farmer Willie Redhouse's fully functioning farm includes feeding the ducks, bottle-feeding the lambs, a visit to aviaries stocked with exotic birds, and a straw maze for the kids. A blacksmith gives demonstrations of his ancient art, and there is a nice tractor ride around the farm. Every Sunday at 3 pm the Sheep Derby takes place, with teddy bears tied astride the animals in the place of jockeys. ✉ *N51, 3 km (2 miles) east of Slane* ⊕ *www.newgrangefarm. com* 🎫 €9 🕙 *Mid-Mar.–early Sept., daily 10–5.*

Slane Castle. The stately 18th-century Slane Castle overlooks a natural amphitheater. In 1981 the castle's owner, Anglo-Irish Lord Henry Mount Charles, staged the first of what have been some of Ireland's largest outdoor rock concerts; REM's show holds the record for attendance, with 70,000, while other stars that have appeared here have included Madonna, Bob Dylan, and the Rolling Stones. A tour of the Gothic-style castle includes the main hall, with its delicate plasterwork and beautiful stained glass, the dazzling neo-Gothic ballroom completed in 1821 for the visit of King George IV. The stunning parklands were laid out by Capability Brown, the famous 18th-century landscape gardener. Slane Castle now produces its own whiskey and has fun tasting tours. ✉ *Slane Castle* ☎ *041/982–0643* 🌐 *www.slanecastle.ie* 🎫 *€7* ⏲ *June 3–Sept. 1, Sun.–Thurs. noon–5.*

Slane Hill. North of Slane is the 500-foot-high Slane Hill, where St. Patrick proclaimed the arrival of Christianity in 433 by lighting the Paschal Fire. From the top you have sweeping views of the Boyne Valley. On a clear day, the panorama stretches from Trim to Drogheda, a vista extending 40 km (25 miles).

WHERE TO STAY

$$$$ B&B/INN Fodor's Choice ★ 🏨 **Tankardstown House.** Voted Ireland's best private house hotel in a national newspaper, Tankardstown is a sumptuous Georgian-era manor house with a classic walled garden and 80 acres of breathtaking parkland. **Pros:** authentic Georgian exterior and interiors; idyllic setting; cottages a great option for families. **Cons:** not cheap; limited facilities for the price. [$] *Rooms from: €330* ✉ *2½ km (1½ mile) from the gates of Slane Castle* ☎ *041/982–4621* 🌐 *www.tankardstown.ie* 🛏 *5 rooms, 2 suites, 7 cottages* 🍴 *Breakfast.*

DROGHEDA

15½ km (9 miles) east of Slane, 45 km (28 miles) north of Dublin.

Drogheda (pronounced dra-*he*-da) is one of the most enjoyable and historic towns on the east coast of Ireland—and a setting for one of the most tragic events in Irish history, the siege and massacre wrought by Oliver Cromwell's English army. The town was colonized in 911 by the Danish Vikings; two centuries later, it was taken over by Hugh de Lacy, the Anglo-Norman lord of Trim, who was responsible for fortifying the towns along the River Boyne. At first, two separate towns existed, one on the north bank, the other on the south. In 1412, already heavily walled and fortified, Drogheda was unified, making it the largest English town in Ireland. Today, 18th-century warehouses line the northern bank of the Boyne. The center of town, around West Street, is the historic heart of Drogheda.

GETTING HERE AND AROUND

Thanks to the M1 motorway, Drogheda is a 45-minute trip north of Dublin. Paid parking is available throughout the town. Bus Éireann operates express and regular service connecting Drogheda to Dundalk (30 minutes), Dublin (40 minutes), Navan (40 minutes), and Belfast (1 hour, 30 minutes), while Irish Rail connects the town to Hueston Station in Dublin (51 minutes), Belfast (1 hour, 40 minutes), and Dundalk (20 minutes) on the same line.The bus station is south of the river on the corner of John Street and Donore Road, and the train station is south of the river and east of the town center on the Dublin Road.

ESSENTIALS

Visitor Information Drogheda Tourist Office ✉ *The Tholsel, West St.* ☎ *041/987–2843* 🌐 *www.drogheda.ie* ⏲ *May–Nov., Mon.–Sat. 9:30–5:30; Dec.–Apr., weekdays 9:30–5:30.*

EXPLORING

TOP ATTRACTIONS

Fodor's Choice ★ **Drogheda Museum Millmount.** It was in Millmount that the townsfolk made their last stand against the bloodthirsty Roundheads of Cromwell. Perhaps in defiance of Cromwell's attempt to obliterate the town from the map, the museum contains relics of eight centuries of Drogheda's commercial and industrial past, including painted banners of the old trade guilds and a circular willow-and-leather coracle (the traditional fishing boat on the River Boyne). Most moving are the mementos of the infamous 1649 massacre of 3,000 people by Cromwell. The exhibit inside the Martello Tower, adjacent to the museum, focuses on the town's military history. The museum is off the Dublin road (N1), south of Drogheda, and shares space in a renovated British Army barracks with several crafts workshops. ✉ *Off Mount Saint Oliver, Millmount* ☎ *041/983–3097* 🌐 *www.droghedamuseum.ie* 🎟 *Museum €3.50, tower €3* 🕒 *Mon.–Sat. 10–5:30, Sun. 2–5.*

St. Laurence's Gate. There were once 11 passages through the city walls, but the 13th-century St. Laurence's Gate is one of the last that remains. With two four-story drum towers, it's one of the most perfect examples in Ireland of a medieval town gate. ✉ *Saint Laurence St.*

WORTH NOTING

Butler's Gate. One of the city's original 11 entrances, Butler's Gate predates St. Laurence's Gate by 50 years or more, making it one of the country's oldest surviving Norman urban structures. It's near the Drogheda Museum Millmount. ✉ *Off Mount Saint Oliver, Millmount.*

St. Peter's. A severe church within an enclosed courtyard, the 18th-century Anglican St. Peter's is rarely open except for Sunday services. It's worth a peek for its setting and for the fine views of the town from the churchyard. ✉ *Fair St.* 🌐 *www.stpetersdrogheda.ie.*

St. Peter's Church. The Gothic-Revival Roman Catholic St. Peter's Church houses the preserved head of St. Oliver Plunkett. Primate of all Ireland, he was martyred in 1681 at Tyburn in London; his head was pulled from the execution flames. ✉ *West St.* 🌐 *www.wix.com/thomasmch/st-peters-parish-drogheda.*

Tholsel. This bank building has an 18th-century square granite edifice with a cupola. ✉ *West St. and Shop St.*

Victorian Railway Viaduct. Among the town's landmarks is its long railway viaduct, which towers over the river. Built around 1850 as part of the railway line from Dublin to Belfast, it's still in use and is a splendid example of Victorian engineering. Its height above the river makes the viaduct Drogheda's most prominent landmark.

WHERE TO STAY

$$ B&B/INN 🏨 **Boyne Valley Hotel and Country Club.** Once owned by a Drogheda brewing family, this 19th-century mansion has been restored in period fashion with Neoclassical pillars, intricate plasterwork, and crystal chandeliers. **Pros:** great facilities; lovely grounds. **Cons:** newer building a touch functional; restaurant only open weekends. [$] *Rooms from: €158* ✉ *Dublin Rd.* ☎ *041/983–7737* 🌐 *www.boyne-valley-hotel.ie* 🛏 *71 rooms* 🍴 *Breakfast.*

3

$ ⛨ **The D Hotel.** A dramatic location on the south bank of the Boyne
HOTEL easily makes up for the slightly functional exterior of this trendy hotel
in the center of medieval Drogheda. **Pros:** dramatic riverside location;
extra-comfy beds; great terrace for people-watching. **Cons:** only some
rooms have great views; restaurant open weekends only off-season.
$ *Rooms from: €99* ✉ *Marsh Rd.* ☎ *041/987–7700* ⊕ *www.thedhotel.
com* ⟿ *104 rooms* ⦿ *Breakfast.*

SPORTS AND THE OUTDOORS
GOLF
County Louth Golf Club. How do they keep this links treasure such a
secret? Covering 190 acres by the Irish Sea at the mouth of the River
Boyne, this wonderful links course really has flown under the radar
of the golfing world, which means smaller crowds in summer. Long
hitters will love the atypical layout, a par-72 that features five par-5s,
but beware the well-protected, undulating greens. ✉ *Off R167, Bal-
tray* ☎ *041/988–1530* ⊕ *www.countylouthgolfclub.com* ✉ *Nov.–Mar.,
weekdays €55, weekends €70; Apr. and Oct., weekdays €75, weekends
€90; May–Sept., weekdays €100, weekends €120* ⚑ *18 holes, 6936
yards, par 72. Practice area, caddies, caddy carts, club rental, catering*
⊙ *Visitors: Mon. and Wed.–Sun.; no weekends Oct.–Dec.*

MELLIFONT ABBEY

10 km (8 miles) northwest of Drogheda.

GETTING HERE AND AROUND
The abbey is a 13-km (8-mile) drive northwest of Drogheda off the
R168. There is ample parking at the site. There is no public transport
to the abbey, but you can get a taxi from Drogheda.

EXPLORING
Fodor'sChoice **Mellifont Abbey.** On the eastern banks of the River Mattock, which
★ creates a natural border between Counties Meath and Louth, lie the
remains of Mellifont Abbey, the first Cistercian monastery in Ireland.
Founded in 1142 by St. Malachy, it was inspired by the formal structure
surrounding a courtyard of St. Bernard of Clairvaux's monastery, which
St. Malachy had visited.

Among the substantial ruins are the two-story chapter house, built
in 12th-century English-Norman style and once a daily meeting place
for the monks; it now houses a collection of medieval glazed tiles.
Four walls of the 13th-century octagonal lavabo, or washing room,
still stand, as do some arches from the Romanesque cloister. At its
peak, Mellifont presided over almost 40 other Cistercian monasteries
throughout Ireland, but all were suppressed by Henry VIII in 1539
after his break with the Catholic Church. Adjacent to the parking lot
is a small architectural museum depicting the history of the abbey and
the craftsmanship that went into its construction. ✉ *Off N2, near Collon, Collon* ⊕ *www.heritageireland.ie* ✉ *€3* ⊙ *May 30–Aug. 28, daily
10–5:15.*

ARDEE

14½ km (9 miles) northwest of Mellifont Abbey.

The road from Mellifont Abbey to Ardee passes through Monasterboice, home to some of Ireland's finest medieval High Crosses. Near the village's Round Tower, you'll find the famed Muireadach Cross and, nearby, the West Cross, the tallest in all the country. Once you take in these noted medieval sculptures, continue on to the market town of Ardee, found at the northern edge of the Pale. Here stand two 13th-century castles: Ardee Castle and Hatch's Castle. The town of Ardee (Baile Átha Fhirdia or Ferdia's Ford), interestingly, was named after the ford where the mythical folk hero Cuchulainn fought his foster brother Ferdia. There's a statue depicting this battle at the start of the riverside walk.

GETTING HERE AND AROUND

Take the M1 motorway north from Dublin and exit at junction 14, then take the roundabout onto the N33 signposted Ardee. There is a regular Bus Éireann service from Dublin. Parking is readily available around the town.

EXPLORING

Ardee Castle. The angular Ardee Castle was founded by Roger de Peppard in 1207, but much of the present building dates to the 15th century and later. The castle faces north—its objective to protect the Anglo-Irish Pale from the untamed Celtic tribes of Ulster. It was converted into a courthouse in the 19th century. ⊠ *Castle St.*

Hatch's Castle. Known for its unusual rounded corners, Hatch's Castle is a private residence and not open to the public. Built in the 13th century, it was given by Cromwell as a gift to the loyal Hatch family. If you look closely you can see it still flaunts two 18th-century cannons at its entrance. ⊠ *Market St.*

Muireadach Cross. Dating to AD 923, the Muireadach Cross stands nearly 20 feet high and is considered to be the best-preserved example of a High Cross in Ireland. Its elaborate panels depict biblical scenes, including Cain slaying Abel, David and Goliath, and a centerpiece of the Last Judgment. (Figurative scenes are not a characteristic of earlier High Crosses, such as those found in Ahenny, County Clare.) The West Cross stands a couple of feet taller than Muireadach's, making it one of the tallest in Ireland. Its engravings are less impressive, many of them having been worn away by centuries of Irish wind and rain. From the adjacent, 110-foot-high round tower, the extent of the former monastic settlement at Monasterboice is apparent. The key to the tower door is kept at the nearby gate lodge. ⊠ *Off M1, Monasterboice.*

St. Mary's Church of Ireland. Parts of a 13th-century Carmelite church burned by Edward the Bruce in 1316, including the holy water font, can be seen at St. Mary's. The current building was constructed in the 19th century. ⊠ *Main St.* ☎ *183/23019.*

WHERE TO EAT AND STAY

$ ✕ **Fuchsia House.** Ardee isn't the first place that comes to mind for
INDIAN great curry, but Bangladeshi owner-chef Sarajit Chanda is an expert
at turning the best local ingredients into South Asian masterpieces.
Critics have fallen in love with the authentic flavors and the family-run
atmosphere—Sarajit runs the place with his Irish wife, Sarah. Have a
drink in the tiny lounge-bar while waiting for your table, then enter
the functional but cozy dining room. The set menu is a real treat for
adventurous diners, with the mixed fritters of eggplant, zucchini, and
cauliflower the perfect starter. For a main dish, try the Bengali fish curry
with sea bass, cauliflower, and potato in a turmeric-and-chili sauce.
Chanda also offers hands-on cooking classes most weeks. $ *Average
main: €18* ✉ *Dundalk Rd.* ☎ *041/685–8432* ⊕ *www.fuchsiahouse.ie*
☺ *Closed Mon. No lunch.*

$ ✕ **The Glyde Inn.** Sitting right on the edge of Dundalk Bay and overlook-
SEAFOOD ing the Cooley and Mourne mountains, this stolid little guesthouse
("inn" is pushing it) features a quality surf-and-turf restaurant. You'd
never know the Glyde was established way back in 1700, as it is now
such a casual, no-fuss place. Happily, the hospitality matches the delicious locally sourced food. The menu ranges from fish pie—comfort
food at its best—to lobster (the poor critters are housed in a tank tiny
enough to make some people lose their appetite). The four-course special is a great deal. There's also a mean Irish breakfast you can enjoy
if you book one of the inn's few B&B rooms. $ *Average main: €16*
✉ *Main St., Annagassan* ☎ *042/937–2350* ⊕ *www.theglydeinn.ie.*

$$$ 🏨 **BrookLodge.** Located in a spectacular valley, there's a green/organic
HOTEL vibe to this serene country house with a get-away-from-it-all feel, but
that doesn't mean it skimps on the luxury. **Pros:** great amenities at
your doorstep; stunning valley location; a chance to spoil yourself on
your trip to Ireland. **Cons:** a little out of the way; can feel busy in high
season. $ *Rooms from: €180* ✉ *Off Aughrim Oaks Rd., Macreddin
Village, Co. Wicklow* ☎ *0402/36444* ⊕ *www.brooklodge.com* 🛏 *86
rooms* ⚋ *Breakfast.*

DUNDALK

*14½ km (9 miles) east of Inniskeen, 20 km (12 miles) northeast of
Ardee, 80 km (53 miles) north of Dublin.*

Perfectly positioned as a hub to explore the region north and south of
the border, Dundalk—only 9½ km (6 miles) from Northern Ireland—is
the main town of County Louth, Ireland's smallest county. Its earliest
settlement dates from the early Christian period, around the 7th century.
In May the town hosts an avant-garde "fringe" drama and visual arts
festival that includes a nice schedule of children's events.

GETTING HERE AND AROUND

From Dublin, take the M1 north and exit at junction 16 onto the round-
about. Take the first exit onto the N52 to Dundalk. Bus Éireann runs
regular buses from Dublin to the town's bus station on Long Walk; the
trip takes one hour and 30 minutes. Routes from Belfast and Drogheda
also connect to Dundalk. Serviced by Irish Rail, Clarke Train Station is

on Carrickmacross Road. There are daily trains from Dublin (1 hour, 20 minutes); Belfast (1 hour, 20 minutes); and Drogheda (20 minutes).

ESSENTIALS

Visitor Information Dundalk Tourist Office ✉ *Market Sq.* ☎ *042/935–2111* 🌐 *www.dundalk.ie.*

THE LEGENDARY CUCHULAINN

The area around Dundalk is closely connected with Cuchulainn (pronounced *coo*-chu-lain)—"a greater hero than Hercules or Achilles," as Frank McCourt, in *Angela's Ashes,* quotes his father. Cuchulainn, the warrior of the Irish epic *Táin Bó Cuailnge* (Cattle Raid of Cooley), heroically defended this area of ancient Ulster against invaders.

EXPLORING

Bell Tower. On Mill Street, the bell tower of a Franciscan monastery dates back to the 13th century. Keep an eye out for the lovely Gothic windows. ✉ *Mill St.*

County Museum Dundalk. Set in a beautifully restored 18th-century warehouse, this museum is dedicated to preserving the history of the dying local industries, such as beer brewing, cigarette manufacturing, shoe and boot making, and railway engineering. Other exhibits deal with the history of Louth from 7500 BC to the present, and include Oliver Cromwell's shaving mirror. ✉ *Carroll Centre, Joycelyn St.* ☎ *042/932–7056* 🌐 *www.dundalkmuseum.ie* 🎟 *€2* 🕒 *Tues.–Sat. 10–5.*

St. Patrick's Cathedral. Built between 1835 and 1847, this grand cathedral was designed when the Gothic Revival was at its height. With its buttresses and mosaics lining the chancel and the side chapels, it was modeled on the 15th-century King's College Chapel at Cambridge, England. The fine exterior was built in Newry granite, and the high altar and pulpit are of carved Caen stone. ✉ *Roden Pl.* ☎ *42/933–4648* 🌐 *www.stpatricksparishdundalk.org* 🕒 *Daily 8–6.*

WHERE TO EAT AND STAY

$$ EUROPEAN 🍴 **Restaurant No. 32.** A cozy local spot with a wonderfully warm welcome, 32 has a great corner location near the county museum. The light-filled dining room has simple decor and ideal people-watching windows. The menu offers adventurous but unfussy fare—to start try the warm shredded pork and sweet noodle stir fry. Follow up with the duck confit, served with glazed shallots, puy lentil cassoulet, and port and ginger jellies. Their early evening menu is an incredibly good value. [$] *Average main: €20* ✉ *32 Chapel St.* ☎ *042/933–1113* 🌐 *www.no32.ie* 🕒 *Closed Sun. No lunch.*

$$ HOTEL 🏨 **Ballymascanlon House Hotel.** Just north of Dundalk, this Victorian mansion with a slightly severe but elegant modern addition sits on 130 acres on the scenic Cooley Peninsula. **Pros:** guest rooms big enough to get lost in; discount golf for guests; good weekend deals. **Cons:** a little pricey for the area; in-room facilities sparse; sometimes crowded with wedding parties. [$] *Rooms from: €160* ✉ *Off R173, 3 km (2 miles) north of Dundalk* ☎ *042/935–8200* 🌐 *www.ballymascanlon.com* 🛏 *90 rooms* 🍽 *Breakfast.*

$ B&B/INN 🏨 **Innisfree House.** An early-20th-century redbrick gem in the heart of Dundalk, Innisfree House is a shockingly good value considering the genteel, stylish atmosphere created by the beautiful Edwardian furniture and antiques throughout. **Pros:** genuine afternoon tea served; option of evening dining; authentic Edwardian furnishings. **Cons:** not in the most picturesque area; maybe a little over-decorated; short on facilities. $ *Rooms from: €65 ⊠ Carrick Rd.* ☎ *042/933–4912* ⊕ *www. innisfreehouse.ie* ⤙ *9 rooms* ❏ *Breakfast.*

COUNTY WICKLOW

Make your way to the fourth or fifth story of almost any building in Dublin that faces south and you can see off in the distance—amazingly, not *that* far off in the distance—the green, smooth hills of the Dublin and Wicklow mountains. On a clear day, the mountains are even visible from some streets in and around the city center. If your idea of solace is green hills, and your visit to Ireland is otherwise limited to Dublin, County Wicklow—or Cill Mhantáin (pronounced kill *wan*-tan), as it's known in Irish—should be on your itinerary.

Not that the secret isn't out; rugged and mountainous with dark, wooded forests, central Wicklow, known as the "garden of Ireland," is a popular picnic spot among Dubliners. It has some of Ireland's grandest 18th-century mansions, including Russborough and Powerscourt, and cradles one of the country's earliest Christian retreats: Glendalough. Nestled in a valley of dense woods and placid lakes, Glendalough and environs can seem (at least during the off-season) practically untouched since their heyday 1,000 years ago. The granite mountains that have protected Glendalough all these years run into the sea along the east coast, which has several popular sandy beaches.

BLESSINGTON

23 km (14 miles) southwest of Dublin.

With its wide main street lined on both sides by tall trees and Georgian buildings, Blessington is one of the most charming villages in the area. It was founded in the late 17th century, and was a stop on the Dublin–Waterford mail coach service in the mid-19th century. Until 1932, a steam train ran from here to Dublin. Just outside the village are two of the marvels of Ireland: 18th-century **Russborough House** *(see "Treasure Hunt: the Anglo-Irish Georgian House")* and the adjacent Poulaphouca Reservoir.

GETTING HERE AND AROUND
You can reach Blessington by car from Dublin via the N81; the drive takes half an hour. Dublin bus runs a daily service to Blessington.

EXPLORING
Poulaphouca Reservoir. Known locally as the Blessington Lakes, Poulaphouca (pronounced pool-a-*fook*-a) is a large, meandering reservoir that provides Dublin's water supply. You can drive around the entire perimeter of the artificial lake on minor roads; on its southern end lies Hollywood Glen, a particularly beautiful natural spot. ⊕ *www. coillteoutdoors.ie/.*

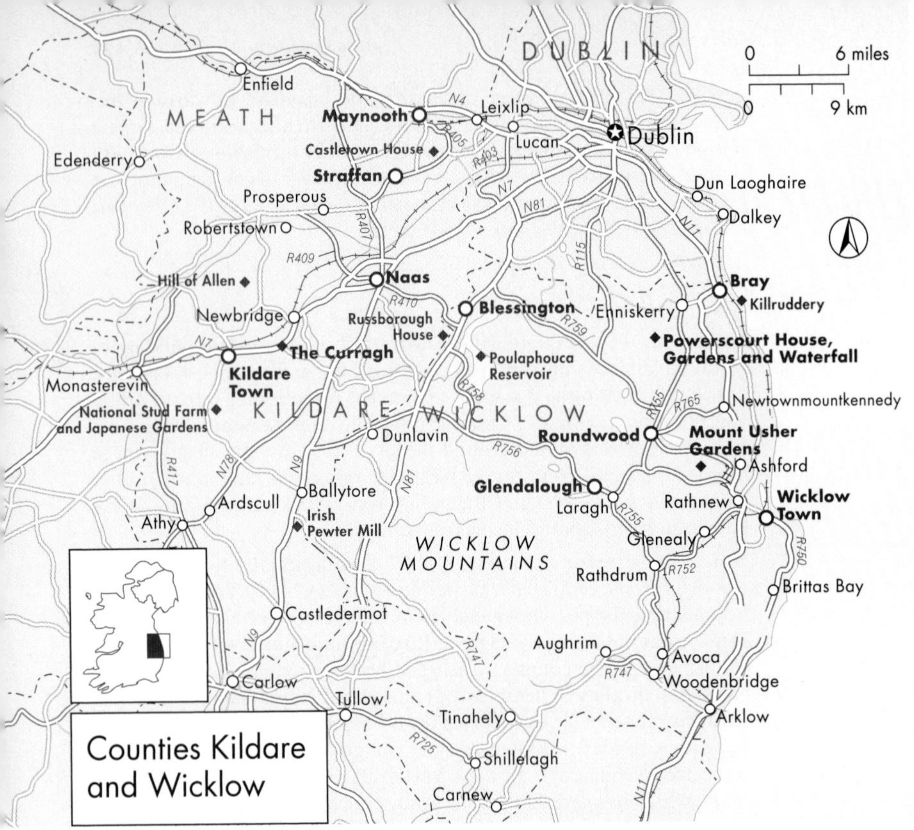

Counties Kildare and Wicklow

OFF THE BEATEN PATH

Piper's Stones. Beyond the southern tip of the Poulaphouca Reservoir, 13 km (8 miles) south of Blessington on N81, look for a small sign for the Piper's Stones, a Bronze Age stone circle that was probably used for worship of the sun. It's just a short walk from the road.

WHERE TO STAY

$$$ HOTEL Fodor's Choice ★

Rathsallagh House. A lovely hotel set on more than 50 acres of parkland, Rathsallagh House first came into being when the low-slung, ivy-covered Queen Anne stables were converted into a farmhouse in 1798. **Pros:** luxurious rooms; superb dining room. **Cons:** books up quickly; some variance in room quality; expensive food. [$] *Rooms from: €200* ✉ *Dunlavin* ☎ *045/403–112* 🌐 *www.rathsallagh.com* 🛏 *29 rooms* 🍴 *Multiple meal plans.*

SPORTS AND THE OUTDOORS

HIKING

Church Mountain. You can take in splendid views of the Blessington Lakes from the top of Church Mountain, which you reach via a vigorous walk through Woodenboley Wood, at the southern tip of Hollywood Glen. Follow the main forest track for about 20 minutes and then take the narrow path that heads up the side of the forest to the mountaintop for about another half hour.

BRAY

22 km (14 miles) south of Dublin on N11, 8 km (5 miles) east of Enniskerry on R755.

One of Ireland's oldest seaside resorts, Bray is a trim town known for its summer cottages and sand-and-shingle beach, which stretches for 2 km (1 mile). When the trains first arrived from Dublin in 1854, Bray became the number one spot for urban vacationers and subsequently took on the appearance of an English oceanfront town. Some Dubliners still flock to the faded glory of Bray's boardwalk to push baby carriages and soak up the sun. Uncrowded trails for hiking and mountain biking crisscross the mountains bordering Bray to the south.

GETTING HERE AND AROUND

From Dublin, take the N81 south to the M50 southbound. Exit onto the M11, and at junction 5 take the second exit at the roundabout to the R761 (signposted Bray). The drive takes about half an hour. The DART train runs regularly to Dublin to Bray, as do a number of city buses. There is plenty of parking around the town. St Kevin's bus from Dublin also stops in Bray.

EXPLORING

FAMILY
Fodor's Choice
★

Killruddery. The 17th-century formal gardens at Killruddery House are precisely arranged, with fine beech hedges, Victorian statuary, and a parterre of lavender and roses. The Brabazon family, the earls of Meath, have lived here since 1618. In 1820 they hired William Morris to remodel the house as a revival Elizabethan mansion. The estate also has a Crystal Palace conservatory modeled on those at the botanic gardens in Dublin. Killruddery Arts organizes year-round events including an old-fashioned Easter egg hunt. The tea house in the old dairy is a perfect spot for a light snack. They have a wonderful farmer's market every Saturday. ⊠ *Bray–Greystones Rd., 3 km (2 miles) south of Bray, Killruddery* ☎ *01/286–3405* ⊕ *www.killruddery.com* ✉ *Gardens €6.50, house and gardens €11* ☉ *Gardens: Apr. and Oct., weekends 9:30–5; May–Sept., daily 9:30–5; house July–Sept., daily 1–4.*

FAMILY
National Sealife. Dedicated to the creatures of the sea, National Sealife emphasizes those that occupy the waters around Ireland. Besides massive tanks that contain all manner of swimming things, there's a major conservation project focusing on breeding sea horses. FinZone is an undersea adventure trail perfect for kids; Nemo's Kingdom is a coral reef tank with all the fish portrayed in the animated movie. Touchscreen computers and video games give the place a high-tech feel. There are also regular feeding demonstrations during the day. In winter, call ahead to confirm opening times. ⊠ *Strand Rd.* ☎ *01/286–6939* ⊕ *www. visitsealife.com/bray* ✉ *€12.50* ☉ *Mar.–Oct., daily 10–5; Nov.–Feb., weekdays 11–4, weekends 10–4.*

One Martello Terrace. Novelist James Joyce (1882–1941) lived here between 1887 and 1891 and used the house as the setting for the Christmas dinner in *A Portrait of the Artist as a Young Man.* Although the residence has been renovated, the dining room portrayed in Joyce's novel

The Wicklow Way

Whether you're a novice or veteran hiker, Wicklow's gentle, rolling hills are a terrific place to begin an Irish walking vacation. Devoted hikers come from all over the world to traverse the 137-km (85-mile) **Wicklow Way** (⊕ www.wicklowway. com), the first long-distance trail to open in Ireland and still one of the best. Wicklow is Ireland's little Alps, with bracing fresh air guaranteed among the (hopefully) blue skies and mountain heather and gorse. Much of the route lies above 1,600 feet and follows rough sheep tracks, forest firebreaks, and old bog roads (rain gear, windproof clothing, and sturdy footwear are essential). The trail starts in the outskirts of Dublin suburbs, in Marlay Park, just south of Dublin city center, then ascends into the Wicklow mountain foothills, before passing glens, farms, and historic sights such as Rathgall, home to the Kings of Leinster, and the Mill of Purgatory—a venerated "wardrobe" in Aghowle Church—before finishing up in Clonegal. It's a great way to see some of

the more scenic villages of County Wicklow, and also a good excuse to sit down for a hearty lunch or dinner at some of their fine eateries—you will have earned it. You'll most likely run into fellow hikers, make new friends, and maybe even walk a few miles together. If you're going to spend a couple of days on the Way it's wise to plan out your accommodation in advance, as it can get busy in peak season. Overall the trail is wild and secluded enough to give you the sense of proper hiking and self-orienteering, but it's also established enough to suit even the first timer. Consider participating in one of the walking festivals held at Easter, in May, and in autumn. If your feet are less than bionic, you might opt for biking, another excellent way to see the area.

The autumn **Footfalls Wicklow Walking Festival** (☎ 0404/45152, ⊕ www.walkinghikingireland.com) is a three-day event based in the Glenmalure area. It costs around €60 for three days' walking.

---

maintains the spirit of his time. ⊠ 1 Martello Terr. ☎ 01/286–8407 TD constituency office, call Thurs. 10–1.

WHERE TO EAT

$$ ✕ **Campo de Fiori.** The most unassuming of exteriors hides one of Ireland's most authentic, award-winning Italian eateries. Owners Laura
ITALIAN and Marco Roccasalvo (he's also the chef) and their Italian staff give this little place a warm, informal vibe. The old posters, fishing nets, and wine bottles on display might hint of tourist trap, but this chilled-out spot is introducing locals to the delights of hearty, no-frills Italian cuisine. The pizza and pasta specials are always worth checking out, as are such fine mains as the lamb cutlets wrapped in pancetta with olives, white wine, and herbs. The wine list is large, and the staff loves to help you match your *vino* to your food. They also have a lovely little deli nearby. $ Average main: €19 ⊠ Strand Rd. ☎ 01/276–4257 ⊕ www. campodefiori.ie.

$$ SEAFOOD Fodor's Choice ★ 🍴 **The Hungry Monk.** The cloisters-and refectory-style decor is definitely tongue-in-cheek at this upbeat, fun restaurant in sleepy Greystones, an old-fashioned seaside resort a couple of miles south of Bray. Owner Pat Keown is a great host, and his laughter and love of good food and fine wine are contagious. Dinner is served by candlelight and the menu specializes in uncluttered seafood dishes in summer and wild game on cold winter nights. The Seafood Symphony is a particular favorite, as is the roast haunch of Wicklow venison with red cabbage roulade. Sunday lunches, in the bar area, are famous for their length (they often last into the early evening) and for the lively atmosphere. [$] *Average main: €22* ✉ *1 Church Rd., Greystones* ☎ *01/287–5759* 🌐 *www.thehungrymonk.ie* 🕓 *Closed Wed. No lunch Thurs.–Sat. No dinner Sun.*

SPORTS AND THE OUTDOORS

Bray Head. A well-marked path leads from the beach to the 10-foot-tall cross that crowns the spiny peak of Bray Head, a rocky outcrop that rises 791 feet from the sea. The fairly difficult one-hour climb affords stunning views of Wicklow Town and Dublin Bay.

POWERSCOURT HOUSE, GARDENS, AND WATERFALL

25 km (16 miles) south of Dublin on R117, 22 km (14 miles) north of Glendalough on R755.

One of the grandest estates and gardens in Ireland, Powerscourt is one of the main reasons that people head to Enniskerry. Within the shadow of the Great Sugar Loaf mountain, Enniskerry remains one of the prettiest villages in Ireland. It's built around a sloping central triangular square with a backdrop of the wooded Wicklow Mountains. But the real draw is the majesty of Powerscourt.

GETTING HERE AND AROUND

Powerscourt is about a half-hour drive from Dublin. Head south from Dublin on the N81 to the M50 southbound. Take the exit for the M11, which becomes the N11, then take the R117 for Enniskerry and continue on to Powerscourt House and Gardens. You can also take the bus from Dublin to Enniskerry and walk the mile to Powerscourt. Alternatively, you can take the Irish Rail's DART train line from Dublin to Bray and then take Dublin bus No. 185c (€1.80) to Powerscourt. Not all No. 185 buses go to Powerscourt, only the 185c buses. Ask the driver whether you have the right bus.

EXPLORING

FAMILY Fodor's Choice ★ **Powerscourt House & Gardens.** They really had the life, those old aristocrats. At more than 14,000 acres, including stunning formal gardens and a 400-foot waterfall, Powerscourt must have been some place to call home. The grounds were originally granted to Sir Richard Wingfield, the first viscount of Powerscourt, by King James I of England in 1609. Richard Castle (1690–1751), the architect of Russborough House, was hired to design the great house. His was an age not known for modesty, and he chose the grand Palladian style. The house took nine years to complete and was ready to move into in 1740. It was truly one of the great houses of Ireland and Britain.

Unfortunately, you won't be able to see much of it. A terrible fire almost completely destroyed the house in 1974, cruelly on the eve of a huge party to celebrate the completion of a lengthy restoration. The original ballroom on the first floor—once "the grandest room in any Irish house," according to historian Desmond Guinness—is the only room that gives a sense of the place's former glory. It was based on Palladio's version of the "Egyptian Hall" designed by Vitruvius, architect to Augustus, emperor of Rome.

Powerscourt Gardens, considered among the finest in Europe, were laid out from 1745 to 1767 following the completion of the house—and were radically redesigned in the Victorian style, from 1843 to 1875, by Daniel Robertson. The Villa Butera in Sicily inspired him to set these gardens with sweeping terraces, antique sculptures, and a circular pond and fountain flanked by winged horses. The grounds include many specimen trees (plants grown for exhibition), an avenue of monkey puzzle trees, a parterre of brightly colored summer flowers, and a Japanese garden. The kitchen gardens, with their modest rows of flowers, are a striking antidote to the classical formality of the main sections. A cute café, crafts and interior design shops, a garden center, and a children's play area are also in the house and on the grounds. Kids love Tara's Palace, a 22-room Georgian-style dollhouse. ☎ *01/204–6000* 🌐 *www.powerscourt.com* 🎟 *€8.50* 🕒 *Daily 9:30–5:30.*

Powerscourt Waterfall. One of the most inspiring sights to the writers and artists of the Romantic generation, the 400-foot Powerscourt Waterfall, 5 km (3 miles) south of Powerscourt Gardens, is the highest in Ireland or Britain. ☎ *01/204–6000* 🎟 *€5.50* 🕒 *Mar., Apr., Sept., and Oct., daily 10:30–5:30; May–Aug., daily 9:30–7; Nov.–mid-Dec. and late Dec.–Feb., daily 10:30–4.*

WHERE TO EAT AND STAY

$ IRISH 🍴 **Poppies Country Cooking.** This cozy café—with a pine-panel ceiling, farmhouse furniture, and paintings of poppies on the walls—is a great place for breakfast, lunch, or late-afternoon tea. Expect potato cakes, shepherd's pie, lasagna, vegetarian quiche, house salads, and soups. The most popular dishes are Poppies chicken (a casserole-like concoction) and homity pie (potpie with potatoes, onion, garlic, and cream cheese). For dessert try the apple pie or the rhubarb crumble, which is so good that the Irish rugby team stops by after practice. [$] *Average main: €8* ✉ *The Square* ☎ *01/282–8869* 🌐 *www.poppies.ie* 🕒 *No dinner.*

$$$ FRENCH 🍴 **Sika.** Star of the bleep-ridden *Hell's Kitchen* TV show, Scottish superchef Gordon Ramsay originally set up this hotel restaurant, but little of his daring or brashness remains in the more conservative, but quality current menu. Low ceilings give the very formal dining room a slightly overbearing feel, but large windows open onto an expansive terrace that is ideal for summer dining. The food focuses on Wicklow produce with a twist, and a favorite starter is the beef consommé with fois gras parfait. You can follow that with the Challans duck breast with savoy cabbage, beetroot, and picked garlic jus. As a treat you can book the Chef's table in the kitchen and watch the team at work as you sample a tasting menu. [$] *Average main: €32* ✉ *Powerscourt Hotel, Powerscourt Estate* ☎ *01/274–9313* 🌐 *www.powerscourthotel.com.*

$$$$ 🏨 **Powerscourt Hotel.** The gargantuan Palladian-style exterior of this
RESORT Xanadu may seem out of place, but luxury always makes itself at home,
Fodor's Choice and no one can carp about the views of the fabled Sugar Loaf peak
★ outside the soaring windows. **Pros:** sumptuous pool and spa; top restaurant; beautiful setting in Powerscourt grounds. **Cons:** some people
have called the exterior over-the-top; garden rooms don't have a great
view; can feel very busy at times. $ *Rooms from: €215* ⊠ *Powerscourt
Estate* ☎ *01/274–8888* ⊕ *www.powerscourthotel.com* ↩ *107 rooms,
93 suites* ❲❘ *Breakfast.*

SPORTS AND THE OUTDOORS
GOLF

Fodor's Choice **Druids Glen Resort.** Known in golfing circles as the "Augusta of Europe,"
★ the beautiful Druids Glen Golf Course has hosted the Irish Open on
four occasions since it opened in 1995. The wonderful landscaping
and the extensive use of water in the layout explain the comparisons
to the home of the Masters. It's essentially an American-style target
course incorporating some delightful changes in elevation, and its forbidding, par-3 17th has an island green, like the corresponding hole
at the Tournament Players Club at Sawgrass. A second course, Druids
Heath, is a marvelous attempt to combine the best of links, heathland,
and parkland golf. ⊠ *Newtownmountkennedy* ☎ *01/287–3600* ⊕ *www.
druidsglenresort.com* ⛳ *Glen: Oct.–Mar. 17, weekdays €50, weekends
€60; Mar. 18–Apr., weekdays €60, weekends €70; May–Sept., weekdays
€75, weekends €90. Heath: Oct.–Mar. 17, weekdays €30, weekends
€40; Mar. 18–Apr., weekdays €35, weekends €40; May–Sept., weekdays €45, weekends €50* ⛳ *Glen Course: 18 holes, 7046 yards, par 71;
Heath Course: 18 holes, 7434 yards, par 71. Practice area, caddies,
caddy carts, buggies, club rental, shoe rental, catering* ☉ *Visitors: daily.*

ROUNDWOOD

18 km (11 miles) south of Enniskerry on R755.

At 800 feet above sea level, Roundwood is the highest village in Ireland. It's also surrounded by spectacular mountain scenery. The Sunday afternoon market in the village hall, where cakes, jams, and other
homemade goods are sold, livens up what is otherwise a sleepy place.
From the broad main street, a minor road leads west for 8 km (5 miles)
to two lakes, Lough Dan and Lough Tay, lying deep between forested
mountains like Norwegian fjords.

GETTING HERE AND AROUND
Drive south from Dublin on the N81 to the M50 southbound, then take
the exit for the M11, which becomes the N11. At junction 12, exit onto
the R772 into Newtownmountkennedy. Turn right onto the R765 for
Roundwood. St. Kevin's Bus runs here from Dublin.

WHERE TO EAT

$ ✕ **Roundwood Inn.** Travel back to the 17th century at this evocatively
IRISH furnished inn, distinguished by its wooden floors, dark furniture, and
Fodor's Choice diamond-shaped windows. The place is best known for its wonderful,
★ hearty, reasonably priced lunches and dinners that are served in a nook

of the bar—try the glorious cream of seafood soup. The restaurant opens only for Friday and Saturday dinner and Sunday lunch. The menu blends Continental and Irish cuisines, reflecting the traditions of the German proprietor, Jurgen Schwalm, and his Irish wife, Aine. Highlights include an excellent seafood platter of salmon, oysters, lobster, and shrimp, along with a very gamey pheasant casserole. $ *Average main: €17* ⊠ *Main St.* ☎ *01/281-8107* ⌲ *Reservations essential.*

> **GENIUS IN A BOTTLE**
>
> Powerscourt's grand Victorian gardens were designed by an eccentric boozer, Daniel Robertson, who liked to be tooled around the gardens-in-progress in a wheelbarrow while taking nips from a bottle of sherry.

GLENDALOUGH

9 km (6 miles) southeast of Roundwood via R755 and R756.

GETTING HERE AND AROUND

If you're driving, consider taking the scenic route along R115, but be prepared for awesome, austere mountain passes. Don't take this route if you're in a hurry—it takes about an hour and 45 minutes, compared to an hour on the N11—and don't expect a lot of signage. Just concentrate on the nifty views.

St. Kevin's Bus has daily service between Dublin and Glendalough, with a stop in Bray. The trip takes 1½ hours. There is no direct train to Glendalough, but you can take the Irish Rail train from Dublin as far as Rathdrum (1 hour, 20 minutes) and then take a taxi (approximately €10) the 11 km (7 miles) from there to Glendalough.

EXPLORING

Fodor's Choice ★ **Glendalough.** Nestled in a lush, quiet valley deep in the rugged Wicklow Mountains, among two lakes and acres of windswept heather, Gleann dá Loch ("glen of two lakes") is one of Ireland's premier monastic sites. The hermit monks of early Christian Ireland were drawn to the Edenlike quality of some of the valleys in this area, and this evocative settlement remains to this day a sight to calm a troubled soul. Stand here in the early morning (before the crowds and the hordes of students arrive), and you can appreciate what drew the solitude-seeking St. Kevin to this spot. St. Kevin—Coemgen, or "fair begotten," in Irish—was a descendant of the royal house of Leinster who renounced the world and came here to live as a hermit before opening the monastery in 550. Glendalough then flourished as a monastic center until 1398, when English soldiers plundered the site, leaving the ruins that you see today.

Glendalough's visitor center is a good place to orient yourself and pick up a useful pamphlet. Many of the ruins are clumped together beyond the visitor center, but some of the oldest surround the Upper Lake, where signed paths direct you through spectacular scenery devoid of crowds. Most ruins are open all day and are freely accessible.

Probably the oldest building on the site, presumed to date from St. Kevin's time, is the **Teampaill na Skellig** (Church of the Oratory), on

Even though destroyed by Viking raids and then disbanded as a monastery by the Reformation, medieval Glendalough remains magical and magnificent.

the south shore of the Upper Lake. A little to the east is **St. Kevin's Bed,** a tiny cave in the rock face, about 30 feet above the level of the lake, where St. Kevin lived his hermit's existence. It's not easily accessible; you approach the cave by boat, but climbing the cliff to the cave can be dangerous. At the southeast corner of the Upper Lake is the 11th-century **Reefert Church,** with the ruins of a nave and a chancel. The saint also lived in the adjoining, ruined beehive hut with five crosses, which marked the original boundary of the monastery. You get a superb view of the valley from here.

The ruins by the edge of the Lower Lake are the most important of those at Glendalough. The **gateway,** beside the Glendalough Hotel, is the only surviving entrance to an ancient monastic site anywhere in Ireland. An extensive **graveyard** lies within, with hundreds of elaborately decorated crosses, as well as a perfectly preserved six-story **round tower.** Built in the 11th or 12th century, it stands 100 feet high, with an entrance 25 feet above ground level.

The largest building at Glendalough is the substantially intact 7th- to 9th-century **cathedral,** where you can find the nave (small for a large church, only 30 feet wide by 50 feet long), chancel, and ornamental oolite limestone window, which may have been imported from England. South of the cathedral is the 11-foot-high Celtic **St. Kevin's Cross.** Made of granite, it's the best-preserved such cross on the site. **St. Kevin's Church** is an early barrel-vaulted oratory with a high-pitched stone roof. ⊠ *Glendalough* ☎ *0404/45325* ⊕ *www.heritageireland.ie* ✉ *Ruins free, visitor center €3* ⊗ *Visitor center mid-Mar.–mid-Oct.,* *daily 9:30–6; mid-Oct.–mid-Mar., daily 9:30–5; last admission 45 mins before closing.*

WHERE TO STAY

$ 🛏 **Derrymore House.** On 6 acres above the Lower Lake in Glendal-
B&B/INN ough Valley, Derrymore is one of the most serene B&Bs in Wicklow. **Pros:** family-owned and -run; music played in the house by family; Victorian beds. **Cons:** room decor is basic; books up quickly; family lives in house. $ *Rooms from: €80* ⊠ *Lake Road* 🕾 *0404/45493* ⊕ *www.glendaloughaccommodation.com* ⤳ *3 rooms* ⊟ *No credit cards* ☾ *Closed mid-Oct.–Mar.* 🍴 *Breakfast.*

MOUNT USHER GARDENS

18 km (11 miles) east of Glendalough via R755 and R763.

GETTING HERE AND AROUND

From Dublin, Mount Usher Gardens is under an hour's drive. Take the N81 to the M50 southbound and exit onto the M11. At junction 15, exit onto the R772 to Ashford and turn left to the signposted Mount Usher Gardens. Bus Éireann runs regular service to Ashford from Dublin.

EXPLORING

Mount Usher Gardens. Covering more than 20 acres on the banks of the River Vartry, the gardens here were first laid out in 1868 by textile magnate Edward Walpole. Succeeding generations further planted and maintained the grounds, which today include more than 5,000 types of plants. The "Robinsonian" (that is, informal) gardener has made the most of the riverside locale by planting eucalyptus, azaleas, camellias, and rhododendrons. The river is visible from nearly everywhere in the gardens; miniature suspension bridges bounce and sway underfoot as you cross the river. Near the entrance, you'll find a cluster of crafts shops (including a pottery workshop) as well as a bookstore and tearoom. The twin villages of Ashford and Rathnew are to the south and east, and Newtownmountkennedy is to the north. ⊠ *Ashford, Co. Wicklow* 🕾 *404/40205* ⊕ *www.mountushergardens.ie* 🎟 *€7.50* ☾ *Mar.–Oct., daily 10:30–5:20.*

WHERE TO STAY

$$ 🛏 **Hunter's Hotel.** On 2 acres of flower gardens (the Knot Garden is an
HOTEL award winner) beside the Vartry River, the beautiful white Hunter's
Fodor's Choice Hotel is the oldest coaching inn in Ireland. **Pros:** pleasing period atmo-
★ sphere; enchanting gardens; fine restaurant. **Cons:** books up easily; bedrooms aren't huge. $ *Rooms from: €140* ⊠ *Newrath Bridge, Rathnew* 🕾 *404/40106* ⊕ *www.hunters.ie* ⤳ *16 rooms* 🍴 *Breakfast.*

WICKLOW TOWN

26 km (16 miles) east of Glendalough, 51 km (32 miles) south of Dublin.

At the entrance to the attractive, tree-lined Main Street of Wicklow Town sprawl the extensive ruins of a 13th-century Franciscan friary.

Wicklow, from the Danish *wyking alo*, means "Viking meadow," testifying to the region's very ancient roots.

The streets of Wicklow ran with blood during the 1798 rebellion when Billy Byrne, member of a wealthy local Catholic family, led rebels from south and central Wicklow against the forces of the Crown. Byrne was eventually captured and executed at Gallow's Hill just outside town. There is a memorial to him in the middle of Market Square.

GETTING HERE AND AROUND

A 50-minute drive south on the N81 and then the N11/M11 takes you from Dublin straight into Wicklow Town. Parking is available throughout the town. There are also daily trains and buses from Dublin.

ESSENTIALS

Visitor Information Wicklow Tourist Office ⊠ *Railto House, Fitzwilliam Sq.* ☎ *0404/69117* ⊕ *www.ireland.com/destinations/republic-of-ireland/wicklow* ⊙ *Weekdays 9:30–1 and 2–5:15.*

EXPLORING

Black Castle. Immediately south of the harbor, perched on a promontory that has good views of the coastline, are the ruins of the Black Castle. This structure was built in 1169 by Maurice Fitzgerald, an Anglo-Norman lord who arrived with the English invasion of Ireland. The freely accessible ruins extend over a large area; with some difficulty, you can climb down to the water's edge. ⊠ *Wicklow Head.*

Friary. Closed down during the 16th-century dissolution of the monasteries, the Friary is a reminder of Wicklow's stormy past, which began with the unwelcome reception given to St. Patrick on his arrival in AD 432. Inquire at the nearby priest's house to see the ruins. ⊠ *Main St.* ☎ *0404/67196 priest's house.*

Protestant Church. Between the River Vartry and the road to Dublin stands the Protestant Church, which incorporates various unusual details: a Romanesque door, 12th-century stonework, fine pews, and an atmospheric graveyard. The church is topped off by a copper, onion-shaped cupola, added as an afterthought in 1771. ⊠ *Dublin Rd.* 🆓 *Free* ⊙ *Daily 10–6.*

Wicklow Harbor. The town's most appealing area is Wicklow Harbor. Take Harbour Road down to the pier; a bridge across the River Vartry leads to a second, smaller pier at the northern end of the harbor. From this end, follow the shingle beach, which stretches for 5 km (3 miles); behind the beach is the broad lough, a lagoon noted for its wildfowl.

Wicklow's Historic Gaol. Just above Market Square, the town's old jail has been converted into a museum and heritage center where it's possible to trace your genealogical roots. Computer displays and life-size models tell the gruesome history of the prison, from the 1798 rebellion to the late 19th century. ⊠ *Market Sq.* ☎ *404/61599* ⊕ *www. wicklowshistoricgaol.com* 🎟 *€7.30* ⊙ *Daily 10:30–4:30.*

WHERE TO EAT AND STAY

$$$$
FRENCH
Fodor'sChoice
★

✕ **The Strawberry Tree.** Claiming to be Ireland's only "certified organic restaurant," this spot has been getting great reviews for its serious approach to all-natural but always stylish cuisine. It's tucked away in a rural valley as part of the BrookLodge Hotel. The glossy decor—midnight-blue walls, mirrored ceiling, and gleaming mahogany furniture—comes as a surprise, but cues you into the classy service and creative menu. Grilled mackerel with smoked chili yogurt, carrot-and-orange sorbet, and wood pigeon with crispy coppa and white tomato foam are part of the feast that can be enjoyed at the Big Table, which seats up to 40. After dessert, check out the spectacular wine cellar. $ *Average main: €35* ✉ *BrookLodge Hotel, Macreddin Rd., Macreddin Village* ☎ *0402/36444* ⊕ *www.brooklodge.com* ⊗ *Nov.–Mar., closed Mon.–Wed.; Apr., May, and Oct., closed Mon. and Tues.; June–mid-July and Sept., closed Mon.*

$$$$
RENTAL
Fodor'sChoice
★

⌂ **Wicklow Head Lighthouse.** This 95-foot-high stone tower—first built in 1781—once supported an eight-sided lantern, and has been renovated by the Irish Landmark Trust as a delightfully quirky lodging. **Pros:** unique lodging; stunning views; inexpensive if you have a group. **Cons:** a lot of stairs; books up quickly; minimum stay is two nights. $ *Rooms from: €240* ✉ *Dunbar Head, Wicklow Head* ☎ *01/670–4733* ⊕ *www.irishlandmark.com* ⇆ *2 rooms* ⦿ *No meals.*

COUNTY KILDARE

Horse racing is a passion in Ireland—just about every little town has at least one betting shop—and County Kildare is the country's horse capital. Nestled between the basins of the River Liffey to the north and the River Barrow to the east, its gently sloping hills and grass-filled plains are perfect for breeding and racing Thoroughbreds. For some visitors, the fabled National Stud Farm just outside Kildare Town provides a fascinating glimpse into the world of horse breeding. And don't forget the Japanese Gardens, adjacent to the National Stud, which are among Europe's finest. You may want to head to this area from Glendalough—the spectacular drive across the Wicklow Gap, from Glendalough to Hollywood, makes for a glorious entrance into Kildare.

MAYNOOTH

21 km (13 miles) southwest of Dublin.

Maynooth itself is a serene university town named for a pre-Christian king of Ireland. The mighty Fitzgerald family inherited the local manor in the 12th century and founded the original Catholic college. A few minutes south of the tiny Georgian town is the hamlet of Celbridge, official address to Ireland's largest country house, **Castletown** *(see "Treasure Hunt: The Anglo-Irish Georgian House").*

GETTING HERE AND AROUND

From Dublin take the N4/M4 in the direction of Galway/Sligo, then exit at junction 7 and take the R406 to Maynooth. The drive takes around half an hour. Dublin Bus serves Maynooth from Merrion Square in the city center, and there is a regular train service from Connolly station in Dublin.

EXPLORING

St. Patrick's College. What was once a center for the training of Catholic priests is now one of Ireland's most important lay universities. The visitor center chronicles the college's history and that of the Catholic Church in Ireland. Stroll through the university gardens—the Path of Saints or the Path of Sinners. At the entrance to St. Patrick's College are the ruins of Maynooth Castle, the ancient seat of the Fitzgerald family. The Fitzgeralds' fortunes changed for the worse when they led the ill-fated rebellion of 1536. The castle keep, which dates from the 13th century, and the great hall are still in decent condition. ⊠ *Main St.* 🕾 *01/628–5222, 01/628–6744 castle tours* ⊕ *www.nuim.ie* ✉ *Free* ☉ *Castle tours: May 24–Sept. 26, daily 10–6 (call for exact times).*

SPORTS AND THE OUTDOORS

GOLF

Carton House Golf Club. This just-outside-of-Dublin estate has quickly become one of the brightest stars in the Irish golfing universe. The parkland Mark O'Meara course makes use of the estate's rolling hills, specimen trees, and the River Rye. The 14th, 15th, and 16th stretch is a highlight: a pair of classy par-3s wrapped around a heroic par-5. The second 18 holes, created by Colin Montgomerie, are an inland links-style course that is flatter and virtually treeless. There's a good mix of long par-4s backed up with tricky short ones. Recessed pot bunkers lie in wait to pick up off-line shots. ⊠ *Off R148* 🕾 *01/651–7720* ⊕ *www.cartonhousegolf.com* ✉ *Apr.–Sept., Mon.–Thurs. €75, Fri.–Sun. €85; Oct.–Mar., Mon.–Thurs. €60, Fri.–Sun. €70* ⚐ *O'Meara Course: 18 holes, 7006 yards, par 72; Montgomerie Course: 18 holes, 7301 yards, par 72. Practice area, caddies, caddy carts, buggies, club rental, shoe rental, catering* ☉ *Visitors: daily.*

STRAFFAN

5 km (3 miles) southwest of Castletown House, 25½ km (16 miles) southwest of Dublin.

Its attractive location on the banks of the River Liffey, its unique butterfly farm, and the Kildare Hotel and Country Club—where Arnold Palmer designed the K Club, one of Ireland's most renowned 18-hole golf courses—are what make Straffan so appealing.

GETTING HERE AND AROUND

To get here by car from Dublin, take the N4/M4 toward Galway and exit at junction 7 to the R406 (toward Naas). At the roundabout take the second exit onto Barberstown Road (signposted Straffan). Bus Éireann runs a regular service here from Dublin.

EXPLORING

The Steam Museum. This museum covers the history of Irish steam engines, handsome machines used both in industry and agriculture—for churning butter or threshing corn, for example. There's also a fun collection of model locomotives. Engineers are present on "live steam days" every Sunday and on bank holidays. The adjoining Lodge Park Walled Garden is included in the price and is perfect for a leisurely summer stroll. ✉ *Lodge Park, Off Baberstown Rd.* ☎ *01/627–3155* 🌐 *www.steam-museum.com* 🎟 *€7.50* 🕒 *June–Aug., Wed.–Sun. 2–6; May and Sept., by appointment only.*

Straffan Butterfly Farm. The only place of its kind in Ireland, this farm has a tropical house filled with exotic plants, colorful butterflies, and even some interesting moths. Mounted and framed butterflies are for sale. ✉ *Off R403* ☎ *01/627–1109* 🌐 *www.straffanbutterflyfarm.com* 🎟 *€8* 🕒 *June–Aug., weekdays noon–5:30, weekends 10–5:30.*

3

WHERE TO STAY

$$$ HOTEL Fodor's Choice ★

🏨 **Barberstown Castle.** With a 13th-century castle keep at one end, an Elizabethan section in the middle, a large Georgian country house at the other end, and a modern wing, Barberstown Castle represents 750 years of Irish history. **Pros:** 20 acres of serene gardens; real fires in public spaces. **Cons:** prices still a little inflated; newer wings have less charm. [$] *Rooms from: €190* ✉ *Baberstown Rd.* ☎ *01/628–8157* 🌐 *www.barberstowncastle.ie* 🛏 *57 rooms* 🍴 *Multiple meal plans.*

$$$$ RESORT

🏨 **Kildare Hotel and Country Club.** Manicured gardens and the renowned Arnold Palmer–designed K Club golf course surround this mansard-roof country mansion. **Pros:** all-around luxury; quality spa; charming rooms. **Cons:** very expensive year-round. [$] *Rooms from: €455* ✉ *Off Baberstown Rd.* ☎ *01/601–7200* 🌐 *www.kclub.ie* 🛏 *60 rooms, 9 suites, 23 apartments* 🍴 *Multiple meal plans.*

SPORTS AND THE OUTDOORS

GOLF

Fodor's Choice ★

The K Club. "Home to the 2006 Ryder Cup" says all a golfer needs to know about the pedigree of the K Club. The Palmer course is named after its designer, the legendary Arnold Palmer, and offers a round of golf in lush, wooded surroundings bordered by the River Liffey. The generous fairways and immaculate greens are offset by formidable length, which makes it one of the most demanding courses in the Dublin vicinity. The Smurfit course is essentially an "inland links" course. The signature 7th hole wows visitors with its water cascades and rock-quarry feature. ✉ *Kildare Country Club, off Baberstown Rd.* ☎ *01/601–7321* 🌐 *www.kclub.com* 🎟 *Palmer, €120–€220; Smurfit, €95–€135* ⛳ *Palmer Course: 18 holes, 7350 yards, par 72; Smurfit Course: 18 holes, 7277 yards, par 72. Practice area, driving range, caddies, caddy carts, club rental, shoe rental, catering* 🕒 *Visitors: daily.*

NAAS

13 km (8 miles) south of Straffan, 30 km (19 miles) southwest of Dublin.

The seat of County Kildare and a thriving market town in the heartland of Irish Thoroughbred country, Naas (pronounced "nace"), is full of pubs with high stools where short men (apprentice jockeys) discuss the merits of their various stables.

Continued on page 198

TREASURE HUNT

THE ANGLO-IRISH GEORGIAN HOUSE

For an up-close look at the lifestyles of the rich and famous, 18th-century style, nothing beats a visit to the great treasure houses of Castletown and Russborough. Set just a half-hour south of Dublin and located only 20 miles apart, they offer a unique peek through the keyhole into the extravagant world of Ireland's "Princes of Elegance and Prodigality."

Castletown House and its impressive grounds.

When the Palladian architectural craze swept across England, the Anglo-Irish—determined not to be outdone—set about building palaces in their own domain that would be the equal of anything in the mother country. Both Castletown House and Russborough House set new benchmarks in symmetry, elegance, and harmony for the Georgian style, which reigned supreme from 1714 to 1830 and was named after the four Georges who successively sat on the English throne.

This style was greatly influenced by the villa designs of the 16th-century Italian architect Andrea Palladio.

Although Castletown remains the largest private house in Ireland, and Russborough has the longest façade of any domicile in the country, Georgian groupies know that the real treasures lie inside: ceilings lavishly worked in Italianate stuccowork, priceless Old Master paintings, and an intimate look at the glory and grandeur of the Anglo-Irish lords.

CASTLETOWN: A GEORGIAN VERSAILLES

★ Fodor's
Choice

Reputedly the inspiration for a certain building at 1600 Pennsylvania Avenue, Castletown remains the finest example of an Irish Palladian–style house.

In 1722, William Conolly (1662–1729) decided to build himself a house befitting his new status as the speaker of the Irish House of Commons and Ireland's wealthiest man. On an estate 20 km (12 miles) southwest of Dublin, he began work on Castletown, designed in the latest Neoclassical fashion by the Florentine architect Alessandro Galilei. As it turns out, a young Irish designer and Palladian aficionado by the name of Sir Edward Lovett Pearce (1699–1733) was traveling in Italy, met Galilei, and soon signed on to oversee the completion of the house. Inspired by the use of outlying wings to frame a main building—the "winged device" used in Palladio's Venetian villas—Lovett Pearce added Castletown's striking colonnades and side pavillons in 1724. It is said that between them a staggering total of 365 windows were built into the overall design of the house—legend has it that a team of four servants were kept busy year-round keeping them all clean.

Conolly died before the interior of the house was completed, and work resumed in 1758 when his great nephew Thomas, and more importantly, his 15-year-old wife, Lady Louisa Lennox, took up residence there. Luckily, Louisa's passion for interior decoration led to the creation of some of Ireland's most stunning salons, including the Print Room and the Long Gallery. Little of the original furnishings remain today, but there is plenty of evidence of the ingenuity of Louisa and her artisans, chief among whom were the Lafranchini brothers, master craftsmen who created the famous wall plasterwork, considered masterpieces of their kind. Rescued in 1967 by Desmond Guinness of the brewing family, Castletown was deeded to the Irish state and remains the headquarters for the Irish Georgian Society.

Above left: Castletown House facade
Above right: The family crest of William Conolly.

CASTLETOWN HOUSE

✉ Celbridge

☎ 01/628-8252

🌐 www.castletownhouse.ie

💳 € 4.50

🕙 Open Mid Mar.–Oct., Tues.–Sun. 10–4:45.

THE ENTRANCE HALL

Studded with 17th-century hunting scenes painted by Paul de Vos, this soaring white-on-white entryway showcases one of Ireland's greatest staircases. Also extraordinary are the walls festooned with plaster-work sculpted by the Brothers Lafranchini, famous for their stuccoed swags, flora, and portraits.

THE LONG GALLERY

Upstairs at the rear of the house, this massive room—almost 80 feet by 23 feet—is the most notable of the public rooms. Hued in a vibrant cobalt blue and topped by a coved ceiling covered with Italianate stuccowork and graced by three Venetian Murano glass chandeliers, it is a striking exercise in the antique Pompeian style.

THE PRINT ROOM

Smaller but even more memorable is the Print Room, the only example in Ireland of this elegant fad. Fashionable young women loved to glue black-and-white prints—here, looking like oversize postage stamps in a giant album—onto salon walls. This was the 18th-century forerunner of today's teens covering their walls with posters of rock-star icons.

Above left: The Grand Staircase. Upper right: 18th-century Italian engravings decorate the Print Room. Bottom right: A marble statue within the Long Gallery. Far right: Mahogony bureau made for Lady Louisa, circa 1760.

WHAT A WAY TO GO

"I do not get any idea of the beauty of my house if I live in it…only if I can gaze upon the house from far off," proclaimed Lady Louisa in 1821 of her beloved Castletown. In her late seventies, she had a tent built on the front lawn so she could study the house at her leisure. After one evening on the lawn she caught a chill and promptly died.

5 OTHER GREAT GEORGIAN HOUSES

Newbridge, County Dublin

Emo Court, County Laois

Westport House, County Mayo

Florence Court, County Fermanagh

Castle Coole, County Fermanagh

RUSSBOROUGH: A TEMPLE TO ART

An Irish Xanadu, Russborough House pulls out all the stops to achieve Palladian perfection.

Another conspicuously grand house rising seemingly in the middle of nowhere—actually the western part of County Wicklow—Russborough was an extravagance paid for by the wages of beer. In 1741, a year after inheriting a vast fortune from his brewer father, Joseph Leeson commissioned architect Richard Castle to build him a home of palatial stature, and was rewarded with this slightly over-the-top house, whose monumental 700-foot-long façade one-upped every other great house in Ireland. Following Castle's death, the project was taken over and completed by his associate, Francis Bindon. Today, the house serves as a showcase for the celebrated collection of Old Master paintings of Sir Alfred Beit, a descendant of the De Beers diamond family, who had bought and majestically restored the property in 1952.

PRINCELY MAGNIFICENCE

The first sight of Russborough draws gasps from visitors: a mile-long, beech-lined avenue leads to a distant embankment on which sits the longest house frontage in Ireland. Constructed of silver-gray Wicklow granite, the façade encompasses a seven-bay central block, from either end of which radiate semicircular loggias connecting the flanking wings—the finest example in Ireland of Palladio's "winged device."

The interiors are full of grand period rooms that were elegantly refurbished in the 1950s by their new, moneyed owner under the eye of the legendary 20th-century decorator, Lady Colefax. The Hall is centered around a massive black Kilkenny marble chimneypiece and has a ceiling modeled after one in the Irish Parliament. Four 18th-century Joseph Vernet marine landscapes—once missing

Top left: A look at the 700-foot façade of Russborough House. Bottom left: The grand Saloon. Above right: The Hall. Opposite, top: Drawing Room. Opposite: Vermeer's Lady Writing a Letter.

RUSSBOROUGH HOUSE

✉ Off N81, Blessington

☎ 045/865–239

🌐 www.russborough.ie

💶 € 10

🕐 Open May–Sept., daily 10–6, Mid Mar.–April and Oct., weekends 10–6

but found by Sir Alfred—once again grace the glorious stucco moldings created to frame them in the Drawing Room. The grandest room, the Saloon, is famed for its 18th-century stucco ceiling by the Lafranchini brothers; fine Old Masters hang on walls covered in 19th-century Genoese velvet. The views out the windows take in the foothills of the Wicklow Mountains and the famous Poulaphouca reservoir in front of the house.

VERMEER, DIAMONDS, AND GANGSTERS

If it can be said that beer paid for the house, then diamonds paid for the paintings. Russborough House is today as famed for its art collection—and the numerous attempts, some successful, to steal it—as for its architecture. Credit for this must go to Sir Alfred Beit (1903—1994), nephew of the cofounder of De Beers Diamonds. One evening in 1974 while Alfred was enjoying a quiet dinner with his wife, the door burst open and in marched Rose Dugdale, an English millionaire's daughter turned IRA stalwart. Her gang "liberated" 19 of the Beit masterpieces, including Vermeer's fabled *Lady Writing a Letter*, hopefully to bargain for the release of two IRA members jailed in London. Once the paintings were recovered a week later, Sir Alfred decided to donate 17 works to the National Gallery of Ireland. Alas, a week before the handing-over ceremony in 1986, Sir Alfred and his wife were again settling down to dine when in marched Martin Cahill, a.k.a. "The General," Dublin's most notorious underworld boss (and subject of three major movies). He made off with the Vermeer and 16 other paintings. They were returned and now sit safely (we hope) in the National Gallery.

STUCCADORES

Sounds better than plaster-workers, no? Baroque exuberance reigns in the house's lavishly ornamented plasterwork ceilings executed by celebrated stuccadores the Brothers Lafranchini, who originally hailed from Switzerland and worked in other great houses in Ireland, including Castletown. Their decorative flair adorns the Music Room and Library, but even these pale compared to the plasterwork done by an unknown artisan in the Staircase Hall—an extravaganza of whipped-cream moldings, cornucopias, and Rococo scrolls: "the ravings of a maniac," according to one 19th-century critic, who guessed that only an Irishman would have had the blarney to pull it off.

GETTING HERE AND AROUND

To get here from Dublin, take the N81 to the N7 toward Limerick. Exit at junction 9 to the R445 (signposted Naas). The drive takes about 35 minutes. Bus Éireann runs a regular service from Dublin. Parking is available throughout the town.

WHERE TO EAT

$ WINE BAR 🍴 **Las Rada.** Originality and inventiveness run riot in this surprising addition to the Naas dining scene. Experienced foodies Jules and Joanne Bradbury have taken the tapas idea and given it an extra touch of fun and local flavor in their Moorish-inspired, brightly colored bar and restaurant. Tapas choices include wonderful sweet potatoes with truffle mayo and cheese, and roasted red peppers stuffed with salmon and crab. The wine list always offers something out of the ordinary. [$] *Average main: €15* ✉ *New Row* ☎ *045/879–978* 🌐 *www.lasradatapas.ie* 🕒 *No lunch.*

SPORTS AND THE OUTDOORS

HORSE RACING

Punchestown Racecourse. A wonderful setting amid rolling plains distinguishes the Punchestown Racecourse, with the Wicklow Mountains providing a spectacular backdrop. Horse races are held regularly, but the most popular event is the Punchestown National Hunt Festival in April, a real pilgrimage for fans of steeplechase racing. ✉ *R411, 3 km (2 miles) south of Naas* ☎ *045/897–704* 🌐 *www.punchestown.com.*

THE CURRAGH

8 km (5 miles) southwest of Naas, 25½ km (16 miles) west of Poulaphouca Reservoir.

The broad plain of the Curragh, bisected by the main N7 road, is the biggest area of common land in Ireland, encompassing about 31 square km (12 square miles) and devoted mainly to grazing.

SPORTS AND THE OUTDOORS

HORSE RACING

Curragh Racecourse. Curragh is Ireland's major racing center, and the Curragh Racetrack is its main showplace. It's a flat racing mecca for enthusiasts from all over the world, and the Irish Derby and other international horse races are run here. ✉ *N7* ☎ *045/441–205* 🌐 *www.curragh.ie* 🎫 *€15.*

KILDARE TOWN

5 km (3 miles) west of the Curragh, 51 km (32 miles) southwest of Dublin.

Horse breeding is the cornerstone of County Kildare's thriving economy, and Kildare Town is the place to come if you're crazy about horses. But, in addition to all things equine, Kildare boasts other stellar attractions, including the famous Japanese Gardens.

GETTING HERE AND AROUND

Kildare Town is about 45 minutes from Dublin; take the N81 south to the N7/M7, exit at junction 13, and take the third exit at the round-about to the R415 (signposted Kildare). Parking is available throughout the town. Kildare Town is a major junction stop for Irish Rail, which has trains to Dublin (45 minutes), Cork (2 hours, 25 minutes), Limerick (1 hour, 45 minutes), and Galway (2 hours). The town's train station is just outside town, but a free bus service drops you into the center of town. Bus Éireann travels here from Dublin.

ESSENTIALS

Visitor Information Kildare Tourist Office ⊠ Heritage Centre, Market Sq. ☎ 0455/21240 ⊕ www.ireland.com.

EXPLORING

Irish National Stud. If you're a horse aficionado, or even just curious, check out this stud farm, a main center of Ireland's racing industry. The Stud was founded in 1900 by brewing heir Colonel William Hall-Walker. It's here that breeding stallions are groomed, exercised, tested, and bred. Spring and early summer, when mares have foals, are the best times to visit. The **National Stud Horse Museum**, also on the grounds, recounts the history of horses in Ireland. Its most outstanding exhibit is the skeleton of Arkle, the mighty Irish racehorse that won major victories in Ireland and England during the late 1960s. The museum also contains medieval evidence of horses, such as bones from 13th-century Dublin, and some early examples of equestrian equipment. ⊠ *Tulley Rd., 1½ km (1 mile) south of Kildare Town* ☎ *045/521–617* ⊕ *www.irish-national-stud.ie* ✆*€12.50, includes Japanese Gardens* ☉ *Mid-Feb.–Dec., daily 9:30–5.*

Fodor's Choice ★ **Japanese Gardens.** Adjacent to the Irish National Stud, the Japanese Gardens were created between 1906 and 1910 by the horse breeder's founder, Colonel Hall-Walker, and laid out by a Japanese gardener, Tassa Eida, and his son Minoru. The gardens are recognized as among the finest Asian gardens in the world, although they're more of an East–West hybrid than authentically Japanese. The Scots pines, for instance, are an appropriate stand-in for traditional Japanese pines, which signify long life and happiness. The gardens symbolically chart the human progression from birth to death, although the focus is on the male journey.

A series of landmarks runs along a meandering path: the Tunnel of Ignorance (No. 3) represents a child's lack of understanding; the Engagement and Marriage bridges (Nos. 8 and 9) span a small stream; and from the Hill of Ambition (No. 13), you can look back over your joys and sorrows. It ends with the Gateway to Eternity (No. 20), beyond which lies a Zen Buddhist meditation sand garden. This is a worthwhile destination any time of the year, though it's particularly glorious in spring and fall. ⊠ *Tully Rd., about 2½ km (1½ miles) south of Kildare Town* ☎ *045/521–617* ⊕ *www.irish-national-stud.ie* ✆*€11, includes Irish National Stud* ☉ *Mid-Feb.–Dec., daily 9:30–5.*

Round Tower. The 108-foot-high Round Tower, dating from the 12th century, is the second highest in Ireland (the highest is in Kilmacduagh in County Galway). Extraordinary views across much of the Midlands await if you're energetic enough to climb to the top. ✉ *St. Brigid's Cathedral, off Market Sq.* ☎ *045/521–229* 🌐 *www.ireland.com* 🎟 *€4* 🕐 *May–Sept., Mon.–Sat. 10–1 and 2–5, Sun. 2–5.*

St. Brigid's Cathedral. The Church of Ireland St. Brigid's Cathedral is where the eponymous saint founded a religious settlement in the 5th century. The present cathedral, with its stocky tower, is a restored 13th-century structure. It was partially rebuilt around 1686, but restoration work wasn't completed for another 200 years. The stained-glass west window of the cathedral depicts three of Ireland's greatest saints: Brigid, Patrick, and Columba. In pre-Christian times Druids gathered around a sacred oak that stood on the grounds and from which Kildare (*Cill Dara*), or the "church of the oak," gets its name. Also on the grounds is a restored fire pit reclaimed from the time of Brigid, when a fire was kept burning—by a chaste woman—in a female-only temple. Interestingly, Brigid started the place for women, but it was she who asked monks to move here as well. ✉ *Off Market Sq.* 🎟 *€2* 🕐 *May–Sept., Mon.–Sat. 10–1 and 2–5, Sun. 2–5.*

WHERE TO STAY

$$ HOTEL 🏨 **Keadeen Hotel.** The luxurious spa and health center are the big attractions at this family-owned hotel on 10 acres of flower-filled gardens. **Pros:** good spa and pool; light-filled rooms. **Cons:** uninspired architecture; crowded with weddings; can feel very busy at times. [$] *Rooms from: €135* ✉ *Off Ballymany, Newbridge* ☎ *045/431–666* 🌐 *www.keadeenhotel.ie* 🛏 *75 rooms* 🍴 *Multiple meal plans.*

THE MIDLANDS

Including Counties Cavan, Laois,
Leitrim, Longford, Monaghan, Offaly,
Roscommon, and Westmeath

WELCOME TO THE MIDLANDS

TOP REASONS TO GO

★ **Stately Clonmacnoise:** Atmospheric and still spirit-warm, this great early Christian monastery survived Viking, Norman, and English invaders over the centuries.

★ **Green Mansions:** While known for its rich farmlands, the Midlands is also home to stately homes and gardens, including fairy-tale Tullynally Castle and Birr Castle.

★ **Hiking the Slieve Bloom Mountains:** Dip in and out of the 32-km (20-mile) Slieve Bloom Trail, ideal hiking country for those with a yen to rise above their surroundings.

★ **Athlone:** The restored 13th-century castle along with the quirky shops and Europe's oldest pub are worth taking time to visit, as is the newly opened Luan Gallery.

★ **The Treasure House of Emo:** A quintessential landmark of 18th-century Palladian elegance, Emo—the former home of the Earl of Portarlington—has a spectacular rotunda inspired by Rome's Pantheon.

1 The Eastern Midlands. Just an hour from Dublin, this region is essentially rich farmland but is studded with even richer sights: grand homes such as Emo Court, Belvedere House, and Tullynally Castle; once-upon-a-time villages such as Abbeyleix; and the historic treats of Fore Abbey and Kilbeggan Distillery. Leaving the ancient kingdom of Leinster, you come to two counties of Ulster: Cavan and Monaghan. Beyond Cavan Town you enter the heart of the Northern Lakelands, dotted with hundreds of beautiful lakes.

2 The Western Midlands. One of the corners of "hidden Ireland," this region is unblighted by crowds. While some of the country's most distinctive boglands are here, cultural treasures also beckon: stately Birr Castle and Strokestown House, and the great early Christian monastery of Clonmacnoise, burial place of the Kings of Tara.

NORTHERN IRELAND

N2

N12

Upper Lough Erne

N54

Monaghan

N3

Clones

MONAGHAN

N2

Butler's Bridge

Cavan Town

Bellananagh

N55

CAVAN

N3

LONGFORD

Longford

Edgeworthstown

Tullynally Castle

MEATH

Fore Abbey

N55

WESTMEATH

Mullingar

Moate

Belvedere House

N6

N80

N62

Tullamore

OFFALY

KILDARE

N80

Portarlington

Portlaoise

Emo Court

Roscrea

N7

LAOIS

Abbeyleix

N8

KILKENNY

0   25 mi

0   25 km

GETTING ORIENTED

4

Perfect for the relaxed visitor who values the subtle over the spectacular, the flat, fertile plain at the center of Ireland is full of relatively undiscovered historic towns, abbey ruins, and grand houses. Though just two hours from the chaotic rush of Dublin, Cork, or Galway, the region is carpeted with countryside perfect for bicycling: no wonder stressed-out Dubliners love to head here to chill out.

CRUISING ON THE SHANNON

Whether you opt for a one-hour or one-week journey—and choose between a guided boat tour or private boat hire—cruising on the River Shannon is a never-to-be-forgotten experience, giving a new perspective on 'ole Ireland.

(top) A great vacation along the Shannon River; (right, top) Many travelers opt to boat 'n' bike downriver to the boating hub of Athlone; (right, bottom) Ireland's "inland sea," Lough Derg

Think of blissful relaxing times on the river, mooring for lunch at a quayside inn, or sampling traditional culture with gregarious lockkeepers. Along the Shannon's 334-km (207-mile) length you can head to major boating hubs like Athlone, or to historic stretches where it meanders past ancient settlements (such as Clonmacnoise), or to lakes aplenty. The biggest is Ireland's "inland sea," Lough Derg, bordered by easygoing villages like Terryglass and Mountshannon that offer appealingly quiet streets, stone-built cottage restaurants, and rustic harborside bars with picnic tables (many with evening music or Irish dancing sessions). Remember, the motto of Shannon cruising is "There's no hurry"—the boats travel at only 11 kph (7 mph), so a river journey is a slow affair with time to drink in the history, wildlife, and inland gems of an older Ireland many thought had disappeared.

WHEN TO GO

Good times to cruise are in May through early June. Rentals are cheaper, the waterways are less crowded, the weather is generally favorable, and daylight stretches well into late evening. Whenever you go, get the scoop on permits, moorings, and river by-laws from Waterways Ireland (⊕ *www. waterwaysireland.org*).

A WONDERFUL DAY ON THE WATER

On the map, the scale of the Shannon may look daunting—it *is* the longest river in Ireland or Britain—but that's one reason why many people opt for an idyllic daylong exploration. If you only have time for a short guided journey, then one of the best is upriver from Athlone to Lough Ree on a three-hour trip on board the *Viking* boat, costing €10–€20. Or opt to go downriver to magnificent Clonmacnoise. You can also board pleasure cruisers at Killaloe and Dromineer. If you're feeling romantic, try an evening cruise with the Moon River company, which operates a luxurious 100-seater from Carrick-on-Shannon. A detailed commentary is provided on these cruises.

Guided Cruises Moon River ⊠ *Carrick-on-Shannon, Co. Sligo* ☎ *071/962–1777* ⊕ *www.moonriver.ie.* **Silver Line Cruisers** ⊠ *Banagher, Co. Offaly* ⊕ *www.silverlinecruisers.com.* **The Spirit of Killaloe** ⊠ *Killaloe, Co. Clare* ⊕ *www.killaloerivercruises.com.* **Viking Ship Cruises** ⊠ *7 St. Mary's Pl., Athlone, Co. Westmeath* ⊕ *www.vikingtoursireland.ie.*

GOING WITH THE SHANNON FLOW

As the Shannon has its own slow-paced signature—a place where you are alive to the layers of history along the riverside and sequestered villages, which are a joy to explore—why not consider your own boat hire? The beauty of a personal cruise is that you can concoct your own itinerary, moving at your own speed and stopping off where the notion, and the motion, takes you.

There are four main boating towns for hiring cruisers: Carrick-on-Shannon, Portumna, Banagher, and Williamstown. From luxury cabin cruisers to barges or smaller boats, a glittering array of vessels is available for rent. Prices range from €650 for a two- to four-berth cruiser for one week in the quieter off-season, and from €1,550 in the more expensive summer months. With most companies, you can also rent for three-night/four-day short breaks. Rates start from €450 for the fall and early spring periods, rising to €1,400 in summer. In addition to guided tours, Silver Line Cruisers offers boat rentals.

Boat Hires Carrick Craft ⊠ *The Marina, Carrick-on-Shannon, Co. Sligo* ☎ *071/962–1777* ⊕ *www.carrickcraft.com.* **Emerald Star** ⊠ *Portumna, Co. Galway* ☎ *071/962–3711* ⊕ *www.emeraldstar.ie.* **Shannon Castle Line** ⊠ *Williamstown Harbor, Whitegate, Co. Clare* ☎ *061/927042* ⊕ *www.shannoncruisers.com.* **Silver Line Cruisers** ⊠ *Banagher, Co. Offaly* ☎ *057/915–1112* ⊕ *www.silverlinecruisers.com.*

Updated by
Paul Clements

The Celtic Tiger–era motorways may have bypassed the alluring towns and villages of the Midlands, but for a slice of authentic Ireland—a chance to see how the country gets on with its daily life—this region is worth lingering in. That's not to say its pleasures are all workaday; visitors can sample first-class food and rural peace in spa hotels or farmhouses, experience festivals, walk or cycle through lush countryside, and follow well-developed tourist trails—all in an area where life moves at a different pace.

And no wonder: the flat plains of the center of Ireland are made up of elegant places rich in delights that attract the culturally curious. Art galleries and heritage museums cluster around the town centers of Birr, Athlone, Tullamore and Cavan. You won't find international coffee chains or behemoth brands, but you will discover age-old industries such as lace making, crystal making, and whiskey making. Slow down and appreciate the gentle pace of time-burnished G&G (Grocery & Guinness) pubs, old-school barbers, or hardware and drapery stores complete with high shelves, long counters, and garrulous owners. Granted, blink-and-you'll-miss-some one-tractor villages, but half the fun is the serendipity of driving down a back road and stumbling on an artisan cheese maker, a teddy bear shop, or craft workers sculpting wood. Spend enough time in the region and you might even get to recognize the difference between a Cavan twang and a Tipperary brogue.

The big set pieces are also here, too. Among them are Clonmacnoise, Ireland's most important monastic ruins; the gorgeous gardens of Birr Castle, now open to the public for tours for the time in its history; and some of Ireland's finest Anglo-Irish houses, including Strokestown Park House and Emo Court. As for scenic pleasures, this region has its fair share of Ireland's 800 bodies of water, and much of the landscape is blanket bog. The River Shannon, one of the longest rivers in Europe and the longest in Britain or Ireland, bisects the Midlands from north to south, piercing a series of *loughs* (lakes): Lough Allen, Lough Ree, and Lough Derg. The Royal Canal and the Grand Canal cross the Midlands from east to west, ending in the Shannon north and south of Lough Ree. The Midlands comprises nine counties: Tipperary, Laois (pronounced leash), Offaly, Westmeath, Longford, Roscommon, Leitrim, Cavan, and Monaghan.

THE MIDLANDS PLANNER

WHEN TO GO

C'mon, this is Ireland, after all—a rain mac or windbreaker should never be far from your side when you visit the Midlands. The best time is the spring and summer when there's at least a better chance of some sunshine, although bring a rain mac just in case.

FESTIVALS AND EVENTS

JULY **Percy French Summer School.** In mid-July, one of Ireland's best-loved songwriters, Percy French, is celebrated in Roscommon town and at Castlecoote House with a summer school, complete with concerts and lectures. French was born at Cloonyquinn House near Elphin; his best-known songs include "Are Ye Right There Michael?" and "Phil the Fluther's Ball." ⊠ *Elphin, Co. Roscommon* ⊕ *www.percyfrench.ie.*

AUGUST **Castle Palooza Festival.** Music dominates at this festival, held at Charleville Castle in Tullamore over the August bank-holiday weekend. ⊕ *www.castlepalooza.com.*

Terryglass Arts Festival. This event in North Tipperary on the shores of Lough Derg presents music, dance, and street theater for five days in the third week of August. ⊠ *Terryglass, Co. Tipperary* ⊕ *www. terryglassartsfestival.ie.*

Tullamore Show. Ireland's biggest agricultural gathering attracts 60,000 annually in early August to the Butterfield estate near Blueball on the road to Birr. An international visitor center caters to the huge crowds of overseas visitors who flock to see the largest assembly of cattle anywhere in Ireland competing in 1,000 classes for 42 national titles. ⊠ *Tullamore, Co. Offaly* ⊕ *www.tullamoreshow.com.*

OCTOBER **Pumpkin Festival.** You'll see some of Europe's largest pumpkins at this annual festival in County Cavan's Virginia, held on the October holiday weekend. ⊠ *Virginia, Co. Cavan* ⊕ *www.virginia.ie.*

PLANNING YOUR TIME

The Midlands is a slice of old Ireland. Spend a few days traveling around the unspoiled countryside with its traditional hay meadows and you will come across ancient humped bridges, handsome square tower-houses, and curious-looking castles.

IF YOU HAVE THREE DAYS

If you come from the Greater Dublin area (the Midlands is easily accessible from the city in less than two hours) or surrounding counties such as Wicklow and Kildare, then a grand kickoff to a tour is at Portarlington to visit the nearby Emo Court and Gardens, a large country house designed by James Gandon, the architect responsible for much

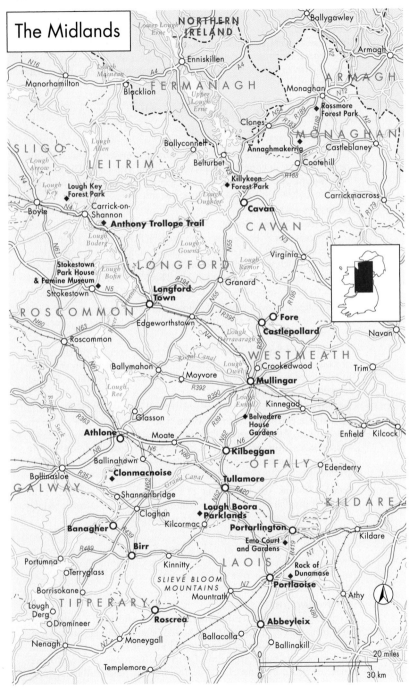

The Midlands

of Georgian Dublin. Head on to Tullamore, stopping at the elegantly restored 19th-century bonded warehouse of Tullamore Dew Irish Whiskey Distillery (based in the heritage center). Consider an overnight in Tullamore, which has a good selection of hotels and bed-and-breakfasts.

On Day 2 drive across to Birr for a morning's exploration of its Georgian architecture and a wander around the castle grounds. The formal gardens contain the tallest box hedges in the world; in spring you will see a dazzling display of flowering magnolias, cherries, crab apples, and naturalized narcissi. Guided tours of the Gothic Revival castle, opened to the public in 2013 for the first time in its 400-year history, take place in the summer, pulling back a curtain into a previously unseen world.

Half-an-hour's drive takes you to Clonmacnoise, Ireland's most important monastic settlement, where it's worthwhile joining a guided tour that will give you a sense of the place and its past in less than an hour. The next day head for Athlone on the River Shannon and walk around the quirky Left Bank, full of crafts and antiques shops as well as secondhand book shops, cafés, and Sean's Bar (which lays claim, sometimes disputed, to be Ireland's oldest). You could easily spend an hour or two touring the exhibits in the wonderfully restored Athlone Castle as well as visiting the nearby Luan Gallery. Make time for a two-hour cruise along the Shannon to get a different perspective on the Midlands.

GETTING HERE AND AROUND

AIR TRAVEL
Dublin Airport is the principal international airport that serves the Midlands; car-rental facilities are available here.

BIKE TRAVEL
One of the best ways to immerse yourself in the Midlands is to meander through the region on a bike. Although the area may not offer the spectacular scenery of the more hilly coastal regions, its level, Netherlands-like terrain means a less strenuous ride.

The twisting roads are generally in good (well, good enough) condition. There are picnic spots galore in the many state-owned forests just off the main roads. The more rural regions of Laois allow you to spend days exploring beautiful glens, waterfalls, nature trails, and wooded regions around the Slieve Bloom Mountains. Try to avoid the motorways that bisect the region. After all, this is an area that deserves thorough and leisurely exploration! Contact the regional and township tourist offices for all the details.

BUS TRAVEL
With a much more extensive network than trains, buses are a better bet for exploring much of the Midlands. Most small towns and villages are serviced by at least one bus per day, while trains are generally limited to towns on main lines linking cities. Bus Éireann runs express buses from Dublin to many Midlands towns, and regular-speed buses connect others. The train stations for Athlone, Cavan, and Longford also act as their bus depots.

Walk the Slieve Bloom Mountains

Crystal-clear freshwater streams, gushing waterfalls, lush forests, and no fewer than 27 glens are all part of the Slieve Bloom Mountain experience. The mountains stretch across the southern end of Offaly and are shared with neighboring County Laois. At one time, the summit—Arderin—was considered to be the highest point in Ireland. Whether you come for serious hiking, a gentle stroll, or just to drink in the spectacular views, you won't be disappointed. Looped walks, some led by guides, range from 4 km (3 miles) to 15 km (12 miles). Popular trailheads start from the villages of Kinnitty, Cadamstown, and Clonaslee, or you can make your base in the beautiful heritage town of Birr. Information and guided walking leaflets are available from the tourist information offices in Birr and Tullamore.

CAR TRAVEL

The roads of the Midlands offer an easier intro to Irish driving than the hairpin bends of West Cork and Connemara. Because the area has a decent network of main arteries and off-the-beaten-track byroads, a car may be your best option for covering the widest itinerary.

Don't be surprised to round a bend only to confront a herd of sheep idly grazing with little hurry about them—do what the locals do, slow to a stop and wait for an opening in the woolly mass to occur. The same goes for cows. Refrain from honking your horn on these occasions—it will only confirm your status as an impatient tourist, and, besides, the cows won't take a bit of notice.

TRAIN TRAVEL

All trains are run by Irish Rail. The main Midlands towns that have train connections lie on cross-country routes linking the cities, either east–west or north–south. Intercity trains make only a few stops at smaller towns, while slower trains stop at small towns and some villages. You can connect from one Midlands town to another by train, but check in advance on the regularity of services. There are no exclusively local train services—they all continue on to cities.

Train Information Sligo Railway Station ☎ 071/916–9888.

For more information on getting here and around, see Travel Smart Ireland.

RESTAURANTS

The Midlands town of Birr may be known as the "belly button of Ireland" because of its central location, not because this region is regarded as one of the cuisine centers of Ireland. No matter that Ireland's best restaurant (according to some)—Neven Maguire's MacNean's, near Cavan town—is in the Midlands, nor the fact that the region is also home to Wineport Lodge, Ireland's first "wine hotel," you'll find that most restaurants here are simple eateries, ranging in price from inexpensive to moderate.

Nevertheless, there are those restaurants that will entice you right in off the street, especially those offering beef—Mullingar, in the center of the Midlands, is the beef capital of Ireland—and fish specialties, as the many lakes and rivers of the region provide an abundance of fresh salmon and trout (in fact, since no place is more than an hour and a half from the sea, expect to find lots of fresh ocean fish).

HOTELS

The Irish bed-and-breakfast offers great value in the Midlands—farmhouses and homes geared to paying guests provide direct contact with local families and the lore of their area. Good beds, decent heating, en suite bathrooms, and the legendary Irish breakfast are now the norm; broadband, flat-screen TVs, and computer games courtesy of the landlady's kids are often part of the bargain.

Although B&Bs may not offer the same kind of privacy as hotels, they still work delightfully well as the ultimate way to meet genuine Irish folk. As commercial progress has blossomed in the Midlands, so, too, have the options in hotels, country houses, and cottage rentals increased.

From June to early September, tourism gets into serious stride, bolstered by the many Irish families using their holiday homes and get-away cottages in the region. Finding accommodation is never a major problem—except for those weekends when a town is holding an annual music festival. *Hotel reviews have been shortened. For full information, visit Fodors.com.*

WHAT IT COSTS IN EUROS				
	$	**$$**	**$$$**	**$$$$**
Restaurants	under €19	€19–€24	€25–€32	over €32
Hotels	under €120	€120–€170	€171–€210	over €210

Restaurant prices are the average cost of a main course at dinner or, if dinner is not served, at lunch. Hotel prices are the lowest cost of a standard double room in high season.

TOURS

To plan a trip within any particular county or area, you're best off starting with the local tourist office. They will have a thorough list of the must-see attractions in their areas.

VISITOR INFORMATION

Four Midlands Tourist Information Offices (TIOs) are open all year: Cavan, Monaghan, Mullingar, and Portlaoise. The Mullingar TIO has information on Counties Westmeath, Offaly, Monaghan, Cavan, and Laois. Another four Midlands TIOs are open seasonally: Athlone (April–October), Birr (May–September), Longford (June–September), and Tullamore (mid-June–mid-September).

Find tourist office addresses, phone numbers, and websites listed under the main town sections throughout this chapter.

THE EASTERN MIDLANDS

The eastern fringe of the Midlands is about an hour's drive from Dublin, and a visit to the area could easily be grafted on to a trip to the Dublin environs. In spite of its proximity to the capital, or perhaps because of it, this area is a bit removed from the regular tourist trail and is a source of constant surprises. Unspoiled Georgian villages, ruined castles, and "towns that time forgot" dot the landscape. There are also plenty of opportunities for hill walking, horseback riding, and other outdoor pursuits. Lovers of stately homes are in for a treat, as Emo Court and Gardens, Charleville Forest Castle, Belvedere House & Gardens, and Tullynally Castle await them. If rare plants, mixed annuals, or specimen trees get you excited then head off on the County Laois Garden Trail, a delightful journey to 10 formal and not-so-formal gardens where you may find a perfumed pergola to stimulate your senses.

The Eastern Midlands fan out from the central point of Mullingar. With richer farmland than is found in the northern area of the Midlands, the eastern region tends toward agriculture. But the Dublin commuter culture means that you're as likely to be delayed on a back road by a badly parked BMW as by a slow-moving tractor on its way home from the dairy.

ABBEYLEIX

99 km (61 miles) southwest of Dublin.

Fodor's Choice One of the most elegant small towns in Ireland, Abbeyleix has retained
★ its Georgian feel and its broad main street, which is lined with well-appointed stone-cut buildings and original shop fronts in the traditionally ornate Irish style. The entire tree-lined village was built in the 18th century, on the orders of the Viscount de Vesci, to house servants and tradesmen working on his nearby estate. Many town houses and vernacular buildings date from the 1850s, but more recent buildings, including the Market House, erected in 1906, and the Hibernian Bank, from 1900, contribute greatly to the town's refined character.

GETTING HERE AND AROUND
Drivers between Cork and Dublin can now bypass Abbeyleix via the N8, which has partially alleviated the town's traffic problems. However, on busy summer holiday weekends, congestion still occurs, so add a little extra time in case of delays. Allow 75 minutes driving time to Dublin or 90 minutes to Dublin airport. The nearest large town is Portlaoise, a 10-minute drive, while Kilkenny is 30 minutes south on the N77. Free on-street car parking and several car parks are available in town. Daily buses connect Abbeyleix to Dublin or Cork; the former is just under 2 hours away, the latter a 2¾-hour trip.

EXPLORING
Heritage House. Also known as the former North Boys School, the Heritage House has fascinating informative displays on the history of Abbeyleix and the de Vescis, an Anglo-Norman family who, in 1699, came to live at an estate nearby. They were instrumental in building and developing the new town of Abbeyleix in 1770. The school was

originally constructed for the education of Catholics (at the other end of the town you'll find the South School, built for Protestants). Also accessible through the Heritage House is the original Sexton's House (no extra charge), which boasts a stylish interior from the turn of the 19th century. Tourist literature is also available. ✉ *Top of town* ☎ *057/873–1653* 🌐 *www.heritagehousemuseum.com* 🎫 *€3* 🕒 *Weekdays 9–5.*

WRECKED RUGS

The carpets for the ill-fated *Titanic* were woven at a now-defunct carpet factory in Abbeyleix.

4

Heywood Gardens. Ballinakill, a pretty Georgian village about 5 km (3 miles) south of Abbeyleix, contains the Heywood Gardens, designed by the English architect Sir Edwin Lutyens in the early 20th century within an existing 18th-century park. The Lutyenses' house burned down, but the gardens, with landscaping most likely attributable to the famed Gertrude Jekyll, are worth a detour. Guided one-hour tours are available through this gardener's paradise, where a formal lawn flanked by traditional herbaceous borders leads to a sunken Italian garden. Highlights include a rose called Natalie Naples and Johnston's Blue geraniums. ✉ *Ballinakill* ☎ *057/873–3563* 🌐 *www.heritageireland.ie* 🎫 *Free* 🕒 *Daily 9–dusk.*

Fodor's Choice ★ **Morrissey's Pub and Grocery Store.** Don't miss Morrissey's. A working public house since 1775, this is one of Ireland's best-loved drinking emporiums and has a dark, wood-panel interior furnished with antique bar fittings. Customers can warm themselves by an ancient potbelly stove. Until 2005 this establishment still functioned as a shop, and while it retains its stocks of groceries, they are no longer for sale. An evocative time capsule, it serves as a reminder of times when you could purchase a pound of butter, the newspaper, and cattle feed while enjoying the obligatory pint of Guinness. They serve soup and sandwiches in the afternoon which you can enjoy alfresco at picnic tables at the front of the bar. A trad band entertains the drinkers from 6 to 8 on Sunday evening. ✉ *Main St.* ☎ *057/873–1281.*

WHERE TO STAY

$ B&B/INN 🏨 **The Foxrock Inn.** The main attraction of this modest 200-year-old guesthouse, set in the tiny village of Clough right in the heart of the County Laois countryside, is the genuinely warm welcome extended by its owners, Sean and Marian Hyland, one that is delightfully seconded by a friendly red setter by the name of Shannon and a terrier called Marley. **Pros:** well off the tourist track but plenty of activities in surrounding area; friendly owners who are knowledgeable about the area. **Cons:** no frills; rooms don't come with any extras. [$] *Rooms from: €70* ✉ *Clough, Ballacolla* ☎ *057/873–8637* 🌐 *www.foxrockinn.com* 🛏 *5 rooms* 🍴 *Breakfast.*

PORTLAOISE

14 km (9 miles) north of Abbeyleix.

Near the heart of County Laois, the rich farmland south and west of Portlaoise is one of Ireland's undiscovered gems. Golf, fishing, hiking, and horseback riding are traditional sports here, and the development of the Grand Canal for recreational purposes is adding to the area's attractions. Explore the pretty villages and romantic, ivy-covered ruins by car, follow one of the many hiking trails, or drive the Garden Trail.

Portlaoise's name is derived from the Irish for "Fort of Laois" and refers to the town's strife-filled history. In terms of its architecture, it's rather eclectic—it feels as if bits of other towns were picked up and dropped randomly on to the site. Once best known for having Ireland's highest-security prison, which housed the IRA's most notorious members during the 1970s and '80s and still looms over the town, Portlaoise is undergoing a renaissance. The main street, which once formed part of the main Dublin–Cork road, is now largely given over to pedestrians; pubs and restaurants are flourishing; and the thriving Dunamaise Arts Centre adds an extra dash of culture.

GETTING HERE AND AROUND

Portlaoise is an hour by train, bus, or car from Dublin. Kilkenny is 45 minutes south on the N8 and then N77. Roads from Portlaoise also lead south and west to Cork, Galway, and Limerick. There is no free parking anywhere in town; paid parking is available on James Fintan Lalor Avenue, next to County Hall, and at shopping centers.

Portlaoise has several daily Irish Rail trains to the capital and is on the main line linking it with Cork, Limerick, and Tralee. The small station is five minutes from the town center. Bus routes leading to Ireland's three main cities—Dublin, Cork, and Limerick—converge at Portlaoise. In addition to Bus Éireann, an independent operator, J. J. Kavanagh & Sons, serves the town, and Dublin Coach offers a route to Dublin Airport. ■ TIP➔ **Staying in Portlaoise gives you a good base from which to explore the surrounding countryside and helps you to avoid the heavy traffic that can clog the main N7 Dublin road.**

ESSENTIALS

Transportation Contacts Dublin Coach ☎ *018/627–566* ⊕ *www.dublincoach. ie.* **JJ Kavanagh** ☎ *056/883–1106* ⊕ *www.jjkavanagh.ie.*

Visitor Information Portlaoise Tourist Office ✉ *James Fintan Lalor Ave.* ☎ *057/862–1178* ⊕ *www.laoistourism.ie.*

EXPLORING

Laois Garden Trail. Connecting 10 of the county's celebrated formal gardens and expertly maintained privately owned ones, this driving route promotes the area's horticultural heritage. There's no set order for visiting the gardens; start the trail wherever you wish, and spend as long as you'd like in each garden. To do unhurried justice to all 10 gardens it'll take you at least two days, better still three if time permits. Stops include the state-run gardens at Emo Court and Heywood House, as well as Gash Gardens in Castletown, which offers a delightful river walk along the banks of the Nore; the demesne gardens of Castle Durrow, with its glorious scented roses; and the organically managed potager-style kitchen garden of Dunmore Country School, just outside Durrow. There is a charge for only one garden—at Ballintubbert; admission to the others is free. ⊠ *Portlaoise* ⊕ *www.laoisgardens.ie.*

Laois Heritage Trail. Stop by the Portlaoise Tourist Office to pick up a map of the Laois Heritage Trail, a signposted, daylong drive on quiet back roads that takes in 13 heritage sites, ranging from Abbeyleix to Emo Court. The circular trail starts in Borris-in-Ossory on the N7. ⊠ *Portlaoise, Co. Laois.*

Rock of Dunamase. A dramatic 150-foot-high limestone outcrop, the famous Rock of Dunamase dominates the landscape east of Portlaoise. For this reason, it was used as a military stronghold. As far back as AD 140 its occupants kept watch against marauders, and it was fought over in turn by the Vikings, Normans, Irish, and English. Today it's crowned by the ruins of a 12th-century castle, once home to Diarmuid MacMurrough, king of Leinster, who precipitated the Norman invasion when he invited the famed and feared Norman leader Strongbow to Ireland to marry his daughter. Some of the castle's thick walls still stand. The main reason for visiting the Rock today is to take the short walk to its summit to enjoy the view of the Slieve Bloom Mountains to the north and the Wicklow Mountains to the south. ⊠ *N80 (Stradbally Rd.), 5 km (3 mi) east of Portlaoise.*

WHERE TO EAT AND STAY

$ EUROPEAN ✕**Relish.** Portlaoise's secret is now unleashed: Monday is half-price night at Relish and if you can plan your visit for that day be advised to make an early table booking since it's mightily busy, all year round. In the upstairs candlelit dining room, plain dressers and cabinets rest on white walls alongside no-fuss wooden tables and chairs. House specials for dinner include char-grilled steak medallions or duck; seared chicken escalope or the Relish gourmet sausage infused with Guinness and leeks and topped with mash and red wine gravy are menu staples. Comfort food scores high here with eight different choices of gourmet burger. Lunches range from sandwiches and wraps to healthy salads such as walnut and pear. $ *Average main: €11* ⊠ *67 Main St.* ☎ *057/866–2200* ⊕ *www.relishbrasserie.com.*

$$ RESORT Fodor'sChoice ★ 🏨**Heritage Golf & Spa Resort.** Step into this hotel's spacious, light-filled atrium with its touches of marble, cherrywood, and mahogany and you quickly realize you have entered another world. **Pros:** a haven of peace, calm, and elegance; the smoked haddock at breakfast is a winner. **Cons:** the grass-cutters start early so prepare for a lawnmower wake-up around 6:30; isolated from any nearby towns. $ *Rooms from: €120* ⊠ *Killenard* ☎ *057/864–5500* ⊕ *www.theheritage.com* ➴ *98 rooms, 13 suites* ❋❋ *Breakfast.*

$ B&B/INN 🏨**Ivyleigh House.** "The best of everything" is the maxim of affable owners Dinah and Jerry Campion and that is certainly evident the minute you step inside this elegant Georgian town house next to the Portlaoise train station—open fires, antiques, and sumptuously cozy sofas await you in the beige-on-brown, wood-accented sitting room. **Pros:** breakfasts are lavish, filling, and imaginative; luxury linens. **Cons:** no baths, so it's a power shower only; the town lacks much in the way of evening activities. [$] *Rooms from: €90* ✉ *Bank Pl., Church St.* ☎ *057/862–2081* 🌐 *www.ivyleigh.com* 🛏 *6 rooms* 🍴 *Breakfast.*

NIGHTLIFE AND THE ARTS

Anchor Inn. Also known as Turley's Bar, this canal-side spot, 10 km (6 miles) east of Portlaoise on N80, is popular for its lively Monday-night traditional-music sessions, which start around 10. Sessions take place more frequently in spring and summer. Fishing, boating, and canal-bank walks are all accessible from this location. ✉ *Grand Canal near Stradbally, Vicarstown.*

Dunamaise Arts Centre. This lively arts center has a 240-seat theater, an art gallery, and a friendly coffeehouse (open daily 8:30–5:30). You may catch a professional production on tour or a local amateur show. The exhibition space displays the work, usually of a surprisingly high standard, of contemporary Irish artists. It's built into the back of the 18th-century stone courthouse on Church Street in a space that used to be the town jail. In September 2013 the center hosted the inaugural James Fintan Lalor School, bringing together those interested in Irish history, politics, heritage, and current affairs. Lalor was an agrarian reformer whose writings inspired many in the fight for land rights. ✉ *Church St.* ☎ *057/866–3355* 🌐 *www.dunamaise.ie.*

Ramsbottom's Bar. For a glimpse of old Ireland, call into Ramsbottom's in Lower Main Street where a log fire burns brightly beside comfy settees. This former grocery-cum-bar now sells only alcohol but reminders of its past are all around. The original bacon-slicing machine from the grocery shop is on display; walls are adorned with sepia-tinted photographs, whiskey and cigarette signs, and record sleeves featuring John McCormack and Bing Crosby, and bank notes from around the world are pinned to the bar. For €2 you can select your own five tunes from the jukebox, sit back, and enjoy a flawless pint. ✉ *Lower Main St.* ☎ *057/866–1298.*

SPORTS AND THE OUTDOORS

GOLF

Heath Golf Club. From early spring the dazzling blaze of yellow furze—also known as gorse—decorates the open heathland at this 18-hole course. The area has a colorful history, too, as the popular Irish politician Daniel O'Connell held meetings here in the mid-1830s. They've been playing golf on the Heath since the 1890s and the club dates from 1930. The course, open to the public, incorporates three natural lakes and is referred to as an "inland links." Good value deals for visitors include special rates combining golf with a meal; or you can settle for a drink in the friendly "19 Hole" bar. ✉ *5 km (3 miles) northeast of Portlaoise on main Dublin Rd., The Heath* ☎ *057/864–6533* 🌐 *www.theheathgc.ie* 🎫 *Weekdays €15, weekends €20* 🏌 *18 holes, 6120 yards, par 72. Two practice areas, putting green, indoor driving range, buggies, pull carts, catering* 🕒 *Visitors: daily.*

The Heritage Golf and Spa Resort. Millions of dollars were spent on developing this Celtic Tiger arrival to the Irish golf scene—and it shows. This 18-hole championship course is a challenge for the pros but somehow manages to be forgiving to the amateur at the same time. Heritage has second-to-none facilities including a 38,000-square-foot clubhouse. A life-size bronze of Seve Ballesteros (by the renowned sports sculptor Paul Ferriter) greets you at the entrance to the course he designed here, which is noted for its mix of challenging doglegs and water traps (including five on-course lakes). Add four demanding par-5s to the mix and the result is a truly world-class parkland course. The development of luxury on-site accommodation has also increased the club's attractiveness to the visiting golfer. ⊠ *Killenard* ☎ *057/864–5500* ⊕ *www. theheritage.com* ✉ *Fees: May–Oct., weekdays €30–€50, weekends €40–€50; Nov.–Apr., weekdays €30, weekends €40* ⅃ *18 holes, 7319 yards, par 72. Practice area, driving range, caddies, caddy carts, buggies, club rental, shoe rental, catering* ◷ *Visitors: daily.*

PORTARLINGTON

13 km (8 miles) northeast of Portlaoise.

Built on the River Barrow in the late 17th century, Portarlington was originally an English settlement. Later, a Huguenot colony developed here, and French surnames are still common in the area. Some good examples of Georgian architecture can be seen in the town.

GETTING HERE AND AROUND

On the road between Mullingar and Portlaoise, Portarlington is a small crossroads town relatively free of traffic—it's well clear of the N7 so it misses out on the motorway trade. Tullamore is a 30-minute drive away, Portlaoise is 20 minutes, and Dublin is a 45-minute drive. There are several free parking lots in town. The Dublin–Cork train stops at Portarlington and there are regular Bus Éireann connections to the bigger towns and to Dublin.

EXPLORING

Fodor'sChoice **Emo Court and Gardens.** A quintessential landmark of Irish Palladian
★ elegance lies just 7 km (4½ miles) south of Portarlington. Emo Court is one of the finest large-scale country houses near Dublin that is open to the public. Even if you elect to skip over much of the Midlands, try to tack on a visit to Emo, especially if you're in Counties Kildare or Wicklow. To come upon the house from the main drive, an avenue lined with magisterial Wellingtonia trees, is to experience one of Ireland's great treasure-house views. Begun in 1790 by James Gandon, architect of the Custom House and the Four Courts in Dublin, Emo (the name derives from the Italian version of the original Irish name Imoe) is thought to be Gandon's only domestic work matching the grand scale of his Dublin civic buildings. Construction continued on and off for 70 years, as family money troubles followed the untimely death of Emo's original patron and owner, the first earl of Portarlington.

In 1994 Emo's English-born owner donated the house to the Irish nation. The ground-floor rooms have been beautifully restored and decorated and are prime examples of life on the grand scale. Among the highlights are the entrance hall, with trompe l'oeil paintings in the apses on each side, and the library, which has a carved Italian-marble mantel. But the showstopper, and one of the finest rooms in Ireland, is the dome rotunda—the work of one of Gandon's successors, the Irish architect William Caldbeck—inspired by the Roman Pantheon. Marble pilasters with gilded Corinthian capitals support the rotunda's blue-and-white coffered dome. A permanent exhibition of photographs featuring the work of the Jesuit priest, Fr. Francis Browne—best known for his images of RMS *Titanic*—is on display in three rooms. Guided tours are held every hour in summer. Emo's 55 acres of grounds include a 20-acre lake, lawns planted with yew trees, a small garden (the Clocker) with Japanese maples, and a larger one (the Grapery) with rare trees and shrubs. ■ TIP→ **Make time for a stroll around the attractive lake walkway, added in 2014 along with two new bridges. Afterwards visit the tearoom serving tasty snacks and light lunches.** ⊠ *Emo* ☎ *057/862–6573* ⊕ *www. heritageireland.ie* 🎫 *Gardens free, house €3* ⊙ *Gardens daily 9–dusk. House Apr.–Sept., daily 10–6; last tour at 5.*

Coolbanagher Church. Coolbanagher Church, the familiar name for the exquisite Church of St. John the Evangelist, was, like Emo Court and Gardens, designed by James Gandon. On view inside are Gandon's original 1795 plans and an elaborately sculpted 15th-century font from an earlier church that stood nearby. Adjacent to the church is Gandon's mausoleum for Lord Portarlington, his patron at Emo. The church is open only by advance telephone arrangement. ⊠ *8½ km (5 miles) south of Portarlington on R419* ☎ *057/864–6538* 🎫 *Free* ⊙ *Advance arrangement by telephone.*

WHERE TO STAY

$ 🏠 **Eskermore House.** A delightful display of rambling summer roses
B&B/INN adorns the doorway of this charming ivy-covered farmhouse, which, located 9 km (6 miles) west of Edenderry on R402, is a good base for hiking in the Slieve Bloom Mountains. **Pros:** great-value accommodation in peaceful surroundings; the open fire is a pure delight. **Cons:** few frills on offer; rooms are basic. $ *Rooms from: €70* ⊠ *Mount Lucas, Edenderry* ☎ *086/824–9574* ⊕ *www.eskermore.com* ➡ *3 rooms* ⊖| *Breakfast.*

$$ 🏠 **Roundwood House.** There's a dreamlike beauty to this chateau-like
B&B/INN mansion set on the slopes of the Slieve Bloom mountains—as you arrive,
Fodor's Choice a dark tree-lined avenue suddenly opens up to reveal a dramatically gorgeous Palladian villa, and a flock of white geese, some ducks, and hens,
★ as well as a Labrador called Rococo often form the welcoming party. **Pros:** friendly hosts; mature woodland is ideal for walks. **Cons:** dinner sometimes served at a communal table; not easy to drag yourself away at stay's end. $ *Rooms from: €140* ⊠ *Mountrath* ☎ *057/873–2120* ⊕ *www.roundwoodhouse.com* ➡ *10 rooms, plus 2 self-catering cottages* ⊖| *Breakfast.*

TULLAMORE

27 km (17 miles) northwest of Portarlington.

The county seat of Offaly, Tullamore is a bustling market town that thrived during Ireland's Celtic Tiger boom that began in the mid-1990s and, like many parts of Ireland, has suffered in the economic downturn. The town's historical success was based on its location on the Grand

In the spring, the gardens at Emo Court rival the splendor of its neoclassical-style salons—here, a section of parkland abloom with bluebells.

Canal, one of Ireland's most important trading links during the 18th and 19th centuries.

GETTING HERE AND AROUND

A medium-size Midlands town, Tullamore is a transportation hub. Six roads converge here, meaning that market days at the end of the week are especially busy and free street parking is first-come, first-served. Dublin is just over an hour's drive, while the neighboring towns of Athlone, Mullingar, and Portlaoise are approximately 30 minutes away. Travelers are reasonably well served by Bus Éireann buses here; routes connect to Dublin (two hours east) as well as towns north, south, and west of Tullamore. By train, Tullamore is 70 minutes from Dublin, 90 minutes from Galway, and two hours from Sligo. Train and bus services coalesce at Cormac Street in town.

EXPLORING

Charleville Forest Castle. One relic of Tullamore's former splendor is found on the southwestern edge of town, where, if you take the road heading to Birr from the center of Tullamore, you'll find a storybook vision in splendid Tin Soldier Fortress style: Charleville Forest Castle. Perhaps the finest Neo-Gothic, British-style 19th-century castle in Ireland, its Flag Tower and turrets rise above its domain of 30 acres of woodland walks and gardens. The Georgian–Gothic Revival house was built as a symbol of English might triumphing over French force (the French revolutionary forces, to be exact, who had become a little too cozy with the Irish locals). In fact, the floor plan is even modeled on the Union Jack. Commissioned by Baron Tullamore and dating from 1812, the castle is a rural example of the work of architect Francis Johnston, who was responsible for many of Dublin's stately Georgian buildings. The interiors are somewhat the worse for wear—most are gigantic chambers with a few sticks of furniture—but the William Morris–designed dining room still has its original stenciled wallpaper.

Descended through the Bury family, who eventually lost their fortune and left no heirs, the castle became an orphan in the 1960s but has been slowly restored. The surrounding forest is said to be haunted by the spirits of the ancient Druids. Guided tours leave every 40 minutes in the summer between 1 and 5 pm. ⊠ *1½ km (1 mile) outside Tullamore on N52 to Birr* ☎ *057/932–3040* ⊕ *www.charlevillecastle. ie* ⊠ *€20 for minimum tour with 4 people; €8 per extra adult member of party* ☉ *Daily 1–5.*

FAMILY **Lough Boora Parklands.** This open expanse of rehabilitated land is a place to potter and ponder. The old commercial, now exhausted, bog has been restored for a variety of leisure activities, from hiking and cycling to coarse angling and bird-watching (more than 150 species make their home here). When it was first established in 2001 there were just 11 breeding pairs of gray partridge in the parkland—now it boasts more than 900 of these ground-nesting birds. You're unlikely to see them, however, as they spend only one minute of each day in the air. Best of all, Lough Boora is home to one of Ireland's most unique sculpture parks. Along the **Sculpture Walk**, where golden plovers, lapwings, and starlings may accompany you, 22 large-scale sculptures made from local materials (including glacial stone, water, and willow) have been created by artists influenced by the legacy of the bogs. The result is some of the most creative environmental outdoor artwork anywhere in Ireland. To cite one instance, the installation artist Mike Bulfin has turned a rusty old bog train into a cartoonish curve whose image will remain imprinted in your mind long after your visit to this magical place. An off-road bike trail runs for 10 km (6 miles). Bikes can be hired for an hour (€3) or half day (€10). Guided walking tours run April–September. ⊠ *Boora, 3 km (2 miles) north of Kilcormac* ☎ *057/934–5978* ⊕ *www. loughbooraparklands.com* ⊠ *Free.*

Fodor's Choice **Tullamore Dew Visitor Center.** Along the banks of the Grand Canal, Tul-
★ lamore Dew Visitor Center—in a 19th century bonded warehouse— trades heavily on its historic Irish identity. The center underwent a major redevelopment in 2012, adding new whiskey tours and tasting sessions. In 2014, a €35-million distillery opened at Clonminch on the outskirts of town, bringing whiskey production back to the area after a gap of 60 years. The company has also embarked on a €10-million global marketing campaign, and today it's the world's second-largest, and fastest-growing Irish whiskey brand. It's all a far cry from humble beginnings in 1829 when Tullamore Distillery was founded. It was greatly expanded under the aegis of Daniel E. Williams, whose family became joint shareholders, and his own initials, D-E-W, were added to the whiskey's name, inspiring the slogan "Give every man his Dew" (which appeared on the bottles for many years). Triple-distilled, and made from a unique blend of single malt, pot still, and grain whiskey, it is regarded by connoisseurs as exceptionally smooth. Different aspects of the production processes are reflected in five short film presentations.

Guided tours include the Original Classic or the Special Reserve tour; or you can smell, sip and savor at your leisure on a self-guided one. ■TIP→ **For an extra special tipple ask for a bottle of the limited-edition Old Bonded Warehouse whiskey, sold exclusively on-site; in the unique lingua franca of aficionados, it's said to have "zesty lemon notes, mellow complexity, a smooth vanilla oakiness, and lingering finish of honey, toffee and wood." At €53 a bottle, this may be one to treasure for a few years before opening.** Check the website for tour and tasting schedules. The center also includes a tourist information point. ⊠ *Bury Quay* ☎ *057/932–5015* ⊕ *www.tullamoredew.com* ✉ *€6 self-guided, €8 guided tour* ⊘ *Mon.–Sat. 9:30–6:15, Sun. 11:30–5.*

WHERE TO STAY

$

B&B/INN

Annaharvey Farm. Just 6 km (4 miles) outside of Tullamore town on the Portarlington road, this family farmhouse dedicated to all things equestrian was once an old-world grain barn, but has been converted into an elegant accommodation, with pitch-pine floors, massive roof beams, and open fireplaces. **Pros:** well away from the main road; secluded location; stargazing in the clear Offaly night skies. **Cons:** bathrooms are small; noisy neighing horses may disturb your slumber. $ *Rooms from: €70* ⊠ *Tullamore* ☎ *057/934–3544* ⊕ *www.annaharveyfarm.ie* ↩ *7 rooms* ⊘ *Closed Dec. and Jan.* ⼁Ol *Breakfast.*

SPORTS AND THE OUTDOORS

GOLF

Esker Hills Golf Club. Studded with natural lakes and woodlands, as well as excellent sand-based greens and valleys, Esker Hills is an 18-hole championship course. Masterfully designed by Christy O'Connor Jr., it is regarded as one of Ireland's leading inland links-type courses. It is playable all year round and welcomes visitors. The club takes its name from eskers, or mounds of sand or gravel left by streams of melted ice, which provide the dramatic undulations, never mind the challenges, of the course. ⊠ *N52, 5 km (3 miles) north of Tullamore, Esker Hills* ☎ *057/935–5999* ⊕ *www.eskerhillsgolf.com* ✉ *Weekdays €25, weekends €30* ⅃ *18 holes, 6626 yards, par 71. Practice putting area, caddies, buggies, catering* ⊘ *Visitors: daily except Sun. morning until 11 am.*

KILBEGGAN

11 km (7 miles) north of Tullamore.

GETTING HERE AND AROUND

The small town of Kilbeggan is on the main M6 Dublin–Athlone route; the nearest large town is Tullamore, 15 minutes south on the N52. There is free parking in town. Regular buses serving the busy Dublin–Galway route stop at Kilbeggan. Athlone is a 15-minute journey by bus, and Dublin is an 80-minute ride.

EXPLORING

Kilbeggan Distillery Experience. It's the whiskey (the Irish spell their traditional tipple with an "e") that brings most people to the unassuming little town of Kilbeggan, home of the Kilbeggan Distillery Experience, the oldest pot-still distillery in the world and the last of its type in

Ireland. Established in 1757, it closed as a functioning distillery in 1954, but has since found new life as a museum of industrial archaeology, illustrating the process of Irish pot-whiskey distillation and the social history of the workers. In 2012 the glorious timber waterwheel was restored and repainted, and is now creaking again. Guided one-hour tours cover the mashing and fermenting process, plus tasting, while a self-guided tour is 40 minutes. The Silver Medal tour (€13) is more wide ranging and includes tasting three whiskies; on the Gold Medal Masterclass tour (€25) you get to taste all four Kilbeggan core brands: Kilbeggan, Greenore single grain, Tyrconnell single malt, and Connemara peated single malt. This tour also takes in old warehouses, casks, and includes meeting distillers. Afterwards you can browse the gift shop and enjoy homemade food in the Pantry restaurant. ⊠ *Main St., Kilbeggan* ☎ *057/933–2134* ⊕ *www.kilbeggandistillery.com* ⊠*€8* ☉ *Apr.–Oct., daily 9–6; Nov.– Mar., daily 10–4.*

> **BRIGHT ELIXIR**
>
> Kilbegganers know "Irish" is a straight pot-still whiskey, and it has a characteristic flavor that distinguishes it from Scotch, bourbon, or rye. Irish is not drunk until it has matured for at least seven years in wooden casks. It's best quaffed without a mixer, so try it straight or with water.

MULLINGAR

24 km (15 miles) northeast of Kilbeggan.

The Irish are great ones for wrapping an insult up in a lyrical turn of phrase. Rather than describe a woman as overweight they'll say with a wink that she's "beef to the heels, like a Mullingar heifer." Of course, the phrase also illustrates Mullingar's role as Ireland's beef capital, a town surrounded by rich countryside where cattle trading has historically been one of the chief occupations. It's also County Westmeath's major town—a busy commercial and cattle-trading center on the Royal Canal, midway between two large, attractive lakes, Lough Owel and Lough Ennel. Although best used as a base to tour the surrounding countryside, Mullingar has some sights worthy of your time.

GETTING HERE AND AROUND

Mullingar is a busy town on the N4 Longford–Dublin route. Although it is bypassed by the highway, traffic in town can still come to a standstill at certain times of the day. The Dublin–Sligo train stops at Mullingar, and buses run to Athlone (one hour) and Dublin (90 minutes).

ESSENTIALS

Visitor Information Mullingar Discover Ireland Centre ⊠ *Market Sq.* ☎ *044/934–8650* ⊕ *www.discoverireland.ie.*

EXPLORING

FAMILY **Belvedere House & Gardens.** A stately mid-18th-century hunting lodge with extensive gardens, Belvedere House occupies a beautiful spot on the northeast shore of Lough Ennel. Access to the mansion is through the servants' entrance—so you can see what life behind the scenes was like back then. The interiors are a quirky mix of Georgian stateliness and Victorian charm. The noted bow and Palladian windows have great parkland views sloping down to the lake and its islands.

Built in 1740 by architect Richard Cassels for Robert Rochfort, first earl of Belvedere, it became a byword for debauchery and dissipation, thanks to the high jinks of Rochfort's wife, the "very handsome" Mary Molesworth. After falling passionately in love with Rochfort's younger brother (and bearing him a child), she was locked up in another family house for decades. Robert regaled guests with the "scandal" while offering sumptuous dinners at this house under its great plasterwork ceilings. He spent much of his family fortune dotting the gardens of the estate with "follies," including the Jealous Wall, a gigantic mock-castle ruin that served to cover up a view of the adjoining estate, owned by another brother, also hated.

You can walk around the 160 acres of the estate and woodland trails; the Narnia Trail brings you through an ancient whispering wood and past the white witch's castle (a Gothic arch folly), while the Belvedere Sacred Tree Trail and Fairy Garden are equally popular. Also on the grounds are a café and two children's play areas. ⊠ *N52, 4 km (2½ miles) south of Mullingar* ☎ *044/934–9060* ⊕ *www.belvedere-house.ie* ⊠ *House and parkland €8* ⊙ *Mar., Apr., Sept., and Oct., daily 10–7; May–Aug., daily 10–8; Nov.–Feb., daily 10:30–3:30.*

Cathedral of Christ the King. The town's largest structure is the Renaissance-style Catholic Cathedral of Christ the King, completed in 1939. Note the facade's finely carved stonework, and the mosaics of St. Patrick and St. Anne by the Russian artist Boris Anrep in the spacious interior. There's a museum in the cathedral, and tours are available in the spring and summer (call for times). ⊠ *Mary St.* ☎ *044/934–8338* ⊕ *www.mullingarparish.ie* ⊙ *Daily 8–8.*

SPORTS AND THE OUTDOORS
GOLF
Delvin Castle Golf Club. This historic 18-hole course in the stately parkland setting of Clonyn Castle demesne has beautiful views across north Westmeath. Mature trees and woodland surround you; the tree-lined fairways mean that a wayward drive will leave some facing a tricky second. A pleasant, rewarding public course, it is playable all year round—the only difficulty may be occasional severe frost in the winter. Keep your camera handy and look out for the ruins of the castle, originally built in 1639, which can be seen from the 9th to 16th holes. ⊠ *Delvin* ☎ *044/966–4315* ⊕ *www.delvincastlegc.com* ⊠ *Weekdays €16, weekends €20* ⓘ *18 holes, 6103 yards, par 70. Practice area, putting green, caddies, buggies, catering* ⊙ *Visitors: daily.*

CASTLEPOLLARD

21 km (13 miles) north of Mullingar.

A pretty village of multihued 18th- and 19th-century houses laid out around a large, triangular green, Castlepollard is also home to

Tullynally Castle and Gardens, the largest castle in Ireland that still functions as a family home.

GETTING HERE AND AROUND

The small rural town of Castlepollard sits at a crossroads between Cavan and Mullingar, which is the nearest large town, 20 minutes south on the narrow R394. Free parking is available in the Square or on side streets. There is a daily bus service to Dublin (the trip takes two hours), and a route once a week to Mullingar.

EXPLORING

Fodor's Choice ★ **Tullynally Castle and Gardens.** It's hard to figure out which is more famous: Tullynally's storybook castle or the magical parklands that surround this fabled family seat. And this is not just any family: the Pakenhams are the famous Irish tribe that has given us Elizabeth Longford (whose biography of Queen Victoria is in most libraries) and Antonia Fraser, wife of the late playwright Harold Pinter and best-selling biographer of Mary, Queen of Scots, among others. In fact, Tullynally—the name, literally translated, means "Hill of the Swans"—has been the home of 10 generations of this family, which also married into the earldom of Longford. Lady Fraser's brother Thomas, a historian, is the current earl but does not use the title. He inherited Tullynally from his uncle and has planted 90,000 trees.

As a result of an 18th-century "Gothicization," the former Georgian house was transformed into a faux castle by architect Francis Johnston; the resulting 600 feet of battlements were not just for show, as the earls were foes of Catholic emancipation. Inside, the family has struggled to make the vast salons warm and cozy—a bit of a losing battle. The house really comes into its own as a stage set for the surrounding park—the gray-stone structure is so long and has so many towers it looks like a miniature town from a distance. The total circumference of the building's masonry adds up to nearly ½ km (¼ mile) and includes a motley agglomeration of towers, turrets, and crenellations that date from the first early fortified building (circa 1655) up through the mid-19th century, when additions in the Gothic Revival style went up one after another.

Today, more attention is given to the beautiful parkland, in part because Thomas Pakenham is a tree-hugger extraordinaire who founded the Irish Tree Society in 1992. He is the author of several books, his most famous being *Meetings with Remarkable Trees* (1996), an exceptional art book that includes many of his magnificent photographs. The estate's rolling parkland was laid out in 1760, much along the lines you see today, with fine rhododendrons, numerous trees (oak, ash, sycamore, Scots pine, beech, silver fir, larch, and spruce, among others), and two ornamental lakes. A garden walk through the grounds in front of the castle leads to a spacious flower garden, a pond, a grotto, and walled gardens. You'll also find a Tibetan garden, a Chinese garden, and a kitchen garden, one of the largest in Ireland, with a row of old Irish yew trees. ■TIP➔ **Don't miss the forest path, which takes you around the perimeter of the parkland and affords excellent views of the romantic castle. After your energetic tour, enjoy a visit to the Tullynally**

Tea Rooms in a renovated Georgian stable block which serves lunches such as lasagna, quiche, and pre-concert supper roasts. Locals rave about the lemon meringue pie. ⊠ *1½ km (1 mile) west of Castlepollard on the R395 road to Granard* ☎ *044/966–1159* ⊕ *www.tullynallycastle. com* ⊠ *€6* ⊗ *Apr.–Sept., Thurs.–Sun. 11–6.*

FORE

5 km (3 miles) east of Castlepollard.

You've heard of the seven wonders of the ancient world, but here in the heart of the Irish Midlands is a tiny village with seven wonders all to itself! According to Irish myth, this is the place where water runs uphill, where there's a tree that will not burn and water that will not boil, among other fantastical occurrences. The village is known not only for its legend, but also for its medieval church and the remains (supposedly the largest in Ireland) of a Benedictine abbey.

GETTING HERE AND AROUND

Fore is on a quiet country road between Castlepollard and Oldcastle on the R195. The nearest main town is Mullingar, a 30-minute drive. There's free parking in the village. Fore cannot be reached by train or bus.

EXPLORING

Fore Abbey. The spectacular remains of Fore Abbey dominate the simple village—its structure is massive and its imposing square towers and loophole windows make it resemble a castle rather than an abbey. ⊠ *Fore.*

CAVAN

36 km (22 miles) north of Fore, 114 km (71 miles) northwest of Dublin.

Like all the larger towns of the region, Cavan is growing and prosperous. It is perhaps best known for its crystal factory. But as one of the main transportation hubs of the Midlands, Cavan has also attracted an impressive array of restaurants and hotels, so this is a fine base for exploring this region, which lies near the border to Northern Ireland. There are two central streets: with its pubs and shops, Main Street is like many other streets in similar Irish towns; Farnham Street has Georgian houses, churches, a courthouse, and a bus station.

GETTING HERE AND AROUND

Cavan is a thriving market town on the main N3 from Navan to Enniskillen in Northern Ireland. There is metered pay-parking in the town center. The town and surrounding south Ulster area, including neighboring Monaghan, relies on an extensive bus network for public transport. Cavan is equidistant from Belfast and Galway with a three-hour travel time to both cities by bus. Bus Éireann serves Cavan on Galway–Belfast, Athlone–Belfast, and Dublin–Donegal Expressway routes, and there is weekday service to small towns throughout Cavan and Monaghan.

Tullynally Castle—the largest in Ireland (just a small portion is shown here)—is surrounded by spectacular parkland, forest paths, and kitchen gardens.

ESSENTIALS

Transportation Information Cavan Bus Office ☎ 049/433–1709.

Visitor Information Cavan Tourist Office ✉ Farnham St. ☎ 049/433–1942 ⊕ www.thisiscavan.ie.

EXPLORING

FAMILY **Bear Essentials Ireland.** A fun stop for children of all ages, you can view the largest collection of teddy bears in Ireland here. Each bear is hand-crafted in the workshop from the finest mohair. The Silver Bear Centre and gift shop is next door. There's a "Teddy Bear Hospital" on-site, where you can bring your damaged teddy for repair or redesign, and the shop also sells "My First Teddy," a baby bear for infants. ✉ Tirnawannagh, 23 km (18 miles) northwest of Cavan town, Bawnboy ☎ 049/952–3461 ⊕ www.bearessentials.ie ✉ Free ⊘ Mon.–Sat. 9–6, Sun. 11–6.

WHERE TO EAT AND STAY

$$$$ ✕ **MacNean's House & Restaurant.** This is one of the best restaurants in
IRISH Ireland. The five-course dinner menu, priced at €72, is an unhurried
Fodor'sChoice affair—it even comes with pre-starters and pre-desserts. Winning appe-
★ tizers include an artistically presented partridge, and Castletownbere sea scallop. Top mains include Thornhill duck breast, strip-loin of dry aged beef, or lobster cannelloni. The Menu Prestige, at €87 (€132, including wine), delivers a staggering nine courses: your taste buds may never again experience such an explosion of epicurean delights. The five-course Sunday lunch at €39 is a great value. Given the remoteness of Blacklion, why not book one of the 19 guest rooms when reserving

a table? As many diners have learned, the 65-km (40-mile) detour to Blacklion makes a lot more sense if you are heading from Dublin northwest to Sligo or Donegal. But be warned: this restaurant is perpetually busy, and there's a waiting list of up to 12 months for weekends. In 2014 Maguire opened a cookery school featuring classes for all skill levels. Breakfast is served. $ *Average main: €72* ⊠ *Main St., Blacklion* ☎ *071/985–3022* ⊕ *www.nevenmaguire.com* ⌲ *Reservations essential* ⌂ *Jacket required* ⊘ *Closed Mon. and Tues. No lunch Wed.–Sat.*

$$$$
IRISH
Fodor's Choice
★

✗ **The Olde Post Inn.** The magic formula of a genuine Irish welcome and immaculate food with a culinary flourish is what draws people to the Olde Post Inn, set in bucolic south Ulster surroundings. A restored, stone, former post office in an elegantly landscaped garden, the restaurant has won a clutch of awards and, as a result, is often booked solid. Sea bass, steak, loin of rabbit, and Peking duck are main-course favorites, and ingredients highlight regional ingredients. To wash it down, choose from a wine selection that will appeal to Europhiles: Valpolicella, Pouilly-Fuissé, Sancerre, or if you feel like a splurge, try the flamboyantly fruity Puligny Montrachet at a cool €85. Artwork by some top Irish artists decorates the redbrick stone walls. To get here, take the N53 to Cloverhill from Cavan town. Staying overnight is strongly advised; six guest bedrooms, all in the original part of the postmaster's residence, have been modernized with fabrics in bright jewel colors alongside contemporary bathrooms and plasma TVs. $ *Average main: €55* ⊠ *Cloverhill* ☎ *047/55555* ⊕ *www.theoldepostinn.com* ⌲ *Reservations essential* ⊘ *Closed Mon. No lunch Tues.–Sat.*

$$$$
MODERN IRISH
Fodor's Choice
★

✗ **Radisson Blu Farnham Estate Hotel.** A blend of stone, wood, and glass, the Farnham Estate—one of the top spots in the Midlands to detox and purify—exudes the promise of contentment, styling itself as a "playground for the senses" as well as offering a superb choice of dining options. Extended from the original big house (dating from 1664), the hotel comes with 1,300 acres that includes a golf course and mature grounds. Guest rooms and corridors are in relaxing neutral themes of beige, silvery greens, and sky blue, echoing the tones in the gardens and grounds. What steals the show however, is the spa, and in particular the Laconium, which re-creates the atmosphere of a Roman sauna. The snail shower, salt grottos, and reflexology footbath are also recommended. ■ TIP→ **Ask at reception for a booklet outlining five nature trails through woods and around lakes, and make sure you see the magnificent Monterey pine in the center of the parkland. Pros:** the revitalizing effect of the spa leaves a healthy golden afterglow; retreat to nature in the cathedral-like silences of the grounds. **Cons:** slow service at peak times; a danger of spoiling yourself too much in the fab Laconium. $ *Average main: €40* ⊠ *Farnham Estate, Killashandra Rd., Farnham* ☎ *049/437–7700* ⊕ *www.farnhamestate.com* ⌲ *Reservations essential.*

$$
HOTEL

⌂ **Cabra Castle.** With its collection of mock-Gothic towers, turrets, and crenellations, along with rumors of paranormal activity, Cabra Castle has been deemed one of the world's scariest hotels; the Irish Ghosthunters Association has confirmed that it was indeed a place visited by spirits. **Pros:** stunning views of the surrounding countryside; a romantic retreat with attentive personal service. **Cons:** emphasis appears to

4

be on weddings; the ghostly goings-on cannot be guaranteed but the signs are positive. [$] *Rooms from: €150* ✉ *Carrickmacross Rd., 65 km (40 miles) south of Cavan, on R179, Kingscourt* ☎ *042/966-7030* 🌐 *www.cabracastle.com* 🛏 *80 rooms, 5 suites, 21 self-catering lodges* 🍴 *Breakfast.*

SPORTS AND THE OUTDOORS

GOLF

County Cavan Golf Club. Visitors are welcome at this beautifully manicured 18-hole course, redesigned in 2012, and set amid parkland in the heart of the south Ulster lakelands. The Cavan Club has a long pedigree stretching back to 1894; it moved to its present location in 1920. The visual reshaping included work on the fairways lined with mature trees and present a challenge, especially on holes 14–18. The 180-meter (197 yards) 10th is difficult from a tee-box in front of the clubhouse to a new green under an old chestnut tree. The club pro, Bill Noble, holds regular lessons. Golfers can sharpen their pitching, chipping, bunker, and putting techniques in a top-notch practice area. ✉ *Armmore House, Drumelis* ☎ *049/433-1541* 🌐 *www.cavangolf.ie* 🎫 *Daily €20* ⛳ *18 holes, 6164 yards, par 70. Practice area, floodlit driving range, buggies, catering* 🕒 *Visitors: daily.*

LONGFORD TOWN

37 km (23 miles) southwest of Cavan, 124 km (77 miles) northwest of Dublin.

Longford, the seat of County Longford and a typical, small, market-town community, is rich in literary associations, though after Oliver Goldsmith, the names in the county's pantheon of writers may draw a blank from all but the most dedicated Irish literature enthusiasts. Longford town provides a good base for exploring the largely untouristed countryside surrounding it. A day trip to the pretty heritage village of Ardagh (10 km [7 miles] southeast of Longford town), with its quaint houses and village green, is a popular option.

GETTING HERE AND AROUND

Longford is on the N4 linking Mullingar and Carrick-on-Shannon. It's easily accessible by car, and town parking is generally not a problem. Shop around, as some parking is free while other streets are metered. Unlike many Midlands towns, Longford is doubly blessed with both train and bus links. Convenient for making connections, buses stop outside Longford train station. Bus Éireann routes fan out in all directions. Dublin airport and city are 2¼–2½ hours away, and Belfast is a 4-hour ride. There's also a cross-border bus from Longford to Derry operated in conjunction with Ulsterbus; journey time is four hours. The town is on the main Irish Rail Dublin–Sligo railway line: Dublin is 1¾ hours away and Sligo is 1¼ hours.

ESSENTIALS

Transportation Information Longford Railway Station ☎ *043/334-5208.*

Visitor Information Longford Town Tourist Office ✉ *Market Sq.* ☎ *043/334-2577* 🌐 *www.longfordtourism.ie.*

EXPLORING

Bogwood Sculptures. A lovely spot near Longford town is Newtowncashel, on the banks of Lough Ree, where you can visit Bogwood Sculptures, a fascinating workshop run by sculptors Michael and Kevin Casey. The center displays sculptures and keepsakes made from bog oak and bog yew, which is hewn from the 5,000-year-old trees submerged and ultimately preserved by the area's ancient peatlands. To get there from Longford drive 14 km (9 miles) on the N63 to Lanesborough, then take the R392 for 2 km (1 mile) and follow signs for Turreen–Newtowncashel. ⊠ *Barley Harbour, Newtowncashel* ☎ *043/332–5297* ⊕ *www.bogoak.ie* 🎟 *Free* ⊗ *Mon.–Sat. 10–6.*

The Genealogy Centre. This genealogy research center is worth visiting to search of your roots. Call in advance. ⊠ *17 Dublin St.* ☎ *043/334–1235* ⊕ *www.longfordtourism.ie.*

Strokestown Park House & Famine Museum. The highlight of a trip to Strokestown in County Roscommon is the Irish National Famine Museum in the stable yard of Strokestown Park House. The museum tells the story of the devastating Irish potato blight in the 1840s, which is now regarded as one of the greatest social disasters in 19th-century Europe. Two million people—about a quarter of the population of Ireland—either died or emigrated and their harrowing story is well worth exploring. Museum exhibits include original famine documents found during the restoration of the house; it's a remarkable contrast to the opulent surroundings of the Georgian Palladian mansion and its 6 acres of garden. The Strokestown Park House landlord, Major Denis Mahon, was assassinated in November 1847 at the height of the famine. Strokestown is a 30-minute drive west of Longford town on the N5. ⊠ *Strokestown, Co. Roscommon* ☎ *071/963–3013* ⊕ *www.strokestownpark.ie* 🎟 *Museum & gardens €13.50. House, museum, or gardens, €9* ⊗ *Daily 10:30–5:30.*

WHERE TO EAT AND STAY

$$ ✕ **The Purple Onion.** Hungry travelers love this Shannon-side resting place
IRISH on the main street of a tiny village to the west of Longford town. Origi-
Fodor's Choice nally a standard public house with low ceilings, nooks, crannies, and
★ snugs, it has been transformed into a gourmet's delight—a special "gastro pub," abustle with locals, cruise-boat tourists, and food lovers from all over. Specialties include Thornhill duck, tender Roscommon lamb, and prime loin of beef from Ballymahon. Potatoes and vegetables are abundant and even served al dente. The good-value Early Bird stretches from 5 to 9:15 Tuesday–Thursday, and 5:30 to 7 Friday and Saturday. ■TIP➔ It's worth leaving space for the Toblerone cheesecake, which has become the sweet talk of Longford. An upstairs gallery has work by some of the finest and best-known Irish artists, including Jack B. Yeats and Paul Henry, among a hundred others. To get here from Longford town drive 10 km (6 miles) west on the N5. $ *Average main: €22* ⊠ *Tarmonbarry* ☎ *043/335–9919* ⊕ *www.purpleonion.ie* ⟁ *Reservations essential* ⊗ *Closed Mon. No lunch Tues.–Thurs.*

$ 🍴 **Keenan's Boutique Hotel.** Barry Keenan is the fifth generation of his
HOTEL family since 1838 to run this first-rate hotel and restaurant overlooking the Shannon, making Keenan's a virtual village within a village.

Pros: hospitable and helpful family-run operation; great tree-lined walks nearby along the riverbank. **Cons:** Tarmonbarry is best as a one-night stand on your way east or west; a long way from the bright lights. $ *Rooms from: €100* ⊠ *Tarmonbarry* ☎ *043/332–6052* ⊕ *www. keenanshotel.ie* ⤶ *12 rooms* ❍ *Breakfast.*

$

B&B/INN

🏛 **Viewmount House.** An exquisite Georgian home once owned by the Earl of Longford, Viewmount has been restored to its former charm; the bedrooms are full of character and have impressive period wallpapers and antique mahogany wardrobes and beds. **Pros:** wonderfully restored house; comfort and hospitality are the order of your stay. **Cons:** 20-minute walk into town; limited amount to do in Longford. $ *Rooms from: €110* ⊠ *Dublin Rd.* ☎ *043/334–1919* ⊕ *www.viewmounthouse. com* ⤶ *12 rooms, 7 suites* ❍ *Breakfast.*

THE WESTERN MIDLANDS

This section of the Midlands covers the area's western fringe, making its way from the heart of the region, the town of Longford, and skirting the hilly landscape of County Leitrim, dappled with lakes and beloved of anglers for its fish-filled waters. The area is the country's most sparsely populated, though it has a light sprinkling of villages and, until his death in 2006, was the home of one of Ireland's leading writers, John McGahern; at the end of July, the John McGahern International Seminar and Summer School—a series of lectures, workshops, and tours—is held in Carrick-on-Shannon in his honor. Moving south through Roscommon, western Offaly, and the northern part of Tipperary, the scenery is generally low on spectacle but high on unspoiled, lush, and undulating countryside. The towns are small and undistinguished, except Birr and Strokestown, both designed to complement the "big houses" that share their names. This is one of the parts of the country where you're most likely to encounter the "hidden Ireland," a place unblighted by the plastic leprechaun syndrome of the more touristy areas to the south and west. The historic highlight of this region is the ancient site of Clonmacnoise, an important monastery of early Christian Ireland while Birr Castle, opened in 2013 to the public for the first time in 400 years, is an essential part of any visitor's itinerary.

ANTHONY TROLLOPE TRAIL

Trail starts in the village of Drumsna, 16 km (10 miles) north of Longford town.

GETTING HERE AND AROUND

The Trollope Trail is centered in Drumsna, a village 10 minutes from Carrick-on-Shannon and 30 minutes from Longford town. Dublin is a two-hour drive along the N4. Sligo lies 30 minutes north on the N4. Head west across the Plains of Mayo and two hours' driving will take you to Galway.

EXPLORING

Anthony Trollope Trail. This trail, created to honor the celebrated English Victorian novelist Anthony Trollope (1815–82), takes in 27 locations throughout Leitrim and incorporates many fascinating topographical spots, including an area along the River Shannon known as Flaggy Bottoms. Trollope, a senior civil servant, was sent to Drumsna in 1843 to investigate the financial affairs of the postmaster. While living there he wrote his first novel *The Macdermots of Ballycloran,* drawing inspiration from the nearby ruin of Headford House. A leaflet and information on the trail is available from the tourist office in Carrick-on-Shannon (☎ 071/962–0170). ✉ *Carrick-on-Shannon, Co. Sligo.*

ATHLONE

4

34 km (21 miles) southeast of Longford town, 127 km (79 miles) west of Dublin, 121 km (75 miles) east of Limerick.

Fodor'sChoice ★ The mighty Shannon flows majestically through the heart of Athlone, yet for years it seemed as if the town was happy to turn its back on one of Europe's great waterways. That trend has been well and truly reversed and there is a real buzz of regeneration. The area around Athlone Castle has been transformed into a veritable "Left Bank" with the bright new Luan Gallery attracting culture vultures from all over Ireland. On both sides of the Shannon, new restaurants and stylishly modern architecture have sprung up on streets lined with 200-year-old buildings that have been given some imaginative repurposing alongside one of Ireland's most architecturally dazzling churches. Once upon a time, tourists were few and far between in what was cuttingly termed the "dead center" of Ireland, but the renaissance has made Athlone an increasingly attractive destination.

GETTING HERE AND AROUND

Athlone is one of the Midlands' largest towns and on busy days its long main street can take 30 minutes to drive end to end. Although the main Dublin N6 motorway has considerably eased congestion, this is still a place where delays are inevitable. Parking is available on the street, in paid lots, and at shopping centers. The drive to Dublin takes two hours, while Galway is 90 minutes west.

With its central location, Athlone is an important Bus Éireann hub with connecting Expressway services to more than 20 principal towns and cities as well as dozens of smaller destinations across Ireland. Some routes are operated in conjunction with Ulsterbus. Trains branch out in three main directions from Athlone: southwest to Galway, west to Westport, and east to Dublin. The east–west intercity Irish Rail Galway–Dublin service takes 1¾ hours to reach Dublin.

ESSENTIALS

Transportation Information Athlone Railway Station ☎ 090/647–3300.

Visitor Information Athlone Tourist Office ✉ *Athlone Castle* ☎ 090/649–4630 ⊕ *www.athlone.ie* ☼ *Apr.–Oct. only.*

EXPLORING

FAMILY **Athlone Castle.** Bold and imposing, Athlone Castle stands beside the River Shannon. A raft of dazzling new exhibitions is housed inside this 13th-century Norman stronghold. After their defeat at the Battle of the Boyne in 1691, the Irish retreated to Athlone and made the river their first line of defense. The castle, which celebrated its 800th anniversary in 2010, has played a strategic role in Irish history. Eight exhibition spaces—in the main building as well as the keep and the armory—detail this enthralling chronological story and that of the town from the earliest settlement up to modern trading times. Sculptural forms convey human figures that bring the characters of Athlone to life in an engaging way. They sit cheek by jowl with 3-D maps, audiovisuals, and weapons such as a bow and arrow that allow hands-on experiences for both children and adults. You will feel right at the center of things with the 360-degree view of events of the Siege of Athlone in 1690. It's not your typical Irish fairy-tale castle, but it is fun, and kids especially love the interactive game "How to Capture a Castle." It's hard to beat on a wet day in the Midlands. The castle gatehouse serves as the town's tourist office. ⊠ *Castle St.* ☎ *090/644–2130* ⊕ *www.athloneartandheritage. ie* ☎ *€8* ⊙ *Mid-Mar.–Oct., Mon.–Sat. 10–5, Sun. noon–6; Nov.–mid-Mar., Tues.–Sat. 11–5, Sun. noon–5.*

A GREAT IRISH TENOR

Count John McCormack (1884–1945) was perhaps the finest lyric tenor Ireland has produced. Born in Athlone, he recorded 600 records from 1914 to 1918 and made the Hollywood film *Song of My Heart*. A memorial bust stands on Grace Road by the Shannon.

Luan Gallery. When it opened in 2012, the Luan Gallery created a much-needed municipal space to showcase the work of local artists from throughout the Midlands. Since then Athlone's cultural status has risen a few notches, and this contemporary visual-arts gallery, idyllically sited on the River Shannon, has been well supported by both townspeople and tourists, helping promote an artistic revival. The gallery, built at a cost of €3.4 million, extends the well-known 1897 Fr. Mathew Temperance Hall, which over the years has held many roles including cinema, town hall, library, and concert hall. While it organizes exhibitions featuring both emerging and established local artists, the Luan also draws on the national and international permanent collection of the Irish Museum of Modern Art in Dublin. ⊠ *Grace Rd.* ☎ *090/644–2154* ⊕ *www.athloneartandheritage.ie* ⊙ *Tues.–Sat. 11–5, Sun. noon–5.*

St. Peter and St. Paul Catholic Church. Sparkling with its restored granite walls, St. Peter and St. Paul Catholic Church is a striking ecclesiastical and architectural Baroque landmark that many come to see. Built in a completely different style from that generally adopted in Ireland, the church opened on June 29, 1937 (the feast day of the patron saints of St. Peter and St. Paul). Repair work on the impressive interior included re-decoration of the vaulted ceiling, walls, floors, and pews. Dominating the skyline for many miles around, the twin campanili symbolize the saints, while the squat copper dome adds to the overall grace of this much-loved building. Look out for the six fine stained-glass windows

CLOSE UP

Goldsmith Country

All that glitters may not be Goldsmith, but that hasn't prevented the Irish tourist board from promoting the Northern Lakelands to the burgeoning literary tourism market as "Goldsmith Country."

Yes, this is the region that gave birth to the writer Oliver Goldsmith (1730–74), celebrated for his farcical drama *She Stoops to Conquer* and his classic novel *The Vicar of Wakefield*. Goldsmith left his homeland as a teenager and returned rarely. However, he is thought to have drawn on memories of his native Longford for his most renowned poem, "The Deserted Village." At Goldsmith's childhood home in Lissoy in County Longford, only the bare walls of the family house remain standing. At Pallas, near Ballymahon in County Longford, his birthplace, there's a statue in his memory but little else. The plot of *She Stoops to Conquer* involves a misunderstanding in which a traveler mistakes a private house for an inn. This actually happened to Goldsmith at Ardagh House, now a college, in the center of the village of Ardagh (just off N55) in County Longford. In the same play the character Tony Lumpkin sings a song about a pub called the Three Jolly Pigeons; today the pub of the same name, on the Ballymahon road (N55) north of Athlone, is the headquarters of the Oliver Goldsmith Summer School.

Every year on the first weekend in June, leading academics from around the world speak on Goldsmith at this pub and other venues, and there are readings by the best of Ireland's contemporary poets and evening traditional music sessions in the tiny, atmospheric, country pub. Call the Athlone Tourist Office (☎ *090/649-4630*) for more information, or visit the website (🌐 *www.goldsmithfestival.ie*).

4

from the famed Harry Clarke Studios in Dublin. The tribute window to St. Patrick is a riot of glorious color. ✉ *Market Sq.* ☎ *090/649–2171* 🌐 *www.drum.ie/parish* 🕒 *Daily 9–6.*

WHERE TO EAT

$ THAI 🍴 **Kin Khao Thai Restaurant.** Many regard this as the leading Thai restaurant in the Midlands, if not all of Ireland. Adam Lyons runs a slick first-floor operation in a 650-year-old building on the west bank. The extensive menu features dishes rarely available outside Thailand, including the Crying Tiger (grilled fillet of beef on a sizzling hot platter with a hot chili sauce) and Jungle Curry (an extremely hot curry made with mixed vegetables and chicken, beef, or prawns). Ceiling fans and balloon bamboo lights help create the perfect gastronomic scene—it's not hard to imagine yourself in Chiang Mai. ■ **TIP→ Keep the water jug handy as the smooth richness of coconut milk doesn't offset this fiery food.** [$] *Average main: €15* ✉ *Abbey La.* ☎ *090/649–8805* 🌐 *www.kinkhaothai.ie* 🕒 *No lunch Mon., Tues., Sat.*

$$ ASIAN Fodor's Choice ★ 🍴 **The Left Bank Bistro.** One of Athlone's culinary highlights, this bistro is noted for its Early-Bird menu which runs through the evening (except Saturday, when it ends at 7 pm), filled with such delights as beef Stroganoff, wild mushroom risotto, or prawn salad with chorizo

and baby potatoes. Later on, the beige-on-brown dining room fills up with people happy to choose dishes from the main dinner menu, which favors steaks, fish, duck, and rack of lamb. For lunch, the most popular dish is tandoori chicken breast on focaccia bread with sautéed potatoes. Irresistible desserts include Mississippi mud pie, pavlova roulade, and lemon-and-lime cheesecake. ■TIP→ **Ask joint-owner Annie McNamara about the Left Bank dressing, a specially bottled vinaigrette that people come from all across Ireland to buy.** $ *Average main: €22* ⊠ *Fry Pl.* ☎ *090/649–4446* ⊕ *www.leftbankbistro.com* ♥ *Closed Sun. and Mon.*

WHERE TO STAY

$

B&B/INN

🛏 **Bastion Bed & Breakfast.** An inviting glow hits you as you step into the long narrow corridor of this unconventional B&B, all nooks and little staircases, and with a high fun quotient. **Pros:** healthy buffet breakfasts offer up cereal, fresh breads, fruit and cheese; minimalist chic and no clutter; historic character of neighborhood. **Cons:** bathrooms are small; no phones, TVs, or elevators. $ *Rooms from: €65* ⊠ *2 Bastion St.* ☎ *090/649–4954* ⊕ *www.thebastion.net* ⟿ *7 rooms* ⦿ *Breakfast.*

$$

HOTEL

Fodor'sChoice

★

🛏 **Glasson Country House Hotel and Golf Club.** With views extending out to Hare Island and beyond to Lough Ree, this 1780 stone manor house has seen its popularity rise with golfers every year since 1993, when the welcoming hosts Tom and Breda Reid turned a 70-acre field into a challenging course. **Pros:** family-run; an enthralling place to de-stress with woodland walks and boat trips all nearby. **Cons:** strong winds whip in off the lake on breezy days—bring a sweater; bunker discussions dominate the conversation at breakfast, so be prepared. $ *Rooms from: €120* ⊠ *Glasson* ☎ *090/648–5120* ⊕ *www.glassoncountryhouse. ie* ⟿ *65 rooms, 9 suites* ⦿ *Breakfast.*

$

HOTEL

🛏 **Radisson Blu Hotel, Athlone.** In a prime location on the banks of the Shannon, this 128-room property has a distinctive water theme; not surprising, as more than half the units have superb views of the meandering river with a lovely look at the Sts. **Pros:** stunning views; top-notch location for exploring the town, castle, and left bank; free parking. **Cons:** precooked breakfasts are mediocre; good pool but no spa. $ *Rooms from: €100* ⊠ *Northgate St.* ☎ *090/644–2600* ⊕ *www.radissonblu.ie/ hotel-athlone* ⟿ *128 rooms, 10 suites* ⦿ *Breakfast.*

$$$

HOTEL

🛏 **Wineport Lodge.** Catch the right sunset and this is one of the most enchanting hideaways in Ireland. **Pros:** magical lake and forest setting; the under-floor bathroom heating is luxurious. **Cons:** the serenity is occasionally broken by jet-skiers on the lough; restaurant service can be slow. $ *Rooms from: €188* ⊠ *Glasson* ☎ *090/643–9010* ⊕ *www. wineport.ie* ⟿ *29 rooms, 14 suites* ⦿ *Breakfast.*

NIGHTLIFE

Sean's Bar. In Athlone's buzzing Left Bank sector, Sean's Bar styles itself as the world's oldest pub (a claim some cynics dispute although a framed certificate from the *Guinness Book of Records* says otherwise), dating to AD 900. Sawdust on the floor of this dimly lighted, low-ceiling, long narrow bar helps give it a rustic look and soaks up spillages. Framed pictures and prints line the walls alongside maps of the Shannon navigation system, and the beer garden stretches almost down to the water. There's traditional music most weekend nights in the summer. ☒ *13 Main St.* ☎ *090/649–2358* ⊕ *www.seansbar.ie.*

SHOPPING

The Left Bank district is a jumble of lanes and small streets lined with pubs, antiques shops, bookstores, and one of the few surviving Irish bookbinders.

WORD OF MOUTH

"If you like an old-fashioned Irish pub that still has some sawdust on the floor, Sean's Bar on the Connaught (western) side of [Athlone] is worth a look and there is usually music of some sort over a holiday weekend. Apart from Clonmacnoise and Birr Castle, Athlone itself has a castle that houses a town museum."
—SeeDee

Ballinahown Irish Designer Craft Village. Make time for a stop at this craft village, home to two separate and distinctive stores, Core Crafted Design and Celtic Roots Studio. Both sell distinctive local crafts, ranging from bog-oak sculpture to honey as well as an outstanding choice of ceramics, jewelry, glasswork, and textiles. It's the last village in Westmeath as you travel to Clonmacnoise. Core is based in the Old Schoolhouse, and Celtic Roots Studio is next door. ☒ *N62, south from Athlone to Limerick* ☎ *090/643–0222* ⊕ *www.irishdesignercraftvillage.com.*

Bastion Gallery. An Aladdin's cave of a place in which to browse, the funky Bastion Gallery sells quirky gifts, books, and toys. It's no surprise to learn that Michael Jackson, on a recording trip to the Irish Midlands, spent two hours in the shop one evening in 2006. ☒ *6 Bastion St.* ☎ *090/649–4948* ⊕ *www.bastiongallery.com.*

John's Bookshop. Owned and run since 1997 by the affable John Donohue, this bookshop is exactly the way a secondhand bookstore should be: cluttered, disorganized, and heaving with rare and signed Irish-related and general books. ☒ *9 Main St.* ☎ *090/649–4151* ⊕ *www.johnsbookshop.com.*

SPORTS AND THE OUTDOORS

BICYCLING

Buckleys Cycles. A combination of unfrequented back roads, lakeside scenery, and flatlands makes this attractive biking country, so head to this place to rent a bike. ☒ *Kenna Centre, Dublin Rd.* ☎ *090/647–8989* ⊕ *www.buckleycycles.ie.*

BOATING

A boat trip reveals the importance of Athlone's strategic location on the River Shannon as well as the beauty of the region. *For the complete scoop on getting out on the water, see our special section on "Cruising on the Shannon."*

Viking Tours. For a unique way to cruise the Shannon, take a ride on the *Viking.* A replica of a Viking longboat, it travels upriver to nearby Lough Ree. Originally built in 1923, it's the longest-serving timber passenger boat in Ireland or the United Kingdom. The cost is €10; sailings take place March through October. Check the website for schedules. ☒ *Quayside* ☎ *086/262–1136* ⊕ *www.vikingtoursireland.ie.*

GOLF

Athlone Golf Club. An 18-hole parkland course, founded in 1892, Athlone is one of Ireland's oldest clubs. The course stretches along the shores of Lough Ree at Hodson Bay with stunning views of the Shannon. Tree-lined fairways, sandy greens, and undulating terrain make for an idyllic location that visitors hold in high regard. A new fertilizer program has improved the quality of the fairway and rough by producing a thicker sward—resulting in a much more playable course. The club hosts national and provincial competitions, and the resident head pro, Irish golfer Kevin Grealy, offers lessons to players of all abilities and specializes in tuition on the short game. ⊠ *Hodson Bay* ☎ *090/649–2073* ⊕ *www.athlonegolfclub.ie* ✉ *Fees: weekdays €22; weekends €25* ⌣ *18 holes, 6001 yards, par 72. Practice area, caddies, caddy carts, buggies, catering* ⊘ *Visitors: daily (some restrictions on Sun.).*

CLONMACNOISE

20 km (12 miles) south of Athlone, 93 km (58 miles) east of Galway.

Many ancient sites dot the River Shannon, but Clonmacnoise is early Christian Ireland's foremost monastic settlement and, like Chartres, a royal site. The monastery was founded by St. Ciarán between 543 and 549 at a location that was not as remote as it now appears to be: near the intersection of what were then two of Ireland's most vital routes—the Shannon River, running north–south, and the Eiscir Riada, running east–west. Like Glendalough, Celtic Ireland's other great monastic site, Clonmacnoise benefited from its isolation; surrounded by bog, it's accessible only via one road or via the Shannon.

GETTING HERE AND AROUND

It takes dedication to get here. As the easiest way to Clonmacnoise is by car, it can be crowded in high season, although many visitors also arrive on tour buses. Get here early—the main parking lot fills up quickly. The site is 20 minutes south of Athlone; take the N62 then turn off onto the narrow R444 in the direction of Shannonbridge. Birr is 35 minutes by car south along the R357 and then the N52. Parking here is free.

Clonmacnoise is well-nigh impossible to reach by public transport. If you don't have a car, it's best to book a trip with companies such as CIE Tours, Paddywagon, Shamrocker, or Midlands Tours. Or opt to board a boat in Athlone for a 90-minute journey to the jetty beside Clonmacnoise visitor center. Trips are run on the *Viking*, and advance booking is necessary. The round-trip is €15.

EXPLORING

Fodor's Choice ★ **Clonmacnoise.** Thanks to its location, this legendary monastery survived almost everything thrown at it, including raids by feuding Irish tribes, Vikings, and Normans. But when the English garrison arrived from Athlone in 1552, they ruthlessly reduced the site to ruin. Still, with a little imagination, you can picture life here in medieval times, when the nobles of Europe sent their sons to be educated by the local monks. The monastery was founded on an esker (natural gravel ridge) overlooking the Shannon and a marshy area known as the Callows, which today is protected habitat for the corncrake, a wading bird.

Numerous buildings and ruins remain. The small **cathedral** dates as far back as the 10th century but has additions from the 15th century. It was the burial place of kings of Connaught and of Tara, and of Rory O'Conor, the last high king of Ireland, who was buried here in 1198. The two round towers include **O'Rourke's Tower,** which was struck by lightning and subsequently rebuilt in the 12th century. There are eight **smaller churches,** the littlest of which is thought to be the burial place of St. Ciaran. Conservation stonework on the Nun's Church was completed during 2012. The church's chancel arch and doorway is a fine example of Romanesque architecture. The High Crosses have been moved into the visitor center to protect them from the elements (copies stand in their original places); the best preserved of these is the Cross of the Scriptures, also known as Flann's Cross. Some of the treasures and manuscripts originating from Clonmacnoise are now housed in Dublin, most at the National Museum.

Clonmacnoise has always been a prestigious burial place. Among the ancient stones are many other graves dating from the 17th to the mid-20th century. The whole place is time-burnished, though in midsummer it can be difficult to avoid the throngs of tourists. There are tours every hour during the summer season. ✉ *Near Shannonbridge, Clonmacnoise* ☎ *090/967–4195* ⊕ *www.heritageireland.ie* 🎫 *€6* ⊘ *Nov.–mid-Mar., daily 10–5:15; mid-Mar.–mid-May and mid-Sept.–Oct., daily 10–6; mid-May–mid-Sept., daily 9–6:30. Last admission 45 mins before closing.*

BANAGHER

31 km (19 miles) south of Clonmacnoise.

"Well, that beats Banagher!" This small Shannon-side town is best known in Ireland because of this common phrase, which dates from the 19th century when the town was the very worst example of a "rotten borough"—a corrupt electoral area controlled by the local landed gentry. In short, if something "beats Banagher" it's either pretty bad or rather extraordinary. Nowadays, Banagher is a lively marina town that is a popular base for water-sports enthusiasts. Charlotte Brontë (1816–55) famously spent her honeymoon here.

GETTING HERE AND AROUND

Midway between Athlone and Roscrea, Banagher is a small crossroads town. Athlone and Birr are both a 40-minute drive, and although the town is busy in summer, parking is generally not a problem. Kearns Transport operates daily services with links from Banagher to Birr (15 minutes), Tullamore (35 minutes), and Dublin (three hours).

ESSENTIALS

Transportation Contacts Kearns Transport ☎ *057/912–0124* ⊕ *www.kearnstransport.com.*

EXPLORING

The River Queen. If you happen to be in Banagher in summer, consider taking a cruise along the Shannon aboard *The River Queen,* an enclosed launch run by Silver Line Cruisers Ltd. that seats 54 passengers and

One of Ireland's greatest monastic settlements, Clonmacnoise was nearly leveled in places—including the Norman Castle seen above—but has other ruins that still inspire awe.

has a full bar on board. ✉ *The Marina* ☎ *057/915–1112* 🌐 *www.silverlinecruisers.com* 🎟 *€12* 🕒 *Cruises July and Aug., Sun. at 2.*

WHERE TO STAY

$ B&B/INN 🏨 **Charlotte's Way.** The sweet aroma of turf smoke percolates in the living room of this historic B&B, where the delightful Nicola Daly welcomes guests to her "home from home." **Pros:** history seeps from its pores; fresh eggs have never tasted better. **Cons:** nighttime activity limited. [$] *Rooms from: €70* ✉ *Kylebeg* ☎ *057/915–3864* 🌐 *www.charlottesway.com* 🛏 *5 rooms* 🍴 *Breakfast.*

NIGHTLIFE

J. J. Hough's. Travelers love Hough's, where on spring and summer nights there's usually a sing-along around the German piano. Note the walls decorated with business cards, testifying to the pub's popularity the world over. Side rooms lead to a beer garden with wooden chairs and tables. You can also join in card games with the locals. ✉ *Main St.* ☎ *057/915–1893.*

SPORTS AND THE OUTDOORS

Shannon Adventure Canoeing and Camping Holidays. Paddling a canoe is a nice alternative to a river cruise. This outfitter rents Canadian-class canoes, which allow you to explore the Shannon and other waterways on your own terms. Flexibility is offered and you can rent for a day, a weekend, or a week. ✉ *The Marina* ☎ *057/915–1411* 🌐 *www.discoverireland.ie* 🕒 *May–Oct., daily.*

CLOSE UP

The Boglands

Like the Eskimos with their 100 different words for snow, the natives of the Midlands retain a historic attachment to their vast boglands and will extol their virtues at length if prompted by a stranger.

In rural parts, turf (peat) still accounts for much of the winter fuel supply and locals can always be counted upon to discuss in great detail the quality and consistency of this uniquely native resource.

"Grand year for the turf" will generally indicate a sunny August—key drying time when the "sods" are cut and allowed to dry along the banks. Conversely, "wicked bad turf" denotes a typically soft Irish summer with poor drying.

Along country lanes, the sight of reeks of cut turf is still commonplace. If you're tired of using the weather as a conversational icebreaker, try turf as an alternative and virtually guaranteed discourse igniter.

No matter that from a distance an Irish peat bog looks like a flat, treeless piece of waterlogged land. A close-up view shows a much more exciting landscape.

Bogs support an extraordinary amount of wildlife, including larks and snipe, pale-blue dragonflies, and Greenland white-fronted geese. Amid the pools and lakes of the peat bog, amazing jewel-like wildflowers thrive, from purple bell heather to yellow bog asphodel, all alongside grasses, lichens, and mosses.

As you pass through the small town of Shannonbridge, 10 km (6 miles) south of Clonmacnoise, on either side of the road are vast stretches of chocolate-brown boglands and isolated industrial plants for processing the area's natural resource.

Bord na Móna, the same government agency that makes commercial use of other boglands, has jurisdiction over the area.

BIRR

12 km (7 miles) southeast of Banagher, 130 km (81 miles) west of Dublin.

Beautifully reminiscent of an English country town with its tree-lined malls and well-preserved houses, the heritage town of Birr has roots that date to the 6th century. Still, the mid-18th-century Georgian building boom sets the tone. Birr Castle is the pièce de résistance and an ideal place to while away a morning on a guided tour or spend the afternoon in an idyllic setting. For those who enjoy a riparian ramble, the Camcor River Walk opened in 2012, complementing the Active Age Park. Birr is also noted for its variety of festivals throughout the year, including the longest-running hot-air balloon championships in the world, held at the end of September.

GETTING HERE AND AROUND

Six main roads meet at Birr. Limerick is 90 minutes south on the N52 and then the N7, while Athlone is 30 minutes north on the N52. There may be traffic delays along the town's narrow central streets. Several paid lots and on-street metered spaces provide parking. Buses leave from Emmet Square for Dublin (3½ hours away) and west for Limerick (75 minutes).

ESSENTIALS

Birr Tourist Office. In keeping with the historic townscape character, it's worth calling in here to see what ranks as one of Ireland's most spectacular locations for a tourist office (open in the summer months only although the building is open all year round). Based in the ground floor of the offices of Birr Town Council (and a former convent) the building was designed by A.W. N. Pugin and completed by his son, Edward in the mid-19th century. Look into the library next door—the former chapel—which has retained the exquisite gothic-style stone mullioned stained-glass windows. Upstairs you will find a one-only facsimile of an early Christian illuminated manuscript, the Gospel Book of MacRegol, also known as the Book of Birr and the Rushworth Gospels, on permanent display. MacRegol was a scribe, bishop, and abbot in Birr. The original manuscript, which is now in Oxford's Bodleian Library, was produced around AD 800 and consists of 169 vellum folios or leaves. ⊠ *Wilmer Rd.* ☎ *057/912–0110* ⊕ *www.discoverireland.ie/ offaly* ⊙ *May–Sept. only.*

EXPLORING

FAMILY
Fodor's Choice
★

Birr Castle Demesne. Summer visitors can join a guided tour of one of Ireland's most elegant stately homes and peer behind the scenes of a previously closed-off world. The Gothic Revival castle (built around an earlier 17th-century castle that was damaged by fire in 1823) is still the home of the earls of Rosse. Castle tours, usually given by family members, bring you through the spectacular Gothic music saloon from 1810 (said by many to be the most beautiful room in Ireland), the library, the yellow drawing room, and reception rooms. Held only in the mornings in May, July, and August, the tours last one hour. Bear in mind that the castle has more than 100 rooms and the tour takes in just a small number of them.

The present earl and countess of Rosse continue the family tradition of making botanical expeditions for specimens of rare trees, plants, and shrubs to fill the demesne's 150 acres. The formal gardens contain the tallest box hedges in the world (at 32 feet) and vine-sheltered hornbeam allées. In spring, check out the wonderful display of flowering magnolias, cherries, crab apples, and naturalized narcissi; in autumn, the maples, chestnuts, and weeping beeches blaze red and gold. ■TIP→ If you are joining a house tour, book in advance; allow at least three hours to see everything in the demesne—there are 3,400 plants and 3,860 varieties of trees from 40 countries (including the largest gray poplar in the world). Remember to build in time to enjoy the astonishing tree house designed in the shape of a fairy-tale castle with round turrets and Gothic-style windows. It features a huge slide, tree decks lined by a rope bridge, and secret tunnels, and along with the adventure playground with its giant bouncing pillow, hobbit houses, scramble nets, and climbing rocks, it has proved a smash hit with families. There's a crafts shop, picnic area, and the Castle Courtyard Café serves daily lunch specials from 10 to 4. The grounds also contain **Ireland's Historic Science Centre,** an exhibition on astronomy, photography, and engineering housed in the stable block with the oldest surviving darkroom in the world. The giant (72-inch-long) reflecting telescope, built in 1845, was the largest in the world for 75 years. New interactive displays appeal to children by linking science with nature. ⊠ *Rosse Row* ☎ *057/912–0336* ⊕ *www.birrcastle.com* ⊠ *Castle tour and gardens €18; gardens €9.50* ⊙ *Gardens: Nov.–Mar., daily 10–4; Apr.–Oct., daily 9–6. Castle tour: May, July, and Aug., Mon.–Sat. 9:30–12:30; limited to 20; no children under 12.*

> **MACREGOL THE SCRIBE**
>
> A facsimile of an early Christian illuminated manuscript—the MacRegol Gospel—is on display in the restored Birr Library. MacRegol was a scribe, bishop, and abbot in Birr. The original manuscript, which is now in Oxford's Bodleian Library, was produced around AD 800 and consists of 169 vellum folios or leaves.

WHERE TO EAT AND STAY

$ ✕ **The Thatch Bar.** Imaginative food and a warm welcome await at this IRISH 300-year old thatched country pub and restaurant 2 km (1 mile) south of Birr, just off the N62 Roscrea road. Inexpensive meals are available at lunchtime (Friday–Sunday only) and early evening (4 to 7:30); later at night, the restaurant offers a choice of a five-course dinner menu or an à la carte menu. Pigeon and rabbit terrines, loin of pork and sirloin steaks with mushrooms in garlic sauce vie for diners' attention with more exotic dishes such as kangaroo and locally farmed ostrich. The pub is run by Des Connole who brings a long pedigree since he is the sixth generation of his family to own it. $ *Average main: €17* ⊠ *Military Rd., Crinkil* ☎ *057/912–0682* ⊕ *www.thethatchcrinkill.com* ⊙ *No lunch Mon.–Thurs.*

$ 🏨 **Dooly's Hotel.** Originally a coach house, this unpretentious country HOTEL hotel began life 275 years ago and has retained its old-style homeliness. **Pros:** huge rooms with space for moving around in; a handy Midlands stopover, if you're on your way to the west coast. **Cons:** the weekend disco in the nightclub goes on until the early hours, so bring your earplugs; stairs can be difficult for the disabled or elderly. $ *Rooms from: €99* ⊠ *Emmet Sq.* ☎ *057/912–0032* ⊕ *www.doolyshotel.ie* ⤳ *17 rooms* ⏐⊙⏐ *Breakfast.*

$ 🏨 **The Maltings.** Sheltered beneath the eaves of Birr Castle on a riverbank, this converted cut-stone storehouse—built to store malt for B&B/INN Guinness in 1810—is a good option for families and offers special FAMILY rates for children. **Pros:** idyllic location; attractive rooms; great breakfasts. **Cons:** showing signs of wear and tear; no dinner available, but there are several restaurants in the area. $ *Rooms from: €70* ⊠ *Castle St.* ☎ *057/912–1345* ⊕ *themaltingsbirr.com* ⤳ *10 rooms* ⏐⊙⏐ *Breakfast.*

ROSCREA

19 km (12 miles) south of Birr.

Fodor'sChoice Every corner you turn in this charming town will offer reminders of ★ its rich and sometimes turbulent past. Ancient castles, towers, and churches dot the skyline, proof of a heritage that dates to the 7th century. The road through town cuts right through the remains of a monastery founded by St. Cronan. It also passes the west facade of a 12th-century Romanesque church that now forms an entrance gate to a modern Catholic church. Above the structure's rounded doorway is a hood mold enclosing the figure of a bishop, probably St. Cronan.

GETTING HERE AND AROUND

Roscrea is on the main N7 road between Dublin and Cork, making it ideal as a stopover en route to the south. Limerick is one hour south on this route and roads from the town lead to all points of the Midlands compass. Cars park free on the main streets, and there is ample parking on side streets and in designated areas. The Bus Éireann Expressway from Dublin to Limerick stops in Roscrea, a 2½-hour journey. The Roscrea–Limerick leg of the route is 70 minutes. From Roscrea you can also catch a bus south to Cashel (2¼ hours) and Cork (3 hours) as well as north to Athlone (70 minutes) or as far northwest as Sligo, a journey of nearly 5 hours. The Irish Rail Dublin–Limerick train stops in Roscrea as well; the town is 90 minutes from each city.

EXPLORING

Roscrea Castle. In the very center of town is Roscrea Castle, a Norman fortress dating from 1314, given by King Richard II to the duke of Ormonde. Inside are vaulted rooms graced with tapestries and 16th-century furniture. A ticket to the castle gains entry to the adjacent **Damer House,** a superb example of an early-18th-century town house on the grand scale. It was built in 1725 within the curtain walls of the castle, at a time when homes were often constructed beside or attached to the strongholds they replaced. The house has a plain, symmetrical facade and a magnificent carved-pine staircase inside; on display are exhibits about local history. The Damer Art Gallery is on the second floor while on the third the Kelly Exhibition showcases furniture and farm implements donated from a local farmhouse. Hour-long guided tours are held in spring and summer. To get here, start with your back to St. Cronan's monastery, turn left, and then turn right on to Castle Street. Your ticket also includes entry to the restored **Black Mills** in Church Street, a small museum with local artifacts, of which the star attraction is St. Cronan's High Cross. ⊠ *Castle St.* ☎ *0505/21850* ⊕ *www. heritageireland.ie* ⬚ *€4* ☉ *Apr.–Sept., daily 10–5.*

THE SOUTHEAST

Including Counties Carlow, Kilkenny,
Tipperary, Waterford, and Wexford

WELCOME TO THE SOUTHEAST

TOP REASONS TO GO

★ **Sacred Ardmore:** St. Declan founded Ireland's first Christian settlement near this beautifully situated fishing village on the Waterford coast.

★ **Kilkenny, Ireland's Medieval Capital:** With its famous 14th-century "witch," Petronilla, *Camelot*-worthy Black Abbey, and fairy-tale Kilkenny Castle, the city still conjures up the days of knights and damsels.

★ **Pretty-as-a-postcard Lismore:** Presided over by the neo-baronial castle of the Dukes of Devonshire, this storybook village has attracted visitors ranging from Sir Walter Raleigh to Fred Astaire.

★ **Cashel of the Kings:** Ireland's "Rock of Ages," this spectacular 200-foot-tall rock bluff was the ancient seat of the Kings of Munster.

★ **Wexford and Waterford:** Big-city lights shine brightest here, thanks to such attractions as the famed Wexford Opera Festival and the reborn Waterford Crystal factory and visitor center.

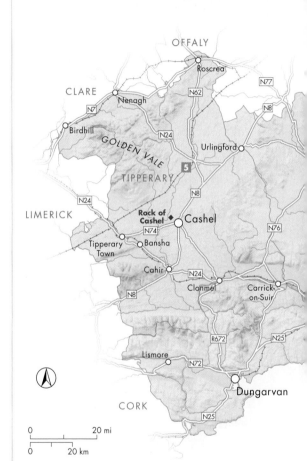

1 Kilkenny City. Creativity is evident in every aspect of this town, from its medieval stonework to its array of modern and traditional craft and design found in galleries and studios. Many festivals and events are held here year-round.

2 Southeast Inlands.
Redolent of the Middle Ages, this once-upon-a-time-ified region is home to some thrilling medieval sights, including Leighlinbridge's Black Castle, the tiny village of Old Leighlin, and Jerpoint Abbey, the most famous Cistercian ruins in Ireland.

4 Southeast Coast.
Combining the best of Ireland's climate with some wonderful sand-and-sea settings, this coastal headland is noted for quaint villages like Ardmore, Kilmore Quay and Ballyhack, the bustling and historic city of Waterford, and beachfront locations that attract Dubliners by the droves.

GETTING ORIENTED

Set around Tipperary—Ireland's largest inland county—the Southeast is a vast region that stretches from the town of Carlow near the border of County Wicklow in the north to Ardmore near the border of County Cork in the south. Although main towns can be packed with camera-wielding tourists, you can easily escape the tour buses thanks to endless expanses of tranquil countryside.

3 Wexford Town. The warm welcome, the ancient Viking streets, and the tiny, atmospheric Theatre Royal add to the cultural pleasures as this proud town puts on its Sunday best for the Wexford Opera Festival, a weeklong binge of arias and charm held every October.

5 County Tipperary and Around. The greatest group of monastic ruins in Ireland—the Rock of Cashel—presides over miles of the idyllic region known as the Golden Vale. There are some relentlessly romantic sights, like the 19th-century village of Lismore plus the dramatic beauty of Lough Derg.

Updated by
Anto Howard

Going to Ireland for the sunshine might sound like a joke, but not if you head to the golden beaches and blue surf of the Southeast. Receiving almost double the rays found anywhere else, the shore resorts buzz with activity from May to October. The Irish like to label their regions, and "Ireland's Sunny Southeast" is the tag they've applied to counties Wexford, Carlow, Kilkenny, Tipperary, and Waterford. The moniker is by no means merely fanciful: the weather station on the coast at Rosslare reports that this region receives more hours of sunshine than any other part of the country. Little wonder the outdoors-loving Irish have made the Southeast's coast a popular warm-weather vacation destination.

Thousands of families take their annual summer holidays here, where picnics and barbecues—often a rain-washed fantasy elsewhere in Ireland—are a golden reality.

The entire Southeast is rich with natural beauty—not the rugged and wild wonders found to the north and west, but a coast that alternates between long, sandy beaches and rocky bays backed by low cliffs, and an inland landscape of fertile river valleys and lush, undulating pastureland. The landscape of the region is diverse, the appeal universal: you'll find seaside fishing villages with thatched cottages, and Tipperary's verdant, picturesque Golden Vale. The region doesn't lack for culture, either. History-rich Ardmore, Carlow Town, the cities of Kilkenny and Waterford, and Wexford Town have retained traces of their successive waves of invaders—Celt, Viking, and Norman.

The most important of these destinations is Kilkenny City, a major ecclesiastic and political center until the 17th century and now a lively market town. Its streets still hold remnants from medieval times—most notably St. Canice's Cathedral—and a magnificent 12th-century castle that received a sumptuous Victorian makeover. Wexford's narrow streets are built on one side of a wide estuary, giving it a delightful maritime air. Waterford, although less immediately attractive than Wexford, is also built at the confluence of two of the region's rivers, the Suir and the Barrow. It offers a rich selection of Viking and Norman remains, some attractive Georgian buildings, and the visitor center and shop at the famed Waterford Glass Factory (which, a few years ago, stopped manufacturing here).

Deeper into the countryside, rustic charms beckon. The road between Rosslare and Ballyhack passes through quiet, atypical, flat countryside dotted with thatched cottages. In the far southwest of County Waterford, near the Cork border, Ardmore presents early Christian ruins on an exposed headland, while, in the wooded splendor of the Blackwater Valley, the tiny cathedral town of Lismore has a hauntingly beautiful fairy-tale castle.

THE SOUTHEAST PLANNER

WHEN TO GO

As well as having some of the richest land in the country, the Southeast is the envy of all Ireland for that most elusive element—sunshine. The region is also one of the driest in Ireland, which is saying something in a country where seldom do more than three days pass without some rain. Compared with an average of 80 inches on parts of the west coast, the Southeast gets as little as 40 inches of rainfall per year, varying from the finest light drizzle (a soft day, thank goodness!) to full-blown downpours.

FESTIVALS AND EVENTS

With practically every hamlet and village across the country glorying in its own festival (excuse for keeping pubs open later), the Southeast delivers some of Ireland's most popular gatherings. Check with the tourist boards for listings and dates of all events, big and small.

JUNE **Eigse Arts Festival.** Carlow's Eigse Arts Festival is a 10-day celebration of visual arts held every June. ⊠ *Waterford City, Co. Waterford* ☎ *059/917–2439* ⊕ *www.eigsecarlow.ie.*

AUGUST **Kilkenny Arts Festival.** Every August, Kilkenny becomes the focus for Ireland's culture vultures when the Kilkenny Arts Festival takes over the city for about two weeks. Street theater, elaborate parades, and even a rock concert set the mood. ⊠ *Waterford City, Co. Waterford* ☎ *056/775–1704* ⊕ *www.kilkennyarts.ie.*

Spraoi. Every August, the Spraoi arts festival presents an exuberant display of music, theater, and other entertainment in Waterford City. You'll find it around the city's extensive pedestrian areas. ⊠ *Waterford City, Co. Waterford* ⊕ *www.spraoi.com.*

OCTOBER **Wexford Opera Festival.** From late October to early November, the two-week-long Wexford Opera Festival is the biggest social and artistic event in the entire Southeast. From mid-September until the final curtain comes down, Wexford becomes home to a colorful cast of international singers, designers, and musicians as they prepare for the annual staging of three grand operas at the Wexford Opera House. Along with an ever-expanding offering of more populist fare performed in small venues and pubs, the festival supplies a feast of concerts and recitals that start at 11 am and continue until midnight. The bad news: nearly every single bed within miles is booked during the festival, and usually for months ahead of time. ⊠ *Wexford Town, Co. Wexford* ⊕ *www.wexfordopera.com.*

Wexford Fringe Festival. Running alongside the opera festival from late October to early November, the chaotic and theatrical Wexford Fringe Festival is an eclectic mix of theater, literature, music, dance, and street events. ⊠ *Wexford Town, Co. Wexford* ⊕ *www.wexfordfringe.ie.*

PLANNING YOUR TIME

IF YOU HAVE THREE DAYS

Distances are not great, but if you are here for a short stay—three days or fewer—you might want to base yourself in one of the region's cities or larger towns: Waterford, Kilkenny, or Wexford. All three are historic locations with plenty of places of cultural and historical interest accessible on foot. They are also growing shopping destinations. Day trips from Waterford and Wexford could include idyllic coastal villages like Ardmore, Dunmore East, and Kilmore Quay. From Kilkenny and Waterford the mountains, glens, and lakes of Tipperary are only a short drive away. Spend a night at a coastal hotel like the Cliff House in Ardmore or the country manor of Ballyduff House in Thomastown.

If you have more time in the region—say three to five days—you might want to drive the whole of the scenic coast from Wexford down around spectacular Hook Head to Waterford and on to the winding road to Ardmore and Dungarvan. You want to take your time, avoid the motorway, and stop off at any village or watering hole that takes your fancy. You'll still have plenty of time for a detour north into Tipperary along some beautiful mountain back roads and on to the historic town of Cashel to see the legendary Rock. From there, head northwest for a touch of water sports on Lough Derg or take the short, scenic hop back to medieval Kilkenny City.

GETTING HERE AND AROUND

AIR TRAVEL

Flybe operates regular flights to Manchester and Birmingham in the United Kingdom, with connections to other major U.K. and European destinations. Waterford Regional Airport is on the Waterford–Ballymacaw road in Killowen. Waterford City is less than 10 km (6 miles) from the airport. A hackney cab from the airport into Waterford City costs approximately €18.

Carrier Flybe ⊕ *www.flybe.com.*

Airport Information Waterford Airport ⊕ *www.waterfordairport.ie.*

BOAT AND FERRY TRAVEL

If you are coming to Ireland from England or the Continent, chances are you'll end up on a ferry bound for Rosslare Harbour, 19 km (12 miles) south of Wexford, one of Ireland's busiest ferry ports. There are two main companies that service Rosslare. Irish Ferries connects Rosslare to Pembroke, Wales (four hours), and France's Cherbourg and Roscoff.

Stena Line sails directly between Rosslare Ferryport and Fishguard, Wales (three hours). They both have small information kiosks in the ultramodern terminal, which also has lockers and a sprawling waiting room. Passage East Car Ferry is a short cut across the Suir Estuary, connecting Ballyhack in Wexford with Passage East in Waterford.

You can purchase ferry tickets at the terminal, but try to reserve a space in advance through the companies' Cork or Dublin office to avoid the frequent sellouts, particularly in summer and any time the Irish soccer team is playing in a major tournament abroad.

Reservations are a must if you're traveling by car or motorcycle because onboard parking space is at a premium. Eurail Pass holders get a 30% discount on ferries from France to Ireland. Departure times vary from season to season, so call ahead.

Boat and Ferry Information Irish Ferries ⊕ *www.irishferries.com.* **Passage East Ferry Company** ⊕ *www.passageferry.ie.* **Stena Line** ⊕ *www.stenaline.ie.*

BUS TRAVEL

Bus Éireann runs frequent buses between Waterford and Dublin, Limerick, Cork, and Rosslare. J. J. Kavanagh & Sons runs daily buses from Dublin to Carlow, Waterford, and Kilkenny.

Bus Information Bus Éireann ⊕ *www.buseireann.ie.* **J.J. Kavanagh & Sons** ⊕ *www.jjkavanagh.ie.*

CAR TRAVEL

With recently completed highways to Waterford and Kilkenny, a car is the best option for covering ground quickly and easily. Waterford City, the regional capital, is easily accessible from all parts of Ireland.

From Dublin, take M7 southwest, change to the M9, and continue along as it bypasses Carlow Town and Thomastown until it end in Waterford. N25 travels east–west through Waterford City, connecting it with Cork in the west and Wexford Town in the east. From Limerick and Tipperary Town, N24 stretches southeast until it, too, ends in Waterford City.

For the most part, the main roads in the Southeast are of good quality and are free of congestion. Side roads are generally narrow and twisting, and you should keep an eye out for farm machinery and animals on country roads.

TAXI TRAVEL

Taxis at Waterford Regional Airport connect to the major cities in the region; to Waterford City costs about €18; to Kilkenny, about €80; and to Wexford, roughly €85. It costs €4.10 to hire a taxi on the street (€4.45 by night) in the larger towns: add €2 to book by phone, and €1.03 per kilometer or part of a kilometer for the first 15 km (9 miles). Reputable companies include Celtic Cabs in Wexford, Taxis Waterford, and Kilkenny Taxi.

Taxi Companies Celtic Cabs ☎ *053/9142434* ⊕ *www.jackswalkingtours. com.* **Taxis Waterford** ⊕ *www.taxiswaterford.com.* **Kilkenny Taxi** ⊕ *www. kilkennytaxi.com.*

TRAIN TRAVEL

Waterford City is linked by daily Irish Rail service to Dublin, with trains making stops at Thomastown, Kilkenny, Bagenalstown, and Carlow Town. The daily train between Waterford City and Limerick makes stops at Carrick-on-Suir, Clonmel, Cahir, and Tipperary Town. The train between Rosslare and Waterford City runs twice daily.

Train Information Irish Rail ⊕ *www.irishrail.ie.* **MacDonagh Station** ⊠ *St. John's St., Kilkenny, Co. Kilkenny.* **O'Hanrahan Station** ⊠ *Redmond Pl., Wexford, Co. Wexford.* **Plunkett Station** ⊠ *Dock Rd., Waterford City, Co. Waterford.*

For more information on getting here and around, see Travel Smart Ireland.

RESTAURANTS

Food is usually prepared in a simple, country-house style, though pleasant surprises abound. A number of ambitious Irish chefs are at work in the Southeast's restaurants and hotels, and at newer joints with inventive offerings that offer a great value. The best of the region's cuisine rests on modern, international interpretations of classic Irish dishes. Leading lights in the area include chef Kevin Dundon at Dunbrody Country House, Paul Flynn of the Tannery, and Martjin Kajuiter at the Michelin-starred Cliff House in Ardmore.

Other than its fabled strawberries, the Southeast is probably best known for its rich seafood, especially Wexford mussels, crabs, and locally caught salmon. Kilmore Quay, noted for lobster and deep-sea fishing, hosts an annual Seafood Festival the second week of July. Many restaurants serve local lamb, beef, and game in season.

HOTELS

Festivals, the good weather, and commerce make the Southeast popular, so plan way ahead for a stay in any of the main towns (and in many country manors, which usually have fewer than six bedrooms and fill up fast). As always, the local tourist offices can offer assistance if you arrive without reservations. *Hotel reviews have been shortened. For full information, visit Fodors.com.*

WHAT IT COSTS IN EUROS				
	$	$$	$$$	$$$$
Restaurants	under €19	€19–€24	€25–€32	over €32
Hotels	under €120	€120–€170	€171–€210	over €210

Restaurant prices are the average cost of a main course at dinner or, if dinner is not served, at lunch. Hotel prices are the lowest cost of a standard double room in high season.

VISITOR INFORMATION

Eight tourist information offices of varying quality in the Southeast are open all year. They are in Carlow Town, Dungarvan, Gorey, Kilkenny, Lismore, Waterford City, Tramore, and Wexford Town. Another four TIOs are open seasonally: Cahir (April–October); Cashel (April–September); Rosslare (April–September); and Tipperary Town (May–October). If traveling extensively by public transportation, be sure to load up on information (schedules, the best taxi companies, etc.) upon arriving at the train and bus stations in Kilkenny City, Wexford Town, and Waterford City.

TOURS

Burtchaell Tours of Waterford City. The knowledgeable and delightful Jack Burtchaell leads a Waterford City walk daily at noon and 2 pm from March through September. Tours depart from the Granville Hotel. ☎ *051/873–711* ⊕ *www.jackswalkingtours.com.*

A Rural Experience. This outfit runs day excursions and extended tours all over the Southeast, and the County Kilkenny tour is especially popular. ☎ *056/772–7590* ⊕ *www.aruralexperience.com.*

Tynan Tours of Kilkenny City. These walking tours of Kilkenny take place daily April through October, and Tuesday through Saturday, November to March. ☎ *087/265–1745* ⊕ *www.kilkennywalkingtours.ie.*

Wexford Walking Tours. Walking tours of historic Wexford Town can be prebooked for groups through town tourist offices. ☎ *086/107-9497* ✎ *mcdonalds05@eircom.net.*

TUNE IN TO THE SOUTHEAST

As you'll no doubt spend a good portion of your time behind the wheel during your travels, tune in to Irish radio for another angle on the country. If you want to feel the true pulse of the nation, check out any of RTÉ Radio 1's morning and afternoon shows. In a country still reeling from the government mismanagement and social damage of the great economic crash, the radio has become Ireland's modern confessional and a serious insight into what makes the Irish tick. Waterford Local Radio (95.1/97.5 FM) and South East Radio (95.6/96.4 FM) are the popular options around Waterford and Wexford respectively.

5

KILKENNY CITY

101 km (63 miles) southwest of Dublin.

Dubbed "Ireland's Medieval Capital" by its tourist board, and also called "the Oasis of Ireland" for its many pubs and watering holes, Kilkenny is one of the country's most alluring destinations. It demands to be explored by foot or bicycle, thanks to its easily circumnavigated town center, a 900-year-old Norman citadel that is now a lovely place of Georgian streets and Tudor stone houses. The city (population 24,500) is impressively preserved and attractively situated on the River Nore, which forms the moat of the magnificently restored Kilkenny Castle. In the 6th century, St. Canice (known as "the builder of churches") established a large monastic school here. The town's name reflects Canice's central role: Kil Cainneach means "Church of Canice." Kilkenny did not take on its medieval look for another 400 years, when the Anglo-Normans fortified the city with a castle, gates, and a brawny wall. Kilkenny City's central location means that it's not too far from anywhere else in Ireland.

GETTING HERE AND AROUND

From Dublin, take the N7/M7 to the M9 and exit at junction 8 for the N10 to Kilkenny. These are major motorways, so the 101-km (62-mile) trip takes only an hour and a half. Cork is a two-hour drive, while Waterford City is only a 40-minute hop. There is plenty of paid parking around the town.

The bus station is a bit down from the train station on St. John's Street, and Bus Éireann runs eight buses a day from Dublin. The two-hour, 10-minute trip costs €12.82 one-way, €1 round-trip. Three buses a day travel from Cork, and that three-hour trip costs €19.48 one-way, €32.78 round-trip. J. J. Kavanagh & Sons runs five buses a day from Dublin city center and airport. The three-hour journey costs €8 one-way, €15 round-trip.

MacDonagh Station, the city train station, is a short walk from the city center at the top of St. John's Street. The station is on the Dublin–Waterford City line, which also serves Athy, Carlow, Bagenalstown, and Thomastown. Irish Rail runs six trains a day from Dublin, and the trip takes about one hour, 45 minutes and costs €15.99 each way if you book online. There is no direct train from Cork, but five trains a day arrive from Newbridge, a nearly five-hour journey that costs a ridiculous €56.

ESSENTIALS

Visitor Information Kilkenny Tourist Office ⊠ *Shee Alms House, Rose Inn St.* ☎ *056/775–1500* ⊕ *www.ireland.com/destinations/republic-of-ireland/kilkenny.*

EXPLORING

Kilkenny's city center is small, and despite the large number of historic sights and picturesque streets—in particular, Butter Slip and High Street—you can easily cover it in less than three hours. One of the most pleasant cities south of Dublin (and one of its most sports-minded—from July to September practically the only topic of conversation is the fate of the city's team at the All-Ireland Hurling Championship), Kilkenny City has become in recent years something of a haven for artists and craft workers seeking an escape from Dublin. At such venues as the Kilkenny Design Centre, you can find an array of quality Irish crafts.

The city has more than 60 pubs, many of them on Parliament and High streets, which also support a lively music scene. Many of the town's pubs and shops have old-fashioned, highly individualized, brightly painted facades, created as part of the town's 1980s revival of this Victorian tradition. So after taking in Kilkenny Castle and the Riverfront Canal Walk—an overgrown pathway that meanders along the castle grounds—mosey down High and Kieran streets. These parallel avenues, considered the historic center of Kilkenny, are connected by a series of horse cart–wide lanes and are fronted with some of the city's

While studded with plenty of historic sights, Kilkenny also welcomes the traveler with traditional and "characterful" pubs.

best-preserved pubs and Victorian flats. Be sure to look up over the existing modern storefronts to catch a glimpse of how the city looked in years past, as many of the buildings still have second-floor facades reflecting historic decorative styles.

Kilkenny holds a special place in the history of Anglo-Irish relations. The infamous 1366 Statutes of Kilkenny, intended to strengthen English authority in Ireland by keeping the heirs of the Anglo-Norman invaders from assimilating into the Irish way of life, was an attempt at apartheid. Intermarriage became a crime punishable by death, and the native Irish were forced to live outside the walls in shantytowns.

By the early 17th century, Irish Catholics began to chafe under such repression; they tried to bring about reforms with the Confederation of Kilkenny, which governed Ireland from 1642 to 1648, with Kilkenny as the capital. Pope Innocent X sent money and arms. Cromwell responded in 1650 by overrunning the town and sacking the cathedral, which he then used as a stable for his horses—thus marking the end of Kilkenny's "Golden Age." However, the succeeding centuries were not uneventful. In 1798 the city was placed under martial law due to a revolt by the United Irishmen; in 1904 King Edward VII paid a visit; and in 1923, at the height of Ireland's civil war, forces opposed to a government peace deal with the British briefly occupied Kilkenny Castle.

TOP ATTRACTIONS

Black Abbey. With a stained-glass, carved-stone interior that seems right out of the musical *Camelot*, the 13th-century Black Abbey is one of the most evocative and beautiful Irish medieval structures. Note the famous 1340 five-gabled Rosary Window, an entire wall agleam with ruby and

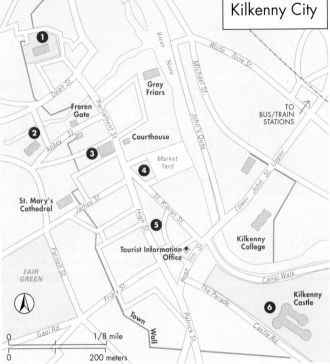

Kilkenny City

sapphire glass, depicting the life of Christ. Home to a Dominican order of monks since 1225, the abbey was restored as a church by the order, whose black capes gave the abbey its name. Interestingly, it's also one of the few medieval churches still owned by the Roman Catholic Church, as most of the oldest churches in Ireland were built by the Normans and reverted to the Church of Ireland (Anglican) when the English turned to Protestantism. Nearby is the Black Freren Gate (14th century), the last remaining gateway to the medieval city. ⊠ *South of St. Canice's Cathedral* ☎ *056/772–1279* ⊒ *Free* ☉ *Daily 9–1 and 2–6.*

Fodor's Choice **Kilkenny Castle.** Built in 1172 and set amid 50 acres of rolling lawns
★ beside the River Nore, Ireland's most recognizable castle is a bewitching marriage of Gothic and Victorian styles. It conjures images of knights and damsels, dukes and duchesses. For more than 500 years, beginning in 1391, Kilkenny Castle served as the seat of one of the more powerful clans in Irish history, the Butler family, members of which were later designated earls and dukes of Ormonde. Around 1820, William Robert, son of the first marquess of Ormonde, overhauled the castle to make it a wonderland in the Victorian Feudal Revival style. In 1859, John Pollen was called in to redo the aptly named Long Gallery—a refined, airy hall with dazzling green walls hung with a vast collection of family portraits and frayed tapestries, and a marvelously decorated

ceiling, replete with oak beams carved with Celtic lacework and brilliantly painted animal heads. The main staircase was also redone in the mid-1800s to become a showpiece of Ruskinian Gothic.

The castle's Butler Gallery, formerly the servants quarters, houses a superb collection of Irish modern art, including examples by Nathaniel Hone, Jack B. Yeats, Sir John Lavery, Louis Le Brocquy, and James Turrell. Be sure to stroll the grounds, and the Celtic-cross-shaped rose garden, after a spot of tea in the old Victorian kitchen. ⊠ *The Parade* ☎ *056/772–1450* ⊕ *www.kilkennycastle.ie* ⊠ *Castle tour €6* ☉ *Apr., May, and Sept., daily 9:30–5:30; June–Aug., daily 9–5:30; Oct.–Feb., daily 9:30–4:30; Mar., daily 9:30–5.*

Kyteler's Inn. The oldest inn in town, Kyteler's is notorious as the place where Dame Alice Le Kyteler, a member of a wealthy banking family and an alleged witch and "brothel keeper," was accused in 1324 of poisoning her four husbands. So, at least, said the enemies of this apparently very merry widow. The restaurant retains its medieval aura, thanks to its 14th-century stonework and exposed beams down in the cellar, built up around Kieran's Well, which predates the house itself. Food and drink in this popular pub are as simple and plentiful as they would have been in Dame Alice's day—but minus her extra ingredients. ⊠ *Kieran St.* ☎ *056/772–1064* ⊕ *www.kytelersinn.ie.*

Fodor's Choice ★ **St. Canice's Cathedral.** In spite of Cromwell's defacements, this is still one of the finest cathedrals in Ireland and the country's second-largest medieval church, after St. Patrick's Cathedral in Dublin. Behind the massive walls of this 13th-century structure (restored in 1866) is an exuberant Gothic interior, given a somber grandeur by the extensive use of a locally quarried black marble. Many of the memorials and tombstone effigies represent distinguished descendants of the Normans, some depicted in full suits of armor. Look for a female effigy in the south aisle wearing the old Irish, or Kinsale, cloak; a 12th-century black-marble font at the southwest end of the nave; and St. Ciaran's Chair in the north transept, also made of black marble, with 13th-century sculptures on the arms.

In recent years, St. Canice's has achieved notoriety as the resting place of President Obama's great-great-great uncle, the Bishop of Ossory. The biggest attraction on the grounds is the 102-foot-high round tower, which was built in 847 by King O'Carroll of Ossory; if you have the energy, climb the tower's 167 steps for the tremendous 360-degree view from the top, as well as for the thrill of mounting 102 steps on makeshift wooden stairs. Next door is St. Canice's Library, containing some 3,000 16th- and 17th-century volumes. ⊠ *Dean St.* ☎ *056/776–4971* ⊕ *www. stcanicescathedral.com* ⊠ *Cathedral €4, tower €3, both €6* ☉ *Cathedral June–Aug., Mon.–Sat. 9–6, Sun. 2–6; Apr., May, and Sept., Mon.–Sat. 10–1 and 2–5, Sun. 2–5; Oct.–Mar., Mon.–Sat. 10–1 and 2–4, Sun. 2–4. Tower access depends on weather.*

WORTH NOTING

Rothe House. There's a feeling of time travel as you step off the busy main street and into one of Ireland's finest examples of a Tudor-era merchant's house. Built by John Rothe between 1594 and 1610, this medieval complex with stone-wall courtyards (one of which houses a medieval well) is owned by the Kilkenny Archaeological Society and houses a collection of Bronze Age artifacts, ogham stones (carved with an early Celtic alphabet), and period costumes. The Burgage Garden recreates, down to the plant types themselves, a typical 17th-century Irish merchant's garden. There's also a genealogical research facility to help you trace your ancestry. ✉ *Parliament St.* ☎ *056/772–2893* 🌐 *www.rothehouse.com* 🎟 *€5, garden only €2* 🕓 *Apr.–Oct., Mon.–Sat. 10:30–5, Sun. 3–5; Nov.–Mar., Mon.–Sat. 10:30–4:30.*

Tholsel. With its distinctive clock tower and grand entrance portico, this limestone-marble building on Parliament Street stands on the site of the execution of poor Petronilla, the "witch" burned at the stake in the 14th century in lieu of her mistress, Dame Alice Le Kyteler. Built in 1761, burned down in 1985, and then completely rebuilt, Tholsel now houses the city's municipal archives. Adjacent to the Tholsel is Alice's Castle, a town jail rather grandly fitted out in 18th-century architectural ornamentation. ✉ *Parliament St., Kilkenny.*

WHERE TO EAT

$$$ FRENCH Fodor's Choice ★

🍴 **Campagne.** When the former head chef of Dublin's celebrated Chapter One returns home and opens a restaurant, people take notice, and the awards start flooding in. Garrett Byrne chose an industrial site beside the disused railway yard and transformed it into a stylish, uncluttered space with a beautiful green canopy that adds a touch of the French bistro. The oak flooring and curved banquettes contrast with the abstract splashes of bright colors on the walls. The menu is the real work of art, with common French themes toyed with and expanded. The monkfish with jerusalem artichoke, suckling pig croquette, cabbage, and mustard sauce is just about perfect. For something lighter, try the Hegarty's cheese soufflé, with marinated beetroot and walnuts. The wine list is long and luxurious. [$] *Average main: €28* ✉ *5 The Arches, Gashouse La.* ☎ *056/777–2858* 🌐 *www.campagne.ie* 🕓 *Closed Mon. No dinner Sun. No lunch Tues.–Thurs.*

$ IRISH Fodor's Choice ★

🍴 **Langton's.** When it comes to restaurants and pubs, this is Kilkenny Central. A landmark since the 1940s, Langton's is a labyrinth of interconnected bars and eateries. Most of the seating areas, all with open fires, have different personalities—from the leather-upholstered gentlemen's club in the Horseshoe Bar to an attempt at art deco in the spacious dining room. Up front is one of Ireland's most famous "eating pubs," often crammed with punters to the rafters of its low ceiling. For more tranquil environs, head out back, where you can chow down in a neo-Gothic garden framed by a stretch of the old city walls. The main restaurant offers well-prepared traditional dishes, including (of course) Irish stew and a mean cod in beer batter. There are 30 art-deco-style hotel rooms upstairs. [$] *Average main: €17* ✉ *69 John St.* ☎ *056/776–5133* 🌐 *www.langtons.ie.*

$$ ITALIAN

🍴 **Ristorante Rinuccini.** A warm glow emanates from this excellent Italian restaurant as you descend the steps into its dining room in the basement of a Georgian town house. Owner-chef Antonio Cavaliere is intensely involved in preparing such luscious pasta dishes as *rigatoni all' arrabbiata* (tubes of homemade egg pasta in a fresh tomato sauce with chili

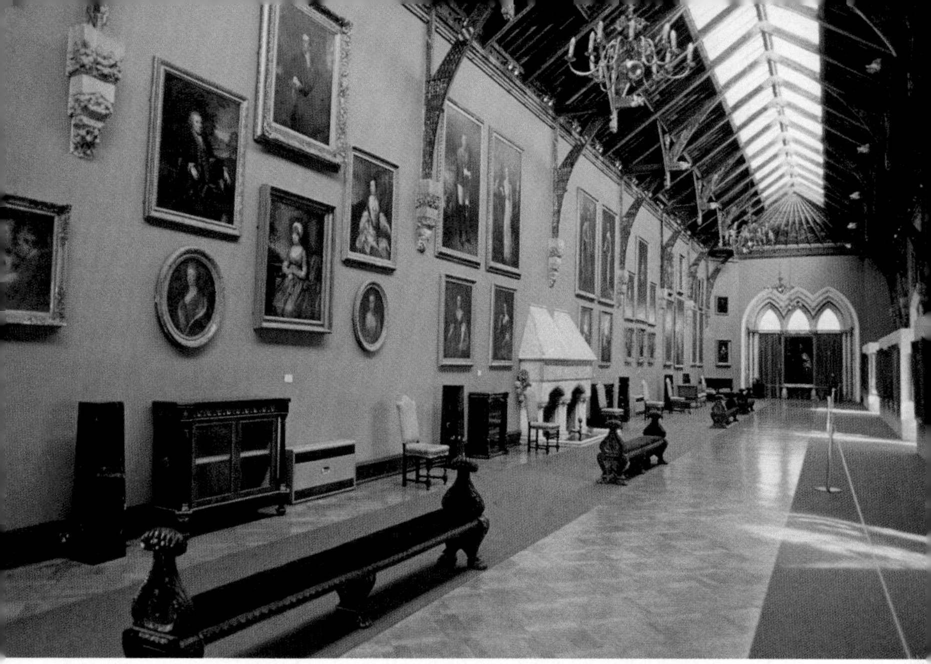

Extending 150 feet, Kilkenny Castle's Long Gallery is lined with family portraits and has a hammer-beam ceiling supported on carved stone corbels with gilded animal and bird heads on the crossbeams.

and garlic). Other specialties, such as Silver Hill Irish Duckling in a fresh-orange-juice-and-Aurum-liquor sauce, go particularly well with Antonio's garlic roasted potatoes—highly recommended as a side dish. A splendid all-Italian wine list complements the menu, and there's a host of delicious homemade desserts. This is one of the best Italian options in town. The restaurant accommodates overnight guests in the town house above. [$] *Average main: €24* ✉ *1 The Parade, across from Kilkenny Castle* ☎ *056/776–1575* 🌐 *www.rinuccini.com* ✍ *Reservations essential.*

WHERE TO STAY

$$ HOTEL 🏨 **Butler House.** Who needs Kilkenny Castle when you can stay at the Dowager Duchess of Ormonde's 18th-century town house, a charming piece of Georgian grandeur with an ivy-covered three-bay facade and an elegant walled garden? **Pros:** live in a castle for a few days; serene walled garden; breakfast in the old stables of Kilkenny Castle. **Cons:** books up quickly; no restaurant or bar; some rooms a lot smaller than others. [$] *Rooms from: €155* ✉ *16 Patrick St.* ☎ *056/776–5707* 🌐 *www.butler.ie* 🛏 *12 rooms, 1 suite* 🍴 *Breakfast.*

$ HOTEL 🏨 **Zuni Townhouse and Restaurant.** This popular family-owned hotel in the center of Kilkenny boasts the gloss of a big-city boutique lodging but not the icy-cool reception you get in some fashionable joints. **Pros:** in the heart of the city; family owned and run; tasty eatery. **Cons:** books up quickly; business clientele can stifle atmosphere; can get noisy outside on weekends. [$] *Rooms from: €110* ✉ *26 Patrick St.* ☎ *056/772–3999* 🌐 *www.zuni.ie* 🛏 *13 rooms* 🍴 *Breakfast.*

NIGHTLIFE AND THE ARTS

John Cleere's. If you're craving a pint, you have a choice of pubs along Parliament and High streets. John Cleere's is the best in town for a mix of live traditional music, poetry readings, and theatrical plays. ⊠ *22 Parliament St.* ☎ *056/776–2573.*

Pumphouse. Offering traditional music during the week, the Pumphouse also features live rock and pop on weekends. ⊠ *26–28 Parliament St.* ☎ *056/776–3924* ⊕ *www.pumphousekilkenny.ie.*

Fodor's Choice
★ **Tynan's Bridge House.** Set on one of Kilkenny's famous "slips," Tynan's Bridge House was first used as an exercise run for dray horses. Inside, you can guess that the pub is more than 200 years old from all the gas lamps, silver tankards, and historic teapots on display. Behind the horseshoe-shaped bar, you'll find antiquities from its time as a grocery and pharmacy, but it's best known these days for its Guinness and good conversation. ⊠ *2 Horseleap Slip* ☎ *056/772–1291.*

Watergate Theatre. With a roster of operas, plays, concerts, and comedy shows, the Watergate hosts affordable local, national, and international productions. ⊠ *Parliament St.* ☎ *056/776–1674* ⊕ *www.watergatetheatre.com.*

SPORTS AND THE OUTDOORS

HURLING

Kilkenny GAA Grounds. The 1366 Statutes of Kilkenny expressly forbade the ancient Irish game of hurling. No matter: today, Kilkenny is considered one of the great hurling counties. Like its neighbor and archenemy, Wexford, Kilkenny has a long history of success in hurling, and as the annual All-Ireland Hurling Championships draws to its final stages during July and August, interest in the county's team runs to fever pitch. Catch the home team at matches held at Kilkenny GAA Grounds. ⊠ *Nowlan Park* ☎ *056/776–5122* ⊕ *www.kilkennygaa.ie.*

SHOPPING

Kilkenny is a byword for attractive, original crafts that combine traditional arts with modern design elements.

CRAFTS

Jerpoint Glass Studio. You can see glass being blown at this noted family-run studio, where the glass is heavy, modern, uncut, and hand finished using traditional tools and methods. The studio's factory shop, 16 km (10 miles) south of Kilkenny, is a good place to pick up a bargain. ⊠ *Main St., Stoneyford* ☎ *056/772–4350* ⊕ *www.jerpointglass.com.*

Kilkenny Design Centre. One of Ireland's favorite sources for Irish handcrafts, the Kilkenny Design Centre sells ceramics, jewelry, sweaters, and

---

THROW AWAY THE KEY

Across the road from Rothe House stands the stern limestone facade of Kilkenny Courthouse, below which lies an extremely spooky dungeon. Until the early 19th century, convicts were locked up four or five to a darkened cell and literally left to rot. Those who managed to live through the experience emerged in a deranged state. You can visit the prison as part of a walking tour of the city, arranged through the city's tourist information office.

Kilkenny Hurling: A Fast and Furious Sport

5

Get chatting with the locals in almost any pub across the Southeast, mention the sport of hurling, and an enthusiastic and often passionate conversation is bound to ensue. The region is the heartland of this ancient sport, whose followers have an almost religious obsession with the game.

Hurling is a kind of aerial field hockey with players wielding curved sticks. Its history comes from Ireland's Celtic ancestors, but it bears about the same relation to field hockey as ice hockey does to roller-skating. It's no accident that prowess on the hurling field is regarded as a supreme qualification for election to public office. A man who succeeds at hurling is eminently capable of dealing with anything that fate and the spite of other politicians can throw at him. Hurling is also an extremely skillful sport. A player must have excellent hand-eye coordination combined with an ability to run at high speeds while balancing a small golf-ball-size ball on his *camán* (hurling stick). Fans will proudly tell you it's also the world's fastest team sport.

Ireland's other chief sporting pastimes, including soccer and hurling's cousin,

Gaelic football, take a backseat in this part of the country. Stars like Kilkenny's Henry Shefflin, rather than professional soccer players, are sporting icons for local kids. Counties Tipperary, Wexford, and Waterford are among the top teams in the region, but Kilkenny (nicknamed "The Cats") have dominated the national scene over the last 20 years. It has won 8 of the last 13 All-Ireland Hurling Champi-onships and is considered one of the best teams in history.

There's an intense rivalry between the counties, especially between old foes Tipperary and Kilkenny. When it gets down to club level, passions run even higher. Almost every parish in the region has a hurling club, and a quick inquiry with locals will usually be enough to find out when the next game is on. Even for the uninitiated, hurling is a great spectator sport. Sporty types wishing to give it a go, be warned; it's fast, furious, and entails more than a hint of danger, as players flail the air to capture the bullet-fast *sliotar* (hurling ball).

handwoven textiles. This spot in the old stable yard opposite the castle has a restaurant specializing in hearty Irish fare. ⊠ *Opposite Kilkenny Castle* ☏ *056/772–2118* ⊕ *www.kilkennydesign.com.*

Fodor's Choice **Nicholas Mosse Pottery.** One of the best-known names in Irish ceramics,
★ Mosse first set up his potter's wheel in an old flour mill in 1975. Since then, the shop's rustic floral-pattern pottery has become instantly recognizable for its "spongeware" designs. A visit to the shop, in a quiet village 16 km (10 miles) south of Kilkenny, allows you to see the pottery being made, and the adjoining factory shop often has good bargains. ⊠ *Off Annamult Rd., Bennettsbridge* ☏ *056/772–7505* ⊕ *www. nicholasmosse.com.*

CLOTHING

Sweater Shop. You'll find a great selection of Irish knitwear and accessories for men, women, and children at this popular shop. ⊠ *81 High St.* ☏ *056/776–3405* ⊕ *www.sweatershop.ie.*

JEWELRY

Murphy Jewellers. This county favorite specializes in silver and diamond jewelry. ⊠ *85 High St.* ☏ *056/772–1127* ⊕ *www.murphyjewellers.com.*

Rudolf Heltzel. Known for striking, modern designs, Rudolf Heltzel mostly showcases gold and silver jewelry. ⊠ *10 Patrick St.* ☏ *056/772– 1497* ⊕ *www.rudolfheltzel.com.*

SOUTHEAST INLANDS

North of Kilkenny City is a region notably rich in historical sights. Travel through the farmlands of the Barrow Valley to the small county seat of Carlow Town, with scenic detours to Leighlinbridge's picturesque castle and Old Leighlin's time-stained cathedral.

LEIGHLINBRIDGE

14 km (9 miles) northeast of Kilkenny City.

GETTING HERE AND AROUND

From Kilkenny take the N77 to the N10 to the M9; exit at junction 7, then take the second exit onto the N9, and exit onto the R448 to Leighlinbridge. The trip takes about half an hour. Bus Éireann runs a regular service to the town from Dublin and Kilkenny. There is no train service.

EXPLORING

Black Castle. Poetically mirrored in the waters of the River Barrow and framed by the bulk of a grandly medieval bridge, the Norman fortress of Black Castle was built in 1181 and has seen countless battles and sieges. You can walk around the hulking, 400-year-old main tower, which all but dares you to set up your easel and canvas on the adjoining towpath. The bridge's five stone arches have spanned the river since 1320, making it one of the oldest functioning bridges in Europe and a magnificent repoussoir for the castle. ⊠ *Off Main St.*

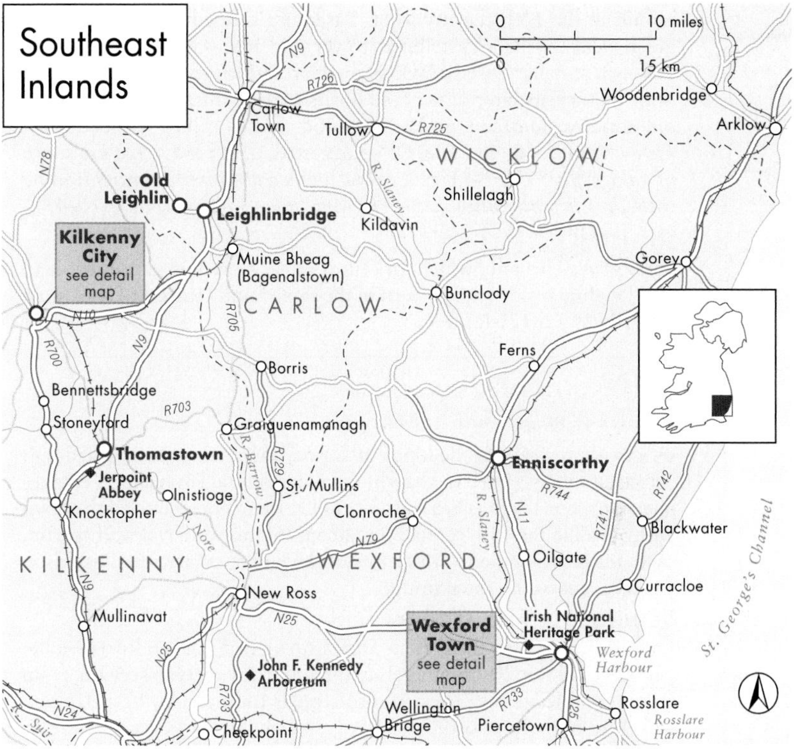

WHERE TO STAY

$$ HOTEL **Lord Bagenal Hotel.** Old and new blend spectacularly at this hotel on the banks of the River Barrow, made up of a famous 19th-century pub and the surrounding buildings dating from the early 1800s. **Pros:** winning mix of ancient and modern; charming walled garden. **Cons:** uncommunicative staff. [$] *Rooms from: €120* ✉ *Main St.* ☎ *059/977–4000* 🌐 *www.lordbagenal.com* 🛏 *39 rooms* 🍴 *Breakfast.*

OLD LEIGHLIN

5¾ km (3 miles) west of Leighlinbridge.

GETTING HERE AND AROUND

From Kilkenny take the N77 to the first exit onto the N78 to Old Leighlin. The trip takes about half an hour. There is no direct bus or train service, but the bus goes to nearby Leighlinbridge. There is parking around the town.

EXPLORING

St. Laserian's Cathedral. Home to one of Ireland's undiscovered gems of late-medieval architecture, the tiny village of Old Leighlin first found fame as the site of a monastery, founded in the 7th century by St. Laserian, that once accommodated 1,500 monks. The old monastery was rebuilt in the 12th century as St. Laserian's Cathedral. Sitting among green fields, with a castellated tower and Irish-Gothic windows, it evokes a stirring sense of Wordsworthian forlornness. Enlarged in the 16th century, its interior is noted for its 11th-century font, a 200-year-old grand wind organ, and a fine wood vaulted ceiling. Guided tours are available. A donation of €1 is suggested. ✉ *Off the N9, 2 km south of village* ☎ *059/972–1570* 🌐 *cashel.anglican.org/information/diocese/cathedrals/leighlin.html* 🎟 *Free* 🕒 *Mid-June–Aug., weekdays 10–4.*

NIGHTLIFE

Carey's Pub. This pub, which for centuries has served up glasses of ale to Old Leighlin residents, has been in the same family since 1542. ✉ *Main St.* ☎ *059/972–1214.*

THOMASTOWN

14½ km (9 miles) south of Kilkenny.

Originally the seat of the kings of Ossory (an ancient Irish kingdom), Thomastown is a pretty, stone-built village on the River Nore. It takes its name from Thomas FitzAnthony of Leinster, who encircled the town with a wall in the 13th century. Fragments of this medieval wall remain, as do the partly ruined 13th-century church of St. Mary. Mullins Castle sits adjacent to the town bridge.

GETTING HERE AND AROUND

From Kilkenny, take the N77 to Thomastown exit. The 16-km (10-mile) trip should take 20 minutes. Bus Éireann runs regular services from Dublin and Kilkenny. There is also regular train service from Dublin, Kilkenny, and Waterford.

EXPLORING

Fodor's Choice ★ **Jerpoint Abbey.** Known for its rearing and massive 15th-century tower, Jerpoint Abbey is one of the most notable Cistercian ruins in Ireland, dating from about 1160. The church, tombs, and the restored cloister are must-sees for lovers of the Irish Romanesque. The vast cloister is decorated with affecting carvings of human figures and fantastical mythical creatures, including knights and knaves (one with a stomach-ache) and the assorted dragon or two. Dissolved in 1540, Jerpoint was taken over, as was so much around these parts, by the earls of Ormonde. The one part of the abbey that remains alive, so to speak, is its hallowed cemetery—the natives are still buried here. Guided tours are available. ✉ *N9, 2 km (1 mile) south of Thomastown* ☎ *056/772–4623* 🌐 *www.heritageireland.ie/en/South-East/JerpointAbbey* 🎟 *€3* 🕒 *Mar.–Sept., daily 9–5:30; Oct., daily 9–5; Nov., daily 9:30–4; last admission 45 mins before closing.*

WHERE TO STAY

$ B&B/INN 🏨 **Ballyduff House.** As the clematis-clad mansion comes into view at the top of a gently curving driveway you can understand why this wonderfully picturesque house was used as a location in the '90s movie adaptation of Maeve Binchy's *Circle of Friends*. **Pros:** family-run lodging; stunningly authentic mansion; guests can use kitchen to prepare a picnic. **Cons:** fills up fast; few modern facilities. [$] *Rooms from: €110*

✉ *Off R700* ☎ *056/775–8488* 🌐 *www.ballyduffhouse.com* 🛏 *4 rooms* 💳 *No credit cards* 🕓 *Closed Dec.–Feb.* 🍴 *Breakfast.*

$$ HOTEL Fodor's Choice ★ 🏨 **Mount Juliet.** For many, the Jack Nicklaus–designed golf course—which has hosted the Irish Open on three occasions—is the main draw, but this lush 1,500-acre estate beside the beautiful River Nore offers so much more. **Pros:** great golf on your doorstep; pampering spa; period elegance with modern amenities; relatively gentle room rates for such luxury. **Cons:** rooms outside main house a little inferior; some charm sacrificed for modern comfort. [$] *Rooms from: €139* ✉ *Off L4206* ☎ *056/777–3000* 🌐 *www.mountjuliet.ie* 🛏 *29 rooms, 2 suites, 11 lodges* 🍴 *Breakfast.*

SPORTS AND THE OUTDOORS

GOLF

Fodor's Choice ★ **Mount Juliet Golf Course.** Attached to a magisterial country-house hotel, this Jack Nicklaus–designed championship parkland course, 19 km (11 miles) from Kilkenny Town, includes practice greens, a driving range, and, for those who feel a little rusty, a David Leadbetter golf academy. The heavily forested course has eight holes that play over water, including the wonderful 3rd hole—a par-3 over a stream from an elevated tee. The back 9 presents a series of difficult bunker shots. Greens fees are above average, and although visitors are always welcome, a weekday round is best, since it's often crowded with members on weekends. ✉ *Mount Juliet Estate, off L4206* ☎ *056/777–3010* 🌐 *www.mountjuliet.ie* 🎟 *May–Sept., Sun.–Thurs. €75–€80, Fri. and Sat. €90; Nov.–Mar., Sun.–Thurs. €65, Fri. and Sat. €75; Apr. and Oct., Sun.–Thurs. €70–€75, Fri. and Sat. €85* ⛳ *18 holes, 7264 yards, par 72. Practice area, driving range, caddy carts, club rental, catering* 🕓 *Visitors: daily.*

ENNISCORTHY

32 km (20 miles) east of Graiguenamanagh.

On the sloping banks of the River Slaney and on the main road between Dublin and Wexford to the south of the popular resort of Gorey, Enniscorthy is a thriving market town that is rich in history.

GETTING HERE AND AROUND

From Wexford, take the N1 to the N30; the 32-km (20-mile) trip takes about half an hour. From Dublin, take the N11/M11 all the way to Enniscorthy; the trip takes about 90 minutes. There is regular bus and train service from Wexford and Dublin.

EXPLORING

Fodor's Choice ★ **Enniscorthy Castle.** The town is dominated by Enniscorthy Castle, built in the first quarter of the 13th century by the Prendergast family. The imposing Norman castle was the site of fierce battles against Oliver Cromwell in the 17th century and during the Uprising of 1798. The castle has reopened after extensive renovations, with an exhibition exploring the development of the building and the town. Exhibits also explore the 1916 Rising in Enniscorthy and the work of furniture designer and architect Eileen Gray, who was born in 1878 just outside town. Gray went on to become one of the founding designers of the modernist movement in the 1920s and now enjoys worldwide fame and staggering prices (one chair she designed brought $22 million at auction). The guided tour is a real treat, with a trip to the dungeon followed by a walk on the roof with impressive views out over the town and beyond. ✉ *Castle Hill* ☎ *053/923–4699* 🌐 *www.enniscorthycastle.ie* 🎟 *€4* 🕒 *Apr.–Sept., daily 9–4:20; Oct.–Mar, weekdays 10–3:20, weekends noon–4:20.*

National 1798 Centre. This small museum tells the tale of the United Irishmen and the ill-fated 1798 rebellion. ✉ *Arnold's Cross* ☎ *053/923–7596* 🌐 *www.1798centre.ie* 🎟 *€7* 🕒 *June–Aug., weekdays 9:30–4, weekends noon–4:30; Sept.–May, weekdays 9:30–4.*

St. Aidan's Cathedral. Standing on a commanding site overlooking the Slaney, the Gothic Revival structure of St. Aidan's was built in the mid-19th century under the direction of Augustus Welby Pugin, famed architect of the Houses of Parliament in London. ✉ *Cathedral St.* ☎ *053/923–5777* 🌐 *www.staidanscathedral.ie* 🎟 *Free* 🕒 *Daily 10–6.*

WHERE TO STAY

$$$ B&B/INN Fodor's Choice ★ 🏨 **Kilmokea Country Manor and Gardens.** A former Georgian rectory dating to 1794, Kilmokea presides over 7 acres of formal walled gardens blooming by the River Barrow. **Pros:** family-owned and -run; incredible gardens; four-poster beds. **Cons:** no Internet in rooms; some rooms are expensive for this region; books up quickly. [$] *Rooms from: €190* ✉ *R733, Campile* ☎ *051/388–109* 🌐 *www.kilmokea.com* 🛏 *6 rooms* 🍴 *Breakfast.*

$ B&B/INN 🏨 **Salville House.** Gordon and Jane Parker have created a hilltop haven where food and bohemian relaxation are the order of the day, thanks to Gordon's way with inspired contemporary cuisine, the spacious guest rooms with plenty of books on the shelves, and the great view of the River Slaney. **Pros:** family-run lodging; wonderful home-style food; great views. **Cons:** only five rooms; no air-conditioning; can be a little tricky to find. [$] *Rooms from: €110* ✉ *Wexford Rd.* ☎ *053/923–5252* 🌐 *www.salvillehouse.com* 🛏 *5 rooms* 💳 *No credit cards* 🍴 *Breakfast.*

SHOPPING

Kiltrea Bridge Pottery. Garden pots and country kitchen crocks are just a few of the goodies at this pottery studio and shop just west of Enniscorthy. ✉ *Kiltealy Rd.* ☎ *053/923–5107* 🌐 *www.kiltreapottery.com.*

WEXFORD TOWN

19 km (12 miles) south of Enniscorthy, 62 km (39 miles) northeast of Waterford City, 115 km (72 miles) southwest of Dublin.

This coastal town is most famed for the Wexford Opera Festival, usually held in October, which has been seducing the world with wonderful productions of rare opera for more than 50 years. The warm and vivacious welcome, the narrow streets, and the atmospheric Theatre Royal add to the pleasure of this event and of any visit to Wexford Town.

From its appearance today, you would barely realize that Wexford is an ancient place, but in fact the Greek cartographer Ptolemy mapped it as long ago as the 2nd century AD. Its Irish name is Loch Garman, but the Vikings called it Waesfjord—the harbor of the mudflats—which became Wexford in English. Wexford developed into an English garrison town after it was captured by Oliver Cromwell in 1649.

Rising above the town's rooftops are the graceful spires of two elegant examples of 19th-century Gothic architecture. These twin churches have identical exteriors, their foundation stones were laid on the same day, and their spires each reach a height of 230 feet. The Church of the Assumption is on Bride Street. The Church of the Immaculate Conception is on Rowe Street.

GETTING HERE AND AROUND

From Dublin take the N11/M11 all the way to Wexford town; the trip takes about two hours and 10 minutes.

Intercity buses arrive at O'Hanrahan Train Station on Redmond Place. Bus Éireann has nine buses a day from Dublin (three hours; €18.05 one-way, €25.17 round-trip), nine from Rosslare (30 minutes; €5.51 one-way, €9.22 round-trip), and six (three on Sunday) from Waterford City (three hours; €10.45 one-way, €19.95 round-trip).

Irish Rail trains arrive at O'Hanrahan Train Station, at the northern end of town on Redmond Place. Wexford is on the Dublin–Roslare line and three trains a day arrive from Dublin; the 2½-hour trip costs €21.99 one-way, €31.98 round-trip. The short hop to Rosslare costs €5.60 and takes 25 minutes. There are no direct trains to Cork or Waterford.

ESSENTIALS

Visitor Information Wexford Tourist Office ⊠ *Crescent Quay* ☎ *053/912–3111* ⊕ *www.ireland.com/destinations/republic-of-ireland/wexford.*

EXPLORING

The River Slaney empties into the sea at Wexford Town. The harbor has silted up since the days when Viking longboats docked here; nowadays only a few small trawlers fish from here. Wexford Town's compact center is on the south bank of the Slaney. Running parallel to the quays on the riverfront is the main street (the name changes several times) and its pleasant mix of old-fashioned bakeries, butcher shops, stylish boutiques, and a share of Wexford's many pubs. It can be explored on foot in an hour or two. Allow at least half a day in the area if you also intend to visit Irish National Heritage Park at nearby Ferrycarrig, and a full day if you want to take in Johnstown Castle Gardens or walk in the nature reserve at nearby Curracloe Beach.

TOP ATTRACTIONS

FAMILY **Irish National Heritage Park.** A 35-acre, open-air, living-history museum beside the River Slaney, this is one of Ireland's most successful and enjoyable family attractions. In about 90 minutes, a guide takes you through 9,000 years of Irish history—from the first evidence of humans on this island, at around 7000 BC, to the Norman settlements of the mid-12th century. Full-scale replicas of typical dwellings illustrate the changes in beliefs and lifestyles. Highlights include a prehistoric home-stead, a *crannóg* (lake dwelling), an early Christian *rath* (fortified farm-stead), a horizontal water mill, a Viking longhouse, and a Norman castle. There are also examples of pre-Christian burial sites and a stone circle. Most of the exhibits are "inhabited" by students in appropriate historic dress who will answer questions. The riverside site includes several nature trails. ⊠ *N11, 5 km (3 miles) north of Wexford Town, Ferrycarrig* ☎ *053/912–0733* ⊕ *www.inhp.com* 🎫 *€9* ☉ *May–Aug., daily 9:30–5; Sept.–Apr., daily 9:30–3.*

Fodor'sChoice
★
Johnstown Castle Gardens. Set in a beautiful garden estate, this Victorian Gothic castle looks like it was designed for a Disney movie but it was in fact built for the Grogan-Morgan family between 1810 and 1855. The magnificent parklands—with towering trees and ornamental gardens—offer a grand frame to the castle. Unfortunately, you can't tour the building (it houses an agricultural college) other than its entrance hall, but the well-maintained grounds are open to the public. The centerpiece is the 5-acre lake, one side of which has a statue-lined terrace where you can take in the panorama of the mirrored castle. Because there's such a variety of trees—Japanese cedars, Atlantic blue cedars, golden Lawson cypresses—there's color through much of the year. Nearby are the Devil's Gate walled garden—a woodland garden set around the ruins of the medieval castle of Rathlannon—and the Irish Agricultural Museum. The latter, housed in the quadrangular stable yards, shows what life was once like in rural Ireland. It also contains a 5,000-square-foot exhibition on the potato and the Great Famine (1845–49). ⊠ *Off N25, 6 km (4 miles) southwest of Wexford Town* ☎ *053/914–2888* ⊕ *www.irishagrimuseum.ie* 🎫 *Gardens and museum €8, museum €6, gardens €3. Gardens free Oct. 20–Mar.* ☉ *Gardens: Apr.–Oct., daily 9–5:30; Nov.–Mar., daily 9–4:30. Museum: Apr.–Oct., weekdays 9–5, weekends 11–5; Nov.–Mar., weekdays 9–12:30 and 1:30–4.*

Westgate Tower. Of the five fortified gateways through the Norman and Viking town walls, Westgate is the only one remaining. The early-13th-century tower has been sensitively restored. Keep an eye out as you wander this part of town for other preserved segments of the old town walls. ⊠ *Westgate.*

Wexford Bull Ring. Once the scene of bull baiting, a cruel medieval sport that was popular among the Norman nobility, this arena was sad wit-ness to other bloody crimes. In 1649, Cromwell's soldiers massacred 300 panic-stricken townspeople who had gathered here to pray as the army stormed their town. The memory of this heartless leader has remained a dark folk legacy for centuries and is only now beginning to fade. ⊠ *Quay St.*

Wexford Opera House. Wexford's grand and hoary landmark, the Theatre Royal, has been entirely rebuilt to serve as the Wexford Opera Theatre for the world-famous Wexford Opera Festival, held here during the last two weeks of October and the beginning of November. The strik-ingly modern, Keith Williams–designed building is custom built for opera and offers fabulous views out over Mt. Lenister to the northwest and Tuskar Rock lighthouse to the southeast. The surprisingly large

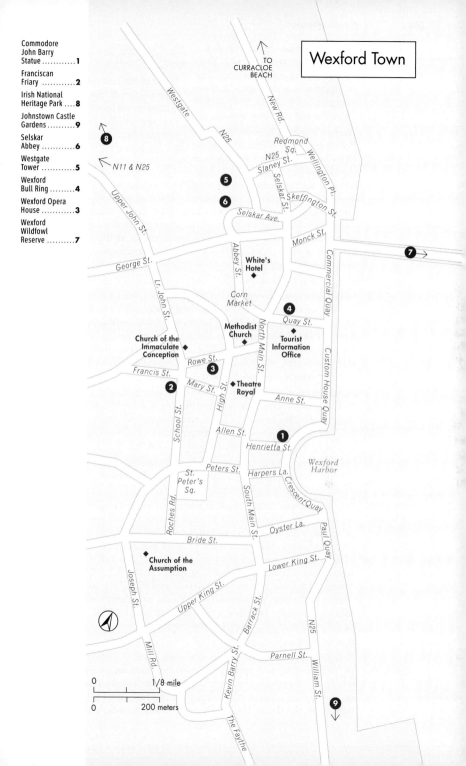

Wexford Town

Commodore John Barry Statue 1
Franciscan Friary 2
Irish National Heritage Park 8
Johnstown Castle Gardens 9
Selskar Abbey 6
Westgate Tower 5
Wexford Bull Ring 4
Wexford Opera House 3
Wexford Wildfowl Reserve 7

TO CURRACLOE BEACH

Westgate

N25

N11 & N25

Upper John St.

George St.

Lr. John St.

Redmond Sq.
N25
Slaney St.
Selskar St.
Wellington Pl.
Skeffington St.

Selskar Ave.

Monck St.

Commercial Quay

Custom House Quay

Abbey St.

White's Hotel

Corn Market

Methodist Church

Quay St.

Tourist Information Office

North Main St.

Church of the Immaculate Conception

Rowe St.

Francis St.

Mary St.

High St.

Theatre Royal

Anne St.

Allen St.

School St.

Henrietta St.

Wexford Harbor

Peters St.

Harpers La.

St. Peter's Sq.

Roches Rd.

South Main St.

Crescent Quay

Oyster La.

Paul Quay

Bride St.

Lower King St.

Church of the Assumption

Joseph St.

Upper King St.

Barrack St.

N25

Kevin Barry St.

Parnell St.

William St.

Mill Rd.

The Faythe

0   1/8 mile
0   200 meters

main auditorium seats 749 with a smaller second space for 172. Year-round, touring companies and local productions are also seen at these venues. ⊠ *27 High St.* ☎ *053/912-2144* ⊕ *wexfordopera.com.*

Wexford Wildfowl Reserve. A nature lover's paradise, Wexford Wildlife Reserve is just a short walk across the bridge from the main part of town. It shelters a third of the world's Greenland white-fronted geese. As many as 10,000 of them spend their winters on the mudflats—known locally as slobs—which also draw ducks, swans, and other waterfowl. Observation hides are provided for bird-watchers, and an audiovisual show and exhibitions are available at the visitor center. ⊠ *Wexford Harbor* ☎ *053/912–3406* ⊕ *www.wexfordwildfowlreserve. ie* ☑ *Free* ☉ *Daily 9–5.*

WORTH NOTING

Commodore John Barry Statue. In the center of Crescent Quay, this large bronze statue commemorates the man who came to be known as the father of the American Navy. Born in 1745 in nearby Ballysampson, Barry (1745–1803) settled in Philadelphia at age 15, became a brilliant naval fighter during the War of Independence (thus avenging his Irish ancestors), and trained many young naval officers who went on to achieve fame. ⊠ *Cresent Quay.*

Franciscan Friary. While Oliver Cromwell made a bonfire of the original 13th-century Friary, this rebuilt 19th-century landmark has a ceiling worth noting for its fine, locally crafted stuccowork and a relic and wax effigy of St. Adjutor—a young martyr slain by his own father. ⊠ *School St.* ☎ *053/912–2758* ☑ *Free* ☉ *Daily 8:30–6:30.*

Selskar Abbey. This 12th-century abbey witnessed the first treaty between the Irish and the Normans signed in 1169. Today only ruins remain. ⊠ *Selskar St., south of Westgate Tower.*

OFF THE BEATEN PATH

Curracloe Beach. Steven Spielberg filmed the terrifyingly gory D-Day landing scenes from his blockbuster *Saving Private Ryan* along this beautiful, soft, white-sand strand. In real life it's a popular swimming place in summer and a quiet home to many migratory birds in winter. It's 9 km (5½ miles) long, with a 1-km (½-mile) nature trail in the seashore sand dunes. There are 500 parking spaces at the White Gap entrance. Amenities are minimal, with lifeguards on duty only in summer on one stretch of the beach. **Amenities:** lifeguards; parking; showers. **Best for:** solitude in winter; swimming; walking; windsurfing. ⊠ *R742, 11 km (7 miles) northeast of Wexford Town* ⊕ *www.wexford.ie.*

WHERE TO EAT AND STAY

$ ✕ **Cistín Eile.** Proud of its modern Irishness, Cistín Eile takes the produce
MODERN IRISH   of local farmers and applies a simple but stunning brand of culinary magic. "Hunger makes a great sauce" reads the Irish-language motto on the wall, so arrive with your appetite fully intact. Little time is wasted on the decor, though the space has a homey, warm feel. The

Viking longboats once docked where fishing trawlers now berth in Wexford's busy harbor.

menu changes depending on what's good in the local market. Favorites include black-and-white pudding with cabbage salad, apple, and mustard, or the slow-cooked beef with onion fondue, spiced turnip colcannon, and peppered cream. How they offer dishes of this quality at such affordable prices is a Wexford miracle. And the name? It just means "another kitchen" in Irish. $ *Average main: €11* ✉ *80 S. Main St.* ☎ *053/912–1616* ☉ *Closed Sun. No dinner Mon. and Tues.*

$ **✕ La Dolce Vita.** You might have to get in line behind a few locals to
ITALIAN get seated in this little Italian deli in a surprisingly serene spot just off the busy shopping area. Hearty food, high standards, and people's prices make it the perfect place to break up a day's sightseeing. Try the genuinely fresh pasta with walnuts and Gorgonzola; you also can't go wrong with the salads. $ *Average main: €12* ✉ *6 Trimmers La.* ☎ *053/917–0806* ☉ *Closed Sun. No dinner.*

$$ **✕ Reed Restaurant.** Fresh-off-the-boat fish is the big draw at this restau-
IRISH rant at the family-friendly Ferrycarrig Hotel. Seafood from Kilmore Quay is a favorite, but the Killurin lamb is just as local and tasty, as is the cider-braised belly of pork with buttered cabbage. Check out the wine list, one of the better ones in the Southeast. While the tables are formally appointed with crisp white linens, the light-filled dining room has a friendly, relaxed vibe. Ask for a table with a romantic and serene riverfront view. $ *Average main: €20* ✉ *Ferrycarrig Hotel, off N11, 4 km (2½ miles) outside Wexford Town* ☎ *053/912–0999* ⊕ *www. ferrycarrighotel.ie/reeds-restaurant.htm.*

$$ **⌂ Ferrycarrig Hotel.** A favorite with families, this spot offers a swimming
HOTEL pool for kids, a peaceful and tranquil riverside location for parents,
FAMILY and a well-equipped health center for both. **Pros:** family-friendly; good

restaurant; riverside location. **Cons:** can get a bit hectic in summer; a little overpriced; some rooms better than others. [$] *Rooms from: €160* ✉ *Off N11, 4 km (2½ miles) outside Wexford Town* ☎ *053/912–0999* 🌐 *www.ferrycarrighotel.ie* 🛏 *98 rooms, 4 suites* 🍴 *Breakfast.*

$ B&B/INN Fodor's Choice ★ 🏨 **McMenamin's Townhouse.** From opera divas to Hollywood stars, they've all stayed at this cozy Victorian town house—and not just because of Kay and Seamus McMenamin's homemade whiskey marmalade. **Pros:** family-run lodging; great breakfast; beautiful antique beds in rooms. **Cons:** only four rooms, so it books up quickly; no TVs in rooms. [$] *Rooms from: €90* ✉ *6 Glena Terr., Spawell Rd.* ☎ *053/914–6442* 🌐 *www.wexford-bedandbreakfast.com* 🛏 *4 rooms* ⏲ *Closed last 2 wks of Dec.* 🍴 *Breakfast.*

NIGHTLIFE AND THE ARTS

Centenary Stores. As the saying goes, if you can find a street without at least one bar on it, you've left Wexford. Centenary Stores is a Victorian-style pub with an adjoining nightclub that makes it popular with the young crowd. Lunch is served Monday through Saturday, and there's traditional music every Sunday morning. ✉ *Charlotte St.* ☎ *053/912–4424* 🌐 *www.thestores.ie.*

The Sky & the Ground. One of the best pubs in town, the Sky & the Ground is a hub for Irish music sessions, which pack in the crowds from Monday through Thursday. ✉ *112 S. Main St.* 🌐 *www.theskyandtheground.com.*

Fodor's Choice ★ **Thomas Moore Tavern.** Dating to the 13th century, the Thomas Moore Tavern is Wexford's oldest pub, named after the renowned Irish poet whose parents lived here. The pub has its original medieval walls and fine old beams along the ceiling, and a spot by the roaring fire is the perfect place for a quiet drink. There's a restaurant attached, and light lunches and snacks are served in the bar on weekdays. ✉ *Cornmarket* ☎ *053/917–4688* 🌐 *www.thomasmooretavern.com.*

SHOPPING

Barkers. Waterford crystal, Belleek china, local pottery, linens, and crafts are found here in tempting array. ✉ *36 S. Main St.* ☎ *053/912–3159.*

Martin's Jewellers. This popular shop specializes in bespoke Celtic jewelry. Have it made before your eyes in the attached workshop. ✉ *Lower Rowe St.* ☎ *053/912–2635* 🌐 *www.martinsjewellers.ie.*

Westgate Design. A good selection of quality Irish crafts, clothing, pottery, candles, and jewelry is found at Westgate Design. There's also a restaurant and deli. ✉ *22A N. Main St.* ☎ *053/912–3787* 🌐 *www.westgatedesign.ie.*

SPORTS

GAELIC FOOTBALL

Wexford Park GAA. Wexford is mostly a hurling county, but you can watch both Gaelic football and hurling at the Wexford Park GAA. ✉ *Clonard Rd.* ☎ *053/914–4808* 🌐 *www.wexford.gaa.ie.*

THE SOUTHEAST COAST

This journey takes you along mainly minor roads through the prettiest parts of the coast in counties Wexford and Waterford, pausing midway to explore Waterford City—home of the dazzling cut glass—on foot. Along the way expect to see long golden beaches, quaint fishing villages like Kilmore Quay and Ballyhack, some of the country's best nature reserves, and the family seaside resort of Tramore. If you're coming from the Continent or England, chances are you'll end up on a ferry bound for Rosslare Harbour, one of Ireland's busiest ferry ports.

ROSSLARE

16 km (10 miles) southeast of Wexford Town.

Sometimes called Ireland's sunniest spot, the village of Rosslare is a seaside getaway with an attractive beach. Many vacationers head here to hike, golf, sun, and swim. But the truth is that most visitors are only here to take the ferry from the Rosslare-Europort terminal, the only reason (some point out) you should find yourself in this otherwise dull little town.

GETTING HERE AND AROUND

As Rosslare is so well connected to the ferry port, the roads to major cities to and from here are very good: N81, N11, and N25. Rosslare is 16 km (9 miles) southeast of Wexford Town on the R470. The trip from Dublin takes around two hours, 12 minutes.

Bus Éireann has service from many cities and towns in Ireland, including Waterford City (€18.42 one-way, €30.88 round-trip; 1½ hours) and Dublin (€18.05 one-way, €25.17 round-trip; 3 hours). Irish Rail runs three trains daily on the Dublin–Rosslare Europort line via Wexford Town. The trip to Dublin takes three hours (€26.50 one-way, €32.50 round-trip) and to Wexford Town only 25 minutes (€5.60 one-way, €8.20 round-trip).

Stena Line Express sails May to September between Rosslare Harbour and Fishguard in Wales (3½ hours; two sailings per day) year-round. The fare in summer starts from €35, or €105 for a car and driver. Irish Ferries sails to Pembroke in Wales (3¾ hours, twice daily). Single summer fares start at €32 for a foot passenger, €125 for a car and driver. Between April and December there are ferries to Cherbourg, France (19½ hours, up to three a week). ■TIP➜ Ferries to and from Rosslare sometimes sell out, so reserve your space in advance.

EXPLORING

Rosslare Harbour. The end of the line for car ferries to and from Fishguard (3½ hrs) and Pembroke (3¾ hrs) in Wales and Cherbourg (19½ hrs) and Roscoff (22 hrs) in France, Rosslare Harbour, is 8 km (5 miles) south of the village. Irish Ferries and Stena Sealink have small kiosks in the ultramodern terminal, which also has lockers, a café, and a sprawling waiting room. You can purchase ferry tickets at the terminal, but reservations are also a must if you're traveling by car because space is at a premium. Connecting bus and rail stations are also here. ⊕ *rossla-reeuroport.irishrail.ie*

WHERE TO STAY

$$$ ⊡ **Kelly's Resort Hotel & Spa.** This place opened its doors 1895, and since
HOTEL then it's become somewhat legendary because of its overflowing sand-
FAMILY bucket of attractions: a stunning beachfront location, second-to-none
entertainment and leisure facilities, a child-friendly approach, and a
reputation for good food. **Pros:** great value for families; lots of activi-
ties; spa on-site. **Cons:** lots of kids make it hectic in summer; fairly
basic amenities in rooms; pricey. $ *Rooms from: €176* ⊠ *Strand Rd.*
☎ *053/913–2114* ⊕ *www.kellys.ie* ⇌ *114 rooms, 4 suites* ⊙ *Closed
Dec.–mid-Feb.* ❍| *Multiple meal plans.*

NIGHTLIFE AND THE ARTS

Porthole Bar. A trendy spot with designer decor, the Porthole Bar is the
main hangout at the Hotel Rosslare. It's particularly popular for live
music on weekends. ⊠ *Hotel Rosslare, Rosslare Harbour* ☎ *053/913–
3110* ⊕ *www.hotelrosslare.ie.*

SPORTS

GOLF

Rosslare Golf Club. Opened in 1905, this 30-hole championship links sits
on a narrow peninsula with the harbor on one side and the Irish Sea on
the other. On the 18-hole Old Course, the "Barber's Pole" is the devil-
ishly tricky par-4 11th hole. The 12-hole Burrow Course was designed
by Irish legend Christy O'Connor Junior. The course is famous for its
stunning flora and birdlife. ⊠ *Rosslare Strand* ☎ *053/913–2203* ⊕ *www.
rosslaregolf.com* ⊠ *Old Course: weekdays €35, weekends €40. Burrow
Course: weekdays €15, weekends €20* ⅄ *Old Course: 18 holes, 6786
yards, par 72; Burrow Course: 12 holes, 3956 yards, par 48.*

KILMORE QUAY

22 km (14 miles) south of Rosslare.

Noted for its fishing industry, this quiet, old-fashioned seaside village
of thatched and whitewashed cottages is also popular with recreational
anglers and bird-watchers. From the harbor there's a pleasant view to
the east over the flat coast that stretches for miles. Recent development
has turned the harbor into a popular leisure marina.

GETTING HERE AND AROUND

From Wexford take the N25 to the R739 and into Kilmore Quay. The
trip should take about 35 minutes. Bus Éireann runs regular services
from Dublin and Wexford. There is parking all over town, but it can
get tricky in summer.

EXPLORING

Saltee Islands. Ireland's largest bird sanctuary, the Saltee Islands make a fine
day trip from Kilmore Quay. You can see kittiwakes, puffins, guillemots,
cormorants, gulls, and petrels, especially in late spring and early summer
when several million seabirds nest among the dunes and rocky scarp on
the southernmost of the two islands. From mid-May to mid-September,

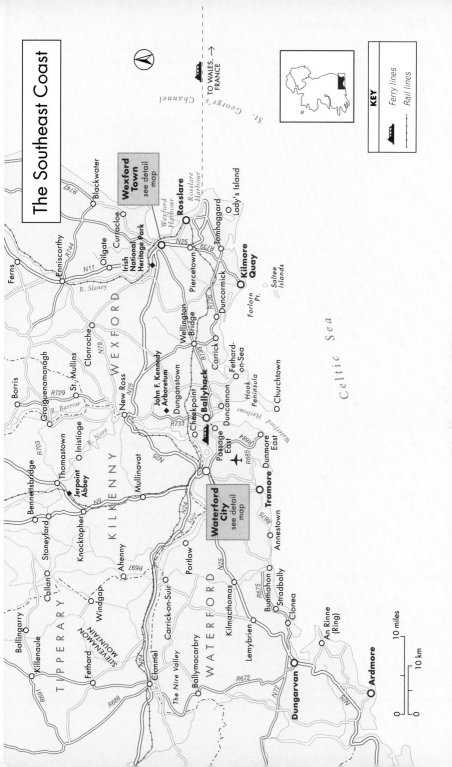

look for boats at the village waterfront or on the marina to take you to the islands, weather permitting. ⊕ *www.discoverireland.ie.*

BALLYHACK

39 km (24 miles) west of Kilmore Quay, 54 km (33 miles) west of Rosslare.

Fodor'sChoice On the upper reaches of Water-
★ ford Harbor, this pretty village with a square castle keep, thatch cottages, and a green, hilly background is admired by painters and photographers.

> ### SLOW BOAT TO WATERFORD
>
> The Knights Templars of St. John of Jerusalem were required to keep a boat at Ballyhack to transport injured knights to the King's Leper Hospital at Waterford.

GETTING HERE AND AROUND

A small car ferry makes the five-minute crossing from Passage East in County Waterford. Driving from Wexford, take the N25 west to the R373. The 48-km (30-mile) trip takes about an hour on these relatively narrow roads. There is regular bus service from Wexford Town.

EXPLORING

Ballyhack Castle. The gray-stone keep of Ballyhack Castle dates from the 16th century. It was once owned by the Knights Templars of St. John of Jerusalem, who held the ferry rights by royal charter. The first two floors now house local-history exhibits. Guided tours are available by appointment. ⊕ *www.heritageireland.ie/en/south-east/ballyahackcastle* ⊠ *Free* ⊙ *Late June–late Aug., daily 10–4:15.*

John F. Kennedy Arboretum. About 12 km (8 miles) to the north of Ballyhack lies the John F. Kennedy Arboretum, with more than 600 acres of forest, nature trails, and gardens, plus an ornamental lake. The grounds contain some 4,500 species of trees and shrubs and serve as a resource center for botanists and foresters. The top of the park offers fine panoramic views. The arboretum is clearly signposted from New Ross on R733, which follows the banks of the Barrow southward for about 5 km (3 miles). The cottage where the president's great-grandfather was born is in Dunganstown; Kennedy relatives still live in the house. About 2 km (1 mile) down the road at Slieve Coillte you can see the entrance to the arboretum. ⊠ *Off R733, Dunganstown* ☎ *051/388–171* ⊕ *www.heritageireland.ie* ⊠ *€3* ⊙ *May–Aug., daily 10–8; Apr. and Sept., daily 10–6:30; Oct.–Mar., daily 10–5.*

WHERE TO EAT AND STAY

$$$$ ✕ **Harvest Room.** Gourmands come in droves to the ruby-red dining room
CONTEMPORARY at Dunbrody House, where master celebrity-chef Kevin Dundon serves up foie gras with toasted brioche and balsamic-marinated strawberries, rack of Wexford lamb, and a chocolate "selection of indulgences." If you're a hands-on type, you can learn how to cook the Harvest Room's delights yourself; Dundon runs a cooking school on weekends. After a dinner that is likely to be memorable sip-to-sup, sit back with a goblet of Irish mist in hand and catch a dramatic sunset fading over the Hook

Peninsula. Sunday lunch here is the stuff of legend. [$] *Average main: €35* ✉ *Dunbrody House, off L4052, Arthurstown* ☎ *051/389–600* 🌐 *www.dunbrodyhouse.com* ✍ *Reservations essential* ⏲ *Closed Mon. and Tues. No lunch Wed.–Sat.*

$$$$ HOTEL Fodor's Choice ★ 🏨 **Dunbrody Country House.** Thanks to Kevin and Catherine Dundon, this sprawling, two-story, 1830s Georgian manor house has plenty of allurements: the gardens are soul-restoring, the public salons are a soigné symphony of mix-and-match tangerine-hue fabrics and stuffed armchairs, the views over the Barrow estuary are grand, and the guest rooms charm with a judiciously luxe combination of period antiques and fine reproductions. **Pros:** authentic Georgian feel; wonderful gardens; great restaurant. **Cons:** expensive for this region; facilities limited for luxury hotel; giant Irish breakfast too good to resist. [$] *Rooms from: €235* ✉ *Off L4052, Arthurstown* ☎ *051/389–600* 🌐 *www.dunbrodyhouse.com* 🛏 *15 rooms, 7 suites* 🍴 *Breakfast.*

WATERFORD CITY

10 km (6 miles) west of Ballyhack by ferry and road, 62 km (39 miles) southwest of Wexford Town, 158 km (98 miles) southwest of Dublin.

The largest town in the Southeast and Ireland's oldest city, Waterford was founded by the Vikings in the 9th century and was taken over by Strongbow, the Norman invader, with much bloodshed in 1170. The city resisted Cromwell's 1649 attacks but fell the following year. It did not prosper again until 1783, when George and William Penrose set out to create "plain and cut flint glass, useful and ornamental," and thereby set in motion a glass-manufacturing industry long without equal. The famed glassworks closed in 2008, but Waterford Crystal has triumphantly risen from the flames in a smaller, leaner version that opened in 2010.

GETTING HERE AND AROUND

From Dublin, take the N7/M7 to the N9/M9 and all the way to Waterford City. This motorway is often quiet, and the trip takes only two hours. The city is only 45 minutes from Kilkenny via the N9 and N10.

It can be a long drive around the coast from Wexford to Waterford and the Passage East Car Ferry Company operates year-round from Passage East in Wexford to Ballyhack, near Waterford City. The five-minute crossings are continuous from 7 am until 10 pm April through September and until 8 pm the rest of the year (with first sailing on Sundays at 9:30 am). The cost is €8 one-way and €12 round-trip for a car and passengers and €1.50 one-way, €2 round-trip for a foot passenger.

Bus Éireann has a station on the waterfront at Merchant's Quay and runs regular buses to cities and towns all over the country, including Tramore (€3.42 one-way, €6.84 round-trip; 30 minutes); Dungarvan (€12.64 one-way, €19.48 round-trip; 50 minutes); Wexford (€10.45 one-way, €19.95 round trip; 1½ hours); and Cork (€21.38 one-way, €28.02 round-trip; 2¼ hours) and Dublin (€15.20 one-way, €19.48 round-trip; 3 hours). Bus Éireann also runs a local city bus service in Waterford City, with five routes that cover the city center.

On the north side of the river, Plunkett Station receives Irish Rail trains from Kilkenny (€10 one-way, €20 round-trip; 45 minutes); Dublin (€10–€21.99 one-way, €20–€42 round-trip; 2¾ hours); and Limerick (€25 one-way, €58 round-trip; 2¾ hours).

ESSENTIALS

Visitor Information Waterford City Tourist Office ⊠ *The Granary, The Quay* ☎ *051/875-823* ⊕ *www.discoverireland.ie.*

EXPLORING

Waterford has better-preserved city walls than anywhere else in Ireland besides Derry. ■ TIP➜ You can spot one of the remaining portions of the city walls along Spring Garden Alley, off Colbeck Street. Initially, the slightly run-down commercial center doesn't look promising. You need to park your car and proceed on foot to discover the city's proudly preserved heritage, in particular the grand 18th-century Georgian buildings that Waterford architect John Roberts (1714–96) built, including the town's Protestant and Catholic cathedrals.

Waterford's compact town center can be visited in a couple of hours. Most visitors consider the Waterford Glass Visitor Centre and the impressive pair of history museums as must-sees in any city tour.

TOP ATTRACTIONS

Christ Church Cathedral. Lovers of Georgian decorative arts will want to visit this late-18th-century Church of Ireland cathedral—the only Neoclassical Georgian cathedral in Ireland—designed by local architect John Roberts. Inside, all is elegance—yellow walls, white-stucco florets and laurels, grand Corinthian columns—and you can see why architectural historian Mark Girouard called this "the finest 18th-century ecclesiastical building in Ireland." It stands on the site of a great Norman Gothic cathedral, which a bishop authorized knocking down after rubble fell in his path a few times (with a little help from potential builders). Medievalists will be sad, but those who prize Age of Enlightenment high style will rejoice. Try to catch one of the regular choral concerts to get the full atmospheric reward. ⊠ *Henrietta St.* ☎ *051/858–958* ⊕ *www.christchurchwaterford.com* ▣ *€3* ⊙ *May–Sept., weekdays 9–5, Sat. 10–4; Apr. and Oct. weekdays 10–5, Sat. 10–4; Nov.–Mar., weekdays 10–3.*

Fodor's Choice ★ **House of Waterford Crystal.** Iconic Waterford crystal is once again being produced in the city, albeit on a much smaller scale than before. The factory tour, which includes the blowing, sculpting, and cutting departments, is a must for anyone who appreciates timeless craftsmanship and unique design. After watching a team of glassworkers create a twinkling masterpiece from a molten blob, you may have trouble resisting the retail store, where you can select from the world's largest collection of Waterford crystal. You can have your purchase engraved on the spot. ⊠ *The Mall* ☎ *051/317–000* ⊕ *www.waterfordvisitorcentre.com* ▣ *Tour €13* ⊙ *Mar., Mon.–Sat. 9–3:15, Sun. 9:30–3:15; Apr.–Oct., Mon.–Sat. 9–4:15, Sun. 10–4:15; Nov. and Dec., weekdays 9:30–3:15; Jan. and Feb., weekdays 9–3:15.*

Medieval Museum. Waterford's newest museum cleverly incorporates two medieval-era structures within its walls. Inside, the focus is on

Waterford City

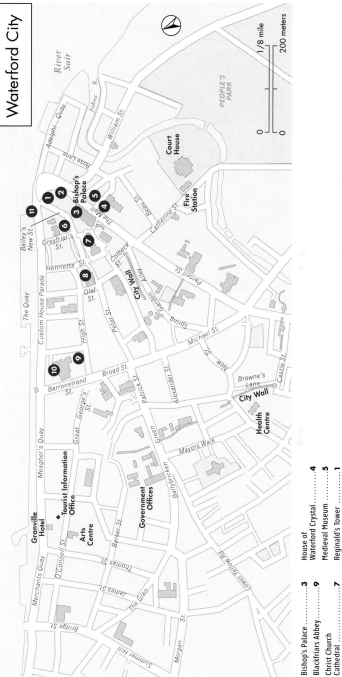

1/8 mile

200 meters

The circular Reginald's Tower, originally built by the Vikings, is one of the eye-catching sights along Waterford's Merchant's Quay, long the center of the city's social and economic scene.

Waterford's rich Norman history. A collection of rare and beautiful artifacts includes the Charter Roll of 1372, a list of all charters granted to Waterford up to that time, written in Latin. Also here you'll find the sword of King Edward IV and 15th-century "Cloth of Gold" religious vestments—a true work of art. There's a detailed audiovisual display to add to the experience. ⊠ *The Mall* ☎ *051/304–500* ⊕ *www. waterfordtreasures.com/medieval-museum* ⊡ *€7* ⊗ *June–Aug., Mon.– Sat. 9:15–6, Sun. 11–5; Sept.–May, Mon.–Sat. 10–5, Sun. 11–5.*

Fodor's Choice ★ **Reginald's Tower.** Restored to its original medieval appearance, Reginald's Tower—a circular structure on the east end of Waterford's quays—is a striking setting for a museum on Waterford's Viking history. Built by the Vikings for the city's defense in 1003, it has 80-foot-high, 10-foot-thick walls; an interior stairway leads to the top. The tower served in turn as the residence for a succession of Anglo-Norman kings (including Henry II, John, and Richard II), a mint for silver coins, a prison, and an arsenal. It's said that Strongbow's marriage to Eva, the daughter of Dermot MacMurrough, took place here in the late 12th century, thus uniting the Norman invaders with the native Irish. The impressive exhibits include the full weapon kit of a local Viking leader. On the top floor there's an audiovisual display and objects to represent every century since the tower was built. ⊠ *The Quay* ☎ *051/304–500* ⊕ *www. waterfordtreasures.com/reginalds-tower* ⊡ *€3* ⊗ *June–mid-Sept., daily 10–6; Easter–May, daily 10–5; mid-Sept.–Easter, Wed.–Sun. 10–5.*

Waterford City Hall. One of Waterford's finest Georgian buildings, Waterford City Hall dates from 1783 and was designed by native son John Roberts. The arms of Waterford hang over the entrance, which leads into a spacious foyer that originally served as a town meeting place and merchants' exchange. The building contains an enormous 1802 Waterford glass chandelier, which hangs in the Council Chamber (a copy hangs in Independence Hall in Philadelphia). The Victorian horseshoe-shaped Theatre Royal is the venue for the annual Festival of Light Opera in September. ⊠ *The Mall* ☎ *051/309–900* 🖾 *Free* ⊘ *Weekdays 9–5.*

WORTH NOTING

Bishop's Palace. Among the most imposing of the city's remaining Georgian town houses, the Bishop's Palace is the home to the Georgian part of the Waterford Treasures exhibition, mapping the history of what was Ireland's second city from 1700 to 1790. The most impressive part of the collection is the elegant silverware and, of course, fine glassmaking, including the oldest piece of Waterford crystal on the planet—a decanter from the 1780s. Try to catch one of the regular tours, where local actors play some well-known scenes from Waterford history. ⊠ *The Mall, alongside Waterford City Hall* ☎ *051/304–500* ⊕ *www.waterfordtreasures.com/bishops-palace* 🖾 €7 ⊘ *June–Aug., Mon.–Sat. 9:15–6, Sun. 11–5; Sept.–May, Mon.–Sat. 10–5, Sun. 11–5.*

Blackfriars Abbey. While you can't go inside, you can get close to the remans of this genuinely medieval abbey. This ruined tower belonged to a Dominican abbey that was founded in 1226 and returned to the Crown in 1541 after the dissolution of the monasteries. It was used as a courthouse until Cromwellian forces destroyed most of it it in the 17th century. ⊠ *High St.*

City Quays. A good place to begin a tour of Waterford City, the City Quays stretch for nearly 2 km (1 mile) along the River Suir and were described in the 18th century as the best in Europe. ⊠ *Custom House Parade and Peter St.*

French Church. Roofless ruins are all that remain of French Church, a 13th-century Franciscan abbey. The church, also known as Greyfriars, was given to a group of Huguenot refugees (hence the "French") in 1695. A splendid east window remains amid the ruins. The key is available at Reginald's Tower. ⊠ *Greyfriars St.*

Holy Trinity Cathedral. This Roman Catholic cathedral has a simple facade and a richly (some would say garishly) decorated interior with high, vaulted ceilings and ornate Corinthian pillars. It was designed in Neoclassical style by John Roberts, who also planned Christ Church Cathedral and Waterford City Hall. Surprisingly, it was built in the late 18th century—when Catholicism was barely tolerated—on land granted by the Protestant city fathers. ⊠ *Barronstrand St., between High St. and*

ONE WAY OR ANOTHER

Although there are several theories about the origin of the phrase, some experts credit Cromwell with coining the expression "by hook or by crook." Planning two siege routes to Waterford—one via Hook Head, the other via Crooke Village on the estuary of the River Suir—Cromwell declared that he would take the city "by Hooke or by Crooke."

5

CLOSE UP

Waterford Crystal

Silica sand + potash + litharge = Waterford crystal. It reads like cold science, but something magical happens when the craftsmen of Waterford produce arguably the top crystal in the world (although France's Baccarat might have something to say about that).

When the Waterford Glass Factory opened in 1783, it provided English royalty and nobility with a regular supply of ornate handcrafted stemware, chandeliers, and decorative knickknacks. Since then, Waterford crystal has graced the tables of heads of state the world over, and Waterford's earlier pieces have become priceless heirlooms.

The best Waterford glass was produced from the late 18th century to the early 19th century. This early work, examples of which can be found in museums and public buildings all over the country, is characterized by a unique, slightly opaque cast that is absent from the modern product.

Crystal glass is not cheap: each piece is individually fashioned by almost two dozen pairs of hands before it passes final inspection and receives the discreet Waterford trademark.

The first thing on the itinerary of any visitor to Waterford was for many years a tour of the glass factory, a buzzing hive of master craftspeople. But the global downturn saw the landmark factory close. Happily, Waterford Crystal arose from the ashes in 2010 and now offers a smaller specialist facility at the Mall (🌐 *www.waterfordvisitorcentre.com*). The adjoining visitor center is already a must-see.

clock tower on quays ☎ *051/875–166* 🌐 *www.waterford-cathedral.com* 🎫 *Free* 🕒 *Daily 8:30–5:30.*

St. Olaf's Church. Built, as the name implies, by the Vikings in the mid-11th century, this church has one sole extant remnant: its original door, which has been incorporated into the wall of a meeting hall. ✉ *St. Olaf's St.*

WHERE TO EAT

$$ MODERN IRISH

🍴 **Bodega Restaurant & Wine Bar.** A casual modern-Irish eatery, Bodega Restaurant is known as the fun place to eat in town. Bright colors and comfortable couches give it a festive feel, while the extensive wine menu gets everyone warmed up for lively dishes such as Kilmore Quay fish cakes with Thai red-curry oil, perhaps followed by chicken with wild mushrooms and Gubbeen-chorizo potatoes. Everything is prepared with locally sourced ingredients. Bodega also hosts intimate gigs by some of Ireland's top folk singers. [$] *Average main: €19* ✉ *54 John's St.* ☎ *051/844–177* 🌐 *www.bodegawaterford.com* 🕒 *Closed Sun. No lunch Sat.*

$$$ FRENCH

🍴 **La Boheme.** In the historic Port of Waterford building, this intimate eatery offers an authentic taste of France and plenty of old-world charm. Owners Christine and Eric Théze restored the arched-ceiling space, including the original flagstone floors and lime-washed walls, and they've made a showplace out of the beautiful pewter bar. The menu is a modern take on traditional French dishes, including a starter of beef carpaccio with a black peppercorn crust, white truffle oil, and rocket (arugula) leaves. For a main course try the Barbary duck breast with melted organic red cabbage, roast apple, and ginger-and-honey sauce. *Average main: €27* *2 George's St.* *051/875–645* *www.labohemerestaurant.ie* *Closed Sun. and Mon. No lunch.*

$$$$ FRENCH Fodor's Choice ★ **Munster Dining Room.** Inside the Waterford Castle Hotel, the Munster Dining Room's luxe decor—with oak paneling darkened with age and ancestral portraits in gilt frames—hints at one of the most sophisticated menus around. The dress code is smart (jackets for the men) and the surroundings suggest a big night out. Options include a fixed-price, three-course menu featuring adventurous starters such as wild rabbit tart with carrot pureé and grain-mustard jus. Main-course winners include the best of Irish steaks or the roasted goose breast with potato-and-orange stuffing and burnt-orange sauce. *Average main: €33* *Waterford Castle Hotel, The Island, 2 km (1 mile) south of Waterford, Ballinakill* *051/878–203* *www.waterfordcastle.com/munster-room-restaurant.html* *No lunch.*

WHERE TO STAY

$$ HOTEL **Dooley's Hotel.** A short stroll from all the main attractions, this unpretentious hotel on the banks of the River Suir is popular both with families and business travelers, while the traditional bar is packed with locals. **Pros:** downtown location; large guest rooms; excellent service. **Cons:** attracts a business clientele; you can get more for same price elsewhere; can be a little noisy. *Rooms from: €129* *30 The Quay* *051/873–531* *www.dooleys-hotel.ie* *113 rooms* *Breakfast.*

$$ B&B/INN Fodor's Choice ★ **Foxmount Country House.** About 15 minutes northeast of Waterford City, this stylish Georgian country house manages to be luxurious and elegant and at the same time warm and personal. **Pros:** authentic vibe; great value; rural but near the city. **Cons:** few facilities; no restaurant. *Rooms from: €130* *Passage East Rd.* *051/874–308* *www.foxmountcountryhouse.com* *4 rooms* *No credit cards* *Some meals.*

$$$$ HOTEL Fodor's Choice ★ **Waterford Castle Hotel & Golf Resort.** Not only does this fairy-tale castle come with an 800-year history, its own 310-acre island, a private ferry, and a highly rated 18-hole golf course, it also caters to lucky guests with the best of Irish service and the grandest of Irish style. **Pros:** historic building; great golf course; awe-inspiring Great Hall. **Cons:** expensive for this region; books up quickly in summer; popular with weddings. *Rooms from: €258* *The Island, 2 km (1 mile) south of Waterford, Ballinakill* *051/878–203* *www.waterfordcastle.com* *14 rooms, 5 suites* *No meals.*

NIGHTLIFE AND THE ARTS

NIGHTLIFE

Geoffs. A dimly lighted pub, Geoffs is frequented by a mixed crowd including students and locals. Big flagstones cover the floors, and seating is on old wooden benches. An outdoor area is available for smokers. A wide selection of food is served until 9 pm every night. *9 John St.* *051/874–787.*

5

Jack Meades. Known to locals as "Meades Under the Bridge," this place is indeed set beneath a time-stained stone bridge. In centuries past it was a stop on the coach road from Waterford to Passage East. There's a pub menu from May through September, and sing-along sessions are held throughout the year on the weekends. In winter the fireplaces roar, illuminating the wood beams and bric-a-brac. ⊠ *Halfway House, Cheekpoint Rd., Ballycanavan* 🕾 *051/873–187* ⊕ *www.jackmeades.com.*

Old Ground. Housed in an 800-year-old building, this pub is highly popular with locals. Lunch is served daily, and traditional-music sessions sometimes break out. ⊠ *10 The Glen* 🕾 *051/852–283.*

T & H Doolan's Bar. Reputed to be one of the oldest pubs in Ireland, Doolan's hosts traditional Irish music most summer nights and Monday through Wednesday nights year-round. ⊠ *32 George's St.* 🕾 *051/872–764* ⊕ *www.thdoolans.com.*

THE ARTS

Forum. A multipurpose entertainment venue, the Forum often hosts local productions or those of traveling theater companies. Two music venues present big names as well as local acts performing all kinds of music. ⊠ *The Glen* 🕾 *051/871–111* ⊕ *www.forumwaterford.com.*

Garter Lane Arts Centre. Culture buffs shouldn't miss the Garter Lane Arts Centre, which has a schedule filled with concerts, exhibits, and theater productions. Garter Lane is home to many productions by Red Kettle (⊕ *www.redkettletheatre.com*), Waterford's most successful theater company. ⊠ *22A O'Connell St.* 🕾 *051/855–038* ⊕ *www.garterlane.ie.*

Theatre Royal Waterford. One of the oldest theaters in Ireland, the elegant Theatre Royal is devoted to large-scale theater and musical productions as well as live music. ⊠ *Waterford City Hall, The Mall* 🕾 *051/874–402* ⊕ *www.theatreroyal.ie.*

SHOPPING

City Square Shopping Centre. With more than 40 shops ranging from small Irish boutiques to international department stores, City Square Shopping Centre presents fashion shows and other forms of entertainment on its stage area. ⊠ *City Sq.* 🕾 *051/853–528* ⊕ *www.city-square.ie.*

Kellys. This is a fine source for excellent souvenirs, including traditional musical instruments, dolls, linen, jewelry, and even Waterford crystal. ⊠ *75–76 The Quay* 🕾 *051/873–557.*

Penrose Crystal. Check out the quality goods at the town's handmade-crystal manufactory. With a little notice, Penrose can have a personally engraved piece waiting for you when you arrive. ⊠ *32 John St.* 🕾 *051/876–537* ⊕ *www.penrosecrystal.com.*

SPORTS

GAELIC FOOTBALL

Waterford GAA Grounds. Watch exciting and spectacular Gaelic football and hurling at the Waterford GAA Grounds. ⊠ *Walsh Park* 🕾 *051/591–5544* ⊕ *www.waterfordgaa.ie.*

GOLF

Faithlegg Golf Club. A perfectly manicured, 20-year-old, 18-hole parkland course, Faithlegg is set in the mature landscape of a 200-acre estate on the banks of the River Suir. Problematic doglegs, blind shots, and nasty sand traps make it a lot trickier than it seems on first glance. The difficult finishing stretch, with Faithlegg House as the backdrop, can catch out the overambitious golfer. ⊠ *Faithlegg House, Checkpoint* ☎ *051/382–241* ⊕ *www.faithlegg.com* 🗓 *Jan. and Feb., daily €25; Mar., Apr., and Oct., weekdays €30, weekends €35; May–Sept., weekdays €35, weekends €40; Nov. and Dec., weekdays €25, weekends €30* ⅃. *18 holes, 6674 yards, par 72.*

Waterford Castle Hotel & Golf Club. Claiming to be Ireland's only true island course, Waterford Castle is completely detached from the mainland on a privately owned 310-acre island. Designed by Irish golfing great Des Smyth, the tricky but playable 18-hole course winds through mature woodland and features four internal water features in addition to the encroaching sea. There are plenty of opportunities to hit one into the drink. ⊠ *The Island, 2 km (1 mile) south of Waterford, Ballinakill* ☎ *051/871–633* ⊕ *www.waterfordcastle.com* 🗓 *Weekdays €25, weekends €30* ⅃. *18 holes, 6372 yards, par 72.*

TRAMORE

FAMILY *11 km (7 miles) south of Waterford City on R675, 4 km (2½ miles) west of Dunmore East.*

Tramore's 5-km-long (3-mile-long) **beach** is a popular escape for families from Waterford and other parts of the Southeast, as the many vacation homes indicate. The beach is adjacent to the giant Tramore Amusement Park, which features all the usual rides, including a Ferris wheel, roller coaster, and old-fashioned dodgems. Kiddie heaven, in other words.

GETTING HERE AND AROUND

From Waterford City, take the R675 south to Tramore. The trip takes about 15 minutes. Bus Éireann runs frequent service from Waterford City (€3.42 one-way, €6.84 round-trip; 30 minutes). The Bus Éireann bus stop is outside the tourist office near Splashworld.

DUNGARVAN

42 km (26 miles) southwest of Tramore, 44 km (27 miles) southwest of Waterford.

With their covering of soft grasses, the lowlands of Wexford and eastern Waterford gradually give way to heath and moorland. The mountains responsible for the wetter climate rise up behind Dungarvan, the largest coastal town in County Waterford. This bustling fishing and resort spot sits at the mouth of the River Colligan where it empties into Dungarvan Bay. It's a popular base for climbers and hikers.

GETTING HERE AND AROUND

From Waterford, take the N25 west to Dungarvan. The trip takes 45 minutes. Bus Éireann drops off passengers on Davitt's Quay. It has regular daily services from Waterford (€12.64 one-way, €19.48 round-trip; 1

hour); Cork (€18.52 one-way, €25.65 round-trip; 1½ hours; 13 daily); and Dublin (€18.05 one-way, €25.17 round-trip).

ESSENTIALS

Visitor Information Dungarvan and West Waterford Tourism ⊠ *The Court-house* ☎ *058/41741* ⊕ *www.dungarvantourism.com.*

EXPLORING

Ring (An Rinn). Unusual in the south and east of the country, Ring (An Rinn) is an unspoiled Gaeltacht area on Dungarvan Bay where you will find the Irish language still in daily use. Courses in Irish have been taught at Coláiste na Rinne, a language college, since 1909. It's a lovely spot for bikers, walkers, and bird-watchers—the area includes An Cuinigear, a long, thin peninsula that thousands of seabirds call home. Helvic, a tiny fishing village, commands great views over the Waterford coastline, with the Comeragh Mountains as a backdrop. ⊠ *Off N674F, 7 km (4½ miles) southeast of Dungarvan.*

WHERE TO EAT AND STAY

$ ✕ **Nude Food.** Louise Clark's eclectic little café specializes in simple,
CAFÉ delicious food with nothing to hide and everything to love. For a pre-mountain-walk breakfast, fortify yourself with the Ballinamult free-range baked egg and Marmite soldiers. When you come back down the mountain, try the traditional Irish stew with pearl barley, lamb, carrots, and homemade soda bread, or the ploughman's platter with honey-glazed ham, farmhouse cheese, and house-made pickles, pre-serves, and griddled sourdough bread. In fact, you might want to skip the mountain altogether so you can stay for the delightful almond tart with clotted cream. Nude has a lovely bakery and deli next door (so you can take a packed lunch to the mountain tomorrow). $ *Average main: €12* ⊠ *86 O'Connell St.* ☎ *058/24594* ⊕ *www.nudefood.ie* ⊗ *Closed Sun. No dinner Mon.–Wed.*

$$$ ✕ **The Tannery.** Clearly, the mountain air in Knockmealdown won-
ECLECTIC ders for the creativity and vision of chef–culinary wizard Paul Flynn;
Fodor's Choice it also whets quite an appetite in the flocks of Dubliners who besiege
★ what is commonly regarded as one of Ireland's leading restaurants every weekend. The menu is rustic but whimsical and always seasonal. Check out the corned beef, potato, and onion fritters with horseradish dress-ing, or, if that doesn't tickle your taste buds, opt for the quail and foie gras pie, with cabbage and quince jelly. Fanatical foodies who want to stay as close to the culinary action as possible can now overnight in the adjoining guesthouse and attend the regular cooking-school classes. $ *Average main: €28* ⊠ *10 Quay St.* ☎ *58/45420* ⊕ *www.tannery.ie* ⊗ *Closed Mon. and 2 wks in Jan. No dinner Sun. Sept.–May. No lunch Tues.–Thurs. and Sat.*

$ ⊞ **Gold Coast Golf Hotel.** Overlooking Dungarvan Bay, this hotel is part of
HOTEL a family-run and family-friendly property that includes self-catering hol-
FAMILY iday cottages and golf villas on the edge of a woodland course on a links setting. **Pros:** great location; owners love kids; great value even in high season. **Cons:** gets a bit hectic with all those kids around; guest rooms are a little mundane; no Internet in rooms. $ *Rooms from: €119* ⊠ *Off*

Clonea Rd. ☎ *058/42249, 058/42416* ⊕ *www.goldcoastgolfresort.com* ⇨ *35 rooms, 2 suites, 16 cottages, 12 villas, 27 lodges* ⚭ *Breakfast.*

NIGHTLIFE AND THE ARTS

Coláiste na Rinne. A few miles outside Dungarvan, you can sit/join in on a *ceilí* (traditional Irish dance), held most nights in summer at Coláiste na Rinne, the school in this Irish-speaking community known for its strong tradition in Irish language, heritage, and culture. ⊠ *Ring* ☎ *058/46104* ⊕ *www.anrinn.com.*

ARDMORE

29 km (18 miles) southwest of Dungarvan.

Fodors Choice ★ Historic spiritual sites, white beaches, dramatic cliff walks, local fishermen—little Ardmore is a picture-postcard Irish town that packs a whole lot of wonder into a small peninsula at the base of a tall cliff. With a few notable exceptions—including John F. Kennedy and Gregory Peck—the cute but very real village is often overlooked by most overseas tourists.

GETTING HERE AND AROUND

From Waterford, take the N25 west and exit left onto the R673. The trip takes about an hour, with the last part traveled on a small country road. There are a few buses a day from Dungarvan and Youghal. Parking can be a problem in the high season.

EXPLORING

Cathedral of St. Declan and Round Tower. There's a story behind every ruin you pass in Ireland; behind many, there's a truly ancient story. Inside the ruined 12th-century Cathedral of St. Declan are some pillar stones decorated with ogham script (an ancient Irish alphabet) as well as weathered but stunningly abstract biblical scenes carved on its west gable. St. Declan is reputed to have disembarked here in the 5th century—30 years before St. Patrick arrived in Ireland—and founded a monastery. The saint is said to be buried in St. Declan's Oratory, a small early Christian church that has been partially reconstructed.

On the grounds of the ruined cathedral is the 97-foot-high Round Tower, which is in exceptionally good condition. Round towers were built by the early Christian monks as watchtowers and belfries but came to be used as places of refuge for the monks and their valuables during Viking raids. This is the reason the doorway is 15 feet above ground level—once inside, the monks could pull the ladder into the tower with them. ⊠ *Off Tower Hill.*

Holy Island. The 6th-century monastic settlement of Holy Island (*Inis Cealtra* in Irish) sits in the middle of Lough Derg, slightly closer to the western shore. Around the year 520 St. Colum, seeking the type of solitude only an island can offer, founded his small monastery here. It was later expanded into a serious seat of Christian learning. The Vikings arrived in 836 and killed many of the monks before making off with most of their treasures, but the monastery survived in different forms until the Reformation. The ruins on the island include a Round Tower, St. Caimin's Romanesque church, and the Saints' Graveyard, which includes 11th-centruy grave markers in Irish, and one headstone for

Cosrach "the miserable one" who died in 898. Access to the island is via boats that leave from Mountshannon, on the western side of the lake. ✉ *Co. Tipperary.*

WHERE TO EAT AND STAY

$$$$ ECLECTIC Fodor's Choice ★ 🍴 **The House Restaurant.** Celebrated Dutch chef Martjin Kajuiter presides over the compact, award-winning dining room of the Cliff House. Go in summer, when you can dine on the expansive terrace, which winds its way down toward the sea. The food is locally sourced and innovatively prepared—"trad" Irish is often the base, but garnishes and sauces lend a festive, nouvelle air. Dinner is a fixed-price, three-course affair with the West Cork scallops with pork belly, purple kale–and–potato preparations, oyster leaves, and crystalized borage flower a stunning starter. And you can't go wrong with the wild sea bass with leek fondue as your main course. The staff will even match the perfect glass of wine to each mind-blowing course. [$] *Average main: €35* ✉ *Cliff House, Cliff Rd.* ☎ *024/87800* 🌐 *www.thecliffhousehotel.com/dining* ⏲ *No lunch weekdays.*

$$$$ HOTEL Fodor's Choice ★ 🏨 **Cliff House.** Tucked into the cliffs overlooking the fishing village of Ardmore, ageless nature confronts modernist design in this luxury hotel and spa—one of the most innovative additions to Irish accommodations in years. **Pros:** the sea is everywhere; great spa and pool; up the road from the wonderful Ardmore Pottery shop. **Cons:** pricey for the region; sometimes has two-day minimum in summer; younger staff still learning the trade. [$] *Rooms from: €280* ✉ *Cliff Rd.* 🌐 *www.thecliffhousehotel.com* 🛏 *24 rooms, 15 suites* 🍽 *No meals.*

SHOPPING

Fodor's Choice ★ **Ardmore Pottery & Craft Shop.** Home to potter Mary Lincoln, a poll of *Irish Times* readers agreed this is one of the most beloved, creative, and cleverly stocked craft shops in the country. They stock everything from Alan Ardiff gold jewelry to Veronica Molloy's famed homemade jams. You can even watch Mary work at the wheel and purchase some of her own beautiful, delicate designs. ✉ *The Cliff* ☎ *024/94152* 🌐 *www.ardmorepottery.com.*

SPORTS AND THE OUTDOORS

Ardmore Adventures. Ardmore and other nearby beaches have become meccas for water-sports lovers, and this shop organizes snorkeling, kayaking, powerboating, and anything else that involves fun and the sea. There's also some rock climbing on local cliffs. ✉ *Main St.* ☎ *083/374–3889* 🌐 *www.ardmoreadventures.ie.*

Killaloe River Cruises. A cute, 12-seater passenger boat takes you on a serene, one-hour cruise of Lough Derg and into the River Shannon. It's a great chance to take in the unique wildlife and natural beauty of the region. Boats leave from the lakeshore at Killaloe, on the Clare bank of the lake. ✉ *Killaloe, Co. Clare* ☎ *086/814–0559* 🌐 *www.killaloerivercruises.com.*

COUNTY TIPPERARY AND AROUND

"It's a long way to Tipperary . . . " So run the words of that famed song sung all over the world since World War I. Actually, Tipperary is *not* so far to go, considering that, as Ireland's biggest inland county, it's within easy striking distance of Waterford and Cork. Moving in from the coastline, you can travel through some of Ireland's lushest pasturelands and to some of its most romantic sights, such as Lismore Castle. The Blackwater Valley is renowned for its peaceful beauty and excellent fishing. Some of the finest racehorses in the world are raised in the fields of Tipperary, which is also where you can find the Rock of Cashel—the greatest group of monastic ruins in all Ireland.

LISMORE

20 km (13 miles) northwest of Dungarvan.

Fodor'sChoice
★
Lismore is one of Ireland's grandest places to get lost in. Popular with both anglers and romantics, the enchanting little town is built on the banks of the Blackwater, a river famous for its trout and salmon. From the 7th to the 12th century it was an important monastic center, founded by St. Carthac (or Carthage), and it had one of the most renowned universities of its time. The village has two cathedrals: a soaring Roman Catholic one from the late 19th century and the Church of Ireland's St. Carthage's, which dates from 1633 and incorporates fragments of an earlier church.

Glamour arrived in the form of the dukes of Devonshire, who built their Irish seat here, Lismore Castle (their main house is Chatsworth in England); in the 1940s, Fred Astaire, whose sister, Adele, had married Lord Charles Cavendish, younger son of the ninth duke, would bend the elbow at the town's Madden's Pub. Other architectural jewels include a quaint library funded by Andrew Carnegie and the Ballysaggartmore "folly"—a Gothic-style gateway to a 19th-century house that was so costly the house itself was never erected.

GETTING HERE AND AROUND

From Waterford take the N25 west to the N72. The trip takes about 55 minutes. There are regular buses from Dungarvan. In summer, parking spots are at a premium around the small town.

ESSENTIALS

Visitor Information Lismore Tourist Office ✉ *Lismore Heritage Centre, West St. and Chapel St.* ☎ *058/54975* ⊕ *www.discoverlismore.com.*

EXPLORING

Knockmealdown Mountains. Leaving Lismore, head east on N72 for 6½ km (4 miles), then north on R669 into the Knockmealdown Mountains. From the summit, called Vee Gap, you'll have superb views of the Galtee Mountains in the northwest and a peak called Slievenamon in the northeast. If the day is clear, you should be able to see the Rock of Cashel, ancient seat of the Kings of Munster, some 32 km (20 miles) away. Just before you enter the Vee Gap, look for a 6-foot-high mound of stones beside the road. It marks the grave of Colonel Grubb, a local

DID YOU KNOW?

One of the earliest landmarks of Christianity in Ireland, St. Declan's Cathedral stands on a cliff top settled by the saint between 350 and 420—decades before St. Patrick arrived. On St. Declan's Day, July 24, pilgrims walk along the 80-km (50-mile) St. Declan's Way to the Rock of Cashel.

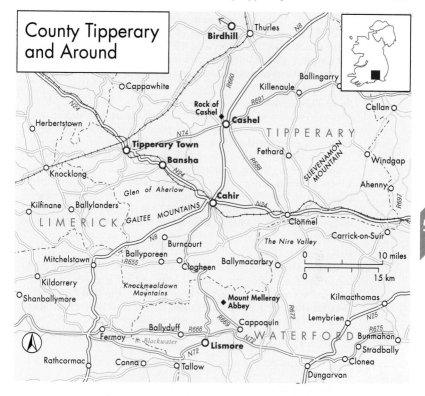

County Tipperary and Around

landowner who liked the view so much that he arranged to be buried here standing up so that he could look out over the scene for all eternity. ✉ *Vee Gap Rd.*

Fodor'sChoice
★ **Lismore Castle and Gardens.** As you cross the bridge entering Lismore, you spot the magnificent Lismore Castle, a vast, turreted building atop a rock overhanging the River Blackwater. There has been a castle here since the 12th century, but the present structure, built by the sixth duke of Devonshire, dates from the mid-19th century. The house remains the estate of the Cavendish family, and most of it is not open to the public. You can see the contemporary-art gallery, designed by Cork architect Gareth O'Callaghan, in the west wing, as well as the upper and lower gardens, which consist of woodland walks, including an unusual yew walk said to be more than 800 years old (Edmund Spenser is said to have written parts of *The Faerie Queene* here), certain months of the year. The gardens have an impressive display of magnolias, camellias, and shrubs, and are adorned with examples of contemporary sculpture. ✉ *Off N72* ⊕ *www.lismorecastle.com* 🎫 *€8* ⏱ *Apr.–Sept., daily 10:30–4:30.*

Lismore Heritage Center. In the former town courthouse, Lismore Heritage Center and its exhibits focus on the town's Celtic origins and its links to famous people from Sir Walter Raleigh to Prince Charles to

Fred Astaire. Lismore Experience, an impressive video presentation, charts the history of the town from its monastic 7th-century origins up to the present day. The center also has a large crafts shop. ✉ *West St. and Chapel St.* ☎ *058/54975* 🌐 *www.discoverlismore.com* 🎫 *€4.80 for Lismore Experience* 🕘 *Apr.–Oct., weekdays 9:30–5:30, Sat. 10–5, Sun. noon–5; Nov.–Apr., weekdays 9:30–5:30.*

Mount Melleray Abbey. The first post-Reformation monastery, Mount Melleray Abbey was founded in 1832 by the Cistercian Order in what was then a barren mountainside wilderness. Over the years the order has transformed the site into more than 600 acres of fertile farmland. The monks maintain strict vows of silence, but you're welcome to join in services throughout the day and are permitted into most areas of the abbey. It's also possible to stay in the guest lodge. There's a small heritage center about the history of Irish monasticism with a few ogham stones and a short film. ✉ *Off R669, 13 km (8 miles) from Lismore, Cappoquin* ☎ *058/54404* 🌐 *www.mountmellerayabbey.org* 🎫 *Free* 🕘 *Daily 8–8.*

WHERE TO STAY

$$ B&B/INN 🏨 **Richmond House.** It's been 300 years since the Earl of Cork and Burlington built this handsome country house, and it still retains its imposing aura of courtly elegance, thanks to owners Claire and Paul Deevy. **Pros:** excellent restaurant; enchanting gardens. **Cons:** limited facilities; place is a little tattered around the edges. [$] *Rooms from: €150* ✉ *Off N72, Cappoquin* ☎ *58/54278* 🌐 *www.richmondhouse.net* 🛏 *10 rooms* 🕘 *Closed late Dec.–mid-Jan.* 🍴 *Breakfast.*

CAHIR

37 km (23 miles) north of Lismore.

Cahir (pronounce it "Care") is a busy but easygoing market town with a pleasant Georgian square at its heart. It is built on the River Suir at the eastern end of the Galtee mountain range. The Suir is known for its good salmon and trout fishing, as is the Aherlow River, which joins it above town.

GETTING HERE AND AROUND

From Dublin, take the N7/M7 south to junction 19 and the N24. At junction 10, take the R670 to Cahir. The trip takes just over two hours. There is regular bus service from Kilkenny and Waterford, as well as train service from Dublin and Kilkenny.

ESSENTIALS

Visitor Information Cahir Tourist Office ✉ *Castle car park* ☎ *052/744–1453* 🌐 *www.ireland.com* 🕘 *Closed Nov.–Mar.*

EXPLORING

Cahir Castle. The unavoidable focal point of the town, Cahir Castle is dramatically perched on a rocky island on the River Suir. Once the stronghold of the mighty Butler family and one of Ireland's largest and best-preserved castles, it retains its dramatic keep, tower, and much of its original defensive structure. An audiovisual show and guided tour are available upon request. ✉ *Castle St.* 🌐 *www.heritageireland.ie* 🎫 *€3*

The duke of Devonshire's Lismore Castle once sheltered Edmund Spenser when he was writing *The Faerie Queene*; today, his parklands are home to avant-garde artworks.

🕐 *Mid-Mar.–mid-June and Sept.–mid-Oct., daily 9:30–5:30; mid-June–Aug., daily 9–6:30; mid-Oct.–mid-Mar., daily 9:30–4:30; last entry 45 mins before closing.*

Fodor's Choice
★

Swiss Cottage. If there's little storybook allure to the brute mass of Cahir Castle, fairy-tale looks grace the first earl of Glengall's 1812 Swiss Cottage, a dreamy relic from the days when Romanticism conquered 19th-century Ireland. A mile south of town on a particularly picturesque stretch of the River Suir, this "cottage *orné*" was probably designed by John Nash, one of the Regency period's most fashionable architects. Half thatch-roof cottage, half mansion, it was a veritable theater set that allowed the lordly couple to fantasize about being "simple folk" (secret doorways allowed servants to bring food without being noticed). Inside, some of the earliest Dufour wallpapers printed in Paris charm the eye. A pleasant way to get here is to hike from Cahir Castle on a footpath along the river. In peak season, crowds can be fierce. ⊠ *Off R670* ⊕ *www.heritageireland.ie* 🎫 *€3* 🕐 *Apr.–late-Oct., daily 10–6.*

WHERE TO STAY

$$
HOTEL
Fodor's Choice
★

🏨 **Aherlow House Hotel & Lodges.** Built in 1928 to replace a house destroyed in Ireland's Civil War, Aherlow is set on the slopes of Sliabh na Muc (Mountain of the Pigs), and comes with its own private forest and incredible views of the magnificent Galtee Mountains and the ancient Glen of Aherlow. **Pros:** rooms are big; families will love the lodges; stunning natural surroundings. **Cons:** popular with local weddings and parties; gets booked up summer weekends. 💲 *Rooms from: €138* ⊠ *Off R663, Aherlow* ⊕ *www.aherlowhouse.ie* 🛏 *29 rooms, 15 lodges* 🕐 *Closed Sun.–Thurs. during Jan.–Mar.* 🍴 *No meals.*

$$
B&B/INN
Fodor's Choice
★

☆ The Old Convent. A wonderfully tucked-away sanctuary—it began life as a prim-and-proper, 19th-century convent set amid spectacular vistas of the Knockmealdown Mountains—this retreat has been tastefully restored by Christine and Dermot Gannon. **Pros:** passionate owners; extra-comfortable mattresses; serenity of natural surroundings. **Cons:** a trek to the nearest town; not ideal for kids. $ *Rooms from: €170* ✉ *Mount Anglesby, Clogheen* ☎ *052/746-5565* ⊕ *www.theoldconvent. ie* ⇋ *7 rooms* ◎ *Some meals.*

TIPPERARY TOWN

22 km (14 miles) northwest of Cahir.

Tipperary Town, a dairy-farming center at the head of a fertile plain known as the Golden Vale, is a good starting point for climbing and walking in the hills around the Glen of Aherlow. The small country town, on the River Ara, is also worth visiting in its own right. In New Tipperary, a neighborhood built by local tenants during Ireland's Land War (1890–91), buildings such as Dalton's Heritage House have been restored; you can visit the Heritage House by calling the offices of Clann na Éireann. You can also visit the old Butter Market on Dillon Street; the Churchwell at the junction of Church, Emmet, and Dillon streets; and the grave of the grandfather of Robert Emmett—one of the most famous Irish patriots—in the graveyard at St. Mary's Church. A statue of Charles Kickham, whose 19th-century novel *The Homes of Tipperary* chronicled the devastation of this county through forced emigration, has a place of honor in the center of town. Adjacent to Bridewell Jail on St. Michael's Street is St. Michael's Church, with its stained-glass window depicting a soldier killed during World War I.

GETTING HERE AND AROUND

From Dublin, take the N7/M7 south to junction 19 and the M8. Take junction 9 to the N74 to Tipperary Town. There is bus service from Dublin, Cork, and Kilkenny, and regular train service from Dublin and Cork. There is ample parking around the town.

ESSENTIALS

Visitor Information Tipperary Tourist Office ✉ *Tipperary Excel, Mitchel St.* ☎ *062/80520* ⊕ *www.tipperary-excel.com.*

Tipperary Excel. This arts and culture center contains the local tourist office and the Tipperary Family History research center—a top spot for all those tracking down their Irish roots. ✉ *Mitchel St.* ☎ *062/80520* ⊕ *www.tipperary-excel.com.*

CASHEL

17 km (11 miles) northeast of Tipperary Town.

Cashel is a market town on the busy Cork–Dublin road, with a lengthy history as a center of royal and religious power. From roughly AD 370 until AD 1101, it was the seat of the Kings of Munster, and it was probably at one time a center of Druidic worship. Here, according to legend, St. Patrick arrived in about AD 432 and baptized King Aengus, who

Continued on page 299

TOWERING GLORY
The Rock of Cashel

Haunt of St. Patrick, Ireland's "rock of ages" is a place where history, culture, and legend collide.

Dormitory

Hall of Vicar's Choral
This was once the domain of the cathedral choristers.

Seat of the Kings of Munster and the hallowed spot where St. Patrick first plucked a shamrock to explain the mystery of the Trinity, the Rock of Cashel is Ireland's greatest group of ecclesiastical ruins. Standing like an ominous beacon in the middle of a sloped, treeless valley, the Rock has a titanic grandeur and majesty that create what one ancient scribe called "a fingerpost to Heaven."

Historians theorize the stupendous mass was born during the Ice Age. This being Ireland, however, fulsome myths abound: There are those who believe it was created when the Devil himself took a huge bite of the Slieve Bloom Mountains only to spit it out right in the middle of the Golden Vale. Today, the great limestone mass still rises 300 feet to command a panorama over all it surveys—fittingly, the name derives from the Irish *caiseal*, meaning stone fort, and this gives a good idea of the strategic importance of Cashel in days of yore.

For centuries, Cashel was known as the "city of the kings"—from the 5th century, the lords of Munster ruled over much of southern Ireland from here. In 1101, however, they handed Cashel over to the Christian fathers, and the rock soon became the center of the reform movement that reshaped the Irish Church. Along the way, the church fathers embarked on a centuries-long building campaign that resulted in the magnificent group of chapels, round towers,

and walls you see at Cashel today. View them from afar on the N8 highway and the complex looks so complete you're surprised upon arriving to discover guides in modern dress and not knights in medieval uniform.

■TIP➜ You have to stay at the Cashel Palace Hotel on Main St. to enjoy the best approach to the rock; along the Bishop's Walk, a 10-minute hike that begins outside the drawing room.

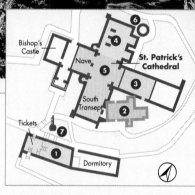

① HALL OF THE VICAR'S CHORAL

Built in the 15th century—though topped with a modern reconstruction of a beautifully corbeled medieval ceiling—this was once the domain of the cathedral choristers.

The Museum Located in the hall's undercroft, this collection includes the original St. Patrick's Cross and fast-forwards you to the present thanks to a striking audiovisual display on the Rock entitled the "Stronghold of the Faith."

② CORMAC'S CHAPEL

The real showpiece of Cashel is this chapel, built in 1127 by Cormac McCarthy, King of Desmond and Bishop of Cashel. A rare jewel in gleaming red sandstone, it is the finest example of Hiberno-Romanesque architecture. The entry archway carries a tympanum featuring a centaur in a helmet with a bow and arrow aimed at a lion, perhaps a symbol of good over evil. Such work was rare in Irish architecture and points to possible European influence. Preserved within the chapel is a splendid but broken sarcophagus, once believed to be Cormac's final resting place. At the opposite end of the chapel is the nave, where you can look for wonderful medieval paintings now showing through old plasterwork.

ST. PATRICK'S CATHEDRAL

With thick walls that attest to its origin as a fortress, this now-roofless cathedral is the largest building on the site. Built in 1169, it was dedicated on March 17th—St. Patrick's Day. On the theory that ancient churches were oriented to the sunrise on the feast day of their dedicated saint, the cathedral points east, a direction agreeing closely with March 17th. The original cathedral, constructed in a flamboyant variation on Irish Romanesque style, was destroyed by fire in 1495. In ❸ **The Choir**, look for the noted Tomb of Myler McGrath. Note the tombs in the ❹ **North Transept** whose carvings—of the apostles, other saints, and the Beasts of the Apocalypse— are remarkably detailed. The octagonal staircase turret that ascends the cathedral's central tower leads to a series of defensive passages built into the thick walls—from

North Transept

the top of the tower, you'll have wonderful views. At the center of the cathedral is the area known as ❺ **The Crossing**, a magnificently detailed arch where the four sections of the building come together.

COMING OF AGE

AD 450—St. Patrick comes to Cashel, bringing the advent of Christianity when King Aengus accepts baptism from Ireland's patron saint.

990—Cashel is fortified by King Brian Boru, the legendary figure who broke the stranglehold of the Danes at the Battle of Clontarf in 1014.

1101—King Murtagh O'Brien, grandson of Brian Boru, proclaims the royal fortress "for God, St. Patrick, and St. Ailbe," making Cashel center of the Irish Church.

1317—The arrival of the Scots: Edward Bruce, brother of Robert I, is inaugurated king of Ireland, and attends Mass on the Rock where he later holds a parliament.

1749—Protestant archbishop Price earns undying infamy by pulling down the roof of the cathedral to rebuild his own church.

Detail of wooden ceiling in the Vicar's Choral, Rock of Cashel

NORTHERN VIEW OF THE ROCK

Bishop's Castle

Central Tower

⑥ THE ROUND TOWER

As the oldest building on the Rock, the Round Tower rises 92 feet to command a panoramic view of the entire Vale of Tipperary. Dating back to 1101, its construction followed the grim reality of the Viking invasions. A constant lookout was posted here to warn of any advancing armies, and food was always provisioned in the tower so as to outlast any prolonged siege. Note the door 10 feet from the ground, allowing ladders to be pulled up to thwart attackers, some of whom attempted to chip the rock at the base, to little effect.

⑦ ST. PATRICK'S CROSS

Directly beyond the Rock's main entrance is this 7-foot-tall High Cross carved from one large block and resting upon what is said to have been the original coronation stone of the Munster kings. The cross was erected in the saint's honor to commemorate his famous visit to Cashel in 450. Upon both sides carved in high relief are two figures—the face of Christ crucified and a robed St. Patrick with his feet resting upon an ox head. Unique among High Crosses, this one has vertical supports on either side, perhaps allusions to the crosses of the good and bad thieves. A sort of early Irish bible class, these large stone crosses (which were sculpted from the 9th to the 12th centuries) were perfect teaching tools for a population that was largely illiterate. This cross is a faithfully rendered replica—the original now rests in the site museum.

The Crossing

Nave

North Transept

THE ST. PATRICK CONNECTION

While many legends surround Saint Patrick, he was an actual historical figure—his writings, a Latin text dating from the 5th century AD, yield the few undisputed facts about him. Born into a wealthy family in Roman-occupied Britain, he was kidnapped as a young man by Irish marauders and enslaved for six years as a sheepherder on the slopes of Slemish in County Antrim. He escaped, and returned to Britain, but a vision called him back to Ireland to convert the people to Christianity. Arriving in 433, he defied the pagan priests of Tara by kindling the Easter fire on Slane but went on in a peaceful conversion of Ireland to Christianity—not a drop of blood was shed—until his death in AD 460.

St. Patrick's conversion of Ireland was characterized by clever diplomacy: his missionaries were careful to combine elements of then-current druidic ritual with new Christian practice. For example, the Irish Christian church popularized the Feast of all Saints, and arranged for it to be celebrated on November 1, the same day as the great Celtic harvest festival, Samhain. Today's Halloween evolved from this linking of Celtic and Christian holidays.

Clearly a skilled negotiator as well as missionary, St. Patrick wisely preserved the social structure of Ireland, converting the people tribe by tribe. He first attempted to establish the Roman system of dioceses and bishops, but—since Ireland had never been conquered by the Romans—this arrangement did not suit a society without large cities. Instead, the Celts preferred a religious institution introduced by the desert fathers: the monastery, an idea of a "family" of monks being easy to grasp in a tribal society. Over 70 monasteries were founded in the 5th and 6th centuries, and by AD 700 abbots had replaced bishops as the leaders of the Catholic church.

In 457 St. Patrick retired to Saul, where he died. The only relic that can be tied to him is the famous 5th-century iron bell in Dublin's National Museum. Even if it was not, as is traditionally believed, used by the saint, he carried one very like it, and used it to announce his approach.

ROCK OF CASHEL INFO

✉ *Rock of Cashel* ☎ *062/61437* ⊕ *www. heritageireland.ie* ☒ *€6* ⊘ *Mid-Mar.– early-June, daily 9–5:30; early-June–early-Sept., daily 9–7; early-Sept.–mid-Oct., daily 9–5:30; mid-Oct.–mid-Mar., daily 9–4:30.*

Above: Dublin, St. Patrick's Day parade

became Ireland's first Christian ruler. One of the many legends associated with this event is that St. Patrick plucked a shamrock to explain the mystery of the Trinity, thus giving a new emblem to Christian Ireland.

GETTING HERE AND AROUND

Cashel is on the busy N8/M8 motorway between Dublin and Cork. Dublin is 162 km (100 miles) northeast of Cashel on the N8/M8 and N7/M7. Cork City is 97 km (60 miles) or 1 hour and 10 minutes south of Cashel on the N8/M8 and the N74. Bus Éireann runs buses from Dublin (€14.25 one-way, €23.27 round-trip; 3 hours; six daily), Cork (€14.25 one-way and €22.27 round-trip; 1½ hours) via Cahir (€5.51 one-way and €9.22 round-trip; 15 minutes) and Fermoy (€14.25 one-way and €23.27 round-trip; 1 hour, 20 minutes). The bus stop for Cork is outside the Bake House on Main Street. The Dublin stop is directly opposite.

To head to the Rock of Cashel directly from Dublin, many travelers use the Irish Rail route that heads to the small town of Thurles, then take a 20-minute bus or taxi ride to Cashel.

5

ESSENTIALS

Visitor Information Cashel Tourist Office ✉ *Cashel Heritage Centre, Main St.* ☎ *062/62511* 🌐 *www.cashel.ie.*

EXPLORING

Fodor's Choice ★ The awe-inspiring, often mist-shrouded **Rock of Cashel** is one of Ireland's most visited sites. *For complete information, see "Towering Glory: The Rock of Cashel."*

Cashel Heritage Centre. In the same building as the tourism office, the Cashel Heritage Centre explains the historic relationship between the town and the Rock and includes a scale model of Cashel as it looked during the 1600s. ✉ *City Hall, Main St.* ☎ *062/62511* 🌐 *www.cashel.ie* 🎫 *Free* 🕒 *Mar.–Oct., daily 9:30–5:50; Nov.–Feb., weekdays 9:30–5:30.*

G. P. A. Bolton Library. Located on the grounds of the St. John the Baptist Church of Ireland Cathedral, this library has a particularly fine collection of rare books, manuscripts, and maps, some of which date to the beginning of the age of printing in Europe. ✉ *John St.* ☎ *062/61944* 🎫 *€2* 🕒 *Mon.–Wed, 10–3, Thurs. 10–2:30.*

WHERE TO EAT AND STAY

$$$ MODERN IRISH Fodor's Choice ★ 🍴 **Chez Hans.** It's rather fitting that this restaurant is in a converted church, as it's become something of a shrine for foodies. Gourmands travel from Dublin and Cork to get their fix of chef Jason Matthia's cuisine, which is contemporary with a hint of nouvelle. He works wonders with fresh Irish ingredients, especially seafood. The seafood cassoulet—half a dozen varieties of fish and shellfish with a delicate chive velouté—is legendary. Another specialty is panfried turbot, with salade Niçoise and Dingle crab mayonnaise. The atmosphere is wonderful, too, with dark wood and tapestries providing an elegant background for the white linen. He's opened a great café next door if you prefer something more informal. [$] *Average main: €29* ✉ *Moore La.* ☎ *062/61177* 🌐 *www.chezhans.net* ✍ *Reservations essential* 🕒 *Closed Sun. and Mon. and late Jan.–early Feb. No lunch.*

$$$ ⌕ **Cashel Palace Hotel.** This grand house is a palace in every sense: red-
HOTEL   pine paneling, barley-sugar staircases, Corinthian columns, and a sur-
Fodor's Choice   feit of cosseting antiques all create an air of Georgian volupté, while
★   outside the majestic manse is gorgeously offset by parkland with foun-
tains and centuries-old trees. **Pros:** glorious period main house; great
strolling gardens; luxurious baths. **Cons:** expensive for this region;
popular for weddings; few in-room facilities. $ *Rooms from: €175*
⊠ *Main St.* ☎ *062/62707* ⊕ *www.cashel-palace.ie* ⌁ *21 rooms, 1 cot-
tage* ⦿| *Breakfast.*

$$ ⌕ **Dundrum House Hotel.** Nestled beside the River Multeen, 12 km (7½
HOTEL   miles) outside busy Cashel, this imposing, four-story, 1730 Georgian
house features elaborate plaster ceilings, attractive period furniture,
open fires, and an old chapel (stained-glass windows intact) converted
to a cocktail bar, as well as a health spa and golf course. **Pros:** good
value for Georgian comfort; wonderful parkland views; lively cocktail
bar. **Cons:** main house rooms superior to others; can get a bit noisy
when full; attracts flush crowd. $ *Rooms from: €130* ⊠ *Off R505,
Dundrum* ☎ *062/71116* ⊕ *www.dundrumhousehotel.com* ⌁ *70 rooms,
16 holiday homes* ⦿| *Breakfast.*

NIGHTLIFE AND THE ARTS

Brú Ború Cultural Centre. Enjoy folksinging, storytelling, trad music, and
dancing at the Brú Ború Centre at the foot of the Rock of Cashel. The
center also has the "Sounds of History" audiovisual exhibition open all
day, and regular arts and music events throughout the year. ⊠ *Rock Lane*
⊕ *www.bruboru.ie* ⦿ *Mid-June–Aug., Mon. 9–5, Tues.–Sat. 9 am–11
pm; Sept.–mid-June, weekdays 9–5.*

BANSHA

16 km (10 miles) south west of Cashel.

This prosperous little farming town at the foot of the Galtee Mountains
is really of interest as a base for the beautiful Glen of Aherlow. The Glen
itself is a lush valley formed where the River Aherlow runs between the
Galtees and the tree-covered ridge of Slievenamuck. Historically, it was
a key passageway for the native Irish between Tipperary and Limerick.

GETTING HERE AND AROUND

From Dublin take the N7/M7 towards Cork. Exit onto the M8 and get
off on the N24 to Bansha. From Cashel take the N74 west, then the
N24 to Bansha. There are regular bus services from Dublin, Limerick
and Waterford.

EXPLORING

The Glen of Aherlow is a hiking and horse riding paradise, with a feast
of national trails ranging from gentle loops to some serious climbs. The
rewards for mountain walking are great, with Lough Curra and Lake
Muskry two stunning corrie lakes with view overlooking the whole of
central and southern Ireland. The Glen hosts two walking festivals on
the last weekend in January and the first weekend in June. For history
buffs, the Tipperary Heritage Way (based on ancient pilgrim walks)
from Cashel to Ardmore also passes through here. The walks will take

you past a number of ancients sights, from St. Pecaun's Holy Well at the eastern end of the Glen to the fascinating and overlooked Darby's Bed passage tomb on the west side of Slievenamuck hill near the village of Galbally. This is also prime horse country and the same trails can often be taken on a locally hired mount with an experienced guide to help along the way. Hillcrest Riding Centre in nearby Galbally can organize treks, including a picnic lunch. For details of walks, activities, and events in the Glen, see the very helpful site, ⊕ *aherlow.com.*

Hillcrest Equestrian Centre ⊠ *Co. Limerick* ☎ *062/37915* ⊕ *www.hillcrest equestriancentre.com.*

WHERE TO STAY

$$
B&B/INN
Fodor's Choice
★

⌕ Lismacue House. The Irish country-house experience reaches its epitome at this beautiful, untarnished Georgian masterpiece just outside the village of Bansha. **Pros:** a family operation; stunning views; genuine Georgian architecture. **Cons:** two bedrooms share a bathroom; isolated. **$** *Rooms from: €170* ⊠ *Lismacue House* ☎ *062/625–4106* ⊕ *www. lismacue.com* ⤳ *5 rooms.*

BIRDHILL

62 km (38 miles) north of Bansha, 24 km (15 miles) northeast of Limerick City.

It's no coincidence that this picturesque little village in undiscovered north Tipperary always does well in the national "Tidy Towns" competition—a village beauty contest that the Irish take very seriously. But the real charm of this cute hamlet is its proximity to the majestic Lough Derg with the mysterious Holy Island at its center.

GETTING HERE AND AROUND

From Bansha take the N24 north to the R455. From Dublin take the N7/M7 south and exit at junction 21 to the R445.

ESSENTIALS

Visitor Information Tipperary Tourist Information ⊠ *Cashel* ⊕ www. tipperary.com.

EXPLORING

Lough Derg is the third-largest lake in Ireland and actually borders three counties: Clare, Tipperary, and Galway. The lake area near Birdhill is some of its least explored territory. It's a haven for anglers and watersports enthusiasts, including wind surfers, sailors, and relaxed cruisers. The Lough Derg Drive is another undiscovered treasure of the area. It meanders around the Lake, through gorgeous little villages in all three counties. You can pull over at numerous lookout points to appreciate the unique setting of the monastic settlement at the center of the lake. The adventure hot spots section of ⊕ *www.discoverireland.ie* has a whole section on Lough Derg and the best providers for waterskiing, wakeboarding, sailing, and other activities. The Watermark Ski Club (based in Terryglass) is one of the best places on the lake to get started and meet fellow water sporters.

Watermark Ski Club ✉ *Lough Derg* ☎ *087/257–3661* ⊕ *www. irishwaterski.com.*

WHERE TO STAY

$$ 🏨 **Coolbawn Quay.** The main appeal of this collection of cottages built in
HOTEL the style of a 19th-century Irish village is their magical setting between
Lough Derg and the surrounding rolling hills and forests. **Pros:** incredible natural setting; great choice of accommodation types; high-quality spa. **Cons:** can book out at weekends; popular for weddings. $ *Rooms from: €150* ✉ *Coolbawn Quay, Lough Derg* ☎ *067/28162* ⊕ *www. coolbawnquay.com* ⇥ *17 cottages* ⫟○⫠ *Some meals.*

6

COUNTY CORK

WELCOME TO COUNTY CORK

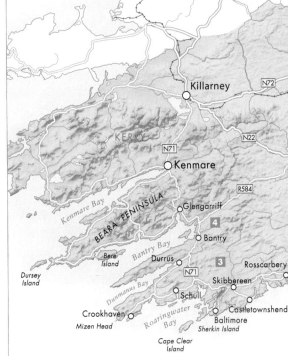

TOP REASONS TO GO

★ **Blarney Castle:** Visitors line up to kiss the Blarney Stone and acquire the gift of gab. This is an impressive 15th-century tower-house castle with unusual gardens, at their best in daffodil season— early to mid-March.

★ **Cobh:** If you have Irish roots, chances are your ancestors left from Cobh. Exhibits in The Queenstown Story at Cobh Heritage Centre commemorate the 2.5 million emigrants who sailed from here.

★ **Kinsale:** This picturesque port, long a favored haven of sailors, is famed for its fine dining in tiny front-parlor eateries. It's also a chic place to see and be seen—the Irish St-Tropez.

★ **The Cork Coastline:** On the drive from Kinsale to Skibbereen, one of the less rugged stretches of the Wild Atlantic Way, you'll encounter charming little villages.

★ **Bantry House:** One of Ireland's finest stately homes, packed with treasures from all over Europe, stands on a breathtaking bluff.

1 Cork City and Around. Identifying Cork as Ireland's second-largest city is misleading—it has just one-tenth the population of Dublin, and its character is more along the lines of a college town, which it is, than a metropolis. That means lively pubs, quirky cafés, and lots of good music, trad and otherwise.

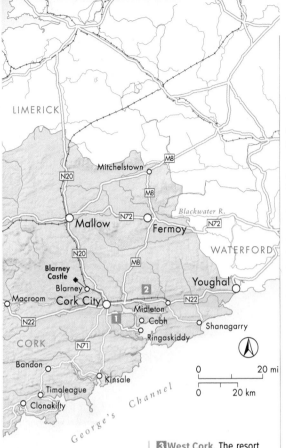

GETTING ORIENTED

After exploring the delights of Cork City, use it as a base to explore the county's famed wonders, including Blarney Castle. Embark on a gastronomic adventure by traveling east to Midleton and Shanagarry—famed respectively for their whiskey and culinary traditions. Shanagarry, in rich farming country, also has a local tradition of craft pottery. Due south is fashionable Kinsale, while westward lies Skibbereen and picture-perfect Bantry. From here a cliff-top road with stunning views leads to ruggedly beautiful Glengarriff.

6

2 East Cork. Products of the rich farming land east of Cork City used to include whiskey: see how it was made at the Jameson Experience in Midleton, just a short drive from Ballymaloe House, pioneer of the New Irish cuisine. The long, flat, sandy beaches here—a summertime favorite with Irish holidaymakers—are great for windswept walks year-round.

3 West Cork. The resort town of Kinsale is the gateway to an attractive rocky coastline east and west of Skibbereen. The area is known for its atmospheric pubs and cottage restaurants.

4 Bantry Bay. At the top of the long sea inlet is the imposing Georgian mansion, Bantry House, just outside Bantry Town. The road between here and subtropical Glengarriff climbs high above the water, offering sweeping views of the bay; the hills of the Beara Peninsula are a scenic highlight.

CORK'S FOOD MARKETS

Long known as "the belly of Ireland," West Cork is celebrated for its rich fishing and even richer farming. Like a world-class picnic, this cook's tour is the tastiest recipe for a day trip through the region.

FINDING THE FEAST

The best places to track down top temptations from Cork's gastronomic cornucopia are the area's food markets, often set in small villages and averaging only about a dozen stalls, and held one morning a week. Low overheads mean bargains for the buyers, who enjoy an amazing array of artisanal foodstuffs, from organic vegetables to sauces and relishes, Breton pancakes, handmade bread, home-cured ham, preserves, smoked salmon, and a great range of local cheeses. And the markets' festive atmosphere (often enlivened by a jazz trio or guitarist) is complemented by the camaraderie of the stall-holders—this is often their main contact with the buying public. Check out (⊕ *www.* *westcorkmarkets.com*) for up-to-date information.

MARKETS

Bantry, Main Square, Friday 9 am to 1 pm

This traditional street market has a strong presence of growers of organic plants and vegetables.

Clonakilty, Friday 10 am to 2 pm

The Friday market (mainly food) is in and around the covered alley beside O'Donovan's Hotel off Main Street.

Kinsale, Market Square, Wednesday 10 am to 1 pm

Snack on a Breton crepe while stocking up on chutneys, smoked salmon, farmhouse cheeses, fresh fish, and organic fruit and vegetables at this cute piazza market.

Midleton, Saturday 9:30 am to 1 pm

One of the liveliest farmers' markets, it's held in a small parking lot, with buskers creating a festive vibe.

Schull, Sunday 9:30 am to 2 pm Easter to December

At its best in summer and at Christmas, this foodie's market showcases superb products from local bakers, fish smokers, and cheesemakers, and Gubbeen smoked pork products.

The English Market, Cork. Today this famous city-center covered market is a thriving hub of artisanal bakers, butchers, fishmongers, and greengrocers. Organic fruit and vegetables, top-quality meat and fresh fish, imported coffees and teas, locally made charcuterie, farmhouse cheeses—even a champagne from the local wine merchant, Bubble Brothers.

OTHER FOODIE FAVES

The Irish deli is unlike any other, perhaps because there is no indigenous tradition of specialty food shops, so those that do exist tend to be one-off expressions of their owners' personalities.

In Clonakilty head for **The Lettercollum Kitchen Project**. Both talented chefs and dedicated vegetable gardeners, Con McLaughlin and Karen Austin are masters of the vegetarian and ethnic repertory (and also offer cooking classes). Their bakery shop sells specialist breads,

cooks' ingredients, sandwiches, and savory tarts.

Mannings' Emporium, with its open-air display of vegetables and outdoor picnic tables, looks as if it belongs on a southern Italian roadside, rather than at Ballylickey, on the road between Bantry and Glengarriff. Val Manning has long championed West Cork's artisan food producers, home bakers, and confectioners, and what was once a corner store selling milk and bread is now a renowned gastronomic outpost. This is the place to try two local hard cheeses, Gabriel and Desmond, the pungent Milleens, Ardsallagh goat's cheese, and Knockalara sheep's milk cheese. Manning's choice of wine is interesting, too.

SUPERMARKETS

In many parts of the world the supermarket and the artisan food tradition are at opposite ends of the spectrum. In West Cork however, they have a complementary relationship, with local supermarkets making a point of supporting small local food producers, and local people enjoying the chance to support their friends and neighbors by buying their produce. **Scally's** of Clonakilty and **Field's** of Skibbereen, both trading under the **SuperValu** logo, are prime examples of this trend.

Updated by Alannah Hopkin

County Cork is the essence of what makes Ireland different. The small-scale city of Cork, with its limestone bridges and Georgian facades, is a friendly place where strangers soon become good friends. The gently lilting accent is mirrored in the green hills that lead to Blarney and its famous castle, but there's drama aplenty on the rugged fingers of land that reach out into the Atlantic Ocean to the west, and on clear nights the glorious sunsets over the wide expanse of Bantry Bay paint a lasting picture in the memory.

With its landscape dotted with small farms, charming towns, mild climate, and deep-rooted history, the county of Cork is perennially popular with visitors. The county may be Ireland's largest, Cork may be Ireland's second-biggest city, and Kinsale the largest beep on the Irish foodie radar screen, but nearly everything else here is small scale and friendly. The towns are tiny and the roads are narrow and twisting. Brightly painted villages and toy harbors encourage you to stop and linger. From Kinsale along the coast to Glengarriff, miles of pretty lanes meander through farmland. Indeed, this is Ireland's picture-postcard country.

But as you look over the fuchsia-laden hedges that ring thriving dairy farms or stop at a wayside restaurant to sample locally sourced beef, it's difficult to imagine that a century and a half ago this area was decimated by famine. Thousands perished in fields and workhouses, and thousands more took "coffin ships" from Cobh in Cork Harbour to the New World. The region was battered again during both the War for Independence and the civil war that were fought with intensity in and around "Rebel Cork" between 1919 and 1921. Economic recovery didn't pick up until the late 1960s, and tourist development did not surge until the mid-1990s.

During the Irish economic boom, large sections of Cork's city center were rebuilt with an array of all-weather shopping malls. However, the landmark buildings survived and the streetscape got a much-needed face-lift in 2005, Cork's year as European Capital of Culture. The lilting up-and-down accent of Cork City's locals will immediately charm you, as will the generally festive air that prevails in its streets, making many visitors assume that some kind of festival is going on, even on those rare occasions when it is not. Cork has a reputation as Ireland's festival city, with jazz, film, and choral music festivals and the Midsummer Arts Festivals all attracting huge, good-natured crowds.

COUNTY CORK PLANNER

WHEN TO GO

The best times to visit County Cork are from mid-March to June and in September and October. July and August are the peak holiday periods. Roads are more crowded, prices are higher, and the best places are booked in advance. March can be chilly, with daily temperatures in the 40s and 50s. The average high in June is 65°F (18°C). May and June are the sunniest months, while May and September are the driest ones. From November to March, daylight hours are short, the weather is damp, and many places close.

FESTIVALS AND EVENTS

Cork is known as Ireland's festival city, with a busy calendar of events, including a number of high-profile festivals. Elsewhere in the county there are annual festivals that are well worth planning your trip around, along with small community events that portray local heritage, local passions, and the character of the local people. These are just a selection.

Ballymaloe LitFest of Food and Wine. Based on Ballymaloe's multigenerational heritage of cookbook writing, this mid-May festival brings a host of food writers and TV presenters to Ballymaloe House and Cookery School to celebrate gastronomy with demonstrations, talks, workshops, tours, and—of course—tastings. ⊠ *Ballymaloe, Co. Cork* ☎ *021/464–5777* ⊕ *www.litfest.ie.*

Cork Film Festival. In the second week of November, this nine-day festival puts on a lively program of world cinema at several city venues, and includes feature films, documentaries, shorts, and other events; 2015 will mark its 60th year. ⊠ *Cork City, Co. Cork* ☎ *021/427–1711* ⊕ *www.corkfilmfest.org.*

Cork International Short Story Festival. Readings, author interviews, workshops, and award presentations are highlights of this five-day literary event in mid-September. ⊠ *Cork City, Co. Cork* ☎ *021/431–2955* ⊕ *www.munsterlit.ie.*

Guinness Cork Jazz Festival. Late October brings an international lineup of jazz and soul musicians to the city, for four days of concerts in the big venues—Opera House, Everyman, Triskel Auditorium, and Triskel Christchurch—bands in pubs and hotels, street music, and various fringe events. ⊠ *Cork City, Co. Cork* ⊕ *www.guinnessjazzfestival.com.*

Kinsale Gourmet Festival. A gourmand's delight, this foodie festival creates a party atmosphere all over town for three days in early October. ⊠ *Kinsale, Co. Cork* ☎ *021/477–3571* ⊕ *www.kinsalerestaurants.com.*

Masters of Tradition. One very good reason to visit County Cork at any time is to hear authentic traditional music, but time your trip to coincide with this mid-August five-day festival in Bantry and you'll hear some of the finest. ✉ *Bantry, Co. Cork* ☎ *027/52788/9* ⊕ *www.westcorkmusic.ie.*

West Cork Chamber Music Festival. Internationally renowned musicians perform in the library of Bantry House for 10 days in late June. ✉ *Bantry, Co. Cork* ☎ *027/52788/9* ⊕ *www.westcorkmusic.ie.*

PLANNING YOUR TIME

When you plan a trip to County Cork, you'll need to make a pick of the ports. The biggest one, Cobh, to the east of the Cork City, was the point of embarkation for most 19th-century Irish transatlantic passengers and it retains a strong whiff of nostalgia. Dominated by its tall-spired cathedral, the town, filled with 19th-century buildings, climbs vertiginously up- and downhill and faces southward out to sea. Kinsale is more of a village than a town, built beside a hill at one end of an unspoiled fjord-like harbor. With its yacht marinas and tempting restaurants, Kinsale has a cosmopolitan air, but it also offers serious history at Charles Fort. Timoleague is a sleepy hamlet, nestled beside the romantic ruins of its abbey. Many visitors regard Castletownshend as the prettiest village, while others prefer the sheltered waters of subtropical Glengarriff.

IF YOU HAVE THREE DAYS

If you're here for a short stay—three days or fewer—you'd do well to base yourself in Cork City, which is easy to explore on foot. Allow a day to take in the sights of the city center, including the Crawford Art Gallery, the indoor English Market, and the boutiques along St. Patrick's Street (also called Patrick Street). On the second day, visit Blarney Castle; from there it's a half-hour drive to Cork Harbour, where you can visit Fota Island and Cobh. On the third day head for Kinsale, worth a day itself, or you can head to the scenic coast of West Cork, which can be comfortably driven in a day. The narrow roads here meander through attractive waterside villages to the splendid prospect of Bantry Bay, overlooked by the stately Bantry House. A few miles farther west is another highlight of the Wild Atlantic Way, the sheltered inlet of Glengarriff. Return that night to Kinsale or Cork, both handy for the airport.

GETTING HERE AND AROUND

AIR TRAVEL

Cork Airport, 5 km (3 miles) south of Cork City on the Kinsale road, has direct flights daily to Dublin, London (Heathrow, Gatwick, and Stansted), Manchester, East Midlands, Paris, and Malaga, and direct flights to many other European cities. Shannon Airport, 26 km (16 miles) west of Limerick City, is the point of arrival for many transatlantic flights, including direct flights from Atlanta, Chicago, Philadelphia, Toronto (summer only), and New York City (from both JFK and Newark). It also has regular flights from the United Kingdom and many European cities.

Airports Cork Airport ☎ *021/431–3131* ⊕ *www.corkairport.com.* **Shannon Airport** ☎ *061/712–000* ⊕ *www.shannonairport.ie.*

AIRPORT
TRANSFERS
Bus Éireann has a bus link between Cork Airport and the Cork Parnell Place Bus Station about every 30 minutes, and a route between the airport and Kinsale roughly every hour. Tickets for both destinations can be bought on the bus.

Shuttles Bus Éireann ☏ *021/450–8188, 021/422–2129 recorded timetable* ⊕ *www.buseireann.ie.*

BUS TRAVEL

Bus Éireann and Aircoach operate express buses from Dublin, Galway, Shannon Airport, Limerick, Tralee, and Killarney to Cork City. Be warned: even so-called express buses from Dublin make at least two off-motorway stops en route, so the journey takes from four to five hours, depending on traffic. Citylink buses serve many Irish cities, including Cork City; book online for the best prices. Local buses tend to stop running in the early evening, which rules out many day trips—unless you want to spend most of the day on the bus. As a general rule, the smaller and more remote the town, the less frequent its bus service. Consult with hotel concierges, tourist board staffers, or the bus lines' websites for bus schedules.

Bus Information Aircoach ☏ *01/844–7118* ⊕ *www.aircoach.ie.* **Bus Éireann** ☏ *01/836–6111 in Dublin, 021/450–8188 in Cork* ⊕ *www.buseireann.ie.* **Citylink** ☏ *091/564–164* ⊕ *www.citylink.ie.* **Cork Bus Station Parnell Place** ✉ *Parnell Pl. and Merchant's Quay, City Center South, Cork City, Co. Cork* ☏ *021/450–8188, 021/422–2129 recorded message (6 pm–9 am).*

CAR TRAVEL

Scenery is the main attraction in County Cork, and unless you're a biker or hiker, the best option for taking it in is to rent a car, although regional buses do run on main roads. Once behind the wheel, plan to adopt the local pace—slow. Covering about 100 km (60 miles) a day is ideal, with many stops along the way. Speed is dictated to some degree by the roads: most are small, with one lane in each direction and plenty of bends and hills.

The main driving route from Dublin is the M7 motorway, connecting with the M8 in Portlaoise to continue 257 km (160 miles) on to Cork City. The journey from Dublin to Cork takes less than three hours. A car is the ideal way to explore this region's scenic routes and attractive but remote towns. Except for Cork City, where you're best off using a garage, parking is relatively easy to figure out.

TAXI TRAVEL

Taxis at Shannon and Cork airports connect with Limerick and Cork respectively. Shannon to Limerick City costs about €40; from Cork to Cork City Railway Station, about €15. The National Transport Authority website has a fare estimator tool.

Taxis and Information Cork Taxi Co-op ☏ *021/427–2222* ⊕ *www.corktaxi.ie.* **National Transport Authority** ☏ *01/879–8300* ⊕ *www.transportforireland.ie/taxi.*

6

TRAIN TRAVEL

Irish Rail–Iarnród Éireann runs direct hourly trains from Dublin Heuston Station to Cork's Kent Station; the trip takes just under three hours. Suburban trains serve Fota Island, Midleton, and Cobh. The journey time to Midleton or Cobh is about 25 minutes.

Train Information **Irish Rail–Iarnód Éireann** 🕾 *01/836–6222 for inquiries and booking, 1850/366–222 in Ireland, 021/450–4777 in Cork ⊕ www.irishrail.ie.*

For more information on getting here and around, see Travel Smart Ireland.

RESTAURANTS

County Cork, home of the famous Slow Food Ireland movement, has become Ireland's top foodie destination. The mecca: Ballymaloe House, where Myrtle Allen pioneered New Irish cuisine and her daughter-in-law, the celebrated cookery author Darina Allen, learned her trade. Adventurous, well-traveled chefs throughout County Cork make the most of the first-rate local specialties: succulent beef and lamb, game in the winter, fresh seafood, and farmhouse cheeses. The best restaurants are not all in towns: even tiny villages might boast a gastropub.

HOTELS

County Cork's great country-house accommodations include Ballymaloe House in east Cork, along with the guest wing at magnificent Bantry House. At the spectrum's other end is the uniquely Irish farmhouse bed-and-breakfast, such as the Glen Country House, where you are welcomed by the family dogs and treated as a long-lost friend. In between are excellent family-owned and -run traditional hotels, such as the Blarney Castle Hotel on Blarney's village green and the Seaview in Ballylickey on Bantry Bay. *Hotel reviews have been shortened. For full information, visit Fodors.com.*

WHAT IT COSTS IN EUROS				
	$	**$$**	**$$$**	**$$$$**
Restaurants	under €19	€19–€24	€25–€32	over €32
Hotels	under €120	€120–€170	€171–€210	over €210

Restaurant prices are the average cost of a main course at dinner or, if dinner is not served, at lunch. Hotel prices are the lowest cost of a standard double room in high season.

TOURS

Adams & Butler. Self-driven or chauffeur-driven group tours with accommodations in private country houses and castles are available. The company also conducts special-interest tours; topics include gardens, architecture, ghosts, and golf. ✉ *The Carriage House, 58 Foster Ave., Mount Merrion, Co. Cork* 🕾 *01/288–9355* ⊕ *www.adamsandbutler.com* ✍ *Call for details.*

Bus Éireann Tours and Trips. A range of daylong and half-day guided bus tours are available from June through August. Book these at the Cork Bus Station Parnell Place or at any tourist office. Bus Éireann also offers open-top bus tours of Cork City on some summer days.

☎ *021/450–8188 in Cork* ⊕ *www.buseireann.ie* 🎟 *€6 Cork City, €16 half day, €32 full day.*

Irish Ways Walking Tours. Group and self-guided walking tours are offered on the Beara Way and the Sheep's Head Peninsula, plus other areas of Ireland. ⊠ *Belfield Bike Shop, University College, Dublin, Co. Dublin* ☎ *01/260–0749* ⊕ *www.irishways.com* 🎟 *From €379 for 3 days, or €685 for 7 days, including accommodations and some meals.*

Kinsale Pottery & Arts Centre. Adrian Wistreich of the Kinsale Pottery & Arts Centre puts together vacation packages that include multi-destination tours, hands-on pottery, jewelry-making, stained-glass, and other workshops. ⊠ *Olcote, Kinsale, Co. Cork* ☎ *021/477–7758* ⊕ *www. kinsaleceramics.com* 🎟 *From €1,443 for 12-day tour.*

SouthWestWalks Ireland. Themed walks take you along the coast of West Cork, around the Sheep's Head and Beara peninsulas in Bantry Bay. ⊠ *Oakpark, Tralee, Co. Kerry* ☎ *066/718–6181* ⊕ *www. southwestwalksireland.com* 🎟 *From €499 for 5 days, or €925 for 11 days.*

VISITOR INFORMATION

Fáilte Ireland tourist information offices are open year-round in Bantry, Clonakilty, Cobh (Cork Harbour), Cork Airport (Arrivals), Cork City, and Skibbereen. Those in Blarney, Glengarriff, Kinsale, and Midleton are open from mid-March to mid-September or the end of October. Fáilte Ireland's Discover Cork website page has details about locations and hours.

Cork City Tourist Information Office ⊠ *Grand Parade, City Center South, Cork City, Co. Cork* ☎ *021/425–5100* ⊕ *www.discoverireland.ie/ places-to-go/Cork.*

CORK CITY AND ENVIRONS

The major metropolis of the South, Cork City makes a great base from which to explore the whole southern region. Though it's Ireland's second-largest city, it runs a distant second, with a population of 123,000, roughly one-tenth the size of Dublin. In the last decade, with high prices and overcrowding in Dublin, Cork became the new hot spot for short city breaks. Groups of Europeans frequently pop over for a weekend of partying, as the city is a spirited place, with a formidable pub culture, a lively traditional-music scene, a respected and progressive university, attractive art galleries, and offbeat cafés. Nearby Blarney, northwest of Cork City on R617, makes a perfect day trip. Blarney's attractions are Blarney Castle and the famous Blarney Stone.

CORK CITY

253 km (157 miles) southwest of Dublin.

Cork City received its first charter in 1185 from Prince John of Norman England, and it takes its name from the Irish word *corcaigh*, meaning "marshy place." The original 6th-century settlement was spread over 13 small islands in the River Lee. Major development occurred during the 17th and 18th centuries with the expansion of the butter trade, and many attractive Georgian-design buildings with wide bowfront windows were constructed during this time. As late as 1770 Cork's present-day main streets—Grand Parade, St. Patrick's Street, and the South Mall—were submerged under the Lee. Around 1800, when the Lee was partially dammed, the river divided into two streams that now flow through the city, leaving the main business and commercial center on an island, not unlike Paris's Île de la Cité. As a result, the city has a number of bridges and quays, which, although initially confusing, add greatly to the port's unique character.

Cork can be very "Irish" (hurling, Gaelic football, televised plowing contests, music pubs, and peat smoke). But depending on what part of town you're in, Cork can also be distinctly itself—the sort of place where hippies, gays, and farmers drink at the same pub.

PLANNING YOUR TIME

You can tour the city's center in a morning or an afternoon, depending on how much you plan to shop along the way. To really see everything, however, allow a full day, with a break for lunch at the Farmgate Café in the English Market. Note that the Crawford Art Gallery and the English Market are closed on Sunday.

GETTING HERE AND AROUND

The drive from Dublin to Cork City on the M7/M8 motorway takes just under three hours. The drive from Shannon Airport to Cork takes under two hours, with motorway for some stretches. Use the tunnel (toll €1.80) to avoid traveling through the center of Limerick. Cork is about an hour-and-a-half drive from Killarney. Cork is well served by express buses. Irish Rail–Iarnród Éireann direct trains from Dublin Heuston Station to Cork's Kent Station run hourly. The trip takes just under three hours.

If you're driving within Cork City, it's advisable to use a multistory parking garage, as on-street parking can be hard to find and the process of paying for it can be difficult to master. Cork's city center is compact and walkable, but if you want to bus the mile to the university campus, pick up a No. 8 outside Debenham's department store on St. Patrick's Street. A great introductory tour is the hop-on, hop-off Cork City Tour run by Cronin's Coaches, a double-decker bus that departs (March–October, €14) from the tourist information office on Grand Parade between 9:30 am and 5 pm.

ESSENTIALS

Transportation Contacts **Cork Bus Station Parnell Place** ✉ *Parnell Pl. and Merchant's Quay, City Center South* ☎ *021/450–8188, 021/422–2129 recorded message (6 pm–9 am).* **Cronin's Coaches** ☎ *021/430–9090* ⊕ *www. croninscoaches.com.* **Kent Station** ✉ *Lower Glanmire Rd., City Center North* ☎ *021/836–6222* ⊕ *www.irishrail.ie.*

As the River Lee flows through Cork's center, delightful bridges and quays add to the city's unique character.

EXPLORING

TOP ATTRACTIONS

Cork Vision Centre@St Peter's. In the renovated St. Peter's Church, an 18th-century building in what was the bustling heart of medieval Cork, this historical society provides an excellent introduction to the city's history and geography. The highlight is a detailed 1:500-scale model of the city, showing how it has changed over the ages. ⊠ *N. Main St., City Center South* ☎ *021/427–9925* ⊕ *www.corkvisioncentre.com* ✉ *Free* ⊙ *Tues.–Sat. 10–5.*

Fodor'sChoice ★ **Crawford Art Gallery.** The large redbrick building was built in 1724 as the customs house and is now home to Ireland's leading provincial art gallery. An imaginative expansion has added gallery space for visiting exhibitions and adventurous shows of modern Irish artists. The permanent collection includes landscape paintings depicting Cork in the 18th and 19th centuries. Take special note of works by Irish painters William Leech (1881–1968), Daniel Maclise (1806–70), James Barry (1741–1806), and Nathaniel Grogan (1740–1807). The café, run by the renowned Allen family of Ballymaloe, is a good place for a light lunch or a house-made sweet. ⊠ *Emmet Pl., City Center South* ☎ *021/480–5042* ⊕ *www.crawfordartgallery.ie* ✉ *Free* ⊙ *Mon.–Sat. 10–5 (to 8 Thurs.).*

Fodor'sChoice ★ **English Market.** Food lovers (and, who, pray, isn't?): be sure to make a beeline for one of the misleadingly small entrances to this large and famous mecca for foodies. Fetchingly housed in an elaborate, brick-and-cast-iron Victorian building, such is the fame of the English Market that Her Majesty Queen Elizabeth insisted on an impromptu walk-about here on her historic first visit to Ireland in May 2011. Among the 140 stalls, keep an eye out for the Alternative Bread Co., which produces more than 40 varieties of handmade bread every day. Tom Durcan's Meats Ltd sells vaccuum-packed local specialties including spiced beef and dry aged beef. The Olive Stall sells olive oil, olive-oil soap, and olives from Greece, Spain, France, and Italy. Kay O'Connell's Fish Stall, in the legendary fresh-fish alley, purveys local smoked salmon. O'Reilly's Tripe and Drisheen is the last existing retailer of a Cork specialty, tripe

(cow's stomach), and *drisheen* (blood sausage). Upstairs is the Farmgate, an excellent café. ✉ *Entrances on Grand Parade and Princes St., City Center South* ⊕ *www.englishmarket.ie* ⊘ *Mon.–Sat. 9:30–5:30.*

Patrick's Bridge. From here you can look along the curve of Patrick Street and north across the River Lee to St. Patrick's Hill, with its tall Georgian houses. The hill is so steep that steps are cut into the pavement. Tall ships that served the butter trade used to load up beside the bridge at Merchant's Quay before heading downstream to the sea. The design of the large, redbrick shopping center on the site evokes the warehouses of old. ✉ *St. Patrick's St., City Center South.*

Paul Street. A narrow stretch between the River Lee and St. Patrick's Street and parallel to both, Paul Street is the backbone of the trendy shopping district that now occupies Cork's old French Quarter. The area was first settled by Huguenots fleeing religious persecution in France. Musicians and other street performers often entertain passersby in the Rory Gallagher Piazza, named for the late rock guitarist, whose family was from Cork. The stores here offer the best in modern Irish design— from local fashions to handblown glass. ✉ *City Center South.*

St. Anne's Church. The church's pepper-pot steeple, which has a four-sided clock and is topped with a golden, salmon-shaped weather vane, is visible from throughout the city and is the chief reason why St. Anne's is so frequently visited. The Bells of Shandon were immortalized in an atrocious but popular 19th-century ballad of that name. Your reward for climbing the 120-foot-tall tower is the chance to ring the bells out over Cork, with the assistance of sheet tune cards. Beside the church, **Firkin Crane,** Cork's 18th-century butter market, houses two small performing spaces. Adjacent is the **Shandon Craft Market.** ✉ *Church St., Shandon* ☎ *021/450–5906* ⊕ *www.shandonbells.ie* 🔊 *Church free, tower €5* ⊘ *Mar.–Oct., Mon.–Sat. 10–4 (to 5 June–Sept.), Sun. 11:30– 4:30; Nov.–Feb., Mon.–Sat. 11–3.*

St. Fin Barre's Cathedral. On the site that was the entrance to medieval Cork, this compact, three-spire Gothic cathedral, which was completed in 1879, belongs to the Church of Ireland and houses a 3,000-pipe organ. According to tradition, St. Fin Barre established a monastery

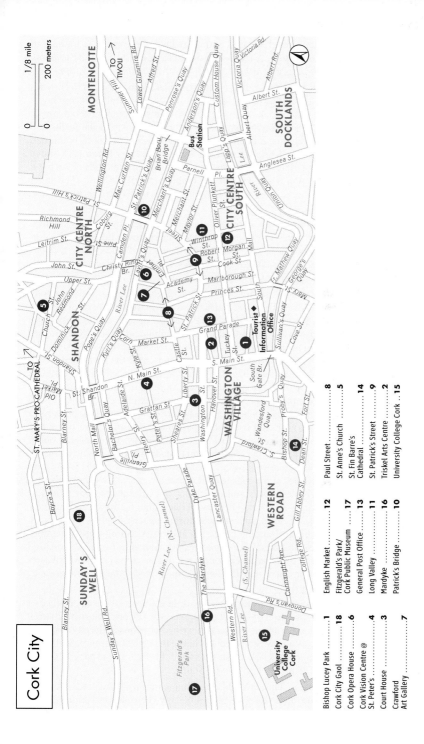

Cork City

Bishop Lucey Park	1	English Market	12	
Cork City Gaol	18	Fitzgerald's Park/		
Cork Opera House	6	Cork Public Museum	17	
Cork Vision Centre @		General Post Office	13	
St. Peter's	4	Long Valley	11	
Court House	3	Mardyke	16	
Crawford		Patrick's Bridge	10	
Art Gallery	7			

Paul Street	8
St. Anne's Church	5
St. Fin Barre's	
Cathedral	14
St. Patrick's Street	9
Triskel Arts Centre	2
University College Cork	15

on this site around AD 650 and is credited with being the founder of Cork. ✉ *Bishop St., City Center South* ☎ *021/496–3387* ⊕ *cathedral. cork.anglican.org* ⊘ *Mon.–Sat. 9:30–5:30; also Sun 12:30–5, Apr.–Nov.*

St. Patrick's Street. Extending from Grand Parade in the south to Patrick's Bridge in the north, Panna (as it's known locally—and also commonly referred to as Patrick Street) is Cork's main shopping thoroughfare. It has been designed as a pedestrian-priority area with wide walks and special streetlights. A mainstream mix of department stores, boutiques, pharmacies, and bookshops lines the way. ■TIP➡ **If you look above some of the plate-glass storefronts, you can see examples of the bow-front Georgian windows that are emblematic of old Cork.** The street saw some of the city's worst fighting during the War of Independence. ✉ *City Center South.*

Triskel Arts Centre. An excellent place to get the pulse of artsy goings-on in town, the Triskel occupies converted town houses and a former church. ✉ *Tobin St., City Center South* ☎ *021/427–2022* ⊕ *www. triskelartscentre.ie* ✆ *Free* ⊘ *Mon.–Sat. 10–5, and during performances.*

Fodor'sChoice
★

University College Cork. The Doric, porticoed gates of UCC stand about 2 km (1 mile) from the city center. The college, which has a student body of roughly 10,000, is a constituent of the National University of Ireland. The main quadrangle is a fine example of 19th-century university architecture in the Tudor-Gothic style, reminiscent of many Oxford and Cambridge colleges. Several ancient ogham stones are on display in the North Quadrangle (near the visitor center), and the renovated Crawford Observatory's 1860 telescope can be visited. The Honan Collegiate Chapel, east of the quadrangle, was built in 1916 and modeled on the 12th-century, Hiberno-Romanesque style, best exemplified by the remains of Cormac's Chapel at Cashel. The UCC chapel's stained-glass windows, as well as its collection of art and crafts, altar furnishings, and textiles in the Celtic Revival style, are noteworthy. Three large, modern buildings have been successfully integrated with the old, including the Boole Library, named for mathematician George Boole (1815–64), who was a professor at the college, and whose bicentenary will be celebrated in 2015. Both indoors and out the campus is enhanced by works of contemporary Irish art. The **Lewis Glucksman Gallery,** a striking new building adjacent to the college's entrance gates, displays works from the college's outstanding collection and hosts cutting-edge contemporary-art exhibitions. ✉ *College Rd., Western Road* ☎ *021/490–3000* ⊕ *www.ucc.ie* ✆ *Free* ⊘ *Visitor center weekdays 9–5; call for hrs Easter wk, July, Aug., and mid-Dec.–mid-Jan.; guided tours by arrangement.*

WORTH NOTING

Bishop Lucey Park. This tiny green park in the heart of the city opened in 1985 in celebration of the 800th anniversary of Cork's Norman charter. During its excavation, workers unearthed portions of the city's original fortified walls, now preserved just inside the arched entrance. Sculptures by contemporary Cork artists are found throughout the park. ✉ *Grand Parade/S. Main St., City Center South.*

FAMILY **Cork City Gaol.** This castle-like building contains an austere, 19th-century prison. Life-size wax figures occupy the cells, and sound effects illustrate the appalling conditions that prevailed into the 20th century. Also here, in the Governor's House, the **Radio Museum Experience** exhibits genuine artifacts from the 1923 radio station, 6CK, and tells the story of radio broadcasting in Cork. ⊠ *Sunday's Well Rd., Sunday's Well* ☎ *021/430–5022* ⊕ *www.corkcitygaol.com* ⛯ *€8, Ghost Tour €10* ⊙ *Mar.–Oct., daily 9:30–5; Nov.–Feb., daily 10–4; Ghost Tour, Thurs. 6 pm, book in advance.*

Cork Opera House. This unattractive concrete hulk erected in 1965 replaced an ornate and much-loved opera house that was ruined in a fire. Later attempts to integrate the opera house with its neighbor, the Crawford Art Gallery, have softened the grim facade. Inside, the huge auditorium hosts theatrical productions and visiting stars of light entertainment, with the occasional opera. The piazza outside has sidewalk cafés and street performers. ⊠ *Emmet Pl., at Lavitt's Quay, City Center South* ☎ *021/427–0022* ⊕ *www. corkoperahouse.ie.*

Court House. A landmark in the very center of Cork, this magnificent classical building has an imposing Corinthian portico and is still used as the district's main courthouse. The exterior has been cleaned and fully restored and looks every bit as good as it did when it was built in 1835. ⊠ *Washington St., City Center South* ☎ *021/427–2706* ⊙ *Weekdays 9–5.*

FAMILY **Fitzgerald's Park.** This small, well-tended park is beside the River Lee's north channel in the west of the city. The park contains the **Cork Public Museum,** a Georgian mansion that houses a well-planned exhibit about Cork's history since ancient times, with a strong emphasis on the city's Republican history. ⊠ *Western Rd., Western Road* ☎ *021/427–0679* ⊕ *www.corkcity.ie/traveltourism* ⛯ *Free* ⊙ *Park: always accessible; museum: Mon.–Sat. 11–1 and 2:15–5; also Sun. 3–5, Apr.–Sept.*

General Post Office. Dominating a street otherwise occupied by boutiques, jewelry stores, and antiques shops, this Neoclassical building with an elegant colonnaded facade was once Cork's opera house. ⊠ *Oliver Plunkett St., City Center South* ☎ *021/427–2000* ⊙ *Weekdays 9–5:30, Sat. 9–5.*

> ### GRANDDAD OF THE COMPUTER
>
> George Boole (1815–64), a University College professor, is one of the heroes of the computer age. Despite growing up in poor circumstances, he developed into a mathematical genius, inventing Boolean algebra—the foundation upon which computer science was built. University College Cork aims to raise his profile considerably during 2015, which has been declared The Year of George Boole, and will host a major conference on his work.

QUICK BITES

Long Valley. The friendly, old Long Valley pub, popular with artists, writers, students, and eccentrics, serves tea, coffee, pints, and sandwiches. The dark, mismatched interior is like a time warp taking you back to early-20th-century Cork. Some of the booths are built from wood salvaged from wrecked ocean liners—ask to be told the story. The generously filled sandwiches,

made to order from home-cooked meat and thickly cut bread, also seem to belong to another age. There's traditional music on Thursday nights. ✉ ***Winthrop St., City Center South*** ☎ ***021/427–2144*** 🌐 ***www.thelongvalleybar.com*** 🕒 ***Daily.***

Mardyke. This popular riverside walk links the city center with Fitzgerald's Park. Beside it is a field where cricket, very much a minority sport in Ireland, is played on summer weekends. ✉ *Western Rd., Western Road.*

REBEL CORK

"Rebel Cork" suffered great damage during the Irish War of Independence (1919–21), when much of its center was burned down. Cork is now regaining some of its former glory as a result of sensitive commercial development and an ongoing program of inner-city renewal.

WHERE TO EAT

$$ VEGETARIAN 🍴 **Café Paradiso.** The Mediterranean–Eastern fusion-style food here is so tasty that even dedicated meat eaters forget that it's vegetarian. Irish owner-chef Denis Cotter, who has won awards for his cookbooks, garners raves for his risottos with seasonal vegetables, and imaginative combinations of flavors—parsnip ravioli, perhaps with ginger brown butter and apple-balsamic syrup. Many of the vegetables are grown especially for the restaurant on a farm nearby, and Denis also sources local cheeses. The stylish dining room is busy and colorful, with enthusiastic young waiters to recite the daily specials, and the food is creatively arranged, adding a sense of occasion. Midway between the courthouse and university, the restaurant are two attractive rooms available (€200 a night including dinner). [$] *Average main: €23* ✉ *16 Lancaster Quay, Western Road* ☎ *021/427–7939* 🌐 *www.cafeparadiso.ie* 🕒 *Closed Sun., and last 2 wks of Aug. No lunch weekdays.*

$ MODERN IRISH 🍴 **The Electric.** The neon-clad exterior of the snazzy Art Deco building, between the legal enclave and the university, announces a casual venue that combines a sense of dining as theater with friendly staff to put everyone at ease. The ground floor is dominated by a square bar with booths and dining niches around the perimeter, while upstairs is a more formal dining area. Food is local, fresh, and made to order. Lunch is good value, with a daily special stew—chicken, mushroom, and potato, or spicy chorizo and chickpeas—or combos of soup and doorstep or ciabatta half-sandwich. The dinner menu is unfussy: mussels in a fennel, shallot, and leek cream sauce; house-made beef burger; or battered fish with twice-fried chips (fries), and served with panache in a lively atmosphere. [$] *Average main: €15* ✉ *41 South Mall, City Center South* ☎ *021/422–2990* 🌐 *www.electriccork.com.*

$ IRISH 🍴 **Farmgate Café.** One of the best—and busiest—informal lunch spots in town is on a terraced gallery above the fountain at the Princes Street entrance to the atmospheric English Market. All ingredients used at the café are purchased in the market below. One side of the gallery opens onto the market and is self-service; the other side is glassed in and has table service (reservations advised). Tripe and *drisheen* (blood sausage) is one dish that is always on the menu; daily specials include less

Great resources like the English Market have made Cork a foodie mecca. Her Majesty Queen Elizabeth II's walkabout here was a highlight of her first visit to Ireland, in 2011.

challenging but no less traditional choices, such as corned beef with *colcannon* (potatoes and cabbage mashed with butter and seasonings) and loin of smoked bacon with *champ* (potatoes mashed with scallions or leeks). $ *Average main: €14* ⊠ *English Market, Princes St., City Center South* ☎ *021/427–8134* ⊕ *www.farmgate.ie* ⊘ *Closed Sun. No dinner.*

$$
ECLECTIC

✗ **Fenn's Quay.** This tiny city-center restaurant, on the ground floor of a 250-year-old Georgian house, is always buzzing with a faithful local clientele—legal eagles from the nearby courthouse at lunch, theater- and moviegoers at dinner. The char-grilled fillet steak with chunky chips has achieved legendary status: some regulars can't bring themselves to order anything else. But there are other good options: fish from the nearby market is given robust, unfussy treatment, and vegetarian offerings include a twice-baked goat cheese soufflé with beetroot carpaccio. Flourless chocolate pudding with white chocolate cream is a memorable dessert. The interior is simple, with bright-red chairs and tan banquettes, but striking modern paintings supply a dose of character. $ *Average main: €23* ⊠ *5 Fenn's Quay, Sheares St., City Center South* ☎ *021/427–9527* ⊕ *fennsquay.net* ⊘ *Closed Sun.*

$$$
FRENCH
Fodor's Choice
★

✗ **Flemings Restaurant.** On a hillside overlooking the river on the eastern edge of the city, this restaurant is in a stately Georgian house with extensive grounds, including a kitchen garden that supplies the restaurant. The food is classical French, and it's served, appropriately, in a dining room decorated in the French Empire style, with plush Louis XV–style chairs, gilt-frame mirrors, and crystal chandeliers. Local ingredients are important: a starter of panfried foie gras is accompanied by black pudding from West Cork and glazed apple; it's a favorite with the regulars. Other standout items include grilled monkfish from Court-macsherry, served with a basil-oil dressing and red-wine sauce, and fillet of beef with wild mushrooms, red-onion confit, and red-wine sauce. As a "restaurant with rooms," dine-and-stay packages are available. [$] *Average main: €29* ⊠ *Silver Grange House, Lower Glanmire Rd., Tivoli* ☎ *021/482–1621* ⊕ *www.flemingsrestaurant.ie* ⊗ *Closed Mon. and Tues. No lunch Wed.–Sat., except by reservation.*

$$
EUROPEAN
Fodor's Choice
★

✕ **Greenes.** Tucked away on a cobbled patio, this surprising haven is part of a Victorian warehouse conversion that houses Hotel Isaacs. Stone and redbrick walls are the backdrop to a minimalist modern interior, while out back a gigantic rock-wall waterfall makes a stunning backdrop to a dining terrace with a very special atmosphere. The menu features the best of local produce, often served with an unusual twist. Start with organic Ummera smoked salmon three ways—with lemon, beetroot, and crème fraîche on organic leaves—or steamed West Cork mussels (mariniere or with chorizo and onion). Popular mains include a 10-ounce rib-eye steak with a brandy pepper sauce, and seared scallops on a crab-and-pea risotto with citrus syrup. Classic vanilla panna cotta comes with ginger foam and crispy strawberries. [$] *Average main: €24* ⊠ *Hotel Isaacs, 48 MacCurtain St., City Center North* ☎ *021/455–2279* ⊕ *www.greenesrestaurant.com* ⊗ *No lunch Sat.*

$
CONTEMPORARY

✕ **Isaacs.** Cross Patrick's Bridge to the River Lee's north side and turn right to reach this large, atmospheric brasserie in a converted 18th-century warehouse. Modern art, muted jazz, high ceilings, and well-spaced tables with colored wooden tops create a popular informal venue, where the food is taken seriously but the atmosphere is fun. The East-meets-Mediterranean menu features fresh local produce, and suits all tastes, making this a favorite venue for multigenerational family gatherings. Among the many tempting dishes are mild madras lamb curry with poppadom and chutney, potato pancake with Clonakilty black pudding, crispy duck confit with caramelized shallots and purée potato, and tempura of king prawns with eggplant, scallions, wasabi, pickled ginger, and soy dipping sauce. Service is friendly and efficient. Reservations are advisable Friday and Saturday evenings. [$] *Average main: €18* ⊠ *48 MacCurtain St., City Center North* ☎ *021/450–3805* ⊕ *www.isaacsrestaurant.ie* ⊗ *No lunch Sun.*

$$$$
CONTEMPORARY

✕ **Ivory Tower.** Don't be put off by the seedy-looking street entrance to this second-floor restaurant: Seamus O'Connell, the American-born owner-chef here, is one of the stars of the Irish culinary scene, describing his approach as "trans-ethnic fusion." He has cooked in Mexico and Japan, and his accomplished menu features quirky, eclectic dishes like wild duck with vanilla, sherry, and jalapeños or pheasant tamale. His mastery of Japanese cooking is impressive, and he works wonders with Irish staples, combining monkfish cheeks with pearl barley risotto, and in early spring serving a memorable nettle-and-wild-garlic soup. Imaginative presentation, including a surprise taster to set the mood, compensates for the stark interior of the dining room, as does the tradition that the maestro himself often serves the dishes he has created. The eight-course Irish tasting menu (€45) is a great introduction to O'Connell's inimitable style. [$] *Average main: €45* ⊠ *35 Princes St.,*

Washington Village ☎ *021/427–4665* 🌐 *www.ivorytower.ie* 💳 *No credit cards* 🕒 *Closed Sun.–Wed. No lunch.*

$$ EUROPEAN Fodor's Choice ★ 🍴 **Jacques.** Behind a plate glass window near the GPO, one of Cork's favorite restaurants has added a street-side eatery serving informal food from 10 am (no reservations taken). It leads to the heart of the original restaurant (which can also be accessed from Phoenix Street at the rear), a curved Art Deco–style bar, that's carefully lighted to soothe away the world outside. It has recently been expanded, with a new entrance serving a tapas menu of light bites from 5 pm. Food is always sourced from local artisan producers, and chef Jacques's cooking allows the flavor to shine through, whether in a starter of smoked chicken, fennel, and orange salad, or a main course of roast breast of duck with potato stuffing, red cabbage, and apricot sauce. For dessert try the fruited bread-and-butter pudding, or indulge in a chocolate-and-hazelnut torte. The two-course dinner menu at €24 is a good value. [$] *Average main: €24* ✉ *23 Oliver Plunkett St., City Center South* ☎ *021/427–7387* 🌐 *www.jacquesrestaurant.ie* 🕒 *Closed Sun. No dinner Mon.*

$ AMERICAN FAMILY 🍴 **Liberty Grill Restaurant.** It may primarily be a burger joint, but it's a burger joint with a difference—all the food is freshly prepared and locally sourced, the classic burger really tastes of beef, and there are also lamb, crab, and tuna varieties. A selection of tapas-style "small plates" is also available, plus char-grilled steaks and daily specials that might include classic duck confit, lamb, and feta cheese burger; a classic Caesar salad; and a vegan salad option. American desserts include key-lime pie and brownies. Black leather banquettes, plain white walls, and a wood-plank floor provide an unassuming background for this busy eatery, popular with kids as well as adults—so popular that reservations are advisable at peak times. [$] *Average main: €15* ✉ *32 Washington St., Washington Village* ☎ *021/427–1049* 🌐 *www.libertygrill.ie* 🕒 *Closed Sun.*

$ MODERN IRISH 🍴 **Market Lane Restaurant & Bar.** All that remains of this building's former identity as a pub is the long mahogany bar. Today it is a popular bistro-style restaurant serving robust, freshly prepared food from an open kitchen. Art Deco touches and a predominantly black-and-white theme set a Parisian mood, and light floods in from two walls of large windows on summer evenings. Most ingredients come from the renowned English Market *(⇨ See Top Attractions)*, for a menu (on no-frills paper tablemats) that is mainly contemporary Irish, majoring on comfort food—braised ox-cheek stew; game pie—and other winners include baked cod with buttered leeks, and house-made sausages with colcannon (potato mash with cabbage) and creamy mustard sauce. Vegetarian? Many options include moussaka of lentils with aubergine and Gruyère, with a feta, orange, and rocket salad. [$] *Average main: €16* ✉ *5/6 Oliver Plunkett St., City Center South* ☎ *021/427–4710* 🌐 *www.marketlane.ie.*

$ IRISH 🍴 **Strasbourg Goose Restaurant.** Tucked away in a pedestrian alley, this is the kind of personable restaurant you dream of finding on vacation and turning into a culinary home away from home. It's cheerful, bustling, basic, and a little odd, with a baronial wooden chimneypiece, dating from 1901, dominating the small, double-height room, which also has tables on an overhead balcony. Photos of Hollywood stars, glass-block room dividers, and piquant lamps add to the pleasantly eccentricity. People not only come here for the style, but also for value. Choose a daily special like twice-cooked crispy lamb, or Barbary duck breast with gratin potatoes, or for a few euros more, go for the extensive 20-euro menu. You can substitute a glass of wine for a dessert, which is good value, given Irish wine prices. [$] *Average main: €15* ✉ *17/18 French Church St., City Center South* ☎ *021/427–9534* ⏲ *Closed Mon. No lunch Tues.–Thurs.*

WHERE TO STAY

$ HOTEL Fodor's Choice ★ 🏨 **Ambassador Hotel.** An imposing redbrick and cut-limestone Victorian-era nursing home is now a comfortable hotel, which maybe not be the fanciest or hippest in Cork, but it has the most character and the best view, encompassing the city and surrounding hills. **Pros:** strong local atmosphere; amazing views. **Cons:** steep hike up from city; some jarring notes in decoration. [$] *Rooms from: €90* ✉ *Military Hill, St. Luke's, City Center North* ☎ *021/453–9000* 🌐 *www.ambassadorhotelcork.ie* 🛏 *70 rooms* 🍴 *Breakfast.*

$$ HOTEL 🏨 **Clarion Hotel Cork.** Occupying a corner block beside the River Lee, the Clarion is a pioneer of Cork's docklands development—as you enter you'll spot black-clad receptionists standing behind simple wooden desks at the far end of the vast, marble-floor lobby, the first indication that this place aspires to boutique-hotel chic. **Pros:** funky; high-luxe rooms; great value. **Cons:** limited parking; neighborhood quiet after dark; some rooms overlook internal atrium/staircase. [$] *Rooms from: €120* ✉ *Lapp's Quay, City Center South* ☎ *021/422–4900* 🌐 *www.clarionhotelcorkcity.com* 🛏 *196 rooms, 2 suites* 🍴 *Breakfast.*

$ B&B/INN 🏨 **Gabriel House.** On a bluff high above the train station and the docks, this huge Victorian house is in Cork's boho north-side quarter among fine 19th-century homes, many of which have seen better days. **Pros:** young, enthusiastic staff; quiet location; oodles of character; rock-bottom prices. **Cons:** nearly hostel-like; some rooms very small; a long hike uphill. [$] *Rooms from: €90* ✉ *Summerhill N., St. Luke's Cross, Montenotte* ☎ *021/450–0333* 🌐 *www.gabriel-house.ie* 🛏 *28 rooms* 🍴 *Breakfast.*

$ B&B/INN 🏨 **Garnish House.** At this pair of large Victorian town houses near the university, owner-manager Johanna Lucey will be offering you tea and homemade cake before you have even crossed the threshold—the kind of old-fashioned hospitality that's fast disappearing in modern Ireland. **Pros:** friendly welcome; genuine Irish experience; short walk from town center. **Cons:** seriously unhip; on a busy road; rooms book up well in advance. [$] *Rooms from: €88* ✉ *Western Rd., Washington Village* ☎ *021/427–5111* 🌐 *www.garnish.ie* 🛏 *21 rooms* 🍴 *Breakfast.*

$$$ HOTEL Fodor's Choice ★ 🏨 **Hayfield Manor.** Ruddy with red brick and brightened by white-sash windows, the exterior hints at the comfy luxury that lies within, and the location—off College Avenue in an undistinguished suburb—is forgotten as soon as you cross the threshold. **Pros:** stylish and chic; good value for luxury accommodation. **Cons:** a taxi or car ride to city center or a dull 15-minute walk; lack of scenic views. [$] *Rooms from: €179*

✉ *Perrott Ave., Western Road* ☎ *021/484–5900* ⊕ *www.hayfieldmanor. ie* ⇗ *88 rooms* ❍ *Breakfast.*

$
HOTEL

🏨 **Hotel Isaacs Cork.** With a tone of boho shabby chic that appeals to the hotel's many regular guests, this stylish renovation transformed an old, city-center warehouse. **Pros:** location near bus and train stations; old-world character. **Cons:** heavy through-traffic outside; interiors a bit worn at the edges; limited parking. **$** *Rooms from: €110* ✉ *48 Mac-Curtain St., City Center North* ☎ *021/450–0011* ⊕ *www.isaacscork. com* ⇗ *50 rooms* ❍ *Breakfast.*

$$
HOTEL

🏨 **Imperial Hotel.** Though she cannot compete in size with the grande-dame hotels of bigger cities, the Imperial, which dates to 1813, plays this role with conviction, with its marble lobby and traditional concierge. **Pros:** central location; genuine Cork experience. **Cons:** some standard bedrooms are very small; quiet rooms have no view; popular venue for wedding receptions. **$** *Rooms from: €139* ✉ *South Mall, City Center South* ☎ *021/427–4040* ⊕ *www.flynnhotels.com/Imperial_Hotel_Cork* ⇗ *126 rooms, 1 suite* ❍ *Breakfast.*

$
B&B/INN

🏨 **Lancaster Lodge.** Free city-center parking, a great location midway between the shopping district and the university, and good value are the main reasons to stay at this modern, four-story inn. **Pros:** great central location; free parking; good value. **Cons:** no bar or wine license. **$** *Rooms from: €96* ✉ *Lancaster Quay, Western Road* ☎ *021/425–1125* ⊕ *www.lancasterlodge.com* ⇗ *48 rooms* ❍ *Breakfast.*

NIGHTLIFE AND THE ARTS

See the *Examiner* or the *Evening Echo* for details about movies, theater, and live music performances.

NIGHTLIFE

PUBS AND
NIGHTCLUBS

Bierhaus. The huge world-beer selection, poker on Tuesday, and a DJ on Saturday lure a young hip crowd here. ✉ *Pope's Quay, Shandon* ☎ *021/455–1648* ⊕ *www.thebierhauscork.com.*

Charlies Bar. This traditional "early bar" is open Monday through Saturday from 7 am, Sunday from 12:30 pm; nightly music sessions are held here, with traditional Irish showcased on Sunday from 3 pm. ✉ *2 Union Quay, South Docklands* ☎ *021/431–8342* ⊕ *www.charliesbarcork.com.*

Corner House. This popular bar, Cork's best local in the opinion of many regulars, is open daily and hosts Cajun, folk, or Irish music from Thursday to Sunday. ✉ *7 Coburg St., City Center North* ☎ *021/450–0655.*

Counihan's. On Sunday evenings this popular music bar features Arundo, with their blend of traditional Irish and Latin-rhythm music, while on Monday from 9:30 pm Ricky Lynch's folk-blues guitar session is legendary. ✉ *11 Pembroke St., City Center South* ☎ *021/427–7850* ⊕ *www.counihans.com.*

Franciscan Well Brewery. This lively, award-winning microbrewery, on the site of an ancient Franciscan monastery, has a heated beer garden and an atmospheric candlelit bar, open daily from 3 pm. ✉ *North Mall, Shandon* ☎ *021/439–3434* ⊕ *www.franciscanwellbrewery.com.*

The Oliver Plunkett. You can hear live music here nightly—trad, blues, rock, swing, and soul. ⊠ *116 Oliver Plunkett St., City Center South* ☎ *021/422–2779* ⊕ *www.theoliverplunkett.com.*

The Pavilion. The bar here draws crowds with live entertainment nightly, while the nightclub kicks off late Thursday to Saturday nights. ⊠ *13 Careys La., City Center South* ☎ *021/427–6230* ⊕ *www.pavilioncork.com.*

Savoy Club and Venue. The major venue for night owls, the Savoy operates Thursday to Saturday from 11 until late. Live acts from Ireland and elsewhere are on offer in the main room and in the lobby, and there are DJ sets in the lobby. ⊠ *St. Patrick's St., City Center South* ☎ *021/427–4299* ⊕ *www.savoytheatre.ie* ⊘ *Closed Sun.–Wed.*

Sin é. Pronounced Shin-*ay*, Irish for "that's it," this is the place for live Irish music—fiddles, flutes, banjos, and bodhráns. ⊠ *8 Coburg St., City Center North* ☎ *021/450–2266.*

THE ARTS

GALLERIES **CIT Wandesford Quay Gallery.** This ground-floor space exhibits works by students and staff of Cork's thriving Crawford College of Art and Design. ⊠ *Wandesford Quay, Washington Village* ☎ *021/455–5210* ⊕ *ccad-research.org/gallery* ⊘ *Wed.–Sat. 10–6.*

The Lavit Gallery. The gallery, off South Mall, showcases artworks and crafts by Cork Arts Society members and other Irish artists. ⊠ *5 Father Mathew St., City Center South* ☎ *021/427–7749* ⊕ *www.lavitgallery. com.*

PERFORM- **Cork Opera House.** The city's major hall for touring productions also
ING ARTS presents dance, theater, and comedy, and music events. ⊠ *Lavitt's Quay,*
AND FILM *City Center South* ☎ *021/427–0022* ⊕ *www.corkoperahouse.ie.*

Everyman Palace Theatre. Modest-size theatrical productions are staged at this theater, which has an ornate Victorian interior. ⊠ *15 MacCurtain St., City Center North* ☎ *021/450–1673* ⊕ *www.everymanpalace.com.*

Triskel Arts Centre. The popular venue presents live music, classic and contemporary films, and readings in the former Christchurch (dating from 1717), and hosts art exhibitions. ⊠ *Tobin St., off S. Main St., Washington Village* ☎ *021/427–2022* ⊕ *www.triskelartscentre.ie.*

SHOPPING

DEPARTMENT STORES

Brown Thomas. Ireland's high-end department store carries items by Irish and international designers. The ground floor has an excellent cosmetics hall and a good selection of menswear and Irish crystal. Refuel at the coffee shop, which sells healthful open sandwiches and homemade soups. ⊠ *18–21 St. Patrick's St., City Center South* ☎ *021/480–5555* ⊕ *www.brownthomas.com.*

Debenham's. Cork's largest department store, a branch of the U.K. chain, occupies a beautiful landmark building with a central glass dome. ⊠ *12–17 St. Patrick's St., City Center South* ☎ *1890/946–779* ⊕ *www. debenhams.ie.*

Marks & Spencer. This British retail giant is as popular for its foods (great for picnics) and housewares as for its clothing basics. ⊠ *6–8 St.*

Thanks to streets lined with cafés, pubs, and shops, a simple stroll around Cork can be a delightful way to while away the hours.

Patrick's St., Merchant's Quay, City Center South ☎ *021/427–5555* ⊕ *www.marksandspencer.com.*

MALLS

Merchant's Quay Shopping Centre. This large mall is conveniently located in the heart of downtown. ⊠ *Merchant's Quay, 1–5 St. Patrick's St., City Center South* ☎ *021/427–5466* ⊕ *www.merchantsquaycork.com.*

Opera Lane. Topshop, Next, Gap, Viyella, Tommy Hilfiger, and other high-street fashion retailers do business in a gleaming covered arcade between St. Patrick Street and the Opera House. Open Sunday from noon to 6 pm. ⊠ *City Center South* ☎ *021/427–5008* ⊕ *www.operalane.com.*

ANTIQUES

Diana O'Mahony. This is a major spot for antique jewelry. ⊠ *8 Winthrop St., City Center South* ☎ *021/427–6599* ⊕ *www.dianaomahonyjewellery.com.*

Meadows & Byrne. You'll find the best of Irish contemporary design for the home here, from cookware to Irish crystal. ⊠ *22 Academy St., City Center South* ☎ *021/427–2324* ⊕ *www.meadowsandbyrne.com.*

Stokes Fine Clocks and Watches. Packed with antique clocks and watches, Stokes often has a barograph or two (to measure atmospheric pressure). ⊠ *48B MacCurtain St., City Center North* ☎ *021/455–1195* ⊕ *www.stokesclocks.ie.*

BOOKS

Connolly's Bookshop. This shop is known for its good selection of Irish-interest titles and extensive stock of new and secondhand books. ⊠ *Paul St. Piazza, City Center South* ☎ *021/427–5366.*

Vibes & Scribes. Loyal, avid readers head here to peruse the extensive stock of new, secondhand, and discount books. The new bargain books are strong on art and Irish interest. ✉ *21 Lavitt's Quay, City Center South* ☎ *021/427–9535* ⊕ *vibesandscribes.ie*

Waterstones. Cork's biggest bookshop carries a wide selection new fiction and nonfiction and stocks many locally published books. ✉ *69 St. Patrick's St., City Center South* ☎ *021/427–6522* ⊕ *www.waterstones.com.*

CLOTHING

Brocade and Lime. A tempting selection of retro-style high fashion from the 1940s to the 1970s hangs in this nicely restored Victorian town house across from Cork's traditional Saturday market. ✉ *4 Cornmarket St., City Center South* ☎ *021/427–8882* ⊕ *www.brocadeandlime.ie.*

The Dressing Room. Fashion lovers adore the eveningwear and business attire at this bijou upscale boutique opposite the entrance to the Cork Opera House. ✉ *4 Emmet Pl., City Center South* ☎ *021/427–0117.*

Kuyichi. The international fashion chain with a sustainable-living ethos occupies a fine Queen Anne house. ✉ *19 Opera La., City Center South* ☎ *021/480–6671* ⊕ *www.kuyichi.com.*

Monica John. In addition to locally designed high-fashion ladies' wear, Monica John carries some imported lines. ✉ *French Church St., City Center South* ☎ *021/427–1399.*

Quills. A good selection of Irish-made apparel for women and men is always available at Quills. ✉ *107 St. Patrick's St., City Center South* ☎ *021/427–1717.*

Samui. Here's a stop for dramatic—often quirky, but always flattering—fashions from Ireland, France, Germany, and the United Kingdom. ✉ *17 Drawbridge St., City Center South* ☎ *021/427–8080* ⊕ *www.samuifashions.com.*

JEWELRY

Designworks Studio. A local favorite, this store is a top showcase for imaginative, modern jewelry. ✉ *Cornmarket St., City Center South* ☎ *021/427–9420* ⊕ *designworksstudio.ie.*

Silverwood. A large selection of Celtic-inspired silver jewelry is sold here, including traditional Claddagh rings. ✉ *84a Oliver Plunkett St., City Center South* ☎ *021/427–8150* ⊕ *www.silverwoodjewellery.com.*

The Swiss Gem. A trove of custom-made gold jewelry, this boutique also specializes in engagement rings. ✉ *21 Winthrop St., City Center South* ☎ *021/422–3892.*

MUSIC

Pro Musica. Along with sheet music, Pro Musica stocks instruments for classical musicians. ✉ *20 Oliver Plunkett St., City Center South* ☎ *021/427–1659* ⊕ *www.promusica.ie.*

BLARNEY

10 km (6 miles) northwest of Cork City.

"On Galway sands they kiss your hands, they kiss your lips at Carney, but by the Lee they drink strong tea, and kiss the stone at Blarney."

This famous rhyme celebrates one of Ireland's most noted icons—the Blarney Stone, which is the main reason most people journey to this small community built around a village green.

GETTING HERE AND AROUND

Blarney is about a 20-minute drive west of Cork City, midway between the N22 Killarney road and the N20 to Limerick. Local buses that depart from Cork Bus Station Parnell Place drop you at the Village Green, adjacent to the castle and the crafts shops. There is a large parking lot (free). Taxis are available from Castle Cabs by phone reservation.

ESSENTIALS

Transportation Contacts Castle Cabs ☎ *021/438–2222.*

Visitor Information Blarney Tourist Office ✉ *Blarney Woolen Mills entrance, The Square* ☎ *021/438–1624* ☉ *Closed Nov.–mid-Mar.*

EXPLORING

Fodor's Choice ★ **Blarney Castle.** In the center of Blarney, the ruined central keep is all that's left of this mid-15th-century stronghold. The castle contains the famed **Blarney Stone**; kissing the stone, it's said, endows the kisser with the fabled "gift of the gab." It's 127 steep steps to the battlements. To kiss the stone, you must lie down on the battlements, hold on to a guardrail, and lean your head way back. It's good fun and not at all dangerous. Expect a line from mid-June to early September; while you wait, you can admire the views of the wooded River Lee valley and chuckle over how the word "blarney" came to mean what it does. As the story goes, Queen Elizabeth I wanted Cormac MacCarthy, Lord of Blarney, to will his castle to the Crown, but he refused her requests with eloquent excuses and soothing compliments. Exhausted by his comments, the queen reportedly exclaimed, "This is all Blarney. What he says he rarely means."

You can take pleasant walks around the castle grounds; Rock Close contains oddly shaped limestone rocks landscaped in the 18th century, and a grove of ancient yew trees that is said to have been a site of Druid worship. In early March there's a wonderful display of naturalized daffodils. ✉ *Village Green, Blarney, Co. Cork* ☎ *021/438–5252* ⊕ *www.blarneycastle.ie* 🎫 *€12* ☉ *May and Sept., Mon.–Sat. 9–6:30, Sun. 9–5:30; June–Aug., Mon.–Sat. 9–7, Sun. 9–5:30; Oct.–Apr., Mon.–Sat. 9–sunset, Sun. 9–5 or sunset.*

WHERE TO EAT AND STAY

$$ ✕ **Blairs Inn.** Surrounded by woods a five minutes' drive from Blarney, EUROPEAN Blair's Inn—noted for its exuberant window-box displays—is the perfect retreat from Blarney's tour-bus crowds. This is a real "local," run by genial owner-hosts and their sons. The bar serves a range of local craft beers and bottled beers. You can dine in the bar or the quieter

6

wood-paneled restaurant. In summer enjoy the beer garden; in winter, warm yourself by a wood fire. Freshly prepared local produce is served in generous portions all day: best bets include Irish stew (lamb, carrots, and potatoes), the house special—hot corned beef with parsley sauce—and a memorable gratin of prawns, crab, and salmon, served piping hot. There's live entertainment every Monday at 9 pm from May to October. $ *Average main: €23* ⊠ *R579, Cloghroe, Co. Cork* ☎ *021/438–1470* ⊕ *blairsinn.ie.*

$

HOTEL

Blarney Castle Hotel. Set on the village green only a minute's walk from the famed castle, this 1837 hotel occupies a traditional gabled building, with guest rooms on two stories above the bar and a quiet residents' lounge on the first floor. **Pros:** ideal touring base; good alternative to Cork City 8 km (5 miles); restaurant on premises; no smoking throughout. **Cons:** bar can get busy on Sunday night; no elevator; some rooms overlook park lot and yard. $ *Rooms from: €100* ⊠ *Village Green, Blarney, Co. Cork* ☎ *021/438–5116* ⊕ *www.blarneycastlehotel.com* ⌂ *13 rooms* ◯◯ *No meals.*

$

B&B/INN

The White House Bed and Breakfast Blarney. On an elevated site on the main road between the N20 and Blarney village (a five-minute walk from the latter), this hacienda-style bungalow has a distant view of the castle from its front door. **Pros:** good value for money; quiet and comfortable; home-cooked breakfast. **Cons:** won't win any style awards. $ *Rooms from: €70* ⊠ *Shean Lower, Blarney, Co. Cork* ☎ *021/438–5338* ⊕ *www.thewhitehouseblarney.com* ⌂ *6 rooms* ◯◯ *Breakfast.*

SHOPPING

Blarney Woollen Mills. With the largest stock and the highest turnover of Blarney's crafts shops, this noted emporium sells everything from Irishmade high fashion to Aran hand-knit items to leprechaun key rings. ⊠ *The Square, Blarney, Co. Cork* ☎ *021/451–6111* ⊕ *www.blarney.com.*

EAST CORK

Most visitors to Cork head west out of the city for the coastal areas between Cork and Glengarriff, but the county's eastern portions—Cork Harbour, Midleton, and Shanagarry, are also worth exploring.

CORK HARBOUR

16 km (10 miles) east of Cork City.

Cork City's nearby harbor district has seen plenty of history. Cork Harbour's draws include Fota Island—with an arboretum, a wildlife park, and the Fota House ancestral estate—and the fishing port of Cobh.

GETTING HERE AND AROUND

Cobh lies 16 km (10 miles) east of Cork City, and is signposted from the N25 (follow signs for Waterford). A suburban train from Cork's Kent Station stops at Fota Island and Cobh, and offers better harbor views than the journey by road.

ESSENTIALS

Visitor Information Cobh Tourist Office ✉ *Sirius Arts Centre, Lower Rd., Cobh* ☎ *021/481–3301* ⊕ *www.visitcobh.com.*

TOURS

Spike Island Guided Walking Tour. Local historian and author, Dr. Michael Martin, leads this half-day trip, an informative and entertaining 2½-hour tour featuring a boat ride to, and exploration of, this historic island fortress (reservations recommended). ✉ *Cobh* ☎ *087/276–7218* ⊕ *www.titanic.ie* ✉ *€13.50* ☉ *June–Aug. daily; May and Sept. weekends; Apr., Sun. Tours depart at 2 pm and return at 4:30.*

The Titanic Trail. Another tour by local historian and author, Dr. Michael Martin (⇨ *see also Spike Island Guided Walking Tour*), this is a 60-minute guided walking tour of Cobh that covers *Titanic* sites and history; it departs daily at 11 am from the Commodore Hotel. ✉ *Cobh* ☎ *087/276–7218* ⊕ *www.titanic.ie* ✉ *€9.50.*

Whale of a Time. This company runs whale- and dolphin-watching trips, coastal sightseeing cruises, and adventure boating experiences. ✉ *East Ferry Marina, Church View, Cobh* ☎ *086/328–3250* ⊕ *www.whaleofatime.ie* ✉ *From €35.*

EXPLORING

Fota House, Arboretum & Gardens. The name of the Smith-Barry ancestral estate is derived from the Irish *Fód te*, which means "warm soil," a tribute to the unique tidal estuary microclimate here and the reason why one of Ireland's most exotic botanical gardens was established here. The original lodge house was built in the mid-18th century for the family, which owned vast tracts of land in South Cork, including the whole of Fota Island. The next generation of the powerful family employed the renowned architects Richard and William Vitruvius Morrison to convert the structure into an impressive Regency-style house that has now been painstakingly restored. The symmetrical facade is relatively unadorned and stands in contrast to the resplendent Adamesque plasterwork of the formal reception rooms (somewhat denuded of furniture). The servants' quarters are almost as big as the house proper. Fota's glories continue in the gardens, which include an arboretum, a Victorian fernery, an Italian garden, an orangerie, and a special display of magnolias. You can also (for an extra charge) visit the Victorian Farmyard. There's a tearoom, and the house hosts a program of concerts and exhibitions: see the website for details. ✉ *Fota Island* ☎ *021/481–5543* ⊕ *www.fotahouse.com* ✉ *€8 house, €5 farmyard, €11 combination ticket; gardens and arboretum free* ☉ *House: Apr.–Sept., daily 10–5 (last tour 3:30). Gardens: daily 9–5.*

Fota Island Wildlife Park. The 70-acre park is 12 km (7 miles) east of Cork via N25 and R624, the main Cobh road, and also accessible by rail from Cork's Kent Station. It's an important breeding center for cheetahs and wallabies, and also is home to monkeys, zebras, giraffes, ostriches, flamingos, emus, and kangaroos. ✉ *Fota Island* ☎ *021/481–2678* ⊕ *www.fotawildlife.ie* ✉ *€14* ☉ *Mid-Mar.–Oct., daily 10:30–6; Nov.-mid-Mar., daily 10:30–4:30 (last entry 1 hr before closing).*

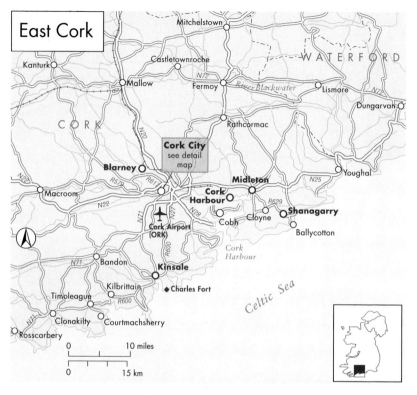

East Cork

0   10 miles
0   15 km

Fodor's Choice **The Queenstown Story at Cobh Heritage Centre.** Many of the people who
★ left Ireland on immigrant ships for the New World departed from Cobh,
which was formerly known as Queenstown. The exhibit, in the old
Cobh train station, re-creates the experience of the 2.5 million emigrants who left from here between 1848 and 1950. It also tells the stories of great transatlantic liners, including the ill-fated *Titanic*, whose
last port of call was Cobh, and the *Lusitania (see box)*. ⊠ *Lower Rd.,
Cobh* ☎ *021/481–3591* ⊕ *www.cobhheritage.com* 🖾 *€7.50* ⊘ *Apr.–
Sept., daily 9:30–6; Nov.–Mar., Mon.–Sat. 9:30–5, Sun. 11–5.*

St. Colman's Cathedral. The best view of Cobh, well worth the uphill
stroll, is from St. Colman's Cathedral, an exuberant neo-Gothic granite
church designed by the eminent British architect E.W. Pugin in 1869,
and completed in 1919. Inside, granite niches portray scenes of the
Roman Catholic Church's history in Ireland, beginning with the arrival
of St. Patrick. ⊠ *Cathedral Close, Cobh* ☎ *021/481–3222* ⊕ *www.
cobhcathedralparish.ie.*

The Titanic Experience Cobh. Cobh was the last port of call for the ocean
liner *Titanic*. At 1:30 pm on April 11, 1912, tenders carried 123 passengers out to the ship from the offices of the White Star Line. These
offices have now been converted into an interactive exhibition (cinema, holographs, touch-screen displays), allowing visitors to follow,

THE SINKING OF THE LUSITANIA

On May 7 every year an event is held on the quayside in Cobh at the *Lusitania* Peace Memorial to commemorate the 1,198 innocent civilians lost at sea on May 7, 1915. The Cunard liner *Lusitania* was torpedoed off the Old Head of Kinsale, 25 miles west of Queenstown (as Cobh was then known). This attack on a nonmilitary target was a major factor in the decision by the United States to declare war in 1917.

The *Lusitania* was the pride of the Cunard fleet. She had set a record in 1907, crossing the Atlantic in four days, 19 hours, 52 minutes, and the transatlantic service continued, despite the outbreak of war in 1914. The vessel was on a voyage from New York to Liverpool when she was struck by a torpedo from the German submarine U20 shortly after 2 pm. She quickly listed to one side, making it difficult to launch the lifeboats, and 18 minutes later, the mighty liner had sunk, leaving hundreds struggling in the water. A flotilla of local boats, tenders, tugs, and fishing vessels rushed to the rescue, while those onshore worked tirelessly to cope with the sudden disaster. Of the 1,959 passengers and crew aboard, only 761 survived. Of the 289 bodies recovered, 169 are buried in Cobh, 45 of them unidentified.

6

literally, in the footsteps of the passengers as they embarked on the fateful voyage. ✉ *The Promenade, Cobh* ☎ *021/481–4412* 🌐 *www.titanicexperiencecobh.ie* 🎟 *€9.50* ⏲ *Daily 10–5:30 (last admission 4:45).*

WHERE TO EAT

$$ CONTEMPORARY 🍴 **Gilbert's Restaurant & Townhouse.** Just below Cobh's cathedral, a short step from the waterfront, this handsome cut-stone house dates to 1824. Locals can be seen lingering over coffee and newspapers through the street-front windows of the café and bar area, and the elegant bistro-style restaurant, with bentwood chairs and contemporary art, has an equally relaxed Continental atmosphere. The food is locally sourced and contemporary in style, with many light dishes on the menu. Start with the spiced beef carpaccio, or smoked salmon, avocado, and feta salad with honey-mustard dressing; mains might include slow-braised shank of venison or linguine with prawns and mussels. White chocolate mousse is a star among the desserts, but the lemon tart is equally popular. Five spacious bedrooms are also available. [$] *Average main: €20* ✉ *11 Pearse Sq., Cobh* 🌐 *www.gilbertsincobh.com.*

MIDLETON

12 km (8 miles) east of Cork City.

Midleton is famous for its school, Midleton College, founded in 1696, and its distillery, founded in 1825 and modernized in 1975, which manufactures spirits—including Irish whiskey—for distribution worldwide. A pleasant market town set at the head of the Owenacurra River estuary, near the northeast corner of Cork Harbour, Midleton has many gray-stone buildings dating mainly from the early 19th century.

GETTING HERE AND AROUND

Midleton is 12 km (8 miles) east of Cork City on the main N25. It also has regular bus and train connections with the city. If you're going to visit the Jameson distillery, it runs a daily shuttle, April through October, from St Patrick's Quay in Cork. In other months, Bus Éireann's daily service from Cork Bus Station Parnell Place is the best option because it stops right outside the distillery (€9 round-trip, 30 minutes). Many trains run from Cork's Kent Station every day (€6.50 round-trip); Midleton train station is about 25 minutes' walk from the distillery.

Bus Éireann ✉ *Parnell Pl., City Center South, Cork City* ☎ *021/450–8188* 🌐 *www.buseireann.ie.*

Irish Rail ✉ *Kent Station, City Center North, Cork City* ☎ *021/450–6766 for timetable* 🌐 *www.irishrail.ie.*

EXPLORING

Jameson Experience. The "experience" here is all about Irish whiskey. On a tour of the Old Midleton Distillery, you'll learn how whiskey—*uisce beatha*, "the water of life"—was made in the old days. The old stone buildings are excellent examples of 19th-century industrial architecture, the impressively large old waterwheel still operates, and the pot still—a copper dome that can hold 32,000 imperial gallons of whiskey—is the world's largest. Early in the tour, requests are made for a volunteer "whiskey taster," so be alert if this option appeals. Tours end with a complimentary glass of Jameson's Irish whiskey (or a soft drink). A gift shop and café are also on the premises. From April to October there is a daily shuttle bus service from St Patrick's Quay Cork; enquire when booking. ✉ *Old Midleton Distillery, Old Distillery Walk* ☎ *021/461–3594* 🌐 *www.jamesonwhiskey.com* 🎟 *€13* 🕒 *Apr.–Oct., daily 10–6; Nov.–Mar., tours daily 11:30, 1:15, 2:30, and 4.*

WHERE TO STAY

$$$$ RESORT FAMILY 🏨 **Castlemartyr Resort.** A gracious 18th-century manor house is the centerpiece of this resort comprising spa, golf course, and rental lodges overlooking ancient pasture grazed by Kerry Bog ponies, and adjacent to a 12th-century castle. **Pros:** enthusiastic staff, some here for generations; top-grade spa and golf; Kids Club; close to beaches and Ballymaloe. **Cons:** a bit off the beaten track; popular as a wedding and conference venue. [$] *Rooms from: €290* ✉ *Castlemartyr* ☎ *021/421–9000* 🌐 *www.castlemartyrresort.ie* 🛏 *92 rooms, 11 suites, 45 lodges* 🍴 *No meals.*

SHANAGARRY

15 km (8 miles) southeast of Midleton, 17 km (11 miles) southeast of Cork Harbour.

There are three reasons to come to Shanagarry, a farming village known chiefly for its Quaker connections: Ballymaloe House, one of Ireland's first and still most famous country-house hotels; Ballymaloe Cookery School Gardens, at a top destination for chefs-in-training; and the gallery and shop of Stephen Pearce, a leading designer of earthenware pottery. All three enterprises are run by Quaker families, testimony to the religious roots of this community.

GETTING HERE AND AROUND

Shanagarry, on a rural back road, is about an hour's drive from Cork City or Cork Harbour on the N25 to the R632; from Midleton, take the R629. Or take the Ballycotton bus (there are five runs daily) from Cork Bus Station Parnell Place. The trip takes an hour and a quarter. The last bus back to Cork leaves Shanagarry at 4:45 pm.

EXPLORING

FAMILY **Ballymaloe Cookery School Gardens.** While Myrtle Allen reigns supreme at Ballymaloe House (⇨ see *Where to Stay*), her daughter-in-law Darina, Ireland's most famous celebrity chef and Slow Food advocate, rules at the Ballymaloe Cookery School, 3 km (2 miles) east. The school offers 12-week residential courses for aspiring professional chefs, and day and half-day courses with famous visiting chefs (including Darina's daughter-in-law, Rachel Allen). The extensive organic gardens here provide herbs and vegetables for the school and the restaurant (glass houses open weekdays), and visitors can ramble through wildflower meadows and admire herbaceous borders leading to an ornately crafted shell house, the potager vegetable garden, a rustic tree house, and a Celtic maze. A farm walk visits cows in their clover field, rare breed pigs, and some 400 hens. ⊠ *Kinoith House* ☏ *021/464–6785* ⊕ *www.cooking-is-fun.ie/gardens/our-gardens* ☐ *€6* ☉ *May–Sept., daily 11–5:30; Oct.–Apr., Mon.–Sat. 11–5:30.*

Shanagarry Design Centre. Run by the Kilkenny Shop, the spacious gallery and showroom (with scrumptious home baking in the café) is in the village center. On display are high-end Irish-made crafts including Newbridge silverware, Orla Kiely handbags, and potter Louis Mulcahy's huge bowls and lamps, as well as Irish-made clothing, woolen goods, Irish linen, and jewelry. Three artists have studios in the basement, where their work is also for sale. ⊠ *Next to Shanagarry Parish Church* ☏ *021/464–5838* ☐ *Free* ☉ *Daily 10–6.*

Shanagarry House. Shanagarry's most famous Quaker native son was none other than William Penn (1644–1718), the founder of the Pennsylvania colony, who grew up in Shanagarry House, still a private residence in the center of the village. The house's most famous tenant since William Penn was Marlon Brando, who stayed here in the summer of 1995 while filming *Divine Rapture* in nearby Ballycotton. ⊠ *Opposite the church.*

Stephen Pearce Pottery. Now returned to the village where he grew up, potter Stephen Pearce has reopened the traditional craft pottery that launched his career in the late 1960s. The showroom sells his distinctive hand-thrown black-and-cream earthenware tableware and the terracotta-and-white line, both beloved of collectors. The tearoom opens daily from May to September, weekends only in winter. Book a pottery tour in advance, and ask about workshops. ⊠ *The Old Pottery* ☏ *021/464–6807* ⊕ *www.stephenpearce.com* ☉ *Mon.–Sat. 10–5, Sun. 11:30–6.*

WHERE TO STAY

$$$$ B&B/INN FAMILY Fodor's Choice ★ 🏨 **Ballymaloe House.** This Georgian manor is a symphony of whites and beiges, its drawing room beckoning with its fine modern Irish paintings—a lovely touch for what is basically a farmhouse family home, albeit a world-famous one: Ballymaloe is the fountainhead of New Irish cuisine. **Pros:** top restaurant; child-friendly atmosphere; quiet rural location. **Cons:** advance booking essential; village not in walking distance. [$] *Rooms from: €240* ✉ *Off R629* ☎ *021/465–2531* 🌐 *www.ballymaloe.ie* 🛏 *29 rooms* 🍴 *Breakfast.*

WEST CORK

The historic old port—and now booming seaside town—of Kinsale is the perfect place to begin the 136-km (85-mile) trip, via Bantry Bay and through a variety of seascapes, to the lush vegetation of Glengarriff. If you tackle this scenic West Cork coastal route nonstop, the drive takes less than two hours, but the whole point of this journey is to linger in places that tickle your fancy. Must-sees include the famed 18th-century manse of Bantry House and the romantic island gardens of Ilnacullin.

KINSALE

29 km (18 miles) southwest of Cork City.

Foodies flock to Kinsale, a picturesque port that pioneered the Irish small-town tradition of fine dining in unbelievably small restaurants. In the early 1980s, Kinsale had a village-size population of 2,000 and at least a dozen top-grade restaurants, mostly run by enthusiastic owner-chefs. Things have leveled out since then—the town has grown, while the number of restaurants has remained nearly the same, and most of the original chefs have moved on—but there is still a great buzz during the annual **Kinsale Gourmet Festival** (🌐 *www.kinsalerestaurants.com*) held in October. Year-round, head to Market Square (Wednesday 10–1) to find Kinsale Market, a cute piazza market where you can snack on a Breton crepe while stocking up on chutneys, smoked salmon, farmhouse cheeses, fresh fish, and organic goodies.

In Kinsale's town center, at the tip of the wide, fjordlike harbor that opens out from the River Bandon, upscale shops and eateries with brightly painted facades line small streets. Kinsale has two yacht marinas, and skippers with deep-sea angling boats offer day charters. The Kinsale Yacht Club hosts racing and cruising events during the sailing season, which runs from March to October for hardy souls and from June to August for everyone else.

GETTING HERE AND AROUND

Kinsale is 29 km (18 miles) southwest of Cork City on the R600, a half-hour drive, and is only a 15-minute drive from Cork Airport. Ground-level parking is easily available. Buses from Cork City stop at the airport and run about every hour. Kinsale's town center is compact, and there is no public transport, but taxis can be booked from Kinsale Cabs.

TOURS

Don & Barry's Kinsale Historic Stroll. On this tour of Old Kinsale you'll learn about the town's links to "Man Friday" and the truth about Kinsale Hookers pirates. It departs from the town's tourist office daily at 11:15, and Monday to Saturday at 9:15 from May to September. ☎ 021/477–2873 ⊕ *www.historicstrollkinsale.com* ✉ €6 ⊗ *Daily 11:5; also Mon.–Sat. 9:15, May–Sept.*

Kinsale Harbour Cruises. For an overview of Kinsale's great natural harbor, take an hour-long cruise on the *Spirit of Kinsale*, offered by Kinsale Harbour Cruises. You'll hear informative commentary and view wildlife, including herons, seals, and otters. ⊠ *Pier Rd.* ☎ 086/250–5456 ⊕ *www.kinsaleharbourcruises.com* ✉ €12.50 ⊗ *Mid-Mar.–Sept., daily, weather permitting.*

Kinsale Heritage Town Walks. Dermot Ryan, a native of Kinsale and a local-history enthusiast, leads guided town walks daily at 10:30 am and 4:30 pm. ☎ 021/477–2729 ⊕ *www.kinsaleheritage.com* ✉ €5.

ESSENTIALS

Transportation Contacts Kinsale Cabs ⊠ *Market Sq.* ☎ 021/477–2642 ⊕ *www.kinsalecabs.com.*

Visitor Information Kinsale Tourist Office ⊠ *Pier Rd.* ☎ 021/477–2234 ⊕ *www.kinsale.ie.*

EXPLORING

FAMILY
Fodor's Choice
★
Charles Fort. The British built Charles Fort on the east side of the Bandon River estuary in the late 17th century, after their defeat of the Spanish and Irish forces. One of Europe's best-preserved "star forts" encloses some 12 cliff-top acres and is similar to Fort Ticonderoga in New York State. If the sun is shining, take the footpath from Kinsale signposted Scilly Walk; it winds along the harbor's edge under tall trees and then through the village of Summer Cove. ⊠ *3 km (2 miles) east of town* ☎ 021/477–2263 ⊕ *www.heritageireland.ie* ✉ €4 ⊗ *Mid-Mar.–Oct., daily 10–6; Nov.–mid-Mar., Tues.–Sun. 10–5.*

Desmond Castle and the International Museum of Wine. This museum occupies a 15th-century fortified town house—originally a custom house—that has a dark history. It was used as a prison for French and American seamen in the 1700s, and was subsequently a jail and then a workhouse. Now it contains displays that tell the story of the wine trade and its importance to the Irish diaspora in France, America, Australia, and New Zealand. ⊠ *Cork St.* ☎ 021/477–4855 ⊕ *www.heritageireland.ie* ✉ €3 ⊗ *Apr.–mid-Sept., daily 10–6.*

Kinsale Museum. Memorabilia from the wreck of the *Lusitania* (⇨ *See box: The Sinking of the Lusitania*) are among the artifacts in this museum, housed in a 17th-century, Dutch-style courthouse. The 1915 inquest into that ship's sinking took place in the wood-paneled courtroom. Downstairs is a fascinating collection of antique tradesman's tools. Because the staff consists of volunteers, it's best to call to confirm opening times. ⊠ *Old Courthouse, Market Sq.* ☎ 021/477–7930 ⊗ *Apr.–Oct., daily 10–4.*

WHERE TO EAT

$ WINE BAR 🍴 **The Black Pig.** A small 18th-century coach house on a backstreet was an unlikely candidate to become the hottest place in a town famed for sophisticated eateries, but that's what happened here, and the uncluttered premises positively buzz with life. Reserve and your name is chalked on the wall beside your table, but the tall squeaky bar stools are just as popular. More than 80 wines are listed, 40 available by the (extra-large) glass, with many interesting organic and biodynamic options. Simple hot dishes of the day might include scallop risotto or a hearty lamb tagine, but most people order the house specials—local charcuterie, farmhouse cheeses, smoked salmon, mixed antipasto—served on slates or wooden platters. End your locavore feast with locally roasted coffee and locally made Koko chocolates. [$] *Average main: €12* ✉ *66 Lower O'Connell St.* ☎ *021/477–4101* 🕒 *Closed mid-Jan.–Mar. and Mon.–Wed. Nov.–mid-Jan. No lunch.*

WORD OF MOUTH

"When you visit Kinsale, if you do nothing else, make *sure* you take Don & Barry's Historic Kinsale Walking Tour. It was the best historical thing we did during our entire stay in Ireland. We had Barry Moloney as our guide and he was just fabulous! Lots of historical happenings in Kinsale to hear about, and loads of laughs." —Maggie1017

$ CONTEMPORARY 🍴 **The Bulman Bar and Toddies.** Kinsale has other pub restaurants, but none with such an idyllic waterside location. In summer, bar food is served on the big stone quay, midway between the town and Charles Fort, which looks back to the town and out to the unspoiled outer harbor. The characterful interior has a large open fireplace and a maritime theme, with a quirky selection of furniture. The bar menu is simple, and features fresh local produce, including lobster and oysters from nearby Oysterhaven Bay. Toddies, the first-floor restaurant, open from 6 pm, has a stunning sea view and a slightly more extensive menu, including fillet steak with Parmesan mash and onion rings, and daily seafood specials. [$] *Average main: €15* ✉ *Summercove* ☎ *021/477–2131* 🌐 *www.thebulman.ie* 🕒 *No food Mon.*

$ ECLECTIC 🍴 **Crackpots.** A grocery store was transformed into Carole Norman's "ceramic café," a simple but elegant eatery with warm yellow walls, an open fireplace, and cozy dining areas. The most popular tables are in the front "shopwindow" area. Behind the restaurant is Carole's pottery workshop; if you like your dinner plate, you can buy it. The eclectic menu has plenty of light dishes in the lower price range, with vegetarian options a strong point. Choices range from mussel-and-leek chowder to baked brill with a tapenade mash or Tuscan bean and curly-kale cassoulet. There's always steak, too. A singing pianist in the big-band tradition (Streisand, Sinatra) entertains on Friday nights. [$] *Average main: €18* ✉ *3 Cork St.* ☎ *021/477–2847* 🌐 *www.crackpots.ie* 🕒 *Closed Mon.–Wed., Nov.–Mar. No lunch.*

$$ SEAFOOD FAMILY Fodor's Choice ★ 🍴 **Fishy Fishy Café.** Originally a café in a fish shop, this place has moved up in the world, with sumptuous indoor-outdoor premises in the town park. Crowds flock to stand in line for lunch (reservations are only available for dinner) because TV chef Martin Shanahan, who trained in San Francisco, brings California pizzazz to his dishes. Look for surf

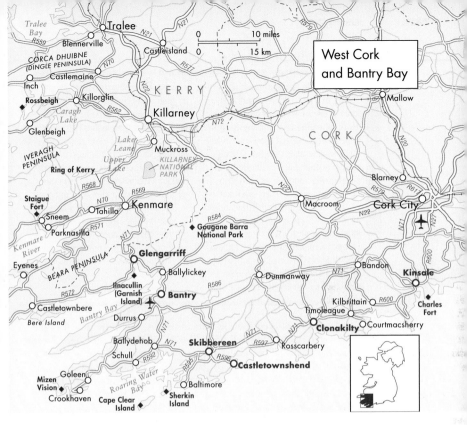

n' turf of scallops and black pudding on parsnip puree; "fishy fishy" pie (white fish, salmon, and leeks in a hot cream sauce and mash au gratin); and the signature warm seafood salad with a sweet chili dressing. Stylish young staffers seem thrilled to be part of the show. Lunch is the big event, although service does continue until 9 pm (except some days in winter). $ *Average main: €23* ⊠ *Crowley's Quay* ☎ *021/470–0415* ⊕ *www.fishyfishy.ie* ☾ *No dinner Sun.–Wed., Nov.–Feb.*

$$
EUROPEAN
✕ **Jim Edwards.** One of Ireland's original bar-restaurants, this is a famous Kinsale institution known for its generous portions of local steak, lamb, duck, and fresh seafood. Choose from the inexpensive daily specials in the busy bar, or have a more leisurely meal among the mahogany tables and dark-red decor of the somewhat baronial restaurant. With seafood this fresh, the preparation is kept simple: Kinsale oysters au naturel or crab claws tossed in garlic butter to start, followed by 10 ounces of prime fillet steak or medallions of monkfish in a scallion, ginger, and lime sauce. Classic homemade desserts (profiteroles, crème brûlée) are substantial and the Irish coffee is renowned. $ *Average main: €22* ⊠ *Market Quay* ☎ *021/477–2541* ⊕ *www.jimedwardskinsale.com.*

$$$
FRENCH
✕ **Max's Wine Bar and Restaurant.** Polished antique tables, a large stone chimney, and bay windows lend considerable charm to the open-plan ground floor of this town house—more a restaurant than a wine bar. Lunches are light and strong on salads. At dinner, owner-chef Olivier

The Battle of Kinsale

Before Kinsale became the foodie capital of Ireland, it was chiefly famous for the Battle of Kinsale in 1601, when the Irish and the Spanish joined forces against the English—and lost. As generations of Irish school-children could tell you, the Battle of Kinsale was a turning point in Irish history. It precipitated an event known as "the Flight of the Earls" (the subject of Brian Friel's play *Making History*), in which the Irish aristocracy left Europe to seek help from the Catholic king of Spain. The Irish earls never returned, leaving their lands to be colonized by the English settlers, who also filled the power vacuum created by their absence. The Spanish influence that can be traced back to this battle can be seen in Kinsale's older houses, which have slate roofs and unusual slate fronts. Because of its geographical position—approximately 800 km (500 miles) of open sea due north of La Coruña—Kinsale continued to trade with Spain, and even today, Spanish trawlers fish in the waters off the coast of County Cork. Kinsale went on to become an important fishing port as well as a British army and naval base.

Queva's classical French background is evident in his treatment of the daily catch, including fresh grilled lobster in the summer, and clever ways with unusual cuts of meat (oxtail, trotters, offal). In winter, the catch of the day is replaced by game: quail, pheasant, wild duck, or venison. The wine list is long and includes a good selection of French and New World wines. [$] *Average main: €27* ⊠ *48 Main St.* ☎ *021/477–2443* ⊕ *www.maxs.ie* ⊗ *Closed Jan.–mid-Mar.*

WHERE TO STAY

$
B&B/INN
Fodor's Choice
★

🏨 **Friar's Lodge.** A large Georgian town house has been tastefully converted into this cheerful guesthouse, with an array of amenities that would do a hotel proud. **Pros:** private parking; quiet location; very attentive service. **Cons:** no restaurant; no bar. [$] *Rooms from: €110* ⊠ *Friar's St.* ☎ *021/477–7384* ⊕ *www.friars-lodge.com* ⇥ *18 rooms* ⊗ *Closed Christmas wk* ⊗ *Breakfast.*

$$
HOTEL

🏨 **Innishannon House.** A pretty country house, built in the châteaux style in 1720 on the banks of the Bandon, Innishannon retains plenty of casual character. **Pros:** scenic riverside location; highly romantic; private car parking. **Cons:** a mile from nearest village; sometimes hosts wedding parties. [$] *Rooms from: €130* ⊠ *Innishannon* ☎ *021/477–5121* ⊕ *www.innishannon-hotel.ie* ⇥ *12 rooms* ⊗ *Breakfast.*

$
B&B/INN

🏨 **Kilcaw House.** With lovely views over the Oysterhaven estuary, this farmhouse-style B&B makes a tranquil and hassle-free base for visiting Kinsale. **Pros:** ample safe parking; friendly hosts; a quiet night's sleep. **Cons:** driving in and out of town; showers a little small. [$] *Rooms from: €70* ⊠ *Pewter Hole Cross* ☎ *021/477–4155* ⊕ *www.kilcawhouse.com* ⇥ *7 rooms* ⊗ *Closed Nov.–mid Mar.* ⊗ *Breakfast.*

$$
HOTEL

🏨 **Trident Hotel.** The modern three-story building may lack old-world charm, but the waterfront location—built around three sides of a former dockyard on the edge of Kinsale's magnificent harbor—more than

Thanks to locals painting their houses with bright colors, the historic seaside village of Kinsale has become one of Ireland's most picturesque photo ops.

compensate. **Pros:** great sea views. **Cons:** bland interiors; pool and spa are at a sister hotel a five-minute walk away. $ *Rooms from: €120* ✉ *Pier Rd., World's End* ☎ *021/477–9300* 🌐 *www.tridenthotel.com* 🛏 *75 rooms* 🍴 *Breakfast.*

NIGHTLIFE

The Folk House. This friendly pub presents live music on weekends year-round, and also midweek from May through October. ✉ *Guardwell* ☎ *021/477–2382* 🌐 *folkhousevenue.com.*

Shanakee. This club is renowned for live music—both rock and Irish traditional. ✉ *Market St.* ☎ *021/477–4472* 🕐 *No music Mon. Nov.–mid-Mar.*

SPORTS AND THE OUTDOORS

Butch Roberts Deep-Sea Angling and Scenic Tours. Whether you want to watch whales, catch a shark, or just enjoy the scenery, Butch will tailor a day or half-day trip—year-round, weather permitting—on his comfortable 38-foot boat, *Sundance Kid.* ✉ *The Marina* ☎ *021/477–8054* 🌐 *www.anglingkinsale.com.*

GOLF

Fodor's Choice ★

Old Head Golf Links. Golf doesn't get much more spectacular than this. On a celebrated 215-acre peninsula, which juts out into the wild Atlantic nearly 300 feet below, you can find an awe-inspiring spectacle that defies comparison. The only golfing stretches that could be likened to it are the 16th and 17th holes at Cypress Point and small, Pacific sections of Pebble Beach, from the 7th to the 10th, and the long 18th. Even if your golf is moderate, expect your pulse to race at the stunning views and wildlife. They've added 15 suites and a spa so you can now stay at the course for a few days. ⊠ *Old Head, off R604* ☎ *021/477–8444* ⊕ *www.oldhead.com* ✉ *€220 May–Sept.; €160 mid-Apr. and Oct.* ⅄ *18 holes, 7215 yards, par 72, practice area, caddies (reserve in advance), caddy carts, club rental, catering* ⊙ *Visitors: mid-Apr.–Oct., daily.*

SHOPPING

ART

The Boathouse Gallery. Many of the works by locally based contemporary artists sold here are small enough to carry home. ⊠ *60 Main St.* ☎ *021/470–9981* ⊕ *www.theboathousegallery.ie.*

Giles Norman Photography Gallery. Black-and-white photographs of Irish scenes are featured at this local gallery. ⊠ *44 Main St.* ☎ *021/477–4373* ⊕ *www.gilesnorman.com.*

BOOKS

Kinsale Bookshop. Irish poetry and books on local history are the specialties of this fine bookshop. ⊠ *8 Main St.* ☎ *021/477–4244* ⊕ *www.kinsalebookshop.com.*

FOOD

Koko Chocolates. Just across the road from the tourist office, the tempting aroma of hot chocolate will lead you to Kinsale's tempting little chocolate shop. Truffles are handmade on the premises and there's a range of novelty chocolates (including a chocolate iPhone), and hot drinks to go. ⊠ *Pier Rd.* ☎ *086/344–5974.*

Quay Food Company. Stock up on the Irish farmhouse cheeses and other local foods here for a great picnic. ⊠ *Market Sq.* ☎ *021/470–4000.*

HOUSEWARES

Granny's Bottom Drawer. A selection of fine linen and lace, in classic and contemporary styles, is carried at this shop, together with luxury designer knitwear. ⊠ *53 Main St.* ☎ *021/477–4839.*

Hilary Hale. This wood turner uses storm-felled locally grown timber to make lamps, bowls, and platters. ⊠ *Rincurran Hall, Summercove* ☎ *021/477–2010* ⊕ *www.hilaryhale.com.*

Kinsale Crystal. This family-run studio sells handblown, hand-cut Irish crystal. ⊠ *Market St.* ☎ *21/477–4493* ⊕ *www.kinsalecrystal.ie.*

JEWELRY

Kinsale Silver. Dominic Dolan is the silversmith who crafts fine jewelry on the premises here. ⊠ *Pearse St.* ☎ *021/477–4359* ⊕ *www.kinsalesilver.com.*

Mary Enright. A fine collection of contemporary jewelry is created on-site by goldsmith Mary Enright. ⊠ *Market Quay* ☎ *021/474–474* ⊕ *www.maryenright.com.*

CLONAKILTY AND ENVIRONS

28 km (19 miles) west of Kinsale.

Clonakilty is a small market town to the west of Kinsale on a scenic, largely coastal road that passes through the village of Timoleague. Many of the storefronts in Clonakilty have charmingly traditional hand-painted signs and wooden facades. Clonakilty marks the western edge of the Seven Heads Peninsula, which stretches back eastward to Timoleague, whose ruined abbey dominates the view. Timoleague sits on the Argideen River estuary, renowned for its birdlife, especially great flocks of wintering migrants. From the abbey, you can see the road to Courtmacsherry, across the water. The sandy beach of this postcard-pretty village attracts many vacationers.

GETTING HERE AND AROUND
Clonakilty is 28 km (19 miles) west of Kinsale on the R600, Timoleague 19 km (12 miles). Follow the signposts from Timoleague to reach Courtmacsherry. Parking is easy in all three towns. There is no public transit between Kinsale and Clonakilty, but you can take a bus (about an hour) from Cork City.

EXPLORING
Michael Collins Centre. It was in the village of Woodfield, 9 km (6 miles) west of Timoleague, that Michael Collins (1890–1922) had his last drink before he was shot in an ambush. The enthusiastic guide at this cottage-museum, signposted off the R600 east of Clonakilty, offers a lively introduction to the controversial hero of Irish independence, using slides, large photos, and film clips. Outside is a reconstruction of the ambush site, complete with Collins's armored Rolls-Royce and a Crossley tender. Directions to other Collins sites in the area are available, as are guided tours (prebooking essential). ⊠ *Castleview, off R600, Clonakilty* ☎ *023/884–6107* ⊕ *www.michaelcollinscentre.com* ⊲ *€5* ⊙ *Mid-June–mid-Sept., weekdays 10:30–5, Sat. 11–2; rest of year by appointment.*

Timoleague Abbey. A mid-13th-century Franciscan abbey at the water's edge is Timoleague's most striking monument. The abbey was built before the estuary silted up, and its main business was the importing of wine from Spain. A tower and walls with Gothic-arch windows still stand, and you can trace the ground plan of the old friary—chapel, refectory, cloisters, and the extensive wine cellar. The English sacked the abbey in 1642, but like many other ruins of its kind it was used as a burial place until the late 20th century, hence the modern gravestones. ■ TIP➔ Walk around the back to find the entrance gate. The view of the sea framed by the structure's ruined Gothic windows is a don't-miss photo op. ⊠ *The Quay* ⊕ *www.timoleague.ie.*

WHERE TO EAT AND STAY
$$
EUROPEAN
FAMILY
✕ **The Pink Elephant.** The legendary Pink Elephant looks out to sea and across the bay to wooded slopes. Huge windows frame the stunning view, and in good weather there is seating outside. The menu incorporates locally produced foods—organic leaves, farmhouse cheeses, smoked salmon, and the freshest fish and meats. Lunch includes a range of open sandwiches and healthy salads. Hearty mains dominate the dinner menu, on which you might find slow-roast shank of lamb with balsamic and red wine jus on scallion mash or roast monkfish with a tomato and mint salsa. Desserts are substantial classics. This is also a popular bar, often lively with banter between the friendly hosts and their clientele. On weekdays call first, or check the website, as opening times

vary. 💲 *Average main: €21* ✉ *R600 between Kinsale and Timoleague, Harbour View, Kilbrittain* ☎ *023/884–9608* ⊕ *www.pinkelephant.ie* ⊗ *No dinner Mon.–Wed.; no lunch weekdays Sept.–June.*

$$
B&B/INN
FAMILY
Fodor's Choice
★

🏠 **The Glen Country House.** Midway between Kinsale and Clonakilty on the scenic R600, this lovely creeper-clad Victorian house is excellent as a touring base or quet retreat—many guests just nestle down and enjoy the sheltered sea estuary and good walks. **Pros:** family atmosphere; gracious surroundings; great value. **Cons:** must drive to nearest shops and eateries. 💲 *Rooms from: €120* ✉ *Kilbrittain* ☎ *023/884–9862* ⊕ *www. glencountryhouse.com* ↩ *5 rooms* ⊗ *Closed Nov.–Mar.* ⊺◯⊺ *Breakfast.*

$
B&B/INN

🏠 **Kilbrogan House.** At the highest point of a rural market town between Kinsale and Clonakilty, this house has been the community's architectural star since it was built in 1818, and makes a peaceful base that's good for touring but off the beaten tourist trail. **Pros:** a haven of civilized style; out of the way; off-street parking. **Cons:** not much nightlife in town; limited restaurant scene in town. 💲 *Rooms from: €80* ✉ *Kilbrogan Hill, Bandon* ☎ *023/884–4935* ⊕ *www.kilbrogan.com* ↩ *5 rooms* ⊗ *Closed Nov.–Feb.* ⊺◯⊺ *Breakfast.*

SPORTS AND ACTIVITIES

BEACHES

Inchydoney Beach. The beach is on an island connected to the mainland by causeways, and accessible by car. It consists of two flat wide stretches of fine white sand divided by a rocky promontory. ■ **TIP→ The east side is the most sheltered and has dunes that can be walked.** The slope to the sea is so gentle that at low tide it's a long walk to find deep water. Busy in July and August, its vast expanses offer exhilarating walks the rest of the year. **Amenities:** lifeguards; parking (free); toilets; water sports. **Best for:** surfing; swimming; walking. ✉ *Inchydoney Island, 3 km (2 miles) south of town, Clonakilty.*

SHOPPING

Edward Twomey. This butcher's shop is famed for its Clonakilty Black Pudding, a breakfast product that's prominently featured on the shop's T-shirts—the ultimate West Cork souvenir. ✉ *16 Pearse St., Clonakilty* ☎ *023/883–4835* ⊕ *www.clonakiltyblackpudding.ie.*

Etain Hickey Collection. Etain Hickey is one of Ireland's leading ceramic artists, and her shop stocks the best of contemporary crafts from local artists, including her partner Jim Turner of Rossmore Pottery, and Fair Trade sources. ✉ *40 Ashe St., Clonakilty* ☎ *023/882–1479* ⊕ *www. rossmorepottery.com.*

Lettercollum Kitchen Project. Owners Con McLaughlin and Karen Austin are masters of the vegetarian and ethnic repertory. Their bakery and deli sells specialty breads, cooks' ingredients, sandwiches, and savory herb tarts. You can assemble a superior picnic here. ✉ *22 Connolly St., Clonakilty* ☎ *023/883–6938* ⊕ *www.lettercollum.ie.*

Scally's SuperValu. Scally's regularly wins awards for its own-label "take and bake" range of soups, lasagna, and pies, its salads, and the wide range of local artisan food available in-store, including charcuterie, smoked fish, and farmhouse cheese. ✉ *Clonakilty Shopping Centre,*

Wolfe Tone St., Faxbridge, Clon-akilty ☎ *023/883–3088* ⊕ *www.supervaluclon.ie.*

Spiller's Lane Gallery. Set in a converted grain store at a pretty mews, this shop sells Irish-made jewelry, cutlery, pottery, and paintings. ✉ *Spiller's La., Bridge St., Clon-akilty* ☎ *023/883–8416.*

Urru. After taking the Ballymaloe Certificate Cookery Course, Ruth Healy left the corporate treadmill behind to open the ultimate cook's shop, which aims to bring urban chic to rural Ireland. Sip a latte while browsing among locally made foodstuffs, including pâtés and patisserie, and a tempting range of cookbooks, cookware, and chocolates. ✉ *The Mill, MacSwiney Quay, Bandon* ☎ *023/885–4731* ⊕ *www.urru.ie.*

GOING NATIVE

If you really want to see Skibbereen at its liveliest, come on a Wednesday when the cattle market is in full swing, and the sounds of men spitting and backslapping fill the air.

SKIBBEREEN

33 km (20 miles) west of Clonakilty.

Skibbereen is the main market town in this neck of southwest Cork. The Saturday country market and the plethora of pubs, punctuated by bustling shops, supermarkets, and coffeehouses, keep the place jumping year-round.

GETTING HERE AND AROUND

Skibbereen is 85 km (53 miles) southwest of Cork City, a drive of an hour and 20 minutes on the N71, the main Bantry road. The town lies 33 km (20 miles) west of Clonakilty—about half-an-hour's drive. There is free parking on street and in several parking lots. Buses depart from Cork Bus Station Parnell Place, but there's no local public transportation. For local excursions, contact Long's Taxis. Skibbereen is a designated hub of the National Cycle Network, with three signposted routes of one-day and half-day trips. Book a bike in advance from Roycroft Cycles.

ESSENTIALS

Transportation Contacts Roycroft Cycles ✉ *Ilen St.* ☎ *028/21235* ⊕ *www.westcorkcycles.ie.* **Skibbereen Cabs & Taxi Service** ✉ *55 Bridge St.* ☎ *028/21258.*

Visitor Information Skibbereen Tourist Office ✉ *North St.* ☎ *028/21766* ⊕ *www.skibbereen.ie.*

EXPLORING

Mizen Vision Visitor Centre. Travel to this visitor center, set in a lighthouse at the tip of the Mizen Head (follow the R591 through Goleen to the end of the road), and you'll wind up reaching the Irish mainland's most southerly point. The lighthouse itself is on a rock at the tip of the headland; to reach it, you must cross a dramatic 99-step suspension footbridge. The lighthouse was completed in 1910; the Engine Room and Keepers' House have been restored by the local community.

The exhilaration of massive Atlantic seas swirling 164 feet below the footbridge and the great coastal views guarantee a memorable outing. ⊠ *Harbour Rd., Goleen* ☎ *028/35115* ⊕ *www.mizenhead.ie* 🖾 *€6* ⊙ *Mid-Mar.–May, Sept., and Oct., daily 10:30–5; June–Aug., daily 10–6; Nov.–mid-Mar., weekends 11–4.*

Nic Slocum Whale Watch West Cork. More than 24 species of whale and dolphin have been spotted off the coast of West Cork. Trips to see at least some of them last three to four hours, with commentary on other local bird- and wildlife, and leave from the harbor at Baltimore, about 13 km (8 miles) southwest of Skibbereen. Reservations are recommended in peak season. ⊠ *Baltimore* ☎ *086/120–0027* ⊕ *www. whalewatchwestcork.com* 🖾 *€50* ⊙ *Apr.–Aug., daily at 9:30 am and 2:15 pm (also 7 pm July and Aug.), or by appointment.*

Skibbereen Heritage Centre. A thoughtful renovation of a stone gasworks building has created an attractive, architecturally appropriate home for the Skibbereen Heritage Center. An elaborate audiovisual exhibit on the Great Famine presents dramatized firsthand accounts of what it was like to live in this community when it was hit hard by hunger. Other attractions include displays on area marine life, walking tours, access to local census information, and a varying schedule of special programs. ⊠ *Upper Bridge St.* ☎ *028/40900* ⊕ *www.skibbheritage.com* 🖾 *€6* ⊙ *Mid-Mar.–mid-May and mid-Sept.–Oct., Tues.–Sat. 10–6; late May–mid-Sept., daily 10–6; mid-Nov.–mid-Mar., by appointment.*

WHERE TO EAT

$$$
SEAFOOD

✕ **Heron's Cove.** Although only minutes by foot from the main road and Goleen's village center, this harborside retreat is a peaceable kingdom— expect to see herons outside the window. "Fresh fish and wine on the harbour" is the motto here. The restaurant, in Sue Hill's modern house (she also offers bed-and-breakfast) is well run and extremely civilized. In summer, fresh local seafood stars on the menu, including John Dory panfried with balsamic butter, and scallops with smoked bacon cream sauce. Lobster is another specialty. Instead of a wine list, you choose a bottle from the annotated racks along the wall. Off-season (November– March) dinner must be booked in advance. Ⓢ *Average main: €25* ⊠ *The Harbour, Goleen* ☎ *028/35225* ⊕ *www.heronscove.com.*

$$$$
EUROPEAN

✕ **Island Cottage.** On Heir Island—a four-minute ferry ride—this unlikely venture is a pilgrimage spot for food lovers, who praise the high standard of cooking and the location. The five-course (no choices) set menu focuses on local produce, some of it picked in the wild on the island. Expect good, honest, unfussy food, representing the best of new Irish Traditional cuisine. The restaurant is country-casual and tables seat 10, so be prepared to share. Cape Clear turbot with sea spinach is typical; for dessert, you might have hot Grand Marnier crepe soufflé with blackcurrant coulis. The proprietors also operate "the world's smallest cooking school" here. Call for details about the ferry. Ⓢ *Average main: €40* ⊠ *Heir Island* ⊕ *Ferry departs from Cunnamore, about 15 km (9 miles) west of Skibbereen; follow signs on the Ballydehob road* ☎ *028/38102* ⊕ *www.islandcottage.com* ⚓ *Reservations essential* ▭ *No credit cards*

⊗ *Closed mid-Sept.–mid-June and Sun.–Tues. mid-June–mid-Sept. No lunch (except for groups).*

SHOPPING

Field's Supervalu. Here in the heart of West Cork's artisan food country you will search in vain for a small deli selling local specialties: this is because the local supermarkets do the job so well. Choose from a range of home-baked breads and cakes, farmhouse cheeses, smoked fish, and local charcuterie. ⊠ *26 Main St.* 🕾 *028/21400* ⊕ *www.fields ofskibbereen.ie.*

Gubbeen Farmhouse Products. About 27 km (17 miles) west of Skibbereen, farmer Tom Ferguson tends a herd of prize cows, whose rich milk is made into creamy cheese by his wife, Giana. The fresh-straw piggery allows its lucky pigs to have a view of Roaring Water Bay, one of the most scenic corners of Ireland. Tom and Giana's son, Fingal, runs the smokehouse (great smoked bacon, chorizo, and salamis), while daughter Clovisse grows organic fruit, vegetables, and herbs. Products are sold at Neal's Yard in London and West Cork's Farmers' Markets. Groups of up to eight people can prebook a tour of the farm, dairy, and smokehouse, culminating in lunch at the kitchen table (€40 per person). ⊠ *Gubbeen, Schull* ✛ *From Skibbereen, take N71 west to Ballydehob, then R592 to Schull. Beyond Schull center, fork left, signposted "Coast Road L4406" and continue to Gubbeen* 🕾 *028/28231, 086/399–1415 Clovisse Ferguson, farm visit and lunch bookings* ⊕ *www.gubbeen.com.*

The Time Traveller's Bookshop & Gallery. Lovers of rare books, out-of-print books, collectable illustrations and photographs, vinyl discs, and CDs will be in heaven at No. 44-45, while those looking for affordable first editions and other carefully selected readable books will head to the second shop farther west on Bridge Street. ⊠ *44–45 and 61–62 Bridge St.* 🕾 *028/22944* ⊕ *www.timetraveller.ie.*

CASTLETOWNSHEND

8 km (5 miles) southeast of Skibbereen.

Castletownshend has an unusual number of large, stone houses, most of them dating from the mid-18th century, when it was an important port. The main street runs steeply downhill to the 17th-century castle (built by the Townshends, a noted family in the region) and the sea. The sleepy town awakens in July and August, when its sheltered harbor bustles. Sparkling views await from cliff-top St. Barrahane's Church, which has a medieval oak altarpiece and three stained-glass windows by early-20th-century Irish artist Harry Clarke.

GETTING HERE AND AROUND

Castletownshend lies southeast of Skibbereen on R596. The best way to get here and around is by car. The 8-km (5-mile) drive takes about 10 minutes.

WHERE TO EAT

$$$ ✕ **Mary Ann's.** Writer Edna O'Brien calls this low-beamed pub—one of
EUROPEAN Ireland's oldest—her favorite in the world. Its mostly wealthy visitors
Fodor's Choice mingle happily with the few locals left in the village in the front bar-
★ room, the quieter back room, or the large garden. The owner-manager
is always on the spot, supervising the operations and contributing to
the *craic* (lively conversation). An all-day bar-food menu is available,
and the upstairs restaurant nearly always buzzes (reservations advised).
Try the trademark baked avocado stuffed with crabmeat, the massively
generous platter of Castlehaven Bay seafood, or the succulent T-bone
steak. This is a good place to sample local farmhouse cheeses, such as
Durrus, Milleens, Gabriel, and Gubbeen. $ *Average main: €26* ✉ *Main
St.* ☎ *028/36146* ⊘ *Phone to confirm hrs open Nov.–Mar. No bar food
Mon., Nov.–Mar.*

BANTRY BAY

Between 9½ and 13 km (6 and 8 miles) wide, Bantry Bay is one of
the largest natural harbors in the world. It was here that the French
attempted to land a force of some 14,000 men in 1796, during the
Napoleonic Wars. A combination of foul winds and naval incompetence
proved their undoing. The chief market town for this part of Cork is
Bantry, which lies at the head of Bantry Bay. This is a quiet rural area
where small family farms, fishing, and shellfish farming are the main
industries besides tourism.

BANTRY

25 km (16 miles) northwest of Skibbereen.

Fodor's Choice The town of Bantry is at the head of Bantry Bay, between the Sheep's
★ Head Peninsula to the southwest and the Beara Peninsula to the north-
west. A somewhat unprepossessing town at first sight, Bantry is centered
on a large square that attracts artisans, craftspeople, and musicians to
its Friday-morning market in summer. If you approach Bantry heading
west on the seaside road, before you reach town you'll spot the park-
ing lot and visitor's entrance to the area's big attraction, Bantry House
and Gardens.

GETTING HERE AND AROUND

Bantry is on the N71, midway between Skibbereen and Kenmare, an
hour-and-a-half drive from Cork and an hour from Killarney. There is
a large parking lot (free) in the main square. Buses from Cork Bus Sta-
tion Parnell Place continue on to Glengarriff *(see Glengarriff).* There is
no other local public transportation.

ESSENTIALS

Ireland can be expensive, but in this part of the country many of the
best things are free. Ask at tourist information offices about the many
coves and small beaches or the looped walks along sections of the
Sheep's Head Walking Route. Information on looped walks in Bantry
town can be found in local bars and hotels and on ⊕ *www.bantry.ie.*

Divided by the Hundred Steps, the gardens of Bantry House are adorned with exotic plants due to the microclimate of its bay setting.

Visitor Information Bantry Tourist Office ⊠ *Wolfe Tone Sq.* ☎ *027/50229* ⊕ *www.bantry.ie.*

EXPLORING

Fodor's Choice

★

Bantry House and Gardens. One of Ireland's most famed manors is noted for its picture-perfect perch, on a hillock above the south shore of Bantry Bay. The fine Georgian mansion is surrounded by a series of stepped gardens and parterres that make up "the stairway to the sky" and spreading out below lies the bay and, in the far distance, the spectacular range of the Caha Mountains—one of the great vistas of Ireland. Built in the early 1700s and altered and expanded later that century, the manor is the ancestral seat of the White family. The house is largely the vision of Richard White, 1st Earl of Bantry, who traveled extensively through Europe and brought a lot of it back with him: fabulous Aubusson tapestries said to have been commissioned by Louis XV adorn the Rose Drawing Room, while state portraits of King George III and Queen Charlotte glitter in floridly Rococo gilt frames in the hypertheatrical, Wedgwood-blue and gold dining room. An antique or two is thought to have belonged to Marie-Antoinette.

Outside, the drama continues in the garden terraces, set with marble statues, framed by stone balustrades, and showcasing such delights as an embroidered parterre of dwarf box. The tearoom serves light lunches, and features local artisan foods. In summer the house hosts concerts in the grand library, notably the West Cork Chamber Music Festival (held during the first week of July). ⊠ *N71* ☎ *027/50047* ⊕ *www.bantryhouse.ie* ⊠ *€11* ☉ *Easter–Oct., daily 10–6 (can vary in spring and Oct.).*

WHERE TO EAT AND STAY

Bantry's hotels offer two distinct dining experiences. The Seaview House is a good place for a quiet meal in elegant surroundings, while the Maritime has a busy bar and restaurant area, and a children's menu.

$$ SEAFOOD 🍴 **O'Connors Seafood Restaurant.** On Bantry's main square, this restaurant is a stone's throw from the sea that provides for the bulk of its menu. The sophisticated taupe-and-bronze frontage with model yachts in the windows reflects the restaurant's serious ambitions, while the unfussy cream-and-beige interior is calming and comfortable. The chef has a way with fish: local oysters are baked with stout and walnuts, and monkfish is served with a wild smoked-venison risotto. Sea-fresh local mussels are served every which way: grilled and topped with garlic and herb bread crumbs, in a Thai coconut sauce, and à la marinara. A more conventional standout is the seafood pie. Meat and vegetarian dishes are also served. [$] *Average main: €24* ✉ *Wolfe Tone Sq.* ☎ *027/55664* 🌐 *www.oconnorseafood.com.*

$$ B&B/INN 🏨 **Bantry House.** When the day-trippers leave, you can play lord and lady of this celebrated manor *(⇨ See Exploring)* for the night, thanks to six guest bedrooms, set in a self-contained wing off a long corridor with views over the famous garden and Bantry Bay. **Pros:** a genuine heritage experience (ask about private guided tours with a family member); unique location; friendly, helpful hosts; not as pricey as you'd think. **Cons:** a longish walk (or a short drive) into town; worth the premium only if you are into history and heritage. [$] *Rooms from: €169* ✉ *N71* ☎ *027/50047* 🌐 *www.bantryhouse.ie* 🛏 *6 rooms* ⏲ *Closed Nov.–Easter* 🍽 *Breakfast.*

$$ HOTEL FAMILY Fodor's Choice ★ 🏨 **The Maritime Hotel.** A legacy of Ireland's boom years, this gleaming, modern, waterfront hotel recalls times when building budgets were lavish, and it's a super-stylish addition to the town, with leisure facilities that make it a good all-weather touring base. **Pros:** great location; high comfort levels; top value for medium-range rates. **Cons:** long, dimly lighted internal corridors; some rooms accessible only via two elevators. [$] *Rooms from: €120* ✉ *The Quay* ☎ *027/54700* 🌐 *www.themaritime.ie* 🛏 *76 rooms, 34 suites* 🍽 *No meals.*

$$ HOTEL 🏨 **Seaview House Hotel.** Among private, wooded grounds overlooking Bantry Bay, this large, three-story, 19th-century country house is an oasis of calm, nestled in its own gardens well away from the main road. **Pros:** sea views; unostentatious comfort; good food; low-key, friendly service. **Cons:** make your own entertainment; the "village" is more a suburb of Bantry, with only one pub. [$] *Rooms from: €140* ✉ *N71, Ballylickey* ☎ *027/50073* 🌐 *www.seaviewhousehotel.com* 🛏 *19 rooms, 6 suites* ⏲ *Closed Nov.–mid-Mar.* 🍽 *Breakfast.*

SHOPPING

Dunbeacon Pottery. Europe's most southwesterly pottery workshop can be found on the scenic Durrus–Mizen Head road just west of Bantry. Helen Ennis produces handmade ceramic tableware in a variety of glazes. ✉ *R591* ☎ *027/61036* 🌐 *www.dunbeaconpottery.com.*

Manning's Emporium. On the road between Bantry and Glengarriff, this shop is a showcase for locally made farmhouse cheeses, pâtés, and salamis—an excellent place to assemble a picnic or just to browse. ✉ *Ballylickey* ☎ *027/50456* ⊕ *www.manningsemporium.ie* ⊘ *Closed Jan. and Feb.*

GLENGARRIFF

14 km (8 miles) northwest of Bantry.

Fodor's Choice ★ One of the jewels of Bantry Bay is Glengarriff, the "rugged glen" much loved by the writers William Thackeray and Sir Walter Scott. The drive from Bantry along the cliff top, with views of the islands of the bay and its shelter belt of mountains, is one of the scenic highlights of West Cork, while the descent into the sheltered wooded village reveals yet another landscape: thanks to the Gulf Stream, it's mild enough down here for subtropical plants to thrive. Trails along the shore are flanked by rhododendrons and offer beautiful views of the nearby inlets, loughs, and lounging seals. You're very much on the beaten path, however, with crafts shops, tour buses, and boatmen soliciting your business by the roadside.

GETTING HERE AND AROUND

Glengarriff is a 10-minute drive, 14 km (8 miles) from Bantry on the N71. There is a large public parking lot at Quill's Woolen Mills; on-street parking is easily found, too. Buses from Cork City stop here, and some continue to the Beara Peninsula. There is no public transportation locally, but you can take a boat trip around the harbor, where huge seals bask in fine weather.

Blue Pool Ferry. Buy a ticket at the kiosk beside the Quill's Woolen Mills car park, and follow the trail to an enchanting hidden harbor that's surrounded by rocks and overhanging trees. Boats leave from here for Garnish Island and Ilnacullin Gardens, traveling via Seal Island. No need to land—you can take a round-trip tour and enjoy the wildlife of the bay, which includes a colony of comical basking seals. Cameras at the ready! ✉ *N71* ☎ *027/63333* ⊕ *www.bluepoolferry.com* 🎫 *€10* ⊘ *Closed Nov.–mid-Mar.*

EXPLORING

Fodor's Choice ★ **Ilnacullin.** Many visitors head to Glengarriff because of that Irish Eden, Ilnacullin. On Garnish Island, offshore from Glengarriff and beyond islets populated by comical-looking basking seals, you can find one of the country's horticultural wonders. In 1910 a Belfast businessman, John Annan Bryce, purchased this rocky isle, and, with the help of famed English architect Howard Peto and Scottish plantsman Murdo Mackenzie, transformed it into a botanical Disneyland. The main showpiece is a wisteria-covered "Casita"—a rather strange-looking half-shed, half-mansion that overlooks a sunken Italian garden. Ilnacullin has a little bit of everything, from a Grecian temple to a Martello tower to a Happy Valley, all bedded with extraordinary shrubs, trees, and many unusual subtropical flowers.

You get to Ilnacullin by taking a Blue Pool ferry (10 minutes), which departs for the island from Glengarriff. George Bernard Shaw found Ilnacullin peaceful enough to allow him to begin his *St. Joan* here; maybe you'll find Garnish inspiring, too. ✉ *Garnish Island* ☎ *027/63040* 🌐 *www.heritageireland.ie/en/south-west* 🎟 *Gardens €4, ferry €10 round-trip* 🕒 *July and Aug., Mon.–Sat. 9:30–6:30, Sun. 11–6:30; Apr.–June and Sept., Mon.–Sat. 10–6:30, Sun. noon–6:30; Oct., Mon.–Sat. 10–4, Sun. 1–5.*

Ring of Beara. Glengarriff is the gateway to this 137-km (85-mile) scenic drive that circles the Beara Peninsula on R572. One of the main attractions is the **Beara Way**, a 196-km (120-mile) marked walking route that takes in prehistoric archaeological sites. **Dursey Island** is a birder's paradise that you reach by cable car. From Dursey Island, head for tiny **Allihies**, the former site of a huge copper mine, celebrated in its own museum. The area is now the home of several leading Irish artists, some of whom invite studio visits (watch for signs). Continue along a breathtaking coastal road to **Eyeries**—a village overlooking Coulagh Bay—and then up the south side of the Kenmare River to Kenmare *(⇨ see The Southwest).* ✉ *R572.*

WHERE TO STAY

$ HOTEL 🏨 **Glengarriff Eccles.** Fronted by a massive wrought-iron balcony, this stately landmark has looked out over the calm water of Glengarriff's harbor since before the Victorian novelist William Thackeray passed through. **Pros:** water's edge location; great sense of history; locals use the bar. **Cons:** five-minute walk from village; a bit eerie when not busy. [$] *Rooms from: €110* ✉ *Harbour* ☎ *027/63003* 🌐 *www.eccleshotel.com* 🛏 *66 rooms* 🕒 *Closed Nov.–Mar.* 🍴 *No meals.*

$ HOTEL 🏨 **Glengarriff Park Hotel.** Smack-dab in the middle of the scenic and busy village of Glengarriff, this is a small, family-run hotel is an excellent base for touring, with some great scenic walks on the doorstep, and sits alongside its sister establishments MacCarthy's Bar and The Park Bistro. **Pros:** great value; knowledgeable local staff; handy one-stop shop for bed, food, and drink; popular destination for Irish people on short breaks. **Cons:** views from bedrooms are disappointing; in high season the village is busy with tourists and tour buses en route to Killarney and the Ring of Kerry. [$] *Rooms from: €80* ✉ *Village Center* ☎ *027/63000* 🌐 *www.glengarriffpark.com* 🛏 *27 rooms, 1 suite* 🍴 *No meals.*

SHOPPING

Gift2. Catherine Hammond runs an acclaimed gallery of contemporary art on the main street of Glengarriff, and she's now added a gift shop with ceramics, glass, and beautiful one-of-a-kind objects at affordable prices. ✉ *Main St.* ☎ *027/63812* 🌐 *hammondgallery.com.*

THE SOUTHWEST

Including Counties Kerry and Limerick

WELCOME TO THE SOUTHWEST

TOP REASONS TO GO

★ **The Ring of Kerry:**
The most brazenly
scenic coastal drive in
Ireland might have been
designed with the visitor
in mind—cameras and
videos at the ready!

★ **Skellig Michael:** Take
a wet and wonderful
ride out to Ireland's most
spectacular island, whose
twin peaks, crowned with
a medieval monastery,
beckon to you along
the Ring of Kerry.

★ **The Gap of Dunloe:** A
half-day tour lets you walk
or ride horseback through
the heart of Killarney's
purple mountains and
cross the glittering blue
lake by rowboat.

★ **Adare:** Discover
Ireland's prettiest village
by taking a walk past its
cute thatched cottages
to the banks of the River
Maigue, where the remains
of priories established by
medieval monks still stand.

★ **"Castle Country":**
Limerick is studded with
top attractions like King
John's Castle on the
banks of the Shannon.

1 Killarney and Around.
Nineteenth-century visitors
found the views of Killarney
every bit as romantic and
uplifting as the mountains
of Switzerland; the unique
combination of glacial
landscape and abundant
subtropical vegetation,
studded by the bright blue
waters of the lakes creates
an unforgettable vista—and
it smells good, too, with
peat-fire smoke mingling
with fresh mountain air.

GETTING ORIENTED

In the Southwest, five-star scenery is everywhere, from the mountains and lakes of Killarney out to Kerry's craggy western peninsulas. Brightly painted villages and small harbors encourage you to stop and linger—and when you do, you're rewarded with exceptional food, particularly in Kenmare and Dingle, towns that boast an extraordinary number of talented chefs in proportion to their size. Off the western coast, the Skelligs rank as the region's most awesome sight, though it takes an often-choppy boat ride to reach them. Adare, midway between Kerry and Limerick, is both picture-book pretty and rich in historical churches and monasteries. The main sights of Limerick's historic center are linked by a riverside walkway.

2 **The Ring of Kerry.** One of Europe's great scenic drives, a highlight of the Wild Atlantic Way, the route runs around the edge of this rocky peninsula, passing from the subtropical splendor of Sneem, on the sheltered Kenmare River, past Waterville, where the twin-peaked Skellig rocks hover on the horizon, to the starker views of Dingle Bay to the north.

3 **Corca Dhuibhne: The Dingle Peninsula.** Dingle Town is a-hopping, between the live traditional music in its numerous bars and the fresh seafood on offer in its eateries; head west to Slea Head for stunning coastal scenery, with pristine sandy beaches, rocky islands, and Iron-Age ruins.

4 **North Kerry and Shannonside.** Beyond the pretty and historic village of Adare with its charming thatched cottages is the great River Shannon. Limerick City bears the scars of history from the 1691 Siege of Limerick—a confrontation with the English.

Updated by Alannah Hopkin

Ever since Killarney was first "discovered" by William Thackeray and Sir Walter Scott, visitors have been searching for superlatives to describe the deep blue lakes, dark green forests, and purple mountainsides of this romantic region. While modern-day tour bus traffic and increased visitor numbers have slightly diminished the experience, the appeal of small-scale lake and mountain scenery, the ever-changing light, and the unusual flora and fauna persist—along with the lingering aroma of turf smoke—and the old tales resurrected by the tour guides continue to cast a unique spell.

To be in a hurry in the Southwest is to be ill-mannered. To truly enjoy the amazing array of scenic delights found here, remember that the locals of the Southwest—this region stretches from the Ring of Kerry in the south, the Dingle Peninsula in the west, through Killarney and north to Adare, and Limerick City—are unusually laid-back, even by Irish standards. They still remember what attracted tourists in the first place: uncrowded roads, unpolluted beaches and rivers, easy access to golf, unspoiled scenery, and, above all, time to stop and talk. So take your cue from them and venture onto the back roads. Meander along at your own pace, sampling wayside delights. Before you know it, you'll be far from Killarney town's crowds and in the middle of the region's tranquil and incredibly stunning landscapes.

If Mother Nature doesn't cooperate, there is always the bounty of man-made attractions. Moving northward, scenery becomes less dramatic but much cozier, with Adare's thatched cottages giving the village the reputation as one of Ireland's prettiest. Head up to Limerick and a busy four-lane highway hurls you back into the 21st century. Metropolitan hub of southwest Ireland (and the republic's third-largest city), Limerick bears the scars of history, most notably from the Siege of Limerick, a face-off with the English that took place in 1691. Its other "scars" of history—described so memorably in Frank McCourt's best seller

Angela's Ashes—lure travelers who discover that this is a compact, vibrant city.

THE SOUTHWEST PLANNER

WHEN TO GO

The best times to visit the Ring of Kerry, Killarney, and Dingle are mid-March to June, and September and October. In July and August it's the peak holiday period, meaning roads are more crowded, prices are higher, and the best places are booked in advance. March can be chilly, with daily temperatures in the 40s and 50s. The average high in June is 65°F (18°C), which is about as hot as it gets. May and June are the sunniest months, while May and September are the driest months. The farther west you go, the more likely you'll get rain. The weather is not such a crucial factor in Adare and the Limerick area, but from November to mid-March daylight hours are short, the weather is damp, and many smaller places on the Kerry coast and in Killarney are closed.

FESTIVALS AND EVENTS

In common with many areas of Ireland, there's plenty going on in the Southwest, with a number of high-profile festivals that are well worth taking into account when deciding when to visit. These are just a few of the highlights; tourist offices will have details of others.

Dingle Food and Wine Festival. On the first weekend in October, this is a major festival, and growing in popularity with every passing year. You can sample local produce on the Taste Trail, enjoy special menus, try your hand at chocolate making, or learn about beekeeping and biodynamic vegetable growing. And, of course, there's entertainment, too. ⊠ *Dingle Town, Co. Kerry* ☎ *066/915–1188 tourist information office* ⊕ *www.dinglefood.com.*

Listowel Writers' Week. Big names and beginners rub shoulders at this major event on the Irish literary calendar, which takes over the small North Kerry town for five days in late May and early June. Workshops for all levels combine with readings and prize-giving events for a range of competitions, including the National Poetry Award. ⊠ *Listowel, Co. Kerry* ☎ *068/21074* ⊕ *www.writersweek.ie.*

Portmagee Set Dancing and Music Weekend. Maybe not high profile on a national scale, but certainly high on local flavor and fun, this is a friendly festival that keeps alive the old traditions of Irish music and dance. Held on the first weekend of May (a holiday weekend), it's based in the local community hall and the Bridge Bar and features dance workshops, traditional music sessions, and the Saturday night "Mighty Céili." ⊠ *Portmagee, Co. Kerry* ☎ *066/947–7108* ⊕ *www.moorings.ie.*

Puck Fair. Expect big crowds at one of Ireland's oldest fairs—it celebrated its 400th year in 2013. It's held over three days in mid-August (with additional events on the day before and the day after) in the streets of Killorglin. A goat is crowned King Puck, horses are traded in the traditional manner, and there are street stalls, a funfair (midway), and lashings of free entertainment, including traditional music and dancing. ⊠ *Killorglin, Co. Kerry* ☎ *066/976–2366* ⊕ *www.puckfair.ie.*

Rose of Tralee International Festival. The town is en fête for five days in mid-August with street theater, parades, fireworks, and big-name concerts. The highlight is a televised two-evening show in which young women from the Irish diaspora compete for the title of Rose, as they have done for the past 55 years. ⊠ *Tralee, Co. Kerry* ☎ *066/712–1322* ⊕ *www.roseoftralee.ie.*

PLANNING YOUR TIME

If you're here for a short stay—three or fewer days—you'd do well to base yourself in Killarney and devote your time to exploring the surrounding area, then heading out to the Ring of Kerry or the Dingle Peninsula. With more time at your disposal, consider a half-day trip to Skellig Michael, an unforgettable remote, rock-hewn monastery, or Adare, one of Ireland's prettiest villages.

You also want to pick your peninsula, for two of Ireland's most scenic destinations sit side by side on the map: the Iveragh Peninsula (also known as the Ring of Kerry, for its scenic drive) and the Dingle Peninsula (also known by its Irish name, Corca Dhuibhne). If you like wild, rugged scenery, archaeological remains, and Irish music, Dingle is for you. In contrast, the Ring of Kerry is a longer drive with more varied scenery, ranging from lush subtropical vegetation to rocky coves and long sandy beaches near Glenbeigh. The scenery is punctuated by a series of small villages, all much quieter than Dingle.

IF YOU HAVE THREE DAYS

Spend day one driving the Ring of Kerry, pausing often to take in the varied coastal scenery. Spend the night in Kenmare or Killarney, then head out the next morning to explore Killarney National Park either on a boat trip or in a horse-drawn jaunting car. Next head for Dingle and drive the Slea Head loop, before enjoying fresh seafood and live traditional music in Dingle Town, a good overnight stop. On your third morning, drive the Conor Pass to Tralee, heading away from the rugged coast to rich farmlands and a short walk around historic Adare. Finish the day with a riverside walk and overnight stay in Limerick City.

GETTING HERE AND AROUND

AIR TRAVEL

The Southwest can be accessed from two international airports: Cork (ORK) on the southwest coast, and Shannon (SNN) in the west (26 km [16 miles] west of Limerick City). Cork Airport is about two hours' drive from both Killarney and Kenmare. Shannon Airport is 135 km (84 miles) from Killarney via Limerick, a journey that takes about two hours. Kerry County Airport (KIR) at Farranfore, 16 km (10 miles) from Killarney, has daily flights from Dublin, London (Stansted and Luton), and Frankfurt (Hahn) operated by Ryanair.

Airport Information Kerry County Airport ☎ *066/976–4644* ⊕ *www.kerry airport.ie.*

AIRPORT TRANSFERS Bus Éireann runs a 40-minute bus route (€5) between Shannon Airport and Limerick City between 8 am and midnight. J. J. Kavannagh & Sons runs a popular bus shuttle to Shannon Airport, connecting with Limerick (€5 one-way; 25 minutes).

Shuttles Bus Éireann ☎ *061/313–333* ⊕ *www.buseireann.ie.* **J. J. Kavanagh &**
Sons ☎ *081/833-3222* ⊕ *www.jjkavanagh.ie.*

BUS TRAVEL

Bus Éireann operates express services from Dublin to Limerick City
and Tralee. Most towns in the region are served by the provincial Bus
Éireann network. The main Bus Éireann bus stations in the region are
at Limerick and Tralee, and there is also a bus station in Killarney. The
bus stations are located outside the railway stations. Buses tend to stop
running in the early evening, which is fine if you want to stay overnight
and leave the next morning, but it rules out many day trips—unless you
want to spend most of the day on the bus. As a general rule, the smaller
the town, and the more remote, the less frequent its bus service: some
of the smaller villages on the remote Corca Dhuibhne (Dingle Peninsula) have bus service only one day a week in winter. Bus Éireann runs
a regular bus service around the Ring of Kerry between mid-June and
mid-September, but there are only two buses a day, leaving Killarney
at 8:45 am or 1:45 pm.

Bus Information Bus Éireann ☎ *01/836–6111 in Dublin, 061/313–333 in*
Limerick, 066/716–4700 in Tralee ⊕ *www.buseireann.ie.*

CAR TRAVEL

A car is the ideal way to explore this region, packed as it is with scenic routes, attractive but remote towns, and a host of out-of-the-way
restaurants and hotels that deserve a detour. Road upgrades have not
kept up with the increased usage; as a result, prepare for peak-hour
traffic jams.

The main driving route from Dublin is N7, which goes 192 km (120
miles) directly to Limerick City. If you land at Shannon Airport, access
to the Southwest is also via Limerick City; from there, pick up the
N21 to Killarney. From Limerick it is about two hours to Killarney
(111 km [69 miles]), and another half hour to Kenmare. An alternate,
more scenic, route from Dublin leaves the N7 at Naas to join the N8 at
Portlaoise, turning off the main Dublin–Cork road at Mitchelstown and
following the N72 to Killarney. Both journeys from Dublin take about
four hours; many people prefer to fly from Dublin to Kerry Airport (40
minutes) and pick up a rental car there.

TAXI TRAVEL

A taxi from Shannon Airport to Limerick City costs about €35. It costs
€4.10 to hire a taxi on the street (€4.45 by night); add €2 to book one
by phone, and €1.03 per kilometer.

Full details of fares and conditions are on the National Transport
Authority's website (⊕ *www.nationaltransport.ie*). Taxis are also found
at train stations in Tralee, Killarney, and Limerick, and at Shannon and
Kerry airports. Otherwise, they must be prebooked by phone: ask for
the number of the local company at your hotel or bed-and-breakfast.

Taxi Companies All Route Taxis ✉ *Limerick* ☎ *061/300–777.* **Killar-**
ney Cabs ✉ *Killarney, Co. Kerry* ☎ *064/663-7444.* **Taxi Regulator** ⊕ *www.*
transportforireland.ie/taxi/. **Tralee Radio Taxis** ✉ *Tralee, Co. Kerry* ☎ *066/712–*
5451 ⊕ *www.traleeradiotaxis.com.*

TRAIN TRAVEL

The region is accessible by train from Dublin Heuston Station and from Cork's Kent Station. From Dublin the region is served by two direct rail links, to Limerick Junction (where you change trains for Limerick City), and on to Tralee (via Mallow and Killarney). The rail network is mainly useful for moving from one touring base to another.

For more information on getting here and around, see Travel Smart Ireland.

RESTAURANTS

The Southwest can almost be described as one big culinary hot spot. Kenmare, Dingle, and Killarney all have a high density of restaurants and gastropubs serving locally raised meat, artisanal cheeses, and local seafood. Kerry mountain lamb has a unique flavor imparted by the wild herbs and grasses that those sheep you see on every hillside are busy munching. Adare also has an array of tempting restaurants: choose between the low-ceilinged charm of the tiny rooms in the thatched-cottage restaurant the Wild Geese, and the genuine old-world hospitality at the blissfully comfortable Dunraven Arms, an old coaching inn still with some of its original antiques, which is now one of Ireland's leading hotels.

HOTELS

For accommodations, the Southwest has some of the great country houses, including Adare Manor in County Limerick; Kenmare's unique duo of the magnificent Sheen Falls Lodge and the stately Park Hotel; the Cahernane House, which recalls Killarney's Victorian heyday; and finally the rambling landmark resort, the Parknasilla Resort in Sneem, a great place for a family break. At the other end of the spectrum is the uniquely Irish experience of a farmhouse bed-and-breakfast, such as Lakelands Farm Guesthouse in Waterville, with rowboats bobbing on Lough Currane at the bottom of the garden. In between is a range of excellent family-owned and -run traditional hotels, such as the Brook Lane Hotel in Kenmare, the Butler Arms in Waterville, and the secluded Carrig Country House at Glenbeigh near Killorglin. *Hotel reviews have been shortened. For full information, visit Fodors.com.*

WHAT IT COSTS IN EUROS			
$	$$	$$$	$$$$
Restaurants	under €19	€19–€24	€25–€32	over €32
Hotels	under €120	€120–€170	€171–€210	over €210

Restaurant prices are the average cost of a main course at dinner or, if dinner is not served, at lunch. Hotel prices are the lowest cost of a standard double room in high season.

TOURS
BUS TOURS

Many of the tours listed here can be booked through the Killarney Tourist Office.

Bus Éireann. A range of daylong and half-day guided tours are offered from June to September. You can book them at the bus station in Killarney, or at any tourist office. The memorable Gap of Dunloe Tour (at €25) includes a coach or vintage bus and boat trip; add €20 for a horse-drawn carriage ride through the Gap. More conventional day trips can also be made to the Ring of Kerry, An Daingean (Dingle), and Ceann Sléibhe (Slea Head), and to Caragh Lake and Rossbeigh. Full-day tours depart at 10:30 am and return at 5 pm, and the price does not include lunch and refreshments. ☎ *061/313–333 in Limerick, 066/716–4700 in Tralee, 064/663–0011 in Killarney ⊕ www.buseireann.ie ✉ Full-day tour around €30; half day from €15.*

Keating Coaches. Day trips and half-day tours of the Shannon region from Limerick City (book in advance; minimum of four people required) include themes such as "castles and gardens"; "waterways, highways, and byways"; and "flying boats, monks, and dolphins." ☎ *069/68201 ⊕ www.limericktours.com ✉ Call for details.*

SPECIAL-INTEREST TOURS

Adams & Butler. This company provides self-driven or chauffeur-driven group tours with accommodations in private country houses and castles. It also conducts special-interest tours, including gardens, architecture, ghosts, and golf. ☎ *01/288–9355 ⊕ www.adamsandbutler.com ✉ Call for details.*

Go Visit Ireland. This Killorglin-based company offers comprehensive packages (including accommodations and meals) for walking, cycling, fishing, golfing, and equestrian holidays on the Ring of Kerry and the Dingle Peninsula with experienced local guides. ☎ *066/976–2094 ⊕ www.govisitireland.com ✉ From €650 per wk.*

Hidden Ireland Tours. Two knowledgeable Ireland-based guides, Con Moriarty of Killarney and Ann Curran of Dingle, will tailor a package to suit your interests for groups of 2 to 16 people, and upward. Consider an eight-day walking tour with bases in Killarney and Dingle, or a luxurious car tour staying in some of the region's best country-house hotels. Slow food, painting, literary tours, or antiques tours can also be arranged. ☎ *087/258–1966 ⊕ www.hiddenirelandtours.com ✉ Call for details.*

WALKING TOURS

Ancient Ways Walks & Talks. Neil O'Sullivan is a local man with a wealth of knowledge on the region's prehistoric sites and traditional plant lore, and offers a three- to four-hour informative stroll. ☎ *087/702–3661 ⊕ www.ancientways.ie ✉ €40.*

Gap of Dunloe. You can customize your tour with this company, and walk or ride on horseback for the central 11-km (7-mile) off-road stretch of the Gap. ✉ *O'Connor's Pub, 7 High St., Killarney, Co. Kerry* ☎ *064/663–0200 ⊕ www.gapofdunloetours.com.*

Irish Ways Walking Tours. Customized walking tours for two or more can explore Dingle, Killarney, and the Ring of Kerry. ☎ *01/260–0749 ⊕ www.irishways.com.*

Killarney Guided Walks. Run by Richard Clancy, a noted historian, these tours feature a two-hour walk in Killarney National Park daily at 11 am; departures are from O'Sullivan's Bike Shop opposite the cathedral in Killarney; book early for November–April. ☎ *087/639–4362* ⊕ *www. killarneyguidedwalks.com* ▦ €9.

Outdoors Ireland. Hill walking and rock climbing in the Kerry hills are the specialty of this tour company based in Beaufort, Killarney. They also lead tours of the Kerry Way. ☎ *086/860–4563* ⊕ *www. outdoorsireland.com.*

SouthWestWalks Ireland. A variety of walks on the Ring of Kerry and around Killarney are available through this company; some include accommodations and evening meals. ☎ *066/718–6181* ⊕ *www. southwestwalksireland.com.*

VISITOR INFORMATION

Fáilte Ireland provides a free information service; its tourist information offices (TIOs) also sell a selection of tourist literature. For a small fee it will book accommodations anywhere in Ireland. Seasonal TIOs in Waterville, Cahirciveen, and Valentia are open from June to September; the TIO in Kenmare is open Easter to October. All of the seasonal TIOs are generally open Monday–Saturday 9–6; in July and August they are also open Sunday 9–6. Year-round TIOs can be found in Adare, An Daingean/Dingle, Killarney, Limerick Shannon Airport, and Tralee. These offices are usually open Monday–Saturday 9–6 and also Sunday 9–6 in July and August.

KILLARNEY AND AROUND

87 km (54 miles) west of Cork City, 19 km (12 miles) southeast of Killorglin, 24 km (15 miles) north of Glengarriff.

One of Southwest Ireland's most attractive locales, Killarney is also the most heavily visited town in the region (its proximity to the Ring of Kerry and to Shannon Airport helps to ensure this).

Killarney is famous for its lakes, not for the town, a point to bear in mind in order to avoid disappointment. Killarney town was one of the first places in Europe to owe its existence almost entirely to the tourism industry. Visitors started seeking out the region's dramatic lake scenery in the early 19th century, and the arrival of the railroad ensured its growing popularity. Today Killarney is a small, low-key town lined with shops and eateries firmly targeted at the numerous visitors, but it's also a popular holiday destination for Irish visitors, and retains the traditional friendliness of less famous towns. There's a lively restaurant scene, and some good craft and clothing shops, but you may want to limit time spent there if discos, Irish cabarets, and singing pubs—the last of a local specialty with a strong Irish-American flavor—aren't your thing.

The nightlife is at its liveliest from May to September; the Irish and Europeans pack the town in July and August. Peak season for Americans follows in September and October. At other times, particularly from November to mid-March, when many of the hotels are closed, the town is quiet to the point of being eerie. Given the choice, go to

Killarney in April, May, or early October.

Light rain is typical of the area, but because of the topography, it seldom lasts long. And the clouds' approach over the lakes and the subsequent showers can actually add to the scenery. The rain is often followed within minutes by brilliant sunshine and, yes, even a rainbow.

GETTING HERE AND AROUND

Killarney is about 2 hours from Cork on the N22, about 3 hours from Shannon Airport, on the N21/23/22, and 2½ hours from Limerick. From Shannon Airport be sure to take the tunnel (toll €1.80) route when approaching Limerick, rather than driving through the center of the city. The main car park in Killarney is near the tourist information office in the town center, and there are others around the town, all operated on a "pay-and-display" basis during business hours. The town is well served by Expressway buses and has a rail link to Dublin (three hours, 20 minutes) and Cork (two hours, 20 minutes). The bus and train stations are adjacent to each other, in the center of town, with taxi ranks. Most B&Bs and hotels offer a pickup service. Elsewhere, taxis should be prebooked by phone.

■TIP➔ There is no local bus service in Killarney town; the traditional way to get around, especially if you plan to visit the car-free Muckross Park, is to hire one of the famous ponies and traps, known as "jaunting cars." The leading jaunting, bus, and boat tour operator is Killarney Jaunting Cars. An hour's "jaunt" for four people costs about €40. Jaunting cars can be prebooked or hired at the junction of Main Street and East Avenue. From mid-March to September you can view the National Park by taking a water-coach cruise on the Lily of Killarney boat from Ross Castle (one hour, €10); book at the Killarney Tourist Office.

ESSENTIALS

Transportation Contacts **Killarney Bus and Train Station** ⊠ *East Ave.* ☎ *064/663–0011, 064/663–1067 for trains.* **Killarney Jaunting Cars** ⊠ *Kinvara House, Muckross Rd.* ☎ *064/663–3358, 087/253–2770* ⊕ *www. killarneyjauntingcars.ie.*

Visitor Information **Discover Ireland Centre** ⊠ *Aras Fáilte, Beech Rd.* ☎ *064/663–1633* ⊕ *www.killarney.ie.*

EXPLORING

With its glacial landscape enhanced by subtropical vegetation, the views found in and around Killarney are legendary. Yes, the lakes really are sapphire blue (at least when the sun is out), and seen from a distance, the MacGillicuddy's Reeks really are purple. Add a scattering of large

7

gray rocks (large, as in big as a car), and acres of lush green flowering shrubs and trees, and you're starting to get the picture.

TOP ATTRACTIONS

FAMILY

Fodor'sChoice

★

Gap of Dunloe. Massive, glacial rocks form the sides of this narrow mountain pass that stretches for 6½ km (4 miles) between MacGillicuddy's Reeks and the Purple Mountains. The rocks create strange echoes: give a shout to test it out. Five small lakes are strung out beside the road. Cars are banned from the gap, but in summer the first 3 km (2 miles) are busy with horse and foot traffic, much of which turns back at the halfway point.

The entrance to the Gap is 10 km (7 miles) west of Killarney at Beaufort on the N72 Killorglin Road. If you drive or are on a tour bus, stop here and either hire a pony and trap or opt to walk. One advantage to an organized tour—and a popular option—is that, without the need to get back to your car, you can amble through the parkland as far as Lord Brandon's Cottage ($\Rightarrow$ *see below*), then get a boat back to Killarney town. ⊠ *N72 Killorglin Rd., Beaufort.*

Kate Kearney's Cottage. At the entrance to the Gap of Dunloe, Kate Kearney's Cottage is a good place to rent a jaunting car or pony. Kate was a famous beauty who sold illegal *poitín* (moonshine) from her home, contributing greatly, one suspects, to travelers' enthusiasm for the scenery. Appropriately enough, Kearney's is now a pub and restaurant, and a good place to pause for an Irish coffee. ⊠ *Gap of Dunloe, Beaufort* ☎ *064/664–4146* ⊕ *www.katekearneyscottage.com* ⊗ *Daily (but not open until 6 pm Mon.–Thurs., Jan.–mid-Mar.).*

Lord Brandon's Cottage. The Gap of Dunloe's southern end, 7 km (4½ miles) west of Killarney, is marked by Lord Brandon's Cottage, a basic tea shop serving soup and sandwiches. From here, a path leads to the edge of Upper Lake, where you can journey onward by rowboat. It's an old tradition for the boatman to carry a bugle and illustrate the echoes. The boat passes under Brickeen Bridge and into Middle Lake, where 30 islands are steeped in legends, many of which your boatman is likely to recount. Look out for caves on the left-hand side on this narrow stretch of water. ⊠ *Gap of Dunloe, Beaufort* ⊗ *May–Sept., daily 10–dusk.*

Killarney National Park. The three Lakes of Killarney and the mountains and woods that surround them make up this beautiful national park. It extends to nearly 25,000 acres, which includes oak holly and yew woodlands, and is populated by red deer. The **National Park Visitor Centre** at Muckross House ($\Rightarrow$ *see below*) offers an audiovisual presentation that is a good introduction to what you can explore on the signposted self-guiding trails that thread the park.

At the park's heart is **Muckross Park** (or Demesne), the entrance to which is 4 km (2½ miles) from Killarney on N71. Cars aren't allowed in Muckross Park; you can either walk, rent a bicycle, or take a traditional jaunting car (pony and a cart).

The air here smells of damp woods and heather moors. The red fruits of the Mediterranean strawberry tree (*Arbutus unedo*) are at their peak in October and November, which is also about the time when the bracken turns rust color, contrasting with the evergreens. In late April and early

May, the purple flowers of the rhododendron *ponticum* put on a spectacular display. ⊕ *www.heritageireland.ie* ✉ *Free* ⊙ *Always accessible.*

Fodor's Choice
★

Ladies' View. If the weather is fine, head southwest 19 km (12 miles) out of Killarney on N71 toward Kenmare to this famed viewpoint, with a panorama of the three lakes and the surrounding mountains. The name goes back to 1861, when Queen Victoria was a guest at Muckross House. Upon seeing the view, her ladies-in-waiting were said to have been dumbfounded by its beauty.

FAMILY
Fodor's Choice
★

Muckross House. Hero of a 1,001 travel posters, the ivy-covered 19th-century Elizabethan-style manor known as Muckross House, 6½ km (4 miles) south of Killarney within the Killarney National Park (⇨ *see above*), now houses the Kerry Folklife Centre. Downstairs, bookbinders, potters, and weavers demonstrate their crafts. Upstairs, elegantly furnished rooms portray the lifestyle of the landed gentry in the 1800s; in the basement you can experience the conditions of servants employed in the house. Next door you'll find the Killarney National Park Visitor Centre.

The informal grounds are noted for their rhododendrons and azaleas, the water garden, and the outstanding limestone rock garden. In the park beside the house, the Muckross Traditional Farms comprise reconstructed farm buildings and outbuildings, a blacksmith's forge, a carpenter's workshop, and a selection of farm animals. It's a reminder of the way things were done on the farm before electricity and the mechanization of farming. Meet and chat with the farmers and their wives as they go about their work. The visitor center has a shop and a restaurant. ✉ *Muckross Rd. (N71)* ☏ *064/667–0144* ⊕ *www.muckross-house.ie* ✉ *House €7.50, farms €7.50, farms and house €12.50, visitor center free* ⊙ *House and visitor center: Sept.–June, daily 9–5:30; July and Aug., daily 9–7. Farms: mid-Mar.–Apr. and Oct., weekends 1–6; May and Sept., daily 1–6; June–Aug., daily 10–6.*

Ross Castle. A fully restored 14th-century stronghold, sited on the lower lake 2 km (1 mile) south of town, this castle was the last place in the province of Munster to fall to Oliver Cromwell's forces in 1652. A later dwelling has 16th- and 17th-century furniture. ✉ *Knockreer Estate, Muckross Rd. (N71)* ☏ *064/663–5851* ⊕ *www.killarneynationalpark. ie* ✉ *€4* ⊙ *Mid-Mar.–Oct., daily 9:30–5:45.*

FAMILY

Torc Waterfall. You reach this roaring cascade by a footpath that begins in the parking lot outside the gates of the Muckross Park, 8 km (5 miles) south of Killarney. After your first view of the Torc, which will appear after about a 10-minute walk, it's worth the climb up a long flight of stone steps to the second, less-frequented clearing. ✉ *Muckross Rd. (N71).*

WORTH NOTING

Aghadoe. Just 5 km (3 miles) west of Killarney on the Beaufort–Killorglin road, this an outstanding place to get a feel for what Killarney is all about: lake and mountain scenery. Stand beside Aghadoe's 12th-century ruined church and round tower, and watch the shadows creep gloriously across Lower Lake, with Innisfallen Island in the distance and the Gap of Dunloe to the west.

Innisfallen Island. The romantic ruins on Innisfallen Island date from the 6th or 7th century. Between 950 and 1350 the *Annals of Innisfallen* were compiled here by monks. (The book survives in the Bodleian Library in Oxford.) To get to the island, which is on Lough Leane, you can rent a rowboat at Ross Castle (€5 per hour), or you can join a cruise (€10) in a covered, heated launch.

WORD OF MOUTH

"We had a great time biking through the gap... rent bikes in Killarney, take the boat across the lakes, unload the bikes and you're on your way. The first part is steep, no shame in walking the bikes up this part, and then you can coast down for a few km's. One of our favorite days from our two visits to Ireland." —bdokeefe

Muckross Friary. The monks were driven out of this 15th-century Franciscan friary by Oliver Cromwell's army in 1652, but it's amazingly complete, although roofless. An ancient yew tree rises above the cloisters and breaks out over the abbey walls. Three flights of stone steps allow access to the upper floors and living quarters, where you can visit the cloisters and what was once the dormitory, kitchen, and refectory. It's located 4 km (2½ miles) south of Killarney. ✉ *Muckross Rd. (N71)* ☎ *064/667–0144* 🌐 *www.heritageireland.ie* 🎟 *Free* 🕒 *Freely accessible daily 8–6 (to 8 pm July and Aug.)*

WHERE TO EAT

$ IRISH 🍴 **Bricín.** In the unlikely event you didn't hit a craft shop in Killarney, you can browse the shelves of Bricín on your way to the restaurant on the second floor. This quirky little eatery set above the ground-floor craft emporium on Killarney's main street makes a change from pub grub, combining a warm welcome with a romantic atmosphere. Candles and an open fire shed light on Persian-style rugs and dark red walls hung with antique engravings of Killarney, while simple country-style wooden tables and stick-back chairs are set within "snug" areas created by stained-glass panels. The good value menu features boxty (Irish potato pancake) with a choice of fillings, including vegetarian. Other options include baked salmon stuffed with crabmeat, char-grilled beef fillet, and roast rack of lamb. [$] *Average main: €18* ✉ *26 High St.* ☎ *064/663–4902* 🌐 *www.bricin.com* 🕒 *Closed Jan.–mid-Mar., Mon. Easter–Oct., and Mon.–Wed. Nov. and Dec. No lunch.*

$$$ SEAFOOD 🍴 **Gaby's Seafood.** Expect the best seafood in Killarney from the Belgian owner-chef here. Behind the rustic exterior is a little bar beside an open fire; steps lead up to the main dining area, where ornate wooden stick-back chairs match a huge wooden dresser. In summer you can sip an aperitif in the small garden. Try the seafood platter (seven or eight kinds of fish in a cream-and-wine sauce) or lobster Gaby (shelled, simmered in a cream-and-cognac sauce, and served back in the shell). Turbot, salmon, and sole are also regular menu items, along with a selection of fillet and sirloin steaks, au poivre or with garlic butter, and herb-scented rack of lamb. [$] *Average main: €32* ✉ *27 High St.* ☎ *064/663–2519* 🕒 *Closed Sun., and Mon.–Wed. Jan.–Mar. No lunch.*

$ **✕ Pay As You Please.** The perfect antidote to touristy Killarney is this
ECLECTIC kind of funky, off-the-wall joint where you pay what you think your
FAMILY meal was worth, putting cash into a jar on the table (no credit cards).
It's off Main Street on a pedestrian alley beside O'Connor's Pub, in a
warehouse-like room with eclectic furniture and silent movies projected
on one wall. In good weather tables sprawl outside. The menu is limited, but features fresh and strongly flavored options—soup of broc-
coli, Cashel blue cheese, and walnuts in a bowl made of bread; pizza
with Serrano ham, arugula, and pecorino; home-baked chocolate or
carrot cake. Wine is reasonably priced, or bring your own for a modest corkage fee. The owners' enthusiasm for fresh wholesome food has
not wavered since opening in 2011. $ *Average main: €12* ⊠ *Old Milk
Market, off Main St.* ☎ *087/190–2567* ▬ *No credit cards* ⊗ *Closed
Mon.–Wed. No dinner Thurs. and Sun.; no brunch Thurs.–Sat.*

$$$ **✕ Treyvaud's.** Step behind the Victorian arched facade here and you'll
EUROPEAN discover a buzzing contemporary restaurant, masterminded by the two
Treyvaud brothers, who are also the chefs. The interior is simple—
pine floorboards, wood-beam ceiling, lines of red-back chairs—so the
food takes center stage. To start try the local smoked salmon with
warm potato cake and crème fraîche, or deep-fried calamari with a
saffron-and-citrus rouille. Follow with bacon and cabbage Treyvaud-
style (smoked loin with buttered cabbage and whole-grain mustard
sauce); homemade smoked haddock fish cakes with garlic aioli; or
the renowned, flavorful beef-and-Guinness pie. In winter this place
is famous for its wide selection of game, including rabbit, wild boar,
pheasant, and quail. $ *Average main: €25* ⊠ *62 High St.* ☎ *064/663–
3062* ⊕ *www.treyvaudsrestaurant.com* ⊗ *Closed Mon. Oct.–Apr.*

WHERE TO STAY

While the immediate region of Killarney has a vast array of accommo-
dations, visitors should consider staying in hotels in Glenbeigh (about
20 minutes' drive away) if they really want to savor the region's peace
and quiet.

$$$$ **Aghadoe Heights.** Once inside this large, modern hotel you'll soon
HOTEL forget its blocklike external appearance, as the entrancing panorama
of Killarney's lakes casts its spell. **Pros:** memorable views; excellent spa;
super-helpful staff. **Cons:** 4 km (2½ miles) out of town; a big hotel by
Irish standards. $ *Rooms from: €240* ⊠ *Off N22* ☎ *064/663–1766*
⊕ *www.aghadoeheights.com* ⤶ *48 rooms, 26 suites* ⊗ *Closed Mon.–
Thurs. Nov.–Dec. 27 and Jan. 7–Mar.* ⏁ *Breakfast.*

$$$ **Cahernane House Hotel.** Get a glimpse of the Killarney that attracted
HOTEL discerning 19th-century visitors at this imposing gray-stone house—
Fodor's Choice if you need a refuge from the touristy buzz of Killarney town, this
★ is the place. **Pros:** great old-world atmosphere; very luxe; fantastic
views. **Cons:** standard rooms are disappointingly plain; lots of weddings. $ *Rooms from: €190* ⊠ *Muckross Rd.* ☎ *064/663–1895* ⊕ *www.
cahernane.com* ⤶ *36 rooms, 2 suites* ⊗ *Closed Dec. 23–mid-Mar.*
⏁ *Breakfast.*

$ **Earls Court House.** In a quiet suburb within walking distance of
B&B/INN Killarney's center, this spacious guesthouse is furnished with interesting antiques collected by Emer Moynihan, who likes to greet her

guests by offering home-baked goods in front of the open fire. **Pros:** quiet location; plenty of parking; warm welcome. **Cons:** long walk or taxi ride to town center; bland suburban location. $ *Rooms from: €110* ✉ *Woodlawn Junction, Muckross Rd.* ☎ *064/663–4009* ⊕ *www.killarney-earlscourt.ie* ⤴ *24 rooms, 6 suites* ⊙ *Closed mid-Nov.–mid-Mar.* ⍩ *Breakfast.*

$
B&B/INN

⊞ **Friars Glen.** Set in its own 28 acres within Killarney National Park (⇨ *see Exploring*), this stone house is a dream retreat for nature lovers. **Pros:** sylvan peace; mountain air; friendly welcome. **Cons:** remote from town; limited choice of restaurants nearby. $ *Rooms from: €110* ✉ *Mangerton Rd.* ☎ *064/663–7500* ⊕ *www.friarsglen.ie* ⤴ *10 rooms* ⊙ *Closed Nov.–mid-Mar.* ⍩ *No meals.*

$$$$
HOTEL
FAMILY

⊞ **Killarney Park Hotel.** This luxurious hotel in landscaped grounds is a few minutes' walk from the train station, shops, and restaurants, making it an excellent base, with or without a car. **Pros:** central location; friendly local staff; excellent cuisine; children's play area. **Cons:** no lake or mountain views; very busy in high season. $ *Rooms from: €320* ✉ *East Ave. (N71)* ☎ *064/663–5555* ⊕ *www.killarneyparkhotel.ie* ⤴ *65 rooms, 3 suites* ⍩ *No meals.*

$$
HOTEL

⊞ **Loch Lein Country House Hotel.** A perfect rural retreat combining warm hospitality with a scenic location, this spacious country house is 3 km (2 miles) out of town near Killarney's famous golf courses. **Pros:** excellent value; friendly hosts; plenty of space. **Cons:** distance from town; closed off-season. $ *Rooms from: €130* ✉ *Off N72, Fossa* ☎ *064/663–1260* ⊕ *www.lochlein.com* ⤴ *25 rooms* ⊙ *Closed mid-Oct.–mid-Apr.* ⍩ *Breakfast.*

NIGHTLIFE AND THE ARTS

DANCE CLUBS

McSorleys Nite Club. A lively late-night venue, McSorleys attracts a younger crowd. ✉ *College St.* ☎ *064/663–9770.*

CABARET

Gleneagles. The place for big-name cabaret—from comedian Dara O'Briain to the High Kings to James Blunt—at the Irish National Events Centre (INEC) within the hotel, Gleneagles also has a late-night disco. ✉ *Muckross Rd.* ☎ *064/667–1555* ⊕ *www.inec.ie.*

PUBS AND BARS

Buckley's Bar. Located in the Arbutus Hotel, this popular spot has traditional Irish entertainment nightly from around 10 pm from June through September, and on Sunday from 1 to 3 pm and weekend evenings year-round. ✉ *Arbutus Hotel, College St.* ☎ *064/663–1037.*

Courtney's Bar. Famous for its selection of more than 30 Irish and Scottish whiskies, this family-run traditional bar in the town center hosts live traditional music on Thursday and Friday and is a magnet for visiting musicians. ✉ *24 Plunkett St.* ☎ *064/663–2689.*

The Danny Mann. Live Irish music is provided by local bands in this friendly hotel bar. Visitors are encouraged to sing along or offer a solo, or even just tell a joke. It's impossible to resist joining in. ✉ *Eviston House Hotel, New St.* ☎ *064/663–1640.*

The beauty-measuring gauge flies off the scale at the Gap of Dunloe, considered by many to be the scenic star of the Lakes of Killarney region.

SPORTS AND THE OUTDOORS

BICYCLING

O'Sullivan's Cycles. A bicycle is the perfect way to enjoy Killarney's mild air, whether within the confines of Muckross Park or farther afield in the Kerry Highlands, and O'Sullivan's (opposite the cathedral) is a top place to rent cycles for either the day or the week. ⊠ *Lower New St.* ☎ *064/663–1282* ⊕ *www.killarneyrentabike.com.*

FISHING

Salmon and brown trout populate Killarney's lakes and rivers.

John Lyne Fishing Tours. Call or email Mr. Lyne before you arrive in Killarney to organize a day or half-day's salmon angling on the lakes. All gear, the license, and even the raincoats and pants are included in the rate of €120 per half day. ⊠ *Gortagullane* ☎ *087/278–9335* ✉ *john-mikelyne@gmail.com.*

O'Neill's. To bag your own salmon or brown trout in Killarney's wondrous lakes and rivers, check out this longtime outfitter of fishing tackle, bait, and licenses. ⊠ *6 Plunkett St.* ☎ *064/663–1970.*

GOLF

Fodor'sChoice ★ **Killarney Golf and Fishing Club.** This club, 3 km (2 miles) west of Killarney on the Kilorglin road, is among a stunning mixture of mountains, lakes, and forests. There are three courses: Mahony's Point, along the shores of Lough Leane; the Lackabane, on the far side of the road from the main entrance; and—the jewel in the crown—water-feature-packed Killeen. Despite the abundance of seaside links, many well-traveled golfers name Killarney their favorite place to play in Ireland. Freshwater fishing is also available here. ⊠ *Mahony's Point, N72* ☎ *064/663–1034*

⊕ *www.killarney-golf.com* ✉ *Fees: Mahony's Point, €65 mid-Apr.–mid-Oct., €35 mid-Oct.–mid-Apr.; Killeen, €100 mid-Apr.–mid-Oct., €55 mid-Oct.–mid-Apr.; Lackabane: currently closed; call for details* 🏌. *Mahony's Point: 18 holes, 6780 yards, par 72; Killeen: 18 holes, 7178 yards, par 72; Lackabane: 18 holes, 7050 yards, par 72. Practice area, caddies, caddy carts, club rental, catering* ◉ *Visitors: Mon.–Sat.*

HIKING

Cronin's Yard. Drive out to Beaufort, 10 km (7 miles) west of Killarney on the N72 Killorglin road, and follow signs to this famed gateway to the MacGillicuddy's Reeks—the traditional starting point for the ascent of Ireland's highest mountain, Carrauntoohil (3,408 feet). Outdoor types will definitely fall in love with Killarney here. Parking at the yard is €2 for the whole day. You can prebook a guide for the ascent, which is about six hours round-trip. For a less strenuous outing, there is a self-guided, signposted 8-km (5-mile) loop of sandy paths and mountain tracks. On your return, enjoy a hot bowl of soup in the tearoom and, especially if the Irish weather has not been kind, luxuriate in a hot shower (small fee). Those with sleeping bags can avail of their wooden "sleeping pods," and wake up to a stunning view. ✉ *Mealis, Beaufort* ☎ *064/662–4044* ⊕ *www.croninsyard.com* ◉ *May–Sept., daily; Oct.–Easter, weekends or by prior arrangement.*

Kerry Way. This long-distance walking route passes through the Killarney National Park on its way to Glenbeigh. You can get a detailed leaflet about the route from the tourist information office. ⊕ *www.kerryway.net.*

Mangerton Mountain. The 2,756-foot summit of Mangerton can be reached on foot in about two hours—less if you rent a pony. It's perfect if you want a fine, long hike with good views of woodland scenery.

Mangerton Walking Trail. You can reach the small tarred road leading to this scenic trail that circles Mangerton Lake (aka Devil's Punch Bowl) by turning left off N71 midway between Muckross Friary and Muckross House (follow the signs).

HORSEBACK RIDING

Killarney Riding Stables. Book a day or half-day of horseback riding on a quiet cob in Killarney National Park, or embark on a three- or six-day Reeks Trail ride through the mountains and woodlands of MacGillicuddy's Reeks. ✉ *N72, Ballydowney* ☎ *064/663–1686* ⊕ *www.killarney-riding-stables.com.*

SHOPPING

ART GALLERIES

Back Lane Gallery. Buy a unique view of Killarney direct from local artists at this "pop-up" gallery. At least one artist will be working in the gallery every day. ✉ *Scott's La.* ☎ *087/321–2948* ⊕ *thebacklanegallery.blogspot.com.*

Frank Lewis Gallery. Visit this noted gallery beside the General Post Office for a good selection of original paintings and sculptures. ✉ *6 Bridewell La.* ☎ *064/663–1108* ⊕ *www.franklewisgallery.com.*

BOOKS

Killarney Bookshop. For a lovely array of local-interest books as well as fiction, biography, and travel titles check out this bookshop. ⊠ *32 Main St.* ☎ *064/663–4108* ⊕ *www.killarneybookshop.ie.*

CLOTHING

Aran Sweater Market. Traditional fisherman's knitwear, designed and knitted in the Aran Islands, can be purchased here. You can acquire an heirloom-quality piece or buy knitting wool and patterns and make your own. ⊠ *College St.* ☎ *064/663–9756* ⊕ *www.aransweatermarket.com.*

Kerry Woollen Mills. This mill was established here in the 17th century and still uses the original buildings. Its traditional woolen products, from knitting yarns to hats and capes, make great gifts. The property is signposted off the main road between Killarney and Killorglin. ⊠ *Beaufort* ☎ *064/664–4122* ⊕ *www.kerrywoollenmills.ie.*

MacBee's. This modern boutique stocks the best of Irish high fashion. ⊠ *26 New St.* ☎ *064/663–3622* ⊕ *macbees.ie.*

Quills Woollen Market. Stop here for the town's largest selection of Irish woolen goods. Quills carries knitwear, tweeds, linens, and Celtic jewelry. ⊠ *Market Cross, 79 High St.* ☎ *064/663–2277* ⊕ *www. irishgiftsandsweaters.com.*

CRAFTS

Bricín Craft Shop. Interesting handicrafts here include candles, ceramics, and woolens. ⊠ *26 High St.* ☎ *064/663–4902.*

The Kilkenny Shop. Peruse this shop's stock of contemporary Irish pottery, ironwork, woodwork, crystal, and jewelry. ⊠ *3 New St.* ☎ *064/663–3309* ⊕ *www.kilkennyshop.com.*

Mucros Craft Shop. Adjacent to Muckross House, the craft center has a wide range of gifts and clothing, as well as a resident weaver, a bookbindery, and Mucros Pottery. Margaret Phelan works on-site producing tableware in attractive blue and honey-colored glazes. ⊠ *Muckross House, N71* ☎ *064/667–0147* ⊕ *www.muckross-house.ie.*

FOOD

Wholesome Fayre. This spacious modern deli showcases the best local artisanal foods, including farmhouse cheeses, charcuterie, and handmade bread, and includes a lively café. ⊠ *Kenmare Pl., East Ave.* ☎ *064/662–6637* ⊕ *www.wholesomefayre.com.*

MUSIC

Variety Sounds. Visit this specialist music shop for Irish CDs, music, and songbooks and a collection of musical instruments including tin whistles and bodhrans. ⊠ *7 College St.* ☎ *064/663–5755.*

OUTLET SHOPPING

Killarney Outlet Centre. Bargain hunters should head for this discount shopping center (adjacent to the Malton Hotel and the train station), which has the Nike Factory Store and the Army Surplus Store among its tenants. ⊠ *Fair Hill* ☎ *064/663–6744* ⊕ *www.killarneyoutletcentre.com.*

BRIGHT WATERS AND DARK SKIES

When planning a day out on the water it is well to bear in mind the long days of the Irish summer. In May the sun rises at 5:40 am and doesn't set until 9:21 pm, while by July the sun is rising at 5:33 and setting at 9:47. The light will linger for another hour or so on clear evenings.

Once the sun has set, you will be beneath some of the clearest night skies in Europe—providing the mist holds off. Southwest Kerry is recognized as the Kerry International Dark Sky Reserve due to the lack of light pollution in the area, and in 2014 the reserve achieved Gold Tier status, representing the highest level of darkness and greatest visibility of night-sky features. Over the Ring of Kerry an unusual array of phenomena are visible, including a great view of the Milky Way. Anyone with even a slight knowledge of astronomy will be thrilled at the array of stars.

THE RING OF KERRY

Running along the perimeter of the Iveragh Peninsula, the dramatic coastal road from Kenmare to Killorglin known as the Ring of Kerry has long been a popular tourist route, and is a highlight of the Wild Atlantic Way. Stunning mountain and coastal views are around almost every turn. The only drawback: on a sunny day, it seems like half the nation's visitors are traveling along this two-lane road, packed into buses, riding bikes, or backpacking. The route is narrow and curvy, and the local sheep think nothing of using it for a nap; take it slowly.

Tour buses tend to start in Killarney and head for Killorglin to ply the Ring counterclockwise, so consider jumping ahead and starting in Killorglin ahead of the Killarney buses, or following the route clockwise, starting in Kenmare (although this means you risk meeting tour buses head-on on narrow roads). Either way, bear in mind that most of the buses leave Killarney between 9 and 10 am. The trip covers 176 km (110 miles) on N70 (and briefly R562 and N71) if you start and finish in Killarney; the journey will be 40 km (25 miles) shorter if you only venture between Kenmare and Killorglin. Because rain blocks views across the water to the Beara Peninsula in the east and the Dingle Peninsula in the west, hope for sunshine. It makes all the difference.

KENMARE

34 km (21 miles) south of Killarney, 336 km (209 miles) southwest of Dublin.

Located slightly inland without a clear view of Kenmare Bay, Kenmare is a natural stopover for Ring of Kerry buses and travelers as it is the closest town to Killarney. Set at the head of the sheltered Kenmare River estuary, this small but bustling market town makes a lively touring base for those who wish to skip hectic Killarney altogether. The town was founded in 1670 by Sir William Petty (Oliver Cromwell's surveyor general, a multitasking entrepreneur), and most of its buildings date

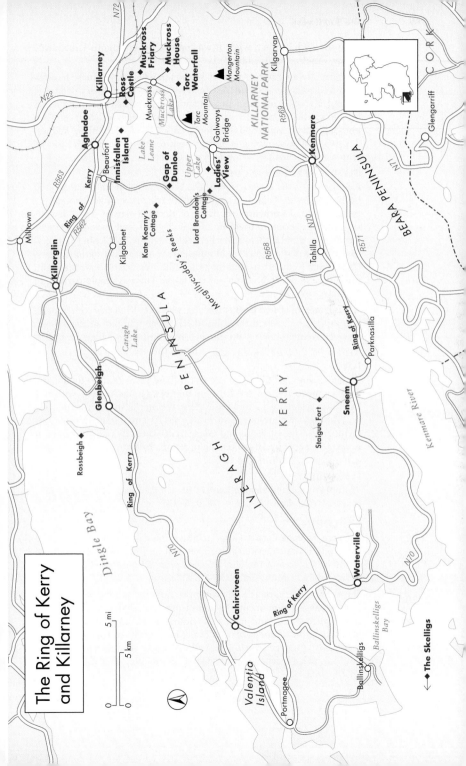

The Ring of Kerry and Killarney

N72

Killarney
N22
Ross Castle
Muckross Friary
Muckross House
Torc Waterfall
Mangerton Mountain
Muckross
Muckross Lake
KILLARNEY NATIONAL PARK
Kilgarvan
CORK

N22
Aghadoe
Beaufort
Innisfallen Island
Gap of Dunloe
Lake Leane
Torc Mountain
Galways Bridge
Ladies' View
Upper Lake
Kenmare
R569
Glengarriff

R563
Ring of Kerry
R562
Kilgobnet
Kate Kearny's Cottage
Lord Brandon's Cottage
Macgillycuddy's Reeks
R568
Tahilla
N70
BEARA PENINSULA
N71
R571

Milltown
Killorglin

Caragh Lake
Ring of Kerry
Parknasilla
R571

IVERAGH PENINSULA

KERRY

Kenmare River

Glenbeigh
Rossbeigh
Ring of Kerry
N70

Dingle Bay

Staigue Fort
Sneem

Waterville
N70

Cahirciveen
Ring of Kerry

Valentia Island
Portmagee
Ballinskelligs
Ballinskelligs Bay

◆ The Skelligs

5 mi
5 km
0

from the 19th century, when it was part of the enormous Lansdowne Estate—itself assembled by Petty.

It's currently a matter of some debate as to whether Kenmare has displaced Kinsale *(see Chapter 6, County Cork)* as the culinary capital of Ireland. Kenmare offers an amazing number of stylish little restaurants for a town its size, and also boasts the top-rated Kenmare Market, with purveyors of organic goods and foodstuffs (March–December, Wednesday 10–5). The shopping is pretty good, too, with Irish high fashion, crafts, and original art vying for your attention.

GETTING HERE AND AROUND
Kenmare is at the intersection of the N71 road that links Bantry and Glengarriff with Killarney, and the N70, which continues around the perimeter road known as the Ring of Kerry. Killarney and Glengarriff are both about 40 to 45 minutes away on scenic mountain roads. Kenmare is a natural stopover between Glengarriff (21 km [13 miles] south) and Killarney (34 km [21 miles] to the north). The mountain pass (N71) from Kenmare to Killarney via Ladies' View is a scenic highlight, offering a stunning first view of the lakes. There is ample parking in Kenmare town center.

A bus route, operated by Bus Éireann, connects Killarney to Kenmare; it continues on around the Ring of Kerry, stopping in all the villages between Kenmare and Killorglin before returning to Killarney. Otherwise, there is no public transportation in this area.

TOURS
Kenmare Coach and Cab. You can opt to base yourself in Kenmare and take a guided tour of the Ring by minibus (June–August) with this local taxi company. Its minibuses depart from the square for the Ring on Monday, Wednesday, and Friday at 10 am. Other destinations include the Ring of Beara and Glengarriff (Tuesday and Thursday). It is best to reserve by 10 pm the night before. ☎ *064/664–1491* ⊕ *www. kenmarecoachandcab.com* 🖻 *€25.*

ESSENTIALS
Visitor Information Kenmare Tourist Office ⊠ *The Square* ☎ *064/664–1233* ⊕ *kenmare.ie* ⊗ *Easter–Oct., Mon.–Sat. 9:30–5:30.*

EXPLORING
Kenmare Heritage Centre. Come to this center in the tourist office to learn about the town's history. They can outline a walking route to Kenmare's places of interest. ⊠ *The Square* ☎ *064/664–1233* 🖻 *Free* ⊗ *Easter–Oct., Mon.–Sat. 9:30–5:30.*

Stone Circle. Perhaps the town's most notable historic sight is this 3,000-year-old monument that dates from the early Bronze Age. Sometimes called the Druid Circle, it is within five minutes' walk of the village square (head down Market Street in front of the tourist office). It consists of 15 large stones arranged in a circle around a huge central boulder, which marks a rare Bronze Age burial site. ⊠ *Market St.* ▭ No *credit cards.*

GIFTS TO BRING HOME

You will soon notice that parts of County Kerry have more sheep than people. Sheep mean wool, and in this part of Ireland wool means sweaters, socks, and wool hats. All three will come in very useful during your stay, and make great gifts, too.

Louis Mulcahy Pottery. Ceramics are a strong point, too, with the Louis Mulcahy Pottery ceramics workshop and showrooms on Slea Head being the most western pottery in Europe. ✉ *Clogher, Ballyferriter, Dingle, Co. Kerry* ☎ *066/915–6229* 🌐 *www.louismulcahy.com.*

Quills Woollen Market. This top gifts-and-souvenirs resource has outlets in Killarney, Kenmare, Sneem, and Dingle. Look out for "blackthorns": a traditional, craggy walking stick made from branches of the blackthorn tree, a handy accessory to have while you're here, and a great souvenir to take home. ✉ *Market Cross, Killarney, Co. Kerry* ☎ *064/663–2277.*

WHERE TO EAT

$$$ EUROPEAN 🍴 **Lime Tree.** An open fire, stone walls, and a minstrel's gallery above the main room lend considerable character to this restaurant. Built in 1823 as a schoolhouse, it is located in its own leafy gardens near the Park Hotel (where many of its staff trained). Tables are set with Irish linen napery, and in the long summer evenings light streams in from tall windows. Try one of the chef patron's imaginative vegetarian options, such as goat's cheese croquettes with beetroot chutney, or roast rack of Kerry lamb with a mini shepherd's pie, with warm crepes with vanilla ice cream and butterscotch sauce to finish. Reservations are advisable. [$] *Average main: €25* ✉ *Shelburne St.* ☎ *064/664–1225* 🌐 *www.limetreerestaurant.com* 🕓 *Closed Nov.–mid-Mar. and weekdays mid- to end Mar. and Oct. No lunch.*

$$ ECLECTIC 🍴 **Mulcahy's.** Previously a pub, this street-level room has stylish contemporary place settings, with leather seats at small wooden tables, and a selection of homemade breads presented on a tray. Chef Bruce Mulcahy's menu reflects his enthusiasm for fresh Irish produce, and his love of Asian cuisine. Start with sushi and sashimi or tempura of crab dumplings, and follow with paupiettes of sole with seafood colcannon or roast Kerry lamb with a cep mushroom and pistachio crust. Bruce runs a relatively modest operation, but many people in the know reckon he is one of Ireland's most talented chefs. The food is plated with such flamboyance that you will want to take a photograph. [$] *Average main: €22* ✉ *36 Henry St.* ☎ *064/664–2383* 🕓 *Closed Tues. and Wed. Oct.–May and last 2 wks Jan. No lunch.*

$$ IRISH 🍴 **Tom Crean Fish & Wine.** Owner Aileen d'Arcy named her restaurant, on the ground floor of a former bank, after her grandfather, the Arctic explorer Tom Crean. You can learn his story while browsing the menu, which is dominated by local produce. Top bets include Sneem black pudding with apple-and-tomato chutney, baked in filo pastry, and local duck breast, panfried and served with roasted root vegetables and Puy lentils. Known for her warm welcome, Aileen learned her trade at Kenmare's famed Park Hotel, and shares the chef duties with

her two sons. The main room is warmed by a large turf fire and has fully upholstered leather chairs. $ *Average main: €20* ✉ *25 Main St.* ☎ *064/664–1589* ⊕ *www.tomcrean.ie* ☉ *Closed early Jan.–end Feb. and Mon.–Wed. Mar., Apr., and Oct.–Dec. No lunch.*

WHERE TO STAY

$$
HOTEL

Brook Lane Hotel. This small hotel may look like a traditional two-story stone building, with pointed gables and bay windows, but in fact it is an Irish-style "boutique" hotel—a product of the economic boom years. **Pros:** one-stop-shop with bar, restaurant, and parking on-site; genuine warm welcome; high standard of comfort. **Cons:** an uninspiring mile-long walk into village; live music in pub may shatter the rural idyll. $ *Rooms from: €140* ✉ *Sneem Rd.* ☎ *064/664–2077* ⊕ *www. brooklanehotel.com* ⤳ *20 rooms* ⫿◎⫾ *Breakfast.*

$$$$
HOTEL
Fodor'sChoice
★

Park Hotel Kenmare. One of Ireland's premier country-house hotels, this 1897 stone château has spectacular views of the Caha Mountains and its 11-acre parkland, where every tree seems manicured, features magnificent terraced lawns sweeping down to the bay. **Pros:** amazingly friendly staff; great spa; impressive grounds. **Cons:** a bit like living in a museum; basic room rates are quite steep. $ *Rooms from: €376* ✉ *Shelburne Rd.* ☎ *064/664–1200* ⊕ *www.parkkenmare.com* ⤳ *35 rooms, 9 suites* ☉ *Closed Nov.–Dec. 23 and Jan. 2–mid-Apr.* ⫿◎⫾ *Breakfast.*

$
B&B/INN

Sallyport House. Across the bridge on the way into Kenmare, this 1932 family home has been enlarged to serve as a comfortable B&B, with spotless rooms and harbor or mountain views. **Pros:** interesting antiques; impeccable housekeeping; quiet location. **Cons:** no credit cards; short opening season. $ *Rooms from: €110* ✉ *Shelbourne St. (N71)* ☎ *064/664–2066* ⊕ *www.sallyporthouse.com* ⤳ *5 rooms* ▭ *No credit cards* ☉ *Closed Nov.–Mar.* ⫿◎⫾ *Breakfast.*

$$$$
HOTEL
Fodor'sChoice
★

Sheen Falls Lodge Kerry Hotel. The magnificence of this bright-yellow, slate-roof stone manor is matched only by its setting on 300 secluded acres of lawns, gardens, and forest between Kenmare Bay and the falls of the River Sheen. **Pros:** fun and informal for the price range; good sport amenities. **Cons:** modern interiors lack traditional character; 2 km (1 mile) from the village. $ *Rooms from: €280* ✉ *Off N71* ☎ *064/664–1600* ⊕ *www.sheenfallslodge.ie* ⤳ *55 rooms, 11 suites* ☉ *Closed Jan. and Sun.–Thurs. Feb.–mid-Mar., Nov., and Dec.* ⫿◎⫾ *Breakfast.*

SHOPPING

Avoca Handweavers. At this scenic spot, midway between Kenmare and Killarney, you'll find wool clothing, mohair throws, and rugs in remarkable palettes and a variety of weaves. ✉ *Moll's Gap (N71)* ☎ *064/663–4720* ⊕ *www.avoca.ie* ☉ *Closed mid-Nov.–early Mar.*

Kenmare Bookshop. A good selection of books of local interest and all the best sellers can be found here. ✉ *Shelburne St.* ☎ *064/664–1578.*

Paul Kelly Jewellers. Striking, modern jewelry in gold and silver is made and sold here. ✉ *18 Henry St.* ☎ *064/664–2590* ⊕ *www.pfk.ie.*

Skyline Gallery. Stunning landscape images by international award-winning Irish photographer Eoghan Kavanagh are showcased here. ✉ *27 Henry St.* ☎ *064/664–8621* ⊕ *www.skyline.ie.*

Sue Designer Knits. Here you'll find Irish-made knitwear in lambswool and cashmere. ⊠ *20 Henry St.* ☎ *064/664–8986* ⊕ *suedesignerknits.com.*

The White Room. Irish lace and linen, both new and antique, are the specialty here. ⊠ *21 Henry St.* ☎ *064/664–0600* ⊕ *www. thewhiteroomkenmare.com.*

SPORTS AND THE OUTDOORS

BICYCLING
Finnegan's Bicycle Hire. Pick up a free copy of the Ring of Kerry Cycle Route brochure from the tourist information office, and then explore the Ring using quiet country roads. The full trip is a blister-inducing 213 km (133 miles). Bikes are available for rent at this shop in town. ⊠ *Henry St.* ☎ *064/664–1083.*

FISHING
Kenmare Angling. Book a day (€300 per boat for up to 10 people) or half-day (€200) fishing trip and get free rods and bait from owner-skipper Sean McCarthy. Fishing is not obligatory—you could just enjoy the scenery, which includes castles, seals, dolphins, and salmon farms. ☎ *087/259–2209* ⊕ *www.kenmareanglingandsightseeing.com.*

WILDLIFE-WATCHING
FAMILY **Seafari Seal and Eagle Watching Cruises.** With complimentary tea and coffee for adults, plus lollipops (suckers) for the kids, Seafari features fun two-hour ecotours with regular sightings of seals and white-tailed sea eagles. Cruises cost €20 per adult, with special family rates. Reservations are essential. They are also an outfitter for kayaking, sailing, and windsurfing. ⊠ *Kenmare Pier, 3 Pier Rd.* ☎ *064/664–2059* ⊕ *www. seafariireland.com* ☉ *Closed Dec.–Mar.*

SNEEM

27 km (17 miles) southwest of Kenmare.

The pretty little village of Sneem (from the Irish for "knot") is settled around an English-style green on the Ardsheelaun River estuary, and its streets are filled with houses washed in different colors. The effect has been somewhat diminished by a cluster of new holiday home developments. The town has a cluster of souvenir shops that play Irish music over loudspeakers when the Ring of Kerry tour buses stop here.

GETTING HERE AND AROUND
It takes about 15 minutes to reach Sneem from Kenmare on N70. There's plenty of free street parking in the town's main square. ■TIP➜ To see the best of Sneem, park near the Blue Bull pub, and walk down the narrow road beside it, signposted "Pier." This quiet byway leads past a carefully tended community garden, terminating about 300 yards farther on at the village pier. Take a seat and look back toward the village to appreciate Sneem's unique location, nestled amid lush subtropical growth between the sea and the hills.

Continued on page 387

GETTING OUTSIDE
THE RING OF KERRY

When you travel Ireland's most popular scenic route, leaving your car behind makes all the difference. Here's how to get far from the madding crowd.

The Ring of Kerry is one of Europe's great drives. The common wisdom, though, is that it suffers from its own popularity: tour buses dominate the road from sunup to sundown. There's more than a grain of truth to this reputation, but that doesn't mean you should scratch the Ring from your itinerary. Instead, plan to turn off the main road and get out of your car. You'll make a blissful discovery: the Iveragh Peninsula—one of the most beautiful locations in all of Ireland—remains largely unspoiled. It's full of fabulous places to hike, bike, and boat—and best of all, there are views the tour bus passengers can only dream of.

Top, Elevated coastal view from the Ring of Kerry; Below left, on horseback in Rossbeigh Strand, Kerry; Below right, cycling around the Ring

AROUND THE RING BY FOOT AND BY BIKE

HIKING THE RING

Option number one for getting outdoors around the Ring of Kerry is to go by foot. There are appealing walking options for every degree of fitness and experience, from gentle, paved paths to an ascent up Ireland's tallest mountain.

THE KERRY WAY

The main hiking route across the peninsula is the Kerry Way, a spectacular 133-mile footpath that's easily broken down into day-trip-size segments. The path winds from Killarney through the foothills of the MacGillicuddy's Reeks and the Black Valley to Glencar and Glenbeigh, from where it parallels the Ring through Cahirciveen, Waterville, Caherdaniel, and Sneem, before ending in Kenmare. The route, indicated by way markers, follows grassy old paths situated at higher elevations than the Ring—meaning better, and more tranquil, views. Hiking the entire Kerry Way can take from 10 to 12 days.

Numerous outfitters organize both guided and unguided tours. For a great day trip, hike the 10 km (6 miles) section from Waterville to Caherdaniel, which has great views of small islands and rocky coves. In the Glencar area near Blackstones Bridge, a series of shorter signposted walks, from 3 km (2 miles) upward, put you in the shadow of Carrauntuohill, Ireland's highest mountain.

TAKING IT EASY: THREE GENTLE STROLLS

MUCKROSS PARK in Killarney is a car-free zone with four signposted nature trails. Try the 4 km (2½ miles) Arthur Young's Walk through old yew and oak woods frequented by sika deer. You can also take an open boat from Ross Castle to the head of the Upper Lake, then walk back along the lakeside to Muckross House—about 10 km (6 miles).

The trails in DERRYNANE NATIONAL PARK, a 320-acre estate, run through mature woodland, bordering on rocky outcrops that lead to wide sandy beaches and dunes. At low tide, you can walk to Abbey Island offshore.

Even in high summer, VALENTIA ISLAND is a peaceful spot for walking, with little traffic. Walk the road from Knightstown through the sub-tropical vegetation of the Knight of Kerry's estate, to the historic Slate Quarry (3 km/2 miles), 900 ft above the sea, with views of the Skelligs offshore.

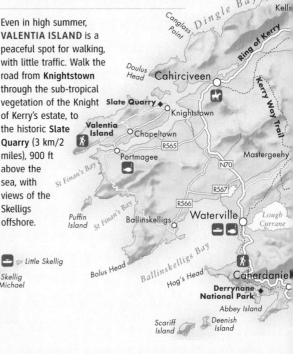

CYCLING THE RING

The Ring of Kerry Cycle Route follows the main road for about a third of its 134 miles, but the rest is on deserted roads, including a long, scenic loop through Ballinskelligs, Portmagee, and Valentia Island. There are significant climbs and strong winds along the way, so good fitness is a prerequisite.

EASY RIDES

From **Killarney**, the N71 road past **Muckross Park** and the **Upper Lake** takes you through ancient woodlands to **Ladies' View** (about 12 km/7.5 miles). From here you have one of the area's best panoramas, with the sparkling blue lakes backed by purple mountains. The scene will be in front of you as you make the ride back.

From **Glenbeigh**, escape the traffic by riding inland to peaceful **Caragh Lake** through a bog and mountain landscape that's rich in wildlife. You might spot a herd of

long-bearded wild goats, or a peregrine falcon hovering above its prey. The full circuit of the lake, returning to Glenbeigh, is about 35 km (22 miles).

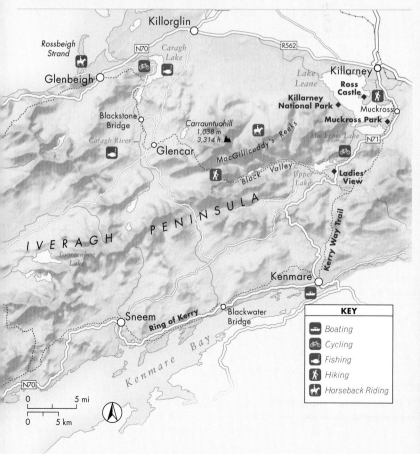

Rossbeigh Strand

Killorglin

N70

Caragh Lake

R562

Glenbeigh

Lake Leane

Killarney

Ross Castle

Killarney National Park

Muckross

Muckross Park

Blackstone Bridge

Carrauntuohill
1,038 m
3,314 ft

MacGillicuddy's Reeks

Muckross Lake

N71

Caragh River

Glencar

Black Valley

Upper Lake

Ladies' View

IVERAGH PENINSULA

Toorneenog Lake

Kerry Way Trail

Kenmare

Sneem

Ring of Kerry

Blackwater Bridge

N70

0   5 mi

0   5 km

Kenmare Bay

KEY

🚤 Boating
🚲 Cycling
🎣 Fishing
🚶 Hiking
🐎 Horseback Riding

RING ACTIVITIES

BOATING AROUND THE RING . . .

Kenmare Bay is the best spot for boating expeditions, on which you can see castles, seals, dolphins, and salmon farms. Boats can take up to 10 people.

. . . AND SWIMMING

Swimming off the beaches around the coast is confined to July and August, when the water temperatures reach 55 to 60 degrees. There are dive centers at **Caherdaniel, Kenmare,** and **Valentia Island;** ⊕ www.scuba.ie is a good information resource.

. . . AND FISHING

There's good fishing here, both inland and at sea. **Portmagee** and **Waterville** are the main deepsea angling centers; outings are generally from small open boats carrying up to 10 rods and run about €30 per person per day. Wreck and reef fishing promises pollock, ling, cod, conger, monkfish, and shark. Inshore there are bass, turbot, dogfish, flounder, and tope.

The **Caragh Lake** and the rivers **Laune, Inny, Roughty,** and **Caragh** are all excellent for wild salmon—and all are beautiful wilderness locations. **Lough Currane** near Waterville is one of the great sea trout fisheries. The season runs from March to September, and fishing permits are available locally from hotels. You'll find tackle shops in Killarney and Waterville. For detailed information before you go, check out the website of the South Western Regional Fisheries Board (⊕ www.swrfb.com).

. . . AND EQUITREKKING

Horses hold a special place in the hearts of the Irish. Horsemanship and breeding are sources of national pride. If you share the Irish passion for all things equine, there's no better way to see the Ring than from the back of a horse. You can gallop along the 3mile stretch of **Rossbeigh Strand,** or take a trek around quiet country roads.

Top left, horses at the Lakes of Killarney; Right, trout fishing; Bottom left, fishing boats in the Dingle harbor

WEATHER, FLORA, AND TOURING TIPS

Swimming at the Ring

THANKS TO
THE GULF STREAM . . .

The warm waters flowing from the Gulf of Mexico across the Atlantic, known as the Gulf Stream, give Ireland a mild climate, and the effects are particularly felt along the Ring of Kerry. The area is frost-free year round, with temperatures averaging 45 degrees Fahrenheit in winter and 60 in summer. But rain is a constant threat, brought in from the Atlantic by the prevailing southwesterly winds. Console yourself with this though: it may be wet, but it is never freezing.

Don't bother touring the Ring in heavy sea mist: you won't see a thing. But don't let other forms of rain deter you. Part of the attraction of the Ring is the interplay of light with sea, mountain, and distant horizons. Rain often enhances the view, and can give delightful effects. The sun is often shining before the rain

has finished, so rainbows abound. Any weather, good or bad, seldom lasts more than half a day: if it's wet in the morning, it will probably be sunny in the afternoon, and vice versa.

SOCK IT TO ME

Bring a rain jacket and a warm fleece or sweater: sea winds can be chilly. Above all, wear sensible footwear. If you're venturing off-road, even in summer, you will be glad of strong, waterproof shoes. And bring plenty of socks. There's nothing more miserable than wet feet!

LAND OF EXOTIC PALMS

With no frost, Killarney and the Iveragh Peninsula are havens for subtropical vegetation. The New Zealand fern tree and the banana tree thrive. The "palm trees" you see here are usually yuccas that have been allowed to grow tall. Flax also grows to enormous size, and is often used as a shelter belt. The leaves of the gunnera can grow to the size of a compact car—look for them in Muckross Park. The lakes of Killarney are surrounded by luxuriant woods of oak, arbutus, birch, holly, and mountain ash, with undergrowth of ferns, saxifrages, and mosses. Rhododendron and azaleas thrive on pockets of acid soil, and are at their best from mid-April to May.

Valentia Island

THE ICE AGE COMETH, AND GOETH

Some 60 million years ago, the great rias, or drowned rivers, that became the bays of Bantry, Kenmare, and Dingle were formed. The sea penetrated far inland, forming the peninsulas of Beara, Iveragh, and Dingle. A million years ago, these lands were gripped by the Ice Age. When the ice receded, some 10,000 years ago, it left corries (or glacial hollows) gouged out of the mountains, great rocks scattered on the landscape (giving rise to legends of giants throwing stones), and outcrops of ice-smoothed sandstone.

7

IN FOCUS GETTING OUTSIDE: THE RING OF KERRY

THE TWIN PEAKS OF YOUR TRIP

Above and below left, ancient monastic site on Skellig Michael with Little Skellig in the background.

The distinctive conical **Skellig Rocks** hover offshore at the western end of the Iveragh Peninsula, surrounded by swirling blue sea. They're a haunting presence that seems to follow along as you travel the mainland from Valentia to Waterville and Caherdaniel.

A venture out to the twin peaks of **Skellig Michael** (shown above, also known as Great Skellig) is a truly awesome experience. Boats leave from Waterville, Ballinskelligs, and Portmagee for a white-knuckle ride lasting about 45 minutes. Along the way you pass Michael's companion, **Little Skellig**, where people aren't allowed but gannets flourish.

Skellig Michael rises steeply for 700 feet; you reach the summit by climbing 600 steps cut into the rockface. Once there, you find, amazingly, the remains of a monastery, occupied by hermit monks from the 7th to 12th century. Looking back to the mainland and out at the wild expanse of open sea, you get an inkling of the monks' isolation from all things worldly. A visit to Skellig Michael may not be the most comfortable outing of you trip, but it will probably be the most memorable.

BIRDS OF THE SKELLIGS

The Ring of Kerry is one of the best places in Europe for observing seabirds, and the Skelligs are a particular treasure for birders. The gannet, with a wing span of 2 yards, is Ireland's largest seabird and up to 22,000 nesting pairs reside on Little Skellig, where they dive for food from heights of up to 120 feet.

If you are lucky enough to get out to Skellig Michael in May, you'll be warned to watch out for comical-looking **puffins** (*below*) nesting in burrows underfoot.

Below, two puffins standing on Skellig rocks

EXPLORING

Fodor's Choice ★ **Derrynane House.** The Ring of Kerry has very few beautiful and historic country houses, so many visitors here enjoy making a special excursion to Derrynane House, located 30 km (18 miles) west of Sneem, near Caherdaniel, off N70. Famed as the home of Daniel O'Connell (1775–1847), "the Liberator," the mansion comes complete with a lovely garden and 320-acre seaside estate, now called the Derryname National Park. The house's south and east wings (which O'Connell himself remodeled) are decorated with much of the furniture and other items associated with the man who campaigned for Catholic Emancipation (the granting of full rights of citizenship to Catholics), which became a reality in 1829. ☎ *066/947–5113* 🌐 *www.heritageireland.com* 🎟 *€3* 🕒 *May–Sept., daily 10:30–6; Apr. and Oct.–late Nov., Wed.–Sun. 10:30–5.*

Staigue Fort. Approximately 2,500 years old, the stone Staigue Fort—signposted 4 km (2½ miles) inland at Castlecove—is almost circular and about 75 feet in diameter, with a single south-side entrance. From the Iron Age (from 500 BC to the 5th century AD) and early Christian times (6th century AD), such "forts" were, in fact, fortified homesteads for several families of one clan and their cattle. The walls at Staigue Fort are almost 13 feet thick at the base and 7 feet thick at the top; they still stand 18 feet high on the north and west sides. Within them, stairs lead to narrow platforms on which the lookouts stood. ⚠ **Private land must be crossed to reach the fort, and a "compensation for trespass" of €1 is often requested by the landowner.** ✉ *Castlecove.*

WHERE TO STAY

$$$ RESORT FAMILY Fodor's Choice ★ 🏨 **Parknasilla Resort.** For more than a century Parknasilla, a towering, gray-stone mansion on a stunningly beautiful inlet of the Kenmare estuary, has been synonymous with old-style resort luxury, attracting guests like George Bernard Shaw, Princess Grace, and Charles de Gaulle. **Pros:** excellent sports amenities and spa; sheltered coastal location; great family destination. **Cons:** grounds and hotel big enough to get lost in; hugely popular with families in July and August. [$] *Rooms from: €209* ✉ *N70* ☎ *064/667–5600* 🌐 *www.parknasillahotel.ie* 🛏 *72 rooms, 11 suites* 🕒 *Closed Jan.–early-Mar.* 🍴 *Breakfast.*

$$ HOTEL 🏨 **Sneem Hotel.** Meet the locals and enjoy spacious accommodations at this waterfront hotel and apartment complex on Goldens Cove, a rocky, sheltered spot with views of distant mountains. **Pros:** large, modern rooms; friendly service. **Cons:** some new development detracts from the views; large bar and restaurant can be a bit eerie when not busy. [$] *Rooms from: €160* ✉ *Goldens Cove* ☎ *064/667–5100* 🌐 *www.sneemhotel.com* 🛏 *69 rooms, 28 apartments* 🕒 *Closed Sun.–Thurs. mid-Nov–mid-Feb.* 🍴 *No meals.*

WATERVILLE

35 km (22 miles) west of Sneem.

Waterville, a seaside village facing Ballinskelligs Bay, is famous for its sportfishing, its 18-hole championship golf course (adopted as a warm-up spot for the British Open by Tiger Woods), and for the fact that Charlie Chaplin and Charles de Gaulle spent summers here. The village, like many others on the Ring of Kerry, has a few restaurants and pubs, but little else. There's excellent salmon and trout fishing at nearby Lough Currane, and the area offers challenging hikes with stunning vistas.

GETTING HERE AND AROUND

Waterville, part of the Ring of Kerry driving loop, is a short half-hour drive from Sneem on the N70. You approach the town driving through the dramatically rocky Coomakesta Pass and Hog's Head. Stop at one of the viewing areas to take in the panoramic sea views, which look out at the distinctive Skellig Rocks. There is plenty of free parking in the village.

ESSENTIALS

Visitor Information Waterville Tourist Office ✉ *Town Center* ☎ *066/947-4646* ⏲ *Closed Oct.–May.*

EXPLORING

Cill Rialaig. West of Waterville and 1 km (½ mile) before the Irish-speaking village of Ballinskelligs is the Cill Rialaig Arts Centre. This is the best place in Kerry to see Irish and international art, along with fine crafts and gifts. Its attractive, thatched, beehive-shaped roof is hard to miss. There's also a café with wholesome homemade food. ✉ *R566* ☎ *066/947–9277* 🌐 *www.cillrialaigartscentre.org* 🎟 *Free* ⏲ *June–Sept., daily 11–6; other months call in advance.*

WHERE TO STAY

$$ HOTEL 🏨 **Butler Arms Hotel.** Charlie Chaplin loved it here—the connection is now commemorated by a mini-film festival here in late August—and a whole host of families return year after year to this rambling old-world landmark, with its white castellated corner tower. **Pros:** charming old-world vibe; near beaches and village. **Cons:** village mainly a golfing and fishing center, dominated by all-male groups; limited nightlife, shopping, dining. [$] *Rooms from: €140* ✉ *N70* ☎ *066/947–4144* 🌐 *www.butlerarms.com* 🛏 *24 rooms, 12 suites* ⏲ *Closed Nov.–Mar.* 🍴 *Breakfast.*

$ B&B/INN 🏨 **Lakelands Farm Guesthouse.** Amid rocky hills, this spacious, Dutch-gable modern house enjoys a stunning location about a mile off the Ring on the shore of Lough Currane (boats for hire) and is hosted by an angling/shooting guide and his wife. **Pros:** good value; great scenery; huge bedrooms; hosts are happy to advise on local dining options. **Cons:** nearly 3 km (2 miles) outside village (look for signpost on the N70 on the south side of the village); won't win any style kudos. [$] *Rooms from: €75* ✉ *Lake Rd.* ☎ *066/947–4303* 🌐 *www.lakelandswaterville.com* 🛏 *12 rooms* ⏲ *Closed Oct. and mid-Jan.–Feb.* 🍴 *Breakfast.*

NIGHTLIFE AND THE ARTS

Inny Tavern. For live Irish music, head to this traditional country pub that's popular among locals. ✉ *Inny Bridge* ☎ *066/947–4512.*

SPORTS AND THE OUTDOORS
GOLF

Waterville Golf Links. Famously adopted by Tiger Woods and Mark O'Meara to practice their swings for the British Open, this 18-hole championship links course remains one of the toughest and most scenic in Ireland or Britain, and as one of Ireland's top five courses, it is considered to be among the best in the world. Consisting of sand dunes, gorse, native grass, and sod-faced bunkers linked by firm fairways and carefully tended greens, Waterville is bordered by the wild Atlantic on two of its three sides. Gary Player described the 11th hole, which runs for 500 yards through majestic dunes, as "the most beautiful and satisfying par 5 of them all." Caddies must be booked in advance. ☎ *066/947–4102* ⊕ *www.watervillegolfclub.ie* ✉ *Fees: Apr.– Oct., weekdays €144, weekends €163; Nov.–Mar. €58* ⅃ *18 holes, 7355 yards, par 72. Practice area, caddies, caddy carts, buggies, catering* ☉ *Visitors: daily, year-round.*

HIKING

SHOPPING

FAMILY **Skelligs Chocolate.** The wild coastal road between Waterville and Portmagee is an unusual location for a chocolate factory, café, and shop, but then this is unusual chocolate, handmade in small batches, and acclaimed by connoisseurs for its excellence. Enjoy the freshly made samples while the kids explore the playground, or order up a picnic for the beach. ✉ *The Glen, Skellig Ring (R566), Ballinskelligs* ☎ *066/947– 9119* ⊕ *www.skelligschocolate.com* ☉ *Closed Jan.*

THE SKELLIGS AND VALENTIA

Islands off the coastal town of Portmagee, 21 km (13 miles) northwest of Waterville; Valentia Island is across a road bridge from Portmagee.

In the far northwestern corner of the Ring of Kerry, across Portmagee Channel, lies scenic Valentia Island, where the eastern end of the first transatlantic telegraph cable was sited, and also known for its well-preserved tetrapod fossil trackways. Visible from Valentia, and on a clear day from other points along the coast, are the Skelligs, one of the most spectacular sights in Ireland. Sculpted as if by the hand of God, the islands of Little Skellig, Great Skellig, and the Washerwoman's Rock are distinctively cone-shaped, surrounded by blue swirling seas. The largest island, the Great Skellig, or Skellig Michael, distinguished by its twin peaks and ancient monastic site, rises 700 feet from the Atlantic. During the journey to these islands you'll pass Little Skellig, the breeding ground of more than 22,000 pairs of gannets. Puffin Island, to the north, has a large population of shearwaters and storm petrel. Puffins nest in sand burrows on the Great Skellig in the month of May.

GETTING HERE AND AROUND

To visit the Skelligs, you can take a half-day trip in an open boat—perfect for adventurers who pack plenty of Dramamine. The entire visit takes 3 to 4 hours, with 1½ hours on Skellig Michael, where visitors are supervised by resident guides, and the remaining time in transit (the duration varies depending on the weather and tides). Note that

the waters are choppy at the best of times, and trips are made when the weather permits. Even in fine weather, it can be a rough, white-knuckle ride (at least 45 minutes) as you cross the swell of the open sea, and it's not suitable for small children. One worthy outfitter to the Skelligs is Sea Quest, on Valentia Island. Valentia is reached via R565 through Portmagee then across a road bridge. ■TIP→ **From April to October the Valentia Island Car and Passenger Ferry operates a daily shuttle for cars and foot passengers between Knightstown on Valentia Island and Renard Point near Cahirciveen. The five-minute ferry ride saves a round-trip of about 25 km (15 miles) by land.**

ESSENTIALS

Transportation Contacts Sea Quest ⊠ *The Pier, Portmagee, Co. Kerry* ⊕ *www. skelligsrock.com* 🖃 *€50* ⊙ *Apr.–Aug., daily 10 am, weather permitting (book in advance).* **Valentia Island Car and Passenger Ferry** ⊠ *Renard Point, Cahirciveen, Co. Kerry* ☎ *066/947–6141.*

Visitor Information Skelligs Tourist Office ⊠ *Skellig Experience, Valentia Island, Co. Kerry* ☎ *066/947–6306* ⊕ *www.skelligexperience.com* ⊙ *June–Sept.*

EXPLORING

Skellig Experience. Located on Valentia Island, just across the bridge from Portmagee, the Skellig Experience offers an alternative for the less adventurous traveler. This center contains exhibits on local birdlife, the history of the lighthouse and keepers, and the life and work of the early Christian monks. There's also a 15-minute audiovisual show that allows you to "tour" the Skelligs without leaving dry land—although the center does offer a 90-minute non-landing cruise around the islands. But if you're up for it, don't miss the boat ride from Portmagee that lets you land on the rocks; Skellig Michael is something you won't soon forget. ⊠ *R565, Valentia Island, Co. Kerry* ☎ *066/947–6306* ⊕ *www. skelligexperience.com* 🖃 *€5, cruise €27.50* ⊙ *Mar.–June and Sept., daily 10–6; July and Aug., daily 10–7; Oct. and Nov., daily 10–6.*

Fodor'sChoice ★ **Skellig Michael.** The masterpiece of the Skellig Islands is the phenomenal Unesco World Heritage Site of Skellig Michael, with its amazing remains of a 7th- to 12th-century village of monastic beehive dwellings that were home to a group of early Christian monks. In spite of a thousand years of battering by Atlantic storms, the church, oratory, and living cells are surprisingly well preserved. The site is reached by climbing more than 600 increasingly precipitous step, offering vertigo-inducing views. The Skelligs boat trip (⇨ *see Getting Here and Around*) includes 1½ hours on Skellig Michael. ■TIP→ **Because of the choppy seas, stiff climb, and lack of facilities, the trip is not recommended for small children.** ⊠ *Skellig Islands, Co. Kerry* ⊕ *www.heritageireland.ie* 🖃 *Free (charge for boat trip)* ⊙ *Mid-May–late Sept. (weather permitting).*

WHERE TO EAT AND STAY

$
IRISH
Fodor'sChoice ★ ✕ **Bridge Bar.** Hungry mariners make a beeline for this simple bar on the windswept waterfront of the tiny fishing village of Portmagee. Overlooking the channel between the mainland and Valentia Island, its dramatic location has led the Bridge to being featured in ads as "the quintessential Irish pub." While not overly historic in style, the

low-beam interior—with red walls, rustic pine, and an open fire—is a sweet place to enjoy the renowned seafood chowder, or daily specials like grilled haddock with lemon butter or steamed mussels with garlic. In July and August the pretty, adjoining Moorings restaurant serves a more ambitious, pricier menu most evenings. There are also 14 rooms overhead and an ace craft shop next door. Between Easter and October call to confirm. [$] *Average main: €14* ✉ *Portmagee, Co. Kerry* ☎ *066/947–7108* 🌐 *www.moorings.ie.*

$ B&B/INN 🏨 **Shealane Country House Bed & Breakfast.** A large, modern house on Valentia Island, beside the bridge to the mainland, Shealane is easily reached but also affords views of cows grazing in the adjoining field and a breakfast room with ocean views. **Pros:** friendly welcome from local family; quiet rural location. **Cons:** outside the village; rooms book far in advance for July and August. [$] *Rooms from: €80* ✉ *Corha-Mor, Valentia Island, Co. Kerry* ☎ *066/947–6354* 🌐 *www.valentiaskelligs.com* 🛏 *5 rooms* 🕑 *Closed mid-Oct.–Mar.* 🍴 *Breakfast.*

CAHIRCIVEEN

18 km (11 miles) north of Waterville.

Cahirciveen (pronounced cah-her-si-*veen*), at the foot of Bentee Mountain, is the gateway to the western side of the Ring of Kerry and the main market town for southern Kerry. Following the tradition in this part of the world, the modest, terraced houses are each painted in different colors (sometimes two or three)—the brighter the better.

GETTING HERE AND AROUND

Cahirciveen is about a 15-minute drive from Waterville on N70, double that if you choose to detour to Portmagee for a visit to the Skellig Rock and Valentia Island. In summer you can return from Knightstown on Valentia Island to Cahirciveen by ferry. There is free parking on the side streets off the main road and outside the Tourist Office.

ESSENTIALS

Visitor Information Cahirciveen Tourist Office ✉ *Church St.* ☎ *066/947–1300* 🌐 *www.destinationringofkerry.com/cahersiveen/* 🕑 *June–Sept.*

EXPLORING

Caherciveen Parish Daniel O'Connell Memorial Church. This large, elaborate, neo-Gothic structure dominates the main street. It was built in 1888 of Newry granite and black limestone to honor the local hero Daniel O'Connell—the only church in Ireland named after a layman. ☎ *066/947–2210* 🌐 *www.caherciveenparish.com.*

Old Barracks Heritage Centre. The converted former barracks of the Royal Irish Constabulary, an imposing, castle-like structure (built after the Fenian Rising of 1867 to suppress further revolts) now houses this museum. Well-designed displays depict scenes from times of famine, the life of Daniel O'Connell, and the restoration of this fine building from a blackened ruin. ✉ *The Barracks, Brendan's Terr.* ☎ *066/947–2777* 🌐 *www.theoldbarracks.com* 🎟 *€4* 🕑 *Weekdays 10–4:30, Sat. 11:30–4:30, Sun. 1–5 pm.*

GLENBEIGH

27 km (17 miles) northeast of Cahirciveen.

The road from Cahirciveen to Glenbeigh is one of the Ring's highlights. To the north is Dingle Bay and the jagged peaks of the Dingle Peninsula, which will, in all probability, be shrouded in mist. If they aren't, the gods have indeed blessed your journey. The road runs close to the water here, and beyond the small village of Kells it climbs high above the bay, hugging the steep side of Drung Hill before descending to Glenbeigh. Note how different the stark character of this stretch of the Ring is from the gentle, woody Kenmare Bay side.

On a boggy plateau by the sea, the block-long village of Glenbeigh is a popular holiday base—the hiking is excellent in the Glenbeigh Horseshoe, as the surrounding mountains are known, and the trout fishing exceptionally good in Lough Coomasaharn. The area south of Glenbeigh and west of Carrantouhill Mountain, around the shores of the Caragh River and the village of Glencar, is known as the Kerry Highlands. The scenery is wild and rough but strangely appealing. A series of circular walks have been signposted, and parts of the Kerry Way pass through here. The area attracts serious climbers who intend to scale Carrantouhill, Ireland's highest peak (3,408 feet).

GETTING HERE AND AROUND

The tiny roadside village of Glenbeigh is about 40 minutes from Cahirciveen on N70. There's free parking on the streets.

EXPLORING

Caragh Lake. A signpost to the right outside Glenbeigh points to Caragh Lake, a tempting excursion south to a beautiful expanse of water set among gorse- and heather-covered hills and majestic mountains. The road hugs the shoreline much of the way.

FAMILY **Kerry Bog Village Museum.** Worth a quick look, this museum, between Glenbeigh and Killorglin on the Ring of Kerry, is a cluster of reconstructed, fully furnished cottages that vividly portray the daily life of the region's working class in the early 1800s. The adjacent Red Fox Bar is famous for its Irish coffee. ⊠ *N70, Ballincleave* ☎ *066/976–9184* ⊕ *www.kerrybogvillage.ie* 🎟 *€6.50* ⏱ *Daily 9–6.*

WHERE TO STAY

$$$ 🏨 **Carrig Country House.** A rambling two-story Victorian house covered in flowering creepers and set on 4 acres of lush gardens along the secluded shore of Caragh Lake, this comes pretty close to most people's dream rural retreat. **Pros:** lovely secluded location; real country-house atmosphere; affable owner-managers. **Cons:** tricky to find first time. 💲 *Rooms from: €190* ⊠ *Caragh Lake, off Ring of Kerry, Killorglin* ⊹ *From Killorglin, take the Ring of Kerry toward Glenbeigh. After 4 km (2½ miles) turn left signposted Caragh Lake; at Caragh Lake School and Shop, turn sharp right and continue to the hotel. From Glenbeigh, turn right near Red Fox Inn onto Caragh Lake road (signposted)* ☎ *066/976–9100* 🛏 *17 rooms* ⏱ *Closed Nov.–early Mar.* 🍽 *Breakfast.*

HOTEL
Fodor's Choice
★

SPORTS AND THE OUTDOORS

BEACHES

FAMILY **Rossbeigh.** On the coast, 2 km (1 mile) west of Glenbeigh, Rossbeigh consists of a tombola (sand spit) of about 3 km (2 miles) backed by high dunes. It faces Inch Strand, a similar formation across the water on the Dingle Peninsula. Popular with families for its safe swimming, it also attracts walkers. **Amenities:** food and drink; lifeguards; parking (no fee). **Best for:** swimming; walking. ⊠ *Rossbeigh Rd.*

BICYCLING

Caragh Lake Cycling Route. Cyclists love this circuit, which is about a 35-km (22-mile) round-trip from Glenbeigh. It is relatively traffic-free compared to the Ring of Kerry, and runs through truly remote bog and mountain landscape that's rich in wildlife. You might spot a herd of long-bearded wild goats, or a peregrine falcon soaring above. But bring your own drinks and snacks: retail outlets are scarce in these parts.

Glenross Caravan & Camping Park. Rent a bike here to explore the coast around Glenbeigh and follow the scenic route around Caragh Lake, one of the most peaceful places on Earth. ⊠ *Ring of Kerry (N70)* ☏ *066/663–1282* ⊕ *www.killarneycamping.com/glenross.html* ☉ *Mid-Apr.–Sept.*

HIKING

FAMILY **Blackstones Bridge.** In this partially wooded area near Glencar, in the shadow of Carrauntuohill, Ireland's highest mountain, and MacGillicuddy's Reeks, a series of looped walks from 3 km (2 miles) upward, are mapped out on picture boards in the parking areas. It's about 12 km (7 miles) southeast of Glenbeigh. ⊠ *Off N70* ⊕ *www.irishtrails.ie.*

Cappanalea Outdoor Education Centre. Canoeing, rock climbing, and orienteering are among the outdoor activities available (book in advance) at this center, located between Caragh and Cappanalea lakes, and can be arranged to meet the needs of all comers. ⊠ *Oulagh West, Caragh Lake, Killorglin* ☏ *066/976–9244* ⊕ *www.cappanalea.ie.*

HORSEBACK RIDING

FAMILY **Burke's Horse Trekking Center.** Gallop a 5-km (3-mile) stretch of Rossbeigh Strand, or take a trek around quite country roads on a horse from this long-established family business. They use mainly quiet colored cobs (black-and-white long-haired all-rounders). Hats and boots are included in the price. Book 24 hours in advance to avoid disappointment. ⊠ *R564* ☏ *087/237–9100* ⊕ *www.beachtrek.ie* ☒ *€20–€30.*

KILLORGLIN

14 km (9 miles) east of Glenbeigh, 22 km (14 miles) west of Killarney.

Killorglin is on top of a hill beside the River Laune. At the "top of the town" is a Continental-style piazza, with outdoor tables in good weather and free entertainment in summer. (This is also the location of the tourist information office.) Venture down the hill to find an old-style traditional pub where you can savor a pint.

Killorglin is famed as the scene of the Puck Fair, three days of merrymaking during the second weekend in August. A large billy goat with beribboned horns, installed on a high pedestal, presides over the fair.

The origins of the tradition of King Puck are lost in time. Horse dealing takes place in an open field on the first morning of the fair. In the village the main attractions are fun fair rides, street traders, street performers, free outdoor concerts, and extended drinking hours. The crowds can be huge, so avoid Killorglin at fair time if you've come for peace and quiet. On the other hand, if you intend to join in the festivities, be sure to book accommodations well in advance.

GETTING HERE AND AROUND

The town is a 10-minute drive on the R70 from Glenbeigh. Street parking is available, and there is a free parking lot near the tourist information office.

ESSENTIALS

Visitor Information **Killorglin Tourist Office** ✉ *Iveragh Rd.* ☎ *066/976–1451* 🌐 *www.killorglinringofkerry.com.*

WHERE TO EAT

$$ IRISH 🍴 **The Bianconi.** This hostelry opened in the 19th century, before the days of railroads, as the coaching inn for the national network of horse-drawn coaches known as Bianconis, after the Italian who set up the business. Today it's a busy pub, with guest rooms as well, at the riverside crossroads at the entrance to town. Its dark-wood Victorian interior has a rambling barroom with a tile floor, leatherette banquettes, and ancient stuffed animals above the booths. The menu includes such favorites as Dingle Bay prawns, local oak-smoked salmon, a steaming mussel pot in garlic sauce, and braised shank of Kerry lamb. Even though it's a pub, advance booking is advisable in summer and on weekends. [$] *Average main: €20* ✉ *Lower Bridge St.* ☎ *066/976–1146* 🌐 *www.bianconi.ie* 🕓 *No lunch Sun.*

7

CORCA DHUIBHNE: THE DINGLE PENINSULA

The gorgeously scenic Dingle Peninsula stretches for some 48 km (30 miles) between Tralee (pronounced tra-*lee*) in the east and Ceann Sléibhe (Slea Head) in the west. Often referred to by its Irish name, Corca Dhuibhne (pronounced Cor-kah-guy-nay), the peninsula is made up of rugged mountains, seaside cliffs, and softly molded glacial valleys and lakes. Long sandy beaches and Atlantic-pounded cliffs unravel along the coast. Drystone walls enclose small, irregular fields, and exceptional prehistoric and early Christian remains dot the countryside. As you drive over its mountain passes, looking out past prehistoric remains to the wild Atlantic sea, Dingle can be a magical destination that makes you feel like you're living in an ancient legend. Unfortunately, Dingle is notorious for its heavy rainfall and impenetrable sea mists, which can strike at any time of year. If they do, sit them out in An Daingean (Dingle Town) and enjoy the friendly bars, cafés, and crafts shops. ■ **TIP→ West of Annascaul, the peninsula is Irish-speaking: English is considered a second language. A good Irish-English map can prove handy.**

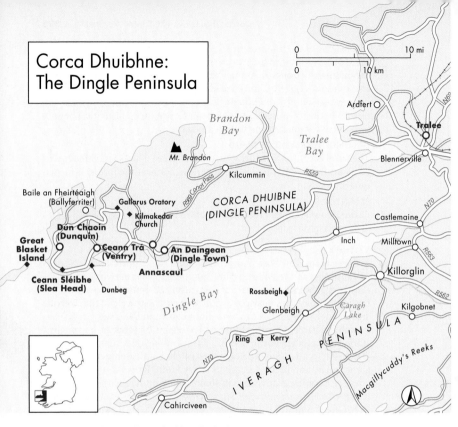

Corca Dhuibhne: The Dingle Peninsula

GETTING HERE AND AROUND

Corca Dhuibhne is less than an hour's drive from Tralee on the N86 or N70, and about an hour from Killarney. From Killarney or Killorglin, take the N70 to Castlemaine, then R561. There are five buses a day from Tralee, which also has the nearest train station, and two from Killarney. Remember, it will be signposted in Irish: "An Daingean." You can cover the peninsula in a long day trip of about 160 km (99 miles). If mist or continuous rain is forecast, postpone your trip until visibility improves.

ANNASCAUL

47 km (30 miles) northwest of Killarney.

An important livestock center until the 1930s, this village near the junction of the Castlemaine and Tralee roads has a wide road, as cattle trading was once carried out in the streets. The town also has many pubs.

GETTING HERE AND AROUND

Annascaul is about one hour from Tralee on the N86, just over an hour from Killarney (take N70 then R561), and less than half an hour's drive from Dingle Town continuing on the main N86. There is abundant free parking in town.

CLOSE UP

Dingle by Any Other Name

Residents of Dingle, especially those involved in the tourist business, fought a battle with the government for the right to continue to call their town and their peninsula by the name of Dingle. The problem arose because the western part of Dingle Peninsula—known in Irish as Corca Dhuibhne, and its main town, Dingle (An Daingean, in Irish)—is officially an Irish-speaking area, part of the Kerry Gaeltacht. The Official Languages Act of 2003 was introduced to strengthen the rights of Ireland's 90,000 Irish speakers to do business with the state in their native tongue—officially Ireland's first language. A side effect of this act was the necessity, under the new law, for all signposts for places where Irish is the official spoken language to be in Irish. So the name Dingle has disappeared from all signposts by official decree, to be replaced by An Daingean, leaving many puzzled visitors on the road from Killarney, Tralee and other places, searching in vain for signs to Dingle. The traders of Dingle claimed that the name of their town is equivalent to an internationally recognized brand name, and demanded that an exception be made in their case. Eventually, following a change of government, their wish was granted, and signs to Dingle reappeared. Nevertheless, when heading for Dingle Town from the Irish-speaking part of the Dingle Peninsula, west of the town, follow signs to An Daingean. Only in Ireland.

7

EXPLORING

The South Pole Inn. This fascinating landmark was built by local hero Tom Crean (1877–1938). Crean enlisted in the English navy at the age of 15, and served on three expeditions to Antarctica—the *Discovery* (1901–04) and the *Terra Nova* (1910–13), both under the command of Captain Robert Falcon Scott, and the *Endurance* (1914–16), where he was second officer to Ernest Shackleton. Crean himself failed to reach the South Pole on any of these expeditions, and named his pub so that in his retirement he could go to work at the South Pole every day.

Memorabilia at the pub fill in the details of Crean's Antarctic adventures. Famed for his amazing strength and resilience, he walked 56 km (35 miles) through an Antarctic blizzard to bring help to his colleagues, with only two bars of chocolate and three cookies for sustenance. For this he received the Albert Medal for Bravery. On another occasion he survived a 15-day journey across 1,280 km (800 miles) of ocean in an open boat.

The pub is the headquarters of the Tom Crean Society, which hosts occasional lectures and festivals and has been addressed by Sir Edmund Hillary and the grandsons of both Scott and Shackleton. ☎ *066/915-7388.*

AN DAINGEAN (DINGLE TOWN)

18 km (11 miles) west of Annascaul, 67 km (42 miles) west of Killarney, 45 km (28 miles) west of Killorglin.

Backed by mountains and facing a sheltered harbor, An Daingean, the chief town of its eponymous peninsula, has a year-round population of 1,400 that more than doubles in summer. Although many expect Dingle (to use its English name) to be a quaint and undeveloped Gaeltacht village, it has many crafts shops, seafood restaurants, and pubs.

Still, you can explore its main thoroughfares—the Mall, Main and Strand streets, and the Wood—in less than an hour. Celebrity hawks, take note: off-season Dingle is favored as a hideaway by the likes of Julia Roberts, Paul Simon, and Dolly Parton. These and others have their visits commemorated on Green Street's "path of stars."

The latest addition to the annual calendar is the **Dingle Food and Wine Festival** (*see The Southwest Planner: When to Go*).

GETTING HERE AND AROUND

Dingle Town is about an hour and 15 minutes' drive from Tralee on the N86, and about two hours west of Killarney via Killorglin and Castlemaine. There are daily buses from Tralee, which also has the nearest train station.

There is no public transportation west of Dingle Town, around Slea Head, where the best scenery is found. If you don't have a car, the 30-km (18-mile) circuit can be toured by minibus (€20 per person for two or more people). Coastline Tours is a good choice for these excursions, or ask at the tourist information office. Bear in mind that there are no gas stations and no ATMs west of Dingle Town, so load up on supplies before you leave.

Most boats to the Blasket Islands leave from Dunquin, 21 km (13 miles) west of town, but Dingle Bay Charters has boats from the marina in Dingle Town making ecotours of the Blasket Islands daily between May and September, weather permitting (€40). They (and several other local operators on the town pier) also run a harbor cruise (€10 for one hour) several times daily between April and September.

ESSENTIALS

Transportation Contacts Coastline Tours ☎ *087/998–2230* ⊕ *www. coastline-tours.com.* **Dingle Bay Charters** ⊠ *Dingle Marina* ☎ *066/915–1344* ⊕ *www.dinglebaycharters.com.*

Visitor Information An Daingean (Dingle Town) Tourist Office ⊠ *The Quay* ☎ *066/915–1188* ⊕ *www.discoverireland.ie.*

EXPLORING

FAMILY **Fungie.** Since 1985, An Daingean's central attraction, apart from its "trad" music scene, has been a winsome bottle-nosed dolphin who has taken up residence in the harbor. The Dingle dolphin, or Fungie, as he has been named, will play for hours with swimmers (a wet suit is essential) and scuba divers, and he follows local boats in and out of the harbor. It's impossible to predict whether he will stay, but boatmen have become so confident of a sighting that they offer trippers their money

An entry in Fodor's "Show Us Your Ireland" contest, this photo by Fodors.com member Michelle Nadal shows the coastal tip of the dramatic Dingle Peninsula.

back if Fungie does not appear. Boat trips (€10) leave the pier hourly in July and August between 11 and 6, weather permitting. ✉ *The Pier.*

WHERE TO EAT

$$$ IRISH Fodor's Choice ★ 🍴 **Chart House.** Host Jim McCarthy is often found in the early evening leaning over the red half door of this low, cabinlike stone building. The exterior gives little hint of the spacious, cleverly lighted dining room within, nor of the beautiful pair of windows at the back that frame lovely views of Dingle Harbor's trawler fleet. Nautical artifacts complement the rusty-red walls and matching tablecloths. The atmosphere is pleasantly informal, but both food and service are polished and professional. Top choices include Dingle Bay crabmeat salad with ginger mayonnaise and mango salsa, or rack of Kerry mountain lamb with red-currant-and-rosemary jus. Finish the meal with a selection of Irish cheeses, served with a glass of port, or a homemade apple-and-clove tartlet with ginger-nut crumble. [$] *Average main: €27* ✉ *The Mall* ☎ *066/915–2255* 🌐 *www.thecharthousedingle.com* ⏲ *Closed Jan. 2–mid-Feb., and Mon. and Tues. in Apr., May, and mid-Sept.–Dec. (call to confirm). No lunch.*

$ EUROPEAN 🍴 **Chowder Cafe.** Look for the bright blue wooden shop front near the pier (about three minutes' walk from the tourist office) to find one of the best budget eateries in town. Enthusiastic young owner-chefs Charlie and Joanna welcome you to their restaurant, nicely brightened with the work of local artists. The chowder is a star, but so is the steak sandwich with home fries, and some adore the goat's-cheese-and-red-onion quiche. When the dinner menu kicks in during high season, more substantial seasonal mains are offered, perhaps slow-braised lamb shank, or cod with chorizo. Slow-fooders will like this place: fresh bread and cakes are home-baked daily. *[$] Average main: €16 ✉ Strand St. ☎ 066/915–1061 ⏲ No dinner Oct.–May.*

$$$ SEAFOOD 🍴 **Out of the Blue.** Every fishing port should have a simple waterfront bistro like this one, serving the best seafood (the owner won't open up if there's no fresh-caught seafood available—which is almost never). Lobster, scallops, and crayfish are specialties, but also expect turbot, black sole, plaice, brill, monkfish, and even the humble pollack on the daily blackboard menu. The duo of French chefs put a modern twist on seafood classics, perhaps pan-seared scallops flambéed in Calvados, with pineapple and chili salsa, or grilled lemon sole fillet with toasted almond and lemon butter. There's a short but well-chosen wine list, and basic dessert selection. The bargain "Fish Deal," with two or three choices per course, is served 5:30 to 6:30 on weekdays. *[$] Average main: €25 ✉ The Pier ☎ 066/915–0811 🌐 www.outoftheblue.ie ✍ Reservations essential ⏲ Closed mid-Nov.–mid-Mar. No lunch Mon.–Sat.*

WORD OF MOUTH

"Dingle is definitely worth two nights . . . The Dingle Loop drive was a great mix of scenery, historical stops to explore, small villages, and beaches. We spent nearly an entire day making the drive. Dingle itself has a great collection of shops, pubs, and eating spots, and is very walkable. We really enjoyed just browsing around the town. Great variety of music to be heard as well." —Maggie1017

WHERE TO STAY

$$ HOTEL FAMILY 🏨 **Dingle Skellig Hotel and Peninsula Spa.** This rambling modern hotel's setting on Dingle Bay offers great views of the water, notably from the restaurant and the spa's outdoor hot tub. **Pros:** waterfront location; creche, kids' dining, and organized entertainment and activities for children; separate floors for child-free guests. **Cons:** still shows signs of its undistinguished 1970s architecture; edge-of-town location a bit bleak in bad weather. *[$] Rooms from: €124 ✉ Dingle Harbour ☎ 066/915–0200 🌐 www.dingleskellig.com 🛏 99 rooms, 14 suites ⏲ Closed Jan. and Mon.–Thurs. in Nov. and Dec. 🍽 Breakfast.*

$ B&B/INN Fodor's Choice ★ 🏨 **Greenmount House.** More like a modern boutique hotel than a B&B, the combination of comfort and elegance in the lobby sets the tone, as do the wonderful views of the town and harbor. **Pros:** plenty of private parking; wine license; wonderful breakfasts; nice common areas. **Cons:** new developments mar the foreground of an otherwise great view; short walk uphill from town center. *[$] Rooms from: €110 ✉ Upper John St. ☎ 066/915–1414 🌐 www.greenmount-house.com 🛏 6 rooms, 6 suites 🍽 Breakfast.*

$$ B&B/INN 🏨 **Heaton's Guesthouse.** On the Slea Head edge of Dingle Town, but just a short walk to the center, this traditional-style yellow house is right on the water's edge. **Pros:** high standard of comfort and interior design; ample parking; only a short walk from town. **Cons:** if it rains you'll be driving, not walking, to nearest bars and restaurants. *[$] Rooms from: €124 ✉ The Wood ☎ 066/915–2288 🌐 www.heatonsdingle.com 🛏 14 rooms, 2 suites ⏲ Closed Dec. 1–28 and Jan. 7–31 🍽 Breakfast.*

NIGHTLIFE AND THE ARTS

Nearly every bar on the Corca Dhuibhne (Dingle Peninsula), particularly in the town of An Daingean, offers live music nightly in July and August.

An Droichead Beag (The Small Bridge). For a lively nighttime spot, try this large, busy pub in the town center, known for live Irish music. ⊠ *Main St.* ☎ *066/915–1723.*

O'Flahertys. An Daingean's pubs are well known for their music, but among them O'Flaherty's, a simple, stone-floor bar at the entrance to town, is something special and a hot spot for traditional musicians. Spontaneous sessions occur most nights in July and August, less frequently at other times. Even without music, this pub is a good place to compare notes with fellow travelers. ⊠ *Bridge St.* ☎ *066/915–1983.*

SHOPPING

Greenlane Gallery. Shows of contemporary Irish art, with an emphasis on local landscapes, are often held here. ⊠ *Holy Ground, Grey's La.* ☎ *066/915–2018* ⊕ *www.greenlanegallery.com.*

Leác a Ré. For handmade Irish crafts, check out this noted emporium. ⊠ *Strand St.* ☎ *066/915–1138.*

Murphy's Ice Cream. One of Ireland's more unusual culinary success stories, Murphy's has won international awards. Find out why at this flagship parlor. ⊠ *Strand St.* ☎ *066/915–2644* ⊕ *www.murphysicecream.ie.*

Weaver's Shop. Lisbeth Mulcahy sells outstanding handwoven, vegetable-dyed woolen wraps, mufflers, and fabric for making skirts here. ⊠ *Green St.* ☎ *066/915–1688* ⊕ *www.lisbethmulcahy.com.*

SPORTS AND THE OUTDOORS

BICYCLING

Foxy John's Hardware. You're likely to remember a bike ride around Slea Head for a long time. You can rent bicycles at Foxy John's, which also has a great old-style bar–cum–hardware store. ⊠ *Main St.* ☎ *066/915–1316.*

HORSEBACK RIDING

Dingle Horse Riding. Up in the hills behind Dingle Town, this stable offers some unforgettable treks. The two-hour rides (€65) follow mountain tracks then proceed through the town to visit the dolphin Fungi before galloping back along the beach. The half-day trek (€100) goes to Ventry Strand. ⊠ *Baile na Buaile* ☎ *086/821–1225* ⊕ *www.dingle horseriding.com.*

CEANN TRÁ (VENTRY)

8 km (5 miles) west of An Daingean (Dingle Town) on R561.

The next town after An Daingean along the coast, Ceann Trá has a small outcrop of pubs and small grocery stores (useful, since west of Dingle Town you'll find few shops of any kind), and a long sandy beach. Between Ventry and Dún Chaoin (Dunquin) are several interesting archaeological sites on the spectacular cliff-top road along Ceann Sléibhe (Slea Head).

GETTING HERE AND AROUND

It takes about 10 minutes to reach Ventry by car on R561 from Dingle Town. Take extra care when driving these narrow scenic roads, which can be busy with cyclists, walkers, and sometimes sheep, as well as many other drivers unfamiliar with the locality.

EXPLORING

Dunbeg Fort. Perched on the very edge of a Dingle Bay cliff, and set in the small district of Fagan (which is part of the larger township of Ventry), this small, well-weathered fort was an important Iron-Age defensive promontory site, inhabited from about AD 800 until around 1200. Its drystone mound was defended against cattle raiders by four earthen rings—note the *souterraine* (underground) escape route, by the entrance. In addition, there are a number of archaeological artifacts here to interest the time traveler.

There is a 10-minute audiovisual show in the adjacent visitor center, but just as fascinating is the building itself, a modern replica of the drystone construction of the *clocháns* (pronounced cluk-*awns*), the famous prehistoric "beehive" cells first used by hermit monks in the Early Christian period. Beside it is a typical *naomhóg* (pronounced "na-*vogue*"), a tarred canvas canoe, resting upside down.

About 1 km (half a mile) farther on is another parking lot, and an interesting group of clocháns can be visited (€2 fee to resident farmer), built of drystone and set on the southern slopes of Mt. Eagle looking out directly across the sea to Skellig Michael. Far from being only prehistoric relics, as the signposts claim, clocháns were being built until a century ago; wood was scarce and stone abounded, so you'll find more than 400 of them between Ceann Sliebne and Dún Chaoin. ⊠ *Fahan, 8 km (5 miles) west of Ventry* ☎ *066/915–9070* ⊕ *www.dunbegfort.com* 🖾 *€3.50* ⊙ *Easter–Apr., daily 9:30–7; May–Oct., 9:30–8; Nov.–Easter, phone in advance.*

SPORTS AND THE OUTDOORS

BEACHES

Ventry Beach. Ventry Beach (or Ventry Strand) is just southwest of the village of Ceann Trá (Ventry). This lovely stretch of golden sand, said by many to be one of Ireland's most beautiful beaches, runs for 8 km (5 miles) and is part of the Dingle Way walking route. There is a dune system with a small lake, wetlands, and a reed swamp, and abundant wildlife. In July and August it attracts families and swimmers. **Amenities:** food and drink; lifeguards; parking (no fee); toilets; water sports. **Best for:** surfing; swimming; walking; windsurfing.

CEANN SLÉIBHE (SLEA HEAD)

16 km (10 miles) west of An Daingean (Dingle Town), 8 km (5 miles) west of Ceann Trá.

From the top of the towering cliffs of Ceann Sléibhe (pronounced kye-own *shla*-va) at the southwest extremity of the Dingle Peninsula, the view of the Blasket Islands and the Atlantic Ocean is guaranteed to stop you in your tracks. Alas, Slea Head—to use its English name—has become so popular that tour buses, barely able to negotiate the narrow road, are causing traffic jams, particularly in July and August. Coumenole, the long sandy strand below, looks beautiful and sheltered, but swimming here is dangerous. This treacherous stretch of coast has claimed many lives in shipwrecks—most recently in 1982, when a large cargo boat, the *Ranga,* foundered on the rocks and sank. In 1588 four ships of the Spanish Armada were driven through the Blasket Sound; two made it to shelter, and two sank. One of these, the *Santa Maria de la Rosa,* is being excavated by divers.

GETTING HERE AND AROUND

Slea Head is a 10-minute drive from Ventry on R559.

SPORTS AND THE OUTDOORS

BEACHES

Clogher Strand. This dramatic, windswept stretch of rocks and sand visible below the coast road to the north of Slea Head is not a safe spot to swim, but it's a good place to watch the ocean dramatically pound the rocks when a storm is approaching or a gale is blowing. It may be familiar from David Lean's 1970 film *Ryan's Daughter*. **Amenities:** none. **Best for:** solitude; sunset; walking. ⊠ *Dunquin.*

DÚN CHAOIN (DUNQUIN)

13 km (8 miles) west of Ceann Trá, 5 km (3 miles) north of Ceann Sléibhe (Slea Head).

Once the mainland harbor for the Blasket islanders (when there *were* islanders, as the Blaskets are deserted now), Dún Chaoin is at the center of the Gaeltacht, and attracts many students of Irish language and folklore.

GETTING HERE AND AROUND

Dunquin is on R559 at the western end of the Dingle Peninsula. Bus Éireann's Dingle–Ballyferriter service (Monday and Thursday only) calls at Dunquin.

EXPLORING

FAMILY

Fodor's Choice
★

Blasket Centre. The Blasket Islands (An Bhlaskaoid Mhóir) are among Ireland's most extraordinary islands. The largest visible from Ceann Sleibne is the Great Blasket, inhabited until 1953. The Blasket islanders were great storytellers and were encouraged by Irish linguists to write their memoirs. The Blasket Centre explains the heritage of these islanders and celebrates their use of the Irish language with videos and exhibitions. ☎ *066/915–6444* ⊕ *www.heritageireland.ie* ⊟ *€4* ☉ *Apr.–Oct., daily 10–6.*

Dún Chaoin's Pier. Signposted from the main road, Dún Chaoin's pier is surrounded by cliffs of colored Silurian rock, more than 400 million years old and rich in fossils. Down at the pier you can see *naomhóga* (open fishing boats traditionally made of animal hide stretched over wooden laths and tarred) stored upside down. Three or four men walk the curraghs out to the sea, holding them over their heads. Similar boats are used in the Aran Islands, and when properly handled they're extraordinarily seaworthy.

Kruger's Pub. Long frequented by artists and writers, including Brendan Behan, Kruger's Pub is known as Dunquin's social center. ☎ *066/915–6127.*

Louis Mulcahy Pottery. Overlooking the beach is the pottery studio of one of Ireland's leading ceramic artists. Louis Mulcahy produces large pots and urns that are both decorative and functional. You can watch the work in progress and buy items at workshop prices. There is also a coffee shop. ⊠ *Clogher Strand, Ballyferriter* ☎ *066/915–6229* ⊕ *www. louismulcahy.com* ☉ *Daily 9:30–6.*

GREAT BLASKET ISLAND

The Great Blasket, which measures roughly 3 km by 1 km (2 miles by ½ mile), has no traffic, no pub, no hotel, and no electricity. Yet this island—centerpiece of the An Bhlaskaoid Mhóir (Blasket Islands)—is one of the most memorable places in Ireland to visit.

Until 1954 a small community of hardy fisherfolk and subsistence farmers eked out a living here.

Today, visitors are usually attracted by the literary heritage of the island—the Irish-language writings of Tomás Ó Criomhthain, Muiris Ó Suilleabhain (also known in English as Tomás O'Crohán and Maurice O'Sullivan), and Peig Sayers—but what makes people return is something else: a rare quality of light and an intense peace and quiet in beautiful, unspoiled surroundings.

The inadequacy of the existing piers limits visitors to the island to a maximum of about 400 per day, a figure that is reached only rarely, with the average less than 200. Most visitors stay for three or four hours, walking, sketching, or taking photographs.

The silence strikes you at once. The seabirds, stonechats, and swallows sound louder than on the mainland; sheep graze silently on the steep hillside. The simple domestic ruins are very touching; you do not need to know the history to work out what happened to their owners (most departed for other places, with many settling in Springfield, Massachusetts).

■ TIP➔ Before you go, read Maurice O'Sullivan's Twenty Years a-Growing, a fascinating account of a simple way of life that has only recently disappeared on the Blaskets. For an overview of the island's more recent history, read Hungry for Home: Leaving the Blaskets: A Journey from the Edge of Ireland by Cole Moreton.

GETTING HERE AND AROUND

These days it takes only 15 minutes from Dún Chaoin (Dunquin) Pier to make the 3-km (2-mile) crossing of the Blasket Sound, but even on a calm day the swell can be considerable. In summer the island is usually accessible most days; in winter the island can be cut off for weeks.

ESSENTIALS

Transportation Contacts Blasket Islands Ferry. The ferry makes the 15-minute crossing from Dún Chaoin Pier to the island daily from April through September, weather permitting, and costs €20 round-trip. The same company runs a four-hour ecotour around the island with the option of landing for €40.

Almost as memorable as the boat ride to the Skellig isles is the excursion out to the unspoiled Blasket Islands, a favorite escape for poets and writers.

Sightings of seals are pretty well guaranteed. ⊕ *www.blasketislands.ie* 🎫 *€20.*
Dingle Bay Charters. A long-established charter boat company that sails from An Daingean (Dingle Town) to the Blaskets is Dingle Bay Charters. The trip usually takes about 40 minutes and costs €30 for a round-trip ticket. They also run a three-hour guided ecotour (€40). ✉ *Dingle Town* ☎ *066/915–1344* ⊕ *www. dinglebaycharters.com.*

TRALEE

67 km (41 miles) west of Ballyferriter, 50 km (31 miles) northeast of An Daingean (Dingle Town) on R559.

County Kerry's capital and its largest town, Tralee (population 22,700), is a superb springboard to explore the adjoining Dingle Peninsula. It is also the transportation hub of the region. As such, people used to joke that the only good things to come out of Tralee were the buses shuttling travelers elsewhere. To a certain extent, that is still the case: apart from some Georgian town houses near the museum there is not much of architectural or antiquarian interest. Modern renovations, including concrete piazzas (which attract crowds of drinkers on weekends) have done little to ameliorate Tralee's medium-size-town-with-little-character feel. Accordingly, however, there are no tourists, so the local folk have been fashioning some worthwhile sights, including the town museum, and the Siamsa Tíre—the National Folk Theatre of Ireland—which stages impressive dances and plays based on Irish folklore.

The town has long been associated with the popular Irish song "The Rose of Tralee," the inspiration for the annual Rose of Tralee International Festival (*see Planning: When to Go*). The second week of August, Irish communities worldwide send young women to join native Irish competitors; one of them is chosen as the Rose of Tralee. Visitors, musicians, and entertainers pack the town then. A two-day horse-racing meet—with seven races a day—runs at the same time, which contributes to the crowds.

GETTING HERE AND AROUND

Tralee is at the junction of the N21 from Limerick (about an hour and a half away), the N21 and N22 from Killarney (about half an hour away), and the N86 from Dingle (an hour and 15 minutes away). It is also the terminus for the train from Dublin (the trip takes three hours and 45 minutes) and is well served by buses from Shannon Airport, Limerick, Killarney, and Dingle. There is a bus service that circles the town every hour, mainly to facilitate students: visit the tourist information office for details.

ESSENTIALS

Transportation Contacts Tralee Bus Station ✉ *John Joe Sheehy Rd.* ☎ *066/716–4700.* **Tralee Rail Station** ✉ *Casement Station, John Joe Sheehy Rd.* ☎ *066/712–3522* 🌐 *www.irishrail.ie/tralee.*

Visitor Information Tralee Tourist Office ✉ *Ashe Memorial Hall, Denny St.* ☎ *066/712–1288* 🌐 *www.discoverireland.ie/TraleeTIO.*

EXPLORING

FAMILY **Kerry County Museum.** Tralee's major cultural attraction traces the history of Kerry's people since 5000 BC, using dioramas and an entertaining audiovisual show. You can also walk through a life-size reconstruction of a Tralee street of the Middle Ages. ✉ *Ashe Memorial Hall, Denny St.* ☎ *066/712–7777* 🌐 *www.kerrymuseum.ie* 🎫 *€5* ⏲ *June–Aug., daily 9:30–5:30; Sept.–May., Tues.–Sat. 9:30–5.*

WHERE TO STAY

$ HOTEL Fodor's Choice ★ 🏨 **Ballygarry House Hotel.** A mile and a half outside town, this family-run hotel with 6 acres of gardens and supremely stylish guest rooms is an excellent choice if you're touring by car. **Pros:** next to a woodland amenity area for runners; spa and outdoor hot tub. **Cons:** no shops or cafés within walking distance. [$] *Rooms from: €90* ✉ *Leebrook* ☎ *066/712–3322* 🌐 *www.ballygarryhouse.com* 🛏 *53 rooms, 11 suites* 🍴 *Breakfast.*

$ B&B/INN 🏨 **Brook Manor Lodge.** Set against a dramatic backdrop of the Slieve Mish Mountain, this large double-gable country house is a nice option, both as a touring base and for avoiding Tralee's notoriously snarled-up traffic and late-night noise. **Pros:** quiet and spacious; friendly personal welcome; delicious breakfast. **Cons:** no nearby village. [$] *Rooms from: €110* ✉ *Fenit Rd. (R558)* ☎ *066/712–0406* 🌐 *www.brookmanorlodge.com* 🛏 *8 rooms* 🍴 *Breakfast.*

NIGHTLIFE AND THE ARTS

The Abbey Inn. Slap-bang in the middle of the town center, this two-story inn stays open late seven nights a week, and has live music and DJs, big-screen sports, and poker classics. ☒ *Bridge St.* ☎ *066/712–3390* ⊕ *www.theabbeyinntralee.com.*

National Folk Theater of Ireland (Siamsa Tíre). Language is no barrier to the supremely colorful entertainment offered by this theater, which re-creates traditional rural life through music, mime, and dance. ☒ *Town Park* ☎ *066/712–3055* ⊕ *www.siamsatire.com* ☼ *Shows June–Aug., Mon.–Sat. at 8:30 pm; May and Sept., Tues.–Sat. at 8:30 pm.*

SPORTS AND THE OUTDOORS
BICYCLING

Tralee Bicycle Supplies. A top outfitter in town, this is a handy place to rent bicycles. ☒ *Strand St.* ☎ *066/712–2018.*

GOLF

Fodor'sChoice ★ **Ballybunion Golf Club.** President Bill Clinton will be eternally associated in Irish golfers' minds with this revered course. In fact, there's even a brass statue of him teeing off in the nearby village, to commemorate his visit here in 1999. On the shore of the Atlantic where the Shannon estuary meets the open sea, Ballybunion has the huge dunes of Lahinch without the blind shots. It's no pushover, but every hole is pleasurable. Watch out for "Mrs. Simpson," a double fairway bunker on the 1st hole, named after the wife of Tom Simpson, the architect who remodeled the course in 1937. (Tom Watson did the same in 1995.) The Cashen Course, which opened in 1985, was designed by Robert Trent Jones Sr. and currently is available at a bargain rate if you've paid for a round on the Old Course. ☒ *Sandhill Rd., Ballybunion* ☎ *068/27146* ⊕ *www. ballybuniongolfclub.ie* ☒ *Old Course, May–Sept. €180, Oct.–Apr. €95; Cashen Course, May–Sept. €65, Oct.–Apr. €55; €200 to play both on same day* ⅃ *Old Course: 18 holes, 6568 yards, par 72; Cashen Course: 18 holes, 6306 yards, par 70. Practice area, driving range, caddies, caddy carts, club rental, catering* ☼ *Visitors: weekdays.*

Tralee Golf Club. Tralee is what all modern-golf-course architects *wish* they could do in the States: find unspoiled, seaside links and route a course on it that's designed for the modern game. This is an Arnold Palmer–Ed Seay design that opened in 1984, and the location is fantastic—cliffs, craters, dunes, and the gale-blowing ocean. Don't let the flat front 9 lull you to sleep—the back 9 can be a ferocious wake-up call. ☒ *West Barrow, Ardfert* ☎ *066/713–6379* ⊕ *www.traleegolfclub. com* ☒ *May–Sept. €175, Apr. and Oct. €85, Nov.–Mar. €55* ⅃ *18 holes, 6975 yards, par 72. Practice area, putting green, caddies, caddy carts, club rental, catering* ☼ *Visitors: Mon., Tues., and Thurs.–Sat.*

NORTH KERRY AND SHANNONSIDE

Until several decades ago, Shannon meant little more to most people—if it meant anything at all—than the name of the longest river in Ireland and Great Britain, running from County Cavan to Limerick City in County Clare. But mention Shannon nowadays and people think

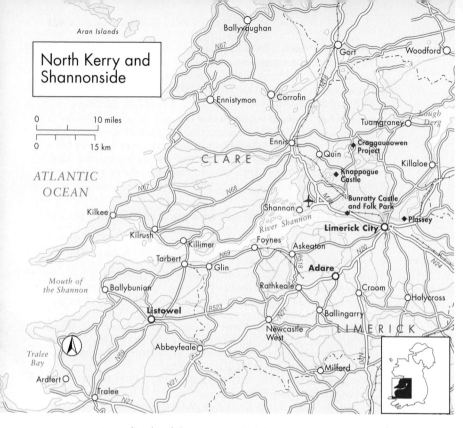

North Kerry and Shannonside

| 0 | 10 miles |
| 0 | 15 km |

ATLANTIC
OCEAN

immediately of the airport, which has become western Ireland's principal gateway. In turn, what also comes to mind are many of the glorious sights of North Kerry and Shannonside: Adare, sometimes called "Ireland's Prettiest Village" (and the neighboring Adare Manor, a grand country-house hotel); and Limerick City, which attracts visitors tracing the memories so movingly captured in Frank McCourt's international best seller *Angela's Ashes*.

If you want to leapfrog over the Shannon Estuary and head directly into the West of Ireland, head north on N69 18 km (11 miles) from Listowel to Tarbert, the terminus for the **Shannon Ferries** (☎ 065/905–3124 ⊕ *www.shannonferries.com*) crossing to Killimer in West Clare, a convenient 20-minute shortcut to the West. The Shannon River is 273 km (170 miles) long, and its magnificent estuary stretches westward for another 96 km (60 miles) before reaching the sea.

ADARE

19 km (12 miles) southwest of Limerick City, 82 km (51 miles) northeast of Tralee.

Fodor's Choice On the banks of the River Maigue, this once-upon-a-time-ified village
★ dotted with thatch cottages is famed as one of Ireland's prettiest spots.

Perhaps it's more correct to say it's actually one of England's: the place was given a beauty makeover by a rich Anglo lord, the third earl of Dunraven, in the 1820s and 1830s, in an effort to create the "perfect rustic village." To a great extent, he succeeded.

Few local feathers were ruffled since Dunraven won goodwill by restoring many villagers' houses. Playing into the mid-19th-century vogue for romantic rusticity, the earl "picturesquely" restored many of the town's historic sights, including the remains of two 13th-century abbeys, a 15th-century friary, and the keep of the 13th-century **Desmond Castle** (now the centerpiece of a private golf course). Adjacent to the Adare Heritage Centre you'll find the **Trinitarian Priory,** founded in 1230 and now a convent. From the main bridge (where you can best view the castle), head to the **Augustinian Priory** and its gracious cloister. The most fetching time-burnished allure is provided by Adare's stone-built, thatch-roof cottages, often adorned with colorful, flower-filled window boxes and built for the earl's estate tenants. Some now house boutiques selling Irish crafts and antiques, along with a fine restaurant called the Wild Geese. Adare Manor, an imposing Tudor–Gothic Revival mansion, which was once the grand house of the Dunraven peerage, is now a celebrated hotel; on its grounds you can view two 12th-century ruins, the **St. Nicholas Chapel** and the **Chantry Chapel.**

GETTING HERE AND AROUND

Adare is on the main road (N21) between Tralee and Limerick, just over an hour from Tralee and about 20 minutes from Limerick. The parking lot is in the center of town behind the Adare Heritage Centre; parking here is free. Buses on the Limerick–Tralee route stop at the Heritage Centre.

EXPLORING

Adare Heritage Centre. This center is home to an array of helpful facilities, including a restaurant and three retail outlets (one sells sweaters, another crafts, and the third heraldry items). There is also an exhibition on Adare's history since 1223, complete with a 15-minute audiovisual display, but some may feel it is not worth the extra fee. Guided tours of Desmond Castle (June–September; €6) can be booked in advance online, and leave the center by bus. ⊠ *Main St.* ☎ *061/396–666* ⊕ *www. adareheritagecentre.ie* ⊠ *Heritage center free, exhibition €4.50* ☉ *Daily 9–6. Historical exhibition Mar.–June, daily 9–5; July–Sept., daily 9–5:30; Oct.–Dec., weekdays 9–4, weekends 11–4.*

WHERE TO EAT AND STAY

$$$

MODERN
EUROPEAN

Fodor'sChoice
★

✕ **The Wild Geese.** There's a charming, old-world atmosphere in the series of small dining rooms in this low-ceiling thatch cottage, one of the prettiest in a village famed for its fairy-tale looks. Co-owner and chef David Foley uses the best local produce to create imaginative and seriously good dishes. Try roast rack of lamb with a potato-and-garlic gratin, or pan-seared Castletownbere scallops with Clonakilty black pudding and deep-fried leeks. Lobster—grilled with snow peas and shallots and topped with a chive mayonnaise—is a popular summer option. The house dessert platter for two lets you sample all desserts, including the fantastic homemade ice cream. For a real bargain, try the Sunday lunch (€25 for three courses). The restaurant is opposite the Dunraven Arms. [$] *Average main: €25* ✉ *Rose Cottage, Main St.* ☎ *061/396–451* 🌐 *www.thewild-geese.com* ⏲ *Closed Mon. and 3 wks in Jan. No dinner Sun. No lunch Tues.–Sat.*

$$$$ HOTEL Fodor's Choice ★ 🏨 **Adare Manor Hotel.** Play king or queen for a day at this spectacular (and, interestingly, American-owned) Victorian Gothic mansion, once the abode of the earls of Dunraven and still a wonderland, thanks to 840 acres of French-style gardens outside and the 36-foot-high, 100-foot-long Minstrels' Gallery inside. **Pros:** an amazing and unforgettable Gothic experience; golf course, designed by Robert Trent Jones Sr., is one of Ireland's best. **Cons:** dominated by golfers; even the rich find it expensive. [$] *Rooms from: €550* ☎ *061/396–566* ✉ *Limerick Rd.* 🌐 *www.adaremanor.ie* 🛏 *57 rooms, 5 suites* 🍴 *Breakfast.*

$$ HOTEL 🏨 **Dunraven Arms Hotel.** Charles Lindbergh stayed here in Room 6 while he advised on the nearby Shannon Airport's design and he might still cotton to this tranquil, antiques-adorned landmark, established as a coach stop in 1792, even though it is now somewhat over-restored and generic. **Pros:** the staff make it a memorable Irish experience; in a pretty village. **Cons:** interior design verges on bland international; expensive for what it is. [$] *Rooms from: €170* ✉ *Main St.* ☎ *061/605–900* 🌐 *www.dunravenhotel.com* 🛏 *56 rooms, 30 suites* 🍴 *Breakfast.*

$$$ B&B/INN Fodor's Choice ★ 🏨 **Mustard Seed at Echo Lodge.** This is the small country hotel of your dreams: a Victorian yellow-stucco jewel set atop a small hill overlooking Ballingarry, a village that time forgot, deep in rural Ireland, yet only 13 km (8 miles) southwest of Adare. **Pros:** quirky, memorable, and extremely comfortable; acclaimed restaurant. **Cons:** in the middle of nowhere; cock crows at dawn. [$] *Rooms from: €180* ✉ *Village Center, Ballingarry* ☎ *069/68508* 🌐 *www.mustardseed.ie* 🛏 *14 rooms, 2 suites* ⏲ *Closed last 2 wks in Jan.* 🍴 *Breakfast.*

SPORTS AND THE OUTDOORS

GOLF

Adare Manor Golf Course. Connected with the celebrated Adare Manor luxury hotel (⇨ *see Where to Stay*), this parkland stretch is on the ancestral estate of the Earl of Dunraven. Its immediate success was virtually guaranteed by the international profile of its designer, Robert Trent Jones Sr. The front 9 is dominated by an artificial 14-acre lake with a $500,000 polyethylene base. It's in play at the 3rd, 5th, 6th, and 7th holes. The dominant hazards on the homeward journey are the River Maigue and the majestic trees, which combine to make the par-5 18th one of the most challenging finishing holes imaginable. ✉ *Limerick Rd.* ☎ *061/395–044* 🌐 *www.adaremanor.com* 🎫 *May–Sept. €125, Oct. and Apr. €95, Nov. €90, Dec.–Mar. €80* ⛳ *18 holes, 7453 yards, par 72. Practice area, caddies, caddy carts, club rental, catering* ⏲ *Visitors: daily.*

SHOPPING

Adare Cottage Shop. A gem of a gift and craft shop, this is found cozily ensconsced in one of the village's thatched cottages. ✉ *Main St.* ☎ *061/396–422.*

As cute as a Fisher-Price toy village, Adare is a thatched-roof jewel laid out with characteristics that conjure up the English rather than the Irish countryside.

George Stacpoole. Head here to find a nice selection of antiques large and small, plus books. ⊠ *Main St.* ☎ *061/396–409.*

Lucy Erridge's. This cottage boutique has Irish-made jewelry and fine ladies' wear from Irish designer labels. ⊠ *Main St.* ☎ *061/396–898.*

LIMERICK CITY

19 km (12 miles) northeast of Adare, 198 km (123 miles) southwest of Dublin.

Before you ask, there's *no* direct connection between Limerick City and the facetious five-line verse form known as a limerick, which was first popularized by the English writer Edward Lear in his 1846 *Book of Nonsense.* The city, at the head of the Shannon estuary and at the intersection of a number of major crossroads, is an industrial port and the republic's third-largest city (population 75,000). If you fly into or out of Shannon Airport, and have a few hours to spare, do take a look around. The attractions around the cathedral and the castle are linked by a riverside footpath, while the western part of the town center is dominated by mid-18th-century buildings with fine Georgian proportions. What's more, the city has undergone considerable revitalization since the days recounted in Frank McCourt's famed childhood memoir, *Angela's Ashes.* Limerick was named Ireland's first national City of Culture for 2014, so expect some ongoing intensified activity in the arts sector.

Looming over Adare's Desmond Castle is the regal Adare Manor Hotel, once home to the town's lord of the manor, the Earl of Dunraven.

GETTING HERE AND AROUND

Limerick is a major gateway to the Southwest and the West of Ireland, and is linked to Dublin by the M7 motorway (the drive is about 2½ hours). Cork is two hours south on the N20. A tunnel under the city links the Cork road with the road to Shannon Airport (N19) and the N18 to Galway (about an hour and a half). There are excellent express bus links to these cities and to Killarney. Limerick has a rail link to Dublin via Limerick Junction, and a smaller commuter line travels via Ennis to Galway (two hours). Citylink buses, bookable online only, serve Dublin, Shannon, and Cork airports.

Within the city there is a regular bus service for shoppers connecting the historic center with the newer Crescent Shopping Centre at Dooradoyle.

In Limerick it's advisable to use a multistory parking garage, as on-street parking can be hard to find. If you do get lucky, you'll have to become familiar with "disk" parking regulations, which involve buying a ticket (or disk) for around €2 an hour from a machine or a shop and displaying it. Beware: car-clamper officers are active!

ESSENTIALS
TOURS

Angela's Ashes Tour. St. Mary's Action Centre offers a tour (on request, with advance booking) encompassing places in the city associated with Frank McCourt's *Angela's Ashes*. ☎061/318–106 ⊕ *www.iol.ie/~smidp/*.

Limerick City Tours. City walks are available from June to September, and can be booked at the tourist office. ☎087/235–1339.

Limerick Civic Trust. To appreciate Limerick's 18th-century heyday, take a 45-minute guided tour of the Georgian Quarter with Limerick Civic Trust. Included on the tour is the Georgian House and Garden *(see Exploring)*. Other tours visit Medieval Limerick and the Masonic Lodge. Advance booking is required. ⊠ *People's Park entrance, Pery Sq.* ☎ *061/313–399* ⊕ *www.limerickcivictrust.ie* ✉ *€6* ⊘ *Weekdays 11 and 2, or by arrangement for small groups.*

Red Viking Tours. Orientation tours of the city are given on a semi-open-top bus, giving fine views of the River Shannon. ⊠ *Liddy St.* ☎ *061/394–033* ⊕ *www.redvikingtours.com.*

Transportation Contacts Limerick Bus Station ⊠ *Colbert Station Forecourt, Parnell St.* ☎ *061/313-333.* **Limerick Rail Station** ⊠ *Colbert Station, Parnell St.* ☎ *061/315-555.*

Visitor Information Limerick City Tourist Office ⊠ *Arthur's Quay* ☎ *061/317-522* ⊕ *www.discoverireland.ie.*

EXPLORING

There has been a huge investment in Limerick's inner city in recent years, and it is finally starting to pay off. The snarled-up traffic that used to bedevil the city center has been eased by the opening of an east–west tunnel that takes much of the heavy traffic along with its noise and pollution under the River Shannon instead of across it. An attractive riverside walk now leads visitors past the Hunt Museum to the city's medieval center which is sited, as in Paris, on a small island surrounded by rushing water. Bars and restaurants have started to colonize the quiet riverside quays between the Hunt Museum and the Absolute Hotel, while the Georgian Quarter now has a focal point in One Pery Square, an elegant 18th-century town house converted into a popular hotel, spa, and bistro. The good-natured sporting passion of Limerick's rugby supporters is legendary, and if you are in town on a match day it will never be forgotten. At any time of year, Limerick's reputation for friendliness is a genuine phenomenon: total strangers will engage you in conversation on the street—relax and enjoy!

TOP ATTRACTIONS

Hunt Museum. In the Old Customs House on the banks of the Shannon in the city center, the Hunt Museum has the finest collection of Celtic and medieval treasures outside the National Museum in Dublin. Ancient Irish metalwork, European objets d'art, and a selection of 20th-century European and Irish paintings—including works by Jack B. Yeats—are on view. A café overlooks the river. ⊠ *Rutland St.* ☎ *061/312-833* ⊕ *www.huntmuseum.com* ✉ *€5 (free Sun.)* ⊘ *Mon.– Sat. 10–5, Sun. 2–5.*

FAMILY **King John's Castle.** First built by the Normans in the early 1200s, King John's Castle still bears traces on its north side of a 1691 bombardment. If you climb the drum towers (the oldest section), you'll have a good view of the city and the Shannon. Inside, a 22-minute audiovisual show illustrates the history of Limerick and Ireland; an archaeology center has three excavated, pre-Norman houses; and two exhibition centers display scale models of Limerick from its founding in AD 922.

⊠ *King's Island* ☎ *061/360–788* ⊕ *www.shannonheritage.com* ⊠*€8* ⊙ *Daily 10–4:30 (to 5 Mar.–Oct.).*

St. Mary's Cathedral. Limerick is a predominantly Catholic city, but the Protestant St. Mary's Cathedral is the city's oldest religious building. Once a 12th-century palace—pilasters and a rounded Romanesque entrance were part of the original structure—it dates mostly from the 15th century. The black-oak carvings on misericords in the choir stalls are from this period. ⊠ *Bridge St.* ☎ *061/310–293* ⊕ *www.cathedral.limerick.anglican. org* ⊙ *Mon.–Sat. 9:30–4:30; open for services only Sun.*

WORTH NOTING

Cruises Street. An inviting pedestrian thoroughfare, this street has chic shops and occasional street entertainers. It's on the opposite side of O'Connell Street from the Arthur's Quay Shopping Centre.

FAMILY **The Frank McCourt Museum.** This imposing redbrick building dating from 1834 was once the school of American-Irish author, Frank McCourt (1930–2009), best known for his "misery memoir" (later a movie) of an impoverished Limerick childhood. See the actual classroom in use in the 1930s, posters and photographs of the Pulitzer Prize–winning author, and a replica of the McCourt home in this modest but oddly touching tribute. ⊠ *Hartstonge St.* ☎ *061/319–760* ⊕ *www. frankmccourtmuseum.com* ⊠ *€3* ⊙ *Weekdays 11–4:30, weekends 2–4.*

Georgian House and Garden. To see how people lived in Limerick's 18th-century heyday, head to this tall, narrow row house, which has been meticulously restored and filled with furnishings from the period. Out back, the garden has been planted in a manner true to the time. ⊠ *Tontine Bldgs., 2 Pery Sq.* ☎ *061/314–130* ⊕ *www.gerogianhouseandgarden.ie* ⊠ *€6* ⊙ *Weekdays 10–4, weekends by appointment.*

Limerick City Gallery of Art. With a major redevelopment of its home in the historic Carnegie Building completed in 2012, this is one of Ireland's finest galleries of contemporary art. Along with a small but charming permanent collection of Irish art, it also mounts exhibits of international contemporary art, and has a small café. ⊠ *Carnegie Bldg., Pery Sq.* ☎ *061/310–633* ⊕ *gallery.limerick.ie* ⊠ *Free* ⊙ *Mon., Wed., and Fri. 10–5:30; Tues. 11–5:30; Thurs. 10–8:30; Sat. 10–5; Sun noon–5.*

O'Connell Street. Here you can find Limerick City's main shopping area, which consists mostly of modest chain stores. However, the street lies one block inland from (east of) the Arthur's Quay Shopping Centre, through which it can be reached. Along with the futuristic tourist information center, this was part of a successful campaign to develop the Shannonside quays.

WHERE TO EAT AND STAY

$$ ✕ **Brasserie One.** The location—a second-floor room in one of Limer-
IRISH ick's finest Georgian houses, recently converted into a luxury hotel—is
Fodors Choice naturally elegant, but the aim here is to serve robust, brasserie-style
★ food in informal surroundings. Cream walls and gilt mirrors are lighted by small crystal sconces and candelabra, while Victorian spoon-back chairs lend a raffish air. Fresh local produce is simply and imaginatively presented: duck-leg praline with duck-liver pâté, or a tart of onion

and Cashel blue cheese, followed by grilled rib-eye steak with fries and béarnaise sauce. Don't miss the rhubarb crème brûlée with butter shortbread for dessert. The bar food, served in a comfortable lounge on the ground floor, is also excellent. $ *Average main: €22* ⊠ *1 Pery Sq.* ☎ *061/402–402* ⊕ *www.oneperysquare.com/brasserie-restaurants* ⊘ *No dinner Sun. and Mon.*

$ **Absolute Hotel and Spa.** Exciting architecture and design and a great
HOTEL   site on a river bend in Limerick's medieval center make this a great choice for city sightseeing, dining, and shopping. **Pros:** on the riverside path; museums and bars within 100 yards; short walk to shopping area; reasonably priced food and drink; spacious rooms. **Cons:** secure private parking is limited (€5 for nearby public parking); not easy to find. $ *Rooms from: €90* ⊠ *Sir Harry's Mall* ☎ *061/463–600* ⊕ *www.absolutehotel.com* ⤳ *99 rooms* ⦿ *No meals.*

$ **Jurys Inn.** Clean, airy, and in good shape (unlike some of Limerick's
HOTEL   other inner-city lodgings), this big, well-run hotel is part of a popular budget chain. **Pros:** good value for couples and families; reliable hotel chain with consistently helpful staff. **Cons:** totally bland experience; "per room" pricing policy makes it expensive for singles; hugely popular with large groups of partying Irish people. $ *Rooms from: €85* ⊠ *Lower Mallow St., Mount Kennett Pl.* ☎ *061/207–000* ⊕ *www.limerickcityhotel.ie* ⤳ *141 rooms* ⦿ *Breakfast.*

$$ **One Pery Square.** One of Limerick's finest Georgian houses—a tall
HOTEL   redbrick structure with classical cut-stone portico, overlooking leafy People's Park—has been converted into a sumptuous boutique hotel with a high reputation for attentive service. **Pros:** genuinely stylish; private parking; excellent service. **Cons:** you need to book well in advance. $ *Rooms from: €165* ⊠ *1 Pery Sq.* ☎ *061/402–402* ⊕ *www.oneperysquare.com* ⤳ *20 rooms* ⦿ *No meals.*

NIGHTLIFE AND THE ARTS

Curragower Pub. Across the river from King John's Castle, this is a favorite haunt of music students from Limerick University. You can hear good traditional music nightly from May through September, and Wednesday through Saturday in winter. ⊠ *Clancy's Strand* ☎ *061/321–788* ⊕ *www.curragower.com.*

Dolan's Pub. A lively waterfront spot, Dolan's has traditional Irish music every night, and dancing classes from September to May. Dolan's Warehouse, under the same management and in the same location, is a live-music venue with top national and international acts. ⊠ *3–4 Dock Rd.* ☎ *061/314–483* ⊕ *www.dolans.ie.*

The Locke Bar & Oyster House. Set on the riverside, this is one of Limerick's oldest bars, dating from 1724, and has live music every night. It's also a great place for outdoor drinking in summer. ⊠ *3 George's Quay* ☎ *061/413–733* ⊕ *www.lockebar.com.*

Nancy Blake's Pub. There's traditional music at this pub year-round Sunday–Wednesday from 9 pm. ⊠ *19 Denmark St.* ☎ *061/416–443.*

William G. South's Pub. An old-fashioned pub, this one is typical of the age of Frank McCourt's *Angela's Ashes.* There's no music, but drop by for hearty bar food or a drink. ⊠ *4 Quinlan St.* ☎ *061/318–850.*

SHOPPING

DEPARTMENT STORES

Brown Thomas. Limerick has a branch of Ireland's upscale department store. ⊠ *O'Connell St.* ☎ *061/417–222* ⊕ *www.brownthomas.com.*

Debenham's. A midrange department store, this is one of Limerick's largest. ⊠ *O'Connell St.* ☎ *1890/946–779.*

Dunnes Stores. This is, perhaps, Ireland's favorite department store chain. ⊠ *Harvey's Quay* ☎ *061/431–200* ⊕ *www.dunnesstores.ie.*

Penneys. Also known as Primark, Penneys sells inexpensive clothing; it's a great place for low-price rain gear. ⊠ *137 O'Connell St.* ☎ *061/416–033.*

SPECIALTY SHOPS

Arthur's Quay. A small indoor shopping mall near the tourist office, Arthur's Quay has a fine choice of Irish crafts and knitwear. ☎ *061/419–888.*

The Milk Market. Occupying a historic site two blocks east of Arthur's Quay (ask at the Tourist Information Office), the Milk Market is a vibrant weekend market selling virtually everything but milk. On Friday the emphasis is on fashion and crafts; Saturday is the big food day, featuring many local artisan producers; and Sunday adds antiques and a flea-market ambience into the mix of food and handcrafts. ⊠ *Cornmarket Row* ☎ *061/214–782* ⊕ *www.milkmarketlimerick.ie* ⊗ *Fri. 10–4, Sat. 8–4, Sun. 11–4.*

O'Mahony's. Known for its good selection of Irish interest, this shop has been selling books since 1902. ⊠ *120 O'Connell St.* ☎ *061/418–155.*

COUNTY CLARE, GALWAY CITY, AND THE ARAN ISLANDS

WELCOME TO COUNTY CLARE, GALWAY CITY, AND THE ARAN ISLANDS

TOP REASONS TO GO

★ **Ancient Aran:** Spend at least one night on one of the Oileáin Árainn (Aran Islands), three outposts of Gaelic civilization, which still have a strong whiff of the "old ways"—and not just the whiff of turf smoke.

★ **Foot-Tapping in Doolin and Ennis:** Tap your foot in time to "trad" Irish music— those heavenly strains of traditional Irish folk music— and sip your pint as you while away an afternoon and maybe an evening as well, in one of Doolin's or Ennis's noted music bars.

★ **High-Style Galway:** A university town and booming, buzzing hive of activity, with great theaters, bars, nightlife, shopping, and restaurants, Galway is the city that loves to celebrate and, as one of Europe's fastest-growing towns, has much to offer.

★ **The Mighty Cliffs of Moher:** Rising straight out of the sea to a height of 700 feet, these cliffs—towering imposingly over the wild Atlantic—give you a new understanding of the word "awesome."

1 **County Clare.** Set with postcard-perfect villages like Ballyvaughan and Lisdoonvarna, the lunar landscape of the Burren, and the towering Cliffs of Moher, County Clare is pure tourist gold. Surfers have discovered the huge waves off Lahinch and the Cliffs of Moher. Its capital, Ennis, is renowned for its annual Fleadh Nua (Fla Noo-a), in which hundreds of singers, dancers, and players of traditional Irish music compete for prizes, while more informal sessions take place in Doolin's three pubs.

GALWAY

WESTMEATH

N17

Athenry

Ballinasloe

N6

N6

M18

Kilcolgan

Loughrea

N65

Kinvara

N66

Portumna

Gort

M18

Lough
Derg

Crusheen

TIPPERARY

Newmarket
on Fergus

N7

M18

Limerick

LIMERICK

GETTING ORIENTED

Once you cross the Shannon in Limerick City you are officially in the West of Ireland. The rocky limestone plateau known as the Burren, dotted with megalithic remains, overlooks Galway Bay, lined with characterful villages like Ballyvaughan and Kinvara, and cradling the Aran Islands that lie across its entrance. Galway City is one of Ireland's liveliest, with a compact historic center bursting with artistic energy and a lively pub culture. This is the place to organize your trip to the Aran Islands, three windswept rocky islands where Irish is still spoken, with an almost total absence of traffic.

2 **Galway City.** This is easily the liveliest city in Ireland after Dublin. You've got to get your fill of its buzz when visiting, best done by checking out its eye-popping "g" Hotel, stylish new boutiques and crafts shops, and dazzling weekend festivals.

3 **Aran Islands.** An hour or less away via ferry are the ageless Aran Islands. Once famed for their isolation, they are now disturbed a bit by some 60,000-plus curious visitors every summer, but even so they retain a distinctive identity, with traditional communities where Irish is still the daily language.

8

Galway Camera

Updated by Alannah Hopkin

The west of Ireland is the most westerly seaboard in Europe, and the part of Ireland least influenced by its neighbor to the east, England. Galway and West Clare are where the Irish go to reconnect with their heritage, whether by practicing their jigs at the Fleadh Nua folk festival, enjoying "the craic" at the Lisdoonvarna Matchmaking Festival, visiting the ancient megalithic tombs of the Burren, or trading news with a Gaeltacht (Irish-speaking) resident. Wherever you go in the West, you'll not only see, but more important *hear*, how the best of traditional Ireland survives.

Even a Jackeen (Dubliner) will tell you that this area is distinctly different from the rest of Ireland and is bent on retaining its unspoiled, rugged way of life. With much of nature's magnificence on display—the majestic Cliffs of Moher, the rocky Burren, and the sublime Aran Islands—it's easy to see why. Visitors continue to relish the unique thrill of standing high above the pounding Atlantic, watching seabirds reel below, as the numerous Cliffs of Moher posts on YouTube demonstrate.

This area lies at the far western extremity of Europe, facing its nearest North American neighbors across thousands of miles of the Atlantic Ocean. Although other areas of Ireland were influenced by Norman, Scots, or English settlers, the West largely escaped systematic resettlement and, with the exception of the walled town of Galway, remained purely Irish in outlook. No wonder these western regions have the highest concentration of Irish-speaking communities and the best traditional musicians in the republic.

West Clare, in fact, is the guardian of Ireland's musical traditions, where people still flock to learn new dance steps and fiddle riffs. The hub of the area remains Galway, the city that loves to celebrate. Saunter through its naturally festive, pedestrianized center and the city's many pubs, and you will find proof of Galway's reputation for good times. Not far away is the town of Ennis, and villages like Doolin and Kinvara, also noted as trad-music hot spots.

Visitors will find, particularly in western County Galway, the highest concentration of Gaeltacht communities in Ireland, with roughly 40,000 native Irish speakers and the country's first Irish-language TV station based in tiny An Spidéal (Spiddle), a suburb of Galway City. You'll see plenty of signs printed in Irish only. This is especially the case out on the isolated Oileáin Árainn (Aran Islands), where many Irish schoolchildren have their first experience of a place where Irish is the main language during summer camps. These limestone islands are actually geological extensions of the mainland expanse known as the Burren, a craggy landscape rich in megalithic remains, unique geological formations, rare flora and fauna, and a rich history of myth and legend.

COUNTY CLARE, GALWAY CITY, AND THE ARAN ISLANDS PLANNER

WHEN TO GO

Be prepared for rain any time of year. Average rainfall in the rest of Ireland is between 31 inches and 47 inches, but here on the west coast, it can exceed 79 inches. Take comfort from the thought that while it may be damp, it is never really cold. In the coldest months, January and February, the mean daily temperature is around 6°C (43°F). That said, Ireland—like much of Northern Europe—has been experiencing colder winters in recent years with significant snow accumulations and prolonged below-normal temperatures. In the warmest months, July and August, average temperatures are around 15°C (60°F). ■TIP→ If you're looking for authentic fun and festivity, skip St. Patrick's Day in March and plan to visit between May and September; yes, it's peak season, but you'll have your choice of local food and music festivals and you'll be able to catch a local hurling or Gaelic football match in the heated lead-up to All-Ireland finals in September.

FESTIVALS AND EVENTS

For visitors and locals alike, festivals provide both free entertainment and a chance to meet people from all backgrounds who share a common interest.

MAY **Fleadh na gCuach.** During the first weekend in May, the scenic village of Kinvara hosts the hugely popular traditional music festival, Fleadh na gCuach (the Cuckoo Fleadh), attracting musicians from far and wide. ⊠ *Main St., Kinvara, Co. Galway* ☎ *091/637–137* ⊕ *www.kinvara.com.*

JULY **The Willie Clancy Summer School.** Named for legendary piper Willie Clancy, and held in Miltown Malbay every July since 1973, the week-long Willie Clancy Summer School is Ireland's largest summer school for traditional musicians, with 135 daily workshops and a full program of recitals, concerts, and dances open to the public. ⊠ *Co. Clare* ⊕ *www.willieclancyfestival.com.*

Galway Arts Festival. Held the middle two weeks of July, the Galway Arts Festival hosts an international array of the best of contemporary theater, film, rock, jazz, traditional music, poetry readings, comedy acts, and visual arts exhibitions. ⊠ *Co. Galway* ⊕ *galwayartsfestival.com.*

The Galway Races. Running for seven consecutive days at Galway Racecourse, starting from the last Monday in July each year, the Galway Races are *the* place for Irish socialites to be seen. More competitive than the thoroughbred horse races is the sport of "Spot the Celebrity" (if you can recognize one under the required fanciful hat). ⊠ *Galway, Co. Galway* ⊕ *www.galwayraces.com.*

AUGUST   **Criuinniú na mBád.** Kinvara's Criuinniú na mBád, meaning "the gathering of the boats," in late August commemorates a time when the Galway hookers—red sailed, black hulled timber boats—hauled turf to trade in Galway. Great opportunity to see restored craft in all their glory and remember a time gone by. ⊠ *Kinvara, Co. Galway* ⊕ *www.kinvara.com.*

SEPTEMBER   **Lisdoonvarna Matchmaking Festival.** Held in September in the spa town of Lisdoonvarna in the Burren, Europe's largest matchmaking fest is a monthlong festival of music, dancing, craic, and—if you're lucky—love! ⊠ *Lisdoonvarna, Co. Clare* ⊕ *www.matchmakerireland.com.*

PLANNING YOUR TIME

There's much to see between Clare and Galway, so prioritizing your time means prioritizing your interests: if you want quintessential Irish castles, scenery, music, and history, spend all three days in Clare, allowing yourself time to stop and explore everything from Bunratty to the Burren and Craggaunowen to the Cliffs, as well as a night on the Aran Islands. If you want a little city buzz with your scenery, save the third day for vibrant Galway City—rich in history and buzzing with artistic activity and festivals—and plan to spend the night so that you can sample the lively pub and music scene.

IF YOU HAVE 3 DAYS

Dedicate your first day to castles, *crannógs* (early Celtic dwellings), and *craic* (a good time). Begin with the magnificently restored Bunratty Castle, flanked by a lively folk village and a famous old riverside pub, Durty Nelly's. Allow a few hours to visit nearby Craggaunowen, where you'll find a medieval castle, a ring fort, Crannóg, and the Brendan Boat—a leather hulled boat built to reenact the voyage of St. Brendan, an early Christian monk said to have discovered America centuries before Columbus. Then, continue the castle theme with a quick visit to Knappogue Castle, a restored medieval manor, home to medieval banquets and beautiful walled gardens—perfect for a predinner stroll. Finally, end the day in Ennis, with a hearty dinner, live music, and a well-earned pint.

Go coastal on Day 2 with an early start and a scenic drive that hugs the coastline of West Clare, taking in the seaside villages of Spanish Point, Lahinch, and Liscannor; the awe-inspiring Cliffs of Moher; the musical hot spot of Doolin; the beach of Fanore (noted for its edible seaweed); and the megalithic remains and limestone landscape of the Burren. ■TIP→ The drive along the coast from Doolin to Ballyvaughan (past Fanore and Black Head) is a favorite Sunday drive for Clare locals and especially lovely. If you're looking for a lively music scene, spend the night in a B&B in Doolin or Ballyvaughan. Otherwise, consider spending the night on the Aran Islands where you'll experience a taste of old Ireland—slow and peaceful. Take the ferry from Doolin; you can book a B&B with your ferry ticket.

Day 3 depends on your interests; if you want more of the raw quiet and countryside that inspired Irish writers like J. M. Synge, Liam O'Flaherty, and Máirtín Ó Díreáin, explore the forts and folklore of the Aran Islands. If you're ready for a little noise and excitement, head for Galway City, park the car, and take in the buzz on the streets. If you can, spend the night to sample Galway's lively and informal fine dining and music scene.

GETTING HERE AND AROUND

AIR TRAVEL

Flights to the Oileáin Árainn (Aran Islands) leave from Aerfort Chonamara (Connemara Airport) at Inverin, 30 km (18 miles) west of Galway on the R336, served by a minibus from Galway City (€3). There are hourly flights in July and August, and off-peak there are up to half a dozen flights a day. These flights call at all three Aran Islands. The journey takes eight minutes and costs about €50 round-trip. The airline will book a B&B for you when you book your flight. In summer (June–August) you can take a scenic flight over the coast and the islands daily at noon (€60). Ask about other special offers at the time of booking.

Carriers Aer Arann Islands ☎ 091/593–034 ⊕ www.aerarannislands.ie.

AIRPORTS The West's most convenient international airport is Shannon, 25 km (16 miles) east of Ennis. Flying time from Dublin is about 30 minutes. Connemara Airport at Inverin, which is 27 km (16 miles) west of Galway on R336, services the Aran Islands. Ask about transport to the airport when buying your ticket: there is usually a courtesy bus from the center of Galway City.

Airport Information Aerfort Chonamara/Connemara Airport ☎ 091/593–034 ⊕ www.aerarannislands.ie. **Shannon Airport** ☎ 061/712–000 ⊕ www.shannonairport.com.

AIRPORT TRANSFERS From Shannon Airport you can pick up a rental car to drive into the West, or you can take a bus to Galway or Ennis. Connemara Airport (for flights to the Aran Islands) is 27 km (16 miles) from Galway City, and is accessible by shuttle bus (€3).

BOAT AND FERRY TRAVEL

FROM KERRY TO CLARE The Tarbert–Killimer Ferry leaves every hour on the half hour and takes 20 minutes to cross the Shannon Estuary from North County Kerry to West County Clare; this saves you a 137-km (85-mile) drive through Limerick City. It is very handy if you are heading from the Ring of Kerry or Dingle area to the Cliffs of Moher. The ferry runs every day of the year except Christmas and costs €18 one-way, €28 round-trip. (Ferries return from Killimer every hour on the hour.)

Boat Companies Shannon Ferries ☎ 065/905–3124 ⊕ www.shannonferries.com.

TO THE ARAN ISLANDS The spell of the famed Oileáin Árainn (Aran Islands) is such that many travelers can't resist their siren call and make for the first ferry leaving from Doolin, which offers rates of €10 one-way. However, locals will tell you to hedge your bets and wait until you are in Galway City to make arrangements; that way, you can postpone your trip if the weather looks bad. You can do a day trip, leaving the city at 9:30 or noon and returning by 6:30, but staying overnight is more rewarding. Everyone wants to go to the islands, and it is made as easy as possible to organize by the various transport companies. They are all genuine and licensed: no one is going to rip you off. Book at the Galway Tourist Information Office in Forster Place, where the ferry companies and Aer Arann Islands have concessions.

The standard ferry deal on offer in Galway City is €25 round-trip and €7 for bus transfer to the ferry port at Ros an Mhíl (Rossaveal). Look out for money-saving offers that may include bed-and-breakfast accommodations, free transfers to Ros an Mhíl or Connemara Airport (both 40 minutes away), bicycle rental on the islands, or a ferry-out, flight-back plan. There are three different ferry operators, and tickets are not transferable, so check the return sailing times of your operator when you get on board. If you opt for the five-minute flight, for safety reasons, you (yes, you; not your bags!) will be weighed at check-in, and allocated an appropriate seat.

Boat Companies Aran Island Ferries ⊠ *Tourist Information Office, Forster St., Eyre Sq., Center, Galway City, Co. Galway* ☎ *091/568–903* ⊕ *www. aranislandferries.com.* **Doolin Ferries** ⊠ *Doolin Pier, Co. Clare* ☎ *065/707–4455* ⊕ *www.doolinferries.com.* **O'Brien Line** ⊠ *Doolin Pier, Co. Clare* ☎ *065/707–5555* ⊕ *www.obrienline.com.*

BUS TRAVEL

Bus Éireann runs several Expressway buses into Ennis and Galway City—the principal depots in the region—from Dublin, Cork City, and Limerick City. All buses mentioned are Bus Éireann (which includes Expressway) unless specified otherwise. Expect bus rides to last about one hour longer than the time it would take you to travel the distance by car. The Cliffs of Moher, Lisdoonvarna, Doolin, Liscannor, and Lahinch have two scheduled services a day (in each direction) from Galway, and only one from Ennis. Guided tours of the Cliffs of Moher and the Burren leave from the bus stations in Galway City and Ennis. Citylink operates frequent buses between Galway City and Shannon Airport as well as Dublin and Dublin Airport.

Bus Depots Ennis Bus Station ⊠ *Station Rd., Ennis, Co. Clare* ☎ *065/682–4177.* **Galway Bus Station** ⊠ *Station Rd., Galway City* ☎ *091/562–000.*

Bus Lines Bus Éireann ☎ *01/836–6111 in Dublin* ⊕ *www.buseireann.ie.* **Citylink** ☎ *091/564–164* ⊕ *www.citylink.ie.*

CAR TRAVEL

To do full justice to this region, you really need a car—and a good map: don't rely on GPS for the many small by-roads.

The 219-km (136-mile) Dublin–Galway trip takes about three hours. From Cork City take N20 through Mallow and N21 in the Limerick City direction, following signs for the tunnel (toll €1.90) before reaching the city, to join the N18/M18 Ennis–Galway road. The 209-km

(130-mile) drive from Cork to Galway takes about three hours. From Killarney the shortest route to cover the 193 km (120 miles) to Galway (three hours) is to take N22 to Tralee, then N69 through Listowel to Tarbert and ferry across the Shannon Estuary to Killimer. From here, join N68 in Kilrush, and then pick up N18 in Ennis.

ROAD CONDITIONS

The West has good, wide main roads (National Primary Routes) and better-than-average local roads (National Secondary Routes), both known as "N" routes. There is one stretch of motorway, the M18 north of Shannon, that bypasses Ennis and finishes north of Gort. If you stray off the beaten track on the smaller Regional ("R") routes, particularly in West Clare, you may encounter some challenging roads. Narrow and twisty, they are also used by hikers and cyclists from April to October, as well as local traffic (which can take the form of huge trucks serving the local agricultural co-ops, school buses, and tractors). The speed limits on these Regional routes is a whacking great 80 kph (50 mph), even for trucks and buses, but use your common sense and adjust your speed accordingly. ■ TIP → If traffic builds up behind you, it is customary to signal to the left and slow down or pull over to let the locals fly by. Your kind gesture will usually be acknowledged with a nod or a wave.

TAXI TRAVEL

Taxis operate on the meter for journeys of up to 30 km (22 miles). For longer journeys, agree on the fare in advance. A Shannon Airport to Galway City journey will cost you about €120.

Taxi Companies AAA Taxis ⊠ *Ennis, Co. Clare* ☎ *065/689–2999.* **Big O Taxis** ⊠ *21 Upper Dominick St., Galway City, Co. Galway* ☎ *091/585–858* ⊕ *www. bigotaxis.com.* **Burren Taxis** ⊠ *Ennis, Co. Clare* ☎ *065/682–3456.* **Galway Taxis** ⊠ *Galway City, Co. Galway* ☎ *091/561–111* ⊕ *www.galwaytaxis.com.*

TRAIN TRAVEL

The region's main rail stations are in Galway City and Ennis. Trains for Galway and Ennis leave from Dublin's Heuston Station (on different lines). Trains run direct to Galway via Athlone, taking about three hours, while for Ennis (which is reached via the Cork and Tralee line) you must change twice. Journey time from Limerick to Ennis is 40 minutes (€11.80 round-trip), while Limerick City to Galway takes about two hours (€20 round-trip).

Train Information Ennis Station ☎ *065/684–0444.* **Galway Station–Ceannt Railway Station** ☎ *091/564–222.* **Irish Rail–Iarnod Éireann** ☎ *01/703-2132 (in Dublin)* ⊕ *www.irishrail.ie.*

For more information on getting here and around, see Travel Smart Ireland.

RESTAURANTS

Because the West provinces have a brief high season—from mid-June to early September—and a quiet off-season, it doesn't have as broad a choice of small, owner-operated restaurants as do other parts of Ireland. Often the best place to eat is a local hotel—Gregans Castle Hotel near Ballyvaughan, for example. But some places landmark the region, including Moran's Oyster Cottage in Kilcolgan near Galway City, where the fare is simple, served in traditional pub surroundings,

8

but sea-leaping fresh. At the other extreme are more dazzling experiments, like when you hit a grand blowout place like the superb formal restaurant at Dromoland Castle. For truly adventurous contemporary Irish cooking, head to happening Galway, where you'll find it at such showcases as Kirwan's Lane, the Malt House, and Ard Bia at Nimmo's; the town center is so compact you can meander around and read the menus on display outside before making your choice.

HOTELS

Some of Ireland's finest country-house and castle hotels are in this area. Dromoland Castle, between Shannon Airport and Ennis, provides a standard of luxury that you should experience at least once, if you can stretch your budget. Star country-house destinations include the creeper-clad Georgian house known as Gregans Castle Hotel, a tranquil retreat with views of the Burren and Galway Bay, and the more modest but also charming Ballinalacken Castle, a shooting lodge set in 100 acres of wildflower meadows next to the ruins of an O'Brien castle. Other memorable destinations include the cliff-top Moy House at Lahinch, and, in total contrast, the exuberantly glitzy "g" Hotel in Galway. Among the newer, mid-range hotels, Vaughan Lodge in Lahinch and The Twelve at Bearna offer exceptional standards of comfort and design. Indoor pools and tennis courts are the exception rather than the rule in this region, where business is largely seasonal and the emphasis is on outdoor pursuits. *Note: During peak events, such as the Galway Festival Race Week, hotel rates in Galway shoot up.*

Hotel reviews have been shortened. For full information, visit Fodors.com.

WHAT IT COSTS IN EUROS				
	$	$$	$$$	$$$$
Restaurants	under €19	€19–€24	€25–€32	over €32
Hotels	under €120	€120–€170	€171–€210	over €210

Restaurant prices are the average cost of a main course at dinner or, if dinner is not served, at lunch. Hotel prices are the lowest cost of a standard double room in high season.

TOURS

Barratt Tours. Barratt Tours offers a day trip by coach visiting the Cliffs of Moher, the Burren, and Galway Bay (€27). Book at Ennis Tourist Information Office, which is also the departure point. The tour runs on Saturday only from February to April, and daily from early May to mid-September. ☎ *087/237–5986* ⊕ *www.4tours.biz.*

Burren Wild Walks. Burren Wild Walks runs a daily bus tour from Galway Bus Station that travels through Kinvara and along the coast of Galway Bay to a farm (with shop and café) in the village of Oughtmama in the Burren (€25). Here you stop for a one-hour guided walk of this unique landscape (included in tour price) before returning to the bus and continuing to the Cliffs of Moher. Burren Wild Walks also has daily guided walks starting from its farm at 10:40 (see website for directions) lasting

1½ hours (€10). Longer afternoon walks with qualified guide John A. Connolly, starting at 12:15 and lasting 2½ hours (€25), can be booked by appointment. ☎ *087/877–9565* ⊕ *www.burrenwalks.com.*

Ennis Tourist Information Office ⊠ *Arthur's Row, Ennis, Co. Clare* ☎ *065/682–8366* ⊕ *www.discoverireland.ie/Places-To-Go/Clare.*

Galway City Tourist Information Office. Come here for details of walking tours of Galway. ⊠ *Forster Pl., Center, Galway City, Co. Galway* ☎ *091/537–700* ⊕ *www.discoverireland.ie/Places-To-Go/galway.*

Galway City Walking Tour and Pub Crawl. Enthusiastic young locals offer a free two-hour tour departing daily at 12:30 from the Skeff Bar in Eyre Square, and will show you their city and tell you its tales—including the dramatic story of the Lynch family who gave the world the verb "to lynch." It's a taster for the Galway Pub Crawl, a great introduction to Galway's nightlife, run every evening by the same outfit, departing from the same venue at 8 pm (€15 per head, including drinks, entries, and entertainment). ☎ *087/784–9035* ⊕ *www.galwaypubcrawl.ie* ⊠ *Walking tour free; pub crawl €15.*

Healy Tours. Healy Tours offers historical sightseeing tours with professional guides, including the Cliffs of Moher and the Burren. Tickets, €25 each, can be purchased from the Galway TIO or on the tour bus. All tours run from mid-March to late September only. Book in advance or from 9 am on the day at Galway City's TIO. Buses leave from the bus station opposite. ☎ *091/770–066* ⊕ *www.healytours.ie.*

Heart of Burren Walks. Heart of Burren Walks has guided walks leaving the Burren Display Center in Kilfenora with author Tony Kirby between April and August on Tuesday, Thursday, Saturday, and Sunday at 2:30 and lasting more than two hours (€20), visiting local antiquities and exploring the region's geology, including the Burren's biggest turlough (seasonal lake). Phone or check the website to confirm the schedule. ☎ *065/682–7707* ⊕ *www.heartofburrenwalks.com* ⊠ *€20.*

Lally Tours. A vintage double-decker bus departs every 90 minutes from Eyre Square, offering hourly tours of Galway City from 10:30 am until 4:30 pm from mid-March to October; tickets cost €12. They also offer daily tours to the Cliffs of Moher and the Burren (each €25), returning to Galway around 4:30. ☎ *091/562–905* ⊕ *www.lallytours.com.*

O'Neachtain Day Tours. Daily tours (€25) with professional guides are available to the Cliffs of Moher and the Burren (each €25), returning to Galway around 4:30. ☎ *091/553–188* ⊕ *www.ontours.biz.*

Salthill TIO ☎ *091/520–500.*

VISITOR INFORMATION

Fáilte Ireland provides free information service, tourist literature, and an accommodations booking service at its TIOs (tourist information offices). The following offices are open all year, generally weekdays 9–6, daily during the high season: Aran Islands (Inis Mór), Ennis, and Galway City. Other TIOs that operate seasonally, generally weekdays 9–6 and Saturday 9–1, are open as follows: Cliffs of Moher (April–October; a concession within the main visitor center, which opens year-round) and Salthill (May–September).

Information on Kinvara, Galway City, and the Aran Islands can be found at Discover Ireland (⊕ *www.discoverireland.ie/places-to-go/galway*). Information on the main sights in County Clare—Ennis, the Burren, and the Cliffs of Moher—can be found at Shannon Region Tourism (⊕ *www.discoverireland.ie/places-to-go/clare*).

COUNTY CLARE

County Clare claims two of Ireland's unique natural sights: the awesome Cliffs of Moher and the stark, mournful landscape of the Burren, which hugs the coast from Black Head in the north to Doolin and the Cliffs of Moher in the south. Yet western County Clare (West Clare for short) is widely beloved among native Irish for a natural phenomenon significantly less unique than these: its sandy beaches. Recently the surf that rolls in on these beaches, and on the rocky shores of the Aran Islands, has been attracting big-wave enthusiasts from all over the world. So whether you're looking for inimitable scenery, the perfect wave, or just a lovely beach to plunk down on to relax in the sun (or rain!) for a few hours, you can delightfully find it in West Clare.

This journey begins within minutes of Shannon Airport at Bunratty Castle and Folk Village, where you can kick-start your visit to the West of Ireland with castles and a famed pub.

BUNRATTY CASTLE

18 km (10 miles) west of Limerick City on N18 road to Shannon Airport.

GETTING HERE AND AROUND

Bunratty is about 15 minutes from Limerick's center on the N18 Galway road. Most Bus Éireann buses to Shannon Airport also stop at Bunratty: confirm when boarding.

EXPLORING

Bunratty Castle and Folk Park. Two of those rare attractions that appeal to all ages, Bunrattty Castle and Folk Park manage to be both educational and fun. Built in 1460, the castle—a stolid, massive affair with four square keep towers—has been fully restored and decorated with 15th- to 17th-century furniture and furnishings. It gives wonderful insight into the life of those times. As you pass under the walls of Bunratty, look for the three "murder holes" that allowed defenders to pour boiling oil on attackers below.

Bunratty medieval banquets are world famous and held nightly (subject to demand) at 5:30 and 8:45; the cost is €59.95. You're welcomed by Irish colleens in 15th-century dress, who bear the traditional bread of friendship. Then you're led off to a reception, where you'll quaff mead made from fermented honey, apple juice, clover, and heather. Before sitting down at long tables in the candlelighted great hall, you can don a bib. You'll need it, because you eat the four-course meal medieval-style: with your fingers. Serving "wenches" take time out to sing a few ballads or pluck harp strings. The banquets may not be authentic, but

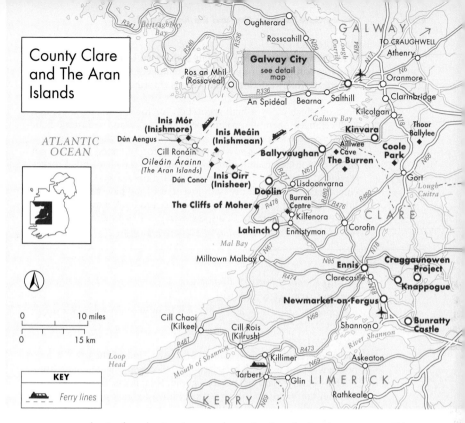

County Clare and The Aran Islands

they're fun; they're also popular, so book as far in advance as possible. The website (⊕ *www.shannonheritage.com*) has good deals for advance booking, and includes a combination of castle visits and banquets.

On the castle grounds the quaint Bunratty Folk Park re-creates a 19th-century village street and has examples of traditional rural housing. Exhibits include a working blacksmith's forge; demonstrations of flour milling, bread making, candle making, thatching, and other skills; and a variety of farm animals. An adjacent museum of agricultural machinery can't compete with the furry and feathered live exhibits. If you can't get a reservation for the medieval banquet at the castle, a *ceilí* folk-music session known as the Traditional Irish Night, held nightly May to September at 7 pm (€49.95) at the Folk Park, is the next-best thing. The program features traditional Irish dance and song and a meal of Irish stew, soda bread, and apple pie. Prices for banquets and entrance to Bunratty are generously discounted if you buy online. ⊠ *Bunratty, Co. Clare* ☎ *061/360–788* ⊕ *www.shannonheritage.com* ☜ *€15* ⊙ *Sept.– May, daily 9–5:30, last entry at 4; June–Aug., daily 9–6, last entry at 5*

Durty Nelly's. No visit to Bunratty is complete without a drink in Durty Nelly's, an old-world (but touristy) pub beside the Folk Park entrance. Its fanciful decor has inspired imitations around the world. ☎ *061/364–072.*

WHERE TO EAT

$ ╳ **J.P. Clarkes Country Pub.** Look left at the bend before Bunratty Castle
MODERN IRISH   and you will see a grouping of low thatched cottages, all gleaming
with fresh whitewash. Inside the various cottages you will find both an
upmarket seafood restaurant, Gallagher's, and its affiliated gastropub,
both of which enjoy a high reputation for food. The pub is an airy,
high-ceilinged open-plan room, the rustic beams and sandstone floor
smartly contrasting with snazzy leather-upholstered chairs. Its menu is
an eclectic crowd-pleaser, with something for all tastes, from the pot
of mussels in garlic and white wine cream to the char-grilled turkey
steak with fiery pepper sauce, or char-grilled rib-eye steak with chunky
chips. Such is its popularity (kids love it, too, and have their own nifty
little menu) that you would be well advised to book a table online on
weekends and holidays. $ *Average main: €14* ✉ *Bunratty, Co. Clare*
☎ *061/363–363* ⊕ *www.gallaghersofbunratty.com.*

KNAPPOGUE

21 km (13 miles) north of Bunratty.

GETTING HERE AND AROUND
Knappogue Castle is about 20 minutes from Bunratty on minor roads;
the route is well marked.

EXPLORING

FAMILY   **Knappogue Castle.** With a name that means "hill of the kiss," Knappogue is one of Ireland's most beautiful medieval tower-house castles.
A 15th-century MacNamara stronghold, Knappogue Castle was renovated in the Victorian era and fitted with storybook details. Restored
by a wealthy American family, the castle has now been retro-ed in
15th-century style.

By day you can enjoy a castle tour, including the walled garden, which
looks like something out of a medieval Book of Hours. In the evenings
(April–October) it hosts fun and fabulous medieval banquets (€44.50).
You're first greeted at the main door by the Ladies of the Castle who
escort you to the Dalcassian Hall, where you enjoy a goblet of mead
(honey wine), listen to harp and fiddle, then proceed to the banqueting
hall for a four-course meal, great Irish choral music, and a theatrical
set-piece in which the Butler and the Earl argue the virtues of Gallantry.
As an added allure, the castle looks spectacular when floodlighted.
✉ *R649, 5 km (3 miles) southeast of Quin* ☎ *061/360–788* ⊕ *www.*
shannonheritage.com 🎫 *€6* ☉ *May–Aug., daily 10–4:30.*

CRAGGAUNOWEN PROJECT

6 km (4 miles) northeast of Knappogue Castle.

GETTING HERE AND AROUND
Craggaunowen Castle is about eight minutes from Knappogue Castle
on minor roads.

EXPLORING

FAMILY **Craggaunowen Castle.** It's a strange experience to walk across the little wooden bridge above reeds rippling in the lake into Ireland's Celtic past as a jumbo jet passes overhead on its way into Shannon Airport—1,500 years of history compressed into an instant. But if you love all things Celtic, you'll have to visit the Craggaunowen Project. The romantic centerpiece is Craggaunowen Castle, a 16th-century tower house restored with furnishings from the period. Huddling beneath its battlements are two replicas of early Celtic-style dwellings. On an island in the lake, reached by a narrow footbridge, is a clay-and-wattle *crannóg,* a fortified lake dwelling; it resembles what might have been built in the 6th or 7th century, when Celtic influence still predominated in Ireland. The reconstruction of a small ring fort shows how an ordinary soldier would have lived in the 5th or 6th century, at the time Christianity was being established here. Characters from the past explain their Iron Age (500 BC–AD 450) lifestyle, show you around their small holding stocked with animals, and demonstrate crafts skills from bygone ages. ✉ *Signposted off road to Sixmilebridge, about 10 km (6 miles) east of Quin Town, Sixmilebridge* ☎ *061/360–788* 🌐 *www.shannonheritage.com* 🎟 *€8* 🕐 *Easter–Aug., daily 10–4:15.*

NEWMARKET-ON-FERGUS

13 km (8 miles) north Shannon Airport on M18.

A small town in County Clare, Newmarket-on-Fergus is chiefly remarkable as the village nearest the famed hotel of Dromoland Castle, formerly the home of Lord Inchiquin, chief of the O'Brien clan.

8

GETTING HERE AND AROUND

Newmarket-on-Fergus is on the R472 between Shannon Airport and Ennis, 32 km (19 miles) west of Limerick. Head west on the M18, take exit 11, and follow the signs. There is a scheduled Bus Éireann service from Shannon Airport taking 25 minutes.

WHERE TO STAY

$$ B&B/INN Fodor's Choice ★ 🏨 **Carrygerry Country House.** Modest and gabled, this 1793 country house is only 8 km (5 miles) from Shannon Airport, but a world apart, with views across the plains where horses calmly graze, as they have done for centuries, to the distant Shannon estuary. **Pros:** real Irish character; abundant wildlife; birdsong; peace and quiet; excellent restaurant. **Cons:** tricky to find; bar food only some nights. [$] *Rooms from: €140* ✉ *Carrygerry* ☎ *061/360–500* 🌐 *www.carrygerryhouse.com* 🛏 *11 rooms* 🕐 *Call to confirm dinner Sun.–Tues. (bar food only when quiet).*

$$$$ HOTEL FAMILY Fodor's Choice ★ 🏨 **Dromoland Castle Hotel and Country Estate.** Dating from the 19th century and now one of Ireland's grandest hotels, Dromoland bristles with towers rising up over a picture-perfect lake like a storybook illustration from King Arthur. **Pros:** real old-fashioned luxury; friendly, helpful staff; genuine castle experience; beautiful grounds. **Cons:** golfers spoiling the romantic idyll; some standard rooms are a little ordinary; you'll want to stay much longer than you can afford. [$] *Rooms from: €454* ✉ *5 km (3 miles) west of Newmarket-on-Fergus, signposted from N18* ☎ *061/368–144* 🌐 *www.dromoland.ie* 🛏 *12 suites, 87 rooms.*

While the opulent interiors of Dromoland Castle will wow all guests, the hotel's parklands are even more enticing thanks to a vast array of sporting facilities.

SPORTS AND THE OUTDOORS

GOLF

Dromoland Golf Course. One of the most scenic courses in the country, Dromoland Golf Club is set in a 700-acre estate of rich woodland, rolling open pasture, and natural water features on the grounds of the famed Dromoland Castle hotel. The parkland course has streams and a natural lake that leaves little room for error on a number of holes. Views of the castle, especially from the 7th hole, are little short of entrancing. Improvers take note: a state-of-the-art golf academy can help you to improve your swing. ✉ *5 km (3 miles) west of Newmarket-on-Fergus, signposted from N18* ☎ *061/368–444* ⊕ *www.dromoland.ie* ✉ *Fees: Apr.–Sept. €77, Oct.–Mar. €68, twilight and early bird €63* 🏌 *18 holes, 6824 yards, par 72. Practice area, driving range, caddies, buggies, catering* ⊗ *Visitors: daily (some restrictions).*

ENNIS

9½ km (6 miles) north of Newmarket-on-Fergus on M18.

A major crossroads and a convenient stop between the West and the Southwest, Ennis is the main town of County Clare. The pleasant market town has an attractively renovated, pedestrian-friendly center, bisected by the fast-flowing River Fergus.

GETTING HERE AND AROUND

Ennis is served by exits 12, 13, and 14 from the M18 Limerick–Galway motorway. It is 37 km (23 miles) northwest of Limerick. There are Expressway bus connections to Cork (3 hours), Limerick (1 hour, 15 minutes), Shannon Airport (1 hour), and Galway (1 hour, 15 minutes). From Ennis there are two Bus Éireann buses a day to the Cliffs of Moher Visitor Centre (50 minutes); the same bus also calls at Lisdoonvarna and Doolin. Ennis Railway Station can be accessed from Limerick City and Galway on the Irish Rail commuter route linking Limerick and Galway; the trip to Limerick takes 40 minutes, and Galway is one hour, 20 minutes.

TOURS

Local bus company Barratt Tours offers a guided tour of the Cliffs of Moher and the Burren leaving from the tourist information office in Ennis (€27; Saturday only from March 21 to early May, then Saturday–Thursday from early May to mid-September). Or opt for taxis whose rates for long trips can be affordable if shared by four people.

ESSENTIALS

Visitor Information Ennis Tourist Office ✉ *Arthur's Row, Town Center* ☎ *065/682–8366* 🌐 *www.discoverireland.ie/places-to-go/clare.*

WHERE TO STAY

$$ HOTEL **Old Ground Hotel.** Enter the original ivy-clad 18th-century manor house (which adjoins a new wing) and you'll see that old-fashioned charm meets contemporary élan at this winning entry to Ennis's hotel stakes—rest on the lobby's inviting brocade sofas as you study paintings on the wall from the hotel's striking collection of new Irish artists, including Donald Teskey, Cecil Maguire, and Mick O'Dea. **Pros:** genuine sense of history; handy town-center location; lively bistro and restaurant. **Cons:** extremely busy bar; hard to find initially due to town's one-way system (follow signs for Town Centre Hotels). [$] *Rooms from: €120* ✉ *O'Connell St.* ☎ *065/682–8127* 🌐 *www.flynnhotels.com* 🛏 *1 suite, 82 rooms.*

$$ HOTEL **Temple Gate Hotel.** Before its conversion, this was a Gothic-style convent, and remnants of its previous existence (including the chapel, which is now a banquet hall) give character to this bright, modern hotel in the town center. **Pros:** more character than most modern hotels; good town-center location. **Cons:** can get very busy with local functions at weekends; standard rooms a bit small; worth upgrading to executive if you need space. [$] *Rooms from: €129* ✉ *The Square* ☎ *065/682–3300* 🌐 *www.templegatehotel.com* 🛏 *70 rooms* 🍴 *Breakfast.*

NIGHTLIFE AND THE ARTS

NIGHTLIFE

Although Ennis is not as fashionable as, say, Galway, it's one of the West's traditional-music hot spots. You're likely to hear sessions at many pubs, but keep in mind that sessions don't necessarily take place every night and that the scene is constantly changing. Phone ahead to check whether a session is happening.

Cruise's. A warm and lively bar in Queen's Hotel, a long-established town landmark near the old Friary, Cruise's has a romantic atmosphere with a roaring fire, candles on the tables, and live music most nights from about 9:30 pm. ✉ *Abbey St.* ☎ *065/682–8963.*

Knox's Pub & Bistro. A Victorian-style high street bar with traditional plate-glass shop front in the town center, Knox's serves bar food until 9 pm, offers live traditional music from 9:30 pm Wednesday–Sunday, and a late bar until 2 am Thursday–Saturday. ⊠ *18 Abbey St.* ☏ *065/682–2871* ⊕ *www.knoxs.ie.*

Michael Kerin's Bar. Known as Mickey's Bar to locals, and far and wide for its Friday-night traditional music sessions, Michael Kerin's is the oldest family-run bar in town and a classic Irish pub in every sense—welcoming, frequented by locals, and home to a decent pint. ⊠ *Lifford Rd.* ☏ *065/682–0582.*

THE ARTS

Glór–Irish Music Centre. Ennis's venue for large concerts, the Glór–Irish Music Centre, hosts competitions of Irish music, song, and dance—including May's wildly popular Fleadh Nua (⊕ *www.fleadhnua.com*)—and big-name touring acts on the Irish music scene, including Mary Black, Paul Brady, and Aslan. There's also an art gallery, café, and free parking. ⊠ *Causeway Link* ☏ *065/684–3103* ⊕ *www.glor.ie.*

Fleadh Nua. Held in Ennis around a long Bank-Holiday weekend in late May, the eight-day-long Fleadh Nua festival is one of the country's biggest traditional music festivals, and offers a great program of workshops, concerts, trad sessions, parades, and street performances, as well as a great opportunity to mix with locals. ☏ *065/682–4276* ⊕ *www.fleadhnua.com.*

SHOPPING

Carraig Donn. A popular spot with locals for its own line of knitwear as well as its mix of Irish and international brands, Carraig Donn is also a sure thing for visitors looking for some contemporary Irish fashion, jewelry, crystal, and pottery. ⊠ *Bank Pl.* ☏ *065/689–3433* ⊕ *www. carraigdonn.com.*

Custy's Traditional Music Shop. This is where Ennis's traditional musicians stock up on sheet music, CDs, DVDs, specialist books, and musical instruments. ⊠ *Cook's La.* ☏ *065/682–1727* ⊕ *www.custysmusic.com.*

Ennis Bookshop. This long-established book store carries a big range of local history and Irish-interest titles. ⊠ *13 Abbey St.* ☏ *065/682–9000* ⊕ *www.ennisbookshop.ie.*

Giftvenue. A wide array of top names is featured here, including Belleek china, Waterford crystal, Newbridge silverware, and Donegal Parian china, as well as Lladró, Hummel, and other collectible china. ⊠ *36 Abbey St.* ☏ *065/686–7891* ⊕ *www.giftvenue.ie.*

Honan Antiques. Established in 1966, and specializing in antique clocks as well as Irish and internationally sourced antiques, this old gem of a shop is handily located in the town center. ⊠ *14 Abbey St.* ☏ *065/682–8137.*

Seoidín. Stop here for a good selection of gold and silver jewelry as well as some lovely Irish-made gifts. ⊠ *52 O'Connell St.* ☏ *065/682-3510* ⊕ *www.seoidin.com.*

SPORTS AND THE OUTDOORS

BICYCLING

Tierney Cycles & Fishing. Follow the scenic Burren Cycleway (69 km [43 miles]) to the famous Cliffs of Moher, or join the Clare 250 Mile Cycle charity event in May, on a bike rented from Tierney Cycles & Fishing. ✉ *17 Abbey St.* ☎ *065/682–9433* 🌐 *www.clarebikehire.com.*

LAHINCH

6 km (4 miles) north of the Cliffs of Moher.

Noted for hotels packed with people touring the nearby Cliffs of Moher, Lahinch is a busy resort village beside a long, sandy beach backed by dunes. It is best known for its links golf courses and—believe it or not—its surfing. In 1972 the European Surfing Finals were held here, putting Lahinch on the world surfing map, and since then, it has achieved YouTube notoriety as the base from which surfers are towed by Jet Ski to surf the huge Atlantic wave known as the Aileens. Still, the center ring here is occupied by golf—with three world-class courses and a dazzling bay-view backdrop, Lahinch is often called the "St. Andrews of Ireland." Between golfers, surfers, and vacationers in general, the permanent winter population of 650 swells to 7,000 in the summer. Other Moher-bound people prefer to stay in Doolin or the nearby village of Lisdoonvarna.

GETTING HERE AND AROUND

Lahinch (also spelled Lehinch, on maps and in GPS systems) is a seaside resort 30 km (18 miles) west of Ennis on the N85. There is ample free parking on the seafront. It can be reached by bus from Ennis (one hour).

8

WHERE TO EAT AND STAY

$ SEAFOOD

🍴 **Morrissey's Seafood Bar and Grill.** Sporting distinctive colorful window boxes, this pretty family-run village pub has been transformed into an enormously popular seafood-and-steak restaurant. Burgundy leather banquettes line the walls, bentwood chairs sit at plain wooden tables beneath brass ceiling fans, while the cream walls are enlivened by a collection of paintings and photos of local scenes. There are no reservations, but you can take a drink at the bar while waiting your turn, or in summer, retreat to the wide deck overlooking the river. Happily, it's worth waiting for the fresh, simply prepared local food: Atlantic jumbo prawns with garlic and herb butter served with homemade breads, or smoked and barbecued salmon with capers, red onion, and crème fraîche. Angus sirloin steak is served with homemade onion rings, and kids love the Morrissey beef burger. There are also seven bedrooms overhead. [$] *Average main: €17* ✉ *Main St., Doonbeg* ☎ *065/905–5304* 🌐 *www.morrisseysdoonbeg.com* 🕓 *Closed Jan. and Feb., Mon. mid-May–Sept., and Mon. and Tues. in Oct., Nov., and Mar.–mid-May.*

$$$ B&B/INN Fodor's Choice ★

🏨 **Moy House.** Built for Sir Augustine Fitzgerald, this enchanting, 18th-century Italianate-style lodge sits amid 15 private acres on an exhilarating, Wuthering Heights–like windswept cliff top that's a three-minute drive from Lahinch. **Pros:** romantic cliff-top location. **Cons:** Lahinch itself feels a bit downmarket in comparison. [$] *Rooms from: €185*

✉ *Milltown Malbay Rd.* ☎ *065/708–2800* ⊕ *www.moyhouse.com* ↻ *9 rooms* ⊘ *Closed Nov.–mid-Apr.* ⓘⓞⓛ *Breakfast.*

$$ 📷 **Vaughan Lodge.** Michael Vaughan is a fourth-generation Lahinch **HOTEL** hotelier, and he and his wife, Maria, uphold the tradition splendidly in their Edwardian-style lodge—set at the quiet end of Lahinch, only a short walk from the busy village, it combines the facilities of a top hotel with the charm of a country house. **Pros:** quiet location; high standard of comfort; excellent restaurant on-site. **Cons:** very popular with golfing groups. Ⓢ *Rooms from: €150* ✉ *Road to Ennistymon* ☎ *065/708-1111* ⊕ *www.vaughanlodge.ie* ↻ *22 rooms* ⊘ *Closed Nov.–Mar.*

NIGHTLIFE AND THE ARTS

Galvin's. Established in 1840, and hosting traditional music sessions ever since, this popular spot has live music most nights in summer and on weekends in winter. ✉ *Church St.* ☎ *065/708–1045.*

O'Looney's. Known as Lahinch's surfers' pub, O'Looney's has a spacious oceanfront location and live music most nights in summer. ✉ *The Promenade* ☎ *065/708–1414* ⊕ *www.olooneys.ie.*

SHOPPING

Lahinch Surf Shop. Tom and Rosemary Buckley's surf shop, the first in Ireland, dates from 1989, and is a landmark on Lahinch's Promenade. You'll find top-quality boards, wet suits, and accessories, as well as lots of local tips and advice. Check their website for daily surf reports and a live webcam. ✉ *The Promenade* ☎ *065/708–1543* ⊕ *www.lahinch surfshop.com.*

SPORTS AND THE OUTDOORS

BEACHES

Lahinch Beach. When the clouds part and the sun shows its prodigal face in Clare, locals drop everything and flock to Lahinch's Blue Flag beach, a wide sandy crescent about 2½ km (1 mile) long, facing southwest onto the Atlantic Ocean. The promenade ends with the village—where if you're in luck, you can find ice-cream, seaweed, and periwinkle vendors—but continues as a footpath behind the beach, leading to a dune system and Lahinch's golf courses. The beach has long been a family favorite, offering safe bathing, and ideal conditions for beginner surfers. Arriving from Ennistymon on the N85, ignore the right hand turn at village entrance for the Cliffs of Moher (R478), and continue straight for about 50 meters (164 ft) to reach the promenade and car park. **Amenities:** food and drink; lifeguards; parking; toilets; water sports. **Best for:** sunset; surfing; swimming; walking; shore fishing. ✉ *Village center.*

GOLF

Doonbeg Golf Club. Despite being held up for a time (due to government legislation to protect a rare local snail), Greg Norman–designed Doonbeg has arrived with a major splash on the Irish links scene. Physically stunning, this tough, unforgiving course stretches along nearly 3 km (2 miles) of pristine Atlantic beach and dunes. The magnificent par-4 15th—with funnel-shaped green surrounded by huge dunes—is at the center of the whole course. Gamblers beware: anything long could easily run off the green and never be seen again. If you make it to the tricky 18th, you'll be rewarded with breathtaking views of the ocean. ⊠ *Doonbeg* ☎ *065/905–5602* ⊕ *www.doonbeglodge.com/golf-ireland.html* 🖳 *Fees: May–Sept., Mon.–Thurs. €145, Fri.–Sun. €175; Oct.–Apr., Mon.–Thurs. €100, Fri.–Sun. €125* 🏌 *18 holes, 6885 yards, par 72. Practice area, caddies, caddy carts, catering* ⊙ *Visitors: daily.*

Lahinch Golf Club. The grand old man of Irish links courses, Old Lahinch was originally designed by Old Tom Morris from St. Andrews in 1894, following the natural contours of the dunes, and is said to have a real Scottish flavor. In the 1920s design maestro Alister MacKenzie improved on the original, creating a memorably challenging 18 holes, with undulating greens, huge bunkers, and maddening blind shots. The Castle Course, built in 1963, is less of a challenge, but has some awkwardly placed bunkers and water hazards to negotiate. ⊠ *The Seafront* ☎ *065/708–1003* ⊕ *www.lahinchgolfclub.com* 🖳 *Fees: Standard: €135 (Old), €35 (Castle); Jan.–Mar. and Nov.–Dec., weekdays.: €50 (Old), €20 (Castle). See website for other seasonal offers* 🏌 *36 holes, 6950 yards (Old), 5700 yards (Castle). Practice area, caddies, club hire, buggies, catering* ⊙ *Visitors: daily (some restrictions).*

SURFING

Lahinch Surf School. Lahinch is a safe place to learn to surf if you stick to the beach. With enough practice—and Ireland's surfing champion, John MacCarthy, and his supercool crew teaching you— maybe it won't be too long before you can join the thrill-seeking surf dudes chasing huge waves (known as Aileens) a little farther up the coast at the Cliffs of Moher. ⊠ *Promenade* ☎ *087/960–9667* ⊕ *www.lahinchsurfschool.com.*

THE CLIFFS OF MOHER

8

10 km (6 miles) northwest of Lahinch.

One of Ireland's most breathtaking natural sights, the majestic Cliffs of Moher rise vertically out of the sea in a wall that stretches over a long, 8-km (5-mile) swath and in places reaches a height of 710 feet. On a clear day you can see the Aran Islands and the mountains of Connemara to the north, as well as the lighthouse on Loop Head and the mountains of Kerry to the south. Get up close and you can study the stratified deposits of five different rock layers visible in the cliff face. But most visitors prefer to take in the grand distant vistas, especially as they open up every turn of the trail along the famous Burren Way that runs from Doolin to the Cliffs.

GETTING HERE AND AROUND

Head north and west from Lahinch through Liscannor on the R478 for 19 km (12 miles)—or west from Lisdoonvarna for about the same distance on the R478—and you will come to the visitor center, a lone feature dominating the otherwise empty landscape, and its huge car park (fee), which is the only parking option, and includes entrance to the visitor center and cliff walkways.

There is a bus service to the Cliffs of Moher Visitor Centre from both Ennis and Galway City. A bus from Ennis to the cliffs takes about 50 minutes. The bus trip from Galway City takes about one hour, 50

DID YOU KNOW?

Almost as much a knock-out as the Cliffs of Moher themselves, their grass-roof, subterranean visitor center showcases the Atlantic Edge exhibition, whose highlight is the Ledge, a vertiginous virtual-reality tour of the Cliffs seen from a bird's-eye point of view.

minutes. ■TIP→ Avoid the parking fees and off-loading buses at the Cliffs of Moher by parking in Doolin and walking over.

TOURS

You'd never know if you just headed to the main car park for the Cliffs of Moher, but one of the most popular ways of viewing these natural wonders is by heading to Doolin (alternative port of departure: Liscannor) to pick up one of the famous Cliffs of Moher cruises. Two of the biggest outfitters heading out from Doolin Pier are Cliffs of Moher Cruises and the O'Brien Line. Cliffs of Moher Cruises has one-hour cruises departing every day, weather permitting, from April to October at noon and 3; tickets go for €20. O'Brien Lines operates mid-March to mid-November, with sailings usually at noon, 3, and 4; tickets go for €15.

ESSENTIALS

Transportation Contacts Cliffs of Moher Cruises ☎ 065/707-5949 ⊕ *www. cliffs-of-moher-cruises.com.* **Ennis Bus Station** ✉ *Station Rd.* ☎ 065/682-4177.**O'Brien Line** ☎ 065/707-5555 ⊕ *www.obrienline.com.*

EXPLORING

FAMILY

Fodor'sChoice
★

Cliffs of Moher. The Cliffs of Moher have a long and almost hallowed history. They were sacred in the Celtic era and were a favorite hunting retreat of BrianBorú, the High King of Ireland. Numerous seabirds, including a large colony of puffins, make their homes in the shelves of rock on the cliffs. Built in 1835 by Cornelius O'Brien—of Bunratty Castle fame and a descendant of the Kings of Thomond—**O'Brien's Tower** is a defiant, broody sentinel on the Cliffs' highest point, built to encourage tourism (yes, there were tourists even back then). Cornelius also erected here a wall of Liscannor flagstones (noted for their imprints of prehistoric eels).

Found on the road from Liscannor to Lisdoonvarna (R478), the grass-roof, subterranean **visitor center** (and adjacent car park) is built into the cliff face and is a good refuge from passing rain squalls. Note that there is no specific address for the Cliffs, which go on for miles, but you cannot miss the only road that gives access to the Cliffs, which is found on the main road from Liscannor to the north, a road which is heavily signposted. The visitor center interior imitates the limestone caves of County Clare and contains a gift shop, public toilets, and a tearoom. The Atlantic Edge exhibition features information panels and interactive consoles for children—the highlight is the Ledge, a vertiginous virtual reality tour of the Cliffs from a bird's-eye point of view. Outside the center extensive hiking paths (some with elevated viewing platforms) gives access to the real thing, including O'Brien's Tower (€2 extra for access to upper levels and O'Brien exhibit) at the northern extremity. ✉ *Cliffs of Moher Visitor Centre (signposted on the R478 north from Liscannor)* ☎ *065/708-6141* ⊕ *www.cliffsofmoher.ie* ⊠ *Parking €6 (includes access to visitor center, cliff-edge paths, and viewing platforms and Atlantic Edge exhibition); €2 optional extra for upper levels of O'Brien's Tower* ⊙ *Visitor center daily 9–dusk; O'Brien's Tower daily 9–dusk (weather permitting).*

DOOLIN

6 km (4 miles) north of the Cliffs of Moher.

Once an enchanting backwater of colorful fishermen's cottages, this tiny village—set at the point where the Cliffs of Moher flatten out and disappear into the sea as limestone plateaus—now seems to consist almost entirely of B&Bs, hostels, hotels, holiday homes, pubs, and restaurants, built on a flat plain about a mile from the pier and the sea. The reason for all this development (much of it newly built during Ireland's Celtic Tiger economic boom) is that Doolin is reputed to have three of the best pubs for traditional music in Ireland: McGann's, McDermott's, and O'Connor's. With the worldwide surge of interest in Irish music since the mid-1990s, the village has become more of a magnet for European and American musicians than it is for young, or even established, Irish artists. Amazingly, there is no tourist board office in Doolin but a sponsored website does offer plenty of listings for the town (⊕ *www.doolin-tourism.com*).

Popularity, of course, brings its own price: when every other person is witnessing the session through a camera screen, it can interrupt the connection and magic between the musicians and the audience. If you're disappointed with the music (or more likely, the crowd) in one pub, there are two more to try.

GETTING HERE AND AROUND
Doolin is on the R479 about 6 km (4 miles) north of the Cliffs of Moher Visitor Centre. There is one bus a day from Ennis and five from Galway. Doolin is not on the express route: be sure to take a local bus.

EXPLORING
Aran Doolin Ferries. Aran Doolin Ferries makes the 30-minute trip from Doolin Pier to Inis Oirr (Inisheer), the smallest of the Aran Islands, from spring until early fall (weather permitting, €20 round-trip). There are at least three round-trip sailings a day, and up to eight in July and August, but inquire on the day you plan to embark, as schedules vary according to weather and demand. There is also a day trip to the Aran Islands which includes a cruise under the Cliffs of Moher (€25). Usually more than one ferry company operates out of Doolin; your return ticket will be valid only with the company that took you out, so when boarding the outbound ferry, be sure to check the return schedule. ☎ *065/707–4455* ⊕ *www.doolinferries.com* ✉ *€15–€25.*

WHERE TO EAT AND STAY
$$
SEAFOOD
✕ **Cullinan's Restaurant & Guesthouse.** The small 25-seat restaurant, set in the back of an attractively renovated traditional farmhouse, is famed for its fresh, simply prepared seafood, but vegetarian and meat dishes are also served. Owner-chef James Cullinan uses fresh local ingredients—Inagh goat cheese, Burren smoked salmon, Doolin crabmeat, and Aran scallops—to form the basis of a light, imaginative menu. Try roast rack of Burren lamb with polenta galette and wild rosemary jus. Desserts are all homemade, or try a plate of farmhouse cheeses. A €27.50 early-bird set menu is served from 6 to 6:45. The floor-to-ceiling windows on two sides of the restaurant overlook the Aille River. The 10 (from €80

double occupancy) cottage-style rooms have simple pine furniture, fresh cotton comforters, pleasant country views, Wi-Fi, and room TVs on request. [$] *Average main: €24* ✉ *Coast Rd.* ☎ *065/707–4183* 🌐 *www.cullinansdoolin.com* ⏲ *Guesthouse closed Dec–mid-Feb.; restaurant closed Nov.–Easter, no dinner Wed. and Sun.*

$ MODERN IRISH 🍴 **Wild Honey Inn.** Owner-chef Aidan McGrath has cooked at some of Ireland's leading hotels, but now runs his own 14-room hotel with his wife, Kate. The bar of the solid Victorian building is warm and welcoming, with an upright piano, original painted wood cladding, assorted wooden tables and bentwood chairs, cheerful cotton-check blinds, and a random selection of bric-a-brac. Try a starter of Liscannor crab claws in garlic and chili butter, or pressed ham-hock terrine. The open crab sandwich on soda bread is a popular lunchtime item, as is the homemade burger with mustard mayo. At dinner braised rabbit is often among the daily specials, or opt for roast monk tail with braised short ribs. The rooms (from €90 B&B for two) are spacious and stylishly decorated in neutral tones with nice Victorian touches such as brass bedside lamps. [$] *Average main: €18* ✉ *Kincora Rd., Lisdoonvarna* ☎ *065/707–4300* 🌐 *www.wildhoneyinn.com* ⏲ *Closed Jan. and Feb. and Mon.–Wed. Mar.–Easter and Oct.–Dec. Kitchen closed Tues. Easter–Sept.*

$ B&B/INN 🏨 **Aran View House Hotel.** This extensively modernized 1736 house on 100 acres of farmland offers magnificent views in nearly every direction: the Aran Islands to the west, the Cliffs of Moher to the south, and the gray limestone rocks of the Burren to the north. **Pros:** well-located; amazing views; bar and restaurant on-site. **Cons:** a rather sprawling development, painted in an odd shade of pink; the exterior is less attractive than the interior. [$] *Rooms from: €110* ✉ *Coast Rd.* ☎ *065/707–4061* 🌐 *www.aranview.com* 🛏 *16 rooms* ⏲ *Closed Nov.–Easter* 🍽 *Breakfast.*

$$ B&B/INN Fodor's Choice ★ 🏨 **Ballinalacken Castle Hotel.** One hundred acres of wildflower meadows surround this restored, low-slung Victorian lodge—built alongside the 16th-century ruins of an O'Brien castle (hence its somewhat bogus name)—making this one of the most memorably sited of Ireland's coastal inns, with panoramic views of the Atlantic, the Aran Islands, and distant Connemara. **Pros:** fabulous location; warm old-fashioned welcome from the O'Callaghan family. **Cons:** not in fact a "castle." [$] *Rooms from: €130* ✉ *Coast Rd., about 1 km (½ mile) outside Doolin on the Lisdoonvarna Rd.* ☎ *086/361–3719* 🌐 *www.ballinalackencastle.com* 🛏 *10 rooms, 2 suites* ⏲ *Closed Nov.–mid-Apr. No dinner Tues.* 🍽 *Breakfast.*

NIGHTLIFE AND THE ARTS

Famous for their traditional-music sessions, Doolin's three traditional pubs are designed to hold big crowds, which means you should expect minimal comfort: hard benches or bar stools if you're lucky, and spit-and-sawdust flooring. The theory is that the music will be so good, you won't notice anything else. However, interesting music-related memorabilia hang on the walls, and all three serve simple bar food from midday until 9 (Irish stew is a good bet). As you might imagine, the word is out about Doolin's trad scene—some nights the pubs overflow with crowds (and the video cams can get really annoying).

Gus O'Connor's. Set midway between the village center and the pier, popular Gus O'Connor's has tables outside near a stream and live music every night after 9:30 pm in the summertime. ✉ *Fisher St.* ☎ *065/707–4168* ⊕ *www.gusoconnorsdoolin.com.*

McDermott's. Popular with locals, McDermott's is a great spot for soul-warming live music and belly-warming grub. Live music nightly early spring to late autumn, and weekends in winter. Note: it's sometimes closed during the day in low season. ✉ *Lisdoonvarna Rd.* ☎ *065/707–4328* ⊕ *www.mcdermottspubdoolin.com.*

McGann's Pub & Restaurant. Across the road from McDermott's, McGann's is the smallest of Doolin's three famous pubs and has been run by the same family for 70 years. The music and food are so hearty you won't want to leave. Luckily, McGann's offers B&B, too (but you will need to book ahead). ✉ *Lisdoonvarna Rd.* ☎ *065/707–4133* ⊕ *mcgannspubdoolin.com.*

THE BURREN

Extending throughout western County Clare from the Cliffs of Moher in the south to Black Head in the north, and as far southeast as Corofin.

As you travel north toward Ballyvaughan, the landscape becomes rockier and stranger. Instead of the seemingly ubiquitous Irish green, gray becomes the prevailing color. You're now in the heart of the Burren, a 300-square-km (116-square-mile) expanse that is one of Ireland's strangest landscapes.

The Burren is aptly named: it's an Anglicization of the Irish word *bhoireann* (a rocky place). Stretching off in all directions, as far as the eye can see, are vast, irregular slabs of fissured limestone, known as *karst,* with deep cracks between them. From a distance, it looks like a lunar landscape, so dry that nothing could possibly grow on it. But in spring (especially from mid-May to mid-June), the Burren becomes a wild rock garden, as an astonishing variety of wildflowers blooms in the cracks between the rocks, among them at least 23 native species of orchid. The Burren also supports an incredible diversity of wildlife, including frogs, newts, lizards, badgers, stoats, sparrow hawks, kestrels, and dozens of other birds and animals. The wildflowers and other plants are given life from the spectacular caves, streams, and potholes that lie beneath the rough, scarred pavements. With the advent of spring, *turloughs* (seasonal lakes that disappear in dry weather) appear on the plateau's surface. Botanists are particularly intrigued by the cohabitation of Arctic and Mediterranean plants, many so tiny (and so rare, so please do not pick any) you can't see them from your car window; make a point of exploring some of this rocky terrain on foot. Numerous signposted walks run through both coastal and inland areas.

GETTING HERE AND AROUND

Take the R476 west from Lisdoonvarna for 9 km (5 miles) to Kilfenora where a visitor center will introduce you to the region. Continue for another 10 km (6 miles), turning left on to the R460 at the striking ruin of Leamaneh Castle (no access) to visit some of the major archaeological sites. Park only in designated car parks (free), which have been built adjacent to the major sites, and proceed by foot to avoid damaging the delicate ecology. The main bus stop for travelers to the Burren area is Lisdoonvarna.

EXPLORING

Burren Centre. Along with a café and a crafts shop with good maps and locally published guides, the tiny Burren Centre has a modest audiovisual display and other exhibits that explain the Burren's geology, flora, and archaeology. ✉ *8 km (5 miles) southeast of Lisdoonvarna on R476, Kilfenora* ☎ *065/708–8030* ⊕ *www.theburrencentre.ie* 🖃 *€5* 🕑 *Mid-Mar.–May, Sept., and Oct., daily 10–5; June–Aug., daily 9:30–5:30.*

WORD OF MOUTH

"After Poulnabrone Dolmen, we decided just to explore and examine The Burren. It is just such a unique landscape, that we couldn't get enough of it. My husband loved looking around at the rocks for fossils, and found quite a few. I just enjoyed looking around and exploring the seeming barren landscape and finding beautiful flowers." —crhq5

The Burren Way. You can explore the Burren area by car, from a bike, or from the back of a bus, but the very best way to soak in the raw beauty of this craggy landscape is on foot. The Burren Way is a 123-km (82-mile) way-marked hiking trail, its highlight being the stretch from Lahinch to Ballyvaughan on the shores of Galway Bay, a distance of 35 km (22 miles). If you're short on time/breath, you may want to focus on the most spectacular and popular section which runs along the top of the Cliffs of Moher from Doolin to the coast near Lisdoonvarna, a distance of about 5 km (3 miles). The trail continues through the heart of the Burren's gray, rocky limestone landscape, with ever-changing views offshore of the Aran Islands and Galway Bay. Buy a map locally. ⊕ *www.burrengeopark.ie.*

Caherconnell Stone Fort. There are several stone forts in the Burren thought to have been in use between AD 400 and 1200, but Caherconnell—1 km (½ mile) south of Poulnabrone—is the best preserved, and the only one excavated and made accessible to visitors. The visitor center has an audiovisual display on the chief archaeological features of the area, including burial places marked by dolmens or cairns. Ongoing excavations continue to fill in the blanks of this impressive structure's history. Be sure to check out the sheepdog demonstrations and café. ✉ *Carron* ☎ *065/708–9999* ⊕ *www.burrenforts.ie* 🖃 *€6* 🕑 *Mar., Apr., and Oct. daily 10:30–5; May, June, and Sept. daily 10–5:30, July and Aug. daily 10–6:30.*

Cathedral of St. Fachtna. Beside the Burren Centre in Kilfenora, the ruins of a small 12th-century church, once the Cathedral of St. Fachtna, have been partially restored as a parish church. There are some interesting carvings in the roofless choir, including an unusual, life-size human skeleton. In a field about 165 feet west of the ruins is an elaborately sculpted high cross that is worth examining, though parts of it are badly weathered. ✉ *Kilfenora.*

8

Poulnabrone Megalithic Tomb. The biggest and most famous of the Burren's megalithic tombs, Poulnabrone ("the hole of sorrows") is a portal grave/dolmen with a massive capstone and a majestic presence amid the craggy limestone fields shouldering the moody gray Burren skies. The monument was built around 4,500 years ago. Stand down the wind and you might hear ancient whispers. There is a designated car park nearby with an historical timeline, and a short gravel walkway to the dolmen (freely accessible). It's open and windy here, so grab an extra layer. ⊠ *On R480, 8 km (5 miles) south of Ballyvaughan, Carron.*

NIGHTLIFE AND THE ARTS
Vaughan's Pub. Known for its traditional-music sessions in a village famed for its ceilí band, Vaughan's has been a local favorite for years. Free set dancing lessons are held in the barn during the summer. ⊠ *Main St., Kilfenora* ☎ *065/708–8004* ⊕ *www.vaughanspub.ie.*

SHOPPING
Burren Perfumery. Shopping opportunities are not abundant in this rocky terrain, so don't miss the chance to buy organic perfumery products at this delightful spot. The Burren is known for its wildflowers, and all the products on sale are made on-site, in small batches. As well as perfume there are soaps, creams, and balms, and you can visit the workshops to see them being made. There is also an organic herb garden, and a flower-bedecked tea room (April—Sept.) selling delicious organic home baking and light lunches. ⊠ *Carron* ☎ *065/708–9102* ⊕ *www. burrenperfumery.com.*

SPORTS AND THE OUTDOORS
BICYCLING
West Ireland Cycling. Either take an organized or self-guided Burren tour or hire a top-of-the-range bike from this Galway-based outfit. They can also deliver up to 80 bikes by trailer for groups, from €15 a day or €80 a week. ⊠ *Earl's Island, Galway, Co. Galway* ☎ *091/588–830* ⊕ *www. westirelandcycling.com.*

BALLYVAUGHAN

16 km (10 miles) north of Lisdoonvarna on N67.

A pretty little waterside village and a good base for exploring the Burren, Ballyvaughan attracts walkers and artists who enjoy the views of Galway Bay and access to the Burren.

GETTING HERE AND AROUND
Ballyvaughan is 16 km (10 miles) north of Lisdoonvarna on the N67. The coastal drive from Doolin is especially scenic.

EXPLORING
FAMILY **Aillwee Cave.** A vast 2-million-year-old cave, Aillwee is the biggest and most impressive chamber in the region accessible to those who aren't spelunkers. Illuminated for about 3,300 feet, the cave contains an underground river and waterfall. Aboveground, there are a big crafts shop, cheese-making demonstrations, a café, and the **Burren Birds of Prey Centre,** which puts on flying displays from eagles, falcons, hawks, and owls daily at noon and 3 pm (weather permitting). ⊠ *5 km (3 miles)*

south of Ballyvaughan on R480 ☎ *065/707–7036* 🌐 *www.aillweecave.ie* 🎫 *Joint ticket for cave tour and birds of prey €18; €12 cave only* 🕓 *Jan.–Nov., daily 10–dusk; Dec. by appointment.*

WHERE TO STAY

$ B&B/INN 🏨 **Drumcreehy Country House.** The delicious breakfast menu offers an unusually wide choice, while the hosts are knowledgeable about the area, and have a good supply of books and maps. The pretty gabled facade with dormer windows is traditional in style, but, in fact, Bernadette Moloney and her German husband, Armin Grefkes, designed and built this house specifically as a B&B. **Pros:** big bedrooms for a B&B; nice waterfront location; peaceful nights. **Cons:** a long (1-mile-plus) walk down a narrow busy road to village. [$] *Rooms from: €100* ☎ *065/707–7377* 🌐 *www.drumcreehyhouse.com* 🛏 *12 rooms* 🕓 *Nov.–Jan. call in advance to confirm.* 🍴 *Breakfast.*

$$$$ HOTEL Fodor's Choice ★ 🏨 **Gregans Castle Hotel.** One of Ireland's best-loved country-house hotels, this quiet, low-key retreat is a romantic, creeper-covered Georgian house, set amid pretty gardens with a splendid view of the rocky Burren hills and Galway Bay beyond. **Pros:** perfectly judged decor; birdsong morning and evening; excellent restaurant. **Cons:** 5 km (3 miles) from nearest village; almost a TV-free zone, only one in-house; no elevator. [$] *Rooms from: €215* ✉ *Base of Corkscrew Hill* ☎ *065/707–7005* 🌐 *www.gregans.ie* 🛏 *15 rooms, 6 suites* 🕓 *Closed Dec.–mid-Feb.* 🍴 *Breakfast.*

$ HOTEL 🏨 **Hyland's Burren Hotel.** A turf fire greets you in the lobby of this unpretentious coaching inn, in the heart of the Burren, which dates from the early 18th century and has become a cheerful, welcoming spot with a reputation for friendliness and good entertainment. **Pros:** central location; bar and restaurant on-site; pleasant staff. **Cons:** won't win any style contests; bar and restaurant very busy July and August. [$] *Rooms from: €90* ✉ *Main St.* ☎ *065/707–7037* 🌐 *www.hylandsburren.com* 🛏 *30 rooms* 🕓 *Closed Nov.–late Mar.* 🍴 *Breakfast.*

NIGHTLIFE AND THE ARTS

Monk's Pub. This friendly pub, near the waterfront, hosts sessions of traditional and folk music on Sunday from 4 pm and most evenings after 9:30 in July and August. The bar food is excellent (the seafood chowder has a cult following), but be warned—the prime location and well-regarded reputation mean it is often a busy spot. ✉ *Main St.* ☎ *065/707–7059* 🌐 *www.monks.ie* 🕓 *Oct.–May, no food Mon.–Thurs.*

KINVARA

13½ km (8 miles) east of Ballyvaughan, 15 km (9 miles) northwest of Gort on N67, 25 km (15½ miles) south of Galway City.

Fodor's Choice ★ The picture-perfect village of Kinvara, just across the border in County Galway, is a growing holiday base, thanks to its gorgeous bayside locale, great walking and sea angling, and numerous pubs. It's well worth a visit, whether you're coming from Ballyvaughan or Gort. The late Seamus Heaney, Ireland's Nobel laureate poet, described this drive along what he called the "Flaggy Shore" in the poem "Postscript": "...the wind/And the light are working off each other/So that the ocean on one side is wild/With foam and glitter." Kinvara is best known for its longstanding early-August sailing event, **Cruinniú na mBád** (Festival of the Gathering of the Boats), in which traditional brown-sail Galway hookers laden with turf race across the bay. Hookers were used until the early part of this century to carry turf, provisions, and cattle across Galway Bay and out to the Aran Islands. A sculpture in Galway's Eyre Square honors their local significance.

GETTING HERE AND AROUND

The N67 coast road, a narrow but scenic route, follows the shore of Galway Bay from Ballyvaughan to Kinvara. From Kinvara, N67 joins the busy national route, the M18 at Clarenbridge and continues into Galway City (25 km [15 miles]). There is free parking in Kinvara. Bus Éireann runs buses between Kinvara and Galway City; the journey takes about 30 minutes. The same bus continues to the Cliffs of Moher, Lisdoonvarna, and Doolin.

EXPLORING

Dunguaire Castle. On a rock north of Kinvara Bay, the 16th-century Dunguaire Castle spectacularly commands all the approaches to Galway Bay. It's said to stand on the site of a 7th-century castle built by the King of Connaught. Built in 1520 by the O'Hynes clan, the tiny storybook castle takes its name from the fabled king of Connaught, Guaire. In 1929 it was purchased by Oliver St. John Gogarty, the noted surgeon, man of letters, and model for Buck Mulligan, a character in James Joyce's *Ulysses*. To his outpost came many of the leading figures of the 19th-century Celtic revival in Irish literature. Today Dunguaire is used for a Middle Ages–style banquet that honors local writers and others with ties to the West, including Lady Gregory, W. B. Yeats, Seán O'Casey, and Pádraic O'Conaire (book on-line for banquet tickets to get substantial discounts). ⊠ *Kinvara* ☎ *061/360–788* ⊕ *www.shannonheritage.com* 🎫 *€6* ☉ *Apr.–Sept., daily 9:30–5.*

WHERE TO EAT AND STAY

$$$$
SEAFOOD
✕ **Moran's Oyster Cottage.** Signposted off the main road on the south side of Clarinbridge, this waterside thatch cottage, the home of six generations of the Moran family (since 1760), houses at its rear a simply furnished restaurant that serves mainly seafood. It's *the* place to sample the local oysters, though chowder, smoked salmon, seafood cocktail, lobster with boiled potatoes and garlic butter, and fresh crab salad are also on offer. In good weather, you can eat outside overlooking the weir and watch the swans float by. The front bar has been preserved in the "old style," which means it's small and cramped, but very interesting if you want to get an idea of what most pubs around here were like 50 years ago. 🅢 *Average main: €33* ⊠ *The Weir, Kilcolgan* ☎ *091/796–113* ⊕ *www.moransoystercottage.com.*

$$
IRISH
✕ **The Pier Head.** Once the village pub, the Pier Head is still a bar, but it sells more food than pints these days. The location is idyllic, at the top (head) of the village's pier. Lunch ($) is served in the bustling, wooden-floored mahogany bar (restaurant lunch Sunday only), with outdoor seating and modest sea views. At dinner you can choose between the

bar and the more formal upstairs restaurant with unforgettable views across Kinvara Bay to Dunguaire Castle. Both have roaring open fires, and friendly staff. Fresh local seafood and locally reared meat (beef, lamb, pork, and duck) feature on the simple, unfussy menu. Start with crab claws in garlic butter, or steamed mussels mariniere, then consider fillet of local lamb on a bed of creamed spinach, or honey-roast half duck with five spice and ginger sauce. Desserts are all made in-house: chocolate and ginger torte with vanilla ice cream perhaps, or a hazelnut pavlova with fresh strawberries and berry coulis. Top it all off with an Irish coffee. Don't forget that in summer there will be enough daylight until around 10 pm to enjoy the view. [$] *Average main: €23* ☎ *091/638–188* 🌐 *www.pierhead.ie* ⏲ *Closed Mon. and Tues. Nov.–mid-Mar.*

$ HOTEL 🏨 **Merriman Inn.** Don't let its traditional looks deceive you: this whitewashed, thatch inn on the shores of Galway Bay is, in fact, a midsize hotel, decorated with locally made, well-designed furniture, and original crafts, paintings, and sculpture. **Pros:** center of village; secure car parking; decent restaurant; choice of other restaurants and bars nearby. **Cons:** bar gets very busy at weekends; bigger windows would be nice, to get more of the view. [$] *Rooms from: €80* ✉ *Main St.* ☎ *091/638–222* 🌐 *www.merrimanhotel.com* 🛏 *32 rooms* ⏲ *Closed Jan. and Feb.* 🍴 *Breakfast.*

NIGHTLIFE AND THE ARTS

Cuckoo Fleadh. The first weekend in May, Kinvara hosts the popular annual Cuckoo Fleadh, or Fleadh na gCuach, a traditional-music festival with a lovely view. ✉ *Main St.* ☎ *091/637–145* 🌐 *kinvara.com/cuckoo.*

Winkles Hotel bar. Traditional music is played most nights at the Winkles Hotel bar, where acclaimed Irish musician Sharon Shannon got her start in the music business. ✉ *The Square* ☎ *091/637–137.*

COOLE PARK

24 km (15 miles) northeast of Corofin on M18.

EXPLORING

Coole Park & Gardens. Located north of the little town of Gort, Coole Park was once the home of Lady Augusta Gregory (1859–1932), patron of W. B. Yeats and cofounder with the poet of Dublin's Abbey Theatre. Yeats visited here often, as did almost all the other writers who contributed to the Irish literary revival in the first half of the 20th century, including George Bernard Shaw (1856–1950) and Sean O'Casey (1880–1964). Douglas Hyde (1860–1949), the first president of Ireland, was also a visitor. The house became derelict after Lady Gregory's death and was demolished in 1941; the grounds are now a wildlife park with a herd of deer and 6 km (4 miles) of nature trails. Picnic tables make this a lovely alfresco lunch spot. The only reminder of its literary past is the Autograph Tree, a copper beech on which many of Lady Gregory's famous guests carved their initials. There's also a visitor center with displays on Lady Gregory and Yeats. A little out of the way, this is one for Yeats fans only. ✉ *Galway Rd.* ☎ *091/631–804* 🌐 *www.coolepark.ie* 🎟 *Park free, visitor center €3* ⏲ *Park: daily 8:30–7:30 (dusk in winter);*

visitor center and tearooms: Easter–June and Sept., daily 10–5; July and Aug., daily 10–6.

GALWAY CITY

Galway is often said to be a state of mind as much as it is a specific place. The largest city in the West today and the ancient capital of the province of Connaught, Galway, with a current population of 72,700, is also one of the fastest-growing cities in Europe. It's an astonishing fact, and you have to wonder where this city can possibly grow. For despite Galway's size, its commercially busy ring road, and its ever-spreading suburbs, its heart is *tiny*—a warren of streets so compact that if you spend more than a few hours here, you'll soon be strolling along with the sort of easy familiarity you'd feel in any small town.

For many Irish people, Galway is a favorite weekend getaway: known as the city of festivals, it's the liveliest place in the republic. It's also a university town: National University of Ireland, Galway—(or NUI Galway as it's locally known)—is a center for Gaelic culture (Galway marks the eastern gateway to the West's large Gaeltacht). A fair share of NUI Galway's 17,000 students pursue their studies in the Irish language. Galway is, in fact, permeated by youth culture. On festival weekends, you'll see as many pierced and tattooed teenagers and twentysomethings here as you'd find at a rock concert. But Galway's students aren't its only avant-garde, as Galway has long attracted writers, artists, and musicians. The latter whip up brand-new jigs while also keeping the traditional-music pubs lively year-round. And the city's two small but internationally acclaimed theater companies draw a steady stream of theater people.

■ TIP➜ If you're looking for the quiet, quaint side of Ireland depicted on travel posters, have a quick look at Galway City and push on to Clifden or Westport.

Although you're not conscious of it when you're in the center of town, Galway is spectacularly situated, on the north shore of Galway Bay, where the River Corrib flows from Lough Corrib to the sea. The seaside suburb of Salthill, on the south-facing shore of Galway Bay, has stunning vistas across the vividly blue bay to Black Head and the Burren on the opposite shore.

Galway's growth and popularity mean that at its busiest moments, its narrow, one-way streets are jam-packed with pedestrians, while cars are gridlocked.

GETTING HERE AND AROUND

Galway is connected to Dublin by motorways M6–M4–M50 (four-lane highways with concrete dividers, some tolls), 20 km (12 miles) with a journey time of about two hours, 20 minutes. There is a similarly good road to Limerick, the M18/N18 (100 km [62 miles]), with a journey time of one hour.

Express bus services to Galway from Dublin are available from both Bus Éireann and Citylink. Both take about three hours, 40 minutes from Dublin City Center. Bus services to Galway from Cork call at

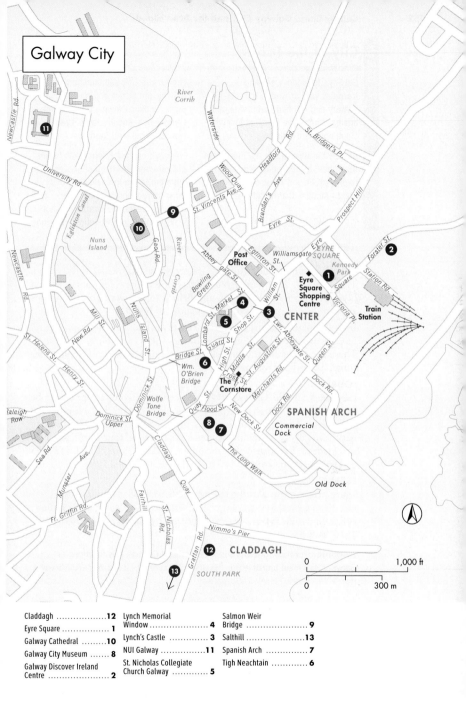

Galway City

River Corrib

Newcastle Rd.

University Rd.

Eglinton Canal

Nuns Island

Newcastle Rd.

Mill St.

New Rd.

St. Helens St.

Henry St.

Raleigh Row

Sea Rd.

Munster Ave.

Fr. Griffin Rd.

Fairhill

Waterside

Wood Quay

St. Vincents Ave.

Gaol Rd.

River Corrib

Nuns Island St.

Dominick St.

Dominick St. Upper

Wolfe Tone Bridge

Claddagh Quay

St. Nicholas Rd.

Grattan Rd.

Nimmo's Pier

SOUTH PARK

12 CLADDAGH

13

Headford Rd.

St. Bridget's Pl.

Prospect Hill

Brendan's Ave.

Eyre St.

Williamsgate St.

Eglinton St.

William St.

Abbeygate St.

Bowling Green

Market St.

Shop St.

Guard St.

High St.

Middle St.

Cross St.

Quay St.

Flood St.

New Dock St.

Merchants Rd.

St. Augustine St.

Lwr. Abbeygate St.

Victoria Pl.

Queen St.

Dock Rd.

Dock Rd.

Forster St.

Station Rd.

Post Office

◆ **Eyre Square Shopping Centre**

EYRE SQUARE

Kennedy Park

Train Station

CENTER

Wm. O'Brien Bridge

Bridge St.

Lombard St.

The Cornstore

SPANISH ARCH

Commercial Dock

The Long Walk

Old Dock

9
10
1
2
3
4
5
6
7
8
11

0   1,000 ft
0   300 m

City of the Tribes

Galway's founders were Anglo-Normans who arrived in the mid-13th century and fortified their settlement against "the native Irish," as local chieftains were called.

Galway became known as "the City of the Tribes" because of the dominant role in public and commercial life of the 14 families that founded it.

Their names are still common in Galway and elsewhere in Ireland: Athy, Blake, Bodkin, Browne, D'Arcy, Dean, Font, French, Kirwan, Joyce, Lynch, Morris, Martin, and Skerret.

The city's medieval heritage, a fusion of Gaelic and Norman influences, is apparent in the intimate two- and three-story stone buildings, the winding streets, the narrow passage-ways, and the cobblestones underfoot.

Limerick and Shannon Airport. Journey time from Cork is 4½ hours. There are also daily buses from Galway to Westport (1½ hours), Ballina (2½ hours), Sligo (2½ hours), and Belfast (6½ hours). For quick hops around the city, use a taxi, such as those of Big O.

Irish Rail–Iarnrod Éireann trains run from Dublin's Heuston Station to Galway City via Athlone. The journey takes two hours, 10 minutes. There are trains from Limerick City via Ennis on the new commuter route, a two-hour journey.

TOURS

Lally Tours. While Galway's historic center is compact and can be explored on foot, many visitors enjoy a quick orientation. Hop aboard Lally Tours' vintage double-decker bus for an hour-long Old Galway City Tour. Every 90 minutes buses leave from the tourist office in Forster Place on the corner of Eyre Square. ⊠ *Lally Tours* ☎ *091/562–905* ⊕ *www.lallytours.com* 💶 *€10* ⊗ *Daily 10:30 am–4:15 pm.*

ESSENTIALS

Transportation Contacts Big O Taxis ☎ *091/585–858* ⊕ *www.bigotaxis. com.* **Ceannt (Bus) Station** ⊠ *Eyre Sq.* ☎ *091/562–000.* **Ceannt (Rail) Station** ⊠ *Eyre Sq.* ☎ *091/564–222* ⊕ *www.irishrail.ie.* **Citylink** ⊠ *Eyre Sq.* ☎ *091/564–164* ⊕ *www.citylink.ie.*

Visitor Information Galway Discover Ireland Centre. This functions as Galway City's main tourist office. ⊠ *Forster St., Eyre Sq.* ☎ *091/537–700* ⊕ *www. discoverireland.ie/Places-To-Go/galway.*

EXPLORING

Most of the city's sights, aside from the cathedral and the university campus, can be found in a narrow sector of the medieval town center that runs in a southwesterly direction from Eyre Square to the River Corrib. Not only is the city center compact, but it's also largely pedestrian-friendly, so the best way to explore it is on foot. It takes only five minutes to walk straight down Galway's main shopping street, the continuation of the north side of Eyre Square, to the River Corrib, where it ends (note that the name of this street changes several times).

TOP ATTRACTIONS

Eyre Square. The largest open space in central Galway and the heart of the city, and a favorite chill-out spot on a sunny day for students, visitors, and lunching locals, Eyre Square on the east side of the River Corrib incorporates a sculpture garden and children's play area on its east side, while its west side is bound by a heavily traveled road. In the center is **Kennedy Park,** a patch of lawn named in honor of John F. Kennedy, who spoke here when he visited the city in June 1963. At the north end of the park, a 20-foot-high steel sculpture standing in the pool of a fountain represents the brown sails seen on Galway hookers, the area's traditional sailing boats. Now a feature of Kennedy Park, the **Browne Doorway** was taken in 1905 from the Browne family's town house on Upper Abbeygate Street; it has the 17th-century coats of arms of both the Browne and Lynch families (2 of Galway's 14 founding families), called a "marriage stone" because when the families were joined in marriage their coats of arms were, too. Keep an eye out for similar if less elaborate Browne doorways as you walk around the old part of town. ⊠ *Galway.*

Galway Discover Ireland Centre (*TIO*). Just off Eyre Square, east of the bus and train station and the Hotel Meyrick, this is the place to make reservations for events around town and find out about the latest happenings. You can also book tickets to the Aran Islands here. ⊠ *Forster Pl., Center* ☎ *091/537–700* ⊕ *www.discoverireland.ie/Places-To-Go/ Galway* ⊗ *Weekdays 9–6, Sat. 9–1.*

Salmon Weir Bridge. The bridge itself is nothing special, but in season— from mid-April to early July—shoals of salmon are visible from its deck as they lie in the clear river water before making their way upstream to the spawning grounds of Lough Corrib. ⊠ *West end of St. Vincent's Ave., Center.*

Salthill. A lively, hugely popular seaside resort, Salthill is beloved for its seaside promenade—the traditional place "to sit and watch the moon rise over Claddagh, and see the sun go down on Galway Bay," as Bing Crosby used to croon in the most famous song about the city. The main attraction of the village, set 3 km (2 miles) west of Galway, is the long sandy beach along the edge of Galway Bay and the promenade above it. The building of big new hotels along the seafront has nevertheless left plenty of room for the traditional amusement arcades (full of slot machines), seasonal cafés, and a fairground.

Spanish Arch. Built in 1584 to protect the quays where Spanish ships unloaded cargoes of wines and brandies, the hefty stone arch is now the central feature of the newly restored Spanish Parade, a riverside piazza located near Wolfe Tone Bridge. It's another reminder of Galway's—and Ireland's—past links with Spain, and is a much-loved local landmark. ⊠ *Spanish Parade, Spanish Arch.*

Fodor's Choice ★ **Tigh Neachtain** (*Naughton's Pub*). Galway City's most famous pub, which stands at a busy little crossroads in the heart of the old town, is treasured for its unrenovated interior. Grab a spot at one of its old-fashioned

A Shopping Tour of Galway

There's no question about it: they have a different look in Galway. People have always dressed differently, because they dress for the Galway weather, which can be wet and windy at any time of year. But ever since Galway was transformed by Ireland's "Celtic Tiger" economic boom, they have also dressed—and decorated—with a real sense of style. Want proof? Just join the locals on the following walk.

Pick up a free map of Galway from the **tourist information office** on Forster Place. Turn left out the front door to reach the **Hotel Meyrick** (formerly the Great Southern), a monumental 19th-century grande dame in cut stone (its lobby is just the place for "scene-iors" to take their coffee or tea). Turn left beyond the hotel and right into Merchants Road, location of the **Blarney Woollen Mills,** for Irish clothing, and (on the top floor) **Meadows & Byrne** for well-designed Irish goods for the home. Turn right out of the Woollen Mills, and take the next turn right along **New Dock Street** into **Flood Street,** the heart of medieval Galway, a tiny area where all the cutest shops are jam-packed together, including **Cobwebs,** abrim with offbeat antique jewelry, old binoculars, and bronze model airplanes. For a feel of the essential Galway, cross the road to the banks of the **River Corrib,** and walk to your left to the **Spanish Arch.** When natives feel homesick, this is the view they think of: white water breaking on the dark surface of the swift-flowing Corrib.

Staying on this side of the Corrib, cross over the bridge and take the riverside footpath past the Jurys Inn and some old warehouses. Turn left over O'Brien's Bridge for the historic **Bridge Mills,** now outfitted with a designer swap shop, a basement restaurant overlooking the river, and **Sam Beardon, Sculptor and Jewellery.** Cross the bridge again, taking the first right into Cross Street and right into Kirwan's Lane. Here, **Design Concourse Ireland/Judy Greene Pottery** has locally made turned-wood objects, basketware, and perfumery.

Medieval Kirwan's Lane leads you on to Quay Street and **Twice as Nice,** a vintage- and antique-clothing boutique with old Irish linen and gold and silver jewelry. Continue up High Street to **Faller's Sweaters and Tweeds,** just the place to buy an Aran sweater, and **The Kilkenny Shop,** Galway's largest emporium of Irish-designed products, with a dazzling selection of chic John Rocha crystal, Newbridge Silver, and Nicholas Mosse pottery.

Farther up on the right, **O'Maille** has some great mohair wraps and *the* essential Galway fashion item, a Jack Murphy raincoat. Top one off with a rainproof Stetson with a feather in it and you'll pass for a local.

High Street leads into William Street, where you'll find **The Treasure Chest,** a three-story shop selling upmarket Irish goods. Its exterior, painted in Wedgwood blue with white swags, just like the famous china, is a favorite with photographers. **Brown Thomas,** on William at the corner of Eglinton, has long been Galway's most upscale department store. The post office is on Eglinton Street. A few steps up Williamsgate Street brings us back to Eyre Square and your starting point at the TIO.

partitioned snugs at lunchtime for an inexpensive selection of imaginative bar food. It's a good place to mingle with local actors, writers, artists, musicians, and students, although it can become sardine-can crowded. ✉ *17 Cross St., Spanish Arch* ⊕ *www.tighneachtain.com.*

WORTH NOTING

Claddagh. On the west bank of the Corrib estuary, this district was once an Irish-speaking fishing village outside the walls of the old town. The name is an Anglicization of the Irish *cladach,* which means "marshy ground." It retained a strong, separate identity until the 1930s, when its traditional thatch cottages were replaced by a conventional housing plan and its unique character and traditions were largely lost. One thing has survived: the Claddagh ring, composed of two hands clasped around a heart with a crown above it (symbolizing love, friendship, and loyalty), was designed some 400 years ago by a goldsmith in this village, and is still used by many Irish, and Irish diaspora, as a wedding ring. Reproductions in gold or silver are favorite Galway souvenirs.

Galway Cathedral. On Nun's Island, which forms the west bank of the River Corrib beside the Salmon Weir Bridge, stands Galway's largest Catholic church, dedicated by Cardinal Cushing of Boston in 1965, and also called of the Cathedral of Our Lady Assumed into Heaven and St. Nicholas. It was built on the site of the old Galway jail; a white cross embedded in the pavement of the adjacent parking lot marks the site of the cemetery that stood beside the prison. A calm and peaceful spot, especially appealing to church-lovers. ✉ *Nun's Island* ☎ *091/563–577* ⊕ *www.galwaycathedral.ie* 🎫 *Free.*

Galway City Museum. The city's civic museum, housed in a modern building behind the Spanish Arch, contains materials relating to local history: old photographs, antiquities (the oldest is a stone ax head carbon-dated to 3500 BC), and other historical gewgaws, including a full-scale Galway hooker (turf-carrying boat) in the stairwell. Its café, The Kitchen, is a lively lunch and coffee spot. ✉ *Spanish Parade, Spanish Arch* ☎ *091/532–640* ⊕ *www.galwaycitymuseum.ie* 🎫 *Free* 🕙 *June–Sept., daily 10–5; Oct.–May, Tues.–Sat. 10–5.*

Lynch Memorial Window. Embedded in a stone wall above a built-up Gothic doorway off Market Street, the window marks the spot where, according to legend, James Lynch FitzStephen, mayor of Galway in the early 16th century, condemned his son to death after the young man confessed to murdering a Spanish sailor who had romanced his girlfriend. When no one could be found to carry out the execution, Judge Lynch hanged his son himself, ensuring that justice prevailed, before retiring into seclusion. ✉ *Market St., Center.*

Lynch's Castle. Now a branch of the Allied Irish Banks, this is the finest remaining example in Galway of a 16th-century fortified house—fortified because neighboring Irish tribes persistently raided the village, whose commercial life excluded them. The decorative details on its stone lintels are of a type usually found only in southern Spain. Historical material about the castle can be seen on the ground floor. ✉ *Shop St., Center.*

NUI Galway. Opened in 1846 to promote the development of local industry and agriculture, NUI Galway today is a center for Irish-language and Celtic studies. The Tudor Gothic–style quadrangle, completed in 1848, is worth a visit, though much of the rest of the campus is architecturally undistinguished. The library here has an important archive of Celtic-language materials, and in July and August the university hosts courses in Irish studies for overseas students. The campus is across the River Corrib, in the northwestern corner of the city. ✉ *Newcastle Rd., University* ☎ *091/524–411* 🌐 *www.nuigalway.ie.*

St. Nicholas' Collegiate Church Galway. Built by the Anglo-Normans in 1320 and enlarged in 1486 and again in the 16th century, the church contains many fine carvings and gargoyles dating from the late Middle Ages, and it's one of the best-preserved medieval churches in Ireland. Legend has it that Columbus prayed here on his last stop before setting off on his voyage to the New World. On Saturday mornings, a street market, held in the pedestrian way beside the church, attracts dozens of vendors and hundreds of shoppers. ✉ *Junction of Mainguard St. and Lombard St., Center* ☎ *091/564–648* 🌐 *www.stnicholas.ie* 🎫 *Free* 🕒 *Daily 8–dusk.*

WHERE TO EAT

$$ EUROPEAN 🍴 **Ard Bia at Nimmo's.** Good food and the friendly, enthusiastic staff make this bustling bistro one of Galway's most popular restaurants. The central location in an old stone boathouse overlooking the Corrib River adds to the pleasure. Downstairs is one of Galway's busiest wine bars and luncheon spots, Ard Bia, which serves casual meals ($), while upstairs is a more sophisticated restaurant. The long, spacious, second-floor room has flamboyant maroon-and-off-white walls, wooden floors, and well-spaced tables, with an eclectic mix of quirky, white-painted, stick- or spoon-back chairs. The menu is short but well balanced, and while presentation is theatrical, the food also tastes good. Try the west-coast scallops with pea-and-truffle sauce to start, then juniper-spiced Kildare venison or spiced monkfish with Lebanese broth, mussels, spinach and sweet peas. Lobster and black sole are available in season. [$] *Average main: €21* ✉ *The Long Walk, Spanish Arch* ☎ *091/561–114* 🌐 *ardbia.com.*

$$$ EUROPEAN 🍴 **Kirwan's Lane.** Look for Mike O'Grady's stylish modern restaurant in a revamped alley at the river end of Quay Street. Tables clad in white damask (covered with paper tablecloths at lunchtime), narrow floor-to-ceiling windows, and a quarry-tile floor set the stage for an informal, bistro-style menu. A seafood bar offers a tapas-style light menu that includes sushi, local oysters, and fresh crab cocktail. On the main menu, a great starter is seared king scallops and crispy pork belly with cauliflower puree and plum preserve. Main courses have similarly imaginative twists—breast of chicken and venison sausage with girolles, farfalle, pear and rosemary puree, or sautéed scallops with smoked garlic-infused spinach, and a vegetarian favorite: wild mushroom and asparagus risotto with truffle oil and Parmesan shavings.

Pedestrian alleys and high-style boutiques help make Galway into a stroller's paradise—keep your eye out for the many 19th-century footscrapers.

$ *Average main: €25* ✉ *Kirwan's La., Spanish Arch* ☎ *091/568–266* ⊕ *kirwanslane.com* ⊗ *Closed Sun. Nov.–Apr. No lunch Sun.*

$$
EUROPEAN

✕ **Malt House.** Hidden away in a flower-filled courtyard off High Street in the center of old Galway is the lunch and dinner venue of choice for the city's movers and shakers. A cool, contemporary space with leather tub chairs, small but with well-spaced wooden-top tables and a wooden floor, the specialty here is seasonal local seafood, with daily specials on the blackboard. Oysters come from Clarinbridge, fresh crab from Miltown Malbay, and smoked salmon from the Burren Smokehouse, Lisdoonvarna. Prawns, crab claws, and scallops are served with samphire, seaweed, and potato boxty, while roast saddle of rabbit is stuffed with spinach, apricots, and pine nuts. Vegetarians can sample pumpkin, spinach, and lentil dahl, or nut-crusted St. Tola's goat cheese with buttered kale. Desserts include blackberry cheesecake with ginger biscuit, or an Irish farmhouse cheese board. $ *Average main: €24* ✉ *Old Malte Arcade, High St., Center* ☎ *091/567–866* ⊕ *themalthouse. ie* ⊗ *Closed Sun.*

$$
ECLECTIC

✕ **Martine's Restaurant Galway.** With its red walls, its mahogany bar topped by a Victorian mirror, and Otis Redding crooning in the background, this cozy bistro-style wine bar is an excellent option for those evenings when you just want a simple meal nicely served in a pleasant ambience. Beyond the tiny wine bar are two more dining areas; go for a window table if you can in order to watch the passersby on busy Quay Street. Typical main courses could be Thai mussels in chili-lemongrass broth with chips, or the tandoori chicken with mint raita, or the splendid beef lasagna. Steaks from the charcoal oven and rack of lamb are

CLOSE UP

The Galway Saturday Market

Locals get up very early on Saturday in Galway in order to get the pick of the goods on offer at the Saturday food market. As many as 90 colorful stall-holders set out their wares in the area behind the Collegiate Church of St. Nicholas in the city center. Take your pick of the Mediterranean goods on offer at the Real Olive Company; sample a wide selection of Irish cheeses from Sheridan's Cheesemongers; treat yourself to an outdoor lunch at the Madras Curry Stall; get sushi from the Japanese-run Da Kappa-ya Sushi; and end on a sweet note with dessert from Yummy Crêpes. Organic-vegetable sellers, plant sellers, herbalists, cheese mongers, and bakers are joined by hat sellers, wood carvers, and knitwear stalls. A selection of Galway's famously wacky buskers entertain with music, juggling, and dance. Come early and hungry! 🌐 *www.galwaymarket.net.*

also menu staples. Service is warm and attentive, even at the busiest times. For dessert, regulars recommend the bread-and-butter pudding, or opt for the fabulous *affogatto*—a scoop of vanilla ice topped with hot espresso. [$] *Average main: €20* ✉ *21 Quay St., Spanish Arch* ☎ *091/565–662* 🌐 *www.winebar.ie.*

$ SEAFOOD 🍴 **McDonagh's Seafood House.** This longtime Galway landmark is partly a self-service fish-and-chips bar ($) and partly a "real" fish restaurant. If you haven't yet tried fish-and-chips, this is the place to start: cod, whiting, mackerel, haddock, or hake is deep-fried in a light batter while you watch. The reasonably priced fish is served with a heap of fabulous freshly cooked chips (which have won a nationwide competition for the best french fries in Ireland), and eaten at communal tables—a great way to meet the locals. Or go for the slightly more expensive Seafood Restaurant menu: Galway oysters au naturel, perhaps, followed by seared scallops with black pudding; or splurge on a seafood platter—local mussels, scallops, prawns, and oysters in a garlic-and-wine sauce. The McDonaghs are one of Galway's biggest entrepreneurial families, in charge of several hotels in addition to this spot. [$] *Average main: €15* ✉ *22 Quay St., Spanish Arch* ☎ *091/565–001* 🌐 *mcdonaghs.net* ⏲ *Restaurant: closed Sun., no restaurant lunch (fish-and-chip bar open noon–9 pm Mon.–Sat.).*

WHERE TO STAY

■ TIP→ If there's a city in Ireland that never sleeps, this must be it. If you want to get some shut-eye, ask for a room in the back of your city-center hotel or simply stay out of town.

$ B&B/INN 🏨 **Adare Guest House.** A five-minute walk from the city center, across the River Coribb, this family-run guesthouse, managed by the son of the original owners, makes a handy base for exploring Galway. **Pros:** convenient, quiet location; free parking; walking distance of pub-restaurant area. **Cons:** exterior of building very plain; bedrooms vary in size; hugely popular: book early. [$] *Rooms from: €110* ✉ *9 Father Griffin*

Pl., Spanish Arch ☎ *091/582–638* ⊕ *www.adareguesthouse.ie* ⤶ *11 rooms* ⦿ *Breakfast.*

$$
HOTEL
Fodor's Choice
★

🏨 **the g Hotel.** "G" is for glamour—or good grief (depending on your taste)—at this flamboyant player at the top end of Galway's hotel scene, whose architects worked with superstar hat designer Philip Treacy (a native of Galway) to create an interior that is every bit as fanciful as Treacy's hats. **Pros:** a must for design lovers; it may be OTT, but it's fun and a much-loved reminder of Celtic Tiger Ireland. **Cons:** will wreck your budget; 1 km (½ mile) from town center; restaurant is ordinary, but expensive. $ *Rooms from: €160* ✉ *Wellpark* ☎ *091/865–200* ⊕ *www.theghotel.ie* ⤶ *101 rooms* ⦿ *Breakfast.*

$
B&B/INN

🏨 **The Huntsman Inn.** Situated 1 km (½ mile) from Eyre Square, across the road from the exotic g Hotel and a stone's throw from Lough Atalia, this pub with rooms makes an excellent base for visiting Galway City if you're traveling by car. **Pros:** free car parking; within walking distance of city center, on bus route; bar is a good place to mix with locals. **Cons:** apart from the window boxes, nothing scenic or romantic about the place; rooms are a bit plain, as you'd expect for the price. $ *Rooms from: €110* ✉ *164 College Rd.* ☎ *091/562–849* ⊕ *www.huntsmaninn. com* ⤶ *12 rooms.*

$
HOTEL

🏨 **Jurys Inn Galway.** Expect good-quality budget accommodations at this four-story hotel set beside the historic Spanish Arch and the river. **Pros:** reliable Irish budget hotel chain; great location for pubs, clubs, and river views. **Cons:** rates subject to demand, so book early; favorite hotel chain for large groups of partying Irish. $ *Rooms from: €95* ✉ *Quay St., Spanish Arch* ☎ *091/566–444* ⊕ *www.jurysinn.com/hotels/ galway* ⤶ *130 rooms.*

$$
HOTEL

🏨 **Park House Hotel.** Even though this is a large, luxury hotel in central Galway, snazzily converted from a 200-year-old warehouse, it feels like a home-away-from-home, thanks to attentive owner-managers. **Pros:** friendly, professional staff; a haven of quiet. **Cons:** tricky to find vehicle entrance first time. $ *Rooms from: €165* ✉ *Forster St., Center* ☎ *091/564–924* ⊕ *www.parkhousehotel.ie* ⤶ *84 rooms* ⦿ *Breakfast.*

$$
HOTEL
Fodor's Choice
★

🏨 **Radisson Blu Hotel and Spa.** The Radisson Blu remains a firm favorite of both business and leisure travelers, with its striking contemporary design overlooking Lough Atalia, an inflow of Galway Bay, a stone's throw from Eyre Square. **Pros:** stylish venue right at the heart of the social scene; sea views in the city center. **Cons:** very busy during Galway's many festivals; arriving by car can be a slow business in peak periods. $ *Rooms from: €149* ✉ *Lough Atalia Rd., Center* ☎ *091/538–300* ⊕ *www.radissonhotelgalway.com* ⤶ *272 rooms* ⦿ *Breakfast.*

$$
HOTEL

🏨 **The Twelve.** Located in a seaside village on Galway Bay's edgy, boho north coast, this boutique hotel is 10 minutes' drive from both the city center and the wilds of Connemara. **Pros:** stylish, buzzy destination with oodles of character; underground parking; choice of excellent restaurants on-site. **Cons:** uninspiring views from bedroom windows. $ *Rooms from: €150* ✉ *Bearna Coast Rd. (R337), Galway* ☎ *091/597– 000* ⊕ *www.thetwelvehotel.ie* ⤶ *26 rooms, 22 suites* ☯ *The West Restaurant closed Sun., Mon., and Tues.* ⦿ *Breakfast.*

NIGHTLIFE AND THE ARTS

Because of its small size and concentration of pubs and restaurants, Galway can seem even livelier at 11 pm than it does at 11 am. On weekends, when there are lots of students and other revelers in town, Eyre Square and environs can be rowdy after pub-closing time—which is 2 am on Friday and Saturday. On the plus side, if you've been staying out in the country and you're ready for a little nightlife, you're certain to find plenty of it here.

NIGHTLIFE

The best spot for traditional music is the area between Eyre Square and the Spanish Arch. Although many pubs are open until 2 am on weekends, there is a big post-pub nightclub scene here, centered in the Eyre Square area.

CLUBS

Electric Garden & Theatre. Galway's liveliest nightclub has several different spaces including Electric, the main room, and the indoor-outdoor Glasshouse. The cocktails are great, as are the sounds, ranging from Balearic beats to house anthems to hip hop Brooklyn Beats nights. ⊠ *Abbeygate St., Center* ☎ *091/565–976* ⊕ *www.electricgalway.com.*

Halo Nightclub. This sophisticated spot for dressy over-23-year-olds has live entertainment in four bars on two floors and two dance floors, as well as quiet booths. It's open Friday, Saturday, and bank holiday Sunday from 11 pm. ⊠ *36 Upper Abbeygate St., Center* ☎ *091/565–976* ⊕ *halonightclub.com.*

PUBS

Áras na nGael. Cross O'Brien Bridge and take the first left to find this Irish-speaking social club/pub, which is a great place to hear traditional music, watch (or join) dancing and language classes, and hear the Irish language in use. Non–Irish speakers are very welcome. ⊠ *45 Dominick St., Centre* ☎ *091/567–824* ⊕ *www.arasnangael.ie.*

The Crane Bar. There's traditional music from 9:30 most nights in a room above this tiny bar, to the west of Claddagh, but come early to get a seat. ⊠ *2 Sea Rd.* ☎ *091/587–419.*

The Dáil Bar. While it looks traditional with its dark-wood decor, the Dáil is actually a recent arrival on the pub scene, and very popular with a younger crowd. ⊠ *42–44 Middle St., Center* ☎ *091/563–777.*

Fibber Magees. Late-night hot spot in town center whose slogan is "cheap drinks and loud music," attracting mainly under 25s. Late nights Friday to Sunday. ⊠ *3 Eyre Sq., Center.*

The Front Door. A lively spot for the twentysomethings, the Front Door has four bars spread over two floors, and a late bar until 2 am Wednesday to Sunday. ⊠ *3 High St., Center* ☎ *091/563–757.*

King's Head. You can usually find a session after about 9 pm at this local favorite. ⊠ *15 High St., Center* ⊕ *www.thekingshead.ie.*

McSwiggan's. A hugely popular Galway City pub with a restaurant upstairs, McSwiggans has everything from church pews to ancient carriage lamps contributing to its eclectic character. ⊠ *3 Eyre St., Wood Quay, Center* ☎ *091/568–917.*

Monroe's. A large and sociable pub, Monroe's has traditional music nightly and set dancing on Tuesday. ⊠ *20 Dominick St., Center* ☎ *091/583–397.*

The Quays. For many people the quintessential Galway bar is The Quays, a tall, narrow pub on three stories with live music upstairs. ⊠ *Quay St., Center* ☎ *091/568–347.*

The Róisín Dubh. A legend in its own right and a serious venue for emerging rock and traditional bands, the Róisín Dubh often showcases big, if still-struggling, talents. ⊠ *Dominick St., Spanish Arch* ☎ *091/586–540* ⊕ *roisindubh.net.*

Sally Longs. For late-night sounds heard from the comfort of your own table, try Sally Longs, Galway's hard-rock pub, much loved by bikers. ⊠ *Upper Abbeygate St., Center* ☎ *091/565–756.*

Taaffe's. In the midst of the shopping district, Taaffe's is very busy on afternoons. ⊠ *19 Shop St., Center* ☎ *091/564–066.*

Tigh Coíli Bar. Up-and-coming young musicians play at this cozy bar in traditional sessions all day long. A great place to experience your first "session" of music. ⊠ *Mainguard St., Center* ☎ *091/561–294.*

Tigh Neachtain. If you're looking for *the* place to check out the quintessential Galway vibe, head here. Find a cozy corner and you'll stay longer than you should. ⊠ *17 Cross St., Spanish Arch* ☎ *091/568–820* ⊕ *www.tighneachtain.com.*

THE ARTS

THEATER

An Taibhdhearc Theatre. Founded in 1928 by Hilton Edwards and Micheál Mac Liammóir as the national Irish-language theater, An Taibhdhearc (pronounced *on tie*-vark) continues to produce first-class shows. Productions are mainly of Irish works in both the English and the Irish languages and it also hosts touring productions. ⊠ *Middle St., Center* ☎ *091/562–024* ⊕ *www.antaibhdhearc.com.*

Druid Theatre Company. Esteemed for its adventurous and accomplished productions, the Druid Theatre Company mainly showcases 20th-century Irish and European plays. The players have performed at Lincoln Center in New York, and several London venues. When they're home, they usually appear at the Town Hall, and they sometimes have a production at Galway Arts Festival in late July. ⊠ *Druid La., Center* ☎ *091/568–660* ⊕ *www.druid.ie.*

Macnas. An internationally renowned, roving Galway-based troupe of performance artists, Macnas has raised street theater in Ireland to new levels. Their participation in the Galway Arts Festival's annual parade is always much anticipated. ⊠ *Fisheries Field, Salmon Weir Bridge, Center* ☎ *091/561–462* ⊕ *www.macnas.com.*

Continued on page 468

Gael Force

THE BOOM IN IRISH
MUSIC & DANCE

Traditional Irish music and dance have taken the world by storm—but you need to journey to the West of Ireland to really get in step.

When the eye-popping spectacular of Riverdance first "tapped" its way into the Irish psyche in 1995 by jazzing up traditional step dancing and moving it from the local parish hall to the stages of Dublin's Point Theatre, it immediately sent its audiences reeling. The first troupe to introduce the Irish jig to world theaters, it has since performed before 18 million people and taken in more than $1 billion at the box office. Along the way, it gave once-languishing, "old-fashioned" arts of Ireland's folkloric music and dance a modern chic: today, thousands of young Irish are learning to play hornpipes, sing the old chanties, and dance the old jigs.

A GAELIC REBIRTH

Irish dancing has always been popular in American-Irish communities, as the first Riverdance stars proved: Jean Butler was born on Long Island to a mother from Mayo, while Michael Flatley was born in Chicago to emigrant parents. In 1995 Flatley founded his own triumphant show, Lord of the Dance, which spawned international troupes and, in turn, was followed by the Feet of Flames show, with more than 100 dancers.

Thanks to all these dance companies, the world has fallen in step—literally—as the passion for Irish dancing has taken hold. The World Irish Dancing Championship of 2014 attracted 5,000 dancers and 24,000 spectators to London for the eight-day competition.

GOING "TRAD"

Competitors, indeed: Irish dancing is now also a competitive sport, with thousands of passionate devotees (see its social networking site, ⊕ www.diddlyi.com) attending *feis* (festivals). Thousands of dollars are invested in costumes, wigs (you thought all those ringlets were real?) and, last but not least, shoes. Irish dancers are now found in far-off lands like Japan and Estonia. Whatever accounts for Irish "Trad's" continuing enormous crossover success—does it appeal because it is a return to a simpler time, or remains a dazzling slice of national culture in a blandly homogeneous age?—it certainly keeps growing more popular.

HARPING ON

Ireland is the only country to have a musical instrument as its national emblem. The harp appears on *garda* (police) caps, Irish Euro coins, and government stationery. The original Irish harp was a small, triangular instrument designed to be held on the knee (not the large version of today's concert halls). The harp was first used as a logo for Guinness stout in 1850. The Guinness harp faces right, while the national emblem faces left.

COME AND MEET THOSE DANCING FEET

Ireland, along with the rest of the world, was swept off its feet by the spectacular success of Riverdance. Thanks to that phenomenon, the thunderous dancing, stomping, clacking feet of today's Irish youth have once again taken up the trigger-quick step dances of old and the traditional music of the past.

Before Riverdance, Irish dancing was something schoolchildren performed chiefly for competitions, and sometimes on civic occasions, with their arms rigidly held by their sides (only the legs would move—a holdover from religious teachings that felt that dancing was sinful), and an expression of grave concentration on their faces. Today, it's a big thing for young people and also, due to those glitzy costumes and contests, a very expensive hobby.

Riverdance was a conscious attempt to project a more modern image of Ireland, and central to its roaring success were two American step dancers, Michael Flatley and Jean Butler. Their dazzling innovations reflected their origin in the more flexible American step dance competition world. Before Riverdance, the only options for prize-winning Irish step-dancers were to teach or to retire—now hundreds of dancers are employed worldwide in touring shows inspired by Riverdance, such as Flatley's Celtic Tiger and Butler's Dancing on Dangerous Ground.

SET DANCING

Set dancing is also the name given to social dancing in which four couples face one another in a square in dances based on the French cotillion and the quadrilles. Nearly every town in Ireland once again has dancing at least one evening a week.

STEPS & SETS

Ireland has a long tradition of solo dancing, first introduced by the jigs, reels, and hornpipes that traveling dancing masters taught in the 18th century. Some are performed in hard shoes, with the dancer beating out rhythms on the floor to complement the music, while others are danced with soft shoes to emphasize their graceful, airborne nature. In both cases, the main interest of the dance is in the foot and lower leg. Some solo dances have specific patterns of steps and are only danced to one tune and are known as "set dances"—in some places, set dances are known as table dances because the dancer often jumped up on the table to display his or her skills.

FANCY FOOTWORK

Because there were no accompanying drums, the sound of the feet on wooden floors has always been an important element in Irish dancing. When dancing really took off in the 18th century, many cabins only had earth floors, so the custom was to remove the top half of the half-door, and dance on that. Dancing masters used to display their prowess on fair days by dancing on soapy barrel lids, so they developed the ability to vary their steps in a confined space. From this came the tradition of dancing solos on one spot.

JUST FOLLOW THE SOUND OF THE MUSIC . . .

If you're interested in "Trad" music, the beat of a bodhrán or the tap of a shoe will likely lead you to Galway and County Clare's great folk *fleadhs* (festivals) and pub *seisiúns* (sessions).

THE BIGGEST FLEADH

The biggest festival of all is a three-day event called the All-Ireland finals of Fleadh Cheoil na hÉireann (pronounced flah-kyole— "festival of music"). The 2014 event was held in Sligo and was attended by nearly 10,000 musicians and 200,000 visitors, many of them second-generation Irish from overseas. This noncommercial festival of traditional music takes over a whole town, whose pubs become centers for casual music making. The All-Ireland rotates to different towns every year, much to the delight of the pub owners in the chosen town (⊕ www.fleadhcheoil.ie).

THE ENNIS BLOW-OUT

During the last week in May, the pleasant country town of Ennis hosts the **Fleadh Nua** (⊕ www.fleadhnua.com/), a massive eight-day-long celebration of dancing and song, with concerts, workshops, competitions, and *céilis*. Many of the events are open-air and free, and there is a great festive buzz. Ennis is home to a growing cadre of musicians: the Custys, Siobhán and Tommy Peoples,

flute player Kevin Crawford, and accordion whiz kid Murty Ryan. Check out **Knox's Pub** (⊠ Abbey St. ☎ 065/682–9264) and **Cruise's Bar** (⊠ Abbey St. ☎ 065/684–1800) for lively evening sessions.

TOE-TAPPING IN MILTOWN

Held during the first week in July, the **Willie Clancy Summer School** (⊕ www.willieclancyfestival.com) is Ireland's biggest traditional music summer school. Classes, lectures, and recitals attract around 1,500 students from 42 countries to this tiny village on the west coast of Clare near Spanish Point. Set dancing is a big draw here, and a surefire way to make friends.

GOOD BEHAVIOR

If you happen on a pub session there are a few ground rules. Don't talk during the solo, and don't stare at the singer; most people look at the floor. Buy the musicians a drink if it's a small session, and if at all possible, have a party piece to contribute yourself. It's the gesture that counts.

A Trad *seisiún*, Sligo, Co. Sligo, Ireland

FIDDLING AROUND

Irish Traditional music is very much the music of the people, played on relatively simple, portable instruments: fiddle, flute, tin whistle, accordion, handheld drum, and, recent additions, guitar or banjo.

SQUEEZE-BOXES & ACCORDIONS

Squeeze-box is a generic term for a variety of melodeons, accordions, and concertinas. The concertina is a small, hexagonal-shaped button-key instrument. The simplest accordion is the one-row button accordion, usually called a melodeon. Styles of playing can vary enormously. Sharon Shannon is rooted in the highly rhythmic East Clare style but can veer into swing and Cajun styles as she plays her wildly energetic dance music.

UILLEANN PIPES

The uilleann (pronounced "illun") pipes, literally "elbow" pipes, are a quieter indoor version of bagpipes. The player sits while playing with a bag under one arm, the bellows under the other, and the "chanter," which plays the melody, on the thigh. A temperamental instrument, it can be heartrenderingly beautiful in the hands of a master like Liam O'Flynn or Paddy Keenan of The Bothy Band.

FLUTES & WHISTLE

The tin whistle is the ideal beginner's instrument, but be sure to buy one in the key of D. It is still called the penny whistle because it costs so little to buy. But the flute used in Irish music is usually a simple wooden flute—hear it at its best in the hands of Matt Molloy and Paddy Moloney of The Chieftains, Mary Bergin, and Olcan Masterson.

FIDDLE

The classical violin all but in name, this is the most popular instrument in Trad music for its singing, swooping versatility, its portability, and its relative affordability. Local fiddle styles still persist, especially in Donegal, Sligo, and the Sliabh Luachra region of Cork and Kerry and virtuosos such as Frankie Gavin of Dé Dannan, Martin Hayes, Tommy Peoples, and Liz Doherty are famed for their rhythm, color, and ornamentation.

BODHRÁN

The Bodhrán (pronounced "bow-rawn") is a simple goat's skin drum played with the back of the hand or a small wooden stick. When played well, by Mel Mercier, John Joe Kelly, or Tommy Hayes, it makes an exciting addition to the running rhythms of Trad music. They make it look easy, but in the hands of an untrained amateur, a badly played bodhrán can wreck a session.

HAPPY LISTENING!

Olcan Masterson, on the whistle

SEÁN Ó RIADA The father of "modern" Trad music, this composer and visionary Irish language enthusiast (1931–71)—noted for his film score *Mise Éire* and his Irish language Mass *Cúil Aodha*—established the prototype traditional Irish group, Ceoltóirí Chualann, in 1963, who evolved into The Chieftains.

DÉ DANNAN This famed group grew from regular sessions in Hughes' bar in Spiddal, Co. Galway, in 1974. Brilliant fiddle and flute player Frankie Gavin, bouzouki whiz Alec Finn, banjo master Carlie Piggot, and Johnny "Ringo" McDonagh on bodhrán were joined by singers Dolores Keane, Mary Black, and Maura O'Connell (all now solo artists). *Dé Dannan* (1975) and *Mist-Covered Mountain* (1980) are their timeless evocations of the West of Ireland.

THE CHIEFTAINS If you've seen a poster of Irish musicians wearing unhip cardigans, baggy trousers, and bad haircuts, it was probably The Chieftains, who went professional in 1975. Outstanding musicians, they include uilleann-piper Paddy Moloney, flute player Matt Molloy, harper Derek Bell (recently deceased), and Seán Keane and Martin Fay (fiddlers). Any of their famous 35 albums are worth owning.

PLANXTY The word *planxty* means a lively tune (without words) written to honor a patron, but it is now forever associated with a "supergroup" formed in 1972 by singer Christy Moore, with Dónal Lunny, Andy Irvine, and Liam O'Flynn. Their haunting debut album, *Planxty* (1972), is a must. Reincarnated in the later '70s as The Bothy Band, their 1975 debut album remains a classic.

ALTAN This Donegal-based band, led by Mairead ní Mhaonaigh (fiddle and vocals), showcase the special Donegal way with fiddle and flute.

ANÚNA This vocal and instrumental ensemble, founded in the 1990s, represents the mystical, spiritual aspect of Celtic music, and is widely known through performances with the original Riverdance production. *Anúna* (1993), their first album, is still their best.

KILA Touted by the under-30s to be the future of Irish music, this group shows African percussion, Andean flute, and Eastern European folk music among the influences on their debut album, *Tóg é go Bog é*—roughly translated as "Take it Easy."

Altan

8

IN FOCUS GAEL FORCE

GALLERIES

Kenny's Gallery. Take the Ballybrit bus (or a 15-minute walk) from the city center to this gallery, which hosts about a dozen shows a year. It's open Monday–Saturday 9–5. ⊠ *Liosbán Retail Park, Tuam Rd. (N17)* ☏ *091/709–350* ⊕ *www.the kennygallery.ie.*

Norman Villa Gallery. Reflecting a passion for modern Irish art, this gallery exhibits work in the gallery owner's home and garden. ⊠ *86 Lower Salthill, Salthill* ☏ *091/521–131* ⊕ *www.normanvillagallery.com.*

NUI Galway. The art gallery at University College has a number of intriguing exhibitions each year. ⊠ *Newcastle Rd., University* ☏ *915/24411* ⊕ *www.nuigalway.ie.*

SPORTS AND THE OUTDOORS

BICYCLING

Bike Hire Ireland. Prebook your bike of choice from a good range if you have strong preferences, then just go. Or opt for a self-guided tour: the company has handy drop-off points in Connemara, the Burren, and Kerry. ⊠ *Seamus Quirke Rd.* ☏ *091/525–007* ⊕ *www.bikehireireland. com.*

FISHING

Galway City is the gateway to Connemara, and Connemara is the place to fish.

Duffy's Fishing. A good range of clothing for anglers, and tackle, is for sale here. ⊠ *5 Mainguard St., Center* ☏ *091/562–367.*

Freeney's Sports. You can get fishing licenses, tackle, and bait, and arrange to hire a traditional fly-fishing guide or book a sea-angling trip at Freeney's Sports. ⊠ *19–23 High St., Center* ☏ *091/568–794.*

GOLF

Galway Bay Golf Resort. An 18-hole parkland course near the village of Renville, 14 km (8½ miles) from the city, Galway Bay Golf Resort is on the shores of Galway Bay, opposite the city, and was designed by former Ryder Cup and World Cup golfer, Christy O'Connor Jr. The Atlantic Ocean forms a dramatic backdrop to a course featuring mature trees, concealed bunkers, and highly praised putting surfaces. ⊠ *Renville, Oranmore* ☏ *091/790–711* ⊕ *www.galwaybaygolfresort.com* ✉ *Fees: weekdays €40 (Fri. €25 via website), weekends €50* 🏌 *18 holes, 7308 yards, par 72. Practice area, caddies, club hire, caddy carts, buggies, catering* ☉ *Visitors: daily (some restrictions).*

Galway Golf Club. Galway Golf Club was established in 1895, and moved to its present location in suburban Salthill in 1925. At that point it was redesigned by course architect Alister McKenzie, who was also responsible for Augusta, home of the U.S. Masters. It has been the home base of two famous Irish pros, Christy O'Connor Sr., and his nephew, Christy O'Connor Jr. In spite of its proximity to the city, there are excellent views of Galway Bay, the Burren, and the Aran Islands. It has an abundance of trees, prickly gorse bushes in the rough, and some tricky fairways that run close to the ocean. ⊠ *Blackrock, Salthill* ☎ *091/522–033* ⊕ *www.galwaygolf.com* ▧ *Fees: €30 year-round, advance booking essential* ⚲. *18 holes, 2995 yards (Championship), par 70. Practice area, caddies, carts, buggies, catering* ⊙ *Visitors: Mon. and Tues.–Sat., some restrictions.*

RIVER CRUISING

Corrib Princess. A lovely way to spend a fine afternoon is to take a Corrib Cruise from Wood Quay, behind the Town Hall Theatre, at the Rowing Club; it lasts 1½ hours and travels 8 km (5 miles) up the River Corrib and about 6 km (4 miles) around Lough Corrib. There's a bar on board, tea and coffee, and a commentary. The trip costs €15, and boats depart daily at 2:30 and 4:30 from May through September, with an additional departure at 12:30 July through August. You can also rent the boat for an evening. ⊠ *Wood Quay, Galway* ☎ *091/592–447* ⊕ *www.corribprincess.ie.*

SHOPPING

ANTIQUES

Tempo Antiques. With an interesting collection of small antiques, Tempo also stocks jewelry, porcelain, and other small collectibles. ⊠ *9 Cross St., Center* ☎ *091/562–282* ⊕ *www.tempoantiques.com.*

Treasure Chest. Browse to your heart's content here for china, crystal, gifts, and classic clothing. ⊠ *31–33 William St., Center* ☎ *091/563–862* ⊕ *www.treasurechest.ie.*

BOOKS

Charlie Byrne's Bookshop. Book lovers should allow at least one hour for browsing at Charlie Byrne's, which not only sells a large, varied selection of new and used books and remainders but also has a wonderful emphasis on Irish interest. ⊠ *Middle St., Center* ☎ *091/561–766.*

CLOTHING

Blarney Woollen Mills. A great place for Irish souvenirs and clothing, Blarney is especially known for their casual Faller & Brown designer line. ⊠ *1–5 Merchants Rd., Center* ☎ *091/539–510.*

Faller's Sweater Shop. The choicest selection of Irish-made sweaters can be found here, and all competitively priced. ⊠ *25 High St., Center* ☎ *091/564–833.*

The Finishing Touch. Accessorize your outfit for the big occasion at this delightful little boutique stocked with a range of jewelry, handbags, clutch bags, wraps, headpieces, combs, and pins. ⊠ *Cross St. Lower, Center* ☎ *091/569–801.*

Galway Hat Shop. Galway City has an excellent hat shop, with stock ranging from ladies' high fashion to men's cloth caps. ⊠ *Corbett Court, Eyre Square Shopping Centre, Eyre Sq., Center* ☎ *091/561–052* ⊕ *www.hatshop.ie.*

8

O'Máille's. In addition to classically tailored clothing, O'Máille's is popular for its selection of Aran sweaters and handwoven tweeds. ⊠ *16 High St., Center* ☎ *091/562–696.*

CRAFTS AND GIFTS

Cloon Keen Atelier. A lovely little boutique stocked beautifully with packaged perfumes and candles, all made locally by dedicated artisans. ⊠ *Kirwan's La., Center* ☎ *091/565–736* ⊕ *www.cloonkeenatelier.com.*

Galway Irish Crystal. A factory outlet on the city's ring road, Galway Irish Crystal sells hand-cut Irish glass, Belleek Pottery, and other fine porcelain. ⊠ *Dublin Rd., Merlin Park* ☎ *091/757–311* ⊕ *www.galwaycrystal.ie.*

Judy Greene Pottery. Ceramics by Judy Greene—a local potter specializing in hand-thrown ceramics depicting Irish flora and landscape—and others can be found in this two-story treasure trove of handcrafts. ⊠ *Kirwan's La., Center* ☎ *091/561–753.*

Kilkenny Shop. Synonymous with good modern design in Ireland, the Kilkenny Shop stocks the best ceramics, crystal, leatherware, clothing, and other craft items from around the country. ⊠ *6/7 High St., Center* ☎ *091/566–110* ⊕ *www.kilkennyshop.com.*

FOOD

McCambridge's. This large, long-established deli on Galway's main street has a large selection of Irish and international specialist foods including home baking, local confectionary, charcuterie, homemade jams and preserves, and farmhouse cheeses. Light snacks are served in the second-floor café. ⊠ *38–39 Shop St., Center* ☎ *091/582–259* ⊕ *www.mccambridges.com.*

Sheridan's Cheesemongers. Together, Seamus and Kevin Sheridan know all of Ireland's artisan cheese makers personally and stock the widest possible range of delectable cheeses, complemented by charcuterie (mainly Italian). The wineshop upstairs will complete your picnic. ⊠ *16 Churchyard St., Center* ☎ *091/564–829* ⊕ *www.sheridanscheesemongers.com.*

JEWELRY

Cobwebs. Phyllis MacNamara's cute two-story boutique is filled with an irresistible selection of antique jewelry (real and costume) and collectibles for men and women, all with a witty twist. ⊠ *7 Quay La.,, Spanish Arch, Centre* ☎ *091/564–388* ⊕ *www.cobwebs.ie.*

Thomas Dillon's Claddagh Gold. Dating from 1750, Thomas Dillon's claims to be the original maker of Galway's famous Claddagh ring. In the back of the shop there's a small but interesting display of antique Claddagh rings and old Galway memorabilia. ⊠ *1 Quay St., Spanish Arch* ☎ *091/566–365* ⊕ *www.claddaghring.ie.*

MALLS

Eyre Square Shopping Centre. On the southwest side of Eyre Square and imaginatively designed to incorporate parts of the old town walls, the Eyre Square Shopping Centre is a good spot to pick up moderately priced clothing, including rain gear. ⊠ *Eyre Sq., Galway* ☎ *091/568–302* ⊕ *www.eyresquarecentre.com.*

Galway Shopping Centre. This spacious indoor mall features more than 60 outlets just 10 minutes' walk from Eyre Square with ample parking. ⊠ *Headford Rd., Centre* ☏ *091/561–803* ⊕ *www.galwaysc.com.*

MUSIC

Kieran Moloney. A display case of the craft of Irish luthiers, this lovely shop stocks acoustic stringed instruments and some wind instruments, including Irish handmade Uillean pipes, and, more tempting for the traveler, pocket-size tin whistles. ⊠ *Olde Malt Arcade, 17 High St., Center* ☏ *091/566–488.*

Opus II. This shop specializes in traditional Irish musical instruments, including the handheld drum, the *bodhrán* (pronounced bau-*rawn*), and CDs by Irish artists. ⊠ *4 High St., Center* ☏ *091/500–300* ⊕ *www. opus2.ie.*

P. Powell and Sons. The knowledgeable staff here can advise shoppers on buying traditional Irish musical instruments and CDs. ⊠ *The Four Corners, William St., Center* ☏ *091/562–295.*

THE OILEÁIN ÁRAINN (ARAN ISLANDS)

No one knows for certain when the Aran Islands—Inis Mór (Inishmore), Inis Meáin (Inishmaan), and Inis Oirr (Inisheer)—were first inhabited, but judging from the number of Bronze Age and Iron Age forts found here (especially on Inis Mór), 3000 BC is a safe guess.

Why wandering nomads in deerskin jerkins would be attracted to these barren islets remains a greater mystery, not least because fresh water and farmable land were (and still are) scarce commodities. Remote western outposts of the ancient province of Connaught (though they are not the country's westernmost points; that honor belongs to the Blasket Islands), these three islands were once as barren as the limestone pavements of the Burren, of which they are a continuation.

Today, the land is parceled into small, human-made fields surrounded by stone walls: centuries of erosion, generations of backbreaking labor, sheep, horses, and their attendant tons of manure have finally transformed this rocky wasteland into reasonably productive cropland. While traditional Irish culture fights a rearguard battle on the mainland, the islanders continue to preserve as best as they can a culture going back generations. Still, the Irish-speaking inhabitants enjoy a daily air service to Galway (subsidized by the government), motorized curraghs, satellite TV, and all the usual modern home conveniences. Yet they have retained a distinctness from mainlanders, preferring simple home decor, very plain food, and tightly knit communities, like the hardy fishing and farming folk from whom they are descended. Crime is virtually unknown in these parts; at your B&B, you'll likely find no locks on the guest-room doors, and the front-door latch will be left open. Many islanders have sampled life in Dublin or cities abroad but have returned to raise families, keeping the population stable at around 1,200. Tourists now flock here to see the ancient sights and savor the spectacular views: the uninterrupted expanse of the Atlantic on the western horizon;

8

CLOSE UP

Aran Rediscovered

During the 1800s, the islands, wracked by famine and mass emigration, were virtually forgotten by mainland Ireland. At the turn of the 20th century, however, the books of J. M. Synge (1871–1909)—who learned Irish on Inishmaan and wrote about its people in his famous play *Riders to the Sea*— prompted Gaelic revivalists to study and document this isolated bastion of Irish culture. To this day, Synge's travel book *The Aran Islands*, first published in 1907, and reissued by Penguin with a brilliant introduction by artist and mapmaker Tim Robinson in 1992, remains the best book ever written about the islands. Liam

O'Flaherty became one of the most famous sons of Inishmore through his novels, such as *Famine*. And in 1934, American director Robert Flaherty filmed his classic documentary *Man of Aran* on Inishmore, recording the islanders' dramatic battles with sea and storm, and bringing the islands into the world spotlight. The film is still highly esteemed by the islanders, and there are frequent showings on Inishmore during the summer months. Flaherty, incidentally, continues to be a common surname on the islands; it is hard to visit the islands *without* meeting a Flaherty.

the Connemara coast and its Twelve Bens to the northeast; and County Clare's Burren and the Cliffs of Moher to the southeast.

There's a small hotel on Inisheer and one on Inishmore, but there's no shortage of guesthouses and B&Bs, mostly in simple family homes. The best way to book is through the Galway City TIO. Each island has at least one wine-licensed restaurant serving plain home cooking. Most B&Bs will provide a packed lunch and an evening meal on request. For general information about visiting the Aran Islands and useful links, try ⊕ *www.discoverireland.ie/ireland-s-islands/the-aran-islands*.

GETTING HERE AND AROUND

The best place to book your trip to the Aran Islands is at the Galway Tourist Information Office.

Decide between a short flight, a 20-minute boat ride on a high-speed catamaran, or an hour-long trip on comfortable ferries.

Aer Arann Islands offers 10-minute flights to the Aran Islands. The fare is €45 round-trip, leaving from Connemara Airport near Inverin, 30 km (19 miles) west of Galway.

The majority of boats for the Aran Islands leave from Ros an Mhíl (Rossaveale), 37 km (23 miles) west of Galway City. (You can also reach the islands from Doolin in County Clare.) Park at Ros an Mhíl, or book a shuttle bus from the city when buying your ticket. There are at least two sailings a day, and four or more in high season, timed to facilitate day trips. Ask when boarding about interisland ferries if you intend to visit more than one island. Inishmore, the biggest island, is the only one with organized transport. Book a tour or taxi in advance (through the TIO in Galway), or hire a bicycle (including electric bikes) or pony and trap on landing. Galway-based Lally Tours sells a bus-and-ferry package.

As you arrive by plane over the Aran Islands, their famous stone-wall fences—built by medieval farmers to clear lands for farms—come into view.

Transportation Contacts Aer Arann Islands ☎ *091/593–034* ⊕ *www. aerarannislands.ie.* **Aran Bike Hire** ✉ *Kilronan Pier, Inishmore, Aran Islands, Co. Galway* ⊕ *www.aranbikehire.com.* **Galway Discover Ireland Centre.** Galway City's tourist office is the best place to go for ferry tickets to Aran Islands. ✉ *Forster St., Eyre Sq., Galway City, Co. Galway* ☎ *091/537–700* ⊕ *www. discoverireland.ie/Ireland-s-Islands/The-Aran-Islands.* **Noel Mahon Luxury Tours** ✉ *Killeany, Kilronan, Inishmore, Aran Islands, Co. Galway* ☎ *087/778– 2775* ⊕ *www.tourbusaranislands.com.*

INIS MÓR (INISHMORE)

31 km (18 miles) southwest of Salthill docks, 48 km (30 miles) west of Galway Docks.

With a population of 900, Inis Mór is the largest of the islands and the closest to the Connemara coast. It's also the most commercialized, its appeal slightly diminished by road traffic.

In summer, ferries arriving at Cill Ronáin (Kilronan), Inis Mór's main village and port, are met by minibuses and pony-and-cart drivers, all eager to show visitors "the sights." More than 8 km (5 miles) long and about 3 km (2 miles) wide at most points, with an area of 7,640 acres, the island is just a little too large to explore comfortably on foot in a day. The best way to see it is really by bicycle; bring your own or rent one from one of the vendors operating near the quay.

GETTING HERE AND AROUND

If you are lucky enough to stay overnight on Inishmore island, try to get away from the crowds of day-trippers in the daytime, who clog up the road between Kilronan and Dún Aengus from 11 am to about 6 pm. Head for the less frequented west of the island, visiting Dún Dúchathair, a dramatically sited promontory fort (freely accessible), only slightly less impressive than Dún Aengus, or walk the secluded east coast. **■ TIP→ Day-trippers: leave your luggage at Inishmore's Tourist Office (€1 per bag), or with the outfit that you are renting your bike from while you explore the island.**

> **ISLAND NIGHTS**
>
> To appreciate the fierce loneliness of the Aran Islands you must spend the night on one. Because all the islands, especially Inishmore, crawl with day-trippers, it's difficult to let their rugged beauty sink into your soul until 10 pm, when the sky is dark and the pubs fill with the acrid smell of peat smoke and Guinness. Once the day-trippers clear out, the islands' stunningly fierce and brooding beauty is disturbed only by the "baa" of the sheep and the incessant rush of the wind.

ESSENTIALS

Visitor Information Oileáin Árainn (Aran Islands)–Inis Mór (Inishmore) Tourist Office ✉ *Cill Ronáin (Kilronan), Co. Galway* ☎ *099/61263* 🌐 *www.discoverireland.ie/Ireland-s-Islands/The-Aran-Islands.*

EXPLORING

Dún Aengus. Even if you have only a few hours to explore Inis Mór, rent a bike (next to the pier) and head straight for Dún Aengus, one of the finest prehistoric monuments in Europe, dating from about 2000 BC. Spectacularly set on the edge of a 300-foot-tall cliff overlooking a sheer drop, the fort has defenses consisting of three rows of concentric circles. Whom the builders were defending themselves against is a matter of conjecture. From the innermost rampart there's a great view of the island and the Connemara coast. In order to protect this fragile monument from erosion, you should approach it only through the visitor center, which gives access to a 1-km (½-mile) uphill walk over uneven terrain—wear sturdy footwear. ✉ *7 km (4 miles) west of Cill Ronáin (Kilronan), Kilmurvey* ☎ *099/61008* 🌐 *www.heritageireland.ie/en/West/DunAonghasa/* 🎟 *€3* 🕒 *Apr.–Oct., daily 9:45–6; Nov.–Mar., daily 9:30–4.*

WHERE TO STAY

$$ B&B/INN 🏨 **Ard Einne Guesthouse.** Almost every window at this B&B on Inishmore looks out to the sea, making it the perfect place to de-stress. **Pros:** great location for getting away from it all; walking distance to pubs (half a mile) and restaurants (a mile and a half). **Cons:** one of the island's biggest guesthouses, thoroughly modernized; no elevator. [$] *Rooms from: €120* ✉ *Cill Ronáin (Kilronan), Co. Galway* ☎ *099/61126* 🌐 *www.ardeinne.com/accommodation/htm* 🛏 *8 rooms* 🕒 *Closed Nov.–Jan.* 🍴 *Breakfast.*

NIGHTLIFE AND THE ARTS

Joe Mac's. Located right off the pier, Joe Mac's is a good place for a pint while waiting for the ferry home. ⊠ *Cill Ronáin (Kilronan)* ☎ *099/61248.*

Joe Watty's. This longtime favorite is a good bet for traditional music virtually every night in summer. ⊠ *Main Rd., Cill Ronáin (Kilronan)* ☎ *099/20892.*

Ostán Oileáin Árainn. Fans-in-the-know say this is the place to head for the best in traditional music on the Aran Islands. ⊠ *Cill Ronáin (Kilronan).*

INIS MEÁIN (INISHMAAN)

3 km (2 miles) east of Inis Mór (Inishmore).

The middle island in both size and location, Inis Meáin has a population of about 300 and can be comfortably explored on foot.

EXPLORING

You have no alternative to walking if you want to reach the island's major antiquities: **Dún Conor (Conor Fort)**, a smaller version of Dún Aengus; the ruins of two **early Christian churches**; and a chamber tomb known as the **Bed of Diarmuid and Grainne**, dating from about 2000 BC. You can also take wonderful cliff walks above secluded coves.

It's on Inishmaan that the traditional Aran lifestyle is most evident. Most islanders still don hand-knitted Aran sweaters, though nowadays they wear them with jeans and sneakers.

SHOPPING

Inis Meáin Knitting. Providing much needed local employment, Inis Meáin Knitting is a young company producing quality knitwear in luxury fibers for the international market, including Liberty of London, Barneys New York, and Bergdorf Goodman. The factory showroom has an extensive selection of garments at discount prices. To get here from the pier, walk five minutes due west. ⊠ *Carrown Lisheen, Co. Galway* ☎ *099/73009* ⊕ *www.inismeain.ie.*

INIS OIRR (INISHEER)

4 km (2½ miles) east of Inis Meáin (Inishmaan), 8 km (5 miles) northwest of Doolin docks.

The smallest and flattest of the islands, Inis Oirr can be explored on foot in an afternoon, though if the weather is fine you may be tempted to linger on the long, sandy beach between the quay and the airfield. Only one stretch of road, about 500 yards long, links the airfield and the sole village.

8

"The back of the island," as Inis Oirr's uninhabited side facing the Atlantic is called, has no beaches, but people swim off the rocks. It's worth making a circuit of the island to get a sense of its utter tranquillity. A maze of footpaths runs between the high stone walls that divide the fields, which are so small that they can support only one cow each, or two to three sheep.

> **EXTRA CREDIT**
>
> In summer, Inis Oirr's population of 300 is augmented by high school students from all over Ireland attending the Gaeltacht, or Irish-language, school.

EXPLORING

Church of Kevin. Signposted to the southeast of the quay, the Church of Kevin is a small, early Christian church that gets buried in sand by storms every winter. Each year the islanders dig it out of the sand for the celebration of St. Kevin's Day on June 14. ✉ *Inis Oirr, Co. Galway.*

O'Brien's Castle. A pleasant walk through the village takes you up to this ruined 15th-century tower on top of a rocky hill—the only hill on the island. ✉ *Inis Oirr, Co. Galway.*

WHERE TO STAY

$ HOTEL 🏨 **Hotel Inisheer.** A pleasant, modern low-rise in the middle of the island's only village, a few minutes' walk from the quay and the airstrip, this simple, whitewashed building with a slate roof and half-slate walls has bright, plainly furnished rooms, with pine-frame beds, pine floors, and white bed linen. **Pros:** island's only all-in-one destination, with pub and restaurant; good location between pier and airstrip; very clean. **Cons:** basic standard of comfort: certainly no frills; very busy July and August. [$] *Rooms from: €86* ✉ *Inis Oirr, Co. Galway* ☎ *099/75020* 🌐 *www.hotelinisoirr.com* 🛏 *14 rooms* 🕒 *Closed Oct.–Mar.* 🍴 *Breakfast.*

CONNEMARA AND COUNTY MAYO

Including Counties Galway and Mayo

WELCOME TO CONNEMARA AND COUNTY MAYO

TOP REASONS TO GO

★ **Captivating Connemara:** An almost uninhabited landscape of misty bogland, studded with deep blue lakes under huge Atlantic skies: painters have strived for generations to capture the ever-changing light.

★ **Cong à la Hollywood:** Fetching ivy-covered thatched cottages—including one commemorating the making of the archetypal "Irish" movie *The Quiet Man*—beside a ruined medieval monastery contrast with the baronial splendor of Ashford Castle, one of Ireland's most luxurious hotels.

★ **Clifden and the Sky Road:** Walk the Sky Road to take in its breathtaking scenery—sea views on one side, the Twelve Bens Mountains on the other—from the compact village of Clifden, the liveliest spot for miles around.

★ **Wordly Westport:** An engagingly old-fashioned town, Westport has an octagonal 18th-century market square and a quayside (on Clew Bay) that offers spectacular sunsets—a highlight of the Wild Atlantic Way.

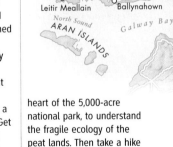

1 **Connemara.** The area between Maam Cross and the rocky coast is the famed Connemara, and consists mainly of rugged, sparsely inhabited hills, enhanced by the ever-changing light of the Atlantic weather, with rainbows every time a shower crosses the sun. Get up close to a bog among the displays at the visitor center in Letterfrack, the heart of the 5,000-acre national park, to understand the fragile ecology of the peat lands. Then take a hike to explore the territory.

GETTING ORIENTED

With the most westerly seaboard in Europe, this region is one of the wildest stretches of the Wild Atlantic Way. While just to the west and north of hip Galway City, this area is famed for its remoteness and rural character. Connemara sits in the northwest corner of County Galway. County Mayo is Ireland's third-largest county, with coast on three of its four sides, and the River Moy and the huge expanse of Lough Conn and Lough Cullin on the fourth. Bright lights are to be found in Clifden and Westport, both lively small towns of great charm.

9

2 County Mayo. Outside the main towns—Castlebar and Ballina—the rest of the county has long-empty roads leading to unspoiled shorelines, and some of the best river and lake angling in Ireland. Apart from Achill Island and Westport, this is a relatively undeveloped destination: head to Mayo's north coast for some spectacular seascapes including the sensational blowholes of Downpatrick Head.

HIKING THE WEST

More and more travelers are discovering that Ireland's western regions are hiking heaven. In fact, hikes or guided walks through Connemara or County Mayo are the best ways to explore these territories at first hand, or rather, foot.

(above) Eco-hiking in spectacular Connemara National Park; *(right, top)* Many way-marked hikes go past beautiful lakes like Lough Corrib; *(right, bottom)* Stop and smell the heather.

Why hike the West? It has some of the finest rugged scenery and dramatic indented coastline in all Ireland. In Connemara serried ranks of heather-clad mountains, interspersed with bright blue lakes, beckon to the walker as dramatic cloud formations scud across huge Atlantic skies. In County Mayo, the huge conical bulk of Croagh Patrick spectacularly looms above Clew Bay. Or what about earning some blisters among the free-range sheep of the Doolough Valley, set in the shadow of Mweelrea Mountain? The attraction lies in the terrific views nearly everywhere you look. Coastal views alternate with mountain vistas, often topped by a perfect rainbow. A daily highlight is the spectacular sunset over the Atlantic, at its biggest and best in late August.

WHAT TO BUY HERE

Walkers on way-marked trails are advised to buy an Ordnance Survey map of the area, which is sold locally. Most tourist offices also have free maps of less ambitious walks on roads and local footpaths. Because of the wind, most Irish walkers wear knitted or fleece hats, often decorated with a Guinness logo or a woolly sheep: shop around locally.

Hiking buffs will be glad to know that the last decade has seen the completion of various "way-marked" (signposted) walking routes, which can be sampled in easy one- or two-hour "loops," or, for more serious walkers, made the focus of a visit.

TOP HIKING DESTINATIONS

The Western Way's County Galway section extends from Oughterard on Lough Corrib through the mountains of Connemara to Leenane on Killary Harbour, a distance of 50 km (30 miles). Its 177-km (110-mile) County Mayo section, known as the Western Way (Mayo), continues past Killary Harbour to Westport on Clew Bay to the Ox Mountains east of Ballina. This trail should be the first choice of serious walkers, as it includes some of the finest mountain and coastal scenery in Ireland. The Great Western Greenway is a traffic-free 42-km (26-mile) cycling and walking trail that follows the line of Mayo's Westport–Mulranny Railway (closed since 1937) along the northern shore of Clew Bay, and offers scenic walking and cycling with very few inclines, suitable for moderately fit people. Another perfect hiking destination is Connemara National Park, which consists of some 5,000 acres of untamed mountain wilderness in and around the Twelve Bens peaks. Allow an hour or two to hike the Diamond Hill

Loop, along 7 km (4 miles) of gravel tracks and paved mountain paths, to a 1,493-foot peak, with a 360-degree vista taking in the distant sea, the turrets of Kylemore Abbey, and the higher peaks in the south. The nearby visitor center (March–October, free) has displays on the flora, fauna, and geology of Connemara.

WALKING IN COMPANY

Walking festivals are highly popular. Achill Island in County Mayo hosts the **Achill Walks Festival** (⊕ *www.achill tourism.com*) in early April, to tempt people out again after the long dark winter, while the **Four Seasons Walking Festival** features excursions from Clifden guided by an archaeologist four times a year—see ⊕ *www.connemara4 seasonswalkingfestival.com*.

BRING WITH YOU

You can't hike Connemara and Mayo in sneakers, due to the combination of bog, rocky terrain, and frequent showers. Wear waterproof hiking boots, quick-drying trousers rather than denim, and carry lightweight, waterproof rainwear (preferably breathable), and a cap. A fleece over a T-shirt gives enough protection from the wind in summer.

9

Updated
by Alannah
Hopkin

A landscape where the thundering Atlantic forms the pounding backbeat to the most westerly seaboard in Europe, this most distinct area of Ireland has been an escape from urban stress since its vast empty landscapes and rocky indented coast was "discovered" by writers and artists in the 19th century. While the bustling town of Westport has assumed the identity of the ultrahip destination of a younger, more confident Ireland, the surrounding countryside still attracts the traditional anglers, golfers, and seekers of rural solitude, along with savvy hikers, cyclists, and birders.

It is a landscape richly endowed with magnificent vistas: Connemara's combination of rugged coastline, mountains, moorland, and lakes; the distinctive conelike shape of Croagh Patrick, towering over the 365 islands of Clew Bay, and the rippling waters of Lough Corrib, Lough Conn, and many smaller lakes. The Irish people are well aware of what a jewel they have in the largely unspoiled wilderness, grazed by sheep and herds of wild ponies, that is the 5,000-acre Connemara National Park, the result of a successful lobby for landscape preservation. Peat lands, or bogs as they are called around here, are at last being valued for their unique botanical character.

Time seems to have a different value out here, as if the 21st century had never begun. It is still not unusual to be stuck behind two cars parked on either side of the white line, drivers' windows open while local news is exchanged, and the drivers oblivious to your revving engine behind them. Unlike most of Ireland where the marks of Viking, Norman, and English invaders blotted out much of the rich heritage of the ancient Irish kingdoms, these western counties retained, by virtue of their remoteness, those essential Celtic characteristics of rebellion and individuality, and the accompanying graces of unstinting hospitality and courtly good manners. These traits survive, despite the purges of Cromwell's English armies and the all-pervasive trauma of the Great Famine (1845–49). That era started a tradition of emigration that continued to deprive the area of the majority of its youth well into the 1960s. The growth of tourism since the 1970s, the building of fine new hotels and the upgrading of traditional ones has helped to provide jobs for the local population. Another boost has come from the development of fish farming, and the fostering of local artisan food producers, whose farmhouse cheese and smoked salmon enhances the menus of the West.

These unspoiled regions possess a spirit that has always spoken to the hidden poet within all who travel here. Images of spectacular red sunsets lingering over the Atlantic, that shocking lapis-lazuli blue of your first Connemara lough, and the fleeting moments when the way ahead was framed by a completely semicircular rainbow will likely haunt your memory long after you leave. As will the ancient whispers, cries, and melodies carried on the Connemara breeze. Here is where the magic lies.

CONNEMARA AND COUNTY MAYO PLANNER

WHEN TO GO
There is a local saying in the Westport area: if you can't see the summit of Croagh Patrick, then it is raining; if you can see it, it is about to rain. Avoid visiting between November and February, when many places close for the winter and the days are short and overcast. In fact, you could have your umbrellas out constantly during all times but the warmest months, July and August, when the average temperatures are around 15°C (60°F).

PLANNING YOUR TIME
Visitors are often geared to a faster pace, but they should allow at least two days for exploring the region, four to six days if you intend to do some serious hiking or cycling, take a boat trip on Lough Corrib, visit Clare Island, and enjoy the village (and pub) life of Clifden and Westport. Although distances between sights are not great, you may want to take scenic—meaning slower—national secondary routes. Covering 80 to 112 km (50 to 70 miles) per day on these roads is a comfortable target.

If you love the outdoors, dramatic scenery, empty roads, and deserted coves, then you'll be in heaven in Connemara and Mayo. If you're a city lover, and tend to fade without daily doses of caffeine and retail therapy, then base yourself in Clifden for the first night, where there is coffee aplenty, and the shopping is surprisingly good for a very small town (Irish designer wear, locally made tweed, traditional hand-knits, and wackier handcrafted knitwear).

IF YOU HAVE 3 DAYS
Allow a full day to meander slowly from Galway City to Clifden, perhaps stopping in Oughterard to take a boat trip to Cong for a little Quiet (Man) time, or climbing the slopes of the heather-clad mountains. Next morning, hire a Connemara pony, or take a stroll along the Sky Road before heading to the lovely Kylemore Abbey and its gardens.

Drive the scenic Doolough Valley to Westport for your second night. Next day, hire a bike to cycle on the traffic-free coastal path, the Great Western Greenway, or drive across the bridge to Achill Island for some magnificent coastal scenery, If the weather grounds you, head up to Turlough and the nostalgic Museum of Country Life (allow two hours), but if it is fine, push on to the north Mayo coast where you can walk in the footsteps of Stone Age farmers, and test your nerve on rugged Downpatrick Head.

GETTING HERE AND AROUND

A car is almost essential in Connemara and Mayo. Trains arrive from Dublin on separate lines to Westport and Ballina, but there is no train service between these towns. The bus network is more flexible, but there are not many services each day, and the entire bus system goes into semihibernation during the winter months, so plan accordingly. If a rental car is out of the question, one option is to make Westport your base, and take a day trip to Connemara and Kylemore Abbey. Then get an Expressway bus to Ballina, and explore the north coast on local buses. And the hardy can always consider making a biking trip through the region, even though it does get periods of strong rain.

AIR TRAVEL

Ryanair flies to Ireland West Airport Knock daily from London's Stansted Airport and Luton Airport; flying time is 80 minutes. Aer Lingus has several flights to Knock from Gatwick and Birmingham daily.

Carriers Aer Lingus ☏ *0818/365–000* ⊕ *www.aerlingus.com.* **Flybe** ☏ *44 01392/683–152 outside U.K.* ⊕ *www.flybe.com.* **Ryanair** ☏ *0818/303–030* ⊕ *www.ryanair.com.*

AIRPORTS The West's most convenient international airport is Shannon, 25 km (16 miles) east of Ennis.

Ireland West Airport Knock, at Charlestown—near Knock, in County Mayo—has direct daily service to London's Stansted, Luton, and Gatwick, and to Manchester and Birmingham, and several flights a week to Paris, Milan, and Frankfurt.

No scheduled flights run from the United States to Knock; use Shannon Airport.

Airport Information Ireland West Airport Knock ☏ *094/936–8100* ⊕ *www.irelandwestairport.com.* **Shannon Airport** ☏ *061/712–000* ⊕ *www. shannonairport.com.*

BOAT AND FERRY TRAVEL

Corrib Cruises runs daily cruises on Lough Corrib from April to October, with great views of Ashford Castle and the Connemara mountains, and an optional visit to the monastic ruins on Inchagoill Island. The boat has indoor and outdoor seating and a licensed bar. Board either at Cong or at Oughterard, on the opposite side of the lake. You can use the cruise as a ferry service from one village to the other, or opt for a historic cruise with guide (both options €20). Its 6 pm traditional music cruise from Cong (June–September) is always popular.

Clare Island in Clew Bay and its smaller neighbor, Inisthturk Island, are increasingly popular day-trip destinations with hikers and natural historians. Clare Island Ferry Company sails to Clare Island and Inishturk between May and September, leaving the mainland at 10:45 am and returning at 4:45 pm (€15 round-trip). O'Malley Ferries is a year-round operator serving Clare Island. Both leave from Roonagh Pier at Louisburgh, a 35-minute drive from Westport. Tickets can be bought at the Westport Tourist Office.

From April through October, Killary Cruises runs 90-minute trips around Killary Harbour (€21), Ireland's only fjord, in an enclosed catamaran launch with seating for 150 passengers, plus a bar and restaurant. It offers a "no-seasickness money-back guarantee."

Boat Companies Shannon Ferries ☎ *065/905–3124* ⊕ *www.shannon ferries.com.*

BUS TRAVEL

Bus Éireann runs several expressway buses into the region from Dublin, Cork City, and Limerick City to Galway City (change for Connemara) and Westport, the principal depots in the region.

Citylink operates frequent buses, with up to 17 departures daily, between Clifden, Galway City, and Dublin and Dublin Airport. The trip costs €15 one-way.

Citylink also makes five daily trips in each direction between Shannon Airport and Galway City, costing €16 one-way.

Within Connemara and Mayo, bus routes are often slow and circuitous, and service can be erratic. The national transport website has an integrated journey planner that is useful for long cross-country trips, for example, Westport to Ballina. To plan local journeys if possible use the Bus Eireann website or phone the bus station (they are always very helpful).

Bus Éireann local buses travel from Galway City to Cong, Clifden, and Westport. There are no buses linking Cong, Clifden, and Westport: you must return to Galway City and take a different bus line out again to visit each place.

Bus Depots Ballina Bus Station ☎ *096/71800* ⊕ *www.buseireann.ie.* **Galway City Bus Station** *(Ceannt Station).* ☎ *091/562–000.* **Westport Bus Station** ☎ *098/25711.*

Bus Lines Bus Éireann ☎ *091/562–000 in Galway, 096/71800 in Ballina, 01/836–6111 in Dublin* ⊕ *www.buseireann.ie.* **Citylink** ✉ *Unit 1, Forster Ct., 17 Forster St., Galway City, Co. Galway* ☎ *091/564–164* ⊕ *www.citylink.ie.* **National Travel Website** ⊕ *www.transportforireland.ie.*

CAR TRAVEL

The 207-km (129-mile) Dublin–Galway trip is on a motorway (four-lane expressway) and takes about two hours, 20 minutes. The 196-km (122-mile) drive from Cork to Galway (opt for the toll tunnel under Limerick) takes about three hours, and another 45 minutes to Oughterard, where the Connemara scenery begins. From Killarney the shortest route to cover the 193 km (120 miles) to Galway (three hours) is to take N22 to Tralee, then N69 through Listowel to Tarbert and ferry across the Shannon Estuary to Killimer *(see "County Clare, Galway*

City, and the Aran Islands"). From here, join N68 in Kilrush, and then pick up the M18.

ROAD CONDITIONS   Connemara and Mayo have good, wide main roads (National Primary Routes) and better-than-average local roads (National Secondary Routes), both known as "N" routes. If you stray off the beaten track on the smaller Regional ("R") or Local ("L") routes you may encounter some hazardous mountain roads. Narrow, steep, and twisty, they are also frequented by untended sheep, cows, and ponies grazing "the long acre" (as the strip of grass beside the road is called) or simply straying in search of greener pastures. If you find a sheep in your path, just sound the horn, and it should scramble away. A good maxim for these roads is: "You never know what's around the next corner." Bear this in mind, and adjust your speed accordingly. Hikers and cyclists constitute an additional hazard on narrow roads. Within the Connemara Irish-speaking area, signs are in Irish only. The main signs to recognize are Gaillimh (Galway), Ros an Mhíl (Rossaveal), An Teach Dóite (Maam Cross), and Sraith Salach (Recess).

TAXI TRAVEL

Within Westport taxis operate on the meter. Outside the town, agree on the fare in advance.

Mickey's Cabs ☏ *087/222–6227* ⊕ *www.westporttaxis.com.*

TRAIN TRAVEL

The region's main rail stations are in Galway City, Westport, and Ballina. Trains leave from Dublin's Heuston Station. The journey time to Galway is 3 hours; to Westport and Ballina, 3½ hours. Rail service within the region is limited. The major destinations of Galway City and Westport/Ballina are on different branch lines. Connections can be made only between Galway and the other two cities by traveling inland for about an hour to Athlone.

Train Information Ballina Station ☏ *096/20229* ⊕ *www.irishrail.ie/Ballina.* **Dublin Heuston Station** ☏ *01/836–6222* ⊕ *www.irishrail.ie/DublinHeuston.* **Galway Station** ☏ *091/564–222* ⊕ *www.irishrail.ie/Galway.* **Irish Rail–Iarnod Éireann** ☏ *098/25253 in Westport* ⊕ *www.irishrail.ie.* **Westport Station** ☏ *098/25253* ⊕ *www.irishrail.ie/westport.*

For more information on getting here and around, see Travel Smart Ireland.

RESTAURANTS

Pubs and informal hotel restaurants are the main places to eat in this sparsely populated rural area. The only places with a choice of stand-alone restaurants are Clifden, the "capital" of Connemara (in fact a small village), and Westport, the chief resort in County Mayo. From Easter into the summer months many menus feature Connemara lamb: the sheep graze on wild herbs on the mountain slopes, which gives the meat a distinctive flavor. The other star is local seafood, including crab and lobster in summer, and superb Atlantic salmon all year round, fresh or smoked. For seafood try the Tavern Bar and Restaurant near Westport, or Mitchell's in Clifden; for country house–style elegance go to Rosleague Manor in Letterfrack, or Mount Falcon near Ballina. For memorable fine-dining experiences, there are three main contenders: dinner beneath the crystal chandeliers at Ashford Castle's George V Restaurant, or the splendid river view from the Owenmore Restaurant in Ballynahinch Castle hotel in the heart of Connemara, or the view of Croagh Patrick from La Fougère Restaurant in Westport's Knockranny House Hotel. Like all hotel restaurants in the area, they are open to nonguests, but it is wise to reserve in advance.

HOTELS

Accommodation in the area tends to the traditional; outside Westport there are few indoor pools and gyms: instead there are informal, friendly places where you will probably end up comparing notes with other travelers over a huge cooked breakfast. Add variety by alternating rural isolation with the lively towns. Both Clifden in Connemara and Westport in Mayo have lively pub scenes. Clifden attracts a younger, mainly single, crowd, especially in July and August, so be prepared: the music might be rock rather than Irish.

Lakeside Cong is a tiny village, but is a magnet for visitors. It is often pointed out that Ashford Castle, one of the most sumptuous of Ireland's castle hotels, is bigger than the village. Abbeyglen Castle Hotel in Clifden is a Victorian manor whose relaxed ambience and good value attract Irish holidaymakers on short breaks. Knockranny House Hotel and Spa in Westport is one of Ireland's premier luxury hotels, situated in its own extensive grounds. Mount Falcon Estate near Ballina offers country house luxury, and caters especially (but not exclusively) for anglers and golfers. *Hotel reviews have been shortened. For full information, visit Fodors.com.*

WHAT IT COSTS IN EUROS				
	$	**$$**	**$$$**	**$$$$**
Restaurants	under €19	€19–€24	€25–€32	over €32
Hotels	under €120	€120–€170	€171–€210	over €210

Restaurant prices are the average cost of a main course at dinner or, if dinner is not served, at lunch. Hotel prices are the lowest cost of a standard double room in high season.

TOUR OPTIONS

All TIOs (tourist information offices) in the West provide lists of suggested cycling tours. The only guided bus tours in the region, which take in the main sights of Connemara (€20), start from Galway and Westport and run only between June and September. Book at the bus station or tourist office.

TOURS

Clew Bay Bike Hire and Outdoor Adventures. Cycling breaks and guided daylong cycle tours in the Westport area are on offer, as well as speedboat rides, sea kayaking, wake boarding, bungee jumps, and other adventure activities. The most popular product, however, is day hire of electric bicycles that take the hard work out of cycling. The company also offers a free drop-off and pick-up service via minibus and cycle trailer, invaluable if the weather takes a turn. ⊠ *Distillery Rd., Westport, Co. Mayo* ☎ *098/37675* ⊕ *www.clewbayoutdoors.ie.*

Connemara Adventure Tours. Self-guided or customized tours for walkers, cyclists, golfers, and horseback riders are on offer from this company. Groups of 8 to 16 people participate in three-, four-, or seven-day programs, staying in a comfortable B&B near Westport, or traveling to a new destination each night with luggage transfer. Walk Clare Island, climb Diamond Hill, or gallop along a sandy beach on Clew Bay. ⊠ *Killary Adventure Centre, Leenane, Co. Mayo* ☎ *095/42276* ⊕ *www.connemaraadventuretours.com.*

Connemara Safari Walking Holidays. Choose between five- and seven-day residential walking holidays starting in either Clifden or Westport. The company specializes in "island hopping" and remote-island hikes. ⊠ *Sky Rd., Clifden, Co. Galway* ☎ *095/21071* ⊕ *www.walkingconnemara.com.*

Croagh Patrick Walking Holidays. This company runs weeklong walking holidays between April and September, based in B&B accommodations near Westport; contact Gerry Greensmyth. ⊠ *Belclare, Westport, Co. Mayo* ☎ *098/26090* ⊕ *www.walkingguideireland.com.*

Galway City TIO ⊠ *Forster Pl., Center, Galway City, Co. Galway* ☎ *091/537–700* ⊕ *discoverireland.ie/places-to-go/Galway.*

Galway Tour Company. This Galway-based company offers a Connemara tour that takes in Clifden, Kylemore Abbey, and Cong, the famed location of the classic movie *The Quiet Man.* Tickets can be purchased from the Galway tourist information office *(see "County Clare, Galway City, and the Aran Islands")* or on the tour bus. ☎ *091/566–566* ⊕ *www.galwaytourcompany.com.*

Lally Tours. Galway City-based Lally Tours runs a €20 day tour through Connemara and County Mayo. ☎ *091/562–905* ⊕ *www.lallytours.com.*

Michael Gibbons Walking Ireland. This Clifden-based company organizes everything from daylong mountain treks to weeklong holidays. ⊠ *Market St., Clifden, Co. Galway* ☎ *095/21379* ⊕ *www.walkingireland.com.*

O'Neachtain Day Tours. This company operates full-day bus tours of Connemara from Galway City's tourist information office for €20. ☎ *091/553–188* ⊕ *www.ontours.biz.*

VISITOR INFORMATION

Discover Ireland provides free information service, tourist literature, and an accommodations booking service at its TIOs (tourist information offices). Oughterard, Castlebar, Ballina, and Westport TIOs are open all year, generally weekdays 9–6, daily during the high season. Other TIOs that operate seasonally, generally weekdays 9–6 and Saturday 9–1, are open as follows: Clifden (March–October), and Cong (May–mid-September). Information on Connemara and Mayo can be found at ⊕ *www.discoverireland.ie/places-to-go.* In addition to this main website, we sometimes also list a town website in individual town sections; this is occasionally an ad-supported site that is unofficial, but still helpful. Generally speaking, tourism has been carefully nurtured in this region. Ferry services to the islands and on Lough Corrib have been upgraded, while walking and cycling holidays are a big growth area.

CONNEMARA

Bordered by the long expanse of Lough Corrib on the east and the jagged coast of the Atlantic on the west is the rugged, desolate region of western County Galway known as Connemara. Like the American West, it's an area of spectacular, almost myth-making geography—of glacial lakes; gorgeous, silent mountains; lonely roads; and hushed, uninhabited boglands. To quote Tim Robinson in his exceptional book *Connemara: Listening to the Wind,* this is a place of "huge, luminous spaces." The glacially carved Twelve Bens mountain range, together with the Maamturk Mountains to their north, lord proudly over the area's sepia boglands. In the midst of this wilderness there are few people, since Connemara's population is sparse even by Irish standards. Especially in the off-season, you're far more likely to come across sheep strolling its roads than another car.

OUGHTERARD

27 km (17 miles) northwest of Galway City.

Bustling Oughterard (pronounced *ook*-ter-ard) is the main village on the western shores of Lough Corrib and one of Ireland's leading angling resorts. Boats can be hired for excursions to the many wooded islands studding the lakes. It is known as a fine center for exploring the beauty spots of the Twelve Bens, and other mountain ranges hereabouts, such as the Maamturk and Cloosh.

GETTING HERE AND AROUND

Oughterard is 27 km (17 miles) west of Galway City on the N59, a busy two-lane main road. The journey normally takes about half an hour by car. There is plenty of free parking. Bus Éireann and Citylink buses traveling from Galway to Clifden stop at Oughterard, a 40-minute journey.

Explore Lough Corrib with Corrib Cruises, which runs daily boat trips from Oughterard Pier from April to October. Take a day trip to Cong on the opposite side of the lake (€28), or opt for a historic cruise with guide (€20).

ESSENTIALS

Transportation Contacts Corrib Cruises ☎ *091/557–798* ⊕ *www. corribcruises.com.*

Visitor Information Oughterard Tourist Inforrmation Point ✉ *The Boat Inn, Main St.* ☎ *091/552–196* ⊕ *www.oughterardtourism.com.*

EXPLORING

The lough is signposted to the right in the village center, less than 1½ km (1 mile) up the road, near the gas station. From mid-June to early September, local boatmen offer trips on the lough, which has several islands. It's also possible to take a boat trip to the village of Cong, at the north shore of the lough. Midway between Oughterard and Cong, Inchagoill Island (the Island of the Stranger), a popular destination for a half-day trip, has several early Christian church remains. The prettiest part of the village is on the far (Clifden) side, beyond the busy

9

commercial center, beside a wooded section of the River Corrib. Stop at the designated parking spot for a stroll beside the river.

FAMILY **Brigit's Garden.** A delightfully imaginative informal garden, with four sections based on the four Celtic festivals that mark the passing of the seasons, Brigit's Garden reopens annually on February 1, St. Brigit's Day, the start of the Celtic spring. The garden introduces Celtic mythology and is adorned with Celtic motifs and planted with healing and culinary herbs as well as native Irish trees. It contains a stone chamber, a ring or fairy fort, giant granite standing stones, a crannóg (thatched rush dwelling), living willow sculptures, and a discovery trail for kids. A popular feature is the wishing tree, where you can leave a written message for a loved one. The garden, designed by award-winning gardener Mary Reynolds, is run by an educational trust and will appeal to the child in everyone. ✉ *Roscahill* ✥ *Signposted 15 km (9 miles) west of Galway on the N59 before Oughterard, ½ km (1/3 mile) off the main road* ☎ *095/550–905* 🌐 *www.brigitsgarden.ie* 🎫 *€5* ⏲ *Garden: Feb.–Oct., daily 10–5:30. Café: May–Sept., daily 10:30–5; Apr. and Oct., Sun. only.*

WHERE TO STAY

$$ HOTEL 🏨 **Ross Lake House Hotel.** Built by James Edward Jackson, land agent for Lord Iveagh at Ashford Castle, this well-off-the-beaten-path, white-trim Georgian house, managed by the enthusiastic Henry and Elaine Reid, has a surprisingly stylish interior, with 19th-century antiques and welcoming open fires. **Pros:** country quiet—silence, in fact—with style; good restaurant on the premises. **Cons:** 5 km (3 miles) out of town; no pubs nearby. [$] *Rooms from: €150* ✉ *5 km (3 miles) from Oughterard, Rosscahill* ☎ *091/550–109* 🌐 *www.rosslakehotel.com* 🛏 *11 rooms, 2 suites* ⏲ *Closed Nov.–mid-Mar.* 🍴 *Breakfast.*

NIGHTLIFE

Faherty's. For good traditional music, drop in to this popular spot. ✉ *Main St.* ☎ *091/552–194.*

RECESS

As you continue northwest from Oughterard on N59, you'll soon pass a string of small lakes on your left; their shining blue waters reflecting the blue sky are a typical Connemara sight on a sunny day. About 16 km (10 miles) northwest of Oughterard, the continuation of the coast road (R336) meets N59 at Maam Cross in the shadow of Leckavrea Mountain. Once an important meeting place for the people of north and south Connemara, it's still the location of a large monthly cattle fair, but for the rest of the time is a rather eerie place, empty unless a tour bus has just arrived, that serves mainly as a handy pit stop on the road between Galway and Clifden.

Beyond Maam Cross, some of the best scenery in Connemara awaits on the road to Recess, 16 km (10 miles) west of Maam Cross on N59. At many points on this drive, a short walk away from either side of the main road will lead you to the shores of one of the area's many small loughs. Stop and linger if the sun is out—even intermittently—for the light filtering through the clouds gives splendor to the distant, dark-gray mountains and creates patterns on the brown-green moorland below. In June and July, it stays light until 11 or so, and it's worth taking a late-evening stroll to see the sun's reluctance to set.

WHERE TO STAY

$$$$ HOTEL Fodor's Choice ★ **Ballynahinch Castle Hotel.** More like a rambling country house than a castle, this magnificent crenellated mansion sits beside a river amid 450 wooded acres with a rugged mountain backdrop. **Pros:** genuine Irish country-house experience; peaceful; stunning surroundings; friendly, enthusiastic staff. **Cons:** doesn't come cheap. [$] *Rooms from: €260* ✉ *Recess, Connemara* ☎ *095/31006* 🌐 *www.ballynahinch-castle.com* 🛏 *3 suites, 37 rooms* 🕓 *Closed Dec. 13–28 and Feb.*

SHOPPING

Joyce's. Joyce's crafts shop is owned by a family famed for its traditional Connemara tweeds. No surprise then that this emporium has a good selection of tweed, and also carries an enticing selection of contemporary ceramics, handwoven shawls, books of Irish interest, original paintings, and small sculptures. ✉ *Maam Cross* ☎ *095/34604.*

CONG

23 km (14 miles) northeast of Maam Cross.

Fodor's Choice ★ Set on a narrow isthmus between Lough Corrib and Lough Mask on the County Mayo border near Maam Cross, the pretty, old-fashioned village of Cong is still as camera-ready as it was when John Ford's *The Quiet Man* was filmed here. Dotted with ivy-covered thatch cottages and lorded over by one immensely posh hotel, Ashford Castle, this tiny village continues to have a worldwide fan base.

Just two blocks long, and bisected by the chocolate-brown River Cong, the village is surrounded on all sides by thickly forested hills. Almost larger than the village itself is the celebrated luxury hotel found here, Ashford Castle, much beloved by billionaires and off-duty celebrities. It was once the country estate of the powerful Guinness family. A public footpath runs from Cong Abbey through the grounds of Ashford Castle and out of its gates and is a pleasant walk of about 3 km (2 miles)—or you could opt to drop by for lunch or dinner, or even afternoon tea, to get a peek at Ashford's aristocratic interior. A still more romantic way to see the castle is on a boat trip run by the local Corrib Cruises.

GETTING HERE AND AROUND

Cong is 23 km (14 miles) northeast of Maam Cross on the N59, a scenic drive skirting the shores of Lough Corrib. The main car parking area is on the edge of the village, a three-minute walk, and is clearly signposted. There is very limited parking in the village itself.

There is a limited Bus Éireann service from Galway Bus Station to Cong—be sure to get a bus that goes to Ryan's, the bus stop in the village center. The journey takes just over an hour. You can also take a delightful day trip to Cong by Corrib Cruises boat from Oughterard between April and October.

ESSENTIALS

Visitor Information **Cong Tourist Office** ✉ *Abbey St.* ☎ *094/954–6542* 🌐 *www.congtourism.com* 🕑 *May–mid-Sept. only.*

EXPLORING

Augustine Abbey. Cong is surrounded by many stone circles and burial mounds, but its most notable ruins are those of the Augustine Abbey, overlooking a river. Dating from the early 12th century when it was founded by Turlough O'Connor, the High King of Ireland, this Abbey still retains some finely carved details and a cloister. Don't miss the fishing hut, an ingenious invention to keep fishermen dry. ✉ *Abbey St.*

Quiet Man Museum and Gift Shop. Cong's 15 minutes of fame came in 1952, when John Ford filmed *The Quiet Man,* one of his most popular films, here; John Wayne plays a prizefighter who goes home to Ireland to court the fiery Maureen O'Hara. (Film critic Pauline Kael called the movie "fearfully Irish and green and hearty.") The Quiet Man Museum, in the village center, is an exact replica of the cottage used in the film, with reproductions of the furniture and costumes, a few original artifacts, and pictures of actors Barry Fitzgerald and Maureen O'Hara on location. O'Hara, a sprightly nonegenarian, and long-term resident of Glengarriff, attended the film's 60th anniversary celebrations in 2012. Margaret and Gerry Collins host Quiet Man tours, leaving the cottage at 11 am daily, and exploring such Cong village sites as the river fight scene, the "hats in the air" scene, and Pat Cohan's Bar. ✉ *Circular Rd., Cong Village Center* ☎ *094/954–6089* 🌐 *www.quietman-cong.com* 🎫 *€5* 🕑 *Daily 10–4.*

WHERE TO STAY

$$$$ HOTEL FAMILY Fodor's Choice ★ 🏨 **Ashford Castle.** Massive, flamboyantly turreted, Ashord is the very picture of a romantic Irish castle and this famed mock-Gothic baronial showpiece, dating from the 13th century, and rebuilt in 1870 for the Guinness family, has been wowing visitors like President Reagan, John Travolta, Brad Pitt, and Pierce Brosnan—who got married here—ever since. **Pros:** baronial flamboyance; no-expense-spared facilities; regal grounds. **Cons:** so luxurious you are cut off from the normal hubbub of Irish life. [$] *Rooms from: €435* ☎ *094/954–6003* 🌐 *www.ashford.ie* 🛏 *72 rooms, 11 suites.*

$ B&B/INN 🏨 **Ryan's Hotel.** With framed fishing ties and specimen fish given pride of place on the lobby wall, you know you are in a hostelry favored by anglers. **Pros:** you don't have to afford Ashford Castle to stay in Cong; central to village; good area for walkers and anglers. **Cons:** uninspiring views from most rooms. [$] *Rooms from: €90* ✉ *Main St.* ☎ *094/954–6243* 🌐 *www.ryanshotelcong.ie* 🛏 *12 rooms.*

CLIFDEN

46 km (29 miles) southwest of Cong, 79 km (49 miles) northwest of Galway.

Fodor's Choice ★ With roughly 1,100 residents, Clifden would be called a village by most, but in these parts it's looked on as something of a metropolis. It's far and away the prettiest town in Connemara, as well as its unrivaled

The village of Cong is world famous as the setting for John Wayne's Oscar-winner *The Quiet Man*, and the Quiet Man Museum takes you behind the scenes.

"capital." Clifden's first attraction is its location—perched high above Clifden Bay on a forested plateau, its back to the spectacular Twelve Bens Mountains. The tapering spires of the town's two churches add to its alpine look.

Clifden is a popular base thanks to its selection of small restaurants, lively bars with music most summer nights, pleasant accommodations, and excellent walks. It's quiet out of season, but in July and August crowds flock here, especially for August's world-famous Connemara Pony Show. Year-round, unfortunately, Clifden's popularity necessitates a chaotic one-way traffic system, and on summer Sunday afternoons loud techno music blasts out of certain bars. So if you're looking for a sleepy country town that time forgot, push on to Westport.

GETTING HERE AND AROUND

Clifden is 66 km (41 miles) southwest of Cong: travel via Maam Cross and take the N59 westwards. The town is 79 km (49 miles) northwest of Galway City on the N59, and takes about an hour and a half. It is a busy main road with only one lane in each direction, and delays can occur. Follow signs to find the car parks (and free parking).

Bus Éireann and Citylink have daily bus service from Galway Bus Station. Bus Éireann's route takes 2 hours (at least half of that through great scenery), while Citylink's service takes 1½ hours and continues from Galway to Dublin and Dublin Airport. Some of these services continue to Letterfrack (about 20 minutes) and Leenane (about an hour). Check with Galway Bus Station on day of travel.

ESSENTIALS

Visitor Information Clifden Tourist Office ⊠ *Galway Rd.* ☎ *095/21163*
⊕ *www.connemara.ie/en/connemara/clifden/* ⊗ *Mid-Mar.–Oct. only.*

EXPLORING

Beach Road. A 2-km (1-mile) walk from the town center (follow signs
from Alcock & Brown's Hotel for The Harbour) along the Beach Road
is the best way to explore the seashore. The road continues along the
seashore into the countryside and back up to the Sky Road if you wish
to extend your walk into a 8-km (5-mile) hike. ⊠ *Beach Rd.*

Clifden Castle. Clifden Castle was built above the town near the aptly
named the Sky Road in 1815 by John D'Arcy, the town's founder,
and High Sheriff of Galway, who wished to establish a center of law
and order in what he saw as the lawless wilderness of Connemara.
Before the founding of Clifden, the interior of Connemara was largely
uninhabited, with most of its population clinging to the seashore.
⊠ *Sky Rd.*

Sky Road. Drive the aptly named Sky Road to really appreciate Clifden's
breathtaking scenery. Signposted at the west end of town, this high,
narrow circuit heads west, giving views of several offshore islands,
before looping back to the N59 after about 10 km (6 miles), giving phenomenal views of Clifden Bay's precipitous shores. ⊠ *Clifden,
Connemara.*

WHERE TO EAT AND STAY

$ ✗ **Mitchell's Seafood.** A town-center shop has been cleverly converted into
SEAFOOD a stylish, two-story eatery. On the first floor, beyond the plate-glass windows, there's a welcoming open fire, and you can eat at the bar or at one
of the polished wood tables. Exposed stone walls and wooden floors are
alluring accents on the quieter second level. Braised whole sea bass with
fennel butter typifies the simple treatment given to seafood. The all-day
menu also features lighter options like homemade spicy fish cakes and
fresh crab salad. There are several meat options, including traditional
Irish stew of Connemara lamb and fresh vegetables. $ *Average main:
€18* ⊠ *Market St.* ☎ *095/21867* ⊗ *Closed Nov.–Feb.*

$$$$ 🏚 **Abbeyglen Castle Hotel.** Creeper covered, as if under a Sleeping Beauty
HOTEL spell, the gorgeous Victorian castle-manor of Abbeyglen sits framed by
Fodor'sChoice towering trees on a height above Clifden town—if time hasn't completely
★ stopped here, it has certainly slowed down, but that's just the way the
relaxed guests want it. **Pros:** laid-back, easygoing atmosphere; pleasantly homey for all its grandeur; friendly hosts and staff. **Cons:** uphill
walk back from Clifden. $ *Rooms from: €218* ⊠ *Sky Rd.* ☎ *095/21201*
⊕ *www.abbeyglen.ie* 🛏 *45 rooms* ⊗ *Closed Jan.* 🍴 *Some meals.*

$ 🏚 **Dún Rí.** An old town house in the lower, quieter part of Clifden has
B&B/INN been extended and converted into a comfortable guesthouse with private parking. **Pros:** hotel-grade rooms at B&B prices; quiet central location. **Cons:** bland decor; parking lot is effectively on-street, not secured.
$ *Rooms from: €100* ⊠ *Hulk St.* ☎ *095/21625* ⊕ *www.dunri.ie* 🛏 *13
rooms* 🍴 *Breakfast.*

$$ B&B/INN Fodor's Choice ★ **The Quay House.** Nineteenth-century time travelers would feel right at home walking into this three-story Georgian house, Clifden's oldest (1820), as ancestral portraits, mounted fish, Victorian engravings, and cosseting fabrics all lend a frozen-in-amber allure. **Pros:** fetching decor; quiet location; harbor views. **Cons:** uphill walk into town. [$] *Rooms from: €150* ✉ *The Quay* ☎ *095/21369* 🌐 *www.thequayhouse.com* 🛏 *14 rooms* 🕓 *Closed Nov.–mid-Mar.* 🍴 *Breakfast.*

THE ARTS

Clifden Arts Festival. Held annually in mid-September for the past 36 years, the Clifden Arts Festival has a great selection of music, arts, and poetry in a friendly informal atmosphere and scenic environment, making it an excellent time to tune in to local culture. 🌐 *www.clifdenartsweek.ie.*

J Conneely's Bar. Irish music is played every night in the summer from 6:30 pm at this popular town-center bar. It gets livelier after 9 pm, when it stops serving food. ✉ *Market St.* ☎ *095/22733.*

Lowry's Bar Lounge. This central pub is famed for its traditional Irish music, played from 10 till late Monday to Friday, and on Sunday from 6 to 8:30. It also has a wide range of whiskeys, and serves pub grub. ✉ *Market St.* ☎ *095/21347.*

SHOPPING

The Clifden Bookshop. As well as selling books of local interest, the bookshop also stocks artists' supplies, and is an informal meeting point for visiting poets, writers, artists, and photographers. ✉ *Main St.* ☎ *095/22020* 🌐 *www.clifdenbookshop.com.*

The Connemara Hamper. A small but well-stocked specialty food shop, this is an ideal place to pick up picnic fare, with its excellent Irish farmhouse cheeses, pâtés, smoked Connemara salmon, and handmade Irish chocolates. ✉ *Market St.* ☎ *095/21054* 🌐 *www.connemarahamper.com.*

Millar's Connemara Tweeds. Millar's is a long-established emporium with a good selection of traditional tweeds and hand knits. ✉ *Main St.* ☎ *095/21038.*

The Outdoor Shop/Faoin Tuath. You didn't pack hiking gear, but now that you're here you want to explore the raw landscape on foot. You'll find everything you need here as well as surfing gear and local knowledge for both activities. ✉ *Market St.* ☎ *095/22838.*

Station House Courtyard. Set around a cobbled courtyard, the Station House has crafts studios, antiques dealers, and designer-wear outlets. ✉ *Old Railway Station, Bridge St.* ☎ *095/21699* 🌐 *www.clifdenstationhouse.com.*

SPORTS AND THE OUTDOORS

BICYCLING

John Mannion & Son. Explore Connemara by renting a bike from this handy outfitter. ✉ *Bridge St.* ☎ *095/21160* 🌐 *www.clifdenbikes.com.*

President Reagan, John Travolta, Brad Pitt, Pierce Brosnan... and now you? Lucky travelers call Ashford Castle their Cong home-away-from-home.

GOLF

Connemara Golf Links. On a dramatic stretch of Atlantic coastline, the links course masterminded by Eddie Hackett, Ireland's finest course designer, is sited between the Twelve Bens mountains and the rugged coast, with unforgettable views of sea, hills, and the huge western sky. The opening hole has a challenging dogleg, while the back 9 offer a memorable golfing experience, considered equal to any in the world. ✉ *9 km (5½ miles) south of Clifden on R341, Ballyconneely* ☎ *095/23502* ⊕ *www.connemaragolflinks.com* ✉ *Nov.–Mar. €35, Apr. and Oct. €45, May–July and Sept. €55, Aug. €70* ♆ *18 holes, 7055 yards, par 72. Practice area, caddies, club hire, catering* ☺ *Visitors: Mon.–Sun. (some restrictions).*

HORSEBACK RIDING

Errislannan Manor Connemara Pony Stud and Riding Centre. Ride a sure-footed Connemara pony in its native habitat at this long-established riding center, where these sturdy ponies are also bred. Treks are tailored to your ability, and the views of coast and hills from the mountain trails will be unforgettable. ✉ *6½ km (4 miles) from Clifden on the Ballyconneely road (R341), Ballyconneely* ☎ *095/21134* ⊕ *www.errislannanmanor.com.*

LETTERFRACK

14 km (9 miles) north of Clifden.

This is the gateway village to the famous Connemara National Park. It also makes a handy base for those visiting spectacular Kylemore Abbey, one of Ireland's grandest ancestral estates.

GETTING HERE AND AROUND

Letterfrack is 14 km (9 miles) north of Clifden on the N59. The journey takes about 15 minutes. There is plenty of free parking in the village center. Bus Éireann has daily routes linking Letterfrack and Clifden, a 20-minute journey. The nonexpress service originates in Galway, and takes about two hours, 30 minutes to reach Letterfrack. Citylink also operates between Letterfrack and Clifden (continuing to Galway).

EXPLORING

Connemara National Park. The 5,000-acre Connemara National Park lies southeast of the village of Letterfrack. Its visitor center covers the area's history and ecology, particularly the origins and growth of peat—and presents the depressing statistic that more than 80% of Ireland's peat, 5,000 years in the making, has been destroyed in the last 90 years. You can also get details on the many excellent walks and beaches in the area. The misleadingly named "park" is, in fact, just rocky or wooded wilderness territory, albeit with some helpful trails marked out to aid your exploration. It includes part of the famous **Twelve Bens** mountain range, which is for experienced hill walkers only. An easier hike is the Lower Diamond Hill Walk, at about 3 km (5 miles). Ask for advice on a hike suited to your abilities and interests at the Park and Visitor Centre, which is on the N59 as you arrive in Letterfrack from Clifden, on your right, clearly signposted, not too far southeast of the center of Letterfrack. ✉ *Park and visitor center, on the N59 near Letterfrack* ☎ *95/41054* 🌐 *www.connemaranationalpark.ie* 🎫 *Free* 🕒 *Park daily, dawn–dusk; visitor center mid-Mar.–Oct., daily 9–5:30.*

9

WHERE TO EAT AND STAY

$ IRISH

🍴 **The Bards Den.** Many visitors to Connemara share a memory of the Den's huge stove, where weary travelers have dried their soaking clothes and warmed frozen hands while sipping restorative glasses of stout. While the low-ceilinged, warrenlike pub has long served food—and great traditional Irish music at night—it now has a restaurant with blackboard menu, a plain, pine-floored room suitable for families with children. The food (last orders at 9 pm) is fresh and local, and includes smoked salmon, Connemara lamb stew, and prime Irish beef T-bone steaks. [$] *Average main: €15* ✉ *Main St.* ☎ *095/41042* 🌐 *www.bardsden.com.*

$$ HOTEL FAMILY Fodor's Choice ★

🏨 **Renvyle House Hotel.** A lake at its front door, the Atlantic Ocean at its back door, and the mountains of Connemara as a backdrop form the enthralling setting for this hotel 8 km (5 miles) north of Letterfrack, home to the Long Room, one of the most eminently civilized salons in Ireland—all polished wood, endless chairs, and pretty pictures. **Pros:** amazing views; secluded end-of-the-world location; recommended for artists and photographers; cheerful, unpretentious version of the country-house hotel experience. **Cons:** driving distance to anywhere

Few landscapes are as quintessentially Irish as the ravishing and rugged ones found in Connemara National Park.

else; bar and restaurant very busy at peak times. $ *Rooms from: €170* ⊠ *Renvyle* ☎ *095/46100* ⊕ *www.renvyle.com* ⇆ *70 rooms* ⊙ *Closed Jan. 6–mid-Feb.* ⊚ *Breakfast.*

$$ 🏨 **Rosleague Manor.** This pink, creeper-clad, two-story Georgian house **HOTEL** occupies 30 lovely acres and has a jaw-dropping view: a gorgeous lawn backdropped by Ballinakill Bay and the dreamy mountains of Connemara. **Pros:** quiet and elegant; mesmerizing views; excellent restaurant. **Cons:** can be very quiet off-season. $ *Rooms from: €150* ⊠ *Rosleague Bay* ☎ *095/41101* ⊕ *www.rosleague.com* ⇆ *20 rooms* ⊙ *Closed Nov.– mid-Mar.* ⊚ *Breakfast.*

NIGHTLIFE

The Bards Den. For traditional music, the best option in this region is the Bards Den. ⊠ *Main St.* ☎ *95/41042* ⊕ *www.bardsden.com.*

Paddy Coyne's Pub. Traditional musicians meet every Wednesday here, at this long-established pub 3 km (2 miles) west of Letterfrack on the scenic Renvyle Peninsula. It's a good bet for music any night in summer. ⊠ *Tully Cross* ☎ *095/43499.*

SHOPPING

Avoca Letterfrack Store. An extensive selection of crafts and women's fashions made by the stellar Avoca Handweavers is showcased here, along with delicious food from the Avoca Pantry range. ⊠ *N59, west of village* ☎ *095/41058.*

Letterfrack Country Shop. A great place to put together a picnic, this is the biggest supermarket for miles around (but still very small by city standards), and has a special line of local, artisanal foods, including smoked Connemara salmon, locally grown salads, handmade breads, and local cheeses. ⊠ *N59, village center* ☎ *095/41851.*

KYLEMORE VALLEY

Runs for 6½ km (4 miles) between Letterfrack and intersection of N59 and R344.

One of the more conventionally beautiful stretches of road in Connemara passes through Kylemore Valley, which is between the Twelve Bens to the south and the naturally forested Dorruagh Mountains to the north. Kylemore (the name is derived from *Coill Mór,* Irish for "big wood") looks "as though some colossal giant had slashed it out with a couple of strokes from his mammoth sword," as artist and author John FitzMaurice Mills has written.

EXPLORING

Fodor's Choice ★ **Kylemore Abbey.** One of the most magical "castles" in all of Europe, much-photographed Kylemore Abbey is visible across a reedy lake with a backdrop of wooded hillside. The storybook Gothic Revival, gray-stone mansion was built as a private home between 1861 and 1868 by Mitchell Henry, a member of Parliament for County Galway, and his wife, Margaret, who had fallen in love with the spot during a carriage ride while on their honeymoon. The Henrys spared no expense—the final bill for their house is said to have come to £1.5 million—and employed mostly local laborers, thereby abetting recovery from the famine (this area was among the worst hit in all of Ireland). Adjacent to the house is a spectacular neo-Gothic chapel, which, sadly, became the burial place for Margaret, who died after contracting "Nile fever" on a trip to Egypt. In 1920, nuns from the Benedictine order, who fled their abbey in Belgium during World War I, sought refuge in Kylemore, and ran a girls' boarding school here until 2010. Three reception rooms and the main hall are open to the public, as are a crafts center and cafeteria. Look out for chocolates, and a range of soaps handmade, labeled and packed by the nuns. There's also a 6-acre walled Victorian garden; a shuttle bus from the abbey to the garden departs every 15 minutes during opening hours. An exhibition and video explaining the history of the house can be viewed year-round at the abbey, and the grounds are freely accessible most of the year. Ask at the excellent crafts shop for directions to the **Gothic Chapel** (a five-minute walk from the abbey), a tiny replica of Norwich Cathedral built by the Henrys. ⊠ *Entrance off N59 about 8 km (5 miles) east of Letterfrack* ☎ *095/52001* ⊕ *www.kylemoreabbeytourism.ie* 🎟 *€13, including shuttle bus to garden* ☉ *Apr.–June and Sept., daily 9–6; July and Aug., daily 9–7 pm; Mar. and Oct., daily 9:30–5:30; Nov.–Feb., daily 10–4:30.*

LEENANE

18 km (11 miles) east of Letterfrack.

Nestled idyllically at the foot of the Maamturk Mountains and overlooking the tranquil waters of Killary Harbour, Leenane is a tiny village

DID YOU KNOW?

To best savor spectacu-
lar Kylemore Abbey take
the serene walk beside its
lake and stroll up the hill
to the life-size statue of
Jesus, usually surrounded by
grazing sheep. The resident
nuns will tell you that the
view over the lake is well
worth the effort.

noted for its role as the setting for the film *The Field,* which starred Richard Harris.

GETTING HERE AND AROUND

Leenane is 18 km (11 miles) east of Letterfrack on the N59. The journey takes just over 15 minutes. There is free parking in the village, on the streets, and in designated car parks. Leenane has at least one Bus Éireann bus a day, traveling to Galway via Clifden, taking about one hour, 15 minutes to Clifden. In summer there is also a bus to Westport, a 45-minute journey.

TOURS

Take a 90-minute trip around Killary Harbour in an enclosed Killary Cruises catamaran launch with seating for 150 passengers, bar, and restaurant.

ESSENTIALS

Transportation Contacts Killary Cruises ✉ *Nancy's Point* ☎ *091/566–736* ⊕ *www.killarycruises.com.*

EXPLORING

Fodor's Choice ★ **Killary Harbour.** Beyond Kylemore, N59 travels for some miles along Killary Harbour, a narrow fjord (the only one in Ireland) that runs for 16 km (10 miles) between County Mayo's Mweelrea Mountain to the north and County Galway's Maamturk Mountains to the south. The dark, deep water of the fjord reflects the magnificent steep-sided hills that border it, creating a haunting scene of natural grandeur. The harbor has an extremely safe anchorage, 13 fathoms (78 feet) deep for almost its entire length, and is sheltered from storms by mountain walls. The rafts floating in Killary Harbour belong to fish-farming consortia that raise salmon and trout in cages beneath the water. This is a matter of some controversy all over the West. Although some people welcome the employment opportunities, others bemoan the visual blight of the rafts. For cruises around the harbor, see Killary Cruises. ✉ *Killary.*

The Sheep and Wool Centre. The Sheep and Wool Centre, in the center of Leenane, focuses on the traditional industry of North Connemara and West Mayo. Several breeds of sheep graze around the house, and there are demonstrations of carding, spinning, weaving, and the dyeing of wool with natural plant dyes. ☎ *095/42323* ⊕ *www.sheepandwoolcentre.com* ▱ *Shop, café free; museum €5* ☼ *Mid-Mar.– Oct., daily 9:30–6.*

LEENANE AND THE ARTS

Martin McDonagh's *Leenane Trilogy,* featuring a cast of tragi-comic grotesques, presents an unflattering view of rural Irish life. An international hit, the plays brought a renown Leenane presumably could have done without. The plot thickened with Kevin Barry's "Fjord of Killary," a hilariously black short story set in a hotel in Leenane and published in the *New Yorker* in February 2010, and in Barry's 2012 collection *Dark Lies the Island* (2012).

WHERE TO STAY

$$$$
B&B/INN
Fodor'sChoice
★

Delphi Lodge. In the heart of what is arguably Mayo's most spectacular mountain and lake scenery, 5 km (3 miles) east of Leenane off N59, this attractive Georgian sporting lodge heavily stocked with fishing paraphernalia has a lovely lakeside setting. **Pros:** beautiful secluded location; abundant peace and quiet. **Cons:** you've got to like fishing or walking—and your fellow guests. $ *Rooms from: €230* ☎ *095/42222* ⊕ *www.delphilodge.ie* ↴ *12 rooms, 5 cottages* ⊙ *Closed mid-Oct.–mid-Mar.* ¶©¶ *Breakfast.*

$$
HOTEL

The Leenane Hotel. Built in the 1790s at the entrance to Leenane village as a coaching inn, only the main road separates this hotel from Killary Fjord—nearly all the bedrooms have a magical view, and it is worth waking at first light to savor the fjord in the early-morning mist. **Pros:** great value; comfortable and atmospheric one-stop base. **Cons:** some of the older bedrooms very small; lighting rather dim in bar and lounge. $ *Rooms from: €120* ☎ *095/42249* ⊕ *www.leenanehotel.com* ↴ *34 rooms* ⊙ *Closed mid-Nov.–mid-Mar.*

SOUTH COUNTY MAYO

County Mayo has long empty roads that stretch along for miles. The Museum of Country Life, the only branch of the National Museum outside Dublin, commemorates a disappearing way of life, and is fittingly located here in Turlough. Castlebar, the county town, has been overshadowed by its neighbor Westport, an elegantly laid-out 18th-century town with quays on the shore of island-studded Clew Bay, under the towering conical peak of St. Patrick's holy mountain, Croagh Patrick. Not only does Westport have scenery, it also has some excellent hotels and bars, some a legacy of the boom years that brought metropolitan chic to the heart of the West.

9

WESTPORT

32 km (20 miles) north of Leenane.

Fodor'sChoice
★

By far the most attractive town in County Mayo, Westport is on an inlet of Clew Bay, a wide expanse of sea dotted with islands and framed by mountain ranges. It's one of the most attractive heritage towns in Ireland, its Georgian origins clearly defined by the broad streets skirting the gently flowing river and, particularly, by the lime-fringed central avenue called the Mall. Built as an O'Malley stronghold, the entire town received a face-lift when the Brownes, who had come from Sussex in the reign of Elizabeth I, constructed Westport House and much of the modern town, which was laid out by architect James Wyatt when he was employed to finish the grand estate of Westport House.

GETTING HERE AND AROUND

Westport is 32 km (20 miles) north of Leenane on the R335, and 78 km (48 miles) north of Clifden, a journey of about an hour. It is 106 km (66 miles) northwest of Galway on the N17, picking up the N60 at Claremorris and the N5 at Castlebar. The journey takes about one hour, 45 minutes. There is ample parking in the town center, on the

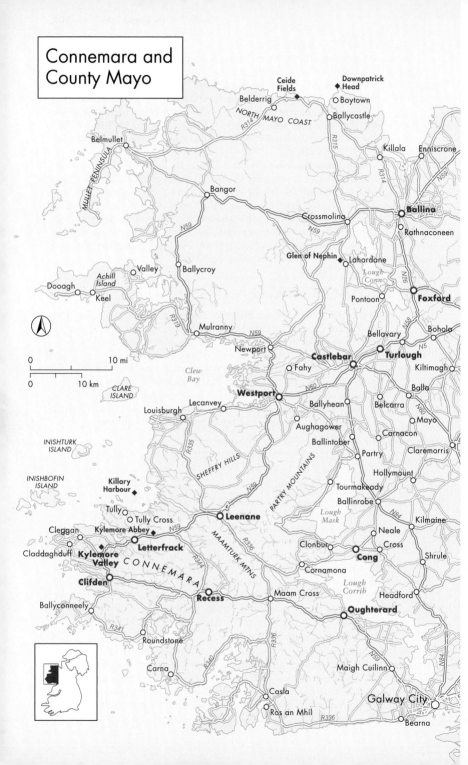

Connemara and County Mayo

streets and in designated lots, with a nominal charge during business hours. There is more parking down on the quays.

There are Bus Éireann buses daily from Westport (the Octagon monument) to Galway, traveling on the nonscenic N17 via Claremorris. The express takes one hour, 50 minutes, while the nonexpress bus takes more than two hours. There are also direct buses from Westport to Ballina, a journey of about an hour. There is no bus station in Westport. Irish Rail trains travel from Dublin's Heuston Station to Westport, a journey of 3½ hours.

ESSENTIALS

Visitor Information Croagh Patrick Information Centre. Located in the car park at the start of the Croagh Patrick ascent, the building houses a café and shop, and has shower and locker facilities. If you have any questions about climbing Croagh Patrick, this is the place to go. ⊠ Murrisk ☎ 098/64114 ⊕ www.croagh-patrick.com. **Westport Tourist Office** ⊠ James St. ☎ 098/25711 ⊕ www.discoverireland.ie/Places-To-Go/Westport.

EXPLORING

Clare Island. Clew Bay is said to have 365 islands, one for every day of the year. The biggest and most interesting to visit is Clare Island, at the mouth of the bay. In fine weather the rocky, hilly island, which is 8 km (5 miles) long and 5 km (3 miles) wide, affords beautiful views south toward Connemara, east across Clew Bay, and north to Achill Island. About 150 people live on the island today, but before the 1845–47 famine it had a population of about 1,700. A 15th-century tower overlooking the harbor was once the stronghold of Granuaile, the pirate queen, who ruled the area until her death in 1603. She is buried on the island, in its 12th-century Cistercian abbey. Today most visitors seek out the island for its unusual peace and quiet, golden beaches, and unspoiled landscape. A walking festival in mid-June had proved very popular. Ferries depart from Roonagh Pier, near Louisburgh, a scenic 19-km (12-mile) drive from Westport on R335 past several long sandy beaches. The crossing takes about 15 minutes. Dolphins often accompany the boats on the trip, and there are large populations of seals under the island's cliffs. ⊠ Clew Bay ☎ 098/25045 O'Malley's Ferries, 098/25212 Pirate Queen boat ⊕ www.clareisland. info ⛴ Ferry €15 round-trip ⊗ May–mid-Sept., sailings usually twice daily, weather permitting

Croagh Patrick. Look out as you travel north for the great bulk of 2,500-foot-high Croagh Patrick; its size and conical shape make it one of the West's most distinctive landmarks. On clear days a small white building is visible at its summit (it stands on a ½-acre plateau), as is the wide path that ascends to it. The latter is the Pilgrim's Path. Each year about 25,000 people, many of them barefoot, follow the path to pray to St. Patrick in the oratory on its peak. St. Patrick spent the 40 days and nights of Lent here in 441, during the period in which he was converting Ireland to Christianity. The traditional date for the pilgrimage is the last Sunday in July; in the past, the walk was made at night, with pilgrims carrying burning torches, but that practice has been discontinued. The climb involves a gentle uphill slope, but you need to be fit and agile to complete the last half hour, over scree (small loose rocks with no trail). This is why most climbers carry a stick or staff (traditionally made of ash, and called an ash plant), which helps you to stop sliding backward. These can sometimes be bought in the parking area. The hike can be made in about three hours (round-trip) on any fine day and is well worth the effort for the magnificent views of the islands of Clew Bay, the Sheeffry Hills to the south (with the Bens visible behind them), and the peaks of Mayo to the north. The climb starts at Murrisk, a village about 8 km (5 miles) before Westport on the R335 Louisburgh road.

Octagon. Westport's streets radiate from its central Octagon, where an old-fashioned farmers' market is held on Thursday morning; look for work clothes, harnesses, tools, and children's toys for sale. Traditional shops—ironmongers, drapers, and the like—line the streets.

FAMILY **Westport House.** The showpiece of the town remains Westport House and Country Park, a stately home built on the site of an earlier castle (believed to have been the home of the 16th-century warrior queen, Grace O'Malley) and most famed for its setting right on the shores of a beautiful lake. The house was begun in 1730 to the designs of Richard Castle, added to in 1778, and completed in 1788 by architect James Wyatt for the Marquess of Sligo of the Browne family. The rectangular, three-story house is furnished with late-Georgian and Victorian pieces. Family portraits by Opie and Reynolds, a huge collection of old Irish silver and old Waterford glass, plus an opulent group of paintings— including *The Holy Family* by Rubens—are on display. A word of caution: Westport isn't your usual staid country house. The old dungeons now house video games and the grounds have given way to an amusement park for children and an adventure center offering zip rides, laser combat games, and archery. In fact, the lake is now littered with swan-shaped "pedaloes," boats that may be fun for families but help destroy the perfect Georgian grace of the setting. If these elements don't sound like a draw, arrive early when it's less likely to be busy. There is also a 1½-km (1-mile) riverside walk, a tree trail, a gift shop, and a coffee shop. ⊠ *Off N59, south of Westport, clearly signposted from Octagon* ☎ *098/27766* ⊕ *www.westporthouse.ie* ✉ *House and gardens €12.50, activities €5–€20, family ticket €60; 10% discount online* ☉ *House, gardens, and attractions: May. and Oct., bank holiday weekends 10–4; 2 wks at Easter, daily 10–4; June, Wed.–Fri. 10–3, weekends noon–6 pm; July and Aug., daily 11–6. Partly closed for weddings and festivals so phone before to confirm.*

WHERE TO EAT AND STAY

$ ✕ **The Tavern Bar and Restaurant.** An outing to this traditional pub in the
SEAFOOD   tiny village of Murrisk—at the foot of Croagh Patrick, just across the
FAMILY   road from the seashore—is a popular excursion from Westport. Its distinctive, fuchsia-pink facade leads into a simple, family-run tavern where the emphasis is firmly on food. Carefully sourced local produce including Clew Bay seafood, Connemara lamb, and farm-house cheese from the nearby village of Carrowholly are served in hearty portions. The bar also has a kids' menu. Connemara lamb sausages with spring-onion mash, or the house-special beef braised in

ACHILL ISLAND

Achill Island is only 20 feet from the mainland and has been connected by a bridge since 1887, the latest (2008) being a €5-million swing bridge, known locally as "our Calatrava-style bridge." At 147 square km (57 square miles), it is Ireland's largest offshore island, with a population of 2,700. The main reason for visiting is to enjoy the wild open spaces of its unspoiled bog and wild heather, its abundant flora, especially rhododendrons in May/June, and fuchsia later in the summer, and to walk its long empty beaches. The best introduction is to follow signs for the 20-km (12-mile) Atlantic Drive. The road runs through Keel, which has a 3-km (2 mile)-long beach with spectacular rock formations in the eastern cliffs. Dugoort, on the north shore of the island is a small village with a beautiful golden strand. Above it, 2,204-foot Slievemore is the island's highest summit. At its base is the Deserted Village, a settlement of 80 ruined one-room stone houses, abandoned since the 1845 famine. Achill has traditionally been an impoverished area with high emigration, but the development of the tourist industry over the past 30 years has helped to stabilize its population, even though the new buildings do nothing to enhance the environment.

Guinness with carrots, onions, and parsnips are two winners. Fishermen arrive regularly with freshly landed langoustine, which are then poached and served in garlic butter. Upstairs a more elaborate à la carte menu ($$$) is served in the restaurant, with a quieter, candlelit atmosphere. $ *Average main: €14* ✉ *Murrisk, 5 km (3 miles) from Westport* ☎ *098/64060* ⊕ *www.tavernmurrisk.com* ☾ *Bar food daily. Restaurant upstairs closed Nov.–mid-Mar., and some weeknights mid-Mar.–Oct; call to confirm.*

$
B&B/INN
⊞ Boffin Lodge. In a quiet part of town, just a short walk from the lively quayside area, the Lodge is a traditional-style two-story gabled house with off-street parking. **Pros:** cozy and quiet; safe parking. **Cons:** a bit of a walk into town, and an uphill walk back from the quays. $ *Rooms from: €80* ✉ *Boffin St, The Quay* ☎ *098/26092* ⊕ *www.boffinlodge.com* ⇄ *10* ⦿ *Breakfast.*

$
HOTEL
⊞ Clew Bay Hotel. In Westport's town center, this hotel welcomes guests with a warmly traditional wooden facade, but once you are inside, a contemporary glass-roofed lobby comprises the centerpiece of a stylish modern interior decorated with original artwork. **Pros:** central location; friendly owner-managers; good value. **Cons:** risk of late-night noise in front rooms; no private parking; bathrooms a bit old-fashioned. $ *Rooms from: €90* ✉ *James St.* ☎ *098/28088* ⊕ *www.clewbayhotel.com* ⇄ *40 rooms.*

$$
HOTEL
Fodor's Choice
★
⊞ Knockranny House Hotel & Spa. Built on a bluff just outside town, with a commanding view of Croagh Patrick, this sumptuous, traditional-style hotel has a mock-Tudor facade leading to a spacious lobby permeated by the inviting aroma of the open log fire. **Pros:** peace and quiet; friendly, attentive staff; great views. **Cons:** a 10-minute walk into town; lots of corridors to negotiate; decor of public rooms a little bland.

9

CONNEMARA'S WILD PONIES

As you drive through Connemara, you will not only see sheep roaming the hillsides (lots of sheep: more sheep than people) but also herds of wild ponies, usually gray (the proper term for white horses) or dun (buckskin) in color.

Connemara ponies are strong, hardy, and companionable, highly intelligent, and also surprisingly elegant: averaging around 13 to 14 hands, they are much sought-after for riding and show jumping. They are assumed to be a cross between a native Irish breed and Spanish-bred Arab horses imported in the Middle Ages.

The breed was only recognized in the early 20th century, and is celebrated on the third weekend in August at the Connemara Pony Show in Clifden. The whole town takes on a festive air and parties long into the night as breeders and competitors from all over Ireland enjoy their annual get-together. The show-jumping competitions are pretty nifty, too.

$ *Rooms from: €150 ⊠ Castlebar Rd. (N5) ☎ 098/28600 ⊕ www.khh. ie ⟿ 84 rooms, 13 suites.*

$$ 🏨 **Mulranny Park Hotel.** Perched on a cliff amid woodland on the north-
HOTEL ern side of Clew Bay, 25 minutes' drive from Westport, overlooking a
FAMILY vast sandy beach, this is a good option if you plan to explore Achill Island, 14 km (9 miles) to the west. **Pros:** great location; genuine sense of history; indoor pool and leisure center for rainy days; Great Western Greenway walking/cycling route on-site. **Cons:** very popular with multigenerational family groups, which can mean noisy children. $ *Rooms from: €150 ⊠ Mulranny ☎ 098/36000 ⊕ www.mulrannyparkhotel.ie ⟿ 41 rooms ☉ Closed Jan. 7–31 ⊙ Some meals.*

$$ 🏨 **Westport Plaza Hotel.** Walk in off the street of this small Irish town,
HOTEL past topiary balls in square wicker holders, to the vast marble lobby with its double-sided gas fire, some 16 giant sofas, and New Age mood music, and you could be in the heart of metropolitan anywhere. **Pros:** all the creature comforts; best of modern design; quiet and central. **Cons:** avoid the few bedrooms with street views; you might forget you're in Ireland. $ *Rooms from: €140 ⊠ Castlebar St. ☎ 098/51166 ⊕ www. westportplazahotel.ie ⟿ 85 rooms, 3 suites.*

NIGHTLIFE

Matt Molloy's. In Westport's town center try this favorite spot; Matt Malloy is not only the owner but also a member of the famed musical group, the Chieftains. Traditional music is, naturally, the main attraction. ⊠ *Bridge St. ☎ 098/26655 ⊕ www.mattmolloy.com.*

The Towers Bar & Restaurant. A good spot for traditional music from 9 pm, the Towers is also known for its good pub grub. In summer there are outdoor tables set up here beside the bay. Children are welcome up to 7 pm. ⊠ *The Quay ☎ 098/26534 ⊕ www.thetowersbar.com.*

SHOPPING

Carraig Donn. A good selection of crystal, jewelry, and ceramics are the main temptations here, along with Carraig Donn's own line of knitwear. ⊠ *Bridge St.* ☎ *098/50300* ⊕ *www.carraigdonn.ie.*

Hewetson Bros. An old-fashioned fishing tackle shop, Hewetson also stocks gear for surfing, climbing, and hiking. ⊠ *Bridge St.* ☎ *098/26018.*

McCormack's. Downstairs is a traditional butcher shop but climb one flight up to find an attractive gallery and café with work by local artists for sale. ⊠ *Bridge St.* ☎ *098/25619.*

O'Reilly/Turpin. Head here for the best in contemporary Irish design for knitwear, ceramics, and other decorative items. ⊠ *Bridge St.* ☎ *098/28151.*

Thomas Moran's. For irresistibly unique gifts, Thomas Moran delivers with its locally made blackthorn sticks, bargain umbrellas, and some high-kitsch souvenirs. ⊠ *Bridge St.* ☎ *098/25562.*

Westport Marine and Treasure Gift Shop. This interesting gift shop with a marine theme carries items from useful boating gear to offbeat souvenirs. ⊠ *Shop St.* ☎ *098/28800.*

SPORTS AND THE OUTDOORS

BICYCLING

Clew Bay Bike Hire. Explore the scenic bike trails of Clew Bay, including the Great Wesetern Greenway, on a top-of-the-range bike, available by the hour, day, or multi-day, and enjoy the minibus and bike trailer that offers a free drop-off and collection service. In addition, kayak hire and escorted trips are available. ⊠ *Distillery Rd.* ☎ *098/37675* ⊕ *www. clewbayoutdoors.ie.*

Electric Escapes. Take the hard work out of cycling and rent an electric bike to explore the Great Western Greenway, or join a guided cycle tour along the Bangor Trail, amid 1,000 square miles of wilderness. Even the young and fit find the electric bike greatly increases the miles you can cover in a day. ⊠ *Distillery Rd.* ☎ *098/56611* ⊕ *www.electricscapes.ie.*

Great Western Greenway. This 42-km (26-mile) off-road cycling and walking trail follows the route of the railway line that ran along the edge of Clew Bay through Newport and Mulranny from 1895 until 1937, connecting Westport to Achill Island. It passes through some of the most spectacular scenery in the west of Ireland, and has given a major boost to tourism in the area. The birdsong and the sound of the wind are praised as highly as the great coastal scenery. It is just as enjoyable to drive out along the N59 and walk a short section as it is to walk or cycle the whole path. ⊠ *Great Western Greenway (N59).*

GOLF

Westport Golf Club. Twice this inland course hosted the Irish Amateur Championship. It lies in the shadows of religious history: rising 2,500 feet above Clew Bay, with its hundreds of islands, is Croagh Patrick, a mountain that legend connects with St. Patrick. The mountain is considered sacred, and it attracts multitudes of worshippers to its summit every year. All the prayers might pay off at the 15th, where your drive has to carry the ball over 200 yards of ocean. ⊠ *Carrowholly*

☎ *098/28262* ⊕ *www.westportgolfclub.com* ▧ *Apr.–Sept. €45; Oct. and Mar., weekdays €35; Nov.–Feb. €25* ⚲ *18 holes, 7000 yards, par 73. Practice area, driving range, caddies, caddy carts, buggies, catering* ⊙ *Visitors: daily.*

CASTLEBAR

18 km (11 miles) east of Westport on N5

The capital of Mayo, situated on its central limestone plain, once the biggest town for miles around, Castlebar is now a commercial and shopping hub for the region, overshadowed by its more scenic neighbor, Westport. Park in one of the many "Pay and Display" car parks, and proceed on foot.

GETTING HERE AND AROUND

Castlebar is 18 km (11 miles) east of Westport on the N5. The journey takes about 15 minutes by car. There are plenty of "Pay and Display" car parks in the town center, which has a one-way traffic system, and is compact and walkable. Bus Éireann has Regional links from here to Galway in the south (three hours, 30 minutes via Westport) and Ballina in the north (one hour). Dublin Airport is a meandering five-hour ride by bus; rail is a better option. The rail connection to Westport in the West takes 18 minutes and it is three hours to Dublin Heuston in the East; change at Manulla Junction for Ballina (one hour).

ESSENTIALS

Castlebar Tourist Information Office ✉ *Linenhall St.* ☎ *094/902-1207* ⊙ *Closed weekends.*

EXPLORING

The Linenhall Arts Centre. The town's arts center has a calendar of exhibitions, concerts, and performances, a craft shop, and a handy coffee shop with home baking. It occupies an imposing building in gray limestone dating from 1790 when the town had a thriving linen industry. ✉ *Linenhall St.* ☎ *094/902–3733* ⊕ *www.thelinenhall.com* ▧ *Free; event ticket prices vary.*

The Mall. At the center of Castlebar is the pleasant tree-lined Mall, with some good 18th-century houses. A memorial honors the French soldiers who died during the 1798 uprising when Castlebar was briefly the capital of "the Provisional Republic of Connaught." The Mall was once a cricket pitch belonging to the local landlord, Lord Lucan, and is now a town park.

WHERE TO EAT

$ ✕ **Café Rua.** This friendly café with its traditional red shopfront (*rua* is
MODERN IRISH Irish for red) is a showcase for locally produced foods, simply served.
FAMILY It's a family business, with the café's founder, Ann McMahon, still providing some of the home-baked cakes, while her daughter Coleen supervises front-of-house. Plain-top wooden tables and assorted chairs give an air of Boho-chic, as does the basket of today's newspapers, while colorful children's drawings adorn the walls. There's an imaginative children's menu, and at lunch there are three daily specials—roast meat, fish, and vegetarian—while many opt for the homemade soup and

panini, a platter of local farmhouse cheeses or a salad of Connemara Smokehouse salmon with locally-grown leaves, the house cucumber relish, and a selection of today's breads. Dinner is served weekends, and is excellent value, but you are advised to book in advance. Park in the SuperValu car park just around the corner. $ *Average main: €10* ✉ *New Antrim St.* ☎ *096/902–3376* ⊕ *www.caferua.com* ⊘ *Closed Sun. No dinner Mon.–Wed.*

TURLOUGH

24 km (15 miles) east of Castlebar.

Before the opening of the Museum of Country Life, Turlough was chiefly visited for its round tower (freely accessible), which marks the site of an early monastery, traditionally associated with St. Patrick, and the nearby ruins of a 17th-century church.

Once a thriving hub, with a village school, two pubs, and a busy shop, Turlough now has a population of about 300, one pub with a small shop attached, and no school. Rather than working on the land, most of the locals commute to jobs in nearby Castlebar.

GETTING HERE AND AROUND
Turlough is 24 km (15 miles) east of Castlebar on the N5 Dublin road. The museum is clearly signposted from the main road. Bus Éireann buses from Westport to Ballina via Castlebar will stop at the Museum of Country Life on request (ask the driver as you board).

EXPLORING

FAMILY
Fodor's Choice
★

Museum of Country Life. To understand the forces that have led to such dramatic changes in Turlough, pay a visit to the Museum of Country Life, which focuses on rural Ireland between 1860 and 1960—a way of life that remained unchanged for many years, then suddenly came to an end within living memory. At this highly acclaimed museum, the only branch of the National Museum of Ireland outside Dublin, you're invited to imagine yourself back in a vanished world, before the internal combustion engine, rural electrification, indoor plumbing, television, and increased education transformed people's lives and expectations. For many, this is a journey into a strange place, where water had to be carried from a well, turf had to be brought home from the bog, fires had to be lighted daily for heat and cooking, and clothes had to be made painstakingly by hand in the long winter evenings. Among the displayed items are authentic furniture and utensils; hunting, fishing, and agricultural implements; clothing; and objects relating to games, pastimes, religion, and education.

The museum experience starts in Turlough Park House, built in the High Victorian Gothic style in 1865 and set in pretty lakeside gardens. Just three rooms have been restored to illustrate the way the landowners lived. A sensational modern four-story, curved building houses the main exhibit. Cleverly placed windows afford panoramic views of the surrounding park and the distant round tower, allowing you to reflect on the reality beyond the museum's walls. Temporary exhibitions, such as one called "Romanticism and Reality," help illustrate the divide between the dreamy image of old rural life and its actual hardships. The shop sells museum-branded and handcrafted gift items as well as a good selection of books on related topics. A café with indoor and outdoor tables is in the stable yard, and you can take scenic lakeside walks in the park. Like all branches of the National Museum of Ireland, admission is free, making it a great rainy day resource. ⊠ *Turlough Park on the N4 (7 km [4 mi] east of Castlebar)* ☎ *094/903–1755* ⊕ *www.museum. ie* ▭ *Free* ☉ *Tues.–Sat. 10–5, Sun. 2–5.*

NORTH COUNTY MAYO

The land between Castlebar and Ballina is rugged and sparsely populated, and leads to one of the most dramatic coastlines in Ireland. Lough Conn and Lough Cullin are two great fishing lakes divided by a landbridge, Pontoon, under which their waters meet. The slopes of Mt. Nephin tower over untilled acres teeming with wildlife, including snipe and woodcock. Pretty Foxford nearby is the center of the local wool industry. Ballina, the largest town in these parts, is on the salmon-rich River Moy, which reaches the sea a few miles to the north in Killalla Bay. Mayo's rugged north coast has a number of sights worth exploring by car.

FOXFORD

As you travel from Turlough northeast to Ballina, you have a choice of two routes. The longer and more scenic is via the tiny, wooded village of Pontoon, skirting the western shore of Lough Conn and passing through the rough bogland of the Glen of Nephin, beneath the dramatic heather-clad slopes of Nephin Mountain (2,653 feet) to Crossmolina and Ballina. The shorter route follows N5 and N58 to Foxford, a pretty village with several crafts and antiques shops.

GETTING HERE AND AROUND
Take N5 and N58 from Turlough.

EXPLORING
Foxford Woolen Mills. A good place for a break is the Foxford Woolen Mills Visitor Center, where you can explore the crafts shop and grab a bite at the restaurant. The "Foxford Experience" tells the story of the wool mill, famous for its tweeds and blankets, from the time of the famine in the mid-19th century—when it was founded by the Sisters of Charity to combat poverty—to the present day. ⊠ *Lower Main St.* ☎ *094/925–6104* ⊕ *www.foxfordwoollenmills.ie* ☉ *Mon.–Sat. 10–6, Sun. noon–6; tour every 20 mins.*

WHERE TO EAT
$ ✕ **Healy's Restaurant and Bar.** Set in a long, creeper-clad two-story building more than 200 years old, Healy's overlooks the waters of Lough Conn, which calmly lap the reeds on its shoreline. Midway between Castlebar and Ballina (14 km [9 miles] south of the latter), this simple rural retreat was previously a lodging favored by serious anglers, but nowadays is known for its good food and wine. Enthusiastic host John

IRISH

Dever meets and greets his guests, many of them old friends, in a hall adorned with numerous glass cases of stuffed game fish, pheasant, and even a mink. The lounge bar has been converted into an informal restaurant with a heart-stopping lake view, while fishermen can still swap tall tales in the traditional pub in the next room. There is a basic all-day menu of smoked salmon, seafood chowder, fish-and-chips, Irish stew, and other bar food staples, while from 5 pm the Lobster Pot Restaurant offers a wider à la carte menu including roast duck with potato stuffing. On weekends (Friday–Sunday 5–9 pm) and Sunday lunch the Lough Cullen dining room opens to cope with the crowds. Situated amid great country for walking, fishing, and golf, Healy's simple fare still attracts an outdoor-loving crowd. $ *Average main: €12* ⊠ *Pontoon* ☎ *094/925–6443* ⊕ *www.healyspontoon.com.*

BALLINA

34 km (22 miles) northeast of Turlough.

Ballina, with a population of around 11,000, is a busy industrial and commercial center, and the second-largest town in Mayo after Castlebar. Built on the River Moy, it's famous for trout and salmon fishing, as well as for being the birthplace of Ireland's first female president (1990–97), Mary Robinson (born 1944). The angling in the town and nearby Lough Conn attracts many visitors. One of the best spots, the Ridge Pool, is right in the town center, and can be reached by crossing the pedestrian Salmon Weir Bridge, a striking structure shaped like a fishing rod that opened in 2009. While not conventionally pretty, the flat, windswept town's solid three- and four-story Victorian buildings house some charmingly old-fashioned pubs and shops.

GETTING HERE AND AROUND

Ballina is 34 km (22 miles) northeast of Turlough, a 45-minute drive. Use designated car parks in the town. During business hours there is a nominal charge. There are four Irish Rail trains a day from Dublin's Heuston Station to Ballina, a journey of 3½ hours.

There are about six buses a day to Dublin (four hours, 20 minutes), and an hourly service to Galway (three hours, 40 minutes). There are three buses a day direct from Ballina to Westport, a journey of about an hour. There is a local bus service four times a day from Ballina to Ballycastle via Killala to explore the North Mayo Coast.

Essentials Ballina Tourist Office ⊠ *41 Pearse St.* ☎ *096/72800* ⊕ *ballina-tourist-office.ballina.tel* ⊗ *Mon–Sat. 10–5.*

EXPLORING

The Jackie Clarke Library & Archives. Jacke Clarke (1927–2000) was a local businessman with a passion for history, and this is his collection of more than 100,000 items from the past 400 years. The well-designed displays will bring Ireland's history to life, with letters, cartoons, proclamations, handbills, maps, and personal memorabilia from the leaders of the 1916 rebellion. Book ahead for a guided tour (free). ⊠ *Pearse St.* ☎ *096/73508* ⊕ *www.clarkecollection.ie* ◨ *Free* ⊗ *Tues.–Sat. 10–5.*

9

WHERE TO STAY

$$$$ B&B/INN Fodor's Choice ★ **Enniscoe House.** Magnificent and magical, this square Georgian mansion is dramatically sited on the shores of Lough Conn under towering Mt. Nephin, about 20 km (12½ miles) west of Ballina. **Pros:** period accents; onsite heritage center; warm hosts. **Cons:** far from town. [$] *Rooms from: €220* ✉ *Castlehill near Crossmolina* ☎ *096/31112* 🌐 *www.enniscoe.com* 🛏 *6 rooms* 🕓 *Closed Nov.–Mar.* 🍴 *Breakfast.*

$$ HOTEL **Ice House Hotel and Spa.** An unusual and elegant combination of modern design and Victorian architecture combined with 19th-century industrial construction awaits visitors to this hotel at the mouth of the River Moy. **Pros:** mesmerizing views of wild swans, ducks, geese, and cormorants in the tidal waters outside the glass wall of your room. **Cons:** a five-minute drive from Ballina: somewhat isolated. [$] *Rooms from: €150* ✉ *The Quay* ☎ *096/23500* 🌐 *www.icehousehotel.ie* 🛏 *32 rooms.*

$$$ HOTEL FAMILY Fodor's Choice ★ **Mount Falcon.** Set in 100 acres between Ballina and Foxford, this baronial 1876 cut-stone house is the centerpiece of a family-owned estate with 45 luxury self-catering lodges, a lake and a river fishery, indoor pool, and spa. **Pros:** spacious, restful surroundings; very high standards of comfort; warm, attentive staff. **Cons:** very busy during Irish school holidays due to self-catering accommodation on-site. [$] *Rooms from: €180* ✉ *Foxford Rd. (N26)* ☎ *096/74472* 🌐 *www.mountfalcon.com* 🛏 *6 suites, 26 rooms.*

SPORTS AND THE OUTDOORS

Ballina Golf Club. Ballina Golf Club is a scenic parkland course only 1½ km (1 mile) from the town center. It is in the heart of the unspoiled Moy Valley, a wide river valley known for its great natural beauty. The course expanded to 18 holes in 1995, and was complemented by a new clubhouse in 2005. In contrast to the more spectacular courses in the West, Ballina, with its lush fairways and carefully manicured greens, interspersed with water hazards and bunkers, prides iteslf on offering a testing but fair game. ✉ *Mossgrove* ☎ *096/21050* 🌐 *www.ballina-golf.com* 🎫 *Fees: Oct.–Mar., weekdays €15, weekends and holidays €20; Apr.–Sept. €15* ⛳ *18 holes, 5933 yards, par 71. Practice area, caddies, caddy carts, buggies, catering* 🕓 *Visitors: Oct.–Mar., daily. Apr.–Sept. Wed. only.*

THE NORTH MAYO COAST

The North Mayo coast is one of the least frequented and most dramatic stretches of the Wild Atlantic Way. Killala, a pleasant little resort with sandy beaches, is the gateway to Mayo's rugged north coast, a dramatic windswept stretch of cliffs, where the wind howls in from the Atlantic directly from Iceland, the nearest landmass. The cliffs at Downpatrick have spectacular blowholes, and have weathered dramatically since the Stone Age farmers built the field systems exposed at the Céide Fields, a unique visitor center showcasing one of the oldest known field systems in the world.

GETTING HERE AND AROUND

Killala, the eastern extremity of the North Mayo coast is 12 km (7½ miles) north of Ballina on the R314. The Ceide Fields near Belderrig is a farther 32 km (20 miles) to the west. A car is the best way to explore this area. There is a commuter bus twice a day from Ballina, Route 445, as far as Ballycastle. Between May and mid-September there is a private bus service visiting Killala, Ballycastle, and the Céide Fields; details from Ballina Tourist Information Office.

EXPLORING

Killala. A pleasant little seaside town overlooking Killala Bay 12 km (7½ miles) north of Ballina, with several big sandy beaches, this was the scene of the unsuccesful French invasion of Ireland, led by Wolfe Tone in 1798. The history of this tiny bishopric goes back much further though, as evidenced by the round tower in the center of the village which dates from the 12th century. Built of large blocks of limestone, it is 84 feet tall, and is one of the most attractive of these monastic remains. ⊠ *Killala* ⊕ *www.roundtowers.org/killala.*

Ballycastle. Anywhere else in Ireland this tiny one-street village would be unremarkable, but out on this wild windswept coast its brightly painted houses in the relatively sheltered valley of the Ballinglen River are a welcome sign of normal life and coziness. Polke's old-fashioned bar-grocery will give you a warm welcome, as will Mary's Tea Rooms, while between May and September you can take in an art exhibition at the Ballinglen Arts Foundation—all within shouting distance of each other. ⊠ *Ballycastle.*

Downpatrick Head. On a clear day you can see the dramatic sea stack at Downpatrick Head in the distance from the Céide Fields Visitor Center. It is worth getting closer however: this rivals the far more famous (and bigger) Cliffs of Moher as an experience of nature in the wild. It is 5 km (3 miles) north of Ballycastle village; Wild Atlantic Way signposts will lead you to a gravel car park a short walk across rough grass from the cliffs. Keep a tight hold on your kids: the unfenced cliffs rise 126 feet above the sea, and the wind can be strong. The sea stack, known in Irish as Dun Briste (the Broken Fort) is 262 feet offshore, and rises to a height of about 164 feet. The sea has undermined the headland, and spouts up to great heights through impressive blowholes: these are fenced off for safety. The rock was inhabited until the 14th century when a landfall turned it into an island. In May and June the cliffs are covered in sea pinks and nesting seabirds.

Céide Fields. One of Europe's most significant megalithic sites, the fields consist of rows and patterns of stones that have been preserved under a 5,500-year-old bog. These stones are the remnants of dwellings places and stone-walled fields built by a peaceful, well-organized faming community more than 5,500 years ago. A glass-and-steel pyramid houses the visitor center, where displays and an audiovisual show bring this landscape to life. Admission includes an optional guided walk through an excavated section of the stones; wet weather gear is provided when necessary. The Céide Fields is on R314, 5 km (3 miles) west of

Ballycastle. ✉ *Ballycastle* ☎ *096/43325* ⊕ *www.heritageireland.ie* 🖅 *€4* ⊙ *Apr., May, and Oct., daily 10–5; June–Sept., daily 10–6.*

SPORTS AND THE OUTDOORS

GOLF

Carne Golf Links. Clinging to the northwest tip of County Mayo, this is literally the last golf course before you hit Boston. Designed by the late Eddie Hackett, this is said to be his greatest course, ducking and diving among towering sand dunes. From the elevated tees you can see a string of Atlantic islands. But don't be distracted by the view: you will need all your wits about you to beat the constant challenge of the high sea winds. (Belmullet is 72 km [45 miles] west of Ballina.) ✉ *Belmullet* ☎ *097/82292* ⊕ *www.carnegolflinks.com/* 🖅 *Fees: Jan., Feb., Nov., and Dec. €35 per day; Mar. €50 per day; Apr.–Oct. €70 per round* 🏌 *18 holes, 6692 yards, par 72. Practice area, caddies, caddy cars, buggies, catering* ⊙ *Visitors: daily (some restrictions).*

THE NORTHWEST

Including Counties Donegal, Leitrim, and Sligo

WELCOME TO
THE NORTHWEST

TOP REASONS
TO GO

★ **Gaeltacht Country:**
Venture to the seaside
village of Ard an Rátha
to listen to the seductive
rhythms of locals convers-
ing in full Irish (Gaelic)
flight. Don't worry: everyone has English at the
ready for lost visitors.

★ **Follow in Yeats's
Footsteps:** From Sligo town's
museums head out to the
majestic Ben Bulben peak
to seek out places special
to the famous brother duo,
W. B. Yeats, the great
poet, and Jack B. Yeats,
one of Ireland's finest
20th-century painters.

★ **Garbo's Castle:** The
legendary screen actress
was just one of the many
notables who enjoyed a
stay at Glenveagh Castle.

★ **Hiking the Slieve League
Cliffs:** To truly humble yourself before ocean, cliff,
and sky, hike these fabled
headlands, the highest sea
cliffs in Europe. The views
will set your heart racing,
and the Atlantic sea winds
are sure to blow away
the cobwebs. The cliffs
are also the spectacular
starting point for the Irish
leg of the International
Appalachian Trail.

1 Sligo and nearby.
What the poet William
Butler Yeats would say
about his native Sligo
town—a once-idyllic spot
now overrun with modern
shopping malls—can only
be imagined, but it makes a
great jumping-off point for
exploring Yeats Country: the
Lake Isle at Innisfree, the
cairn-crowned Knocknarea
(a peak often painted by
brother Jack), and Drumcliff,
where W. B. lies buried
under the shadow of Ben
Bulben.

2 Donegal Bay. Donegal
town, with its fine medieval
castle and abbey, is the
gateway to County Donegal,
regarded by many as the
runner-up to Kerry as
Ireland's most scenic region.

This is the ever-shrinking
heart of the Donegal
Gaeltacht (Irish-speaking
region), where the moody
hamlet of Gleann Cholm
Cille and the majestic Slieve
League Mountains beckon,
as does the Belleek china
of Ballyshannon. The nearby
town of Bundoran has
become synonymous with
international surfing and
hosts many championship
events. Since 2010, a new
50-foot wave called Prowl-
ers has brought surfers from
all over the world to hit this
monster Atlantic swell.

3 Northern Donegal.
This is the far Northwest,
Ireland's back-of-the-
beyond. The gateway town
is Letterkenny, presided over
by the 212-foot-high spire
of St. Eunan's Cathedral.
Westward lies Glenveagh
National Park, where you'll
find the storybook lair
and gardens of Glenveagh
Castle.

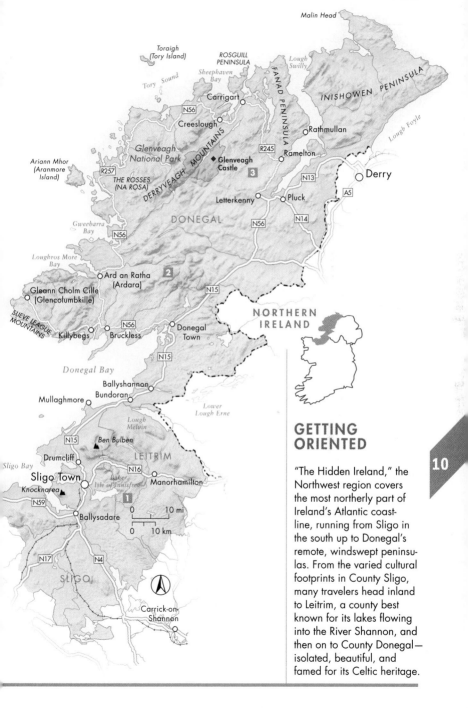

Malin Head

Toraigh
(Tory Island)

ROSGUILL
PENINSULA

Sheephaven
Bay

Tory Sound

FANAD PENINSULA

Lough
Swilly

INISHOWEN PENINSULA

Carrigart

N56

Creeslough

Rathmullan

Lough Foyle

Glenveagh
National Park

DERRYVEAGH MOUNTAINS

R245

Ramelton

Ariann Mhor
(Aranmore
Island)

R257

THE ROSSES
(NA ROSA)

◆ Glenveagh
Castle

3

N13

Derry

Letterkenny

Pluck

A5

Gweebarra
Bay

N56

DONEGAL

N56

N14

Loughros More
Bay

Ard an Ratha
(Ardara)

2

N15

**NORTHERN
IRELAND**

Gleann Cholm Cille
(Glencolumbkille)

SLIEVE LEAGUE MOUNTAINS

Killybegs

N56

Bruckless

Donegal
Town

N15

Donegal Bay

Ballyshannon

Mullaghmore

Bundoran

Lower
Lough Erne

Lough
Melvin

**GETTING
ORIENTED**

N15

Ben Bulben

LEITRIM

Drumcliff

N16

Sligo Bay

Sligo Town

Lough
Isle of Innisfree

Manorhamilton

Knocknarea

N59

1

Ballysadare

0   10 mi

0   10 km

N17

N4

SLIGO

Carrick-on-
Shannon

10

"The Hidden Ireland," the
Northwest region covers
the most northerly part of
Ireland's Atlantic coast-
line, running from Sligo in
the south up to Donegal's
remote, windswept peninsulas. From the varied cultural
footprints in County Sligo,
many travelers head inland
to Leitrim, a county best
known for its lakes flowing
into the River Shannon, and
then on to County Donegal—
isolated, beautiful, and
famed for its Celtic heritage.

Updated by
Paul Clements

With its towering cliffs, secluded expanses of golden beaches and sun-tinted waters, the Northwest is an untamed and wild part of Ireland, shaped, influenced, and tormented by the sea. Wide skies make it the perfect place to appreciate the shape-shifting light, slowly moving cloud formations, and crimson sunsets. As you drive around counties Sligo, Leitrim, and Donegal you will discover roads curve this way and that, following the course of the indented coastline, a mountain valley, glen, or stream. But the only traffic-jam you're likely to encounter will be a herd of heifers, reducing you to cow-speed.

A place of nature on a grand scale, the Northwest should be appreciated in a leisurely way. Catch a cloudless evening and you may be enchanted by a night sky display of the Aurora Borealis, the Northern Lights; and amid this celestial light show, or even an astonishing star-filled sky, you will find a silence that kindles the imagination.

Like nowhere else, this region influenced the writer William Butler Yeats and his brother Jack Butler Yeats, a painter. Both immortalized this splendidly lush and rugged countryside in their work, and "Yeats Country" still attracts fans. Twenty-first-century Sligo pulses not only in the present but also with the charge of history, for it was the Yeats' childhood home, the place that, more than any other, gave rise to their particular geniuses—or, as Jack B. put it: "Sligo was my school and the sky above it."

Northwest Ireland is overwhelmingly rural and underpopulated. That's not to say there isn't a bit of action here with plenty to experience. Sligo town, with its winding streets and Italian Quarter is as busy as Galway—an amazing feat for a town of only 18,000.

After you've drunk in the best views in Europe, washed by the Atlantic Ocean at Slieve League, you can pick up unique tweed in Donegal, look out for golden eagles at fairy-tale Glenveagh Castle, delve into the past at Glencolumbcille Folk Village, or sample burstingly fresh local seafood. Savor the boating town of Carrick-on-Shannon in Leitrim, a place full of architectural delights, or stroll through the county's glens and hillsides—a completely undiscovered part of the country.

THE NORTHWEST PLANNER

WHEN TO GO

When it rains, it really pours. Forget about the winter months, when inclement weather and a heavy fog swing in from the Atlantic and settle in until spring, masking much of the beautiful scenery. But in all seasons remember to pack a warm and waterproof coat (especially if you're headed to the coast) and bring a good pair of walking shoes. It's not all doom and gloom: the weather can be glorious in the summer months—just don't bet your house on it.

Try to plan your visit around one of the many festivals held in the Northwest. Each village tends to have its own *féile* (festival) during the summer months, and it's often worth the money and effort to attend. Music festivals abound, from the traditional Irish Sligo Feis Ceoil in mid-April, or the chamber music festival in May, Music in Drumcliff, to the country-and-western Bundoran Music Festival in June, and the jazz-and-blues weekend féile in Gortahork, County Donegal, in April. But being an Irish-speaking stronghold, the emphasis is on Irish traditional music. Every summer weekend you are guaranteed a bit of *craic* (fun) with lively sessions in most pubs. Sligo town, Ard an Rátha (Ardara), Ballyshannon, and Letterkenny are all hot spots. There are village festivals dedicated to hill walking, fishing, poetry, art, and food. As the saying goes, "any excuse for a féile."

PLANNING YOUR TIME

The Northwest is one of Ireland's most compact regions, and beautifully designed so that you can see the best of it with a three- or five-day trip. The best starting place, of course, is the gateway town where all the trains deposit you: Sligo, an excellent base thanks to its first-class hotels and facilities.

IF YOU HAVE 3 DAYS

Start your tour with Sligo's walking trail, a signposted trail of the town with a free tourist-board booklet to help you identify the important buildings and architectural surprises. Whatever else you do, don't forget to call into Hargadons time-burnished bar—unchanged in 160 years—for some fresh mussels and a glass of stout. You can drive or take an organized tour in the afternoon to the Lake Isle of Innisfree, south of Sligo town. Start early on day two for a short trip out to catch the sea breezes at Rosses Point or Mullaghmore, followed by an onward drive north to Donegal. Stop en route at Drumcliff churchyard to pay your respects at Yeats's grave. Donegal town, with its Irish tweed shops, is good for a spot of shopping followed by a tour of the 15th-century

Gaeltacht: Understanding the Language

County Donegal was part of the ancient kingdom of Ulster, not conquered by the English until the 17th century. By the time the British withdrew in the 1920s, they had still not eradicated rural Donegal's Celtic inheritance. It thus shouldn't come as a surprise that it contains Ireland's largest Gaeltacht (Irish-speaking) area. Driving in this part of the country, you may either be frustrated or amused when you come to a crossroads whose signposts show only the Irish

place-names, often so unlike the English versions as to be completely incomprehensible. To make things more confusing, some shop and hotel owners have opted to go with the English, not Irish, variant for their establishment's name. All is not lost, however, as maps generally give both the Irish and English names.

And locals are usually more than happy to help out with directions (in English)—often with a colorful yarn thrown in.

Donegal Castle. After an hour's drive west over twisting roads and amid glorious mountain scenery via the fishing port of Killybegs, you will come to the "back of the beyonds," aka Glencolumbkille, where you can happily putter around the Folk Village Museum. You can overnight here or drive north to Letterkenny, a modest-sized town with decent hotels, cafés, and restaurants. After a morning exploring Letterkenny's streets you should devote the entire afternoon to Glenveagh: tour the castle and rhododendron-filled gardens, follow one of the short nature trails in search of the golden eagles that are found here, or join a ranger-guided hill walk and take a picnic with you.

GETTING HERE AND AROUND

AIR TRAVEL

The principal international air-arrival point to Northwest Ireland is Ireland West Airport Knock, 55 km (34 miles) southwest of Sligo town. City of Derry Airport, a few miles over the border, receives flights from London Stansted, Birmingham, Liverpool, and Glasgow. City of Derry (also called Eglinton) is a particularly convenient airport for reaching northern County Donegal. Donegal Airport, in Carrickfinn, typically receives flights from Dublin. Ryanair has daily flights to Ireland West Airport Knock from London Stansted and London Gatwick, and also serves City of Derry Airport daily from London.

Airport Information City of Derry Airport ☎ 028/7181–0784 ⊕ www. cityofderryairport.com. **Donegal Airport** ✉ Carrickfinn, Kincasslagh, Letterkenny, Co. Donegal ☎ 074/954–8232 ⊕ www.donegalairport.ie. **Ireland West Airport Knock** ✉ Knock, Co. Mayo ☎ 094/936–8100 ⊕ www.irelandwestairport.com.

Carriers Aer Arann ☎ 0818/365–044, 0871/718–2020 in U.K. ⊕ www. aerlingus.com. **British Airways City Express** ☎ 0844/493–0787 ⊕ www. britishairways.com. **Ryanair** ☎ 0871/246–0000 ⊕ www.ryanair.com.

AIRPORT TRANSFERS   If you aren't driving, Ireland West Airport Knock becomes less attractive; there are no easy public transport links, except the once-a-day (in season) local bus to Charlestown, 11 km (7 miles) away. You can get taxis—both cars and minibuses—right outside Ireland West Airport Knock. The average rate is around €1.50 per kilometer. If you're not flying into Knock, you may have to phone a taxi company. Phone numbers of taxi companies are available from airport information desks and are also displayed beside pay phones.

BUS TRAVEL

Getting around by bus is easy enough if you plan to visit only the larger towns. Bus Éireann's routes are regular and reliable and there are also several privately run local bus companies, including McGeehan Coaches.

Bus Éireann helpfully offers a flexible Open Road bus pass ideally suited for travelers in the Northwest. A three-day tourist travel pass costs €57 and for five days it's €89. You can go anywhere in the republic on the nationwide network of services with this pass, but it is not valid across the border in Northern Ireland. For up-to-the-minute, real-time arrival and departure information with Bus Éireann, log on to ⊕ *www. whensmybus.ie.*

Bus Information Bus Éireann ☎ *01/836–6111 in Dublin, 071/916–0066 in Sligo, 074/912–1309 in Letterkenny* ⊕ *www.buseireann.ie.* **Bus Feda** ☎ *074/954–8114* ⊕ *www.feda.ie.* **Londonderry & Lough Swilly Railway Company** ☎ *028/7126–2017* ⊕ *www.loughswillybusco.com.* **McGeehan Coaches** ☎ *074/954–6150* ⊕ *www.mcgeehancoaches.com.* **North West Busways** ☎ *074/938–2619* ⊕ *www.foylecoaches.com.*

CAR TRAVEL

There is only one way to fully explore the rural Northwest of Ireland and that's by car. Once here, you can always rent a car at Ireland West Airport Knock or Sligo town. But if coming from Dublin, many opt to rent from one of the bigger companies at the larger airports. If arriving from Northern Ireland, there are rental agencies aplenty in Derry or Belfast, but be sure to tell your agency if you are planning to cross the border.

The roads between the larger towns are fairly well maintained and signposted, but go slightly off the beaten track and conditions can vary from bad to dirt track. As long as you're not in a mad rush, this can add to the delight of your journey. This is rural Ireland, and if the scenery doesn't make this blissfully clear, then the suspension on your rented car certainly will!

In the Irish-speaking areas, signposts are written only in the Irish (Gaelic) language, which can be confusing. Make sure that your map lists both English and Irish place-names.

TRAIN TRAVEL

Sligo town is the northernmost direct rail link to Dublin. If you want to get to Sligo town by rail from other provincial towns, you must make some inconvenient connections and take roundabout routes. The rest of the region has no railway service.

Train Information Irish Rail ☎ *01/836–6222, 071/916–9888 Sligo train station* ⊕ *www.irishrail.ie.*

THE WILD ATLANTIC WAY

The Wild Atlantic Way, Ireland's first long-distance driving route, runs from north Donegal down to west Cork, traversing isolated headlands, inlets, and little-visited peninsulas. The route follows the tortuous twists of roads that hug this indented coastline for more than 1,500 km (932 miles), but is arguably at its most dramatic in the Northwest. Donegal, with nearly 30% of all Ireland's sandy beaches, has the lion's share of golden strands. Malinbeg beach or Rossnowlagh are places to get out of the car, listen to the booming breakers, and absorb the tingling fresh air that has crossed 3,000 miles (4,828 km) of sea. All along the coast "Discovery Points" showcase areas of interest (including bars and restaurants), provide information on heritage and culture, and suggest viewpoints at which to breathe in the dramatic scenery and watch the interplay of light. Secret places to visit along the way are said to be "where the locals go" and generally speaking, local knowledge is the best advice to go on. The driving route is well signposted with new information boards pointing you in the right direction. Information is also available from tourist offices in Sligo, Donegal, and Letterkenny where you can pick up copies of the Fáilte Ireland North West Tourist Pocket Guide which includes details of the route. In the Northwest, highlights include the following favorite stopping points:

■ The spectacular stretch of coastline from **Bunbeg to Carrigart** includes Horn Head where squabbling seabirds converge, while across Sheephaven Bay, the rugged splendor of the Rosguill peninsula is ideal for a short looped walk or bike ride.

■ Famed for its musical connection and walls filled with memorabilia, Leo Crolly's Tavern at **Meenaleck** in west Donegal is the home of the singer Enya, Clannad, and Moya Brennan. It is the place to see dancers kick their heels in the air. (⊕ www.leostavern.com).

■ A narrow strip of Atlantic coastline at **Streedagh** beach in north County Sligo provides unique access to rocks encrusted with fossils as well as the site of three Spanish Armada shipwrecks. (⊕ www.seatrails.ie).

■ Fancy a hearty gallop on a young horse along a deserted beach? Then canter along on your own private island that crosses an Atlantic Channel to O'Connor's and Dernish Islands at **Grange** near Sligo. (⊕ www.islandviewridingstables. com).

■ One of Ireland's original coastal thatched pubs, the Beach Bar at **Aughris** in County Sligo is the place for a warming bowl of chowder surrounded by 300 years of maritime history. It's a pub where locals will happily spin you a yarn in exchange for a pint. (⊕ www.the beachbarsligo.com).

For more information on getting here and around, see Travel Smart Ireland.

RESTAURANTS

Donegal mountain spring lamb, Glen Bay crab, Donegal Bay oysters and mussels, Lough Swilly wild salmon, Enniscrone lobster, freshly baked scones, crusty homemade brown bread, and Guinness cake are just some of the delicious reasons why you will not go hungry traveling through the Northwest. Sligo town has established itself as a sort of last stop for food lovers, with a number of tempting shops promoting local produce that are well worth a visit. In 2012 an Italian Quarter was established in Sligo, and its cluster of restaurants and cafés serving up well-above-average food in memorable settings has created an epicurean vibe. It's even come up with its own culinary-and-arts festival, Sligo Food and Cultural Festival, held each May, and brimful of activities. You're likely to find the finest food at the higher-quality country houses, where chefs elegantly prepare local meat, fish, and produce in a hybrid Irish-French haute cuisine. In Donegal town, be sure to ask for what are officially Europe's top sausages, made by McGettigan's butchers. McGettigan's hickory-and-maple pork sausage won the 2012 European Championship title for sausage making, while the pork, curry, and banana and mango sausages picked up a Grand Prix of Excellence award.

HOTELS

True, it's the farthest-flung corner of Ireland, but thanks to the area's popularity, good bed-and-breakfasts and small hotels are abundant. In the two major towns—Sligo town and Donegal town—and the small coastal resorts in between, many traditional provincial hotels have been modernized (albeit not always elegantly). Yet most manage to retain some of the charm that comes with older buildings and personalized service. Away from these areas, your best overnight choice is usually a modest guesthouse that includes bed, breakfast, and an evening meal, though you can also find first-class country-house hotels with that gracious professionalism found elsewhere in Ireland. Consider staying in an Irish-speaking home to get to know some of the area's Gaeltacht population—Glencolumbkille's excellent Oideas Gael cultural center specializes in this; the local tourist information office (TIO) can be helpful in making a booking with an Irish-speaking family. *Hotel reviews have been shortened. For full information, visit Fodors.com.*

10

WHAT IT COSTS IN EUROS			
	$	$$	$$$	$$$$
Restaurants	under €19	€19–€24	€25–€32	over €32
Hotels	under €120	€120–€170	€171–€210	over €210

Restaurant prices are the average cost of a main course at dinner or, if dinner is not served, at lunch. Hotel prices are the lowest cost of a standard double room in high season.

TOURS

Bus Éireann has budget-price, guided, one-day bus tours of the Donegal Highlands and to Glenveagh National Park; they start from Bundoran, Sligo town, Ballyshannon, and Donegal town.

Bus Tours Bus Éireann ☎ *01/836–6111* ⊕ *www.buseireann.ie.*

VISITOR INFORMATION

The tourist information office (TIO) in Sligo town provides a 24-page booklet detailing a signposted walking tour of Sligo, information about bus tours of Yeats Country, and details of boat tours of Lough Gill. It's also the main visitor information center for Northwest Ireland. Open hours are September to mid-March, weekdays 9–5; mid-March to August, weekdays 9–6, Saturday 10–4, and Sunday 11–3. If you're traveling in County Donegal in the north, try the TIO at Letterkenny, about 1½ km (1 mile) south of town. It's open September to May, weekdays 9–5; June to August, Monday–Saturday 9–6 and Sunday noon–3. The office at Bundoran is open only in summer (usually the first week in June to the second week in September).

SLIGO AND NEARBY

Just as James Joyce made Dublin his own through his novels and stories, Sligo and its environs, known locally as Yeats Country, are bound to the work of W. B. Yeats (1865–1939), Ireland's first of four Nobel laureates, and to the work of his brother Jack B. Yeats (1871–1957), one of Ireland's most important 20th-century painters, whose expressionistic landscapes and portraits are as emotionally fraught as his brother's poems are lyrical and plangent. The brothers intimately knew and eloquently celebrated in their art not only Sligo town itself, but the surrounding countryside, with its lakes, farms, woodland, and dramatic mountains that rise up not far from the center of town. On the Sligo to Drumcliff route, you will often see glimpses of Ben Bulben Mountain, which looms over the western end of the Dartry range. The areas covered here are the most accessible parts of Northwest Ireland, easily reached from Galway.

SLIGO TOWN

60 km (37 miles) northeast of Ballina, 138 km (86 miles) northeast of Galway, 217 km (135 miles) northwest of Dublin.

Sligo, the only sizable town in the whole of Northwest Ireland, is the best place to begin a tour of Yeats Country. Squeezed on to a patch of land between Sligo Bay and Lough Gill, Sligo town is clustered on the south shore between two bridges that span the River Garavogue, just east of where the river opens into the bay. Thanks to the pedestrian zone along the south shore of the river (between the two bridges), you can enjoy vistas of the river while right in the center of town.

Sligo was often a battleground in its earlier days. It was attacked by Viking invaders in AD 807; later, it was invaded by a succession of rival Irish and Anglo-Norman conquerors. In 1642 the British soldiers of

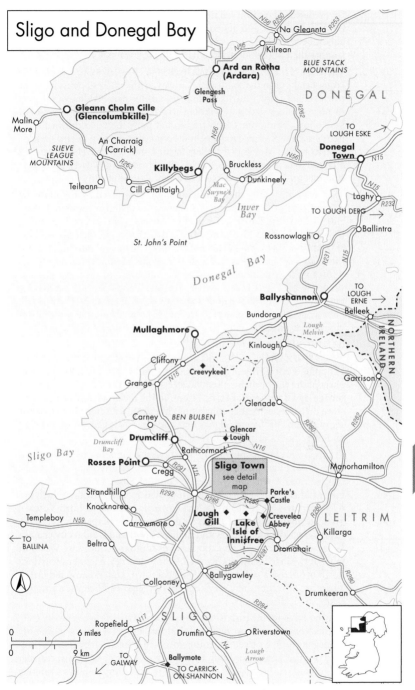

Sligo and Donegal Bay

Na Gleannta

N56 N560 R253

Kilrean

N56

BLUE STACK
MOUNTAINS

**Ard an Ratha
(Ardara)**

Glengesh
Pass

D O N E G A L

**Gleann Cholm Cille
(Glencolumbkille)**

R262

Malin
More

SLIEVE
LEAGUE
MOUNTAINS

An Charraig
(Carrick)

N56

TO
LOUGH ESKE

R263

**Donegal
Town**   N15

Killybegs

Bruckless

N56

N15

Teileann

Cill Chaitaigh

Mac
Swyne's
Bay

Dunkineely

Laghy

R232

Inver
Bay

TO LOUGH DERG

Ballintra

St. John's Point

Rossnowlagh

R231

N15

Donegal Bay

TO
LOUGH
ERNE

Ballyshannon

Belleek

Bundoran

Lough
Melvin

N
O
R
T
H
E
R
N

I
R
E
L
A
N
D

Mullaghmore

Kinlough

Cliffony

N15

♦ Creevykeel

Garrison

Grange

Glenade

R282

Carney

BEN BULBEN

R280

Drumcliff
Bay

Drumcliff

Glencar
♦ Lough

Sligo Bay

Rathcormack

N16

10

Rosses Point

R291

Manorhamilton

Cregg

N15

Sligo Town
see detail
map

Strandhill

R292

R286

R285

Parke's
♦ Castle

Knocknarea

Lough ♦

♦

♦ Creevelea
Abbey

R280

L E I T R I M

Templeboy

N59

Carrowmore ○

Gill

**Lake
Isle of
Innisfree**

Killarga

← TO
BALLINA

Beltra

N4

R287

Dromahair

Colloony

Ballygawley

Drumkeeran

R290

R287

R280

S L I G O

R294

Ropefield

N17

0   6 miles

Drumfin

Riverstown

0   9 km

TO
GALWAY

Ballymote
TO CARRICK-
ON-SHANNON

Lough
Arrow

N4

Sir Frederick Hamilton fell upon Sligo, killing every visible inhabitant, burning the town, and destroying the interior of the beautiful medieval abbey. Between 1845 and 1849, more than a million inhabitants of Sligo County died in the potato famine or fled to escape it.

The Sligo of the 21st century is as lively and crowded as its considerably larger neighbor to the southwest, Galway, with locals, students from the town's college, and tourists bustling past its historic buildings and along its narrow sidewalks and winding streets, and crowding its one-of-a-kind shops, restaurants, and traditional pubs. Long-established businesses such as Lyons department store and its upstairs wood-paneled café, as well as Mullaney Brothers fashion shop and travel agency, with a Burmese-teak-and-Italian-marble shop front, and Wehrly's Jewellers (founded in 1875), are redolent of a more graceful age.

They certainly enjoy their music in Sligo. Organized by the umbrella group Con Brio, event highlights encompass chamber music in Drumcliff in May, the Baroque Festival of Music at the end of September, the weeklong Sligo Live Music Festival at the end of October, and the annual Choral Festival in November. Informal musical offerings include the Sligo Sea Shanty Festival at Rosses Point. If you want some social lubricant, try traditional music in the pubs; one of the most popular venues is the Harp Tavern, where the Jazz Ladds perform on Sunday afternoons, as they have done for many years. During 2015 Sligo will once again play host to the All-Ireland Fleadh Cheoil, the most prestigious event on the Irish traditional music and cultural calendar.

GETTING HERE AND AROUND

Sligo's two main pay car parks are in Wine Street and in the Quayside Shopping Centre. Prices are between €1 and €1.20 per hour. In other parts of the town, such as Temple Street (by the cathedral), you pay €3 for the day if you park before 11 am. In the morning, school runs and store deliveries can cause congestion, but the town is mostly free of any serious traffic problems. Sligo is two hours north of Galway on the N17 and three hours driving time to Dublin on the N4.

Trains are in short supply in the Northwest region, but buses are plentiful. From Sligo town, buses spider out frequently in all directions, serving rural towns and villages in counties Sligo, Leitrim, and much farther afield. The main service is operated by Bus Éireann, which has 47 departures daily from its McDiarmada Station at Lord Edward Street to many points of the Irish geographical compass. Seven daily express services link Sligo with Dublin Airport and Dublin city center's Busaras Station. There are daily services south to Ballina and Westport in County Mayo. Galway City is a 2½-hour journey. Main bus corridors north of Sligo run to Bundoran, Donegal town, Letterkenny, and Derry. There are also four daily services between Sligo and Belfast, a trip that takes about three hours.

Iarnród Éireann, the Irish Rail company, operates efficient intercity train connections from Sligo to Dublin. However, other towns in County Donegal are not served by trains, nor are other nearby cities in Ireland: even if you're traveling to Galway or Belfast, you must transfer in Dublin first. Eight daily services run to and from Dublin's Connolly

Station, taking three hours and five minutes to reach Sligo. ■TIP➜ **Standard class round-trip fares are considerably cheaper if booked online.** Sligo's McDiarmada Station is a 10-minute walk to the city center (walk downhill and turn left).

TOURS

In the summer a good way to get your bearings is to join one of the guided walking tours of Sligo that leave from the tourist office on O'Connell Street. During June, July, and August (Tuesday–Friday 11 am–1 pm) these free two-hour tours are led by a knowledgeable guide and cover cultural history as well as stopping at many of the architectural highlights featured in the historic sites listed here.

WALKING IN COUNTY SLIGO

Sligo's environs, made up of coast, mountains, forest, and lakes, offer some of the best walking anywhere in the Northwest. A detailed website featuring a series of suggested local walks covers everything from the long-distance Sligo Way to the Miners' Way & Historical Trail. It includes information on Sligo's flowers and fauna, and what to look out for when you pull on your walking boots. View a PDF of the color brochure online at ⊕ *www.sligowalks.ie.*

BIKING IN COUNTY SLIGO

For those who prefer two wheels, you can hire bicycles in Sligo town—a fun way to explore the streets or venture into the surrounding countryside on a short ride to the coast. A top-class route is the 40-km (25-mile) signposted cycle loop of Lough Gill that passes through some of Sligo's most scenic areas and is mainly flat on quiet roads. Hire bicycles from Chain Driven Cycles (✉ *23 High St., Sligo* ⊕ *www.chaindrivencycles.com).*

ESSENTIALS

Transportation Information Sligo Railway Station ☎ *071/916–9888.*

Visitor Information County Sligo Tourism ✉ *Old Bank Bldg., O'Connell St.* ☎ *071/916–1201* ⊕ *www.sligotourism.ie.*

EXPLORING

TOP ATTRACTIONS

Fodor'sChoice ★ **The Model: Home of the Niland Collection.** The main attraction at the Model, housed in a school built in 1862, is one of Ireland's largest collections of works by 20th-century artists from home and abroad. And after a €6 million renovation, this gallery can claim to be a leading contemporary art venue. Periodically, the gallery displays works by famed Irish painter Jack B. Yeats, who once said, "I never did a painting without putting a thought of Sligo in it." At the heart of the collection is the work amassed by the woman whose name the gallery now bears, Nora Niland, who was the Sligo librarian from 1945 until the late 1970s and who recognized the importance of Yeats's work. Only a small selection of this work is on display at any time but you can view the whole collection of 300 images on the Model's website.

Paintings by John Yeats (father of Jack B. and W. B.), who had a considerable reputation as a portraitist, also hang here on a rotation basis, as do portraits by Sean Keating and Paul Henry. As part of the renovation, new performance and workshop spaces were built, a new gallery

10

was opened to increase and complete the circuit on the first floor, and seven artists' studios were added. Free informal curators' tours are held along with talks by the artist-in-residence. There is also a 180-seat cinema with a program run in conjunction with the Irish Film Institute. A revamped main entrance and the Model Cafe complete the dynamic makeover. ⊠ *The Mall* 🕾 *071/914–1405* ⊕ *www.themodel.ie* 🖃 *Free* ⊙ *Tues.–Sat. 10–5:30, Sun. noon–5.*

Sligo County Museum. The showpiece of this museum is its Yeats Hall, which houses a collection of W. B. Yeats's writings from 1889 to 1936, various editions of his plays and prose, the Nobel prize medal awarded to him in 1923, and the Irish tricolor (flag) that draped his coffin when he was buried at nearby Drumcliff. W. B. Yeats's letters to James Stephens and Oliver St. John Gogarty offer insight into Yeats's obsessive love for Sligo, the landscape of his poetic imagination. ⊠ *Stephen St.* 🕾 *071/911–1850* ⊕ *www.sligolibrary.ie* 🖃 *Free* ⊙ *May–Sept., Tues.– Sat. 9:30–12:30 and 2–4:45; Oct.–Apr., 9:30–12:30.*

Yeats Memorial Building. An active hub for lectures, poetry readings, discussion and literary events, and research, the Memorial Building on Hyde Bridge makes for a suitably imposing address for the Yeats Society. On the first floor, a gallery hosts a rotating exhibition of contemporary art. In addition, the Yeats International Summer School is conducted here every August, and in 2014 celebrated its 55th School. A permanent photographic exhibition, "Yeats and his Circle," is on display and can be viewed along with a 15-minute film as well as a digital slideshow, "The Yeats Country." Ask to see *Cast a Cold Eye*, a film about Yeats seen through the eyes of his son, daughter, and various literary figures. The Yeats Poetry Circle meets on Wednesday morning while the Poet's Parlor come together on the last Thursday of each month to foster an appreciation of Irish poetry. A new generation is also keeping the flame alive: Young Yeats, founded in 2013, meets on Wednesday afternoon. Research scholars can explore the Yeats Reference Library which has more than 3,000 titles. ■ TIP➜ On the ground floor, drink in the essence of the great man at the delightful Lily's & Lolly's Café, re-dedicated in 2013 in honor of Yeats's sisters. Across the street is Rowan Gillespie's photo-worthy sculpture of the poet, draped in a flowing coat overlaid with excerpts from his work. It was unveiled in 1989 by Michael Yeats, W. B.'s son, in commemoration of the 50th anniversary of his father's death. ⊠ *Hyde Bridge* 🕾 *071/914–2693* ⊕ *www.yeatssociety.com* 🖃 *€2* ⊙ *Weekdays 10–5, Sat. 10–2.*

WORTH NOTING

Sligo Abbey. A massive stone complex that is still redolent of "auld grandeur" and famed for its medieval tomb sculptures, Sligo Abbey is the town's only existing relic of the Middle Ages. Maurice FitzGerald erected the structure for the Dominicans in 1253. After a fire in 1414, it was extensively rebuilt, only to be destroyed again by Cromwell's Puritans under the command of Sir Frederick Hamilton, in 1642. Today the abbey consists of a ruined nave, aisle, transept, and tower. Some fine stonework remains, especially in the 15th-century cloisters. The visitor center is the base for guided tours, which are included with admission.

Sligo's most famous native son, poet W. B. Yeats, is honored by many memorials and statues found throughout the town.

✉ *Abbey St.* ☎ *071/914–6406* ⊕ *www.heritageireland.ie* ✉ *€3* ⊙ *Apr.– Oct., daily 10–6.*

St. John's Church. Designed in 1730 by Richard Castle—the architect who gave us the spectacular Powerscourt and Russborough stately houses in County Wicklow—this Church of Ireland structure has a handsome square tower and fortifications. In the north transept is a copper bronze memorial plaque to Susan Mary Yeats, mother of W. B. and Jack B. A beautiful stained-glass window commemorates William and Elizabeth Pollexfen, Yeats's maternal grandparents. Next door is the larger and newer Roman Catholic Cathedral of the Immaculate Conception (with an entrance on Temple Street), consecrated in 1874. Tours of St. John's can be arranged through the Yeats Society Memorial Building. ✉ *John St.*

WHERE TO EAT

$ ✗ **A Casa Mia.** A Casa Mia opened in 2013, and with its long communal
MODERN ITALIAN   table that seats 36, it has been a dynamic social and culinary triumph of the local scene: the place to get the lowdown on what's happening around town. If you don't feel like getting to know your neighbor and prefer a more intimate experience, you can opt for an individual table for breakfast, lunch, or dinner. Rural Italian dishes steal the show—the delightful piattini menu features small taste explosions of ravioli, calamari, spiced meatballs, and prawns pil-pil, as well as tapas dishes that include patatas bravas. To accompany these, try their tempting ciabatta bread or panini with warm or mixed-leaf salads. Ⓢ *Average main: €10* ✉ *Tobergal La.* ☎ *071/914–1690.*

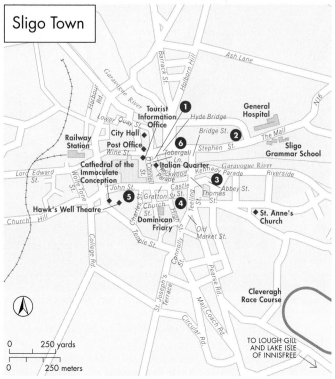

$ ✕ **Bistro Bianconi.** Based in the heart of Sligo's burgeoning Italian Quar-
ITALIAN ter, Bistro Bianconi has built on its 20-year-strong reputation for top-
Fodor's Choice class pizzas baked in a wood-burning oven. Inventive gourmet pizzas
★ include the Michelangelo (goat cheese, caramelized onions, pepperoni,
and a sprinkling of Parmesan), the Vegetariano, and the old reliable
Quatro Formaggi. The menu is heavy on classic fresh pasta and lasagna, while chicken *bocconcini*, (chicken with glazed ham and cheese)
the signature dish, is as popular as ever. Let the aromas of basil pesto,
garlic, and Tuscan bread wash over you as you sip a glass of Chianti
or Montepulciano—you could just as easily be in Florence. Upstairs,
a sister restaurant, **Gulliver's Wood Fire Grill** offers a complete dining
contrast: porterhouse steak, lamb kebab skewers, pork, tuna steak, or
monkfish cooked on a bespoke hand-forged wood grill made by a local
blacksmith. $ *Average main: €15* ⊠ *Tobergal La.* ☎ *071/914–1744*
⊕ *www.bistrobianconi.ie.*

$$ ✕ **Eala Bhán.** Swans will be a leitmotif of your visit to Sligo: you will
MODERN IRISH come across them in Yeats's poetry, see them in the Garavogue River,
find them folded in the shape of white napkins and depicted taking flight
on the walls of Eala Bhán (meaning "White Swan") restaurant. The
decor is modern but comfortable, and the food is Irish with a French
twist. Steak and seafood are prominent on the evening dinner menu,
as well as vegetarian dishes. Highlights include Tobercurry lamb and

Manor Farm stuffed chicken breast. The early-bird menu (5–6:30) is good value with a choice of two or three courses, including, for mains, "posh" fish-and-chips (cooked in tempura and with pea puree), beef burgers, or roasted squash risotto. Don't let the preening swans, visible from the dining-room window, distract you from the dessert menu. $ *Average main: €19* ⊠ *Rockwood Parade* ☎ *071/914–5823* ⊕ *www. ealabhan.ie* ⊘ *No lunch Mon.*

$ ✕ **Osta Café & Wine Bar.** Osta Café's philosophy is a straightforward one: IRISH locally sourced food, preferably organic, simply prepared. The seasonal vegetables are from the Crimlin Farm, free-range and organic eggs are supplied by Bluebell Farm, Le Fournil in Sligo delivers fresh bread each day, honey is from Knocknaree, and the meat is supplied by Clarkes and Sheerins butchers. Salads come from local organic growers. Sheep, cow, and goat cheese is made by Silke Cropp in Belturbet, while Carraig na Breac Smoke House in Drumshanbo provides smoked chicken and smoked cheddar cheese. Their 30-mile breakfast is named for the proud fact that all ingredients are from within that distance—with the exception of the fair-trade and organic Mexican and Peruvian Arabica coffee (though it's ethically sourced). The Osta Platter—homemade brown bread with roast ham, cheese, smoked chicken, and apple chutney—packs a filling lunchtime punch. Lunches are the main reason to come here but they also offer an early evening tapas menu, Monday–Wednesday until 7 pm and Thursday–Saturday until 8 pm. $ *Average main: €10* ⊠ *Garavogue Weir, Stephen St.* ☎ *071/914–4639* ⊕ *www.osta.ie.*

WHERE TO STAY

$$$$ ☷ **Coopershill.** Step beyond the elegant, symmetrical stone facade with HOTEL its central Palladian window, and wander through an appealing mix of Fodor's Choice antique bureaus, marble busts, mounted deer heads, and 19th-century ★ paintings that fill the large reception rooms of this three-story Georgian farmhouse. **Pros:** enter a delightful haven of peace, sink into the roll-top bath or four-poster bed, and lose yourself in luxury; free newspapers and mineral water. **Cons:** rooms can be chilly on cold days; quite a trek to the nearest pub or shops. $ *Rooms from: €218* ⊠ *Off N4, 17 km (11 miles) southeast of Sligo, Riverstown* ☎ *071/916–5108* ⊕ *www. coopershill.com* ☛ *8 rooms* ⊘ *Closed Nov.–Mar.* ❖ *Breakfast.*

$$$ ☷ **The Glasshouse.** Cosmopolitan modernists will love this funky, six-HOTEL story riverside hotel—it elevates accommodations in Sligo to a brash Fodor's Choice new level: just take a look at the towering exterior, which has been ★ designed to resemble a ship docked at the harbor. **Pros:** excellent location: Sligo's bustling heart is around the corner; underground car parking is included; complimentary Wi-Fi in all rooms. **Cons:** bring your shades, as colors will dazzle until you adjust; lacks leisure facilities such as gym or pool. $ *Rooms from: €200* ⊠ *Swan Point, Sligo* ☎ *071/919–4300* ⊕ *www.theglasshouse.ie* ☛ *116 rooms, 4 suites* ❖ *Breakfast.*

$$ ☷ **Markree Castle.** One of the most beautiful fortress fronts in Ireland HOTEL greets you on arrival at Markree, Sligo's oldest inhabited castle and the Fodor's Choice home of the Cooper family for 350 years. **Pros:** nature lovers will be at ★ home with walks across parkland and down to the Unsin River; luxurious but comfortable. **Cons:** bathroom water taps are slow; check-out on time (11:30 am) or wind up with a €50 surcharge per hour. $ *Rooms*

10

from: €140 ✉ *11 km (7 miles) south of Sligo town, off N4, Collooney* ☎ *071/916–7800* 🌐 *www.markreecastle.ie* 🛏 *30 rooms* 🍴 *Multiple meal plans.*

$ HOTEL **Sligo Park Hotel & Leisure Club.** Expect a modern establishment designed for a contemporary traveler and those who want to tour Yeats Country: a first-rate fitness center, dancing and piano entertainment some evenings, and the Hazelwood restaurant as well as the popular Rathana bar. **Pros:** functional rooms; good facilities include a modern leisure center and ample car parking. **Cons:** as it's a suburban hotel, it's a 30-minute walk into town if you're feeling energetic; the dining focus is on pub grub rather than restaurant meals. [$] *Rooms from: €110* ✉ *Pearse Rd. off N4* ☎ *071/919–0400* 🌐 *www.sligopark.com* 🛏 *136 rooms* 🍴 *Multiple meal plans.*

NIGHTLIFE AND THE ARTS

NIGHTLIFE

Fodor's Choice ★ **Hargadons Bar.** Part of the social fabric of Sligo since it opened more than 150 years ago, Hargadons Bar preserves its unique historic character and local chef-owner Joe Grogan maintains high standards in a much-loved institution. Wood paneling, cozy snugs (small booths) for private powwows, marble-top counters, and little glass doors on hinges make this place especially conducive to that intangible Irish element, the craic. Check out the walls, covered with historical black-and-white photos as well as fading invoices from the bar's early days. Hearty food at great prices is served at lunchtime, and the evening dinner menu (4–9 pm), featuring oysters, mussels, burgers, steak sandwiches, or chicken wings, lists local suppliers. The bar specializes in Irish craft beers with Shandon Stout and Eight Degrees among a wide selection. On Friday night musicians often hold center stage with a range of country-rock, pop, folk, and Irish traditional. Walk through the bar and in separate premises at the back you will find the well-stocked Hargadons Wine Shop in Johnston Court. ✉ *4–5 O'Connell St.* ☎ *071/915–3709* 🌐 *www.hargadons.com.*

Thatch. A few miles south of town is a popular spot with the locals, the Thatch pub, which has traditional music sessions in the summer from Thursday to Sunday. ✉ *Thatch, Ballysadare* ☎ *071/916–7288.*

Toffs. A sizable dance floor at Toffs teems with Sligo's younger set moving to a mix of contemporary dance music and older favorites. It stays open later than most places. ✉ *Kennedy Parade* ☎ *071/916–1250* 🌐 *www.toffs.eu.*

THE ARTS

THEATER **Hawk's Well Theatre.** With a jam-packed calendar year-round, Hawk's Well Theatre hosts amateur and professional companies from all over Ireland (and occasionally from Britain) in an eclectic mix of shows. Shows run €10–€30; the box office is open weekdays 10–5:30, Saturday 2–5, and on Sunday two hours before the performance. ✉ *Temple St.* ☎ *071/916–1518* 🌐 *www.hawkswell.com.*

Sligo Live Music and Arts Festival. If you're visiting in the fall, don't miss the Sligo Live Music and Arts Festival, held at various venues around town. Established in 2005, the festival runs over the bank-holiday weekend

Famed as a Sligo landmark since it opened its doors 150 years ago, Hargadons Bar has a time-burnished interior and also some of the freshest mussels around.

at the end of October and has links with North America, particularly with WGBH in Boston. It's elbow-room only as hotels, pubs, and cafés are crammed with scores of live sessions while fiddlers, dancers, jugglers, and puppeteers fill the streets. For dates and details of gigs, visit the website, where you can buy tickets. ⊠ *Sligo* ⊕ *www.sligolive.ie.*

Yeats Festivals. There's no getting away from events linked to the illustrious Yeats family. The Yeats International Summer School has been a permanent fixture for 55 years and is a prestigious academic talking shop. It runs for 12 days from the end of July. The Yeats Winter School is held over a weekend in January and includes lectures and tours. Details of these are at *www.yeatssociety.com.* Not to be outdone, W. B.'s brother Jack B., the painter, is increasingly being brought into the limelight. Tread Softly, a mix of theater, music, film, art, and readings, takes place at the same time as the summer school and explores the link between the brothers: *www.treadsoftly.ie.* June 13th has been designated Yeats Day, when costumed actors take to the streets for poetry readings and a host of other events. ⊠ *Sligo* ⊕ *www.yeatssociety.com and www.treadsoftly.ie.*

SHOPPING

Sligo town has Northwest Ireland's most thriving shopping scene, with lots of food-related, crafts, and hand-knits shops. Two useful websites are ⊕ *www.sligotourism.ie* and the excellent Sligo Craft Trail ⊕ *www.madeinsligo.ie;* leaflets can also be picked up from the tourist office.

Carraig Donn. In addition to Irish knitwear, Carraig Donn carries pottery, glassware, linens, and Aran knits for children. ⊠ *41 O'Connell St.* ☎ *071/914–4158* ⊕ *www.carraigdonn.com.*

The Cat & the Moon. The Cat & the Moon specializes in eclectic and stylish Irish-made crafts, jewelry, pottery, ironwork, and scarves; it's named after the play by W. B. Yeats. Upstairs is the Hamilton gallery, featuring work by contemporary Irish artists. ⊠ *4 Castle St.* ☎ *071/914–3686* ⊕ *www.thecatandthemoon.com.*

Cosgrove and Son. The upscale deli Cosgrove and Son sells everything from Parma ham to carrageen moss boiled in milk (a local cure for upset stomachs). Stock up here for a picnic with excellent muesli, boiled ham, and salads. ⊠ *32 Market St.* ☎ *071/914–2809.*

Cross Sections. Along with lovely tableware, this is the place to head for fine glassware and kitchenware. ⊠ *2 Grattan St.* ☎ *071/914–2265.*

Tír na nÓg. Tír na nÓg, Irish for "Land of the Ever-young," sells organic foods, including local cheeses and honeys, and other health-oriented items. A sister store across the street sells cards and posters. ⊠ *Grattan St.* ☎ *071/916–2752.*

LOUGH GILL

1½ km (1 mile) east of Sligo town.

Lough Gill means simply "Lake of Brightness." In fine weather the beautiful river-fed lough and its surroundings are serenity itself: sunlight on the meadows all around, lough-side cottages, the gentle sound of water, salmon leaping, a yacht sailing by.

GETTING HERE AND AROUND

To get to the lake from Sligo town, take Stephen Street, which turns into N16 (signposted to Manorhamilton and Enniskillen). Turn right almost at once onto R286. Within minutes you can see gorgeous views of the lake so adored by the young W. B. Yeats.

EXPLORING

Creevelea Abbey. A few minutes' walk along a footpath south of Parke's Castle lie the handsome ruins of Creevelea Abbey. In fact not an abbey but a friary, Creevelea was founded for the Franciscans in 1508 by a later generation of O'Rourkes. It was the last Franciscan community to be founded before the suppression of the monasteries by England's King Henry VIII. Like many other decrepit abbeys, the place still holds religious significance for the locals, who revere it. One curiosity here is the especially large south transept; notice, too, its cloisters, with well-executed carvings on the pillars of St. Francis of Assisi. ⊠ *R288, Dromahair.*

Parke's Castle. This fortified house was built on the eastern shore of Lough Gill in the 17th century by an English Planter (a Protestant colonist settling on Irish lands confiscated from Catholic owners) who needed the strong fortifications to defend himself against a hostile populace. His relations with the people were made worse by the fact that he obtained his building materials mainly by dismantling a historic fortress on the site that had belonged to the clan leaders, the O'Rourkes of Breffni (once the name of the district). Don't miss the blacksmith's forge which has been rebuilt and the nearby tiny circular sweathouse

Continued on page 541

SHOPPING FOR
A PIECE OF
THE SHAMROCK

Prepping dishes for Spongeware patterns

With its Belleek porcelains and Waterford crystals, Ireland has always been a treasured island for shoppers. Today, its traditional crafts—centuries old yet very much alive—are enjoying a revival of the fittest.

A CRAFT REVIVAL

Remember all those traditional leprechaun figurines with "Made in China" stickers on their bottoms? Today, Irish traditional crafts are flourishing as never before. In a land where until a generation ago, many villages were still redolent of a preindustrial age, "trad" culture has become commerce— big commerce. Claddagh friendship rings, spongeware pottery, heirloom Aran sweaters, Belleek china wedding plates, Carrickmacross lace, and Waterford crystal (so finely cut you'll need to don anti-brilliance eye goggles) are all objects endowed with vibrant personality. If Ireland has never been a country of great artists, it has always been one of great artistry.

Above: Claddagh ring.
Below: Louis Mulcahey at work on his pottery.
Dingle Peninsula, Southwest Ireland

WHERE TO BUY
While the entire country is blooming with craftsworkers, the Northwest region offers some seventh-level shopping, thanks to hand-knit Aran sweaters, fine Parian china, and handwoven tweeds. Those who want to make browsing—and buying—easy will find the famous multidealer town cooperatives (such as Midleton's Courtyard Crafts or Doolin's Celtic Waves) tempting. But, in general, the more interesting craftspeople are found outside the main cities, and intrepid consumers should head for smaller towns where overheads are lower (and the scenery is better). Don't buy the first blackthorn walking stick you see. Take a good look around and visit any number of crafts shops— you'll probably end up with a bogwood paperweight and basketweave china tureen as well!

CHERISHED COLLECTIBLES

WATERFORD CRYSTAL

Founded in 1783, Waterford crystal is noted for its sparkle, clarity, and heft. Thicker glass means that each piece can be wedge-cut on a diamond wheel to dramatic effect (as you can see during the famous factory tour held at the Waterford factory in Southeast Ireland). Waterford artisans apprentice for *eight* years.

BELLEEK CHINA

China has been made in Belleek, a village just on the border with County Fermanagh, Northern Ireland, since 1857. This local product is a lustrous fine-bone china with a delicate green or yellow-on-white design and often incorporates weave-effect pottery. Americans love it. Old Belleek is an expensive collector's item, but modern Belleek is more reasonably priced and very likely to appreciate in value over the years (according to some experts).

TRADITIONAL LACEMAKING

Traditional Irish crochet and lace-making use a fine cotton and date back to the 1840s when they originated in the cottage homes and lace schools of Carrickmacross.

SPONGEWARE POTTERY

One of Ireland's most beautiful collectibles, Irish Spongeware first appeared in 18th-century potteries. With the use of a cut sponge, patterns and images—often "rural" in flavor, like plants and sheep—are applied to the lovely cream-colored surface.

CLADDAGH RINGS

Born in the Claddagh area of Galway during the 17th century, the Claddagh ring incorporates three symbols: a heart (for love), a pair of hands (for friendship), and a crown (for loyalty). Worn on the right hand, with crown and heart facing out, it symbolizes the wearer is still "free"; worn on the left, with symbols tucked under, indicates marriage.

IN FOCUS A PIECE OF THE SHAMROCK

10

ARAN: FROM FLEECE TO FASHION

Made of plain, undyed wool and knit with distinctive crisscross patterns, sometimes referred to as *báinín* sweaters or "ganseys," the Aran sweater is a combination of folklore and fashion.

Since harsh weather made warmth and protection vital out in the Atlantic Ocean, the women of Aran long ago discovered the solution to this problem in this strong, comfortable, hand-knit sweater. Indeed, these Arans can hold 30 percent of their weight in water before they even start to feel wet. The reason? Traditionally, the wool used was unwashed and retained its water-repellent natural sheep's lanolin.

LOOK FOR THE PATTERN

Not so long ago, these pullovers were worn by every County Donegal fisherman, usually made to a design belonging exclusively to his own family. It's said that a native can tell which family the knitter belongs to from the patterns used in a genuine Aran sweater. Often the patterns used religious symbols and folk motifs, such as the Tree of Life, the Honeycomb (standing for thrift and thought to be lucky), the SeaHorse, the Blackberry—all are patterns in the almost sculptured, deeply knitted work that characterizes the Aran method. Their famous basket stitch represents the fisherman's basket, a hope for a *curragh* (fisherboat) heavy with catch. A colorful belt called a *crios* (pronounced "criss")

is handcrafted in many traditional designs as a useful accessory.

MAKING YOUR PURCHASE

Most of the Aran sweaters you'll see throughout Ireland are made far north of the islands themselves, in County Donegal, an area most associated with high-quality, handwoven textiles. The best are painstakingly knitted by hand, a process that can take weeks. As a result, prices are not cheap, and if you think you've found a bargain, check the label before buying—it's more likely a factory copy. Still, the less expensive, lighter-weight, hand-loomed sweaters (knitted on a mechanical loom, not with needles) are less than half the price, and more practical for most lifestyles. But the real McCoy is still coveted: some of the finest examples woven by Inis Meáin are sold at luxury stores like Bergdorf Goodman and Wilkes Bashford. And young Irish designers like Liadain De Buitlear are giving the traditional Aran a newer-than-now spin, highly popular in Dublin boutiques.

Above left: A large selection of styles and sizes; Above right: Spun yarns ready to be knit into Aran sweaters

(an early druid sauna). The entrance fee includes a short video show on the castle and local history; guided tours are available. In summer, boat tours of the lough leave from here. **■TIP→ For a breathtaking view of the nearby Lough Colgagh, drive west from Parke's Castle, keeping the lake on your left. You will find a small car park from where you can drink in the spectacular views.** ✉ *R288, Fivemile Bourne* ☎ *071/916–4149* 🌐 *www.heritageireland.ie/en/north-west/parkescastle* 🎟 *€3* ⏲ *Apr.–Sept., daily 10–6.*

WHERE TO STAY

$ B&B/INN 🏨 **Stanford Village Inn.** With a 200-year-old pedigree and in the same family for six generations, this rustic stone-front inn is one of the few stops for sustenance near Lough Gill. **Pros:** blissful, pastoral location. **Cons:** hard-to-find location; service can be hit or miss on busy days. [$] *Rooms from: €50* ✉ *7 km (5 miles) from Parke's Castle, 19 km (12 miles) from Sligo town, off R288, Dromahair, Co. Leitrim* ☎ *071/916–4140* 🛏 *9 rooms* 🍴 *Breakfast.*

LAKE ISLE OF INNISFREE

15 km (9 miles) south of Sligo town via Dromahair.

In 1890 W. B. Yeats was walking through the West End of London when, seeing in a shop window a ball dancing on a jet of water, he was suddenly overcome with nostalgia for the lakes of his Sligo home. It was the moment, and the feeling, that shaped itself into his most famous poem, "The Lake Isle of Innisfree":

I will arise and go now, and go to Innisfree,

And a small cabin build there, of clay and wattles made:

Nine bean-rows will I have there, a hive for the honey-bee,

And live alone in the bee-loud glade.

And I shall have some peace there, for peace comes dropping slow.

Though there's nothing visually exceptional about Innisfree (pronounced *in-nish*-free), the "Lake Isle" is a must-see if you're a Yeats fan. To reach Innisfree from Dromahair, take R287, the minor road that heads back along the south side of Lough Gill, toward Sligo town. Turn right at a small crossroads, after 4 or 5 km (2 or 3 miles), where signposts point to Innisfree. A little road leads another couple of miles down to the lakeside, where you can see the island just offshore.

CARRICK-ON-SHANNON

31 km (24 miles) southwest of Sligo town.

Carrick-on-Shannon grew up around the river that still plays an important role in the town's confidence. Its original Irish name, Cora Droma Rúisc, means "the stony ford of the ridge in the marsh." Today's prosperous town, with a population of 3,500, takes pride in its past and is full of architectural surprises. In the first decade of the 21st century many old buildings were given life again, in some cases being turned into cultural or arts centers, offices, or restaurants. Bistro bars, stylish hotels, delis, and boutiques sit cheek by jowl with old-world pubs and family-run shops. In 1613 King James I granted the town a Royal Charter by which it became a Royal Borough with a corporation made up of a Provost, Burgesses, and Commonalty. It had the right to send two members to the Irish Parliament and continued to do so up to the Act of Union in 1800 when the Parliament voted itself out of existence.

GETTING HERE AND AROUND

The main N4 Sligo–Dublin road that skirts Carrick-on-Shannon carries heavy traffic throughout the day, but the town avoids serious congestion. There is ample free car parking in the Townspark area, between the Bush and Landmark hotels. An hourly metered charge applies for parking on the main street where a one-way traffic system operates. Sligo is an hour's drive west while Dublin is just over two hours southeast on the N4.

Seven daily *Bus Éireann* departures leave Carrick-on-Shannon for Dublin (airport and city center); journey time is 2½–3 hours, and the fare is €18 round-trip to the city center. Sligo is an hour's bus journey with seven departures in each direction Monday–Saturday (five on Sunday) and costs €12 one-way. Regular daily services from Carrick also run to Boyle, Longford, Mullingar, and Athlone. There is no bus station in Carrick, so the pickup point is at the waterfront near the Landmark Hotel.

Carrick-on-Shannon's railway station is well served by Irish Rail. The town is on the main Dublin–Sligo intercity rail line and eight trains run weekdays with a restricted service on weekends. From Dublin, trains take just over two hours to reach Carrick (€30.10 one-way, €43.50 round-trip). From Sligo, the journey takes 44 minutes and costs €15.80 one-way, €18.20 round-trip. The small station is on the outskirts of town, so if you're laden with luggage, you'll need a cab for the final leg into town. You can also catch a train from Carrick to neighboring towns such as Ballymote, Collooney, Boyle, Longford, and Mullingar.

ESSENTIALS

Visitor Information Fáilte Ireland Tourist Information Office ⊠ *Old Barrel Store, The Quays* ☎ *071/962–0170* ⊕ *www.leitrimtourism.com.*

EXPLORING

Attic Memorial at Carrick Workhouse. Follow the stylized footprints of a mother and child from St. George's Heritage Centre to the Attic Memorial at Carrick Workhouse to step back into tragic Leitrim. This workhouse opened in 1842 to accommodate hundreds who sought refuge here from the 1845–46 Great Famine. With bare floorboards and whitewashed walls it looks pretty much as it did in the 1840s. Wexford artist Alanna O'Kelly's multimedia installation "No colouring can deepen the darkness of truth," brings a new dimension to this thought-provoking place which also houses a reading room. A sensory garden was opened in 2012. Nearby is a Great Famine Commemoration Graveyard. ⊠ *Summerhill* ☎ *071/962–1757* ⊕ *www.carrickheritage. com* ☏ *€7* ⊗ *Daily 10–4.*

Costello Memorial Chapel. Ask at the tourist office for a free copy of the signposted historical walking town trail booklet and accompanying map. A top sight is one of Ireland's tiniest: the Costello Memorial

Chapel, built in 1879, is the smallest church in Ireland and a testament to a man's love for his wife. Built by local businessman Edward Costello in memory of Mary Josephine, its tiny dimensions are a mere 16 feet long, 12 feet wide, and 30 feet high. The church was extensively renovated in 2009. ✉ *Bridge St.*

Fodor's Choice ★ **St. George's Heritage & Visitor Centre.** Restored by a local heritage group, St. George's Heritage & Visitor Centre occupies St. George's (Church of Ireland), built in 1827. The bright interior houses the Telford Organ (built in 1846), the magnificent altarpiece entitled *The Adoration of the Shepherds* (painted in 1831 by the Swedish artist Carl Gustave Plagemann), and dazzling displays of ecclesiastical silver. But many eyes will be focused on the array of motorized banners choreographed to rise and fall to classical organ music, as they unfurl the names of more than 270 Leitrim men killed during World War I. A central theme is "Twin Traditions," the mingling of Gaelic and Planter cultures entwined for the past 400 years. Next door, the story of Leitrim is told in a lyrical 10-minute film, "Leitrim: Enduring and Enchanting" in the **Visitor Centre** (☎ *071/962–1757*). ✉ *St. Mary's Close* ☎ *071/962–1757* 🌐 *www.carrickheritage.com* 🎟 *€7* 🕒 *Daily 10–4.*

WHERE TO EAT AND STAY

$$ IRISH 🍴 **The Oarsman Bar & Restaurant.** Carrick is renowned for a rich selection of characterful pubs, many of which serve excellent food. The best and most impressive menu is found at this gastropub run by brothers Conor and Ronan Maher. A Carrick institution, it's very popular, so advance reservations for dinner are usually needed. Upstairs, a more expensive restaurant opens only on Friday and Saturday nights. Try some of their craft beers or ciders that include Carrig craft brew and Rower's ale or Galway Hooker pale ale. **■ TIP→ Keep a space for the rhubarb and vanilla mascarpone cheesecake with ginger biscuit base and petit meringues.** [$] *Average main: €20* ✉ *Bridge St.* ☎ *071/962–1733* 🌐 *www.theoarsman.com.*

$$ IRISH 🍴 **Victoria Hall Restaurant.** Set in a former church hall near the waterfront, this place is stylish and soothing. For starters, choose from such delights as sushi and smoked salmon or duck spring roll with homemade BBQ sauce. Main courses, starting at €18, include such classics as sea-bass fillet with king prawns, a delicious green chicken curry, or mouthwatering Thai-style stir-fried beef with garlic. Table settings are minimalist, service is prompt and friendly, and you can bring your own wine for a corkage charge. [$] *Average main: €21* ✉ *Quay Rd.* ☎ *071/962–0320* 🌐 *www.victoriahall.ie.*

$$ HOTEL 🏨 **Bush Hotel.** With roots stretching back to 1794, this historic and convivial hotel enjoys a central location in the heart of Carrick. **Pros:** superb organic breakfast fixings; relaxing place to appreciate the layers of Irish history. **Cons:** room lights slow to warm up but all in an eco-friendly cause; hotel bar lacks charisma. [$] *Rooms from: €129* ✉ *Main St.* ☎ *071/967–1000* 🌐 *www.bushhotel.com* 🛏 *60 rooms* 🍽 *Multiple meal plans.*

$$
HOTEL
Fodor's Choice ★

🏨 **The Landmark Hotel.** If you want to watch the River Shannon cast its calming spell as you sip the best cocktails in Leitrim, head to this waterfront landmark where guest rooms are sleek, spacious, spotlessly well-appointed, and most have riverside views. **Pros:** top location; careful and personal attention to guests' needs. **Cons:** service slow at peak times; traffic noise from busy bypass road. [$] *Rooms from: €130* ✉ *The Waterfront* ☎ *071/962–2222* 🌐 *www.thelandmarkhotel.com* 🛏 *60 rooms* 🍴 *Multiple meal plans.*

NIGHTLIFE AND THE ARTS

Dock Arts Centre. Carrick's impressive Dock Arts Centre is a former courthouse and now a happening place to take in a concert, play, or arts event. Sympathetically restored as Leitrim's first integrated arts center, it houses a chic theater with seating for more than 100 and a café bar. Shows run €12–€35. ✉ *St. George's Terr.* ☎ *071/965–0828* 🌐 *www.thedock.ie.*

SHOPPING

Leitrim Design House. In the same building as the Dock Arts Centre you'll find the Leitrim Design House, which promotes modern Irish craftsmanship. It sells bespoke jewelry, ceramics, glass, textiles, and sculpture as well as contemporary fashion, all helping to conserve the rich cultural identity of Leitrim. ✉ *St. George's Terr.* ☎ *071/965–0550* 🌐 *www.leitrimdesignhouse.ie.*

Market Yard Centre. Carrick's architectural gem, the Market Yard Centre is in the heart of the town; known as the Shambles in 1839, it is now home to a popular weekly market (Thursday10–2:30) and local history center. ✉ *Under the Clock Tower, Main St.* ☎ *071/965–0816* 🌐 *www.themarketyardcentre.com.*

Trinity Rare Books. Many small independently owned shops line Carrick's main streets catering for all tastes, from lovers of fashionable boutiques to antiques hunters and bibliophiles. Hidden-away Trinity Rare Books is run by a garrulous Canadian with a depth of knowledge of both the Irish and international book market. ✉ *Bridge St.* ☎ *071/962–2144* 🌐 *www.antrinityrarebooks.com.*

ROSSES POINT

8 km (5 miles) northwest of Sligo town.

It's obvious why W. B. and Jack B. Yeats often stayed at Rosses Point during their summer vacations: glorious pink-and-gold summer sunsets over a seemingly endless stretch of sandy beach. Coney Island lies just off Rosses Point. Local lore has it that the captain of the ship *Arathusa* christened Brooklyn's Coney Island after this one, but there's probably more legend than truth to this, as it's widely agreed that New York's Coney Island was named after the Dutch word *konijn* (wild rabbits, which abounded there during the 17th century).

GETTING HERE AND AROUND

Rosses Point is an 8-km (5-mile) drive west of Sligo town on the R291 around the northern arm of Sligo Harbour. There's a free car park with dramatic views overlooking Drumcliff Bay. Bus Éireann operates a service from Sligo bus station to Rosses Point and drops you off at the Catholic church. The bus serves Rosses Point beach only in July and August.

SPORTS AND THE OUTDOORS
GOLF

Fodor's Choice
★
County Sligo Golf Club. Founded in 1894 on land leased from an uncle of W. B. Yeats, and one of Ireland's grand old venues, the popular County Sligo coastal links course is situated in the heart of Yeats Country at Rosses Point, a seaside village 8 km (5 miles) north of Sligo town. Ominous Ben Bulbin Mountain (best viewed from the par-5 3rd hole) dominates the northern views on this infamously windy course, which will test any player's ability to keep the ball low off the tee. The 17th is the signature hole—a long par-4 with a steeply uphill green. Another feature of the course is the array of wildlife; it teems with flora and fauna, a wonderful distraction for visitors. Big-hitting names in the golfing world, including Sir Nick Faldo, Padraig Harrington, and Rory McIlroy, are honorary members. ⊠ *Rosses Point, Sligo* ☎ *071/917–7134* ⊕ *www.countysligogolfclub.ie* ⛳ *18 holes, Apr.–Oct. €95; 9 holes, Apr.–Oct. €25* 🏌 *18 holes, 6947 yards, par 71. Practice: putting, chipping, and bunker practice, caddies, buggies, pull and electronic carts, catering* ⊙ *Visitors: daily, restricted hrs on weekends 12:06–1:26 and 2:30–5.*

SAILING

Sligo Yacht Club. With a fleet of some 90 boats, the Sligo Yacht Club has sailing and social programs, and regularly hosts races. ☎ *071/917–7168* ⊕ *www.sligoyachtclub.ie.*

DRUMCLIFF

15 km (9 miles) northeast of Rosses Point, 7 km (4½ miles) north of Sligo town.

W. B. Yeats lies buried with his wife, Georgie, in an unpretentious grave in the cemetery of Drumcliff's simple Protestant church, where his grandfather was rector for many years. W. B. died on the French Riviera in 1939; it took almost a decade for his body to be brought back to the place that more than any other might be called his soul-land. In the poem "Under Ben Bulben," he spelled out not only where he was to be buried but also what should be written on the tombstone: "Cast a cold eye / On life, on death. / Horseman, pass by!" It is easy to see why the majestic Ben Bulben (1,730 feet), with its sawed-off peak (not unlike Yosemite's Half Dome), made such an impression on the poet: the mountain gazes calmly down upon the small church, as it does on all of the surrounding landscape—and at the same time stands as a sentinel facing the mighty Atlantic.

Drumcliff is where St. Columba, a recluse and missionary who established Christian churches and religious communities in Northwest Ireland, is thought to have founded a monastic settlement around AD 574. The monastery that he founded before sailing off to the Scottish isle of Iona flourished for many centuries, but all that is left of it now is the base of a round tower and a carved high cross (both across N15 from the church) dating from around AD 1000, with scenes from the Old and New Testaments, including Adam and Eve with the serpent and Cain slaying Abel.

GETTING HERE AND AROUND

Follow the main N15 north of Sligo town, taking the signposts for Donegal, and you will come to Drumcliff. There is ample parking at the church. It's a 15-minute drive from Sligo to Drumcliff. The Sligo–Donegal town bus stops at Drumcliff and sets down passengers at the post office from where it's a five-minute walk to the grave of W. B. Yeats. Journey time is 15 minutes and a round-trip costs €6.20.

HILLTOP DOINGS

The massive flat-dome plateau of Ben Bulben dominates the surrounding bogland. Dating to 574 when St. Colmcille founded a monastery on its peak (these fellows were seriously into inaccessibility), it became a major religious destination until Oliver Cromwell extinguished it. The 1,730-foot climb has superb views, but remember: it is always windy on top and frequently soggy underfoot.

Drumcliff Tea House and Craft Shop. A good place to buy local crafts, books of W. B. Yeats's poetry, and books about the poet's life, the Drumcliff Tea House and Craft Shop also sells light lunches and snacks, including soup, sandwiches, and panini. ⊠ *Next to Protestant church* ☎ *071/914–4956* ⊗ *Mon.–Sun. 9–6.*

DONEGAL BAY

As you drive north to Donegal town, the glens of the Dartry Mountains (to which Ben Bulben belongs) gloriously roll by to the east. Look across coastal fields for views of the waters of Donegal Bay to the west. In the distant horizon the Donegal hills beckon. This stretch, dotted with numerous prehistoric sites, has become Northwest Ireland's most popular vacation area. There are a few small and unremarkable seashore resorts, and in some places you may find examples of haphazard and fairly tasteless construction that detracts from the scenery. In between these minor resort developments, wide-open spaces are free of traffic. The most intriguing area lies on the north side of the bay—all that rocky indented coastline due west of Donegal town. Here you enter the heart of away-from-it-all: County Donegal.

MULLAGHMORE

37 km (24 miles) north of Sligo town.

In July and August, the sleepy fishing village of Mullaghmore becomes congested with tourists. Its main attractions: a 3-km-long (2-mile-long) sandy beach; and the turreted, fairy-tale Classie Bawn—the late Lord Louis Mountbatten's home (he, his grandson, and a local boy were killed when the IRA blew up his boat in the bay in 1979; the castle is still privately owned and not open to the public). A short drive along the headland is punctuated by unobstructed views beyond the rocky coastline out over Donegal Bay. When the weather is fair, you can see all the way across to St. John's Point and Drumanoo Head in Donegal.

GETTING HERE AND AROUND

Mullaghmore is a 30-minute drive from Sligo along the N15 main road to Donegal. Look for the turnoff signpost at the village of Cliffony; from there it's a five-minute drive along a narrow country road to reach Mullaghmore. There is a large free car park.

EXPLORING

Creevykeel. One of Ireland's best megalithic court-tombs, Creevykeel contains a burial area and an enclosed open-air court where rituals were performed around 3000 BC. Bronze artifacts found here are now in the National Museum in Dublin. The site (signposted from N15) lies off the road, just beyond the edge of the village of Cliffony. ⊠ *3 km (2 miles) southeast of Mullaghmore off N15.*

BALLYSHANNON

23 km (15 miles) north of Mullaghmore, 42 km (26 miles) northeast of Sligo town.

The former garrison town of Ballyshannon rises gently from the banks of the River Erne and has good views of Donegal Bay and the surrounding mountains. Come early August, this quiet village springs to life with a grand fest of traditional music, the **Ballyshannon Folk Festival** (☎ 086/252–7400 ⊕ *www.ballyshannonfolkfestival.com*), Ireland's longest-running music gathering. The town is a hodgepodge of shops, arcades, and hotels. Its triangular central area has several bars and places to grab a snack. The town was also the birthplace of the prolific poet William Allingham. Another son of Ballyshannon, the legendary rock guitarist Rory Gallagher, who died in 1995, is also honored with an annual summer musical tribute. More than 10,000 visitors pour into the town to ensure his spirit lives on in the hearts of many fans 20 years after his death. **The Rory Gallagher International Tribute Festival** (⊕ *www.rorygallagherfestival.com*) is held over the June bank holiday week. A few kilometers down the road are several factories where, for generations, master craftsmen have made eggshell-thin Irish porcelain. It's said that if a newlywed couple receives a piece of this china, their marriage will be blessed with everlasting happiness.

GETTING HERE AND AROUND

Ballyshannon is on the main N15 Sligo–Donegal route, about 20 minutes south of Donegal town. There are several free car parks around the town, but parking on the main street is metered.

EXPLORING

Belleek Pottery Ltd. For generations the name Belleek has been synonymous with much of Ireland's delicate ivory porcelain figurines and woven china baskets (sometimes painted with shamrocks). Belleek Pottery Ltd. is the best known of the producers, in operation since 1857. The main factories are in Northern Ireland (which is why their prices are quoted in pounds sterling, not euros) just down the road from Ballyshannon. Watch the introductory film, take the 30-minute tour, stop

10

by for refreshment in the tearoom, or just head to the on-site shop. The factory-museum-store is near the border with Northern Ireland. Company products can also be found in the shops of Donegal and Sligo. ⊠ *6 km (4 miles) east of Ballyshannon, 3 Main St., Belleek* ☎ *028/6865–9300 in Northern Ireland* ⊕ *www.belleek.com* ⊠ *£4* ☉ *Jan. and Feb., weekdays 9–5:30, closed weekends; Mar.–June, Mon.–Sat. 9–5:30, Sun 2–5:30; July–Sept., weekdays 9–6, Sat.10–6, Sun. noon–5:30; Oct.–Dec., weekdays 9–5:30, Sat. 10–5:30, Sun. noon–5.*

Celtic Weave China. The fourth generation (since 1866) of the Daly family hand crafts and paints the elaborate floral and basket-weave designs at Celtic Weave China. Because it's a small, personal operation, they can make a single piece of china to your specifications. They also carry out design work for Tiffany Jewelers of New York and have worked with the Los Angeles–based architect Frank Gehry. Prices start at €12, and most pieces cost less than €125, although you can spend up to €3,000 on a double photo frame. ⊠ *R230, 5 km (3 miles) east of Ballyshannon, Cloghore* ☎ *071/985–1844* ⊕ *www.celticweavechina.com* ⊠ *Free* ☉ *Weekdays 8–6, Sat. 9–5.*

OFF THE BEATEN PATH

Lough Derg. From Whitsunday to the Feast of the Assumption (June to mid-August), tens of thousands beat a path to the shores of Lough Derg, ringed by heather-clad slopes. In the center of the lake, Station Island—known as St. Patrick's Purgatory (the saint is said to have fasted here for 40 days and nights)—is one of Ireland's most popular pilgrimage sites and a haven for those seeking spiritual renewal. It's also the most rigorous and austere of such sites in the country. Pilgrims stay on the island for three days without sleeping, and ingest only black tea and dry toast. They pay €70 to walk barefoot around the island on its flinty stones and pray at a succession of shrines. Non-pilgrims may not visit the island from June to mid-August. You can also visit the island for a "Quiet Day" trip (10–4) that costs €40 including the boat journey and lunch. In the Basilica of St. Patrick's Purgatory look for the astonishing work of the Irish stained-glass artist Harry Clarke whose 14 windows feature the apostles, St. Paul, and the Virgin Mary. To find out how to become a pilgrim, write to the Reverend Prior. To reach the shores of Lough Derg, turn off the main N15 Sligo–Donegal road in the village of Laghy on to the minor R232 Pettigo road, which hauls itself over the Black Gap and descends sharply into the border village of Pettigo, about 21 km (13 miles) from N15. From here, take the Lough Derg access road for 8 km (5 miles). During pilgrim season, buses connect Pettigo with Ballyshannon and Enniskillen from Thursday to Monday. There are no services on Tuesday or Wednesday. It's a 30-minute journey from both towns and the return taxi fare is €30. There is also a direct Bus Éireann service in the Pilgrim Season from Dublin to Lough Derg from Thursday to Monday. Journey time is just over four hours. ⊠ *Pettigo* ☎ *071/986–1518* ⊕ *www.loughderg.org.*

NIGHTLIFE

Dicey Reilly's. "Dicey's," as the locals call it, has been selling beer in a variety of forms since 1856. Also noted for its selection of quality wines from around the world, in 2014 Dicey's branched into handcrafted beers and opened a microbrewery beside their bar. It's no surprise that

Donegal Blonde, with the merest hints of biscuit and malt and a fine balance of hop flavors, is one of their most popular beers. If this isn't to your liking though there are a staggering 450 world beers from which to choose. Pub grub such as soup and sandwiches is on offer during the day. Guided tours of the brewery lasting 40 minutes are held in summer; it's best to check the website in advance for details. ⊠ *Market St.* ☎ *071/985–1371* ⊕ *www.donegalbrewingcompany.com.*

Seán Óg's. One of the biggest and most popular pubs, Seán Óg's, has live music on Friday, Saturday, and Sunday evenings. ⊠ *Market St.* ☎ *071/985–8964.*

DONEGAL TOWN

21 km (13 miles) north of Ballyshannon, 66 km (41 miles) northeast of Sligo town.

With a population of about 3,000, Donegal is Northwest Ireland's largest small village—marking the entry into the back-of-the-beyond of the wilds of County Donegal. The town is centered on the triangular Diamond, where three roads converge (N56 to the west, N15 to the south and the northeast) and the mouth of the River Eske pours gently into Donegal Bay. You should have your bearings in five minutes, and seeing the historical sights takes less than an hour; if you stick around any longer, it'll probably be to do some shopping—arguably Donegal's top attraction.

The town of Donegal was previously known in Irish as *Dún na nGall,* "Fort of the Foreigners." The foreigners were Vikings, who set up camp here in the 9th century to facilitate their pillaging and looting. They were driven out by the powerful O'Donnell clan (originally Cinel Conail), who made it the capital of Tyrconail, their extensive Ulster territories. Donegal was rebuilt in the early 17th century, during the plantation period, when Protestant colonists were planted on Irish property confiscated from its Catholic owners.

The **Diamond,** like that of many other Irish villages, dates from this period. Once a marketplace, it has a 20-foot-tall obelisk monument (1937), which honors the town monks who, before being driven out by the English in the 17th century, took the time to copy down a series of old Irish legends in what they called *The Annals of the Four Masters.*

10

GETTING HERE AND AROUND
Donegal is a 60-minute drive from Sligo north along the N15. The main pay car park is at the quay beside the tourist information office on the approach road from the south. Catch the wrong day in the height of summer and Donegal town is a bottleneck. Fortunately, that doesn't occur very often—the reason may be a local wedding, a festival, a funeral, or a Gaelic football match. The main delays focus on the one-way system operating around the Diamond. Try to avoid this area around 5 pm.

Public transport throughout Donegal is limited to buses. Bus Éireann operates direct daily services from Donegal town to Dublin Airport and the city center, which also stop in the nearby towns of Ballyshannon and

Belleek. It runs regular services between the bigger towns linking Donegal town with Bundoran, Letterkenny, and west to Killybegs, Glencolumbkille, Glenties, and Dungloe. There is no bus station, but buses stop outside the Abbey Hotel in the Diamond. A raft of smaller independently run buses crisscrosses Donegal's roads—including McGeehan Coaches, Patrick Gallagher Coaches, Feda O'Donnell Coaches, John McGinley Coach Travel, and Donegal Coaches—and these companies pick up and drop off in Quay Street.

ESSENTIALS

Visitor Information Discover Ireland Centre, Donegal Town ⊠ *The Quay* ☎ *074/972–1148* ⊕ *www.discoverireland.ie.*

EXPLORING

Donegal Castle. Donegal Castle was built by clan leader Hugh O'Donnell in the 1470s. More than a century later, this structure was the home of his descendant Hugh Roe O'Donnell, who faced the might of the invading English and was the last clan chief of Tyrconail. In 1602 he died on a trip to Spain while trying to rally reinforcements from his allies. Its new English owner, Sir Basil Brooke, modified the little castle in 1610, fitting Jacobean towers and turrets to the main fort and adding a Jacobean mansion (which is now a ruin). Inside, you can peer into the garderobe (the restroom) and the storeroom, and survey a great banqueting hall with an exceptional vaulted wood-beam roof. Also of note is the gargantuan sandstone fireplace nicely wrought with minute details. Mind your head on the low doorways and be careful on the narrow trip stairwell. The small, enclosed grounds are pleasant. ⊠ *Tirchonaill St., near north corner of Diamond* ☎ *074/972–2405* ⊕ *www.heritageireland.ie* ⊠ *€4* ⊙ *Apr.–Sept., daily 10–6; Oct.–Mar., Thurs.–Mon. 9:30–3:45.*

Franciscan Abbey. The ruins of the Franciscan Abbey, founded in 1474 by Hugh O'Donnell, are a five-minute walk south of town at a spectacular site perched at the end of the quay above the Eske River, where it begins to open up into Donegal Bay. The complex was burned to the ground in 1593, razed by the English in 1601, and ransacked again in 1607; the ruins include the choir, south transept, and two sides of the cloisters, between which lie hundreds of graves dating to the 18th century. The abbey was probably where *The Annals of the Four Masters,* which chronicles the whole of Celtic history and mythology of Ireland from earliest times up to the year 1618, was written from 1632 to 1636. The Four Masters were monks who believed (correctly, as it turned out) that Celtic culture was doomed by the English conquest, and they wanted to preserve as much of it as they could. At the National Library in Dublin, you can see copies of the monks' work; the original is kept under lock and key. ⊠ *Off N15, at the end of the quay* ⊠ *Free* ⊙ *Freely accessible.*

WHERE TO EAT AND STAY

$ ✕ **Blueberry Tea Room and Restaurant.** Proprietors Brian and Ruperta Gallagher serve breakfast, lunch, afternoon tea, and a light early evening meal—always using homegrown herbs. Daily specials—Irish lamb stew, pasta dishes, and quiche—are served from 9 to 7. Soups, sandwiches, salads, and fruit are on the regular menu, along with homemade desserts, breads, scones, sticky cakes, and jams. Upstairs is an Internet café

CAFÉ

but check in downstairs first. It's across the street from Donegal Castle. Get there early for lunch, as the lines stretch out on to the street on busy days. $ *Average main: €10* ⊠ *Castle St.* ☎ *074/972–2933* ✆ *Closed Sun.*

$

HOTEL

Fodor's Choice

★

☷ **The Central Hotel, Donegal.** With its bright white shutters and boldly red facade, this pretty-as-an-Irish-picture inn sits smack on Donegal's central square, more correctly called the "Diamond." **Pros:** top marks for convenience for exploring the town and its history; friendly and knowledgeable staff. **Cons:** no frills; relentless surge of taxis and motorbikes circling the Diamond. $ *Rooms from: €110* ⊠ *The Diamond* ☎ *74/972–1027* ⊕ *www.centralhoteldonegal.com* ⇆ *112 rooms* ⏍ *Multiple meal plans.*

$$

HOTEL

Fodor's Choice

★

☷ **Harvey's Point Country Hotel.** Set in a remote and breathtaking location in landscaped gardens on the shores of Lough Eske at the foot of the Blue Stack Mountains, Harvey's Point has, since 1989, been a spirit-lifting escape. **Pros:** luxury and style in timeless grandeur; peaceful surroundings; great concierge Brendan Brien. **Cons:** older rooms lack the opulence of new ones; long walk to ATM. $ *Rooms from: €140* ⊠ *6 km (4 miles) northwest of Donegal town, off N15, Lough Eske* ☎ *074/972– 2208* ⊕ *www.harveyspoint.com* ⇆ *64 rooms, 12 suites* ⏍ *Some meals.*

$$$

HOTEL

Fodor's Choice

★

☷ **Solis Lough Eske Castle.** Most guests gasp as they come down the sweeping drive through ancient woodland and arrive at this magnificent Tudor-style baronial castle—complete with Sleeping Beauty tower and crenellations and a suitably regal backdrop of Lough Eske and the Blue Stack Mountains. **Pros:** calming sheltered oasis in stunning location; attentive, slick, and impressive service. **Cons:** queues form at busy breakfast times; limited choice on the dinner menu. $ *Rooms from: €195* ⊠ *3 km (2 miles) north of Donegal town, Lough Eske* ☎ *074/972–5100* ⊕ *www.solishotels.com/lougheske* ⇆ *96 rooms, 16 suites* ⏍ *Some meals.*

NIGHTLIFE

The Abbey Hotel. Visit for music every night in July and August and a disco every Saturday and Sunday night throughout the year. ⊠ *The Diamond* ☎ *074/972–1014* ⊕ *www.abbeyhoteldonegal.com.*

O'Donnell's Bar. On summer weekends, people pack O'Donnell's Bar to hear contemporary music. ⊠ *The Diamond* ☎ *074/972–1049.*

SPORTS AND THE OUTDOORS

BEACHES

Silver Strand Beach. The Silver Strand Beach, or in Irish *An Trá Bhán*, at Gleann Cholm Cille lives up to its name. It's a beautifully enclosed small silvery-white sandy beach, quiet and hidden from view/visitor traffic. Peaceful solitude is the name of the game here but if your hair is standing on your arms it's because you're being watched; there are a few peeping sheep on the surrounding hillsides. ■TIP➡ **When you've had your fill of sand and serenity, explore the ruined promontory fort, Dun Allt, directly above the beach. It was built around 300 BC, and archaeologists believe it was used as a defensive fortification when the community was in danger of attack. Amenities:** small car park (no fee); short walk to nearby shop. **Best for:** paddling; swimming; walking; sunbathing; hiding from the crowds. ⊠ *Gleann Cholm Cille.*

10

GOLF

Donegal Golf Club. Highly rated by both local and visiting golfers, this course, on the shores of Donegal Bay, is approached through a forest. The windswept links are shadowed by the Blue Stack Mountains, with the Atlantic as a dramatic backdrop. The greens are large, but the rough is deep and penal, and there's a constant battle against erosion by the sea. The par-3 5th, fittingly called the "Valley of Tears," begins a run of four of the course's biggest challenges, which could have you discreetly hiding your scorecard by the time you reach the 18th. ⊠ *Murvagh, Laghey* ☎ *074/973–4054* ⊕ *www.donegalgolfclub. ie* ✉ *Mar.–Oct., weekdays €70, weekends €80; Nov.–Feb., weekdays €35, weekends €40* ⚑ *18 holes, 6753 yards, par 73. Practice area, caddy carts, buggies, club rental, catering* ☉ *Visitors: daily.*

SHOPPING

Long the principal marketplace for the region's wool products, Donegal town has several smaller shops with local hand weaving, knits, and crafts.

Donegal Craft Village. Explore this small cluster of workshops where you can buy pottery, handwoven goods, jewelry, and ceramics from young, local craftspeople. You can even watch the items being made Monday to Saturday 9–5:30 and Sunday from noon. The Aroma Café in the Craft Village is a top-class spot for homemade cakes and breads, and also serves dishes with a Mexican twist. ⊠ *N15, 1½ km (1 mile) south of town* ☎ *074/972–3222* ⊕ *www.donegalcraftvillage.com.*

Four Masters Bookshop. For the best selection of local history books on Donegal and Ireland in general, Ordnance Survey maps, and travel guides, as well as CDs, DVDs, and Celtic jewelry, the Four Masters Bookshop is a great place to browse. ⊠ *The Diamond* ☎ *074/972–1526.*

Magee's. The main hand-weaving store in town, Magee's carries renowned private-label tweeds for both men and women (jackets, hats, scarves, suits, and more), as well as pottery, linen, and crystal. ⊠ *The Diamond* ☎ *074/972–2660* ⊕ *www.mageeireland.com.*

EN ROUTE As you travel west on N56, which runs slightly inland from a magnificent shoreline of rocky inlets with great sea views, it's worthwhile to turn off the road from time to time to catch a better view of the coast. About 6 km (4 miles) out of Donegal town, N56 skirts Mountcharles, a bleak hillside village that looks back across the bay.

KILLYBEGS

28 km (17 miles) west of Donegal town.

Trawlers from Spain and France are moored in the harbor at Killybegs, one of Ireland's busiest fishing ports. Though it's one of the most industrialized places along this coast, it's not without some charm thanks to its waterfront location. Killybegs once served as a center for the manufacture of Donegal hand-tufted carpets, examples of which are in the White House and the Vatican.

GETTING HERE AND AROUND

Killybegs is a 45-minute drive west of Donegal town along the N56. It's a busy fishing and tourist port in the summer months but there are plenty of parking spaces at the harbor front or along the side roads off the main street, which is a one-way system. Regular daily bus connections link Killybegs with Donegal town or north to Ardara. Services west to Glencolumbkille along the narrow and twisty R263 are much less frequent.

EXPLORING

Killybegs International Carpet Making and Fishing Centre. High-quality handknotted and hand-tufted carpets are produced at this factory to order: a square foot costs around €186 per sq. foot. Visitors are welcome to commission a piece, but examples of the carpets are not sold off the peg. In the fishing center—refurbished in 2012—interpretative panels take you through a detailed history of the fishing industry in Killybegs; local fishermen (when not hauling in the catch) will show you how to mend nets and recount some fishy tales. For €1 you can play with the Ship Simulator and steer your own boat through the tricky waters of the harbor. ⊠ *Kilcar Rd.* ☎ *074/974–1944* ⊕ *www.visitkillybegs.com* ⊡ *€5* ⊗ *Weekdays 9:30–5:30, weekends 11–4.*

Slieve League Cultural Centre. Stop off at Tí Linn, the Slieve League Cultural Centre, where they serve Italian Illy coffee. Sample their delectable traditional home-baked cakes that include carrot, banana and date, and coconut, as well as the apple sultana pancakes with maple-syrup butter. The tomato, orange, and lentil soup is also a lunchtime winner. At the same time you can stock up on information about the cultural history of the region. Paddy Clarke runs the center and is a rich source of information about the area, especially the archaeological heritage. ⊠ *Cliffs Rd., Teileann, Carrick* ☎ *074/973–9077* ⊕ *www.slieveleaguecliffs.ie* ⊗ *Daily 10:30–5.*

Fodor's Choice ★   **Slieve League Mountains.** The dramatic Slieve League cliffs and mountains have become the starting point for the Irish leg of the International Appalachian Trail, an extension to the original route stretching from Georgia to Maine and then on to Newfoundland. And what more spectacular setting could you have for such a renowned trail linking two pieces of land separated by thousands of kilometers of ocean?

Make no mistake, the landscape hereabouts is awe-inspiring. The narrows and twists of R263 afford terrific views of Donegal Bay before descending into pretty Cill Chartaigh (Kilcar), a traditional center of tweed making. Signposted by its Irish name, the next village, An Charraig (Carrick), clings to the foot of the Slieve League Mountains, whose color-streaked ocean cliffs are, at 2,000 feet, the highest in Ireland. Slieve League (Sliah Liec, or Mountain of the Pillars) is a ragged, razor-back rise bordered by the River Glen. To see the cliffs, follow the little road to the Irish-speaking village of Teileann, 1½ km (1 mile) south from Carrick. Then take the narrow lane (signposted to the Bunglass Cliffs) that climbs steeply to the top of the cliffs. The mountain looks deceptively easy from the back (the inaccessible point borders the Atlantic), but once the fog rolls in, the footing can be perilous. If you

10

want to take in this thrilling perspective—presuming you're hardy and careful—walk along the difficult coastal path from Teilann: not for the dizzily squeamish. The cliffs have been made more accessible by widening the road to the top and enhancing it with parking lots, turnouts, fencing, and an information panel as part of the Donegal Interpretative Project, the first of its kind anywhere in Ireland. A viewing point over the sea cliffs ensures visitors can appreciate one of the finest panoramas in Europe in safety.

If you've a mind for a hike, then follow the Appalachian Trail through County Donegal, head eastwards along the Bluestacks Way, cross the Irish border on to the Ulster Way and end up on the Causeway Coast Way, finishing your trek at Ballycastle in the far north of County Antrim. Now that's a walk that'll require a certain amount of advance training—never mind a little stamina and some planning. And, if you feel like an even grander challenge, then Scotland—just a few miles across the sea—has also signed up for the Trail. ✉ *Teilann.*

WHERE TO EAT AND STAY

$ IRISH **Kitty Kelly's.** If you're driving, one of the best places to stop for seafood on the Wild Atlantic Way is this gloriously restored 200-year-old farmhouse about 10 minutes by car from Killybegs. The lunchtime bistro offers mussels in white wine or Irish lamb stew while the evening dinner menu might include seafood platter or black sole. In the main tourist season, starting at Easter, the bistro is open each night while dinner is served in the upstairs restaurant. Traditional music sessions are held on Monday, Wednesday, and Friday evenings. [$] *Average main: €14* ✉ *Largy* ☎ *074/973–1925* 🌐 *www.kittykellys.com* ⏲ *Closed end of Sept.–Easter.*

$ HOTEL **Tara Hotel.** A sterling reputation for professional and friendly service defines this modern, bright, and airy harborside hotel—an ideal base to explore this alluring corner of south Donegal. **Pros:** attractive guest rooms; leisure club is one of the finest in County Donegal. **Cons:** no pool; noisy when big sporting events bring out supporters. [$] *Rooms from: €110* ✉ *Harbor front* ☎ *074/974–1700* 🌐 *www.tarahotel.ie* *31 rooms* *Multiple meal plans.*

GLEANN CHOLM CILLE (GLENCOLUMBKILLE)

27 km (17 miles) west of Killybegs on R263, 54 km (27 miles) west of Donegal town.

Fodor's Choice ★ "The back of beyond" at the far end of a stretch of barren moorland, the tiny hamlet of Gleann Cholm Cille clings dramatically to the rock-bound harbor of Glen Bay. Known alternatively as Glencolumbkille (pronounced glen-colm-*kill*), it remains the heart of County Donegal's shrinking Gaeltacht region and retains a strong rural Irish flavor, as do its pubs and brightly painted row houses. The name means St. Columba's Glen; the legend goes that St. Columba, the Christian missionary, lived here during the 6th century with a group of followers before many of them moved on to find greater glory by settling Scotland's Isle of Iona. Some 40 prehistoric cairns, scattered around the village, have become connected locally with the St. Columba myths. The village

To make the Slieve League mountains—Ireland's highest—more accessible, a viewing station allows access to one of Europe's grandest sea vistas.

has a website (⊕ *www.gleanncholmcille.ie*) where hopeful overnighters can track down one of the village B&Bs. There are no hotels in town, but walking lodges, friendly inns that cater to hikers, are worth checking out.

Cliffs surrounding Gleann Cholm Cille rise up to more than 700 feet, including Glen Head; many cliffs are studded with ancient hermit cells. Also of note is a squat martello tower, built by the British in 1804 to protect against an anticipated French invasion that never happened. Another good walk is the 8-km (5-mile) trek to Malinbeg, reached by the coast road running past Doon Point. Look for the ruins of no less than five burial cairns, a ring fort, a second martello tower, and one of the best beaches in Ireland, renowned for its calm waters, dramatic scenery, and lovely golden sand.

GETTING HERE AND AROUND

It's a roller-coaster mountain road to Glencolumbkille, and you need your wits about you on the R263 from Killybegs. The journey time is 30 minutes (at a top speed of 65 kph [40 mph]). Once you get to Glencolumbkille, car parking is not a problem. Ardara, to the northeast along the R230, is a 45-minute drive (but it'll take much longer if you stop to drink in the stunning scenery).

The main Donegal town–Dungloe Bus Éireann service does not go to Glencolumbkille, but there is a morning Bus Éireann service (Tuesday, Thursday, and Saturday only) that leaves Donegal town for Glencolumbkille year-round. There is also a Monday–Saturday bus from Glencolumbkille to Donegal town at 7:20 am. From early July to August 22, a Hills of Donegal Bus Éireann scheduled service runs Tuesday–Saturday from Donegal town to top attractions like Glencolumbkille, Teelin Village (for the Slieve League cliffs), and Glenveagh National Park. The standard fee for any location is €20 per day.

ESSENTIALS

Transportation Contacts Stranorlar Bus Station ☎ *074/913–1008.*

EXPLORING

Glencolmcille Folk Village Museum. Walk through the beachfront Folk Village Museum to explore rural life. This *clachan,* or tiny village, comprises eight cottages, all of which are whitewashed, thatch-roofed, and extremely modest in appearance. Three showcase particular years in Irish culture: 1720, 1820, and 1920; pride of place goes to the 1881 schoolhouse and the re-created *shebeen* (pub). Two exhibition houses, a fisherman's cottage and a traditional pub-grocery and shoemaker's shop, opened in 2011, and in 2013 two cottages were rethatched. The complex was built after local priest Father McDyer started a cooperative to help combat rural depopulation. You'll also find an interpretive center, tea shop, and crafts shop selling local handmade products. In summer the museum hosts traditional music evenings. Three small cottages, with bare-earth floors, represent the basic living conditions over three centuries. In 2013 a signposted circular nature and history trail, which closed in the early 1990s, was reopened. It's a tranquil and reflective place that includes a sweat house (early Irish sauna), replica lime kilns, and mass rocks. ⊠ *Near beach* ☎ *074/973–0017* ⊕ *www. glenfolkvillage.com* 💷 *€4.50* 🕓 *Easter–Sept., Mon.–Sat. 10–6, Sun. noon–6.*

House of St. Columba. Atop the cliff rising north of the village, House of St. Columba is a small oratory said to have been used by the saint himself. Inside, stone constructions are thought to have been his bed and chair. Every year on June 9, starting at midnight, local people make a 3-km (2-mile) barefoot procession called An Turas (the journey) around 15 medieval crosses and ancient cairns, collectively called the stations of the cross. ⊠ *Gleann Cholm Cille.*

Oideas Gael: Sport & Culture. If you fancy expanding your mind and horizons, both from a sporting and cultural point of view, then Oideas Gael, based in Gleann Cholm Cille—the Irish-speaking Gaeltacht area of southwest Donegal—has an excellent selection of courses for the culturally curious holidaymaker. Since it was formed in 1984, Oideas Gael has run acclaimed Irish-language classes, as well as programs on hill walking, archaeology, landscape, and the environment. Other activities include painting, traditional music, dance, digital photography, and even tapestry hand weaving—one of Donegal's renowned crafts. The courses, which attract thousands of participants from all over the world, run from April to October. Accommodation is based in self-catering hostels or with local families. For a rundown on the schedule and prices, check the website. ☎ *074/973–0248* ⊕ *www.oideas-gael.com.*

WHERE TO STAY

$
B&B/INN

🖥 **Ionad Siúl Walking Lodge.** Lovely Gleann Cholm Cille has enough charms to entice loads of travelers but, until recently, it was short a few beds for those same travelers. **Pros:** set in spectacular countryside;

To step back in time, just head to Gleann Cholm Cille—if you're lucky you'll catch the locals rethatching their roofs.

friendly service; good value. **Cons:** rooms are basic; local facilities are limited. $ *Rooms from: €50* ✉ *Gleann Cholm Cille* ☎ *074/973–0302* ⊕ *www.ionadsiul.ie* ⇌ *12 rooms* ⦿ *No meals.*

ARD AN RÁTHA (ARDARA)

28 km (17 miles) northeast of Gleann Cholm Cille, 40 km (25 miles) northwest of Donegal town.

At the head of a lovely ocean inlet, the unpretentious, old-fashioned hamlet of Ard an Rátha (Ardara) is built around the L-shaped intersection of its two main streets. (If you come from Glencolumbkille, expect a scenic drive full of hairpin curves and steep hills as you cross over Glengesh Pass.) For centuries, great cloth fairs were held on the first of every month; cottage workers in the surrounding countryside still provide Ard an Rátha (and County Donegal) with high-quality, hand-woven cloths and hand knits. The village was thrust into the spotlight on St. Patrick's Day 2012 when it set a record for the most St. Patricks gathered in one place. A total of 229 such saints turned up with their crosiers, including visiting saint clones from Europe.

GETTING HERE AND AROUND

Three main roads from the north, east, and south converge on Ardara, which really only gets busy in the summer months. There is ample, free, on-street car parking in the town. It's 30 minutes from Killybegs and 75 minutes from Donegal town to the south and east. Letterkenny is a 75-minute drive north along the N56 to Glenties, then switch to the narrower R250.

Donegal Tweed

When it comes to Donegal tweed, weavers—inspired by the soft greens, red rusts, and dove grays of the famed Donegal landscape—have had centuries of experience. In long-gone days, crofters' wives concocted the dyes to give Donegal tweed its distinctive flecks, and their husbands wove the cloth into tweed. Traditional Donegal tweed was a salt-and-pepper mix, but gradually weavers began adding dyes distilled from yellow gorse, purple blackberries, orange lichen, and green moss. Today most tweed comes from factories. However, there are still about 25 local craftsmen working from their cottages. Chic fashion designers such as Armani, Ralph Lauren, and Burberry all use handwoven Donegal tweed—obviously, more fashionable than ever. As with Aran sweaters, Donegal tweed is today regarded as a badge of iconic chic—a 21st-century symbol of Irish folk art.

WHERE TO EAT AND STAY

$$
IRISH
✕ **Nesbitt Arms Hotel.** Offering casual pub grub and more substantial fare, this old-fashioned inn gets understandably busy in summer. Decor harks back to the days when Ard an Rátha was Donegal's foremost weaving and wool center. If you want a quick bite, check out the daily specials in the Weavers Bistro. Upstairs in the dining room, steaks such as Irish rib eye are popular, as is the sirloin steak night each Friday. There's music in the bar every Saturday night. The hotel also rents simple rooms. $ *Average main: €20* ✉ *Main St.* ☎ *074/954–1103* ⊕ *www.nesbittarms.com.*

$
B&B/INN
Fodor's Choice
★
⌂ **Woodhill House.** The cream-color exterior of John Yates's spacious manor house is Victorian, but parts of the interior and the coach house date from the 17th century. **Pros:** quiet location; beautifully maintained house where visitors fall in love with the gardens. **Cons:** some don't like the library-like breakfast-time silences; complaints about poor TV reception. $ *Rooms from: €110* ✉ *Wood Rd.* ☎ *074/954–1112* ⊕ *www. woodhillhouse.com* ⇆ *13 rooms* ⊗ *Closed Christmas wk* ❙○❙ *Breakfast.*

NIGHTLIFE

For a small, old-fashioned village, Ard an Rátha has a surprising number of pubs, many of which have traditional music in the evening.

The Corner Bar. You'll likely find this place packed as it features music almost every night in July and August and on weekends the rest of the year. ✉ *Main St.* ☎ *074/954–1736.*

Nancy's Pub. One of the smallest bars in the Republic, Nancy's makes you wonder if you've wandered into the owner's sitting room, but it occasionally finds space for a folk group. Seafood, in the form of oysters, smoked salmon, prawns, and mussels, dominates the menu served noon to 9. ✉ *Front St.* ☎ *074/954–1187.*

SHOPPING

Many handwoven and locally made knitwear items are on sale in Ard an Rátha. Some stores commission goods directly from knitters, and prices are about as low as anywhere. Handsome, chunky Aran hand-knit sweaters (€80–€130), cardigans (similar prices), and scarves (€25) are all widely available.

Campbells Tweed Shop. Stores such as Campbells are treasure troves of ready-to-wear tweeds—sports jackets can run up to €120. ⊠ *Front St.*

C. Bonner and Son. Factory knitwear from €30 to €120 is for sale here, as well as pottery, tweeds, jewelry, and gifts. There's also a good selection of hand-knit Aran sweaters and cardigans available. ⊠ *Front St.* ☎ *074/954-1302.*

E. Doherty (Ardara) Ltd. This store showcases handwoven tweeds, from scarves for €25 to capes for €195, from Ard an Rátha and other parts of the country. ⊠ *Front St.* ☎ *074/954–1304* ⊕ *www.handwoventweed.ie.*

John Molloy. High-quality handwoven Donegal tweed and hand-knit Aran sweaters are on sale at this factory shop, on the Killybegs Road, on the outskirts of town. After a 10-minute factory tour during which you can watch the handweaving and knitting processes, the Weavers coffee shop is an ideal place for a break. ⊠ *Killybegs Rd.* ☎ *074/954–1133* ⊕ *www.johnmolloy.com.*

NORTHERN DONEGAL

Traveling on northern County Donegal's country roads, you've escaped at last from the world's hurry and hassle. There's almost nothing up here but scenery, and plenty of it: broad, island-studded loughs of deep, dark tranquility; unkempt, windswept, sheep-grazed grasses on mountain slopes; ribbons of luminous greenery following sparkling streams; and the mellow hues of wide boglands, all under shifting and changing cloudscapes. This trip begins in Letterkenny, the largest town in the county (population 6,500), and makes a beeline to the Irish Xanadu of Henry P. McIlhenny's Glenveagh Castle. Just one word of warning—don't be surprised if you find a sheep standing in the middle of a mountain road looking as though you, rather than it, are in the wrong place.

LETTERKENNY

55 km (34 miles) northeast of Ard an Rátha, 51 km (32 miles) northeast of Donegal town, 35 km (21 miles) west of Derry.

Letterkenny, like Donegal to the south, is at the gateway to the far Northwest; you're likely to come through here if you're driving west out of Northern Ireland. Letterkenny's claim to fame has been that it has the longest main street in the whole country but there is more to it than that.

In a tourist board survey in 2013, Letterkenny was nominated as one of the top 10 towns in Ireland for making a difference to tourism and has been striving hard to maintain that goal. The Tourism Town Awards helped build confidence, igniting a fresh enthusiasm and encouraging new businesses. The result is a bustling modest-size Irish town with family-run shops and a good place to get a warm sense of local identity.

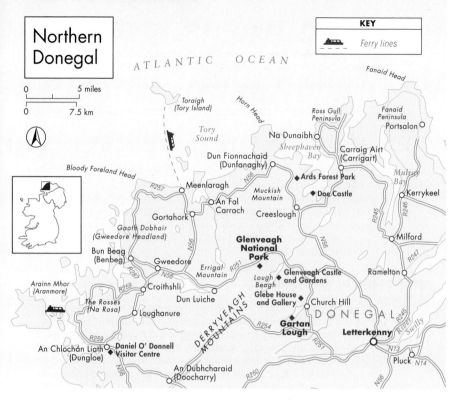

Northern Donegal

KEY
Ferry lines

0 — 5 miles
0 — 7.5 km

ATLANTIC OCEAN

Fanaid Head

Toraigh (Tory Island)
Horn Head
Ross Gull Peninsula
Fanaid Peninsula
Portsalon

Tory Sound
Na Dunaibh
Sheephaven Bay
Carraig Airt (Carrigart)
Mulroy Bay

Bloody Foreland Head
Dun Fionnachaid (Dunfanaghy)
Ards Forest Park
Kerrykeel

Meenlaragh
Muckish Mountain
Doe Castle

An Fal Carrach
Creeslough
Milford

Gortahork
Gaoth Dobhair (Gweedore Headland)
Glenveagh National Park

Bun Beag (Benbeg)
Gweedore
Errigal Mountain
Glenveagh Castle and Gardens
Ramelton

Arainn Mhor (Aranmore)
Croitshli
Lough Beagh

The Rosses (Na Rosa)
Dun Luiche
Glebe House and Gallery
Church Hill
DONEGAL

Loughanure
Gartan Lough
Letterkenny

An Chlochán Liath (Dungloe)
Daniel O' Donnell Visitor Centre
Pluck

An Dubhcharaid (Doocharry)

GETTING HERE AND AROUND

Standing at the intersection of the main roads linking Derry and Donegal town, Letterkenny is at the southern end of Lough Swilly and serves as a handy refueling stop for many drivers. Parking along the main street is free for the first 30 minutes only; use the pay-and-display ticketing system at €1 per hour when your free time is up. There are three main car parks that also have a metered charge but you can park free in the grounds of the cathedral.

Derry is just 30 minutes away along the N13 on a wide fast road, while Donegal is 60 minutes south. The area's major tourist attraction, Glenveagh National Park, is a 30-minute drive northwest along the N56 and then R256.

Bus Éireann runs nine daily services to and from Dublin city center (via Dublin Airport) and Letterkenny with a journey time of four hours. This part of Donegal is served well by independent operators, with many routes connecting with Derry and the Inishowen Peninsula. Most buses leave Derry city's bus station in Foyle Street.

ESSENTIALS

Visitor Information Fáilte Ireland Northwest Tourism Office ⊠ Neil T. Blaney Rd. ☎ 074/912–1160 ⊕ www.discoverireland.ie/northwest.

EXPLORING

An Grianán Theatre. The 380-seater An Grianán Theatre hosts a wide variety of cultural and artistic events. Their program includes drama, comedy, music, and dance while changing exhibitions feature the work of local artists and photographers. The Eatery serves snacks and drinks at lunchtime and before evening shows. ✉ *Port Rd.* ☎ *074/912–0777* 🌐 *www.angrianan.com.*

St. Eunan's Cathedral. With its 212-foot-high spire St. Eunan's Cathedral is the most outstanding building in Letterkenny, dominating the town, especially when illuminated at night. This striking, ornate neo-Gothic Revival structure was finally finished in 1901, and is the only cathedral in the county. Designed by William Hague of Dublin and built of white Donegal sandstone, the exterior of the building is said to be in perfect classical-rule proportion. Inside, the intricate decorative ceilings and ceramic floor mosaics are the work of an Italian artist Signor Amici of Rome. The main and side altars are carved from the finest Italian marble, while the great nave arch depicts in a series of panels in bas-relief the lives of St. Eunan and St. Columba in meticulous detail. ✉ *Convent Rd.* ☎ *074/912–1021.*

FAMILY **Tropical World.** Drama from the world of nature, in the form of an amazing butterfly house, is on display at Alcorn's Tropical World and mini zoo, near Letterkenny. You will also find an eclectic collection of lizards, geckos, bearded, dragons and even slimy snakes—who said St Patrick banished them all from Ireland's fair shores? There's a covered play area for children and a café. ✉ *Loughnagin* ☎ *074/912–1541* 🌐 *www.tropicalworld.town.ie* 🎟 *€7.50* 🕐 *Apr.–Sept. daily, last admission 4:30.*

WHERE TO EAT AND STAY

$ CAFÉ 🍴 **Taste Buds.** Hot steak baguettes are the favored dish at this cozy café, the ideal place for a snack. But you can also choose from club sandwiches, panini, or homemade scones and cakes, all washed down with fine Bewely's coffee or flavored lattes and teas. [$] *Average main: €9* ✉ *95 Lower Main St.* ☎ *074/912–7401* 🕐 *Closed Sun.*

$ B&B/INN 🏨 **Ardeen House.** Overlooking Lough Swilly and the River Lennon and set at the edge of Ramelton, 13 km (8 miles) north of Letterkenny, Ardeen House makes an ideal base for exploring the region, especially Glenveagh National Park. **Pros:** handsome house in a town brimming with the juxtaposition of new and old Ireland; well run with finely appointed rooms. **Cons:** one bathroom is private but not en suite; no bar, but try Conway's thatched pub where you're likely to stumble across a music session. [$] *Rooms from: €80* ✉ *Ramelton* ☎ *074/915–1243* 🌐 *www.ardeenhouse.com* 🛏 *8 rooms, 3 self-catering* 🕐 *Closed Oct.–Mar.* 🍽 *Breakfast.*

$ HOTEL 🏨 **Clanree Hotel.** Formerly a Holiday Inn, this hotel has reinvented itself with flair, and the spacious entrance hall strikes the right welcoming note. **Pros:** fully equipped health and fitness center; friendly and helpful staff. **Cons:** room service lackadaisical; be prepared to queue for the breakfast buffet. [$] *Rooms from: €60* ✉ *Derry Rd.* ☎ *074/912–4369* 🌐 *www.clanreehotel.com* 🛏 *120 rooms* 🍽 *Multiple meal plans.*

GARTAN LOUGH

21 km (13 miles) northwest of Letterkenny on R251.

Gartan Lough and the surrounding mountainous country are astonishingly beautiful. St. Columba was supposedly born here in AD 521, and the legendary event is marked by a huge cross at the beginning of a footpath into Glenveagh National Park. (Close to Church Hill village, Gartan Lough is technically within the national park and is administered partly by the park authorities.)

EXPLORING

Glebe House and Gallery. On the northwest shore of Gartan Lough just off R251 is Glebe House and Gallery, a sweetly elegant redbrick Regency manor with 25 acres of gardens. For 30 years, Glebe House was the home of the distinguished landscape and portrait artist Derek Hill, who furnished the house in a mix of styles with art from around the world; in 1981 he gave the house and its contents, including his outstanding art collection, to the nation. Highlights include paintings by Renoir and Bonnard, lithographs by Kokoschka, ceramics and etchings by Picasso, and the paintings *Whippet Racing* and *The Ferry, Early Morning* by Jack B. Yeats, as well as Donegal folk art produced by the Toraigh islanders. The decoration and furnishings of the house, including original William Morris wallpaper, are also worth a look. ✉ *Church Hill* ☎ *074/913–7071* ⊕ *www.dun-na-ngall.com/glebe* 🖼 *€3* ☉ *Easter, June, Sept., and Oct., Sat.–Thurs. 11–6:30; July and Aug., daily 11–6:30.*

GLENVEAGH NATIONAL PARK

21 km (13 miles) northwest of Letterkenny.

GETTING HERE AND AROUND

Glenveagh National Park is 30 minutes northwest of Letterkenny along the N56 through Kilmacrenan and then left on to the R255, a road that leads on to Gweedore on the west Donegal coastline. There is a free car park at the visitor center.

EXPLORING

Fodor'sChoice **Glenveagh National Park.** Bordered by the Derryveagh Mountains (Derryveagh means "forest of oak and birch"), Glenveagh National Park encompasses 24,000 acres of wilderness—mountain, moorland, lakes, and woods—that has been called the largest and most dramatic tract in the wildest part of Donegal. Within its borders, a thick carpet of russet-color heath and dense woodland rolls down the Derryveagh slopes into the broad open valley of the River Veagh (or Owenbeagh), which opens out into Glenveagh's spine: long and narrow, dark and clear Lough Beagh.

The lands of Glenveagh (pronounced glen-*vay*) have long been recognized as a remote and beautiful region. Between 1857 and 1859, John George Adair, a ruthless gentleman farmer, assembled the estate that now makes up the park. In 1861 he evicted the estate's hundreds of poor tenants without compensation and destroyed their cottages. Nine years later Adair began to build **Glenveagh Castle** on the eastern shore

Oh Danny Boy: Donegal's Singing Son

"Daniel O'Donnell is to Donegal what Tourism Ireland is to the whole country," or so says the local paper, the *Donegal Democrat.* He has appeared 18 times in the U.S. Billboard World Album Charts and in a career spanning more than three decades, sold 10 million albums. Now Donegal's famed singing star, and poster boy for an Ireland long gone, has become a popular tourist attraction: the eponymous Daniel O'Donnell Visitor Centre in Dungloe (An Clochán Liath) welcomes thousands of fans eager to celebrate his life story and glittering musical career. A 12-minute video explains Daniel's humble beginnings and rise to international stardom; memorabilia includes gold discs, videos, stage outfits, his wedding suit and his wife's wedding dress, and even his first schoolbag. Originally from Kincasslagh in west Donegal, O'Donnell is as big a hit with North American audiences as he is in Ireland—although his clean-cut image has also won him his share of homegrown detractors. Each winter, O'Donnell is the star attraction in the showbiz town of Branson, Missouri, where he appears in the Moon River Theater set up by Andy Williams. The Daniel O'Donnell Visitor Centre is at Main Street, Dungloe, and is open April to September, Monday–Saturday 10–6, Sunday 11–6. 🖂 €5 ☎ *074/952-2334* ⊕ *www.daniel odonnellvisitorcentre.com.*

of Lough Veagh, but he soon departed for Texas. He died in 1885 without returning to Ireland, but his widow, Cornelia, moved back to make Glenveagh her home. She created four gardens, covering 27 acres; planted luxuriant rhododendrons; and began the job of making this turret-and-battlement-laden 19th-century folly livable. At the end of a dramatic 3-km-long (2-mile-long) entryway, perched over the lake waters, this is a true fairy-tale castle. Like a dollhouse Balmoral, its castellated, rectangular keep, battlemented ramparts, and a Round Tower enchantingly conjure up all the Victorian fantasies of a medieval redoubt.

The gardens and castle as they appear today are almost entirely an American invention, the product of the loving attentions of Glenveagh's last owners, including Kingsley Porter, a venerated professor of medieval art history at Harvard. He then passed the property over to U.S. millionaire Henry P. McIlhenny, who bought the estate in 1937 and, beginning in 1947, lived here for part of every year for almost 40 years. An avid art collector and philanthropist (his collection of Degas, Toulouse-Lautrec, and Ingres masterworks now resides at the Philadelphia Museum of Art), McIlhenny decorated every inch of the house himself in faux-baronial fashion and entertained lavishly.

Beyond the castle, footpaths lead into more remote sections of the park, including the **Derrylahan Nature Trail,** a 1½-km (1-mile) signposted trail where you may suddenly catch sight of a soaring golden eagle or chance upon a shy red deer. You may also hear the story of Black Francie, a legendary highwayman who made the place his home. A newly designed 4-km (2½-mile) gravel path, leading from the visitor center to

10

the castle and gardens, is ideal for bikes and prams. ■TIP→ Take time to visit the 2½-acre Pleasure Grounds, a sunken garden at the heart of the estate with a sinuous lawn and Japanese maples.

The visitor center has a permanent exhibition on the local way of life and on the influence of climate on the park's flora and fauna. Have a bite to eat in the castle tearooms, or enjoy your own picnic on the extensive estate grounds, which are free for walkers. A shuttle bus runs from the visitor center to the castle, and on weekends a bus service drops you off at the start of the 90-minute Bridal Path—a walking route so-named because local men used to look for brides on it. ⊠ *R251, Church Hill* ☎ *076/100–2551* ⊕ *www.glenveaghnationalpark.ie* ⊠ *Castle tour €5, shuttle bus €3, weekend bus €2* ☉ *Mar.–Oct., daily 9–6; Nov.–Feb., daily 9–5.*

NORTHERN IRELAND

Including Counties Antrim, Armagh,
Derry, Down, Fermanagh, and Tyrone

WELCOME TO NORTHERN IRELAND

TOP REASONS TO GO

★ **Belfast, Gateway City:** As the locals put it, "Despite what you've probably heard, Belfast is not what you expect"—so get ready to love this bustling city that bristles with Victorian shop fronts, hip restaurants, and the Titanic Belfast Visitor Centre.

★ **The Giant's Causeway:** This spectacular remnant of Ireland's volcanic period will steal you away from your 21st-century existence and transport you to a time when the giant Finn McCool roamed the land.

★ **Nine Glens of Antrim:** Fabled haunt of "the wee folk," the glacier-carved valleys have a beauty that has become synonymous with Irishness. Don't miss Glenariff, dubbed "Little Switzerland" by Thackeray.

★ **Ulster-American Folk Park:** A tale of two countries joined by a common people is told at this impressive open-air museum, which re-creates a 19th-century Tyrone village and boasts the Mellon Centre for Migration Studies.

1 Belfast. Belfast's location is striking, nestled on the coast, buffered by green water on one side and by heath-covered hills on the other. Once you tour the Victorian city, head to its outskirts to visit three marvels: Belfast Castle, the Mount Stewart estate, and the Ulster Folk and Transport Museum.

2 The Giant's Causeway Coast. North of the famously beautiful Glens of Antrim—still considered "gentle" (supernatural) in spirit—the coast continues up to Northern Ireland's premier attraction, the Giant's Causeway. Farther along the North Antrim coast are Bushmills, the oldest distillery in the world; Dunluce Castle, spectacularly perched over its "Mermaid's Cave"; and the heart-stopping Carrick-a-Rede rope bridge.

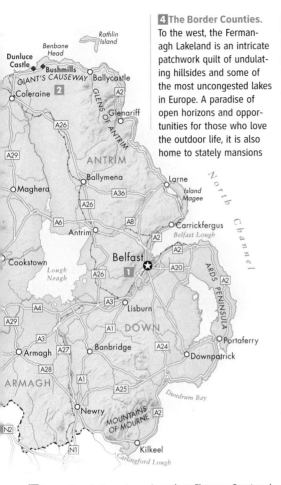

Rathlin Island

Benbane Head

Dunluce Castle

Bushmills

GIANT'S CAUSEWAY Ballycastle

Coleraine **2**

Glenariff

GLENS OF ANTRIM

A2

A26

A29

ANTRIM

Ballymena

Maghera

A36

A26

A6

A8

Antrim

Cookstown

Lough Neagh

Belfast **1**

A26

A3

A20

A4

Lisburn

A29

A3

A1

DOWN

Banbridge

Armagh A27

A24

Portaferry

A28

Downpatrick

ARMAGH

A1

A25

Dundrum Bay

Newry

MOUNTAINS OF MOURNE

A2

N2

N1

Kilkeel

Carlingford Lough

Larne

Island Magee

North Channel

Carrickfergus

Belfast Lough

A2

A2

ARDS PENINSULA

4 The Border Counties.
To the west, the Fermanagh Lakeland is an intricate patchwork quilt of undulating hillsides and some of the most uncongested lakes in Europe. A paradise of open horizons and opportunities for those who love the outdoor life, it is also home to stately mansions

GETTING ORIENTED

With peace—precious peace—nearly always now abiding, Northern Ireland has been going about the business of charming visitors full-time. North of the vibrant Victorian city of Belfast, you'll find the ageless wonders of the Causeway Coast while south of the inspiring skyline of Derry lie the border counties, where tiny "Ulster" towns dot the scenic landscapes around the Lakes of Fermanagh and Mountains of Mourne. Occasional outbreaks of violence and protest do erupt still in Northern Ireland, so it's best not to stray into trouble areas featured on the news; if in doubt ask at the tourist offices for guidance.

3 Derry. A walk through Ireland's only walled city provides a unique way to view the layout of the 17th-century inner town, particularly noticeable in the streets and alleys that fan outward from the Diamond, where fine examples of Georgian and Victorian architecture rub shoulders with old-style pubs and museums.

such as Florence Court and Castle Coole, the Ulster-American Folk Park in next-door County Tyrone, and Belleek, a town famous for its porcelain. South of Belfast past the Ards Peninsula is St. Patrick Country: Downpatrick, reputed to be the burial place of the saint; Armagh's two St. Patrick cathedrals; and the seaside Mountains of Mourne.

ALL ABOUT IRISH WHISKEYS

Located on the Antrim coast, the small town of Bushmills lays claim to the world's oldest distillery. Today, its name is synonymous with the best in whiskey. Taste one drop and you may never drink Jim Beam or Jack Daniels again.

(above) Liquid history on view at Bushmills Distillery; *(right, top)* Learn how malted barley and yeasts are alchemized into whiskey; *(right, bottom)* Drink Bushmills neat.

Some 125 years ago, Ireland had 28 whiskey distilleries in what was a great industry. Today, only four working ones remain: Bushmills in Antrim, Midleton in Cork, Kilbeggan in Westmeath, and Cooley in Louth. For some, Bushmills is the best, literally: at the 2009 San Francisco Wine and Spirit Awards, it won the Best Irish Whiskey title. And to celebrate its 400th anniversary in 2008, it was selected as the icon of Northern Ireland, and was featured on Bank of Ireland notes. Where does the whiskey drinker start? Some prefer the classic melt-in-the-mouth Black Bush (drunk neat) to the more expensive malt. Other delights include the limited-edition 1608, the Original, and four single malts: aged 10 years, 12 years, 16 years, and 21 years.

OLD BUSHMILLS

✉ *2 Distillery Rd., Bushmills, Co. Antrim*
☎ *028/2073-3218*
⊕ *www.bushmills.com*
💷 *£7.50* ☯ *Tours Apr.–Oct., Mon.–Sat. 9:15–5, Sun. noon–5; Nov.–Mar., weekdays 9:30–3:30, weekends 12:30–3:30. For more information on the Distillery tours, see our listing for Bushmills, under the Giant's Causeway Coast.*

THE "WATER OF LIFE"

Whiskey is a word that comes from the Irish *uisce beatha,* meaning "water of life." Water is a major factor influencing the flavor of any whiskey. For Bushmills, it flows from the crystal-clear St. Columb's Rill, taking its character from the basalt and turf bed of the River Bush. Another key ingredient is malted barley, which is here ground into grist in the mash house and added to boiling water in vats to become wort. Yeast is then added to the mix, and the fermentation turns the sugars to alcohol. The wash goes into a copper pot and is distilled three times, each distillation making the alcohol purer. By comparison, American whiskey is distilled only once. The spirit is diluted, then matured in oak casks, and seasoned by sherry, bourbon, or port. A small portion, about 2% of the distillate, evaporates and is affectionately known as the Angels' Share. Remember to first try Bushmills neat and then add water in teaspoonful increments, as a soupçon of water unlocks the flavor while knocking a little fire out of the whiskey—there's a crucial tipping point so don't dilute too much!

WHAT'S IRISH ABOUT WHISKEY?

First off, it is spelled with an "e," to distinguish it from Scotch whisky. "Irish" has a characteristic flavor that distinguishes it from Scotch, bourbon, or rye; try it straight or with water, as it is best without a mixer. And don't

go chasing after *poitín* (pronounced "potcheen"), the famed Irish moonshine. Any attempts by a "stranger" to procure it will result either in meeting a brick wall or a wild goose chase. Just as well: it produces one of the worst hangovers known to man or woman.

TOURING THE DISTILLERY

Set in an area of natural beauty a short distance from the Giant's Causeway, Bushmills was granted its first license in 1608, although records refer as far back as 1276. Visitors to the distillery are shown around a higgledy-piggledy collection of redbrick and whitewashed buildings that include 11 warehouses brimming with 187,000 barrels of whiskey. Look out for the long rows of Oloroso sherry casks, where the drink is aged in some instances for more than 25 years (they favor a generous gestation here). Tours run every half hour and cost £7.50. If you're in the mood to splurge, take the two-hour deluxe Bush Experience tour, which offers eight varieties of whiskey and costs £70 (reservations required, with a minimum of six). Tasting sessions all take place in the 1608 pub where American troops were once billeted during World War II.

Updated by
Paul Clements

Never in its history has Northern Ireland enjoyed such peace, stability, and investment, all of which is making it the envy of Europe. Once a region torn apart by civil strife and sectarian violence, today it has changed beyond recognition. A dizzying rate of regeneration has led to the glossy rebirth of its two major cities, Belfast and Derry, bursting with confidence and contemporary cool. A creative and cultural renaissance has brought an astonishing surge of interest from many parts of the world, and new super-luxury hotels, trendy bars, and chic restaurants have created a huge number of opportunities for holidaymakers.

The Six Counties that make up Northern Ireland cover less than 14,245 square km (5,500 square miles)—the country is about half the size of Delaware and less than one-fifth the size of the Republic of Ireland, its neighbor to the south. But within Northern Ireland's boundaries are some of the most unspoiled scenery you could ever hope to find on this earth: the granite Mountains of Mourne; the Giant's Causeway, made of extraordinary volcanic rock; more than 320 km (200 miles) of coastline beaches and hidden coves; and rivers and leaf-sheltered lakes, including Europe's largest freshwater lake, Lough Neagh, that provide fabled fishing grounds. Ancient castles and Palladian-perfect 18th-century houses are as numerous here as almost anywhere else in Europe, and each has its own tale of heroic feats, dastardly deeds, and lovelorn ghosts.

Northern Ireland not only houses this heritage within its native stone, but has also given the world perhaps an even greater legacy: its roster of celebrated descendants. Nearly one in six of the millions of Irish who journeyed across the Atlantic in search of fortune in the New World came from Ulster (the historic name for this part of Ireland that geographically—although not politically—includes Donegal, Cavan and Monaghan which are part of the Republic) and of this group (and from their family stock), more than a few left their mark in America: Davy Crockett, President Andrew Jackson, General Ulysses S. Grant, President Woodrow Wilson, General Stonewall Jackson, financier Thomas Mellon, merchant J. Paul Getty, writers Edgar Allan Poe and Mark Twain, and astronaut Neil Armstrong.

In the 1970s, '80s, and early '90s, Northern Ireland was synonymous with conflict; sectarian killings and car bomb explosions were an almost daily occurrence from 1969 to 1994, amounting to the deaths of more than 3,500 people. The "peace process," begun with the help of President Clinton, has been a long journey but the two communities now live in relative harmony as a younger generation embraces life without violence.

Present-day Northern Ireland, a province of just 1.8 million people that along with Great Britain comprises the political entity of the United Kingdom, retains its sense of separation, both in the vernacular of the landscape and, some would say, in the character of the people. The hardheaded and industrious Scots-Presbyterians, imported to make Ulster a bulwark against Ireland's Catholicism, have had a profound and ineradicable effect on the place. For all that, the border between north and south is of little consequence if you're just here to see the country, and though political divisions still exist, peace reigns in Northern Ireland today. There are no border road checkpoints, no one is stopped or questioned, no passports are checked, and there isn't even a sign announcing you are passing from the north into the south. Visitors—even ones with English accents—are not hassled in any way, and Americans are more than warmly welcomed. The "peace dividend" has led to massive investment and revitalization in many towns and cities; on the whole, Northern Ireland now approximates a land flowing with milk and honey.

It's a golfing powerhouse, with courses (and golfers) that are some of the world's best; its young bands are renowned; its writers and poets, such as Seamus Heaney who died in 2013, have been internationally acclaimed; and Belfast is home to the Titanic Belfast Centre, one of Europe's leading visitor attractions which has brought in tens of thousands of tourists since the 100th anniversary commemorations in 2012. In 2013 County Fermanagh hosted the G8 summit of world leaders— something that would have been unthinkable 20 years ago. A measure of the newfound confidence and self-belief can be gauged from the opening in 2014 of a dazzling new £1.8-million Belfast Welcome Centre. The North is truly open for business and on the travel map as never before.

NORTHERN IRELAND PLANNER

WHEN TO GO

If the weather is good—and most of the year it isn't—touring Northern Ireland can be a real pleasure. But the place is so green for a reason: lots of rain, which means you should certainly pack your Burberry. Because you're on the coast, even on bright summer days you can feel the chill from the sea, so it's best to wear layers. Needless to say, the weather from May to September is a little friendlier to tourists.

When planning your visit, remember that Northern Ireland is a great place for festivals: almost every town has its own theme festival of some sort. The **Belfast Festival** (⊕ *www.belfastfestival.com*), held in October at Queen's University, is one of the biggest, with a packed program of arts, music, and literature. Belfast's **Cathedral Arts Quarter Festival** (⊕ *www.cqaf.com*), held late April–early May, uses established, new, and unusual venues throughout the oldest part of the city center for two weeks of music, theater, and visual arts. In early April the Titanic Festival commemorates the anniversary of the sinking in 1912 of RMS *Titanic,* built in Belfast and the focus of renewed interest following the opening of the new Belfast Titanic Visitor Centre in 2012. **Féile an Phobail,** the West Belfast Festival (⊕ *www.feilebelfast.com*), held in early August, is a 10-day schedule of events with a political and international theme. **Hillsborough International Oyster Festival** (⊕ *www. hillsboroughoysterfestival.com*), held in September, is three days of good food and entertainment. For a rundown on many other festivals, contact the Northern Ireland Tourist Board.

PLANNING YOUR TIME

Though Northern Ireland may not look that big on paper, tackling a fair share of its many attractions in less than a week isn't possible without exhausting yourself in the process. If your time is limited, choose the eastern half (Belfast, the Antrim Coast, and the Mountains of Mourne) or the western half (Derry and the border counties). The cities are small enough to tour in a day or two. But remember that the rural wonders—the Antrim Coast, the Fermanagh lakes, the Mountains of Mourne—cast their spell easily. You may head out to enjoy them for a day trip and find yourself wishing that you'd factored in more time to explore the endless string of postcard-worthy villages, misty glens, and rugged mountains. And although distances are not great, neither are the roads—you'll spend most of your time traveling smaller roads, not major express highways. If you have three days, then spend an extra night and day in Derry. The city has many shiny new attractions such as Ebrington Square, the refurbished Guildhall and the Peace Bridge, and its old shirt factories and warehouses have been sandblasted and reinvented as bistros, wine bars, and arts centers. A half-day side trip should also be made to the top-class Ulster-American Folk Park at Omagh, where the contribution of Northern Irish people to American history is traced.

GETTING HERE AND AROUND

Because Northern Ireland is so small, one option is to simply base yourself in the two main cities, Belfast and Derry, and make day trips out. However, one of the real glories is the endless supply of spectacular rural scenery. The good news is that bus travel is both quick and fairly priced, with express buses operating on all the high-traffic routes. The bad news is that rail options are somewhat limited: there are just three main routes out of Belfast. That said, you can easily access much of the country by bus or train, though in some areas, including the wildly popular Causeway Coast, you'll may end up on smaller bus routes such as the Causeway Coast Express if you don't drive a car.

AIR TRAVEL

Scheduled services from the United States and Canada are mostly routed through Dublin, Glasgow, London, or Manchester. Frequent services to Belfast's two airports are scheduled throughout the day from London Heathrow, London Gatwick, and Luton (all of which have fast coordinated subway or rail connections to central London) and from 17 other U.K. airports.

AIRPORTS Belfast International Airport at Aldergove is the North's principal airport, 30½ km (19 miles) north of town. George Best Belfast City Airport is the secondary airport, 6½ km (4 miles) east of the city. It receives flights from U.K. provincial airports, from London's Gatwick and Heathrow, and from Stansted and Luton (both near London). City of Derry Airport is 8 km (5 miles) from Derry and receives flights from Dublin, Glasgow, London, and Manchester. United Airlines and several Europe-based airlines are the major carriers serving Northern Ireland's airports.

Airport Information Belfast International Airport at Aldergove ⊠ *Ireland* ☎ *028/9448–4848* ⊕ *www.belfastairport.com.* **City of Derry Airport** ⊠ *Ireland* ☎ *028/7181–0784* ⊕ *www.cityofderryairport.com.* **George Best Belfast City Airport** ⊠ *Ireland* ☎ *028/9093–9093* ⊕ *www.belfastcityairport.com.*

Airline Information Aer Arann ⊠ *Ireland* ☎ *018/447–700* ⊕ *www.aerlingus. com.* **Aer Lingus** ⊠ *Ireland* ☎ *0871/718–5000* ⊕ *www.aerlingus.com.* **British Airways** ⊠ *Ireland* ☎ *0844/493–0787* ⊕ *www.britishairways.com.* **EasyJet** ⊠ *Ireland* ☎ *084/3104–5000* ⊕ *www.easyjet.com.* **Flybe** ⊠ *Ireland* ☎ *0871/700–2000* ⊕ *www.flybe.com.* **Jet2** ⊠ *Ireland* ☎ *0871/226–1737* ⊕ *www.jet2.com.* **Ryanair** ⊠ *Ireland* ☎ *0871/246–0000* ⊕ *www.ryanair.com.* **United** ⊠ *Ireland* ☎ *0845/607–6760* ⊕ *www.united.com.*

AIRPORT TRANSFERS Ulsterbus, a branch of Translink, operates Airport Express 300 buses (one way £7, round-trip £10) several times an hour between Belfast International Airport and Belfast city center (6:50 am–6:15 pm), and Airport Express 600 buses between George Best Belfast City Airport and the city center (one-way £2.20, round-trip £3.30; weekdays every 20 minutes, 6 am–10:05 pm). From the City Airport, you can also travel into Belfast by train from Sydenham Halt to Central Station or catch a taxi from the airport to your hotel. Value Cabs serves both Belfast airports. The fare from Belfast International to Belfast city center is around £25; from Belfast City Airport to the city center is around £6.

If you arrive at the City of Derry Airport, you may need to call a taxi to get to your destination. The fare for Foyle cabs is about £12 to the city center. A direct bus service, the Airporter, links Derry with both Belfast International and George Best Belfast City airports (one-way £17.50, round-trip £27.50).

Airport Transfer Contacts Airporter ⊠ *Ireland* ☎ *028/7126–9996* ⊕ *www. airporter.co.uk.* **City Cabs** ⊠ *Derry* ☎ *028/7126–4466* ⊕ *www.citycabsderry. com.* **Foyle Taxis** ⊠ *Newmarket St., Derry* ☎ *028/7127–9999* ⊕ *www.foyletaxis. com.* **Eglinton Taxis** ☎ *028/7181–1231.* **Translink Airport Services** ⊠ *Belfast*

☎ *028/9066–6630* ⊕ *www.translink.co.uk/services/other-translink-services.*
Value Cabs ✉ *Belfast, Co. Antrim* ☎ *028/9080–9080* ⊕ *www.valuecabs.co.uk.*

BOAT AND FERRY TRAVEL

P&O Ferries has a one-hour sailing from Cairnryan, Scotland, to Larne, and a two-hour ferry, both with train (more convenient) or bus connections to Belfast, 35½ km (22 miles) to the south. Stena Line has eight-hour daytime or overnight car ferries that connect Belfast with the English west-coast port of Liverpool every day. Stena Line also operates a fast catamaran (1½ hours) between Belfast and Stranraer, Scotland.

Boat and Ferry Information P&O Ferries ✉ *Ireland* ☎ *0871/664–4777* ⊕ *www.poferries.com.* **Stena Line** ✉ *Victoria Terminal 2, W. Bank Rd., Belfast* ☎ *028/9077–9090* ⊕ *www.stenaline.co.uk.*

BUS TRAVEL

Northern Ireland's main bus company, Ulsterbus, operates direct Goldline service—superior express buses with modern, comfortable seats—between Dublin and Belfast. Bus Éireann runs direct service to Belfast from Dublin, calling at Dublin Airport. The ride takes three hours; both company's buses arrive at Belfast's Europa Buscentre, just behind the Europa Hotel.

You can take advantage of frequent and inexpensive Ulsterbus links between all Northern Ireland towns. If you want to tour the North by bus and train, contact Translink: an iLink ticket allows unlimited travel on bus or train (£15.50 per day, or £57 per week; it costs £1 to buy the card). Best buy: the Sunday Rambler Ticket, from 9:15 am for £9 for unlimited travel on all scheduled Ulsterbus services.

Bus Depot Europa Buscentre ✉ *Great Victoria St., Golden Mile, Belfast* ☎ *028/9066–6630.*

Bus Lines Bus Éireann ✉ *Dublin* ☎ *01/836–6111 in Dublin* ⊕ *www.buseireann. ie.***Translink Ulsterbus** ✉ *Glengall St.* ☎ *028/9066–6630* ⊕ *www.translink. co.uk/ulsterbus.*

CAR TRAVEL

The fast N1/A1 road connects Belfast to Dublin in 160 km (100 miles) with an average driving time of two hours. When in Belfast, it's best to avail yourself of the many parking garages. If you opt for street meter-ticket parking, check the posted regulations because many spots become no-parking during rush hours. Throughout Northern Ireland, there are plenty of parking lots in the towns, and you should use them.

TAXI TRAVEL

Most taxis operate on the meter; ask for a price for longer journeys. You can order in advance. The minimum fare is usually £2.40 and £1.15 per mile thereafter.

Taxi Companies FonACAB ✉ *Belfast* ☎ *028/9033–3333* ⊕ *www.fonacab.com.* **Foyle Taxis** ✉ *10a Market St., Derry* ☎ *028/7126–3905* ⊕ *www.foyletaxis.com.* **Value Cabs** ✉ *Belfast* ☎ *028/9080–9080* ⊕ *www.valuecabs.co.uk.*

TRAIN TRAVEL

The Dublin to Belfast Enterprise Service, run jointly by Northern Ireland Railways (a company operated by Translink) and Irish Rail—Iarnród Éireann (which only services the Republic of Ireland), operates trains, the fastest of which take about two hours, between Dublin and Belfast's Central Station. A single journey costs £30; a same-day return is £32. You can change trains at Central Station—which, in fact, is not that central—for the city-center Great Victoria Street Station, which is adjacent to the Europa Buscentre.

Northern Ireland Railways (NIR) runs four rail routes from Belfast's Central Station: northwest to Derry via Coleraine; east to Bangor along the shore of Belfast Lough; northeast to Larne (for the P&O European ferry to Scotland); and south to Dublin. Nine daily weekday trains operate between Belfast and Derry, with seven trains on Saturday and five on Sunday. The journey time is about two hours, and a round-trip ticket costs £17.50. If you travel after 9:30 am, you'll get a third off the standard fare. Best buy: the £7 Sunday Day Tracker gives you unlimited travel on all scheduled train services within Northern Ireland.

There are frequent connections to Central Station from the city-center Great Victoria Street Station and from Botanic Station in the university area. If you want to tour the North by train, contact Translink: an iLink ticket allows unlimited travel on bus or train (£15.50 per day, or £57 per week; it costs £1 to buy the card).

Train Info Enterprise Service ⊠ *Central Station, E. Bridge St., Belfast* ☎ *028/9066–6630* ⊕ *www.translink.co.uk/Enterprise.* **Iarnród Éireann** ⊠ *Dublin, Co. Dublin, Ireland* ☎ *1850/366–222 timetables* ⊕ *www.irishrail.ie.* **Northern Ireland Railways** ⊠ *Central Station, E. Bridge St., Belfast* ☎ *028/9066–6630* ⊕ *www.translink.co.uk/ni-railways.*

Train Stations Botanic Station ⊠ *Botanic Ave., Belfast* ☎ *028/9089–9400.* **Central Station** ⊠ *E. Bridge St., Belfast* ☎ *028/9089–9400* ⊕ *www.translink.co.uk.*

RESTAURANTS

Belfast has experienced an influx of au courant and internationally influenced restaurants, bistros, wine bars, and—as in Dublin—European-style café-bars where you can get good food most of the day and linger over a drink. Local produce and seasonal creativity are the order of the day with top-quality fresh local meat and experimental chefs constantly trying out new ideas. Traditional dishes, of course, still dominate some menus and include Guinness-and-beef pie; steak, chicken and pork; champ (creamy, buttery mashed potatoes with scallions); oysters from Strangford Lough; Ardglass herring; mussels from Dundrum; and smoked salmon from Glenarm. A widespread favorite is the Ulster fry, an inexpensive pub plate of bacon, black pudding, mushrooms, sausages, tomatoes, and eggs, served with potato or soda bread—one of the reasons Northern Ireland has a high rate of heart disease. The delights of ethnic restaurants, including Chinese, Japanese, Indian, Persian, and Thai, are available in Belfast, Derry, and in some smaller cities and towns. By the standards of the Republic or the United States, or even the rest of the United Kingdom, restaurant prices can be surprisingly moderate. A service charge of 10% may be indicated on the bill; it's customary to pay this, unless the service was bad.

HOTELS

Major hotel chains based in both the Republic and abroad have invested in Northern Ireland's cities. In Belfast's surrounding area, you can also choose from the humblest terraced town houses or farm cottages to the grandest country houses. Dining rooms of country-house lodgings frequently match the standard of top-quality restaurants. All accommodations in the province are inspected and categorized by the Northern Ireland Tourist Board Information Centre, which publishes hostelry names, addresses, and ratings in the free guidebooks *Hotel and Guest House Guide* and *Bed & Breakfast Guide*, also available online. Hundreds of excellent-value specials—single nights to weekend deals, the most intimate bed-and-breakfasts to Belfast's finest hotels—become available in the low season, from October to March. Assume that all hotel rooms reviewed have in-room phones and TVs, along with private bathrooms, unless otherwise indicated. *Hotel reviews have been shortened. For full information, visit Fodors.com.*

WHAT IT COSTS IN POUNDS STERLING				
	$	**$$**	**$$$**	**$$$$**
Restaurants	under £15	£15–£18	£19–£22	over £22
Hotels	under £82	£82–£115	£116–£160	over £160

Restaurant prices are the average cost of a main course at dinner or, if dinner is not served, at lunch. Hotel prices are the lowest cost of a standard double room in high season.

MONEY

Northern Ireland uses British currency. Euros are accepted in some shops along the border areas and in some shopping centers in Belfast. You may sometimes be given bank notes, drawn on Ulster banks. Be sure not to get stuck with a lot of these when you leave, because they're accepted with reluctance, if at all, in the rest of the United Kingdom and will be difficult to change at banks back home.

TOURS

BUS TOURS   **Allens Tours.** Allen's Tours (from £15) and McComb's/MiniCoach operate day tours of Belfast (£8–£16) and to the Giant's Causeway, Bushmills Distillery, and Carrickfergus (£17.50). ☎ 028/9091–5613 ⊕ *www.allensbelfastbustours.com.*

Ulsterbus Tours. Half- or full-day trips (prices vary) are on offer during the summer from Belfast to the Glens of Antrim, the Giant's Causeway, the Fermanagh lakes, Lough Neagh, the Mountains of Mourne, and the Ards Peninsula. Ulsterbus has also teamed up with the Old Bushmills Distillery on an open-top tour bus running in summer from Coleraine (via Bushmills to observe whiskey making) to the Giant's Causeway and the coastal resorts. ☎ 028/9066–6630 ⊕ *www.ulsterbustours.com.*

CYCLE TOURS   **Belfast City Bike Tours.** Guided bike rides of many areas are offered by Belfast City Bike Tours. Cycle lanes are provided on most main roads and excellent paths link up all sections of the towpath and riverbank with signposted trails. ☎ *078/5033–7366* ⊕ *www.belfastcitybiketours.com.*

Iron Donkey Bicycle Touring. Some of the most scenic parts of Northern Ireland are opened up by Iron Donkey Bicycle Touring which organizes multiday tours. Their itinerary includes the Mourne Mountains, Glens of Antrim, Causeway Coast, the Sperrin Mountains, and other destinations. ☎ *028/9081–3200* ⊕ *www.irondonkey.com.*

Mourne Cycle Tours. This company runs bike tours complete with hotel accommodations (bikes are delivered to the hotel). Their routes, through spectacular countryside, cover a network of mountain and woodland trails as well as quiet country roads. ☎ *028/4372–4348.*

VISITOR INFORMATION

The Northern Ireland Tourist Board provides information about attractions, accommodations, and activities online and at its central and regional tourist information offices (TIOs). The offices in Belfast and Derry are open year-round; other useful TIOs are in Enniskillen, Armagh, Newcastle, Carrickfergus, and at the Giant's Causeway on the North Antrim coast.

Contact Northern Ireland Tourist Board ⊠ *59 North St., Belfast, Co. Antrim* ☎ *028/9023–1221* ⊕ *www.discovernorthernireland.com.*

BELFAST

The city of Belfast was a great Victorian success story, an industrial boomtown whose prosperity was built on trade—especially linen and shipbuilding. Famously (or infamously), the *Titanic* was built here, giving Belfast, for a time, the nickname "Titanic Town."

For many years it wasn't talked about, but in 2012 the city commemorated the 100th anniversary of the liner's sinking on April 15, 1912, by opening a dazzling Titanic Belfast exhibition center. With nine galleries spread over six floors, the enormous multi-prow-shaped building—about the same height as *Titanic* and twice the size of City Hall—the center certainly has the wow factor. It has generated international interest, bringing in much-needed revenue and creating jobs at a difficult economic time.

Tourist numbers have increased as never before and this dramatically transformed city is enjoying an unparalleled renaissance. The record-breaking number of visitors speaks for itself: Titanic Belfast exceeded all expectations, welcoming more than 1.3 million people in its first year; the Metropolitan Arts Centre, which opened in 2012, doubled its attendance expectations in the first 12 months; and the Ulster Museum, which was revamped in 2011, has enjoyed record numbers through its doors.

This is all a welcome change from the period when news about Belfast meant reports about "the Troubles." Since the 1994 ceasefire, Northern Ireland's capital city has benefited from major hotel investment, gentrified quaysides (or strands), a sophisticated new performing arts center, and major initiatives to boost tourism. Although the 1996 bombing of

TRACING YOUR ROOTS

A staggering 3 million documents are stored in the archives of the **Public Record Office of Northern Ireland** (PRONI) with 900,000 official government files and 300,000 maps—a wonderful place to stir the imagination of researchers and visitors. Most records date from around 1600 to the present. For those interested in roots tourism, or anyone with ancestors from the northern third of Ireland, it is an amateur genealogist's dream; those precious transcripts could provide a vivid piece of the family jigsaw. ⊠ *PRONI, Titanic Blvd., Queen's Island, Titanic Quarter, Belfast* ☎ *028/9053-4800* ⊕ *proni.gov.uk; groni.gov.uk.*

The Ulster Historical Foundation, near Queen's University, has a skilled team to help with genealogical research. In recent years, with many more records available online, there is greater access to them, and the staff is adept at unearthing information about those elusive Irish or Scots-Irish ancestors. The UHF offers personal consultation, assessment, and research, as well as document retrieval. Its research offices are at ⊠ *49 Malone Rd., Belfast* ☎ *028/9066-1988,* ⊕ *ancestryireland.com.*

For a different take on Ulster-Scots history and language it's worth calling into the **Ulster-Scots Visitor Centre**. This government-funded agency promotes the study of Ulster-Scots as a living language as well as its culture and history. You can tour the new Discover Ulster-Scots Centre and view exhibition panels on dialect and heritage. ⊠ *Ulster-Scots Agency, Corn Exchange, 31 Gordon St., Belfast* ☎ *028/9023-1113,* ⊕ *ulster-scotsagency.com.*

offices at Canary Wharf in London disrupted the 1994 peace agreement, the ceasefire was officially reestablished on July 20, 1997, and this embattled city began its quest for a newfound identity.

Since 2008, the city has restored all its major public buildings such as museums, churches, theaters, City Hall, Ulster Hall—and even the glorious Crown Bar—spending millions of pounds on its built heritage. A gaol that at the height of the Troubles held some of the most notorious murderers involved in paramilitary violence is now a major visitor attraction.

Belfast's city center is made up of three roughly contiguous areas that are easy to navigate on foot. From the south end to the north it's about an hour's leisurely walk.

GETTING HERE AND AROUND

CAR TRAVEL   Belfast is 167 km (104 miles) north of Dublin. Motorways, or dual carriageways, lead into Belfast's city center from the main airports and seaports, and the fast N1/A1 motorway links the city with Dublin. The trip takes about two hours. The drive from Derry takes 90 minutes. The main arterial routes into central Belfast are busy only at peak commuter times, between 8 and 9 am and 5 and 6 pm.

Street parking costs £1.30 per hour for a pay-and-display ticket from a meter. The maximum parking time is two hours for such street spaces.

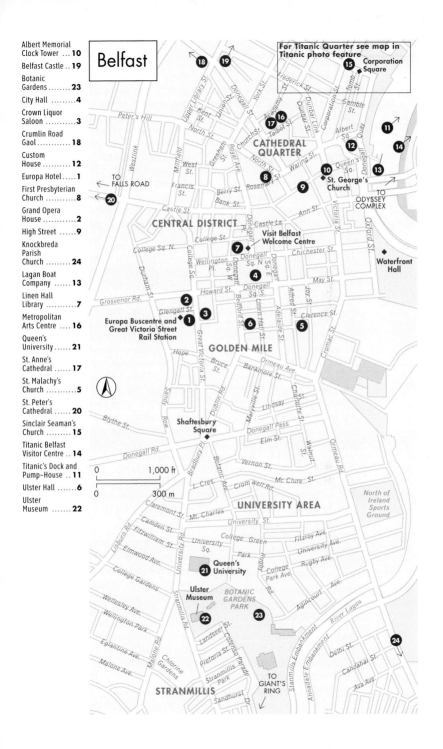

Belfast

Albert Memorial Clock Tower ... **10**
Belfast Castle .. **19**
Botanic Gardens **23**
City Hall **4**
Crown Liquor Saloon **3**
Crumlin Road Gaol **18**
Custom House **12**
Europa Hotel **1**
First Presbyterian Church **8**
Grand Opera House **2**
High Street **9**
Knockbreda Parish Church **24**
Lagan Boat Company **13**
Linen Hall Library **7**
Metropolitan Arts Centre **16**
Queen's University **21**
St. Anne's Cathedral **17**
St. Malachy's Church **5**
St. Peter's Cathedral **20**
Sinclair Seaman's Church **15**
Titanic Belfast Visitor Centre .. **14**
Titanic's Dock and Pump-House .. **11**
Ulster Hall **6**
Ulster Museum **22**

For Titanic Quarter see map in Titanic photo feature

Corporation Square

CATHEDRAL QUARTER

St. George's Church

Waterfront Hall

CENTRAL DISTRICT

Visit Belfast Welcome Centre

GOLDEN MILE

Europa Buscentre and Great Victoria Street Rail Station

Shaftesbury Square

TO FALLS ROAD

TO ODYSSEY COMPLEX

0   1,000 ft
0   300 m

UNIVERSITY AREA

North of Ireland Sports Ground

Queen's University

Ulster Museum

BOTANIC GARDENS PARK

TO GIANT'S RING

STRANMILLIS

THE TROUBLES

Northern Ireland's historic conflict between Catholic and Protestant, Irish and English, had its roots in the first Norman incursions in the 12th century, when the English endeavored to subdue the potential enemy they saw in Ireland. The northern province of Ulster proved the hardest to conquer, but in 1607, its Irish nobility fled, their lands then given by the English to "the Planters"— staunch Protestants from England and Scotland.

Fast-forward through three centuries of smoldering tensions and religious strife to the overwhelming 1918 Nationalist vote across Ireland for Sinn Féin ("Ourselves Alone"), the party that believed in independence for all of Ireland. In Ulster, however, 22 (out of 29) seats went to the Unionists, who believed in maintaining British rule. After 50 years of living with a Unionist majority, students in Belfast's Queen's University launched a civil rights protest in 1968, claiming equal rights in jobs, housing, and opportunity. They were met by brutal British suppression, which, in turn, awoke the Irish Republican Army (IRA), dormant for decades. Britain then imposed Direct Rule. This struggle tragically came to a head on Bloody Sunday, January 30, 1972, when British paratroopers opened fire on people participating in a nonviolent protest in Derry against the British policy of internment without trial. When the smoke cleared, 13 people, all Catholic and unarmed, had been killed.

Decades of guerrilla conflict ensued between the IRA, the UDA/UVF (Protestant/Loyalist paramilitaries), and the British government and continued until 1998's Good Friday Agreement, which finally gave the province its own parliament. But a mere two months later, the province's fragile peace was shattered when a massive car bomb exploded in the quiet market town of Omagh on August 15. A minority of dissident Republicans had succeeded in killing 31 people. Despite this appalling act, the peace process continued and Unionists eventually entered government proceedings with Sinn Féin at the end of 1999.

In September 2005, the IRA decommissioned all its weapons. In 2009, the Loyalist paramilitaries, the Ulster Volunteer Force and its splinter group, the Red Hand Commando, destroyed their weapons. By 2010, the biggest Loyalist paramilitary group, the Ulster Defence Association, decommissioned all weapons and was closely followed by two Irish Republican paramilitary groups—the extreme Irish National Liberation Army and the Official IRA—who also announced they had put weapons beyond use. The endorsement of what everyone had hoped to be a "final political deal" culminated in the Hillsborough Castle Agreement (2010), securing the stability of the Northern Ireland Assembly.

For many nationalists, the icing on the political cake came with the announcement in June 2010 by the British government apologizing for Bloody Sunday and saying it "had been unjustified and unjustifiable." For the people of Derry this has been liberating and has brought about a wind of change that has had a positive impact on the city.

WHAT'S NEXT FOR THE NORTH?

11

Though the 2010 Agreement was a huge breakthrough for Northern Ireland, the question of how to deal with the legacy of the troubled past has proved divisive. Sporadic incidents and the occasional resurgence of sectarian violence grab the headlines while issues such as who can march where, what flag flies where and when, remain contentious. In 2013 the U.S. envoy and mediator Dr. Richard Haass tried to negotiate a deal with the Stormont political parties but some problems remain intractable and the talks ended without conclusion.

Whatever the political bickering and small-scale protests over the non-flying of flags from government buildings, the vast majority of ordinary people get on with the business of leading their lives and are opposed to violence. Northern Ireland is enjoying the greatest prosperity and longest period of peace in its history. Talk to anyone on the streets of Belfast or Derry and they're likely to tell you that while the situation may not be perfect, it is infinitely better than the dark days of the "Troubles."

Be careful not to overstay, as zealous clamping wardens operate. Multistory car park garages are at the Victoria Square and Castle Court shopping centers. Some, but not all, hotels have car parking. If you'll need parking, ask a hotel or inn prior to booking.

BUS TRAVEL Pink-and-white Metro buses are the best way to get around. Fares range from £1.40 to £2, depending on the zone. If you're staying a few days, buy a Smartlink Travel Card for more than five journeys, which is a 30% saving; a weekly card is £15.50, plus £1.50 for the card. A Metro day ticket costs £3.70 (£3.20 after 9:20 am) and takes you anywhere on the network. Most bus routes start from Donegall Square or adjoining streets, where the Metro Kiosk, on Donegall Square West, has details and timetables.

TRAIN TRAVEL As the capital city of Northern Ireland, Belfast is well served by an efficient train network. Most trains arrive and leave from Central Station, a 15-minute walk from the city center.

Transportation Contacts Belfast Metro Service ✉ *Donegall Sq. W* ☎ *028/9066–6630* ⊕ *www.translink.co.uk/metro.* **Central Rail Station** ✉ *E. Bridge St.* ☎ *028/9089–9400.*

TOURS

BUS TOURS **Allen's Tours.** Allen's Tours (from £15) operate day tours of Belfast (£8–£16) and to the Giant's Causeway, Bushmills Distillery, and Carrickfergus (£17.50). A city tour and Causeway combo costs £23. ✉ *Donegall Rd., Golden Mile* ☎ *028/9091–5613* ⊕ *www.allensbustoursbelfast.com.*

Belfast City Sightseeing. Belfast City Sightseeing runs the most comprehensive open-top tour through Belfast. The Belfast City Tour covers the City Hall, University Quarter, Shipyard, Titanic Quarter, Stormont, Shankill Road, peace line, and Falls Road, and goes past the Grand Opera House on Great Victoria Street. You can hop off and hop on as you please at any of the 22 stops. The entire route, without stops, takes about an hour and a half. ✉ *City Tour departs from Castle Pl. (opposite McDonald's), Central District* ⊕ *www.belfastcitysightseeing.com* ✈ *City Tour £12.50, valid 48 hrs on a hop-on, hop-off basis* ☉ *City Tour Mar.–Sept., daily 10–4 every 15 mins; Oct.–Feb., daily every 30 mins.*

Bespoke Tours. Historical walking and driving tours that come with tales of myths and legends are the specialty of Bespoke Tours. The company also runs excursions outside Belfast to some of Northern Ireland's major tourist attractions. The owner tailors his tours to suit individual interests and requirements. ✉ *Central District* ☎ *079/1229–0935* ⊕ *www.bespoke-tours.com.*

Hidden Belfast. Focusing on buildings and history, Hidden Belfast walking tours last one hour and meet at the front gates of Belfast City Hall; look for the Hidden Belfast Umbrella. Tours leave three times a day in July/August; check website for departure times and phone in advance to confirm. ✉ *Meet outside front gates of City Hall, Donegall Sq. N, Central District* ☎ *077/7164–0746* ⊕ *experiencebelfast.com* ✈ *£5* ☉ *July and Aug., daily at 10, 12:15, 2; Feb.–June and Sept.–Nov., Mon., Wed. at 11, weekends at noon (no tours Dec. and Jan.).*

McComb's Coach Travel. As well as the standard open-top bus tours of Belfast and trips to the Giant's Causeway, McComb's also offer more specific tours that include a Game of Thrones tour. Parts of the series were filmed in Belfast and other areas of Northern Ireland. The day-long tour visits some of the stunning locations where filming took place. ✉ *22 Donegall Rd., Central District* ☎ *028/9031–5333* ⊕ *www.minicoachni.co.uk/tours.cfm.*

Richard Hayward's Belfast. This foot-stepping tour takes in places that were written about by one of Ireland's leading 20th-century cultural figures. Hayward, who died in 1964, wrote 12 travel books about Ireland in addition to being a singer and film star. The two-hour guided walking tour leaves from the Crown Bar on Saturday at 2 pm and Thursday at 7 pm. There's a free gift at the end of the tour. ✉ *Depart from outside the Crown Bar, 46 Great Victoria St., Golden Mile* ☎ *077/6237–9303* ⊕ *www.visit-belfast.com* ✈ *£7* ☉ *Apr.–Oct., Sat. at 2, Thurs. at 7 pm; must be booked in advance by phone.*

TAXI TOURS **Belfast City Black Taxi Tours.** Black taxi tours are an excellent way to experience the city's history. Belfast City Black Taxi Tours conducts 75-minute tours in a London-style black taxi, visiting both Loyalist and Nationalist sights. The Loyalist tours leave from North Street or Bridge Street and prices can vary depending on pick-up point; the Nationalist tours pick you up at your hotel. ☎ *077/1267–3178* ⊕ *www.belfastcityblacktaxitours.com* ✈ *£25 for 1–2 passengers, £30 for 3, and £35 for 4.*

The Official Black Taxi Tours. All the main political highlights and trouble spots of the 1970s and 80s, such as the Falls and Shankill roads, are covered by the comprehensive Official Black Taxi Tours. Pick-ups are available from your hotel, B&B, or from bus and train stations. ☎ *028/9064–2264* ⊕ *www.belfasttours.com* ✈ *£30 1–2 passengers, £12 per additional person.*

Parliament Buildings Tour. Free tours of Parliament Buildings are held twice every weekday at 10 and 3. Take a stroll around the home of the Northern Ireland Assembly to see one of the city's most striking pieces of architecture. ⊠ *Upper Newtownards Rd., Stormont, East Belfast* ☎ *028/9052–1802* ⊕ *www.niassembly.gov.uk* ⊙ *Tours last 45 mins, at 10 am and 3 pm.*

TaxiTrax Tours. The itinerary of the popular TaxiTrax Tours provides a balanced history lesson covering the "Troubles" and includes the peace wall and the city's famed murals. ⊕ *www.taxitrax.com* ☞ *£30 1–3 passengers, £10 per additional person.*

ESSENTIALS

The Belfast Welcome Centre, the city's main tourist office, is located at 8–9 Donegall Square North, directly opposite the front of City Hall. The center sells the Belfast Visitor pass—good for unlimited travel within a specified zone, as well as for discounts on tours and entrance to major attractions such as Titanic Belfast Visitor Centre, the Ulster Folk & Transport Museum, Crumlin Road Gaol, and W5 at the Odyssey. The pass costs £6.50 for one day, £10.50 for two, and £14 for three, plus an initial £1.50 charge.

VISITOR INFORMATION **Visit Belfast Welcome Centre.** Meeters and greeters welcome you at this sparklingly new £1.8-million center, opened in 2014, the epitome of the glossy new Belfast. Directly opposite city hall, it's the first stop to find out what's on, buy tickets for events and tours, or book accommodation and travel. Features include a series of "islands" telling the story of Belfast on plasma TVs through people, places, experiences, and events. Striking video wall graphics reflect the city center while digital maps explore the hidden quarters of the city. Multimedia information touch-screens and self-service kiosks provide a signposting service for more than 400 attractions throughout Northern Ireland. You can pick up leaflets and brochures galore on all manner of places and activities from the Antrim coast to Fermanagh lakelands. A gift shop sells maps, books, and locally themed products such as Titanic Rock and Irish Linen from the McCaw Allan firm which has been making it since 1820. A Translink desk will help plan and organize your travel within Northern Ireland and farther afield. There's also free Wi-Fi access, a bureau de change, and left-luggage facilities. ⊠ *8–9 Donegall Sq. N, Central District* ☎ *028/9024–6609* ⊕ *www.visit-belfast.com* ⊙ *June–Sept., Mon.–Sat. 9–7, Sun. 11–4; Oct.–May, Mon.–Sat. 9–5:30, Sun. 11–4.*

EXPLORING

Magnificent Victorian structures still line the streets of the city center, but instead of housing linen mills or cigarette factories, they are home to chic new hotels and fashionable bars. Smart restaurants abound, and the people of Belfast, who for years would not venture out of their districts, appear to be making up for lost time. Each area of the city has changed considerably in the new peaceful era, but perhaps none more than the docklands around the Harland and Wolff shipyards, whose historic and enormous cranes, known to the locals as Samson and Goliath, still dominate the city's skyline. New developments—such as the Titanic Quarter—are springing up all around deserted shipyards, ranging from luxury hotels to modern office blocks. And in the center of the city, Victoria Square is a gigantic shopping and residential complex, replete with a geodesic dome, floors of glossy shops, and renovated Victorian row houses. In the west of the city, the physical scars of the Troubles are still evident, from the peace line that divides Catholic and Protestant West Belfast to the murals on every gable wall. Visitors are discovering that it's safe to venture beyond the city center, and taxi tours of these once-troubled areas are very popular.

Before English and Scottish settlers arrived in the 1600s, Belfast was a tiny village called Béal Feirste ("sandbank ford") belonging to Ulster's ancient O'Neill clan. With the advent of the Plantation period (when settlers arrived in the 1600s), Sir Arthur Chichester, from Devon in southwestern England, received the city from the English Crown, and his son was made Earl of Donegall. Huguenots fleeing persecution from France settled near here, bringing their valuable linen-work skills. In the 18th century, Belfast underwent a phenomenal expansion—its population doubled in size every 10 years, despite an ever-present sectarian divide. Although the Anglican gentry despised the Presbyterian artisans—who, in turn, distrusted the native Catholics—Belfast's growth continued at a dizzying speed. Having laid the foundation stone of the city's university in 1845, Queen Victoria returned to Belfast in 1849 (she is recalled in the names of buildings, streets, bars, monuments, and other places around the city), and in the same year, the university opened under the name Queen's College. Nearly 40 years later, in 1888, Victoria granted Belfast its city charter. Today its population is nearly 300,000.

GOLDEN MILE

The arrowhead-shaped district extending from Howard Street in the north to Shaftesbury Square at the southern tip, and bordered on the west by Great Victoria Street and on the east by Bedford Street and Dublin Road, is a great area from which to begin an exploration of Belfast. Although it doesn't glow quite the way the name suggests, the bustling Golden Mile and its immediate environs harbor noteworthy historic buildings. In addition, the area is filled with hotels and major civic and office buildings, as well as some restaurants, cafés, and shops. Even if you don't end up staying here, you're likely to pass through it often.

TOP ATTRACTIONS

Fodor's Choice ★ **City Hall.** Built of Portland stone between 1898 and 1906 and modeled on St. Paul's Cathedral in London, this Renaissance Revival–style edifice—the cynosure of central Belfast—was designed by Brumwell Thomas (who was knighted but had to sue to get his fee). Before you enter, take a stroll around Donegall Square to see statues of Queen Victoria and a column honoring the U.S. Expeditionary Force, which landed in the city on January 26, 1942—the first contingent of the U.S. Army to arrive in Europe during World War II. A monument commemorating the *Titanic* stands in the grounds, and in 2012 a granite memorial was unveiled in a *Titanic* memorial garden opened for the 100th anniversary of the ship's sinking. The memorial, on the east side of the grounds, lists the names of everyone who died in the tragedy. Enter the building under the porte cochere at the front. From the entrance hall (the base of which is a whispering gallery), the view up to the heights of the 173-foot-high Great Dome is a feast for the eyes. With its complicated series of arches and openings, stained-glass windows, Italian-marble inlays, decorative plasterwork, and paintings, this is Belfast's most ornate public space—a veritable homage to the might of the British Empire. After an £11 million restoration, the modernized building has been brought into the 21st century and is now home to the Bobbin café and the "Waking a Giant" exhibition, in which historic photographs tell the story of Belfast's industrial development. Another permanent exhibition, "No Mean City," an interactive and photographic display, celebrates 68 inspirational people of the last 100 years, including Thomas Andrews (the designer of the *Titanic*), singer Van Morrison, and footballer George Best. In the courtyard a 60-jet fountain has been dedicated to Belfast City Council members killed during the Troubles. Free, guided one-hour tours of the building are offered. There's also a tourist information point on the ground floor. ⊠ *Donegall Sq.* ☎ *028/9027–0456* ⊕ *www.belfastcity.gov.uk* ◫ *Tours free* ☉ *Tours weekdays at 11, 2, and 3; Sat. at 2 and 3.*

Fodor'sChoice
★

Crown Liquor Saloon. Belfast is blessed with some exceptional pubs but the Crown Bar is one of the city's glories. An ostentatious box of delights, the Crown which is owned by the National Trust (the United Kingdom's official conservation organization), has been immaculately preserved. Opposite the Europa Hotel, it began life in 1826 as the Railway Tavern and is still lighted by gas; in 1885 the owner asked Italian craftsmen working on churches in Ireland to moonlight on rebuilding it, and its place in Irish architectural pub history was assured. Richly carved woodwork around cozy snugs (cubicles—known to regulars as "confessional boxes"), leather seats, color tile work, and an abundance of mirrors make up the decor. But the pièce de résistance is the embossed ceiling with its swirling arabesques and rosettes of burnished primrose, amber, and gold, as dazzling again now as the day it was installed. The Crown claims to serve the perfect pint of Guinness—so no need to ask what anyone's drinking—and you can order a great plateful of warming Irish stew. When you settle down in your snug, note the little gunmetal plates used by the Victorians for lighting their matches as well as the newly restored antique push-button bells for ordering another round. Ageless, timeless, and classless—some would say the Crown is even priceless. ⊠ *46 Great Victoria St.* ☎ *028/9024–3187* ⊕ *www.crownbar. com* ☉ *Mon.–Wed. 11:30 am–11 pm, Thurs.–Sat until midnight, Sun. 12:30–10.*

FAMILY
Fodor'sChoice
★

Crumlin Road Gaol. Since opening full-time in 2012, Crumlin Road Gaol has become one of Belfast's hot tourist tickets. Designed by Charles Lanyon in 1841, the gaol originally opened in 1846 and at its height held more than 500 prisoners. Throughout its 150-year lifetime, around 25,000 convicts passed through its doors. During the worst years of the Troubles, between 1969 and 1996 (when the prison closed), it held some of the North's most notorious murderers, including many involved in paramilitary violence. The building has undergone a £10 million restoration, and, with its cream-walled corridors and black railings, has been transformed to reflect the way it looked in Victorian days. The engrossing 75-minute tour takes in the holding, punishment, and condemned cells—the latter where the prisoners were held before being taken to the gallows for execution. The highlight is the execution chamber, hidden behind a moving bookcase where the guide explains the gory details of how the long-drop method was used to break the prisoner's neck. Exhibits in the museum include handcuffs, uniforms, a flogging rack with the birch used for punishment, photographs, and maps. The gaol is said to be one of the most haunted buildings in Belfast, and paranormal tours are also held regularly. Check the website for details of the schedule. ⊠ *53–55 Crumlin Rd.* 🕾 *028/9074–1500* ⊕ *www.crumlinroadgaol.com* 🖅 *£8.50* 🕙 *Daily 10–5:30; last tour 4:30.*

Grand Opera House. Belfast's opera house exemplifies the Victorians' fascination with ornamentation, opulent gilt moldings, and intricate plasterwork. The renowned theater architect Frank Matcham beautifully designed the building in 1894. Facilities include a foyer bar, café, restaurant, and party room. Contemporary Irish artist Cherith McKinstry's exquisite angel-and-cherub-laden fresco floats over the auditorium ceiling. The theater regularly hosts musicals, operas, plays, and concerts. ⊠ *2 Great Victoria St.* 🕾 *028/9024–1919* ⊕ *www.goh.co.uk.*

St. Malachy's Church. Opened in 1844, St. Malachy's Church is one of the most impressive redbrick Tudor Revival churches in Ireland. One of the interior highlights is the densely patterned fan-vaulted ceiling, a delightfully swirling masterpiece of plasterwork—whose inspiration was taken from the chapel of Henry VII at Westminster Abbey in London—tastefully repainted in cream. The high altarpiece featuring Pugin's *Journey to Calvary* was originally carried out by the portraitist Felix Piccioni whose family were refugees to Belfast from Austrian Italy. In 1868 the largest bell in Belfast was added to the church but after complaints that its deafening noise was interfering with the maturing of whiskey in the nearby Dunville distillery, it was wrapped in felt to soften its peal and vibration. Along the southeast wall of the church gazing out in contemplative mood with his brown eyes and torn chocolate brown coat is the delicate Statue of the Ragged Saint. St. Benedict Joseph Labre, the patron saint of the unemployed, welcomes visitors into the ethereal elegance of one of Belfast's most architecturally romantic buildings. ⊠ *Alfred St.* 🕾 *028/9032–1713* ⊕ *www.saintmalachys.ie* 🖅 *Free.*

Ulster Hall. It has hosted Charles Dickens, the Rolling Stones, and Rachmaninov as well as a diverse range of Irish politicians from Charles Stewart Parnell to Ian Paisley. Built in 1862 as a ballroom, the Ulster Hall, affectionately known as the Grand Dame of Bedford Street, celebrated its 150th anniversary in 2012 and has continued to thrive since an £8.5 million renovation in 2009. Much of W.J. Barre's original decor has been restored and 13 historic oil paintings reflecting the history and mythology of Belfast by local artist Joseph Carey are on display in their original magnificence in the Carey Gallery. Another highlight is an interpretative display featuring poetry, pictures, and sound telling the history of the hall through personal reminiscences. During World War II the building was used as a dance hall by U.S. troops based in Northern Ireland. The hall is also the permanent home of the Ulster Orchestra.

Stop by the Café Grand Dame, drink in some of Belfast's colorful history, and reflect on the fact that it was here in March 1971 that Led Zeppelin performed the stage debut of "Stairway to Heaven." At the box office you can buy tickets for all upcoming events at both Ulster Hall and Waterfront Hall. ⊠ *Bedford St.* ☏ *028/9033–4400* ⊕ *www.ulsterhall.co.uk* ☉ *Guided tours by appointment.*

WORTH NOTING

Europa Hotel. A landmark in Belfast, the Europa is a monument to the resilience of the city in the face of the Troubles. The most bombed hotel in Western Europe, it was targeted 11 times by the IRA starting in the early 1970s and was refurbished every time; today it shows no signs of its explosive history. Indeed, even with this track record, President Bill Clinton and his wife, Hillary, chose the hotel for an overnight visit during their 1995 visit—for 24 hours the phones were answered with "White House Belfast, can I help you?" The president's room is now called the Clinton Suite and contains memorabilia from the presidential stay. An Italian marble lobby was installed in 2008 and the Europa expanded to 272 rooms, including six suites. A photographic timeline was added in 2011 to commemorate the hotel's 40th anniversary. The property is owned by the affable Ulster millionaire and hotel magnate Billy Hastings. ⊠ *38 Great Victoria St., at Glengall St.* ☏ *028/9027–1066* ⊕ *www.hastingshotels.com.*

> **VICTORIAN GRISLY**
>
> Most of Belfast's landmarks were built during the reign of Queen Victoria. Once considered unappealing—"Victorian Grisly" was the epithet used by more than one critic—today they are marvelous remnants of an age that considered show, pomp, and circumstance paramount. Most of these buildings are found within 20 blocks of each other and a time-travel walk can hit many of them, including City Hall, Linen Hall Library, the Grand Opera House, Crown Liquor Saloon, Ulster Hall, St. Malachy's Church, and St. Anne's Cathedral.

CENTRAL DISTRICT

Belfast's Central District, immediately north of the Golden Mile, extends from Donegall Square north to St. Anne's Cathedral. It's not geographically the center of the city, but it's the old heart of Belfast. It's a frenetic place—the equivalent of Dublin's Grafton and Henry streets in one—where both locals and visitors shop. Cafés, pubs, offices, and shops of all kinds, from department stores to the Gap and Waterstones (there's even a Disney store), occupy the redbrick, white Portland-stone, and modern buildings that line its narrow streets. Many streets are pedestrian-only, so it's a good place to take a leisurely stroll, browse, and see some sights to boot. It's easy to get waylaid shopping and investigating sights along the river when taking this walk, so give yourself at least two hours to cover the area comfortably.

The Central District contains what locals call the **Cathedral Quarter**: radiating out from the new mock neo-Palladian development of St. Anne's Square. Along its narrow, cobbled redbrick streets a former banana warehouse is now a circus school; an architectural firm has moved into a converted jute sack warehouse; and a busy bar and restaurant has taken over a derelict spirits bonded warehouse. Small privately owned art galleries, alongside the Black Box—a major performance venue—line the side streets and are crammed in alongside a new wave of bars and lively bistros, making it the new restaurant central. Crowning it all is the dramatic Metropolitan Arts Centre, Northern Ireland's new flagship location for the arts opened in 2012. With its bright, airy galleries, the MAC unashamedly contrasts with the neighboring Victorian warehouses and mills. It looms over its quarter the way the Titanic Belfast looms over the Titanic Quarter. Both are important new landmarks for a reinvigorated city.

TOP ATTRACTIONS

Albert Memorial Clock Tower. Tilting a little to one side, not unlike Pisa's more notorious leaning landmark, this clock tower was named for Queen Victoria's husband, Prince Albert. The once-dilapidated Queen's Square on which it stands has undergone a face-lift and a restoration has brought the clock back to its original glory. The tower itself is not open to the public. ⊠ *Queen's Sq*

First Presbyterian Church. The First Presbyterian Church dates from 1783 and has an interesting elliptical interior. It hosts lunchtime concerts in July and August. Tours are held on Wednesday morning. ⊠ *Rosemary St., Central District.*

High Street. Off High Street, especially down to Ann Street (parallel to the south), run narrow lanes and alleyways called entries. Though mostly cleaned up and turned into chic shopping lanes, they still hang on to something of their raffish character, and have distinctive pubs with little-altered Victorian interiors. Among the most notable are the Morning Star (Pottinger's Entry off High Street), with its large windows and fine curving bar; White's Tavern (entry off High Street), Belfast's oldest pub, founded in 1630, which, although considerably updated, is still warm and comfortable, with plush seats and a big, open fire; and the delectable Muriel's Café Bar in Church Lane, with its damask drapes and velvet seats, themed on a 1920s hat shop. Look into St George's Church, at one end of High Street, a beautiful building with a magnificient portico transported by canal from the house of the eccentric Earl Bishop of Derry. Across the road, McHugh's (in Queen's Square), in what is reckoned to be the city's oldest extant building, dating from 1711. ⊠ *High St., Central District.*

Knockbreda Parish Church. Belfast has so many churches you could visit a different one nearly every day of the year and still not make it to all of them. The oldest house of worship is the Church of Ireland Knockbreda Parish Church. This dark structure was built in 1737 by Richard Cassels, who designed many of Ireland's finest mansions. It quickly became *the* place to be buried—witness the vast 18th-century tombs in the churchyard. ⊠ *Church Rd. off A24, Central District* ☎ *028/9064–5372* ⊕ *www.knockbredaparish.org.*

Lagan Boat Company N.I. Ltd. A 75-minute *Titanic* harbor tour takes in the shipyard where the famous liner was built. The Lagan company also runs a separate two-hour boat trip, the Belfast Lough Tour at 3:30 on Sunday (June–October, £12.50). The departure point for both tours is from Donegall Quay near the Big Fish sculpture (a gigantic salmon covered in tiles and printed with text and imagery about Belfast). Tickets can be bought in the Maritime Emporium shop beside the Obel tower at Donegall Quay. ✉ *66 Donegall Quay* ☎ *028/9024–0124* ⊕ *www.laganboatcompany.com* ⛴ *Tours £10* ☾ *Titanic tour Apr.–Oct., daily at 12:30, 2, and 3:30; Nov.–Mar., weekends at 12:30 and 2.*

Metropolitan Arts Centre. Eye-catchingly beautiful, and flooded with light, the Metropolitan Arts Centre (MAC) is Northern Ireland's flagship home for the arts, and has reenergized the Cathedral Quarter's flourishing creative scene since opening in 2012. Six stories tall, and with two theaters, three art galleries, and artists' studios—along with a café, a bar, and a restaurant—the MAC is the centerpiece of the neo-Palladian St. Anne's Square development. The MAC makes an astonishing statement with redbrick and dark basalt, oak furnishings, Danish fabric panels, steel balustrades, bronze window frames, and dark-gray terrazzo flooring. Downstairs is a 350-seat auditorium, while upstairs is a 120-seat studio. The galleries present up-and-coming Northern Irish artists as well as attention-grabbing temporary exhibitions incorporating the works of world-renowned artists. Ushers, known as MACtivists, are on hand to help point you in the right direction, and curator tours are held regularly—check the website for dates. ✉ *St. Anne's Sq., Exchange St.* ☎ *028/9023–5053* ⊕ *www.themaclive.com* ⛴ *Galleries free* ☾ *Daily 10–7, later on performance nights.*

Sinclair Seamen's Church. By the riverfront is one of the most appealing churches, Presbyterian Sinclair Seamen's Church. Designed by Charles Lanyon, the architect of Queen's University, it has served the seafaring community since 1857. The pulpit is shaped like a ship's prow; the bell is from HMS *Hood,* sunk in 1916; and even the collection plates are shaped like lifeboats. ✉ *Corporation Sq. off Donegall Quay* ☎ *028/9071–5997 tours on Wed. 2–4:30 all year.*

St. Peter's Cathedral. The elegant neo-Gothic "twin spires" of St. Peter's Cathedral dominate the skyline of West Belfast. Finding this Roman Catholic cathedral is difficult, but worth the effort. Built in 1866, when the Catholic population was rapidly increasing, St. Peter's acted as a focal point for the community. ✉ *St. Peter's Sq., Central District* ☎ *028/9032–7573* ⊕ *www.stpeterscathedralbelfast.com.*

FAMILY
Fodor's Choice
★

Titanic Belfast Visitor Centre. This world-class attraction headlines a Titanic Experience exhibition along with showcasing nine linked interpretative galleries that outline the *Titanic*'s dramatic story as well as the wider theme of Belfast's seafaring and industrial heritage. The stunning bow-shaped facade of the six-story building reflects the lines of the great ship, the shard-like appearance created from 3,000 different-shaped panels each folded from silver anodized aluminum sheets into asymmetrical geometries. The ultimate, startling effect is of light caught by a cut diamond. As you wander through Titanic Belfast you will learn about the thriving boomtown at the turn of the 20th century; the ride through the reconstruction of the shipyards echoes with the sounds and sensations of 100 years ago. In one of the galleries, the ship's saga is brought up to the present with the discovery of the wreck and into the future with live links to contemporary undersea exploration. Also on-site is a movie theater designed by the *Titanic* explorer Robert Ballard (he discovered the wreck in 1985), which shows films about the ship. From time to time new exhibits are added; one of these is the original plan used during the British Titanic Inquiry held one month after the sinking. The historic plan was a vital reference tool and contains markings indicating where the liner struck the iceberg. The inquiry concluded that the loss of the liner had been brought about by "excessive speed." Tours of the center are self-guided; audio guides are available in seven languages and cost £3. ■TIP➡ Tickets can be bought online (5% cheaper); the least crowded time to go is on Sunday morning. Every Sunday afternoon teas by the grand staircase in the Titanic Suite are held and must be booked in advance. They cost £23, or £29 with a glass of Heidseck Monopole Champagne, the official champagne of RMS Titanic. On the first Friday of each month, "After Hours at Titanic Belfast" offers an atmospheric experience in the gallery with Titanic characters in period costume. ✉ *Olympic Way, 6 Queen's Rd., Titanic Quarter* ⊕ *titanicbelfast.com* 🎫 *£15.50* ☉ *Apr.–Sept., daily 9–7, last admission to tour 5:20; Oct.– Mar., Mon.–Sun. 10–5, last admission to tour 3:20.*

Fodor'sChoice ★ **Titanic's Dock and Pump-House Tour.** The atmospheric 900-foot-long dock where *Titanic* was built—in its time the biggest in the world—is open to the public and ranks as one of *the* great attractions in Northern Ireland. Since 2012, and the events held for the 100th anniversary, *Titanic*'s Dock—officially known as the Thompson Dry Dock—has been accessible to visitors. Steps lead deep down 44 feet to the floor of the dock, where you can bask in the evocative spirit of this remarkable place well below sea level. In its heyday in the early 20th century, the dock could hold 21 million gallons of water. Today it is Belfast's outstanding relic of *Titanic*'s legacy and strikingly represents the ship's physical footprint. Built by 500 men over a period of seven years, it was the beating heart of the shipyard's operation during the construction of the great White Star Liners—*Britannic, Olympic,* and RMS *Titanic.* But it was a tight squeeze; the *Titanic* barely fitted in. The original steel-casing gate (now showing some signs of rust) that enclosed the dock and kept ships watertight weighs a staggering 1,000 tons. The best way of accessing the dock and pump-house is to join one of Colin Cobb's fascinating, fact-filled walks that help visitors—through visual aids of the *Titanic*—imagine, relive, and reflect on both a singular marvel of engineering and the importance of shipbuilding in Belfast's heritage. ■TIP➡ The tours are 10% cheaper if booked online; early booking is recommended. Taking Metro Bus No. 26, 26b, or 26c from City Hall is the easiest way to get to the Dock and Pump-House; you can take a train to the new Titanic Quarter stop or opt for a 20-minute walk from Belfast city center to Queen's Road (home to the Odyssey Arena and W5 science center). ⊠ *Queen's Rd.* ☎ *028/9073–7813* ⊕ *www.titanicsdock. com* ⛴ *£7* ⊗ *Tours daily (check website as times vary).*

NEED A BREAK?

Kelly's Cellars. Steeped in history, Kelly's Cellars, just off Royal Avenue, is a circa-1720 pub brimful of character. It serves a filling bowl of tasty beef stew at lunchtime. Two centuries ago it was the meeting place of a militant Nationalist group, the Society of United Irishmen, whose leader, Wolfe Tone (who was a Protestant), is remembered as the founder of Irish Republicanism. Traditional music and plenty of local banter make the pub particularly lively on weekends although there's music every night except Monday. ⊠ **30–32 Bank St., Central District** ☎ **028/9024–6058.**

FAMILY **W5: WhoWhatWhereWhyWhen.** A staggering 250 hands-on exhibits allow children to explore the world through games and activities. Part of the Odyssey complex in Belfast's docks, the W5 science discovery center takes a high-tech approach to interpreting science and creativity for adults and children. Video displays and flashing lights enhance the futuristic feel and you can do everything from explore the weather to build houses, bridges, and robots. After a £250,000 investment in 2013, the Start exhibits for the under-eights were rethemed featuring subjects such as spying, forensics, and nature. ■ TIP→ Make your way to the upper floors for spectacular views over the city and beyond. ⊠ *2 Queen's Quay* ☎ *028/9046–7700* ⊕ *www.w5online.co.uk* ⛴ *£7.90* ⊗ *Weekdays 10–5, Sat. 10–6, Sun. noon–6; last entry 1 hr before closing.*

WORTH NOTING

Custom House. The 19th-century architect Charles Lanyon designed the Custom House. This building, along with many others in Belfast, including Queen's University and the unusual Sinclair Seaman's Church, bear the hallmarks of his skill. It's not open to the public, but it's worth circling the house to view the lofty pediment of Britannia, Mercury, and Neptune on the front, carved by acclaimed stonemason Thomas Fitzpatrick. A blue plaque records the fact that the 19th-century novelist Anthony Trollope worked in the building as a post-office surveyor. During the historic Dockers' Strike of 1907, the labor organizer Jim Larkin addressed crowds of up to 20,000 people from the steps of the Custom House. The steps became known as "Speaker's Corner." A life-size bronze statue with arms raised commemorates the orator and his cause. ⊠ *Donegall Quay.*

Fodor's Choice ★ **Linen Hall Library.** With its distinctive grayish-yellow brick, this library— the oldest subscription library in Ireland—is a comfortable place to escape the bustle of the city streets. The library has an unparalleled collection of 80,000 documents and books relating to the Troubles, regarded as the definitive archive and attracting scholars from all over the world. One early librarian, Thomas Russell, was hanged in 1803 for supporting an Irish uprising; another early user, Henry Joy McCracken, a founding member of the United Irishmen, went to the scaffold owing the library £1.30 in subscriptions arrears, a debt that was eventually paid by a descendant in 2001. On the walls are paintings and prints depicting Belfast views and landmarks. Much of this artwork is for sale. Look out for the beautiful stained-glass windows on the first floor featuring portraits of men eminent in literature and science. It's an ideal hideaway for relaxing with a newspaper, enjoying the library's café, and falling into conversation. ⊠ *17 Donegall Sq. N, Central District* ☎ *028/9032–1707* ⊕ *www.linenhall.com* ✉ *Free* ⊙ *Weekdays 9:30–5:30, Sat. 9:30–4.*

St. Anne's Cathedral. At the center of the eponymously named Cathedral Quarter, St. Anne's is a turn-of-the-20th century edifice in the Irish neo-Romanesque style. Lord Carson (1854–1935), who was largely responsible for keeping the six counties inside the United Kingdom, is buried here by virtue of a special Act of Parliament. His is the only tomb. The guides on duty will show you around free of charge, but if you want more detailed historical and architectural information it's worth spending £5 on the guidebook. The 175-foot stainless-steel Spire of Hope was erected in 2007 atop the cathedral's roof, adding a new feature to the city's skyline and shining brightly as a beacon of newfound optimism for the future. In 2012, as part of the *Titanic* centennial, an elegant Titanic Funeral Pall was unveiled. The German Luftwaffe bombed this section of Belfast during World War II; on the cathedral's Talbot Street side, at No. 21, the Northern Ireland War Memorial has an interactive exhibit about the war. ⊠ *Donegall St., Cathedral Quarter* ☎ *028/9032–8332* ⊕ *www.belfastcathedral.org* ✉ *Free* ⊙ *Mon.–Sat. 8–5, Sun. services at 8, 10, 11, 3:30.*

UNIVERSITY AREA

At Belfast's southern end, the part of the city around Queen's University is dotted with parks, botanical gardens, and leafy streets with fine, intact, two- and three-story 19th-century buildings. The area evokes an older, more leisurely pace of life. The many pubs and excellent restaurants make this area the hub of the city's nightlife. However, remember that Belfast is a student town and this is the main university area—the pace of life here can be fast (and sometimes a little furious) during school-term weekends.

Botanic Gardens. In the Victorian heyday, it was not unusual to find 10,000 of Belfast's citizens strolling about here on a Saturday afternoon. These gardens are a glorious haven of grass, trees, flowers, curving walks, and wrought-iron benches, all laid out in 1827 on land that slopes down to the River Lagan. The curved-iron and glass Palm House is a conservatory marvel designed in 1839 by Charles Lanyon. Inside, the hot stove wing is a mini jungle of exotic plants such as the bird of paradise flower and heavily scented frangipani. ⚠ **Please note: During 2015 the Tropical Ravine House will be closed for the entire year for a root-and-branch renovation to conserve its rare plant collection and there will be no access.** There's still plenty to explore though in the main grounds. Wander around the arboretum and the 100-year-old rockery, or in summer savor the colors and scents of the herbaceous borders. ■TIP➜ A fun challenge is to follow the Tree Trail which leads you around 20 trees, many planted in the 19th century, with specimens such as the Tree-of-Heaven, Japanese red cedar, and

Continued on page 598

Queenstown • Southampton
New York
Cherbourg
Titanic

THE *TITANIC*: BORN IN BELFAST

"The *Titanic* has at last sailed home." That, in the words of one newspaper headline, fittingly described the 2012 Centennial commemorations held in Belfast to honor the 1912 sinking of the *Titanic*. Not far from the famous shipyards that built her, the city has opened a gloriously dramatic Titanic Belfast Visitor Centre (cost: an eye-watering £77 million), a towering building stuffed with spectacular exhibits, virtual tours, GCI effects, and even a ride through 1912 Belfast. This center might well do for Belfast what the Guggenheim did for Bilbao.

BELFAST TITANIC VISITOR CENTRE

Tragically touted as "unsinkable," the RMS *Titanic* set sail from Belfast's famed Harland & Wolff shipyards on April 2, 1912. Five miles of decks, twenty-nine boilers, a sixteen-ton forward anchor . . . and just 62 seconds to launch. But four days into her maiden voyage to New York—at precisely 11:40 pm on the night of April 14th—lookouts alarmingly sounded the ship's bell: "Iceberg, Straight Ahead!"

Too late: even though the Marconi wireless service on-board had received iceberg warnings from other ships—disregarded in favor of messages for first-class passengers—the ship hit the huge iceberg, which sliced open five watertight compartments (only four and the ship would have stayed afloat). With a 300-foot gash in her hull, the doomed liner sank two hours and forty minutes later—at 2:20 am—the next morning. Of the 2,201 passengers and

crew, only 711 survived . . . because there were not enough lifeboats.

THE WORLD'S LARGEST TITANIC ATTRACTION

Opened on March 31, 2012, and designed by Eric Kuhne Associates, the eye-catching, multi-prow shaped Titanic Belfast Visitor Centre rises right on the spot where the ship was built. Many Titanoraks (the term for Titanic groupies) feel it is a great success, if only because it has reclaimed Belfast's Titanic legacy. In the past, the tragedy had cast a shadow across the city's great shipyards (thanks to whispers about low-quality steel and a rushed production schedule) but the recent centenary uncovered the true story.

THE REAL REASONS SHE SANK

Surviving relatives of key players only revealed in 2012 the real missteps: due to a mix-up between steam-ship and sailing-ship steering systems, Second Officer Charles Lightoller's direction to steer "hard a-starboard" meant that Quartermaster Robert Hitchins panicked and steered right into the ice. But for the fact that Bruce Ismay, owner

Top, left: view of Gallery 7's *Titanic* lifeboat; Top, right above: *Titanica* sculpture on main Plaza; Top, right below: the Fit-Out gallery—how the most elegant ship afloat was furnished; Right page, top: view of the museum exterior.

of the White Star Line, then gave the order to dislodge the berg, the *Titanic* would never have sunk.

TOURING THE GALLERIES

Gallery 1: Walk through the Harland & Wolff shipyard gates to discover Boomtown Belfast, as newspaper billboards and other memorabilia transport you back to 1912.

Gallery 2: Rise to the top of the Arrol Gantry as a six-seater fiberglass cart whisks you on a 5-minute ride through the busy shipyard.

Gallery 3: Through innovative special effects, experience the exciting launch on May 31, 1911, when 100,000 people saw *Titanic* hit the water for the first time.

Gallery 4: The Fit-Out is a custom-designed CGI show that takes you on a virtual tour of the liner from the engine room to the opulent restaurant (where a string orchestra serenades you).

Gallery 5: On the Maiden Voyage, get to know the passengers (of 38 nationalities) as the liner sails from Belfast via Southampton, Cherbourg, and Queenstown.

Gallery 6: The Sinking is portrayed through a dramatically chilly room that re-creates the harrowing last moments as *Titanic* plunges to disaster.

Gallery 7: In the Aftermath gallery a poignant wall of 400 life-vests leads to visual and audio displays centered on a 25-foot replica of a *Titanic* lifeboat. Use the touch-screen passenger and crew database. The original historic plan used during the British Titanic Inquiry—held one month after the sinking—has been restored and added to the display. Bought at auction by a private bidder for $220,000 (one of the most expensive pieces of *Titanic* memoribilia in the world), it was donated to the center in 2012.

Gallery 8: Sort fact from fiction amid the plethora of films, plays, song, poetry, novels and non-fiction works.

Gallery 9: Titanic Beneath dives to the wreck, two-and-a-half miles below the surface of the North Atlantic, by letting visitors stand on a transparent floor; nearby a film explores Robert Ballard's 1985 discovery of the wreck.

THE TITANIC TRAIL: TOURING THE LANDMARKS

Titanic's Dock and Pump-House

Running along Queen's Road, the new Titanic Trail passes the main landmarks of the giant Harland & Wolff shipyards, the actual birthplace of the *Titanic*. Note that several attractions can only be seen as part of an organized tour. (*See the sightseeing outfits listed in the Belfast Tour Options Close-Up box.*) For others, you can only view the exteriors. Several of these Titanic tours pass the largest waterfront development in Europe, the eponymously named Titanic Quarter. It is budgeted at £1 billion and is remaking the former shipyard region in the Queen's Island sector (accessed by the Queen Elizabeth or Queen's bridges), northeast of the city center, into a mini-city (15 years in the building) of repurposed Victorian harbor buildings, plus hotels and marinas.

Heart of Titanic Quarter

❶ Titanic Belfast Visitor Centre. Completed in March 2012, this world-class attraction showcases nine linked interpretive galleries that outline the dramatic saga as well as the wider theme of Belfast's seafaring heritage. Framed by "Titanica"—a life-size female sculpted by Rowan Gillespie—and a gigantic 15-ton Titanic sign, the entrance plaza is embedded with the world's largest map, dotted with LED lights that track the *Titanic*'s route. To do justice to the center, allow up to three hours. Audio guides in seven languages are available for rent. ✉ Titanic House, 6 Queen's Rd., Queen's Island, Titanic Quarter ☎ 028/9076–6386 (ticket inquiries: 028/9076–6399) ⊕ www.titanicbelfast.com ☞ £15.50 ⊙ Apr.–Sept., Mon.–Sun., 9–7; Oct.–Mar., daily 10–5.

❷ Titanic's Dock and Pump-House. Titanic's Dock was opened to the public in 2012 and, along with the Pump-House, can be accessed only as part of a tour. Steps lead down 14m (44 ft.) to the floor of the deck taking you to the liner's physical footprint where she last rested on dry ground.

❸ Titanic and Olympic Slipways. Set in the Titanic Quarter, these massive twin slipways at Queen's Yard, where RMS *Titanic* and *Olympic* were built, are a part of the walking trail, but they can best be studied on one of the harbor boat tours.

Samson and Goliath

SS *Nomadic*

A 1911 view of the Queen's Yard Slipways

The 30-foot-tall Reconstructed Bow, built to scale

❹ Harland & Wolff Drawing Offices. This long and elegant three-story former drawing office block (not open to the public) in sandstone and brick is where the concept design and detailed construction drawings for *Titanic* were laid out. Nearby is the Paint Hall, built in 1974, and now used to film international movies such as *City of Ember, MickyBo & Me* and *Breakfast on Pluto.*

❺ SS *Nomadic*, Hamilton Dock. Right next door to Titanic Belfast lies the tender ship to *Titanic* and last White Star Line ship in existence, SS *Nomadic*. It operated as a shuttle ship delivering 142 first-class passengers—including John Jacob Astor and Benjamin Guggenheim—to *Titanic* in Cherbourg (whose harbor was too small for the big liners to berth) before its departure for New York. Inside, interpretive galleries bring to life a time capsule of what it was like for workers and passengers. The ship is berthed at the Hamilton Graving Dock, and in 2013 was restored and opened for tours. ⌧ Hamilton Graving Dock, Hamilton

Rd., Titanic Quarter ☎ 028/9024–6609 ⊕ www. nomadicbelfast.com ⊙ Apr.–Sep, daily 10–6; Oct–Mar., daily 10–5. Check website for admission prices.

❻ Reconstructed Bow. *Titanic* enthusiasts will love a replica 30-ft. section of the bow of the liner, a new permanent "sculpture" unveiled in 2010. A team of engineers rebuilt the bow section using both modern and Edwardian techniques. It's on display on Queen's Island right beside the dock where the ship was built.

❼ Samson and Goliath. Towering over everything, the giant yet noble yellow gantry cranes provide a top photo-op for tourists; sadly you can't climb them as there is no public access. The Belfast Lough and Harbour Tour, run by Lagan Boat Company, gives visitors an insight into their history—a relatively recent addition to the yard as these replacements to the originals were built in 1969. ☎ 028/9033–0844 ⊕ www.titanicboattours. com ⌧ £12.50 ⊙ June–Sept., Sun., 3:30.

the wonderful Ginkgo biloba from China. The trail was set up by the Friends of Botanic Gardens and you can download a detailed version of it by visiting ⊕ *www.fobbg.co.uk*. ✉ *Stranmillis Rd., University Area* ☎ *028/9031–4762* ⊕ *www.belfastcity.gov.uk* 🖾 *Free* ☉ *Gardens daily dawn–dusk; Palm House Apr.–Sept., weekdays 10–5, weekends 1–5; Oct.–Mar., weekdays 10–4, weekends 1–4.*

Queen's University Belfast. Dominating University Road is Queen's University. The main buildings, modeled on Oxford's Magdalen College and designed by the ubiquitous Charles Lanyon, were built in 1849 in the Tudor Revival style. The long, handsome, redbrick-and-sandstone facade of the main building features large lead-glass windows, and is topped with three square towers and crenellations galore. University Square, really a terrace, is from the same era. The Seamus Heaney Library is named after the Ulster-born 1997 Nobel Prize–winning poet who died in 2013. The McClay Library in College Park features a multistory open atrium, 1.5 million volumes, and the Brian Friel Theatre, named in honor of one of Ireland's most illustrious playwrights. The C.S. Lewis reading room on the first floor has a replica of the wardrobe door used in the film *The Lion, the Witch, and the Wardrobe.* The Queen's Welcome Centre hosts a program of exhibitions and serves as a visitor information point. Guided tours are available but must be booked in advance. ✉ *University Rd., University Area* ☎ *028/9097–5252* ⊕ *www.qub.ac.uk* 🖾 *Free* ☉ *Welcome Centre weekdays 8–6, weekends 11–4.*

FAMILY

Fodor'sChoice

★

Ulster Museum. Right next door to the Botanic Gardens, the rejuvenated Ulster Museum, with its spacious light-filled atrium and polished steel, is a big hit with visitors. The museum's forte is the history and prehistory of Ireland using exhibitions to colorfully trace the rise of Belfast's crafts, trade, and industry, and offering a reflective photographic archive of the Troubles. In addition, the museum has a large natural history section, with a famed skeleton of the extinct Irish giant deer, and a trove of jewelry and gold ornaments recovered from the Spanish Armada vessel *Girona*, which sank off the Antrim coast in 1588. Take time to seek out the *Girona*'s stunning gold salamander studded with rubies and still dazzling after 400 years in the Atlantic. The museum includes a first-rate collection of 19th- and 20th-century art from Europe, Britain, and America. The art, history, and nature discovery zones are jam-packed with hands-on activities for children. Kids also enjoy the Peter the Polar Bear exhibit, and the famed Egyptian mummy, Takabuti. There's an innovative 360-degree light-and-sound immersive experience, museum shop, café, and restaurant. ■ **TIP→ Sunday morning is the quietest time to visit so get in early before the crowds, and take a picnic to the Gardens next door.** ✉ *Stranmillis Rd., University Area* ☎ *028/9044–0000* ⊕ *www.nmni.com/um* 🖾 *Free* ☉ *Tues.–Sun. 10–5. Closed Mon., except for Northern Irish holidays.*

DAY TRIPS FROM BELFAST

The sights along the Ards Peninsula and the north coast are a short drive from Belfast—an hour or less, perfect for day trips.

Belfast Castle. In 1934 this spectacularly baronial castle, built for the Marquis of Donegall in 1865, was passed to the Belfast Corporation. Although the castle functions primarily as a restaurant, it also houses, in the cellar, the Cave Hill Visitor Centre, which provides information about the castle's history and its natural surroundings in Cave Hill Country Park. Tours are self-guided and take in the reception rooms built by the Earls of Shaftesbury. For a fine introduction to the castle and its park, check out the excellent eight-minute video "Watching over Belfast." In fact, the best reason to visit the castle is to take a stroll in its ornamental gardens and then make the ascent to McArt's Fort. This promontory, at the top of sheer cliffs 1,200 feet above the city, affords an excellent view across Belfast. Take the path uphill from the parking lot, turn right at the next intersection of pathways, and then keep left as you journey up the steep-in-places hill to the fort. ■ TIP➜ After your walk, the Tavern Bar is a great place for drinks, snacks, and meals. ⊠ *Antrim Rd., 4 km (2½ miles) north of Belfast* ☎ *028/9077–6925* ⊕ *www.belfastcastle.co.uk* ✇ *Free* ⊙ *Visitor center, Tues.–Sat. 9 am–10 pm, Sun. and Mon. 9–6.*

Belfast Zoo. From the superstar Chilean flamingos and a silverback gorilla to spot-necked otters, West African chimps, and Goodfellow's tree kangaroos, you can enjoy the spectacle of more than 150 types of the world's most exotic creatures on a visit to Belfast Zoo. Great strides have transformed this place into a friendly environment for the animals. Note that it's on the steep side of Cave Hill and getting around the zoo involves a strenuous uphill walk for even the most energetic (not ideal for anyone with mobility problems)—a stroller would be advisable for small children. A popular attraction at the Rainforest House, a walk-through exhibition with dense tropical landscaping, is the toco toucan, with its huge, bright, yellow-orange bill. The zoo is also noted for its children's farm and underwater views of the resident penguins and sea lions. An Adventurers' Learning Centre opened in summer 2014. It includes sculptures linked to the zoo's animals as well as themed areas, such as a giraffe plain, meerkat mound, crocodile creek, hippo haunt, and gorilla glade. ■ TIP➜ The Treetop Tearoom affords the perfect view over Belfast Lough and is surrounded by the Malayan sun bear and cheetah. It's near Belfast Castle—just hop on a pink Metrobus (Number 1A, 1B, 1C, or 1D) at Donegall Square West, by City Hall. ⊠ *Antrim Rd.* ☎ *028/9077–6277* ⊕ *www.belfastzoo.co.uk* ✇ *£10* ⊙ *Apr.–Sept., daily 10–7; Oct.–Mar., daily 10–2:30.*

Mount Stewart. With an extensive £7 million conservation and renovation program slated for completion in 2015, new life is being breathed into Mount Stewart, the grandest stately home near Belfast now in the care of the National Trust. It was the country estate of the Marquesses of Londonderry, whose fame, or infamy, became known around the world thanks to the historical role played by the second Marquess. Known as Castlereagh, this Secretary of Ireland put down the Rising of 1798, helped forge the Act of Union, and killed himself by cutting his own throat. Mount Stewart was constructed in two stages where an earlier house had stood: George Dance designed the west facade (1804–05), and William Vitruvius Morrison designed the Neoclassical

Anchoring Freedom Corner are loyalist murals found on Lower Newtownards Road, near the center of Protestant East Belfast.

main part of the building (1845–49), complete with an awe-inspiring Grecian portico facade. The seventh Marchioness, Edith, managed to wave her wand over the interior—after a fashion: Chinese vases, Louis-Philippe tables, and Spanish oak chairs do their worst to clutter up the rooms here. Still, the house does have some noted 18th-century interiors, including the Central Hall and the grand staircase hung with one of George Stubbs's most famous portraits, that of the celebrated racehorse Hambletonian, after he won one of the most prominent contests of the 18th century—this is perhaps the greatest in situ setting for a painting in Ireland. Since 2012, a team of builders, conservation architects, and specialist engineers and joiners, assisted by more than 40 local volunteers, have carried out important repair and restoration work on the building and its contents, including valuable paintings and other treasures. The result is that eight rooms previously unseen are now open to the public and feature on the 75-minute guided tour.

On the grounds, don't miss the octagonal folly Temple of the Winds (open only Sunday 2–5), a copy of a similar structure in Athens, and the remarkable bathhouse and pool at the end of the wooded peninsula just before the entrance to the grounds. The *Mount Stewart Garden Guide* costs £2.50 and shows the scale and diversity of the 18 named garden walks—you'll need more than one day to explore them and the exotic plants that have survived because of Strangford Lough's mild microclimate. ■**TIP➔ Opening times change here—it's prudent to phone ahead or log on to the website for the complete schedule. The house is open from noon every day and visitors have a choice of tours and times. The last tour is 4 pm.** ⊠ *Portaferry Rd., Newtownards, Co. Down*

Belfast's Wall Murals

In Northern Ireland they say the Protestants make the money and the Catholics make the art, and as with all clichés, there is some truth in it. It's a truth that will become clear as you look up at the gable walls of blue-collar areas of Belfast on which the two communities—Catholic and Protestant—have expressed themselves in colorful murals that have given rise to one of the more quirky tours of the city.

Although the wildly romantic Catholic murals often aspire to the heights of "Sistine Chapel lite," those in Protestant areas (like the tough, no-nonsense Shankill and the Newtownards Road) are more workmanlike efforts that sometimes resemble war comics without the humor. It was not always this way.

In Protestant areas, murals were once painted by skilled coach builders to mark the July 12 celebrations of the defeat of the Catholic King James by King William at the Battle of the Boyne. As such, they typically depicted William resplendent in freshly laundered scarlet tunic and plumed cap, sitting on a white stallion that has mastered the art of walking on water. On the banks of the Boyne sits a mildly disheveled James, the expression on his face making him look as if he has just eaten an overdose of anchovies. Other popular themes in Protestant areas are the Red Hand of Ulster, symbolizing the founding of the province, and, on Carnmore Street, the 13 Protestant apprentice boys shutting the gates of Derry against King James in 1688, leading to the famous siege.

More recently, though, Protestant murals have taken on a grimmer air, and typical subjects include walleyed paramilitaries perpetually standing firm against increasing liberalism, nationalism, and all the other isms that Protestants see eroding their stern, Bible-driven way of life. Nationalist murals, on the other hand, first sprang up in areas like the Falls Road in 1981, when IRA inmates of the Maze prison began a hunger strike in an unsuccessful bid to be recognized by the British government as political prisoners rather than common criminals. Ten died, and the face of the most famous, Bobby Sands, looks down now from a gable wall on the Falls Road alongside the words "Our revenge will be the laughter of our children."

Since then, themes of freedom from oppression and a rising nationalist confidence have expressed themselves in murals that romantically and surreally mix and match images from the *Book of Kells*, the Celtic Mist mock-heroic posters of Irish artist Jim Fitzpatrick, assorted phoenixes rising from ashes, and revolutionaries clad in splendidly idiosyncratic sombreros and bandannas from ideological battlegrounds in Mexico and South America. Irish words and phrases that you will see springing up regularly include the much-used slogan *Tiocfaidh ár lá* (pronounced *chuck-y ohr law* and meaning "Our day will come") and the simple cry *Saoirse* (pronounced *seer-she*), meaning "Freedom."

The murals in both Protestant and Catholic areas are safe to view in daylight and outside the sensitive week of the July 12 marches by Protestant Orangemen. However, the most sensible way to view them would be to take a guided tour with Belfast City Sightseeing or one of the other bus or taxi tour companies.

☎ *028/4278–8387* ⊕ *www.national trust.org.uk* ✉ *£7.30* ⊙ *Gardens: daily 10–6. House: by guided tour, Mar.–Oct., daily noon–6; closed Nov.–Feb.*

Grace Neill's Bar. Reputed to be the oldest pub in Ireland, Grace Neill's served its first pint in 1611 and has hosted such luminaries as Peter the Great, Franz Liszt, and John Keats. Behind the original pub, a cubby under the stairs with bar stools, is a larger bar where you can try slow-roasted steak-and-Guinness pie, Gracie's seafood pie, or chicken tagliatelle. There's live music on Friday and Saturday nights. There's no food on Monday—it's the chef's day off. ✉ *33 High St., 22 km (13 miles) from Mount Stewart, Co. Down* ☎ *028/9188–4595* ⊕ *www.graceneills.com.*

DORMANT ED ISN'T DEAD

The Ulster Museum's showstopper, *Edmontosaurus*, is the most complete dinosaur fossil on display in Ireland. "Ed," as he's affectionately known, roamed America about 70 million years ago and would have looked a bit like a plucked turkey. At 20 feet long, Ed has settled into his 21st-century home and is now a big attraction.

Fodor'sChoice ★   **Ulster Folk and Transport Museum.** Devoted to the province's social history, the excellent Ulster Folk and Transport Museum vividly brings Northern Ireland's past to life. The museum first invites you to visit Ballycultra—a typical Ulster town of the early 1900s—which comes alive thanks to costumed guides who practice such regional skills as lace making, sampler making, spinning, weaving, wood turning, forge work, printing, open-hearth cooking, carpentry, basket making, and needlework. The setting is evocative: a score of reconstructed buildings moved here from around the region, including a traditional weaver's dwelling, terraces of Victorian town houses, an 18th-century country church, a village flax mill, a farmhouse, and a rural school. The museum also houses special collections and archives of interest to researchers on topics such as folklife, Ulster dialect, an oral history of linen, and radio and television archives of BBC Northern Ireland. Across the main road (by footbridge) is the beautifully designed Transport Museum, where exhibits include locally built airplanes and motorcycles, as well as the iconoclastic car produced by former General Motors whiz that John DeLorean in his Belfast factory in 1982. The museum is on the 70 acres of Cultra Manor, encircled by a larger park and recreation area. ✉ *153 Bangor Rd., 11 km (7 miles) east of Belfast on A2, Cultra, Co. Down* ☎ *028/9042–8428* ⊕ *www.nmni.com/uftm* ✉ *£7.50 single-site ticket, £9 dual-site ticket* ⊙ *Mar.–Sept., Tues.–Sun. 10–5; Oct.–Feb., Tues.–Fri. 10–4, weekends 11–4; last entry 1½ hrs before closing; public holiday Mon. 10–5.*

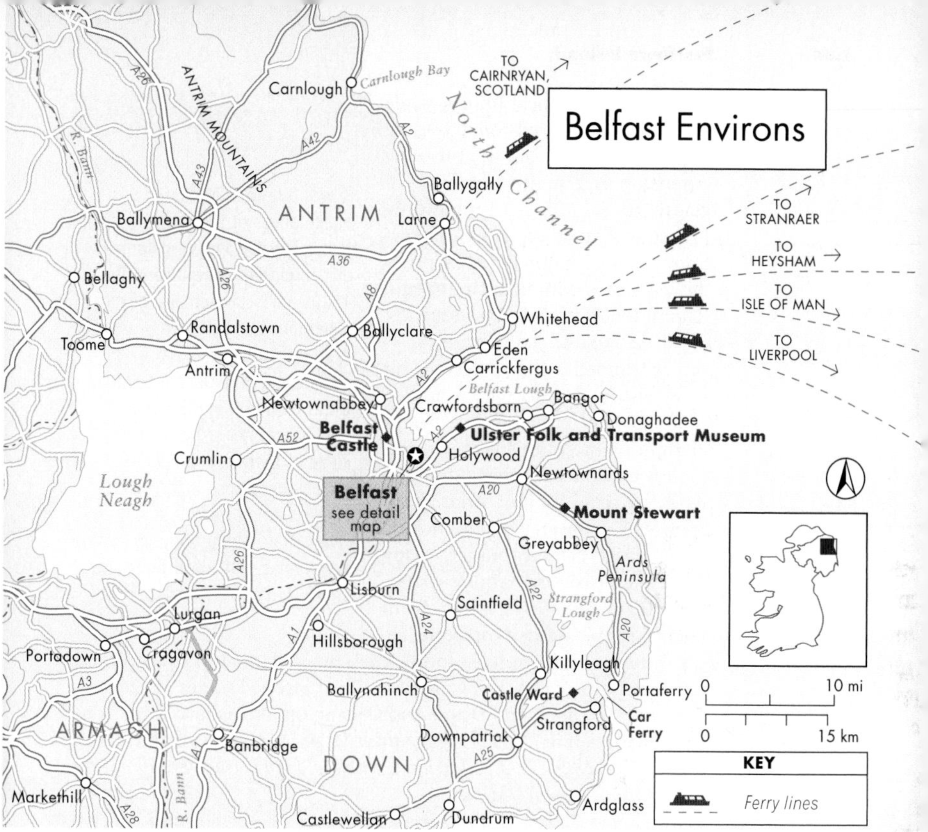

WHERE TO EAT

CENTRAL DISTRICT AND GOLDEN MILE

$ 🍴 **Coppi.** The small dishes known as cicchetti, beloved of Venetian bars and a counterpart to tapas, are drawing the crowds to Coppi, one of the new breed of restaurants that has sprung up in the Cathedral Quarter. Named after a world-champion Italian racing cyclist, Angelo Fausto Coppi, it serves flavorful Mediterranean cuisine amid modern industrial decor. Entrées might include pasta (the one with *guanciale* is masterful), sea bass, risotto and mushroom puff, and steak Florentine. The tiramisu is deliciously light; there's a choice of eating at the counter on high chairs or at cozy booths with rustic wooden tables. No surprise that Italian wines feature prominently, with Chianti, Valpolicella Ripasso, and Montepulciano leading the way. Candles flicker in dim light while the statue of St. Anne salutes the diners from her perch in the buzzy square right beside the MAC. [$] *Average main: £13* ✉ *St Anne's Sq., Cathedral Quarter* ☎ *028/9031–1959* 🌐 *www.coppi.co.uk.*

ITALIAN

$$$ 🍴 **Deanes Restaurant.** For more than 20 years Michael Deane has been the leader of the Belfast culinary pack, and in 2014 he reinvented his flagship operation with no fewer than three distinct restaurants in one building. The Meat Locker, which has 80 covers, is a new beef-driven grill room inspired by London's Hawksmoor steak-house chain.

EUROPEAN

Fodor's Choice ★

Menus come on meat hooks, while a "salt wall" is used for dry-aging locally sourced beef. In the new extension is the upscale Eipic, a classy round table, evening-only (Tuesday–Saturday) 20-seater restaurant and Champagne bar offering a £60 six-course tasting menu. Running beside these two eateries, in an elongated conservatory, is the rebranded seafood restaurant Love Fish. A less formal approach is taken here, capturing a bright Hamptons or south European feel with Brentood steel chairs and artwork by local painter Brian John Spencer. Lunchtime staples include a soy-glazed salmon burger, crispy fried monkfish or *moules frites,* with main courses starting from £6.50. Truly one of Northern Ireland's most extraordinary food experiences. The Deanes empire also includes Deanes Deli Vin Café in Bedford Street, Deanes at Queens in the university area, and Deane and Decano on the Lisburn Road (check website for details). [$] *Average main: £19* ✉ *28–40 Howard St., Central District* ☎ *028/9033–1134* 🌐 *www.michaeldeane.co.uk* 🕒 *Eipic restaurant closed Sun. and Mon.*

THE GREENING OF BELFAST

It was due to Edith, the 7th Marchioness of Londonderry, that Mount Stewart was transformed into a garden showplace in the 1920s. Taking advantage of the salubrious microclimate of the Ards Peninsula, she created, in short order, a Shamrock Garden, Dodo Garden (note the stone figures that honor her close circle of friends—the "Warlock" is Winston Churchill), and Lady Mairi's Garden, complete with a "Mary, Mary, Quite Contrary" statue surrounded with silver bells and cockleshells.

$$ MODERN IRISH Fodor's Choice ★

🍴 **The Ginger Bistro.** Modern Irish classics with an international twist attract the foodie crowd to this cheerful bistro just off Great Victoria Street. A short but perfectly balanced menu emphasizes locally sourced seafood and lean meats. Fishy dinner highlights include plaice, sea bass, or fillet of hake; escalope of chicken with a Merguez sausage or braised-then-roasted belly of pork with fennel are popular. But the flavorsome fried squid far outsells anything else on the menu, and don't forget the parsnip chips to go with it. For lunchgoers in a hurry there is an excellent-value menu offering haddock and chips, fish pie, and rib-eye steak. The wines are outstanding, or try malt-flavored handcrafted Belfast ales or lagers from the Mourne Mountains, made with Saaz hops and yeast from the Old Belfast Brewery. Desserts include the delectable crème brûlée with raspberry compote, the soft-centered chocolate cake with berries, and the unforgettable sticky-toffee pudding. [$] *Average main: £16* ✉ *7–8 Hope St., Golden Mile* ☎ *028/9024–4421* 🌐 *www.gingerbistro.com* 🕒 *Closed Sun. No lunch Mon.*

$$$ EUROPEAN Fodor's Choice ★

🍴 **The Great Room.** Inside the lavish Merchant Hotel, beneath the grand dome of this former bank's great hall and Ireland's biggest chandelier, you'll find the perfect setting for a memorable dinner of adventurous European fare. Exceptional dishes include glazed turbot, roast partridge breasts, and salt-aged rib of beef, or, for vegetarians, pappardelle pasta with black truffles and olive oil. The wonderful extravaganza of profiterole swans swimming delicately in a small lake of chocolate sauce is

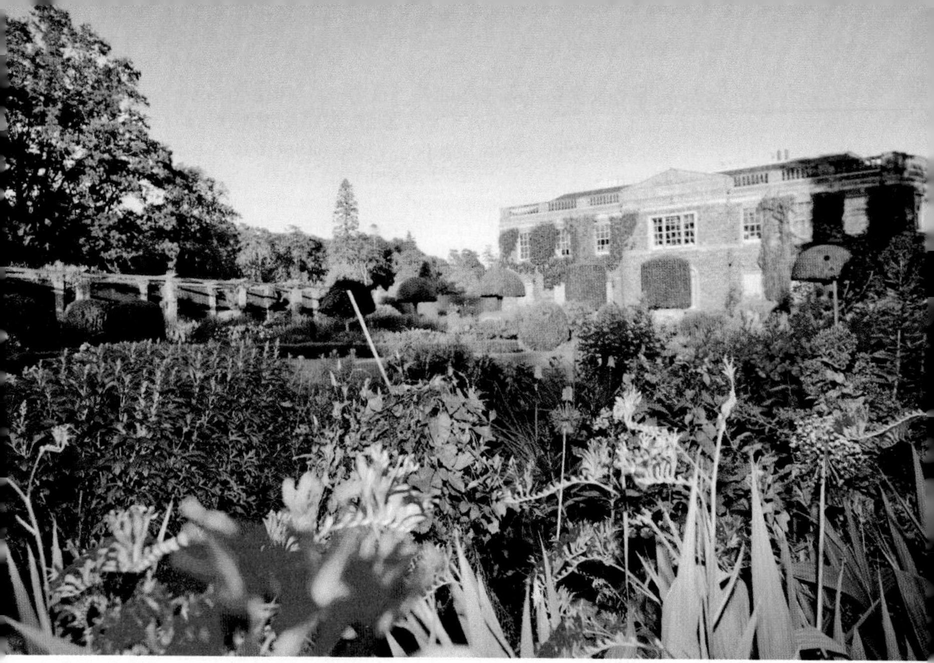

In the early 20th century, the marchioness of Londonderry remade her Mount Stewart estate into the horticultural showplace of Northern Ireland.

just one delight found on the dessert trolley. First-class service in truly opulent surroundings makes this restaurant worth a detour. The two-course dinner is £19.50 and three courses are £24.50 and are exceptional value considering the surroundings. There's also a tasting menu at £85 with wine or £65 without. [$] *Average main: £21* ✉ *35 Waring St., Cathedral Quartert* ☎ *028/9023–4888* 🌐 *www.themerchanthotel.com.*

$ MODERN IRISH 🍴 **James Street South Bar & Grill.** Devotees refer to it as JSS, and locally sourced food comes with a magical weave of flavors in this city center big hitter. Based in a former linen mill, exposed brick walls and leather banquettes set the scene for a terrific appetizer of cured beef with Stilton fritters. Mainstays are steaks—choose from rump, sirloin, rib eye, or beef fillet—and the Comber potatoes, characterized by their sweet buttery flavor and harvested earlier than other potatoes; May and June are peak months to enjoy them. Such is their importance they have been given a European designation of protection: something that JSS should also have. [$] *Average main: £13* ✉ *21 James St. S, Central District* ☎ *028/9560–0700* 🌐 *www.belfastbargrill.co.uk.*

$ IRISH 🍴 **Long's.** Hearty eaters adore Long's which in 2014 celebrated 100 years of serving fish-and-chips in its completely basic Athol Street premises, close to the city center. Garbage collectors, business execs, schoolboys from the nearby Royal Belfast Academical Institution, and patrons from every sector in between flock here for the secret-batter-recipe fish, served with chips, bread and butter, and a mug of tea. Best value in town for what you get. Long's closes at 6:30 pm. [$] *Average main: £8* ✉ *39 Athol St., Golden Mile* ☎ *028/9032–1848* 💳 *No credit cards* 🕓 *Closed Sun. No dinner.*

$ MODERN IRISH Fodor's Choice ★ 🍴 **Made in Belfast: Cathedral Quarter.** Touted as "violently chic" yet with a bohemian, casual vibe, and with a menu packed with classic old favorites, this self-styled "restolounge" in the happening Cathedral Quarter is one of Belfast's buzziest bistros. Decorated in a giant mishmash of vintage lamps and fabrics, and 50s collectibles, this outlet follows the Cuisinart school of restaurant design, mix n' matching all sorts of antiques and objects, including a ceiling adorned with glossy magazine photographs. It's truly one of Belfast's most eye-popping decors. The typewritten menu, set on clipboards, showcases "seasonal" and retro dishes, best downed with one of the fab cocktails such as Apple Poshmopolitan or an Irish martini (made with Jameson's whiskey and cloves). Start with the pear-and-goat-cheese fritters or delectable tomato jam and Guinness wheaten bread. Mains average £11, with the choice ranging from Irish venison pie to champ, a mix of mashed potatoes with butter, milk, and chopped spring onion. And you thought New York City was hip! [$] *Average main: £11* ✉ *23 Talbot St., Cathedral Quarter* ☎ *028/9024–4107* 🌐 *www.madeinbelfastni.com.*

$ IRISH Fodor's Choice ★ 🍴 **The Morning Star.** Halfway down a narrow lane is the 19th-century Morning Star, one of the city's most historic pubs, first built as a coaching stop for the Belfast to Dublin post. There's a traditional bar downstairs and a cozy velvet and wood-panel restaurant upstairs. On the menu you might find venison and game in winter, lamb in spring, and grilled haddock with dark rum or roast Antrim pork in summer. Also notable is the steak menu; you'd be hard-pressed to find a larger assortment of aged-beef cuts. And they are enormous: sizzling steaks, some up to 64 ounces, arrive at the table in red-hot cast-iron skillets and are served with a flourish by the friendly staff. There's also a great value buffet at which you select from chicken, seafood, and pork. This place tends to the pangs of visitors, on Sunday enticing Australians with a Jolly pie and a pint for £6, and providing BBQ sauce daily to keep the Americans happy. [$] *Average main: £9* ✉ *17–19 Pottinger's Entry, Central District* ☎ *028/9023–5986* 🌐 *themorningstarbar.com.*

$ SEAFOOD 🍴 **Mourne Seafood Bar.** Connoisseurs of fresh fish and shellfish will love Mourne Seafood, hidden down a side street and established as a firm favorite. Mussels, oysters, and cockles are sourced from the owner's shellfish beds in Carlingford Lough while fresh seafood comes direct each day from the local ports of Annalong and Kilkeel. Daily specials might include seafood dumplings or seared king scallops with butternut squash risotto and crispy sage. The dogfish, hake, and sea bream are all done to perfection, but the standout dish for many is the gurnard, a whole fish served with bacon and clam velouté. To complement your meal try a glass of Mourne Oyster Stout (don't ask for Guinness here) made by the Whitewater brewery in Kilkeel. Resonant with rich hop flavors, its ingredients include roasted barley, rolled oats, and chocolate and black malts. [$] *Average main: £14* ✉ *34–36 Bank St., Central District* ☎ *028/9024–8544* 🌐 *www.mourneseafood.com* ⏲ *No dinner Sun.*

$ EUROPEAN 🍴 **The Northern Whig.** Housed in an elegant former newspaper building in Belfast's historic Cathedral Quarter, the Northern Whig is spacious and stylish. Three 30-foot-high statues of Soviet heroes that once topped Communist Party headquarters in Prague dominate the wood-and-leather interior. In the evenings, one wall slides away so you can watch a jazz band, or a DJ playing laid-back blues, soul, or retro music. The food is brasserie style—not astonishing, but good. The environment, the wine selection, and the bar are the main draws, though. [$] *Average main: £12* ✉ *2–10 Bridge St., Central District* ☎ *028/9050–9888* 🌐 *www.thenorthernwhig.com.*

$$ MODERN IRISH Fodor's Choice ★

🍴 **Ox Restaurant.** In a city with a plethora of new restaurants jostling for business, the less-is-more Ox has emerged as one of, if not *the,* best of the lot since opening in 2013. Minimalism rules at lunch with small plates (£10) of salmon or beef served without carbs; great if you're following a diet but, if not, then follow up with the lemon polenta cake. Dinner entrées—unadulterated with butter or cream—could be châteaubriand, rabbit saddle, Rademon estate pigeon, brill, or perch. Gasp-worthy five-course tasting menus are on offer for dinner on weekends with European wine pairing matched to each course from the amuse-bouche to the Valrhona chocolate. You'd be hard-pressed to eat this well, for so little money, in such relaxed surroundings anywhere else in Northern Ireland or indeed the whole island. And to cap it all, views through the large windows stretch over the River Lagan to the glowing 56 foot-tall Ring of Thanksgiving beacon by the Scottish artist Andy Scott. [$] *Average main: £18* ✉ *1 Oxford St., Central District* ☎ *028/9031–4121* 🌐 *www.oxbelfast.com* 🕘 *Closed Sun. and Mon.*

$$ CHINESE

🍴 **Red Panda.** The set lunch box at £7.50 is a real winner at this long-established central eatery. It's made up of a multi-combination dish with starter of fresh fruit or salad, and a main course dish of your choice with rice. In the evening the set dinner might include crispy aromatic duck pancakes as an appetizer followed by Kung Pao chicken, or roasted duck Cantonese style. Seafood dishes, such as monkfish in Mongolian sauce or stir-fried king prawns with cashew nuts, are especially popular. This venue (there's another in Odyssey Arena complex) is large, spacious, and modern. [$] *Average main: £16* ✉ *60 Great Victoria St., Golden Mile* ☎ *028/9080–8700* 🌐 *www.theredpanda.co.uk* 🕘 *No lunch Sat.*

$ IRISH

🍴 **The Terrace at Robinson & Cleaver.** Stunning views, thoughtfully produced food, and attentive aproned staff are the reasons to eat at The Terrace, a landmark six-story sandstone building opposite city hall. Older Belfastians remember the name Robinson & Cleaver from its 20th-century days as one of Ireland's most famous department stores. Though still popular with well-heeled ladies, it's been reinvented as a classy restaurant whose hallmark is elegant simplicity. **TIP→ Ask for a terrace table (the halogen heaters will keep you warm on a chilly day) from where you can watch the progress of city life as you deliberate over slow-cooked pork belly, Inch Abbey rib-eye steak, or wild-mushroom-and-sage risotto.** Downstairs in the bright Urban Deli, sharing plates at lunchtime include a Taste of Ulster with Belfast ham, Oakwood cheese, and plum and apple chutney; from the Express menu you can order a soup-and-sandwich combo, hot deli sandwich, or chicken Caeser salad. Kitchen closes at 9:30 pm. [$] *Average main: £12* ✉ *Cleaver House, 1–3 Donegall Sq. N, Central District* ☎ *028/9031–2666*

🌐 *www.robinsonandcleaver.com* ⏲ *Terrace restaurant closed for dinner Sun.–Tues.*

$ BRITISH 🍴 **Yard Bird.** The humble chicken is the raison d'être of Yard Bird, at the site of a linen warehouse built in the 1750s. Start your visit with an aperitif in the Dirty Onion bar downstairs (ask the bartender about the pub's name) which retains the wonderfully evocative original tree-trunk-sized beams, bare floors, and walls of the 18th-century past. The faultless avocado salad with cos leaves, a dressing of lime and lemon juice with olive oil, and finely spiced tomato salsa is a smashing warm-up act. Free-range chickens, marinated overnight in lemon, buttermilk, and paprika, are cooked on the rotisserie, then cut in half and shared between two. Return to the Dirty Onion for a nightcap; with its smoky turf fire, timber decor, and craft beers from Europe and North America, it has a speakeasy feel and is vibrant with live traditional and bluegrass music every night of the week. [$] *Average main: £14* ✉ *3 Hill St., Cathedral Quarter* ☎ *028/9024–3712* 🌐 *www.yardbirdbelfast.com.*

$$ JAPANESE 🍴 **Zen.** The standout dish at Belfast's finest Japanese restaurant is the rare (and expensive) Chilean sea bass, also known as the Patagonian toothfish, served tender on a hot plate with spring onion, ginger, and chilies. Choose between wooden booths, or, if you're prepared to hunker down on the floor Japanese-style, the traditional dining area. Handpick your meal at the downstairs sushi bar, or opt for a discreet table for two under the serene gaze of (reputedly) Ireland's largest Buddha. Finish with a Japanese malt whiskey: Nikka Black is smoky and mellow and will round off the perfect dinner. ■ **TIP→ For a very late lunch (6–7:30 pm) Geisha Fridays are fun; guests receive a complimentary bottle of Asahi beer or glass of house wine with their meal.** [$] *Average main: £16* ✉ *55–59 Adelaide St., behind City Hall, Central District* ☎ *028/9023–2244* 🌐 *www.zenbelfast.co.uk* ⏲ *No lunch Sat.*

UNIVERSITY AREA

$ IRISH 🍴 **Drennans Restaurant.** A magnificently restored stained-glass window featuring St. Cecilia (the patron saint of musicians) playing her pipes and looking down on diners sets the mood in this restaurant run by Lawrence Delaney, who has years of experience pleasing hungry customers. Delaney is interested in Irish history and named his restaurant after Dr. William Drennan, who coined the sobriquet the "Emerald Isle." Reminiscent of a Parisian-style bistro, it offers an early-bird menu (£12.95 for two courses) laden with fillet and rib-eye steak, buttered chicken, pork belly, lamb, and fish. Options from the regular dinner menu include sea bass over tagliatelle with asparagus and Parmesan shavings. For dessert, the warm sticky toffee pudding in butterscotch sauce will linger long on the taste buds. The restaurant is BYOB. As befits a place with a musical saint, each night a pianist switches effortlessly between blues, pop, and jazz. [$] *Average main: £14* ✉ *43 University Rd., University Area* ☎ *028/9020–4556* ✍ *Reservations essential.*

EAST BELFAST

$ EUROPEAN 🍴 **Neill's Hill Cafe & Brasserie.** Named after a long-forgotten railway station in East Belfast, this casual brasserie has established itself as a calming spot in buzzy Ballyhackmore, where lunchtimes can get crowded.

Dishes change monthly but typical main courses for dinner are burgers, steaks, pork fillet, and sea bass from Walter Ewing, Belfast's top fish supplier. Brunches include a malted waffle with fruit or bacon and maple syrup, scrambled eggs with Irish smoked salmon, or granola with fresh fruit and natural yogurt. Small plates such as quail scotch eggs with haggis, monkfish involtini (with dates and bacon), and hot wings with a cool dip, are an excellent value. Since you're in the area where they built the RMS *Titanic*, relax with a bottle of Titanic Iceberg beer, a Belfast Blonde ale, or, if you prefer, Fentiman's Curiosity Cola and Shandy. [$] *Average main: £14* ✉ *229 Upper Newtownards Rd., East Belfast* ☎ *028/9065–0079* 🌐 *www.neillshill.com.*

CARBING UP

When it comes to food, Northern Ireland is most famed (or notorious) for its Ulster Fry, a fried-up, carbohydrate blowout of a breakfast that is a cardiologist's nightmare. Sausage, bacon, eggs, black pudding, fried soda bread, and potato bread (and perhaps a grilled tomato or fried mushrooms) all make a meal that sounds as dangerous to your health as bungee jumping without a rope. After a night on the Guinness, however, you'll understand why this breakfast is so popular: it makes a great cure for a hangover.

WHERE TO STAY

CENTRAL DISTRICT AND GOLDEN MILE

$ HOTEL 🏨 **Benedict's of Belfast.** Friendly, lively, and convenient, Benedict's looms large on Bradbury Place—guest rooms on the second floor are bright and colorful, and have wooden floors; the simple but comfortable carpeted rooms on the third floor are darker, with an Asian influence. **Pros:** buzzy; great inexpensive dining. **Cons:** guests have experienced late check-in due to rooms not being ready; some parts of hotel show wear and tear. [$] *Rooms from: £75* ✉ *7–21 Bradbury Pl., Golden Mile* ☎ *028/9059–1999* 🌐 *www.benedictshotel.co.uk* 🛏 *32 rooms* 🍴 *Breakfast.*

$$$ B&B/INN 🏨 **Holiday Inn Belfast.** A short stroll from the city center, the Holiday Inn offers outstanding facilities at a reasonable price with a huge choice of restaurants, bars, and cafés in the immediate vicinity. **Pros:** value deals; health club and facilities are top-notch; TV celebrities often spotted in front of nearby BBC studios. **Cons:** lines at busy times at check-in and checkout; no car-parking spaces available. [$] *Rooms from: £140* ✉ *22 Ormeau Ave., Golden Mile* ☎ *028/9023–8511* 🌐 *www.hibelfasthotel.co.uk* 🛏 *170 rooms* 🍴 *Multiple meal plans.*

$ HOTEL 🏨 **Jurys Inn Belfast.** This inn has a spacious lobby and is within walking distance of the main city-center attractions—pubs, cinemas, shops, restaurants, and the Grand Opera House are all nearby. **Pros:** reasonably priced cocktails; staff helpful and friendly; spacious rooms. **Cons:** reception lobby is dark and corridors dimly lighted; lack of car parking. [$] *Rooms from: £75* ✉ *Fisherwick Pl., at Great Victoria St., Golden Mile* ☎ *028/9053–3500* 🌐 *www.jurysinns.com* 🛏 *190 rooms* 🍴 *Breakfast.*

$$$$ HOTEL Fodor's Choice ★ **Malmaison.** Malmaison certainly lives up to the claim to be "a hotel that dares to be different"—this transformed 19th-century grain warehouse now features low-slung, soft velour sofas, a chaise longue, and velvet drapes, creating a modern Gothic feel. **Pros:** imaginative and glamorous; five-minute walk to major Belfast shopping. **Cons:** lack of car parking; if you don't like the bar's subtle darkness, bring a flashlight. [$] *Rooms from: £180* ✉ *34–38 Victoria St., Central District* ☎ *028/9022–0200* 🌐 *www.malmaison.com* 🛏 *62 rooms, 2 suites* 🍴 *No meals.*

$$$ HOTEL Fodor's Choice ★ **The Merchant Hotel.** A mix of Victorian grandeur and Art Deco–inspired modernity, this hotel—regarded by some as Ireland's most spectacular—was built as the headquarters of Ulster Bank in the mid-19th century and since opening in 2006 has led the way in style and sophistication. **Pros:** opulent, with attentive reception and friendly bar staff; deep King Koil mattresses leave a mellow afterglow; history and architecture buffs will love it. **Cons:** revelers from pubs and clubs in the surrounding streets detract from the internal serenity; at £15, breakfast room service is for high rollers only. [$] *Rooms from: £160* ✉ *16 Skipper St., Cathedral Quarter* ☎ *028/9023–4888* 🌐 *www.themerchanthotel.com* 🛏 *63 rooms, 5 suites* 🍴 *No meals.*

$$$ HOTEL **Ten Square.** You don't get much more downtown or contemporary than this fashionable boutique hotel (a former post office) right behind City Hall. **Pros:** luxurious surroundings; attention to detail in the attractive rooms; super-king beds; convivial feel to the Grill Room. **Cons:** the noisy bar can be sweaty; sit outside, but only if you don't mind the traffic fumes. [$] *Rooms from: £139* ✉ *10 Donegall Sq. S, Golden Mile* ☎ *028/9024–1001* 🌐 *www.tensquare.co.uk* 🛏 *22 rooms* 🍴 *Multiple meal plans.*

UNIVERSITY AREA

$ B&B/INN **All Seasons.** Enjoying a superb location on the fashionable Lisburn Road in the south of the city, this spot is steps from some of the city's most stylish boutiques and trendiest bars. **Pros:** top-notch location for exploring the Lisburn Road; warm, welcoming, and inviting owner. **Cons:** family rooms can be a tight squeeze; few toiletries and no hair dryers. [$] *Rooms from: £50* ✉ *356 Lisburn Rd.* ☎ *028/9068–2814* 🌐 *www.allseasonsbelfast.com* 🛏 *7 rooms, 1 apartment* 🍴 *Breakfast.*

$ HOTEL **Dukes at Queens.** Although retaining its distinguished redbrick Victorian facade, the inside of this handsome hotel on bohemian Botanic Avenue has been revamped in a cool contemporary style. **Pros:** stylish, with excellent service; good value for money; convenient location. **Cons:** area is thronged at lunchtime with office workers and even busier at night—noise is an ever-present reality. [$] *Rooms from: £70* ✉ *65–67 University St.* ☎ *028/9023–6666* 🌐 *www.dukesatqueens.com* 🛏 *32 rooms* 🍴 *Breakfast.*

$ HOTEL **Madison's Hotel.** Surrounded by the shops and cafés of tree-lined Botanic Avenue, this gracious hotel is an ideal base for an exploration of Belfast. **Pros:** location; friendly service; Madison's Irish-whiskey–and–white chocolate-cheesecake. **Cons:** late-night student rowdiness on Botanic Avenue; some standard rooms on the smallish side. [$] *Rooms from: £78* ✉ *59–63 Botanic Ave.* ☎ *028/9050–9800* 🌐 *www.*

madisonshotel.com ⇆ *35 rooms* 🍴 *Breakfast.*

AROUND BELFAST

$$$$ HOTEL Fodor's Choice ★ **Culloden Estate & Spa.** This imposingly grand vision in Belfast stone presides over the forested slopes of the Holywood hills and the busy waters of Belfast Lough—antiques and silk-and-velvet fabrics grace guest rooms both in the original section and in a newer wing; all rooms have fine views. **Pros:** building oozes character and personality; top-class service. **Cons:** restaurant can be stuffy; massages, manicures, and vintage champagne don't come cheap. [$] *Rooms from: £240* ✉ *142 Bangor Rd., 8 km (5 miles) east of Belfast on A2, Holywood* ☎ *028/9042–1066* 🌐 *www.hastingshotels.com/culloden-estate-and-spa* ⇆ *105 rooms, 22 suites* 🍴 *Multiple meal plans.*

$$ HOTEL **Dunadry Hotel.** This spacious, whitewashed former mill on 10 acres of land is a hotel of considerable charm. **Pros:** historic location; large bedrooms; 10-minute drive from Belfast International Airport. **Cons:** those wedding parties can get boisterous. [$] *Rooms from: £90* ✉ *2 Islandreagh Dr., off M2, Dunadry* ☎ *028/9443–4343* 🌐 *www.dunadry.com* ⇆ *80 rooms* 🍴 *No meals.*

$$$ HOTEL **Hilton Templepatrick Hotel & Country Club.** A convenient location for the international airport as well as many of Belfast and County Antrim's leading visitor attractions, the Hilton is ideally situated. **Pros:** relaxing surroundings; great location near the airport and short distance from Belfast; championship golf course. **Cons:** bland chain lacks individual character; large parties equal noisy nights. [$] *Rooms from: £120* ✉ *6 km (4 miles) from Belfast Airport on A57, Castle Upton Estate, Templepatrick* ☎ *028/9443–5500* 🌐 *www.hilton.com/templepatrick* ⇆ *129 rooms, 1 suite* 🍴 *No meals.*

$ B&B/INN Fodor's Choice ★ **The Old Inn.** Set in the village of Crawfordsburn, this 1614 coach inn, reputedly Ireland's oldest, certainly looks the part: it's pure 17th-century with a sculpted thatch roof, half doors, and leaded-glass windows. **Pros:** a proverbial step back in time; lots of character; comfortable rooms. **Cons:** slow service; breakfasts not always up to snuff. [$] *Rooms from: £80* ✉ *15 Main St., 16 km (10 miles) east of Belfast on A2, Crawfordsburn* ☎ *028/9185–3255* 🌐 *www.theoldinn.com* ⇆ *31 rooms, 8 suites* 🍴 *Breakfast.*

$$$ B&B/INN **Rayanne House.** Since the 100th anniversary of the sinking of the *RMS Titanic* in 2012 this country house has enjoyed unparalleled success by recreating the liner's "last meal," a highlight of any stay here. **Pros:** well-appointed bright and comfortable rooms; handsome furnishings, tastefully presented; the *Titanic* dinner is a true conversation piece. **Cons:** Holywood nightlife is limited to a few bars. [$] *Rooms from: £125* ✉ *60 Demesne Rd., 8 km (5 miles) east of Belfast on A2, Holywood* ☎ *028/9042–5859* 🌐 *www.rayannehouse.com* ⇆ *11 rooms* 🍴 *Multiple meal plans.*

HIDEOUT HISTORY

If you're lucky enough to stay in the oldest parts of the Old Inn, you still may be able to uncover a secret hiding place for contraband, as smugglers, like the famous highwayman Dick Turpin, made this one of their favored homes away from home.

$ ⬚ **Roseleigh House.** This Victorian guesthouse on a tree-filled avenue in
B&B/INN residential south Belfast is a friendly option. **Pros:** the breakfasts are
healthy and robust; terrific suburban location well away from city-
center noise and just a 15-minute bus ride into town. **Cons:** no bar,
but around the corner on the fashionable Ormeau Road you'll find
pubs aplenty. $ *Rooms from: £80* ✉ *19 Rosetta Park, South Uni-
versity* ☎ *028/9064–4414* ⊕ *www.roseleighhouse.co.uk* ⇥ *6 rooms*
⦿| *Breakfast.*

NIGHTLIFE AND THE ARTS

NIGHTLIFE

Belfast has dozens of pubs packed with relics of the Victorian and
Edwardian periods. Although pubs typically close around 11:30 pm,
many city-center–Golden Mile nightclubs stay open until 1 am.

GOLDEN MILE

The glorious Crown Liquor Saloon is far from being the only old pub
in the Golden Mile area—some, but by no means all of Belfast's evening life, takes place in bars and restaurants here. At several replicated
Victorian bars, more locals and fewer visitors gather.

Robinsons. A popular pub two doors from the Crown Liquor Saloon,
Robinsons draws a young crowd with folk music in its Fibber Magees
bar on Sunday and funk in the trendy BT1 karoke bar on weekends.
Food is served daily from 12:30 to 9 pm. ✉ *38–42 Great Victoria St.,
Golden Mile* ☎ *028/9024–7447* ⊕ *www.robinsonsbar.co.uk.*

CENTRAL DISTRICT

Apartment. Beside City Hall, the Apartment serves drinks and brasserie-
style pub grub to Belfast's cool young things. Extensive but inexpensive
wine and cocktail lists attract a good crowd. ✉ *2 Donegall Sq. W, Central District* ☎ *028/9050–9777* ⊕ *www.apartmentbelfast.com.*

Bittles Bar. Colorful drawings of political, cultural, and social life adorn
the walls of this triangular Victorian pub on the fringes of the Cathedral Quarter. The drawings are by talented local artist Joe O'Kane, a
regular drinker in the pub. Bittles serves pub grub at lunchtime as well
as a selection of local craft brews such as MacIvor's cider, Hilden ales,
McGrath's beer, and Hollenhammer ale from the Whitewater Brewery
in County Down. ✉ *70 Upper Church La.*

Fodor'sChoice **Café Vaudeville.** The glamorous and ornate Café Vaudeville is an orgy of
★ leopard-spot chairs, ravishing textiles, and grandly canopied daybeds,
while its inner sanctum, located upstairs, is the ab-fab House of Champagne, a hot spot for local celebrities and the beautiful people. You can
have lunch (noon–3), dinner (5–9), or just pop into the coffee lounge for
a relaxing break. ✉ *25 Arthur St., Central District* ☎ *028/9043–9160*
⊕ *www.cafevaudeville.com* ⊘ *Closed Sun.*

The John Hewitt Bar. A must for every traveler's hit list, this bar named
after one of Ulster's most famous poets (who ironically wasn't a big
drinker) is traditional in style with a marble counter, waist-high wooden
paneling, high ceilings, and open fire. It channels Hewitt's socialist sen-
sibility, as it's owned by the Belfast Unemployed Centre (which it helps

fund with its profits)—top pub grub is served at lunch and live music is featured most nights, including the excellent Panama Jazz Band on Friday (except the first Friday of each month). ⊠ *51 Donegall St., Cathedral Quarter* ☎ *028/9023–3768* ⊕ *www.thejohnhewitt.com.*

Kremlin. A massive statue of Lenin above the front door greets patrons of the city's oldest and most outrageous gay-oriented club, and the over-the-top Soviet theme continues inside. Superstar DJs regularly fly in to perform. ⊠ *96 Donegall St., Cathedral Quarter* ☎ *028/9031–6060* ⊕ *www.kremlin-belfast.com.*

The National Grande Café. The ethos of this hostelry (in a former bank called the National) is to mirror Continental counterparts; you can order everything from a draught glass of Belfast Black to a Walnut Champs-Elysées cocktail, or just hang out with a fancy coffee. The drink and the craic are more important than the food, though there's a limited, but nonetheless enticing, menu that includes a cheese and charcuterie platter served on brioche, Catalan flatbreads, or sourdough breads made next door in the delightful Patissiere Mimi. It's best accompanied by a sweet dark sherry, Pedro Ximénez. If you prefer something more substantial to eat, beef brisket and butter bean ragu or braised lamb with artichokes are on the evening menu. It's worth dropping in to capture the industrial *genius loci* of this listed building: all exposed brick and granite quoins. The high ceiling drips with ivy hanging baskets, and hidden away at the back is Belfast's biggest beer garden. ⊠ *62–68 High St., Central District* ☎ *028/9031–1130* ⊙ *Mon.–Wed. 8:30 am–9 pm, Thurs. 8:30 am–1 am, Fri. and Sat. 9:30 am–1 am, Sun. 9:30 am–midnight.*

Madden's Bar. A popular locals favorite near the Castle Court mall, Madden's has live music nightly and traditional tune fests with set dancing on Wednesday night. ⊠ *Berry St. behind Castle Court, Central District* ☎ *028/90244114.*

McHugh's. In Belfast's oldest building (1711), McHugh's has three floors of bars and restaurants, and live music on weekends. Food is served from lunchtime in the downstairs bar while dinner, including their special "on the rock" steaks, is available from 6 pm in the upstairs restaurant. McHugh's retains the character of an early-18th-century dockside inn and exudes a homely feel with open fires. To mark the bar's 300th anniversary, Whitewater Brewery created the McHughs 300 Beer. ⊠ *29–31 Queen's Sq., Central District* ☎ *028/9050–9999* ⊕ *www.mchughsbar.com.*

Union Street Pub. A gay-friendly bar near the Cathedral Quarter, Union Street is housed in a converted 19th-century shoe factory. The three-story redbrick Victorian is one of the city's few "gastropubs," with a more formal upstairs restaurant that's popular with local foodies. ⊠ *8–14 Union St., Central District* ☎ *028/9031–6060* ⊕ *www.unionstreetpub.com.*

White's Tavern. Enjoy traditional Irish sessions on Friday nights at White's Tavern, which claims to be the oldest public house in Belfast. In winter a roaring fire greets you as soon as you enter the bar. Friendly staff serve pub grub until 7 pm, including the famous creamy, buttery,

Get your perfect pint of Guinness at the Crown Liquor Saloon, a Victorian extravaganza of embossed ceilings, gilded arabesques, and carved woodwork.

cholesterol-laden potato champ. ✉ *2–12 Winecellar Entry, Central District* ☎ *028/9024–3080* ⊕ *www.whitestavern.co.uk.*

UNIVERSITY AREA

Fodor's Choice ★ **Belfast Empire Music Hall.** Inside a deconsecrated church, the Music Hall is the city's leading music venue. Most nights are devoted to concerts from groups such as local heroes Snow Patrol. Stand-up comedy nights are usually on Tuesday—Patrick Kielty was a regular until he hit the big time in London. The Rab McCullough blues nights on Thursday are popular, as are Friday Glamaramas, devoted to Queen, Bowie, and the like. ✉ *42 Botanic Ave., University Area* ☎ *028/9024–9276* ⊕ *www. thebelfastempire.com.*

Botanic Inn. Known as "the Bot" to its student clientele, the Botanic is a big, popular disco-pub. ✉ *23–27 Malone Rd., University Area* ☎ *028/9050–9740* ⊕ *www.thebotanicinn.com.*

Chelsea Wine Bar. Packed with affluent professionals determined to prove that life begins at 30, the Chelsea, which underwent a complete top-to-bottom refit in 2013, serves contemporary cuisine that is reasonably priced and has a 100-plus wines on its list. There's live jazz muich on Sunday night and a house DJ on Thursday and Saturday. ✉ *346 Lisburn Rd., University Area* ☎ *028/9068–7177* ⊕ *www.chelseawinebar.com.*

Cutters Wharf. Down by the river south of the university, this bar and restaurant is at its best on summer evenings and during music performances on Sunday after 6. Spacious and light inside, it rarely gets too packed; if seating is limited, try the picnic tables and chairs on the wooden deck outside. ⊠ *4 Lockview Rd., University Area* ☎ *028/9066–3388* ⊕ *www.cutterswharf.co.uk.*

M-Club. Belfast's place for dedicated clubbers, M-Club even flies in celebrities to mix with the local nighthawks. It's open Tuesday, Friday, and Saturday. ⊠ *23–31 Bradbury Pl., University Area* ☎ *028/9023–3131* ⊕ *www.mclub.co.uk.*

Metro Bar. The stylish Metro Bar is a venue for fashionable wine-sipping and live music. From Thursday to Saturday night, bands play a mix of acoustic, pop, and Irish traditional while an after-work session on Friday draws the crowds. ⊠ *Crescent Town House, 13 Lower Crescent, University Area* ☎ *028/9032–3349* ⊕ *www.crescenttownhouse.com.*

THE ARTS

Culture Northern Ireland. A useful resource for visitors, this organization's website provides information about music, film, multimedia, literature, heritage, sports, and the visual and performing arts, and it has searchable "What's On" listings. ☎ *028/9064–4333* ⊕ *www.culturenorthernireland.org.*

ARTS CENTERS

The Crescent Arts Centre. Based in a beautifully restored rambling stone building—a former girls' high school—the Crescent presents an all-year- round series of events. Experimental dance and theater, concerts and workshops are all part of the program. The center also hosts the Belfast Book Festival (in the second week of June) during which writers participate in lively talks, lectures, and readings. Light meals and snacks are available at lunchtime in Dante's Café where storyboards tell the history of the building and famous locals connected to it. ∎ **TIP→ Nature note: between May and July, common swifts fly in from southern Africa to nest above the center's stone walls. Special "swift bricks" have been installed to provide nesting sites.** ⊠ *2 University Rd., University Area* ☎ *028/9024–2338* ⊕ *www.crescentarts.org.*

Cultúrlann McAdam Ó Fiaich. A £2 million renovation and extension has breathed new life into this venue. Celebrating Gaeilge (Irish language) and culture, this cosmopolitan arts center hosts exhibitions, book launches, concerts, theater, and poetry readings. Two choirs—one from a children's drama school and the other from resident theater company Aisling Ghéar—are based here. For travelers interested in the Gaeltacht experience, this is a great place to start. On the ground floor, the Dillon Gallery, named after the Falls Road artist Gerard Dillon, who spent much time painting in Connemara in the west of Ireland, mounts shows by top local and international artists. A shop sells Irish-language and English books as well as crafts and the all-important West Belfast Mural Map. Also here are a tourist information point, Wi-Fi access, and Restaurant Bia. The center's staff can arrange regional tours and book accommodation. Ask for information here about the Gaeltacht Way, a 4-km (2½-mile) walking route that takes in the major Irish language-related sites of the area. ⊠ *216 Falls Rd., West Belfast* ☎ *028/9096–4180* ⊕ *www.culturlann.ie* ☉ *Daily 9–9.*

ARTS FESTIVALS

Arts Council of Northern Ireland. The country's main arts agency supports a range of cultural events, including many Belfast festivals, and has information about them. ⊠ *MacNeice House, 77 Malone Rd., University Area* ☎ *028/9038–5200* ⊕ *www.artscouncil-ni.org.*

Belfast Festival at Queen's. The long-established festival at Queen's University lasts for three weeks (from late October into early November) and is the city's major arts festival. ⊠ *Festival office, 8 Fitzwilliam St., University Area* ☎ *028/9097–1034* ⊕ *www.belfastfestival.com.*

Cathedral Quarter Arts Festival. This early-May festival, always buzzing with energy, attracts local, national, and international visual and performing artists. Its base of operations is the Black Box on Hill Street, at the heart of the Cathedral Quarter, where a café serves snacks during the day and light lunches. The same organization runs a very successful Out to Lunch festival in January. ⊠ *Hill St., Cathedral Quarter* ☎ *028/9023–2403* ⊕ *www.cqaf.com.*

GALLERIES

Central Belfast, especially in Cathedral Quarter, is awash with small, quirky galleries that exhibit painting, sculpture, photography, and prints, as well as installations of digital and video work. Check ⊕ *www.belfastgalleries.com* for detailed listings.

Craft Northern Ireland Gallery. Opposite the Merchant Hotel, this gallery is a hotbed of crafts where street performers at Cotton Court regularly entertain crowds on summer Sundays. ⊠ *42 Waring St., Cathedral Quarter* ☎ *028/9032–3059* ⊕ *www.craftni.org.*

Golden Thread Gallery. One of Belfast's best arts venues, the Golden Thread has exhibited at the Venice Biennale and the International Symposium for Electronic Art. The gallery presents visual art from paintings on canvas to the latest digital arts. ⊠ *84–94 Great Patrick St., Cathedral Quarter* ☎ *028/9033–0920* ⊕ *www.goldenthreadgallery.co.uk.*

The Red Barn. Popular with visitors, the Red Barn often exhibits photographs reflecting the history of the Troubles as well as social documentary. The gallery also presents installations by students from Belfast Metropolitan College and watercolor paintings by local artists. ⊠ *43b Rosemary St., Central District* ☎ *028/9023–1901* ⊕ *www.rbgbelfast.com.*

THEATER

Belfast Waterfront. Everyone in Belfast sings the praises of this striking civic structure. From the looks of it, the hall is an odd marriage of *Close Encounters* modern and Castel Sant'Angelo antique. It houses a 2,235-seat concert hall (for ballet and classical, rock, and Irish music) and a 500-seat studio space (for modern dance, jazz, and experimental theater). The Arc Brasserie and two bars make the Waterfront a convenient place to eat, have a pint, and enjoy the river views before or after your culture fix. On the ground floor, the We Make Café serves snacks and quick bites such as fresh coconut scones, shortbread, and pancakes. ⊠ *2 Lanyon Pl., E. Bridge St.* ☎ *028/9033–4400* ⊕ *www.waterfront.co.uk.*

Fodor's Choice
★

Grand Opera House. Shows from all over Ireland and Britain—and sometimes farther afield—play at this beautifully restored Victorian theater. Though it has no resident company of its own, major West End musicals and plays pass through, plus the occasional opera or ballet. It's worth attending a show just to enjoy the gigantic and splendid opera house itself. The Baby Grand—a theater within a theater—hosts comedy, live music, and educational workshops as well as film and special events. On the second floor you can peruse a theater-history exhibition.

Luciano's Café Bar (named after the opera giant Pavarotti) serves snacks and light lunches. For a more extensive choice the Hippodrome Restaurant on the third floor opens two hours before the show and allows you to split your meal: have a main course before the performance and come back for puddings at the interval. ⊠ *2 Great Victoria St., Golden Mile* ☏ *028/9024–1919* ⊕ *www.goh.co.uk.*

Fodor's Choice
★

Lyric Theatre. One of Northern Ireland's most prized cultural organizations, the Lyric presents a diverse repertory of classical, popular, and contemporary drama, frequently showcasing the work of local playwrights. With its angular brick bulk topped by three distinctive sloping roofs, the theater, renovated in 2011, is an impressive modernist achievement. To fund it, a total of £18 million was raised with money from local companies as well as the Lyric's famed patron Liam Neeson, who made his 1976 stage debut here in Brian Friel's *Philadelphia, Here I Come!* Strong emphasis is placed on the use of natural light, with a glass-walled Long Hall running the length of the first floor and looking out over the River Lagan. The main auditorium is lined with iroko wood and has 33 different styles of brick, all specially fired so each one is complete and uncut. In addition to the main 390-seat venue, presided over by the Danske Bank Stage, the Naughton Studios, a theater space, holds up to 125 people. ⊠ *55 Ridgeway St., University Area* ☏ *028/9038–5685* ⊕ *www.lyrictheatre.co.uk.*

Odyssey Arena. The Belfast Giants hockey team is the main tenant of the 10,000-seat Odyssey Arena, but Northern Ireland's biggest indoor venue also hosts rock, pop, and classical concerts. The adjacent Odyssey Pavilion complex has bars, restaurants, shops, and nightclubs. ⊠ *2 Queen's Quay, Titanic Quarter* ☏ *028/9076–6000* ⊕ *www.odysseyarena.com.*

Ulster Hall. The historic Ulster Hall (it once hosted Rachmaninov) is the permanent home of the Ulster Orchestra. The classical music season runs here from September through April. Concerts are mostly held on Friday, but you can call or check online (⊕ *www.ulsterorchestra.com*) to learn about other dates and free open rehearsals and 50-minute lunchtime concerts. Apart from classical, the hall presents rock, folk, traditional Irish, blues, jazz, and other forms, along with comedy and cabaret acts. With its superb acoustics, Ulster Hall provides the perfect listening and foot-tapping experience. ⊠ *Bedford St., Central District* ☏ *028/9033–4455* ⊕ *www.ulsterhall.co.uk.*

SHOPPING

Belfast's main shopping streets include High Street, Donegall Place, Royal Avenue, and several of the smaller streets connecting them. Except for buses and delivery vehicles, the area is mostly traffic-free. The long thoroughfare of Donegall Pass, running from Shaftesbury Square at the point of the Golden Mile east to Ormeau Road, contains a mix of biker shops, ethnic restaurants, and antiques arcades. Another retail haven is Lisburn Road, jam-packed with nearly a hundred trendy designer shops, lifestyle emporia, galleries, and antiques stores. The Lisburn Road Business Association (LRBA) has special offers on its website (⊕ *www.thelisburnroad.com*). For a break from shopping, let the Victorian-style Maryville House Tea Rooms (⊕ *www.maryvillehouse. co.uk*), just off Lisburn Road, transport you back to another era, starting with the foyer's 1792 map of Ireland dedicated to His Majesty King George III. The 20 different house teas range from a zesty rooibos citrus to lemongrass with ginger twist.

GOLDEN MILE AND CENTRAL DISTRICT

CLOTHING

Smyth and Gibson. This noted shop makes and sells beautiful, luxurious linen and cotton shirts and accessories. Upstairs you'll find a small and lovely café. ⊠ *Bedford House, Bedford St., Central District* ☎ *028/7131–2343* ⊕ *www.smythandgibson.com.*

FOOD

Sawers Deli. From feta cheese to foie gras, Sawers is a dazzling experience that will thrill your senses. Founded in 1897, it carries a huge selection of artisanal foods from local and international suppliers. Browse the shelves for a trip through some of the finest Northern Irish produce. You will find Robert Ditty's Irish oak cakes rolled with County Armagh oats; salty and flavor-filled Kearney blue cheese from the Ards peninsula; the lemony, zesty bolie log, a soft goat cheese from the famed Fivemiletown creamery in County Tyrone; the delectable Bella Jo's curry-flavored relish from Ballycastle in County Antrim; a raft of jams and marmalades from Margaret Brownlee's Cottage Pride in Armagh; preserves from Jayne Paget in Fermanagh; and potted herrings from Ardglass—all set alongside a selection of wheaten and focaccia breads. And don't forget the Suki Tea made by the Belfast Brew company, which specializes in loose-leaf teas and old-fashioned teapots to go with it. ⊠ *Fountain Centre, 5–6 College St., Central District* ☎ *028/9032–2021* ⊕ *www. sawersbelfast.com.*

GIFTS

Smyth's Irish Linens. Looking for linen souvenirs? Smyth's Irish Linens carries a large selection of handkerchiefs, tablecloths, napkins, knitwear, Belleek china, Galway crystal, and other traditional goods. It's opposite the Castle Court mall. ⊠ *65 Royal Ave., Central District* ☎ *028/9031–4272.*

Utopia. Stocked with everything from toys to costume jewelry, Utopia sells intricate silver pendants and earrings made by local designer Alpha Zed. Also worth a look are the wooden, alabaster, and metal chess sets. ⊠ *Fountain Centre, College St., Central District* ☎ *028/9024–1342.*

JEWELRY

The Steensons. Locally designed, the superb jewelry sold here has a worldwide fan base. ⊠ *Bedford House, Bedford St., Central District* ☎ *028/9024–8269* ⊕ *www.thesteensons.com.*

MARKETS AND MALLS

Castle Court. The city's second-largest shopping mall is euro-friendly, with most shops accepting both sterling and euros. International stores such as Gap can be found under Castle Court's glass roof, alongside British clothing chains such as Miss Selfridge, Warehouse, and Blue Inc. For one-stop shopping, head for Debenham's department store, which has everything from cosmetics to kitchenware. ✉ *10 Royal Ave., Central District* ☎ *028/9023–4591* ⊕ *www.castlecourt-uk.com.*

Fodor's Choice
★
St. George's Market. For an authentic blast of Belfast life make your way to the renovated St. George's Market, an enormous indoor market on Friday, Saturday, and Sunday mornings. When it opened in the 1890s, this historic market sold butter, eggs, poultry, and fruit. In those days Belfast was known as the "City of Seven Smells": these came from such fixtures as gasworks, slaughterhouses, and soap factories. Today the market is a vibrant place with 150 traders selling everything from apples to zippers and antiques to shark meat. The Friday Variety Market starts at 6 am and runs until 2 pm; the Saturday City Food and Garden Market is from 9 to 3, and the Sunday Food, Craft and Antique market is 10–4. Salivating foodies love the treats at Aunt Sandra's Candy Factory stall, with its fudge and flavored sweets, as well as the organically grown produce throughout the market. At Piece of Cake Bakery, you can choose from 25 terrific breads, including rye, spelt, olive, walnut, and banana, or sample the delicious baklava or white sourdough with seaweed dulse. Next door is S.D. Bell's coffee stand; the company is older than the market, as it was set up in 1887 and has been brewing nonstop ever since. ✉ *May St., Central District* ☎ *028/9043–5704* ⊕ *www.belfastcity.gov.uk/stgeorgesmarket.*

Fodor's Choice
★
Victoria Square. Occupying an eight-block site in central Belfast, Victoria Square has changed the Belfast skyline. The flagship 800,000-square-foot shopping complex, all glittering steel, is presided over by a vast geodesic glass dome eight stories high. The House of Fraser department store is the main anchor tenant and designer shops such as Cruise, Hugo Boss, River Island, and Kurt Geiger provide shoppers their fix of happiness. Coffee shops, fast-food restaurants, and an eight-screen cinema are also on-site. Offering a delightful architectural contrast, the complex incorporates noted Victorian landmarks such as the McErvel's Seed Warehouse and the Royal Belfast Ginger Ale Manufactury. ■TIP➔ **Make your way up to the viewing gallery for great views of Belfast—admission is free and a guide will show you the sights.** The **Q-Park** (⊕ *www.q-park.co.uk*) provides 1,000 parking spaces and is open 24/7. ✉ *Chichester, Montgomery, and Ann Sts., and Victoria Sq., 1 Victoria Sq., Central District* ☎ *028/9032–2277* ⊕ *www.victoriasquare. com* ☉ *Mon. and Tues. 9:30–6, Wed.–Fri. 9:30–9, Sat, 9–6, Sun 1–6.*

UNIVERSITY AREA

BOOKS

No Alibis. Just the way a bookstore should be, No Alibis specializes in British and American crime thrillers, as well as general fiction and non-fiction, plus a smattering of the work of local novelists and poets. All in all, it's a bibliophile's delight with knowledgeable staff and regular book launches and literary readings, some of which are held in the nearby

Ulster Museum. The shop hosts jazz, blues, and other music events on Friday nights. ✉ *83 Botanic Ave., University Area* ☎ *028/9031–9607* ⊕ *www.noalibis.com.*

THE GIANT'S CAUSEWAY COAST

Starting in Belfast, stretching for 80 km (50 miles) along Northern Ireland's Atlantic shore, the Causeway Coast holds many of the province's don't-miss attractions. The man-made brilliance of the castle at Dunluce, the endless string of whitewashed fishing villages along the sea, and the world-famous natural wonder that is the Giant's Causeway are just some of the delights to be discovered here. The sparkling visitor center opened in 2012. Once your car or mountain bike (ideal for the Causeway's flat terrain) makes its way past some fair-size towns, you'll enter the splendid Glens area—one of the more "gentle" (an Irish turn of phrase for supernatural) places in all Ireland. Here, ageless villages, still inhabited by descendants of the ancient Irish and the Hebridean Scots who hailed from across the narrow Sea of Moyle, are set in peaceful, old-growth forests that have become synonymous with Irishness. But once past the Giant's Causeway you'll find more cosmopolitan pleasures, including Bushmills—the oldest licensed distillery in the world—and the old walled city of Derry.

CARRICKFERGUS AND LARNE

16 km (10 miles) northeast of Belfast.

Carrickfergus, on the shore of Belfast Lough, grew up around its ancient castle. When the town was enclosed by ramparts at the start of the 17th century, it was the only English-speaking town in Ulster. Not surprisingly, this was the loyal port where William of Orange chose to land on his way to fight the Catholic forces at the Battle of the Boyne in 1690. However, the English did have one or two small setbacks, including the improbable victory in 1778 of John Paul Jones, the American naval hero, over the British warship HMS *Drake*. Although a long way from home, this stands as the first naval victory of America's fledgling naval fleet. After this battle, which was waged in Belfast Lough, the inhabitants of Carrickfergus stood on the waterfront and cheered Jones when his ship passed the town castle, demonstrating their support for the American Revolution. Carrickfergus's past can still be seen in some of its old buildings. St. Nicholas's Church, built by John de Courcy in 1205 (remodeled in 1614), and the North Gate in the town's medieval walls are worth checking. Dobbins Inn on High Street has been a hotel for more than three centuries and is a popular local watering hole.

GETTING HERE AND AROUND

CAR TRAVEL A 15-minute drive northeast of Belfast on A2, Carrickfergus, is an easy town to negotiate. There's a huge free car park beside the castle, and parking on the main streets is free, though limited to one hour. Pay-and-display car parks, costing 40 pence per hour, operate at Joymount, Bride, and Lancastrian streets.

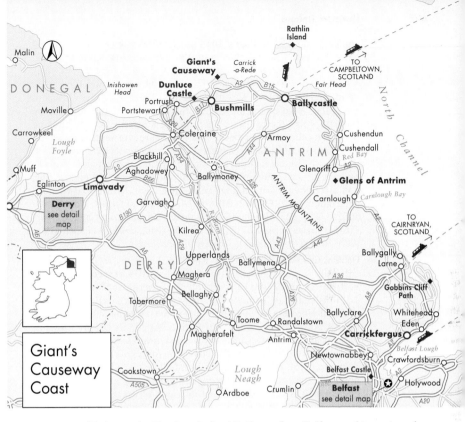

Giant's
Causeway
Coast

Derry see detail map

Belfast see detail map

TRAIN TRAVEL Trains run by Northern Ireland Railways from Belfast on this section of the Antrim coast go only as far as the 40 km (25 miles) to Larne. Daily service stops at a number of towns, including Carrickfergus, Whitehead, and Glynn. A round-trip ticket from Belfast's Yorkgate or Central Station to Carrickfergus costs £6.40 (£4 after 9:20 am); from Belfast to Larne, it's £10.50 (£7 after 9:20 am).

ESSENTIALS

Visitor Information Carrickfergus Borough ⊠ *11 Antrim St., Carrickfergus, Co. Antrim* ☎ *028/9335–8049* ⊕ *www.carrickfergus.org.*

EXPLORING

Andrew Jackson Cottage and U.S. Rangers Centre. The center tells the tale of the U.S. president, whose parents emigrated from here in 1765. This thatch cottage just outside of town is a reconstruction of an 18th-century structure thought to resemble their home. Interpretive panels, illustrating Jackson's story as well as Ulster–Scots history, have been added. Free tea and coffee are offered to visitors. The cottage is open year-round, but access is by arrangement through Carrickfergus tourist office. ⊠ *1½ km (1 mile) northeast of Carrickfergus, Larne Rd., Co. Antrim* ☎ *028/9335–8049* ⊕ *www.carrickfergus.org* ⊠ *Free.*

Fodor's Choice **Carrickfergus Castle.** Built atop a rock ledge in 1180 by John de Courcy,
★ provincial Ulster's first Anglo-Norman invader, Carrickfergus Castle is

still in good shape and since 2014 has sparked renewed visitor appeal with the opening of its dungeons. Apart from being captured briefly by the French in 1760, the castle—one of Ireland's largest —stood as a bastion of British rule until 1928, at which time it still functioned as an English garrison. Walk through the 13th-century gatehouse into the Outer Ward and continue into the Inner Ward, the heart of the fortress, where the five-story keep stands, a massive, sturdy building with walls almost 8 feet thick. And make sure you venture down the steps into the dark stone dungeons, opened as part of a renovation project which also saw the roof of the Great Tower replaced and the opening of an ammunitions room. If you're here at the end of July, you can enjoy the annual Lughnasa festival, a lively medieval-costume entertainment. ⊠ *Off A2, Marine Hwy., Carrickfergus, Co. Antrim* ☎ *028/9335–1273* ⊕ *www.discovernorthernireland.com/Carrickfergus-Castle-Carrickfergus-P2814* 🖃 *£5* ⊙ *Apr.–Sept., daily 10–6; Oct.–Mar., daily 10–4 (last admission 30 mins before closing).*

Gobbins Cliff Path. Thrillseekers will love this newly-revived dramatic cliff walk in east county Antrim, opened in 2014 at a cost of £6 million. The Gobbins Cliff Path, cut into the towering rock on the eastern side of Islandmagee peninsula, is linked with a new metal staircase and is one of Northern Ireland's best-kept secrets. Originally built in 1902 by the railway magnate Berkeley Deane Wise, in its heyday it was as popular as the Giant's Causeway but fell into disrepair and closed to the public after World War II. Today it merits a government-approved acronym, ASSI: Area of Special Scientific Interest, and is noted for its noisy colonies of puffins, razorbills, fulmars, peregrine falcons, and guillemots. On a clear day panoramic views across the North Channel stretch from the Scottish Outer Hebrides in the north to the English Lake District in the south. Legends associated with the Gobbins include mythical figures such as Gobbin Saor, a giant who lived in the cliffs. An exhibition room with interpretation, a café and craft shop, and a tourist information point are located at the site. ⊠ *Islandmagee, Larne, Co. Antrim* ☎ *028/2826–0088* ⊕ *www.larne.gov.uk.*

GLENS OF ANTRIM

Beginning 24 km (15 miles) north of Carrickfergus at Larne.

North of Carrickfergus after Larne, the coast of County Antrim becomes spectacular—wave upon wave of high green hills that curve down to the hazy sea are dotted with lush glens, or valleys, first carved out by glaciers at the end of the last ice age. Before you tackle the Glens though, it's worth considering a short detour from Larne to the nearby peninsula of Islandmagee where the newly reopened Gobbins path is a dramatic cliff-face walk cut into the towering rock. Nine wooded river valleys occupy the 86 km (54 miles) between Larne and Ballycastle, the two largest towns in the Glens of Antrim. Until the building of the narrow coastal road in 1834, the Glens were home to isolated farming communities whose residents adhered to the romantic, mystical Celtic legends and the everyday use of the Irish language. Steeped in Irish mythology, the Glens were first inhabited by small bands of Irish monks as early as AD 700. Some residents proudly note that Ossian, the greatest of the Celtic poets, is supposedly buried near Glenaan. The Glens are famed beauty spots and popular destinations: for tourist offices, head to the larger towns such as Larne, Ballymena, and Ballycastle. Cushendall's tourist information office opens all day during the summer months and mornings only in the winter (✉ *Mill St.* ☎ *028/2177–1180*). But Cushendun and Carnlough are extremely small and can't support tourist offices even in high season.

McKillop's (✉ *14–16 Main St.* ☎ *028/2888–5236*), a shop in Carnlough, has leaflets describing local attractions, and the folks there are happy to offer tips about the Glens. Also helpful is the Causeway Coast and Glens website.

GETTING HERE AND AROUND

CAR TRAVEL Oft-lauded as one of Ireland's most scenic drives—on a clear day you can see Scotland—the A2 Antrim coastal route is a delightful narrow, winding, two-lane road that hugs the slim strip of land between the hills and sea, bringing you to the magnificent Glens of Antrim. In most towns, cars park free of charge on the main street or in parking lots overlooking the harbor. The road is busy in summer, so allow extra travel time.

BUS TRAVEL The scenic Antrim Coaster Goldline buses from Belfast traverse the entire County Antrim coastline all the way to Coleraine—a 160-km (100-mile), four-hour journey (£17.50, and worth every penny) with many stops en route. The service operates Monday–Saturday year-round and on Sunday, too, from early July to mid-September. Because reservations are not accepted, arrive early in summer to be assured a window seat. Departures are from the Europa Buscentre in Belfast.

Visitor Information Ballymena Tourist Information Office ✉ *The Braid, Ballymena Town Hall Museum and Arts Centre, 1–29 Bridge St., Ballymena* ☎ *028/2563–5900* ⊕ *www.gatewaytotheglens.com.* **Causeway Coast and Glens** ⊕ *www.causewaycoastandglens.com.* **Larne Tourist Information Office** ✉ *Narrow Gauge Rd., Larne* ☎ *028/2826–0088* ⊕ *www.larne.gov.uk.*

EXPLORING

The Glens merit several days of serious exploration. Supernarrow B-roads curl west off A2, up each of the beautiful glens, where trails await hikers. You'll need a full week and a rainproof tent to complete the nine-glen circuit (working from south to north, Glenarm, Glencloy, Glenariff, Glenballyeamon, Glenaan, Glencorp, Glendun, Glenshesk, and Glentasie); or you could just head for Glenariff Park, the most accessible glen.

Carnlough. A little resort made of white limestone, Carnlough overlooks a small harbor that is surrounded by stone walls. The harbor can be reached by crossing over the limestone bridge from Main Street, built especially for the Marquis of Londonderry. The small harbor, once a port of call for fishermen, now shelters pleasure yachts. Carnlough is surrounded on three sides by hills that rise 1,000 feet from the sea. McKillop's shop serves as an a tourist information point and dispenses maps and local literature. ⊠ *24 km (15 miles) north of Larne on A2, 14–16 Harbor Rd., Carnlough* ☎ *028/2888–5236.*

Cushendall. Turnley's Tower—a curious, fortified square tower of red stone, built in 1820 as a curfew tower and jail for "idlers and rioters"—stands in Cushendall, at a crossroads in the middle of the village. Cushendall is called the capital of the Glens because it has a few more streets than the other villages hereabouts. The road from Waterfoot to Cushendall is barely a mile long and worth the stroll or cycle out to see the coastal caves (one of which had a resident for many years, a local woman named Anne Murray) that line the route. ⊠ *3 km (2 miles) north of Glenariff on A2, Cushendall* ⊕ *www.cushendall.info.*

> ### CAVE DWELLING
>
> The coastal caves of Cushendall have been used for various purposes, including housing. One of the more colorful residents was a lady called Anne Murray who lived in one cave for 50 years, supplementing her income as one of the region's best *poitín* brewers. The damp and windy conditions obviously agreed with her—as did perhaps a taste of her own brew?—for she lived to the ripe old age of 100.

Fodor's Choice ★ **Cushendun.** Off the main A2 route, the road between Cushendall and Cushendun turns into one of a Tour-de-France hilliness, so cyclists beware. Your reward, however, will be the tiny jewel of a village, Cushendun, which was designed in 1912 by Clough Williams-Ellis (who also designed the famous Italianate village of Portmeirion in Wales) at the request of Ronald John McNeill, Baron Cushendun. Up sprang a series of cottages and a village square of seven houses, all done up in the Cornish taste courtesy of the Penzance-born wife of the baron. To top it all off, the baron had Glenmona House built in the regal neo-Georgian style. From this part of the coast you can see the Mull of Kintyre on the Scottish mainland. Hikes along the beachy strand have inspired poets and artists, including John Masefield. ⊠ *2 km (1½ miles) north of Cushendall on Coast Rd., Cushendun.*

EN ROUTE The precipitous Antrim Coast Road cuts off from A2 and heads north from Cushendun past dramatically beautiful Murlough Bay to Fair Head and on to Ballycastle. In this area are Drumnakill, a renowned pagan site; Torr Head, a jutting peninsula; and three state parks that allow for some fabulous hikes, fine hill-walking, and great views of Scotland from Fair Head. Or you can rejoin A2 at Cushendun via B92 (a left turn). After a few miles the road descends, passing ruins of the Franciscans' 16th-century Bonamargy Friary, into Ballycastle.

Fodor's Choice ★ **Glenariff Forest Park.** Head to this natural preserve to explore the most beautiful and unsettled of Antrim's glens. Glenariff was christened "Little Switzerland" by Thackeray for its spectacular combination of rugged hills and lush vales. The main valley opens on to Red Bay at the village of Glenariff (also known as Waterfoot). Inside the park are picnic facilities and dozens of good hikes. Bisecting the park are two lovely rivers, the Inver and the Glenariff, which help sculpt the rocky gorges here and culminate in the famous 5½-km (3½-mile) **Waterfall Trail**, marked with blue arrows, which passes outstanding views of Glenariff River, its three waterfalls, and small but swimmable loughs. Escape from the summer crowds by taking one of the longest trails, such as the **Scenic Hike**. Pick up a detailed trail map at the park visitor center, which also has a small cafeteria. ✉ *98 Glenariff Rd., 7 km (5 miles) north of Carnlough, off A2, Glenariff* ☎ *028/2955–6000* 🌐 *www.heartof thecausewaycoastandglens.com* 🎫 *Vehicles £4.50, pedestrians £2* 🕓 *Apr.–Sept., daily 8:30–8; Oct.–Mar., daily 10–dusk.*

WHERE TO STAY

$$$$ HOTEL

🏨 **Ballygally Castle.** Connoisseurs of sea views love this baronial castle, built by a Scottish lord in 1625 to rise dramatically beside Ballygally Bay, and newly expanded in 2014 with some top-notch rooms. **Pros:** guests are well looked after; handy stopover en route to the Giant's Causeway of Glens of Antrim. **Cons:** can fill up quickly, leading to delays particularly at peak holiday times. [$] *Rooms from: £180* ✉ *274 Coast Rd., Ballygally* ☎ *028/2858–1066* 🌐 *www.hastingshotels.com* 🛏 *54 rooms* 🍴 *Breakfast.*

$$$ RESORT Fodor's Choice ★

🏨 **Galgorm Resort & Spa.** The original Italinate house dates from the 1850s, but a £10-million renovation in 2015 has pushed this manor house resort into the premier league. **Pros:** an elegant mix of the cozy and luxurious; perfect place for pampering; pool and gym. **Cons:** if you're not a golfer, swimmer, or spa fan, there's not a lot to do apart from relaxing; hovers on the edge of remoteness and a long walk to shops. [$] *Rooms from: £150* ✉ *136 Fenaghy Rd., 40 km (25 miles) east of Larne on A36, Ballymena* ☎ *028/2588–1001* 🌐 *www.galgorm.com* 🛏 *123 rooms* 🍴 *Multiple meal plans.*

$ HOTEL Fodor's Choice ★

🏨 **The Londonderry Arms Hotel.** What awaits at this lovely traditional inn are ivy-clad walls, gorgeous antiques, regional paintings, prints and maps, and lots of fresh flowers—all time-burnished accents well befitting an estate once inherited by Sir Winston Churchill. **Pros:** fine historic vibe; cheerful staff; free newspapers. **Cons:** chattering birds in the ivy sometimes provide unscheduled early wake-up call; old-fashioned hotels (and creaky floorboards) aren't to everyone's taste. [$] *Rooms from: £80* ✉ *20 Harbor Rd., Carnlough* ☎ *028/2888–5255* 🌐 *www.glensofantrim.com* 🛏 *35 rooms* 🍴 *Multiple meal plans.*

BALLYCASTLE

86 km (54 miles) northeast of Larne.

Ballycastle is the main resort at the northern end of the Glens of Antrim. People flock here in summer, but apart from peak season, this is a quiet town. Ballycastle is shaped like an hourglass, with its strand and dock on one end, its pubs and chippers on the other, and the 1-km (½-mile) Quay Road in between. Beautifully aged shops and pubs line its Castle, Diamond, and Main streets.

GETTING HERE AND AROUND

CAR TRAVEL   Ballycastle is an hour's drive north of Belfast on the M2, which leads on to A26 before branching off to the narrower A44. You can park free along the seafront and at the marina. Other car parks are on Quay Road and Ann Street.

BUS TRAVEL   Regular bus services link Ballycastle with the main towns of Bushmills, Coleraine, Ballymoney, and Ballymena. Translink buses run daily between the towns. The Antrim Coaster 252 also stops in Ballycastle.

ESSENTIALS

Visitor Information Ballycastle Visitor Information Centre ⊠ *Portnagree House, 14 Bayview Rd., Ballycastle, Co. Antrim* ☏ *028/2076–2024* ⊕ *www. heartof thecausewaycoastandglens.com.*

EXPLORING

Fodor'sChoice   **Carrick-a-Rede.** Adrenalin junkies love the rope bridge—off the coast
★   at Ballintoy in Larrybane—which spans a 60-foot gap between the mainland and tiny Carrick-a-Rede Island. The island's name means "rock in the road" and refers to how it stands in the path of the salmon that follow the coast as they migrate to their home rivers to spawn. The bridge is open to the public daily, weather permitting. More than 265,000 visitors cross it (or at least take a look at it) each year, looking down on heart-stopping views of the crashing waves 100 feet below. For an exhilarating cliff-top experience, the rope bridge walk is hard to beat. The island's small two-roomed Fishermen's Cottage, where they mended nets and kept materials, has been restored and opened to the public. The whole area is designated a Site of Special Scientific Interest because of its unique geology, flowers, and fauna. ■TIP→ **Hour-long guided tours take in the bridge and the rest of the site, including the cottage, and have priority—best to book in advance.** ⊠ *119a White Park Rd.(8 km [5 miles] west of Ballycastle on B15), Ballintoy, Co. Antrim* ☏ *028/2076–9839* ⊕ *www.nationaltrust.org.uk* ☋ *£5.60 to bridge; £7 for guided tour of entire site* ☉ *Nov.–Jan., daily 9:30–3:30; Feb.–May, Sept., and Oct., daily 9–6; June–Aug., daily 9–7:30; last entry 45 mins before closing.*

The Ould Lammas Fair. Every year since 1606, on the last Monday and Tuesday in August, Ballycastle has hosted the Oul' Lammas Fair, a modern version of the ancient Celtic harvest festival of Lughnasa (Irish for "August"). Ireland's oldest fair, this is a very popular two-day event with entertainers, several hundred shopping stalls, and even a pony show. Treat yourself to the fair's traditional snacks, dulse (sun-dried seaweed), and yellowman (rock-hard yellow toffee). ⊠ *Ballycastle, Co. Antrim* ⊕ *www.irishcultureandcustoms.com/ACalend/ LammasFair.html.*

Rathlin Island. There's a sense of dreamy loneliness about this spot, rising 8 km (5 miles) offshore beyond the tide-rip of *Sloch na Marra* (Valley of the Sea). One hundred people still live on Northern Ireland's only offshore island, among the twin delights of history and wildlife. In 1306 the Scottish king Robert the Bruce took shelter in a cave (under the east lighthouse)

> **SHOOT THE CHUTE**
>
> If you summon up the nerve to cross the famous 60-foot-long Carrick-a-Rede rope bridge, which sways over a rocky outcrop and the turbulent sea, be mindful that you have to do it again to get back to the mainland.

and, according to the popular legend, was inspired to continue his armed struggle against the English by watching a spider patiently spinning its web. It was on Rathlin in 1898 that Guglielmo Marconi set up the world's first cross-water radio link, from the island's lighthouse to Ballycastle. Hiking and bird-watching—look out for the Atlantic nomads: choughs, puffins, guillemots, and razorbills nesting on the cliffs and sea stacks in the summer—are the island's main activities. In 2014, four new way-marked walking trails, covering 32 km (20 miles) were opened and have been given quality status, meaning they are among the best available. You can download the maps to these Rathlin walks at ⊕ *www.walkni.com.* The **Boathouse Visitor Centre** (☎ *028/2076–2024*) houses a collection of photographs, tools, and implements from the island's past. The center is open from April through mid-September, and admission is free. A high-speed double-decker catamaran, the M.V. *Rathlin Express,* cuts the 10-km (6-mile) journey time crossing over the Sea of Moyle to 25 minutes; from July to September it runs six round-trips daily (£12.50; reservations 24 hours ahead essential). Unless the sea is extremely rough, the M.V. *Canna* ferryboat also makes four daily round-trips (£12.50, reservations also essential). This more leisurely trip can take up to 45 minutes; be mindful of the weather to ensure that you can return on the same day. The last return to Ballycastle is at 4:15 pm for the *Rathlin* and 5:30 pm for the *Canna.* ⊠ *Rathlin Island, 9½ km (6 miles) from Ballycastle, Ballycastle, Co. Antrim* ☎ *028/2076–9299* ⊕ *www.rathlinballycastleferry.com.*

GIANT'S CAUSEWAY

19½ km (12 miles) west of Ballycastle.

GETTING HERE AND AROUND

CAR TRAVEL The Causeway is just off the A2 coast road. The nearest towns are Coleraine (a 20-minute drive), Ballycastle (10 minutes), and Ballymoney (35 minutes). In summer, the roads are congested, particularly on bank holidays and festival weekends. You can park your car at the center itself, which has 400 spaces (the parking fee is included in the admission price), or leave it in nearby Bushmills, where a park-and-ride service operates. The National Trust, which runs this site, has introduced a Green Travel Admission Ticket for visitors arriving by park and ride or public transportation; you'll save £1.50 off the standard adult admission price.

BUS TRAVEL   The Antrim Coaster 252 bus (£17.50 round-trip) is a great way to take in the dramatic coastline. The bus departs at 9:05 am for the Giant's Causeway from Belfast's Europa Buscentre. The Coaster stops on the Nook Main Road, where you can catch a shuttle bus (£2 round-trip) down to the Causeway itself. If coming from Coleraine, a fun way to access the Causeway is aboard the Translink North Coast Open Topper Service, a double-decker bus (£5.20) that runs in July and August, weather permitting. Kids love it. This bus also links with the Translink Causeway Rambler high-frequency service (from June to mid-September), which hits all the main visitor attractions, including Bushmills Distillery, the Giant's Causeway, and the Carrick-a-Rede rope bridge. An all-day Rambler ticket allows you to hop on and off as many times as you like. It costs £4.50 and is valid only the day of purchase—at the Europa Buscentre in Belfast or at any Translink station. For a more direct bus between Belfast and Coleraine, catch the Translink Goldline Express service for £17.50.

TOURS   Two bus tours from Belfast (among many) are the Giant's Causeway Tour by Allen's Tours and a same-named offering from McComb's.

TRAIN TRAVEL   No regular public trains serve the Giant's Causeway, but a fun passenger link is provided on a narrow-gauge train running from Bushmills. The Giant's Causeway and Bushmills Railway leaves Runkerry Road, Bushmills, for the 3-km (2-mile) journey along the track bed of the former causeway tram. The train operates every weekend from Easter until the end of June, and daily in July and August. The nearest Translink train stations are 21 km (14 miles) away in Portrush or 18 km (11 miles) west in Coleraine, where the main Belfast–Derry train stops (£17.50 round-trip). If you buy a one-day iLink ticket, you can ride buses and trains to get to and from the Giant's Causeway.

ESSENTIALS

Transportation Contacts Allen's Giant's Causeway Tour. Allen's Tours operate day tours to the Giant's Causeway as well as to the nearby Bushmills Distillery (£17.50). ☎ 028/9091–5613 ⊕ www.allensbelfastbustours.com. **Giant's Causeway and Bushmills Railway** ☎ 028/2073–2844 ⊕ www.freewebs. com/giantscausewayrailway. **McComb's Giant's Causeway Tour.** McComb's/MiniCoach operate day tours of Belfast (£8–£16) and to the Giant's Causeway, Bushmills Distillery, and Carrickfergus (£17.50). ☎ 028/9031–5333 ⊕ www. minicoachni.co.uk.

Visitor Information Giant's Causeway Tourist Office ✉ Visitor Centre, Giant's Causeway Centre, 44 Causeway Rd., Bushmills ☎ 028/2073–1855 ⊕ nationaltrust.org.uk/giants-causeway. **Causeway Coast and Glens Tourism Partnership** ✉ 11 Lodge Rd., Coleraine, Bushmills ☎ 028/7032–7720 ⊕ www. causewaycoastandglens.com.

EXPLORING

FAMILY   **Giant's Causeway.** Northern Ireland's only UNESCO World Heritage Site,
Fodor's Choice   the Giant's Causeway is a mass of almost 40,000 mostly hexagonal pillars
★   of volcanic basalt, clustered like a giant honeycomb and extending hundreds of yards into the sea. This "causeway" was created 60 million years ago, when boiling lava, erupting from an underground fissure that stretched from the north of Ireland to the Scottish coast, crystallized as

Grand Prize winner of Fodor's "Show Us Your Ireland" contest, this entry by Fodors.com member Traveling shows the famed Carrick-a-Rede rope bridge.

it burst into the sea. As all Ulster folk know, though, the truth is that the giant Finn McCool, in a bid to challenge Benandonner, his rival across the sea in Scotland, created the columns as stepping-stones. In taunting his rival, Finn pulled out a huge chunk of earth and flung it toward Scotland. The resulting hole became Lough Neagh, and the sod landed to create the Isle of Man. ■ TIP→ **In the peak summer months it can be very busy—get there early or leave your visit until late afternoon, when it's generally quieter.**

To reach the causeway, you can either walk 1½ km (1 mile) down a long, scenic hill or take the Causeway Coaster minibus. A popular option with many visitors is to take the 20-minute walk downhill to the main causeway and catch the shuttle bus back uphill. ■ TIP→ **Small children need to be properly supervised.**

A good place to start is the sparkling **Giant's Causeway Visitor Experience,** made of locally quarried basalt from the very same lava flows that formed the causeway. The glass front ensures spectacular coastal views, and the building is sunken into the ground, blending so effectively into the landscape that the indigenous grasses on the roof restore the natural ridgeline and provide a habitat for wildlife.

Inside the building, a stunning exhibition, complete with the 21st-century commercialization of Finn McCool, is made up of five parts: coastal map, geological history, people and their stories, natural life, and the power of the landscape. Guided one-hour tours of the stones are included in admission price, and visitors are issued a handheld device with recorded snippets of oral history. Tours leave every hour during the day. You can also take a self-guided geological tour that outlines the timescale of the site and helps differentiate the rocks. ■TIP➔ Kids love the center, so make sure you allow enough time on your visit to let them take in everything.

Outside, be aware that not all stones are created equal. Be sure to take a seat in the "Wishing Chair" and also look out for the "Giant's Boot," "Camel," "Harp," and the "Giant's Organ" pipes. Heading west, keep an eye out for Port-na-Spania, the spot where the 16th-century Spanish Armada galleon *Girona* went down on the rocks. The ship was carrying an astonishing cargo of gold and jewelry, some of which was only recovered in 1967. Beyond this, Chimney Point is the name given to one of the causeway structures on which the Spanish fired, thinking that it was Dunluce Castle, which is 8 km (5 miles) west.

You can park at the center—the fee is included in the admission price—or use the park-and-ride service between Bushmills and the causeway. Visitors who opt for the park and ride, or who arrive by public transportation, save £1.50 on the standard adult admission price (£3 per family) as part of a Green Travel Admission Ticket. ■TIP➔ Booking online far enough in advance to receive email confirmation of your date and time slot is recommended and saves you £1 on the adult admission price. ⊠ *44 Causeway Rd., Bushmills, Co. Antrim* ☎ *028/2073–1582* ⊕ *www.nationaltrust.org.uk/giantscauseway* ⊠ *£8.50* ☉ *Visitor center Feb., Mar., and Oct., daily 9–6; Apr.–June and Sept., daily 9–7; July and Aug., daily 9–9; Nov.–Jan., daily 9–5.*

BUSHMILLS

3 km (2 miles) west of Giant's Causeway.

GETTING HERE AND AROUND

CAR TRAVEL Bushmills is on the A2 coastal route and an ideal stopping place for refueling. It has the best parking facilities if you'll be exploring the Giant's Causeway. A park-and-ride service operates from the town to the visitor center and saves you the trouble of finding a space. If you're visiting Bushmills Distillery, there's a large free car park out front. Parking is free in the town along main streets.

EXPLORING

Bushmills. Reputedly the oldest licensed distillery in the world, Bushmills was first granted a charter by King James I in 1608, though historical records refer to a distillery here as early as 1276. Bushmills produces the most famous of Irish whiskeys—its namesake—and what is widely regarded as the best, the rarer black-label version known to aficionados as Black Bush. On the guided tour you will discover the secrets of the special water from St. Columb's Rill, the story behind malted Irish barley, and learn about triple distillation in copper stills and aging (which happens for long years in oak casks). You begin in the mashing and fermentation room, proceed to the maturing and bottling warehouse, and conclude, yes, with the much anticipated, complimentary shot of *uisce beatha*, the "water of life." ■TIP➔ Try to join a less-crowded early-morning tour. You can also have a light lunch in the Distillery Kitchen or buy souvenirs in the Distillery gift shop. *For more on Bushmills, see our*

Spotlight feature, "All About Irish Whiskeys" in this chapter. ✉ *2 Distillery Rd., off A2, Bushmills, Co. Antrim* ☎ *028/2073–3218* 🌐 *www.bushmills.com/visit* 🎟 *£7.50; children under 8 not permitted on tour* 🕒 *Tours Apr.–Oct., Mon.–Sat. 9:15–5, Sun. noon–5; Nov.–Mar., weekdays 10–4:45, weekends noon–4:45.*

> **WORD OF MOUTH**
>
> "I really didn't feel like walking all the way down to the Giant's Causeway. And the thought of walking back up was even less fun. So it's a good thing that they have the Causeway Coaster bus that goes every 10th minute. Cost £1 for a single ticket, £2 for a return ticket." —anyegr

WHERE TO STAY

$$$$ B&B/INN 🏨 **The Bushmills Inn.** A perfectly enchanting old coach inn welcomes with peat fires, a dazzlingly inventive dinner menu, and cozy rooms; the master distillers' suite even comes with fluffy slippers and bathrobes. **Pros:** the proximity to the distillery and the Giant's Causeway; comfortable rooms; tourists and chatty locals cross paths in the bar. **Cons:** if you're tall, look out for the low timber beams; it's hard to leave—even with the distractions of the surrounding area. [$] *Rooms from: £178* ✉ *9 Dunluce Rd., Bushmills, Co. Antrim* ☎ *028/2073–3000, 028/2073–2339* 🌐 *www.bushmillsinn.com* 🛏 *41 rooms, 9 suites* 🍴 *Breakfast.*

$$ HOTEL 🏨 **Causeway Hotel.** Owned by England's National Trust and flaunting a stunning location overlooking the Atlantic Ocean, this 1840s hotel is less than a half mile from the celebrated Giant's Causeway. **Pros:** bracing coastal walks (often chilly even in summer but you'll feel the warmth when you enter); worth it for the views. **Cons:** too many family parties; service can be a tad churlish. [$] *Rooms from: £99* ✉ *40 Causeway Rd., Bushmills, Co. Antrim* ☎ *028/2073–1210* 🌐 *www.giants-causeway-hotel.com* 🛏 *28 rooms* 🍴 *Some meals.*

DUNLUCE CASTLE

3 km (2 miles) west of Bushmills.

GETTING HERE AND AROUND

CAR AND BUS TRAVEL Dunluce is midway between Bushmills and Portrush. There is a small, free car park at the castle but it isn't big enough to accommodate large numbers at busy times. A tip: park free in Bushmills or Portrush, both a 10-minute drive away, and hop on the Causeway Rambler bus, which operates in summer along the A2 coastal route and will drop you at the castle. Coleraine is the nearest big town. Derry is an hour's drive west.

EXPLORING

FAMILY **Dunluce Castle.** Dramatically perched on a 100-foot-high basalt-rock cliff, halfway between Portrush and the Giant's Causeway, Dunluce Castle is one of the north's most evocative ruins. Even roofless, this shattered bulk conjures up a strength and aura that is quintessentially Antrim. Originally a 13th-century Norman fortress, Dunluce was captured in the 16th century by the local MacDonnell clan chiefs—the so-called Lords of the Isles. They enlarged it, in part using profits from salvaging the Spanish galleon *Girona*, and made it an important base for ruling northeastern Ulster. Perhaps the MacDonnells expanded the castle a bit too much, for in 1639 faulty construction caused the kitchens (with all the cooks) to plummet into the sea during a storm. Between 2009 and 2012, archaeologists uncovered belt buckles, thimbles, dress fastenings, jewelry, clay pipes, animal bones, and shards of pottery that are now on display in the Discovery Room. An eight-minute introductory film explores the castle's history, and a 10-minute film details the excavations. Audio guides are available in seven languages.Guided tours are held every day in the summer months and last 45 minutes. ■ **TIP→ Children love the sand pit where they handle tools and dress up.** ✉ *87 Dunluce Rd., Co. Antrim* ☎ *028/2073–1938* 🌐 *www.discovernorthernireland.com* 🎟 *£5* 🕒 *Apr.–Sept., Mon.–Sun. 10–6; Oct., Nov., Feb., and Mar., Mon–Sun. 10–5; Dec. and Jan., Mon–Sun. 10–4; last entry 30 mins before closing.*

WORD OF MOUTH

"We spent two nights at Bushmills, the old Irish Whiskey–owned inn right in the town of Bushmills: wonderful old rooms, cozy atmosphere, superb restaurant, even a room with a 'secret' revolving bookcase. Since it poured rain, we canceled plans to hike the Giant's Causeway and went to Bushmills. I became an 'official taster': Suffice it to say that I have been drinking Irish whiskey instead of Scotch ever since." —Patrick

WHERE TO EAT

$ ECLECTIC FAMILY 🍴 **Ramore Wine Bar.** Creative, moderately priced fare, alongside panoramic views in an elegant setting, attract locals and tourists to this popular restaurant and wine bar complex. The light-filled Mermaid Kitchen and Bar with white wooden paneling conjures up a beachside feel evocative of somewhere on the coast of Maine, except you're looking out on Portrush's West Strand (although admittedly Belfast is only 100 km [60 miles] south). Dominating the menu is the bountiful produce of the sea with eight different types of grilled fish including sea bass, halibut, and dover sole. If you're in the mood for a smaller plate try fresh white crab, spicy fried monkish, or salt chili prawns, each priced at £5.95—all delicious, especially when washed down with a steely Sancerre and accompanied by a north-coast sunset. There is also an ample selection of steak, pork, chicken, and lamb. The more informal Harbour Bistro serves burgers and chicken and ham pie, while the Coast Restaurant specializes in pizzas and pasta. [$] *Average main: £11* ✉ *The Harbor, Portrush, Co. Antrim* ☎ *028/7082–4313* 🌐 *www.ramorerestaurant.com.*

SPORTS AND THE OUTDOORS

BEACHES

Portstewart Strand. Portstewart Strand is signposted as "The Strand" at all major junctions in town. The magnificent 3 km (2 miles) of golden sand is one of the north coast's finest beaches suitable for all ages. Owned by the National Trust, well maintained and clean, it's the ideal spot for picnics, swimming, or long walks into sand dunes that are a haven for wildflowers and butterflies. Lifeguards are on duty at Easter and from June to August. The beach has an undertow at certain points and small sections have seaweed, but it's not a big nuisance.

While cliff erosion has played havoc with what's left of its battlements, Dunluce Castle still remains one of Northern Ireland's most intensely beautiful sights.

Two-hour guided walks are held on weekends during the summer. On hot days the beach fills with cars, but its size ensures that it is never completely crowded. ■TIP→ To cool down take the delightful 20-minute walk along the cliff-top path into Portstewart for an ice-cream sundae at the famed Morelli's shop along the promenade. **Amenities:** car park; changing rooms; toilets; outdoor shower; lifeguards; shop; café. **Best for:** swimming; sunbathing; snorkeling; windsurfing; kite-surfing; walks; sand dunes. ⊠ *118 Strand Rd., Portstewart* ☎ *028/7083–6396* ⊕ *www.nationaltrust.org.uk/portstewartstrand* ⊑ *£4.50 per car* ⊙ *Facilities Mar. and Oct., daily 10–4; Apr. and Sept., daily 10–5; May, daily 10–6; June–Aug., daily 10–7.*

GOLF

Portstewart Golf Club. More than a century old, Portstewart may scare you with its opening hole, generally regarded as the toughest starter in Ireland. Picture a 425-yard par-4 that descends from an elevated tee to a small green tucked between the dunes. The greens are known for uniformity and speed, and seven of the holes have been redesigned to toughen the course. If you want a break from the grand scale of the Strand championship links, there's the Old Course and the Riverside, 36 holes of downsize, executive-style golf. A modern clubhouse has a bar and restaurant. ⊠ *117 Strand Rd., Portstewart* ☎ *028/7083–2015* ⊕ *www.portstewartgc.co.uk* ⊑ *The Strand: weekdays £100, weekends £120; Old Course: weekdays £10, weekends £15; Riverside: weekdays £22, weekends £27* ⚑ *The Strand: 18 holes, 6895 yards, par 72; Old Course: 18 holes, 4730 yards, par 64; Riverside: 18 holes, 5725 yards,* *par 68. Practice area, caddies, caddy carts, buggies, catering ⊗ Visitors: daily, Sat. after 2 pm.*

Fodor's Choice
★

Royal Portrush Golf Club. With its profile raised after hosting the British Amateur Championships in 2014 and the British Open in 2012, Royal Portrush has confirmed its position as one of the leading courses in Ireland or Britain. Darren Clarke plays his golf here when he's at home and it's where Graeme McDowell, former U.S. Open champion, learned his golf at an early age. The championship Dunluce course is named for the ruins of a nearby castle and is a sea of sand hills and curving fairways. Despite its understated appearance it poses many and varied challenges. "White Rocks," the par-5 5th hole, is quite literally a cliff-hanger. It's a wicked dogleg with the green perched on the edge of a cliff. "Calamity," the aptly named 14th hole, demands total precision to carry the ball over a huge ravine. The Valley course is a less exposed, tamer track. Both are conspicuous for their lack of bunkers. In a poll of Irish golf legends, Dunluce was voted the best in Ireland. ⊠ *Dunluce Rd., Portrush, Co. Antrim* ☎ *028/7082–2311* ⊕ *www.royalportrushgolfclub.com* ✉ *Fees: May.–Sept. weekdays £155 (Dunluce), £55 (Valley); weekends £175 (Dunluce), £45 (Valley). Apr. and Oct. £75 (Dunluce), £42.50 (Valley), Nov.–Mar. £60 (Dunluce), £42.50 (Valley)* ⚑ *36 holes, 7143 yards (Dunluce), 6304 (Valley), par 72 (Dunluce), 75 (Valley). Practice area, caddies, caddy carts, buggies, catering ⊗ Visitors: daily (some restrictions).*

LIMAVADY

27 km (17 miles) east of Derry.

In 1851, at No. 51 on Limavady's Georgian main street, Jane Ross wrote down the tune played by a traveling fiddler and called it "Londonderry Air," better known now as "Danny Boy." While staying at an inn on Ballyclose Street, William Thackeray (1811–63) wrote his rather lustful poem "Peg of Limavady" about a barmaid. Among the many Americans descended from Ulster emigrants was President James Monroe, whose relatives came from the Limavady area.

GETTING HERE AND AROUND

CAR TRAVEL   On the main route between Derry and Coleraine, Limavady is well served with car parking. Motorists park free on the main street with a one-hour time limit. Pay-and-display parking, costing £0.40 per hour, is available at Newtown Square (off Linenhall Street) and on Connell Street.

BUS TRAVEL   Translink buses leave Limavady every hour during the day for Derry; journey time is 35 minutes. There is no train station, but you can connect with the train to Belfast by taking a bus to Coleraine or Ballymena.

ESSENTIALS

Visitor Information Limavady Tourist Office ⊠ *Roe Valley Arts Centre, 24 Main St.* ☎ *028/7776–0650* ⊕ *www.roevalleyarts.com.*

WHERE TO STAY

$$$
RESORT
🏨 **Roe Park Resort.** A country estate serves as the model for this modern deluxe resort on 155 acres straddling the banks of the River Roe—the place is relatively large and impersonal, although the lobby is welcoming and guest rooms have simple, clean-line beds in woods and rich earth tones. **Pros:** ideal location for pampering and relaxation; lively bars good for post-golf analysis. **Cons:** can be noisy with evening wedding parties; older rooms have a somewhat tired appearance. $ *Rooms from: £155* ✉ *Roe Park* ☎ *028/7772–2222* ⊕ *www.roeparkresort.com* ⬐ *118 rooms, 5 suites* ❍ *Multiple meal plans.*

DERRY

Wrapped in historic walls and hilly cobbled streets, Derry/Londonderry (as it's also known) oozes character. It's a small city on the rise, with the imprint of the past around every corner, proud of its 400-year-old walls and architectural heritage as well as the multimillion-pound beautification project that has seen landmark buildings emerge in recent years. Derry's remarkable history is told in expressive visual terms: walls and stained glass, a compelling open-air gallery of 21st-century political murals, the rejuvenated Guildhall, and a spectacular Peace Bridge that opened in 2011 across the River Foyle. The bridge links the city center with Ebrington Square, a redeveloped military parade ground now turned into a spacious playground filled with concerts and tai chi practitioners. The base figured in World War II's Battle of the Atlantic and its developers are slowly building a gallery, art center, studios, bars, shops, and a maritime museum.

Collectively, the changes of recent years are viewed as progress born of the peace process, and there is great desire to continue to build on this message that this city's communities, so long divided, now desire to work together.

GETTING HERE AND AROUND

CAR TRAVEL
The city's two main shopping centers, Foyleside and Quayside, have multistory car parking garages. Collect a ticket on entry and pay at a machine on departure. Other main car parks, which are mostly pay-by-the-hour via metered ticket machines, are located at Foyle Street, Carlisle Road, William Street, Society Street, Queens Quay, Alfred Street, and Victoria Market. Derry is a 75-minute drive from Belfast; A6 takes you over the mountainous Glenshane Pass. Roads lead south to Strabane and Omagh on A5 and on to Dublin (about four hours away, depending on road conditions and traffic). Derry is also the jumping-off point for exploring the Inishowen peninsula by car and the beautifully remote northern Donegal region.

BUS TRAVEL
Fast Translink Goldline Express buses (£17.50 same-day return, £20 open return) link Derry and Belfast on a trip over the Glenshane Pass. Journey time is one hour and 40 minutes. Weekend service, especially on Sunday, is less frequent. An alternative, slightly longer route, operated by Translink Goldline between Belfast and Derry, travels along the M1 motorway and through County Tyrone—it takes about two

hours. Translink buses run from Derry to neighboring towns, with fares averaging about £14.50 round-trip. You can also catch a bus from City of Derry Airport into the Foyle Street bus station in the city center (£8 round-trip). The Airporter Coach, which leaves from Bay Road, operates between Derry and Belfast International Airport and George Best Belfast City Airport. Tickets to both airports cost £29.50 round-trip. If you're traveling across the border from Derry into Donegal, then you have a choice of using Bus Éireann or the Lough Swilly Bus Company.

> **WALKING DERRY**
>
> It's easy to find your own way around Derry's streets and riverside. Walkers and cyclists can explore the new traffic-free Waterside Greenway, a 3½-km (2-mile) route through parkland from the east bank of the Foyle over the Peace Bridge to the Foyle Bridge. Or follow the Pathway to Peace, an initiative that emerged after the unveiling of Ireland's first peace flame in Derry by Martin Luther King III in 2013. Ask at the tourist office for details.

TRAIN TRAVEL   One of the most relaxing ways to arrive in Derry is by train. Frequent daily services on Northern Ireland Railways link it with Coleraine, Ballymena, Antrim, and Belfast. For the final 20-minute section of the journey—along the County Derry coastline—the track runs parallel to the sea and is one of Ireland's most stunning routes. The journey time from Belfast to Derry is about two hours (£17.50 round-trip). The main station is in the Waterside area of the city—catch a free 10-minute shuttle bus across Craigavon Bridge to get to the West Bank, where most attractions are concentrated.

Transportation Contacts Airporter Coach ☎ *028/7126–9996* ⊕ *www. airporter.co.uk.* **Lough Swilly** ☎ *074/912–2873.*

TOURS

City Tours. These walks (£4) led by Martin McCrossan, leave daily at 10, noon, and 2. From April to October there is an additional tour at 4. For more than two decades, Martin has shared his great passion for Derry with visitors. His tour, which departs from 11 Carlisle Road (just show up; reservations not necessary), lasts one hour and incorporates not only history and centuries-old stories but also architecture and engaging bits of local lore and humor. The same company also organizes City Bike Tours (£15, includes bike rental and gear). The 75-minute ride, on a mostly flat route, takes in city sights and some out-of-the-way delights and ends with a gentle pedal along the Derry city walls. ⊠ *11 Carlisle Rd., West Bank* ☎ *028/7127–1996* ⊕ *derrycitytours.com.*

Top Tours Ireland ☎ *028/7137–0067* ⊕ *toptoursireland.com.*

Tours 'n' Trails ☎ *028/7136–7000* ⊕ *www.toursntrails.co.uk.*

VISITOR INFORMATION   **Visit Derry.** Derry's sparkling new tourist information office is right in the heart of the city, on the ground floor of the elegant former Ulster Bank Buildings. Staff can advise on tours, travel, and accommodations. In addition to leaflets on Derry and the rest of Northern Ireland, you can pick up literature and maps on many other parts of Ireland. ⊠ *Ulster Bank Bldgs., Waterloo Pl., West Bank* ☎ *028/7126–7284* ⊕ *www. derryvisitor.com.*

EXPLORING

Derry's name shadows its history. Those in favor of British rule call the city Londonderry, its old plantation-period name: the "London" part was tacked on in 1613 after the Flight of the Earls, when the city and county were handed over to the Corporation of London, which represented London's merchants. The corporation brought in a large population of English and Scottish Protestant settlers, built towns for them, and reconstructed Derry within the city walls (which survive almost unchanged to this day). Derry's sturdy ramparts have withstood many fierce attacks—they have never been breached, which explains the city's coy sobriquet, "The Maiden City." The most famous attack was the siege of 1688–89, begun after 13 apprentice boys slammed the city gates in the face of the Catholic king, James II. Inhabitants, who held out for 105 days and were reduced to eating dogs, cats, and laundry starch, nevertheless helped to secure the British throne for the Protestant king, William III. Whatever you choose to call it—and the latest name is Derry/Londonderry—the city is no longer an underrated place.

TOP ATTRACTIONS

Derry City Walls. Established under a charter by James I in 1613, Derry is among a small but distinctive coterie of places throughout Europe which have preserved their ancient ramparts. Built between 1614 and 1618, the walls today allow you toget a feel for Derry's deep history by strolling along the parapet walkway and pausing on a platform. Pierced by eight gates (originally four) and as much as 30 feet thick, the gray-stone ramparts are only 1½ km (1 mile) all around. On your walk, take a break at a strategically placed café or simply drink in the atmosphere of this most photogenic of cities. In summer when the walls are awash with tourists, ambassadors are on hand to help show you around. ⊠ *West Bank* ⊕ *www.derryswalls.com.*

Derry Wall Murals. Dramatic wall murals throughout Derry testify to the power of art as historical document, while also serving as a reminder of painful pasts. Symbolic of the different communities, the murals attract considerable curiosity from tourists. The Bogside Gallery of Murals, painted by William Kelly, Kevin Hasson, and Tom Kelly, are made up of 12 wall paintings known collectively as "The Peoples Gallery." They include the *Bloody Sunday Commemoration, The Death of Innocence, Civil Rights, The Hunger Strikes,* and a poignant one featuring the Nobel Peace Prize–winning Derry politician John Hume along with Martin Luther King Jr., Nelson Mandela, and Mother Teresa—all beside Brooklyn Bridge. The paintings span the length of Rossville Street in the heart of the Bogside. Some of the guided walking tours that leave from the tourist information center include the story of the murals. On the other side of the political divide, close to the city walls, the Protestant Fountain estate is home to one of the oldest King Billy murals along with other colorful ones linked to the siege of Derry. ⊠ *Rossville St., Bogside* ☎ *028/7126–7284.*

Ebrington Square. Since its reincarnation as a venue for open-air concerts and other outdoor events, Ebrington Square, a former military barracks on the River Foyle's east bank, has become an established cultural hub.

It was named for Lord Ebrington, the Lord Lieutenant of Ireland during the years 1839–41 when many of the military buildings here were erected, including the Star Fort, one of the architectural highlights. During World War II, the barracks became part of a naval base that later functioned as an anti-submarine training school for the Allied navies operating from the city. Derry's contribution to the Battle of the Atlantic was acknowledged with the unveiling in 2013 of a bronze International Sailor statue in the square which pays tribute to seamen from the 12 Allied nations who protected shipping convoys. It is a replica of the Mariner statue in Halifax, Nova Scotia. The base closed in 2004 and is being slowly redeveloped, with shops, a hotel, and a maritime museum planned over the next five years. ⊠ *Ebrington Sq., East Bank* 🕾 *028/7126–7284* ⊕ *www.ilex-urc.com* ✉ *Free.*

FAMILY
Fodor's Choice
★

Guildhall. The rejuvenated Victorian Guildhall, fresh from a three-year £10-million makeover, is an outstanding example of the city's ornate architecture. It has been refashioned as a visitor center with interactive exhibits telling the story of the plantation of Ulster and the construction of the walled city, and how these events shaped present-day Derry. Touch-screen displays explain the building's special features such as elaborate ceilings, baronial wood paneling, and magnificent organ. For children, hands-on displays include a puzzle to re-create a 1598 map of Ulster or they can spin a wheel to find out about the different London companies and how land was divided. Kids can also build a *bawn*, stone house, or castle using wooden blocks, or dress up in the clothes of planters or Irish people of the period. Look out, too, for the delightful scale model of the city in 1738 showing just a few thatched cabins outside the perimeter wall. A conserved page (a folio) from the Great Parchment Book of 1639 detailing the account of the plantation is also on display. With the gleaming restoration, one of the most famous of all Derry's local sayings, "You've more faces than the Guildhall clock" (not to be taken as a compliment), has renewed resonance. ■TIP→ Enjoy an alfresco coffee in the Guild Café at the harbor square entrance overlooking the Foyle, an ideal spot to catch the riverine light and reflect on 400 turbulent years of history. ⊠ *Guildhall Sq., West Bank* 🕾 *028/7137–5151* ⊕ *www.derrycity.gov.uk* ✉ *Free* ☉ *Daily 10–5:30.*

Museum of Free Derry. At Free Derry Corner stands the white gable wall where Catholics defiantly painted the slogan "You are now entering Free Derry" as a declaration of a zone from which police and the British Army were banned until 1972, when the army broke down the barricades. That year, on January 30, 13 civil-rights marchers were shot and killed by British soldiers. Thirty-eight years later, the British government released its official report on the shootings from Lord Saville, which resulted in an official apology from Prime Minister David Cameron saying that he was "deeply sorry" for what happened on Bloody Sunday and that it "had been unjustified and unjustifiable." Historical homage to this tragic moment in time is rendered by the Museum of Free Derry, housed in a derelict block of flats right on the spot where Bloody Sunday happened; the building still retains bullet scars and was conserved to preserve the "line of sight" that fateful day. Inside, visitors will find a real-time recording of the event as well as a gallery

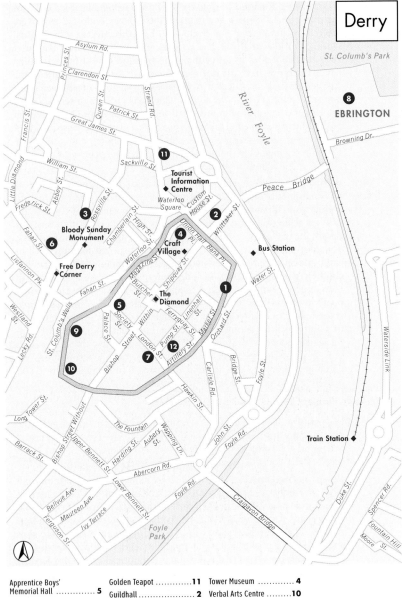

with newspaper reports, photographs, and posters about the "Battle of the Bogside." One-hour Free Derry Walking Tours (£5) leave from here at 10, noon, 2, and 4 each day in the summer months. ⚠ **Please note that due to a £2-million renovation program, the museum will be housed in temporary premises in another location in the Bogside until the summer of 2015.** Phone in advance. ⊠ *55 Glenfada Park, off Rossville St., West Bank* ☎ *028/7136–0880* ⊕ *www.museumoffreederry.org* ☞ *£4* ⊘ *Weekdays 9:30–4:30; also Apr.–Sept., Sat. 1–4; and July–Sept., Sun. 1–4.*

St. Augustine's Church. This is a small jewel of a church wedged just inside the ramparts of the walls. In the ancient graveyard a large board map registers the location of 163 gravestones in alphabetical order. The site was known as "God's Little Acre," indicating a much larger graveyard, but now sits in an area of a quarter of an acre. It has been a sacred spot since Columba founded his first abbey here in AD 546. The oldest gravestone—in the church porch—is that of Richard Carrec, an Elizabethan soldier dating from circa 1609. Immerse yourself in the serenity of the graveyard under the shadow of the cherry trees, tune into the birdsong, a world away from the tour groups being corralled around the walls. Visitors can tour the church and adjoining graveyard from May to October and are welcome at worship on Sunday or at morning communion on Tuesday at 10:30 am. ⊠ *Palace St., West Bank* ☎ *028/7130–8185* ⊕ *www.saintaugustines.co.uk* ⊘ *May–Oct., daily.*

St. Columb's Cathedral. The first Protestant cathedral built in the United Kingdom after the Reformation, this houses the oldest and largest bells in Ireland (dating from the 1620s). It's a treasure house of Derry Protestant emblems, memorials, and relics from the siege of 1688–89; most visitors come to see the keys that locked the four main gates of the city during the siege. The church was built in 1633 in simple Planter's Gothic style, with an intricate corbeled roof and austere spire. In the vestibule is the 270-pound mortar ball that was fired over the wall during the Siege of Derry, with an invitation to surrender sent by King James. Legend has it that when it was read, every man, woman, and child in the city rushed to the walls and shouted, "No surrender!"—a Protestant battle cry to this day. The attached Chapter House Museum has the oldest surviving copy of a map of Derry (from 1600) and the Bible owned by Governor George Walker during the siege. View the information panels and artifacts in display cases that include the original keys to the city and other relics from the past. In recent years the tower and spire have been restored and the stonework and stained-glass windows repaired. A new LED lighting system reveals the beauty of the elegant Canadian pine ceiling. Knowledgeable tour guides are on hand and audio guides are available. In the nearby Cathedral House, visitors can view the CFA Experience, an exhibition about the lives and work of the poetess and hymn writer Cecil Frances Alexander and her husband, Archbishop William Alexander. ⊠ *London St., off Bishop St., West Bank* ☎ *028/7126–7313* ⊕ *www.stcolumbscathedral.org* ☞ *£2 suggested donation* ⊘ *Mon.–Sun. 9–5.*

Tower Museum. The history of Derry is chronicled in this tall, medieval, and magical granite tower that houses the Tower Museum. The original building was constructed in 1615 by the O'Dohertys for their overlords, the O'Donnells, in lieu of tax payments. Partly refurbished in 2012 and with a new Discovery Zone on the first floor, the museum has excellent information celebrating the life and legacy of St. Columba. The vivid "Story of Derry" covers the city's history, from its origins as a monastic settlement in an oak grove up to the Troubles, which began in 1969 after years of institutionalized discrimination in jobs and public housing. (A well-known Derry joke is that the skeleton in the city's coat of arms was actually a Catholic waiting for a house.) There's also an exhibition, spread over four floors, on the Spanish Armada, thanks to the fact that its fourth-largest ship, *La Trinidad Valencera*, foundered in Kinnagoe Bay, in County Donegal, in 1588. ✉ *Union Hall Pl., West Bank* ☎ *028/7137–2411* ⊕ *www.derrycity.gov.uk/museums* 💷 *£4* 🕒 *June–Sept., Mon.–Sun. 10–6; Oct.–May, Tues.–Sat. 10–5; last entry 30 mins before closing.*

WORTH NOTING

Apprentice Boys' Memorial Hall. Imposing in its Scottish Baronial fortified grandeur, this is a meeting place for the exclusively Protestant organization set up in 1715 to honor 13 Apprentice Boys who slammed the city gate in the face of the Catholic King James in 1688, sparking the Siege of Derry; ever since, it has remained a symbol of Protestant stubbornness. During the early part of 2015 the Memorial Hall will be undergoing renovation and at the same time, next door to the Hall, a new £2-million building, the grandiosely titled "Siege Heroes Museum and Shared Space Visitors Centre" is slated to open. The new center tells the fascinating story of the105-day siege and chronicles the history of the Apprentice Boys. A look-alike sandstone scale model of Walker's Pillar—blown up by the IRA in 1973—has been re-created. ⚠ **Check with the tourist office or call the center before visiting.** Guided hour-long tours of the city walls, focusing on the siege, are also being offered by the organization during the summer of 2015. ✉ *13 Society St., West Bank* ☎ *028/7126–3571* ⊕ *www.apprenticeboys.co.uk* 💷 *£3* 🕒 *Daily 10–4:30.*

Walker Memorial. The memorial, a statue of George Walker, the governor of Derry during the siege, is a symbol of the city's divided nature. It was blown up by the IRA in 1973, and the story goes that the statue's head rolled down the hill into the Catholic Bogside, where it was captured by a local youth. He ransomed it back to the Protestants for a small fortune, and today it sits on the shoulders of a replica of the original statue beside the Apprentice Boys' Memorial Hall. ✉ *Apprentice Boys' Memorial Hall, Society St., West Bank.*

WHERE TO EAT

$$ ✕ **Browns in Town.** Candles on tables, leather upholstered horseshoe
IRISH booths with calming cream, and brown timber shades have been attracting the crowds to this central restaurant since it opened in 2013. The three-course early evening dinner menu at £19.95 showcases pan-seared fillet of Greencastle monkfish, free-range chicken, or braised shoulder of Lough Erne lamb. If you have space for a dessert, then indulge in the chocolate meringue with dark chocolate sorbet or the

black treacle and almond tart. Run by local chef hero Ian Orr—he also cooks at Browns flagship restaurant and champagne lounge on Bonds Hill and has put Derry on the culinary map—this is an über-cool spot. Attentive service and comfort means you will leave here with a mellow afterglow that will linger long. $ *Average main: £17* ⊠ *23 Strand Rd., Central District* ☏ *028/7136–2889* ⊕ *www.browns restaurant.com* ⊘ *Closed Mon.*

> **THE HIGH AND THE FLIGHTY**
>
> Aviation fans, take note: Derry was where Amelia Earhart touched down on May 21, 1932, after her historic solo flight across the Atlantic. Local lore has it that the first man to reach her airplane greeted her in typically unfazed Derry fashion: "Aye, and what do you want, then?"

$

CAFÉ

× **Claudes Cafe.** "Say nothin' till ye see Claude," was a famous old Derry saying. Claude Wilton, a solicitor and civil rights campaigner representing all classes and creeds died in 2008, but his name lives on in mugs and T-shirts in this central cafe. Make up your own tortilla wrap or try one of their baked potatoes with a salad filling, accompanied by a specialty tea or freshly roasted Segafredo Italian coffee. ■ TIP→ While you're enjoying your coffee, log on to one of their computers or just browse a copy of the Derry Journal, a paper that has been reporting the news for nearly 250 years and is the essence of the city. $ *Average main: £5* ⊠ *4 Shipquay St., Central District* ☏ *028/7127–9379* ⊕ *www.claudescafederry.co.uk.*

$

EUROPEAN

Fodor'sChoice

★

× **Custom House Restaurant.** The food is first-class and the river views are stunning, but at this restaurant on Derry's quays it's the chandelier that truly wows diners. Made in Italy from thousands of octagonal glass crystals and weighing over 330 pounds, it is illuminated by 30 color-changing LEDs. Such is the weight of the chandelier that workmen had to strengthen the ceiling to accommodate it. Signature dishes for dinner, served upstairs in the main dining area, include crispy pork belly, black pudding, crispy hen's egg, and delicious salt-and-chili squid. Snacks and bar food are available in the more informal downstairs lounge. The restaurant occupies an 1876 building where taxes were collected from ships arriving at the port. $ *Average main: £13* ⊠ *Custom House St., Queen's Quay, Central District* ☏ *028/7137–3366* ⊕ *www.custom houserestaurant.com.*

$$

IRISH

× **The Exchange Restaurant and Wine Bar.** Tucked in along Queen's Quay, this is *the* chic place to be seen in Derry and can be extremely busy on weekend evenings. Unfortunately, reservations are not taken, so be prepared to wait at the bar—with a chilled glass of Sauvignon Blanc from the excellent wine list, it's no hardship. The standout dish of the locally caught seafood served here is the medallions of monkfish with tiger prawns. Service is super-efficient but can be a touch brisk. At £10.95, the early-bird menu (Monday–Thursday) is a great value. $ *Average main: £15* ⊠ *Exchange House, Queen's Quay, Central District* ☏ *028/7127–3990* ⊕ *www.exchangerestaurant.com* ⊘ *No lunch Sun.*

$

EUROPEAN

FAMILY

× **Fitzroy's.** Satisfying, great-value portions of burgers, steaks, and Caesar salads are dinner favorites at this popular city-center brasserie. The lunch dishes may include seafood chowder or the delectable chicken melter, made up of cheese, tobacco onions, and bacon with Mexican spices. Fitzroy's frequently offers discount deals, including half-price meals on Monday and Tuesday—check the website for the latest specials. $ *Average main: £13* ✉ *2–4 Bridge St., Central District* ☎ *028/7126–6211* ⊕ *www.fitzroysrestaurant.com.*

$ ✕ **Thompson's Restaurant.** On the banks of the River Foyle, the main res-
IRISH taurant of the City Hotel takes its name from the old Thompson's Mill
Fodor'sChoice that once occupied this site. The decor is airy and cool. Menu might
★ include medallions of pork fillet, oven-baked salmon, or supreme of chicken with a herb stuffing. Thanks to its popularity, reservations are recommended (and practically essential on weekends). The Two's Company menu, based on two people sharing two courses, is £35 for two people. Throw in an impressive but not expensive wine list, and this adds up to a fine place to chill while taking in some great river views. Breakfast is served daily, but lunch only on Sunday. $ *Average main: £13* ✉ *City Hotel on Queen's Quay, Central District* ☎ *028/7136–5800* ⊕ *www.cityhotelderry.com* ☾ *No lunch Mon.–Sat.*

WHERE TO STAY

$ ⊞ **The Merchant's House.** Number 16 Queen Street was originally a Victo-
B&B/INN rian merchant's family town home built to Georgian proportions, then
Fodor'sChoice a rectory and bank, before Joan Pyne turned it into the city's grand-
. ★ est B&B—garnet-color walls, elaborate plasterwork, and a fireplace make the parlor warm and welcoming. **Pros:** graceful and elegant; great value; for the discriminating traveler. **Cons:** rooms next to kitchen noisy in morning; small bathrooms. $ *Rooms from: £70* ✉ *16 Queen St., West Bank* ☎ *028/7126–9691* ⊕ *www.saddlershouse.com* ⌁ *9 rooms in Merchant's House; 7 rooms with shared bath in Saddler's House* ⦿*Breakfast.*

$$ ⊞ **Tower Hotel.** The only hotel within Derry city's historic walls, this
HOTEL modern building has more to offer than its unequaled location; guest rooms are decorated in vibrant shades of red and green, with pine furnishings and well-stocked bathrooms, while the Walls Restaurant has delights such as Irish salmon with horseradish and parsnips. **Pros:** top-notch location for exploring Derry's walls, sights, shops, and idiosyncrasies; practical, clean, and tastefully decorated rooms with modern facilities. **Cons:** limited parking available; wedding guests and conference delegates spill over into the sometimes noisy, crowded lobby. $ *Rooms from: £99* ✉ *Tower Hotel, Butcher St., Central District* ☎ *028/7137–1000* ⊕ *www.towerhotelderry.com* ⌁ *90 rooms, 3 suites* ⦿*Multiple meal plans.*

NIGHTLIFE AND THE ARTS

NIGHTLIFE

Gweedore Bar. Traditional Irish and folk music sessions are held most nights in the main downstairs bar. There's a different musical personality in Upstairs Gweedore where you're likely to hear everything from indie and house music to rock and chart disco. ✉ *59–63 Waterloo St., West Bank* ☎ *028/7137–2318* ⊕ *www.peadars-gweedorebar.com.*

Sandinos Cafe Bar. For a funky afternoon pit stop, try Sandinos, a haunt of radicals and writers (posters of Che Guevara and Nicaraguan writers decorate the walls). Sample the dozen or so world beers, or try the rare Connemara peated single-malt Irish whiskey. There's traditional Irish music on Sunday from 5 to 9. ⊠ *Water St., West Bank* ☎ *028/7130–9297* ⊕ *www.sandinos.com.*

Sugar Nightclub. Many night owls consider this *the* place for dance music in Derry. ⊠ *33 Shipquay St., West Bank* ☎ *028/7126–6017.*

THE ARTS

If there's one thing about Derry, it certainly knows how to throw a good party. A maelstrom of creative energy was released by the city's role in 2013 as U.K. City of Culture, and through that cultural transformation the city strengthened its musical mojo. Long celebrated as a place of music, Derry has always expressed its soul in words and songs. Phil Coulter, its most famous musical son, wrote "Ireland's Call," the politically neutral anthem played at Irish rugby, cricket, and hockey internationals, and composed a new song, "Bright, Brand New Day" to celebrate the cultural year. Other celebrated musical offspring of the city include Feargal Sharkey and his band the Undertones, and Nadine Coyle from Girls Aloud.

Music festivals take pride of place in the annual calendar of events. During the City of Derry Big Band Jazz Festival in May, it's a case of boogie all over town: R&B, swing, jive, soul, and blues singers as well as tribute acts take over bars, cafés, hotels, restaurants, and community centers. Music also tops the bill at the Foyle Folk Festival, the Walled City Music Festival, and the Maiden City Festival. Literature, drama, and film are all given prominence throughout the year. On October 31, the Banks of the Foyle Halloween Carnival morphs into what the tourism bureau calls "the largest street party in Ireland." The city has also reinvented itself with cultural centers and new galleries sprouting up—excellent places for visual snacking.

ART GALLERIES | **CCA Derry/Londonderry.** Irish and international artistic collaborations are part of the credo of this cutting-edge gallery. It has featured shows by emerging Irish artists and enjoys connections with galleries in Cairo and Seoul, as well as London and Dublin. There's a free public library where you can browse and take advantage of the tea and coffee machine. ⊠ *10–12 Artillery St., West Bank* ☎ *028/7137–3538* ⊕ *www.cca-derry-londonderry.org.*

THEATER AND OPERA | **Millennium Forum.** This catch-all venue hosts everything from boy bands and comedians to plays, musicals, tattoo conventions, and even weddings (invitations required). The Encore Brasserie on the ground floor serves good-value pretheater meals (on show nights) as well as lunches and snacks every day. ⊠ *Newmarket St., West Bank* ☎ *028/7126–4455, 028/7137–2492 reservations* ⊕ *www.millenniumforum.co.uk.*

Playhouse. With its impressive auditorium and workshop spaces, the Playhouse stages traditional and contemporary plays and also holds concerts. ⊠ *5–7 Artillery St., West Bank* ☎ *028/7126–8027* ⊕ *www.derryplayhouse.co.uk.*

Verbal Arts Centre. You would usually expect to see it in Dublin, but the complete manuscript of James Joyce's *Ulysses* has been handwritten on to the walls of the Verbal Arts Centre by Colin Dark. You won't, of course, have time to read all of it, but while you're here, admire the marble floor designed by the celebrated Irish artist Louis le Brocquy, who died in 2012. The center is a hotbed of literary activity promoting the spoken and written word, and presents storytelling re-created in the old Irish tradition of fireside tales. Book hounds love to chill at Blooms Café, a delightful spot looking out over Derry's walls. ⊠ *Stable La. and Mall Wall, Bishop St., West Bank* ☎ *028/7126–6946* ⊕ *www. theverbal.co.*

SHOPPING

Although the major retail department stores are here, shopping is generally low-key. There are some upscale examples of Irish craftsmanship to be found, however. Stroll up Shipquay Street to discover small arts-and-crafts stores and an indoor shopping center. Walk through the Craft Village (just off Shipquay Street) to see the way the city used to look. The Village, with its newly installed glass canopy, re-creates life between the 16th and 19th century and sells Derry crystal, handwoven cloth, ceramics, jewelry, and books. Not to be outdone by Belfast, Derry has set up its own Cathedral Quarter. In the heart of the old city, streets leading from the cathedral—Pump Street, Artillery Street, and Bishop Street—are busy with craft workers, goldsmiths, and jewelers; art galleries sit cheek by jowl with nail bars, solariums and treatment spas. Bedlam, a maze of rooms on Pump Street, is a humming nest of 14 traders under one roof in a former convent. Vintage clothes, antiques, retro furnishings, and New Age products are on sale while Little Acorns bookstore stocks a selection of Irish literature as well as books from the local Guildhall Press.

To appreciate the beauty and scale of the area's Georgian architecture, walk slowly along Pump Street, with a copy of *City of Derry*, an excellent historical gazetteer to the built heritage (published in 2013)—it has a wealth of information and color about each individual building and is available at the bookstore in Bedlam. As you wander around the streets, look out for the Golden Teapot—a 19th-century trade sign in the shape of a gilded copper teapot—restored in 2013 and hanging outside Faller's jewelers on Strand Road; catch the right moment and a plume of environmentally friendly smoke is discharged from its spout. The only other one in the world is in Boston.

BOOKS

Foyle Books. Derry's largest selection of secondhand and antiquarian titles can be found here. The specialties include English lit, Irish-language books, criticism, poetry, biography, local history, travel, music, and sports. ⊠ *12 Magazine St., West Bank* ☎ *028/7137–2530* ⊕ *www. derrycraftvillage.com/foylebooks.html.*

CLOTHING

Trip. Off Shipquay Street, Trip is a teenage-clothing shop that specializes in knitwear. ⊠ *29 Ferryquay St., West Bank* ☎ *028/7137–2382.*

CRAFTS, GIFTS AND JEWELRY

Faller The Jeweller. It's worth calling in to hear the history of the restored Victorian golden teapot hanging outside this long-established family-run shop. Faller's specializes in brooches and charms reflecting local landmarks in their Drop of Derry range; you can even buy a small replica of the famed teapot. The city's cultural history, music, and sporting life is featured in designs as well as Roaring Meg cannon, the Peace Bridge, the Guildhall, and city walls. Even more popular are the high crosses of Inishowen in nearby Donegal; ancient Celtic crosses such as St. Mura, Donagh, and Cooley are all available as pendants. ⊠ *12 Strand Rd., West Bank* ☎ *028/7136–2719* ⊕ *www.faller.com.*

Occasions. This remains one of Derry's best showcases for Irish crafts and gifts. ⊠ *48 Spencer Rd., East Bank* ☎ *028/7132–9595.*

Pauline's Patch. Stop at this gift shop for the perfect knickknack, or gifts such as hand-embroidered bags and locally made crafts. A café serves soups, sandwiches, and cakes. ⊠ *32 Shipquay St., West Bank* ☎ *028/7127–9794* ⊕ *www.paulinespatch.com.*

Thomas the Goldsmith. Head here for exquisite work by international jewelry designers. Ask about their Peace Bridge Collection, handcrafted and individually designed in the workshop. ⊠ *7 Pump St., West Bank* ☎ *028/7137–4549* ⊕ *www.thomasgoldsmiths.com.*

THE BORDER COUNTIES

While blissfully off the beaten track, this region contains some dazzling sights: the Ulster-American Folk Park; the great stately houses of Castle Coole and Florence Court; the pottery town of Belleek; the breathtaking Mountains of Mourne; and the blessed St. Patrick sites in Armagh and Downpatrick. During the worst of the Troubles, the counties of Armagh and Down, which border the republic, were known as "bandit country," but now you can enjoy a worry-free trip through the calm countryside and stop in at some very "Ulster" towns, delightfully distinct from the rest of Ireland.

OMAGH

55 km (34 miles) south of Derry.

Omagh, the county town of Tyrone, lies close to the Sperrin Mountains, with the River Strule to the north. The playwright Brian Friel was born here. Sadly, it's better known as the scene of the worst atrocity of the Troubles, when an IRA bomb killed 31 people in 1998. On the 10th anniversary of the bombing, the Garden of Light, a touching memorial by artist Sean Hillen and landscape architect Desmond Fitzgerald, was opened. A heliostatic mirror in the memorial park tracks the sun and directs a beam of light onto 31 small mirrors, each etched with the name of a victim. They in turn bounce the light via another hidden mirror onto a heart-shaped crystal in an obelisk at the bomb site in Market Street. An entire room in Omagh Library, housing 800 books of condolence and reflecting worldwide media coverage, is dedicated to the memory of the attack. Ask about access to this archive at the tourist office which is in the Strule Arts Centre, a good place for a relaxing snack or meal, and where you may also find out about any events or shows being held.

GETTING HERE

CAR TRAVEL Omagh, 55 km (34 miles) south of Derry on A5, is a busy hub. Free car parking on the town's two main central streets, High and Market, is available for one hour. Pay-and-display ticket machines, costing 40 pence per hour, operate in car parks at Mountjoy Road (beside the bus station) and Kevlin Avenue. You can also park free for two hours in the retail park at the Showgrounds, on Sedan Avenue.

BUS TRAVEL The Translink Goldline service operates buses aplenty between Derry and Belfast and traverses a delightful incantation of mellifluous-sounding Tyrone towns, from Strabane to Ballygawley, and thence along the M1 into Belfast. Journey time is just under two hours (£17.50 round-trip). Services in both directions stop on request at the popular Ulster-American Folk Park.

EXPLORING

Fodor's Choice
★

Ulster American Folk Park. The excellent Ulster American Folk Park re-creates a Tyrone village of two centuries ago, a log-built American settlement of the same period, and the docks and ships that the emigrants to America would have used. The centerpiece is an old whitewashed cottage, now a museum, which is the ancestral home of Thomas Mellon (1813–1908), the U.S. banker and philanthropist. Another thatch cottage is a reconstruction of the boyhood home of Archbishop John Hughes, founder of New York's St. Patrick's Cathedral. There are full-scale replicas of Irish peasant cottages, a New York tenement room, immigrant transport ship holders, plus a 19th-century Ulster village, complete with staff dressed in period costumes. The Mellon Centre for Migration Studies contains 16,000 books and periodicals, an Irish emigration database including passenger lists from 1800 to 1860, emigrant letters, and maps of geographical regions of both Ireland and America. The center has separate opening hours to the folk park: 10:30 am to 4:30 pm.

Other notable exhibits include William Murray's drapery store and W. G. O' Doherty's original candy store on the bustling Ulster Street where visitors can explore the world of retail therapy in the early 1900s.

■TIP➜ As you wander around the folk park you will detect its sensory side, especially in the delightful enclosed herb garden next to the Pennsylvania log farmhouse. Elsewhere the park is imbued with wood smoke from the burning fires as well as apple butter and cinnamon spices from the cornmeal bread being baked in the houses: all part of the education of a good nose. ⊠ *Mellon Rd., Castletown, 10 km (6 miles) north of town on A5* ☎ *028/8224–3292* ⊕ *www.nmni.com/uafp* ⊠ *£7* ⊗ *Mar.–Sept., Tues.–Sun. 10–5; Oct.–Feb., Tues.–Sun. 10–4; weekends 11–4.*

BELLEEK

42 km (25 miles) southwest of Omagh.

World-famous Belleek Pottery is made in the old town of Belleek, on the northwestern edge of Lower Lough Erne, at the border with Northwest Ireland. Other porcelain-ware makers are a few kilometers across the border.

An annual bluegrass music festival at the Ulster-American Folk Park reaffirms the strong links between Northern Ireland and the United States.

GETTING HERE AND AROUND

Belleek is on A46, a scenic route running along the southern shore of Lower Lough Erne between Enniskillen (a 30-minute drive), in County Fermanagh, and Ballyshannon (15 minutes), in County Donegal. There is ample car parking at the pottery factory—the reason most people come here—with no time restrictions. You can also park free along main or side streets.

EXPLORING

Fodor's Choice
★ **Belleek Pottery.** On the riverbank stands the visitor center of Belleek Pottery Ltd., producers of Parian china, a fine, eggshell-thin, ivory porcelain shaped into dishes, figurines, vases, and baskets. There's a factory, showroom, exhibition, museum, and café. On tours of the factory you can get up close and talk to craftspeople—there's hardly any noise coming from machinery in the workshops. Everything here is made by hand just as workers did back in 1857. The showroom is filled with beautiful but pricey gifts: a shamrock cup-and-saucer set costs about £45, and a bowl in a basket-weave style (typical of Belleek) runs £100 and up. The company has a jewelry portfolio called Belleek Living featuring designs inspired by the Irish landscape. ✉ *3 Main St.* ☎ *028/6865–8501* ⊕ *www.belleek.ie* ✍ *£5* ⊙ *Mar.–Oct., weekdays 9–5:30, Sat. 10–5:30, Sun. noon–5:30; Nov. and Dec., weekdays 9–5:30, Sat. 10–5:30; Jan. and Feb., weekdays 9–5:30.*

WHERE TO EAT

$ ╳ **The Thatch.** Housed in a lovely building dating to the 18th century,
CAFÉ this simple café is worth a visit—not just for the excellent soups, sandwiches, baked potatoes, and similarly light fare—but also because it's

Beautiful Belleek

The origins of Belleek china are every bit as romantic as the Belleek blessing plates traditionally given to brides and grooms on their wedding day—that is, if you believe the legends. The story goes that in the mid-1800s, John Caldwell Bloomfield, the man behind the world-famous porcelain, accidentally discovered the raw ingredients necessary to produce china. After inheriting his father's estate in the Fermanagh Lakelands on the shore of the Erne River, he whitewashed his cottage using a flaky white powder dug up in his backyard. A passerby, struck by the luminescent sheen of the freshly painted cottage, commented on the unusual brightness of the walls to Bloomfield, who promptly ordered a survey of the land, which duly uncovered all the minerals needed to make porcelain. The venture was complete when Bloomfield met his business partners— London architect Robert Armstrong and the wealthy Dublin merchant David McBirney. They decided to first produce earthenware, and then porcelain. And the rest, as they say, is history. The delicate, flawless porcelain (Bloomfield declared that any piece with even the slightest blemish should be destroyed) soon attracted the attention of Queen Victoria and many other aristos. Other companies tried to mimic the china's delicate beauty, but genuine Belleek porcelain is recognizable by its seashell designs, basket weaves, and marine themes. It has become a favored tradition in Ireland to give a piece of Belleek china at weddings, giving rise to a saying: "If a newly married couple receives a piece of Belleek, their marriage will be blessed with lasting happiness."

the only thatch-roof establishment in the entire county. Full of locals and the sounds of easy banter, it's the perfect place to glean insider knowledge and gossip about the surrounding area. $ *Average main: £12* ⊠ *20 Main St.* ☎ *028/6865–8181* ⊘ *Closed Sun.*

ENNISKILLEN

5 km (3 miles) south of Devenish Island, Lower Lough Erne.

Enniskillen is the pleasant, smart-looking capital of County Fermanagh and the only place of any size in it. The town center is, strikingly, on an island in the River Erne between Lower and Upper Lough Erne. The principal thoroughfares, Townhall and High streets, are crowded with old-style pubs, family-run shops, and rows of redbrick Georgian flats. The tall, dark spires of the 19th-century St. Michael's and St. Macartin's cathedrals, both on Church Street, tower over the leafy town center.

GETTING HERE

CAR TRAVEL   Enniskillen is 85 km (52 miles) south of Derry on A32 and A5. The town has many car parks, including ones at East Bridge, Eden, Market, and Townhall streets. Be warned: parking attendants clamp down on all drivers lacking a ticket for the required duration of their stay. On the street there are few free street spaces, so be careful where you park.

BUS TRAVEL   Translink's Goldline Express buses connect Enniskillen with Belfast, 145 km (90 miles) east. Buses run from early morning to late evening, with a two-hour journey time (£17.50 round-trip). Local service operates from the bus depot on Wellington Road, beside the tourist information office; an all-day ticket is £2.50. The bus to visit some of Fermanagh's attractions, such as Castle Coole historic house, costs £1.50. The driver will drop you off on request at the entrance gates. Enniskillen also has a slew of cross-border services in many directions. Bus Éireann operates Expressway routes west to Sligo.

Your first stop should be the tourist information office on Wellington Road for an excellent array of brochures, leaflets, maps, and guidebooks. Ask for a Voucher Booklet, which allows discounted entry and two-for-one deals on Fermanagh's major attractions; these include National Trust properties, museums, Belleek Pottery, and free access to climb the 108 spiral steps to the top of Coles Monument, from where you can survey the town and surrounding countryside. Pick up color brochures on History and Heritage Trails, and Natural Heritage Trails throughout County Fermanagh in the tourist office, or see ⊕ *www. fermanaghlakelands.com.*

TOURS

Erne Tours. Fancy a dreamy boat tour on Lough Erne? This company operates tours, about 100 minutes long on the lower lough, aboard the *Kestrel*, a 56-seat water bus. The boat leaves from Round O Pier at Enniskillen. On weekdays it stops for 35 minutes at Devenish Island. From early May to the end of September the company also has a Saturday-evening dinner cruise departing at 6:30. The three-course meal costs £25, and the cruise, which leaves from the Killyhevlin Hotel near Enniskillen, lasts three hours. ⊠ *Round O Pier* ☎ *028/6632–2882* ⊕ *www.*

ernetours.com 🖳 *100-min tours £10* ⏱ *100-min tours May and Sept.,*
Tues. and weekends at 2:15 and 4:15; June, daily at 2:15 and 4:15; July
and Aug., daily at 10:30, 12:15, 2:15, and 4:15.

ESSENTIALS

Visitor Information Fermanagh Visitor Information Centre ✉ *Lakeland*
Visitor Centre, Wellington Rd. ☎ *028/6632–3110* ⊕ *www.fermanagh.gov.uk.*

EXPLORING

Blake's of the Hollow. Among the several relaxed and welcoming old pubs
in Enniskillen's town center, the one with the most appeal is Blake's,
a place hardly altered since it opened in 1887. Its name derives from
the fact that the heart of the town lies in a slight hollow and the pub's
landlord is named William Blake. To celebrate its 125th anniversary
in 2012, the bar produced an old bottle cap with the family coat of
arms etched on to glasses and beer mats. ■ TIP→ The front bar, which
eschews loud music and television, is best for local gossip and stories.
✉ *6 Church St.* ☎ *028/6632–2143.*

Buttermarket. Sixteen wonderful arts and crafts shops selling Fermanagh pottery, jewelry, and paintings are gathered at the Buttermarket,
a restored dairy market built in 1835. It also has a café and a fishing-
tackle shop. ✉ *Down St.* ☎ *028/6632–3117.*

Enniskillen Castle. Enniskillen's main sight is its waterfront castle, one of
the best-preserved monuments in the north. This stronghold, built in
the early 15th century by the friendly-sounding Hugh "The Hospitable"
Maguire, was sited on an important route leading into Ulster. Today,
the Fermanagh Heritage Centre displays pottery and lace on the ground
floor of the County Museum which stands within the castle walls. The
polished paraphernalia of the Inniskillings Museum, which includes
weapons, badges, medals, and engravings, is held in the castle keep.
Pride of place is given to the bugle sounded at the charge of the regiment
at the Battle of the Somme in 1916. The keep has been redeveloped with
new exhibitions and interactive displays, and a Roll of Honor contains
the names of the 9,100 people from all over Ireland who died in World
War II. ✉ *Castlebarracks* ☎ *028/6632–5000* ⊕ *www.enniskillencastle.*
co.uk 🖳 *£4* ⏱ *Apr., May, June, Sept., and Oct., Mon. and Sat. 2–5,*
Tues.–Fri. 10–5; July and Aug., Mon. and weekends 2–5, Tues.–Fri.
10–5; Nov.–Mar., Mon. 2–5, Tues.–Fri. 10–5.

Portora Royal School. Beyond the West Bridge is Portora Royal School,
established in 1608 by King James I. On the grounds are some ruins
of Portora Castle. Writers educated here included Samuel Beckett and
Oscar Wilde, the pride of the school (until his trial for homosexual-
ity). The life and writings of Beckett, the droll existentialist and arch-
modernizer born near Dublin in 1906, is celebrated at the Happy Days
International Beckett Festival held at the school over the bank holiday
weekend at the end of August. The multidisciplinary festival incorporates literature, theater, visual arts, film, and comedy, and offers a
chance to savor some of Beckett's killer lines, such as this one from
Waiting for Godot: "Let us not then speak ill of our generation, it
is not any unhappier than its predecessors." ✉ *Derrygonnelly Rd.*
☎ *028/6632–2658* ⊕ *www.happy-days-enniskillen.com.*

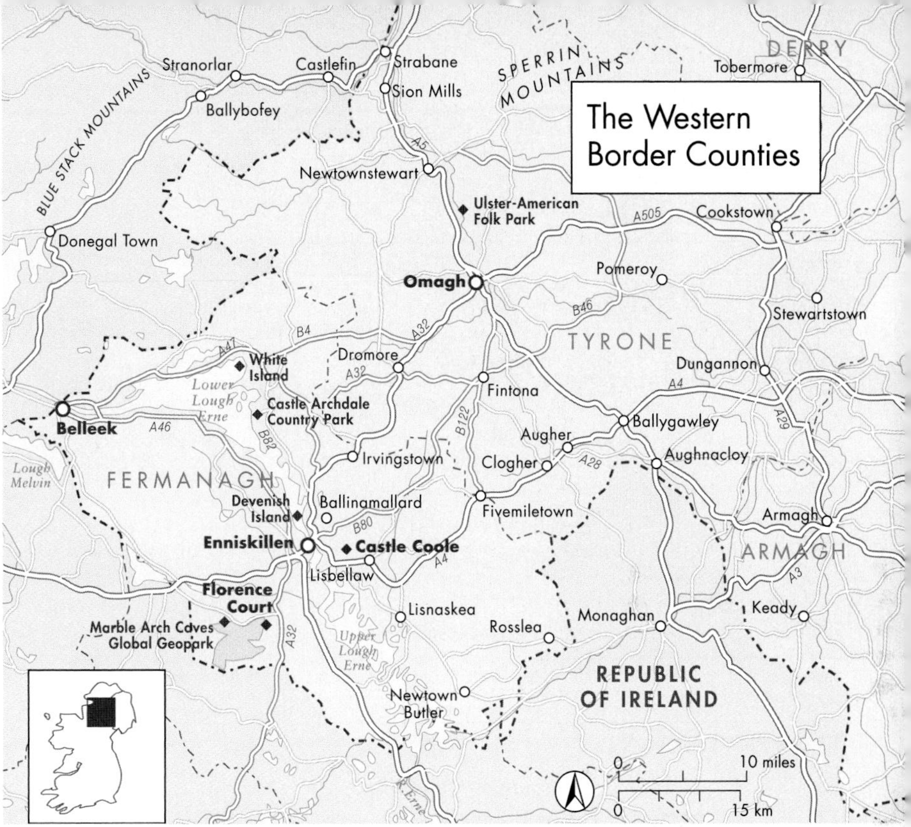
The Western Border Counties
Stranorlar
Castlefin
Strabane
Sion Mills
Ballybofey
BLUE STACK MOUNTAINS
SPERRIN MOUNTAINS
DERRY
Tobermore
Newtownstewart
Ulster-American Folk Park
Cookstown
Donegal Town
Pomeroy
Omagh
Stewartstown
TYRONE
White Island
Dromore
Dungannon
Lower Lough Erne
Fintona
Castle Archdale Country Park
Belleek
Augher
Ballygawley
Irvingstown
Clogher
Aughnacloy
Lough Melvin
FERMANAGH
Devenish Island
Ballinamallard
Fivemiletown
Armagh
Enniskillen
Castle Coole
ARMAGH
Lisbellaw
Florence Court
Lisnaskea
Keady
Marble Arch Caves Global Geopark
Rosslea
Monaghan
Upper Lough Erne
REPUBLIC OF IRELAND
Newtown Butler
10 miles
15 km

Water Gate. At the Erne riverside, the 16th-century Water Gate, between two handsome turrets, protected the town from invading armies. The flag of St. George flies over the building, a tradition that dates back to the 17th century when local soldiers of the Inniskilling Regiments fought for the Protestant William of Orange against the Catholic James II.

WHERE TO STAY

$$$ RESORT Fodor's Choice ★ 🏨 **Lough Erne Resort.** Set between two serene lakes on the small island of Ely, the manicured lawns of the Lough Erne Resort with its backdrop of shimmering Castlehume Lough were thrust into the spotlight in 2013 when it played host to the G8. **Pros:** binoculars in rooms for bird-watching; velour slippers and bathrobe; luxury Irish bed linen; Egyptian cotton towels. **Cons:** luxury comes at a steep price; lines at busy breakfast times. [$] *Rooms from: £150* ✉ *Belleek Rd., 5 km (3 miles) north of Enniskillen* ☎ *028/6632–3230* 🌐 *www.lougherneresort.com* 🛏 *120 rooms, 6 suites, 25 lodges* 🍴 *Breakfast.*

Fabled haunt of "the little people," the stately abode of Florence Court sits in a vale reputedly populated by leprechauns and fairies.

FLORENCE COURT

11 km (7 miles) south of Enniskillen.

GETTING HERE AND AROUND

CAR TRAVEL Take A4 south from Enniskillen and continue south on A32 (also signed as Swanlinbar Road) to reach Florence Court. The drive takes 10 minutes. There is ample car parking at Florence Court, and in summer an overflow car park operates. The admission price to the house and grounds includes parking.

BUS TRAVEL There is no direct bus service, but the main Enniskillen–Swanlinbar Translink bus will pull over on request to allow you to hop off at the Creamery Corner stop. From there, it's a 3-km (2-mile) walk to the estate's entrance, and a further long walk along the avenue to reach the main house.

EXPLORING

FAMILY **Florence Court.** When it comes to Early Irish Georgian houses, there
Fodor'sChoice are few as magical as Florence Court. Less known than some showier
★ estates, this three-story Anglo-Irish mansion was built around 1730 for John Cole, father of the first earl of Enniskillen. Topped off about 1760 with its distinctive two flanking colonnaded wings, the central house is adorned with a surfeit of Palladian windows, keystones, and balustrades thanks to, as one architectural historian put it, "the vainglo-riousness of a provincial hand." Even more impressive is its bucolically baroque setting, as the Cuilcagh Mountains form a wonderful contrast to the shimmering white-stone facade. Showstoppers in terms of decor are the rococo plasterwork ceilings in the dining room; the Venetian

Room; and the famous staircase, all ascribed to Robert West, one of Dublin's most famous *stuccadores* (plaster workers). For a peek at the "downstairs" world, check out the restored kitchen and other service quarters. You can browse a gift shop and secondhand bookstore; holiday accommodation is available at the Butler's Apartment and Rose Cottage. In July and August children's tours, lasting 30 minutes, cost £2, and they can also enjoy activities based around the third earl's fossil collection. ⊠ *11 km (7 miles) south of Enniskillen on A4 and A32* ☎ *028/6634–8249* ⊕ *www. nationaltrust.org.uk/florence-court* ☜ *£4.50 house, £4.50 grounds* ⊙ *Grounds: Nov.–Feb., daily 10–4; Mar.–Oct., daily 10–7. House: Mar. and Oct., weekends 11–5; Apr., daily 11–5; May and Sept., Thurs., and Sat. 11–5; June–Aug., daily 11–5.*

> **LISTEN CLOSELY AND YOU SHALL HEAR . . .**
>
> Florence Court's ancestral park is one of Northern Ireland's glories—dotted with noted heirloom trees (including the Florence Court weeping beech). It also has nooks and dells where, legend has it, you can hear the "song of the little people."

OFF THE BEATEN PATH

Marble Arch Caves Global Geopark. To celebrate its 30th anniversary in 2015, this geopark—one of Europe's finest show caves—is developing a new interpretative center and upgrading trail walking routes in the surrounding mountainous uplands. The only UNESCO geopark in Northern Ireland, it's an ideal half-day underground activity, especially if it's a wet day in Fermanagh. Stalactites glisten above streams as you admire fragile mineral veils and cascades of calcite-coated walls and waterfalls. Guided boat tours, run by knowledgeable Geopark Ambassadors, last 75 minutes. ■ TIP➔ **Bring walking shoes and a warm sweater. Tours begin at Marlbank Scenic Loop Centre, Florence Court. There are frequent events that are suitable for children, such as fossil fun days—check the website for details of these. There's also a restaurant and souvenir shop.** ⊠ *43 Marlbank Rd., Florence Court* ⊕ *www. marblearchcavesgeopark.com* ☜ *£8.75* ⊙ *Mar.–June and Sept., daily 10–4:30; July and Aug., daily 10–5.*

CASTLE COOLE

3 km (2 miles) east of Enniskillen.

GETTING HERE AND AROUND

CAR TRAVEL A five-minute drive from Enniskillen on A4, Castle Coole has a car park (£2.50 per car) that overflows in the summer.

BUS TRAVEL There is no bus service to Castle Coole. You can request the driver to stop on the Translink Enniskillen–Clones route only. The main express bus services heading for Belfast will not stop here.

EXPLORING

Castle Coole. This "uncommonly perfect" mansion (to quote the eminent architectural historian Desmond Guinness) is on its own landscaped oak woods and gardens at the end of a long tree-lined driveway. Although the Irish architect Richard Johnston made the original drawings in the 1790s, and was responsible for the foundation, the castle was, for all intents and purposes, the work of James Wyatt, commissioned by the first Earl of Belmore. One of the best-known architects of his time, Wyatt was based in London but visited Ireland only once, so Alexander Stewart was drafted as the resident builder-architect. The designer wasn't the only imported element; in fact, much of Castle Coole came from England, including the main facade, which is clad in Portland stone and hauled here by bullock carts. And what a facade it is—in perfect symmetry, white colonnaded wings extend from either side of the mansion's three-story, nine-bay center block, with a Palladian central portico and pediment. It is perhaps the apotheosis of the 18th century's reverence for the Greeks.

Inside, the house is remarkably preserved; most of the lavish plasterwork and original furnishings are in place. The saloon is one of the finest rooms in the house, with a vast expanse of oak flooring, gilded Regency furniture, and gray scagliola pilasters with Corinthian capitals. Life Below Stairs features tours of the servants' rooms and service quarters; above stairs is the present Earl of Belmore, who still lives on the estate. ⊠ *Dublin Rd., A4* ☎ *028/6632–2690* ⊕ *www.nationaltrust.org.uk/castle-coole* ⬛ *House £5; grounds £2; car (per adult): £3* ⊗ *House Mar.–May and Sept., weekends 11–5 (open daily Easter wk); June–Aug., daily 11–5. Grounds Nov.–Feb., daily 10–4; Mar.–Oct., daily 10–7.*

ARMAGH

75 km (42 miles) east of Enniskillen.

The spiritual capital of Ireland for 5,000 years, and the seat of both Protestant and Catholic archbishops, Armagh is the most venerated of Irish cities. St. Patrick called it "my sweet hill" and built his stone church on the hill where the Anglican cathedral now stands. On the opposite hill, the twin-spire Catholic cathedral is flanked by two large marble statues of archbishops who look across the land. Despite the pleasing Georgian terraces around the elegant mall east of the town center, Armagh can seem drab. It suffered as a trouble spot in the sectarian conflict, though it's now the scene of some spirited and sympathetic renovation.

GETTING HERE AND AROUND

CAR TRAVEL Armagh is a one-hour drive from Belfast along A3 before joining the M1 at Portadown. Dublin is just over two hours south via Newry on A28 and A1, before crossing the Irish border to join the motorway for the rest of your journey. There are several pay-and-display car parks in Armagh city center. The main one is next to the tourist office, on English Street. You can also park at the mall, and there is free parking on side streets.

BUS TRAVEL Buses link Armagh with neighboring towns as well as Belfast, an 80-minute journey. You can catch a Translink Goldline Express from the Buscentre on the Lonsdale Road in Armagh (£16 round-trip, one-third discount after 9:20 am). Cross-border buses also operate out of Armagh—you can hop aboard the Belfast–Galway Bus Éireann bus that runs via Cavan town and Athlone. Round-trip to Galway is £35.15.

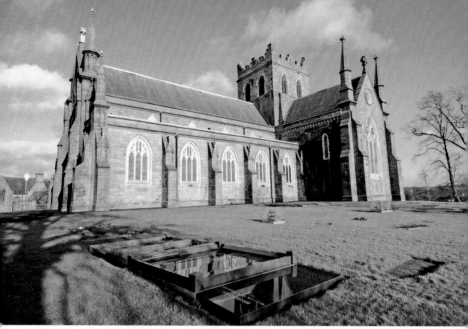

Thackeray admired the Church of Ireland's St. Patrick's Cathedral which, with St. Patrick's Roman Catholic Cathedral, jointly presides over Armagh.

Bus Éireann Expressway connections run from Dublin to Portrush on the north coast and stop in Armagh. The Armagh–Dublin bus journey (three times each day at 8 am, noon, and 8 pm), takes 2¾ hours and costs £21.65 round-trip.

ESSENTIALS

Visitor Information Armagh Visitor Information Centre ✉ *40 English St.* ☎ *028/3752–1800* ⊕ *www.armagh.co.uk.*

EXPLORING

FAMILY **Armagh Planetarium.** Displayed here in all its nickel-iron glory is Ireland's largest meteorite, an astonishing 4.5 billion years old and weighing 24 stone (336 pounds). Elsewhere, you'll find a spaceship, satellite models, and the Digital Theater—sit back and navigate the night sky in the company of experts. Children's activities include building and launching rockets. Outside, stroll through the solar system and into the Milky Way at the huge scale model of the Universe. ✉ *College Hill* ☎ *028/3752–3689* ⊕ *www.armaghplanet.com* ✉ *£6* ⊙ *Mon.–Sat. 10–5; July and Aug., also Sun. 10–5.*

FAMILY **Navan Centre and Fort.** Just outside Armagh is Ulster's Camelot—the region's ancient capital. Excavations date evidence of activity to 700 BC. The fort has strong associations with figures of Irish history. Legend has it that thousands of years ago this was the site of the palace of Queen Macha; subsequent tales call it the barracks of the legendary Ulster warrior Cuchulainn and his Red Branch Knights. Remains dating from 94 BC are particularly intriguing: a great conical structure, 120 feet in diameter, was formed from five concentric circles made of 275 wooden posts, with a 276th, about 12 yards high, situated in the center. In a ritual whose meaning is not known, it was filled with brushwood and set on fire. Young children can dig into the past in the Archeo Pit, dress up as a Celt, and touch history with "feely boxes." In the summer guided tours are held every two hours and last 40 minutes. Ecology trails, opened in 2014, bring the environmental aspects of Navan to life. There's a bug hotel, listening posts, bird boxes, a viewing hide, and Armagh's only "bug and beastie" viewer. An Eco Warrior shows the children around and introduces them to the hidden life found in crevices, stones, and hedges. ⊠ *81 Killyleagh Rd., 3 km (2 miles) west of Armagh on A28* ☎ *028/3752–9644* ⊕ *www.navan.com* ✉ *Apr.–Sept., £6.20; Oct.–Mar., £5.20* ☉ *Apr.–Sept., daily 10–6:30; Oct.–Mar., daily 10–4.*

St. Patrick's Anglican Cathedral. Near the city center, a squat battlement tower identifies the cathedral, in simple, early-19th-century, low-Gothic style. On the site of much older churches, it contains relics of Armagh's long history. Brian Boru, the High King (King of All Ireland) is buried here. In 1014, he drove the Vikings out of Ireland but was killed after the battle was won. Some memorials and tombs here are by important 18th-century sculptors such as Roubilliac and Rysbrack, and in 2012, the cathedral opened its atmospheric crypt to visitors. Dating from the Middle Ages, this sanctuary where law-abiding citizens safely stored their valuable goods—a few archbishops are buried here, too—is worth a look. ⊠ *43 Abbey St., Cathedral Close* ☎ *028/3752–3142* ⊕ *www. stpatricks-cathedral.org* ✉ *£3* ☉ *Nov.–Mar., daily 10–4; Apr.–Oct., daily 10–5.*

St. Patrick's Roman Catholic Cathedral. The pale limestone St. Patrick's, the seat of a Roman Catholic archdiocese, rises above a hill to dominate the north end of Armagh. The cathedral's rather gloomy interior is enlivened by a magnificent organ, the potential of which is fully realized at services. Construction of the twin-spire structure started in 1840 in the neo-Gothic style, but the Great Famine brought work to a halt until 1854, and it wasn't completed until 1873. An arcade of statues over the main doorway on the exterior is one of the cathedral's most interesting features. The altar is solid Irish granite and the woodwork is Austrian oak. ⊠ *Cathedral +Rd.* ☎ *028/3752–2813* ⊕ *www.armaghparish.net.*

THE MOUNTAINS OF MOURNE

52½ km (32½ miles) southeast of Armagh on A28, 51 km (32 miles) south of Belfast.

Subjects of a song that is sung on every Irish occasion from baptisms to funerals, the Mountains of Mourne must surely qualify as one of Ireland's best-known ranges. According to those lyrics by Percy French, the Mountains of Mourne "sweep down to the sea," from 2,000-foot summits. East of the unprepossessing border city of Newry, this area was long considered ungovernable, its hardy inhabitants living from smuggling contraband into the numerous rocky coves on the seashore. Much of the Mourne range is still inaccessible except on foot. The countryside is gorgeous: high, windswept pasture and moorland threaded with bright streams, bound by a tracery of drystone walls and dotted

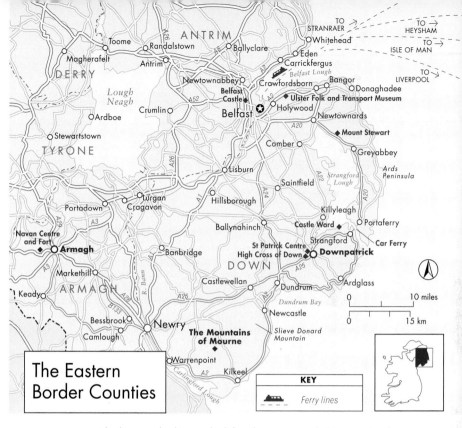

The Eastern Border Counties

with sheep and whitewashed farmhouses snuggled in stands of syca-more. It's the perfect landscape for away-from-it-all walkers, cyclists, and serious climbers.

GETTING HERE AND AROUND

CAR TRAVEL Newcastle is a 45-minute drive south of Belfast on A24 through Bally-nahinch. A one-way system operates through the town and is especially crowded during summer. Car parks are at the seafront near the Slieve Donard Hotel, beside the bus station, and at Donard Park. The nearest city is Newry, a 35-minute drive west on A25.

BUS TRAVEL Newcastle bus station on Railway Street is the arrival and departure point for all routes to one of the most scenic parts of Northern Ireland. Ulsterbus service leaves Belfast regularly for the 48-km (30-mile) trip to Newcastle (70 minutes, £14 round-trip). If you wish to appreciate the panoramic glory of the Mountains of Mourne, take a bus from Newcastle along the coast to the foothill towns of Annalong and Kil-keel (£7.60 round-trip). To truly get an up-close feel for the mountains, board the Mourne Rambler (info found on Rambler Services on the Translink website), a 23-seat rural bus that transports you to the heart of Mourne country. A complete circuit on the Rambler, which runs only in July and August, takes 90 minutes (£6.50). You can also catch a bus from Newcastle to Dublin. This service starts from Downpatrick and runs from Newcastle to Castlewellan, Newry, and across the border to Dublin (£20 round-trip).

EXPLORING

Castlewellan Forest Park. A huge maze, grown to symbolize Northern Ireland's convoluted path to peace, is the latest addition to Castlewellan Forest Park, which comprises 1,150 acres of forested hills running between the Mourne Mountains and Slieve Croob. With the maze, lake, secluded arbors, and arboretum, the park makes an excellent introduction to the area. ⊠ *Castlewellan, Co. Down* ☎ *028/4377–8664* ⊕ *www. forestserviceni.gov.uk* 🖃 *Free; vehicles £4.50* ☉ *Daily 10–dusk.*

Newcastle. A bracing Victorian cold-water bathing station, Newcastle is the main center for visitors to the hills. There's a good selection of cafés, pubs, and restaurants to choose from after a walk along the elegant seafront promenade. ⊠ *Newcastle, Co. Down* ☎ *028/4372–2222* ⊕ *www.downdc.gov.uk.*

Silent Valley. The road to the Silent Valley reservoir park leads to mountain views and excellent photo ops. Also here is a visitor center with an informative exhibition explaining the history of Silent Valley. Look into the "Locals Room" which celebrates the men who worked on the building of the reservoir as well as the Mourne Wall. You can also pick up information on walking trails. ⊠ *6 km (4 miles) north of Kilkeel off B27, right turn, Kilkeel, Co. Down* ☎ *028/9035–4716* ⊕ *www. visitmournemountains.co.uk* 🖃 *£1.60; vehicles £4.50* ☉ *June–Aug., daily 10–6:30; Oct.–Apr., daily 10–4.*

Slieve Donard. Looming above Newcastle is Slieve Donard, its panoramic, 2,796-foot-high summit grandly claiming views into England, Wales, and Scotland "when it's clear enough"—in other words, "rarely," say the pessimists. It's not possible to drive up the mountain, so leave your car in the Donard parking lot. It should take roughly three hours to climb to the summit and no longer than two hours to descend. Experienced hikers should not find it difficult, but if you prefer an easier trek, follow the trails signposted in Tollymore Forest Park. Hiking boots are essential and, as the weather can be unpredictable, it's advisable to take an extra layer of clothing, even in summer. ⊠ *Mourne Mountains, Newcastle, Co. Down.*

Tollymore Forest Park. Covering 1,200 acres and entered through Gothic gateways, Tollymore Forest Park extends up the valley of the River Shimna. Many pretty stone bridges cross over the sparkling waters here. The arboretum at Tollymore has the widest range of tree species of any park in Ireland. Apart from the better known oak, birch, beech, and sitka spruce, the eucalyptus from Australia and Tasmania stand out and bring a cheerful note. ⊠ *Tullybrannigan Rd., Newcastle, Co. Down* ☎ *028/4372–2428* ⊕ *www.forestserviceni.gov.uk* 🖃 *£2; vehicles £4.50* ☉ *Daily 10–dusk.*

WHERE TO STAY

$$

B&B/INN

Fodor's Choice

★

🏠 **Glassdrumman Lodge.** For those who wish to be pampered as well as immersed in the ancient Kingdom of Mourne, brothers Johnny and Ben Hall's eclectically simple and stylish lodge is the place. **Pros:** stunning location in the heart of the mountains with the sea on your doorstep;

A four-hour ascent of the Slieve Donard peak—queen of the magnificent Mountains of Mourne—offers vistas that reach as far as Scotland and the Isle of Man.

rooms well appointed with pleasant en suite bathrooms. **Cons:** some say the restaurant is overrated; pity they've stopped churning their own butter. [$] *Rooms from: £95* ✉ *85 Mill Rd., Annalong, Co. Down* ☎ *028/4376–8451* 🌐 *www.glassdrummanlodge.com* 🛏 *10 rooms, 2 suites* 🍴 *Breakfast.*

$$$ RESORT Fodor's Choice ★ 🏨 **Slieve Donard Resort & Spa.** A lavish redbrick monument to Victoriana, this turreted hotel, built in 1898, stands like a palace on green lawns at one end of Newcastle's 6½-km (4-mile) sandy beach; the traditional furnishings may make you feel as if you're stepping back in time to the town's turn-of-the-20th-century heyday as an elegant seaside resort, though the bright guest rooms have modern comforts. **Pros:** appealing mix of luxury, history, and style; fireplaces in lobby welcome on chilly days. **Cons:** housekeeping slow with requests; occasional cacophony from wedding receptions. [$] *Rooms from: £150* ✉ *Downs Rd., Newcastle, Co. Down* ☎ *028/4372–1066* 🌐 *www.hastingshotels.com/slieve-donard-resort-and-spa* 🛏 *178 rooms, 6 suites* 🍴 *Multiple meal plans.*

SPORTS AND THE OUTDOORS

Tollymore National Outdoor Centre. If you need advice on mountain climbing, canoeing, and hiking trails, this impressive center is the place to head. ✉ *Bryansford, Newcastle, Co. Down* ☎ *028/4372–2158* 🌐 *www.tollymore.com.*

GOLF

Fodor's Choice ★ **Royal County Down.** With a stunning backdrop of mountains and sea, Royal County Down is a links course with craterlike bunkers and small dunes; catch it on the right day at the right time and you may think you're on the moon. And for better players, every day is the right one.

Back in his day, Harry Vardon labeled it the toughest course in the Emerald Isle, and if you can't hit your drive long and straight, you might find it the toughest course in the world.

There are no visitor playing days on Wednesday or Saturday. ✉ *36 Golf Links Rd., Newcastle, Co. Down* ☎ *028/4372–3314* ⊕ *www. royalcountydown.org* ✉ *Championship: weekdays £185 am, £170 pm, weekends £185; Annesley: £28* ⚑ *Championship: 18 holes, 7204 yards, par 71; Annesley: 18 holes, 4617 yards, par 66. Practice area, caddies, caddy carts, catering* ⊙ *Visitors: Sun.–Tues., Thurs., and Fri. (Championship); daily (Annesley).*

DOWNPATRICK

21 km (14 miles) east of Newcastle.

Downpatrick once was called plain and simple "Down" but had its name changed by John de Courcy, a Norman knight who moved here in 1176. De Courcy set about promoting St. Patrick, the 5th-century Briton who was captured by the Irish and served as a slave in the Down area before he escaped to France, where he learned about Christianity and bravely returned to try to convert the local chiefs. Although it's not true that Patrick brought a new faith to Ireland—there was already a bishop of Ireland before Patrick got here—he must have been a better missionary than most because he did indeed win influential converts. The clan chief of the Down area gave him land at the village of Saul, near Downpatrick, to build a monastery. You could happily spend a morning here visiting a trio of top-class sites: Down Cathedral, Down County Museum (now housing the ancient High Cross of Down), and the Saint Patrick Center are all clustered within a few minutes' walk of each other.

GETTING HERE AND AROUND

CAR TRAVEL Downpatrick is 21 km (14 miles) east of Newcastle on A2 and A25 and 30 km (22 miles) south of Belfast on A24. On-street parking is free but restricted to either 30 or 60 minutes. The car park at the Grove shopping center is pay and display and costs £0.40 per hour. There is free parking on English and Market streets and beside the bus station.

BUS TRAVEL Buses arrive at the main station in Downpatrick from many points of County Down and beyond. Frequent Translink Goldline Express services run to and from Belfast. The journey time is one hour (£10.50 round-trip or £7 after 9:45 am). Some services link up with the Belfast Metro network of suburban routes. To visit Strangford, there are daily services from Downpatrick (£6.10 round-trip); to visit Castle Ward, ask the driver to stop by the roadside. Buses also leave Downpatrick for Dublin; the journey takes just over three hours (£20.85 round-trip; £19.50 to Dublin airport).

ESSENTIALS

Visitor Information Downpatrick Visitor Information Center ✉ *53A Market St., Downpatrick, Co. Down* ☎ *028/4461–2233* ⊕ *www.downdc.gov.uk.*

EXPLORING

Down Cathedral. The Cathedral of the Holy Trinity, or Down Cathedral as it's commonly known, is one of the disputed burial places of St. Patrick. In the churchyard, a somber flat stone slab inscribed "Patric" is supposedly the saint's tomb. It might be here, at Saul, or, some scholars argue, more likely at Armagh. The stone was quarried in 1990 at Slieve-na-Largie near Castlewellan and took 12 men 14 days to cut from the quarry. The church, which lay ruined from 1538 to 1790 (it reopened in 1818), preserves parts of some of the earlier churches and monasteries that have stood on this site, the oldest of which dates to the 6th century. Even by then, the cathedral site had long been an important fortified settlement: Down takes its name from the Celtic word *dun*, or fort. Information panels tell the history of the building through a time-line, showing the connection with St. Patrick, and give details on the war memorials. There's also a shop selling souvenirs. ⊠ *35 English St., Downpatrick, Co. Down* ☎ *028/4461–4922* ⊕ *www.downcathedral. org* ⊠ *£3 (suggested donation)* ⊗ *Mon.–Sat. 9:30–4, Sun. 2–4.*

Fodor's Choice
★
Down County Museum. With the transfer of the 1,100-year-old Mourne granite High Cross as the centerpiece of an elaborate extension due for completion in mid-2015, this museum is gaining serious cachet. The Downpatrick High Cross had stood in front of nearby Down Cathedral since the late 19th century, but had suffered deterioration through weather damage—never mind the Viking pillagers—and has been moved permanently indoors. The original location of the intricately patterned cross, carved around AD 900 as a "prayer in stone," is believed to have been the early medieval monastery on the Hill of Down. Elsewhere look into the small cells in the gaol along a narrow whitewashed corridor. The history of the gaol is told through a 40-minute reenactment in a film drama *Prisoners of the Past*. The other main exhibition is "Down through Time," while frequently photographic exhibitions and artwork are on display in other rooms. Behind the building, a short signposted trail leads to an example of a Norman motte and bailey. ⊠ *The Mall, English St., Downpatrick, Co. Down* ☎ *028/4461–5218* ⊕ *www.downcountymuseum.com* ⊠ *Free* ⊗ *Weekdays 10–5, weekends 1–5.*

FAMILY **The Saint Patrick Centre.** The interactive exhibits here bring the ancient myths and stories of early Christian Ireland to life. You can explore how St. Patrick's legacy developed in Early Christian times, examine the art and metalwork that was produced during this golden age, and listen to modern debates about Ireland's patron saint. Interpretative boards outline local sites linked with the saint. Self-guided tours of local sites linked with the saint last about an hour, with a handheld audio device that takes you across a bridge over the River of Words. ■TIP➔ **If time is short you can opt to watch the IMAX cinema presentation, a 17-minute, 180-degree audiovisual flight that whizzes you around Irish sites linked to the saint; a highlight of the entire exhibition.** In summer the center hosts a "Plantation Kiosk" providing visitors the opportunity of finding out more about Ulster-Scots culture and hearing the master highland piper William Wallace. The center includes a café, the Grove gift store an art gallery, terraced gardens, and a well-stocked tourist information office. ✉ *St Patrick's Sq., 53A Lower Market St., Downpatrick, Co. Down* ☎ *028/4461–9000* 🌐 *www.saintpatrickcentre.com* 🎫 *£5.50* 🕘 *Mon.–Sat. 9–5; July and Aug., Sun. 1–5.*

St. Patrick's Trail. After returning to Ireland in the year AD 432, Ireland's patron saint seems to have popped up everywhere on his peregrinations. You can explore places associated with him along St. Patrick's Trail, a 92-mile signposted driving route linking 15 historic and ecclesiastical sites across the beautiful drumlin hills of counties Down and Armagh. ■ TIP→ Pick up a trail map at the tourist office in Armagh or Downpatrick, and at major attractions on the route you qualify for 2-for-1 entry through March 2016. ✉ *Downpatrick, Co. Down* 🌐 *www.discovernorthernireland.com/stpatrick.*

A DAY LIKE ANY OTHER

St. Patrick's Day—March 17—is a great time to visit Downpatrick, as the whole town turns out in carnival dress for the holiday parade. But why is St. Paddy fêted on March 17? Legend has it he died on that date, perhaps in AD 461. Others point to the fact that this date marked one of the great pagan festivals celebrating the onset of spring and the sowing of crops.

WHERE TO EAT AND STAY

$ IRISH

🍴 **Denvir's Coaching Inn.** In this wonderfully atmospheric whitewashed coaching inn dating to 1642, exposed oak beams, stone floors and a large open fireplace testify to the antiquity. The Snug bar top was crafted from timbers of ships wrecked in Lough Foyle. Back in the mists of time, it was a member of the same Denvir family who gave their name to a small settlement in Colorado, later modified to Denver. The six spacious guest rooms have been modernized sympathetically while still retaining the old inn's character and feature original wooden floors, mahogany sleigh beds, and pristine white linen. On the menu, solid traditional dishes dominate—fish from Ardglass, char-grilled steak, burgers, pork, and spring lamb. But the most popular dish is Denvir's Famous Chicken Wings with a hot buffalo sauce and a cooling Cashel Blue cheese dip. An excellent selection of draught beers includes Bee's Endeavour, a delicious golden craft ale from the Whitewater brewery infused with honey and ginger that leaves a warm glow. Live music in the bar mixes traditional Irish with old classics on Thursday and weekend nights. [$] *Average main: £11* ✉ *14–16 English St., Downpatrick, Co. Down* ☎ *028/4461–2012* 🌐 *www.denvirshotel.com.*

$ B&B/INN Fodor's Choice ★

🏨 **Dufferin Coaching Inn.** An elegant Georgian inn dating from 1803, this historic building sits next to picture-perfect, grandly gracious Killyleagh Castle—reputedly the longest-inhabited castle in Ireland and arguably the country's prettiest. **Pros:** ideal for exploring Strangford Lough attractions; good value for the money. **Cons:** far from the bright city lights; no elevator. [$] *Rooms from: £65* ✉ *33 High St., 10 km (6 miles) north of Downpatrick, Killyleagh, Co. Down* ☎ *028/4482–1134* 🌐 *www.dufferincoachinginn.com* 🛏 *7 rooms* 🍴 *Breakfast.*

TRAVEL SMART
IRELAND

GETTING HERE AND AROUND

▌AIR TRAVEL

Flying time to Ireland is 6½ hours from New York, 7½ hours from Chicago, 10 hours from Los Angeles, and 1 hour from London.

Flying into Ireland involves few hassles, although an increase in traffic in the last decade has caused a slight increase in flight delays and time spent waiting for baggage to clear customs. There are few domestic flights within Ireland. Government subsidies were withdrawn following the completion of the highway (motorway) system, and an increase in express train services. The only survivor is the Kerry to Dublin route. Checking in and boarding an outbound plane tends to be civilized. Security is professional but not overbearing, and airport staffers are usually helpful and patient. In the busy summer season the lines can get long, and you should play it safe by arriving a couple of hours before your flight.

Airlines and Airports Airline and Airport Links.com. This website has links to many of the world's airlines and airports. ⊕ *www. airlineandairportlinks.com.*

Airline Security Issues Transportation Security Administration. Everything you need to know about security before you go to an airport, including access to fast track in USA, can be found here. ⊕ *www.tsa.gov.*

AIRPORTS

The major gateways to Ireland are Dublin Airport (DUB) on the east coast, 10 km (6 miles) north of the city center, and Shannon Airport (SNN) on the west coast, 25 km (16 miles) west of Limerick. Two airports serve Belfast: Belfast International Airport (BFS) at Aldergrove, 24 km (15 miles) from the city, handles local and U.K. flights, as well as international traffic; George Best Belfast City Airport (BHD), 6½ km (4 miles) from the city, handles local and U.K. flights only. In addition, the City of Derry Airport (LDY) receives flights from Liverpool, London Stansted, and Glasgow in the United Kingdom. If you plan to visit mainly the Southwest of Ireland, use Cork Airport (ORK), which handles flights from the United Kingdom, as well as from Paris, Malaga, and Rome.

Airport Information Belfast International Airport ☎ *028/9448–4848* ⊕ *www. belfastairport.com.* **City of Derry Airport** ☎ *028/7181–0784* ⊕ *www.cityofderryairport. com.* **Cork Airport** ☎ *021/431–3131* ⊕ *www. corkairport.com.* **Dublin Airport** ☎ *01/814– 1111* ⊕ *www.dublinairport.com.* **George Best Belfast City Airport** ☎ *028/9093– 9093* ⊕ *www.belfastcityairport.com.* **Shannon Airport** ☎ *061/712–000* ⊕ *www. shannonairport.com.*

FLIGHTS

From North America and the United Kingdom, Aer Lingus, the national flag carrier, has the greatest number of direct flights to Ireland.

Aer Lingus flies to Shannon and Dublin from New York's JFK (John F. Kennedy Airport), Chicago's O'Hare, Boston, San Francisco, and Orlando. Delta has a daily departure from New York's JFK to Dublin, and American Airlines flies to Dublin from New York's JFK and Chicago. United flies direct to Dublin, Shannon, and Belfast, departing daily from Newark Liberty International Airport in New Jersey. Except for special offers, prices for the four airlines tend to be similar. London to Dublin is one of the world's busiest international routes. Aer Lingus, British Airways, Flybe, and CityJet all have several daily flights. Ryanair—famous for its cheap, no-frills service—offers several daily flights from London Gatwick, Luton, and Stansted airports to Dublin, Kerry, Shannon, Cork, and Ireland West Airport Knock. With such healthy competition, bargains abound. British Airways, Flybe, and EasyJet offer regularly scheduled flights to Belfast from Birmingham,

Manchester, London Gatwick, Luton, and Stansted airports.

Within Ireland, Aer Lingus Regional provides service from Dublin to Kerry. Flybe flies from Dublin to Donegal.

Airline Contacts Aer Lingus ☎ *800/474-7424, 353/818-365000* ⊕ *www.aerlingus. com.* **American Airlines** ☎ *800/433-7300, 353/818-286597* ⊕ *www.aa.com.* **British Airways** ☎ *800/247-9297, 353/1890-626747* ⊕ *www.ba.com.* **CityJet** ☎ *818/776-057* ⊕ *www.cityjet.com.* **Delta Airlines** ☎ *800/221-1212* ⊕ *www.delta.com.* **EasyJet** ⊕ *www.easyjet.com.* **Flybe** ☎ *44/1392-268315 from rest of world, 01392/268-315 within U.K.* ⊕ *www.flybe.com.* **Ryanair** ☎ *44/871-2460002 from rest of world, 1520/444-004 within Ireland, 0871/246-0000 within U.K.* ⊕ *www.ryanair.com.* **United Airlines** ☎ *800/864-8331* ⊕ *www.united.com.*

■ BOAT TRAVEL

TO AND FROM IRELAND

Ferries are a convenient way to travel between Ireland and elsewhere in Europe, particularly the United Kingdom. There are six main ferry ports in Ireland; four in the republic at Dublin Port, Dun Laoghaire, Rosslare, and Cork, and two in Northern Ireland at Belfast and Larne. The cost of your trip can vary substantially, so compare prices carefully. Bear in mind, too, that flying can be cheaper, so look into all types of transportation before booking.

Irish Ferries operates the *Ulysses,* the world's largest car ferry, on its Dublin to Holyhead, Wales, route (3 hrs, 15 mins); there's also a swift service (1 hr, 50 mins) between these two ports. There are several trips daily. The company also runs between Rosslare and Pembroke, Wales (3 hrs, 45 mins), and has service to France. Stena Line sails several times a day between Dublin and Holyhead (3 hrs, 15 mins) and has swift service to Dun Laoghaire (2 hrs). The company also runs a fast craft (2 hrs) and a superferry (3 hrs) between Belfast and Stranraer, Scotland,

as well as a fast craft (2 hrs) between Rosslare and Fishguard, Wales. There are several trips daily on both routes.

P&O Irish Sea vessels run between Larne and Troon, Scotland (2 hrs), a couple of times a day. The company also sails from Dublin to Liverpool twice daily (8 hrs), with a choice of daytime or overnight sailings.

WITHIN IRELAND

There is regular service to the Aran Islands from Ros an Mhíl (Rossaveal) in County Galway and Doolin in County Clare. Ferries also sail to Inishbofin (off the Galway coast) and Arranmore (off the Donegal coast), and to Bere, Whiddy, Sherkin, and the Cape Clear Islands off the coast of County Cork. Bere and Whiddy have a car ferry, but the other islands are all small enough to explore on foot, so the ferries are for foot passengers and bicycles only. Other islands—the Blaskets and the Skelligs in Kerry, Rathlin in Antrim, and Tory, off the Donegal coast—have seasonal ferry services between May and September, less frequently the rest of the year. Fáilte Ireland publishes a free guide and map with ferry details, *Ireland's Islands,* or visit ⊕ *www.irelandsislands.com.*

FARES AND SCHEDULES

You can get schedules and purchase tickets, with a credit card if you like, directly from the ferry lines. You can also pick up tickets at Dublin tourism offices and at any major travel agent in Ireland or the United Kingdom. Payment must be made in the currency of the country of the port of departure. Bad weather can delay or cancel ferry sailings, so it's always a good idea to call before departing for the port.

Information Irish Ferries ☎ *0818/300-400 in Ireland, 0871/730-0400 in U.K.* ⊕ *www. irishferries.com.* **P&O Ferries** ☎ *01/407-3434 in Ireland, 0871/664-5645 in U.K.* ⊕ *www. poferries.com.* **Stena Line** ☎ *01/204-7777 in Ireland, 028/9074-7747 in Northern Ireland, 0844/770-7070 in U.K.* ⊕ *www.stenaline.co.uk.*

▌ BUS TRAVEL

In the Republic of Ireland, long-distance bus service is operated by Bus Éireann, which also provides local service in Cork, Galway, Limerick, and Waterford. There's only one class, and prices are similar for all seats. Note, though, that outside of the peak season, service is limited; some routes (for example, to the Ring of Kerry) disappear altogether.

Bus Éireann's Expressway buses go directly, in the straightest available line, from one biggish town to another, stopping at a limited number of designated places. There's sometimes only one trip a day on express routes.

Rural bus service, which rambles around the countryside passing through as many villages as possible, shuts down at around 7 or 8 pm. To ensure that a bus journey is feasible, buy a copy of Bus Éireann's timetable—€3 from any bus terminal—or check online. Many of the destination indicators are in Irish (Gaelic), so make sure you get on the right bus.

Citylink, a Galway-based company, has service between Galway, Limerick, Cork, and Dublin, as well as Cork and Dublin airports. Prices are competitive, with the two hour, 45 minute journey from Dublin Airport to Galway costing no more than €16.50 one way. This can be cut to two hours 30 minutes by using the Citylink's Eireagle service which travels direct to the airport, bypassing the city center. All buses have complimentary Wi-Fi.

Aircoach operates a similar service, with Wi-Fi on most buses, between Dublin, Cork, and Belfast and their respective airports. The three-hour journey from Cork to Dublin costs €16 one way. Online fares can be cheaper, and booking online guarantees you a seat and priority boarding, ahead of those paying in cash.

IN NORTHERN IRELAND

All buses in Northern Ireland are operated by the state-owned Translink. Goldline is the long distance bus division, while Ulsterbus run local services. Service is generally good, with particularly useful links to towns not served by train. Ulsterbus also offers tours. Goldline and Eurolines buses run from London and from Birmingham, making the Stranraer–Port of Belfast crossing.

■ TIP→ Prepaid tickets don't apply to a particular bus time, just a route, so show up at least 30 minutes early to get a seat.

FARES AND PASSES

You can buy tickets online, at tourist offices, at bus stations, or on buses (though it's cash only for the latter option). A round-trip from Dublin to Cork costs €22, and a Dublin to Galway round-trip is €19.

You can save money with multiday passes, some of which can be combined with rail service. Consider the **Irish Explorer Rail and Bus Pass,** which gives you 8 days out of 15 of bus and rail travel for €245. An **iLink Card** costs £55 for seven days of unlimited bus and rail travel in Northern Ireland—a great deal when you consider that a one-day ticket costs £15.

Some cost-cutting passes include both Northern Ireland and the Republic of Ireland. An **Irish Rover** bus ticket for travel on Ulsterbus and Bus Éireann covers Ireland, north and south. It also includes city-center bus travel in Cork, Waterford, Limerick, Galway, and on the Metro services in Belfast—but not Dublin.

Bus Information Aircoach ☎ 01/844–7118 ⊕ www.aircoach.ie. **Bus Éireann** ☎ 01/836–6111 in Republic of Ireland ⊕ www.buseireann.ie. **Citylink** ☎ 091/564–164 within Ireland ⊕ www.citylink.ie. **Eurolines** ☎ 08717/818–178 in U.K. ⊕ www.eurolines.co.uk. **Ulsterbus** ☎ 028/9066–6630 in Northern Ireland ⊕ www.translink.co.uk. **Translink Goldline** ☎ 028/9033–7002 in Northern Ireland ⊕ www.translink.co.uk.

▌ CAR TRAVEL

U.S. driver's licenses are recognized in Ireland.

Roads in the Irish Republic are generally good, with four-lane highways, or motorways, connecting Dublin with Waterford, Cork, Limerick, Shannon Airport, Galway, and Newry on the border with Northern Ireland. Service areas with restrooms and food are gradually being added; meanwhile you may have to leave the motorway for comfort stops, usually located in gas stations. National routes and minor roads are slower, but much more scenic. On rural roads, watch out for cattle and sheep. Reckless drivers (surveys say that Irish drivers are among the worst) are also a problem in the countryside, so remain alert.

ROAD SIGNS

Road signs in the republic are generally in both Irish and English; destinations in which Irish is the spoken language are signposted only in Irish. The most important one to know is An Daingean, which is now the official name of Dingle Town. ■TIP→ Get a good bilingual road map, and know the next town on your itinerary; neither the signposts nor the locals refer to roads by official numbers. Traffic signs are the same as in the rest of Europe. On the newer green signposts, distances are in kilometers; on some of the old white signposts they're still miles. Most important, speed limits are posted in the republic (but not in Northern Ireland) in kilometers.

There are no border checkpoints between the Irish Republic and Northern Ireland, where the road network is excellent and, outside Belfast, uncrowded. Road signs and traffic regulations conform to the British system.

CAR FERRIES

All ferries on both principal routes to the Irish Republic welcome cars. Fishguard and Pembroke are relatively easy to reach by road. The car trip to Holyhead, on the other hand, is sometimes difficult: delays on the A55 North Wales coastal road aren't unusual.

GASOLINE

You can find gas stations along most roads. Self-service is the norm, and major credit cards and traveler's checks are usually accepted. Prices are near the lower end for Europe, with unleaded gas priced around €1.25 in Ireland and £1.12 a liter in Northern Ireland—gasoline prices in the United States are a bit more than half the price in Ireland. Prices vary significantly from station to station, so it's worth driving around the block (if you have enough gas!).

ROAD CONDITIONS

Most roads are paved and make for easy travel. Roads designated with an *M* for "motorway" are double-lane divided highways with paved shoulders; *N*, or "national," routes are generally undivided highways with shoulders; and *R*, or "regional," roads tend to be narrow and twisty.

Rush-hour traffic in Dublin, Cork, Limerick, Belfast, and Galway can be intense. Rush hours in Dublin run 7 to 9:30 am and 5 to 7 pm; special events such as soccer matches will also tie up traffic in and around the city, as will heavy rain.

ROADSIDE EMERGENCIES

If you're involved in an accident, note the details of the vehicle and the driver and report the incident to a member of the Garda Síochána (the Irish Police) or the Police Service of Northern Ireland as soon as possible. Since traffic congestion is chronic in Dublin, emergency services are more likely to be dispatched quickly to help you and to clear the road.

If your car breaks down, try to stop in a well-lighted area near a public phone. If you're on a secondary road, remain in your car with the doors locked after you call for assistance. If you break down on the motorway, pull onto the hard shoulder and stay out of your car with the passenger side door open and the other doors locked. This will allow you to jump into the car quickly if you sense any trouble. Make sure you check credentials of anyone who offers assistance—note the license-plate number and color of the assisting vehicle before you step out of the car.

The Automobile Association of Ireland, a sister organization of its English counterpart, is highly recommended. The AA can help you or your vehicle only if you are a member. If not, contact your car-rental company for assistance.

Emergency Services An Garda Síochána (Police) ☎ *112, 999* ⊕ *www.garda. ie.* **Automobile Association of Ireland** ☎ *01/617–9999 in Ireland, 0800/887–766 in Northern Ireland, 08457/887–766 from cell phone in Northern Ireland, 1800/667–788 roadside help in Ireland* ⊕ *www.aaireland.ie.* **Police Service of Northern Ireland** ☎ *999* ⊕ *www.psni.police.uk.*

RULES OF THE ROAD

The Irish, like the British, drive on the left-hand side of the road in whatever direction they are headed (not, as in America, on the right-hand side). Safety belts must be worn by the driver and all passengers, and children under 12 must travel in the back unless riding in a car seat. Motorcyclists must wear helmets. Speed limits in Ireland are posted in kilometers per hour and in Northern Ireland in miles per hour. In towns and cities, the speed limit is 50 kph (31 mph). On Regional (R) and Local (L) roads, the speed limit is 80 kph (50 mph), indicated by white signs. On National (N) roads, the speed limit is 100 kph (62 mph), indicated by green signs. On Motorways (M), the speed limit is 120 kph (74 mph), indicated by blue signs.

Drunk-driving laws are strict. The legal limit is 50 mg of alcohol per 100 ml of blood. Ireland has a Breathalyzer test, which the police can administer anytime. If you refuse to take it, the odds are you'll be prosecuted anyway. As always, the best advice is don't drink if you plan to drive.

Speed cameras and radar are used throughout Ireland. Speeding carries an on-the-spot fine of €80, and if you're charged with excessive speeding you

could be summoned to court. This carries a much higher fine, and you will be summoned within six months (meaning you could be required to return to Ireland).

Note that a continuous white line down the center of the road prohibits passing. Barred markings on the road and flashing yellow beacons indicate a crossing where pedestrians have right-of-way. At a junction of two roads of equal importance, the driver to the right has right-of-way. On a roundabout, vehicles approaching from the right have right-of-way. Left turns aren't permitted on a red light. ■TIP→ If another motorist flashes their headlights, they are giving you right-of-way.

Despite the relatively light traffic, parking in towns can be a problem. Signs with the letter *P* indicate that parking is permitted; a stroke through the *P* warns you to stay away or you'll be liable for a fine of €20–€65; if your car gets towed away or clamped, the fine is around €180. In Dublin and Cork, parking lots are your best bet.

In Northern Ireland there are plenty of parking lots in the towns (usually free, except in Belfast). In Belfast, you can't park your car in some parts of the city center, more because of congestion than security problems.

RENTAL CARS

When you reserve a car, ask about cancellation penalties, taxes, drop-off charges (if you're planning to pick up the car in one city and leave it in another), and surcharges (for being under or over a certain age, for additional drivers, or for driving across state or country borders or beyond a specific distance from your point of rental). All these things can add substantially to your costs. Request car seats for children and extras such as GPS when you book.

Rates are sometimes—but not always—better if you book in advance or reserve through a rental agency's website. There are other reasons to book ahead, though: for popular destinations, during busy times of the year, or to ensure that you get certain types of cars (vans, SUVs, exotic sports cars).

■ TIP→ **Make sure that a confirmed reservation guarantees you a car. Agencies sometimes overbook, particularly for busy weekends and holiday periods.**

If you're renting a car in the Irish Republic and intend to visit Northern Ireland (or vice versa), make this clear when you get your car, and check that the rental insurance applies when you cross the border.

Renting a car once you're in Ireland is far more expensive than if you had arranged for one before you left home. Rates in Dublin for an economy car with a manual transmission and unlimited mileage are from about €35 a day and €160 a week to €50 a day and €190 a week, depending on the season. This includes the 13.5% tax on car rentals. Rates in Belfast begin at £25 a day and £130 a week, including the 17.5% tax on car rentals.

Both manual and automatic transmissions are readily available, though automatics cost extra. Typical economy car models include Volkswagen Lupo, Ford Focus, Fiat Panda, and Nissan Micra. Minivans, luxury cars (Mercedes or Alfa Romeos), and four-wheel-drive vehicles (say, a Jeep Cherokee) are also options, but the daily rates are high. Argus Rent A Car and Dooley Car Rentals have convenient locations at Dublin, Shannon, Belfast, and Belfast City airports, as well as at ferry ports.

Most rental companies require you to be over 24 to rent a car (a few will rent to those over 21) and to have had a license for more than a year. Some companies refuse to rent to visitors over 70, or in some cases 74.

Drivers between the ages of 21 and 26, and 70 and 76 will probably be subject to an insurance surcharge—if they're allowed to drive a rental car at all. An additional driver will add about €8 a day, and a child seat costs about €20 and require 24-hour advance notice.

CAR RENTAL RESOURCES

Local and international car rental companies in both the Republic and Northern Ireland are listed on ⊕ *www.carhireireland.com*.

Local Agencies Argus Rent A Car ☎ *023/888–3002 in Ireland* ⊕ *www.argus-rentacar.com*. **Dooley Car Rentals** ☎ *800/331–9301 in U.S., 062/53103 in Ireland* ⊕ *www.dan-dooley.ie*.

Major Agencies Avis ☎ *800/331–1212 in U.S., 021/428–1111 in Ireland* ⊕ *www.avis.com*. **Budget** ☎ *800/472–3325 from U.S., 01/837–9611 in Ireland* ⊕ *www.budget.com*. **Dollar** ☎ *800/800–6000 in U.S., 01/670–7890 in Dublin* ⊕ *www.dollar.com*. **Hertz** ☎ *800/654–3001, 01/676–7476 in Ireland* ⊕ *www.hertz.com*.

Wholesalers Auto Europe ☎ *888/223–5555 in U.S., 1800/472–3325 in Ireland* ⊕ *www.autoeurope.com*. **Europe by Car** ☎ *800/223–1516, 212/581–3040 in U.S.* ⊕ *www.europebycarblog.com*. **Eurovacations** ☎ *877/471–3876* ⊕ *www.eurovacations.com*. **Kemwel** ☎ *800/678–0678* ⊕ *www.kemwel.com*.

■ TRAIN TRAVEL

Irish Rail trains are generally reliable, reasonably priced, and comfortable. You can easily reach all the principal towns from Dublin, though service between provincial cities can be roundabout. To get to Cork City from Wexford, for example, you have to go via Limerick Junction. It's often quicker, though perhaps less comfortable, to take a bus. Most mainline trains have one standard class. Round-trip tickets are usually cheapest. The best deals are available online, booking at least one week in advance.

Northern Ireland Railways has three main rail routes, all operating out of Belfast's Central Station: north to Derry via Ballymena and Coleraine, east to Bangor along the shores of Belfast Lough, and south to Dublin and the Irish Republic. Note that

Eurail Passes aren't valid in Northern Ireland.

There's only one class of train travel in Ireland (with the exception of the express trains between Dublin and Belfast, which have first-class and standard-class tickets). Seat reservations are part of the package if you book online on Dublin–Cork and Dublin–Belfast routes, but otherwise it's first come, first served. ■TIP➜ Get to the station at least 30 minutes ahead to ensure you'll get a seat. It's not uncommon on busier routes to find all the seats are occupied.

FARES AND PASSES

Tickets can be purchased online or at the train station. Cash, traveler's checks, and credit-card payments are accepted. You must pay in the local currency. Dublin, Connolly, and Heuston stations have automated ticket machines that accept cash or credit-card payments, offering a convenient way to avoid long lines at ticket windows.

Sample fares? A round-trip ticket from Dublin to Cork will cost around €60; Dublin to Belfast is approximately €55. Considerable savings can be made by booking ahead online where off-peak tickets cost as little as €10 each way.

Ireland is one of 24 countries where you can use an **InterRail Pass,** which provides unlimited rail travel in all of the participating countries for the duration of the pass. If you plan to rack up the miles, get a Global pass. These are available from Rail Europe for 15 days (€528), 21 days (€682), and one month (€838). In addition to standard Eurail Passes, ask about special plans, including the **Eurail Youth Pass** (for those under age 26), the **Eurail Saver Pass** (which gives a discount for two or more people traveling together). Whichever pass you choose, you must purchase your pass before you leave for Europe. For these passes, order through your travel agent or contact ⊕ *www.raileurope.com.*

The **Irish Explorer Rail & Bus Pass** covers all the state-run and national railways and bus lines throughout the republic. It does not apply to the North or to transportation within cities. An 8-day ticket for use on buses *and* trains during a 16-day period is €245. In Northern Ireland, the **iLink Card** entitling you to up to seven days' unlimited travel on scheduled bus and rail services throughout Northern Ireland is available from main Northern Ireland Railways stations. It costs about £55.

Information and Passes Eurail ⊕ *www.eurail.com.* **Fáilte Ireland** ⊕ *www.discoverireland.com.*

Train Information Irish Rail (*Iarnrod Éireann*). ☎ *01/836–6222* ⊕ *www.irishrail.ie.* **Northern Ireland Railways** ☎ *028/9066–6630* ⊕ *www.translink.co.uk/Services/NI-Railways.*

Train Station Information Belfast Central Station ✉ *E. Bridge St., Belfast, Northern Ireland* ☎ *028/9089–9400* ⊕ *www.translink.co.uk.* **Connolly Station** ✉ *Amiens St., Dublin, Co. Dublin* ☎ *01/703–2358* ⊕ *www.irishrail.ie.* **Galway Station** ✉ *Station Rd., Galway City, Co. Galway* ☎ *091/564–222* ⊕ *www.irishrail.ie.* **Heuston Station** ✉ *St. John's Rd. W (N4), Dublin, Co. Dublin* ☎ *01/836–6222* ⊕ *www.irishrail.ie.* **Kent Station** ✉ *Lower Glanmire Rd., City Center North, Cork City, Co. Cork* ☎ *021/450–4777* ⊕ *www.irishrail.ie.*

ESSENTIALS

■ ACCOMMODATIONS

From cottages to castles, Ireland has a vast range of accommodations. And while some of them rank among Europe's prettiest and priciest, the recent economic downturn has meant one thing: bargains galore. One minute of research will uncover deals like two nights at a B&B for about half price, sometimes with a third night free, and many hotels have also slashed their prices due to an excess of supply over demand. So remember to ask for a discount and see what they offer.

In Dublin and other cities, boutique hotels blend luxury with contemporary (and often truly Irish) design. Manors and castles offer a unique combination of luxury and history. Less impressive, but equally charming, are the provincial inns and country hotels with simple but adequate facilities.

You'll meet a cross section of Irish people by hopping from one bed-and-breakfast to the next, or you can keep to yourself for a week or two in a thatched cottage. B&Bs approved by Tourism Ireland display a green shamrock outside. Hotels and other accommodations in Northern Ireland are similar to those in the Republic of Ireland.

Fáilte Ireland has a grading system and maintains a list of registered hotels, guesthouses, B&Bs, farmhouses, hostels, and campgrounds. For each accommodation, the list gives a maximum charge that can't be exceeded without special authorization. Prices must be displayed in every room; if the hotel oversteps its limit, don't hesitate to complain.

Prices in the reviews are the lowest cost of a standard double room in high season.

Local Agents Fáilte Ireland ☎ 1890/324–583 in Ireland ⊕ www.discoverireland.ie.

ONLINE BOOKING RESOURCES

Contacts At Home Abroad ☎ 212/421–9165 ⊕ www.athomeabroadinc.com. **Barclay International Group** ☎ 516/364–0064, 800/845–6636 ⊕ www.barclayweb.com. **Interhome** ☎ 800/882–6864 ⊕ www.interhomeusa.com. **Villas & Apartments Abroad** ☎ 212/213–6435, 800/433–3020 ⊕ www.vaanyc.com. **Villas International** ☎ 415/499–9490, 800/221–2260 ⊕ www.villasintl.com.

BED-AND-BREAKFASTS

B&Bs are classified either as town homes, country homes, or farmhouses. Most B&Bs have private bathrooms for most bedrooms, but don't expect this as a matter of course. Some B&Bs are on farms, but the "farmhouses" are more likely to be modern bungalows or undistinguished two-story houses than creeper-clad Georgian mansions. However, there *are* some mansions offering B&B rooms, and they are priced accordingly.

At the lower end of the price scale, expect to pay an average of €30–€40 per person per night. Ask for a reduction if you are staying more than one night. Many travelers don't bother booking a B&B in advance. They are so plentiful in rural areas that it's often more fun to leave the decision open, allowing yourself a choice of final destinations for the night. Long holiday weekends are the exception to this rule, with B&Bs often getting booked up far in advance, so keep an eye on the calendar. If you want to be sure of staying in a family home, check out the places listed by Family Homes of Ireland.

To qualify as a guesthouse, establishments must have at least five bedrooms. Some guesthouses are above a bar or restaurant; others are in someone's home. As a rule, they're cheaper (some include an optional evening meal) and offer fewer amenities than hotels. But often that's where the differences end. Most have high standards of cleanliness and hospitality, and most have a bathroom, a TV, and a direct-dial phone in each room. Premier Guesthouses are generally small inns, run by the owner, and hard to distinguish from hotels.

Local Services B&B Ireland ☎ *071/982–2222* ⊕ *www.bandbireland.com.* **Family Homes of Ireland** ☎ *091/552–000* ⊕ *www.familyhomes.ie.* **Premier Guesthouses of Ireland** ☎ *01/205–2826* ⊕ *www.premierguesthouses.com.*

CASTLES AND MANORS

Among the most magical experiences on an Irish vacation are stays at some of the country's spectacular castle-hotels, such as Dromoland (County Clare), Ashford (County Galway), and Waterford Castle (near Waterford City). For directories to help you get to know the wide array of manor house and castle accommodations, including a goodly number of private country estates and castles, contact Ireland's Blue Book of Country Houses & Restaurants, or Hidden Ireland.

Reservations Services Hidden Ireland ☎ *01/662–7166* ⊕ *www.hiddenireland.com.* **Ireland's Blue Book** ☎ *01/676–9914* ⊕ *www.irelands-blue-book.ie.*

COTTAGES

Vacation cottages, which are usually in clusters, are rented by the week. Although often built in the traditional style, most have central heating and other modern conveniences. It's essential to reserve in advance.

Reservations Services Discover Northern Ireland ✉ *59 North St., Belfast, Northern Ireland* ☎ *44 28/9024–6609* ⊕ *www.discovernorthernireland.com.* **Irish Cottage Holiday Homes** ✉ *Bracken Court, Bracken Rd., Sandyford, Dublin, Co. Dublin* ☎ *01/205–2777* ⊕ *www.irishcottageholidays.com.*

HOTELS

Standard features in most hotels include two twin beds (you can usually ask for a king-size instead), TVs (often with DVD), free parking, and no-smoking rooms. All hotels listed have private bath unless otherwise noted.

Information Discover Ireland ☎ *1890/324–583 within Ireland* ⊕ *www.discoverireland.com.* **Irish Hotels Federation** ☎ *1800/989–909 within Ireland, 353/1293–9170 from other countries* ⊕ *www.irelandhotels.com.* **Northern Ireland Hotels Federation** ☎ *028/9077–6635* ⊕ *www.nihf.co.uk.*

Prices in the reviews are the lowest cost of a standard double room in high season. For expanded reviews, facilities, and current deals, visit Fodors.com.

▌ COMMUNICATIONS

INTERNET

If you're traveling with a laptop, carry a spare battery and adapter. Most laptops will work at both 120V and 220V, but you will need an adapter so the plug will fit in the socket. In the countryside, a surge protector is a good idea.

Going online is becoming routine in Dublin, thanks, in part, to the Wi-Fi hot spots popping up across the city. Net House, an Internet café chain, has the most locations around the country, with nine in Dublin and one in Cork.

Many independent Internet cafés can be found across the country. Prices vary from the low end in Dublin of €2.50 per hour to €5 per hour in smaller cities. There are also many Wi-Fi hot spots throughout the country, such as the Insomnia Coffee/Sandwich Bar chain in Galway. Dublin Airport and Dun Laoghaire Harbor have Wi-Fi access. Most hotels now offer hot spots in the lobby or lounge. A Wi-Fi connection in your room can sometimes incur an hourly charge. In most cases, however, Wi-Fi access is free if you are using the facilities of the hotel or café.

Contacts Cybercafes. More than 4,000 Internet cafés worldwide are listed on this website. ⊕ *www.cybercafes.com.*

PHONES

Ireland's telephone system is up to the standards of the United Kingdom and the United States. Local phone numbers have five to eight digits. You can make international calls from most phones, and some cell phones also work here, depending on the carrier.

Do not make calls from your hotel room phone unless it's absolutely necessary. Practically all hotels add 200% to 300% to the cost. As expensive as mobile phone calls can be, they are still usually a much cheaper option than calling from your hotel.

The country code for Ireland is 353; for Northern Ireland, which is part of the United Kingdom telephone system, it's 44. The local area code for Northern Ireland is 028. When dialing Northern Ireland from the republic you can simply dial 048 without using the U.K. country code. When dialing an Irish number from abroad, drop the initial 0 from the local area code.

If the operator has to connect your call, it will cost at least one-third more than direct dial.

Directory Information Northern Ireland
☎ *118–118 for directory inquiries in Northern Ireland, 118–505 for international directory inquiries, which includes the republic, 155 for the international operator, 100 for operator assistance for calls in Northern Ireland.* **Republic of Ireland** ☎ *11811 for directory inquiries and operator assistance in the republic and Northern Ireland, 11818 for U.K. and international numbers.*

CALLING WITHIN IRELAND

Public phones take either coins or cards, but not both. Card phones are rapidly replacing coin-operated phones, and are also cheaper. Phone cards can be bought at newsagents, convenience stores, and post offices in units of €5 upward. It's worth carrying one, especially in rural areas where coin-operated phones are a rarity. In the republic, €0.40 will buy you a three-minute local call; around €1.50 is needed for a three-minute long-distance call within the republic. In Northern Ireland, a local call costs 20p.

To make a local call, just dial the number direct. To make a long-distance call, dial the area code, then the number. The local code for Northern Ireland is 028, unless you're dialing from the republic, in which case you dial 048 or 004428, followed by the eight-digit number.

CALLING OUTSIDE IRELAND

The international prefix from Ireland is 00. For calls to Great Britain (except Northern Ireland), dial 0044 before the exchange code, and drop the initial zero of the local code. For the United States and Canada dial 001, for Australia 0061, and for New Zealand 0064.

Access Codes AT&T Direct ☎ *1800/550–000 from Republic of Ireland, 0500/890–011 from Northern Ireland.* **MCI WorldPhone** ☎ *1800/551–001 from Republic of Ireland, 0800/890–222 from Northern Ireland using British Telecom (BT), 0500/890–222 using Cable & Wireless (C&W).* **Sprint International Access** ☎ *1800/552–001 from Republic of Ireland, 0800/890–877 from Northern Ireland using British Telecom (BT), 0500/890–877 using Cable & Wireless (C&W).*

CALLING CARDS

"Callcards" are sold in post offices and newsagents. These range in price from €5 to €30. They can only be used at public phones operated by the national operator Eircom, which have become harder to find in recent years.

CELL PHONES

If you have a multiband phone (some countries use different frequencies from those used in the United States) and your service provider uses the world-standard GSM network (as do T-Mobile and Verizon), you can probably use your phone abroad. Roaming fees can be steep, however: 99¢ a minute is considered reasonable. And overseas you normally pay the toll charges for incoming calls. It's almost always cheaper to send a text message than to make a call, since text messages have a very low set fee (often less than 5¢).

If you just want to make local calls, consider buying a new SIM card (note that your provider may have to unlock your

LANGUAGE DO'S AND TABOOS

In the old days, Ireland's native language was called Gaelic and some people chuckled that it was the world's most perfect medium for prayers, curses, and lovemaking. These days, Gaelic is called Irish and no one is joking any longer.

In 2005, legislation was passed to restore the sovereignty of Irish, originally a Celtic language related to Scots Gaelic, Breton, and Welsh, as Ireland's official national language. English is technically the second language of the country but it is, in fact, the everyday tongue of 95% of the population.

However, the western coastlands of Ireland are still home to the Gaeltacht (pronounced *gale*-taukt). These Irish-speaking communities are found mainly in sparsely populated rural areas along the western seaboard, on some islands, and in pockets of West Cork and County Waterford.

Donegal and Galway have passed laws mandating Irish as the sole language for signage. In these areas, English is now outlawed on road signs and official maps. As the Associated Press reported, "Locals concede the switch will confuse foreigners in an area that depends heavily on tourism, but they say it's the price of patriotism."

The Gaeltacht includes some big tourist destinations. For instance, if travelers are in Killarney and now wish to go to Dingle, they will have to follow signposts that say "An Daingean," which is Dingle in Irish. Other instances include: Oileáin Árainn (Aran Islands); Corca Dhuibne (Dingle Peninsula); and Arainn Mhor (Aranmore Island).

As this changeover affects more than 2,000 other place-names, have an updated or Irish-friendly map if touring these Gaeltacht regions. Don't rely on official Ordnance Survey maps, which can now print only Irish place-names in these areas. This is even in cases where the English versions remain popular in local parlance (many hotels will retain their English names, such as the Dingle Bay Hotel).

Main place-names are given in both Irish and English in this guidebook for the affected regions.

Outside these Gaeltacht areas, Ireland remains officially bilingual in its road signs.

With just 55,000 native Irish speakers in a population of 4 million, a major national debate has sprung up, with local councils and tourist authorities beginning to protest the new laws.

Of course, some basic Irish vocabulary certainly wouldn't hurt: *fir* (men) and *mná* (women) should prove useful when using public restrooms.

phone for you to use a different SIM card) and a prepaid service plan in the destination. You'll then have a local number and can make local calls at local rates. If your trip is extensive, you could also simply buy a new cell phone in your destination, as the initial cost will be offset over time.

■ TIP➜ **If you travel internationally frequently, save one of your old cell phones or buy a cheap one on the Internet; ask your cell phone company to unlock it for you, and take it with you as a travel phone, buying a new SIM card with pay-as-you-go service in each destination.**

Renting a phone has the advantage that you get your number in advance and pick it up at the airport or have it mailed to you in advance. But at €69 for the first week, it's expensive compared to buying a SIM card for around €10 and using pay-as-you-go service.

Contacts Cellular Abroad. This company rents and sells GMS phones and sells SIM cards that work in many countries. ☎ 800/287–5072 ⊕ www.cellularabroad.com. **Mobal.** You can rent cell phones and buy GSM phones (starting at $49) from Mobal that will operate in 140 countries. Per-call rates vary throughout the world. ☎ 888/888–9162 ⊕ www.mobal. com. **Planet Fone.** This company rents cell phones, but the per-minute rates are expensive. ☎ 888/988–4777 ⊕ www.planetfone. com. **Rentaphone-Ireland.com** A phone will be awaiting your arrival at Dublin Airport if you rent from this company. ☎ 087/683–4543 ⊕ www.cell-phone-ireland.com. **Vodafone.** Call for details of SIM-card purchase (€10) and price of calls on pay-as-you-go plans. ☎ 01/203–8232 ⊕ www.vodafone.ie.

■ CUSTOMS AND DUTIES

You're always allowed to bring goods of a certain value back home without having to pay any duty or import tax. But there's a limit on the amount of tobacco and liquor you can bring back duty-free, and—if you are traveling to additional destinations after your visit to Ireland—some countries have separate limits for perfumes; for exact figures, check with your customs department. The values of so-called "duty-free" goods are included in these amounts. When you shop abroad, save all your receipts, as customs inspectors may ask to see them as well as the items you purchased. If the total value of your goods is more than the duty-free limit, you'll have to pay a tax (most often a flat percentage) on the value of everything beyond that limit.

Duty-free allowances have been abolished for those traveling between countries in the EU. For goods purchased outside the EU, you may import duty-free: (1) 200 cigarettes or 100 cigarillos or 50 cigars or 250 grams of smoking tobacco; (2) 2 liters of wine, and either 1 liter of alcoholic drink over 22% volume or 2 liters of alcoholic drink under 22% volume (sparkling or fortified wine included); (3) 50 grams (60 ml) of perfume and ¼ liter (250 ml) of eau de toilette; and (4) other goods (including beer) to a value of €175 per person (€90 per person for travelers under 15 years of age).

Goods that cannot be freely imported to the Irish Republic include firearms, ammunition, explosives, indecent or obscene books and pictures, oral smokeless tobacco products, meat and meat products, poultry and poultry products. Plants and plant products (including shrubs, vegetables, fruit, bulbs, and seeds) can be imported from other countries within the EU only, provided they are eligible under the EU's plant passport scheme. Domestic cats and dogs from outside the United Kingdom and live animals from outside Northern Ireland must be quarantined for six months, unless they are traveling under the EU's Pet Travel Scheme.

Information in Ireland Customs and Excise ✉ Government Bldgs., St Conlon's Rd., Nenagh, Co. Tipperary ☎ 067/63400 ⊕ www.revenue. ie. **HM Customs and Excise** ✉ Crownhill Ct., Tailyour Rd., Plymouth, England ☎ 0845/010–9000 ⊕ www.hmrc.gov.uk. **Pet Travel Scheme** ⊕ www.agriculture.gov.ie.

U.S. Information U.S. Customs and Border Protection ⊕ www.cbp.gov.

▌EATING OUT

MEALS AND MEALTIMES

No longer will you enjoy your favorite tipple in the blue haze of a smoke-filled pub. In 2004, the Republic of Ireland became the first European country to ban smoking in all pubs and restaurants. Northern Ireland followed in 2007.

Breakfast is served from 7 to 10, lunch runs from 12:30 to 2:30, and dinners are usually midevening occasions. Unless otherwise noted, the restaurants listed here are open daily for lunch and dinner.

Pubs are generally open Monday and Tuesday 10:30 am–11:30 pm and Wednesday–Saturday 10:30 am–12:30 am. On Sunday, pubs are open 12:30 pm–11 pm or later on certain Sundays. All pubs close on Christmas Day and Good Friday, but hotel bars are open for guests.

Pubs in Northern Ireland are open 11:30 am–11 pm Monday–Saturday and 12:30 pm–2:30 pm and 7 pm–10 pm on Sunday (note that Sunday openings are at the owner's or manager's discretion).

PAYING

Traveler's checks and credit cards are widely accepted, although it's cash-only at smaller pubs and takeout restaurants.

Prices in the reviews are the average cost of a main course at dinner or, if dinner is not served, at lunch.

For guidelines on tipping see Tipping.

RESERVATIONS AND DRESS

Regardless of where you are, it's a good idea to make a reservation if you can. In some places, it's expected. We mention them specifically only when reservations are essential (there's no other way you'll ever get a table) or when they are not accepted. For popular restaurants, book as far ahead as you can (often 30 days), and reconfirm as soon as you arrive. (Large parties should always call ahead

to check the reservations policy.) We mention dress only when men are required to wear a jacket or a jacket and tie.

WINES, BEER, AND SPIRITS

All types of alcoholic beverages are available in Ireland. Beer and wine are sold in shops and supermarkets, and you can get drinks "to go" at some bars, although at inflated prices. Stout (Guinness, Murphy's, Beamish) is the Irish beer; whiskey comes in many brands, the most notable being Bushmills and Jameson, and is smoother than Scotch.

▌ELECTRICITY

The current in Ireland is 220 volts, 50 cycles alternating current; wall outlets take plugs with three prongs.

Consider making a small investment in a universal adapter, which has several types of plugs in one lightweight, compact unit. Most laptops and mobile phone chargers are dual voltage (i.e., they operate equally well on 110 and 220 volts), and so require only an adapter. These days the same is true of small appliances such as hair dryers. Always check labels and manufacturer instructions to be sure. Don't use 110-volt outlets marked "for shavers only" for high-wattage appliances such as hair dryers.

Contacts Steve Kropla's Help for World Travelers. This website has information on electrical and telephone plugs around the world. ⊕ www.kropla.com.

∎ EMERGENCIES

The police force in the Republic of Ireland is called the Garda Síochána ("Guardians of the Peace," in English), usually referred to as the Gardaí (pronounced gar-*dee*). The force is unarmed and is headed by a government-appointed commissioner, who is answerable to the Minister for Justice, who in turn is accountable to the Dáil (the Irish legislature). Easily identified by their fluorescent yellow blazers in winter, or, if weather permits in summer, by a dark blue shirt and peaked cap, the Gardaí are generally very helpful. They, and all other emergency forces, can be contacted in the Republic of Ireland by dialing 999 (112, the European standard, is also used). These numbers connect you with local police, ambulance, and fire services. Expect a prompt response. The Garda Síochána website provides contact information for local stations.

In Northern Ireland the police force is the Police Service of Northern Ireland (PSNI). They are distinguished by their dark blue coats and white shirts. They can be contacted by dialing 999.

Contacts Consulate General of the United States ✉ *Danesfort House, 223 Stranmills Rd., Belfast, Northern Ireland* 📞 *028/9038–6100* ⊕ *belfast.usconsulate.gov.* **United States Embassy** ✉ *42 Elgin Rd., Ballsbridge, Dublin, Co. Dublin* 📞 *01/668–8777* ⊕ *dublin. usembassy.gov.*

General Emergency Contacts Ambulance, fire, police 📞 *999 Republic and Northern Ireland, 112 Republic only.* **An Garda Síochána** ⊕ *www.garda.ie.* **Police Service of Northern Ireland** ⊕ *www.psni.police.uk.*

∎ GUIDED TOURS

Guided tours are a good option when you don't want to do it all yourself. The companies here all offer tours to Ireland on a "land-only" basis. A land-only tour includes all your travel (by bus, in most cases) once you arrive in the destination country, but not necessarily your flights to your destination. And remember that you'll be expected to tip your guide (in cash) at the end of the tour.

GENERAL TOURS

CIE Tours International is one of the biggest and longest-established tour operators in the Irish market. It offers a selection of fully inclusive, escorted bus tours, or independent fly-drive vacations. An eight-day itinerary with car rental and confirmed hotel bookings starts at $1,026 per person. Starting in Dublin, the Heritage Tour is a seven-day bus tour that takes in Bunratty Castle and Folk Park, Blarney Castle, the Cliffs of Moher, the Skellig Experience, and the Lakes of Killarney, among other attractions, with accommodations in top hotels.

Discovering Ireland Vacations, a young company set up by three friends, aims to create the best holiday experience by using enthusiastic local guides. A customized seven-day self-drive tour across Ireland starts at $399 per person. The price includes six nights at a B&B, car rental, and toll-free calls to your vacation specialist. Escorted bus tours include the Irish Spirit, which includes one day in Dublin, a drive to Blarney Castle via the Rock of Cashel, Killarney, the Ring of Kerry, and the Cliffs of Moher. Rates begin at $1,068 per person.

Contacts CIE Tours International 📞 *800/243–8607* ⊕ *www.cietours.com.* **Discovering Ireland Vacations** 📞 *1800/963–9260* ⊕ *www.discoveringireland.com.*

SPECIAL-INTEREST TOURS

BIKING

Irish Cycling Safaris. This company pioneered cycling holidays in Ireland, and offers easygoing to moderate cycling trips along rural back roads with luggage transfer and accommodations in small family-run hotels and guesthouses. A weeklong tour of West Cork and Kerry, including Killarney, costs €735 per person sharing. Tour groups are accompanied by a local guide who drives the support van. Alternatively, you can opt for a self-led tour that includes bike rental, itinerary, and prebooked accommodations, €715 per person sharing. ✉ *Belfield Bike Shop, UCD, Dublin, Co. Dublin* ☎ *01/260–0749* ⊕ *www.cyclingsafaris.com.*

Iron Donkey. Fodor's readers give this company rave reviews. Offering something for everyone from novices to hammerheads, their mainstay are guided group tours: for instance, the Clare and Burren itinerary sets out from Ennis and includes Kilkee, Loop Head, Spanish Point, the Cliffs of Moher, the Burren coastline, and Bunratty Castle (cost is about €1,545 per person sharing). But others swear by the super-thorough and well-run custom tours, where they meet you at the first lodging (all great options, incidentally) with your bikes and size them to you, go over your route, and beautifully prep you for the ride. ☎ *028/9081–3200* ⊕ *www.irondonkey.com.*

■**TIP→** Most airlines accommodate bikes as luggage, provided they're dismantled and boxed.

CULTURE

Adams & Butler. Ireland's leading purveyor of customized vacations, Adams & Butler has an unbeatable range of contacts in the upper end of the market. Most of its tours are for groups in chauffeur-driven cars or on small luxury buses. It can offer you a week in Ireland with a self-drive car, an itinerary, and stays in houses of character from $750; up that price to around $4,000 per person for a luxury hotel with driver-guide and five-star accommodations. ☎ *01/288–9355* ⊕ *www.adamsandbutler.com.*

GOLF

Executive Golf & Leisure. These Scotland-based golf specialists offer customized golf breaks or packages, such as an eight-day golf tour of Ireland for about $7,400 with luxury accommodations, transfers, and rounds on some of the finest courses: the K Club, Old Portmarnock, Waterville, Ballybunion, Killarney, and the Old Head of Kinsale. ☎ *01786/832–244,*

1-877/295–2247 in the U.S., 1-866/392–5021 in Canada ⊕ *www.execgolf-leisure.com.*

Golfbreaks.com. This company will customize a golf tour for you, and also have tours of different regions of Ireland. Their Northern Ireland and the Northwest package includes rounds at the legendary Royal County Down and Royal Portrush courses. ☎ *0808/274–9415 in U.K., 1753/752–900 from other countries* ⊕ *www.golfbreaks.com.*

HIKING

Isle Inn. A long-established company offering self-drive holidays and escorted tours, Isle Inn also has an interesting range of activity holidays and escorted hiking holidays averaging 16 to 19 km (10 to 12 miles) a day. You stay in family-run guesthouses and characterful small hotels while walking through scenic areas, including the Donegal coast, the Glens of Antrim, Achill island, and Mayo. Escorted hiking holidays start from $1,384. A chauffeur-driven itinerary (from $1,649) combines culture and cuisine, offering six nights at top hotels with gourmet dinners and a driver to escort you. ☎ *800/237–9376* ⊕ *www.isleinntours.com.*

RAIL

Railtours Ireland. This top outfitter uses the Irish railroad network for major transfers, and tour buses for sightseeing at the destination, avoiding long, leg-numbing stretches of bus travel. The five-day tour starts with a train ride from Dublin to Cork (2 hours, 45 minutes) including breakfast, and continues with a bus tour to Blarney, train to Killarney, bus tour of the Ring of Kerry, and also visits Galway, the Cliffs of Moher, and Connemara, starting at €679 per person, with accommodations in B&Bs and modest hotels. ☎ *01/856–0045 in Ireland, 800/5008–0200 toll free from U.S.* ⊕ *www.railtoursireland.com.*

▌ HOURS OF OPERATION

Museums and sights are generally open Tuesday–Saturday 10–5 and Sunday 2–5. Business hours are 9–5, sometimes later in the larger towns. In smaller towns, many establishments close from 1 to 2 for lunch. If a holiday falls on a weekend, most businesses are closed on Monday. There are some 24-hour gas stations along the highways; otherwise, hours vary from morning rush hour to late evenings.

In the Republic of Ireland, banks are open 10–4 weekdays. They remain open until 5 one afternoon per week, usually Thursday. Post offices are open weekdays 9–5 and Saturday 9–1. In Northern Ireland, bank hours are weekdays 9:30–4:30. Post offices are open weekdays 9–5:30, Saturday 9–1.

Pharmacies are usually open Monday–Saturday 9–5:30 or 6. Larger towns and cities often have 24-hour establishments. Most shops are open Monday–Saturday 9–5:30 or 6. Once a week—normally Wednesday, Thursday, or Saturday—shops close at 1 pm. These times do *not* apply to Dublin, where stores generally stay open later. Larger malls usually stay open late once a week—generally until 9 on Thursday or Friday. Convenience stores, supermarkets, and gas stations in both Dublin and rural Ireland are generally open until 8 or 9 pm.

Shops in Belfast are open weekdays 9–5:30, with a late closing on Thursday, usually at 9. Elsewhere in Northern Ireland, shops close for the afternoon once a week, usually Wednesday or Thursday.

HOLIDAYS

Irish national holidays in 2015 are as follows: January 1 (New Year's Day); March 17 (St. Patrick's Day); April 3 (Good Friday); April 5 (Easter Monday); May 4 (May Day); June 1 and August 3 (summer bank holidays); October 26 (autumn bank holiday); and December 25 and 26 (Christmas and St. Stephen's Day). If you plan to visit at Easter, remember that theaters and movie theaters are closed for the last three days of the preceding week.

In Northern Ireland, the following are holidays in 2015: January 1 (New Year's Day); March 17 (St. Patrick's Day); April 3 (Good Friday); April 5 (Easter Monday); May 4 (early May bank holiday); May 25 (late-spring bank holiday); July 12 (Battle of the Boyne); August 31 (summer bank holiday); and December 25 and 26 (Christmas and Boxing Day).

▌ MAIL

Outside of Dublin and Northern Ireland, postal codes aren't used; what's more important here is the county, so be sure to include it when addressing an envelope.

Letters by standard post take a week to 10 days to reach the United States and Canada, 3 to 5 days to reach the United Kingdom.

Airmail rates to the United States and Canada from the Irish Republic are €0.82 for letters and postcards. Rates are €0.90 for letters and postcards to Europe. Mail to overseas can be sent economy or airmail. Letters and postcards within the island of Ireland cost €0.60.

Rates from Northern Ireland are 88p for letters and postcards (not over 10 grams) to continental Europe, the United States, Canada, Australia, and New Zealand. To the rest of the United Kingdom and the Irish Republic, rates are 60p for first-class letters and 50p for second-class.

Mail can be held for collection at any post office for free for up to three months. It should be addressed to the recipient "c/o Poste Restante." In Dublin, use the General Post Office. The postal service in the Republic of Ireland, known as An Post, has a website with a branch locator and lots of other postal information. In Northern Ireland mail service is run by the Royal Mail.

Contact **An Post** ☎ *01/705–7600* ⊕ *www. anpost.ie.* **General Post Office** ⊠ *O'Connell St., Dublin, Co. Dublin* ☎ *01/705–8833.*

▌ MONEY

A modest hotel in Dublin costs about €120 a night for two; this figure can drop below €90 if you stay in a registered guesthouse or inn, and to about €70 by staying in a suburban B&B. Lunch, consisting of a one-dish plate of bar food at a pub, costs €10–€14; a sandwich at the same pub costs about €5. In Dublin's better restaurants, dinner will run €45–€60 (dinner being a three-course meal) per person, excluding drinks and tip.

Theater and entertainment in most places are inexpensive—about €20 for a good seat, and triple that for a big-name pop-music concert. For the price of a few drinks and (in Dublin and Killarney) sometimes also a small entrance fee of about €5, you can spend a memorable evening at a *seisun* (pronounced say-*shoon* when referring to this folk music session), in a music pub. Entrance to most public galleries is free, but stately homes and similar attractions charge anywhere from €4 to a whopping €16 per person.

Just about everything is more expensive in Dublin, so add at least 10% to these sample prices: cup of coffee, €2.20; pint of beer, €5; soda, €2.40; and 2-km (1-mile) taxi ride, €8. Due to the exchange rate, Americans, Australians, New Zealanders, and U.K. residents will find Ireland a little pricey when they convert costs to their home currency.

Hotels and meals in Northern Ireland are less expensive than in the United Kingdom and the Republic of Ireland. Also, the lower level of taxation makes gasoline, alcoholic drinks, and tobacco cheaper.

Prices throughout this guide are given for adults. Substantially reduced fees are almost always available for children, students, and senior citizens.

▌TIP➜ Banks never have every foreign currency on hand, and it may take as long as a week to order. If you're planning to exchange funds before leaving home, don't wait until the last minute.

ATMS AND BANKS

Your own bank will probably charge a fee for using ATMs abroad; the foreign bank you use may also charge a fee. Nevertheless, you'll usually get a better rate of exchange at an ATM than you will at a currency-exchange office or even when changing money in a bank. And extracting funds as you need them is a safer option than carrying around a large amount of cash.

▌TIP➜ PINs with more than four digits are not recognized at ATMs in many countries. If yours has five or more, remember to change it before you leave.

ATMs are found in all major towns and are the easiest way to keep yourself stocked with euros and pounds. Most major banks are connected to Cirrus or PLUS systems; there's a four-digit maximum for your PIN.

CREDIT CARDS

It's a good idea to inform your credit-card company before you travel, especially if you're going abroad and don't travel internationally very often. Otherwise, the credit-card company might put a hold on your card owing to unusual activity—not a good thing halfway through your trip. Record all your credit-card numbers—as well as the phone numbers to call if your cards are lost or stolen—in a safe place, so you're prepared should something go wrong. Both MasterCard and Visa have general numbers you can call (collect if you're abroad) if your card is lost, but you're better off calling the number of your issuing bank, since MasterCard and Visa usually just transfer you to your bank; your bank's number is usually printed on your card.

If you plan to use your credit card for cash advances, you'll need to apply for a PIN at least two weeks before your trip. Although it's usually cheaper (and safer) to use a credit card abroad for large purchases (so you can cancel payments or be reimbursed if there's a problem), note that some credit-card companies *and* the banks that issue them add substantial percentages to all foreign transactions, whether they're in a foreign currency or not. Check on these fees before leaving home, so there won't be any surprises when you get the bill.

When using your credit card, check that the merchant is putting the transaction through in euros or pounds sterling. If he or she puts it through in the currency of your home country—a transaction called a dynamic currency conversion—the exchange rate might be less favorable and the service charges higher than if you allow the credit-card company to do the conversion for you. Be sure to ask at the time, and insist on being billed in euros to get the most advantageous rate and avoid the service charge.

Reporting Lost Cards American Express ☎ 800/992–3404 in U.S., 336/393–1111 collect from abroad ⊕ www.americanexpress. com. **Diners Club** ☎ 800/234–6377 in U.S., 303/799–1504 collect from abroad ⊕ www. dinersclub.com. **MasterCard** ☎ 800/622–7747 in U.S., 636/722–7111 collect from abroad ⊕ www.mastercard.com/ie. **Visa** ☎ 800/847–2911 in U.S., 410/581–9994 collect from abroad ⊕ www.visa.com.

CURRENCY AND EXCHANGE

The Irish Republic is a member of the European Monetary Union (EMU). Euro notes come in denominations of €500, €200, €100, €50, €20, €10, and €5. The euro is divided into 100 cents, and coins are available as €2 and €1 and 50, 20, 10, 5, 2, and 1 cent.

The unit of currency in Northern Ireland is the pound sterling (£), divided into 100 pence (p). The bills (called notes) are £50, £20, £10, and £5. Coins are £2, £1, 50p, 20p, 10p, 5p, 2p, and 1p. The bank of Northern Ireland prints its own notes, which look different from the English or Scottish sterling.

Check out today's rates at ⊕ www.oanda. com.

At this writing, €1 is equal to U.S. $1.37. One pound sterling is equal to U.S. $1.66.

Rates fluctuate regularly, particularly for the euro, so monitor them closely.

■TIP➔ Even if a currency-exchange booth has a sign promising no commission, rest assured that there's some kind of huge, hidden fee. (Oh . . . that's right. The sign didn't say no fee.) And as for rates, you're almost always better off getting foreign currency at an ATM or exchanging money at a bank.

TRAVELER'S CHECKS AND CARDS

Some consider this the currency of the caveman, and it's true that fewer establishments accept traveler's checks these days. Nevertheless, they're a cheap and secure way to carry extra money, particularly on trips to urban areas. Both Citibank (under the Visa brand) and American Express issue traveler's checks in the United States, but Amex is better known and more widely accepted. Whatever you do, keep track of all the serial numbers in case the checks are lost or stolen.

▮ PACKING

In Ireland you can experience all four seasons in a day. There can be damp, chilly stretches even in July and August, the warmest months of the year. Layers are the best way to go. Pack several long- and short-sleeve T-shirts (in winter, some should be thermal or silk), a sweatshirt, a lightweight sweater, a heavyweight sweater, and a hooded, waterproof windbreaker that's large enough to go over several layers if necessary. A portable umbrella is absolutely essential, and the smaller and lighter it is, the better, as you'll want it with you every second. You should bring at least two pairs of walking shoes; footwear can get soaked in minutes and then take hours to dry.

The Irish are generally informal about clothes. In the more expensive hotels and restaurants, people dress formally for dinner, and a jacket and tie may be required in bars after 7 pm, but very few places operate a strict dress policy. Old or tattered blue jeans and running shoes are forbidden in certain bars and dance clubs.

If you're used to packing things or stowing dirty clothes in plastic shopping or drawstring bags, bring your own. About the only place you can find the latter here is in the closets of better hotel rooms (for on-site dry cleaning and laundry). Plastic bags carry a 22¢ government levy and can be sold by supermarkets, but it's illegal to give them away. Most stores use paper bags or recycle boxes.

▌PASSPORTS

All U.S. citizens, even infants, need a valid passport to enter Ireland for stays of up to 90 days. Citizens of the United Kingdom, when traveling on flights departing from Great Britain, do not need a passport to enter Ireland, but it's advisable to carry some form of photo ID. Passport requirements for Northern Ireland are the same as for the republic.

U.S. passports are valid for 10 years. You must apply in person if you're getting a passport for the first time; if your previous passport was lost, stolen, or damaged; or if your previous passport has expired and was issued more than 15 years ago or when you were under 16. All children under 18 must appear in person to apply for or renew a passport. Both parents must accompany any child under 14 (or send a notarized statement with their permission) and provide proof of their relationship to the child.

▌TIP➔ Before your trip, make two copies of your passport's data page (one for someone at home and another for you to carry separately). Or scan the page and email it to someone at home and/or yourself.

There are 13 regional passport offices, as well as 7,000 passport acceptance facilities in post offices, public libraries, and other governmental offices. If you're renewing a passport, you can do so by mail. Forms are available at passport acceptance facilities and online.

The cost to apply for a new passport is $100 for adults, $85 for children under 16; renewals are $75. Allow six weeks for processing, both for first-time passports and renewals. For an expediting fee of $60 you can reduce this time to about two weeks. If your trip is less than two weeks away, you can get a passport even more rapidly by going to a passport office with the necessary documentation. Private expediters can get things done in as little as 48 hours, but charge hefty fees for their services.

U.S. Passport Information U.S. Department of State ☎ *877/487–2778* ⊕ *travel.state.gov/ passport.*

U.S. Passport and Visa Expediters A. Briggs Passport & Visa Expediters ☎ *800/806–0581, 202/338–0111* ⊕ *www. abriggs.com.* **American Passport Express** ☎ *800/455–5166, 603/559–9888* ⊕ *www. americanpassport.com.* **Passport Express** ☎ *800/362-8196* ⊕ *www.passportexpress.com.* **Travel Document Systems** ☎ *800/874–5100, 202/638–3800* ⊕ *www.traveldocs.com.* **Travel the World Visas** ☎ *202/223–8822, 866/886–8472* ⊕ *www.world-visa.com.*

▌RESTROOMS

Public restrooms are in short supply in Ireland. They'll be easy enough to find in public places such as airports, train stations, and shopping malls, but if you don't find yourself in one of these locations your best bet is to look for the nearest pub (never more than a few minutes away in Ireland!). Restrooms are often labeled in Irish—*fir* (men) and *mná* (women). Pubs are increasingly putting up signs saying that restrooms are for customers only—but this is difficult to enforce. If it's outside of shopping or pub hours, your last option may be the nearest hotel. Most gas stations will have toilets available. Only toilets in hotels or shopping centers will be up to a polished North American standard. Although many toilets look well worn, they are generally clean. Unfortunately, few restrooms are heated and an open window is typically used for ventilation, making for uncomfortably cold experience in the colder months.

▌ TAXES

When leaving the Irish Republic, U.S. and Canadian visitors get a refund of the value-added tax (V.A.T.), which currently accounts for a hefty 23% of the purchase price of many goods and 13.5% of those that fall outside the luxury category. Apart from clothing, most items of interest to visitors, right down to ordinary toilet soap, are rated at 23%. V.A.T. is not refundable on accommodations, car rental, meals, or any other form of personal services received on vacation.

Many crafts outlets and department stores operate a system that enables U.S. and Canadian visitors to collect V.A.T. rebates in the currency of their choice at Dublin or Shannon Airport on departure. Some stores give you the rebate at the register; with others you claim your refund after you've returned home.

Refund forms, known as tax-free shopping cheques, must be picked up at the time of purchase, and they must be stamped by customs, and mailed back to the store before you leave for home. It may take months for your refund to be processed. Many merchants work with a service such as Global Blue, which has offices at major ports and airports, and will refund your money immediately in return for a 4% fee.

If a store gives you a refund at the register, you'll also be given papers to have stamped by customs; you'll then put the papers in an envelope (also provided by the store) and mail it before you leave. Most major stores deduct V.A.T. at the time of sale if goods are to be shipped overseas; however, there's a shipping charge.

When leaving Northern Ireland, U.S. and Canadian visitors can also get a refund of the 17.5% V.A.T. by the over-the-counter and the direct-export methods. Most larger stores provide these services on request and will handle the paperwork. For the over-the-counter method, you must spend more than £75 in one store. Ask the store for Form V.A.T. 407 (you must have identification—passports are best), to be given to customs when you leave the country. The refund will be forwarded to you in about eight weeks (minus a small service charge) either in the form of a check or as a credit to your charge card. The direct-export method, where the goods are shipped directly to your home, is more cumbersome. V.A.T. Form 407/1/93 must be certified by customs, police, or a notary public when you get home and then sent back to the store, which will refund your money.

Global Blue ☎ 866/706–6090 in U.S. ⊕ www. global-blue.com.

▌ TIME

Dublin is five hours ahead of New York and eight hours ahead of Los Angeles.

▌ TIPPING

In some hotels and restaurants, a service charge of around 10%—rising to 15% in plush spots—is added to the bill. If in doubt, ask whether service is included. In places where it's included, tipping isn't necessary unless you have received particularly good service. If there's no service charge, add a minimum of 10% to the total. Taxi drivers or hackney cab drivers, who make the trip for a prearranged sum, don't expect tips. There are few porters and plenty of baggage trolleys at airports, so tipping is usually not an issue; if you use a porter, €1 is the minimum. Tip hotel porters at least €1 per suitcase. Hairdressers normally expect about 10% of the total spent. You don't tip in pubs, but for waiter service in a bar, a hotel lounge, or a Dublin lounge bar, leave about €1. It's not customary to tip for regular concierge service.

TIPPING GUIDELINES FOR IRELAND	
Bellhop	€1 to €2, depending on the level of the hotel
Hotel Concierge	€5 or more if he or she performs a special service for you
Hotel Doorman	€1–€2 if he helps you get a cab
Hotel Maid	€1–€3 a day (either daily or at the end of your stay, in cash)
Hotel Room-Service Waiter	€1 to €2 per delivery, even if a service charge has been added
Restroom Attendant	Restroom attendants in more expensive restaurants expect some small change or €1.
Taxi Driver	10%, or just round up the fare to the next euro amount
Tour Guide	10% of the cost of the tour
Valet Parking Attendant	€1–€2, but only when you get your car
Waiter	Just small change (up to a euro or two) to round out your bill if service is already included, otherwise add 10%.

▌ VISITOR INFORMATION

For information on travel in Ireland, contact Tourism Ireland, the international marketing authority for both Fáilte Ireland (pronounced *fal*-cha), as the tourism development authority is called within the Republic of Ireland, and the Northern Ireland Tourist Board. Tourism Ireland's website is designed for international travelers planning their trip. Fáilte Ireland runs the network of tourist information offices under the logo Discover Ireland. It's especially useful for those already in the country looking for activities and seasonal events. Information on travel in the north is available from the Northern Ireland Tourist Board.

Information Discover Ireland ☎ *1890/324–583* ⊕ *www.discoverireland.ie.* **Northern Ireland Tourist Board** (*NITB*). ✉ *59 North St., Belfast, Northern Ireland* ☎ *028/9023–1221* ⊕ *www.discovernorthernireland.com.* **Tourism Ireland** ⊕ *www.ireland.com.* **Tourism Ireland New York Office** ✉ *345 Park Ave., 17th fl., New York, New York, USA* ☎ *212/418–0800, 800/SHAMROCK* ⊕ *www.ireland.com.*

ONLINE TRAVEL TOOLS

For lots of entertaining bits—Irish and otherwise—visit ⊕ *www.irishabroad.com.* The website ⊕ *www.ireland-information. com* is dedicated to providing as many free resources and as much free information about Ireland as possible on an array of topics from genealogy to shopping. For a central directory of links to all things Irish, log on to ⊕ *www.finditireland.com.* Comhaltas Ceoltóirí Éireann is an association that promotes the music, culture, and art of Ireland, and its website ⊕ *www. comhaltas.ie* has helpful news about the Irish traditional music scene.

For listings of all music, film, and theater events and festivals, see ⊕ *www. entertainment.ie.* For general information on current affairs, sports, entertainment, and more, log on to ⊕ *www.ireland. com.* Keep in mind that many of the leading newspapers of Ireland have websites, which can be gold mines of timely information. See, for example, the *Irish Times*'s website, ⊕ *www.irishtimes.com.* To keep Irish people abroad up to date on events at home, visit ⊕ *www.irishcentral.com.*

Officially designated Heritage Towns are featured on ⊕ *www.heritagetowns.com.* A range of discounted heritage attractions are flagged on ⊕ *www.heritageisland. com,* while ⊕ *www.heritageireland.ie* is the website for the prime heritage attractions under state management, from the Rock of Cashel to Killarney National Park.

The website ⊕ *www.visitdublin.com* has all you need to know about the capital. Portions of the Tourism Ireland's eloquent magazine, *Ireland of the Welcomes*, are available online at ⊕ *www.irelandofthewelcomes.com.* Castle lovers will enjoy ⊕ *www.celticcastles.com*, while foodies should check out ⊕ *www.bordbia.ie* and ⊕ *www.goodfoodireland.ie.*

BASICS

Currency Conversion Google. Google does currency conversion. Just type in the amount you want to convert and an explanation of how you want it converted (e.g., "14 Swiss francs in dollars"), and then voilà. ⊕ *www.google.com.* **Oanda.com.** On this site, you can also print out a handy table with the current day's conversion rates. ⊕ *www.oanda.com.* **XE.com.** This is a good currency conversion website. ⊕ *www.xe.com.*

Safety Transportation Security Administration (*TSA*). ⊕ *www.tsa.gov.*

Time Zones Timeanddate.com. This site can help you figure out the correct time anywhere. ⊕ *www.timeanddate.com/worldclock.*

Weather Accuweather.com. This is one of the better independent weather-forecasting services. ⊕ *www.accuweather.com.* **Weather.com.** This is the website for the Weather Channel. ⊕ *www.weather.com.*

Other Resources CIA World Factbook. A good website if you need some quick facts and figures, this noted resource has profiles of every country in the world. ⊕ *www.cia.gov.*

INDEX

PHOTO CREDITS

Front cover: Giorgio Raffaelli/Flickr Open/Getty Images [Description: Sheep on the road near Cushendun, County Antrim, Ulster]. Back cover (from left to right): Patryk Kosmider/Shutterstock; (c) Mustang79 | Dreamstime.com; Holger Leue/Tourism Ireland. Spine: nhtg/Shutterstock. 1, Gareth McCormack/age fotostock. 2, Milosz_M/Shutterstock. 5, The Irish Image Colle/age fotostock. Chapter 1: Experience Ireland: 8-9 ARCO/Ludaescher/age fotostock. 10, Dublin Tourism. 11 (left), Charles Bishop/wikipedia.org. 11 (right), Lawyer50, Fodors.com member. 12, fhwrdh/Flickr.13 (left), Holger Leue/Tourism Ireland. 13 (right), Northern Ireland Tourist Board. 16, Brian Morrison/Northern Ireland Tourist Board. 17 (left), Brian Morrison/Northern Ireland Tourist Board. 17 (right), Jonathan Hession/Tourism Ireland. 18 (left), Michal Rozanski/iStockphoto. 18 (top right), James Harris/wikipedia.org. 18 (bottom right), Joe Gough/Shutterstock. 19 (top left), wikipedia.org. 19 (bottom left), Joe Gough/Shutterstock.19 (top center), Thomas Barrat/Shutterstock. 19 (right), Chris Hill/Tourism Ireland. 20, Alan O Connor/Tourism Ireland. 21 (left), photo$/Flickr. 21 (right), Holger Leue/Tourism Ireland. 22, kulicki/iStockphoto. 23, vito arcomano/age fotostock. 24, David Mason/iStockphoto. 25, Kathleen Noehren, Fodors.com member. 26, Chris Hill/Tourism Ireland. 27 (left), Chris Hill/Tourism Ireland. 27 (right), Nic McPhee/wikipedia.org. 28, (c) Bkhamitsevich | Dreamstime.com. 29, (c) Silberkorn | Dreamstime.com. 30, P. Jayne Grote, Fodor's.com member. 32, Shannon Development/Tourism Ireland. 34, Jane Sallee, Fodors.com member. 35 (left), Brian Morrison/Tourism Ireland. 35 (right), carolel, Fodors.com member. 38, Peter Forde, Fodors.com member. 39, Chris Hill/Tourism Ireland. Chapter 2: Dublin: 41, IIC/age fotostock. 42, beamillion/Flickr. 43, Ros Kavanagh.44, upthebanner/Shutterstock. 55, Hochgeladen von Tormod/wikipedia.org. 62 (top), clu/iStockphoto. 62 (bottom), Beinecke Rare Book and Manuscript Library, Yale University. 63 (top left), Random House, Inc.. 63 (bottom left), wikipedia.org. 63 (top right), Jean-Pierre De Mann/age fotostock. 63 (bottom middle), Arrow Books. 63 (bottom right), Macmillan. 64, si_arts/Shutterstock. 65, janetmck/Flickr. 66 (top), Georgios Kollidas/iStockphoto. 66 (middle), Library of Congress Prints and Photographs Division. 66 (bottom), National Portrait Gallery, London/wikipedia.org. 67 (top), wikipedia.org. 67 (middle), Lebrecht Music and Arts Photo Library/Alamy. 67 (bottom), Ida Kar Collection/Mary Evans Picture Library. 68 (top left), Alex Ehrenzweig/wikipedia.org. 68 (bottom), Jack_Dawkins/Flickr. 68 (top right), Homer Sykes/age fotostock. 70, Rob Wilson/Shutterstock. 73, Razvan Stroie/Shutterstock. 78, Alvaro Leiva/age fotostock. 79, MATTES Ren./age fotostock. 80 (left), Richard Cummins/age fotostock. 80-81, peterme/Flickr. 82 (top left), OMS Photography/age fotostock. 82 (bottom), Beamish & Crawford. 82 (middle), Murphy Brewery. 82 (top right), www.studioseventyseven.com. 83 (top), Blaine Harrington/age fotostock. 83 (bottom), WordRidden/Flickr. 91, Neale Clarke/age fotostock. 106, Nico Tondini/age fotostock. 107 (left), Antonio V. Oquias/Shutterstock. 107 (right), Ye/Shutterstock. 139, Martin Child/age fotostock. 145, Vincent MacNamara/Alamy. Chapter 3: Dublin Environs: 153, fi neartfotography/Shutterstock. 154 (bottom), photo$/Flickr. 154 (top), Chris Hill/Tourism Ireland. 155, bencrowe/Flickr. 156, Joe Fox/age fotostock. 157 (bottom), Amanda Bullock. 157 (top), Pyma/Shutterstock. 158, Chris Hill/Tourism Ireland. 168, Una Photo/Shutterstock. 175, Gail Johnson/Shutterstock. 184, Eireann/Shutterstock. 186, Warrenfish/wikipedia.org. 192-93, The Irish Image Colle/age fotostock. 194 (left), Department of the Environment, Heritage and Local Government, Ireland. 194 (right) and 195 (all), Joe Cornish/Dorling Kindersley. 196 (all) and 197 (top), Russborough. 197 (bottom), public domain. Chapter 4: The Midlands: 201, Andrea Seemann/Shutterstock. 202 (bottom), NL Buttonfreak/wikipedia. org. 202 (top), Peter Gavigan/wikipedia.org. 203, Holger Leue/Tourism Ireland. 204, The Irish Image Colle/age fotostock. 205 (bottom), ARCO/Krieger C/age fotostock. 205 (top), The Irish Image Colle/age fotostock. 206, Holger Leue/age fotostock. 219 and 226, The Irish Image Colle/age fotostock. 238, Javier Mediavilla Ezquibela/wikipedia.org. Chapter 5: The Southeast: 243, Kai Loos/age fotostock. 244 (top), kelvin wakefield/iStockphoto. 244 (bottom), Panaspics/Shutterstock. 245, Panaspics/Shutterstock, 246, Chris Hill/ Tourism Ireland. 253, Kevin Galvin/age fotostock. 257, Kevin Galvin/age fotostock. 259, IIC/age fotostock. 269, Martin Moos/age fotostock. 278, Terry Murphy/Tourism Ireland. 288, Richard Cummins/age fotostock. 291, walshphotos/Shutterstock. 293, George Munday/age fotostock. 294-95, Patryk Kosmider/Shutterstock. 294 (bottom), Irish Typepad/Flickr. 296 (top), Patryk Kosmider/Shutterstock. 296 (bottom left), Christian Handl/age fotostock. 297 (top), Danilo Donadoni/age fotostock. 297 (bottom), Marc C. Johnson/Shutterstock. 298, The Irish Image Colle/age fotostock. Chapter 6: County Cork: 303, The Irish Image Colle/age fotostock. 304, Holger Leue/Tourism Ireland. 305, Andrew Bradley/Tourism Ireland. 306, Gubbeen Farmhouse Products. 307 (top), Jaroslaw Grudzinski/Shutterstock. 307 (bottom), Rick Senley/age fotostock. 308, John Woodworth/iStockphoto. 315, Richard Cummins/age fotostock. 321, RIEGER Bertrand/age fotostock. 327, RIEGER Bertrand/age fotostock. 332-33, walshphotos/Shutterstock. 343, IIC/age fotostock. 351, Christian Handl/age fotostock. Chapter 7: The Southwest: 355, Gareth McCormack/age fotostock. 356 (bottom), JohnArmagh/